# Reliability and Risk Analysis in Civil Engineering 1

Proceedings of ICASP5, the Fifth International Conference on Applications of Statistics and Probability in Soil and Structural Engineering, University of British Columbia, Vancouver, B.C., Canada
May 25 - 29, 1987

Edited by N.C. Lind
Institute for Risk Research
University of Waterloo

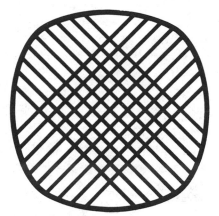

**Canadian Cataloguing in Publication Data**

International Conference on Applications of
Statistics and Probability in Soil and Structural
Engineering (5th : 1987 : Vancouver, B.C.)
Reliability and risk analysis in civil engineering

Papers presented at a conference held in Vancouver,
B.C., May 25-29, 1987.
Includes bibliographies and index.
ISBN 0-969287-00-3 (set) ISBN 0-969287-01-1 (v. 1)
ISBN 0-969287-02-X (v. 2)

1. Structural engineering - Statistical methods -
Congresses. 2. Soil mechanics - Statistical
methods - Congresses. 3. Probabilities -
Congresses. 4. Reliability (Engineering) -
Congresses. I. Lind, N. C. (Niels Christian),
1930- . II. University of Waterloo. Institute
for Risk Research. III. Title.

TA630.I58 1987 624.1'07'2 C87-093667-0

technical editor : A. Mahood
cover design : D. Bartholomew
printer and
binder : Edwards Brothers Inc.

RELIABILITY AND RISK ANALYSIS IN CIVIL ENGINEERING

 For information
address Institute for Risk Research,
University of Waterloo, Waterloo, Ontario,
Canada N2L 3G1

Volume 1 - ISBN 0-9692-870-1-1
Volume 2 - ISBN 0-9692-870-2-X
Set - ISBN 0-9692-870-0-3

**PREFACE**

These volumes contain the manuscripts of the general and special lectures and the text of the contributed papers to be presented at the Fifth International Conference on Applications of Statistics and Probability in Soil and Structural Engineering, held at the University of British Columbia in Vancouver, B.C. on May 25 - 29, 1987.

This conference follows earlier ICASP conferences held in Hong Kong 1971, Aachen 1975, Sydney 1979, and Firenze 1983. It comes at a time when society everywhere expects greater accountability of professionals, including engineers. The applications of statistics and probability have expanded, matured and become accepted for civil engineering structures. These developments have occurred at an opportune time, in view of the perceived need in society for rational safety procedures.

The ICASP conferences were founded with a particular objective in mind: That uncertainty in design be taken rationally into account in a way that is uniform and can be justified. The probabilistic rationales for the design of a structure and its foundations should agree; only by the dialogue between soil and structural engineers, such as ICASP promotes, can our procedures and philosophies be reconciled.

Reflected in these volumes and the preceding proceedings we see the growth of our discipline. It is a source of gratification that in particular the proportion of papers from the area of soil mechanics and foundation engineering has grown substantially and is now comparable with those arising from structural engineering and mechanics. The proportion of papers of general and civil engineering interest has also increased considerably, reflecting the process of generalization of civil engineering reliability and risk analysis as a field in its own right.

A broader perspective is now emerging, demanding a synthesis of risk analysis and reliability analysis in all contexts of technology and, in particular, within disciplines of related technology such as civil engineering. This runs counter to the general trend of fields expanding with the increase of knowledge, becoming subdivided by the specialization that is the logical response to this expansion.

Each of the contributed papers in these volumes was reviewed in extended abstract form by at least two independent anonymous reviewers. This should assure the quality and permanent value of the contents of these proceedings - to the extent that such can ever be assured! We have unfortunately had to restrict the length and the number of papers accepted because of scientifically invalid and arbitrary, but unavoidable, constraints (such as the time available for the conference and the funds available for printing). Regrettably, some fine papers have had to be excluded from the proceedings on such grounds.

I would like to thank all the authors for their excellent contributions and their fine cooperation in the face of many restrictions on space, format and timing. Special thanks are due to the members of the Board of Editors and other referees who carefully reviewed the material. I thank the International Scientific Committee and the National Committee for their guidance on policy, advice on procedure and just plain hard work in putting this conference and these proceedings together. On behalf of all of us as a team, I express the hope that our work will be considered by the organizers of the next conference as a challenge for them to improve upon.

Niels C. Lind
Waterloo, Ontario
February 1987

## BOARD OF EDITORS

## INTERNATIONAL SCIENTIFIC COMMITTEE

**Niels C. Lind**, Waterloo, Ontario (Chairman)
**Giuliano Augusti**, Roma, Italy
**K. Biernatowski**, Wroclaw, Poland
**Victor F.B. de Mello**, Sao Paulo, Brasil
**Luis Esteva**, Mexico D.F., Mexico
**A.M. Hasofer**, Sydney, Australia
**Owen G. Ingles**, Tasmania, Australia
**Peter Lumb**, Hong Kong
**M. Matsuo**, Nagoya, Japan
**A. Nowak**, Ann Arbor, Michigan
**Robert G. Sexsmith**, Vancouver, British Columbia
**Erik H. Vanmarcke**, Cambridge, Massachusetts

## NATIONAL COMMITTEE

**Richard Campanella**, University of British Columbia, Vancouver (Co-Chairman)
**Ricardo Foschi**, University of British Columbia, Vancouver (Co-Chairman)
**Niels C. Lind**, University of Waterloo, Waterloo, Ontario
**Robert G. Sexsmith**, Buckland and Taylor Ltd., Vancouver
**Colin Brown**, University of Washington, Seattle

## ICASP5 SPONSORING ORGANIZATIONS

Air Canada
Canadian Geotechnical Society
Canadian National Group of the IABSE
Canadian Pacific Airlines
Canadian Society for Civil Engineering
Civil Engineering Department, Carleton University, Ottawa
Civil Engineering Department, University of British Columbia
Civil Engineering Department, University of New Brunswick
Civil Engineering Department, University of Waterloo
Institute for Risk Research, University of Waterloo
Natural Sciences and Engineering Research Council
U.S. National Science Foundation

# CONTENTS

## VOLUME 1

## VOLUME 2

## Index of Authors

# Keyword Index of Titles

# THE STRUCTURAL SYSTEM RELIABILITY PROBLEM. QUALITATIVE CONSIDERATIONS

Ove Ditlevsen
Department of Structural Engineering, Technical University of Denmark.

ABSTRACT

Most of the presently available methods of general system reliability modelling and analysis are impenetrable as far as the question of whether the methods overestimate or underestimate the reliability of the structure with respect to the adverse event of collapse is concerned. The discussion is confined to frame or truss structures. The lack of a clear physical interpretation on the loading side of the current structural reliability analysis models and methods is highlighted and it is argued that the question of what is realistic modelling of the failure criteria is disputable.

It is claimed that the rigid-plastic theory is still worth-while. Criteria for the objectivity of the reliability analysis methodology are discussed on basis of works by Popper and Matheron.

## INTRODUCTION

In the context of structural reliability theory a structural system reliability problem is characterized by the simultaneous presence of several different possibilities of adverse structural behavior. For a given mechanical and probabilistic model all the possibilities contribute jointly to the probability of occurrence of the total event of adverse behavior. For statically indeterminate structures of more than some few degrees of indeterminacy the disjoint or overlapping adverse elementary events (often called failure modes) are in general very large in number. The definitions of the single elementary events as well as the number of these depend strongly on the properties of the constitutive laws adopted in the mechanical model (i.e. properties like ductility, brittleness, strain hardening, strain deteoriation etc.). Furthermore, the set of elementary events depends strongly on details of the action model, and in particular on the time evolutionary character of the action as defined in a random process formulation.

In recent years a considerable effort has been put into attempts to develop methods of calculating approximations to the probability of the total adverse event defined for any so-called realistic structural system and action model. However, often there is an inverse relation between the claimed realism of the constitutive part of the model and the realism of the action history model for which the calculation is practicable. In fact, most present works are not at all concerned with the problem of how the action grows from zero to the random valued configuration and magnitude assigned to it at any given time. The need for the help of a monster like a giant ten-armed octopus to keep the structure from failing during the phase of transfer of the load to the structure seems to be of minor concern.

The writer's uneasy feeling of doubt and confusion about what is actually calculated in current structural system reliability analyses makes him hold the attitude that the theory of ideal rigid plasticity theory, be it realistic in its elements or not, is nevertheless worth-while as a consistent mechanical basis for model formulation aiming at the study of system reliability effects in redundant structures with ductile failure behavior. In fact, the convenient help from the ten-armed octopus monster is almost equivalent to assuming the validity of the static theorem of the theory of ideal plasticity with associated flow rule for the surviving stable part of the structure.

The followint text is a qualitative discussion of the system reliability problem. A list of relevant references is given in (Ditlevsen and Bjerager, 1986) which is a part of a state of the art report prepared by the RILEM-Technical Committee SMS 72 on Stochastic Methods in Material and Structural Engineering. To put the problem in the relevant framework of concepts the main steps of the probabilistic reliability analysis are summarized in the next section. This summary reveals both the common elements with deterministic structural analysis and the conceptual differences between them.

STEPS OF SOLUTION OF THE STRUCTURAL RELIABILITY PROBLEMS

1) Identification of the relevant basic physical variables:
   1.1) MATERIAL VARIABLES (strengths, stiffnesses) and GEOMETRICAL VARIABLES identified through the process of designing the structural system lay-out and the corresponding formulation of the constitutive models in particular with respect to failure behavior,
   1.2) ACTION VARIABLES identified through the process of designing the structural system lay-out, the study of the environmental conditions, and the formulation of the corresponding spatial and temporal load history models.
2) Identification of events for design:
   2.1) identification of one or more adverse events that are considered to be important for the structural desing decisions,
   2.2) the mathematical formulation of these adverse events in terms of the models formulated in 1), that is, limit state modelling.
3) Choice of the joint probabilistic structure of all the relevant basic variables.
4) Formulation of model for quantifying the model uncertainty and the statistical uncertainty related to the points 1), 2), and 3). Description and evaluation in terms of this model of the actual model uncertainty of the limit state definitions of the identified adverse events.
5) Calculation of the probabilities of the adverse events:
   5.1) conditional probabilities given the limit states without model uncertainty (sensitivity to model uncertainty demonstrated through calculations in several hypothetical cases),
   5.2) removal of conditioning by calculating the total probabilities on basis of a weighting of the model hypotheses against each other (Bayesian evaluation of model uncertainty).

   Alternative to 5.1) and 5.2): If the model uncertainty is transferred by suitable probabilistic modelling in point 4) into amplified uncertainty of the basic physical variables, then the total probabilities of the adverse events are calculated directly. This pragmatic way of dealing with the model uncertainty will, except for simple cases, not be exactly equivalent to the analysis considered in 5.1) and 5.2). This is due to the different ways the element of professional assessment of model uncertainty is made use of in the two procedures.
6) Comparison of the calculated probability with a standard or with a specific reliability requirement for the considerd structure. Alternatively the calculated probability (or rather a set of calculated probabilities) may be passed as input to a decision model based on utility optimization principles. This step raises a philosophical problem: in which sense can an objective meaning be given to the very small probabilities of adverse events characterizing highly reliable structures? This nontrivial problem of the objectivity of the reliability analysis methodology will be discussed in the last section.

In principle any considered adverse event is completely defined within the full model formulated in 1) and 2). However, the defining characterization will in general not be given directly in terms of a sufficient number of equations (relations) or algorithms that quantitatively define the limit state in the space of the physical variables. The characterization is often a verbal statement that necessitates the carrying out of a structural analysis procedure before the probability calculation can be started. At first glance this structural analysis part contains no probabilistic elements. It follows usual deterministic methods. However, this is only so for simple structural systems for which it is reasonably easy to identify the complete limit state surface. For systems of realistic size it becomes almost out of the question to do a detailed identification of all parts of the limit state surface. In a usual deterministic analysis for design with a given load configuration and proportional loading this complete identification is not needed because the multidimensional problem is turned into the scalar problem of determining the load factor that corresponds to the limit state situation. Thus, only one point of the limit state surface is relevant for the considered deterministic load configuration and strength variable values.

The opposite holds for a probabilistic analysis. Here the entire limit state surface is needed in order to provide an exact calculation of the probability of the adverse event. As mentioned, this is often impracticable and also it is not necessary if only approximate results are needed for guiding the design decisions.

Instead the efforts are concentrated on the identification of subsets (subevents) and supersets (superevents, the opposite of subevents) of the adverse events and calculation of the probabilities on these bounding sets. In passing, it is noted that model uncertainty considerations can be included in this bounding procedure. The practical design situation usually defines a standard for the required narrowness of the bounding in terms of the probabilities.

The process of identifying sub- and supersets involves both structural analysis methods and probabilistic considerations. The probability of the event corresponding to the set difference between the superset and the subset of the adverse event is the measure of the accuracy. Thus, the search strategy for bounding sets should focus on determining bounding approximations that are close in the vicinity of those parts of the limit state surface at which the joint probability density of the basic variables takes the largest values.

REMARK 1: Such a strategy is used in the so-called FORM and SORM methods of probability calculation. These methods consider a representation of the limit state surface in a standardized Gaussian space (zero mean vector, unit covariance matrix). In this space the limit state surface is approximated by simpler surfaces at one or more points of local minimum of the distance from the origin. In single point or multiple point FORM (first order reliability method) the limit state surface is replaced at each of these points by a hyperplane at the same distance from the origin as the limit state surface. The set of these hyperplanes defines a convex polyhedral set for which several different approximate probability calculation methods are available. This polyhedral set is taken as an approximation to the complement S of the set of the adverse event. However, the polyhedral set is not necessarily either a subset or a superset of S. Thus, a general relation between the calculated probability and the exact probability cannot be specified. The experience shows that the approximation is often very good in particular when the probability of the adverse event is small. Asymptotic considerations support this experience. Similar remarks apply to single point or multiple point SORM (second order reliability method) in which second degree hypersurfaces are used instead of hyperplanes. Furthermore, these remarks apply when a point of local minimum of the distance from the origin on the limit state surface is a singular point with respect to differentiability. For this case a single (or multiple) point multiple FORM or SORM can be applied if the singularity is of a type which can be defined completely by a finite number q of different tangential hyperplanes meeting at the point. Multiple FORM considers the surface defined solely by these q hyperplanes while multiple SORM includes second degree surfaces in all directions orthogonal to the linear space spanned by the q normal vectors to the hyperplanes that define the type of singularity.

* * *

It follows from Remark 1 that the requirement that the approximating sets are subsets or supersets to the set of the adverse event in some respects is not critical. In particular, this is the case if the requirement is violated only in regions of low probability density.

DISCRETIZED STRUCTURAL SYSTEM RELIABILITY MODEL

In order to make a reliability analysis of a redundant frame or truss structure practicable it is usually necessary to set up an idealized model of the structural system with respect to its possibilities of failure. For a frame structure, for example, this may be done by choosing a finite number of points in the structure at which local yielding or carrying capacity degradation can take place. Between these failure points the beams of the structure are modelled to be infinitely strong. Of course, the sensitivity of the calculated reliability to this discretization should be judged. If the loads are assumed to act indirectly on the structure, the set of points of action may be taken to be finite. The distribution of internal moments along the members of the structure then have local extremes at these points of load action. Together with points of geometrical singularity they are natural candidates as failure points. Besides these points there may be points of built-in weakness which should also be included in the set of potential failure points.

When a reasonable idealization of the structural failure system has been established in this way, and the set of possible post failure unit strain rates at the failure points is finite, it is in principle possible to identify all failure modes of the system. A failure mode is here defined as a mechanism by which a part of or the entire structure is at least infinitesimally moveable with rigid structural parts between the points of yielding or failure. If there is a joint effect with respect to failure from the different internal force components at the potential failure point (interaction), the number of possible unit strain rates is infinite. Then there is an infinity of different failure modes. Usually this is the case for spatial frame structures.

By this discretization modelling of the structure the possibility of failure point formation at other points than those belonging to the selected finite set of points is disregarded. The effect is that the idealized discretized model leads to an overestimation of the reliability as obtained from a less idealized model of the real structure.

If the model allows for any type of behaviour ranging from ideal plasticity in some failure points through specified strength degradation depending on the angular rotation and the displacement in other failure points to complete disintegration in the rest of the failure points, the set of possible failure modes and the resistance capacity of these failure modes at any given time depend on the load history. This necessitates quite restrictive idealizations usually achieved by requiring the load path to be of a specified simple mathematical form. In any case, if not all failure modes are identified and included in the reliability analysis, the calculated result will be an upper bound on the reliability, that is, it gives an unconservative result.

RIGID-IDEAL PLASTIC MODEL

The only simple case of modelling where the load history has no influence on the set of failure modes and their resistances is the case of rigid-ideal plastic behavior in all the potential failure points and infinitely rigid structural elements between the potential failure points. The potential failure points are then called potential yield hinges.

The definition of ideal plasticity used here implies a strain-independent convex yield condition with the associated flow rule (the normality condition). This ensures the validity of a lower bound theorem which states that the structure is able to carry the load if and only if there exists a statically admissible set of internal forces in all the potential yield hinges such that these internal forces nowhere violate the yield condition.

The "if" part of this lower bound theorem is not valid if the flow rule is rejected. Thus, a reliability analysis based on calculations with statically admissible internal forces without adopting the flow rule has no status as far as being on the safe side is concerned unless the entire internal force history as function of the load history is taken into account in the analysis.

Ideal plasticity theory also contains an upper bound theorem which states that the structure will not be able to carry the load if and only if there exists a kinematically admissible set of rates of rotations and displacements (strain rates) imposed at the yield hinges so that the corresponding plastic dissipation is at most equal to the rate of work done by the external forces moving in accordance with this imposed strain rate field.

The "only if" part of this upper bound theorem is not valid if the flow rule is rejected. Thus the flow rule is not necessary for the validity of an upper bound reliability analysis. However, results of such an analysis may become unconservative.

GENERAL STRUCTURAL SYSTEMS. SEQUENTIAL SAFE SET

Structural system reliability theory often shows overwhelming difficulties due to complicated redistributions of the load effects after each element failure. Thus, the failure probabilities can be dependent on the ordered sequence of element failures. This implies that the entire random load path can affect the reliability of the structural system. However, most current methods of calculating the reliability of general structural systems do not contain load path assumptions. They are solely intended as purely time independent random variable models without concern about the question of how the load vector is gradually transferred to the structure.

In fact, with q potential failure points, referred to in the following as failure elements, most of these models define the full system failure event as the union of the q! formal "system failure" events that correspond to the q! different ordered sequences of failure elements. During computation, the structural model is changed step by step from the model of the original linear elastic structure of full integrity through a sequence of models corresponding to a more and more damaged structure. In order to give a specific definition of the safe set let $\underline{x}$ be a value of the vector of all basic variables $\underline{X}$ in the structural problem, and consider a given sequence of first, second, ..., qth potential failure element. First the basic model is considered. It is the model of the undamaged linear elastic structure completely defined by $\underline{x}$. If the limit state of the first potential failure element is not passed, the structure is said to be statically stable under $\underline{x}$ in the considered sequence. Otherwise the pre-failure constitutive properties of the first failure element are replaced by its post-failure constitutive properties. Often the failed element is simply removed completely and replaced by an "equivalent" external set of forces kept at fixed residual strength values (zero for ideal brittle failure, yield strength for ideal plastic failure). The statics of this second model of the sequence is computed at the value $\underline{x}$. If there is a static solution, it is

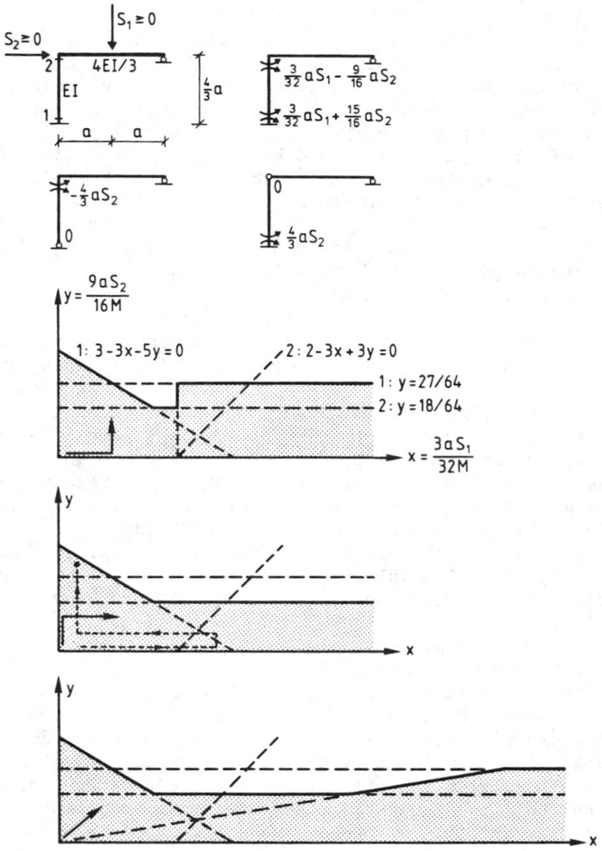


Fig. 1. Illustration of the load path dependency neglected by the sequential stable configuration definition of the safe set. The structure is a simple linear elastic frame as shown in the upper left corner (the example is taken from (Bennett and Ang, 1986)). The points 1 and 2 are the potential failure elements. They are ideal brittle with moment capacities $\pm M$ and $\pm 2M/3$ respectively. Upon failure the points turn into moment-free hinges. The bending moments of the intact failure elements are shown in the upper right corner. Next row of drawings show the bending moments after failure at point 1 or point 2 respectively. The three x,y-coordinate systems show the safe sets corresponding to the indicated loading paths: ($S_1$ first, then $S_2$), ($S_2$ first, then $S_1$), ($S_1$, $S_2$ growing proportionally from zero) respectively. The safe set of the second load path is the smallest of the three and it coincides with the sequential safe set of the structure. It has been claimed, e.g. in (Bennett and Ang, 1986), that the sequential safe set is always a subset of the safe set obtained for models with load paths. For this to be true certain restrictions must be imposed on the load path types. In this example it is only needed to take a piecewise linear load path like $(x,y) = (0,0) \rightarrow (0.9,0) \rightarrow (0.9,0.1) \rightarrow (0.1,0.1) \rightarrow (0.1,0.5)$ in order to get failure. The path is entirely in the sequential safe set.

checked whether the second potential failure element has passed its limit state. If not, the structure is, as above, said to be statically stable under $\bar{x}$ in the considered sequence. Otherwise the computation is carried on for the second element as for the first element and the third model of the sequence is formulated. Computing and modelling recursively in this way either reveals that the structure is statically stable under $\bar{x}$ in the considered sequence or that one of the models of the sequence exhibits statical instability, i.e. that there is no static solution (at the latest the qth model). The value $\bar{x}$ is in this modelling universe said to belong to the safe set of the structural system if and only if the structure is statically stable under $\bar{x}$ in all the q! different sequences. This definition of the safe set will be referred to as the sequential stable configuration definition and the corresponding formal safe set will be called the sequential safe set of the structural system. Its complement is called the sequential failure set.

The definition of the sequential safe set has a certain intuitive appeal. However, in general it lacks physical interpretation in relation to load path specifications. Except for the two special cases mentioned in the following it seems difficult to characterize the sequential safe set as being either a subset or a superset of the "real" safe set defined in a physically interpretable sense in an extended model that contains load path specifications.

Let A be the following property: There is at least one stable structural configuration under $\bar{x}$. From the definition of the sequential safe set it is obvious that if $\bar{x}$ is in the sequential safe set, then property A holds. However, if A holds, it cannot be concluded that $\bar{x}$ is in the sequential safe set. A model in which the safe set is defined as the set of points $\bar{x}$ for which property A holds may be called a stable configuration type of model. For such a model the safe set is a superset of the safe set corresponding to any extended model with load path dependency. The stable configuration type of model is suitable for structures with rigid-ideal plastic failure elements (the lower bound theorem).

For a structural model where all failure elements are elastic-ideal brittle (element removed by failure) it can be shown by a simple proportioning argument that the sequential safe set is a subset of the safe set in a model where the load is grown proportinally and monotonically from zero to its final value contained in $\bar{x}$ as a subvector of $\bar{x}$.

WHAT IS "REALISTIC" CONSTITUTIVE MODELLING IN SYSTEM RELIABILITY ANALYSIS?

Realistic modelling of element stress-strain behavior in structures like large spatial frame structures made of tubular elements is beset with several difficulties. First the information on which the modelling is based as a rule comes from laboratory experiments with idealized elements under idealized loading conditions. Second, the number of relevant test results is usually very modest and the results show large scatter. Third, it is often not clear according to which mechanical principles realistic element failure conditions should be formulated, in particular in cases where internal force interactions play a significant role. One must add to this the problem of how the strain rates after local failure should be modelled.

It is not rare that recourse to the methods and restrictions of ideal plasticity theory is had in these problems. For example, it is established design practice to "decompose" turbular connections in off-shore jacket structures into connections for which experimental results are available. Each of the compotent connections take a "safe part" of the stresses. The capacity of the composite connection is then calculated by adding over all components with the proviso that the carrying capacity of a material part is not used more than once. This method is seen to be simply an application of the static theorem of ideal plasticity theory.

In spite of such common practice, it is a widespread opinion that plasticity theoretical solutions are of limited validity for real structures. For some part this opinion is based on a scepticism about the necessary extensive idealizations of the stress-strain behavior including the requirement of sufficient plastic strain capacity. As far as these provisions are concerned it is interesting to observe that developments in reinforced concrete plasticity theory show that the theory works surprisingly well as a regression model for predicting failure loads even in cases where the idealizations seem to be far-fetched (e.g. for shear failures). The biases of the predictions are well corrected by regression analysis using an effectivity factor $\nu$ applied to the test cylinder concrete strength which depends on the type of failure. Reprints of figures from (Nielsen, 1984) illustrating this are shown in Figs. 2 and 3.

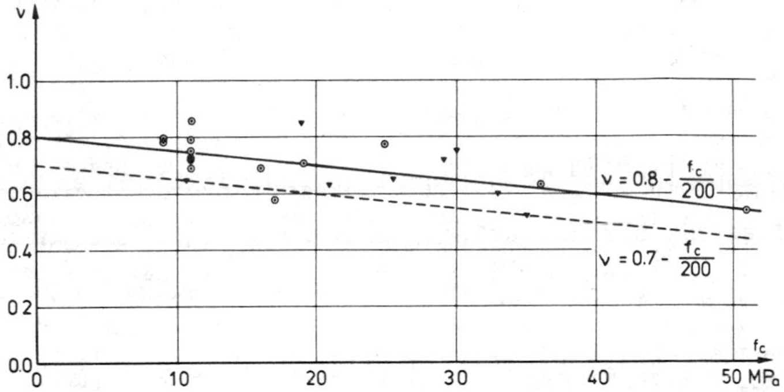


Fig. 2. Reprint of Figure 5.26 in (Nielsen, 1984) showing experimentally determined effectiveness factors $\nu$ for shear reinforced concrete beams failing in the shear mode. The horizontal axis represents the concrete cylinder compression strength $f_c$. The full straight line is obtained by linear regression.

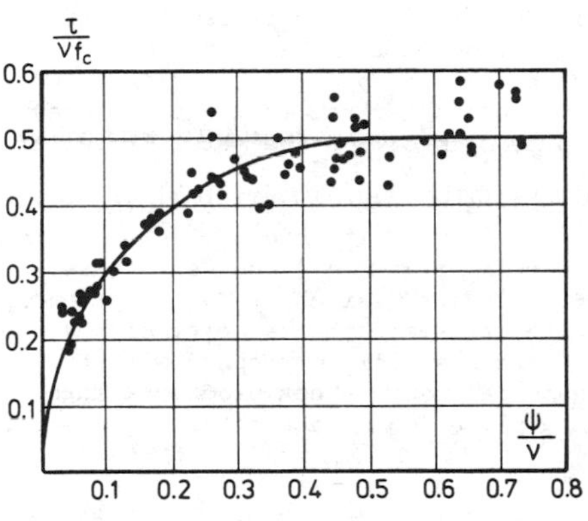


Fig. 3. Reprint of Figure 5.27 in (Nielsen, 1984) showing the experimentally obtained shear carrying capacity $\tau$ normalized by the effective concrete strength $\nu f_c$ as a function of the degree of shear reinforcement $\psi$ (see (Nielsen, 1984) for details). The effectivity factor $\nu$ is taken from the linear regression in Fig. 2. The curve is obtained as the rigid plastic solution to the carrying capacity problem.

It may, perhaps, be possible to extend this effectivity factor approach to a model uncertainty approach in random vector form for system reliability analysis based on a consistent formulation in terms of the ideal plasticity theory. In any case, it should be remembered that the rejection of the ideal plasticity theory in order to achieve more realism in the modelling of the structural member behaviour simultaneously implies a severe lack of realism with respect to the load modelling for which the reliability analysis can be carried through. Also a price of substantial increase of the complexity of the analysis has to be paid.

The last 5 to 10 years of development of effective methods of calculating probabilities on complicated sets of small probability content including the development of search methods for identifying the most important parts of the sequential failure set has provided the necessary prerequisites for the analysis of structural system models that include load path dependence. However, the model formulation problems and the computational difficulties seem to be of a nature that makes it worth-while to proceed with further studies of the ideal-plastic models subjected to random load histories. For more general and realistic structural systems substantial development in the not too far future is for quite restrictive load paths of deterministic shape (proportional loading).

## OBJECTIVITY OF THE RELIABILITY ANALYSIS METHODOLOGY

According to Popper (1972) the crucial criterion of objectivity of a model mirroring some real world phenomenon is that the model can in principle be put to the test of falsification. Structural reliability theory aims at calculating probabilities of adverse events defined within the models of the theory. These adverse events correspond to features in the real world of structures and the calculated probabilities are anticipated in some sense to contain information of empirical value. Following Matheron (1978) (see also Hasofer (1984)), Popper's falsification criterion has been given in statistical modelling the form of hypothesis testing: If a prespecified event has a calculated probability of very small magnitude, then the model is considered falsified if the event actually occurs in the corresponding real experiment. Since adverse events in structural reliability are given very small probabilities, a reliability model used for design of a structure should be considered falsified if one of the adverse design events actually occurs. The interpretation of this is that if a structural failure after close investigation cannot be attributed to a radical error (mistake, gross error) resulting in a deviation from the theoretical design, then the reliability model is falsified, i.e. it contains a radical error.

Structural reliability models differ in their nature fundamentally from other types of probabilistic models in that their targets of interest are events of very small probability. Furthermore, the interest is not in the absolute probability value, except that it has to be small, but in the relative probability values between different adverse events for the same or different structural solutions of a given building construction problem. That is, the probabilities of the adverse events primarily serve as indicators of a reliability ordering. This ordering makes it possible to formulate a statement like "these two structures are equally reliable with respect to the adverse event A". The point dividing the probability scale into sufficiently reliable and insufficiently reliable structures with respect to event A is purely conventional and obtained by declaring a comparison standard defined as a given structural design to be just sufficiently reliable with respect to event A. This declaration is given on the basis of a general consensus within an authorized code committee. Clearly the numerical value of the dividing point on the scale depends on the chosen reliability model. Matheron's formulation of the falsification criterion is seen to need an extension since it is otherwise not possible to falsify the imposed reliability ordering.

The requirement of objectivity necessitates at least a strategy of code committee action that in the long run eventually will put the reliability model to a test of falsification. One such strategy of action, and perhaps the only one, is to gradually change the comparison standard in the direction of less reliability. Eventually the reliability model will lead to designs that with some observable frequency will exhibit adverse behavior. From data of observations of such adverse events it is in principle possible to set up a falsification test of the reliability ordering. It is crucial, however, for the long run objectivity of the reliability analysis method that the methodology is kept free of arbitrary choices of elements to which the reliability measure is sensitive. Only emperical or internally objective choices (Matheron, 1978) of elements should be left to the designer. This implies that the objectivity requirement necessitates the existence by general consensus of a code of standardizations of certain elements of the reliability model. These standardizations should at least include assumptions about distributional tails to be used in the reliability analysis.

The practical difficulty of performing the test of falsification due to the extremely rare adverse events under study enforces the principle of anticipatory modelling (Matheron, 1978). The striving for objectivity necessitates that the total reliability model be built from partial models that can be much more easily put to the test of falsification and which are combined by operational rules that can be claimed to be objective, i.e. natural laws, rules of geometry, rules of probability calculus etc. The partial models may very well be built as simplifying idealizations of more complicated models. So even if a model is falsified by some comparison with the part of the real world of which it is intended to be some mirror image, the model may be accepted for practical use on account of the error not being misleadingly large. The point is that a falsifiable model for the error can still be formulated.

Returning to the ductile structural systems the objectivity of an ideal plastic model, which in principle is calibrated to the anticipatory model of the more realistic stress-strain behavior by use of random effectivity factors, is ensured by the possibility of making comparative simulation calculations. Future investigations should provide the necessary information on effectivity factors for typical examples of ductile structural systems, and thereby open the doors for realistic anticipatory modelling in terms of ideal plasticity theory. In all this it should be remembered that in stochastic modelling there is no need for detailing the behavior of the individual outcomes of the random experiment beyond what can be captured by the probabilities of the events of practical relevance. More than that tends to overstep the threshold of objectivity (Matheron, 1978).

ACKNOWLEDGMENT

The author appreciates interesting discussions with A.M. Hasofer on this philosophical matter during his visit to the Department of Structural Engineering, Technical University of Denmark during the winter of 1986-87.

REFERENCES

Bennett, R.M. and A.H.-S. Ang (1986). "Formulations of Structural System Reliability". Journal of Engineering Mechanics, ASCE, 112, pp. 1135-1151.

Ditlevsen, O. and P. Bjerager (1986). "Methods of Structural Systems Reliability". Structural Safety, 3, pp. 195-229.

Hasofer, A.M. (1984). Objective Probabilities for Unique Objects, in Risk, Structural Engineering and Human Error, M. Grigoriu (ed.), University of Waterloo Press, Waterloo, Ontario, Canada, pp. 1-16.

Matheron, G. (1978). Estimer et choisir, Les Cahiers du Centre de Morphologie, Mathématique de Fontainebleau, Facicule 7. Translated into English: Estimating and Choosing, by A.M. Hasofer (1987).

Nielsen, M.P. (1984). Limit Analysis and Concrete Plasticity. Printice Hall, Inc., Englewood Cliffs, New Jersey.

Popper, K.R. (1972). The Logic of Scientific Discovery, Hutchinson, London.

# STATISTICS & PROBABILITY: THE ENGINEER - CLIENT INTERACTION PROBLEM

O.G. Ingles*
*Owen Ingles Pty.Ltd., Risk Management Consultants, Swan Point, Tasmania 7251 Australia

## ABSTRACT

The last 20 years have seen major advances in risk analysis for the use of structural and geotechnical engineers. At the same time, legal interpretation of their responsibilities has provoked a much greater awareness of fallibility in the execution and performance of engineering work. To reduce the risk of functional failures, or worse, engineers have now quantified their incidence identified their sources and communicated the findings throughout the civil engineering profession by means of interactive exchanges such as the ICASP and ICOSSAR conferences. In short, research and *professional* dissemination of the risk inherent in engineering work is now well advanced; but unfortunately, its public relations aspect is not; to the point where significant engineer-client interaction problems have become visible.

This paper examines some of those problems; for example, of definitions, of the value of life, of spurious inference, of inhomogeneous data, of other data insufficiencies (e.g. quality, record, quantity), of extrapolations, of human error, of communications, and of perpetual supervision. Possible solutions to some (but not all) of these problems are suggested. The urgency for a better engineer-client understanding is stressed, and paths thereto indicated.

## INTRODUCTION

Advances made over the last 20 years in the application of statistics and probability to soil and structural engineering show a considerable theoretical potential to improve engineering practice. But this potential is not being adequately utilised in practice, seemingly because of inadequate communication between engineers and their clients (also perhaps, within the profession).

It is the purpose of this paper to consider why these advances have not yet passed more widely into practice, and to suggest means whereby their adoption might be speeded up. It is important that this be done as soon as is possible so that the profession can face, in a more confident way, the challenges posed by widening interpretations of legal liability which are now inhibiting good practice. The public interest and self-interest now coincide in requiring a better appreciation of the various problems which must be addressed and solved if the risk exposure both for citizen and for engineer is to be minimised.

To illustrate the many pitfalls of legal liability now facing a practising civil engineer, several notable books have recently become available ( Jackson and Powell, 1982; Huffmann, 1986; Sutter & Hecht, 1974 and supplements thereto in 1982, 1985 and 1986. Notice that the last-named reference details *only* the landslide and subsidence liability, in California, in *four volumes !*).

In what follows here, a range of practical and philosophical problems which are inhibiting proper communication between the engineer and his client or the general public are considered. Almost certainly the coverage is not complete but it does cover those matters which, from my own practice in risk management, seem to be the most pressing.

## DEFINITIONS

If we wish to assess soil and structural performance in the field, deciding between the bad and the good, seeking to reduce the former without at the same time accentuating the latter so much that uneconomic designs are produced in future work, then we must have a sensitive and precise definition of *failure*.

We cannot talk about risk analysis and the probability of failure unless we have first agreed what we mean by the event (i.e. failure) which we purport to quantify by probability methods. It must not be forgotten that the symbol $P_f$, so frequently used is a composite in which the "f" is just as important as the "P".

Unhappily, "failure" still has many definitions, ranging from the strong to the weak. At the stronger end, we might find its sense overlapping with such words as "disaster" and "catastrophe"; at the weaker end it might cover a mere visual imperfection of no structural significance. There is a continuum of all possible definitions of failure, wherein we need one or more fixed points which have been agreed internationally. This should not be a difficult task, since it has been achieved long ago: for instance, by soil engineers when they divided up the continuum of particle grain sizes into gravel, sand, silt, and clay at arbitrary but agreed effective diameters. All that is required in the present case (where there is no *quantitative scale* - as yet - like that of the soil particle diameters) is to establish a graded series of named steps, with precisely worded definitions of each. Thus, and only thus, will our data be comparable, and quantitative scales become possible.

I propose, therefore, the following four step scale for its practical value in communications both with client and public, as explained shortly:-

*Fault* - any imperfection, visual or functional, not anticipated by those who commissioned the work (note: this embraces errors of design as well as of execution and performance. It implies that an engineer should only accept work which he believes he can execute to full satisfaction).

*Failure* - a functional imperfection in the completed work (i.e. *performance* below the standard expected by the engineer. Note the wording "by" and not "of", since from here onwards professional judgment should prevail). This definition will present a conservative view, always favorable for good client relations, insofar as performances will exceed expectations.

*Collapse* - total loss of function, following an inability to prevent it (note that where remedial measures can be applied in time, only failure is recorded. Collapse is *not* envisaged to exclude events leading to loss of life, which form the next category).

*Disaster* - a total loss of function causing loss of human life (note: injury and monetary loss are not seen as disasters, since they are both recoverable).

This scale is, to the best of our present knowledge, logarithmic in respect of risk: since disasters are about 1 % of all collapses, collapses are about 1 % of all failures, failures are about 1 % of all faults, and fault occurs in about 1 % of all work (cf. Melchers & Harrington, 1982; Ingles, 1984 and 1985); i.e., the risk is approximately $10^{-2}$, $10^{-4}$, $10^{-6}$, and $10^{-8}$ per structure per annum, proceeding down the scale.

This raises the next problem of definition: in what units should *incidence* of these events be measured ? Most statistics have hitherto been based upon fatalities per annum, since such data is fairly readily available. But several variants derived from this basic data appear in the literature: e.g. average life reduction (usually in days); fatalities per stated number of work hours; etc. The complexity of this problem is perhaps best illustrated by reference to road accident statistics - should they be expressed as fatalities per unit time, or per vehicle, or per unit distance travelled ? Should they be based on total population, or only vehicle passengers ? Might not injury, or perhaps even financial loss, be measures as important as fatalities ?

There has to be an agreed basis for incidence statistics. The scale above has been carefully framed to refer to *completed works* (functional structures) so that only a time unit needs to be specified - per annum is suggested. Money loss, injury, or death, are *results* of the structural malfunction, and so are seen as secondary - albeit important - statistics for client information.

Recent studies (e.g. Matousek & Schneider, 1976) have provided quite clear evidence that the dominant cause of imperfection, failure, or worse, is human error. Since human error accounts for some 80 % or more of all failures, this must be the starting point in the search for error reduction methods. But, how can we study it, whilst it remains undefined ? Nowadays, almost anything would be traceable to human error:thanks, perversely, to the statistician ! Owing to the confidence the engineer now places on his calculations of the occurrence of rare events (return flood, for example), when the rare event exceeds those expectations and the structure is destroyed, is this not now a human error ?

To choose the wrong distribution theory for analysing a statistical tail is probably already negligence (human error) in the eye of the Law. Indeed, we have the interesting situation where legal interpretation of responsibility in this century has effectively redefined "human error", much to the engineer's disadvantage, due to faith in advanced technology and an aversion to risk both by public and professional, of which neither may be justifiable. What once was known as an "Act of God" the risk of which was ever present and accepted, has now become a human error liable to the severest penalties of the law.

Since human error is being constantly redefined by the laws of tort and of negligence, engineers cannot expect to frame an accepted definition. All that we can do is to be careful that we classify as human error only those things which the law at that time has so ruled. But the promotion of good practice in engineering - that is, neither underdesign nor wastage by overdesign - demand that engineers should seek urgently to correct public misapprehensions of risk and promote the determination and dissemination of economically justified risk levels for their work.

In short, human error should *not* be defined so as to discourage economic good practice. But the client *must* be made aware of the risk, however small, attaching to any planned project. It must be his choice whether the cost of additional safety measures or alternative methods is warranted by the various social and other factors which arise from completion of the planned work. It has been my experience that clients, given a choice between methods differing in risk and cost, as often as not have chosen a method of lower cost but more risk (provided the risk is not excessive). That is the client's right; it is the engineer's duty to present those risks as fairly and factually as he does the costs.

## THE VALUE OF LIFE

A decision between alternative procedures having different values of risk-cost-benefit inevitably contains in engineering practice some element, however small, of danger to life and limb. A final decision can only be reached if we equate this risk of injury or death with some monetary loss, however repugnant this may seem on philosophical grounds. Legislation already does this, under worker's compensation law for example; why then should not the engineer also ?

The literature contains some grossly different estimates for this important "value of life" (cf. Abraham & Thedié, 1960; Heathcote & Thom, 1979; Wigan, 1982). These estimates are based on the mistaken idea that we are entitled to place a value on *someone else's* life. The reality is that in any community there are both risk-takers and the risk-averse, and social factors have strong influence on their relative proportions. Philosophically preferable would be a *self-estimate* of the value of life, polled as widely as possible across the whole community; from which a base value for engineering calculations can be drawn according to an agreed statistic (mean, mode, median, or some percentile would all be entitled to consideration; though the median might seem the most democratic).

It has been shown (Ingles, 1985) that this self-estimate can be obtained in principle by polling acceptable losses and acceptable risks ( a better method than direct polling of a "value of life", which is likely to produce responses more emotive than objective). Then,

The Value of Life (\$) = Acceptable Loss ($\$.t^{-1}$) $\div$ Acceptable Risk ($t^{-1}$)    (1)

A small survey has validated the above method, confirming the wide range of community values and also that the median of those values lies (for Australia) not far from the compensation law amount - an indication of the sensitivity of legislative response to public demand ? (This estimate was \$ 50,000 $\pm$ 20,000 in 1982 Australian dollars).

The literature is almost silent on trying to assign a value to injury. The "3-day disability" measure proposed by Senneck (1973) has been criticised for subjectivity, and the problem seems intractable at present. If, indeed, worker compensation law provides a fair measure of the community's value of life, it might be reasonable to assume that it also does so in respect of injuries. But in recent years legal awards for damages (personal injury) have been grossly in excess of compensation law provisions, so that the whole basis for decision making has been subverted.

The engineer's initial response to this legal assault on his work has been to fall back on insurance values for the decision making process, since these are commercially based on claims experience, which in turn reflects both court awards and incidences of malfunction. Grossly excessive verdicts have placed even this recourse at peril, and a major public relations exercise, especially directed at the legislature, is urgently needed. Responsible decision making in civil engineering - responsible in the sense that community resources have been optimised thereby - depends far more on achieving a rational approach to the value of life than on any elegant probabilistic treatment of the risk that is being incurred.

As a guide to those in practice, it is perhaps worth mentioning that it has been held in England (Tremain v. Pike, 1969) that a fatality risk of $3 \times 10^{-6}$ per person per annum is not negligent. I recently had a case in Australia in which the provable risk was $10 \times 10^{-6}$ (i.e. $1 \times 10^{-5}$) per person per annum but unfortunately this was settled out-of-court so that a nearer definition of the upper and lower limits defining legal negligence was not obtained.

By such criteria, collapses and disasters ought not to be held as negligent work without strong reasons therefor. Normally, their incidence is well below the ambient everyday hazard level (circa $10^{-5}$; Ingles, 1985).

In summary, since engineering decisions inevitably involve risk to life and limb, there should be an agreed, *rational*, basis to them. The CIRIA approach (CIRIA, 1977) might be one good starting point. Insurer confidence, client confidence, and ultimately public confidence depend on a consistent approach by engineering planners to the valuation of life and injury. One way in which this might rationally be attempted has been suggested above.

HUMAN ERROR

Mention has already been made of the critical importance of human error and the problems of defining it. It was specifically addressed in a major recent Workshop (Nowak, 1986). Clients must be assured that it is under control both in planning and construction phases, to the best of our ability. Conventional procedure has been to use checking (of designs, material strengths, etc.), but this is still far from foolproof, as illustrated for example by the collapse of the bridge at Pulle (Vandepitte, 1983).

A better procedure may be to use hazard scenarios (Nowak, p.214), but this wider superposition technique still needs research. And however successful we are in reducing error in the planning phase, which of us recalls a project where nothing went wrong during construction ?

It is thought that our design safety factors are such as will cover us from the consequences of human error in the completed works. Ingles (1985) offers evidence that social and technical pressures have produced safety factors very close in their results to the public risk tolerance level. This may be good engineering; but if we can reduce the human error component cheaply, we will be doing even better.

How much room there is for improvement is very evident from the magnitudes of some current safety factors, e.g. 3 to 5 for piping gradients in dams, and 2 to 3 for shearing failure of onshore foundations (Meyerhof, 1982). In many cases it may be better to tell a client what safety factor(s) have been used rather than stating a risk level, because the former acts as a more powerful deterrent to overloading. During diagnosis of engineering failures it is not uncommon to find that something which is found to work well ultimately tempts a client try and get more from the work than that for which it was designed.

Typical examples which I have encountered are the overloading of factory floors, the raising of dam heights, and the removal of traffic load limits on roads. Potential landslip areas, which are safe with good engineering method, are easily destabilised by foolish owners. It would be enormously expensive, and a waste of community resources, to provide against abuse by unintelligent end-users. So what can be done ?

Obviously, the client should be given one or both of two things: either a written set of operating instructions, setting out clearly what should be done or should not be done, or else an inbuilt monitoring system designed to give early warning of dangerous condition during the working life of the structure.

Since most complicated and expensive machinery comes with a user instruction manual, might this not also be attempted for engineering work ? Heavy vehicle load limits are placed on roads, for example; and it becomes the duty of the owner authority to police them. I have seen far too many cases of structural damage - often severe - to buildings, which has been caused by unintelligent work in their near vicinity (not always excavations, as those working in areas of potential landslip or expansive soils or collapsing soils will know).

Monitors for potential distress are now often included in large dams. But how many other major structures are protected in this way ? I would recommend a monitoring system against any anticipated major hazard as a matter of course for important works, but there are two present shortcomings to this. The first arises from the very durability of most engineering structures, whose lifetime will often reach or exceed 100 years. Probabilistic and statistical research has provided a wealth of papers on how to design for the occurrence of rare events with long return periods, but I recall only one paper (Lumb, 1968) that looks at the problem of long term instrument reliability. Obviously, monitor reliability should exceed that of the structure being monitored; and research in this field is urgently needed.

The second shortcoming is in the quality of response. This does not refer solely to the response of the monitor, important though it is that this should be much faster than the time required to institute countermeasures. Equally important is that the *right response* be made. I have seen too many instances where competent engineers - but inexperienced in failure - have not been able to apply the correct remedial measures in time: either because they were not aware of them, or the necessary materials were not available. Dam failure is a common case of this type. Last year, a tailings dam failure ( preventable ) occurred barely 15 miles from my home in a remote part of the country. Those on the spot were unaware of the potential assistance so close at hand, and the nearby river was contaminated with a substantial cyanide discharge.

To ensure the right response at the right time, Australia has backed up its State Emergency Services with a Counter Disaster College, operated by a Natural Disasters Organisation within the Department of Defence, which has produced a Directory (McDermott, 1985) of disaster research workers classified according to their fields of expertise, with their contact telephone number and address. This is an important step forward, but only a first one, in reducing the risk generated by errors.

There is, however, one final point here of great importance. No matter how much safety is improved by probabilistic design (e.g. limit states), improved response techniques, or whatever, the engineer must be particularly careful not to convey any false sense of security about his work. This is an excellent prescription for carelessness either in execution or in use. It is a disservice both to the public and the profession not to publish failures, both details and incidences, as widely as possible. Here is another compelling reason why we must settle the problems of definition, discussed above, as soon as possible.

INFERENCE

Few engineers have been trained in logical inference, though some excellent books (e.g. Blockley, 1980) specifically directed to engineering practice are now available.

Much care is needed in discussing cause and effect, or in the construction of valid relationships within and between data sets, even when some standard mathematical technique has been used. Many years ago, when investigating dam failures in Queensland, I noticed that the failures had all occurred at places whose name began with a "B" or an "M", and the localities of sound dams visited did not. Now clearly it would be foolish to infer, whatever confidence level the statistics might grant, that an inappropriate locality name would lead to dam failure ! The point of this is, that rare coincidences *do* sometimes occur - as they must if our statistical theory is good - and we must always be ready to apply the test of common sense even to what might seem quite plausible.

But common sense is by no means an efficient check on spurious inference. A recent finding by Rüsch (1979) puts a considerable question mark over "common sense" amongst engineers. He found a lack of transitivity between cause and effect, inasmuch as the engineers questioned were prepared to accept concrete beams 20 % deficient to the design strength (on average) before insisting on their replacement, but refused to allow any overload at all (on average) for a beam of fully compliant strength.

Where ample data is available, *significance tests* are used to infer causes or effects with little hesitation. But consider the following case taken from my own practice: An earth dam had failed by piping near an outlet conduit. It was known that air voids in the compacted soil, if excessive, will result in failure; consequently measurements were made of air voids both in the conduit trench failure zone and elsewhere along the main wall, with the results shown in Table 1. Is it necessary to reconstruct the entire wall, or can the trench alone be reinstated with safety ?

Table 1. Air Voids in an Earth Dam (Failed) (%)

| | |
|---|---|
| Main Embankment | 12.6, 4.6, 14.2, 2.3, 5.6, 13.0 |
| Conduit Trench | 8.4, 8.6, 3.9, 7.1, 7.0, 5.4, 4.4, 5.3, 10.9, 18.5, 19.7, 11 |

For the Embankment: $n = 6$, $\bar{x} = 8.7$, $s = 5.1$
For the Trench: $n = 12$, $\bar{x} = 9.2$, $s = 5.2$

Now significance testing of the results in Table 1 tell us that there is no difference in the quality of work as between trench and main embankment, so it will be necessary to replace both. This is, however, a false conclusion, even though the mathematics are sound. To understand how this can be so, an engineer must be thoroughly familiar with the principles of soil compaction and thereby know that a poorer compaction *effort* can subsequently wet up to the same *air* voids condition as a well-compacted soil.

With this knowledge, the moisture contents of the test samples from Table 1 were called from the files and showed the data of Table 2, post. Though an F test is here inconclusive, a t test clearly distinguishes between the conduit trench and the main embankment, showing inadequacy only in the former.

Table 2. Moisture Content in an Earth Dam Wall (as %, difference from optimum)

| | |
|---|---|
| Main Embankment | -1.0, -1.1, +0.2, +1.9, -0.6, -2.7 |
| Conduit Trench | +2.6, +4.7, +9.6, +4.3, +5.3, +4.3, +9.9, +2.8, +1.9 |

| | | | |
|---|---|---|---|
| For the Embankment: | n = 6, | $\bar{x}$ = -0.55, | s = 1.53 |
| For the Trench: | n = 9, | $\bar{x}$ = +5.05, | s = 2.88 |

The moral to these foregoing examples is, that *before drawing conclusions, be sure that the right question has been asked.* The difference between a good engineer and a bad engineer may depend less on the methods he uses than on the quality of his inference; or, experience counts !

Is there a sound way to avoid spurious or biased (e.g. the transitivity gap noted between cause and effect) inference ? Probably not, other than by using the most highly experienced personnel or consultants and, in the longer term, substantially reviewing the course content in engineering education to provide a greater exposure to practice, and grounding in logical analysis.

As Shaw and D'Appolonia (1977) pointed out ten years ago, in an excellent paper which should have been prescribed reading for engineering students, most engineers must make decisions based on *the available information*, and this is almost always inadequate. This is why we would like to use the probabilistic methods now available, especially those based on Bayes' Rule, which permit an optimum decision to be made from poor information, and then to be constantly upgraded as further information comes to hand (e.g. during construction).

Moreover, the use of Bayesian probability ensures that *consistent* decisions will be made, which should make engineering construction more insurable, thus more economical too. Why then has the use of these probabilistic methods not spread more rapidly through the profession ? Probably because such methods do not ensure that the stated result will be *true*, merely that it is the best estimate of truth at any given time and - what is not well recognised in the literature - *by a specific engineer.*

If Bayesian probability is to be more widely used, some of the subjectivity must be extracted; yet this is at the very basis of the method. To do this it is necessary to recognise that the posterior probability is greatly influenced both by the prior and by the liklihoods; thus if the former is vague and the latter is strong (much sample data), the latter will dominate the posterior; whereas if the former is strong and the latter is weak (sparse data), then the former will dominate.

Therefore, if the data is minimal, it is not wise to inject strong opinions through the prior; and likewise it is best to set some lower limit to the data (say, three values) to ensure that the liklihoods are not too weak.

The problems of inference rest largely within the profession itself, not at the engineer-client interface. What has been said here should however make it clear that one engineer-client problem should always be uppermost in the mind of any responsible engineer: that although probabilistic methods can optimize the use of poor information, *they can never replace good information.* Clients notoriously try to skimp the investigation budget because the engineer has not been sufficiently persuasive of its need and merits. The poorer the initial information, the greater is the risk of error; and this point must constantly be stressed to the client, and in the literature.

DATA INADEQUACIES

Apart from the common situation of the available data being numerically insufficient, other inadequacies must also be addressed if "consumer" confidence is to be encouraged. These concern the nature of the data, and the usages to which it is put.

NATURE OF THE DATA. Some comment has already been made about the quantity of data and the need to secure as much as possible (providing it is relevant! - data costs money, and must never be collected without good reason. A first step in data assembly should be to consider carefully what are the criteria for good performance, then what will best measure them. The correctness of cause and effect inference underlies it all !).

When the data is meagre, there is no real alternative to a Bayesian method of analysis and a substantial safety factor to cover lack of knowledge of the form of its distribution, its quality, and whether in fact it covers all the critical variables satisfactorily.

When the data is abundant, it may often contain meaningful subsets or even repetitions which should be extracted and used *provided they are recognized.* (For example, Vines (1986) claims to have detected 10 - 11 year return times for severe bushfire in Australia, linked with an immediately antecedent year or more of drought, in the present century. This refers to *the same area* and is probably associated with the time for regrowth. If one looks at a larger area, such as the whole State of Victoria, one finds a return period of about 5½ years between bushfires which have caused fatalities. These are a useful extension of basic fatality data from bushfire, which indicates a risk of 0.9 x $10^{-6}$ per person per annum in Victoria since 1850).

Obviously, with abundant data, the form of its distribution must be first checked (by histogram or otherwise). Care must be taken to recognise bimodal or multimodal distributions - which may be strongly overlapping - as well as outliers which can be rejected. Some geomechanics tests, such as plasticity index or linear shrinkage can yield truncated distributions, and these also need to be recognised.

All of the above can be handled by standard statistical methods. And yet, we remain vulnerable to the *quality* of the data. Good processing methods can do little to improve the output from poorly recorded or unwittingly biased data. Test methods should be chosen to yield usable information, measured as directly as possible (i.e., in the field if possible) on the chosen criteria. No probabilistic processing can make a silk purse of a sow's ear - and so I always incorporate carefully selected but generally unstated checks over all incoming data; as one simple example, the comparison of compaction data with a zero air voids line, and a desirable coefficient of variation.

More attention is needed on how to detect poor data. For the many standard test methods, we now need published coefficients of variation (cf. Lee et al. 1983), perhaps even specific to the material; as this would provide at least a rough check on data quality.

More must be done about the quality of data, and statisticians in recent years have, fortunately, concerned themselves with robustness. Bickel (1978) has reviewed 15 years of progress in robustness theory (a) against any gross errors in location models (b) for extending the technique to estimation and test of parameters in linear models. Brewer (1978) has described the use of robust techniques for large scale surveys. McNeil (1978) reports about the development of a robust regression package. These are but a few of the new contributions robustness has offered for upgrading the quality of engineering data, and unless they are used there is always a risk of self-deception or, worse, client deception (McNeil's paper describes one sad case of the latter).

Another problem concerning the nature of data, implicit in what has been said above but deserving of a quite specific comment, is the matter of data homogeneity. Accusations that data is inhomogeneous are easy to make and difficult to defend because most measured quantites can be perceived as being subject to an infinite range of influence sources. In the final analysis,the only homogeneous sample has a size of *one*.

This situation is palpably absurd; apples, pears and plums are all *fruit*, and providing they are called fruit one is entitled to make statements about the distribution of observed properties. If that property happens to be shape however, we will find a multimodal distribution: only then are we entitled to say something about an inhomogeneous distribution. And even within the class of apples, we could by other criteria find many different varieties. And so on ad infinitum. Indeed, it could rightly be alleged that the original category of *fruit* was not a representative sample if only apples, pears and plums were present.

The lesson of this little allegory is, that there is really no such thing as inhomogeneous data, only claims and statements made about that data which do not describe its content fairly and precisely. Unfortunately, claims which exceed the ambit of the observed data have become so common that they are now straining the credibility of the engineer in the public eye.

THE USE (AND ABUSE) OF DATA. The chief area where engineers are currently obliged to exceed the ambit of their data is in the estimation of the return period for rare events. Economy in design is very closely linked to accurate knowledge of the probability that a flood, or earthquake, or cyclone, of given magnitude will occur within the lifetime of the structure.

Now there is no shortage of statistics to describe the probability of rare events in the tail of a distribution: Weibull, Fréchet, Gumbel, etc. (cf.Tiago de Oliveira, 1975): but engineering structures suffer from one considerable difficulty - that they are extremely long-lived. This almost invariably means that an *extrapolation* outside the ambit of recorded data is needed.

Such extrapolations are underpinned by a lot of questionable assumptions of which one of the commonest is that there are no trends in time (i.e. the data which has been accumulated in the past is also true of the future. Even when trends in time have been allowed, as is done with traffic projections for road pavement design, the trend itself is based on past data which is unable to cope with changes arising from unanticipated events like the oil shock ).

Not uncommonly, the extrapolations are very gross. In Australia, a design flood with recurrence period of some hundreds of years will often be based on stream gauging and rainfall records covering a few tens of years. In all such cases, we are really quite unable to anticipate what are in effect *unforeseen* events.

The extent of this delusion can be seen in the statistics for dam failures. Table 3 compares data published by Vogel (1984) for dams worldwide with data published by Ingles (1984) for Australian dams. (The former discusses only 15m and higher dams, the latter 7m and higher).

Table 3. Causes of Failure in Dams (as % of failed dams)

| Cause | OV | FF PF | SF | CRF | COF | CAF | SEF | HF | Unknown |
|---|---|---|---|---|---|---|---|---|---|
| World wide (Vogel, n=309) | 35.9 | 33.7 | 9.1 | 2.9 | 1.9 | 1.3 | nil | 1.6 | 13.6 |
| Australia (Ingles, n=33) | 21.2 | 42.4 | 18.2 | 3.1 | 15.1 | nil | nil | nil | nil |

OV = Overtopping, FF = Foundation failure, PF = Piping failure, SF = Slope instability, CRF = Cracking failure, COF = Construction failure (in Ingles' data, this includes severe seepage and spillway erosion), CAF = Calculation failure, SEF = Seismic failure, HF = Hostile action failure.

It is apparent that overtopping is at least the second, and probably most, prevalent form of dam failure. Dam failures, moreover, are not uncommon. An incidence of between 0.2 and 0.3 % per annum is reported (Tavares and Serafim, 1983; Ingles, 1984). But overtopping is surely not to be expected, if a flood return period has been correctly calculated ?

It is, of course, not wholly fair to suggest some inadequacy in the extreme value theory - which has been in use only a few years - on the basis of field data which has been accumulated over a much longer period. Nevertheless, only many years of future observation will confirm whether or not it (theoretically derived rare event prediction) will agree reasonably well with actuality.

Until that time, which may well be as much as 100 years away, it would seem wise to cover the probabilistic estimates by a factor of safety of, say, 2.

In many respects, it is a grave disservice to public relations if engineers talk about the "500-year flood" or the "100-year hurricane" etc., because this creates a sense of security which may prove to be quite unjustified, and will certainly provide no consolation to those caught up in the event when finally it arrives. In short, we have no proof that we have solved the problem of data extrapolation into distribution tails, so surely it is better to change the emphasis and speak of risk levels at or near the limits of our data field ?

However desirable it may be to look at actual events rather than unrealized (probable ?) ones, because failures are often much less publicised than success (in full technical detail) due mostly to lengthy legal proceedings, the study of failures is much hindered by lack of record.

It is fortunately true that good technical records exist within the class of disaster, as previously defined, because these have generally been subject to Commissions of Enquiry. Thus for example, the findings of Royal Commissions Select Committees and Boards of Enquiry into Road, Rail and Mining Disasters in Australia since 1858 show 53 % directly attributed to human error (some are described as "gross negligence") and a further 20 % to possible human errors (Ingles, 1986). Allowing rail collisions as inevitably human error sourced, the Macquarie Book of Events (Fraser & Weldon, 1983) shows 18 out of 32 (56 %) of rail disasters in Australia between 1857 and 1977 being due to human error. (Three cases of possible human error and five unsourced are not included in the above. The fatality rate over 120 years of railway accidents in Australia is approximately $1 \times 10^{-6}$ per person per annum).

It is full records of collapses and failures which are lacking. Obviously they will be much more frequent than disasters. And it has been suggested quite rightly that it would be even better still if we had records of all occasions where failure or collapse has been *averted* by timely action.

So there are substantial gaps in the records which we need if we are to be able to make data-based as opposed to theory-based predictions, and to direct meaningful efforts towards risk reduction.

Of course, not all the available records are written or historical: there is also at times a useful geological record. I would like to conclude by citing a recent case of my own which exemplifies many of the various points that have been discussed above.

A valuable subdivision in the outer suburbs of a developing city was under consideration. Substantial parts of the city were known to suffer from land instability (landslip); building being prohibited in some areas because of it.

At the subdivision in question one substantial slip was apparent, but the geologic and geomorphic evidence indicated an age of 10,000 years or more. No instability of more recent date than this could be seen, despite the clearing of the slopes (deforestation is a destabilisation factor of major effect for landslip-prone areas) about 100 years ago. Should building (of private homes) proceed in this subdivision ?

Holding over, for the moment, the soil test data we have a very interesting situation: the actual evidence is for a risk of slip of $1 \times 10^{-4}$ or less (per annum basis). This is at the threshhold of acceptability, and would be just marginally acceptable by public opinion and by comparison with the performance of other engineering structures (see Ingles, 1983). It is quite unacceptable legally, if the $10^{-6}$ threshhold quoted earlier was applied. And if we look at it from the point of view of return periods, it is very acceptable indeed, for what structure is designed on the basis of a 10,000 year return event ?

So what should be the engineer's decision at this site ? As an information bonus, it might be added that the geomorphology suggested that the ancient slip was the result of seismic activity, and that the present risk rating for this area is Modified Mercalli IV with a 10 % chance of being exceeded in 50 years. (This is a very low risk seismicity).

For those still undecided, it can now be added that soil testing yielded a cohesion value in the range 10 - 40 kPa, and a friction angle in the range of 29° - 33°; whereas the major area to be subdivided had slopes of 8° or less. A shallow surface creep was evident on slopes of 15° or more, but these were not recommended for subdivision.

This case illustrates that the interests of client, of general public, and the engineer himself, can be widely different. The client may be a risk-taker but the engineer is not (if he wishes to stay in practice !). The public may stand somewhere in between or at either extreme according to circumstances. A dispassionate view of the public interest can be difficult to achieve without thorough, understandable communication at all levels.

CONCLUSION

A case has been argued that technical advances in the engineering field due to the shedding of the old deterministic approach to data, although excellent in themselves, require more attention to communications especially at a client level. There is, moreover, an urgent need to address philosophical questions and matters of definition before these advances can be fully mobilised for day to day use.

Since theoretical prediction of very rare events cannot be tested against real data, clients should be made aware of the best estimates of risk that can be made within the data field, not merely those beyond it. It is not uncommon that clients, given the choice of risks and of costs reckoned as carefully as possible, choose a lower cost - higher risk option. That is their prerogative provided the risks are not excessive.

There is an urgent need for the standardization of terminology in failures, and for the keeping and dissemination of records, not only for failure events, but also for those events where timely action has averted failure. At present the latter go largely unrecorded. It is suggested that monitoring systems are an essential part in all large engineering works, and their wider use may well provide some of the records which are desirable. Neither the monitor systems nor their reliability are sufficiently researched at the present time.

REFERENCES

Abraham C. and Thedié J. (1960). "The Price of a Human Life in Economic Decisions", Revue Francais de Recherche Operationelle, 157 -168.

Bickel P.J. (1978). "Robustness Considerations Enter New Fields", Proc. Fourth Australian Statistical Conference, Canberra, July.

Blockley D.I. (1980). The Nature of Structural Design and Safety, Ellis Horwood Chichester, UK.

Brewer K.R.W. (1978). "A Class of Robust Sampling Designs for Use in Large Scale Surveys", Proc. Fourth Australian Statistical Conference, Canberra.

CIRIA (Construction Industry Research and Information Association) ( 1977 ). "Rationalisation of Safety and Serviceability Factors in Structural Codes", Report 63, London, UK.

Fraser B. and Weldon K. (1983). The Macquarie Book of Events, Griffin Press, S.A., Australia.

Heathcote R.L. and Thom B.G. (1979). Natural Hazards in Australia, Australian Academy of Sciences, Canberra, Australia.

Huffmann J. (1986). Government Liability and Disaster Mitigation, University Press of America Inc., US.

Ingles O.G. (1983). "Measurements of Risk and Rationality in Civil Engineering" In G. Augusti, A. Borri and G. Vannuchi (Eds.), Proceedings of ICASP 4,

Pitagora Editrice, Bologna, I, 357-373.
Ingles O.G. (1984). "A Short Study of Dam Failures in Australia, 1857 - 1983", Civil Engineering Systems, 1, 190-194.
Ingles O.G. (1985). Human Error and its Role in the Philosophy of Engineering, Thesis, School of History and Philosophy of Science, University of N.S.W. Australia.
Ingles O.G. (1986)."Where Should we look for Error Control", In A.S. Nowak(Ed) Proceedings of NSF Workshop on Modeling Human Error in Structural Design & Construction, ASCE Construction Division, New York, US, pp. 13-21.
Jackson R.M. and Powell J.L. (1982). Professional Negligence, Sweet & Maxwell, London, UK.
Lee I.K, White W. and Ingles O.G. (1983). Geotechnical Engineering, Pitman Books Ltd., London, UK.
Lumb P. (1968). "Statistical Aspects of Field Tests", In Proceedings of Fourth Conference Australian Road Research Board, Melbourne, Aust., pp. 1761-1770.
Matousek M. and Schneider J. (1976). Untersuchungen zur Struktur des Sicherheitproblems bei Bauwerken, ETH Zürich, Bericht Nr. 69.
McDermott I. (1985). Australian Disaster Research Directory, 2nd Edn., Aust. Counter Disaster College, Mount Macedon, Australia.
McNeil D.R. (1978). "An Embarrassing Experience with a 249 cm Man", Proc. 4th Australian Statistical Conference, Canberra, July.
Melchers R.E. and Harrington M.V. (1982). "Human Error in Simple Design Tasks" Dept. of Civil Engineering, Monash University, Aust., Research Report 3.
Meyerhof G.G. (1982). "Limit States Design in Geotechnical Engineering", in Structural Safety, 1, 67-71.
Nowak A.S. (1986). (Ed.) Proceedings of NSF Workshop on Modeling Human Error in Structural Design and Construction, ASCE Construction Division, New York US.
Rüsch H. (1979). "Kritische Gedanken zu Grundfragen der Sicherheitstheorie" , in Festschrift, Carl Cordina gewidmet, Johannes Eibl, München, Germany.
Senneck C.R. (1973). "Over 3-day Absences and Safety", Applied Ergonomics,6(3) 147-153.
Shaw D.E. and D'Appolonia E. (1977). "Probabilistic Methods in Engineering Decisions", In D. A-Grivas (Ed.) Proceedings of NSF Workshop on Probability Theory and Reliability Analysis in Geotechnical Engineering, Rensselaer Polytechnic Institute, Troy, US, pp. 180-190.
Sutter J.H. and Hecht M.L. (1974). Landslide and Subsidence Liability, Regents of the University of California, Berkeley, US.
Tavares L.V. and Serafim J.L. (1983). "Probabilistic Study on Failure of Large Dams", Journal of Geotechnical Engineering, ASCE, 109(11), 1483-1486.
Tiego de Oliveira J. (1975). "Statistical Decision for Extremes", Trabajos de Estadistica y de Investigacion Operativa, XXVI, 433-471.
Tremain v. Pike & Anor. (1969). All England Law Reports, 3, 1303.
Vandepitte D. (1983). "The Collapse of the Bridge at Pulle", Ghent University, Belgium.
Vines R. (1986). "Is Weather Random ?", Address to Australian Counter Disaster College, Hazard Analysis Workshop, Mount Macedon, 19th November.
Vogel A. (1984). "Failures of Masonry and Concrete Dams in Europe", In "Safety of Dams", J. Laginha Serafim (Ed.), A.A.Balkema, Rotterdam, Netherlands , pp. 45-54.
Wigan M.R. (1982). "Accident Valuation: Indexation Options", In Proceedings of 11th Conference Australian Road Research Board, 11(5), 250-271.

# WHAT SHOULD WE DO WITH STRUCTURAL RELIABILITIES

Emilio Rosenblueth*
*Instituto de Ingeniería, Universidad Nacional Autónoma de México, Ciudad Universitaria, México 04510 D F.
*Fundación Javier Barros Sierra, Carretera al Ajusco 203, México 14000 D F.

## ABSTRACT

We shall soon be able to compute some structural reliabilities accurately and efficiently. In a few instances socially acceptable risk sets a lower limit. In others we shall have to compute the optimum reliability and hence to determine the social cost of nonmonetary values. Ethical principles on which this task should be based are discussed. They are applied to assessing the value of human lives using results of Delphi exercises. Application to optimize earthquake resistant design in Mexico City discloses a serious discrepancy with perceived social impact and lack of relation to socially acceptable risk, thus stressing the need for research into social attitudes toward risk.

## INTRODUCTION

The time approaches when we shall be able to compute structural reliabilities accurately and efficiently for some structures. The time is therefore ripe for asking what we do with the reliabilities. Only in extreme cases have we apparently objective bases for deciding that a proposed design be modified to make it more conservative. Saying that we should always choose the optimum reliability or maximize the utility is stating a truism. What becomes a fascinating challenge is the task of quantifying the optimum. Questions that demand an answer in the process are: what we understand by utility, whose utility is of concern, how we discount utility with time, and the values of human lives and of other intangibles, especially social impact. Search for these answers takes us into distant territories, from philosophy and psychology to decision making and the hard sciences. We need a formal, quantitative treatment of these subjects as applied to reliability optimization.

For some social benefits, such as ordinary recreation, the direct recipients pay the entire cost. These benefits are easy to translate into monetary value. Higher forms of culture are generally subsidized, though, which complicates their evaluation. This is particularly true of the preservation of historical objects, as the present generation pays for its own benefit and for that of future generations. Old is beautiful. It will become more so. Yet this very fact raises questions whose surface we have not begun scratching: How much should the present generation pay? How do we set priorities? To what extent is it desirable to affect historic buildings upgrading their earthquake resistance? Even the objectives remain undefined (Luft, 1985).

## THE MEANING OF UTILITY

We will take *utility* to be a logical scalar measure of the intensity of preference. We will adopt the axiom of von Neumann and Morgenstern (1943) that makes utility synonymous with expected utility. Of the various meanings that can be assigned to the term *preference* we choose the normative one: what we ought morally to prefer. Hence we must always choose the option with highest utility; we must always optimize.

We will distinguish between preference in terms of present desires and (hypothetical) preference in terms of happiness, after having experienced all possible outcomes of the potential decisions. The former is often based on ignorance and tainted by passion. The latter would coincide with what we would prefer had we perfect knowledge about our reactions to those outcomes. We can approach this ideal through our serene examination of our preferences with the aid of expert opinions in several disciplines. Being a bit cryptic we may say that we must discriminate between prior and preposterior preferences.

As I will explain later, I choose preposterior preferences as basis for decision making. Hence I will take *utility* in its sense of a logical scalar measure of the intensity of happiness and will call it *felicity*. However, the intensities of our prior preferences have a decisive bearing on our felicity. For one thing there are time limitations, the value of intuition, the limitations of reason, the cost of exhaustive analysis, and the fallibility of experts. Then, even though decision making and implementation are means toward the end of achieving the results of decisions, all means have extrinsic as well as intrinsic values, so that all means are ends in themselves (Ackoff, 1975); indeed in some contexts the manner of making and that of implementing decisions are more important than the results of the decisions. This stand is reinforced by the role that aesthetics should play in decision making and our inability to quantify aesthetic values (Ackoff, 1975). Also, we should not underestimate the pleasure of deciding for ourselves rather than having others decide for us, nor the virtue that a society learn, through participation, to decide optimally so that it evolve and cope with rapid changes in the environment and in society's own values as molded by experience. The evolution of engineering practice and building codes would benefit from a conscious increase in duly informed participation of the profession and the lay public.

WHOSE UTILITY

As with the acceptance of a scientific theory we can accept an ethical system if it pleases us, is self-consistent, and does not contradict our convictions. We cannot prove its veracity (Churchman, 1961; Ferrater-Mora and Cohn, 1983). On these bases I postulate felicity as the form of utility to maximize. Let us infer the implications of this postulate when our concern is with members of a group -- a community.

We shall need interpersonal comparisons of felicity. This has led some decisions theorists to discard all utilitarianism.. Yet similarities are more striking than differences among humans. Introspection and observation and the study of aesthetics, psychology, sociology, history, and biology (Ferrater-Mora and Cohn, 1983) give much insight. Then there are questionaires and surveys. Above all there is participation, at least of representative members of the community, in decision making, and our identifying ourselves with them through "compassion" (Rousseau, 1762), "extended sympathy" (Arrow, 1977), or acting their roles (Gordon Pask, personal communication).

Following Harsanyi (1978) we can show that if our concern is with individual felicities, we should maximize some positive linear combination of the felicities of all members of society. In turn the felicity of each is a function, among other factors, of the perception the member has of her own felicity and of those of others and of how just or unjust she thinks our decisions have been. For reasons of symmetry and of perceived justice we should give equal weights to the felicities of all the members. As a first extension of this result, if not all are full members, the weights assigned should be proportional to the degree in which each individual belongs to the community, in the sense of fuzzy sets. Secondly we introduce time by considering every infinitesimal segment of a subject's life as one subject. The quantity to maximize is then the time integral of the weighted sum of individual felicities per unit time. Finally there are reasons for discounting these quantities as in monetary transactions. This is because our uncertainty about the effects of our decisions on felicities decreases with time; we are not sure of the very existence of the community in the distant future; less so of the needs and scales of values of its members. And in a sense the extent to which someone belongs to the group decreases with time. Thus the quantity we should maximize is the utility

$$U = E\int_0^\infty \Sigma_i \beta_i f_i \, dt \qquad (1)$$

where E· denotes expectation quantified by the decision maker, subscripts refer to the ith individual, the sum extends over all full and partial members of the community, $\beta_i = \beta_i(t)$ is of the form $\beta_i(0)e^{-\gamma t}$ with $\gamma$ = discount rate, f = f(t) is felicity per unit time, and t is time counted from the instant of decision making. One may often defend assigning $\gamma$ a value close to that used in monetary operations after correcting for inflation, $\gamma \cong 0.05$/yr in recent decades. Still, intergeneration trade-offs should not be questions to be brushed aside so easily as by adopting a certain yearly discount rate (Burke, 1986), but let us not delve into the matter.

When all members of society are full members, eq 1 can be written as

$$U = \Sigma_i U_i \qquad (2)$$

where

$$U_i = E\int_0^\infty f_i e^{-\gamma t} \, dt \qquad (3)$$

is the expected present value of i's utility in the sense of felicity.

Considerations of perceived justice and their mellowing of rigid, casuistic utilitarianism of the action can be subsumed in principles of utilitarianism of the rule, which responds to the assumption "If everyone in my circumstances did as I do" (Harsanyi, 1978).

The bland brand of utilitarianism, lightened and enlightened, that I advocate is, in broad lines, consistent with the Golden Rule, intuitionism, contractualism, and other schools of ethics (see Ferrater-Mora and Cohn, 1983).

The ethics advocated is relativistic: good is good relative to a group. It becomes absolute only when eq 1 comprises the felicities of all sentient beings with equal weights. We might be tempted to elect the absolute ethics as the only valid one. Several facts conspire against this stand. First, a tendency prevails among most people to favor their own groups, the more so the smaller the groups, be they determined by biological, working, sporting, political, or cultural affinity. Only of quite mature persons can an attitude consistent with absolute ethics be expected. Second, our uncertainties are great concerning the effects of our decisions on the felicity of distant living beings. Finally we are often implicitly or explicitly committed with specific groups; again for reasons of perceived justice, but also of our effectiveness in these and future occasions, we should ordinarily fulfill our commitments. Divided loyalty, between the groups we must and those we would like to serve, is a normal state of affairs.

Divided loyalty pervades everyday practice. We are committed to serve society by serving our clients, but our clients' interests often differ much from those of society. The optimum base shear coefficient in the design of a building on a seismic area can be less than half from the viewpoint of an investor intending an early sale than from society's viewpoint. This is illustrated in Fig. 1, where a negative utility implies it is undesirable to erect the building. The investment is desirable for our client only if the base shear coefficient or some other design parameter lies between A and B. For society these limits are $A_s$ and $B_s$. The purpose of a building code is to favor the interests of society bringing the design value closer to society's optimum. If the engineer, out of loyalty to society, whether with or without a code limitation goes as far to the right as her client tolerates, she will soon find herself out of clients through whom to serve society. The same will happen if in trying to increase her income to favor her family she produces quick, careless designs. Or she can then find her license revoked, as when she goes overboard in meeting her clients' wishes.

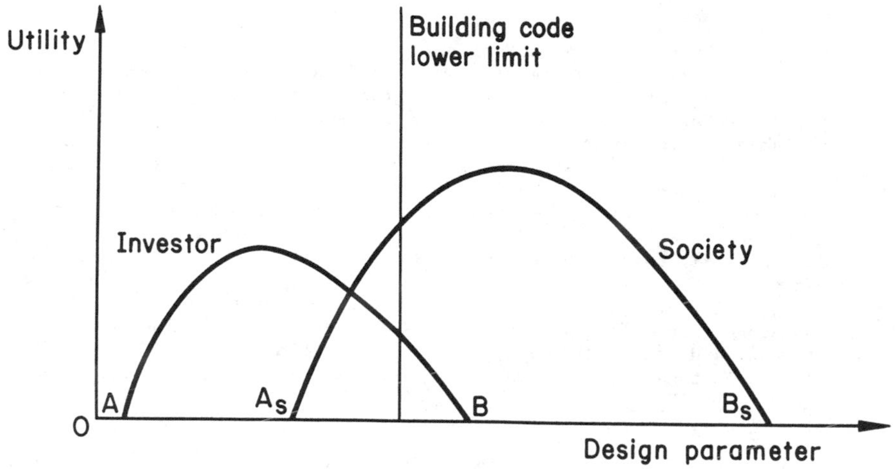


Fig 1. Utility for investor and utility for society

ACCEPTABLE RISK

There is apparently a value of the yearly probability that a person die when exposed to a given set of circumstances, beyond which the risk is unacceptable, or the disutility increases pronouncedly. Starr (1969) quotes $10^{-6}$ per year of involuntary exposure. If this were rigorously so, then with no need of formal calculations we could usually anticipate that the optimal risk would not significantly exceed this value. If rough calculations indicated that it would lie slightly below, it would be satisfactory to design for a value of say $10^{-7}$. Yet the precise meaning of acceptable in terms of utility is not clear.

MONETARY OPTIMIZATION

Reliability optimization often produces designs that differ markedly from design for a fixed reliability. Suppose that in the range of interest we can take utility to be a linear function of money and that there is a single limit state. Thus the optimum of some design parameter x, such as central safety factor, will minimize C + D where C = initial cost and D = expected present value of losses due to failure.

Consider first a structure that is to resist a single application of a static load. Suppose that the load and the resistance are normally distributed with respective coefficients of variation 0.2 and 0.1, that $C = C_0 + cx$ where $C_0$ and c are constants, and that $D = (100 + x)cP$. We find the optimum failure probability $P = 3.22 \times 10^{-3}$, with $x = 2.264$. If we double the coefficients of variation and retain P we must raise x to 6.450. Yet the optimum x is 4.190, with P more than nine-fold the former value.

Suppose now we are to design a structure to resist earthquakes idealized as a Poisson process. Let $\lambda$ = exceedance rate of the design spectral acceleration a, $\lambda \propto a^{-2}$, $C = C_0 + ca^{1.7}$, L = expected loss at the time of failure, L independent of a. Design for a constant failure rate gives $a \propto \lambda^{-1/2}$ while in optimum design $a \propto \lambda^{1/3.7}$. Doubling $\lambda$ requires increasing a by 41% if we keep the failure rate constant, but by only 21% if we design optimally.

The foregoing examples oversimplify practical conditions (see Newmark and Rosenblueth, 1971; Rosenblueth, 1976, 1979, 1987) but serve to illustrate differences between both criteria.

INDIVIDUAL UTILITY AS A FUNCTION OF MONEY

Here we are interested in the average relations between money and utility in the sense of felicity, among groups of individuals rather than for specific persons. As an approximation we will be content with examining the relation between expected present values of the quantities of interest and we will assume that the subjects are rational and have perfect knowledge. We will examine the restrictions that U(S) must then satisfy, where U and S are expected present values of utility and of wealth and income, respectively.

Let $S_o$ denote the value of S required for survival and let U = 0 correspond to a dead person. Obviously $U(S) = 0$ if $S < S_o$, $U'(S) > 0$ if $S \geq S_o$, where the prime denotes derivative with respect to S. Also, $U''(S) < 0$ if $S \geq S_o$, for if there were two or more members of a community with $U'' > 0$ they would bet among themselves until there was at most one individual having a convex utility curve. From the condition that risk aversion, as measured by $-U''/U'$, be nonincreasing with S (Keeney and Raiffa, 1976) we infer that $U''^2(S) < U'(S)U'''(S)$ if $S \geq S_o$ (Rosenblueth, Bustamante, and Morales, 1984). Finally, from the finiteness of human nature,

$$\lim_{S\to\infty} U(S) = U_m < \infty.$$

$U_o = U(S_o)$ is a measure of the happiness of being alive, independently of wealth and income. Introspection leaves no doubt as to the reality of the joy of living and of engaging in activities that do not involve monetary expenditure or practically none, such as human company, contemplation of nature, and experience of art and discovery. Still, $U_o$ can be negative, as it is in many individuals deprived of dignity, liberty, or good health. They would rather be dead than alive but would prefer not to die. In Schelling's (1968) words, "... a life is more than a living."

There is, besides, clearly and necessarily a significant disutility associated with experiencing death. We will call the it *personal impact* and denote it by $I_o$. We use $I_o$ to denote the net personal impact, after discounting the expected present value of the impact should the person not die as a consequence of the decision being analyzed, that is, if the person should die what we will call a natural death.

In addition to the constraints enunciated earlier, we must have $U_o + I_o > 0$, and the condition that U(S) not be convex imposes the limitation $U' < (U_o + I_o)/S_o$ (Fig. 2).

A rich family of utility curves that satisfies all requirements is

$$\begin{aligned} U(S) &= 0 \text{ if } S < S_o \\ &= U_o + (U_m - U_o)(1 - \alpha_1 e^{-\delta_1 s} - \alpha_2 e^{-\delta_2 s}) \end{aligned} \qquad (4)$$

where $s = S/S_o - 1$ and the $\alpha$s and $\delta$s are positive parameters such that $\delta_1 \neq \delta_2$, $\alpha_1 + \alpha_2 = 1$, and $\alpha_1\delta_1 + \alpha_2\delta_2 < (U_o + I_o)/(U_m - U_o)$.

A Delphi exercise in Mexico City (Rosenblueth, Bustamante, and Morales, 1984) gave $U_o \cong 0.50U$ on the average and allowed expressing $U_m$ as a function of age and socioeconomic group.

A reassessment of $I_o$ suggests $I_o \cong U_o$ on the average after subtracting the expected present value of the impact due to natural death.

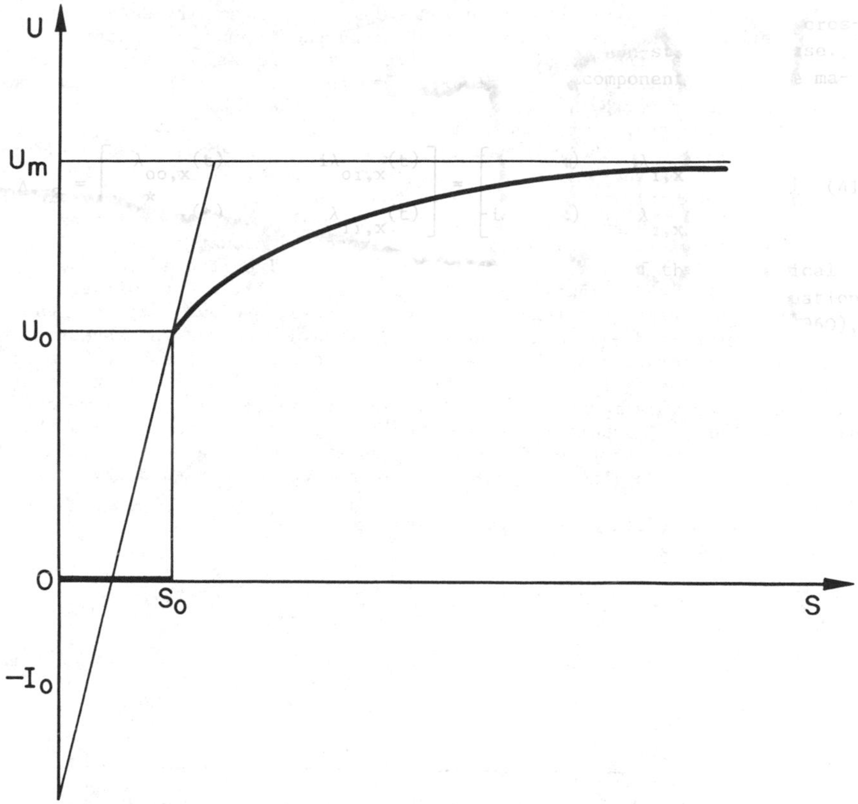


Fig. 2. Typical utility curves

VALUE OF HUMAN LIVES

To optimize the reliability we must often quantify the value that a human life has for society. We begin with the amount that a person should be willing to pay to reduce by some amount an originally small risk of losing her life. In this range we take U(S) to be linear. Then the person will be indifferent between a) accepting the full risk, and b) reducing it by $\Delta P$ through payment of an amount $\Delta S = (U + I_o)\Delta P/U'$. Thus she values her life at

$$H = (U + I_o)/U' \tag{5}$$

Although we do not know the $\alpha$s and $\delta$s we can find a lower bound to H by replacing the second part of eq 4 with

$$U(S) = U_o + (U_m - U_o)(1 - e^{-\delta s}) \text{ if } S \geq S_o \tag{6}$$

where $\delta$ is such as to minimize H. We find $H > (3e^{2S} - 1)/2$ if $S \leq 1.429S_o$ and $H > 7.08(S - S_o)$ if $S \geq 1.429S_o$.

In what follows we will consider exclusively communities having only full members. The value of the ith person's life to a community depends on how the cost of reducing the risk is distributed among the community members. We will take this cost as the sum of what individual members are willing to contribute. Hence, to a community of N members the ith life is worth $H_i = \Sigma_j H_{ij}$ and an anonymous life is worth $H = (1/N)\Sigma_i\Sigma_j H_{ij}$, where the sums extend from 1 to N and $H_{ij}$ is the value that j assigns to i's life.

Utilitarianism of the rule dictates that survivors should be willing to pay to reduce the risk that i's U and $I_o$ be lost. Indeed, everyone would expect the rest of the commuinity to defray the cost of reducing the danger of his losing his life should he abstain from doing so himself, say out of ignorance of the risk he was running. An obvious lower limit to the amount that on this ground j should assign to i's life is $(1/N)(U_{oi} + I_o^j)U_j^!$. Then there are the impact to the victim's kin and friends, $I_c^i$, the social impact $I_s^i$, and the funeral costs $F^i$, after reducing these quantities by their expected present values should the victim eventually die a natural death. We should also add the expected present value of the production $Z_i$ that i would have contributed to society, minus the monetary equivalent $Y_i$ of the lowering in the survivors' quality of life for there being one more member in society, had the victim lived. If we believe that the current population-growth policy is optimum, we can find the yearly value of this monetary equivalent by equating to zero the value of an unconceived child's life, for it is then a second-order quantity; then we can compute $Y_i$.

Averaging over all of society we find

$$H = \frac{1}{N}\Sigma_i\left[\frac{U_i + I_o^i + I_c^i + I_s^i}{U_i^!} + \frac{1}{N}(U_o^i + I_o^i)\Sigma_j\frac{1}{U_j^!} + F_i + Z_i - Y_i\right] \tag{7}$$

The Delphi exercise referred to gave $I_c \cong I_o/2$ and $I_s \cong 3I_o$ on the average.

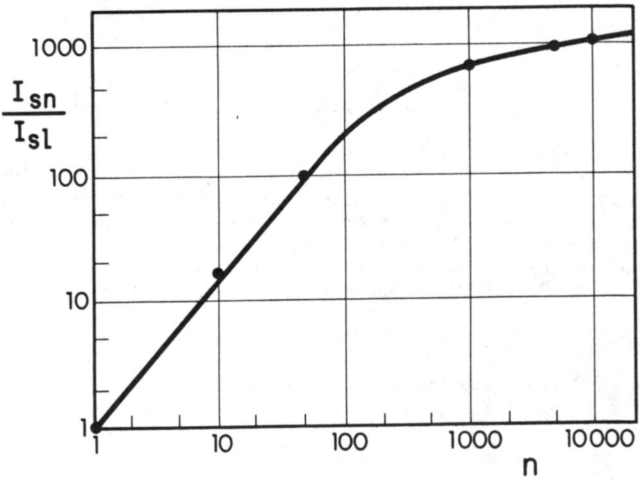


Fig. 3. Social impact in terms of number of victims

When a single event can cause the death of n anonymous persons, $n << N$, all components in eq 7 are proportional to n except $I_s$. Keeney (1980) has postulated an attractive aprioristic model. However, results of our Delphi exercise do not confirm it. They are shown in Fig. 3 together with the curve

$$I_{sn}/I_{s1} = n^{1.173} \quad \text{if } n \leq 80$$
$$= 80^{1.173} \exp\left(\frac{\ell}{1+0.37\ell}\right) \quad \text{if } n \geq 80 \qquad (8)$$

which fits them nicely. Here $I_{sn}$ = social impact due to n deaths and $\ell = 1.173 \ln(n/80)$. Eq 8 is such that $I_{sn}/I_{s1} \geq n$ if and only if $n < 604$.

EARTHQUAKE RESISTANT DESIGN ON MEXICO CITY'S SOFT GROUND

The Michoacán earthquake of 85.9.19 caused, in Mexico City, a number of victims estimated at from less than 5 000 to over 20 000. For present purposes we will take this number as 10 000. Those injured numbered perhaps three times more. Economic loss has been estimated as between $2 \times 10^9$ and $2 \times 10^{10}$ US dollars depending on whether one neglects or includes the value of lost jobs and reduction in industrial production and in the tourist trade (Müchinger Re, 1986). Of the order of 200 000 lost their homes, though the majority found shelter with relatives. I will take the total economic loss plus the equivalent of all disutilities except deaths and injuries as $\$8 \times 10^9$.

As in Whitman et al (1975) I will assume that the mean cost of an injury is 1/30 of the cost of an individual life. Using economic and actuarial data for Mexico together with eqs 6-8 we find $H > \$120\,000 + I_{sn}/n$, $I_{s1} > \$120\,000$. According to eq 8, for n = 10 000 we get $I_{sn} = 1064 I_{s1}$. Consequently the total loss to society was not smaller than $\$8 \times 10^9 + (10^4 + 1064)1.2 \times 10^5 \times 1.1 = \$9.46 \times 10^9$. However, had the earthquake occurred at a less favorable time of day than when it took place (7:20), the number of victims would have been much greater. I will take its expectation as 40 000. Then we find that the expected loss for an earthquake like that of 85.9.19 but occurring at a random time of day is greater than $\$1.34 \times 10^{10}$ but probably not much greater. Let us take it equal to $\$1.5 \times 10^{10}$. (This does not include the cost of damage to public utilities.) Depending on whether we assume n = 10 000 or 40 000, the computed monetary value of the social impact is 1.5% or 1.2% of the total loss to society. Yet the psychological effect was profound on everyone. I venture to say that these values underestimate the social impact by a factor of perhaps a few hundred.

The vast majority of the losses took place in an area where the prevailing ground period is close to 2 s and which is inhabited by some $5 \times 10^6$ people. It is desired to find the optimal base shear coefficient for design in this section of the city.

A month after the earthquake a set of Emergency Regulations was issued superseding the earthquake resistant provisions of the 1976 Building Code. The regulations raised the base shear coefficient 67% in the area of interest. They also lowered several strength reduction coefficient and introduced other clauses. The net increase in resistance to lateral was about 125% for most types of structures relative to the resistance achieved with code provisions in effect since 1957, and somewhat more for the most vulnerable ones. A new code has been proposed. At the time of submitting this paper the proposal is being examined by professional societies. The final version will be as much a function of detailed analysis as of the societies' feedback.

I estimate the cost of all the buildings in the area at $\$10^{11}$. On the basis of some trial designs the cost of a new building will vary approximately as $0.95 + 0.05z^{1.73}$ times the cost it would have if designed according to pre-1985 Emergency Regulations with z = 1, where z is proportional to its design lateral force resistance (concerning the 1.73 exponent see Rosenblueth, 1986).

It is important to take into account the non-Poisson nature of Mexican subduction earthquakes. The arrivals in Mexico City of earthquakes having other sources can be approximated as Poisson. Using the approach in Rosenblueth and Ordaz (1986) the probability distribution of times to exceedance of various values of z have been computed in a crude, preliminary manner. For new construction these distributions depend on the time of erection. It is assumed that during the next ten years, when the 1987 Building Code will be changed unless a major earthquake occurs earlier, the construction rate is a yearly constant 1% of the total amount in existence today. The computed smoothed spectral ordinates, the ratio of actual ordinates to the smoothed spectral values, and the ratio of actual to nominal lateral force resistances are assigned independent lognormal distributions with respective standard deviations of the natural logarithms equal to 0.25, 0.15, and 0.40. It is assumed that 2% of the structures extant in 1985 collapsed or were demolished, 5% have been brought up to the Emergency Regulations standards, and the rest fit the probability distribution of lateral force resistances without truncation to account for their having withstood the 1985 event. This last assumption is intended to account for damage accumulation in the latter structures.

The optimum z is found to be 1.15. Now let $Q = \int_0^\infty [\bar{n}(t)/N(t)]e^{-\gamma t}\,dt$ = expected present value of individual risk, where $\bar{n}(t)$ = expected number of victims per unit time at time t. If the optimum z were adopted, $Q = 2.1 \times 10^{-2}$, as against $2 \times 10^{-5}$ that corresponds to the limit of acceptable risk, $10^{-6}$ per individual per year of exposure. At first sight one ought to adopt z = 1.15, inform the people that this is optimum for society, and hope that they accept it. One would thereby ignore that Q would be unacceptable. Even if new construction were absolutely invulnerable, one would not reduce Q below $1.8 \times 10^{-2}$. To bring Q down to $2 \times 10^{-5}$ would require retrofitting the most hazardous existing buildings in the area despite their not having been damaged or not severely so in 1985. If the entire zone under consideration were demolished and rebuilt with z = 2.25, Q would still be as high as $3.75 \times 10^{-5}$. Notice that if an absolute limit is set on Q it should apply as constraint not only in the entire zone with five million inhabitants but in every individual building as well.

The significance of Q is obscured by the fact that "acceptable risk" implies acceptable perceived risk, and it is unrealistic to assume that the lay public has any idea of the actual seismic risk.

The optimal z would be smaller than computed if measures were taken to insure better compliance with the code than in the past and/or better rescue operations were implemented after a disaster than in 1985.

Let $P_s$ denote the computed expected present value of social impact. At "optimum" (z = 1.15) it is found equal to a mere $\$4.1 \times 10^8$, as against the expected present value of all losses, which is $\$3.14 \times 10^{10}$. The discrepancy between the computed $P_s$ and the perceived social impact of the earthquake casualties should deserve a closer look. Notice that the economic value of the social impact caused by a single death is not strongly contingent on the analytical and Delphi studies used, considering Mexico's 1985 internal national product per capita (about $1700). the values ordinarily assigned to human life in first-world countries (less than $1000). and that $P_s$ for one life lost is taken as half of the social value of a human life. It is of the essence that this contradiction be solved. It is of the essence that we look in depth at social attitudes toward risk.

CONCLUSIONS

Rapid, accurate calculation of structural reliabilities is in the horizon. Rather than on arbitrarily fixed reliabilities, design will have to be based on socially acceptable risk and reliability optimization. The latter will require assessment of the social cost of nonmonetary values. Ethical principles on which to base the assessment have been discussed. A relativistic, softened utilitarianism has been proposed which pays heed to utilitarianism of the rule.

It is applied to quantify the social value of human lives.

The value per anonymous life lost is found to depend on the number of victims, on the expected present values of individual utilities, their derivatives with respect to the expected present value of income, personal impact, impact to kin and friends, social impact, funeral costs, and foregone production minus expenses and lowering in the quality of life of the rest of society. Results are applied to earthquake resistant design in Mexico City.

Apparently Delphi exercises seriously underestimate social impact. Of concern also is the lack of relation between social impact and socially acceptable risk. There is a clear need for in-depth studies of social attitudes toward risk.

ACKNOWLEDGMENTS

This work was partly supported by the Federal District Department. I am grateful to Mario Ordaz for his magnificent help in the preparation of the paper.

REFERENCES

Ackoff R.L. (1975). "Does Quality of Life Have to Be Quantified?", Systems and Management Annual, pp. 551-66.

Arrow K. (1977). "Extended Sympathy and the Possibility of Social Choice", The American Economic Reviews, 67, pp. 219-25.

Burke F.E. (1986). "Risk Management and Welfare Theory: Dilemmas in Pragmatism", Risk Abstracts, 4, 3, pp. 113-17.

Churchman C.W. (1961). Prediction and Optimal Decision: Philosophical Issues of a Science of Values, Prentice-Hall, Inc., New York, NY.

Ferrater-Mora J. and P. Cohn (1983). Etica Aplicada: del Aborto a la Violencia, Alianza Editorial, Madrid.

Harsanyi J. (1978). "Bayesian Decision Theory, Rule Utilitarianism, and Arrow's Impossibility Theorem", Justice and Economic Distribution, J. Arthur and W. H. Shaw, eds., Prentice-Hall, Inc., Englewood Cliffs, NJ.

Keeney R.L. (1980). "Evaluating Alternatives Involving Potential Fatalities", Operations Research, 28, 1, pp. 188-205.

Keeney R.L. and H. Raiffa (1976). Decisions with Multiple Objectives: Preferences and Value Trade-offs, John Wiley & Sons, New York, NY.

Luft R.W. (1985). "Preservation and Rehabilitation of Historic Buildings", Proc. Workshop on Reducing Seismic Hazard in Existing Buildings, Federal Emergency Management Agency, FEMA 91, Washington, DC, pp. 141-62.

Münchener Re (1986). "Terremoto de México '85", Münchener Rückversicherungs-Gesellschaft, Munich.

Newmark N.M. and E. Rosenblueth (1971). Fundamentals of Earthquake Engineering, Prentice-Hall, Inc., Englewood Cliffs, NJ.

Rosenblueth E. (1976). "Optimum Design for Infrequent Disturbances", Journal of Structural Division, ASCE, 102, ST9, pp. 1807-25.

Rosenblueth E. (1979). "Optimum Design to Resist Earthquakes", Journal of Engineering Mechanics Division, ASCE, 105, EM1, pp. 159-76.

Rosenblueth E. (1986). Discussion of "Economics of Seismic Design for New Buildings", by J.M. Ferritto, submitted for publication in Journal Structural Engineering.

Rosenblueth E., J.I. Bustamante, and J. Morales (1984). "Valor de la Vida Humana", Centro de Investigación Prospectiva, Fundación Javier Barros Sierra, A.C., Mexico.

Rosenblueth E. and M. Ordaz (1986). "Use of Seismic Data from Similar Regions", accepted for publication in Earthquake Engineering and Structural Dynamics.

Rousseau J.J. (1762). Le Contrat Social, Amsterdam.

Schelling T.C. (1979). "The Life You Save May be Your Own", Problems in Public Expenditure, S.B. Chase, ed, Brookings Institution, Washington, DC.

Starr C. (1969). "Societal Benefit Versus Technological Risk", Science, 165, pp. 1232-48.

von Neumann J. and A. Morgenstern (1943). Theory of Games and Economic Behavior, Princeton University Press, Princeton, NJ; 2nd ed, 1953.

Whitman R.V., J.M. Biggs, J.E. Brennan III, C.A. Cornell, R. de Neufville, and E.H. Vanmarcke (1975). "Seismic Design Decision Analysis", Journal of Structural Division, ASCE, 101, ST5, pp. 1067-84.

# DIRECTIONAL SIMULATION WITH APPLICATIONS TO OUTCROSSINGS OF GAUSSIAN PROCESSES

A.M. Hasofer*
*School of Mathematics, University of New South Wales,
P.O.Box 1, Kensington, N.S.W. 2033, AUSTRALIA

ABSTRACT

An exact method for calculating the reliability of structures with a class of Gaussian vector process physical variables is described. The two main ideas are: (1) representation of the processes with predetermined accuracy by random trigonometric polynomials. (2) Calculation of the structure reliability by the efficient "directional sampling" method. Results are exact and can be evaluated numerically on a Personal Computer with reasonable accuracy. The method works best for those values of the parameters for which the approximate methods presently in use are the least reliable. It thus provides a valuable check on their validity.

## 1. INTRODUCTION

In recent years there has been much progress made in the analysis of structure reliability under random loads. The static case, when loads and resistances are taken to be time invariant, can now be treated with good accuracy. For a recent review, see Ditlevsen and Bjerager (1986). However, most loads and resistances fluctuate with time, and their interaction may affect the reliability of the structure in a significant way.

The modelling of the physical variables effecting the reliability of a structure as a vector-valued stochastic process was proposed as early as 1977 by Veneziano et al (1977). Significant further work is contained in papers by Ditlevsen (1983), Lindgren (1984) and Hohenbichler and Rackwitz (1986), as well as in the references quoted therein.

The basic difficulty in dealing with the vector-process model as compared with the static model lies in the fact that while in the static case only a finite number of random variables appears in the model, in the case of vector processes there is a non-denumerable infinity of random variables exhibiting a complex pattern of dependence. In the papers quoted above, the difficulty has been circumvented by focussing the attention on the outcrossing rate of the vector process from the safe domain. The mean outcrossing rate can be calculated comparatively easily. If in addition it is assumed that successive outcrossings are approximately Poisson distributed, the time-dependent reliability of the structure can be calculated. The disadvantage of this method is that the error committed cannot be ascertained easily. Upper bounds for the reliability are available, but no easily calculated lower bounds.

In this paper, an exact method for calculating the reliability of some structures with a class of vector process physical variables will be presented. It is based on two main ideas:

(1) Representation of the vector process with predetermined accuracy by random trigonometric polynomials.

(2) Calculation of the structure reliability by an efficient Monte Carlo method using the recently introduced method of "directional sampling".

The method can be implemented on a personal computer and works best for those values of the process parameters for which the accuracy of the outcrossings method is the most doubtful. Thus it complements the outcrossings method and in the range of overlap can provide a precise check on its accuracy. For a further treatment of the scalar case, see Hasofer (1982), Hasofer (1987) and Hasofer and Ghahremen (1985). For an exposition of directional sampling see Bjerager (1987) and the references quoted therein.

## 2. THE SCALAR CASE

Before embarking on the presentation of the general case, the scalar case will be presented.

Let $X(t)$ be a Gaussian, zero-mean, stationary stochastic process, that can be thought of as a random load, and let the safe region be $X(t)\leq u$, and the time span of interest be $(0,T)$. Then the reliability of the structure is given by

$$P(\max_{0\leq t\leq T} X(t)\leq u) \quad . \tag{1}$$

Let $R(t) = E[X(\tau)X(\tau+t)]$ be the covariance function of $X(t)$, and let $\lambda_0 = R(0)$, $\lambda_2 = R''(0)$. Then the upcrossing rate at level $u$, $\nu_u$, is given by Rice's formula

$$\nu_u = \frac{1}{2\pi}\sqrt{\frac{\lambda_2}{\lambda_0}}\, e^{-\frac{1}{2}\cdot\frac{u^2}{\lambda_0}} \tag{2}$$

To calculate the reliability, one makes two crucial assumptions:

(1) Prob.$\{X(0)>u\}$ is negligible.

(2) The point process of upcrossings is approximately Poisson with intensity $\nu_u$.

The reliability of the structure is then the same as the probability of no upcrossings, namely $\exp(-\nu_u T)$.

There are, among others, two important situations where one or both of the above two assumptions break down:

(a) Processes with a narrow band spectrum. For then the sample functions of $X(t)$ take the form of a modulated wave, and upcrossings tend to be "bunched" or "clumped". The Poisson assumption is then unrealistic.

Attempts have been made to overcome the problem by replacing $X(t)$ in that case by its envelope. But then it turns out that for high levels $u$ some of the envelope crossings are "empty" i.e. do not contain crossings of the process. A further correction may be introduced by considering only "qualified" envelope crossings (Vanmarcke 1975).

(b) Low levels $u$. For then both assumptions break down. On the other hand, the Rice formula provides a very easily calculated upper bound for the failure probability. The bound is

$$P(\max_{0\leq t\leq T} X(t)>u) \leq P(X(0)>u) + \nu_u T \ . \qquad (3)$$

For a "double-barrier" problem the following bound, which will be used in the sequel, holds

$$P(\max_{0\leq t\leq T} |X(t)|>u) \leq P(|X(0)|>u) + 2\nu_u T \ . \qquad (4)$$

(see e.g. Hasofer 1982)

The basic idea of the procedure is simply to split the stochastic process X(t) into two parts: One that depends only on a finite number of random variables and to which the methods developed for static reliability may be used, and another, a small residual, whose magnitude can be bounded by the use of the above-mentioned bound (4).

The following procedure is followed:

(1) Without loss of generality, the interval of interest is taken to be (-T,+T).

(2) The covariance function R(t) of the process X(t) is expanded in a cosine Fourier series over (-2T,2T) (since R(t) is even and t ranges over (-2T,2T) when X(t) ranges over -T,+T):

$$R(t) = \sum_{n=0}^{\infty} \alpha_n \cos \frac{n\pi t}{2T} \ . \qquad (5)$$

Note that some of the $\alpha_n$ may turn out to be negative, because Bochner's theorem only applies to expansions over $(-\infty,+\infty)$.

However, if T is large, the negative coefficients tend to be few and very small.

(3) Put $a_n^2 = \alpha_n^+$, $b_n^2 = \alpha_n^-$. Then

$$R(t) + \sum_n b_n^2 \cos \frac{n\pi t}{2T} = \sum_n a_n^2 \cos \frac{n\pi t}{2T} \ . \qquad (6)$$

(4) Set

$$W(t) = \sum_n a_n (V_n \cos \frac{n\pi t}{2T} + W_n \sin \frac{n\pi t}{2T}) \ , \qquad (7)$$

$$Y(t) = \sum_n b_n (V_n \cos \frac{n\pi t}{2T} + W_n \sin \frac{n\pi t}{2T}) \ , \qquad (8)$$

where $V_n$ and $W_n$ are independent standard normal variables independent of X(t). Then

$$X(t) + Y(t) \underset{=}{d} W(t) \qquad (9)$$

where $\underset{=}{d}$ denotes equality in distribution. Formula (9) follows from the fact that both sides are Gaussian, have zero mean and the same covariance function.

(5) Choose a minimal set of integers N such that

$$\sum_{n\in\bar{N}} a_n^2 \ll \sum_{n\in N} a_n^2 \ , \qquad (10)$$

where $\bar{N}$ is the complement of N in the set of non-negative integers. Write

$$W_N(t) = \sum_{n\in N} a_n(V_n\cos\frac{n\pi t}{2T} + W_n\sin\frac{n\pi t}{2T}) , \quad (11)$$

$$W_N'(t) = \sum_{n\in \bar{N}} a_n(V_n\cos\frac{n\pi t}{2T} + W_n\sin\frac{n\pi t}{2T} . \quad (12)$$

Then

$$X(t) + Y(t) \underset{=}{d} W_N(t) + W_N'(t) . \quad (13)$$

In equation (13) $W_N(t)$ is to be thought of as the "finite trigonometric approximation" to X(t) while Y(t) and $W_N'(t)$ are remainder terms which may be made as small as required by taking T and N sufficiently large.

*Example* (Hasofer 1987)

Let the spectral density function of X(t) be the popular narrow-band bell-shaped spectrum

$$f(\omega) = (8\pi\sigma^2)^{-\frac{1}{2}}\{\exp[-(\mu-\omega)^2/2\sigma^2] + \exp[-(\mu+\omega)^2/2\sigma^2]\} \quad (14)$$

and choose the following numerical values:

$$\mu = 15\pi , \sigma = 2\pi , 2T = 1 .$$

It then turns out that there are no significant negative $\alpha_n$, so that Y(t) is negligible.

To obtain a very close approximation to X(t) it is enough to take the set N to be

$$N = \{5, ... ,24\} \quad (15)$$

i.e. 20 coefficients. The remainder-process then has values of the spectral moments $\lambda_0 = 8.58\times10^{-7}$ and $\lambda_2 = 4.98\times10^{-3}$ as against $\lambda_0 = 1$ and $\lambda_2 = 2260$ for X(t), i.e. a ratio of about $10^{-6}$ in both cases.

The values of the coefficients obtained are shown in Table 1.

Table 1: Fourier coefficients for $W_N(t)$

| n | $\alpha_n = a_n^2$ | n | $\alpha_n = a_n^2$ |
|---|---|---|---|
| 5 | $7.43\times10^{-7}$ | 15 | 0.199 |
| 6 | $7.99\times10^{-6}$ | 16 | 0.176 |
| 7 | $6.69\times10^{-5}$ | 17 | 0.121 |
| 8 | $4.36\times10^{-4}$ | 18 | $6.48\times10^{-2}$ |
| 9 | $2.22\times10^{-3}$ | 19 | $2.69\times10^{-2}$ |
| 10 | $8.76\times10^{-3}$ | 20 | $8.76\times10^{-3}$ |
| 11 | $2.70\times10^{-2}$ | 21 | $2.22\times10^{-3}$ |
| 12 | $6.48\times10^{-2}$ | 22 | $4.36\times10^{-4}$ |
| 13 | 0.121 | 23 | $6.69\times10^{-5}$ |
| 14 | 0.176 | 24 | $7.99\times10^{-6}$ |

(6) The error committed by finding the distribution of the maximum of $W_N(t)$ instead of that of $X(t)$ can now be bounded by using the following inequality (Hasofer 1982) which holds for any k:

Let

$$M_x = \max_{-T \le t \le T} X(t) , \tag{16}$$

$$M_1 = \max_{-T \le t \le T} W_N(t) , \tag{17}$$

$$M_2 = \max_{-T \le t \le T} |W'_N(t)| . \tag{18}$$

Then

$$P(M_1 > x+k) - P(M_2 > k) \le P(M_x > x) \le P(M_1 > x-k) + P(M_2 > k) \tag{19}$$

Knowing $\lambda_0$ and $\lambda_2$ for $M_2$, it is easy to find an upper bound for $P(M_2>k)$, using (4). Note that as k increases $P(M_2>k)$ decreases, while the difference between $P(M_1>x+k)$ and $P(M_1>x-k)$ increases, so there is an optimum value of k for which the outer members of (19) are closest. This optimum value can easily be found by trial and error.

It remain to find the distribution of $M_1$, the maximum of $W_N(t)$. Suppose that the set N contains q integers. Then $W_N(t)$ depends on 2q standard normal variables. One may think that it might be possible to calculate the value $P(M_1>x)$ by using the methods developed for the static case that rely on the so-called β-point, such as FORM and SORM (for references see the bibliography in Ditlevsen and Bjerager 1986). Unfortunately it turns out that the "failure surface" in that case is the envelope of an infinity of (2q-1) dimensioned hyperplanes, each of which is tangent to a hypersphere of radius x in $\mathbf{R}^{2q}$, the points of tangency forming a curve on the surface of the hypersphere that is the (2q-1)-dimensional equivalent of a Lissajou figure! Thus the number of β-points in this case is infinite, and the β-point method is not suitable for this case.

A crude Monte-Carlo method would be quite unfeasible, for to achieve estimation of a probability p with a coefficient of variation c, the number of simulations required is about $(pc^2)^{-1}$. For $p = 10^{-6}$ and c = 0.05, the number required is $4\times10^8$.

The problem can be resolved by using the method of *directional simulation*. A short account of the method will now be given. Its application to the problem of finding the distribution of $M_1$, as well as the numerical results obtained, will then be discussed.

## 3. DIRECTIONAL SIMULATION

The method of directional simulation calculates the probability that a vector $\underset{\sim}{X}$ of length m of standard normal variables will lie outside a safe region S. The region S is assumed to be star-shaped. The formalism of the method is best stated in terms of a special form of the failure function defined as follows:

Let $\underset{\sim}{x}$ be any point in $\mathbf{R}^m$. Draw the line from the origin to $\underset{\sim}{x}$ and extend it to +∞. If the line does not intersect the failure region $S^c$, put $g(x) = 0$. If it does intersect it at a point $\underset{\sim}{x}_0$, set $g(\underset{\sim}{x}) = ||\underset{\sim}{x}|| / ||\underset{\sim}{x}_0||$. It is then very easy to check that

(i) the region $S^c$ is characterized by $g(\underset{\sim}{x}) \geq 1$,

(ii) $g(\lambda \underset{\sim}{x}) = \lambda g(\underset{\sim}{x})$ for any $\lambda \geq 0$,

i.e. $g(\cdot)$ is homogeneous of degree one.

Let now $R^2 = X_1^2 + \ldots + X_m^2$, where $X_1, \ldots, X_m$ are the components of $\underset{\sim}{X}$. Then $R^2$ has the chi-squared distribution with m degrees of freedom, and is independent of the vector $\underset{\sim}{X}/R$.

Let p be the required probability. Then

$$p = P\{g(\underset{\sim}{X}) \geq 1\} = P\{Rg(\frac{\underset{\sim}{X}}{R}) \geq 1\}. \tag{20}$$

Let $g(\frac{\underset{\sim}{X}}{R}) = M^{-1}$. Then

$$p = P(RM^{-1} \geq 1) = P(R \geq M)$$

$$= E[P(R^2 \geq M^2 | M)]$$

$$= E[1 - \chi_m^2(M^2)], \tag{21}$$

where $\chi_m^2(\cdot)$ is the distribution function of the chi-squared distribution.

The estimation of p by formula (21) is carried out as follows:

(1) A set of $\Omega$ standard normal vectors $\underset{\sim}{X}_i$, $i = 1, \ldots, \Omega$ are generated.

(2) For each $\underset{\sim}{X}_i$ the corresponding $R_i$ is calculated.

(3) The value of $M_i = [g(\underset{\sim}{x}_i/R_i)]^{-1}$ is computed.

(4) For each i, $p_i = 1 - \chi_m^2(M_i^2)$ is computed.

(5) The unbiassed Monte Carlo estimator of p is then

$$\hat{p} = \frac{1}{\Omega} \sum_{i=1}^{\Omega} p_i , \tag{22}$$

and the estimated standard deviation $\hat{\sigma}(\hat{p})$ is given by $\hat{\sigma}(p_i)/\Omega^{\frac{1}{2}}$, where

$$\hat{\sigma}^2(p_i) = \frac{1}{(\Omega-1)} \sum_{i=1}^{\Omega} (p_i - \hat{p})^2 . \tag{23}$$

The reason for the efficiency of directional simulation compared with the crude Monte Carlo method is that while in the crude Monte Carlo method a fraction 1-p (very near to 1) of the simulation is wasted, in directional simulation the sampling is carried out effectively on the surface of the unit sphere in $R^m$, and for each simulation $\underset{\sim}{X}$ the conditional probability of the whole part of the line from the origin to $\underset{\sim}{X}$ that lies in $S^c$ is calculated exactly.

The above explanation highlights the domain of applicability of directional simulation as compared with FORM and SORM. It is particularly suitable when there are an infinity of β-points and when it is difficult to discover favoured directions of sampling. The following results, (Table 2), taken from Bjerager (1987), illustrate this point. They refer to the probability outside the ellipsoid in $R^m$

$$\sum_{i=1}^{m} (x_i/c_i)^2 = 1 \tag{24}$$

where $c_i = c_0+(i-1)\Delta/(m-1), \quad i = 1, \ldots ,m.$

The results are given in β-notation, that is, the values given are $\beta = \Phi^{-1}(1-p)$, where Φ is the normal distribution function. The corresponding FORM and SORM results are given for comparison.

Table 2: Results from directional simulation on an ellipsoidal failure surface.

| m = 12 | $(c_0,\Delta)=(6.5,1.0)$ | $(c_0,\Delta)=(6.2,2.0)$ | $(c_0,\Delta)=(5.8,4.0)$ | $(c_0,\Delta)=(5.2,8.0)$ |
|---|---|---|---|---|
| Ω=100 | 4.52,4.56(0.07) | 4.55,4.63(0.14) | 4.59,4.77(0.33) | 4.35,4.76(0.58) |
| Ω=500 | 4.54,4.55(0.03) | 4.59,4.62(0.07) | 4.65,4.74(0.17) | 4.46,4.67(0.38) |
| Ω=1000 | 4.53,4.54(0.02) | 4.57,4.60(0.05) | 4.62,4.68(0.11) | 4.45,4.57(0.20) |
| Ω=5000 | 4.53,4.54(0.01) | 4.58,4.59(0.02) | 4.63,4.66(0.06) | 4.46,4.52(0.12) |
| Ω=10000 | 4.54,4.54(0.01) | 4.58,4.59(0.02) | 4.63,4.66(0.04) | 4.44,4.49(0.09) |
| FORM, SORM | 6.39,4.30 | 6.09,4.62 | 5.68,4.73 | 5.07,4.52 |

The two numbers separated by a comma give an 80% Confidence Interval for β, while the number in brackets represents the coefficient of variation of $\hat{p}$.

As is to be expected, FORM and SORM work well for elongated ellipsoids, while directional simulation works best for almost spherical shapes.

The efficiency of directional simulation as compared with crude Monte Carlo can be well appreciated here. A coefficient of variation of less than 5% is achieved for all but the last ellipsoid with less than 10,000 simulations, while crude Monte Carlo would require about $10^8$ simulations!

4. THE DYNAMIC CASE.

Suppose now that the failure function is still $g(\underset{\sim}{X})$, where $\underset{\sim}{X}$ is a vector of length m, but now let each component $\tilde{X}_i$ be a stochastic process $X_i(t)$. We may also let $g(\underset{\sim}{X})$ be a function of t, and denote it by $g_t(\underset{\sim}{X}(t))$, where $\underset{\sim}{X}(t) = [X_1(t), \ldots ,X_m(t)]$. Suppose now that $\underset{\sim}{X}(t)$ can be represented over (-T,+T) in the form

$$\underset{\sim}{X}(t) = \sum_{i=1}^{K} Y_r \underset{\sim}{\xi}_r(t) \tag{25}$$

where the $\underset{\sim}{\xi}_r(t)$ are vector-valued deterministic functions of time. The probability of failure p during the time-span (0,T) will then be given by

$$p = P\{ \max_{-T\le t\le T} g_t[\sum_{r=1}^{K} Y_r \underset{\sim}{\xi}_r(t)] \ge 1\} . \tag{26}$$

Let as before $R^2 = Y_1^2 + \ldots + Y_K^2$, and let $U_r = Y_r/R$. Then

$$p = P\{R \max_{-T\le t\le T} g_t[\sum_{r=1}^{K} U_r \underset{\sim}{\xi}_r(t)] \ge 1\} . \tag{27}$$

Let

$$\max_{-T\leq t\leq T} g_t\left[\sum_{r=1}^{K} U_r \xi_r(t)\right] = M^{-1} . \tag{28}$$

Then

$$\begin{aligned} p &= P(R\geq M) \\ &= \mathbf{E}[P(R\geq M|M)] \\ &= \mathbf{E}[1 - \chi_K^2(M^2)]. \end{aligned} \tag{29}$$

The simulation can then proceed as in the static case.

5. APPLICATION TO THE SCALAR GAUSSIAN PROCESS

The remaining problem in the case of the scalar Gaussian process was to find the distribution of $M_1$, given by

$$M_1 = \max_{-T\leq t\leq T} W_N(t).$$

Now

$$W_N(t) = \sum_{n\in N} a_n\left(V_n\cos\frac{n\pi t}{2T} + W_n\sin\frac{n\pi t}{2T}\right),$$

and this is exactly of the form (25).

Let $R^2 = \sum(V_n^2 + W_n^2)$, $A_n = V_n/R$, $B_n = W_n/R$,

$$T_N(t) = \sum_{n\in N} a_n\left(A_n\cos\frac{n\pi t}{2T} + B_n\sin\frac{n\pi t}{2T}\right) . \tag{30}$$

Then $W_N(t) = R\,T_N(t)$. Let now

$$M^{-1} = \max_{-T\leq t\leq T} T_N(t) .$$

As before

$$\begin{aligned} p = P(M_1>u) &= E[P(R>uM|M] \\ &= E[1 - \chi_{2k}^2(uM)]. \end{aligned} \tag{31}$$

The simulation then proceeds as before.

6. NUMERICAL RESULTS

Directional simulation was applied to the stochastic process described in the Example of Section 2. The results are given in Table 3.

The values of $\hat{p}$ and $\hat{\sigma}(p_i)$ are as given in equations (22) and (23) respectively. $\Omega(5\%)$ refers to the number of simulations required to achieve a coefficient of variation of 5% and $\beta$ is $\Phi^{-1}(1-\hat{p})$.

Correction for the remainder in the case of u = 3 was carried out, using equation (19). The optimal value of k was 0.005. The result was

$$0.0624 \leq P(M_x>3) \leq 0.0654.$$

Table 3: Distribution of $M_1$ for the stochastic process of the Example.

| u | $\hat{p}$ | $\hat{\sigma}(p_i)$ | $\Omega(5\%)$ | $\beta$ |
|---|---|---|---|---|
| 4 | $1.82\times10^{-3}$ | $1.8\times10^{-2}$ | 40,000 | 2.94 |
| 5 | $9.68\times10^{-6}$ | $2.03\times10^{-4}$ | 175,900 | 4.28 |
| 6 | $2.92\times10^{-9}$ | $6.22\times10^{-8}$ | 182,700 | 5.83 |

For the same process and time interval, and for u = 3 Rice's formula yields 0.0806, a value significantly too high. The crude envelope formula yields 0.0801, a very insignificant improvement. In fact Varmarcke's correction shows that 20% of all envelope crossings are empty. The qualified envelope formula gives 0.0648, which is rather satisfactory in this case. This example highlights the importance of testing the validity of the approximate formulae in the various parameter ranges.

## 7. REPRESENTATION OF GAUSSIAN VECTOR PROCESSES

The random trigonometric polynomial representation of a zero-mean, stationary Gaussian process given in Section 2 can be generalized to a vector-valued process as follows. Let

$$\underset{\sim}{X}(t) = [X_1(t), \ldots, X_m(t)] \qquad (32)$$

with $E[\underset{\sim}{X}(t)] = 0$ and $\underset{\sim}{X}$ stationary.

The covariance function is now a matrix

$$R(t) = E[\underset{\sim}{X}(\tau+t)\underset{\sim}{X}^T(\tau)] \qquad (33)$$

where $\underset{\sim}{X}^T$ denotes the transpose of $\underset{\sim}{X}$, and each element can be expanded in a Fourier series over (-2T,+2T). It then turns out that, similarly to the scalar case, $\underset{\sim}{X}(t)$ can be approximated as closely as needed by a random vector-valued trigonometric polynomial of the form

$$\underset{\sim}{W}_N(t) = \sum_{n\in N} (C_n\underset{\sim}{U}_n + D_n\underset{\sim}{V}_n)\cos\frac{n\pi t}{2T} + (C_n\underset{\sim}{V}_n - D_n\underset{\sim}{U}_n)\sin\frac{n\pi t}{2T} \qquad (34)$$

where $\{\underset{\sim}{U}_n\}$ $\{\underset{\sim}{V}_n\}$ are sequences of independent vectors, whose elements are all independent standard normal variables, and $C_n$ and $D_n$ are constant matrices.

A full description of the method as well as numerical results will be given in a forthcoming paper.

## 8. REPRESENTATION OF NON-STATIONARY GAUSSIAN PROCESSES

The representation $\underset{\sim}{X}(t) = \sum_{r=1}^{K} Y_r\,\underset{\sim}{\xi}_r(t)$ given in Section 4, which permits the use of directional simulation, is not confined to stationary Gaussian processes. In fact, the celebrated Karhunen-Loève expansion (see e.g. Wong 1971) is exactly of the required form. A short presentation follows for the scalar case, although a similar expansion holds for the vector case. Let C(t,u) be the covariance function of the non-stationary process K(t), and consider the restriction of the process to the interval (-T,+T). The

Fredholm integral equation

$$\int_{-T}^{T} C(t,u)\phi(u)du = \lambda\phi(t), \quad (-T \leq t \leq T) \tag{35}$$

has a denumerable number of eigenvalues $\{\lambda_n\}$, real and positive, with corresponding eigenfunctions $\{\phi_n(t)\}$ which can be scaled so as to satisfy the orthogonality condition

$$\int_{-T}^{T} \phi_i(t)\overline{\phi_j(t)}dt = \delta_{ij}.$$

It can then be shown that K(t) can be represented by the expansion

$$K(t) \overset{d}{=} \sum_{n=0}^{\infty} \lambda_n^{\frac{1}{2}} X_n \phi_n(t) \tag{36}$$

where the $X_n$ are independent standard normal. Moreover the series converges in mean-square, so that it can be truncated to obtain any required degree of approximation. For an application of the Karhunen-Loève expansion to a first-passage time problem see Hasofer and Ghahreman (1987).

## 9. OTHER TYPES OF PROCESSES

Another type of process that has received much attention for modelling actions has been the Ferry Borges-Castanheta (FBC) process (Ferry Borges and Castanheta 1972). It consists of a sequence of independent rectangular pulses of fixed duration following immediately after each other. An FBC n-combination problem is a combination of n mutually independent FBC processes having pulse durations that are all integral multiples of a basic duration. An approximate solution has been given by Rackwitz and Fiessler (1978).

Directional simulation is applicable to solve completely the FBC n-combination problem when the load pulses of the FBC processes are Gaussian or clipped Gaussian. The FBC model may in that case be extended to include dependence between pulses and between processes. For details see Ditlevsen et al (1985) and Ditlevsen et al (1987).

## 10. CONCLUSIONS

Directional simulation, together with the representation of a vector-valued stochastic process in the form $\underset{\sim}{X}(t) = \sum Y_r \underset{\sim}{\xi}_r(t)$ has a wide field of applicability in the determination of the time-dependent failure probability of structures. The method works best for those values of the parameters for which the approximate methods used so far (FORM, SORM, outcrossings) are the least reliable, and its exact nature provides a valuable check of their validity.

ACKNOWLEDGEMENT

This paper was written while the author was a Visiting Professor in the Department of Structural Engineering of the Technical University of Denmark.

REFERENCES

Bjerager P. (1987). "Probability integration by directional Simulation", To appear.

Ditlevsen O. (1983). "Gaussian outcrossings from safe convex polyhedrons", J. Eng. Mech. Div., ASCE, Vol. 109, pp. 127-148.

Ditlevsen O., R. Olesen and A.M. Hasofer (1985). "Load combination by Deak simulation", Proceedings of SMIRT 8 (Structural Mechanics in Reactor Technology), Division M1: Structural Reliability. Brussels.

Ditlevsen O. and P. Bjerager (1986). "Methods of Structural systems reliability", Structural Safety, 3, pp. 195-229.

Ditlevsen O., R. Olesen and G. Mohr (1987). "Solution of a class of load combination problems by directional simulation", Structural Safety, 4, pp. 95-109.

Ferry Borges J. and M. Castanheta (1972). "Structural Safety", 2nd Edition, Laboratorio Nacional de Engenharia Civil, Lisbon.

Hasofer A.M. (1982). "Simple trigonometric models for narrow-band stationary processes", Essays in Statistical Science, J. of Applied Prob. Special Vol. 19A, pp. 333-344.

Hasofer A.M. (1987), "Distribution of the maximum of a Gaussian process by a Monte Carlo method", J. Sound and Vibration. To appear.

Hasofer A.M. and S. Ghahreman (1985), "Simulation of random vibrations on a small computer", Proceedings of International Conference on Education, Practice and Promotion of Computational Methods in Engineering using Small Computers (EPMESC), Macao, pp. 449-457.

Hasofer A.M. and S. Ghahreman (1987), "On the Slepian process of a random Gaussian trigonometric polynomial". Submitted for publication.

Hohenbichler M. and R. Rackwitz (1986), "Asymptotic crossing rate of Gaussian vector processes into intersections of failure domains", Prob. Eng. Mech., Vol. I, No. 3, pp. 177-179.

Lindgren G. (1984), "Extremal ranks and transformation of variables for extremes of functions of multivariate Gaussian processes", Stochastic processes and their applications, Vol. 17, pp. 285-312.

Rackwitz R. and B. Fiessler, "Structural reliability under combined random load sequences", Computers and Structures, Vol. 9, pp. 489-494.

Vanmarcke, E.H. (1975), "On the distribution of the First-Passage Time for Normal Stationary Random Processes", J. Appl. Mechanics, Vol. 42, pp. 215-220.

Veneziano D., M. Grigoriu and C.A. Cornell (1977), "Vector-process models for system reliability", J. Eng. Mech. Div., ASCE, Vol. 103, No. EM3, pp. 441-460.

Wong E. (1971), "Stochastic Processes in Information and Dynamical Systems". McGraw-Hill, New York.

# STRUCTURAL RELIABILITY ASSESSMENT AND HUMAN ERROR

R.E. Melchers
Department of Civil Engineering and Surveying, The University of Newcastle, N.S.W., 2308, Australia.

## ABSTRACT

Realistic assessment of reliability must take account of the possibility of human error in the design and execution of the project of interest. This is also true for structural reliability assessment, even though for some applications, such as design code writing, a nominal reliability measure, largely ignoring human error, may well be sufficient.

The present paper reviews, briefly, the principles by which human error information may be taken into account in reliability assessment, and, in a little more detail, both empirical models and data for some types of human error which may arise in structural design processes. Attention is also given to three forms of checking: independent, self- and overview checking. Only recently has some indicative data for checking processes become available; in all aspects the reported research must seem as preliminary rather than definitive.

## INTRODUCTION

Reliability assessment will generally have little absolute meaning, and perhaps not even relative or "nominal" meaning (in the code calibration sense) unless account is taken, in the assessment, of the possible influence of human error. This has been recognized, particularly for non structural engineering assessments such as in the operation of nuclear power plants and in the aerospace industry. Considerable effort has, and is still being expended in estimating human error rates in these industries.

There is both anecdotal and statistical evidence and experience to indicate the importance of human error in the structural/construction engineering field. Available evidence suggests that many (but not all) human errors which led to structural failure were committed in the execution of relatively simple tasks, as might not at first be expected [Matousek & Schneider, 1976]. Since most structures do not "fail", (although many show some signs of minor distress or malfunction after some years), it seems that serious errors are not committed very often; and those that are might well have been detected before becoming permanently incorporated in the structure. Error detection as well as error initiation is therefore a matter of concern in incorporating human error in reliability assessment. Both these matters will be reviewed herein.

It is important at the outset to note that the available research suggests that most human errors are not due to unforeseeable events, but are due to a variety of quite preventable causes [Walker, 1981]. Since it is unlikely that only unforeseeable events can be prevented, and since it appears reasonable to suppose that such events are generally tolerated to some degree by society, there is little that can or need be done about them, except, perhaps to be constantly aware that truly unforeseeable events are extremely rare [Sibly & Walker, 1977]. For the purpose of reliability assessment, a useful, but not very precise, restriction is therefore to consider only errors involving foreseeable events.

The research work carried out over the last few years at Monash University (and now being continued at The University of Newcastle) has focussed on human error in structural engineering design processes. Both design and construction figure highly in error surveys, but because design was seen as a more homogeneous process, it was selected as the target for initial study.

THEORETICAL FRAMEWORK

The theoretical basis for the work has developed from a consideration of the individual tasks in design processes - socalled "micro-tasks" - their relation to one another and their relation to the structure or structural element being designed - the socalled "macro-task". The inter-relation between micro-tasks and the macro-task is through event trees which describe the decision and process steps to achieve the macro-task. A typical component sequence of a micro-task and its related checking process is shown in Figure 1, [Melchers & Stewart, 1985].

By setting up an event tree model of a specific macro-task, such as the determination of wind loading on a structure, or the design of one of its components, the micro-task data can be used to predict the error rate distribution in performing the macro-task. This has been attempted already in a preliminary fashion using crude control (checking) models and compared to survey results for macro-task error rates [Melchers & Harrington, 1984].

Clearly error initiation in the micro-task, error control (either at the time the micro-task is completed or subsequently) and error consequence in relation to the particular structure being designed are important components of any modelling. It is clear, from the work completed to date, that these components are not always strictly separable, although this has been a convenient assumption in order to make progress. A somewhat similar model incorporating error initiation, error control and error consequence has been advocated by Kupfer & Rackwitz (1980).

The basic mathematics are then as follows. Consider a number of error states, i = 0, 1, ...., n (after checking and control, etc.) with i = 0 denoting no error content in the micro task sequence. Then the probability of failure for any one sequence is $p_{f|i}$. The probability of this error sequence occurring is $p_i$: clearly a histogram of error magnitude for this sequence can also be drawn. The total probability of failure for the structure is the sum over all error sequences:

$$p_f = \bigcup_{i=0}^{n} [p_i \cap p_{f|i}] \qquad (1)$$

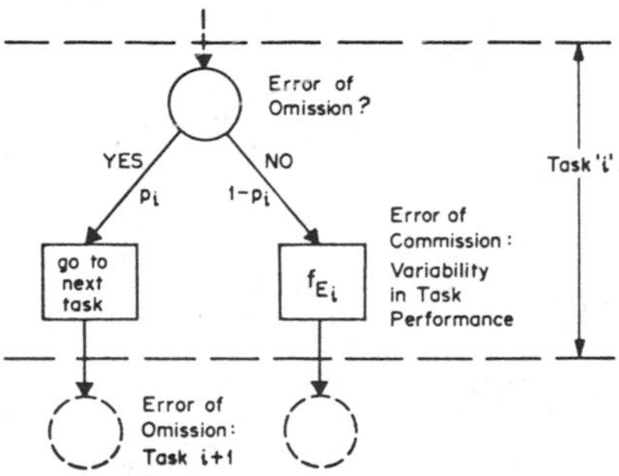


FIGURE 1: Typical Micro-task and Control

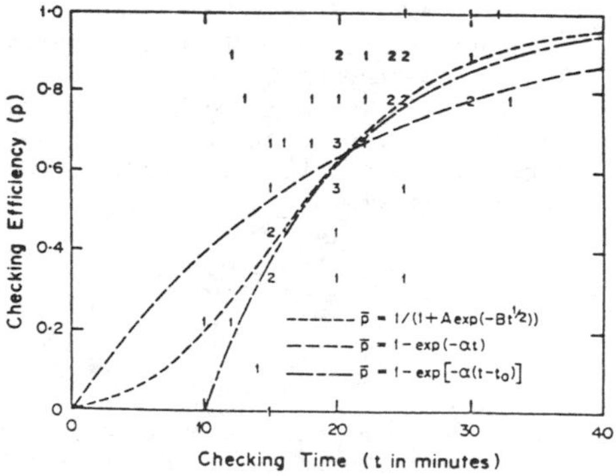


FIGURE 2: Typical Error Detection Data and Model

which for independent sequences and independence between sequence and its occurrence becomes simply:

$$p_f = \sum_{i=0}^{n} p_i \, p_{f|i} \tag{2}$$

In considering equation (1) or (2), more than one failure mode may need to be considered. It is also required that the calculations themselves be carefully made; in particular the correct limit state equations must be used [Kupfer & Rackwitz, 1980].

The calculation of $p_{f|i}$ needs to consider the intersection of the probabilities of occurrence of all errors in the sequence, together with the effect such errors may have on the resistance (and occassionally the loading) on the structure. A particularly useful and simple formulation of the relevant limit state has been given by Baker & Wyatt (1979) as:

$$Z = ER - KS \tag{3}$$

where E represents a random variable of error applied to the random variable of resistance R and K represents a discrete-valued model uncertainty (such as might occur when extrapolating beyond existing knowledge).

The error variable E should strictly be viewed as the structural outcome of a human error or errors, such as the misplacement of reinforcement, or incorrect location of a bolt, etc. A variety of human error(s) may have caused this particular outcome (e.g., omission, incorrect number, etc.). There is thus room to explore the dependence of safety (expressed, for example, through Z) and its dependence on structural errors [Nowak, 1979] as well as the latter's dependence on human errors.

In addition, it is possible to explore the variation in error magnitude for particular structural errors; for example, histograms of bending moment variation have been obtained in preliminary work [Melchers & Harrington, 1984].

## ERROR OCCURRENCE

ERROR MODELS: To apply the relative simple ideas given above, it is necessary to have some idea of the type of human errors which occur in design processes, their frequency of occurrence for different tasks and their magnitude. Such data exists in the human factors literature [e.g., Harris & Chaney, 1969], for psychomotor tasks such are involved in the aerospace and nuclear industries. A model commonly suggested [Rackwitz, 1983; Nessim & Jordaan, 1983] for occurrence of design errors is the Poisson process, in which design errors are assumed to occur randomly over a time period t, say, at an average rate per unit time of $\lambda$:

$$P_{N|A}(n, \lambda) = \frac{e^{-\lambda t} (\lambda t)^n}{n!} \qquad n = 0, 1, 2 \tag{4}$$

where $P_{N|A}(n, \lambda)$ denotes the probability that the number of errors N is actually n given that the average rate of error occurrence is $\lambda$. Clearly the latter is usually uncertain due to variations between tasks, between persons or team etc., and hence may also need to be modelled as a random variable. Unfortunately it is very doubtful that design errors are completely random; this is also suggested by recent empirical evidence.

Initially research by the author's group concentrated on the description of error initiation or occurrence [Melchers & Harrington, 1982, 1984]. Typical micro tasks include algebraic calculations, table look-up, table interpolation, etc. These tasks may be performed erroneously (error of commission) or not performed at all (error of omission). It is possible to have other types of errors, but these are generally of lesser importance [Melchers & Stewart, 1985].

A review of some typical data is given below.

CALCULATION ERRORS: The aggregated error rate for calculation errors was reported as about 0.01 for engineering students [Melchers & Harrington, 1982]. A more extensive survey was conducted with calculations of differing lengths to ascertain if there was a trend with calculation length. Sampling of engineering design calculation suggests that typically only 1-3 mathematical operations are involved in calculations, but that much longer calculations do occur [Melchers & Harrington, 1984].

The results were analysed for three types of error: round-off, decimal and computational. Although there was considerable scatter in the results there was a definite trend for the error rate to increase with the number of mathematical steps in the calculation. If 5% is used to discriminate between round off and other errors, the trend for overall error is approximately

$$P_E = 0.027\,n$$

while for 2.5% discrimination,

$$P_E = 0.0225\,n$$

where n is the number of mathematical steps. In both cases the error in these expressions can be up to 100%, particularly for low values of n.

TABLE READING ERRORS: Error rates for table-look-up and for number ranking were reported previously [Melchers & Harrington, 1982]. Typically, an error rate of 1-2% was obtained. In addition, a study on 15 fourth-year civil engineering students using a broad-based selection of table-look-up tasks as well as table-look-up with interpolation tasks, produced altogether 238 responses during the task time (20 minutes). 16 incorrect responses were counted, giving an error rate of 0.067. This quite high rate was attributed to the repetitiveness of the task.

For each of seven table interpolation tasks, Table 1 gives the number of "gross errors" in 15 samples used for each task [Melchers, 1986]. A "gross error" was in this case considered to be a response outside the interpolation range given in the appropriate table. This would therefore include the incorrect choice of location within the table. With this rather arbitrary definition, the gross error rate was found to be 0.08.

TABLE 1: Table Interpolation Results

| Task no. | No. of "gross errors" | Response mean | Standard Deviation | Coefficient of Variation |
|---|---|---|---|---|
| 1 | - | 161.47 | 2.55 | 0.016 |
| 2 | 1 | 34.0 | 1.63 | 0.048 |
| 3 | 1 | 87.11 | 1.64 | 0.019 |
| 4 | 1 | 80.08 | 1.57 | 0.02 |
| 5 | 2 | 36.52 | 1.63 | 0.045 |
| 6 | 2 | 20.6 | 0.60 | 0.29 |
| 7 | 1 | 688.25 | 21.45 | 0.031 |

No probabalistic models appear to be obviously able to describe the empirical data.

ERROR DETECTION

INDEPENDENT CHECKING: Independent checking is a widely used technique to control errors in design; it has been estimated that 0.5 - 1.0% of total project cost is spent on independent checking. Yet remarkably little appears to be known about its effectiveness or about the most appropriate practices.

Several models have been proposed to model error detection [Lind, 1983]: apart from the most recent these are based on relevant empirical data. Attention will therefore be restricted here to the latest findings.

Restricting attention also to checking of design calculations, the author's group used a mailed questionnaire technique targetted at consulting structural engineers, government agencies and semi-government agencies to elicit preliminary data on design checking efficiency [Stewart & Melchers, 1985]. A reasonably realistic sample of design loading calculations for a steel portal frame structure was used as the test vehicle. Written responses were examined and note taken of corrections made or errors otherwise indicated. Only errors of commission were used in the test vehicle. Respondents were asked to indicate the time taken to complete the checking work.

Although the data showed considerable scatter, it appeared to have a trend which suggested an S- or learning-curve [Stewart & Melchers, 1985]: for checking effectiveness $\bar{p}$ as a function of time:

$$\bar{p}(t) = 1/[1 + A \exp(-Bt^{1/2})] \qquad (5)$$

where constant A must be sufficiently large to ensure $\bar{p}(t) = 0$ at $t = 0$ and B is inversely proportional to task complexity and proportional to the expertise of the checker. Such a curve has appeal since the initial growth may be attributed to the checker attempting to come to an understanding of the designer's work, both concept and procedure. The next period involves actual checking of each micro task, and perhaps an overall review of the sensibility of the result; it seems obvious that the error detection rate will fall, in general, with time spent. Figure 2 indicates such a curve, and the survey data.

With increased experience, the initial part of the curve becomes less pronounced, at least in situations where training can be effective [Harlow, 1959]. In the limit a negative exponential curve, derived from search theory,

$$\bar{p}(t) = 1 - \exp(-\alpha t) \qquad (6)$$

might then become appropriate [Kupfer & Rackwitz, 1980]. It is unlikely, however, that this situation would arise in realistic structural design checking practice. A shifted negative exponential curve might be a reasonable approximation:

$$\bar{p}(t) = 1 - \exp[-\alpha(t - t_0)] \qquad (7)$$

where $t_0$ is the time before which no effective checking takes place (see also Figure 2).

Checking efficiency as a function of error magnitude was also considered for each micro task. As expected, larger errors were more easily detected than smaller ones, with a fifth power function $c_0 h(x) = x^{1/5}$ appropriate for $\alpha$ in equation (7) where $c_0$ is a constant. Equation (5) may similarly be adjusted to

$$\bar{p}(x, t) = 1/[1 + A \exp(-h(x) Bt^{1/2}] \quad (8)$$

with $h(x) = x^{1/10}$ giving a reasonable fit to the data. No obvious explanation of the powers on x can yet be given.

SELF CHECKING: It was recognized that self checking by the designer is an important process, yet not an easy one to investigate. Direct survey techniques appeared not to be feasible, and the data collected from previous surveys did not contain sufficient evidence of self checking to be meaningful. It was decided therefore to resort to undergraduate student examination scripts in basic structural engineering and dynamics topics [Stewart & Melchers, 1986]. The results obtained were corrected to allow for rate of error occurrence using previous data [Melchers & Harrington, 1984]. Figure 3 shows a typical histogram of percentage error magnitude for errors for which self checking occurred. It is evident that many more small errors were corrected than large errors; which seems at first contrary to expectation. However, it may mean that self checking is not effective for larger errors because the subject is unable to sufficiently divorce himself from the calculations. Of course, the present results may simply not apply to experienced designers: at present no evidence appears to exist either way.

OVERVIEW CHECKING: Overview checking occurs whenever a design (calculations or drawings or both) is reviewed by another engineer (or other persons) without specifically carrying out checking calculations or following through the design calculations. Such checking takes place perhaps already by the designer but normally occurs during the process by which the design is "approved" by various persons and organisations, and eventually, in a different fashion, in going to tender and construction.

An insight into overview checking has recently been obtained using practising engineers as subjects [Stewart & Melchers, 1987]. Each respondent indicated for each of eleven simple beam designs whether he considered the proposed design to be "undersized", "correct" or "oversized" for the given loading configuration or whether he was "unsure". It was clearly stated in the questionnaire that the decisions were to be based on personal judgement only. Respondents were also asked to indicate their response time and their number of years of structural engineering experience.

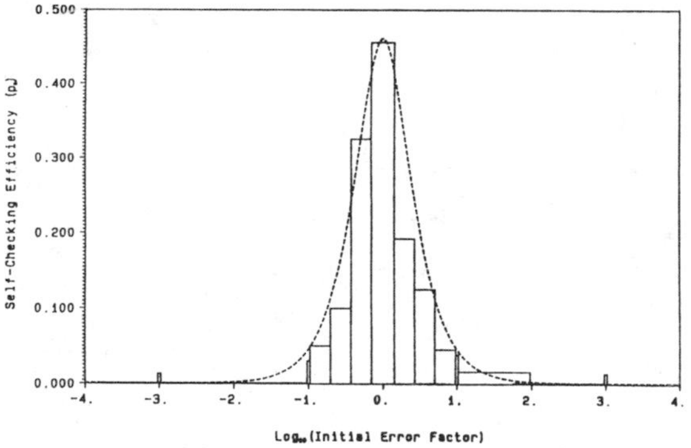


FIGURE 3: Histogram for Self Checking

Space does not permit a detailed discussion here, but suffice it to note that:

1. There was a greater proportion of "unsure" responses for the reinforced concrete beams compared with the mild steel beams;

2. The decision process for an overview checker appeared to be:
   a. is the member adequate?
   b. if so, is it overdesigned?;

3. Experience appeared not be of importance in making decision 2a, but was important in being able to select oversized members (decision 2b). (This last observation appears not to entirely support popularly held views about experience!);

4. There appeared to be no correlations between time taken and decisions made, nor with experience.

A model based on the F-distribution appeared to fit the data for item 2a, and one based on the t-distribution for item 2b, however no theoretical basis for these choices currently exist. Details are given elsewhere [Stewart & Melchers, 1987]. Figure 4 shows the survey data and one of the proposed models for estimating the probability of "safe" (or adequate) as a function of error size.

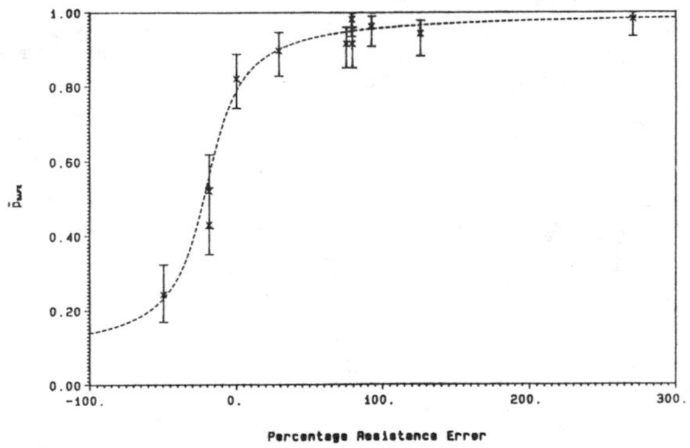


FIGURE 4: Survey Data and Model for Overview Checking

## DISCUSSION

The work outlined above must still be seen as rather tentative first steps in our attempts to understand the nature and the control of human errors in design processes. As noted earlier it is hoped that by understanding various elemental human error aspects, it will be possible to build-up a model which will help in estimating the importance of human error for a realistic design process. This may then be used to estimate reasonably realistic structural reliability levels.

The methods employed to date can be criticized on a number of grounds [Stewart & Melchers, 1985]; the important point, however, is that we cannot hope to proceed in our understanding unless we make an effort, even under quite imperfect conditions.

## CONCLUSION

Some of the results given herein indicate trends that, to some extent, appear quite obvious. However, virtually no data has previously been collected or theoretical models developed. The present paper reviews this work and its place in structural reliability assessment.

## ACKNOWLEDGEMENTS

The work reported herein was supported by The Australian Research Grants Scheme, under Grant No. F81 15110.

## REFERENCES

Baker, M.J. and Wyatt, T.A., (1979), Methods of Reliability Analysis for Jacket Platforms, Proc. 2nd Int. Conf. Behaviour of Off-shore Structures, London.

Harlow, H.F., (1959), Learning Set and Error Factor Theory, in: Psychology: A Study of Science, Koch, S. (Ed.), McGraw-Hill, pp. 492-537.

Harris, D.H. and Chaney, F.B., (1969), Human Factors in Quality Assurance, Wiley.

Kupfer, J. and Rackwitz, R., (1980), Models for Human Error and Control in Structural Reliability, Final Report, 11th Congress, IABSE, Vienna, pp. 1019-1024.

Lind, N.C., (1983), Models of Human Error in Structural Reliability, Struct. Safety, Vol. 1, No. 3, April, pp. 167-175.

Matousek, M. and Schneider, J., (1976), Untersuchungen zur Struktur des Sicherheitsproblems bei Bauwerken, Bericht Nr. 59, Institute fur Baustatik und Konstruktion, Zurich, Feb.

Melchers, R.E. and Harrington, M.V., (1982), Human Error in Simple Design Tasks, Research Report 3/1982, Department of Civil Engineering, Monash University.

Melchers, R.E. and Harrington, M.V., (1984), Human Error in Structural Reliability I - Investigation of Typical Design Tasks, Research Report 2/1984, Department of Civil Engineering, Monash University.

Melchers, R.E. and Stewart, M.G., (1985), Data-Based Models for Human Error in Design, Fourth International Conference on Structural Safety and Reliability, Kobe, Japan, Vol. II, pp. 51-60.

Melchers, R.E., (1986), Human Influences in Quality Assurance, Introductory Report, Tokyo Symposium, IABSE, pp. 107-110.

Nessim, A.M. and Jordaan, I., (1983), Decision Making for Error Control in Structural Engineering, 4th ICASP, Florence, pp. 713-728.

Nowak, A.D., (1979), Effects on Human Error on Structural Reliability, J. Amer. Conc. Inst., Proc. Vol. 76, No. 9, pp. 959-972, September.

Rackwitz, R., (1983), Planning for Quality - Concepts and Numerical Tools, Workshop on Quality Assurance within the Building Process, Rigi, Switzerland, pp. 49-64.

Sibly, P.G. and Walker, A.C., (1977), Structural Accidents and Their Causes, Proc. Inst. Civil Engrs., Pt. 1, Vol. 62, pp. 191-208.

Stewart, M.G. and Melchers, R.E., (1985), Human Error in Structural Reliability - IV: Efficiency in Design Checking, Research Report No. 3/1985, Department of Civil Engineering, Monash University.

Stewart, M.G. and Melchers, R.E., (1986), Human Error in Structural Reliability - V - Efficiency in Self Checking, Research Report No. 018.12.86, Department of Civil Engineering and Surveying, The University of Newcastle.

Stewart, M.G. and Melchers, R.E., (1987), Human Error in Structural Reliability - VI - Overview Checking, Research Report No. 019.01.87, Department of Civil Engineering and Surveying, The University of Newcastle.

Walker, A.C., (1981), Study and Analysis of the First 120 Failure Cases, in: Structural Failures in Buildings, The Institution of Engineers.

## SPECTRAL MOMENTS AND ENVELOPE FOR NON-STATIONARY NON-SEPARABLE PROCESSES

M. DI PAOLA* and G. MUSCOLINO*
*Dipartimento di Ingegneria Strutturale e Geotecnica. Univ. di Palermo, Viale delle Scienze, 90128, Palermo, Italy.

ABSTRACT

Many time varying loadings to structures can be considered as stochastic processes and both excitation and response are modeled as stationary or non-stationary ones. In this framework we are concerned with the evaluation of the structural safety, which involves the evaluation of the spectral moments (Vanmarcke 1972) and the statistics of the envelope process (Dugundji 1958).

Recently Di Paola (1985) has shown that in the time domain the spectral moments are variances of complex physical processes in which the imaginary parts are related to the real ones by means of the Hilbert transform operator; consequently the envelope process is defined as the modulus of such processes in a natural way. In this new representation of physical stochastic processes a critical review of well-known concepts, especially in the non-stationary case, must be made.

In previous works (Di Paola 1985, Di Paola and Muscolino 1986) the spectral moments and the statistical properties of the envelope process of separable processes have been treated. Here the extension of the previous concepts to the more general case of non-separable processes using the spectral representation made by Priestley (1961) is presented. The mean rate threshold crossing process of the envelope is evaluated for such processes in a closed form solution.

### PHYSICAL PROCESSES

Let f(t) be a non-stationary zero mean process given in the spectral representation (Priestley 1967) as follows:

$$f(t) = \int_{-\infty}^{\infty} e^{-i\omega t} A(t,\omega)\, dN(\omega), \qquad (1)$$

i being the immaginary unit ( $i = \sqrt{1}$ ), $A(t,\omega)$ a slowly varying deterministic function and $N(\omega)$ a stochastic process having orthogonal increments, i.e such that

$$E[dN(\omega_1)\, dN^*(\omega_2)] = \delta(\omega_2-\omega_1)\, d\psi(\omega_1), \qquad (2)$$

where $\delta(\cdot)$ is the Dirac's delta, the star means complex conjugate, $E[\cdot]$ means stochastic average and $\psi(\omega)$ is a deterministic function;if $\psi(\omega)$ is differentiable then the relationship:

$$d\psi(\omega) = G(\omega)\, d\omega \qquad (3)$$

hold true, $G(\omega)$ being a power spectral density function of the process $dN(\omega)$.

If f(t) is a physical process, then its frequency content must be defined only in the positive frequency range (Di Paola 1985). It follows that the appropriate description of a physical process is given as:

$$\tilde{f}(t) = \int_{-\infty}^{\infty} e^{-i\omega t} A(t,\omega)\, d\tilde{N}(\omega) = \frac{2}{\sqrt{2}} \int_{0}^{\infty} e^{-i\omega t} A(t,\omega)\, dN(\omega), \tag{4}$$

$d\tilde{N}(\omega)$ being expressed as:

$$d\tilde{N}(\omega) = (1 + \mathrm{sgn}(\omega))\, dN(\omega)/\sqrt{2} \tag{5}$$

where $\mathrm{sgn}(\omega)$ is the signum function. In this way both $d\tilde{N}(\omega)$ and the corresponding $d\tilde{\psi}(\omega)$ exhibit power only in the positive frequency range and if $\tilde{\psi}(\omega)$ is differentiable then the power spectral density function of $d\tilde{N}(\omega)$ coincides with the well-known one-sided power spectral density function.

Notice that if we consider a physical process $\tilde{f}(t)$, then its time domain representation is a complex one, i.e.

$$\tilde{f}(t) = r(t) + i\, \bar{r}(t) \tag{6}$$

where:

$$r(t) = \frac{2}{\sqrt{2}} \int_{0}^{\infty} \{\mathrm{Re}[A(\omega,t)]\mathrm{Re}[e^{-i\omega t} dN(\omega)] - \mathrm{Im}[A(\omega,t)]\mathrm{Im}[e^{-i\omega t} dN(\omega)]\} \tag{7a}$$

$$\bar{r}(t) = \frac{2}{\sqrt{2}} \int_{0}^{\infty} \{\mathrm{Re}[A(\omega,t)]\mathrm{Im}[e^{-i\omega t} dN(\omega)] + \mathrm{Im}[A(\omega,t)]\, \mathrm{Re}[e^{-i\omega t} dN(\omega)]\} \tag{7b}$$

It can easily be shown that $\mathrm{Im}[e^{-i\omega t} dN(\omega)]$ is the Hilbert transform (HT) of (-1) $\mathrm{Re}[e^{-i\omega t} dN(\omega)]$ and vice-versa. The $HT[\cdot]$ operator is defined as:

$$HT[g(t)] = \hat{g}(t) = \frac{1}{\pi} \int_{-\infty}^{\infty} \frac{g(\rho)}{t - \rho}\, d\rho \tag{8}$$

For the sake of completeness the two relevant processes-stationary and separable -are examined.

STATIONARY PROCESS: This case can be obtained by putting $A(\omega,t) = 1 \forall\, t,\omega$. It follows that:

$$r(t) = \frac{2}{\sqrt{2}} \int_{0}^{\infty} \mathrm{Re}[e^{-i\omega t} dN(\omega)] \tag{9}$$

$$\bar{r}(t) = \frac{2}{\sqrt{2}} \int_{0}^{\infty} \mathrm{Im}[e^{-i\omega t} dN(\omega)] = -\hat{r}(t) \tag{10}$$

and $\tilde{f}(t)$ can be written as:

$$\tilde{f}(t) = r(t) - i\, \hat{r}(t) \tag{11}$$

Equation (11) shows that a stationary physical process is an analytic one,

(Papoulis 1984), i.e. such that the imaginary part is the Hilbert transform of the corresponding real part.

NON-STATIONARY SEPARABLE PROCESS. This case can be obtained by putting $A(t,\omega) = F(t)\,Q(\omega)$. Without loss of generality, we assume that F(t) is a real deterministic function. It follows that equation (7) can be written as:

$$r(t) = F(t) \int_0^\infty \frac{2}{\sqrt{2}} \{Re[Q(\omega)]Re[e^{-i\omega t}dN(\omega)]-Im[Q(\omega)]Im[e^{-i\omega t}dN(\omega)]\} \tag{12a}$$

$$\bar{r}(t) = F(t) \int_0^\infty \frac{2}{\sqrt{2}} \{Re[Q(\omega)]Im[e^{-i\omega t}dN(\omega) +Im[Q(\omega)]Re[e^{-i\omega t}dN(\omega)]\} \tag{12b}$$

It is worth noting that the integrals in equation (12) represent complex·stationary processes such that:

$$r(t) = F(t)\, n(t) \; ; \qquad \bar{r}(t) = -F(t)\, \hat{n}(t) \tag{13}$$

$n(t)$ and $\hat{n}(t)$ being the stationary processes defined by the integrals in equations (12a) and (12b) respectively. It follows that the representation of a physical separable process is given as:

$$f(t) = F(t)[n(t) - i\, \hat{n}(t)] \tag{14}$$

The response of linear systems to this kind of processes has been treated in a previous paper (Borino et al.1987, Di Paola 1985).

INPUT-OUTPUT RELATIONSHIPS OF LINEAR SYSTEMS.

The equation of motion of a single degree of freedom (SDOF) linear system may be written in the canonical form as follows:

$$\ddot{x} + 2\xi_o \omega_o \dot{x} + \omega_o^2 x = \tilde{f}(t) \tag{15}$$

where $\xi_o$ and $\omega_o$ are the damping ratio and the natural radian frequency respectively; the upper dot means time differentiation, and x(t) is the response of the oscillator to the physical process $\tilde{f}(t)$, namely:

$$x(t) = y(t) + i\, \bar{y}(t) \tag{16}$$

where y(t) and $\bar{y}(t)$ are the response of the oscillator (15) to the inputs r(t) and $\bar{r}(t)$ respectively. It follows that x(t) can be cast as follows:

$$x(t) = \frac{2}{\sqrt{2}} \int_0^\infty e^{-i\omega t} k_o(\omega,t)dN(\omega) \tag{17}$$

where $k_o(\omega,t)$ is the truncated Fourier transform of the product of $h(\tau)$ by the function $A(t-\tau,\omega)$, i.e.

$$k_o(\omega,t) = \int_0^t h(\tau)\, e^{i\omega\tau}\, A(t-\tau,\omega)\, d\tau \tag{18}$$

$h(\tau)$ being the impulse response function:

$$h(\tau) = \frac{1}{\omega_D} e^{-\xi_o \omega_o \tau} \sin \omega_D \tau, \; \tau \geq 0; \quad h(\tau) = 0, \quad \tau < 0 \tag{19}$$

and

$$\omega_D = \omega_o \sqrt{1 - \xi_o^2} \tag{20}$$

The various derivatives of the response $x(t)$ can be written in the form:

$$\frac{d^r x(t)}{dt^r} = \int_o^\infty e^{-i\omega t} k_r(\omega,t) \, dN(\omega) \tag{21}$$

where

$$k_r(\omega,t) = \int_o^t \frac{d^r h(\tau)}{d\tau^r} e^{i\omega\tau} A(t-\tau,\omega) d\tau \tag{22}$$

Notice that if $r > 1$ then the r-th derivative of the impulse response function must be written as:

$$\frac{d^r h(\tau)}{d\tau^r} = \alpha_r h(\tau) + \beta_r g(\tau) + \sum_{\substack{s=0 \\ r>2}}^{r-2} \frac{\beta_{r-s-1}}{\omega_D} \frac{d^s \delta(\tau)}{d\tau^s} \tag{23}$$

$\delta(\tau)$ being the Dirac delta, and

$$g(\tau) = \frac{1}{\omega_D} e^{-\xi_o \omega_o \tau} \cos \omega_D \tau, \; \tau \geq 0; \quad g(\tau) = 0, \; \tau < 0, \tag{24}$$

In equation (23) the coefficients $\alpha_r$ an $\beta_r$ are given in recursive form as follows:

$$\alpha_r = - \xi_o \omega_o \alpha_{r-1} - \omega_D \beta_{r-1} \; ; \; \beta_r = - \xi_o \omega_o \beta_{r-1} + \omega_D \alpha_{r-1} \tag{25}$$

with:

$$\alpha_o = 1; \quad \beta_o = 0 \tag{26}$$

Using equation (23) no Leibnitz rule must be used (see Nigam (1983) appendix B).

Notice that the response $x(t)$ and its time derivatives to the physical process $\tilde{f}(t)$ are physical too, and exhibit power only in the positive frequency range.

## ENVELOPE PROCESS AND NON-STATIONARY SPECTRAL MOMENTS.

The process $x(t)$ can be considered as a point in the rectangular coordinates of the plane $y(t)$, $i\,\overline{y}(t)$. In polar coordinates this process $x(t)$ can be rewritten in the form:

$$x(t) = a(t) \exp[i\ \theta(t)] \tag{27}$$

where a(t) and θ(t) are a pair of stochastic processes called the amplitude and the phase respectively. It is to be noted that y(t) and $\bar{y}(t)$ are given in polar coordinates in the form:

$$y(t) = a(t) \cos \theta(t); \qquad \bar{y}(t) = a(t) \sin \theta(t) \tag{28}$$

in equations (27) and (28) following the main definition given by Yang (1972), a(t) is the so-called non-stationary envelope function and is the modulus of the complex process x(t), i.e.

$$a(t) = \sqrt{y^2(t) + \bar{y}^2(t)} \tag{29}$$

while θ(t) is given as:

$$\theta(t) = \tan^{-1} \left[\frac{\bar{y}(t)}{y(t)}\right] \tag{30}$$

Notice that a(t) is defined in the range 0 ÷ ∞, while θ(t) is defined in the range 0 ÷ 2π (uniformly). It is to be emphasized that in the stationary case $\bar{y}(t) \equiv \hat{y}(t)$ and the envelope coincides with the modulus of the analytic response process according to the definition by Dugundji (1958) and Cramer and Leadbetter (1967).

In order to obtain the various statistics of the envelope process and of the given complex process the vector of state variable $\underset{\sim}{Z}_m(t)$ is introduced in the form:

$$\underset{\sim}{Z}_m^T(t) = [x(t)\ dx(t)/dt \ldots . d^{m-1}x(t)/dt^{m-1}] / \sqrt{2} \tag{31}$$

where the apex T means transpose. If $\tilde{f}(t)$ is a zero mean Gaussian process, then the joint probability density function (JPDF) of the vector $\underset{\sim}{Z}_m(t)$ is also Gaussian and is expressed as follows:

$$P_{\underset{\sim}{Z}_m}(\underset{\sim}{Z}_m^T; t) = \frac{1}{(2\pi)^m |\underset{\sim}{\Lambda}_{m,\underset{\sim}{Z}}(t)|} \exp\{-\underset{\sim}{Z}_m^{*T}(t)\ \underset{\sim}{\Lambda}_{m,\underset{\sim}{Z}}^{-1}(t)\ \underset{\sim}{Z}_m(t)\} \tag{32}$$

where the symbol |·| means determinant of, and $\underset{\sim}{\Lambda}_{m,\underset{\sim}{Z}}$ is the cross-covariance of the complex processes defined above, i.e.

$$\underset{\sim}{\Lambda}_{m,\underset{\sim}{Z}}(t) = E\ [\underset{\sim}{Z}_m(t)\ \underset{\sim}{Z}_m^{*T}(t)] \tag{33}$$

In an explicit form the hermitian matrix $\underset{\sim}{\Lambda}_{m,\underset{\sim}{Z}}$ can be written in the form

$$\underset{\sim}{\Lambda}_{m,\underset{\sim}{Z}}(t) = \begin{bmatrix} \lambda_{00,x}(t) & i\lambda_{01,x}(t) & -\lambda_{02,x}(t)\ldots\ldots \\ -i\lambda^{*}_{01,x}(t) & \lambda_{11,x}(t) & i\lambda_{12,x}(t)\ldots\ldots \\ -\lambda^{*}_{02,x}(t) & -i\lambda^{*}_{12,x}(t) & \lambda_{22,x}(t)\ldots\ldots \\ \ldots & \ldots & \ldots \end{bmatrix} \tag{34}$$

where the various entries of the matrix $\underset{\sim}{\Lambda}_{m,\underset{\sim}{Z}}(t)$ are given as follows

$$(-1)^k\ i^{k+s}\ \lambda_{ks,x}(t) = E\left[\frac{d^k x(t)}{dt^k}\ \frac{d^s x^{*}(t+\tau)}{d(t+\tau)^s}\right]_{\tau=0} \tag{35}$$

The introduction of the symbol $\lambda_{ks,x}(t)$, that usually means spectral moment is due to the fact that in the stationary case the following relationship holds true

$$E\left[\frac{d^k x(t)}{dt^k}\ \frac{d^s x^{*}(t+\tau)}{d(t+\tau)^s}\right] = (-1)^k\ i^{k+s}\int_0^{\infty}\omega^{k+s}\ |H(\omega)|^2\, d\psi(\omega) \tag{36}$$

where $H(\omega)$ is the transfer function of the oscillator given as

$$H(\omega) = \frac{1}{\omega_o^2 - \omega^2 + 2\, i\xi_o\omega_o\omega} \tag{37}$$

and the integrals in equation (36) are the moments of the one-sided power spectral density function, i.e. well-known spectral moments introduced by Vanmarcke (1972). It is worth noting that the spectral moments in the non-stationary case must be defined as variances of the physical processes and not as moments of the one-sided evolutionary power, because the latter definition has no physical meaning.

It is to be emphasized that in the non-stationary case two indices are necessary in order to define the spectral moments since, in general

$$\lambda_{ij,x}(t) \neq \lambda_{jk,x}(t); \qquad i + j = s + k,\ i \neq s,\ j \neq k \tag{38}$$

However, if $j + i < 2$, then a single index is sufficient to define the non-stationary spectral moment in a perfectly clear manner. Hence

$$\lambda_{01,x}(t) = \lambda^{*}_{10,x}(t) \tag{39}$$

Substituting equation (21) in equation (36) the non-stationary spectral moments are written in the form:

$$\lambda_{ks,x}(t) = \frac{(-1)^k}{i^{k+s}}\int_0^{\infty} K_k(\omega,t)\ K^{*}_s(\omega,t)\ d\psi(\omega) \tag{40}$$

To conclude this section, we can state that the introduction of the complex physical processes, instead of the more familiar real ones, is necessary not only to define the envelope function as the modulus of such processes but also to give an adequate definition of the non-stationary spectral moments.

MEAN RATE THRESHOLD CROSSING

As an application of the physical processes the mean rate threshold crossing of the enevelope process is here obtained in the non-stationary case. The vector of state variables has for this case two components, and the matrix $\Lambda_{2,Z}$ is given as:

$$\Lambda_{2,Z} = \begin{bmatrix} \lambda_{oo,x}(t) & i\lambda_{o1,x}(t) \\ -i\lambda^{*}_{o1,x}(t) & \lambda_{11,x}(t) \end{bmatrix} = \begin{bmatrix} \lambda_{o,x}(t) & i\lambda_{1,x}(t) \\ -i\lambda^{*}_{1,x}(t) & \lambda_{2,x}(t) \end{bmatrix} \tag{41}$$

The mean number of upcrossing per unit time $\nu^{+}_{a}(\eta,t)$ of the cylindrical barrier (Vanmarcke 1975) $\eta$ of the envelope process a(t) defined in equation (29), following the main definition by Rice (1955) and Middleton (1960), can be written in the form:

$$\nu^{+}_{a}(\eta,t) = \int_{o}^{\infty} p_{a\dot{a}}(\eta,\dot{a};t)\,\dot{a}\,d\dot{a} = \int_{o}^{\infty}\left[\int_{o}^{2\pi}\int_{\infty}^{\infty} p_{a\dot{a}\theta\dot{\theta}}(a,\dot{a},\theta,\dot{\theta};t)\,d\theta d\dot{\theta}\right]\dot{a}\,d\dot{a} \tag{42}$$

where $p_{a\dot{a}}(a,\dot{a};t)$ is the JPDF of the envelope and its time differentiation.

By means of the usual coordinate transformation

$$p_{a\dot{a}\theta\dot{\theta}}(a,\dot{a},\theta,\dot{\theta};t) = |J_2|\; p_{Z_2}(Z_2^T;t) \tag{43}$$

where $|J_2| = a^2(t)$ is the Jacobian of the transformation, after some algebra we obtain a closed form solution for $\nu^{+}_{a}(\eta;t)$ involving all terms (real and imaginary ) of the spectral moments, i.e.:

$$\nu^{+}_{a}(\eta;t) = \frac{\eta}{\lambda_{o,z}(t)}\sqrt{\frac{|\Lambda_{2,Z}(t)|}{2\pi\lambda_{o,z}(t)}}\;\exp\left[-\frac{\eta^2}{2}\,\frac{\lambda_{o,z}(t)\lambda_{2,z}(t)-(Re[\lambda_{1,z}(t)])^2}{\lambda_{o,z}(t)\,|\Lambda_{2,Z}(t)|}\right]$$

$$\{1+\psi_{1,z}(t)\,\eta\,\sqrt{\pi}\left[\exp(\psi_{1,z}(t)\eta)^2(1+\Phi(\psi_{1,z}(t)\eta))\right]\} \tag{44}$$

where

$$\psi_{1,z}(t) = Im[\lambda_{1,z}(t)]/\sqrt{2\lambda_{o,z}(t)\,|\Lambda_{2,Z}(t)|}\;;\quad \Phi(b) = \frac{2}{\sqrt{\pi}}\int_{o}^{b} e^{-\rho^2}d\rho. \tag{44}$$

It is worth noting that, introducing the complex processes instead of the real ones, the exact mean rate upcrossing given in equation (44) has been obtained,while only approximate expression are available in literature.

CONCLUSIONS

In this paper the importance of defining the physical stochastic processes is pointed out for the general class of non-stationary non-separable processes. Considering that the physical processes must have power in the positive frequency range the corresponding time domain representation is complex. By contrast considering the stochastic processes as real ones in the time domain, their corresponding frequency representation exibits power in both positive and negative ranges. Here is used the complex stochastic representation in the time domain, obtaining the envelope as the modulus of the stochastic complex process, and the non-stationary spectral moments as covariances of the physical processes. In this way an exact solution for some problems can be obtained: as an example the mean rate threshold crossing is given in a closed form solution. The latter problem could not be solved by considering the processes in the time domain as real ones.

REFERENCES

Borino G., Di Paola M. and Muscolino G. (1987). " Non-Stationary Spectral Moments of Base Excited MDOF Systems", to appear on Earth.Engng. & Struct. Dynamics.

Corotis, R.B., Vanmarcke E.H. & Cornell C.A. (1972), " First Passage of Non-Stationary Random Processes", J. of Engng. Mech.Div.,ASCE,98 (2),401-414.

Cramer H. & Leadbetter M.R. (1967), " Stationary and Related Stochastic Processes", John Wiley & Sons, Inc. New York, N.Y.

Di Paola M., (1985), " Transient Spectral Moments of Linear Systems", SM Archieves, 10,225-243.

Di Paola M. & Muscolino G.,(1986), " On the convergent Part of High Spectral Moments for Stationary Structural Response", Journal of Sound and Vibration, 110 (2),233-245.

Dugundji J.(1958), " Envelope and Pre-Envelope of Real Waweforms", IRE Transaction on Information Theory, 4, 53-57.

Middleton D., (1960), " An Introduction to Statistical Communication Theory", McGraw-Hill, Inc., New York, N.Y.

Nigam N.C., (1983), " Introduction to Random Vibrations", Mit Press Series in Structural Mechanics.

Papoulis A., (1984), " Signal Analysis", McGraw-Hill,Inc. New York, N.Y.

Priestley M.B., (1967), " Power Spectral Analysis of Non-Stationary Random Processe", Journal of Sound and Vibration, 6,301-328.

Rice S.O., (1955), " Mathematical Analysis of Random Noise", Selected Papers on Noise and Stochastic Processes, N.Wax ed.Dover Pub.Inc.New York, N.Y.

Vanmarcke E.H., (1972), " Properties of Spectral Moments with Applications to Random Vibration", Journal of the Engineering Mechanics Division, ASCE, 98 (2), 425-446.

Vanmarcke E.H., (1975), " On the Distribution of the First-Passage Time for Normal Stationary Random Processes",Journal of Applied Mechanics Division, ASME,42,215-220.

Yang J.N.,(1972), " Non-Stationary Envelope Process and First Excursion Probability", Journal of Structural Mechanics, 1,231-248.

# PROBABILISTIC SERVICEABILITY ANALYSIS OF R.C. STRUCTURES

Dr. F. Bljuger*
*Building Research Station, Faculty of Civil Engineering, Technion - Israel Institute of Technology, Haifa, Israel.

ABSTRACT

The serviceability limit state of R.C. structures should be characterized by the expected probability of its appearance. The evaluation methodology of probability distributions of crack appearances and deflections in R.C. structures is considered. The behaviour of statically-determinate and indeterminate structures is analysed.

The main variable parameters are the mean tensile strengths of the concrete in different areas of the structure and the lengthwise variability of concrete strength. Numerical examples are provided.

Probabilistic design analysis of serviceability of structures, with recourse to probabilistic criteria, is recommended.

## INTRODUCTION

The evolution of the methodology of structural design is primarily characterized by more and more refined approaches and models, permitting improved evaluation of the reliability of the structure. The serviceability of R.C. structures is assured by limitations on the appearance or excessive width of cracks and on excessive deflections or displacements. In all cases the dominant variable characteristic of the structure is the tensile strength of the concrete.

The traditional deterministic approach to estimation of structural serviceability, universally accepted in practice, is based on use of probabilistic characteristics of certain parameters (load, concrete, strength), dispensing with a uniform reliability level for all structures having the same purpose (CEB-FIP Code, 1978; ACI Standard, 1983; SNiP, 1985). In fact, in simple cases, all variable structural parameters are practically constant, while in other cases appearance of cracking or deformations in a structure is characterized by considerable dispersion.

The traditional approach has, in principle, two disadvantages: its criteria are deterministic and the characteristic deformation or crack appearance is calculated for a single deterministic structural system. In reality, for all structural systems, cracking or deformation is a probabilistic function, and the natural criterion of structural serviceability should be a probabilistic limit. Such a limit may be a set of several values of deformations, a definite probability of their appearance in the structure population; it may also be a definite function of the distribution of limit states, fallint outside their expected distribution in the population in question.

The variable characteristics of the structure parameters may be given in terms of distribution, and the attendant calculation difficulties can be overcome by recourse to a computer.

## CRACK APPEARANCE

The problems of serviceability limit state of statically-determinate structures relative to crack appearance, are considered by Bljuger (1983; 1985a; 1985b). For the relevant probabilistic analysis of such structures, the main characteristics are the lengthwise variability of concrete strength over the structure, and the mean concrete strength of the members within their general population. Potential cracks in the considered model of a member in bending may appear with 40mm spacing in its middle part. According to Bljuger (1985b), with normal distribution of concrete strength, the probability of crack appearance in the x-section is (see Fig. 1):

$$P_x = \frac{\Delta_i}{\sqrt{2\pi}} \sum_{i=-3}^{j} \exp(-i^2/2) \qquad (1)$$

where $\Delta_i$ is the summation step (taken as 0.3), i is an independent parameter, j is given by:

$$j = [(\frac{M_x}{W} - f_p)/f_{cm} - 1]/C_{vl} \qquad (2)$$

and the moment $M_x$ in the x-section for a uniformly distributed load p is:

$$M_x = \frac{p}{2} (\ell x - x^2) \qquad (3)$$

$f_p$ - residual prestress in most stressed fibre.
$f_{cm}$ - mean concrete strength in member.
$C_{vl}$ - coefficient of lengthwise strength variation.

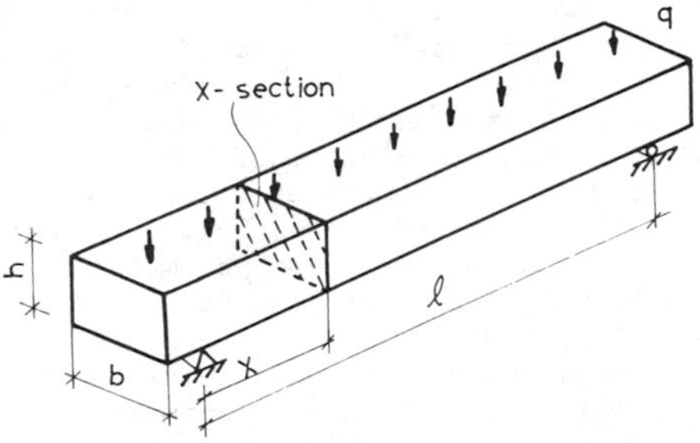


Fig. 1. Member for numerical analysis

The probability of crack appearance in the considered member with specific mean concrete strength is:

$$P_{rm} = 1 - \prod_{x_1}^{x_2} (1 - P_x) \qquad (4)$$

$x_1$ and $x_2$ denoting the limiting sections under consideration, and the spacing of potential cracks, taken as 40mm (Bljuger, 1985a).

The probability of crack appearance in a member with a given grade of concrete is evaluated by:

$$P_r = \sum_m P_{rm} \cdot P_m \qquad (5)$$

where

$P_m$ - probability of occurrence of the specific mean concrete strength, namely:

$$P_m = \frac{\Delta_m}{\sqrt{2\pi}} \exp(-m^2/2) \quad (6)$$

The mean concrete strength is defined as:

$$f_{cm} = f_{cmm} (1 + m\, C_{vo}) \quad (7)$$

where

$f_{cmm}$ - mean flexural tensile strength for given grade of concrete,
$C_{vo}$ - variation coefficient of above mean concrete strength in member population,
m - independent parameter.

The member shown in Fig. 1 (h=.2m, b=.3m), made of C-30 grade concrete, is analysed as a common R.C. structure ($f_p$=0), as well as a prestressed one ($f_p$=4 MPa).

On the basis of literature data (CEB-FIP Code, 1978), the variation coefficient of tensile concrete strength can be taken as:

$$C_v = 0.215 - 0.2 \cdot f_{ck}^{-0.465} \quad (8)$$

where $f_{ck}$ - characteristic concrete strength in compression, in MPa.

Different variabilities of the mean concrete strength in members, make for significant differences in the probability of crack appearance (Fig. 2), and in the load corresponding to the 5% probability level ($q_{.05}$). It should be noted that $C_{vl} = \sqrt{C_v^2 - C_{vo}^2}$ ; the case $C_{vo}=C_v$ ($C_{vl}$ = 0) is essentially the deterministic one (CEB-FIP Code, 1978).

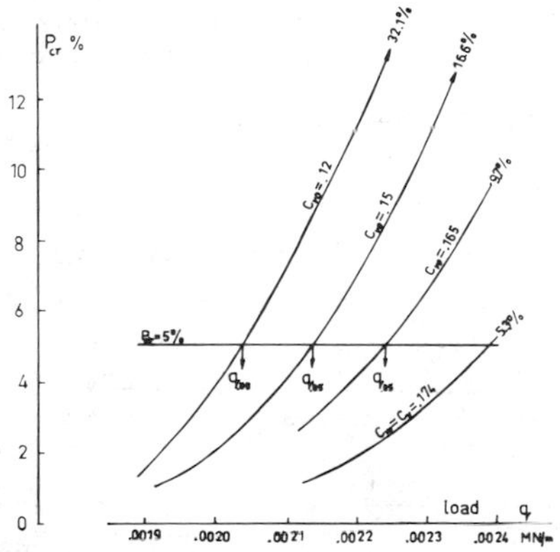


Fig. 2. Probabilities of crack appearance in members with different variabilities of mean concrete strength.

The prestressed case (Fig. 3, $f_p$=4 MPa) is analogous to the above, except that the effect on $q_{.05}$ is slight.

Lengthwise variability of concrete strength makes for drastic increase of the probability of crack appearance in all statically-determinate structures.

In statically-indeterminate structures, the probabilities of crack appearance in certain zones should be taken into account. For each

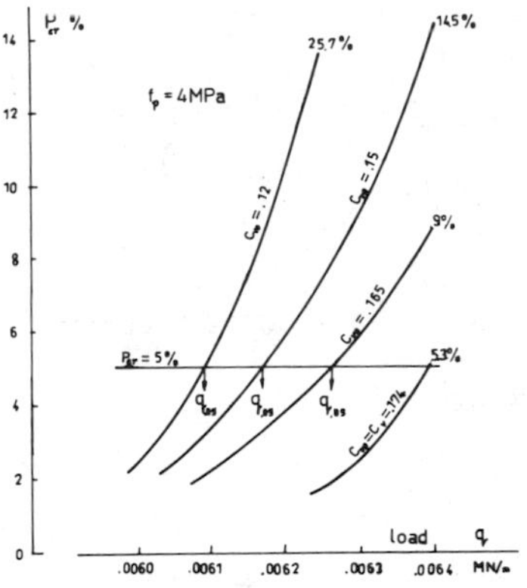


Fig. 3. Probabilities of crack appearance in prestressed members with different variabilities of mean concrete strength.

combination of variable parameters in the different zones, the appropriate moment distribution is evaluated. This procedure is obviously only feasible by iteration. The structure should preferably be taken to consist of a set of parts with variable stiffness, the latter being a function of concrete strength and also of the position of the considered section in the member. With such an approach, all distinctive features of loading and support of structure can be taken into account.

Consider, for example, the two-span composite structure shown in Fig. 4. The probability of crack appearance, at least in one section of a member, is evaluated by (4), with $M_x$ given by:

$$M_x = 4M\cdot[\frac{x}{\ell} - (\frac{x}{\ell})^2] - \frac{x}{\ell}\cdot M_s \qquad (9)$$

where $M=q\ell^2/8$ and $M_s$ is the support moment, evaluated iteratively.

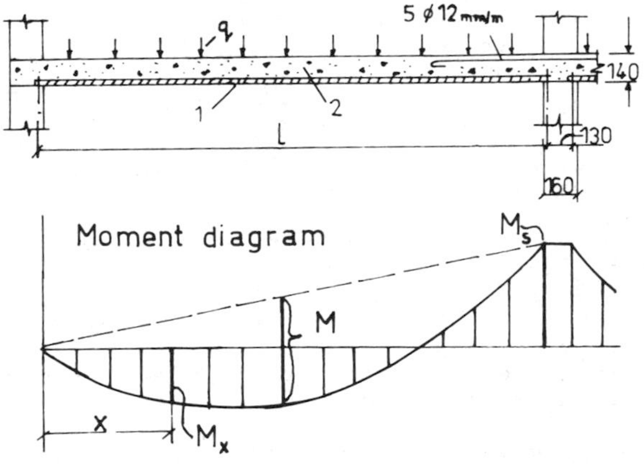


Fig. 4. Continuous member for numerical analysis, 1 - prestressed plank, 2 - cast-in-situ concrete.

The discrete probability of crack appearance in the span of a considered member with given mean concrete strength, is evaluated by:

$$P_o = P_{rm} - \Sigma P_{xo} \qquad (10)$$

where $\Sigma P_{xo}$ - sum of probabilities of crack appearance in all cases with mean strength less than the given one; $P_{rm}$ is evaluated by (4).

The overall probability of crack appearance, for the given grade of concrete, is:

$$P_r = \sum_{m2} [(\sum_{m1} P_o \cdot P_1) \cdot P_2] \qquad (11)$$

where $P_1$ and $P_2$ are the probabilities of mean concrete strength in the span and of concrete strength at the support, respectively, m1 and m2 - independent parameters. Numerical analysis of the slab in Fig. 4 [b=1m, h=.14m, residual stress in wires $\sigma_p$ = 1000 MPa, grades of concrete: planks ($h_1$ =40mm) - C40 ($f_{ctk}$=2.4 MPa, $E_c$=35 GPa), cast-in-situ - C20 ($f_{ctk}$=1.6 MPa, $E_c$=29 GPa), $\ell$=5.22m, loads: q=3.36 kN/m, p=2.5 kN/m, $p_t$ = 1.3kN/m; coefficients of variation: $C_v$ = 0.17, $C_{vo}$ = 0.12]. The final results are presented in Fig. 5.

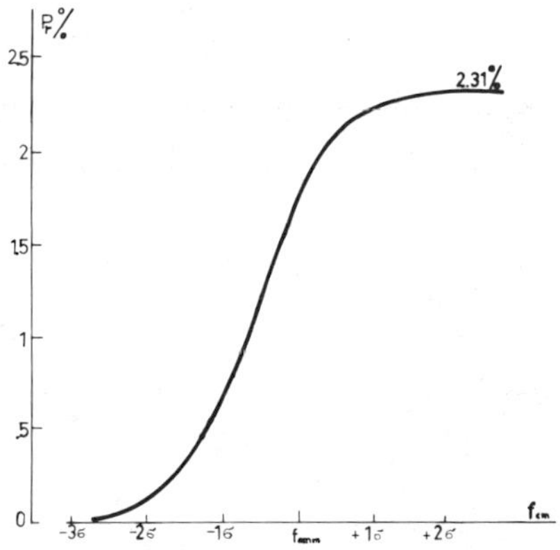


Fig. 5. Probability function of crack appearance in span versus mean strength of cast-in-situ concrete in member ($f_{cmm}$ - mean strength of given concrete).

Under the traditional approach, the design probability of crack appearance in the span is taken as the product of two probabilities of characteristic strengths of the concretes: .05x.05 = .0025, i.e. only 0.25%, while under the probabilistic approach the expected probability is higher, namely 2.31%.

DEFLECTION

In probabilistic analysis of deflections, considerable importance attaches to choice of the design model. In principle, two models are available: (1) the simple one presented in ACI Standard (1978), in which the deflection is a function of the cracking moment, and (2) the more sophisticated one presented in (SNiP, 1985; Carreira, 1986), and based on evaluation of section curvatures. Both are valid for the stage with the acting moment significantly in excess of the cracking moment, but in slabs, as a rule, this stage is irrelevant. The second model is preferable in that it permits incorporation of the probabilities of crack appearance.

Consider a model (Fig. 6) comprising $n_1 = \frac{\ell}{2}/h$ parts of member. The deflection is computed by summation of products:

$$a = 2\frac{\ell}{n_1} \cdot \sum_{n_1} k_x \cdot x \tag{12}$$

where $k_x$ - curvature of x-part, $n_1$ - number of parts in one-half of member, x - distance from support to centre of considered part.

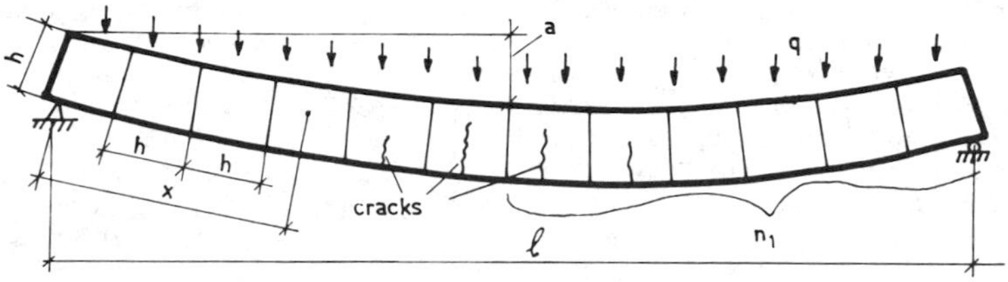


Fig. 6. Model of member for evaluation of deflections

The curvature of the cracked part is evaluated by SNiP (1985):

$$k_x = \frac{M_x\left(\frac{\psi}{E_s A_s} + \frac{0.9}{x_c \cdot b \cdot E_c \cdot \nu}\right)}{d(d - x_c/3}\tag{13}$$

where $\psi$ - bond coefficient between concrete and reinforcing steel

$$\psi = 1.25 - S \cdot M_{cr}/M_x \tag{14}$$

$$M_{cr} = W(f_p + f_c) \tag{15}$$

$M_x$ - as per (3).
$x_c$ - height of compressed part of section.
d - distance from extreme compressed fibre to centroid of tension reinforcement.

The curvature of the non-cracked part is:

$$k_x = M_x \cdot C/E_c I_g \tag{16}$$

C,S and $\nu$ - coefficients creep of concrete (for short-term loads: C=1, S=1.1, $\nu$=.45).

Different types of members with height 150mm and span 4m were analysed. As appearance of a crack or two causes an insignificant increase of the deflections (only one or two summands of the total of $n_1$ in (12) are increased), the lengthwise variation of concrete strength may be disregarded. The probability functions of $a/\ell$ for members with different reinforcement rations and variability of mean concrete strength are plotted in Fig. 7.

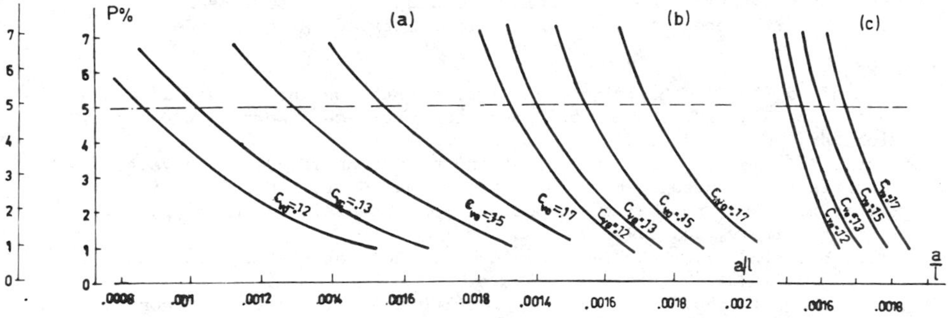


Fig. 7. Probability functions of relative deflections in members with different reinforcement ratios: (a) $\rho$ = 0.3%, (b) $\rho$ = 0.5%, (c) $\rho$ = 1%.

The graphs are compared with cases of deflection $\ell/600$ for short-term load on members with $C_{vo}$=.173*. As the variability of mean concrete strength decreases, there is a steep drop in the probability of the corresponding deflection.

The deflection ratio $a/a_o$ (member with given $C_v$ to the reference C =.173), for structures with different reinforcement ratios, is plotted against $C_{vo}$ in Fig. 8.

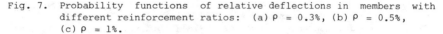

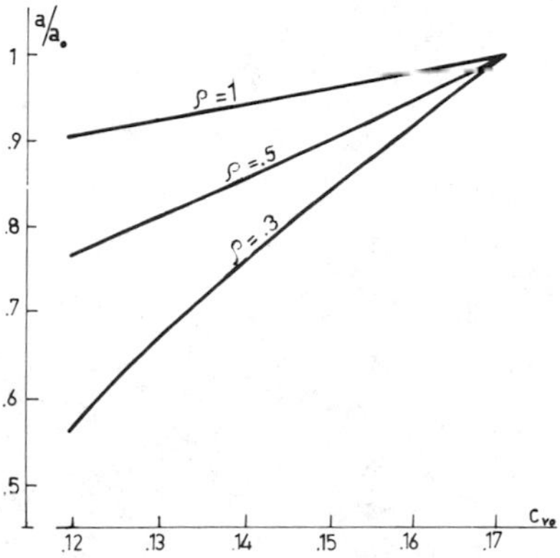


Fig. 8. $a/a_o$ vs. coefficient of variation of mean concrete strength ($C_{vo}$) in member.

The proposed probabilistic approach is applicable for continuous structures, as well as in crack-width analysis.

*The corresponding long-term load causes a deflection of $\ell/200$, which is equal to the criterion.

## CONCLUSION

The traditional approach to estimation of structural serviceability yields, essentially, different reliabilities in terms of crack formation or excessive deformation. Probabilistic analysis of serviceability of structures, with recourse to probabilistic criteria, is recommended.

## REFERENCES

ACI Standard (1983). Building Code Requirements for Reinforced Concrete (ACI 318-77), ACI Manual of Concrete Practice, part 3, Detroit, Michigan, pp. 218-330.

Bljuger, F. (1983). Lengthwise strength variability in analysis of concrete structures, Proc. of 4th Intern. Conf. on Applications of Statistics and Probability in Soil and Structural Engineering, V.1, Florence, Italy, pp. 377-389.

Bljuger, F., (1985a). Cracking Resistance of Concrete Members in Bending, ACI Journal, July-August, pp. 467-474.

Bljuger, F., (1985b). Reliability cracking analysis of two-way concrete slabs, Proc. of 4th Intern. Conf. on Structural Safety and Reliability, Kobe, Japan, pp. III-652-658.

Carreira, D.J. and Kuang-Han Chu, (1986). The Moment-Curvature Relationship of R.C. Members, ACI Journal, pp. 191-198.

CEB-FIP Code for Concrete Structures (1978), 3rd Edition. Comite Euro-International du Beton/Federation Internationale de la Precontrainte, Paris, 471 pp.

SNiP 2.03.01-84 (1985). Building Code for Design of Reinforced and Non-Reinforced Concrete Structures, S.I., Moscow (in Russian).

# LIFETIME SYSTEM RELIABILITY MODELS WITH APPLICATION TO HIGHWAY BRIDGES

Gongkang Fu and Fred Moses
Dept. of Civil Engineering
Case Western Reserve Univ.
Cleveland, OH 44106, U.S.A.

ABSTRACT

Structural system reliability needs to model lifetime safety strategies including redundancy, inspection, maintenance and load control. It is pointed out that redundancy is not related to survival probability. A compatible index in terms of probabilistic analysis is a proposed damage index, which describes the redundancy concept quantitatively. The reliability as well as the damage index are needed to describe a structure system for both system survival and system damage tolerance. Applications to highway bridges are presented. Parameters such as safety factors, structural configurations and statistical correlations between resistances are studied for their influence on the system reliability and the damage index.

## 1 INTRODUCTION

For application to routine designs, theoretical and practical developments in structural reliability have emphasized component safety. It is well recognized that the system reliability may be different from the component reliability. The importance of structural system reliability analysis has thus been attracting intensive attention from engineers and researchers in recent years. A major impetus for structural system reliability has occurred in evaluating existing structures either due to incurred damage or changes in load conditions. The economic advantage of salvaging an existing structure by using sophisticated system reliability is clearly evident. The validation of reliability models from observed performance histories also recognizes the computed system reliabilities rather than component reliabilities.

In this paper, several concepts addressed are reliability, redundancy and damage index in the context of structure systems. They are concerned in both new structure design and existing structure evaluation. A structure system should possess both reserve strength and residual strength to be accepted as safe. The former is defined as the capacity to carry higher loads than expected in design, while the latter indicates the ability to tolerate incurred component damage without loss of major system serviceability.

It is intended in this paper to describe redundancy and damage tolerance in terms of probabilistic analysis by introducing the concept of damage index, developed by Gorman and Moses [1981] and modified here. A simple illustration is included, and also a practical problem in highway bridge design.

A further application of system reliability is modelling of lifetime safety strategies encompassing design, redundancy requirements, inspection, maintenance and load controls. Fu and Moses [1986] reviewed developments in this direction and introduced a general lifetime system reliability model by using Markov processes for resistance modelling. Thus, the damage index presented can also quantify system redundancy over its lifetime.

## 2 RELIABILITY, REDUNDANCY AND DAMAGE INDEX

<u>Reliability</u> - The term reliability has been more widely accepted as "probability of success in service as desired in the design". It quantifies the safety and admits the limit of designers' knowledge about the structure, which is termed "uncertainty" of both loads and structure capacity. The

introduction of structural reliability has impacted traditional concepts of structure safety. Mathematically speaking, it implies a stochastic or probabilistic analysis. Some classic deterministic concepts about structures such as redundancy and multiple load paths have to be carefully modified or redefined to avoid confusion.

According to its definition above, system reliability is a probabilistic description of system reserve strength, but not that of system residual strength. It quantifies the survival possibility or occurrence possibility of the loads not exceeding the capacity. This view explains why reliability cannot cover the aspect of damage tolerance related to redundancy to be discussed later.

System reliability analysis consists of A) identification of possible failure modes of the system formulated by the failure mode equations

$$g_m(\underset{\sim}{X}) = 0 \quad ( m=1,2,...,M ) \tag{1}$$

where $\underset{\sim}{X}$ is the basic random variable vector consisting of load effects and component resistances; function $g_m(\underset{\sim}{X})$'s are less than or equal zero when the corresponding modes occur; B) calculation of each failure mode occurrence probability and C) estimation of overall system failure probability:

$$P_{f(sys)} = \text{Prob}\,[\text{any } g_m(\underset{\sim}{X}) \leq 0] = \int_{\text{all } \underset{\sim}{x}} G(\underset{\sim}{x})\, f_{\underset{\sim}{X}}(\underset{\sim}{x})\, d\underset{\sim}{x} \quad ( m=1,2,...,M ) \tag{2}$$

in which $f_{\underset{\sim}{X}}(\underset{\sim}{x})$ is the joint probability density distribution of random vector $\underset{\sim}{X}$, and $G(\underset{\sim}{X})$ is the system failure indicator function, i.e.

$$G(\underset{\sim}{X}) = \begin{cases} 1 & \text{any } g_m(\underset{\sim}{X}) \leq 0 \\ 0 & \text{no } g_m(\underset{\sim}{X}) \leq 0 \end{cases} \quad ( m=1,2,...,M ) \tag{3}$$

In the case of numerous failure modes for a complex system, identification of dominant modes out of all possible failure modes should be included in step A) to avoid costly computation in estimation of the failure probability $P_{f(sys)}$. In another words, M failure modes in (1) and (2) include only those that make significant contributions to $P_{f(sys)}$. Step C) can be performed by various bounds or simulation techniques such as advanced methods of Importance Sampling [Fu & Moses 1986].

In this paper, a highway bridge system problem is investigated based on system reliability criteria. Factors influencing system reliability are studied such as statistical correlation between resistances, safety factors for loads and resistances, component safety level and structure configurations.

Redundancy - Redundancy is, by Webster III, defined as a "lavish or excessive supply". It is usually, in structural engineering, understood as those components that are not neccessary for load carrying in terms of statical determinancy. It is often referred by the capacity to prevent failure of an entire structure system upon failure of a single component. However, the word redundancy in structural engineering still remains fuzzy and even confusing. This can be observed by the variety of definitions and quantifications of redundancy.

The concept of redundancy often impacts a general concept of safety or reliability to structures, since it also provides residual strength to the structural system after it is damaged. This is one of the most serious confusions about redundancy among engineers and researchers. Based on its definition above, reliability does not completely cover our general concept of "being reliable". Redundancy addresses the system residual strength but is not able to deal with problems of reserve strength covered by system reliability defined previously.

It is thus neccessary to introduce a new index to cover the system residual strength in terms of probabilistic analysis. The damage index is suggested here for this.

Damage Index - For a structure system, the damage index is defined here as

$$\text{Damage Index} = E[d(\underset{\sim}{X})] = \int_{\text{all } \underset{\sim}{x}} d(\underset{\sim}{x})\, f_{\underset{\sim}{X}}(\underset{\sim}{x})\, d\underset{\sim}{x} \tag{4}$$

where $d(\underset{\sim}{X})$ is a system damage function of the random vector $\underset{\sim}{X}$ defined in eq.(1), $E[d(\underset{\sim}{X})]$ is its expectation. The system damage ratio d is given a value of 1.0 for system failure and 0 for no damage or failure to any component of the system. For example, d can be the damage state of a structure system or the repair cost for that state. d is understood as a function of the system capacity as well as the load effects according to the definition above. It is a generalization of the damage index introduced by Gorman and Moses [1981] and used by Moses and Ghosn [1981]. For simplification, damage d was defined earlier as a function of load level only, although another integration would cover the participation of system capacity. For multiple loads and multiple failure modes, that definition cannot handle such intractable problems.

More specifically, the damage function d depends on damage states defined by partial failure modes as developed by Rashedi and Moses [1983]. The damage index also provides damage tolerance information for the structure system and covers the important features of redundancy in terms of probabilistic analysis.

The definition (4) offers some calculation advantages. It can be observed by noticing the similarity between eq.(4) and (2). In fact, (2) is a special case of (4) by setting

$$d(\underset{\sim}{X}) = G(\underset{\sim}{X}) \tag{5}$$

This indicates an extreme case of damage measure that only system failure or its repair cost is taken into account and that the system has zero damage tolerance. Thus many techniques for system reliability can be utilized here for damage index estimation.

A proposed redundancy index RI, as a measure of reserve and/or residual strength for a structure system, can be introduced based on the damage index concept:

$$RI = [P_d - P_{f(sys)}]/P_{f(sys)} \tag{6a}$$

where

$$P_d = \text{Prob}[\ d(\underset{\sim}{X})>0\ ] \tag{6b}$$

is the probability of any damage occurrence to the system. The redundancy index, RI, is the probability of damage without system failure scaled by the system failure probability. An RI of zero means zero redundancy or "brittle" system. Another alternative to RI definition is to replace $P_d$ in eq.(6) with the damage index $E[d(\underset{\sim}{X})]$.

## 3 AN ILLUSTRATIVE EXAMPLE

A simple example of a structural system problem is first presented. Consider two parallel bar system under a deterministic load S (Fig.1). The resistances, $R_1$ and $R_2$, are assumed normally distributed with a common COV (coefficient of variation ) of 20% and a correlation coefficient $\rho$ . Under the assumption of equal load sharing between the two bars, the system failure modes are

$$g_{(sys)} = R_1 + R_2 - S \tag{7}$$

for ductile components and

$$g_{(sys)} = \text{Min}[\ \text{Max}(2R_1, R_2), \text{Max}(R_1, 2R_2)\ ] - S \tag{8}$$

for brittle components. The damage ratio d is considered as the repair cost of the corresponding damage state:

$$d = \begin{cases} 0 & \text{no bar fails} \\ 1/n_d & \text{1 bar fails only} \\ 1 & \text{2 bar fail (system failure)} \end{cases} \tag{9}$$

The factor $n_d$ reflects repair and/or other cost for partial failures. $n_d$ should exceed 1.0 in practice. The mean resistances are determined by a safety factor S.F.: $\overline{R}_1=\overline{R}_2=0.5*S.F.*S$

For S.F.=2.2, Fig.1 shows the damage index E[d] with the correlation coefficient $\rho$ for both brittle and ductile materials and different values of $n_d$. The integrations of (2) and (4) were carried out by using the tables of binormal integration [National Bureau of Standards 1959]. It should be noticed that $E[d]=P_{f(sys)}$ when $n_d \rightarrow \infty$. In Fig.1, two material models lead to different system influence for damage index E[d] and system failure probability $P_{f(sys)}$:

1) $P_{f(sys)}$ for brittle model is not monotonic with $\rho$, while it is for ductile. This system is compared with a single component case with the same component safety level, which is shown in Fig.1 by the constant $E[d]=P_{f(sys)}$. This comparison confirms that a structure with "redundant" load paths may not always be more reliable. 2) The damage index curves also characterize the system behavior with respect to damage tolerance. This is seen in the smaller differences between E[d] and $P_{f(sys)}$ for brittle model than for ductile one. 3) The damage tolerance or the range between E[d] and $P_{f(sys)}$ decreases with $\rho$ for both material models. It is more evident, however, for the brittle model. For $\rho>0.65$, the system with brittle material displays almost perfect brittle behavior, since the damage indices E[d] are the same as $P_{f(sys)}$, no matter what $n_d$ is. Thus, highly correlated resistances do not provide effective redundant load paths to a structure system of brittle components. The failure of one load path means statistically simultaneous failure of the other one, even though there is statical indeterminancy. 4) For a ductile system, maximum expected damage may occur at $0<\rho<1$, depending on $n_d$ or the definition of d. This happens here when $n_d=3$ and 4, which correspond to relatively higher costs for partial (1 bar) failure.

The observations described above are also present for S.F.=1.7 and 2.7 although not shown here due to space limits. Fig.2 shows the redundancy index RI defined in eqs.(6) vs. $\rho$ for the three values of S.F. The safety factor affects system reliability and redundancy index in the following ways: 1) The maxima of $P_{f(sys)}$ for the brittle model occurs at higher $\rho$ as the safety factor increases. This may be important in practical designs. 2) The system redundancy quantified by RI increases with the safety factor. This increase is more significant for the brittle material, especially when $\rho$ is close to 1.

This simple example illustrates the application of system reliability and damage index. It also explores the importance of the safety factor S.F. and the correlation coefficient $\rho$.

# 4 APPLICATIONS TO HIGHWAY BRIDGES

Consider a 2-lane highway bridge with steel girders shown in Fig.3. Three configurations are investigated for the design. Loads D, $L_1$ and $L_2$ are dead load and live (vehicle) loads 1 and 2, whose nominal sum is the design load. The loads are lognormally distributed with COV of 7% (D) and 30% ($L_1$ and $L_2$) respectively. The dynamic effects are included, and the two live loads are considered fully correlated. $r_1$ and $r_2$ are location factors representing the deviations of vehicle centers from the lane centers, and are normally distributed with 0 mean values and standard deviation of 0.025. Moment effects on the girders are considered in the system reliability study with ductile girder failures. A bridge system of n girders fails if n-1 girders have failed. The nominal girder resistances are determined by the following design equation for the most heavily loaded girder and then setting the rest the same:

$$R_n = \gamma_D\, g_D\, D_n + \gamma_L\, g_L\, (L_{1n}+L_{2n}) \tag{10}$$

The resistances are also lognormally distributed and correlated to each other by $\rho$, with COV of 12%. In (10), $\gamma_D$, $\gamma_L$, $g_D$ and $g_L$ are load factors and girder distribution factors for dead and live loads respectively. They are given values in Fig.4 according to AASHTO bridge specifications [1983]. The subscript n in eq.(10) denotes the nominal value that relates to the corresponding mean value by the bias (mean divided by nominal).

The failure modes are identified by structure analysis of continuous beams in tranverse direction. The integrations of failure probabilities are computed by employing Importance Sampling in simulations. The partial failure modes are defined by the number of failed girders. The following damage definitions are estimated for 4-girder (4-g) bridges

$$d = \begin{cases} 0 & \text{no girder fails} \\ 1/n_d & \text{only 1 girder fails} \\ 1.5/n_d & \text{only 2 girders fail (the factor 1.5 is assumed)} \\ 1 & \text{system (3 girders) failure} \end{cases} \tag{11}$$

for 3-girder (3-g) bridges

$$d = \begin{cases} 0 & \text{no girder fails} \\ 1/n_d & \text{only 1 girder fails} \\ 1 & \text{system (2 girders) failure} \end{cases} \tag{12}$$

and for 2-girder (2-g) bridges

$$d = \begin{cases} 0 & \text{no girder fails} \\ 1 & \text{system (1 girder) failure} \end{cases} \tag{13}$$

The damage indices for these systems are plotted vs. $\rho$ in Fig.4 for three values of $n_d$ for a hypothetical 70 ft. span with $L_n/D_n$ equal to 1.08. The bias of D, L and R are equal to 0.95, 0.90 and 1.2 respectively. Also shown in Fig.4 are the system failure probabilities. In fact, $E[d]=P_{f(sys)}$ for 2-g case and when $n_d \rightarrow \infty$ for the others. It may be obsered that: 1) The 3-g bridge has a higher damage index which is almost constant with $\rho$. The highest load carrying girder in the center most likely fails, which causes the higher expected damage. This girder also dominates the expected damage so that the statistical correlation of girders does not affect the damage assessment. 2) For 4-g bridge, E[d] is lower and decreases with $\rho$. 3) The system reliability of 4-g bridge is more sensitive to $\rho$ than the others. It is expected that the more girders are used, the more affected is the bridge system reliability by the correlation between girders. 4) the 2-g bridge is a system in series, so that the correlation of the two girders is helpful in reliability.

Fig.5 contains plots of the redundancy index RI for 3-g and 4-g systems of the same cases. The 2-g system has a RI of zero not shown because of the logarithm plot. These curves show us higher damage tolerances for 3-g case than the 4-g one. This reflects the greater reserve in the 3-g case after failure of the center girder at least for the parameters used in the example.

5 CONCLUSIONS

This paper addresses concepts of reliability, redundancy, damage index and lifetime modelling of structural systems. The introduction of the damage index provides a probabilistic measure of system damage tolerance and redundancy. Applications to the two parallel bar system and the highway bridge system bring us some results of parametric studies. 1) The reliability of the parallel system with brittle components is not monotonic with the resistance correlation coefficient. 2) Safety factors contribute to both system reliability and damage tolerance characterized by the damage index. 3) The statistical correlation between girders has more influence on the reliability of bridge systems with more parallel girders. 4) Further research is needed to investigate validation of the damage index when considering accidental and repeating type loadings. 5) Additional work is also needed in practically defining the damage ratio d.

ACKNOWLEDGEMENT

The support for this work from National Science Fundation of U.S.A. (Grant No. ECE85-16771) is gratefully appreciated.

REFERENCES

AASHTO. Standard Specifications for Highway Bridges 13th Edition 1983

Fu,G. & Moses,F. "Application of Lifetime System Reliability" Preprint No.52-1 of Structures Congress'86 New Orleans, LA Sep.1986

Gorman,M.R. & Moses,F. "Partial Factors for Structural Damage" Probabilistic Methods in Structural Engineering (Ed.) by Shinozuka,M. & Yao,J.T.P. St.Louis, MI Oct.1981 p.251-257

Moses,F. & Ghosn,M. "Requirements for a Reliability Based Bridge Code" Probabilistic Methods in Structural Engineering (Ed.) by Shinozuka,M. & Yao,J.T.P. St.Louis, MI Oct.1981 P.61-80

National Bureau of Standards, Tables of the Bivariate Normal Distribution Function and Related Functions, Applied Math. Series 50 June 1959

Rashedi,M.R. & Moses,F. "Studies on Reliability of Structural Systems" Report No.R83-3 Dept. of Civil Engineering Case Western Reserve Univ. Cleveland, OH Dec.1983

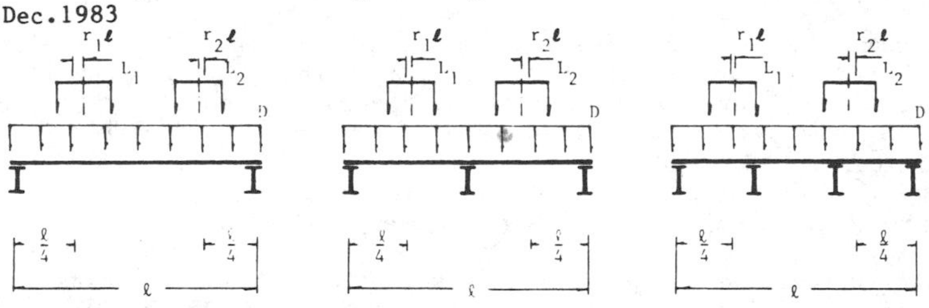

Fir. 3 2-Lane Highway Bridge System

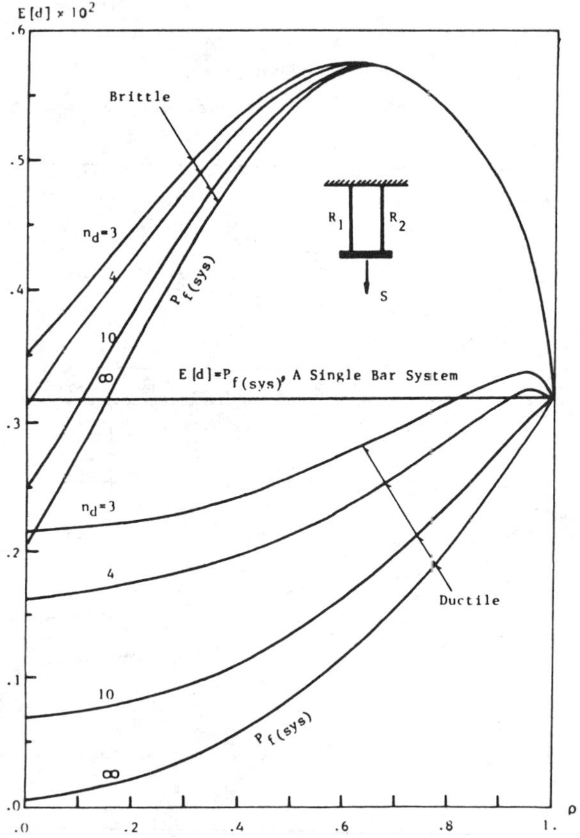


Fig.1 Damage Index vs. Correlation ρ for the Two Bar Parallel System

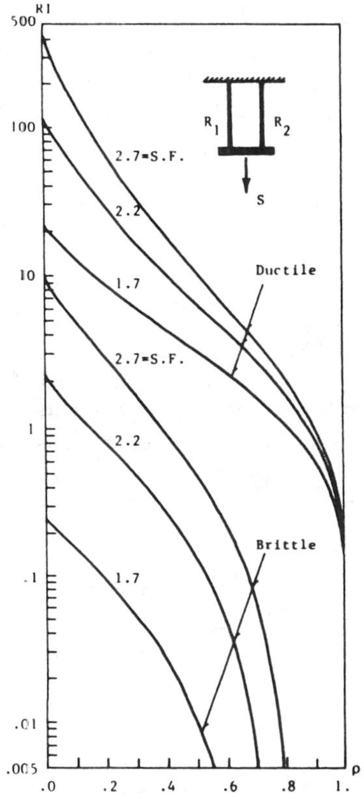


Fig.2 Redundancy Index vs. Correlation ρ for the Two Bar Parallel System

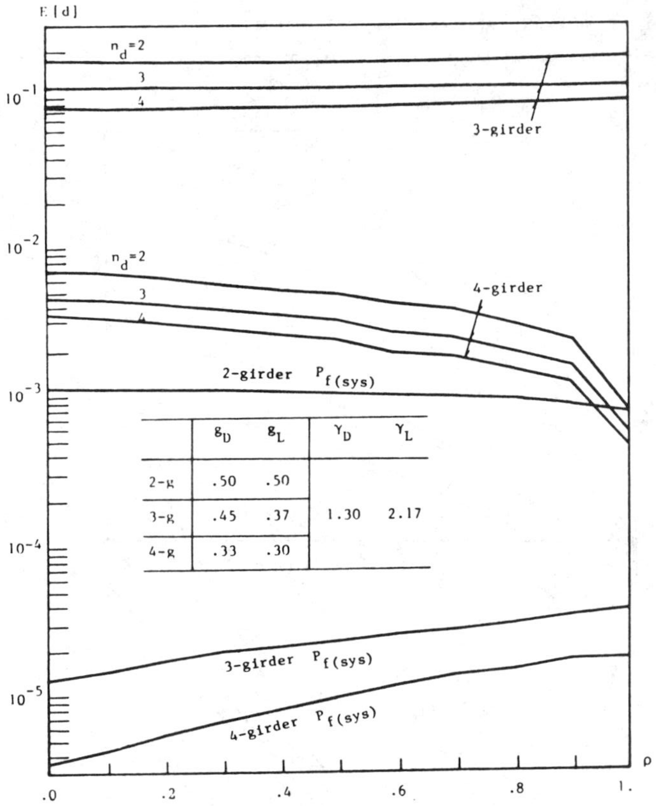


| | $g_D$ | $g_L$ | $\gamma_D$ | $\gamma_L$ |
|---|---|---|---|---|
| 2-g | .50 | .50 | | |
| 3-g | .45 | .37 | 1.30 | 2.17 |
| 4-g | .33 | .30 | | |

Fig.4 Damage Index and $P_{f(sys)}$ vs. Correlation ρ for the Bridge System Examples

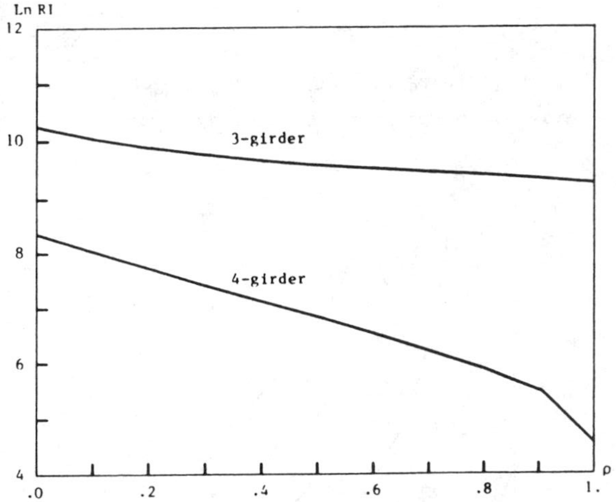


Fig.5 Redundancy Index vs. Correlation ρ for the Bridge System Examples

# PROBABILISTIC STABILITY ANALYSIS OF COLUMNS AND FRAMES*

Magdi H. Mansour[1], M.CSCE & Chandra S. Putcha[2], M.ASCE

## ABSTRACT

This paper deals with the variability associated with the critical buckling load of columns and frames due to the uncertainities existing in the parameters which affect the deterministic analyses of such problems. The aim of this study is to provide a designer with formulas able to account for the variability of the buckling load, to any desired degree of confidence, at the earliest possible stage in the design process. These formulas are first derived using the basic principles of probability theory. Thereafter, they are modified as appropriate using Monte-Carlo simulations. The variabilities of the input random variables are assumed to follow Gaussian (normal) distributions. It is found that the formulas derived describe the variability of the buckling load successfully, provided that the variabilities of the input parameters are small.

## INTRODUCTION

In the past few years, interest in structural analyses, based on the applications of the probabilistic concepts, has been growing rapidly. The trend in this line of research lies mainly in the aspect of establishing safety indices for the various elements of structures. Rosenblueth and Esteva (1972) are among the first pioneers who developed techniques of establishing such indices. Their technique was used by Galambos and Ravindra (1973) to develop a load and resistance factor for a steel design code. Many researchers (Hasofer and Lind, 1974, Rackwitz and Fiessler, 1977, Putcha, 1986, and others) have contributed to the safety index concept. However, the link between these indices and their use in the design steps of a particular structure is not available in many design cases. Furthermore, at present, there exists no explicit relationship between the coefficient of variation of the critical load (of columns or frames) and the coefficients of variation of the input parameters.

In this study, an attempt is made to establish such relationships. Thus, a designer would be able to account for the variability of the buckling load during the steps of the design, having estimated the uncertainities in the deterministic values of the input parameters. Formulas derived in this paper are based on the basic principles of probability theory. For input parameters with normal distribution variability functions, the variability of the output parameter can be estimated using the partial derivative method (Haugen, 1968), provided that the coefficients of variation are small and the deterministic anaslysis is not highly non-linear. These relationships are then examined using Monte-Carlo simulation and modified accordingly. The modifications, carried out

---

* This work was done while the second author was at California State University, Fullerton, California, U.S.A.

[1] Assistant Professor, Department of Engineering, Dalhousie University, Halifax, Nova Scotia, Canada, B3H 3J5 .

[2] Member of the Technical Staff, TRW Defense System Group, 134/9858, One Space Park, Redondo Beach, CA. 90278. U.S.A.

through the determination of correction factors, are due to the high degree of non-linearity in the deterministic solution, especially in the case of frames.

**DETERMINISTIC ANALYSES**

**COLUMNS.** The critical buckling load of a column, $P_{cr}$, with any end conditions, is given by Chajes (1974) in the form:

$$P_{cr} = \pi^2 EI/(eL)^2 \qquad (1)$$

where E is the modulus of elasticity of the column's material, I is the cross-section's moment of inertia about the axis where buckling is expected, L is the column's length, and e is the effective length coefficient. Fig. 1-a shows a schematic sketch of a pin-ends column.

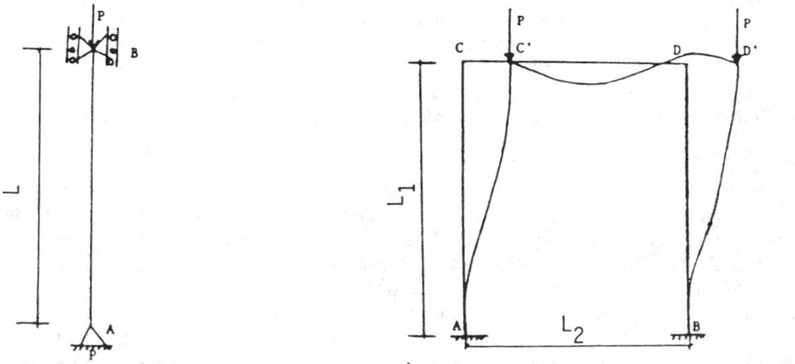


a) A Pin-Ends Column b) A Frame with Sidesway Buckling

Fig. 1: Diagramatic Sketch of a Column and a Frame

**FRAMES.** In the case of frames, the degree of non-linearity in the deterministic analysis depends upon the frame type and its geometrical constraints. As a first attempt to establish an explicit functional relationship based on probabilistic concepts, only the one-panel, single storey frames with permitted sidesway buckling, is considered here. Referring to Fig. 1-b, the critical buckling load, which satisfies the moment equilibrium equations (Chajes, 1974), may be written in the form:

$$P_{cr} = \theta^2 EI_1/(L_1)^2 \qquad (2)$$

where $\theta$ in this case is the solution of the trigonometric equation:

$$\tan\theta + \alpha\theta = 0\ , \qquad (3)$$

and

$$\alpha = I_1 L_2/6 I_2 L_1\ . \qquad (4)$$

The subscripts 1 and 2 in these relations refer to the column and beam respectively. Looking closely at these equations, one can regard $\alpha$ as being a strength parameter for the frame. Fig.2 shows the solution of equation (3) for a practical range of values of $\alpha$. Furthermore, the case $\alpha = 0$ is a special case for which the frame is reduced to a column.

STATISTICAL ANALYSES

**PARTIAL DERIVATIVE FORMULA.** As indicated by Haugen (1968), if the mean value $\bar{y}$, of a random variable y, is related to the mean values of the random variables $x_1$, $x_2$, ..., by the relation $\bar{y} = f(\bar{x}_1, \bar{x}_2, ...)$, then the standard deviation, $\sigma_y$, in case where $x_1$, $x_2$, ..., have small variabilities according to a Gaussian distribution, is given by :

$$\sigma_y = [(\sigma_{x1}\partial f/\partial x_1)^2 + (\sigma_{x2}\partial f/\partial x_2)^2 + \ldots]^{.5} \quad . \tag{5}$$

In the case of a column, the mean value of the critical buckling load, $\bar{P}_{cr}$, is given in terms of the mean values, $\bar{E}$, $\bar{I}$, and $\bar{L}$. To simplify the typing of this text, the bar sign on the top of a variable will be ommitted from now on. Thus, $P_{cr}$ denotes the mean value of the buckling load or its deterministic value as appropriate.

In order to estimate the variability of $P_{cr}$ in terms of the variabilities of E, I, and L, one may apply equation (5), using equation (1). Furthermore, in terms of coefficients of variation, V ($V_y = \sigma_y/y$ for example), one may write at once :

$$V_{Pcr} = [(V_E)^2 + (V_I)^2 + (2V_L)^2]^{.5} \tag{6}$$

In turn, the moment of inertia, I, and its variation, $V_I$, are functions of the geometric dimensions of the cross-section and their variations, respectively. Thus, I and $V_I$ depend on the shape of the cross-section. For example, in case of a circular column of diameter D, and the uncertainity in D is represented by $V_D$, then $I = \pi D^4/64$, and by equation (5), $V_I = 4V_D$. For a rectangular (or square) column of cross-sectional dimensions bxd, $I = db^3/12$, and $V_I = [(V_d)^2 + (3V_b)^2]^{.5}$ . In addition, it is practically appropriate to assume that the coefficients of variation of the various dimensions of a given cross-section are approximately equal (i.e., $V_b = V_d = V_G$, for example), where $V_G$ denotes the coefficient of variation of any geometrical dimensions of a cross-section. Thus, one may write:

$$V_I \simeq \sqrt{10}\, V_G \tag{7}$$

Another shape for the cross-section, which is widely used, is the I-section (whether it is an S, W, and/or a built-up section). Fig.3 shows a typical I-section, and by using the symbols defined on the sketch, the

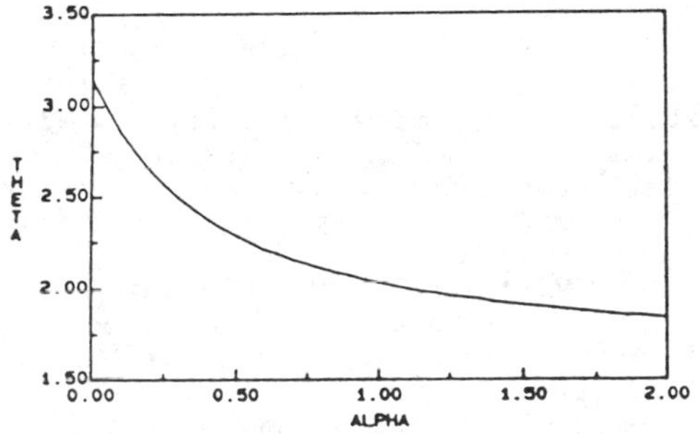


Fig. 2: Values of Θ for the Deterministic Solution of a Frame

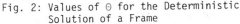

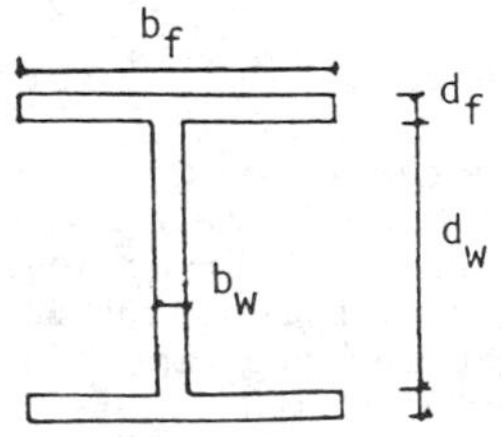


Fig. 3: A Typical I-Section

moment of inertia can be expressed in the form:

$$I = [2d_f b_f^3 + d_w b_w^3]/12 \tag{8}$$

Equation (5) may now be used with equation (8) to predict the standard deviation of I. In terms of coefficients of variation, one may write:

$$V_I = \{10[1 - (1 + d_w b_w^3/2d_f b_f^3)^{-2} d_w b_w^3/d_f b_f^3]\}^{.5}\ V_G \tag{9}$$

For cross-sections of this type, $b_w$ is much smaller than $b_f$ or $d_w$, numerically, and therefore, $(d_w b_w^3/d_f b_f^3) << 1$. Hence, the series in equation (9) may be expanded, and by neglecting terms of higher orders than unity, equation (9) reduces to:

$$V_I = [10(1 - d_w b_w^3/d_f b_f^3)]^{.5}\ V_G \tag{10}$$

It is interesting to note here that equation (10) is, to a high degree of accuracy, equivalent to equation (7). This is due to the same reason that the term inside the bracket is very close to unity. Thus, equation (7) serves for both cross-sections; the rectangular and I-sections.

In case of frames with buckling load given by equation (2), the partial derivative equation (5) yields, in terms of coefficients of variation, to

$$V_{Pcr} = [(2V_\theta)^2 + (V_E)^2 + (V_I)^2 + (2V_L)^2]^{.5}\ . \tag{11}$$

The standard deviation of the parameter $\theta$ may be expressed using equations (3) and (5), in the form $\sigma_\theta = [(\sigma_\alpha\, d\theta/d\alpha)^2]^{.5}$, where $d\theta/d\alpha$ can be determined by taking the derivative of equation (3) with respect to $\alpha$. Thus,

$$V_\theta = \alpha\, V_\alpha /(\sec^2\theta + \alpha). \tag{12}$$

Finally, one may express $V_\alpha$ in terms of $V_I$ and $V_L$, using equation (4), in the form:

$$V_\alpha = [2(V_I)^2 + 2(V_L)^2]^{.5}, \tag{13}$$

bearing in mind that $V_{I1} = V_{I2}$ and $V_{L1} = V_{L2}$. Hence, equations (12) and (13) may be substituted in (11) to arrive at the general expression:

$$V_{Pcr} = [(V_E)^2 + (1+2a^2)(V_I)^2 + 4(1+.5a^2)(V_L)^2]^{.5}\ , \tag{14}$$

where, $a = 2\alpha/(\sec^2\theta + \alpha)$ .

Furthermore, the term $V_I$ in the above equation may be substituted by its appropriate relation in terms of $V_G$, as discussed in the case of columns. Thus, equations (6) and (14) give closed-form expressions for the variability of the buckling load in columns and frames, respectively, in terms of the variabilities of the input parameters.

**MONTE-CARLO SIMULATION.** In order to check the validities of equations (6) and (14), Monte-Carlo analysis is carried out on pin-end columns and some frames. The technique used in this simulation is as outlined by Mansour (1984). A summary of this technique is given below:

- By discretizing the area under a normal distribution curve, one may construct a sample of a predefined size of an event, such that the sample follows the normal distribution curve very closely.

- Following the above procedure, one may construct independent samples which follow a Gaussian distribution, each according to a given mean value and a standard deviation. In case of a column with I-section for example, six samples will be constructed; four samples to simulate the dimensions of the cross-section; one to simulate the column's length; and one for the material's modulus of elasticity.
- At random, one value from each sample may be picked up. These values together represent the input parameters of a particular case, with which the deterministic analysis can be carried out.
- Repeat the above step until all elements of the samples are used.
- Calculate the statistical properties of any desired output parameter.
- Repeat the above steps for various cases, as it may seem appropriate.

In fact, the above technique permits the use of a fairly small sample size. A sample size of 450 proved to be adequate for this study.

**RESULTS AND DISCUSSION**

**COLUMNS.** Monte-Carlo simulation has been used on a steel pin-ends column. The column's cross-section is W36x300, and its geometric dimensions are:

$b_f$ = 16.655 in. (423.04 mm) , $b_w$ = 0.945 in. ( 24.00 mm) ,
$d_f$ = 1.680 in. ( 42.67 mm) , $d_w$ = 33.380 in. (847.85 mm) ,
L = 360.00 in. (9144.00 mm), and E = 29,000.00 ksi (199,955.00 MPa).

Thus, the deterministic value of the critical buckling load as determined by equation (1), for e = 1, is given by $P_{cr}$ = 2862.02 kips (12,730.26 kN).

In order to check the validity of equation (6), the variability of the input parameters are considered one at a time. It is noted that, if only one coefficient of variation has a non-zero value, while the others are zeros, equation (6) reduces to a linear equation. Fig. 4 shows these equations together with the results of Monte-Carlo simulations. For example, if $V_I = 0 = V_L$, then $V_{Pcr} = V_E$. This is a straight forward result of the basic principles of the probability theory. Furthermore, Monte-Carlo technique as described here is supported by this result, and thus, confidence in the technique has been gained. In case of $V_E = 0 = V_L$, equation (6) reduces to $V_{Pcr} = V_I$, where $V_I$ is given in terms of $V_G$ as stated by equation (7). Thus, it is evident from Fig.4 that the approximate relation (7) relates the variability of the moment of inertia of an I-section to the variability of its geometric dimensions to a very good degree of accuracy. Finally, by setting $V_E = 0 = V_I$, equation (7) reduces to $V_{Pcr} = 2V_L$. Fig. 4 also shows that this relation is suitable only for a small variation in the column's length. For a level of variation $V_L > 0.1$, the results obtained from Monte-Carlo simulation do not match the straight line relationship. Ellyin and Ghannoum (1972) had shown that a practical value of $V_L$ would be 0.0033. Thus, equations (6), and (7), as presented, estimate the variability of the column buckling load very accurately, from a pratical point of view.

When all input random variables are permitted to vary

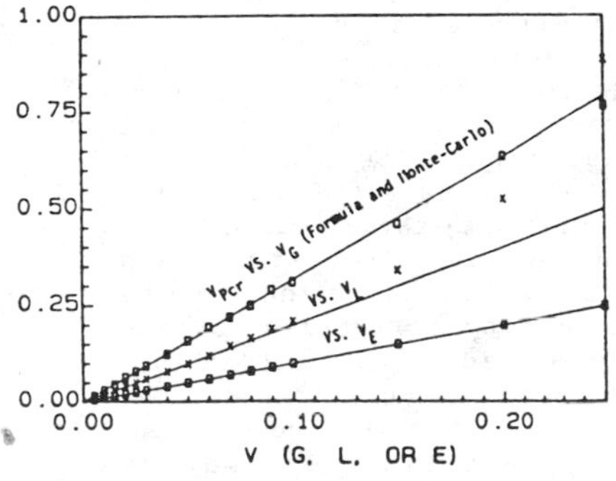


Fig. 4: Comparison Between Proposed Formula and Monte-Carlo Simulation for a Column

simultaneously, equation (6) can be used to estimate the overall variability in the critical buckling load. This is better illustrated by a numerical example. In accordance to the level of variations presented by Ellyin and Ghannoum (1972), the following coefficients of variation are assumed: $V_G = 0.0042$, $V_L = 0.0033$, and $V_E = 0.1$. Using equation (6) together with equation (7), one may estimate $V_{Pcr}$ as 0.1011 . In addition, when Monte-Carlo analysis is used with the same set of data, the mean value of $P_{cr}$ is found to be 2862.73 kips (12,733.42 kN) compared to the deterministic value of 2862.02 kips (12,730.26 kN), which is almost the same. $V_{Pcr}$ in this case is found to be 0.1029, which is only 1.78% above the value predicted by relation (6). Thus, a designer may use this relation with a great deal of confidence.

It might be worth mentioning here that, even at such small variabilities in the input parameters, a reduction in the critical buckling load, for a safe design, is neccessary. For example, if about 95% range of confidence is adopted in the design procedure, the buckling load will be reduced by almost two standard deviation below the mean value (which is the same as the deterministic value). Thus, a 20.22% reduction is neccessary for a safe design.

**FRAMES.** A similar study as in the case of columns is conducted for the frames. First, both column and beam are chosen to be similar and identical to the column discussed above. Thus, the frame has a strength parameter $\alpha$ = 1/6 . Fig.5 shows a comparison between the results of Monte-Carlo simulation and the derived relation (14). Again, each input random variable is allowed to vary at a time and therefore equation (14) is reduced to a straight line equation in each case. When E is only allowed to vary, the variation of the load has exactly the same variation as E. This is due to the same reason discussed previously. However, when either G or L is allowed to vary, equation (14) over estimates the variability in the buckling load. This is perhaps due to the multi-accounts for the effects of the variability in the length and geometrical dimensions as presented in the given analysis, because of the high non-linearity in the deterministic solution. However, the trend of the straight line relationship is maintained in every case. Similar comments can be made when other frame dimensions are considered. This has been carried out by changing the ratio of the beam length to the column length, to produce a new strength parameter $\alpha$ . Figuers 6-a and 6-b show representative results of this investigation, where the straight line trend is supported again. Therefore, equation (14) needs only to be modified, so that its straight lines would coincide with those obtained from Monte-Carlo analysis. This modification can be achieved by introducing correction factors into equation (14). These factors are such that the slopes of the straight lines will be reduced. Hence, equation (14) may be modified to the form:

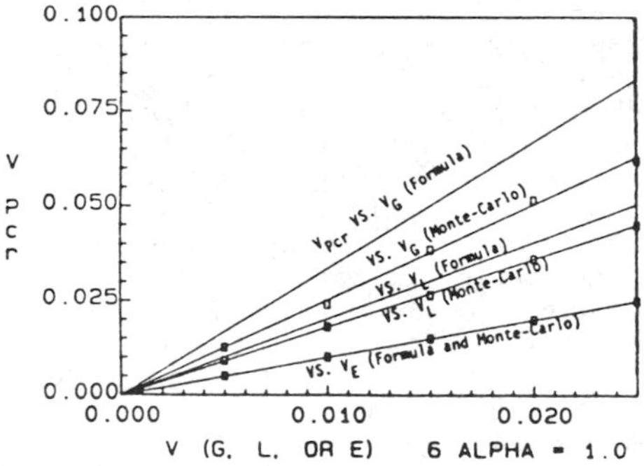


Fig. 5: Comparison Between Proposed Formula and Monte-Carlo Simulation for $\alpha$ = 1/6

$$V_{Pcr} = [(V_E)^2 + (1+2a^2)(C_G V_I)^2 + (1+.5a^2)(2C_L V_L)^2]^{.5} , \qquad (15)$$

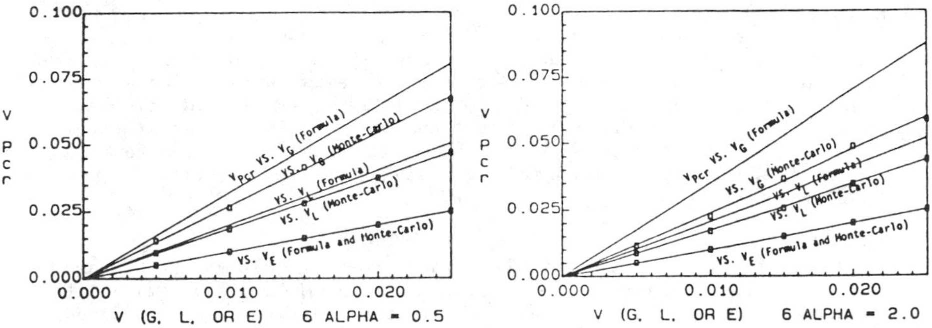


a) Frame with $L_2/L_1$ = 0.5 b) Frame with $L_2/L_1$ = 2.0

Fig. 6: Representative Results for $V_{Pcr}$ VS. $V_G$, $V_L$, and $V_E$

where $C_G$ and $C_L$ are the correction factors and to be determined. Looking closely at the differences in the slope of the lines in Figuers 5, 6-a and 6-b, one may notice at once that $C_G$ and $C_L$ are functions of the strength parameter $\alpha$ . Thus, the correction factors can be obtained corresponding to a given value of $\alpha$ , by finding the ratios between the slopes of the straight lines resulting from Monte-Carlo analysis and those of the derived formula (14). Fig. 7 shows these factors plotted against various values of $\alpha$ . It is noted from this figuer that, when $\alpha = 0$, (i.e., the frame is reduced to a column) no correction factors are neccessary, which again supports equation (6). Surprisingly, these factors changes with $\alpha$ in a parabolic shapes. A least square polynomial, with a second order, is used to fit the points shown in Fig.7. The following expressions are obtained:

$$\left.\begin{aligned} C_G &= 1.0 - 0.34\,(6\,\alpha) + 0.09\,(6\,\alpha)^2 \\ C_L &= 1.0 - 0.15\,(6\,\alpha) + 0.04\,(6\,\alpha)^2 \end{aligned}\right\} \qquad (16)$$

Thus, equations (15) and (16), as well as equations (6) and (7) discussed earlier, are recommended for possible adoption by design codes of practice, to account for the variability encountered in these types of design problems.

The use of these equations is a straight forward matter and depends only on deterministic values. For example, if a critical buckling load is to be determined for a frame with a strength parameter $\alpha$ = 1/6, and let the column dimensions are as mentioned previously, then from Fig.2, corresponding to the given value of $\alpha$ , $\theta$ is found to be 2.716. Hence, from equation (2), the deterministic value of $P_{cr}$ is given as 2139.8 kips (9,517.83 kN). Now using

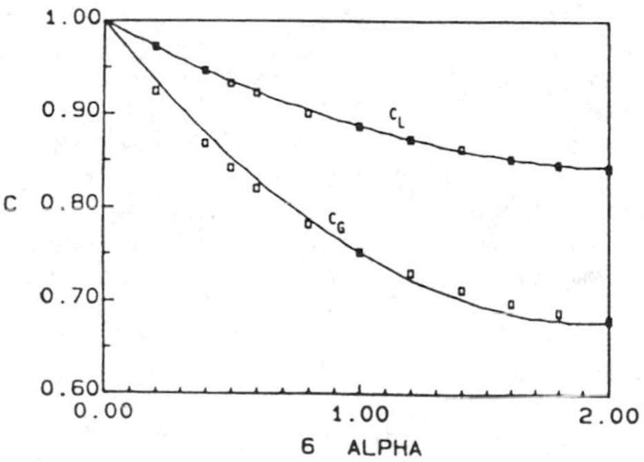


Fig. 7: Correction Factors $C_G$ and $C_L$ VS. $6\alpha$

equations (16), the correction factors for the shape and length variabilities are .75 and .89 respectively. For the same levels of variabilities as given in the column section, equation (15) gives $V_{Pcr}$ = 0.1007 . This can be used to any range of confidence to estimate the actual critical buckling load. When Monte-Carlo analysis is used for this problem, the mean value of the critical load is found to be indistinguishable from the deterministic value and $V_{Pcr}$ = 0.1004, which is 0.3% below the formula value. Indeed, the derived formula describes the variability of the buckling load very closely.

**CONCLUSIONS**

The variability of the critical buckling load of columns and a frame due to variabilities in the cross-sectional dimensions, length and material properties, has been considered. When all random variables are considered to follow a normal distribution variability functions, with small coefficient of variations, it is possible to relate the variability of the buckling load to the other variabilities through equations (6), (7), (15) and (16). The formulas are cross-checked using Monte-Carlo simulations and have been proven to be able to account for such variability with great deal of accuracy. Thus, they are proposed for possible inclusion in design codes of practice.

**ACKNOWLEDGEMENT**

The authors would like to thank the computer centers at both Dalhousie University and California State University for providing computing facilities to carry out this research work. Thanks are also due to the Natural Sciences and Engineering Research Council of Canada for its financial support in the form of an operating research grant.

**REFERENCES**

Chajes, A. (1974). Principles of Structural Stability, Prentice Hall, Inc. Englewood Cliffs, NJ.

Ellyin, F. and Ghannoum, E. (1972)."An Assessment of Reliability of Structures", Transaction of Engg. Institute of Canada, 15(A-1).

Galambos, T.V. and Ravindra, M.K. (1973). "Tentative Load and Resistance Factor Design Criteria for Steel Buildings", Research Report, No. 18, Structural Division, Washington University, St. Louis.

Hasofer, A.M. and Lind, N.C. (1974). "An Exact and Invariant First Order Reliability Format", ASCE, J. Eng. Mech. Div., Vol. 100, No.EM1.

Haugen, E.B. (1968). Probabilistic Approach to Design, John Wiley & Sons, Inc., New York, NY.

Mansour, M.H. (1984). "Statistical Analysis of the Transverse Load Distribution in Simple Timber Bridges", Ph.D. Thesis, Technical University of Nova Scotia, Halifax, NS.

Putcha, C.S. (1986). "A Numerical Method for Safety Indices Evaluation of Single Storey Steel Frames", Proc., First Canadian Conference on Computer Applications in Civil Engineering/Micro-Computers, Hamilton, Ont., pp.211-219.

Rackwitz, R. and Fiessler, B. (1977). "An Algorithm for the Calculation of Structural Reliability Under Combined Loading", Technische Universitat-Mumchen, Heft, 17.

Rosenblueth, E. and Esteva, L. (1972). "Reliability Basis for Some Mexican Codes in Probabilistic Design of Reinforced Concrete Buildings", American Concrete Institute, SP.31.1.

## STOCHASTIC FATIGUE OF NONLINEAR OFFSHORE STRUCTURAL SYSTEMS

A. Haldar* and H. B. Kanegaonkar*
*School of Civil Engineering, Georgia Institute of Technology, Atlanta, Georgia 30332, U.S.A.

### ABSTRACT

Fatigue is an important consideration in the design of offshore structural systems. Commonly, the wave loading is considered to be a Gaussian random process. Assuming linear structural behavior, the stress resultants become Gaussian. Fatigue analysis under these conditions is well known. However, if nonlinearities are introduced in the loading, support conditions, and geometric and material behavior to realistically model the system, the simple standard method of fatigue analysis can not be used. Nonlinearities in the loading and in the stiffness are considered here. Nonlinearities in the wave loading due to nonlinear wave kinematics and free surface fluctuation are considered for a jacket-type platform. The first four moments of the response are estimated using the mean square estimation technique via conditional distribution. Nonlinear stiffness is considered for a guyed tower system. Approximating the loading by the ARMA process, Ito stochastic differential equations for the response moments are solved up to fourth order where the system of equations is closed by neglecting the fifth and higher order cumulants. The response moments are considered to be a mixture of Gaussian and non-Gaussian distributions. By mapping a Gaussian process into this response process, the expected rate of positive crossings is estimated, leading to the probability density of the peaks. Palmgren-Miner's hypothesis for fatigue damage accumulation is used. It is shown that the conventional method is unconservative when the response distribution is leptokurtic.

### INTRODUCTION

A wide variety of offshore structural systems are used, and each of them resists the wave loading by different mechanisms. Structural systems such as jackets, gravity platforms, semisubmersibles, articulated platforms, and guyed tower have been employed. Jackets are space frame structures fixed to the sea bed which resist the forces by bending. The cyclic wave load causes fatigue, especially at the joints. The structure behaves linearly; however, if the wave loading is modeled realistically by considering nonlinearities in the drag and wave kinematics and the intermittency of the loading, it becomes nonlinear and thus non-Gaussian (Tung, 1984). Consequently, the response in terms of stress resultants at the joints is non-Gaussian (Haldar and Kanegaonkar, 1986). For a guyed tower system, the wave loading is resisted by a set of guylines. Each guyline is a multicomponent cable system comprising a fairlead line, a clump weight and a trailing line. The catenary produced by the guyline provides nonlinear stiffness to the structure. Even if the load is considered to be Gaussian, the response of the tower to wave loads is non-Gaussian because of the nonlinear stiffness (Kanegaonkar and Haldar, 1987). The cable tensions in the guylines are non-Gaussian. The tension fatigue of the cables, and the fatigue of the joints in jackets have one thing in common: both are under non-Gaussian stress resultants.

A method is described here which takes into account the non-Gaussian behavior of the structural responses for fatigue damage estimation. Using the methods for dynamic analysis described in the following sections, the first four moments of the responses of the jackets and guyed towers are obtained. With the help of the third and fourth moments, the optimal marginal distribution of the response is modeled as a mixture distribution, i.e., weighted sum of Gaussian and a non-Gaussian distribution. When the marginal distribution is known, level crossings and the probability density of the peaks are obtained by mapping a Gaussian process into this response process using the double inversion technique. Palmgren-Miner's hypothesis is then used for estimation of the accumulated damage.

JACKET PLATFORM

The response of a jacket platform shown in Fig. 1 is estimated by considering the nonlinearity in the wave loading due to nonlinearity in wave kinematics and free surface fluctuations. The governing equation of motion with linearized drag can be expressed as

$$[m]\{\ddot{x}\} + [C]\{\dot{x}\} + [K]\{x\} = [CD]\{\dot{u}\} + [CM]\{\ddot{u}\} \tag{1}$$

in which [m] = mass matrix inclusive of added mass; [C] = damping matrix inclusive of hydrodynamic damping; [K] = stiffness matrix; [A] and [V] = the lumped effective projected areas and volumes at the nodes, respectively; $x$, $\dot{x}$, $\ddot{x}$ = displacement, velocity, and acceleration of the structure, respectively; $u$, $\dot{u}$, $\ddot{u}$ = displacement, velocity and acceleration of the water particle, respectively; $C_d$ and $C_m$ = drag and inertia coefficients, respectively; $\rho$ = mass density of water; $CD_j = \sqrt{8/\Pi}\ \sigma_{(\dot{u}-\dot{x})}\ \frac{1}{2}\rho\ C_d\ A_j$; and $CM_j = \rho C_m V_j$.

Depending upon whether or not the point near the mean sea level is below the sea surface, the members near the mean sea level are intermittently loaded. The actual wave velocity can be represented by (Tung, 1984)

$$\dot{u}'_j = \dot{u}_j\ H(\eta - z_j) \tag{2}$$

in which $\eta$ = sea surface elevation with origin at mean sea level; H(.) = Heaviside unit step function; and $z_j$ = vertical ordinate of node j. Stokes' second order wave theory can be used to estimate $u_j$.

Quasi-static response is observed at higher sea states where the load is correlated over a much larger period than the natural period of the structure (Haldar and Kanegaonkar, 1986). The wave load, f, with effective velocities and accelerations can be represented as

$$\{f\} = [CD]\ \{\dot{u}'\} + [CM]\{\ddot{u}'\} \tag{3}$$

in which $\dot{u}'$ and $\ddot{u}'$ are effective velocity and acceleration, respectively, obtained from Eq. 2. For quasi-static behavior the deflection $x_i$ at node i can be estimated as

$$x_i = \sum_{j=1}^{N} F_{ij}\ f_j \tag{4}$$

in which $F_{ij}$ = flexibility coefficients; and N = total number of nodes.

From Eqs. 2 and 3, it can be seen that $f_i$'s are non-Gaussian. To completely define the probability distribution of $x_i$, therefore, the higher order moments of $x_i$ are required. Assuming all the random variables are ergodic, the first four moments of response $x_i$ can be obtained by calculating the expected values of $x_i$, $x_i^2$, $x_i^3$ and $x_i^4$, respectively. Expansion of $x_i$ to higher powers can be obtained using the multinomial theorem (Bernard and Child, 1936) along with Eq. 4. $x_i$ is a summation of 2N terms involving effective velocity and acceleration as random variables, hence, the expectations of $x_i$, $x_i^2$, $x_i^3$ and $x_i^4$ are functions of the expectations of corresponding powers and combinations of $\dot{u}'$ and $\ddot{u}'$. Typically, it can be shown from Eq. 2 that

$$E[\dot{u}'] = -\sigma_{\dot{u}}\ Z(\beta) \tag{5}$$

$$E[\dot{u}'^2] = \sigma_{\dot{u}}^2\ [\beta\ Z(\beta) + Q(\beta)] \tag{6}$$

$$E[\dot{u}'^3] = -\sigma_{\dot{u}}^3\ [Z(\beta)\ (2 + \beta^2)] \tag{7}$$

$$E[\dot{u}'^4] = \sigma_{\dot{u}}^4\ \{\beta^3 Z(\beta) + 3[\beta Z(\beta) + Q(\beta)] \tag{8}$$

where $\sigma$ = standard deviation; $\sigma = Z/\sigma_\eta$; $Z(\beta) = 1/\sqrt{2\Pi}\ \exp(-\beta^2/2)$; and $Q(\beta) = \int_\beta^\infty Z(\beta)\ d\beta$.

The combination expectation formulae can be found elsewhere (Haldar and Kanegaonkar, 1986). Once the first four moments of the response are known, the central moments can be estimated by standard methods. Since the displacement and stress are linearly related, the skewness and kurtosis will remain invariant and the mean and the root mean square of the stresses can be obtained by standard static analysis procedures. Stress concentration factors at the joints can be estimated using empirical formulae (Kuang, Potvin and Leick, 1975) to obtain hot-spot stress statistics at the joints. Procedures to estimate fatigue life with these statistics will be explained later in this paper.

## GUYED TOWER PLATFORM

Non-Gaussian response can also be caused by nonlinear stiffness. As discussed earlier, the guyed tower has nonlinear stiffness due to the nonlinear behavior of multicomponent guylines. Thus, even if the loading is considered to be Gaussian, the response will be non-Gaussian. An idealized guyed tower platform used in this study is shown in Fig. 2. The tower is assumed to be hinged at the base with all restoring forces to be provided by the mooring lines and buoyancy tanks only. The methodology to estimate the stiffness provided by these mooring lines using catenary equations is now well established (Ansari, 1979). Using the least square regression equation for restoring force and the angle of rotation of the tower, the nonlinear stiffness can be expressed as a sum of linear and cubic terms.

The governing equation of motion of the platform can be developed by taking the moment of all the forces about the base, i.e.,

$$J\ddot{\Theta} + cd^2\dot{\Theta} + (z_c c_1 - DW_p - Ddw_T - z_c c_1' + F_b z_b)\Theta + z_c\ (c_2 - c_2')\ \Theta^3 = F(t)\cdot h \quad (9)$$

where $c_1, c_2$ = regression constants for horizontal restoring force expressed as a sum of linear and cubic terms of tower rotation; $c_1', c_2'$ = regression constants for vertical reaction at the point of attachment expressed as a sum of constant and square terms. All other terms in Eq. 9 are explained in Fig. 2. The right hand side of Eq. 9 represents the moment of the wave load about the base. This can be estimated by dividing the tower into a number of sections, finding the moment of the load acting on each section and summing it up. The moment due to load on each section, M(t), can be expressed as

$$M(t) = [0.5\ C_d\ \rho\ A\ \sqrt{8/\Pi}\ \sigma_{(\dot{u}-\dot{x})}\ \dot{u} + C_m\ \rho V\ \ddot{u}]\ h_s \quad (10)$$

in which $h_s$ = distance between the base and the center of the section.

Using Eq. 10, the spectral density function for the total moment $S_{MM}(\omega)$ can be obtained. This spectarl density is then approximated by a rational spectral density function given by

$$S_{MM}(\omega) = \frac{\overline{G}\ \omega^2}{(\omega^2 - \omega_0^2) + (C_0\omega)^2} \quad (11)$$

The parameters $\overline{G}$, $\omega_0$, $C_0$ are then obtained by using the least square minimization algorithm (IMSL, 1982).

When the spectral density function of the wave load moment is fitted to the form of Eq. 11, using the results of Lipster and Shiryayev (1978), the governing differential equation, Eq. 9, can be expressed in terms of four first order stochastic differential equations given by

$$d\Theta_1 = \Theta_2 dt \quad (12)$$

$$d\Theta_2 = -\ (a\Theta_2 + b\Theta_1 + \varepsilon\Theta_1^3) + \Theta_3 dt \quad (13)$$

$$d\Theta_3 = \Theta_4\ dt + \sqrt{G_0}\ dW(t) \quad (14)$$

$$d\Theta_4 = -\ (C_0\Theta_4 + \omega_0^2\ \Theta_3)\ dt - C_0\ \sqrt{G_0}\ dW(t) \quad (15)$$

in which $\Theta_1$, $\Theta_2$ = angular displacement and velocity of the tower, respectively; $a = (cd^2 + c_{hd}h_{eff})/J_0$, $b = (z_c c_1 - DW_p - Ddw_T - z_c c_1' + F_b z_b)/J_0$; $\varepsilon = z_c\ (c_2 - c_1')/J_0$; $J_0 = J + C_m \rho V h_{eff}^2$; $h_{eff}$ = height above the base where effective force is acting;

$$c_{hd} = \sum_{j=1}^{\text{all sections}} \tfrac{1}{2} C_d \rho A\ \sigma_{(\dot{u}-\dot{x})}; \text{ and } G_0 = \overline{G}\ /J_0^2.$$

Using Eqs. 12 to 15, differential equations for moxed moments of $\Theta_1$, $\Theta_2$, $\Theta_3$, $\Theta_4$ up to the fourth order can be written (Ito, 1951; Bolotin, 1984). In all, sixty five equations for the second, third and fourth moments can be developed. Because of the cubic term in Eq. 13, the fourth order moment equations contain sixth order moment terms. By assuming that the cumulants of the fifth and sixth order are zero, the moments of the fifth and sixth order are expressed in terms of the first four moments. For steady state stationary response, the moments are constants and the differential equations become algebric equations and can be solved using standard algorithms (IMSL, 1982). Thus, the first four moments of the response are known, from which the central moments can be obtained.

OPTIMAL MARGINAL DISTRIBUTION

The first four moments of the responses of both the jacket and guyed tower are known at this stage. The unknown non-Gaussian distribution, $F_r$, of the response can be assumed to be a mixture of two known distributions with weighting factors as

$$F_r = \sum_{l=0}^{L} p_l \, F_l; \text{ with } p_l > 0 \text{ and } \sum_{1}^{L} p_l = 1 \tag{16}$$

The distributions $F_l$ have the same mean and variance. Weighting factors are obtained by minimizing $\eta$ under the constraints of Eq. 16, where

$$\eta = \sum_{k=3}^{4} (\psi_k - \bar{\psi}_k)^2 \tag{17}$$

$\psi_k$, $\bar{\psi}_k$ = kth order dimensionless moments of the response and the mixture distribution, respectively.

FATIGUE ANALYSIS

For the jacket platforms, the hot-spot stress statistics are now known along with the probability distribution. Once the probability distribution and statistics for the guyed tower displacement are known, the guy line tension being a function of the tower displacement, the statistics for the guyline tension can be easily found from elementary probability laws (Papoulis, 1984). If $F_S$ is the non-Gaussian distribution function of the stress, the mean rate of threshold crossing at level s can be estimated as (Grigoriu, 1984)

$$\nu_s = \frac{\sigma_{\dot{S}}}{\sqrt{2\Pi}} \phi(s') \tag{18}$$

where $s' = \Phi^{-1}\{F_S[S = \frac{s-m_S}{\sigma_S}]\}$; $\Phi$, $\phi$ = Gaussian distribution and density function, respectively; and $m_S$, $\sigma_S$ = mean and r.m.s. of the stress process.

The probability distribution function of the hot-spot stress peaks is calculated using the heuristic assumption for a narrow band process (Lin, 1967) as

$$F_{pS} = 1 - \nu_s/\nu_m \tag{19}$$

in which $\nu_s$ = expected rate of crossings at level s and $\nu_m$ = expected rate of crossings at the mean. The probability density function, $f_{pS}$, is obtained by differentiating the function $F_{pS}$

numerically.

Using Palmgren- Miner hypothesis, the total damage per year due to a sea state can be obtained as

$$D = \frac{N_c}{K_s} \int_0^{\infty} (2s)^m f_{pS}(s)\, ds \qquad (20)$$

in which $N_c$ = total number of cycles per year in the sea state: and $K_s$ and m = constants from S-N curve. Damage thus can be summed up over all the sea states and the fatigue life can be estimated.

## RESULTS AND DISCUSSION

A jacket platform (Fig. 1) and a guyed tower (Fig. 2) are analyzed using the methods presented earlier. The random waves are characterized by the Pierson-Moskowitz spectrum to estimate the load on both structural systems. For jacket platform analysis, Stokes' deep water second order wave theory is used and drag and inertia coefficients are assumed to be 1.0 and 2.0, respectively. For guyed tower analysis, Airy's wave theory is used and drag and inertia coefficients are assumed to be 1.0 and 1.5, respectively. Accumulated fatigue damage for a sea state is estimated using the AWS-X curve for joints in jacket platform. For mooring line fatigue, tension fatigue curves (Ronson, 1980) are used. Table 1 gives the fatigue damage estimate per year for the jacket for the two sea states for joint A near the mean sea level considering the stress process to be Gaussian as well as non-Gaussian. The non-Gaussian distribution is modeled as a sum of Gaussian and shifted

Table 1 Damage/Year at Joint A Near Mean Sea Level

| Sea State | | | Probability Dist. | | Fatigue Damage | |
|---|---|---|---|---|---|---|
| $H_s$ m | $T_z$ sec | % occurrence | % Gaussian | % Shifted Exponential | Gaussian ($10^{-3}$) | non-Gauss. |
| 6.86 | 10.0 | 2.65 | 54.06 | 45.94 | 0.4642 | 0.7580 |
| 8.38 | 11.5 | 1.35 | 30.78 | 69.22 | 0.3059 | 0.6212 |

exponential distributions. It is observed that the non-Gaussian distribution of the stresses gives significantly higher fatigue damage depending on the deviation from Gaussian. For jacket platform at higher sea states the damage estimate using Gaussian stresses may be unconservative by a factor of two or more. Table 2 shows the fatigue damage for guylines under two different sea states. For the guyed tower the nonlinearity is in the stiffness. For the two sea states described in Table 2, the tower displacemnet has coefficients of excess of 0.24 and 0.36, respectively. The fatigue behavior of the cables is estimated from the statistics on cable tension and the breaking load of the cable. Since the deviation of the probability distribution of the cable tensions from the Gaussian is less compaired to the stresses in the joints of the jacket platform, the ratio of non-Gaussian fatigue damage to the Gaussian fatigue is not as high as for the jacket platforms. The results are seen to be in close agreement with simulation results (Lutes et al., 1984). Some of the other major

Table 2 Damage/Year for the Guyline

| Sea State | | | Probability Dist. | | Fatigue Damage | |
|---|---|---|---|---|---|---|
| $H_s$ ft | $T_z$ (sec) | % occurrence | % Gaussian | % Laplace | Gaussian | Non-Gaussian $x(10^{-3})$ |
| 31.84 | 13.8 | 2.5 | 92 | 8 | 0.8690 | 0.8913 |
| 41.58 | 15.5 | 1.0 | 88 | 12 | 0.2952 | 0.3067 |

conclusions will be made during the presentation.

ACKNOWLEDGEMENTS

This material is based upon work partly supported by the National Science Foundation under Grants No. MSM-8352396, MSM-8544166 and MSM-8644348. Any opinions, findings and conclusions or recommendations expressed in this publication are those of writers and do not necessarily reflect the views of the National Science Foundation.

REFERENCES

Ansari, K.A. (1979). "How to Design a Multicomponent Mooring System," Ocean Industry.

Bernard, S. and Child, J.M. (1936). Higher Algebra, McMillan, London.

Grigoriu, M. (1981). "Contribution to Approximate Reliability Analysis," Report 81-15, Department of Civil Engineering, Cornell University, N.Y.

Haldar, A. and Kanegaonkar, H.B. (1986). "Stochastic Fatigue Response of Jackets Under Intermittent Wave Loading," 18th Offshore Technology Conference, Houston, OTC 5332, Vol. 4, pp. 377-386.

International Mathematics and Statistics Library, Inc., IMSL. (1982). Library Reference Manual Volume 4, Edition 9, Houston, Texas.

Kanegaonkar, H.B. and Haldar, A. (1987). "Non-Gaussian Stochastic Response of Nonlinear Compliant Platforms," to appear in the Journal of Probabilistic Engineering Mechanics.

Kuang, J.G. Potvin, A.B. and Leick, R.D. (1975). "Stress Concentration in Tubular Joints," Proceedings of Seventh Offshore Technology Conference, Houston, OTC 2205, Vol. 1, pp. 593-612.

Lin, Y.K. (1967). Probabilistic Theory of Structural Dynamics, McGraw Hill Book Co., New York.

Lipster, R.S. and Shiryayev, A.N. (1978). Statistics of Random Processes, Applications., Springer-Verlag.

Lutes, L.D. Corazao, M. Hu, S.J. and Zimmerman,J. (1984). "Stochastic Fatigue Damage Accumulation," Journal of Structural Engineering, ASCE, Vol. 110, No. 11, pp. 2585-2601.

Papoulis, A. (1965). Probability, Random Variables and Stochastic Processes, McGraw Hill Book Co., New York.

Ronson, K.T. (1980). "Ropes for Deep Water Mooring," Twelth Offshore Technology Conference, Houston, OTC 3850, pp. 485-496.

Tung, C.C. (1984). "Statistical Properties of Non-Linear Waves," Proceedings of the 4th Spec. Conference on Prob. Mech., ASCE.

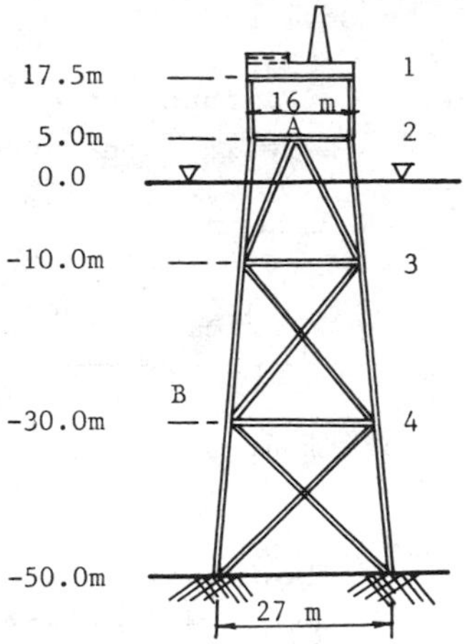


STRUCTURAL DATA

| | | |
|---|---|---|
| Deck Legs Diameter | D | = 2.0 m |
| Thickness | t | = 50 mm |
| Jacket Legs and Diag. | D | = 1.2 m |
| Vert. Plane | t | = 16 mm |
| Bracings and Diag. | D | = 0.80 m |
| at Level +5 m | t | = 8 mm |
| Bracings and Diag. | D | = 1.2 m |
| at Level -10 m | t | = 14 mm |
| Bracings | D | = 1.2 m |
| at Level -30 m | t | = 14 mm |
| Diagonals | D | = 1.2 m |
| at Level -30 m | t | = 16 mm |

Youngs Modulus (steel) = 205 Gpa
Yield Stress (steel) = 240 MPa
Mass Density (steel) = 7800 $kg/m^3$
Mass of Deck = 4800 ton

Fig. 1 Jacket Platform

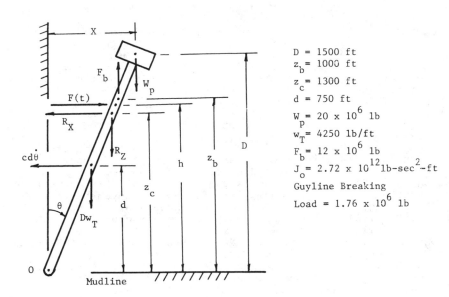

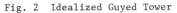

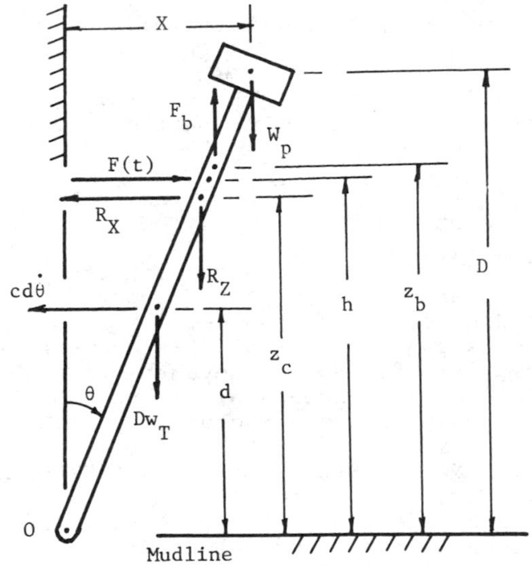


$D = 1500$ ft
$z_b = 1000$ ft
$z_c = 1300$ ft
$d = 750$ ft
$W_p = 20 \times 10^6$ lb
$w_T = 4250$ lb/ft
$F_b = 12 \times 10^6$ lb
$J_o = 2.72 \times 10^{12}$ $lb\text{-}sec^2\text{-}ft$
Guyline Breaking
Load $= 1.76 \times 10^6$ lb

Fig. 2 Idealized Guyed Tower

# Risk Based Code Formats For Evaluating Existing Bridges

D. Verma, S. Raju and F. Moses
Department of Civil Engineering
Case Western Reserve University
Cleveland, Ohio 44106, USA

## ABSTRACT

A large percentage of highway bridges in the United States were built more than several decades ago. Due to environmental effects combined with deferred maintenance and repair, many of these bridges have deteriorated. At the same time, there has been a significant increase in the weight and volume of the truck traffic using the highways. Due to these trends of decreased strength, heavier traffic and increased volume, over 125,000 highway bridges have been listed as structurally deficient with many either posted for reduced loadings or closed. Due to limited funds for bridge replacement, it has been found necessary to more accurately predict the safe load carrying capacity and safe remaining life of these older bridges. For many bridge engineers the potential of using risk criteria to assist in the decision strategy is evident.

The aim of this study was to accurately model uncertainties and assess bridge reliability. A range of appropriate load and resistance factors are derived and can be selected by a bridge engineer based on site-specific inspection and observations, and on the level of evaluation effort.

In addition to a reliability criteria for selecting factors the procedures incorporate the results of recent research in load distribution, load spectra, live load modelling, fatigue strength for bridges and site-specific bridge data obtained from an inspection and/or traffic survey.

## INTRODUCTION

Evaluation provisions for highway bridges in the U.S. evolved from the AASHTO design specifications which are necessarily conservative since they cover a wide variety of situations. This conservatism accounts for the high degree of uncertainty associated with each of the design parameters. However, these uncertainties are lower in evaluation as the structure already exists. Moreover, the fatigue provisions are not suitable for evaluation as they do not reflect the actual fatigue conditions in the members.

Use of reliability principles has enabled explicit consideration of the uncertainties of relevant variables and the development of safety factors which are correlated both to these uncertainties and the nominal values used. The success of such methods has been amply demonstrated in the Ontario OHBDC in 1979 which applied formal reliability logic to calibrate safety factors to uncertainty levels. The loading effects and resistance were modelled as random variables and target reliability satisfied by selecting appropriate load factors and resistance factors for different steel, concrete and timber components. The application of reliability to bridge rating has also been incorporated in an alternative to the CSA code in Canada. The limitations have been that until recently the data base for assessing the true load spectrum effect has been limited. Work by the last author using Weigh-In-Motion (WIM) has in recent years provided an extensive data base for such needed load and load effect modelling.

## RELIABILITY MODEL FOR STRENGTH EVALUATION

For strength evaluation, failure means that the load effect S (bending, axial, shear) is greater than, R, the resistance of the member being checked.

Another way of expressing this is to define a failure function z which is given by

$$z = R - S \tag{1}$$

Failure takes place then if z is less than zero. Both the resistance and the load effects are random variables with a mean given by $\bar{z}$ and a standard deviation $\sigma_z$. A conventional measure of safety (Thoft-Christensen and Baker, 1982) is given by the safety index defined as

$$\beta = \bar{z}/\sigma_z \tag{2}$$

That is, the safety index is the number of standard deviations that the mean of the safety margin is away from zero (or failure).

Use of a safety index is very convenient since it does not make direct use of the probability of failure. Hence all the results will be modelled in terms of this safety index.

For the case of strength evaluation, the failure function can be written even more explicity as

$$z = R - D - L \tag{3}$$

D = Dead load effect
L = Live load effect
The analysis is then to assemble statistics for the three random variables (R,D and L) mentioned in eqn. (3).

LIVE LOAD MODELLING FOR BRIDGES

In short to medium span bridges, the maximum live load effect is usually due to the simultaneous occurrence of two or more heavy trucks on the bridge. A number of researchers have attempted to obtain a live load model which accurately predicts this load effect (Larrabee, Harman, Ghosn). The live load model used for this study has been developed by Ghosn and Moses (1984). It is given by

$$M = amHW_{.95}ig \tag{4}$$

where
M = maximum load effect (moment, shear...)
a = a deterministic influence quantity given by the load effect of the normalized reference vehicle
$W_{.95}$ = characteristic truck weight at a site
H = An amplification factor which takes into account both multiple presence of vehicles on a bridge and the extreme tail of the truck weight histogram. H can been found by simulation or analytical techniques.
m = Effect of axle weight and spacing of actual traffic as compared to the reference evaluation vehicle
i = dynamic amplification or impact
g = girder distribution or other structural analysis variable

For purposes of evaluation, no load growth is assumed to occur over a typical interval of inspection, say two years. One advantage of this live load model is that the statistics are available from the extensive data base of the WIM (Weigh-In-Motion) system. Since this method of data acquisition is undetectable to the drivers, the truck weight and traffic data obtained are unbiased as compared with that obtained from static weigh stations. In addition to load data, WIM has provided extensive data on load effects including dynamic response, member force distribution and stresses.

## ESTABLISHING A TARGET SAFETY INDEX

A target safety index is defined as the acceptable level of safety from decisions based on economics to those based on performance studies. In code proposals, the safety indices implicit in current performance are calculated. However, this approach is complicated by the wide variety of evaluation practices prevailing in different states. Differences arise because of various legal vehicles, different methods of rating (working stress or load factor) and most important the various stress levels used for rating i.e. operating (which is 0.75 of yield) or inventory (which is 0.55 of yield stress). Since states which have consistently used the operating stress level for rating have not reported a significant number of bridge failures, this level will determine, herein, the target safety index.

To provide more uniform reliability, the operating level is used, but only for redundant spans where the load redistribution and multiple load paths clearly exist. For the case of a nonredundant span, the failure of an element would be more critical and hence reliabilities based on inventory stress levels are used. Using the model in equations (3) and (4) the operating ratings are found to have a safety index in the range of 2.5 while for inventory ratings this is of the order of 3.5. Hence these will be taken as the respective target safety indices.

## THE RATING EQUATION

The rating check is in the load and resistance factor format:

$$\phi R_n = \gamma_D D + \gamma_L L_n (1 + I) R.F. \tag{5}$$

where

$\phi$ = capacity reduction factor
$\gamma_D$ = dead load factor
$\gamma_L$ = live load factor
$R_n$ = nominal computed member resistance
$D$ = dead load effect
$L_n$ = nominal live load effect
$I$ = Impact
R.F.= rating factor

This format correlates the factors to the relative uncertainty of each variable and also allows the reliability levels to be more finely tuned to attain uniformity. Load and resistance factors are selected so that target safety levels are closely attained. These depend on <u>both</u> the bias (ratio of mean value to nominal value) and the uncertainty (a measure of which is given by the coefficient of variation "COV" defined as the ratio of the standard deviation to the mean value). The statistics of the relevant variables are presented in the next section.

## DATA BASE

The statistics for the resistance of both steel and prestressed concrete members in good condition is assembled from existing literature (Ellingwood et al, Nowak and Zhou 1984). For slightly to badly corroded steel members, however, there is not much data availabe. So the bias and COV are estimated, with sensitivity studies conducted to examine the implications of the assumed values. The statistics are tabulated below

| | Bias | COV |
|---|---|---|
| (a) Good condition | 1.1 | 12% |
| (b) slightly corroded, some loss of section | 1.05 | 16% |
| (c) heavily corroded | 1.0 | 20% |
| (d) prestressed concrete | 1.05 | 9% |

The impact of maintenance and inspection on the resistance factors is introduced by noting that a better inspection would lead to more certainty in the section loss (if any) which raises the capacity reduction factor. Similarly a better maintenance schedule can lead to quicker identification of any potential problems and can be rewarded with more beneficial capacity reduction factors. As an illustration, the proposed specifications allow an increase of 0.05 in $\phi$ for cases where a vigorous inspection is conducted to determine the condition of that particular element of the bridge.

Thus, a flexibility is introduced in the evaluation procedure. All the above mentioned options are available to the engineer who can use them depending on the site-specific need and the evaluation resources available.

Shifting our attention to the load side of the equation, the dead load factor accounts for variabilities in material weights and analysis uncertainties. An overall bias of 1.0 with a COV of 10% is fixed (Ellingwood et al., Nowak and Zhou). However, the asphalt wearing surface (which comprises about 20% of the total dead load) has a COV of 25% as noted by Nowak and Zhou. So if no additional measurements of asphalt thickness are made (in the form of cores), an added factor for wearing surface dead weight is introduced.

Finally, the live load statistics are established according to eqn. (4). The factor 'a' is deterministic and depends on the choice of the rating vehicles. The three AASHTO legal trucks are chosen, so the value of 'a' for simple spans can be determined as the maximum load effect due to the vehicle divided by its total weight.

The mean and COV of the random varialbe 'm' are determined from data collected from WIM studies. It varies with span length and vehicle, with COV of'm'approaching zero for longer spans. The bias of 'm' reflects the scatter in axle weights and distribution of random traffic as compared to the reference vehicles and approaches the value of 1 with increasing spans.

The two factors H and $W_{.95}$ as defined previously are combined into a single random variable which gives the measure of the maximum loading at the bridge over the inspection interval. Sites having a $HW_{.95}$ value greater than 100 kips for singles and 180-kips for combinations are assumed to be unenforced. This was based on comparisons of data with corresponding legal limits in the U.S. Also, an ADTT of 1000 and above corresponds to heavy traffic. Hence, this leads to a rational methodology for categorizing sites based on truck volume and degree of enforcement.

Impact to a large degree depends on the roughness of the bridge and approach spans. The values for I are a mean of 1.1 for smooth, 1.2 for medium roughness and 1.3 for very rough surfaces. A COV of 10% in all cases is used. Member force analysis uncertainty known as girder distribution as given by the AASHTO specifications has a bias of 0.9 (conservative) and the COV depends on the method of analysis. This factor is introducted to encourage more accurate methods of analysis ranging from finite elements to field measurement.

## CALIBRATION

With the statistics assembled above, the load and resistance factors are selected such that the target safety index is attained. The dead load factor is chosen to be 1.2 with an additional 20% increase for asphalt if no detailed thickness measurements are made. Corresponding to the different categories of enforcement and volume, live load factors ranging from 1.4 to 1.95 are chosen. Corresponding to the different resistance categories the following capacity reduction factors are illustrated.

| | CAPACITY REDUCTION FACTOR |
|---|---|
| a) Good condition | 0.95 |
| b) Slightly corroded | 0.85 |
| c) Heavily corroded | 0.75 |
| d) Prestressed concrete | 0.90 |
| e) Non-redundant | 0.75 |

RELIABILITY MODEL FOR FATIGUE EVALUATION

In addition to strength evaluation, many agencies are concerned that heavier trucks are leading to potential fatigue problems. Already, some states are rating steel bridges with fatigue specifications.

A failure function for fatigue evaluation can be written as,

$$z = Y_F - Y_S \tag{6}$$

where $Y_F$ - life at which the member fails (a random variable),
$Y_S$ - Specified or desired safe life (deterministic)

Using a linear miner cumulative damage rule assumption, $Y_F$ can be written in terms of other random variables. $Y_F$ can be written as

$$Y_F = XN_T/(365(ADTT)C) \; [Z_x R_s S/(WGIMH)]^3 \tag{7}$$

where X - a random variable reflecting the uncertainty in the model (mainly Miner's rule)
$N_T$ - number of cycles (deterministic); $N_T = ADTT(365)Y_sC$
ADTT - Average daily truck traffic in vehicles per day
C - Equivalent stress range cycles per truck crossing
$Z_x$ - A random variable reflecting the scatter in true section modulus compared to computed section modulus
$R_s$ - Factor of safety specified after calibration of the risk. This safety factor ensures an acceptable risk for the computed fatigue life of the member
S - Ratio of the true stress range the member can sustain at $N_T$ cycles, compared to the nominal (or design) value of stress range at $N_T$ cycles (a random variable)
W - Ratio of equivalent fatigue truck weight (defined as the truck weight that causes the same damage as the damage caused by the entire truck spectrum on the bridge) to the design value of the fatigue truck (a random variable)
G - Ratio of true member load distribution factor to it's nominal value
I - Ratio of true impact factor to its nominal value
M - Ratio of the average influence factor (maximum moment/gross weight) due to truck spectrum to the influence factor of the design fatigue truck
H - A random variable accounting for closely spaced or multilane presence of vehicles which amplify the moment

The cubic exponent in Eq. (7) results from the slope of the fatigue curve on a log-log plot which is usually close to 3. Hence, stress range affects the life with a cubic exponent. The terms in Eq. (7) relate the true value of a variable to the nominal value selected in an analysis procedure. In addition to stress terms, the Eq. for $Y_F$ also contain the terms affecting the number of stress cycles. The random variables include material terms, X and S, truck variables, W, ADTT, H, M and C and analysis uncertainties $Z_x$ I and G. The function in equation (7) is input to a reliability program which requires statistical parameters and distribution functions for each of the ten variables. For a given value of the safety factor $R_s$, the reliability program obtains the safety index, $\beta$ . Conversely, if a target safety index is fixed, a safety factor can be derived to give the required safety index.

## DATA BASE

Random variable X has a mean value of 1.0 (unbiased) and a coefficient of variation of 15% (Nyman and Moses, 1985). This means that there is a 95% chance that the predicted value will be within 70-130% ($\pm$ 2 sigma) of the true value. Statistical data on random variable S is obtained from test results reported by Lehigh University (Fisher and Keating, 1985). A fatigue truck (Schilling, 1982) is selected to represent the variety of trucks of different types and weights in actual traffic. This above vehicle was found to have an influence factor closest to the average influence factor due to the entire truck spectrum on the bridge for various span lengths. WIM data (Snyder, Likins and Moses, 1985) collected from 30 sites nationwide with over 27,000 truck samples yielded an effective fatigue truck gross weight of 54 kips.

Actual recorded weigh-in-motion truck data from 12 sites was used to obtain statistical parameters of M. As the gross weight of fatigue truck matches the effective fatigue truck weight, the random variable W has a mean value of 1.0. A cov of 10% is assumed for W implying a 95% chance that the effective fatigue truck weight for the site will be between 43 kips-65 kips. This is based on results of WIM studies (Synder, Likins and Moses, 1985). Best estimates of girder distributions and impact factors are to be used as nominal values. Hence the mean values of G and I are equal to 1.0. The cov's of G and I are taken as 13% and 11% respectively (Nyman and Moses, 1985). The best estimate of the average daily truck traffic is used with the mean value obtained from a knowlege of site conditions. The cov of ADTT is assumed as 10%. The random variable H is found to have a mean value of 1.03 and a cov of 0.6% (Nyman and Moses, 1985).

The mean value of random variable C for different spans and span types was studied by Schilling. The cov of C is assumed as 5%. The method used to calculate the equivalent number of cycles considers that damage is proportional to the cube of stress range.

## TARGET BETA SELECTION AND SAFETY FACTORS

The target beta is selected as an average of the betas implicit in present fatigue design practice. This implies there is no obvious need to either raise or lower existing calibration risk levels based on performance experience. This was the philosphy adopted in the recent AISC-LRFD and is also appropriate for fatigue evaluation of bridges herein. Thirteen typical AASHTO design cases for redundant details with different volumes, fatigue categories, spans, impact factors, girder distributions and support conditions (simply supported or continuous) were used to evaluate an average beta implicit in the present AASHTO design practice. The existing safety indices were found to vary between 1.0-3.5. The average safety index was found to be approximately 2.0 and hence the target safety index of 2.0 was fixed for redundant members. Similar analysis lead to a target safety index of 3.0 for nonredundant members. The reliability program determined that a safety factor of 1.35 was required for redundant members while safety factor of 1.75 was required for nonredundant members. These values assume a precise nominal checking format which in most parts is similar to present AASHTO rules as illustrated below.

ESTIMATION OF REMAINING LIFE

A nominal stress range is calculated, using the standard fatigue truck. If the site conditions are expected to cause unusual bunching of trucks, gross weight is increased by 15%. This is based on actual measurements at five different sites (Moses, Ghosn and Gobieski, 1985). An impact factor to account for the dynamic effect is taken as 1.10 for smooth surfaces and 1.10-1.30 for rough surfaces (Moses and Nyman 1985). The maximum moment range due to the given fatigue truck is then calculated. This maximum moment range when multiplied by lateral distribution factor gives the maximum moment range on a component. The section modulus is calculated including the deck for composite girders (as per AASHTO specifications) or using the steel section alone for noncomposite girders. The moment range on the girder divided by the section modulus gives the nominal stress range on the girder. The nominal stress range is then multiplied by a reliability (or safety) factor to obtain the factored stress range.

In addition, partial safety factors are introduced to make the evaluation procedure flexible enough to allow the engineer to incorporate site specific data. For example, a partial safety factor is used when nominal stress range is obtained through site measured stress range spectrum. Another partial safety factor is associated with the estimation of the gross weight of fatigue truck. As an alternative to using the standard fatigue truck with a gross weight of 54 kips, the evaluator may modify the gross weight with some knowledge of local traffic conditions or WIM measurements. The third partial safety factor relates to girder distribution factor. The basic method in the proposed procedures estimates the girder distribution by a simple conservative formula obtained from grillage analogy studies proposed by Bakht. As an alternative, the evaluator may use rigorous methods like finite element methods to estimate girder distribution. Partial safety factors are calibrated to maintain the same target reliability levels but "reward" the evaluator with less conservative safety factors based on methods which reduce the uncertainties. These factors are discussed in detail in NCHRP project 12-28(3). In addition, field measurements are used to recognize that computed stresses often overestimate measured values due to conservativeness in the section modulus. This is especially true for existing noncomposite deck sections which in fact exhibit considerable composite behavior.

The factored stress range (nominal stress range x safety factor) is used to compute the remaining safe life of structure $Y_F$, using the evaluation chart or the following equation:

$$Y_f = K \times 10^6/T_a C(R_s S_r)^3 - a \qquad (8)$$

where $K$ - detail constant based on attachment category

$T_a$ - estimated lifetime average daily truck volume in outer lane

$R_s\ S_r$ - Factored Stress Range

$a$ - Present age of bridge

As an alternative, more complicated equations are available to enable the evaluator to divide the total life into 2 or more periods in which truck volume or equivalent truck weights remain constant. Equations are also presented to take into account annual truck traffic growth rates.

CONCLUSIONS

Flexible risk-based evaluation specifications for strength and fatigue life evaluation of existing bridges have been developed. These approaches have options ranging from an initial screening level to obtaining site specific data through a full fledged site investigation. The level of data acquisition of course depends on the economic importance of the structure and the amount of time, effort and money the evaluator is willing to spend.

Results for both the strength evaluation and fatigue life assessment have been completed. These include:

1) A bridge load model suitable for evaluation using current site-specific traffic and bridge characteristics.
2) A risk criteria which provides consistent and uniform reliability levels for evaluation decisions.
3) A safe fatigue life estimation also using site data input.
4) A flexible approach in which load and resistance factors depend on the level of effort instituted by the evaluation engineer.
5) A set of guidelines suitable for strength evaluation and fatigue life assessment. These have been submitted to appropriate bridge code committees.

ACKNOWLEDGEMENTS

The authors express their appreciation of support for this research contributed by Federal Highway Administration, Ohio DOT and Transportation Research Board (NCHRP). The conclusions and recommendations, however, in the paper are solely those of the authors.

REFERENCES

Nowak A.S. and Zhou J. (1985) "Reliability Models for Bridge Analysis", Department of Civil Engineering, University of Michigan.

Ellingwood Bruce et. al. (1980) "Development of a Probability Based Load Criterion for American National Standard A58". NBS special publication 577.

Thoft-Christensen P. and Baker M.J. "Structural Reliability Theory and its Application". Springer Verlag New York (1982).

Moses F. and Ghosn M. (1985) "A Comprehensive Study of Bridge loads and Reliability". Department of Civil Engineering, Case Western Reserve University.

Keating, P.B., and Fisher J.W. (1985), "Review of Fatigue Tests and Design Criteria on Welded Details", Fritz Engineering Laboratory report 488-1 (85), Lehigh University, Bethlehem, PA October, 1985.

Ghosn, M., Moses, F. and Gobieski, J., (1985) "Evaluation of Steel Bridges Using In-Service Testing" TRB Research Record 7072, Washington, D.C Dec., 1986.

Nyman and Moses F., (1985) "Calibration of Bridge Fatigue Design Model", Journal of Structural Engineering, ASCE, Vol. 111, No. 6, June 1985.

Schilling (1982), "Lateral Distribution Factor for Fatigue Design", proceedings, ASCE, Vol. 108, No. ST9, September, 1982.

Schilling C.G., (1984) "Stress Cycles for Fatigue Design of Steel Bridges, "Journal of Structural Engineering, ASCE, Vol. 110, No. 6 June, 1986.

Snyder, R.E., Likins, G.E., and Moses F., (1985), "Loading Spectrum Experienced by Bridge Structures in the United States", Report FHWA/RD-85/012, Bridge Weighing systems, Inc., Warrensville, OH, February, 1985.

# RELIABILITY OF WOODEN TRUSSES

E. Varoglu* and F. Lam*
*Wood Engineering Department, Forintek Canada Corp.
Western Laboratory, 6620 N.W. Marine Drive,
Vancouver, B.C., Canada V6T 1X2

## ABSTRACT

A comprehensive study of the short-term reliability of wood pitched trusses is presented. Fink trusses with 4/12 roof slopes built from visually graded No. 2 Spruce-Pine-Fir (SPF) and machine stress rated (MSR) 1650f-1.5E lumber were considered in this study. Computer simulation techniques were employed to evaluate the short-term ultimate load capacity of trusses with 16 to 32 ft. span.

Based on reliability analysis of the short term strength limit state of these truss systems, allowable truss spans have been determined under balanced snow loads from two locations in Canada for a target reliability index of 3.5. The impact of utilization of lumber produced by better quality control procedures, such as 1650f-1.5E MSR lumber, in truss manufacturing as compared to visually graded No. 2 SPF graded lumber have been demonstrated by the considerable increase in allowable truss spans.

## INTRODUCTION

Structural design philosophy has undergone major changes in recent years. Previous studies have demonstrated that Reliability-Based Design (RBD) methods offer a means to quantify safety in a better and more uniform way in comparison to allowable stress design methods. As a result, significant advances have been made in the application of RBD methods for concrete and steel structures. Although the application of RBD methods for wood structures has been limited, the current direction in structural wood design code development is towards adopting RBD procedures.

The use of wood trusses in light frame structures represents a potentially significant share in both residential and non-residential roof and floor construction markets. It is important to develop RBD procedures for the proper assessment of the safety of trusses so that more reliable and efficient use of wood in these engineered systems can be realized.

A key step in the development of RBD procedures for trusses is the use of computer simulation techniques to randomly generate trusses built from a given population of lumber. In this study, a structural analysis methodology using a probabilistic approach has been developed to evaluate the short-term ultimate load capacity distribution of a truss family with a given span, built from wood members of a given stiffness and strength distribution. The amplitude of the load to which these trusses will be subjected during their lifetime is also considered as a random variable and is defined by the snow load information at the geographical location of construction. By comparing the short-term resistance distribution to the load distribution using the Rackwitz-Fiessler algorithm, the reliability of truss systems can be established. Thus, the effect of variability in stiffness and strength properties of the lumber on the performance and safety of wood trusses under snow load in a given geographic location can be taken into account in a rational way.

A comprehensive study of the short-term reliability of a Fink truss configuration with 4/12 slope under balanced snow load has been undertaken. Preliminary experimental strength and stiffness data for visually graded No. 2 SPF lumber and the properties of MSR lumber (1650f-1.5E) were used in the computer simulations. Based on these preliminary material properties data, allowable spans were determined for a target reliability index of 3.5 associated with the strength limit state, for Vancouver and Quebec City in Canada.

THE SHORT-TERM RELIABILITY OF TRUSSES

Strength of wood depends on duration of loading. Duration of load tests for SPF lumber in bending, compression and tension are in progress in Canada. The results of these tests when completed may be used to study the long-term reliability of wood structural systems by taking into account the duration of load effect on the strength of lumber. Stiffness and short-term bending, tension and compression strengths of a given grade of lumber, obtained from short-term ramp load tests, exhibit large variability. For instance, for visually graded lumber and MSR lumber, the coefficient of variation in bending strength exceeds 35% and 20%, respectively. Here, the short-term reliability of trusses under balanced snow loads has been investigated by considering only the variability in stiffness and strength properties of wooden truss members from a given grade of lumber.

Several truss spans, ranging from 16 to 32 ft. with 4/12 roof slope, were examined. A representative truss configuration of a 28-ft. span is illustrated in Figure 1. The spacing of the trusses on the roof was taken as 24 in. on centre. The sizes of the truss plates are also given in Figure 1. At all joints, 18 gauge metal truss plates were used. For trusses of 32 ft. span, the single lower chord splice is replaced by two similar splices located symmetrically at a distance of 8 ft. from the centre of the lower chord. Also when the span is greater than 28 ft., each side of upper chord can no longer be built from one piece of lumber; therefore, one splice is used in each side of the upper chord.

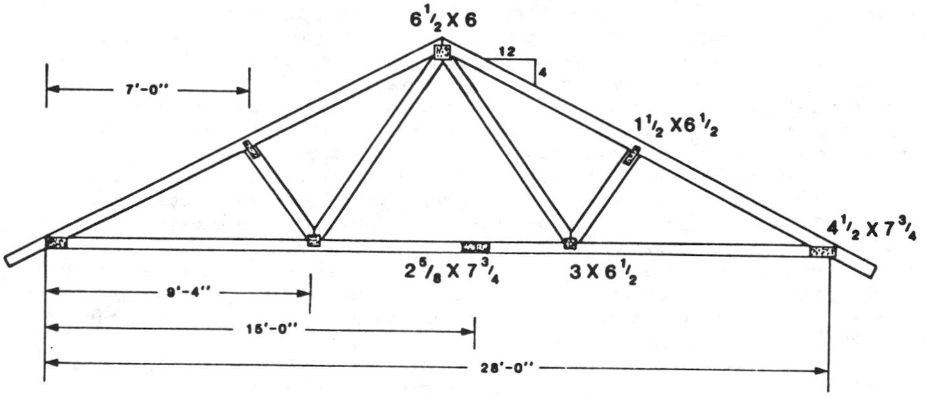


Figure 1. 4/12 Truss Configuration Used in the Short-Term Reliability Analysis.

The flow chart in Figure 2 illustrates the steps in simulations required to establish the load carrying capacity distribution for the truss family of a given span. The computer program, SIMGEN, was used to randomly generated material properties data for the truss members from a given population representing either visually graded or MSR lumber. A random value of Modulus of Elasticity (MOE) and an associated random bending, compression, and tension strengths (MOR) selected from normal distributions were assigned to each truss component. For each span, material properties data for a total of 300 truss replications were generated. Two types of material were considered in this study: visually graded, No. 2, Spruce-Pine-Fir (SPF) lumber, and machine stress rated lumber 1650f-1.5E.

The distributions representing the variability of MOE and the short-term strengths of visually graded lumber in bending, tension and compression, as well as the correlation between MOE and the mean strengths were based on the preliminary results of stiffness and short-term ramp load tests of the material under consideration.

Values of MOE for each truss component (web and chord members) were randomly selected from a normal distribution:

$$MOE = \overline{MOE} \ ( 1 + K \ C_{MOE} ) \qquad (1)$$

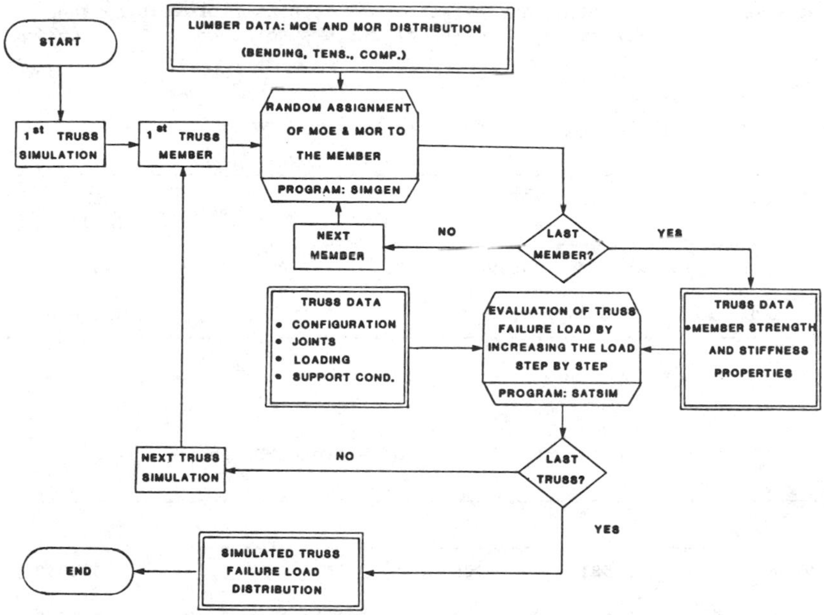


Figure 2. Determination of Load Carrying Distribution of a Given Truss Family

Here, K is a randomly chosen standard normal variable. The values of the mean ($\overline{MOE}$), the coefficient of variation ($C_{MOE}$), and the maximum and the minimum values of MOE representing the preliminary stiffness test results are given in Table 1.

Variability of the bending and compression strength for a fixed value of MOE was assumed to be normal with a mean Modulus of Rupture, $\overline{MOR}$, and coefficient of variation, $C_{MOR}$, which are expressed as functions of MOE:

$$\overline{MOR} = A\ MOE\ 10^{-6} + B \tag{2}$$

$$C_{MOR} = a\ [10^{-6}(MOE - MOE_{min})]^{b}\ [10^{-6}\ (MOE_{max} - MOE)]^{c} \tag{3}$$

Variability of the tension strength for a fixed value of MOE was assumed to be lognormal with a mean, $\overline{\ln MOR}$, and coefficient of variation, $C_{\ln MOR}$, which are expressed as functions of MOE:

$$\overline{\ln MOR} = A\ MOE\ 10^{-6} + B \tag{4}$$

$$C_{\ln MOR} = a\ [10^{-6}\ (MOE - MOE_{min})]^{b}\ [10^{-6}\ (MOE_{max} - MOE)]^{c} \tag{5}$$

For the modulus of ruptures in bending, compression and tension, the values of parameters A, B, a, b, and c are given in Table 2. These parameters were evaluated employing the preliminary experimental results representing the correlation between stiffness and modulus of rupture for each failure mode of the lumber sample.

Table 1 Modulus of Elasticity (MOE) Distribution.

| Material | $\overline{MOE}$ (psi) | $C_{MOE}$ (%) | $MOE_{max}$ (psi) | $MOE_{min}$ (psi) |
|---|---|---|---|---|
| Visual Grade No. 2 | 1,300,000 | 21 | 2,000,000 | 700,000 |
| MSR 1650f-1.5E | 1,500,000 | 11 | 1,650,000 | 1,350,000 |

Table 2 Parameters to define the Correlation Between MOE and MOR's.

| | A | B | a | b | c |
|---|---|---|---|---|---|
| Bending | 5,581 | -905 | 0.3626 | 0.0577 | 0.6358 |
| Compression | 2,907 | 109 | 0.2224 | 0.0084 | 0.3690 |
| Tension | 1.298 | 6.272 | 0.0680 | 0.3485 | 0.5060 |

The same test results were utilized in the case of MSR lumber with additional constraints defined by the MSR grading rules in the random selection of MOE and strength values for the truss components. For example, the randomly generated bending strength data for truss components was adjusted, if necessary, so that the fifth percentile bending strength of the truss components is not less than 1650 x 2.1 psi.

As shown in Figure 2, the truss simulation program SATSIM was used to perform the structural analysis of the simulation study. SATSIM has the capability to perform the structural analysis of trusses by directly accessing the member properties of trusses, randomly generated by SIMGEN. The theoretical background of the structural analysis portion of SATSIM has been published by Foschi (1977). Only a brief description of it will be presented here. The truss is modelled as a linear, elastic frame joined by linear members called truss plates. The connection between the truss plates and wood frame members is through the teeth of the truss plates. And the connector is assumed to have nonlinear load-deformation characteristics.

Each truss with randomly generated material properties and uniformly distributed load on the upper chord was analyzed. The load applied to upper chord was increased step by step until truss failure. For each replication, failure load, failure type and maximum truss deflections were recorded. The results obtained from the analysis for each span and material type are summarized in Table 3. The mean failure load is expressed as the load per unit length of the upper chord.

Table 3 Failure Load and Maximum Truss Deflections.

| Material | Slope | Span (ft.) | Failure Load Mean (lb./in.) | Failure Load Coefficient of variation (%) | Maximum deflection (in.) | Percentage of connection failure (%) |
|---|---|---|---|---|---|---|
| Visual | 4/12 | 16 | 22.41 | 11.33 | 0.831 | 65 |
| graded | | 19 | 21.01 | 12.84 | 0.896 | 64 |
| No. 2 SPF | | 22 | 17.83 | 13.53 | 0.948 | 66 |
| | | 26 | 14.54 | 18.54 | 1.069 | 42 |
| | | 28 | 11.59 | 22.88 | 1.273 | 25 |
| MSR | 4/12 | 24 | 17.79 | 0.40 | 0.800 | 99 |
| lumber | | 26 | 16.71 | 2.00 | 1.073 | 99 |
| 1650f-1.5E | | 32 | 9.49 | 1.00 | 1.055 | 100 |

RELIABILITY STUDY

After the truss resistance distribution for a given span has been determined from the failure loads of 300 truss replications, the resistance distribution was compared with the load distribution. Weather data provided information about the statistical distribution of the annual maximum snow depth for a given geographic location. Quebec City and Vancouver were chosen for this study because the snow load in Vancouver has a high variability but low magnitude and the snow load in Quebec City in contrast to Vancouver has a high magnitude but low variability. The snow loads at these cities were represented by Gumbel Type I distributions. The failure function, G, for the strength limit state can be expressed as

$$G = R - (D + S) \tag{6}$$

for a given span. Here, R is the failure load (resistance) and D and S are the dead load and 30 year maximum snow load respectively for the given geographic location. The dead load was taken as 10 psf on the roof surface which corresponds to a uniformly distributed load D = 1.58 lb/in on the upper chord of the truss. The 30 year maximum snow load distributions were represented by Gumbel Type I distributions for both locations. The distribution of 30 years maximum snow load per unit length of upper chord was taken as

$$S = 0.1265 \; [\; U + (\; -\ln\; (\; -\ln P^{1/30}\; ))\; ] \; / \; C \tag{7}$$

U and C are distribution parameters given by Environment Canada. The distribution parameters for Quebec City are U = 39.30 and C = 0.140; and the corresponding values for Vancouver are U = 2.69 and C = 0.181. P is a random number, uniformly distributed from 0 to 1, giving the probability of having a snow load less than or equal to S (lb/in), the load per unit length of upper chord of the truss.

The reliability index for the failure function was calculated using the Rackwitz-Fiessler algorithm. The algorithm requires the distribution of random variables R and S in the failure function so that the slope and the values of the cumulative distribution functions can be computed for any given value of the random variables. These calculations were performed numerically for R, working directly with the ranked values of failure loads obtained from the simulations. For S, the above Gumbel Type I distribution was used for each location. Iterations for the most likely failure point were terminated when two successive values of reliability safety index, $\beta$, differed by less than 0.001. The reliability safety index values as a function of truss span are presented in Figure 3. The allowable spans which give a target reliability index ( $\beta$ = 3.5) were calculated by interpolation of extrapolation, and the results are presented in Table 4.

DISCUSSION OF RESULTS

The percentages of failures which occurred at connections, characterized by either tooth withdrawal or tension yielding at the truss plates, are presented for each span in the last column of Table 3. For trusses built from visually graded lumber, the percentage of connection failures increased from 25% to about 65% when the span length decreased from 28 ft. to 16 ft. In the case of trusses built of MSR lumber, with spans from 24 ft. to 32 ft., connection failure was

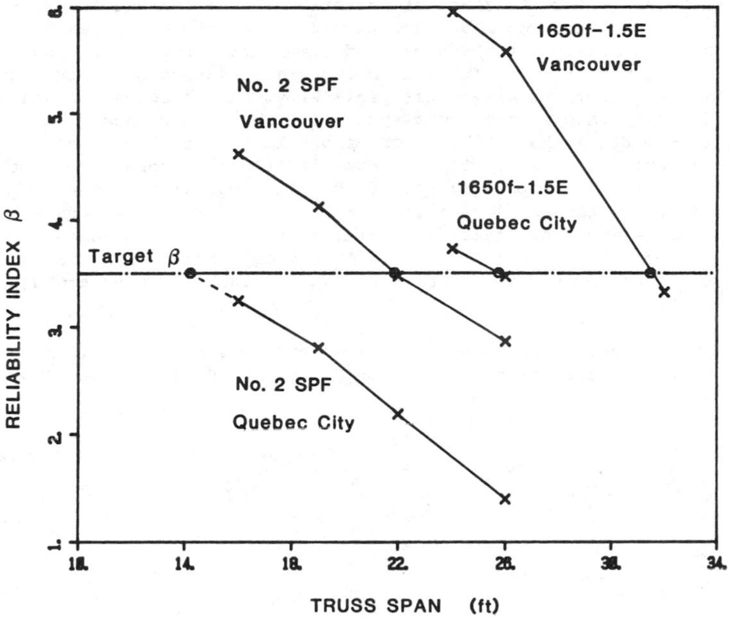


Figure 3. Reliability Index Versus Truss Span

Table 4 Allowable Truss Spans Yielding a Target Reliability Index of 3.5 for the Strength Limit State.

| Material | Slope | Location | Span (ft) |
|---|---|---|---|
| Visually graded No. 2 SPF | 4/12 | Vancouver | 21.86 |
| | | Quebec City | 14.21 |
| MSR 1650f-1.5E | 4/12 | Vancouver | 31.48 |
| | | Quebec City | 25.74 |

the main failure mode. The coefficient of variation of the failure loads of MSR lumber truss systems was very small because almost all of these trusses experienced connection failure at the same load level, irrespective of the variability in member properties. The joints for truss systems built from MSR lumber may be improved by increasing truss plate sizes and thicknesses, which may lead to substantial gain in the truss system's total performance.

It is clear from Table 4 that utilization of MSR lumber results in higher allowable spans in both locations. The increase in allowable spans due to the utilization of MSR lumber is approximately 10 ft. The reliability index concept can be extended to study the serviceability limit state of maximum truss deflection. In this study, serviceability limit state was not considered since the maximum truss deflections at failure were less than span/240 for all replications except for few cases of the 16 ft. span visually graded trusses.

REFERENCES

Foschi, R.O. (1977). "Analysis of wood diaphragms and trusses. Part I: Diaphragms, Part II: Truss Plate", Canadian Journal of Civil Engineering, 4(3), 345-362.

# LOAD SPACE REDUCTION OF RANDOM STRUCTURAL SYSTEMS AND FAILURE COST DESIGN

Mehrdad Soltani* and Ross B. Corotis**

*Civil and Arch. Engrg., Univ. of Miami, Coral Gables, FL 33124

**Civil Engrg., The Johns Hopkins Univ., Baltimore, MD 21218

ABSTRACT

The reliability of redundant random structural systems is evaluated by simulation of load vectors as load variables are reduced. It is concluded that a three-dimensional load space formulation appears to provide a reasonable approximation of system reliability of structural systems.

The reduction of load space dimensions enables a systematic approach to design, based on applying weights to modes of failure and minimization of the total expected cost using single and multiobjective programming. The result is a trade-off curve between future (or failure) cost and initial cost.

## INTRODUCTION

Reliability of ductile structural systems is often computed using limit state functions based on simple plastic theory (Moses, 1982). In this paper, a recently developed more accurate procedure for the failure probability of the whole structural system and failure mode probabilities is discussed (Corotis and Soltani, 1985; Kam, Corotis and Rossow, 1983; Kam, Rossow and Corotis, 1983; Lin and Corotis 1985).

System probability of failure is evaluated by the integration of the joint probability density function of the applied loads over the region lying outside the limit state curve (or surface) in load space (Lin and Corotis, 1985). Similarly, failure probabilities of individual or characteristic modes of failure (combination of several similar individual modes, e.g., those associated with beam mechanisms of certain floors) may be computed by integration of loads over sections of the limit state curve (or surface) associated with these modes of failure in load space shown in Figure 1 (Corotis and Soltani, 1985). The n-dimensional integration is performed by load simulation and identification of safety or failure.

A study of system probabilities of failure of a typical frame structure as load space dimensions are decreased (by the assumption of positive perfect correlation amongst certain floor loads) from seven to three and two is performed. A three-dimensional load space seems to provide a close approximation of the system reliability.

New codes which have incorporated load and resistance factor design are based on a target probability of failure for a given structural element (CISC, 1978; AISC, 1983), and therefore elements of the same nature, such as beams or columns, are treated similarly. An approach is developed by which collapse modes with greater impact (in case of failure) control the reliability of the system using an optimization procedure. Single and multiobjective linear programming with objectives of future (or failure) costs and initial cost and constraints on system probability of failure is used for this purpose (Corotis and Soltani, 1985). The result is a trade-off

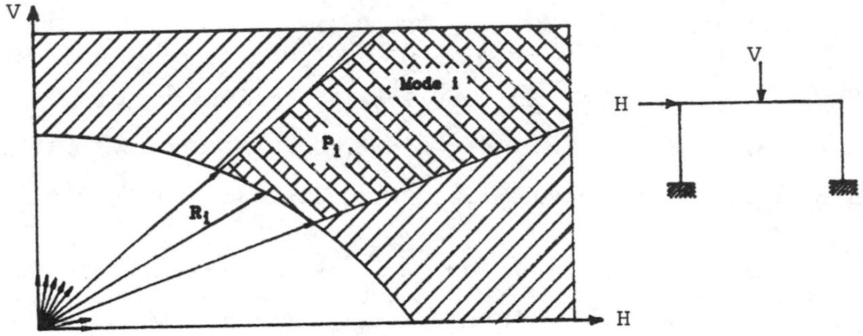


Figure 1 - Typical Limit State Curve

curve relating initial cost to future (or failure) cost (Soltani, 1986).

PROBABILITY OF FAILURE

The evaluation of structural system reliability based on the failure mode method requires the identification of either all (Gorman and Moses, 1979; Stevenson and Moses, 1970; Vanmarcke, 1973) or at least the major modes of failure (Ma and Ang, 1981). Generally, however, the number of possible failure modes is extremely large, and it is difficult to identify the major modes of failure.

The method for computation of failure probability, P, used in this research is based on that developed by Lin and Corotis (1985). In this method, a nonlinear structural analysis program (Kam et al, 1983) and an incremental load procedure are used to define progressive limit state functions. Structural variability is modeled by randomization of the limit state function in load space without requiring any additional structural analysis (Lin and Corotis, 1985; Rashedi and Moses, 1983).

LOAD SPACE STRUCTURAL RELIABILITY

System reliability is evaluated from the joint probability density function of the applied loads over the region lying within the limit state curve (or surface) in load space. The load space approach has several advantages for the computation of reliability. First, It permits a separate examination of load and strength parameters. Strength values are fixed and an incremental load procedure is applied to the deterministic structure. The randomization of the strength is permitted without any additional structural analysis (which is very costly). Second, the dimensions of the load space are kept small, even for large structures. Only load combinations with high likelihoods of causing failure need be used. For instance, for a typical office building, one may use a lateral wind load in combination with a lifetime maximum live load in one suite of offices and an arbitrary point-in-time live load in all other offices. The assumed location of the suite of offices experiencing lifetime maximum may also be treated as a random variable. Third, different load probability distributions may be associated with the axes in load space for different load combinations. The first crossing of the elastic limit state is independent of load path, and ultimate limit states are insensitive to load path (unless significant load reversal into the inelastic region exists) (Chou, 1983). This means that proportional loading starting at the origin rather than the expected point of all load variables may be justified. It is therefore possible to use the limit states determined from a single ensemble of loading paths for various load combinations.

## n-DIMENSIONAL LIMIT STATE SURFACE

The limit state is approximated by interpolation between the computed failure points. It is obvious that a better approximation of the limit state curve may be achieved by increasing the number of failure points. If the number of failure points is held constant and a limit state independent of load distributions is desired (for different possible load combinations), one objective may be to keep failure points equally spaced on the limit state curve, thereby reducing the chance of clustering in a certain region.

Consider an n-dimensional sphere, or n-sphere. A point Q on the sphere is defined as

$$Q:\{\theta_1, \theta_2, \ldots, \theta_n, \rho \mid \sum_{i=1}^{n} \cos^2 \theta_i = 1\} \qquad (1)$$

or

$$Q:\{\theta_1, \theta_2, \ldots, \theta_{n-1}, \rho\} \qquad (2)$$

with corresponding rectangular coordinates

$$X_i = \rho \cos \theta_i \qquad \text{for } i=1,2,\ldots,n-1 \qquad (3)$$

$$X_n = \rho \left(1 - \sum_{i=1}^{n-1} \cos^2 \theta_i\right)^{1/2} . \qquad (4)$$

where $\theta_i$ , i=1,2,...,n are direction angles of point Q and $\rho$ is the distance from the origin to point Q.

The value of $\Delta\theta$ , the interval of direction angles, influences the accuracy of the interpolation of the limit state. A study of the effect of $\Delta\theta$ on the failure probability as well as on the number of failure points suggests that equal angles, $\Delta\theta_i = \Delta\theta = 15$ degrees for i=1,2,3,...,n-1, may be used to define directions of failure points on an n-sphere of radius 1 (Soltani, 1986). The coordinates of these failure points will be used as direction cosines of load vectors to be applied to the actual structure.

## n-DIMENSIONAL INTEGRATION

Probability of failure, P, is

$$P = \int\int\ldots\int_{\text{(failure region)}} f_{L_1, L_2, \ldots, L_n}(\ell_1, \ell_2, \ldots, \ell_n)\, d\ell_1 d\ell_2 \ldots d\ell_n \qquad (5)$$

in which the kernel is the joint probability density function of loads $L_i$. Note that P is actually the probability of failure of the system given a limit state surface in which resistance is deterministic. Loads in this study will be assumed to be statistically independent. It has been shown from load survey data that the live load in one suite in an office building is almost independent of the live loads in various other suites of offices (Corotis and Jaria Aldea, 1979), and live loads and wind loads may be assumed to be independent. The joint density function in Equation (5) may then be replaced by the product of marginal density functions.

P is computed using simulation (Thoft-Christensen and Baker, 1982). Realistic load distribution functions (Ellingwood et al, 1980; 1982; Galambos et al, 1982) are used to describe $f_L(\ell)$ and the n-dimensional integration is performed by the Monte Carlo method (Mihran, 1972; Rubinstein, 1981). The procedure is as follows:

1. Proportional load path orientations are determined from associated points on an n-dimensional hypersphere.
2. The nonlinear structural analysis is run for each proportional loading direction as determined in step 1, using mean plastic moment capacities. The resulting vector in direction k from the origin to the limit state surface is denoted

$$\underset{\sim}{R}_k = \{R_{1k}, R_{2k}, \ldots, R_{nk}\}. \tag{6}$$

3. n loads are simulated from their respective distribution functions. The result is the vector

$$\underset{\sim}{L}_j = \{L_{1j}, L_{2j}, \ldots, L_{nj}\}. \tag{7}$$

4. The simulated load is identified as being either inside (safe region) or outside (failure region) of the limit state boundary. To determine this, the closest $\underset{\sim}{R}_k$ vector to the simulated load vector, i.e., that k with the smallest angle between the two vectors $\underset{\sim}{R}_k$ and $\underset{\sim}{L}_j$, is identified. Since the limit state is approximated by hyperspherical regions in the neighborhood of $\underset{\sim}{R}_k$, failure is specified if $L_j > R_k$, where $L_j$ and $R_k$ are lengths of the two vectors $\underset{\sim}{L}_j$ and $\underset{\sim}{R}_k$.
5. Steps 3 and 4 are repeated many times and the number of points falling in the failure region is stored and P is computed by

$$P = \frac{\text{no. of points in the failure region}}{\text{total no. of simulated points}}. \tag{8}$$

System probability of failure, P, computed using the above procedure is really P given R, failure probability with random loads and deterministic resistance. Lin and Corotis (1985) have employed a technique of incorporating the randomness in resistance by modification of Moses' "unzipping method" (1982). The randomization of resistance incorporated in this study is performed using a slight modification of the same technique.

The mean and the standard deviation of resistance, $R_k$, in a sector k are defined in terms of the statistics of the structural elements, i.e., mean, standard deviation, and coefficient of correlation of moment capacity and functions of structural geometry.

A two parameter distribution form is calibrated for $f_R(r)$ in sector k (the normal distribution is generally adequate) for the computation of P. Lin (1984) showed that the exact form of the distribution of $R_k$ is not critical (in two- and three-dimensional load space). Normal and lognormal distributions are assumed to model $R_k$ in this study, and the effect on P is presented.

A maximum of n = 7 dimensions is considered, requiring 1616 structural analyses in the seven-dimensional load space for $\Delta\theta=15°$. The large number of computer runs are carried out on a CRAY "supercomputer", which reduces the CPU time to a reasonable level.

The values of P are evaluated as the dimension of the load space is reduced. Approximations in the computation of P as the number of load dimensions is reduced result from:

1. Reduction of the number of independent loads, i.e., two or more independent loads are assumed perfectly correlated.
2. Reduction of the limit state surface; i.e., only a part of the limit state surface is used, and some generality is lost.

Realistic wind and live load distributions, but with nominal values 2.5 times those calculated for the structure using the ANSI procedure (1982), are applied. The increase in load magnitude was necessary to obtain reasonable probability estimates on the order of $10^{-8}$ (Lin, 1984, showed that probabilities of failure of $10^{-17}$ are common in the case of deterministic resistance).

There was a change of one order of magnitude as the 7-D load space of the frame in Figure 2, i.e., PIW (pseudo instantaneous wind load, PML (pseudo life time maximum live load) on beam $L_1$ and PIL (pseudo instantaneous live load) on all other beams, was reduced to 3-D as shown in Table 1. Results of this loading condition as well as various other loading conditions (e.g., PIW, PML on beam $L_2$ and PIL on all other beams) seem to indicate that approximations induced in the three-dimensional load space (or two-dimensional load space for the case pseudo life time maximum wind load and PIL on all beams) are not serious since errors of this magnitude are generally acceptable in computation of point estimates of system failure probability (Soltani, 1986).

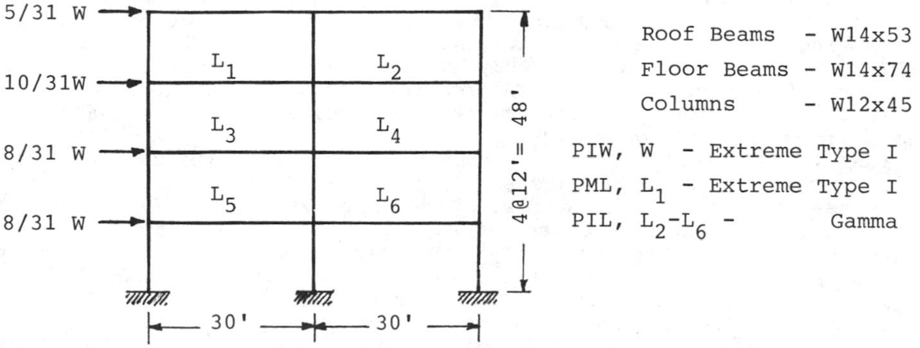


Figure 2 - Two-Bay Four-Story Structure

Table 1 - Probability of Failure Versus Load Space Dimension

| n | | 7 | 6 | 5 | 4 | 3 |
|---|---|---|---|---|---|---|
| Det. | P | $4.7x10^{-7}$ | $2.8x10^{-7}$ | $1.9x10^{-7}$ | $9.8x10^{-8}$ | $6.8x10^{-8}$ |
| | ratio to 7 | | 0.60 | 0.40 | 0.21 | 0.14 |
| Normal | P | $9.8x10^{-5}$ | $6.8x10^{-5}$ | $4.8x10^{-5}$ | $3.0x10^{-5}$ | $9.7x10^{-6}$ |
| | ratio to 7 | | 0.69 | 0.49 | 0.31 | 0.10 |
| Log-normal | P | $9.4x10^{-5}$ | $6.3x10^{-5}$ | $4.5x10^{-5}$ | $3.0x10^{-5}$ | $9.7x10^{-6}$ |
| | ratio to 7 | | 0.67 | 0.48 | 0.32 | 0.10 |

It was noted that for the loading condition shown the values of P for deterministic and random resistance are considerably different (on the order of 2 or 3 degrees of magnitude). This indicates that variability in strength must not be ignored, and approximations of failure probabilities of deterministic systems, no matter how sophisticated, are far from the true values of P. The exact distribution of the resistance seems not to be critical since values of P for the two cases of normally and lognormally distributed resistance were very close.

## SINGLE AND MULTIOBJECTIVE FORMULATION

Structural system reliability is used to identify critical structural components and modes of failure. A design formulation based on a long term investment (cost) of the structural system is considered, with total cost the sum of initial cost and the expected costs of failure in different modes.

The ideal objective is to establish a criterion for selecting a design which will maximize its utility for operation while minimizing its expected loss in case of failure (Au, Shane and Hoel, 1972). The cost of failure includes not only the replacement cost, but also the cost of compensation for possible damage caused by failure, making the calculation extremely difficult, especially if human lives are endangered.

The multicriteria design problem involves initial cost and failure costs. These two costs contradict each other, i.e., if one increases the other decreases. An approximate trade-off curve showing the decrease of expected loss from multiple modes with the increase of initial cost for a simple frame subjected to two random loads is presented by Soltani (1986). A decision maker, e.g., designer or owner, may benefit from such a trade-off curve. The multiobjective scheme described here may be applied to structures with objectives such as cost of failure, initial cost, failure probability associated with collapse in various modes, and failure probability associated with different levels of unserviceability (e.g., excessive deflection, inelastic behavior, partial failure).

REFERENCES

(AISC proposed) Load and Resistance Factor Design Specification for Structural Steel Buildings. (1983). Trial Document, American Institute of Steel Construction.

Au, T., Shane, R. M. and Hoel, L. A. (1972). Fundamentals of System Engineering, Probabilistic Models. Addison Wesley Publishing Co., Reading, MA.

Chou, K. C. (1983). "Stochastic Load Processes with Nonlinear Structural Response." thesis submitted to Northwestern University in partial fulfillment of the requirement for the degree of Doctor of Philosophy.

(CISC) Limit State Design Steel Manual. (1978). Canadian Institute of Steel Construction, 1st Edition.

Corotis, R. B. and Soltani, M. (1985). "Structural System Reliability; Limit States and Modal Consequences." 4th International Conference on Structural Safety and Reliability, Kobe, Japan, I107-116.

Corotis, R. B. and Jaria Aldea, V. (1979). "Stochastic Nature of Building Live Loads." Journal of the Structural Division, ASCE, 105(3), 493-510.

Ellingwood, B. R., Galambos, T. V., Macgregor, J. G. and Cornell, C. A. (1980). "Development of a Probability Based Load Criterion for American National Standard A58." National Bureau of Standards Special Publication 577.

Ellingwood, B. R., Macgregor, J. G., Galambos, T. V. and Cornell, C. A. (1982). "Probability Based Load Criteria; Load Factors and Load Combinations." Journal of the Structural Division, ASCE, 108(5), 978-997.

Galambos, T. V., Ellingwood, B. R., Macgregor, J. G. and Cornell, C. A. (1982). "Probability Based Load Criteria: Assessment of Current Design Practice." Journal of the Structural Division, ASCE, 108(5), 995-977.

Gorman, R. M. and Moses F. (1979). "Reliability of Structural Systems." Report No. 79-2 Case Western Reserve University, Cleveland, Ohio.

Kam, T. Y., Corotis, R. B. and Rossow, E. C. (1983). "Reliability of Nonlinear Framed Structures." Journal of the Structural Division, ASCE, 109(7), 1585-1601.

Kam, T. Y., Rossow, E. C. and Corotis, R. B. (1983). "Inelastic Tangential Stiffness for 2-D Frames." Journal of Structural Engineering, ASCE, 109(11), 2685-2697.

Lin, T. S. (1984). "Load Space Formulation of Reliability for Nonlinear Random Structural Systems." thesis submitted to The Johns Hopkins University in partial fulfillment of the requirement for the degree of Doctor of Philosophy.

Lin, T. S. and Corotis, R. B. (1985). "Reliability of Ductile Systems with Random Strengths." Journal of Structural Engineering, ASCE, 111(6), 1306-1325.

Ma, H. F. and Ang, A. H. (1981). "Reliability Analysis of Redundant Ductile Structural Systems." Civil Engineering Studies, Structural Research Series No. 494, University of Illinois.

Mihran, G. A. (1972). Simulation: Statistical Foundations and Methodology. Academic Press, New York, N. Y.

Minimum Design Loads for Buildings and Other Structures. (1982). American National Standards Institute, ANSI A58.1, New York, N.Y.

Moses, F. (1982). "Structural Reliability Developments in Structural Engineering." Structural safety, Elseveir Scientific Publishing Co., Amsterdam, 1, 3-13.

Rashedi, M. R. and Moses, F. (1983). "Studies on Reliability of Structural Systems." Department of Civil Engineering Report No. R 83-3, Case Western Reserve University, Cleveland, Ohio.

Rubinstein, R. Y. (1981). Simulation and the Monte Carlo Method. John Wiley & Sons, New York, N.Y.

Soltani, M. (1986). "Reliability of Random Structural Systems and Failure Cost Design." thesis submitted to The Johns Hopkins University in partial fulfillment of the requirement for the degree of Doctor of Philosophy.

Stevenson, J. and Moses, F. (1970). "Reliability Analysis of Frame Structures." Journal of the Structural Division, ASCE, 96(11), 2409-2427.

Thoft-Christensen, P. and Baker, M. J. (1982). Structural Reliability Theory and Its Applications. Springer-Verlag, New York, N. Y.

Vanmarcke, E. H. (1973). "Matrix Formulation of Reliability Analysis and Reliability Based Design." Computers and Structures, 3, 757-770.

# SYSTEM RELIABILITY OF RIGID PLASTIC FRAMES

A.M. Nafday*
Post-doctoral fellow
*Department of Civil Engineering, The Johns Hopkins University, Baltimore, MD, 21218
R.B. Corotis**
Willard and Lillian Hackerman Professor and Chairman
**Department of Civil Engineering, The Johns Hopkins University, Baltimore, MD, 21218
J.L. Cohon***
Professor and Vice Provost for Research
***The Johns Hopkins University, Baltimore, MD 21218

## ABSTRACT

The methods for time-invariant system reliability assessment of frames are systematically classified into two basic categories, such that the alternative formulations are linked by elegant structural and mathematical duality relations. Potential problem steps in each categcry are explored, difficulties identified and proposed solutions reviewed. A new approach for the estimation of system reliability of rigid plastic frames is presented. The proposed method replaces the safe region of the structure with an analytically tractable region of equivalent volume, where this volume may be of different order and dimension. The system reliability can be computed from the properties of the substituted region. A hyperspherical equivalent region is used for polytopic limit surfaces, and the system reliability can be directly obtained from probability tables.

## INTRODUCTION

In considering the ultimate collapse of frames, the methods for time invariant system reliability estimation can be divided into two basic categories:

(1) Random Variable cr Direct Approach, and

(2) Random Events or Indirect Approach

All known methods can be considered to belong to one of these categories. The two approaches are linked by static-kinematic duality and, if the problem is expressed in mathematical programming format, by mathematical duality [Nafday, Corotis and Cohon 1987d].

In the random variable approach, system reliability is estimated with respect to the limit state surface or performance function, explicitly or implicitly defined. This function is dependent on the basic variables and divides the region into discrete states corresponding to safety and failure. Loads, strengths and geometric variables constitute the basic random variables in structural problems. The reliability is defined as the probability that the set of basic random variables produces an outcome in the safe state. In the random events approach, one enumerates a finite number of events, representing either the failure or stable configuration modes, and computes the reliability as the probability of their unions and intersections. The available techniques in each category are limited, however, from the point of computational suitability.

RANDOM VARIABLE APPROACH

The main problem in the random variable approach are:

(a) The mathematical formulation of the global limit state surface for the structural frame (Deterministic Problem D1), and

(b) The computation of probability of random variables having an outcome in the safe set (Probabilistic Problem P1).

The random variable approach has not been pursued by many researchers in the field of system reliability because generating the global limit state surface for the entire frame has been considered a daunting task. So far, limit surfaces have only been generated for elements of the systems or for systems up to three dimensions.

An early attempt to derive the global limit surface for an entire structure is due to Symonds and Prager [1950], who generated two- and three-dimensional interaction surfaces for trusses in stress space from geometric arguments. Although intuitively appealing, the geometric approach cannot be used for higher dimensional spaces. Lin and Corotis [1985] established an approximating limit surface in two- and three-dimensional load spaces by repeated analysis of structures for a large number of proportional loading paths. For each analysis, a single point on the limit state surface was identified, and the limit surface was approximated by interpolation. This method is only approximate since it is not possible to identify the true limit state surface from a set of arbitrary points on this surface. Smith [1974] suggested generation of an inner bound approximating surface from the convex combination of certain arbitrary points on the limit surface, obtained by repeated use of a single parameter optimization scheme. Alternatively, he proposed an outer bound approximating surface based on enumeration of several of the possible collapse modes. However, this is not realistic for any except the simplest structures.

Recently, a method for the generation of an exact global limit state surface in the linear case has been developed by the authors [1987b, 1987c], where each maximal facet of the polyhedral surface has been shown to represent a unique failure mode. Similar analytical procedures for nonlinear surfaces are yet to be found. However, even if the limit state surface is available, direct integration of the joint probability density function of the basic variables over the safe set is not feasible except for very small problems. Some approximations based on the assumption of a multinormal distribution have been proposed in this regard [Ditlevsen and Bjerager 1986]. Simulation procedures may also be used for this. Soltani [1986] used simulation procedures to estimate reliability in seven-dimensional load space by generating some of the failure points on the surface, without explicitly generating the entire failure surface. Grigoriu [1982/83] suggested the fitting of an approximating polynominal surface passing through some such generated points, and computing reliability by estimating its distribution function from the information about the first few moments, but no realistic numerical experience was demonstrated. Second moment procedures have also been proposed [Rackwitz and Fiessler 1978] but the problem of convergence of numerical algorithms in higher dimensions is not resolved. Moreover, the methods generally do not work for piecewise differentiable functions, which is the most likely form for most global limit surfaces.

Thus, except for elements of systems and for linear systems, there is no method available for generating global limit surfaces, nor is there any viable method, except simulation, for computing the failure probability of larger systems. Therefore, direct methods have generally been used for elements of the systems rather than the entire systems.

RANDOM EVENTS APPROACH

For the random events category, the chief difficulties concern:

(a) The identification of all the failure modes (Deterministic Problem D2),

(b) Computation of the probability of failure of individual modes (Probabilistic Problem P2), and

(c) The evaluation of point or range estimates of system reliability from modal probabilities (Combination Problem C2).

There have been a number of methods proposed for identifying the failure modes of structure frames with elastic-perfectly plastic or rigid-plastic component behavior that fail by formation of a plastic mechanism [see Nafday, Corotis and Cohon 1987a for details]. All of these methods are essentially based on one of the three basic ideas, viz., enumeration, repeated structural analysis or optimization. An appraisal of procedures indicates that rather than follow a systematic algorithmic approach, they are variously dependent on simulation, trial and error, perturbation, human judgement, complex heuristic strategies or approximation, either for choosing the appropriate starting points or for continuing the method at various stages.

Engineers generally tend to use the words 'method,' 'procedure,' and 'algorithm' synonymously. However, if the problem is to be solved by a digital computer, the three words have distinct meanings. A 'method' finds the solution to a problem, irrespective of whether it can be solved by a computer or not. A 'procedure' has to be describable by a finite number of steps, be unique, take finite interval to perform each step and be closed, i.e., use information only from the previous steps. An 'algorithm' can be defined as a procedure that terminates in a finite number of steps. Assuming that failure modes must always be solved by using a computer, one of the most important characteristics for any proposed procedure must be the existence of an algorithm for its solution. Once this basic requirement of a procedure being algorithmic is satisfied, different procedures can be rationally compared by evaluating their time and space complexity instead of using empirical tests.

The NP-hard nature of the failure mode problem (D2) has led to proposals for generation of only a few of the stochastically dominant modes. An efficient algorithm for the special case of perfectly correlated member resistances [Nafday, Corotis and Cohon 1987a] has recently been proposed. Problem P2 is identical to P1 from a mathematical point of view, even though the sizes of the two problems vary.

Theoretically, from the upper bound theorem of plasticity, it is necessary to account for all the modes to get an exact reliability. Also as collapse modes in general are correlated through common material properties, plastic hinges and loads, exact evaluation of system failure probability is almost impossible. Therefore, various approximating techniques for point and range estimates of system reliability have been proposed [see Ditlevsen and Bjerager 1986 for a comprehensive review]. Most of these depend on the generation of only a few significant modes, and further approximations are introduced in evaluations of modal probabilities (for example, obtaining only first order estimates) and in the estimation of system reliability.

EQUIVALENT VOLUME METHOD FOR SYSTEM RELIABILITY EVALUATION

Of the two basic approaches for structural system reliability evaluation, the random events approach appears to be impractical for highly redundant structures because of the very large number of failure modes. Since only a subset of failure modes can be reasonably used, the methods always give an upper bound on reliability, which is an undesirable characteristic for design decisions. Therefore, the random variable approach is used here to develop an approximate method for system reliability assessment of rigid plastic frames.

Considering the difficulties in attempting an exact solution of the system reliability problem, it is only realistic to seek an approximate solution. Approximations in the random variable methods can be introduced at two stages. The first concerns the suitable simplification of the safe set so that the probability content of an analytically tractable modified safe set is as close as possible to the actual set. The proposed Equivalent Volume Method follows this procedure. The second stage of approximation is in the actual process of probability evaluation. Many of the existing methods introduce approximations at both stages [Ditlevsen and Bjerager 1986].

The limit state surface for a rigid plastic frame under flexure has a polytopic form, i.e., a set of hyperplanes (linear safety margins) enclose the bounded convex safe set. Often, such convex polytopes may be used even for nonlinear cases by replacing the actual surface by a series of tangent hyperplanes on the boundary of the surface. For such a safe set, if the number of bounding hyperplanes is $\rho$, the values of partial reliability indices $\beta_1, \beta_2, \ldots, \beta_\rho$ associated with each linear safety margin can be easily determined, along with their mutual correlations. Using the minimum value of $\beta$ for such a limit state ignores all failure modes except one. Obviously, such first order methods can be grossly inaccurate and fail to capture the characteristics of the entire limit state surface.

Methods based on the assumption of a joint multinormal distribution for the $\beta$'s, and the appropriate approximations for its evaluation, are extensively discussed in [Ditlevsen and Bjerager 1986]. Alternatively, it is possible to find the value of $\beta_{min}$ and to use an inscribed hypersphere of this radius to estimate the lower bound reliability from the Chi-square distribution, implicitly assuming normal distributions for the basic variables. Similarly, an upper bound can be computed from $\beta_{max}$. Ditlevsen [1976] used inscribing and circumscribing rotational paraboloids to develop sharper bounds. Hyperspheres, rotational ellipsoids, and hyperboloids, with the same maximum or minimum curvature at the checking point, have also been investigated [Fiessler, Neumann and Rackwitz 1979]. Veneziano's [1974] multiple point checking method can also be modified to estimate the reliability in this fashion.

In all these procedures, the essential characteristics of the safe set are captured by one or more discrete parameters. The proposed Equivalent Volume Method is designed for polytopic limit states and captures the entire information from the continuum of the safe set. The basic premise is quite simple: the actual polytopic region is replaced by an analytically tractable region of equivalent volume, where the term volume is interpreted in a broad sense, since the volume may be of different dimensions and order.

The volume of a convex set in $R^n$ is its n-dimensional Lebesgue measure, and it depends on the dimension of the space. For example, volume of a set in $R^2$ is usually referred to as area, and the volume of a set in $R^1$ is its length. Also note that volume of a set is zero if it is contained in a lower dimensional subspace. Thus, volume of a plane in 3-dimensional space is zero.

Zero-order volume is obtained when equal weighting is given to all the points in the region and is the commonly understood meaning of the term. The first-order volume weights each point according to its distance from the mean, and the second-order according to the square of that distance. These basically correspond to the commonly understood moment of area and moment of inertia, respectively. Similarly, higher order volumes can be defined.

An equivalent region can be a parallelotope, hypersphere, hyperellipsoid, or any other suitable form. Analytical expressions for the volumes of such regions in higher dimensions are either available in the literature [Kendall 1961, Somerville 1959] or can be easily computed. Thus, the problem reduces to finding the volumes of the original safe sets, i.e., polytopes.

Until recently, except for Monte Carlo simulation there was no known method for finding the volumes of polytopes in higher dimensional spaces. Developments in computer science, where such volumes are required for program analysis, has led to some proposals in this regard [Cohen and Hickey 1979, Lasserre 1983]. Cohen and Hickey [1979] apparently were the first to develop systematic procedures for computing polyhedral volumes in $R^n$ and gave two algorithms for this purpose.

The first algorithm is based on the decomposition of an n-dimensional (n-D) polytope into a finite number of n-D simplices. An n-D simplex is an n-D convex polytope with n+1 extreme points, i.e., it is the smallest possible n-D unit. Thus, points are zero-dimensional (0-D) simplices, edges are 1-D simplices, triangles are 2-D simplices and tetrahedra are 3-D simplices. It is well known that the volume of a simplex can be found from the determinant of the associated square matrix defining the simplex. Thus, summing the volumes of simplices that form the polytope will give the total volume. This method gives exact volume, but the number of simplices and determinants grows exponentially with the dimension of the space, and as such it is only suitable for spaces of low dimensions, e.g., no more than 10.

The second algorithm is approximate and is applicable to any convex body, including those with nonlinear boundaries. It is based on summing the volumes of increasingly smaller parallelotopes which can fit into the polytope. Convex problems are easier since it is known that if all vertices of an n-parallelotope (n-P) lie in a given n-D polytope, then all of the points in n-P lie in the polytope. Thus, it is not necessary to check the points within n-P. As a guide, it is often useful to find the smallest parallelotope enclosing the entire polytope, which can be easily done by linear programming.

Lasserre [1983] has given an analytical expression for the volume of a convex polyhedron A x = b as a function of b. The method follows from Euler's theorem on homogeneous functions and gives a simple recursive identity. Based on this, an efficient algorithm is presented. This algorithm is also able to identify and eliminate redundant constraints. The advantage of this method is that there is no need to partition the polytope into elementary simplices or parallelotopes, and evaluations of the determinants is not required. The method is claimed to be efficient if coded in a languge that allows recursivity, such as PL1 or ALGOL.

Assume that a polytopic limit state surface in the n-D space of standardized normal variables is given. The zero$^{th}$ order volume, V, for this polytope can be computed by any of the above procedures. Let the equivalent region be a hypersphere of radius $\beta_e$, which is defined by $\sum Y_\ell^2 = \beta_e^2$, where $Y_\ell$ denote the standardized normal random variables, ($\ell$= 1,n). Then, from the expression for zero order volume of the hypersphere [Kendall 1961, Somerville 1959], one can write

$$V = \frac{2\beta_e^n}{n} \frac{\pi^{\frac{n}{2}}}{\Gamma(\frac{n}{2})} \tag{1}$$

For example, with n = 2 one obtains $\pi\beta_e^2$, the area of a circle; with n = 3 one has $\frac{4\pi\beta_e^3}{3}$, the volume of a sphere and so on. From (1), the value of $\beta_e$ is

$$\beta_e = \left\{ \frac{V\, n\, \Gamma(\frac{n}{2})}{2\pi^{\frac{n}{2}}} \right\}^{\frac{1}{n}} \tag{2}$$

Using the value of $\beta_e$ given by (2), one can find an approximate value for the probability of failure, $P_f$, for the system as

$$P_f \approx 1 - X_n^2\,(\beta_e^2) \tag{3}$$

where $X_n^2$ (.) = the Chi-square distribution for n-degrees of freedom. This will give a value intermediate between the upper and lower bounds on $P_f$, which were obtained by using $\beta_{min}$ and $\beta_{max}$, respectively.

First order volumes will give a better approximation since weighting by distance can account for variation of probability density. The algorithms discussed above will have to be modified for this case. Similar results for higher order volumes and for different types of equivalent regions can also be derived. Some of these aspects and numerical results are being prepared for a future paper.

REFERENCES

Cohen J. and T. Hickey (1979). "Two Algorithms for Determining Volumes of Convex Polyhedra," Journal of the Association for Computing Machinery, Vol. 26, No. 3, pp. 401-414.

Ditlevsen O. (1976). "Evaluation of the Effect on Structural Reliability of Slight Deviations from Hyperplane Limit State Surfaces," Proceedings, Second International Workshop on Code Formats in Mexico City, DIALOG 2-76, Denmarks Ingeniørakademi, Lyngby, Denmark.

Ditlevsen O. and P. Bjerager (1986). "Methods of Structural System Reliability," Structural Safety, Vol. 3, pp. 195-229.

Fiessler B., Neumann H.J. and Rackwitz R. (1979). "Quadratic Limit States in Structural Reliability," Journal of the Engineering Mechanics Division, ASCE, Vol. 105, No. EM4, pp. 661-676.

Grigoriu M. (1982/83). "Methods for Approximate Reliability Analysis," Structural Safety, Vol. 1, No. 2, pp. 155-165.

Kendall M.G. (1961). A Course in Geometry of n Dimensions, Hafner Publishing Co., New York.

Lasserre J.B. (1983). "An Analytical Expression and an Algorithm for the Volume of a Convex Polyhedron in $R^n$," Journal of Optimization Theory and Applications, Vol. 39, No. 3.

Lin T.S. and R.B. Corotis (1985). "Reliability of Ductile Systems with Random Strengths," Journal of the Structural Division, Vol. 111, No. 6, pp. 1306-1325.

Nafday A.M., R.B. Corotis and J.L. Cohon (1987a). "Failure Mode Identification for Structural Frames," Journal of Structural Engineering, ASCE, accepted for publication.

Nafday A.M., R.B. Corotis and J.L. Cohon (1987b). "Multiparametric Limit Analysis of Frames: Part I - Model," Journal of Engineering Mechanics, ASCE, submitted.

Nafday A.M., J.L. Cohon and R.B. Corotis (1987c). "Multiparametric Limit Analysis of Frames: Part II - Computations," Journal of Engineering Mechanics, ASCE, submitted.

Nafday A.M., R.B. Corotis and J.L. Cohon (1987d). "Geometrical Structure of the Failure Modes for Ductile Frames," technical report under preparation for conference presentation.

Rackwitz R. and B. Fiessler (1978). "Structural Reliability under Combined Load Sequences," Computers and Structures, Vol. 9, pp. 489-494.

Smith D.L. (1974). "Plastic Limit Analysis and Synthesis of Structures by Linear Programming," thesis presented to the University of London, U.K. in partial fulfillment of the requirements for the degree of Doctor of Philosophy.

Soltani M. (1986). "Reliability of Random Structural Systems and Failure Cost Design," A dissertation submitted to The Johns Hopkins University, Baltimore, in partial fulfillment of the requirements for the degree of Doctor of Philosophy.

Somerville D.M.Y. (1959). An Introduction to the Geometry of N Dimensions, Dover Publications, New York.
Symonds P.S. and W. Prager (1950). "Elasto-Plastic Analysis of Structures Subjected to Loads Varying Arbitrarily between Prescribed Limits," Journal of Applied Mechanics, Vol. 17, pp. 315-323.
Veneziano D. (1974). "Contributions to Second Moment Reliability Theory," Research Report R74-33, Department of Civil Engineering, M.I.T., Cambridge, Massachusetts.

# SECOND MOMENT ANALYSIS OF LARGE STRUCTURES WITH RANDOM APPLIED LOADS AND DISPLACEMENTS

Robert R. Dickinson and Gordon J. Savage,
University of Waterloo, Dept. of Systems Design Engineering, Waterloo, Ont., Canada, N2L 3G1

## ABSTRACT

Until recently, little attention has been given to automated second moment analysis of large complex structures. In this paper, we give some results that can be used as a basis for augmenting existing deterministic software systems, when the variability arises from uncertainty in the applied loads and displacements. A second moment model building process is described, that takes as input, specifications of the topology and statistics of applied loads and displacements. We also extend the well-known concept of substructuring to account for random loads. Incidence matrices are used to advantage throughout the theory, but it is shown that these are not required in practice.

## NOTATION

Lower case is used for scalars and upper case for vectors and matrices. Bold face characters are used for random variables and random vectors.

**Characters:**

| | |
|---|---|
| $k$ | 2-terminal constitutive coefficient |
| $K$ | matrix of constitutive coefficients |
| $I$ | incidence matrix |
| $F$ | system graph |
| $A$ | coefficient matrix of MNT |
| $G$ | constitutive sub-matrix of MNT |
| $\mathbf{B}$ | excitations vector of MNT |
| $\mathbf{\Phi}$ | nodal variables (displacements) |
| $\eta_.$ | mean of . |
| $\sigma_.$ | standard deviation of . |
| $r_{..}$ | correlation coefficient of . with . |
| $C_.$ | covariance of . |
| $\mathbf{x}$ | across variable (eg. displacement) |
| $\mathbf{y}$ | through variable (eg. force) |

**Subscripts:**

| | |
|---|---|
| $\cdot_a$ | across driver variables |
| $\cdot_t$ | through driver variables |
| $\cdot_0$ | user specified driver value |

**Diacritical marks:**

| | |
|---|---|
| $\bar{}$ | (bar) multi-terminal component |
| $\tilde{}$ | (tilde) a multi-dimensional variable |
| $\_$ | (underscore) the summing effect $I_t$ |

**Miscellaneous:**

| | |
|---|---|
| $\otimes$ | Kronecker product operator |
| $[.]^{-1}$ | inverse of . |
| $[.]^T$ | transpose of . |
| $U_.$ | unit matrix of order . |
| E{.} | expectation (mean) of . |
| S.D.{.} | standard deviation of . |
| Cov[**X**] | auto-covariance of **X** |
| Cov[**X**,**Y**] | cross-covariance of **X** with **Y** |

## 1. INTRODUCTION

The use of second moment analysis is well-known in the fields of stuctural safety and uncertainty modeling (Vanmarcke1973, Ditlevsen1981, Hart1982, Augusti1984, Madsen1986). In this paper we go beyond simple examples that can be analysed on a hand calculator, and show that these techniques can be readily implemented in software for large structures.

This work is intended for use in *technical models* as opposed to *research models*. Technical models are used as tools in design and as aids to decision making — "the mechanical model is simplified considerably" (Duddeck1977). Research models try to minimize the difference between the reliability of an idealized system and that of the real system.

The results herein provide for the efficient analysis of subjectively estimated second order statistics of the loads and displacements that are applied to a given structure. This tends to be less restrictive than subjective estimation of probability density functions (Blockley1983).

The techniques described have been developed for augmenting graph-theoretic models for probabilistic system analysis. Deterministic graph-theory has been applied to structural engineering problems in the past (Kron1955,Lind1962,Fenves1966,Kaveh1986), but since many readers are likely to be more familiar with the domain-specific terminology of matrix structural analysis (eg:Bhatt1981), we have minimized the use of graph theory terminology in the present paper. Where it is used, it is mainly to demonstrate the applicability of the concepts to a wide range of engineering systems.

## 2. THE BASIC PROBABILISTIC SYSTEM MODEL

**Overview:**

The model we present for analysis purposes is a general network model. That is, the system is assumed to be modeled by a network of distinct components, each with any number of terminals of interconnection. Each component is modelled by both a *terminal graph* and a set of *terminal equations.* The terminal equations relate the system's "through" and "across" variables with the orientation of "measurement" given by the direction of the arrow of the relevant graph edges. A set of generic components and their terminal equations for general steady state problems is:

1. across driver, $\mathbf{x}_a = \mathbf{x}_{a0}$, (eg. specified forces)
2. through driver, $\mathbf{y}_t = \mathbf{y}_{t0}$, (eg. specified displacements)
3. two-terminal constitutive component, $\mathbf{y}_k = k\mathbf{x}_k$, (eg. truss element)
4. multi-terminal constitutive component, $\overline{\mathbf{Y}}_K = [\overline{K}]\overline{\mathbf{X}}_K$ (eg. substructure)
5. hybrid, $\begin{Bmatrix} \mathbf{y}_{d1} \\ \mathbf{x}_{d2} \end{Bmatrix} = \begin{bmatrix} d_{11} & d_{12} \\ d_{21} & d_{22} \end{bmatrix} \begin{Bmatrix} \mathbf{y}_{d2} \\ \mathbf{x}_{d1} \end{Bmatrix}$ (eg. friction component)

Time dependent components are excluded due to space limitations. Some other examples of "driver components" whose parameters are typically uncertain, are given in Table 1.

**Table 1. Examples of through and across drivers.**

| Physical system | Across driver | Through driver |
|---|---|---|
| Elastic frames | Prescribed rotations | Applied moments |
| Electric networks | Voltage source | Current source |
| Pipe networks | Fixed-head pumps | Fixed-flow pumps |

In view of the present readership, we will be use the term "applied force" in lieu of "across driver"; and "prescribed displacement" in lieu of "through driver" for the remainder of this paper.

The "topology" of a physical system is defined as the interconnection pattern of its components. If the terminal graphs of each component are interconnected in a one-to-one correspondence with the components, then the system graph $F$ is obtained. A simple structural example is shown in Fig. 1.

The graph $F$ can be expressed in terms of an "incidence matrix", $I$. In turn, $I$ is used to obtain the *graph equations*. In structural analysis terms, these represent equilibrium: $I.\mathbf{Y} = 0$, and compatibility: $\mathbf{X} = I^T\mathbf{\Phi}$, where $\mathbf{X}$, $\mathbf{Y}$ and $\mathbf{\Phi}$ are random vectors. $\mathbf{\Phi}$ represents the displacements measured relative to the datum node. Each row of $I.\mathbf{Y} = 0$ represents the balance of all the forces at a given node. Each row of $\mathbf{X} = I^T\mathbf{\Phi}$ constrains the sum of displacements around a closed loop to zero. For small systems, clearly defined correlation structures within $\mathbf{X}$ and $\mathbf{Y}$ are easy to investigate via the graph equations alone, without reference to the terminal equations.

**Mixed Nodal Tableau:**

The mixed nodal tableau (MNT) provides an efficient matrix structure for assembling the equilibrium, compatibility, and terminal equations. For steady state problems the MNT takes the specific form:

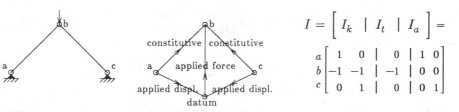

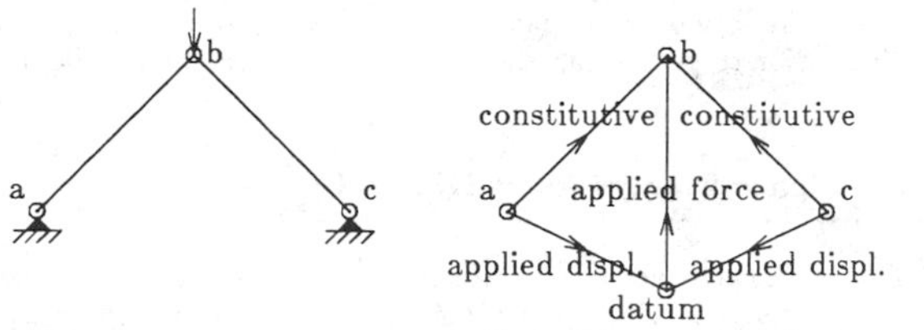


$$I = \left[\, I_k \mid I_t \mid I_a \,\right] = \begin{array}{c} a \\ b \\ c \end{array}\left[\begin{array}{cc|c|cc} 1 & 0 & 0 & 1 & 0 \\ -1 & -1 & -1 & 0 & 0 \\ 0 & 1 & 0 & 0 & 1 \end{array}\right]$$

**Fig. 1** The interconnection pattern of the physical system on the left, including the excitations, is described by its system graph in the centre. This is mathematically described by the incidence matrix on the right, which is partitioned into constitutive components, applied forces, and prescribed displacements.

$$\begin{bmatrix} I_k K I_k^T & I_{d2} + I_{d1} D_{11} & I_a \\ I_{d2}^T - D_{22} I_{d1}^T & -D_{21} & 0 \\ I_a^T & 0 & 0 \end{bmatrix} \begin{Bmatrix} \mathbf{\Phi} \\ \mathbf{Y}_{d2} \\ \mathbf{Y}_a \end{Bmatrix} = \begin{Bmatrix} -I_t \mathbf{Y}_{t0} \\ 0 \\ \mathbf{X}_{a0} \end{Bmatrix}. \qquad (1)$$

where, $I_k$, $I_a$, $I_{d1}$, $I_{d2}$, and $I_t$ are sub-matrices of $I$, $K$ is a block diagonal matrix of ordered constitutive sub-matrices, $D_{11}$, $D_{12}$, $D_{21}$ and $D_{22}$ are block diagonal matrices of ordered hybrid sub-matrices, and $\mathbf{Y}_{t0}$ and $\mathbf{X}_{a0}$ are known (or subjectively estimated) random vectors representing the respective applied forces and displacements.

**Automatic formation of the MNT:**

From equation (1), it is easy to show that once the component type, its topology, and its parameter values are known, its contribution can be added to, or "stamped" into the MNT automatically. In the more familiar *stiffness method* the usual procedure is to form only the *nodal equations* where the "unknown" vector contains only $\mathbf{\Phi}$. However, this smaller set of equations requires some manipulation to set prescribed displacements and it does not readily permit the specification of correlations between any pair of dissimilar excitations.

**Second moment representation of the MNT:**

Writing (1) more compactly as $[A].\mathbf{Z} = \mathbf{B}$ its second moment representation is

$$[A]\ .\ \mathrm{E}\{\mathbf{Z}\} = \mathrm{E}\{\mathbf{B}\}\quad , \quad \text{and} \qquad [A]\ .\ \mathrm{Cov}[\mathbf{Z}]\ .\ [A]^T\ = \mathrm{Cov}[\mathbf{B}]\ .$$

Symbolically, the solution vector $\mathbf{Z}$ is then given by

$$\mathrm{E}\{\mathbf{Z}\} = [A]^{-1}\ .\ \mathrm{E}\{\mathbf{B}\}\quad , \quad \text{and} \qquad \mathrm{Cov}[\mathbf{Z}] = [A]^{-1}\ .\ \mathrm{Cov}[\mathbf{B}]\ .\ [A]^{-T}\ . \qquad (3,4)$$

If desired, alternatives to the explicit inversion of $[A]$ can be developed for defining $\mathrm{Cov}[\mathbf{Z}]$ in terms of $\mathrm{Cov}[\mathbf{B}]$ (eg:Dickinson1986).

**Automatic formation of** $\mathrm{Cov}[\mathbf{B}]$**:**

In order to make second moment analysis available to design engineers in an easy to use format, we need to be able to automatically build covariance matrices from user specified component properties. For each uncertain excitation, we require specifications of its standard deviation and any non-zero correlation coefficients that statistically relate this excitation with any other excitation. It is also desirable to routinely permit several uncertain forces to be incident upon the same node, each of which may have different correlation coefficients with other excitations.

It can be shown using matrix algebra and the definition of covariance, that $\mathrm{Cov}[\mathbf{B}]$ is the sum of individual (user specified) variances and covariances. On this basis, "stamps" can be derived to obviate the apparent need for incidence matrices (Dickinson1986a). These are listed in Tables 2 and 3 below. In Table 3, it is assumed that the standard deviations and topology of a given pair of correlated excitations have been specified, prior to specifying the relevant correlation coefficient.

**Table 2. Mean and Variance Stamps for** $\mathrm{E}\{\mathbf{B}\}$ **and** $\mathrm{Cov}[\mathbf{B}]$**.**

| Excitation | Terminal Graph | Parameters (user input) | Mean Stamp | Variance Stamp |
|---|---|---|---|---|
| Applied Force | 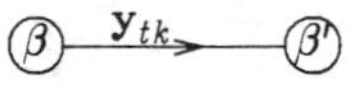  | $\eta_{tk} \equiv \mathrm{E}\{\mathbf{y}_{tk}\}$, $\sigma_{tk} \equiv \mathrm{SD}\{\mathbf{y}_{tk}\}$ | $\begin{matrix} \beta' \\ \beta \\ \\ \end{matrix} \begin{Bmatrix} \eta_{tk} \\ -\eta_{tk} \\ \cdot \end{Bmatrix}$ | $\begin{matrix} & \beta' & \beta & \\ \beta' & \sigma_{tk}^2 & -\sigma_{tk}^2 & \cdot \\ \beta & -\sigma_{tk}^2 & \sigma_{tk}^2 & \cdot \\ & \cdot & \cdot & \cdot \end{matrix}$ |
| Prescribed displacement | 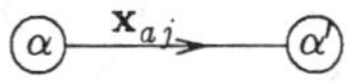  | $\eta_{aj} \equiv \mathrm{E}\{\mathbf{x}_{aj}\}$, $\sigma_{aj} \equiv \mathrm{SD}\{\mathbf{x}_{aj}\}$ | $\begin{matrix} \\ \\ a_j \end{matrix} \begin{Bmatrix} \cdot \\ \cdot \\ \eta_{aj} \end{Bmatrix}$ | $\begin{matrix} & & & a_j \\ & \cdot & \cdot & \cdot \\ & \cdot & \cdot & \cdot \\ a_j & \cdot & \cdot & \sigma_{aj}^2 \end{matrix}$ |

## 3. EXTENSION TO VECTOR NETWORKS

The "stamps" in Tables 2 and 3 are implicitly limited to single process, scalar systems. That is, each graph edge is associated with a single pair of scalar across and through variables. But these tables can be readily extended for multi-process systems and vector networks (eg: 2 and 3-D truss systems), by making use of the algebraic properties of the Kronecker Product operator (eg:Graham1981). Space limitations do not permit a detailed derivation of such tables. Instead, we explicitly derive the link between the MNT formulation described herein, and the *stiffness method*, as an example of the concepts involved.

Prior to the specification of constraints, the stiffness method essentially produces a coefficient matrix of the form

$$\tilde{G} = \tilde{I}_k.[\tilde{K}].\tilde{I}_k^T \tag{5}$$

where the tilde indicates the extension to a vector network, $\tilde{I}_k = I_k \otimes U_q$, $q$ is the number of dimensions (eg. 2 or 3), and the symbol " $\otimes$ " is used for the Kronecker Product operator. (To avoid confusion, it should be noted that this operator is not the same as the "star-multiplication" operator referred to in Ditlevsen1981). Expanding (5) we obtain:

$$\tilde{G} = (I_k \otimes U_q).[\tilde{K}].(I_k^T \otimes U_q) \tag{6}$$

For simple 2-terminal components, (eg. truss-elements) equation (6) can be re-arranged to express $G$ as a sum of $N$ contributions from $N$ components:

$$\tilde{G} = \sum_{e=1}^{N} (I_e.I_e^T) \otimes \tilde{k}_e \tag{7}$$

where $\tilde{k}_e$ is a $q^2$ matrix defining the constitutive properties of the $e^{\text{th}}$ component (graph edge) in $q$-dimensional space. $I_e$ is the "incidence vector" corresponding to column $e$ of $I_k$. If $I_e$ is written as $[\,1 \;\; -1\,]^T$ and $N = 1$, equation (7) expands to the familiar *element stiffness matrix* of order $2q^2$. For $q = 2$:

**Table 3. Covariance stamps for** Cov.[**B**].

| Correlated Excitations | Terminal Graphs (user input: $r_{..}$) | Covariance Stamp |
|---|---|---|
| Applied Forces | 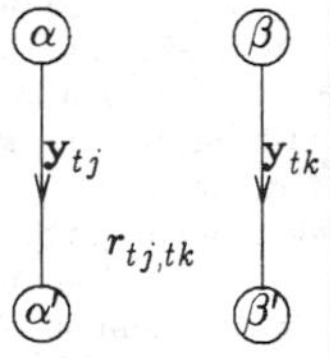  | $\begin{array}{c} \\ \alpha' \\ \beta' \\ \alpha \\ \beta \\ \\ \end{array}\begin{array}{ccccc} \alpha' & \beta' & \alpha & \beta & \\ \cdot & C_{tj,tk} & \cdot & -C_{tj,tk} & \cdot \\ C_{tj,tk} & \cdot & -C_{tj,tk} & \cdot & \cdot \\ \cdot & -C_{tj,tk} & \cdot & C_{tj,tk} & \cdot \\ -C_{tj,tk} & \cdot & C_{tj,tk} & \cdot & \cdot \\ \cdot & \cdot & \cdot & \cdot & \cdot \end{array}$ |
| Prescribed displacement correlated with an Applied Force | 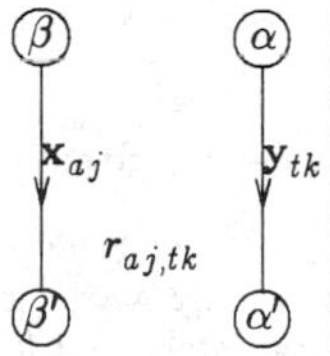  | $\begin{array}{c} \\ \alpha' \\ \alpha \\ a_j \end{array}\begin{array}{ccc} \alpha' & \alpha & a_j \\ \cdot & \cdot & C_{aj,tk} \\ \cdot & \cdot & -C_{aj,tk} \\ C_{aj,tk} & -C_{aj,tk} & \cdot \end{array}$ |
| Prescribed displacements | 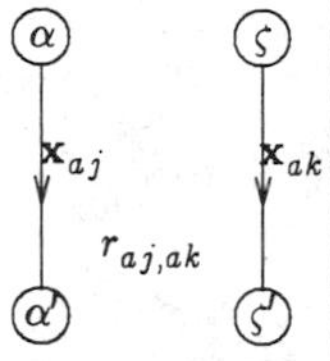  | $\begin{array}{c} \\ \\ a_j \\ a_k \end{array}\begin{array}{ccc} & a_j & a_k \\ \cdot & \cdot & \cdot \\ \cdot & \cdot & C_{aj,ak} \\ \cdot & C_{aj,ak} & \cdot \end{array}$ |

$$\tilde{G} = \begin{bmatrix} 1 & -1 \\ -1 & 1 \end{bmatrix} \otimes \begin{bmatrix} k_{11} & k_{12} \\ k_{21} & k_{22} \end{bmatrix} = \begin{bmatrix} k_{11} & k_{12} & -k_{11} & -k_{12} \\ k_{21} & k_{22} & -k_{21} & -k_{22} \\ -k_{11} & -k_{12} & k_{11} & k_{12} \\ -k_{21} & -k_{22} & k_{21} & k_{22} \end{bmatrix} .$$

Similar operations can be used to produce second order stamps for uncertain excitations of vector networks and coupled systems (Dickinson1986a).

## 4. EXTENSION TO SUBSTRUCTURES

There are obvious computational savings to be gained if repetitive sub-systems or "substructures" can be identified. In addition to this, modern software systems can be designed to take advantage of multiprocessing by solving various parts of a system in parallel with other user input tasks. Further, more efficient use can be made of modern graphical input techniques if substructuring is used. Substructuring also reduces memory requirements — a significant consideration in second moment analysis compared to solving deterministic systems of comparable sizes. Finally, to the extent that the statistical dependence between applied loads will often tend to decrease with spatial separation, it is likely that independent substructures can be indentified accordingly.

If it is assumed that the substructure consists of deterministic constitutive components and random applied forces, it is possible to derive a second moment model from the second moments of the applied forces (Dickinson1986a), using the theory of multi-terminal representations (Savage1980). The conceptual result is that a set of "multi-terminal" equations can be computed, that represent the behaviour of an entire sub-system in terms of its nodes of interconnection with other substructures:

$$\overline{\mathbf{Y}} = \overline{K}.\overline{\mathbf{X}} + \overline{\mathbf{Y}}_{t0} \tag{8}$$

where, in structural analysis terms, the "element stiffness matrix" is given by:

$$\overline{K} = G_{bb} - G_{bi}G_{ii}^{-1}G_{ib} \tag{9}$$

and the "equivalent applied forces" at the boundary nodes are given by:

$$\overline{\mathbf{Y}}_{t0} = M \cdot \underline{\mathbf{Y}}_{it0} + \underline{\mathbf{Y}}_{bt0} \tag{10}$$

where $M = -G_{bi}G_{ii}^{-1}$, $\underline{\mathbf{Y}}_{it0} = I_{it}\mathbf{Y}_{t0}$, and $\underline{\mathbf{Y}}_{bt0} = I_{bt}\mathbf{Y}_{t0}$. Again, the underscore indicates the summing nature of the incidence matrix, $I_t$. The subscripts $i$ and $b$ indicate internal and boundary nodes partitions of $G$.

**Second moment multi-terminal equations:**

The important attribute of the above derivation is that only linear operations are involved if the constitutive properties are linear. Hence the second moment multi-terminal equations can be written as

$$\mathrm{E}\{\overline{\mathbf{Y}}_{t0}\} = M \cdot \mathrm{E}\{\underline{\mathbf{Y}}_{it0}\} + \mathrm{E}\{\underline{\mathbf{Y}}_{bt0}\} \tag{11}$$

and

$$\begin{aligned}\mathrm{Cov}[\overline{\mathbf{Y}}_{t0}] &= M.\mathrm{Cov}[\underline{\mathbf{Y}}_{it0}].M^T + M.\mathrm{Cov}[\underline{\mathbf{Y}}_{it0}\underline{\mathbf{Y}}_{bt0}] \\ &\quad + \mathrm{Cov}[\underline{\mathbf{Y}}_{bt0}\underline{\mathbf{Y}}_{it0}]M^T + \mathrm{Cov}[\underline{\mathbf{Y}}_{bt0}]\end{aligned} \tag{12}$$

where the covariance matrices on the right hand side are sub-matrices of $\mathrm{Cov}[\underline{\mathbf{Y}}_{t0}]$, which can be automatically assembled using the procedures described earlier.

**An application:**

Consider the simplified transmission tower in Fig. 2(b), comprised of four instances of the substructure shown in Fig. 2(a), and some cable restraints. A second moment model of this system was built and analysed using an interactive matrix computations system (Dickinson1986a).

The analysis involved: (a) random wind loads, uniformly distributed (perfectly correlated) with respect to height above the ground; (b) the dead weight of truss elements (deterministic); (c) random live loads from transmission equipment; and (d) random displacements applied parallel to the direction of each cable, to model pretensioning and the various sources of uncertainty (eg: thermal expansion) that might arise in practice.

Without substructuring, $G$ and $\mathrm{Cov}[\underline{\mathbf{Y}}_{t0}]$ for the overall system model are of order 216×216. With substructuring, the corresponding matrices are of order 54×54.

Space restrictions do not permit detailed discussion of solution statistics, but conceptually, complete second order information about all member stresses and nodal deflections is readily obtained. Such results can, of course, be readily used as input to the computation of second moment reliability indices.

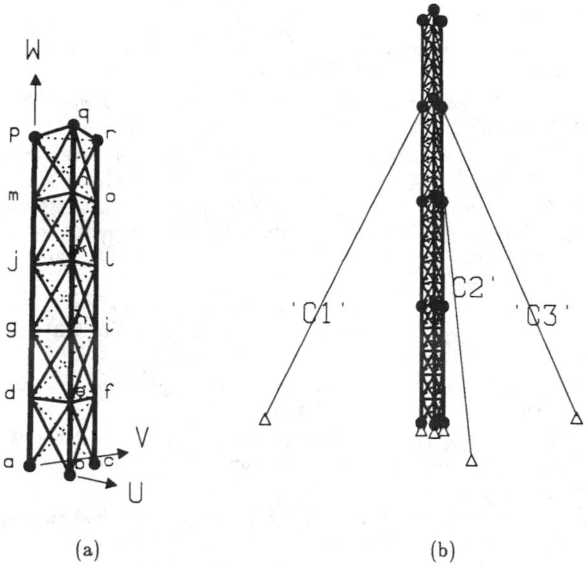


**Fig. 2** (a) A 3-D truss substructure with 6 boundary nodes and 12 internal nodes. (b) A structural system comprising four instances of the sub-structure in (a), and 3 cable restraints.

## 5. SUMMARY AND CONCLUSIONS

In has been shown that well known second moment analysis concepts found in basic text books on Structural Safety can be readily implemented in software for large structural analysis systems. Some aspects that are of interest include the use a "stamps" and implicit connectivity table concepts in lieu of incidence matrices; the use of sub-structuring to break down large and complex systems into smaller and conceptually simpler sub-systems; and the efficient manner in which uncertain applied displacements can be specified.

A practical advantage is that in a single analysis, the second moment solution gives a large amount of useful information for evaluating the performance of a structure in terms of its various limit states. To obtain the same information using traditional sensitivity analysis and Monte Carlo methods is cumbersome and requires extensive file management facilities.

While the theoretical presentation given here is expressed largely in terms of system theoretic concepts, it is clear that analogous procedures can be used to augment more traditional methods. This would substantially increase the usefullness of existing "technical models".

The authors are currently involved in extending these concepts to systems involving uncertain and non-linear constitutive components. But the results presented in this paper are of particular interest in that the excitation parameters are often the greatest source of uncertainty, and that their incorporation into existing (deterministic) software systems is straightforward.

**Acknowledgment:** This research was supported under grant number A4700 by the Natural Sciences and Engineering Research Council of Canada.

**References**


Augusti1984. G. Augusti, A. Baratta, and F. Casciati, *Probabilistic methods in structural engineering,* Chapman and Hall (1984).

Bhatt1981. P. Bhatt, *Problems in structural analysis by matrix methods,* The Construction Press (1981).

Blockley1983. D.I. Blockley, Comments on "Model uncertainty in structural reliability" by Ove Ditlevsen, *Structural Safety* **1** pp. 233-235 (1983).

Dickinson1986. R.R. Dickinson, G.J. Savage, T.E. Unny, and T. Prasad, Techniques for handling finite element like models with stochastic boundary conditions, pp. 77-82 in *Innovative Numerical Methods in Engineering,* ed. R.P. Shaw et al, Springer-Verlag (1986).

Dickinson1986a. R.R. Dickinson, *Second moment analysis of uncertain systems: theory and applications,* Dept. of Systems Design Eng., Uni. of Waterloo, Ont., Canada (1986).

Ditlevsen1981. O. Ditlevsen, *Uncertainty modeling with applications to multidimensional civil engineering Systems,* McGraw-Hill (1981).

Duddeck1977. H. Duddeck, The role of research models and technical models in engineering science, *Proceedings ICOSSAR'77,* pp. 115-118 Werner Verlag, Dusseldorf, (1977).

Fenves1966. S.J. Fenves, Structural analysis by networks, matrices, and computers, *Jnl. structural division, ASCE* **92**(ST1) pp. 199-221 (1966).

Graham1981. A. Graham, *Kronecker Products and Matrix Calculus with Applications,* Ellis Howard Ltd., Chichester (1981).

Hart1982. G.C. Hart, *Uncertainty analysis, loads, and safety in structural engineering,* Prentice-Hall (1982).

Kaveh1986. A. Kaveh, Graph theoretic methods for efficient flexibility analysis of planar trusses, *Computers and Structures* **23**(4) pp. 559-564 (1986).

Kron1955. G. Kron, Solving highly complex elastic structures in easy stages, *Jnl Applied Mechanics* **22** pp. 235-244 (1955).

Lind1962. N.C. Lind, Analysis of structures by system theory, *Jnl. structural division, ASCE* **88**(ST2) pp. 1-22 (1962).

Madsen1986. H.O. Madsen, S. Krenk, and N.C. Lind, *Methods of structural safety,* Prentice-Hall (1986).

Savage1980. G.J. Savage and H.K. Kesevan, The graph theoretic field model - II: Application to multi-terminal representations of field problems, *Jnl. Franklin Institute* **309**(4) pp. 241-266 (1980).

Vanmarcke1973. E.H. Vanmarcke, Matrix formulation of reliability analysis and reliability-based design, *Computers and Structures* **3** pp. 757-770 (1973).

# STOCHASTIC RESPONSES OF STRUCTURES WITH BILINEAR HYSTERESIS

R. Y. Tan* and D. Y. Jiang*
*Department of Civil Engineering, National Taiwan University, Taipei, ROC, 107

## ABSTRACT

A finite element-based approach is developed to estimate the stochastic responses of nonlinear continuum with bilinear hysteresis. The system is a simple plane-stress structure whose support base is subjected to a separable nonstationary excitation. The global motion equation is derived on the basis of the linearized constitutive equation in each element. The complex modal analysis is then employed to obtain the covariance matrices of responses. The result is compared with that from Monte Carlo techniques. With the aid of the least-squares algorithm, only a few number of simulation samples is needed. Numerically this paper confirms that the proposed analytical procedure is feasible in determining the stochastic response of a nonlinear structure.

## INTRODUCTION

Various techniques have been developed to estimate the nonlinear structural responses under random excitation. For instance, perturbation methods, the Fokker-Planck equation approach, equivalent linearization methods, and Monte Carlo simulations are commonly employed. However, those methods are generally limited in their application to structures with only a few degrees of freedom.

Since the finite element method which enables us to convert a problem with an infinite number of degrees of freedom to one with a finite number in order to simplify the solution process, is the best approach available for the numerical analysis of continua, it has been utilized for dealing with various sorts of stochastic problems in the last decade. Among others, finite element analysis is performed to predict the effect of spatial variability on differential settlement. Soil variability is modeled as one realization of a second-order stationary random field (Baecher and Ingra, 1981). A finite element analysis of a class of nonstationary random diffusion problems with random initial condition and random external excitation is carried out (Tasaka and Matsuoka, 1982). The role of the stochastic finite element method in the field of structural safety and reliability is also discussed (Hisada and Nakagiri, 1985). On the basis of the stochastic linearization of constitutive equations, the finite element equations are derived to obtain the desired response statistics (Mochio and et al., 1985).

The last reference mentioned above seems to provide us with a straightforward approach suitable for the reliability analysis of general multi-degree-of-freedom structures under random excitations. However, the nonlinear force-displacement relationships used in that paper are unnecessarily complex. That the auxiliary variables are included in the motion equation not only increases the number of degrees of freedom but also has to solve two complex modal matrices. In addition, the accuracy of results based on the stochastic equivalent linearization remains to be examined.

This paper focuses on developing a finite element-based approach to obtain the stochastic responses of nonlinear structures with bilinear hysteresis. As a preliminary investigation, this study considers a simple plane-stress structure whose support base is subjected to a separable nonstationary excitation. On the basis of ordinary equivalent linearization techniques, an approximate stress-strain relationships in each element are obtained. This makes it possible that the motion equation is formulated by the standard direct stiffness method. The covariance matrix of responses is then obtained through the complex modal analysis. The analytical outcome is compared with that from Monte Carlo simulation to explore the validity of linearization. To reduce the numerical labor of simulation, a regression curve of responses on time, based on a fewer samples, is produced and deemed as the true value of responses.

## FINITE ELEMENT FORMULATION

The restoring force, H (x, z), which exhibits bilinear hysteresis is described as:

$$H(x, z) = \alpha k_o\, x + (1 - \alpha) k_o\, z \qquad (1)$$

where x = displacement, $k_o$ = initial slope, $\alpha k_o$ = post-yield slope after yield displacement Y, and z = auxiliary variable which implicitly describes the hysteretic nature of the system. For the state of plane stress, the stress vector $\tau$ and strain vector $\epsilon$ can be written approximately as follows:

$$\tau = D_L \, \epsilon + D_N \, z \tag{2}$$

where

$$D_L = \frac{E}{1-\nu^2} \begin{bmatrix} \alpha_1 & \nu & 0 \\ \nu & \alpha_2 & 0 \\ 0 & 0 & \alpha_3 \cdot \frac{1-\nu}{2} \end{bmatrix} \quad D_N = \frac{E}{1-\nu^2} \begin{bmatrix} 1-\alpha_1 & 0 & 0 \\ 0 & 1-\alpha_2 & 0 \\ 0 & 0 & (1-\alpha_3)\frac{1-\nu}{2} \end{bmatrix} \tag{3}$$

It is noted that E = Young's modulus, and $\nu$ = Poisson's ratio. For each stress component, Eqs. 2 to 3 consider only the nonlinear effect due to the corresponding strain component.

An appropriate linearization of Eq. 2 is necessary in order to follow the finite element formulation. Within a finite element, each component in Eq. 2 will be linearized as $k_i\epsilon_i + c_i\dot{\epsilon}_i$, i = 1, 2, and 3. With those linearized constitutive equations, we apply the virtual work principle to each element. The following system motion equation is produced through proper nodal equilibrium and superposition.

$$M\ddot{d} + C\dot{d} + K d = F \tag{4}$$

where d is the nodal displacement vector, M is the system mass matrix, C is the equivalent damping matrix, and K is the system stiffness matrix. the force vector F is assumed to be induced by support excitation which consists of a stationary Gaussian process g (t), with zero mean and spectrum S ($\omega$), multiplied by a deterministic envelope function, e (t).

**EQUIVALENT LINEARIZATION**

The method of stochastic linearization is a useful and popular approximate method for probabilistic analysis of nonlinear structural dynamics problems. The reason stems from the scarcity or nonavailability of the exact solutions, e.g. the solution of the associated Fokker-Planck equation, and the significant computational cost of Monte Carlo simulations. However, indiscriminate use of this method is inadvisable due to the fact that for most of the reported studies the stochastic linearization technique yields solutions which underestimate the exact statistical moments of the response (Spanos, 1981). On the other hand, a broad class of general linearization techniques is widely used ranging from those based on harmonic response behavior to those based on random response behavior. The accuracy of various techniques has been examined (Iwan and Gates, 1979).

Since the present study strives for a systematic application of the linearization method to the analysis of finite-element type models of randomly excited nonlinear structural systems, only those approaches which are deemed suitable and simple, but are somewhat less rigorous, will be pursued here.

We assume that each peak response is equal to a harmonic response amplitude so that the results of a harmonic analysis can be related to the earthquake response problem. The equivalent linear stiffness, $k_i$, is defined as the simple average of the secant stiffness for all response amplitudes up to $x_i$ and is given as (Jiang, 1986):

$$k_i(x_i) = k_o\,[(1-\alpha_i)(1+\ln \mu_i)/\mu_i + \alpha_i] \quad \mu_i > 1 \tag{5}$$

The parameter $\mu_i = x_i/Y_i$ is referred to the ductility ratio of response in the i-th component and is a measure of the degree of yielding of a hysteretic system.

An equivalent damping coefficient in the i-th component $c_i$, can be found by equating the cyclic energy dissipated by the hysteretic system to that of the equivalent linear system with assumed harmonic motion. It is expressed as (Jiang, 1986):

$$c_i = \frac{2k_o}{\pi\omega}(1-\alpha_i)(1-\frac{1}{\mu_i})\,[2/\mu_i + \alpha_i(1-\frac{1}{\mu_i})] \quad \mu_i > 1 \tag{6}$$

where $\omega = \sqrt{\Sigma k_{ii}/\Sigma m_{ii}}$. Note that $k_{ii}$ and $m_{ii}$ are the diagonal elements in element stiffness matrix and mass matrix, respectively.

Since the support excitation is random rather than sinusoidal, the ductility ratio in Eqs. 5 and 6 can logically be replaced by its probable quantity, more specifically, by its expected value (Liu, 1969). With appropriate assumptions that the random response, x(t), is slowly varying and approximately Gaussian with standard deviation $\sigma_x$, the probability distribution of peak value $x_i$ can be Rayleigh. It follows that

$$E[\mu_i] = E[x_i]/Y_i = \sqrt{\pi/2} \cdot \sigma_x/Y_i \tag{7}$$

**COMPLEX MODAL ANALYSIS**

The matrix C in Eq. 4 is not necessarily orthogonal with respect to the mass matrix and the stiffness matrix, therefore the complex modal analysis method will be used. Eq. 4 is written as:

$$B\dot{y} + A\,y = P \tag{8}$$

where $y = [d^T\ \dot{d}^T]^T$, $P = [F\ O]^T$. The matrices A and B consist of M, C, and K.

The response matrix y of Eq. 8 can then be expanded into

$$y = \phi\, Q = \Sigma\, \phi_i Q_i \tag{9}$$

where $\phi$ = modal matrix. Q is the generalized coordinate vector whose components are obtained from uncoupling equations. We have

$$E[Q_m Q_n] = p_m p_n \int_{-\infty}^{\infty} H_m(t,\omega)\, H_n^*(t,\omega)\, S(\omega)\, d\omega \tag{10}$$

where $p_m$ = modal participation factor of the m-th mode, $H_n^*$ = conjugate of $H_n$, and

$$H_m(t,\omega) = \int_0^t \exp[\lambda_m(t-\tau) - i\omega\tau] \cdot e(\tau)\, d\tau \tag{11}$$

In which $\lambda_m$ = eigenvalue of the m-th mode. Thus, the covariance matrices of y and other response quantities can be obtained once Eq. 10 is evaluated.

**SIMULATION SOLUTIONS**

The above analytical solution is checked against the simulation solution from Monte Carlo techniques. For each sample function of loading, the step-by-step integration procedure is employed to perform the nonlinear analysis. Indeed, the linear acceleration method proposed by Newmark is used to evaluate the structural response for a series of short time increments. The assumption of this method is that the acceleration varies linearly during each time increment while the properties of the system remain constant during this interval. The condition of dynamic equilibrium is established at the beginning and end of each interval, and the motion of the system during the time increment is evaluated approximately on the basis of above assumed mechanism. Two aspects concerning the nonlinear analysis are worth a note. First of all, the gorverning motion equation should be derived on the basis of Eq. 2 rather than linearized constitutive equations. In addition, the changing values of material property in a nonlinear problem requires the decomposition for each time step to solve standard simultaneous equations. This represents a major computational effort dealing with a large system.

To avoid numerous repetitions of decomposition, we have introduced the auxiliary variable z in Eq. 1, so that the system matrices will be constant. The values of z for each time step can be determined by a few cycles of iteration.

To generate sample function of F, the generation of g(t) is accomplished digitly with the aid of Fast Fourier Transform techniques (Shinozuka, 1971). The envelope function is taken to be

$$e(t) = \beta\,[\exp(-at) - \exp(-bt)] \tag{12}$$

with b = 0.5/sec, a = 0.25/sec and $\beta$ being a normalizing factor to make the maximum value of e(t) equal to unity.

It is well known however that simulations usually consume a great deal of computation time when the number of samples increases. To alleviate this difficulty, the least-squares theory is employed to estimate the simulation solution based on a few number of samples. The justification stems from the concept that the least-squares technique provides us with a mathematical procedure by which a model can achieve a best fit to experimental data in the sense of minimum-error-squares.

A system consisting of single Q4 element is shown in Fig. 1. The parameter values used for the numerical analysis are: $E = 10^6$ N/m$^2$, $\nu = 0.3$, $\rho = 2 \times 10^3$ kg/m$^3$, $\alpha_i = 0.4$, $Y_1 = Y_2 = 0.001$, $Y_3 = 0.003$, and $S = 0.02$ m$^2$/sec$^3$. On the basis of different number of samples, Fig. 2 shows the standard deviations of $\epsilon_1$ as a function of time. The numbers of samples are 8, 100, and 150 in Figs. (a), (b), and (c), respectively. The smoothed curve in (b) and (c) is a fourth order polynominal curve obtained by performing the least-square technique on (a). From the viewpoint of engineering practice, it seems that the present regression curve well reflects the simulation solution. In the sequel, such regression result is deemed as the true value of responses with which the analytical one can be compared.

The stochastic responses of the structures shown in Fig. 3 are considered. The data are as follows: $E = 1.2 \times 10^6$ N/m$^2$, $\nu = 0.3$, $\rho = 1.5 \times 10^3$ kg/m$^3$, $\alpha_1 = 0.4$, $\alpha_2 = \alpha_3 = 1.0$, $Y_i = 0.001$, and $S = 0.04$ m$^2$/sec$^3$. In Figs. 4(a) and 4(b), standand deviation of $\epsilon_1$ and $\epsilon_2$ in the first element are delineated. The simulation result is obtained from the regression analysis with number of samples being ten. The analytical solution based on linearization technique is fairly close to the true one and, for most cases, is on the conservative side. The result for other elements is similar and not shown here.

## CONCLUSIONS

The finite element method is employed to estimate the stochastic responses of plane-stress structures whose support base is subjected to a separable nonstationary excitation. The responses is obtained on the basis of ordinary linearization on stress-strain relationship and complex modal analysis. The analytical outcome is compared with that from the regression-based simulation approach. Numerical results show that the technique developed here possibly provides us with a practical approach to assess the nonlinear responses of a complex structure under random excitations.

## REFERENCES

Baecher G.B. and T.S. Ingra (1981). "Stochastic FEM in Settlement Prediction", J. Geo. Eng. Div., ASCE, 107, 449-463.

Hisada T. and S. Nakagiri (1985). "Role of the Stochastic FEM in Structural Safety and Reliability", Fourth ICOSSAR, Kobe, Japan, pp. I 375-384.

Iwan W.D. and N.C. Gates (1979). "Estimating Earthquake Response of Simple Hysteretic Structures", J. Eng. Mech. Div., ASCE, 105, 391-405.

Jiang D.Y. (1986)."Stochastic FEM in Structural Responses Analysis", M.S. Thesis, Department of Civil Engineering, National Taiwan University, Taipei, China.

Liu S.C. (1969). "Earthquake Response Statistics of Nonlinear Systems", J. Eng. Mech. Div., ASCE, 95, 397-419.

Mochio T and et al. (1985). "Stochastic Equivalent Linearization for Finite Element-Based Reliability Analysis", Fourth ICOSSAR, Kobe, Japan, pp. I 375-384.

Shinozuka M. (1971). "Simulation of Multivariate and Multidimensional Random Processes", J. of the Accoustical Soc. of America, 49, 357-367.

Spanos P.D. (1981). "Stochastic Linearization in Structural Dynamics", Applied Mech. Reviews, 34, 1-8.

Tasaka S. and O. Matsuoka (1982). "Finite Element Analysis of Nonstationary 1-D Random Diffusion Problems", Int. J. Numerical Methods in Eng., 18, 1045-1054.

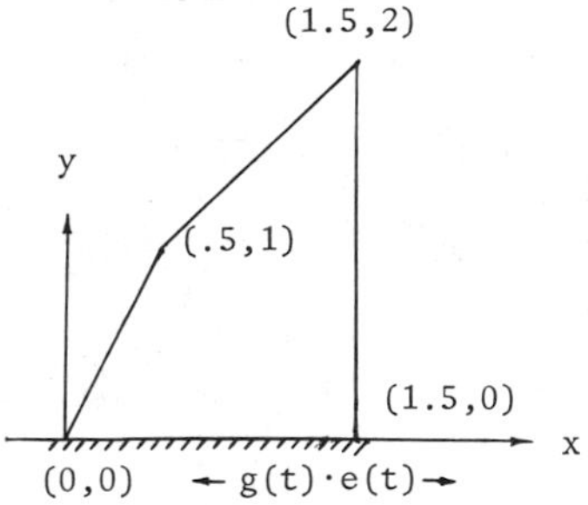


Fig.1 Single Q4 element

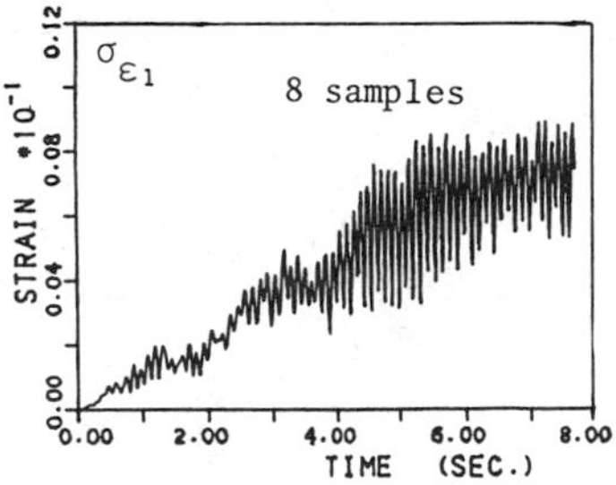


Fig. 2a

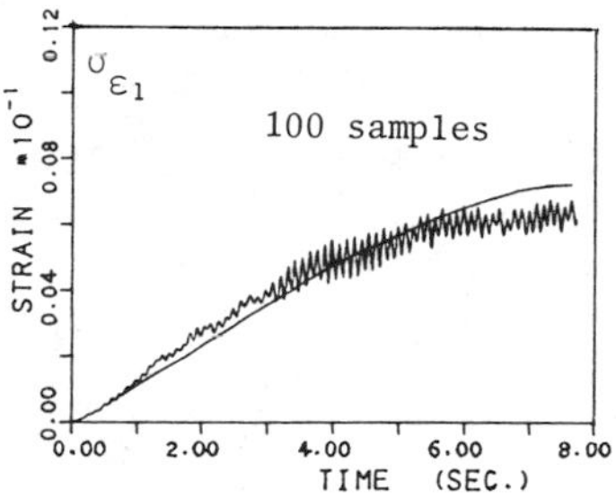


Fig. 2b

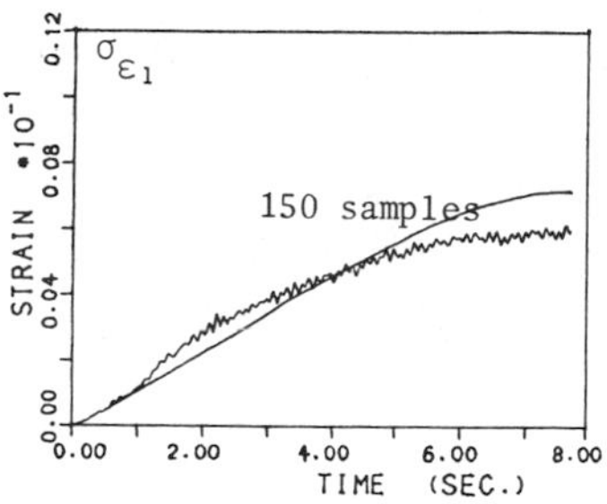


Fig. 2c

Fig. 2 Regression-based simulation solutions

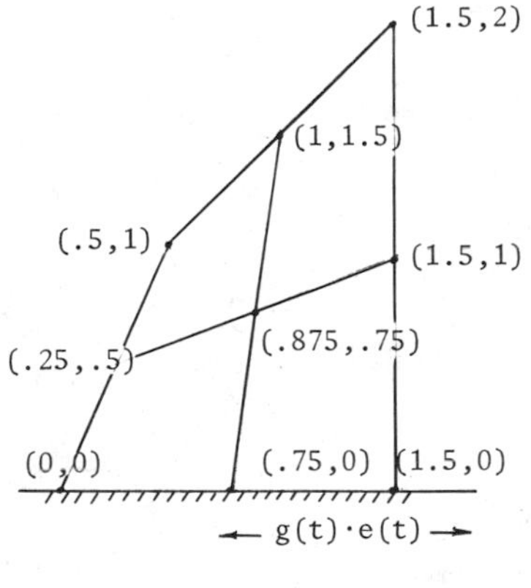


Fig.3 Mesh configuration of system

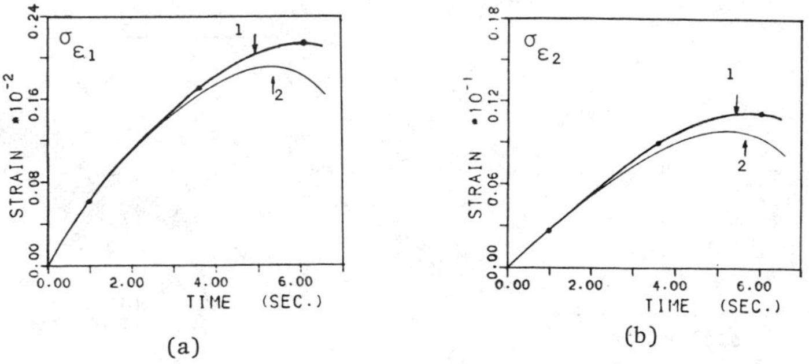


Fig.4 Comparison of analytical solutions with simulation ones ( 1: analytical 2: simulation)

# RELIABILITY OF PRESTRESSED HIGH-STRENGTH CONCRETE BEAMS IN FLEXURE

R. A. Hamann*
*Formerly, Department of Civil Engineering, Michigan Technological University
W. M. Bulleit**
**Department of Civil Engineering, Michigan Technological University, Houghton, MI 49931

## ABSTRACT

The objective of the work reported in this paper was to examine the relative reliability for underreinforced prestressed high-strength concrete beams with bonded tendons designed in accordance with ACI-318. Monte Carlo simulations of the ultimate moment capacity were performed. The capacity was calculated using a nonlinear analysis which included the shape of the concrete and steel stress-strain curves. The first four statistical moments of the moment capacity were determined from the simulation data.

The reliability index, $\beta$, was then determined using advanced first-order, second moment methods. Only one load combination, dead load plus snow load, was considered. The maximum lifetime snow load was considered to be lognormally distributed. The moment capacity had either a lognormal, normal or Johnson S(u) distribution depending on the third and fourth statistical moments; although the choice of distribution had little effect on the reliability. The existing ACI design procedure produced a reliability index of approximately 3.0 which, for most cases, tended to increase slightly as the specified concrete strength increased.

## INTRODUCTION

The development of probability-based load factors in the U.S. (Ellingwood et al. 1980) has spurred on the generation of probability-based material design codes. The proposed AISC steel design code (1978) is an example. The new codes are calibrated to the existing codes in an effort of avoid over or under conservatism by including the "experience" in the present codes. The manner in which this has been done is to determine the notional reliability levels in the present code and then match these as closely as possible in the new code. If the present code exhibits any unexpected inconsistencies, the new code may be somewhat adjusted.

The objective of the work reported in this paper was to examine the relative reliability for prestressed high-strength concrete beams with bonded tendons designed to ACI-318 (1983). The ratio between the mean versus nominal moment capacity is presented for different cross-section beams. The nominal moment capacity is the capacity determined using ACI-318. The coefficient of variation is also presented. These are used to examine the reliability of the beams under dead load plus snow load.

## MOMENT CAPACITY

The statistics for the moment capacity were obtained from Monte Carlo simulation results. The simulations were performed using a nonlinear model for moment capacity which included the shape of the concrete and steel stress-strain diagrams (Naaman 1983). The analysis procedure is shown in Naaman (1983, 1985). The equation for the concrete stress-strain behavior was taken from Wang (1977) and is shown in Equation (1), with the constants in Table 1.

$$Y = (AX + BX^2)/(1 + CX + DX^2) \tag{1}$$

where X = $\varepsilon$(c)/ $\varepsilon$(m), Y = f(c)/f'(c) and (m) = 0.001648 + 0.000114 f'(c) (f'(c) in ksi). $\varepsilon$(c) is the concrete strain, f(c) is the concrete stress corresponding to $\varepsilon$(c) and f'(c) is the maximum concrete stress.

Table 1. Constants for Stress-Strain Curve of Concrete

| f'(c) | (c) | | (m) | |
|---|---|---|---|---|
| ksi | A | B | C | D |
| 5.0 | 1.50886 | -0.52920 | -0.49114 | 0.47080 |
| 7.0 | 1.40631 | -0.69984 | -0.59369 | 0.30016 |
| 9.0 | 1.35586 | -0.76976 | -0.64414 | 0.23024 |

| f'(c) | (c) | | (m) | |
|---|---|---|---|---|
| ksi | A | B | C | D |
| 5.0 | 0.78813 | -0.05030 | -1.21187 | 0.94970 |
| 7.0 | 0.37260 | -0.01859 | -1.62740 | 0.98141 |
| 9.0 | 0.22156 | -0.00959 | -1.77844 | 0.99041 |

The equation for the prestressing steel stress-strain behavior (Menegotto and Pinto, 1973) is

$$f(ps) = E(ps)\ \varepsilon(ps)\ [Q + (1-Q)/(1 + (E(ps)\ \varepsilon(ps)/Kf(py)^N)^{1/N}] \tag{2}$$

where f(ps) is the stress in the steel, E(ps) is the prestressing steel modulus, $\varepsilon$(ps) is the strain in the prestressing steel and f(py) is the yield stress. The constants, N, K and Q are 7.344, 1.0618 and 0.01174 respectively (Naaman, 1985).

SIMULATION

Monte Carlo simulation of the moment capacity was performed on an IBM PC using a computer program written in FORTRAN (Hamann, 1986). The statistical properties of the random variables were taken from Naaman and Siriaksorn (1982) and are shown in Table 2.

Table 2. Statistical Properties of the Random Variables in the Simulations

| Variables | | Mean, | COV, V | Remarks |
|---|---|---|---|---|
| b | = width | b(n) | 0.045 | |
| h | = height | (h(n)-0.125) | 0.045 | |
| d | = effective depth | d(n) | 0.04 | |
| A(ps) | = strand area | 1.01176 A(psn) | 0.0125 | A(psn)=0.153 in$^2$ |
| f(pu) | = ultimate stress | 1.0387 f(pun) | 0.0142 | f(pun)=270 ksi |
| E(ps) | = strand modulus | 1.011 E(psn) | 0.01 | E(psn)=29000 ksi |
| f(py) | = strand yield | 1.027 f(pyn) | 0.022 | f(pyn)=240 ksi |
| C(Ec) | = constant | 33.6 | 0.1217 | C(Ec) nominal=33 |

$E(C)=(C(Ec))(\gamma)^{1.5}(f'(c))^{1/2}$

| | | | |
|---|---|---|---|
| (c) | = concrete unit wt. | $\gamma$(cn) | 0.03 |
| f(pe) | = effective prestress | C(fsi)C(fse)f(pu) | 0.114 |
| f'(c) | = maximum concrete stress | 0.67f'(cn) to 1.17f'(cn) | 0.1-0.25 |

All the random variables were assumed to be normally distributed (Naaman and Siriaksorn, 1982). The coefficient of variation of the effective prestress, V(fpe), is determined from

$$f(pe) = C(fsi)C(fse)f(pu) = (0.7)(0.83)f(pu) \quad (3)$$

where C(fsi) is the variable which relates f(pu) to the initial prestress and (fse) is the variable which relates the initial prestress to the effective prestress. The coefficient of variation for C(fsi) and C(fse) is 0.08. Thus

$$V(fpe) = \quad (0.08)^2 + (0.08)^2 + (0.0142)^2)^{1/2} = 0.114 \quad (4)$$

Note that in Table 2 the nominal modulus of the prestressing steel, E(psn), was taken as 29000 ksi. This follows Naaman and Siriaksorn (1982) and Siriaksorn and Naaman (1980) and originally came from Tide and VanHorn (1966). In retrospect, it seems that this should have been E(psn) = 27,000 ksi for strands. The possible effect of this will be discussed below.

RELIABILITY ANALYSES

The reliability was measured using the advanced first-order, second-moment method with distributional information included using the equivalent normal tail concept (Throft-Christensen and Baker, 1982). For comparison purposes, only one load combination was considered, dead load moment plus snow load moment. The dead load statistics used were D/D(n) = 1.0 and V(D) = 0.10 where D is the mean dead load effect, D(n) is the nominal dead load effect and V(D) is the coefficient of variation of the dead load. It was assumed to be normally distributed. The snow load statistics were S/S(n) = 0.69 and V(S) = 0.44 with a lognormal distribution (Thurmond et al., 1984). Two snow load to dead load ratios were considered, S(n)/D(n) = 2.0 and 3.0.

The distribution of the moment capacity was selected by considering the third and fourth moments of the simulation data (Hahn and Shapiro, 1967). In some cases, the capacity seemed to be either normal or lognormal. But in a few cases, the skewness and kurtosis were such that a left skewed, highly peaked distribution was required. In these cases, a Johnson S(u) distribution (Hahn and Shapiro, 1967) was used.

RESULTS AND DISCUSSION

The simulation results for moment capacity are shown in Table 3 for f'(cn) equal 7 and 9 ksi. The results are shown in terms of the ratio of mean to nominal moment capacity, M/M(n), and the coefficient of variation of the moment capacity, V(M). The extremes of f'(c) are considered, i.e. low and high V, 0.1 and 0.25 respectively, and low and high mean, 0.67f'(cn) and 1.17f'(cn) respectively. Four basic sections, from b = 12 inches and h = 24 inches to b = 48 inches and h = 48 inches, were considered.

Table 3. Moment Capacity Results for Various Cross-Sections

| Section | | b=12, h=24 | | b=12, h=48 | | b=48, h=24 | | b=48, h=48 | |
|---|---|---|---|---|---|---|---|---|---|
| f'(c) (ksi) | | 7 | 9 | 7 | 9 | 7 | 9 | 7 | 9 |
| Low mean | M/M(n) | 1.056 | 1.046 | 1.040 | 1.037 | 1.056 | 1.060 | 1.116 | 1.126 |
| Low V | V(M)(%) | 5.5 | 5.1 | 5.1 | 5.0 | 5.1 | 5.0 | 5.3 | 5.2 |
| Low mean | M/M(n) | 1.039 | 1.036 | 1.033 | 1.032 | 1.050 | 1.056 | 1.106 | 1.119 |
| High V | V(M)(%) | 8.0 | 6.7 | 5.9 | 5.5 | 5.6 | 5.3 | 6.1 | 5.5 |
| High Mean | M/M(n) | 1.111 | 1.095 | 1.071 | 1.073 | 1.082 | 1.101 | 1.142 | 1.180 |
| Low V | V(M)(%) | 5.1 | 5.1 | 5.0 | 5.1 | 5.0 | 5.2 | 5.2 | 5.6 |
| High Mean | M/M(n) | 1.107 | 1.093 | 1.072 | 1.074 | 1.086 | 1.105 | 1.150 | 1.188 |
| High V | V(M)(%) | 6.0 | 5.8 | 5.4 | 5.6 | 5.4 | 6.0 | 5.8 | 7.0 |

Table 3 shows no unexpected trends. M/M(n) ranges from 1.04 to 1.19. V ranges from 5% to 8%. Under plant control conditions, it's likely that the high mean and low V are representative which means that M/ M(n) ranges from 1.07-1.18 and V ranges from 5.0% to 5.6%.

Concrete with f'(cn) = 5 ksi was examined only for the smallest section, b = 12 inches and h = 24 inches. For this case, with low mean f'(c) and high V, M/M(n) was 1.03 and V(M) was 10.4%. The lower the specified concrete strength the more its variability affects the moment capacity.

Before considering the reliability results, a brief discussion is in order on the distributions used for the moment capacity. When the concrete strength variation was high and the section width was small (i.e. 12") the moment capacity distribution tended to be left-skewed with a peakedness greater than the normal or lognormal distribution. An empirical distribution which meets this criteria is the Johnson S(u) distribution (Hahn and Shapiro, 1967). This distribution was fit to the moment capacity data when appropriate. All distributions considered were fit to the simulation data using the method of moments.

The reliability index was determined for each case using advanced first-order, second-moment methods. Since the coefficient of variation of the moment capacity data is small the choice of distribution had little effect on the reliability index. As would be expected for small variation, the normal and lognormal distributions gave virtually identical results. Since it is left-skewed and more peaked, the Johnson S(u) gave reliability indices slightly greater than the other two. The difference in reliability indices between the S(u) and the normal or lognormal was less than 0.10. Due to this, it was felt that the use of the S(u) distribution was not warranted and the results discussed below will be for a normal distribution for moment capacity.

As more representative of existing structures, the S(n)/D(n) ratio of 3.0 will be discussed. The reliability indices for S(n)/D(n) of 2.0 are slightly greater; the difference between the two is about 0.10. Table 4 shows the reliability indices for sections with b = 12 in. and h = 24 in. for all three concrete strengths considered.

Table 4. Reliability Indices for S(n)/D(n) = 3.0

| f'(c) (ksi) | 5 | 7 | 9 |
|---|---|---|---|
| Low mean<br>Low V | 2.89 | 2.94 | 2.92 |
| Low mean<br>High V | 2.78 | 2.88 | 2.89 |
| High mean<br>Low V | 3.17 | 3.08 | 3.04 |
| High mean<br>High V | 3.14 | 3.07 | 3.04 |

The relative reliability results are somewhat difficult to generalize. Table 4 shows the reliability of ACI designs increasing with specified concrete strength when the mean concrete strength is low with respect to the specified strength and vice versa when the mean concrete strength is high. But, this trend does not hold when the section size changes. The one item to note in Table 4 is the reduced effect of concrete strength variability as the specified concrete strength and/or the mean concrete strength increased. For 9 ksi concrete with a high mean, the reliability index remains unchanged irrespective of high or low V.

Table 5 shows the relative reliability results for the various sections considered with specified concrete strengths of 7 and 9 ksi when S(n)/D(n) = 3.0.

Table 5. Reliability Indices for Various Cross Sections with S(n)/D(n) = 3.0

| b x h | 12" x 24" | | 12" x 48" | | 48" x 24" | | 48" x 48" | |
|---|---|---|---|---|---|---|---|---|
| f'(c) (ksi) | 7 | 9 | 7 | 9 | 7 | 9 | 7 | 9 |
| Low mean<br>Low V | 2.94 | 2.92 | 2.90 | 2.90 | 2.95 | 2.96 | 3.09 | 3.12 |
| Low mean<br>High V | 2.86 | 2.87 | 2.87 | 2.88 | 2.92 | 2.94 | 3.06 | 3.10 |
| High mean<br>Low V | 3.08 | 3.04 | 2.98 | 2.99 | 3.01 | 3.06 | 3.16 | 3.24 |
| High mean<br>High V | 3.06 | 3.03 | 2.98 | 2.98 | 3.02 | 3.06 | 3.17 | 3.23 |

Examination of Table 5 shows that as the sections get larger, the reliability tends to increase with increasing specified f'(c). The exception occurs for shallow sections, particularly narrow, shallow sections. The reduced effect of concrete strength variability on the reliability is also evident in Table 5.

From the reliability analyses, it appears that the ACI design procedure, rectangular stress block and approximate steel stress at ultimate, is fully adequate. One possible exception is narrow sections with poor concrete strength relative to specified. Under plant control conditions this should not be a problem.

The effect of using a strand modulus of 29,000 ksi instead of 27,000 ksi needs to be discussed. If the steel stress is actually somewhat lower than what would have been used in this analysis, then the depth of concrete in compression is probably reduced. This would increase the internal moment arm which would increase the moment capacity. Thus, the difference in moment capacity is likely to be slight if 29,000 is used instead of 27,000 ksi. Furthermore, the sections considered in this study were underreinforced which means that the steel stress was very likely in the inelastic region of the stress-strain curve. In that region, the difference between assuming 29,000 or 27,000 ksi is very small if the ultimate tensile stress doesn't change significantly.

CONCLUSION

Monte Carlo simulations for underreinforced prestressed high-strength concrete beams with bonded tendons were performed. A non-linear analysis which included the concrete and steel stress-strain curves was used. The ACI-318 moment capacity calculation procedure using the rectangular stress block and an approximation for the steel stress was adequate. The procedure gave slightly low reliabilities for shallow sections when the average concrete strength was low relative to specified concrete strength. The ACI procedure produced a reliability index of approximately 3.0 which, for most cases, tended to increase slightly as the specified concrete strength increased.

REFERENCES

ACI (1983). Building Code Requirements for Reinforced Concrete, ACI 318-83, American Concrete Institute, Detroit, Michigan.

AISI (1978). Proposed Criteria for Load and Resistance Factor Design of Steel Building Structures, Bulletin No. 27, American Iron and Steel Institute, Washington, D.C.

Ellingwood, B., T. V. Galambos, J. G. MacGregor, J. G., and C. A. Cornell (1980). Development of a Probability Based Load Criterion for American National Standard A58: Building Code Requirements for Minimum Design Loads Buildings and Other Structures, NBS Special Publication 577, U.S. Department of Commerce, Washington, D.C.

Hahn, G. J. and S. S. Shapiro (1967). Statistical Models in Engineering, John Wiley & Sons, Inc., New York, London, Sydney.

Menegotto, M. and P. E. Pinto (1973). Method of Analysis for Cyclically Loaded R. C. Plane Frames, IABSE Preliminary Report for Symposium on Resistance and Ultimate Deformability of Structures Acted on a Well-Defined Repeated Load, Lisbon, Portugal, 15-22.

Naaman, A. E. (1983). An Approximate Nonlinear Design Procedure for Partially Prestressed Concrete Beams, Computers & Structures, Vol. 17, No. 2, 287-299.

Naaman, A. E. (1985). Partially Prestressed Concrete: Review and Recommendations, PCI Journal, Vol. 30, November-December, 30-71.

Naaman, A. E. and A. Siriaksorn (1982). Reliability of Partially Prestressed Beams at Serviceability Limit States, PCI Journal, Vol. 27, November-December, 66-85.

Siriaksorn, A., and A. E. Naaman (1980). Reliability of Partially Prestressed Beams at Serviceability Limit States, Thesis presented to the University of Illinois at Chicago Circle in partial fulfillment of the requirements for the degree of Doctor of Philosophy, Chicago, Illinois.

Throft-Christensen, P., and M. J. Baker (1982). Structural Reliability Theory and its Applications, Springer-Verlag, Berlin, Heidelberg, New York.

Thurmond, M. B., F. E. Woeste and D. W. Green (1984). Roof Loads for Reliability Analysis of Lumber Properties Data, Wood and Fiber Science, Vol. 16, April, 278-297.

Tide, R. H. R. and D. A. VanHorn (1966). A Statistical Study of the Static and Fatigue Properties of High Strength Prestressing Strand, Progress Report No. 2, Bond in Prestressed Concrete, Fritz Engineering Laboratory Report No. 309.2, Lehigh University, Bethlehem, PA.

Wang, P. T. (1977). Complete Stress-Strain Curve of Concrete and its Effect on Ductility of Reinforced Concrete Members, Ph.D. Thesis, University of Illinois at Chicago Circle, Chicago, IL.

# RECENT ADVANCES IN THE APPLICATION OF STRUCTURAL SYSTEMS RELIABILITY METHODS

**P. Thoft-Christensen**
**University of Aalborg, Sohngaardsholmsvej 57, DK - 9000 Aalborg, Denmark**

## ABSTRACT

Structural systems reliability methods are now in a state where practical applications are relevant. This is due to the fact that it is now possible to include a large number of important failure modes in the systems reliability analysis. However, a number of unsolved problems still exists. In this paper a number of failure elements investigated at the University of Aalborg is presented. Further application of systems reliability theory in optimal design and in optimal maintenance strategies are described. Finally, some unsolved problems are listed. It is concluded that estimation of the reliability of structural systems can now be performed for many important structures with a sufficient degree of accuracy.

## INTRODUCTION

In the last decade structural systems reliability theory has changed from being a subject of research to being a subject of interest for engineers. This fact is clearly demonstrated in the growing number of research projects being funded by private companies, especially within offshore engineering. At the University of Aalborg, Denmark, a number of research projects oriented towards the development of applicable methods for evaluating the reliability of structural systems has been established. In this paper some of the recent advances obtained through these projects are presented with special emphasis on the

- introduction of new failure elements
- optimal design of structures with reliability constraints
- optimal strategies for inspection and repair of structures.

A number of methods by which the reliability of structural systems can be estimated has been derived lately. The failure elements and the optimal design and optimal maintenance strategies presented here are all derived in relation to the so-called $\beta$-unzipping method which is described in detail by Thoft-Christensen & Murotsu (1986). However, they can be used without difficulties by any systems reliability method based on the concept of a failure element. A failure element is simply a local failure mode for a structural element. Therefore, a given structural element will usually have a number of different failure elements (failure modes) such as failure in bending, instability failure, etc. Note that a structural element can be e.g. a beam or a plate, but also a tubular joint. To conclude this description of failure elements it can be mentioned that a tubular joint in an offshore platform typically has at least four different types of failure elements, namely failure in yielding, punching, buckling and fatigue.

For some structures it is relevant to consider the individual structural elements separately and define failure of such a structural element as failure of any failure element in the structural element. Likewise, for a structural system failure can be defined as failure in any failure element in the structural system. Estimation of the reliability of a structural system based on this failure definition is called reliability modelling at level 1 and the estimation of the probability of failure of the structural system is based on a series systems approach.

However, for a redundant structure failure in a single failure element will in general not be considered as failure of the complete structural system. It seems to be more useful to define failure of a structural system as failure of two failure elements (level 2 modelling) or as failure of three elements (level 3 modelling) etc. By the $\beta$-unzipping method the most significant failure elements, pairs of failure elements, triples of failure elements etc. can be identified. For the sake of completeness failure of an elasto-plastic structure defined as formation of a mechanism should also be mentioned here. However, this definition is of less interest from an application point of view.

On the following pages a number of different types of failure elements is mentioned, namely:

- Tension/compression failure elements (yielding)
- Bending failure elements (yielding)
- Combined load effect failure elements (yielding)
- Strain softening failure elements
- Instability failure elements
- Buckling failure elements
- Global instability failure elements
- Fatigue failure elements
- Punching failure elements
- Slab failure elements.

Some of these failure elements have been described earlier and will therefore only be briefly discussed here. Only the new failure elements will be presented in some detail.

## TENSION/COMPRESSION FAILURE ELEMENTS

Let $R^+$ and $R^-$ be random variables describing the (yield) strength capacity in tension and compression of a cross-section of a bar/beam and let S be the corresponding load effect (force). Then failures in tension and in compression are described by the following two safety margins

$$M^+ = R^+ - S \tag{1}$$

$$M^- = R^- + S \tag{2}$$

corresponding to two failure elements. Let the corresponding probabilities of failure be $P_f^+$ and $P_f^-$. Then in practice $P_f^+$ is much smaller than $P_f^-$ or vice versa. In such cases sufficient accuracy can be obtained by combining the failure elements into one failure element with the safety margin

$$M = \begin{cases} R^+ - S & \text{if } P_f^- < P_f^+ \\ R^- + S & \text{if } P_f^- > P_f^+ \end{cases} \tag{3}$$

## BENDING FAILURE ELEMENTS

Failure of beam elements in pure bending can be treated in a way similar to failure in tension/compression. The same safety margin (1) - (3) can be used. $R^+$ and $R^-$ are now the bending strength capacity in positive and negative bending and S the corresponding bending moment. Torsion failure elements are treated in the same way.

In the most well-known structural systems reliability methods only the above-mentioned failure elements are normally included. This fact puts severe limits to the applicability of these methods.

## COMBINED LOAD EFFECT FAILURE ELEMENTS

It is in general not easy to include combined load effects in a systems reliability analysis. Consider e.g. the interaction between axial forces N and bending moments B with regard to failure (yielding), see figure 1. This interaction is not taken into consideration when the above-mentioned failure elements are used. The »unsafe» approximation in figure 1 corresponds to using the above-mentioned tension/compression and bending failure elements. The »safe» approximation is linear and corresponding failure elements can therefore without difficulties be used. Failure elements based on the »exact» interaction curve are much more complicated to use unless the formation of a mechanism is used as systems failure definition. The problem is that the actual point on the interaction curve must in general be determined by an iterative process taking into account not only the interaction curve but also the associated flow rule (orthogonality condition). One of the earliest investigations in this area was performed by Høj & Loklindt (1983). They introduced a failure element based on the »exact» non-linear interaction curve in figure 1 and were able to apply this failure element to some simple examples. The iterative method used is complicated and it seems to be difficult to extend their method to more general interaction curves. The same failure element has been used by Thoft-Christensen, Sigurdsson & Sørensen (1986) in estimation of the reliability of an elasto-plastic structure (mechanism level). This analysis was much simpler because knowing the mechanism the actual point of the non-linear interaction curve is known for all cross-sections. They applied this failure element to three examples and showed that the effect of using the »exact» interaction curve compared with the »unsafe» approximation was negligible for these examples. Combined load effects have also been investigated by Murotsu et al. (see e.g. Thoft-Christensen & Murotsu (1986), section 5.4).

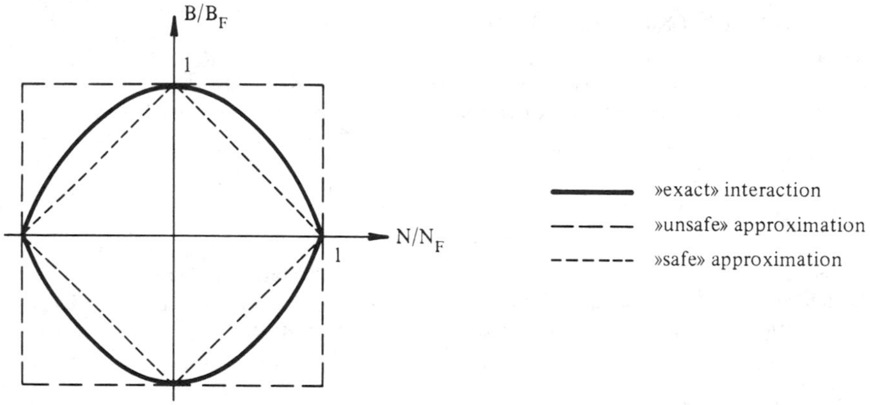


Figure 1. Interaction curves. $N_F$ and $B_F$ are the strength capacity in pure axial loading and pure bending.

## STRAIN SOFTENING FAILURE ELEMENTS

Paczkowski (1986) has introduced a failure element with special attention to softening of bar elements. The non-linear relation between the axial force P and the axial deformation of the bar $\Delta$ is linearized as shown in figure 2. $X_1$, $X_2$ and $X_3$ are assumed to be random variables. All other quantities necessary to define the failure element are deterministic. This failure element can be incorporated in the $\beta$-unzipping method, but monitoring of nodal displacement for each element of the truss is necessary. The fictitious load F for the softening part is shown in figure 2. Failure is

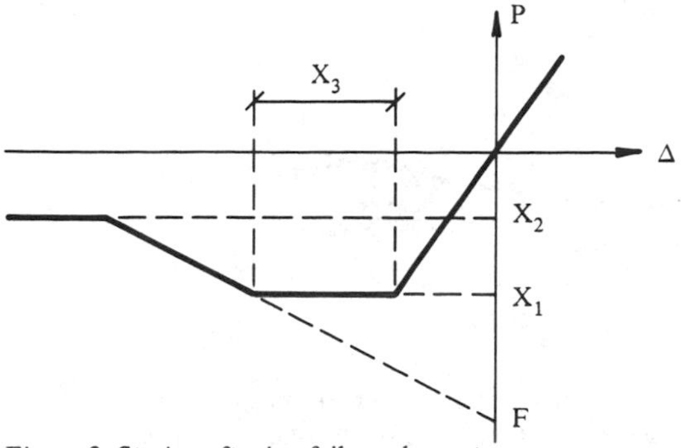

Figure 2. Strain softening failure element.

defined as collapse and the analysis is performed at the increasing levels (0, 1, 2, . . . ) till the collapse is detected.

## INSTABILITY FAILURE ELEMENT

Faber & Thoft-Christensen (1987) have introduced the so-called instability failure element. Consider a single beam which is a member of a complicated structural system. The failure mode modelled by the instability failure element is local instability failure taking into account the influence of the axial load P in the beam on the stiffness of the beam and the uncertainty related to the interaction between this beam and the remaining part of the structure. The stiffness matrix $\bar{\bar{k}}$ (6×6 matrix) is divided into two matrices

$$\bar{\bar{k}} = \bar{\bar{k}}_m + \bar{\bar{k}}_c \tag{4}$$

where $\bar{\bar{k}}_m$ is the modified stiffness matrix and $\bar{\bar{k}}_c$ the condensed stiffness matrix. The matrix $\bar{\bar{k}}_m$ is formulated on the basis of the so-called stability functions s(P) and c(P). The restraints imposed on the structural member by the remaining part of the structure are represented by the condensed stiffness matrix $\bar{\bar{k}}_c$. The smallest value of P resulting in singularity of $\bar{\bar{k}}$ is equal to the elastic instability load $P_{cr}$ of the beam. A simple way to model the uncertainty related to the interaction between the beam (column) and the remaining part of the structure is to introduce a model uncertainty variable Z into (4)

$$\bar{\bar{k}} = \bar{\bar{k}}_m + Z\bar{\bar{k}}_c \tag{5}$$

The reliability of the column with respect to instability can then be estimated on the basis of the safety margin

$$M = P_{cr} - P \tag{6}$$

or alternatively,

$$M = \det(\bar{\bar{k}}) = \det(\bar{\bar{k}}_m + Z\bar{\bar{k}}_c) \tag{7}$$

It is a simple matter to include instability failure elements in the estimation of the reliability of a structural system, see Faber & Thoft-Christensen (1987).

BUCKLING FAILURE ELEMENT

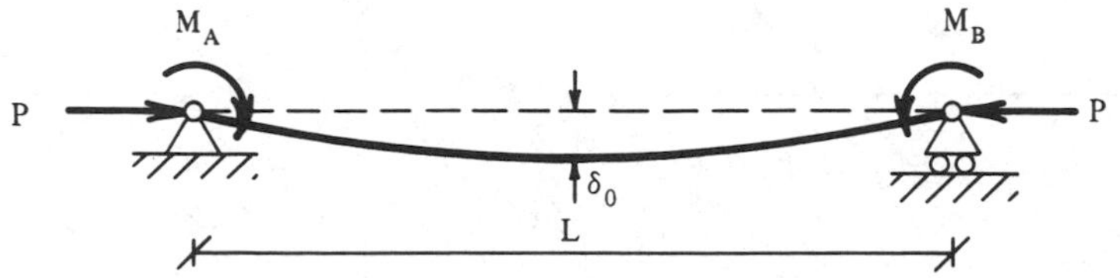


Figure 3. Beam-column with imperfection.

A simple buckling failure element has been introduced by Faber & Thoft-Christensen (1987). The purpose of this failure element is to model buckling failure due to an initial out of straightness imperfection of a beam-column and to include deflections due to end moments (see figure 3). The shape of the imperfection is assumed to be a sine curve. Buckling failure is assumed to take place when the axial load exceeds the peak value of the axial load - lateral deflection curve. The load-carrying capacity of the beam column is obtained by Newmark's method, see Chen & Han (1985). The total deflection is $w = w_i + w_0 + w_a$, where $w_i = \delta_0 \sin(\pi x/L)$ is the initial imperfection, $w_0$ the deflection due to end moments and $w_a$ the deflection applied by the axial force P. By formulating the equilibrium equation and assuming that a non-linear moment-axial-load relationship is known it is a simple matter to obtain the buckling load $P_b$.

For beam columns the eccentricity of P (and therefore the end moments $M_A$ and $M_B$) and the imperfection $\delta_0$ are usually uncertain parameters. The buckling reliability of such beam columns with end moments and the imperfection modelled by stochastic variables can then be estimated by the following safety margin

$$M = P_b - P \tag{8}$$

Buckling failure of the tubular members forming a tubular joint has been investigated by Thoft-Christensen & Sørensen (1987) on the basis of the API model for stability strength, see Miller (1981). A buckling failure element with the safety margin

$$M = Z - (\frac{N}{N_B} + \frac{B}{B_B}) \tag{9}$$

is introduced, where $N_B$ and $B_B$ are functions of the yield stress and where Z is a model uncertainty variable.

## GLOBAL INSTABILITY FAILURE ELEMENTS

To illustrate the concept of a global instability failure element consider the plane structure shown in figure 4. The structure is loaded with two concentrated forces $P_1$ and a distributed load $P_2$. Details of the structure and the loading are given by Thoft-Christensen (1984). This structure is analysed for a number of different load histories of the 3 types shown in figure 5a and by taking into account only geometrical non-linearities. For each type of load history the horizontal deflection u of the top of the structure is calculated as a function of the loading. Consider as an example the type I load history where, during the first step, $P_2 = 0$ and $P_1$ is increased from zero to some given value $P_1^*$. Then during the second step $P_1 = P_1^*$ and $P_2$ is increased from zero until the $P_2$-u relation reaches a maximum. This maximum value for $P_2$ and the $P_2$-values corresponding to u = 3.0 and u = 2.0 are used to obtain points of the three failure curves shown in figure 5b.

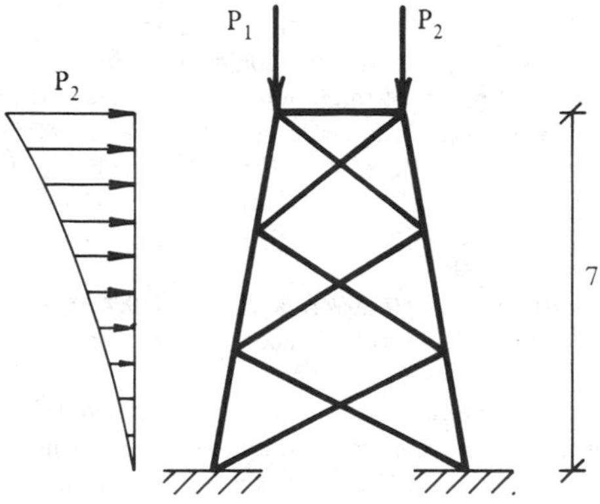


Figure 4.

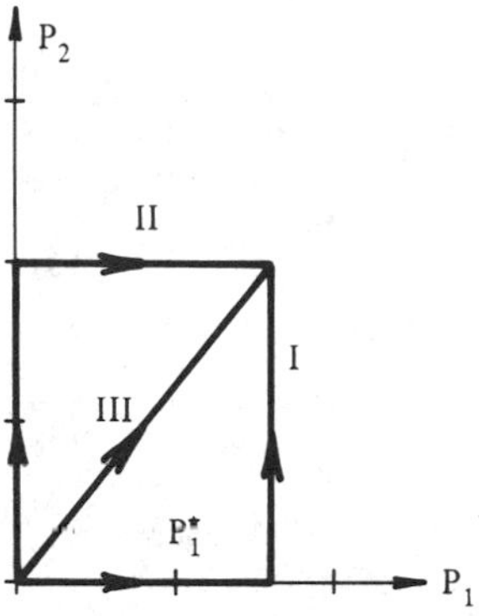


Figure 5a. Load history.

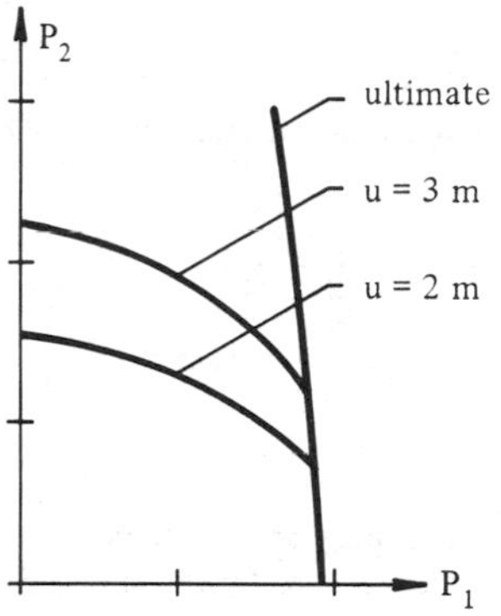


Figure 5b. Failure function.

The invariance of these points with regard to load history is investigated by performing analogous calculations for load histories of the types II and III. Only minor deviations were discovered for this structure. Let a failure function corresponding to a given deflection u or corresponding to the ultimate curve in figure 5b be given by the equation $f(P_1, P_2) = 0$. By assuming $P_1$ and $P_2$ to be random variables global reliability with regard to »instability» is estimated on the basis of the following safety margin

$$M = f(P_1, P_2) \tag{10}$$

To take into account the uncertainty related to the determination of the failure function f a number of model uncertainty variables can be included in the safety margin M in the usual way.

## FATIGUE FAILURE ELEMENTS

Thoft-Christensen & Sørensen (1987) have used a simple fatigue failure element in relation to estimation of the reliability of tubular joints in offshore structures. The fatigue load is modelled as a stationary narrow-banded zero-mean Gaussian process with standard deviation $\sigma_p$ and zero-up-crossing rate $\nu_p$. Stress concentration factors for the hot points of the tubular joint are calculated from formulas suggested by Kuang et al. (1985). The damage accumulation is determined by Miner's rule and the following safety margin for each hot spot is derived, see Wirshing (1984)

$$M = Z_1 - (Z_2)^m K^{-1} (\max(t/32, 1))^{M_1} \cdot g \tag{11}$$

where m (= 3) and K are constants in the S - N relation used in Miner's rule. K is modelled as a random variable, t is the wall thickness, $M_1$ is a random variable and g is a constant. $Z_1$ and $Z_2$ are model uncertainty variables.

In a recent paper by Corotis & Sheekam (1986) the damage accumulation in wood is investigated on the basis of creep rupture damage accumulation models proposed by Barrett & Foschi (1978). Only one of these models (model II) is referred to here. The rate of change of damage $\dot{\alpha}$ is expressed as a function of the current stress $\sigma$ and the damage level $\alpha$ in the following way

$$\dot{\alpha} = \begin{cases} a(\sigma - \sigma_0)^b + c\alpha & \text{when } \sigma > \sigma_0 \quad (12a) \\ 0 & \text{when } \sigma \leqslant \sigma_0 \quad (12b) \end{cases}$$

where $\sigma_0$ is a treshold stress and a, b and c constants. Failure occurs for $\alpha = 1$. For constant stress (12a) gives

$$\alpha(t) = a c^{-1} (\sigma - \sigma_0)^b (e^{ct} - 1) \tag{13}$$

so that the time to failure T is given by

$$T = c^{-1} \ell n[1 + c^{-1} a^{-1} (\sigma - \sigma_0)^{-b}] \tag{14}$$

The constants a, b and c are determined by curve-fitting and can be modelled by random variables. Likewise, $\sigma$ is modelled by a random variable. A failure element for fatigue failure (creep rupture) of wood can therefore be defined by the safety margin

$$M = T - T_0 \tag{15}$$

where $T_0$ is the target lifetime of the wood element in question. Model uncertainty can be included as usual by introducing a number of model uncertainty variables.

## PUNCHING FAILURE ELEMENTS

An important failure mode for tubular joints is punching failure in the braces. Based on a punching criterion by Yura et al. (1980) the following safety margin for a punching failure element has been formulated by Thoft-Christensen & Sørensen (1987)

$$M = Z_1 - [\,|\frac{N}{Z_2 N_U}| + (\frac{|B|}{Z_3 B_U})^{1.2}\,] \tag{16}$$

where $N_U$ and $B_U$ are ultimate punching capacities in pure axial loading and pure bending, respectively.

SLAB FAILURE ELEMENTS

For many building structures failure of concrete slabs must be included in the estimation of the reliability of the building. Upper bounds for the load-carrying capacity of a concrete slab can be determined by the work equation method, see Nielsen (1984). By this method a geometrically admissible yield line pattern is selected and the work $W_i$ dissipated in the yield lines is calculated and equated with the work $W_e$ performed by the external load. The solution of this so-called work equation $W_i = W_e$ is then an upper bound for the load-carrying capacity. A simple slab failure element can now be introduced by assuming the strength properties and the load to be random. The safety margin is

$$M = ZW_i - W_e \tag{17}$$

where Z is a model uncertainty variable connected with the choice of yield line pattern. The safety margin (17) can be used to estimate the reliability of the slab given a yield line pattern. The optimal yield line pattern within a set of patterns can be determined in this way as the pattern with the lowest reliability.

SOME APPLICATIONS

As mentioned earlier the reliability of TUBULAR JOINTS has been investigated by Thoft-Christensen & Sørensen (1987). Four types of failure elements are included in their analysis of a K-joint, namely yielding in the four tubes, punching in the two braces, buckling in the four tubes, and fatigue in two hot points. So the total number of failure elements for the K-joint is 12. The random variables involved are the load, the yield stress, a number of model uncertainty variables, the constant K in Miner's rule and $M_1$ in equation (11). The reliability of a single K-joint of an offshore platform at levels 1 and 2 was estimated. Further, optimal design of a tubular joint with reliability constraints was performed.

OPTIMAL DESIGN with reliability constraints has been considered by Sørensen et al., see e.g. Sørensen (1986) and Sørensen & Thoft-Christensen (1986). In reliability-based structural optimization a number of formulations can be used. Here, only two will be mentioned. Let the object function (e.g. the cost or the weight of the structure) be $F(\bar{x})$ where $\bar{x} = (x_1, \ldots, x_n)$ are the variables. Then the first formulation is to minimize $F(\bar{x})$ subject to the constraints that

$$\beta_S(\bar{x}) \geqslant \beta_S^0 \quad \text{and} \quad \bar{x}_\ell \leqslant \bar{x} \leqslant \bar{x}_u \tag{18}$$

where $\beta_S^0$ is the target value for the systems reliability index $\beta_S$. $\bar{x}_\ell$ and $\bar{x}_u$ are lower and upper bounds for $\bar{x}$. In the second formulation the constraints (18) are changed for

$$\left.\begin{array}{ll} \beta_i(\bar{x}) \geqslant \beta_i^0 & i = 1, \ldots, m \\ x_i^\ell \leqslant x_i \leqslant x_i^u & i = 1, \ldots, n \end{array}\right\} \tag{19}$$

where $\beta_i^0$ is the minimum permissible reliability index for the safety element i. A number of optimization procedures to solve these problems has been proposed. For the problem (18) a method based on the solution of a sequence of easily solved element reliability index optimization problems seems to very efficient. This method uses Lagrange multiplier estimates to adjust the element reliability index.

An OPTIMAL STRATEGY FOR INSPECTION AND REPAIR of structural elements and systems is proposed by Thoft-Christensen & Sørensen (1986). The total cost of inspection and repair is minimized with the constraint that the reliability of elements and/or of the structural system are acceptable. The design variables are the time intervals between inspections and the quality of the inspections. The maintenance strategy model can easily be used by anyone having experience in estimating reliability of systems and using non-linear optimization methods.

## CONCLUSIONS

In this paper it is shown that the traditional methods of estimating the reliability of structural systems can be generalized to include various failure elements. A number of new failure elements is presented. Some recent application of systems reliability methods are briefly discussed. Several important applications in relation to offshore structures and earthquake loading could also have been included here.

Structural systems reliability theory is applicable in many situations. However, more research is needed before widespread applications can be expected. A number of unsolved problems can be mentioned here, e.g.

- reliability of non-linear systems
- reliability of dynamically sensitive systems
- inclusion of gross errors.

## REFERENCES


Barrett, J. D. & R. A. Foschi (1978). »Duration of Load and Probability of Failure in Wood. Part II. Constant, Ramp, and Cyclic Loadings». Canadian J. of Civ. Engrg., Vol. 5, pp. 505-532.

Chen, W. F. & D. J. Han (1985). »Tubular Members in Offshore Structures». Pitman Advanced Publishing Program. Boston/London/Melbourne.

Corotis, R. B. & D. P. Sheeham (1986). »Wood Damage Accumulation by Stochastic Load Models». ASCE, J. of Structural Engineering, Vol. 112, No. 11, pp. 2402-2415.

Faber, M. H. & P. Thoft-Christensen (1987). »Instability and Buckling Failure Elements for Columns». Structural Reliability Theory, Paper no. 25, University of Aalborg, Report R8702.

Høj, N. P. & E. Loklindt (1983). »Estimering af svigtsandsynlighed for rammekonstruktioner» (in Danish). Institute of Building Technology and Structural Engineering. University of Aalborg. Report 8302.

Kuang, J. G., Potvin, A. B. & R. D. Leick (1975). »Stress Concentrations in Tubular Joints». OTC, Houston, Texas, OTC 2205.

Miller, C. D. (1981). »Buckling Design Methods for Steel Structures - A State-of-the-Art». In D. Faulkner et al.: Integrity of Offshore Structures. Applied Science Publishers, London, pp. 397-418.

Nielsen, M. P. (1984). »Limit Analysis and Concrete Plasticity». Prentice Hall, Inc., Englewood Cliffs, New Jersey.

Paczkowski, W. (1986). »Strain Softening Elements in the β-Unzipping Method». Structural Reliability Theory, Paper no. 20, University of Aalborg, Report R8617.

Sørensen, J. D. (1986). »Reliability-Based Optimization of Structural Elements». Structural Reliability Theory, Paper no. 18. University of Aalborg, Report R8608.

Sørensen, J. D. & P. Thoft-Christensen (1986). »Recent Advances in Optimal Design of Structures from a Reliability Point of View». 9th ARTS, Bradford, 1986. To be published in Journal of Quality and Reliability Management.

Thoft-Christensen, P. (1984). »Structural Reliability Theory». Proc. ESRA Pre-Launching Meeting on Safety and Reliability in Europe, Ispra, October 1984, pp. 82-99.

Thoft-Christensen, P. & J. D. Sørensen (1986). »Optimal Strategy for Inspection and Repair of Structural Systems». Structural Reliability Theory, Paper no. 22, University of Aalborg, Report R8619.

Thoft-Christensen, P., Sigurdsson, G. & J. D. Sørensen (1986). »Development of Applicable Methods for Evaluating the Safety of Offshore Structures, Part 3». Structural Reliability Theory, Paper no. 17, University of Aalborg, Report R8604.

Thoft-Christensen, P. & J. D. Sørensen (1987). »Reliability Analysis of Tubular Joints in Offshore Structures». Reliability '87, Birmingham, England, April 1987.

Wirshing, P. H. (1984). »Fatigue Reliability for Offshore Structures». ASCE. J. Structural Engineering. Col. 110, No. 10, pp. 2340-2356.

Yura, J. A., Zettlemayer, N. & I. F. Edwards (1980). »Ultimate Capacity Equations for Tubular Joints». OTC, Houston, Texas, OTC 3690, pp. 113-125.

# TOWARDS RISK ANALYSIS THROUGH KNOWLEDGE BASED SYSTEMS

D.I. Blockley
Department of Civil Engineering, University of Bristol
Bristol, BS8 1TR, UK

## ABSTRACT

It is becoming increasingly clear that controlling, rather than predicting, the chances of human error and risk is a central issue. Known predictive methods are incomplete and likely to remain so. It is argued that knowledge based systems will have an important role in advising engineers about risky decisions. It is suggested that a class of problems exist for which there are no significant scientific models but which can be described linguistically and that the knowledge can be captured in an advice system. Support logic, an open world inference technique, is introduced.

## INTRODUCTION

In a recent Workshop (Novak 1986) on the modelling of human error in structural engineering, there was considerable emphasis on the control of error. The report of a working group on occurrence of errors suggested that engineering analysts have perhaps become over zealous at modelling extreme natural events. This, it was suggested, tends to give the general public the impression that everything is under control and so complete responsibility is placed on the engineer

It is increasingly becoming clear from a number of studies Blockley (1980), Novak (1986) that control of human error is complex and that all known predictors of risk are deficient and likely to remain so. Methods of analysis for parts of the risk problem (eg load overcoming strength) have been developed to very sophisticated levels but unfortunately these models do not represent the whole problem. It is perhaps fortuitous that just as this is being realised, a new field of knowledge engineering is emerging in the general research field of artificial intelligence (AI). Knowledge based systems KBS, and expert systems may provide a vehicle for capturing the complexities of engineering knowledge in an organised way and thus become an important tool in the control and management of risk.

## ADVICE SYSTEMS

An expert system is a computer program which attempts to emulate the manner of problem solving and decision taking of an expert in some (restricted) context. The central modules of such a system are the "knowledge base" and the "inference engine". It is clearly important that the nature of the knowledge contained in the system is clarified. In particular the problem of the "completeness" of such knowledge is a central issue. The perspectives of the various experts who input knowledge into an engineering risk assessment might be very different. In particular the technical, financial and environmental factors which are part of any project risk assessment will have differing relative importance for various experts. The responsibilities of the expert and the computer are also important; the term "expert" systems is a misnomer. No computer program can be an expert in the real sense that it cannot be held legally liable for its recommendations. An engineer is an expert to the extent he is a responsible decision maker. These programs ought therefore to be called advice systems.

ADVICE AND CRITIQUING

Miller (1984) has suggested a similar approach for medical management. A computer system ATTENDING is used to critique a physician's plan for a patient's anesthetic management. Miller argues that in anesthesiology, as in most medicine, the decisions a physician makes involve a substantial amount of subjective judgement at several levels.

The traditional approach to expert system design has been to design a system which simulates an expert's decision making process. Such a system is supposed to gather data, as an expert might, and then attempts to come to similarly expert conclusions. When applied in practice this traditional approach has the effect of trying to tell the decision maker what to do ie how to practice medicine, or engineering.

In contrast a critiquing system like ATTENDING assumes that the user has already evaluated a plan of action and rather than simulating it the system critiques it, discussing the pros and cons of the proposed approach as compared to alternatives which might be reasonable or preferred.

ENGINEERING KNOWLEDGE

The critique approach, it may be argued, is all very well for highly subjective problem areas, but when one is dealing with problems subject to precise scientific analysis, it is unnecessary. The attitude that engineering consists only of the application of precise scientific theories is now totally outdated(Blockley 1980). It is recognised that the engineer's theoretical tools are many and various and vary enormously in precision and dependability. An engineering advice system therefore must be based on uncertain data and knowledge which must be manipulated in such a way as not to involve difficult hidden assumptions on behalf of the user. Central to this issue are the notions of "completeness" of systems(even within a restricted problem area) and dependence between factors within a system.

A so-called closed world model is "complete". It represents total knowledge about everything in a particular system and everything is either true or false with no undefined or inconsistent states possible. An open world model represents partial knowledge where some things are true, some false and others simply unknown. Many facts that are deducible might not be represented.

Unfortunately probability theory forces a closed world model by the restrictive nature of its axions. It is, therefore, essential to relax these axioms(Blockley 1985) and to obtain a method of uncertainty analysis which allows an open world model. Of course the result of this is that the model is recognisably incomplete and must be used with that recognition at the forefront of the user's attention. Hence the need to stress that the engineer should use risk control advice systems responsibly.

For the purposes of this discussion engineering knowledge will be divided into three categories, facts, scientific models and descriptive models. Generally facts are obvious; they are what is. However facts are often established by measurement and analysis which contains hidden assumptions. Statistical data are particularly susceptible to various interpretations. In general terms it is too simplistic to think of a fact as being absolutely true or dependable there must be an associated degree of belief.

A scientific hypothesis is usually defined as a general proposition which asserts a universal connection between properties of observables or concepts built up on observables which can be thoroughly tested. However a theory always has limitations which restrict the scope of its application and therefore it is perhaps more useful to think of all scientific hypotheses as models. It is of course the limitations of a theoretical model and its relationship with a given practical problem which makes up system uncertainty (Blockley 1980). Conventional quantitative assessments of risk rely on scientific models of capacity (R) and demand (S) and use probability theory to assess margins of safety. As has been discussed previously (Blockley 1980) reliability theory copes well with uncertainty in the familiar parameters (strain, deflection settlement etc) because they can be identified clearly and measured dependably in repeatable experiments. However, factors which are difficult to define clearly and measure repeatably (such as workmanship etc) are often dominant in the causes of actual failures.

There is another class of engineering problems where no significant scientific models of demand and capacity exist. One example to be reported fully in a future paper is the subsidence of undermined ground in the West Midlands of England. Although there are no significant scientific models describing the mechanisms of general subsidence or of crown hole formation it is not true to say that these mechanisms are not understood. Engineers and geologists can more or less agree on a linguistic description, but are unable to capture that description in any formal system for risk comparisons or risk, cost, benefit comparisons. It may be in this class of problems that risk analysis through knowledge based systems will have the greatest impact.

## MEASURES OF UNCERTAINTY

A new method of uncertain inference called support logic has recently been introduced (Blockley, Baldwin 1987) and included in FRIL (Fuzzy Relational Inference Language). In early versions of FRIL (Blockley, Pilsworth, Baldwin 1983 a) only the rules of fuzzy logic were implemented. It has since been stressed (Blockley, Pilsworth, Baldwin 1983 b, Blockley 1985) that when choosing an inference technique to help solve a problem it is the responsibility of the engineer to choose a technique which in his opinion, models the problem in the most appropriate manner. In other words, just as physical systems can be modelled in various ways (eg pinned vs fixed joints in structural frameworks) so can inference mechanisms.

In particular probability and fuzzy measures are special cases of a more general result involving intervals of possibilities. For propositions A, B with uncertainty measures

$p(A) = p,\ p(B) = q,\ p \in (0,1),\ q \in (0,1)$, then

$p(A \,\&\, B) \leqslant \min(p, q) \leqslant \max(p, q) \leqslant p(A \text{ or } B)$

and in the case where the measures over the universal set sum to unity

$\max(0, p+q-1) \leqslant p(A \,\&\, B) \leqslant \min(p,q)$

$\max(p,q) \leqslant p(A \text{ or } B) \leqslant \min(1, p+q)$

Thus the special cases are

fuzzy logic: $p(A \,\&\, B) = \min(p,q)$

$p(A \text{ or } B) = p + q - \min(p, q) = \max(p, q)$

probability logic: $p(A \,\&\, B) = p.q$

$p(A \text{ or } B) = p + q - p.q$

Note that in both cases $p(A/B) = p(A \text{ and } B)/p(B)$

and $p(\text{not } A) = 1 - p(A)$

The fuzzy logic rules lead to bound values which have maximum inertia or involve least change. The probability rules result from an assumption of independence and correspond to maximum entropy or least bias.

Using the interval values other results follow, for example if
$p(A/B) = a$, $p(B) = b$ then

$$p(A) = p(A/B)p(B) + p(A/\bar{B})p(\bar{B})$$
$$= a\beta + \theta\ (1-b)$$

and $0 \leqslant \theta \leqslant 1$

Thus $ab \leqslant p(A) \leqslant 1-b + ab$

Now clearly in general terms the uncertain inputs to a given inference are upper and lower bounds on an interval so that

$A : [a_L, a_U]$

means that proposition A has a lower bound uncertainty measure of $a_L$ and an upper bound of $a_U$.

Now if $B : [b_L, b_U]$

then $A \& B : [\max(0, a_L + b_L - 1), \min(a_U, b_U)]$

$A \text{ or } B : [\max(a_L, b_L), \min(1, a_U + b_U)]$

Similarly if
A if B is interpreted as A/B

$A \text{ if } B : [a_L, a_U]$

$B : [b_L, b_U]$

---

then $A : [c_L, c_U]$

and $c_L = a_L b_L$, $c_U = 1 - b_L + a_U b_L$

Interval Inference

It is clearly possible to use the results of the previous section to make inferences. In this way the assumptions of fuzzy, probability or any other theory can be avoided. Unfortunately in practise the intervals rapidly expand to fill the total interval (0, 1) and hence be of little practical use. For example:

| | | |
|---|---|---|
| X if (A & B) | : | [0.6, 0.7] |
| Y if (C or D) | : | [0.9, 1.0] |
| Z if (X & Y) | : | [0.5, 0.7] |
| A | : | [0.7, 0.7] |
| B | : | [0.7, 0.8] |
| C | : | [0.5, 0.6] |
| D | : | [0.9, 1.0] |
| X | : | $[x_L, x_U]$ |
| Y | : | $[y_L, y_U]$ |
| Z | : | $[z_L, z_U]$ |

It is required to calculate $x_L$, $x_U$, $y_L$, $y_U$, $z_L$, $z_U$, the steps are as follows:

1. A & B : [max(0,0.7+0.7−1), min (0.7, 0.8)]
   A & B : [0.4, 0.7]
   $x_L = 0.4 \times 0.6$; $x_U = 1 - 0.4 + 0.7 \times 0.4$
   X : [0.24, 0.88]
2. C or D : [max(0.5,0.9), min (1, 1+0.6)]
   C or D : [0.9,1.0]
   $y_L = 0.9 \times 0.9$; $y_U = 1 - 0.9 + 1 \times 0.9$
   Y : [0.81, 1]
3. X & Y : [max(0, 0.24 + 0.81−1), min (0.88, 1)]
   X & Y : [0.05, 0.88]
   $z_L = 0.05 \times 0.5$ $z_U = 1 - 0.05 + 0.7 \times 0.05$
   Z : [0.025, 0.985]

The inference results in a wide range for the uncertainty interval on Z and is therefore of very limited practical use.

It is worth noting that the uncertainty interval arises from two sources, the unknown dependence between the propositions, and the difficulty of dealing with negation. Thus the previous results apply to two propositions whose interdependence is unknown. If that dependency is known (for example from a conditional proposition) then of course it should be used. There is great difficulty however in dealing with the relationship between A/B and A/$\bar{B}$ for most practical problems. If both of these can be assessed then the problem is

A if B : $[a_L, a_U]$
A if $\bar{B}$ : $[\bar{a}_L, \bar{a}_U]$
B : $[b_L, b_U]$

---

A : $[c_L, c_U]$

$c_L = a_L b_L + \bar{a}_L (1-b_U)$; $c_U = a_U b_u + \bar{a}_U (1-b_L)$
and of course if $a_L = a_U = a$, $\bar{a}_L = \bar{a}_U = \bar{a}$, $b_L = b_U = b$
then $c_L = c_U = ab + \bar{a}(1-b)$ as in standard probability theory

## Support Logic

Support logic is a development of these ideas into a practical inference technique which has been already described in some detail. It is recognised that, in order to obtain a useful result, the user of the inference technique has to choose point estimates on the intervals discussed in the previous section. The fact of having to make a choice will make the user aware of the assumptions being made. This will have the effect, hopefully, of enabling the user to make better judgements concerning the effectiveness of a given inference and this in turn will lead to better decision making.

However, the central development of this treatment is to realise that the mathematical rigour of the rule for negation is too restrictive for measures of uncertain subjective belief. The measure of support for a proposition and the measure of support for the negation of the proposition are therefore dealt with separately. Two measures called the necessary (N) and possibility (P) values are associated with a proposition A as

A : [N, P] or with a rule
A if B & C : [N, P] written in a modified prolog form of
A:-B,C : [N, P]

The necessary support N is the measure that represents the maximum level on a scale (0, 1) that it is believed the proposition (or rule) is necessarily (certainly) true or dependable. The possible support P is such that the measure (1-P) represents the maximum belief in a scale (0, 1) that the proposition or rule is necessarily (certainly) not true. It is assumed that a proposition cannot be certainly true (ie N = 1) and certainly not true (ie 1-P = 1 or P = 0) at the sametime. Following on from that it is assumed that by convention $N + (1-P) \leqslant 1$ or $P \geqslant N$. This means that the sum of the necessary support ($N \leqslant 1$) for a proposition plus the necessary support ($1-P \leqslant 1$) against a proposition is at most equal to one. Thus example support pairs (N, P) are

(0, 0) represents certainly false or certainly undependable
(1, 1) represents certainly true or certainly dependable
(0, 1) represents "don't know" because the necessary or certain support is zero both for and against

Of course in problems of sparse and conflicting information the ability to model "don't know" is very important.

Note that the sum of the necessary supports for a proposition and its negation do not sum to one. The necessary support for the negation of a proposition is not determined from the necessary support for the proposition.

Support for Compound Propositions

These have been described in detail(Blockley, Baldwin 1987) and so it is sufficient here to quote the main results. Two alternative models have been proposed, the multiplication model and the minimum model. For propositions A, B with supports N (A), P (A), N(B), P(B) then for the multiplication model

N (A and B) = N (A).N(B)
and for the minimum model N (A and B) = min [N(A), N(B)]
for both models N (A or B) = N(A) + N(B) - N(A and B)
P (A or B) = P(A) + P(B) - P(A and B)

The multiplication model corresponds to the distribution which maximises the entropy which means the measures are distributed with least bias. The relationship of this with classical probability theory can be understood from the following argument:

A:-B : [N(A/B), P(A/B)]
A:-$\bar{B}$ : [N(A/B), P(A/B)]
B : [N(B), P(B)]
A : [N(A), P(A)]

Now N(A) = N (A:-B) and B) + N(A:-$\bar{B}$) and B)
= N (A/B). N(B) + N(A/$\bar{B}$). (1-P(B)) Similarly
P(A) = 1-[(1-P(A/B)). N(B) + (1-P(A/$\bar{B}$)) . (1-P(B))]
and of course if N ( ) = P ( )
then N (A) = P(A) = P(A/B).P(B) + P(A/$\bar{B}$).(1-P(B))
as in standard probability theory.

Combination of Evidence for the Same Conclusion

This again has been described in some detail (Blockley, Baldwin 1987). Clearly in any particular knowledge base it may be possible to obtain support for a particular conclusion from a number of sources. Thus the problem is:

A : [N1, P1]
A : [N2, P2]
A : [N, P]

and it is required to find (N, P) in terms of (N1, P1) and (N2, P2). A measure of conflict has been derived
conflict (A) = N2.(1-P1) + N1.(1-P2)
for the multiplication rule. If the conflict is removed by normalising then
if K = 1- conflict (A)
N = (N1.P2 + N2.P1 - N1.N2)/K
P = 1-((1-P1) (1-N2) + (1-P2) (P1-N1))/K
similar formulae have been derived for the minimum rule.

FRISP

A computer programme FRISP (Fuzzy Relational Inference with SuPport logic) has been written in prolog-2 and Cprolog. The prolog-2 programme was developed by the author on an IBM-PC-AT with a 30M byte CDC fixed hard disc and the disk operating system DOS 3.00. Although the IBM-PC-AT has a very large fixed disk storage capacity and an enormous amount of data can be stored within the machine, the amount of working store available for processing a single prolog predicate is limited to 64K bytes. Prolog-2 is written so that "modules" of information can be stored in "virtual memory" on the disc. Application files containg the particular knowledge data and rules are set up in accordance with the modified prolog form described earlier. Thus a typical rule might be:

good-design (Nec, Pos, Design) :-safe (Nec1, Pos1, Design, Saf_fac), economic (Nec2, Pos2, Cost): [0.9, 1.0].
which says that a particular Design will belong to the concept good_design with necessity and possibility values (Nec,Pos) IF the Design has a safety factor (Saf_fac) which belongs to the concept safe with (Nec1, Pos1) AND has a cost (Cost) which belongs to the concept economic with (Nec2, Pos2). This rule has a support of (0.9, 1.0).

The programme is written so that it can operate in two modes. The first is simply from prolog itself so that with all of the system and application modules open any particular FRISP predicate can be accessed. For example to ask a query of the knowledge base one would type
query ([A, B](safe (A,B) or economic (A,C)).
This is asking for the values of the attributes (A,B) together with their (N,P) values which satisfy the goal safe or economic. In this case the attributes A, B, C are Design, safety factor and cost. Other predicates are available although there is insufficient space here to describe them in detail.

The second mode of operation for the programme is by using a menu which targets the "current relation" or current clause in the knowledge base. The menu is shown in Figure 1. Again there is insufficient space to describe each option in detail. However the user may explore the knowledge base by moving to new "current relations" and by asking questions and for explanations of the answers.

CONCLUSIONS

It has been argued that knowledge based systems may have an important role to play in risk management. The term"expert system" should be replaced by the term "advice system". The role of advice systems to provide critiques of decision plans should be explored.

Engineering knowledge which can be linguistically described but for which there are no established or significant scientific models may be the most fruitful source of engineering examples for testing a knowledge based risk management system.

In order to utilise such systems an open world uncertainty analysis technique is required. Support logic has been introduced.

REFERENCES

Blockley D.I. (1980). The Nature of Structural Design and Safety, Ellis Horwood, Chichester, UK.
Blockley D.I. (1985). "Fuzziness and Probability: a discussion of Gaines' Axioms", Civ. Engng. Syst., Vol 2, Dec, 195-200.
Blockley D.I., Baldwin J.F. (1987). "Uncertain Inference in Knowledge Based Systems" to appear Proc. Am. Soc. Civ. Engrs.
Blockley D.I., Pilsworth B.W., Baldwin J.F. (1983a). "Structural Safety as inferred from a Fuzzy Relational Knowledge Base",In G. Augusti, A. Borri and G. Vannucchi (Eds.), Proc. ICASP-4, Pitagora Editrice, Bologna.
Blockley D.I., Pilsworth B.W., Baldwin J.F. (1983b). "Measures of Uncertainty", Civ. Engng. Syst. Vol.1, Sept., 3 -9
Miller P.L. (1984) A Critiquing Approach to Expert Computer Advice:ATTENDING, Pitman Advanced Publishing Program, MA.
Novak A. (Ed) (1986) Modeling Human Error in Structural Design and Construction, Proc. NSF Workshop, Ann Arbor, MI, June,Published by Am.Soc.Civ.Engrs

```
Prolog 2 V1.21 TLI                                              Insert
        CURRENT RELATION                                frinp     littc
        roof(nec,pos,index,cz_name,mine_nm,risk_sz,treatmt,assessr)

                  ********** Option Menu **********

                  1. Display relation in English
                  2. Display relation in PROLOG/FRIL
                  3. Report on current Relation
                  4. Proceed to next relation
                  5. Back to previous relation
                  6. Specify a new current relation
                  7. Ask a general query
                  8. Do a WHAT IF query
                  9. Ask WHY
                  10.Reset a WHAT IF query
                  11.Set explanation mode
                  12.Cancel explanation mode
                  13.Calculate measure of conflict
                  14.Return to Prolog2
                  15./16.Switch on/Switch off Printer

        Please enter choice number followed by a .
```

Fig 1

# RELIABILITY OF COMPLEX STRUCTURES UNDER WAVE LOADS

H.Y. Chan and R.E. Melchers
Department of Civil Engineering and Surveying, The University of Newcastle, N.S.W., Australia, 2308.

## ABSTRACT

The reliability analysis of multi-membered structures such as steel tubular offshore platforms has been largely confined to considerations of structural member behavior and given loading uncertainty. However realistic modelling of wave forces may require account to be taken of the effect of wave forces varying with the incident wave location as it passes through the structure. Such an analysis is described in the present paper, using the Truncated Enumeration technique previously described. Main emphasis is given to structures composed of elastic-brittle members: the analysis for elastic-plastic structures degenerates to that of a probabilistic adaptation problem.

## INTRODUCTION

Offshore structures are highly redundant structural systems constantly subjected to hostile environmental loadings. These loadings result from the wind, wave and current environment as well as from ship impact and possibly from ice forces. All are largely random in nature. This has been recognized for a long time and has led to techniques such as extreme value analysis to attempt to set design loadings for a sufficiently remote chance of structural overload and hence possible structural failure. With the recognition that the structure itself also contains many aspects about which knowledge is uncertain (e.g. material strength, imperfect sizes, fabrication variations), has come the need to take into account more than just loading uncertainty in safety assessment. Reliability analysis provides a tool to do this. The basic techniques available for reliability analysis and special techniques for complex (many-membered) structures have been reviewed elsewhere. The present paper describes the collapse failure analysis of a multi-member steel tubular jacket platform under extreme wave load conditions, with particular attention focussed on the effect of wave loading varying as the extreme wave passes through the structure.

## REVIEW

The deterministic method of calculating wave loading on small diameter piles or tubular members is the traditional approach. It also forms the basis for a reliability analysis and involves the following steps:

(i) choosing a design wave appropriate to the climatic conditions at the particular location and having a sufficiently low probability of occurrence. The design wave is described by the parameters "wave height" and "wave period";

(ii) choosing an appropriate wave theory to relate the fluid particle kinematics to the wave parameters;

(iii) using the well-known Morison equation with appropriate drag coefficient $C_D$ and mass coefficient $C_m$ to calculate the forces on members from the fluid particle kinematics.

Various studies such as those by Hogben et al (1977) and Bea and Lai (1978) give a detailed description of the state of knowledge of wave loading. It is clear from these that there are considerable uncertainties associated with each of the above steps. Of main concern is the intrinsic random nature of wave motion and the insufficient knowledge of the complex mechanism of fluid loading. The latter affects mainly $C_D$ and $C_m$. A probabilistic description of loading is needed to accommodate these uncertainties: in addition the material and member strengths of the structure are uncertain and a probabilistic description for these is also appropriate.

In the first order second moment (FOSM) reliability analysis to be employed later, it is sufficient to know only the first two moments of a random variable. The first two moments of the wave load can be deduced once the probability distributions of the wave height and the wave period are known. For waves having a narrow band spectrum, it is often sufficient to assume that the wave period is deterministic (Borgman, 1965) or in the case of an extreme wave being used for design, a deterministic relationship between wave height might be assumed (Weigel, 1964). This is reasonable as one can deduce from a joint probability density function of wave height and wave period, that the higher the wave height, the less variable the wave period (Longuet-Higgins, 1975). Such an assumed relationship between wave height and period is convenient because the resulting wave loads can then be treated as a single parameter function with wave height as the only random variable and this, together with the fact that extreme waves usually have long periods, means the loadings acting at different parts of the structure can be assumed to be perfectly correlated.

The failure probability of a general structural system may be given by the following expression:

$$p_f = P(\bigcup_{i=1}^{m} \bigcap_{j=1}^{n} F_{ij}) \tag{1}$$

where $F_{ij}$ = failure of jth member in the structure in the ith failure mode.

A failure mode is attained when sufficient structural members have failed to cause the structural stiffness matrix to become singular. Each failure mode consists of a sequence of member failures. Except for the special case of ideal plastic member behavior, each failure mode is sequence dependent. At this point, it is important to note that while the members are in the process of failing progressively, the wave which causes the applied loading is itself moving through the structure at the same time. The loading is therefore not a static phenomenon, as has been often assumed (Murotsu, 1985). Since offshore platforms are highly redundant structures, the number of failure modes can be numerous. Procedures such as the incremental load method, the truncated enumeration method or a combination of both have been developed to determine only the most dominant failure modes (Melchers & Tang, 1984; Murotsu, 1985). These techniques will be adapted herein to examine the effect, on the reliability analysis of multimembered offshore platforms, of progressive wave loading.

## WAVE LOAD MODELLING

A common approach in selecting the loading for extreme wave conditions is to take the maximum total load on the structure resulting from the maximum wave train of the considered sea state as input into the reliability analysis (Murotsu, 1985). However, it will be realized that the maximum load effect on a particular member does not necessarily occur at the same time as the maximum total external load. As the wave train moves through the structure, the relative magnitudes of loads acting on the members change. What is important for obtaining the maximum load on each member is the interaction of local fluid particle velocity components and local $C_D$ and $C_m$ values. The global (i.e. total structural) forces have little relevance. In addition, there are distinctly local effects which may also need to be considered, for example, wave slamming on horizontal members near mean water level and change in buoyancy of a structure occurring with the passing of a wave through the structure (Hogben et al, 1977). It follows that the critical patterns of loading are not necessarily the same for each member. Therefore instead of using just one load pattern for the entire reliability analysis, a complete cycle of load patterns caused by the passing of a wave might be input into the analysis. If this is done, the member failure probability under n load patterns from the same wave becomes

$$p_f = P[E_1 \cup E_2 \cup \ldots E_n] \tag{2}$$

where $E_i$ = the event "failure under load pattern i". Since all n load patterns result from the same wave (as it passes through the structure), they are perfectly correlated so that the member failure probability can be written as:

$$p_f = \max \{P[E_i]\} \tag{3}$$

The load pattern, but not the wave force magnitude, will be assumed independent of wave height. Thus the worst load effect for a member is independent of the wave height.

The failure probability for a sequence (A, B, C) of member failure is given by:

$$p_f = P[A \cap B \cap C] \tag{4}$$

where event A corresponds to $P[A] = \max \{P[A_i]\}$ $i = 1,n$
B corresponds to $P[B] = \max \{P[B_j]\}$ $j = 1,n$
C corresponds to $P[C] = \max \{P[C_k]\}$ $k = 1,n$
and $A_i$ = failure of A under load pattern i and similarly for $B_j$, $C_k$.

The formulation suggests that the members fail progressively as their maximum load effects are reached. An implicit assumption in (4) is that the waves are periodic and thus that the load pattern repeats itself after each cycle. This is entirely reasonable for the sea state of interest. The means of the load patterns themselves can be obtained from a deterministic analysis given the mean wave height and mean period. Details of calculation can be found in Sarpkaya & Isaacson (1982) as can details of calculation of variances.

## SYSTEM RELIABILITY ANALYSIS

As pointed out in Tang & Melchers (1984), the Incremental Load and Truncated Enumeration techniques can be combined to give an economical system reliability analysis which can cater for a wide range of member behavior. These procedures were adopted in the present study to generate the dominant failure modes. In selecting the failure path, the member (node) failure probability is given by (3). The limit state equation of a member having resistance R is obtained by solving the incremental equation:

$$\underline{\underline{B}} \cdot \underline{R} - \underline{\underline{C}} \cdot \underline{Q} = \underline{\underline{A}} \cdot \underline{r} \tag{5}$$

where matrix $\underline{\underline{A}}$ is termed the "utilization" matrix and represents the relationship between member strength R and load increments vector $\underline{r}$. Matrix $\underline{\underline{B}}$ represents the effect which partial or total unloading of a failed member has on the remaining or unfailed members in the structure. Matrix $\underline{\underline{C}}$ is constructed on the basis of the equilibrium conditions of the intact structure and relates the load vector $\underline{Q}$ to the load increments vector $\underline{r}$. It is important to note that all the entries in the matrix $\underline{\underline{A}}$ must be based on the load pattern applicable to the current state of the structure (with perhaps some member failed). They will generally be different from those of the previous state. Such different states will be called "stages". The following example illustrates this point and the construction of the limit state equations at various stages.

EXAMPLE: Consider a failure path $i \rightarrow j$ under the actions of wave load $Q_1$ (several patterns) and load $Q_2$. $Q_1$ is taken as the incremental load (Melchers & Tang, 1984; Tang & Melchers, 1984). The incremental equations (5) become:

$$\begin{bmatrix} 1 & 0 \\ -\left(\dfrac{a_{j1}^{(2)} - a_{ji}^{(1)}}{a_{i1}^{(1)}}\right)-\mu & 1 \end{bmatrix} \begin{bmatrix} R_i \\ R_j \end{bmatrix} - \begin{bmatrix} a_{i2}^{(1)} \\ a_{j2}^{(1)} \end{bmatrix} = \begin{bmatrix} a_{i1}^{(1)} & 0 \\ a_{j1}^{(1)} & a_{j1}^{(2)} \end{bmatrix} \begin{bmatrix} r_1 \\ r_2 \end{bmatrix} \tag{6}$$

where $a_{i1}^{(1)}$ = action in member i due to unit load $Q_1$ at stage 1

$a_{j1}^{(2)}$ = action in member j due to unit load $Q_1$ at stage 2 (member i "failed")

$\mu$ = unloading factor (0 for ideal plastic member behavior, 1 for brittle member behavior)

$r_1$, $r_2$ = load increments at stage 1 and 2.

For the first member to fail, i.e. at stage 1, the incremental equation reduces to the first row entries only. Thus the load increment $r_1$ is:

$$r_1 = (R_i - a_{i2}^{(1)}\,Q_2)/a_{i1}^{(1)} \tag{7}$$

The limit state equation corresponding to this load increment is:

$$Z_i^{(1)} = r_1 - Q_1 \tag{8}$$

or

$$= (R_i - a_{i2}^{(1)}\,Q_2)/a_{i1}^{(1)} - Q_1 \tag{8a}$$

Multiplying by $a_{i1}^{(1)}$ changes both sides of the equation; since Z = 0 at the instant of failure, it is permissible to retain Z for $a_{i1}^{(1)}Z$, hence:

$$Z_i^{(1)} = R_1 - a_{12}^{(1)}Q_2 - a_{i1}^{(1)}Q_1 \tag{9}$$

In this equation, $a_{i2}^{(1)}$ (due to dead load) remains unchanged (unless the dead load changes) while $a_{i1}^{(1)}$ (due to wave load) changes as different wave load patterns are input into the analysis.

Using the limit state equations for each of the members, the safety index β for each member under different load patterns can be computed using well known methods (Melchers, 1987). For any one member, the β values can then be compared. According to equation (3), the member failure probability then corresponds to the lowest β value in this set. For consideration of the second member to fail, i.e. at stage 2, the whole matrix equation (6) is solved, yielding:

$$r_1 + r_2 = (1-\mu)\left(\frac{a_{j1}^{(2)} - a_{j1}^{(1)}}{a_{i1}^{(1)}}\right)\frac{R_1}{a_{j1}^{(2)}} + \frac{R_j}{a_{j1}^{(2)}} - \left(\frac{a_{i2}^{(1)}\,a_{j1}^{(2)} - a_{i2}^{(1)}\,a_{j1}^{(1)} + a_{j2}^{(1)}\,a_{i1}^{(1)}}{a_{i1}^{(1)}}\right) \times Q_2/a_{ji}^{(2)}$$

$$= (1-\mu)\left(\frac{a_{j1}^{(2)} - a_{j1}^{(1)}}{a_{i1}^{(1)}}\right)\frac{R_1}{a_{j1}^{(2)}} + \frac{R_j}{a_{j1}^{(2)}} - \frac{a_{i2}^{(1)}}{a_{j1}^{(2)}}\left(\frac{a_{j1}^{(2)} - a_{j1}^{(1)}}{a_{i1}^{(1)}}\right)Q_2 - \frac{a_{j2}^{(1)}}{a_{j1}^{(2)}}\,Q_2 \tag{10}$$

The appropriate limit state equation is then:

$$Z_j^{(2)} = r_1 + r_2 - Q_1$$

which becomes, on multiplying by $a_{j1}^{(2)}$:

$$Z_j^{(2)} = (1-\mu)\left(\frac{a_{j1}^{(2)} - a_{j1}^{(1)}}{a_{i1}^{(1)}}\right) R_i + R_j - a_{i2}^{(1)} \left(\frac{a_{j1}^{(2)} - a_{j1}^{(1)}}{a_{i1}^{(1)}}\right) Q_2 - a_{j2}^{(1)} Q_2 - a_{j1}^{(2)} Q_1 \qquad (11)$$

Here the term $\frac{a_{j1}^{(2)} - a_{j1}^{(1)}}{a_{i1}^{(1)}}$ represents the internal action in member j contributed by unit change of resistance of member i. As noted in Tang & Melchers (1984), this term is independent of the load selected as the incremental load. Clearly, this term is therefore also independent of the load pattern used in the present analysis. The arguments for the failure sequence to be independent of the loading selected for incrementation have been given earlier (Tang & Melchers, 1984), in essence, however, the incrementation technique is purely an artifice to generate possible failure modes. The contribution which such modes may make to the total estimate of structural failure probability depends on other considerations (see Melchers & Tang, 1984), including the actual statistics of all the loads and the member resistances. Any failure mode obtained by the incrementation procedure only has a limited probability of occurrence; as expressed generally by equation (4). In a sense, therefore, the structure at stage 2 only "records" the damage at stage 1 and not the load that caused it to happen. Again, as the loading magnitude changes, the only term that changes should be $a_{j1}^{(2)}$, assuming the load pattern at the previous stage(s) to be equal to the current one.

It follows fairly readily that it does not matter even if the loading used incrementation is changed from one load to another; and a complete cycle of loads could be used, for instance. Hence in terms of the present analysis involving cyclic wave loading, instead of using a single load pattern for the entire analysis, it would be possible at each stage of the analysis to run through the whole cycle of load patterns for each eligible member. In this way, the critical pattern can be identified for each member in turn.

EXAMPLE: A 2-dimensional truss tower modified from the spatial truss tower studied by Bjerager (1984) will be considered. It will be assumed that the member capacity is described by elastic-residual strength, without post-yield stiffness. It will also be assumed that the wave train consists of a sinusoidal pattern of given (deterministic) wave length of 350m. This corresponds to realistic storm conditions. The wave height will be the only uncertain load parameter : this has been converted to uncertainty of the loading $Q_2$, and hence to the actual loads $L_i$ shown in Fig. 1 through the relationship:

Wave Load $L_i$ = vertical variation x sinusoidal curve x peak load (12)
(a sinusoidal load profile is assumed, for convenience, in this example)

The resulting values for $L_i$ and $\sigma L_i$ are given in Table 1A and 1B, together with statistics of member resistance $R_i$ and the loadings $Q_1$ and $Q_2$. The relationships for $L_i$ corresponding to equation (12) are also shown. Note that $\phi_i$ represents the phase angle difference between joints, with joint (1) taken as the reference joint. The angle $\theta$, which varies from 0 to $\Pi$ represents the generic variable for wave height (see Fig. 2). All loads are assumed, for convenience, to act at the truss joints only.

The results from the reliability analysis are given in Tables 2 - 4. Table 2 indicates the change in bounds on the system reliability index $\beta_S$ as a function of location of the wave. It is seen that the lowest bounds on $\beta_S$ (highest nominal system failure probability) occur for $\theta$ in the range 67.5 - 90$^o$

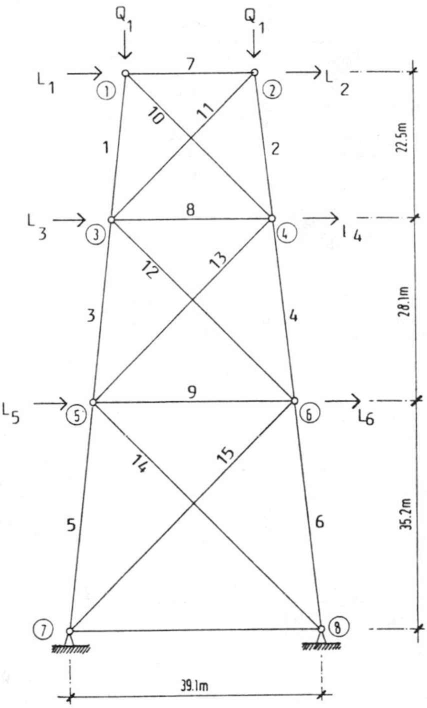


Fig. 1. Truss Tower and Wave Loading

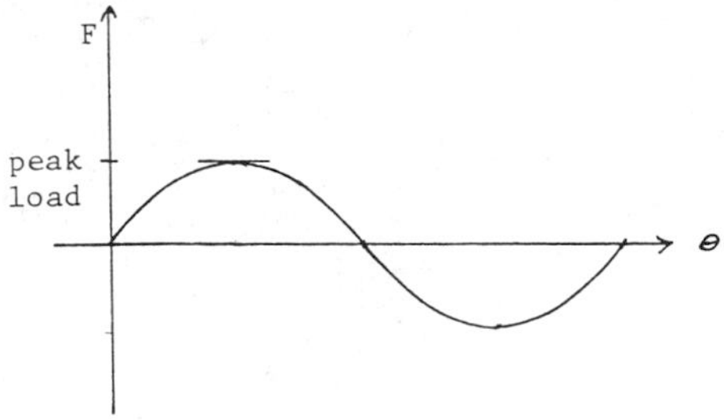


Fig. 2. Sinusoidal load profile

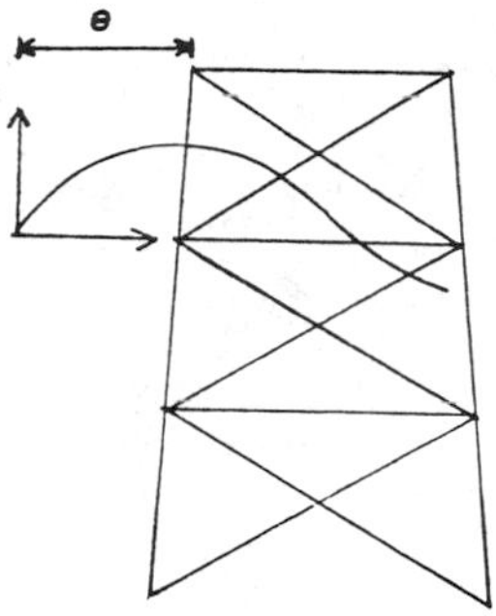


Fig. 3. Position of wave relative to structure

(see Fig. 3). This is rather greater than suggested by Murotsu et al (1984). However still lower bounds result from considering the complete cycle of loading as described in the present paper. The error for the present example is small, however, less than one percent.

Table 3 shows the most dominant modes of failure for ideal plastic behavior with an unloading factor of 0.25. It is evident that members involved in the dominant modes are those from the top two storeys. Further, in the majority of cases, only two members were required to fail to cause local structural failure. Thus the overall redundancy of 3 turns out to be largely irrelevant due to the local nature of the failures.

Finally from Table 4 it may be observed that as the individual member behavior changes from ideal plastic to partially unloaded and to elastic-brittle the bounds on the system reliability index $\beta_S$ generally diminish in value. This shows that the nominal safety of the structure is lowered considerably when a transition from plastic to brittle behavior occurs. This might happen, for example, in cold weather conditions and with metals having a rather high transition temperature.

## DISCUSSION

The system reliability analysis described herein can be applied to offshore platforms provided a realistic load model is used. The proposed wave load model is an attempt in this direction, and takes into account the movement of a wave through the structure. Improvement to the load modelling which might also be considered include the change in buoyancy due to changes in water elevation

Table 1a. Wave Load

| $\gamma_i$ | Wave load position $\theta^o$ 0 | 22.5 | 45 | 67.5 | 90 | 112.5 | 135.0 | 157.5 |
|---|---|---|---|---|---|---|---|---|
| $\gamma_1$ | 0.0 | 0.3827 | 0.7071 | 0.9239 | 1.0 | 0.9239 | 0.7071 | 0.3827 |
| $\gamma_2$ | 0.3514 | 0.6829 | 0.9105 | 0.9994 | 0.9362 | 0.7305 | 0.4136 | 0.0337 |
| $\gamma_3$ | -0.0299 | 0.2274 | 0.4500 | 0.6042 | 0.6663 | 0.6271 | 0.4923 | 0.2826 |
| $\gamma_4$ | 0.2621 | 0.4769 | 0.6190 | 0.6670 | 0.6133 | 0.4663 | 0.2484 | -0.0075 |
| $\gamma_5$ | -0.0128 | 0.0362 | 0.0796 | 0.1109 | 0.1254 | 0.1207 | 0.0977 | 0.0598 |
| $\gamma_6$ | 0.0560 | 0.0949 | 0.1194 | 0.1257 | 0.1129 | 0.0829 | 0.0402 | -0.0085 |

$\bar{L}_i = \gamma_i \bar{Q}_2$ $\qquad$ $i = 1, 6$

$\gamma_1 = \sin\theta$ $\qquad$ $\gamma_4 = 0.667 \sin(\theta+\phi_4)$

$\gamma_2 = \sin(\theta+\phi_2)$ $\qquad$ $\gamma_5 = 0.126 \sin(\theta+\phi_5)$

$\gamma_3 = 0.667 \sin(\theta+\phi_3)$ $\qquad$ $\gamma_6 = 0.126 \sin(\theta+\phi_6)$

Table 1b. Numerical data of truss tower

| Member i | $\bar{R}_i$ (kN) | Area $A_i$ ($m^2$) | Diameter $D_i$ (m) |
|---|---|---|---|
| 1 - 6 | 51890.0 | 0.324 | 2.5 |
| 7 | 8400.0 | 0.053 | 1.0 |
| 8 | 18535.0 | 0.116 | 1.5 |
| 9 | 33600.0 | 0.210 | 2.0 |
| 10 - 11 | 6675.0 | 0.042 | 0.9 |
| 12 - 13 | 11535.0 | 0.074 | 1.2 |
| 14 - 15 | 18535.0 | 0.116 | 1.5 |

Dead load = 40,000 kN $\qquad$ $Cov_{Q1} = 0.05$

Peak wave load = 278 kN $\qquad$ $Cov_{Q2} = 0.3$

$cov_{Ri}$ = 0.15 for all members

Correlation coefficients $\rho_{RiRj}$ = 0.5 for all members for member strength

Table 2. Bounds on system reliability index for various wave positions

| Wave position $\theta^o$ | Bounds on system reliability index $\beta_s$ | |
|---|---|---|
| 0 | 1.2266 | 0.9922 |
| 22.5 | 1.2240 | 0.9771 |
| 45.0 | 1.2169 | 0.9650 |
| 67.5 | 1.2066 | 0.9582 |
| 9.0 | 1.2064 | 0.9582 |
| 112.5 | 1.2163 | 0.9650 |
| 135.0 | 1.2248 | 0.9769 |
| 157.5 | 1.2278 | 0.9924 |
| Complete cycle | 1.1980 | 0.9296 |

Table 3. Dominant failure modes

| Unloading factor $\mu'$ | Failure path (member number) | | | Reliability index $\beta_s$ |
|---|---|---|---|---|
| 0 | 2 | 10 | | 1.8906 |
| | 1 | 11 | | 1.9485 |
| | 4 | 12 | | 2.1383 |
| | 4 | 13 | | 2.2227 |
| | 3 | 13 | | 2.2768 |
| | 6 | 14 | | 2.5030 |
| 0.25 | 4 | 12 | | 1.6266 |
| | 2 | 10 | | 1.6539 |
| | 3 | 13 | | 1.6851 |
| | 4 | 13 | | 1.8355 |
| | 4 | 8 | 11 | 1.8786 |
| | 4 | 8 | 10 | 1.9220 |

Table 4. Effect of unloading on system reliability index

| Unloading factor $\mu$ | Bounds on system reliability index $\beta_s$ | |
|---|---|---|
| 0 (ideal plastic) | 1.4919 | 1.4708 |
| 0.1 | 1.1399 | 0.9954 |
| 0.25 | 1.0537 | 0.8642 |
| 0.5 | 1.0277 | 0.8563 |
| 1.0 (elastic-brittle) | 1.0192 | 0.8809 |

and wave slamming. The variation in period of the wave which was ignored herein might also be considered, particularly as this would affect the degree of correlation between the loadings at different points in the structure.

As the extreme loading acting on offshore structures occurs relatively infrequently, phenomena such as low cycle fatigue, shake-down and alternating plasticity might occur for structures composed of members having plastic-type behavior. These effects have been ignored herein as has possible high cycle fatigue under lower, but more frequently occurring loading. Techniques to deal with these aspects are currently under investigation.

## CONCLUSION

A wave load model which takes into consideration a complete wave cycle has been proposed herein for integration into well developed structural system reliability analysis techniques. It is demonstrated using an example that the method produced an absolute minimum on the structural system reliability index using a reasonably realistic wave loading model. It remains to show whether this is always true. Further, it was shown that changing the member behavior from ideal plastic to elastic-brittle has a significant effect on the overall system reliability index. This indicates the importance of realistic member behavior modelling.

## REFERENCES

Bea R.G. and N.W. Lai (1978). "Hydrodynamic Loadings on Offshore Platforms", OTC Paper No 3064, Houston, Texas.

Borgman L.E. (1965). "Wave Forces on Piling for Narrow-Band Spectra". Journal of the Waterways and Harbors Division, ASCE, Vol. 91, No. WW3, pp.65-90.

Bjerager P. (1984). "Reliability Analysis of Structural Systems", Department of Structural Engineering, Technical University of Denmark, Lyngby, Denmark.

Hogben N. et al (1977). "Estimation of Fluid Loading on Offshore Structures", Proceedings I.C.E., Part 2, Vol. 63, pp.515-562.

Longuet-Higgins M.S. (1975). "On the Joint Distribution of the Periods and Amplitudes of Sea Waves". Journal of Geophysical Research, Vol. 80, No. 18, pp.2688-2694.

Melchers R.E. (1987). Structural Reliability Analysis and Prediction. Ellis Horwood/J. Wiley.

Melchers R.E. & L.K. Tang (1984). "Dominant Failure Modes in Stochastic Structural Systems". Structural Safety, Vol 2, pp.127-142.

Murotsu Y. et al (1985). "Probabilistic Collapse Analysis of Offshore Structure", 4th OMAE, Dallas.

Sarpkaya T. and M. Isaacson (1982). Mechanics of Wave Forces on Offshore Structures. Van Nostrand Reinhold.

Tang L.K. and R.E. Melchers (1984). "Reliability of Structural Systems with General Member Behaviour". Research Report No. 1, Department of Civil Engineering, Monash University.

Wiegel R.L. (1964). Oceanographical Engineering, Prentice-Hall, Englewood Cliffs, New Jersey.

ANALYSIS OF THE SAFETY OF A PRESTRESSED BOX GIRDER BRIDGE BY THE MONTECARLO TECHNIQUES

C. Floris [1]

ABSTRACT

This paper concerns the study at the third probabilistic level (CEB-CECM-FIP-IABSE-RILEM, 1978) of the safety of a simply supported box girder bridge: i.e. the probability of failure $P_{fail}$ is calculated. Since the bridge is subjected to loads normal to its axis, only the bending moment $M_S$ and the shear $V_S$ are present: as the shear span is very large, the failure is supposed to be caused only by $M_S$. Fatigue effects are disregarded.
The knowledge of the probability density functions (p.d.f.) of the external moment $M_S$ ($f_S$) and of the resisting moment $M_R$ ($f_R$) is necessary in order to calculate $P_{fail}$ : these two unknown functions are determined by the computer with a numerical simulation.
The external moment $M_S$ depends on the dead load of both box girder bridge and the vehicles on it: the event "bridge fully loaded by the vehicles" is simulated by the so-called Montecarlo Techniques (or Method). The basic random variables (r.v.), $M_S$ depends on, are the traffic composition, the type of vehicle ( car, light truck, heavy vehicle), its dead load and length and the dead load of the bridge. Some samples for the r.v. $M_S$ are generated with so large a number of realizations $n_R$ for sample as to calculate reliable values for the statistical parameters. The histograms of the samples are plotted and the mathematical function that gets the best fitting, is adopted as p.d.f. $f_S$ .
A similar way, i.e. numerical simulation with Montecarlo Techniques, is followed in order to determine $f_R$ . Finally $P_{fail}$ is calculated in consequence of the number $r$ of repetitions of the load.

## 1. NATURE OF THE PROBLEM.

The box girder of Fig.1 is given: the probability of failure $P_{fail}$ under the indicated loads must be calculated. It is assumed that :

-the influence of the shear can be disregarded owing to the large shear span;
-the bridge has constant resistance in statistical sense along its span and with a perfect positive dependence;
-the dead load is statistically constant along the span;
-the effects of the fatigue are not taken into account;

then the failure occurs when the stressing moment $M_S$ exceeds the moment of resistance $M_R$; moreover $P_{fail}$ of the bridge coincides with $P_{fail}$ of the most stressed section. $M_S$ and $M_R$ are random variables with joint probability density function $f_{RS}$ (r,s) : so $P_{fail}$ is expressed by

$$P_{fail} = P(M_R - M_S \leqslant 0) = \int_{D_f} f_{RS}(r,s) \cdot dr \cdot ds \qquad (1)$$

where $D_f$ is the failure domain with $M_R - M_S \leqslant 0$.
$M_R$ and $M_S$ are dependent r.v.: as a matter of fact $M_R$ is determined by the cross-section dimensions, that are primary variables of $M_S$ with the specific weight.But the dead load also affects the prestressing strain,on which $M_S$ depends.Should $M_R$ and $M_S$ be considered dependent, the computer program would become much involved,since a unique routine would be necessary to determine $M_R$ and $M_S$ at the same time. Moreover the statistical dependence between these variables is not well known: then $M_R$ and $M_S$ are assumed independent in

1 Department of Structural Engineering, Politecnico di Milano,Milano,Italy

order to avoid useless complications and arbitrary statements. In any case, since the bridge is precast, its cross-section dimensions have a limited variation along the span and hence a limited influence on the basic r.v.
Let $M_R$ and $M_S$ be independent r.v. : so $f_{RS}(r,s) = f_R(r) \cdot f_S(s)$. Introducing the last expression in (1), we obtain

$$P_{fail} = \int_{D_f} f_R(r) \cdot f_S(s) \cdot dr \cdot ds = \int_0^{+\infty} ds \cdot \int_0^{s} f_R(r) \cdot f_S(s) \cdot dr =$$

$$= \int_0^{+\infty} F_R(m) \cdot f_S(m) \cdot dm = \int_0^{+\infty} [1 - F_S(m)] \cdot f_R(m) \cdot dm \qquad (2),$$

where m is the common final variable of integration.
It is necessary to point out (e.g. see Freudenthal-Garrelts-Shinozuka [1966], Ferry Borges-Castanheta [1971], Migliacci[1974]) that, when the load is repeated $r$ times, the functions $f_S$ and $F_S$ become

$$f_{S,r} = r f_{S,1} \qquad (3), \qquad\qquad F_{S,r} = (F_{S,1})^r \qquad (4),$$

where $F_{S,1}$ and $f_{S,1}$ are respectively the C.D.F. and the p.d.f. for one application of the load. Subsequently $f_{S,1}$ will be determined with the Montecarlo Techniques, whilst the $r$ repetitions will be taken into account in evaluating the integral (2).

## 2. EVALUATION OF THE p.d.f. $f_S$ OF THE STRESSING MOMENT BY MONTECARLO TECHNIQUES.

A probabilistic treatise of the safety of bridges was already made by some authors: we remember Radogna-Materazzi (1983-1985) and Takaoka (1982). While the first two of them examine the failure due to the fatigue, Takaoka is interested in the problem of the ultimate limit state for bending moment: the load on the bridge is treated as a stochastic process, the autocorrelation function and the variance of which are determined by the Montecarlo Techniques. The autocorrelation function and the variance of the stress are derived starting on those of the load using the well known relation $d^2M/dx^2 = -q$. The stress is also statistically determined directly by the Montecarlo Method, disregarding the stochastic process: the results are compared and found quite in accordance to each others. In this paper the p.d.f. $f_S$ is found by omitting the stochastic characteristic

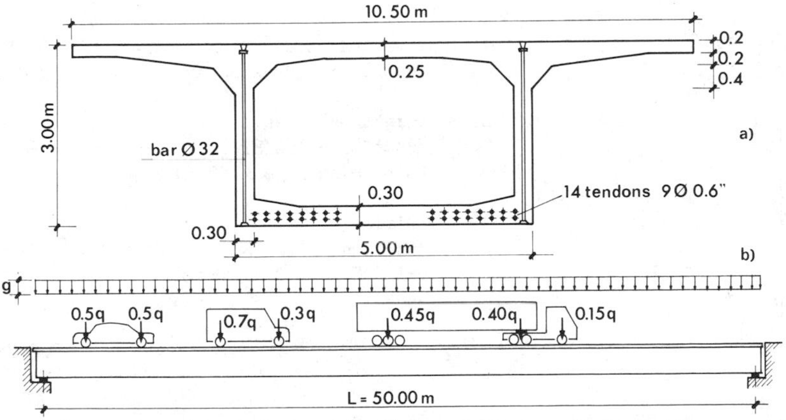


Fig.1 - a) cross-section of the box girder; b) span of the bridge; g = dead load : $\bar{g}$ = 162.59 KN/m, $\sigma_g$ = 6.25 KN/m.

of the load : as a matter of fact , if the load varies in the time really as a stochastic process, the flexural resistance of the bridge is " attacked " only a finite number of times during the structural life, since the bridge is fully loaded by the vehicles only in a discrete sequence of instants,according to the intensity and evolution of traffic. The bridges on highways surrounding Milan are fully loaded twice a day during 2 or more hours ( see ANAS, 1983 ) : in evaluating the integral (2) this fact must be taken into account, since $f_S$ will be determined for the single event " bridge fully loaded ".
Would it be possible to count and to weigh the vehicles crossing a bridge, $f_S$ could be experimentally determined, but this way is not feasible.Alternatively the event " bridge fully loaded " can be simulated by the computer: since most of the variables in question are random ones, the Montecarlo Techniques are suitable; as a matter of fact with these techniques it is possible to generate series of pseudo-random values of whatever r.v. ( see Rubinstein [ 1981 ] and Ang-Tang [1984] ).
The following r.v. are considered for the single realization of " bridge fully loaded " :

-the composition of the traffic : the first random number generated from the uniform statistics in 0 — 1 is turned into a variate for N ( 0.72, 0.12 ) , where 0.72 is the average percentage of cars and light trucks on lombard highways ( ANAS, 1983 );

-the type of the vehicle ( cars, medium weight vehicles, heavy vehicles );

-the weight $Q$ of the vehicles : three different statistics,all with truncated normal density (Fig.2), has been considered according to the data of the vehicles in Italy (ANFIA [1985], TAM [1985], TUTTOTRASPORTI [1986]). It must be emphasized that the data on loads of heavy vehicles are still widely uncertain;

-the length $l$ of the vehicles : this r.v. is assumed dependent on the r.v. $Q$. Let Q be the random value generated for the weight: thus a random number generated from the uniform statistics in 0 —— 1 is transformed for the statistics of mean $\bar{l}$ expressed by

$$\bar{l} = l_{min} + [(l_{max} - l_{min}) / (Q_{max} - Q_{min})] \cdot (Q - Q_{min}) \quad (5)$$

this statistics has a p.d.f. of normal type, but it exists only between $-\alpha\sigma$ and $\alpha\sigma$ : $\alpha$ is 1.5 for cars and medium weight vehicles, 3.0 for heavy vehicles ; the c.o.v. is respectively 0.15 for the first two cases, 0.25 for the third ; lmin and lmax are respectively 4 and 21 m for the heavy vehicles ;

-the dead load $g$ of the bridge : this statistics is assumed to be of normal

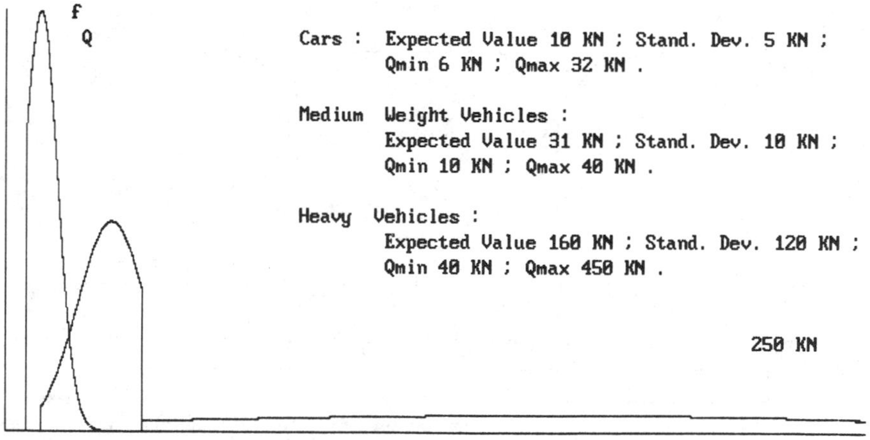


Fig.2 - Statistics of the dead load (comprehensive of surcharge) of the three different types of vehicles.

type with $\bar{g}$ and $\sigma_g$ (Fig.1) calculated according to CEB-CECM-CIB-FIP-IABSE (1971) rules on actions.

Random vehicles are generated in such a number as to fill the three lanes of the bridge and the bending moment is calculated in many cross-sections. This procedure is repeated $n_R$ times, so that a sample of $n_R$ values for the bending moment $M_S$ is generated : some sets of 5 samples are generated, each of them having equal $n_R$ ; starting from $n_R = 250$ , $n_R$ is increased so much as to reach convergence for the statistical parameters. A simple but effective criterion of convergence is adopted: for each set the mean of the mean values $\bar{M}_S$ and the mean of $\sigma_{MS}$ are calculated :

$$\bar{\bar{M}}_S = \frac{1}{5} \sum_i \bar{M}_{Si} \ , \quad \bar{\sigma}_{MS} = \frac{1}{5} \sum_i \sigma_{MSi} \ ( i= 1,5 ) \qquad (6)$$

when, for $n_R = n^*$,

$$( \bar{\bar{M}}_S - \min \bar{M}_{Si} \ , \ \max M_{Si} - \bar{\bar{M}}_S ) \leqslant ( 0.002 \div 0.003 ) \bar{\bar{M}}_S$$

$$( \bar{\sigma}_{MS} - \min \sigma_{MSi} \ , \ \max \sigma_{MSi} - \bar{\sigma}_{MS} ) \leqslant ( 0.01 \div 0.02 ) \bar{\bar{M}}_S \ , \qquad (7)$$

the convergence is reached for $\bar{M}_S$ and $\sigma_{MS}$. On achieving convergence, some sets of 5 samples, all with $n_R = n^*$, are generated : $\bar{\bar{M}}_S$ and $\bar{\sigma}_{MS}$ must be almost equal from one set to another. Moreover the coefficient of skewness $\gamma_a$ and the excess $e$ must be of the same order of greatness for all the samples of each set.

It must be noted that the midspan section is always the most stressed. The following results have been got for one of the series with $n_R = 10000$ (the others are like these) :

Table 1

| sample | - $\bar{M}_S$ (mean ; KN m) | - $\sigma_{MS}$ (KN m) | - $\gamma_a$ | - $e$ |
|---|---|---|---|---|
| 1 | - 59687.8 | - 3256.03 | - -.0395 | - -.1513 |
| 2 | - 59651.0 | - 3315.90 | - -.0105 | - -.2062 |
| 3 | - 59638.9 | - 3256.38 | - -.0010 | - -.1558 |
| 4 | - 59679.6 | - 3262.24 | - -.0171 | - -.1317 |
| 5 | - 59655.2 | - 3315.21 | - -.0044 | - -.1060 |

$\bar{\bar{M}}_S = 59662.49$ ; $\bar{\sigma}_{MS} = 3281.15$ ; $\bar{\gamma}_a = -.0145$ ; $\bar{e} = -.1502$

It is easy to verify that the conditions of convergence are all satisfied.
The histograms of the samples have been plotted (Fig.4): the curve N ($\bar{\bar{M}}_S, \bar{\sigma}_{MS}$) gives a very good fitting; in fact in a sample extracted from a normal statistics the stand. dev. of $\gamma_a$ is $\sqrt{6/n_R}$ : with $n_R = 10000$ $\sigma_{\gamma a} = .0245$, therefore the asymmetry is not statistically relevant.

## 3. DETERMINATION OF THE P.D.F. $f_R$ OF THE MOMENT OF RESISTANCE $M_R$.

The cross-section of the box girder (Fig.1) is schematized for the theoretical analysis with the double T section of Fig. 3. The relations that determine $M_R$ are as follows :

$$M_R = \int_0^{x_c} \sigma_c(\varepsilon_c) \cdot b(\xi) \cdot (h/2 - \xi) \cdot d\xi + \sigma_{sp1}(\varepsilon_{s1} + \varepsilon_{o1}) \cdot A_{sp1} \cdot ( h/2 - d_{p1}) + \sigma_{sp2}(\varepsilon_{s2} + \varepsilon_{o2}) \cdot A_{sp2} \cdot ( h/2 - d_{p2} ) \qquad (8)$$

$$\int_0^{x_c} \sigma_c(\varepsilon_c) \cdot b(\xi) \cdot d\xi - \sigma_{sp1}(\varepsilon_{s1} + \varepsilon_{o1}) \cdot A_{sp1} - \sigma_{sp2}(\varepsilon_{s2} + \varepsilon_{o2}) \cdot A_{sp2} = 0 \qquad (9)$$

$$\sigma_c = f_{cu} ( 1000\ \varepsilon_c - 250000.\ \varepsilon_c^2 ) \text{ for } 0 \leq \varepsilon_c \leq 0.002$$
$$\sigma_c = f_{cu} \qquad \text{for } 0.002 \leq \varepsilon_c \leq \varepsilon_{cu} , \qquad (10)$$

while the constitutive law for the prestressed steel is schematized by the broken curve of Fig.3 ;

$$\varepsilon_c = 0.01\xi/(h-\xi-d_{p1}) \text{ (field I Fig.3)};\ \varepsilon_{s1} = \varepsilon_{cu}(h-x_c-d_{p1})/x_c \text{ (field II)} \qquad (11).$$

Tichy and Vorlicek (1972) proved how it is impossible to evaluate the p.d.f. $f_R$ of $M_R$ starting on these relations with a development in series owing to their high nonlinearity and their expressions different from a field to another. The numerical simulation by computer with Montecarlo Techniques is again used in order to evaluate $f_R$ : some samples with $n_R$ values of $M_R$ are generated ; the procedure of this computer program and the criterion of convergence are the same as those for $M_S$ .
The basic r.v. are $f_{cu}$ (compressive strength of the concrete), $\varepsilon_{cu}$ (its ultimate compressive strain), $f_{pt}$ (tensile strength of the steel) and $\varepsilon_{su}$ (its ultimate tensile strain). $f_{cu}$ and $f_{pt}$ are the primary r.v. and are of normal type (see caption of Fig.3), whilst $\varepsilon_{cu}$ and $\varepsilon_{su}$ depend respectively on the other 2 : 4 random numbers are generated, two of which are transformed for the statistics of $f_{cu}$ and $f_{pt}$; the third into a variate for the statistics $N(\bar{\varepsilon}_{cu}, 0.08\ \bar{\varepsilon}_{cu})$, where $\bar{\varepsilon}_{cu}$ is a quadratic function of the random value extracted $f_{cu}$ (see Rüsch [1955, 1962] for this function). The fourth random number is transformed for the statistics $N(\bar{\varepsilon}_{su} , 0.08\bar{\varepsilon}_{su})$, where $\bar{\varepsilon}_{su}$ is a linear function of the extracted value $f_{pt}$ (see Munari-Piroddi [1986] for this function). The dimensions of the cross-section are deterministic as well as the prestressing, of which a reliable statistical-stochastic model is not well known. The Eq.9 is satisfied by a numerical procedure of bisection. The conditions of convergence are reached for $n_R$ = 10000; the values got for one of these series are in the table 2. Some histograms are plotted in Fig.4: as p.d.f. $f_R$ the Student's t and the log-normal have been tested; both give a good fitting.

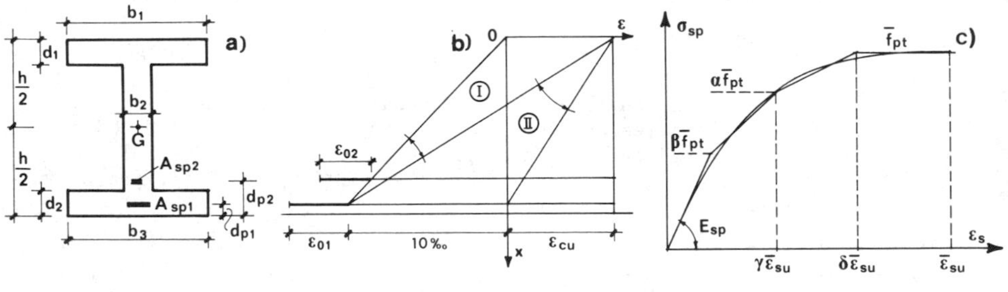


Fig.3 - a) cross-section adopted for the theoretical analysis: $b_1$ = 1050cm ; $b_2$ = 60; $b_3$ = 500; h = 300; $d_1$ = 35; $d_2$ = 30; $d_{p1}$ = 8.5; $d_{p2}$ = 20.5; $A_{sp1}$ = $A_{sp2}$ = 175.14; concrete $f_{cu}$ = 45 MPa, $\sigma_{fc}$ = 7.2 MPa.
b) failure fields: $\varepsilon_{01} = \varepsilon_{02}$ = 0.005. c) mean stress-mean strain curve for the prestressing steel : $f_{pt}$ = 1765.8 MPa, $\sigma_{fpt}$ = 141.3 MPa, $\alpha$ = .865, $\beta$ = = .757, $\gamma$ = .35, $\delta$ = .571, $E_{sp}$ = 196200. MPa.

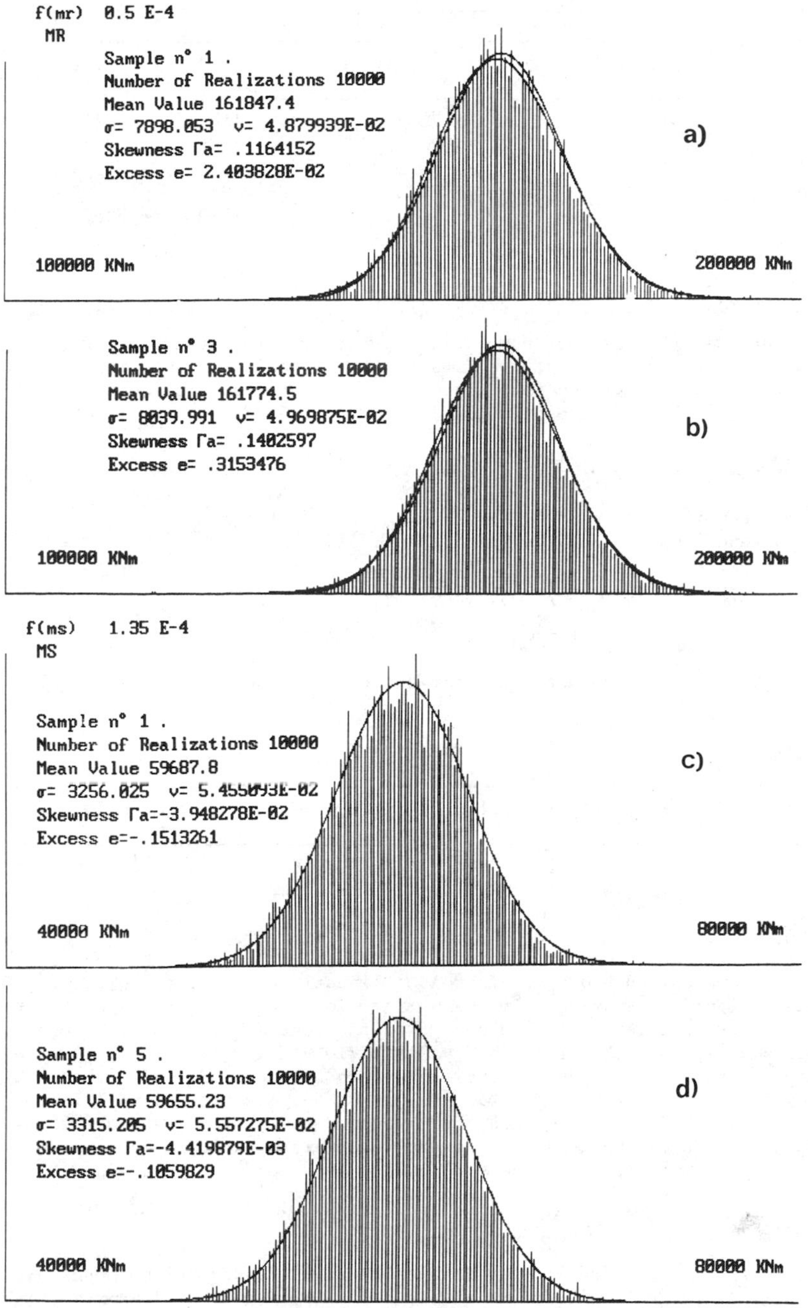


Fig.4 - Examples of histograms : a) and b) resistance with interpolating curves lognormal and Student's t (the highest); c) and d) stress with interpolating curve $N(\overline{M}_S, \overline{\sigma}_{MS})$.

Table 2

| sample | - $\bar{M}_R$ (mean; KN m) | - $\bar{\sigma}_{MR}$ (KN m) | - $\gamma_a$ | - $e$ |
|---|---|---|---|---|
| 1 | - 161847.4 | - 7898.05 | - .1164 | - .0240 |
| 2 | - 161823.6 | - 8015.96 | - .1057 | - .3404 |
| 3 | - 161774.5 | - 8039.99 | - .1403 | - .3154 |
| 4 | - 161764.4 | - 7978.15 | - .0949 | - .2108 |
| 5 | - 161741.5 | - 8044.18 | - .1570 | - .2653 |

$\bar{\bar{M}}_R$ = 161790.28 ; $\bar{\sigma}_{MR}$ = 7995.26 ; $\bar{\gamma}_a$ = .1229 ; $\bar{e}$ = 0.2312

4. CALCULATION OF THE PROBABILITY OF FAILURE $P_{fail}$. CONCLUDING REMARKS.

The integral (2) has been numerically evaluated by a suitable computer program using Simpson's formula; the first form and the Eq.4, that is only approximated, have been employed (see Freudenthal and others, Migliacci). The analytical expressions of $f_R$ are as below : for the Student's t

$$f_R\ (m) = \frac{1}{\sqrt{\pi\nu}}\ \frac{\Gamma\ (\nu\ +1/2)}{\lambda\cdot\Gamma(\nu/2)}\ \left(1 + \frac{t^2}{\nu}\right)^{-(\nu+1)/2} \tag{12}$$

where $\nu = 4 + 6/\bar{e}$, $\sigma^2_{t\nu} = \nu/\ (\nu-2)$ , $\lambda = \bar{\sigma}_{MR}\ /\sigma_{t\nu}$ , $t= (m-\bar{\bar{M}}_R)/\ \lambda$ and $\Gamma$ is the eulerian function . For the lognormal p.d.f.

$$f_R\ (m) = \frac{1}{\sqrt{2\pi}\ \zeta m}\ \exp\left[ -\frac{1}{2}\left(\frac{\ln m - \lambda}{\zeta}\right)^2\right] \tag{13},$$

where $\zeta^2 = \sigma^2_{\ln\ MR} = \ln\ (\ 1 + \bar{\sigma}^2_{MR}\ /\ \bar{\bar{M}}_R{}^2\ )$ and $\lambda = \ln \bar{\bar{M}}_R - \frac{1}{2}\ \zeta^2$

The integration has been performed for different values of $r$ : the results are here below

Table 3

| $r$ | - $P_{fail}$ ($f_R$ Student's t) | - $P_{fail}$ ($f_R$ lognormal) |
|---|---|---|
| 1 | - $1.574184 \cdot 10^{-14}$ | - $3.648886 \cdot 10^{-51}$ |
| 1000 | - $1.574184 \cdot 10^{-11}$ | - $3.648886 \cdot 10^{-48}$ |
| 10000 | - $1.574184 \cdot 10^{-10}$ | - $3.648886 \cdot 10^{-47}$ |
| 50000 | - $7.870921 \cdot 10^{-10}$ | - $1.824443 \cdot 10^{-46}$ |

It must be emphasized how $P_{fail}$ increases linearly with $r$ : the present rules for the design of the bridges impose nominal loads that do not depend quite at all on the traffic intensity and on $r$ ; on the contrary they should depend. $P_{fail}$ is much smaller than the prescribed value of $10^{-6}$ for a statically determined structure : this fact is due to the prevalence of the dead load with a small c.o.v. The lognormal p.d.f. gives incorrect values of $P_{fail}$ since its tail is too low. The author thinks that the method here proposed has proved its feasibility : only the data records of the loads of the heavy vehicles should be more precise and reliable; much work must be done for a wider knowledge of the loads.

REFERENCES

ANAS ( Italian Administration for National Roads ) (1983)."Piano Decennale della Viabilità di Grande Comunicazione : Relazione Generale", Vol.2,Roma,pp.1-40 , 177-190.

ANFIA (Italian Association between Cars Manufacturers) (1985)."Automobile in cifre", Torino.

Ang A.H.S. and W.H. Tang (1984). "Probability Concepts in Engineering Planning and Design", Vol.2, John Wiley & Sons, New York.

CEB-CECM-CIB-FIP-IABSE (1971). "Basic Notes on Actions", Bulletin CEB No.112,Paris.

CEB-CECM-CIB-FIP-IABSE-RILEM (1978)."Common Unified Rules for Different Types of Construction and Material", Vol.I, CEB, Paris.

Ferry Borges J. and M. Castanheta (1971). "Structural Safety", LNEC, Lisbon.

Freudenthal A.M., J.M. Garrelts and M. Shinozuka (1966). "The Analysis of Structural Safety", Journ. of Struct. Eng., ASCE, Vol.92, No. ST1.

Migliacci A. (1974)."Applicazione dei Principi Probabilistici alla Progettazione Strutturale", Tamburini,Milano, Chap. II-III.

Munari M. and D. Piroddi (1986)."Calcolo della Probabilità di Rovina di una Trave in C.A.P.",Graduate Thesis, Dept.of Structural Engineering, Politecnico di Milano.

Radogna E.F. and A.L. Materazzi (1983). "Considerazioni Critiche sul Problema della Sicurezza alla Fatica di Travi in Cemento Armato Parzialmente Precompresso", Trans of Spec. Conf. on Partially Prestressed Structures (L'Aquila,Italy), AICAP, pp. 318-339.

Radogna E.F. and A.L. Materazzi (1985). "Considerazioni Critiche sulla Verifica a Fatica nel Caso di Ponti in C.A. Parzialmente Precompresso", Trans. of Spec. Conf. on advanced Technologies and Researches on Prestressed Concrete (Riva del Garda,Italy), AICAP, Vol.I, pp. 355-366.

Rubinstein,R.Y. (1981)."Simulation and the Montecarlo Method", John Wiley & Sons, 1981.

Rusch H. (1955). "Versuche zur Festigkeit der Biegedruckzone", D.A.f.S., Heft 120, W. Ernst & Sohn, Berlin.

Rusch H. (1962). "Principes du Calcul du Béton Armé sous des Etats de Contraintes Monoaxiaux", in CEB-Bulletin No. 36, Paris.

Takaoka P.N. (1982). "Reliability Analysis of Highway Bridges", in "Analysis of Random Capacity of Structures", Editor J. Murzewski,Polska Akademia Nauk,Warsaw, pp. 105-135.

TAM-Tutte le Auto del Mondo (1985). Domus Editor, Milan.

Tichy M. and M. Vorliçek (1972). "Statistical Theory of Concrete Structures", Irish University Press, Shannon, pp. 223-226.

Tuttotrasporti (1986). No. 69, November,Domus Editor,Milan.

SYMBOLS

No unusual symbols have been used. The r.v. have been indicated with italic characters.

# IDENTIFICATION OF NONLINEAR STRUCTURAL SYSTEMS

Masaru Hoshiya
and
Osamu Maruyama

Department of Civil Engineering
Musashi Institute of Technology
Tokyo,Japan

**Abstract**

A method was developed to identify parameters on a hysteretic restoring system of non-degrading type by appling the Extended Kalman filter incorporated with a weighted global iteration.The method is based on a simplified versatile hysteretic model by Bouc and Wen. By this method a nonlinear model of non-degrading type equivalent to any hysteretic system may be identified in terms of the model's parameters at the stage of their stable convergency to optimal ones. Numerically simulated data were used for the verification of the method.

## 1.INTRODUCTION

This paper presents an identification method on a hysteretic restoring system by appling the Extended Kalman filter incorporated with a weighted global iteration, shortly the EK-WGI method(Hoshiya and Saito,1984,1986).By this method, a nonlinear model of non-degrading type equivalent to any hysteretic system may be identified in terms of the model's parameters, at the stage of their convergency to optimal ones after weighted global iterations of the Extended Kalman filtering. However, because of the advantage of renewing the parameters by sequentially processing observed data by the method, even general hysteresis curve of a system with deterioration in strength or stiffness or both may be traced out during the global iterations. For the numerical verification, a single degree of freedom hysteretic system was employed and the parameters were identified by using data simulated on responses of the known system.

## 2.STATE VECTOR FORMULATION IN IDENTIFICATION

For the EK-WGI method to be applied to system identification problems, a set of the state vector equation and observation equation must be properly formulated. The equivalent nonlinear model under the present study is a single degree of freedom hysteretic system represented by

$$\ddot{u}(t)+2h_o\omega_o\dot{u}(t)+\omega_o^2\Phi(u(t))=-\ddot{f}(t) \qquad (1)$$

$$\dot{\Phi}(u(t))=A\dot{u}(t)-\beta|\dot{u}(t)||\Phi(u(t))|^{n-1}\Phi(u(t))-\gamma\dot{u}(t)|\Phi(u(t))|^{n} \qquad (2)$$

where $\ddot{f}(t)$=input excitation, ho = fraction of critical viscous damping for small amplitudes,$\omega_o$ =undamped natural circular frequency of small amplitude response(=pre-yielding natural circular frequency)

Equation(2) is a non-degrading restoring force model simplified from a versatile model proposed by Bouc and Wen (Bouc,1967;Wen,1981), and the parameters A,$\beta$,$\gamma$ and n govern the amplitude, shape of the hysteretic restoring force characteristic and transition from elastic to inelastic ranges.

Equations(1) and (2) are put into a state vector representation by introducing the state variables $X_1=u(t)$,$X_2=\dot{u}(t)$,$X_3=\Phi(u(t))$, $X_4=ho$, $X_5=\omega o$, $X_6=\beta$ ,$X_7=\gamma$ and $X_8=A$:

$$\begin{bmatrix}\dot{X}_1\\ \dot{X}_2\\ \dot{X}_3\\ \dot{X}_4\\ \dot{X}_5\\ \dot{X}_6\\ \dot{X}_7\\ \dot{X}_8\end{bmatrix} = \begin{bmatrix} X_2\\ -2.0*X_4*X_5*X_2-X_5^2*X_3-\ddot{f}(t)\\ X_8*X_2-X_6*X_2*X_3^{n-1}*X_3-X_7*X_2*X_3^n\\ 0\\ 0\\ 0\\ 0\\ 0\end{bmatrix} \tag{3}$$

If observation data for the response displacement u(t) and the response velocity $\dot{u}(t)$ are available, the observation vector equation is given by

$$\begin{bmatrix}Y_1\\ Y_2\end{bmatrix} = \begin{bmatrix}1,0,0,0,0,0,0,0\\ 0,1,0,0,0,0,0,0\end{bmatrix}\mathbf{X} + \mathbf{V} \tag{4}$$

where **V** is a noise vector of zero mean, white Gaussian processes with the covariance, $E[\mathbf{V}(tk)*\mathbf{V}^T(tj)]=\mathbf{R}(k)\delta kj$, and $\delta kj$ is the Kronecker delta.

The identification by the EK-WGI method is based on eqs(3) and (4), and if observation response data and input excitation are given to the EK-WGI algorithm, an unknown system may be identified within the scope of the equivalent model by eqs(1) and (2).

The brief outline of the EK-WGI method is that if the initial state vector $\hat{X}(to/to)$ and error covariance matrix P(to/to) are given, then as the observation data Y(t) are processed, it is possible to estimate the state vector $\hat{X}(tk/tk)$ and the error covariance P(tk/tk) by the iterative calculation of the Extended Kalman filter. For a stable estimation, the weighted global iteration of the algorithm is necessary. The detail of the EK-WGI method is given in References(Hoshiya and Saito, 1984,1986, and Hoshiya and Maruyama,1986).

It is noted that the state variables $X_4$ to $X_8$ are the parameters to be identified in this study. Regarding the parameter n appeared in eq(3), it is to be treated as a predetermined constant value for the range of 1 to 10 sacrificing to some degree the accuracy of an equivalent modelling.

## 3.NUMERICAL VERIFICATION OF IDENTIFICATION METHOD

In order to verify the method of identifing parameters for the simplified versatile hysteretic restoring model by eqs(1) and (2), and to investigate the potentiality of the method incorporated with the EK-WGI procedure in the study of elucidating nonlinear characteristics of structural systems, numerical analyses were carried out with observed data which were simulated on the responses of a known hysteretic system.

The system was a single degree of freedom bilinear hysteretic system with the undamped natural circular frequency of small amplitude responses ωo of 7.07 rad/sec, the ratio of post-yielding stiffness to pre-yielding stiffness α of 0.4 and the yielding displacement Ue of 2.5 cm. The viscous damping term of the coefficient ho of 0.1 was also considered in the system.

The responses of this system were evaluated at a discrete time of 0.01 sec due to an Imperial Valley Acceleration record of the maximum value of 213.1 gal and of the time duration of 30 sec.

Figure 1 shows the input and output time histories as well as the hysteretic restoring force characteristic of the system. In the identification analyses, the displacement and velocity responses were used as observation data. For this known system, the stability and convergency of estimated parameters and hysteretic behavior of the system could be correctly examined.

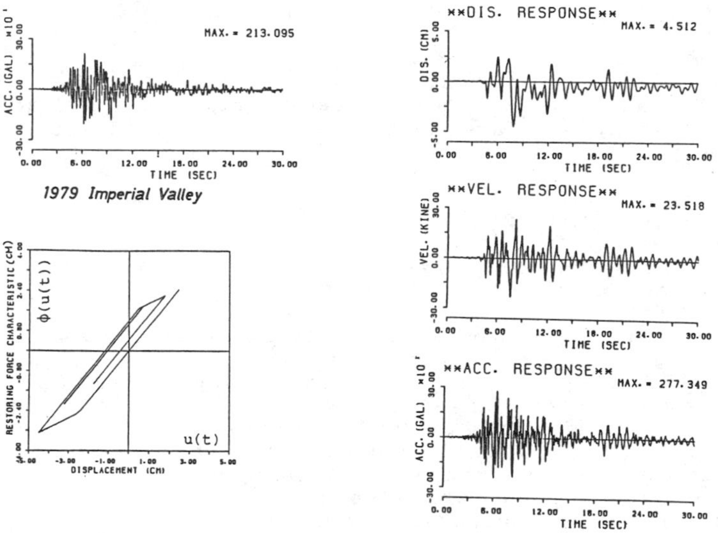


Figure 1. Input and Observation Data

The identification procedure was divided into two stages. At the first stage, the parameters ωo and ho were identified using the first portion of 4 sec duration of the observation data on the assumption that the responses were linear during the initial stage of oscillation. Thus, predeterming $X_6(=\beta)=0.0$, $X_7(=\gamma)=0.0$ and $X_8(A=1.0)$ for the linear characteristic of the hysteretic model of eq(2), the parameters $X_4$(=ho) and $X_5$(=ωo) were identified. The initial conditions for this analysis are given in Table 1.

Table 1. Initial Condition for Linear Model

| Initial Conditions | $X_1$ | $X_2$ | $X_3$ | $X_4$(ho) | $X_5$(ωo) |
|---|---|---|---|---|---|
| $\hat{X}$(to/to) | 0.0 | 0.0 | 0.0 | 0.5 | 5.0 |
| P(to/to) | 1.0 | 1.0 | 1.0 | 100.0 | 100.0 |

Note: Covariance of **V**=100.0

The results are shown in Figures 2 and 3 where we find that the coefficient of viscous damping $X_4$(=ho) and the natural circular frequency $X_5$(=ωo) were stably estimated at the first iteration by the EK-WGI procedure. It was also found that the results were invariant as the number of the global iterations increased, where the weight of 100 was used in the global iterations.

Figure 3 shows the variational trends of each parameter at the first iteration and the fifth iteration respectively.

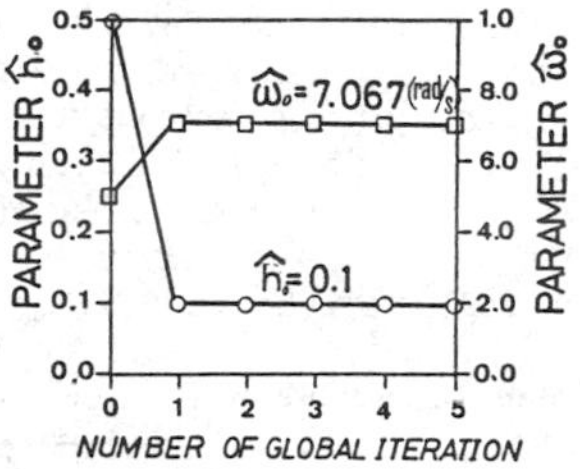


Figure 2. Convergency Process in Number of Iterations

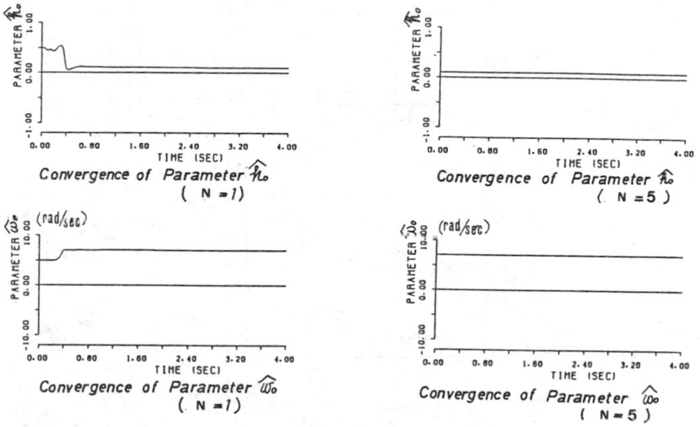


Note: N =Number of Global Iterations

Figure 3. Convergency Process in Single Iteration

For the second stage of identification procedure, the identified values at the first stage 0.1 and 7.067 rad/sec respectively for $X_4$ and $X_5$ were fixed, and the parameters $X_6$(=β ), $X_7$(=γ ) and $X_8$(=A) which govern the hysteresis were estimated for the initial conditions; $\hat{X}_6$(to/to)=0.0, $\hat{X}_7$(to/to)=0.0 and $\hat{X}_8$(to/to)=1.0. The values of covariances involved in the observation vector equation and of the error covariances were same as in the first stage.

Figures 4 to 6 show the results. In Figure 4, the first column shows the known hysteretic behaviors at each period in the proceeding order. The second and third columns show the corresponding estimated behaviors in the first iteration and the tenth iteration respectively, where the parameter n of the model was taken as n=5.

Figure 5 shows how the convergency is attained by means of number of the weighted global iterations.

Figure 6 shows the convergency processes in detail of parameters at the first and tenth iterations respectively.

It was found that the identification of the hysteretic restoring force characteristics was successfully obtained within the scope of an equivalent nonlinearity to the given system (Figure 4). It should be easily conceivable that the identification procedure could also be applied to even a system of degrading type, which was not the case in the present analyses, since the procedure was essentially a method of sequential least squares estimation on parameters and therefore upon the change of the system,parameters to be estimated may be adapted and transfered to true values as data are processed(Figure 6).

It is also encouraging to note the first few iterations were sufficient for this analyses(Figures 5 and 6).

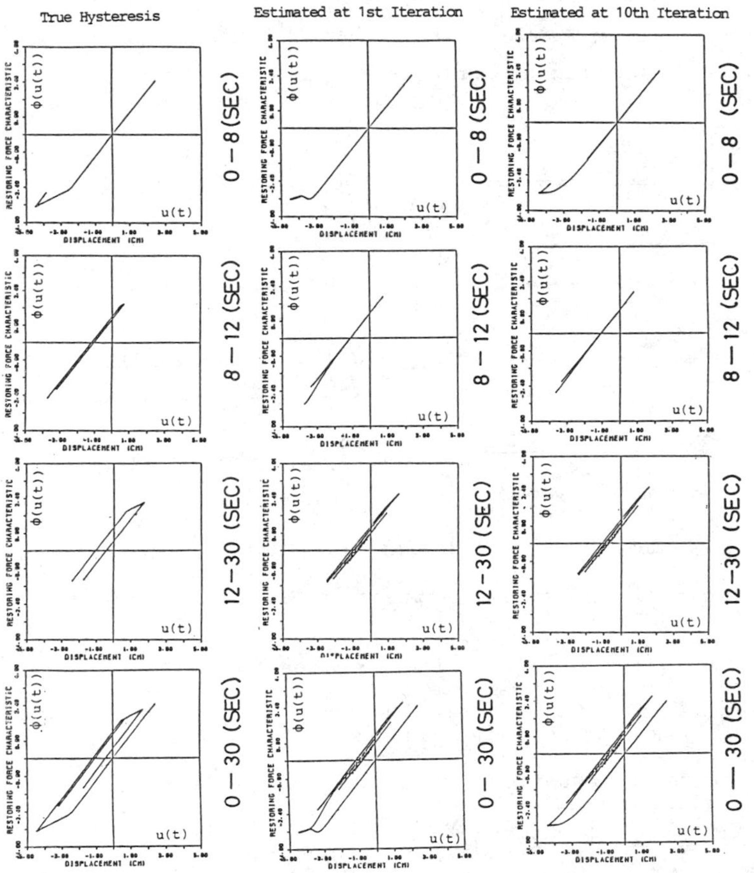


Figure 4. Estimated Hysteresis Restoring force Characteristics

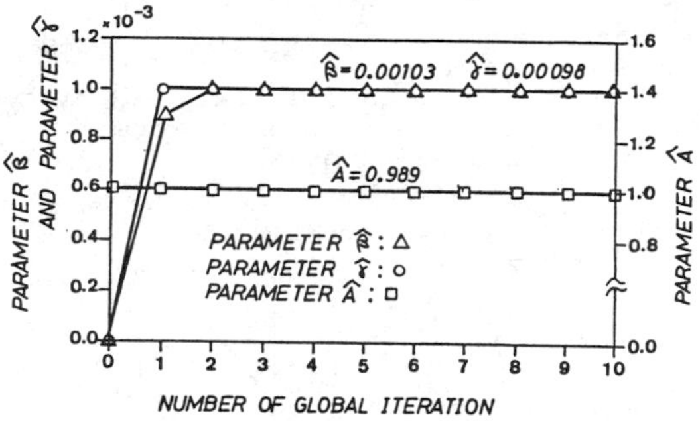


Figure 5. Convergency Process in Number of Iterations

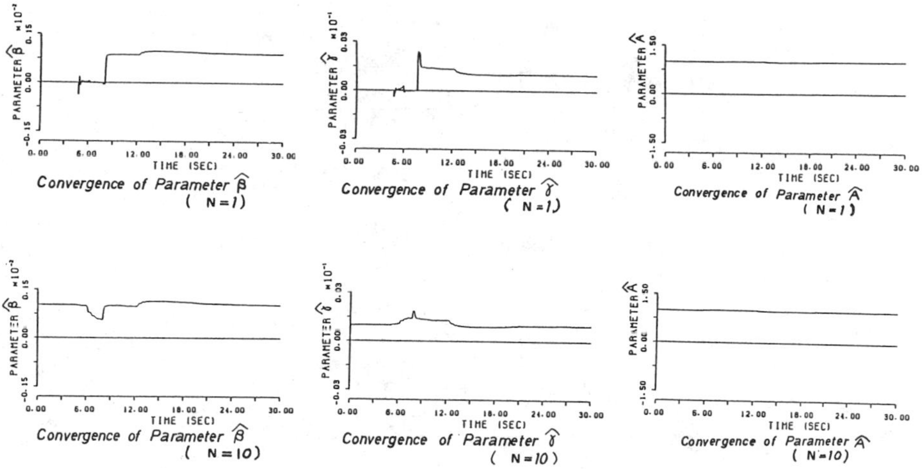


Figure 6. Convergency Process in Single Iteration

In order to further discern the results, response analysis was performed for a system having the following identified parameter values;ho=0.1, $\omega o$ =7.067 rad/sec, $\beta$=0.00103, $\gamma$=0.00098, A=0.989 and n=5.

It is clear form Figure 7 that each response time history in the second column of Figure 7 was almost identically realized corresponding to the true one in the first column respectively. When the amplitude of the excitation time history was reduced to the half of the original one, responses on the same system were obtained as in Figure 8. On the other hand, for the twice amplified excitation time history, the results were obtained in Figure 9.

Figure 8 shows linear responses because of the small amplitude of the excitation as expected, whereas for the stronger excitation, the hysteretic behavior was estimated largely different from the true hysteresis in Figure 9. This large difference is due to the fixed value of n.

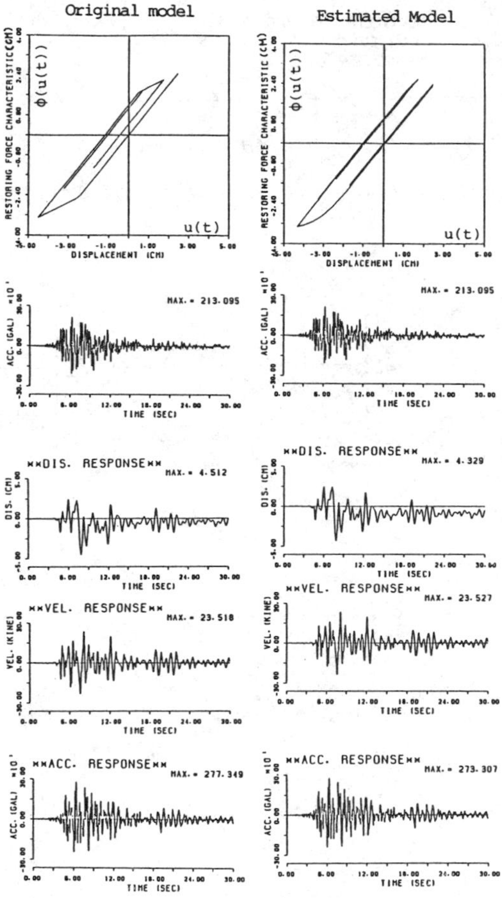


Figure 7. Responses in Comparison

## 4. CONCLUSIONS

An identification procedure is proposed for a hysteretic restoring system by using the Extended Kalman filter with weighted global iterations. The identification is based on a set of a properly formulated state vector equation and an observation vector equation which stem from the versatile hysteretic restoring model by Bouc and Wen.

It is found from numerical analyses that (1) by

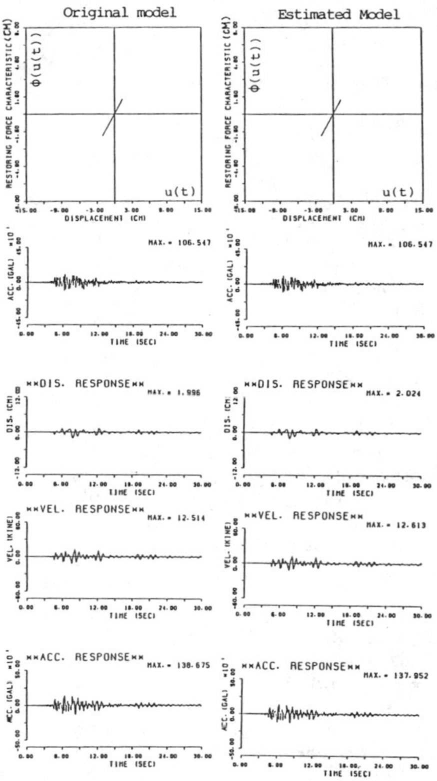


Figure 8. Responses in Comparison
(0.5*original input excitation)

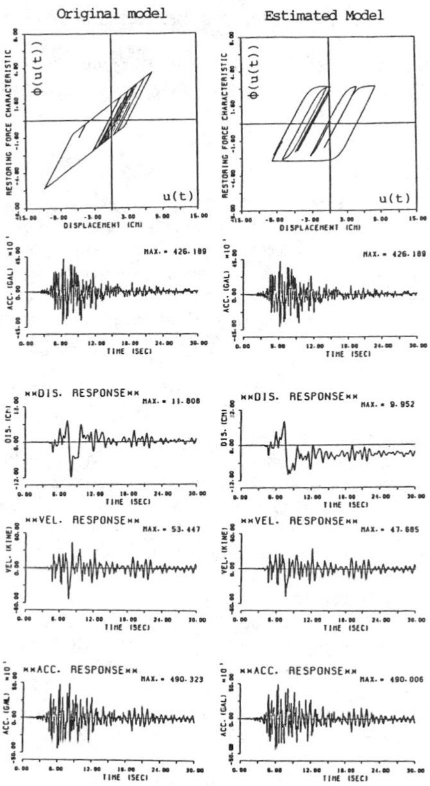


Figure 9. Responses in Comparison
(2*original input excitation)

the identification procedure, we may estimate properly the hysteretic restoring force characteristic of a nonlinear system, since parameters to be estimated catch up adaptively with the varying true values as the identification is proceeded, and (2) an equivalent hysteretic model may be properly identified to an unknown system by employing estimated parameter values when they are in convergency after the weighted global iterations.

## 5.REFERENCES

Baber,T.T.,and Wen,Y.K.,(1981),Random Vibration of Hysteretic Degrading System,Jour. of Eng. Mech.,Vol.107,No.EM6,ASCE.

Bouc,R.,(1967),Forced Vibration of Mechanical System with Hysteresis,Proceedings of the Fourth Conference on Nonlinear Oscillation (Abstract),Prague,Czechoslovakia.

Hoshiya,M., and Maruyama,O.,Identification of a Running Load and Beam System,Jour. of Eng. Mech.,ASCE,(to be appeared)

Hoshiya,M., and Saito,E.,(1984),Structural Identification by Extended Kalman Filter,Jour. of Eng. Mech.,Vol.110,No.12,ASCE.

Hoshiya,M.,and Saito,E.,(1986),Linearized Liquefaction Process by Kalman Filter, Jour.of Geotech.Eng.,Vol.112,No.2,ASCE.

# RELIABILITY ANALYSIS OF DAMAGED STRUCTURES

Naruhito Shiraishi* and Hitoshi Furuta*
*Department of Civil Engineering, Kyoto University, Kyoto 606, Japan

## ABSTRACT

In order to establish an appropriate maintenance program, it is necessary to evaluate the reliability of existing structures. However, the estimation of their damage states, which is inevitable in the reliability assessment, may not be carried out in a clear manner due to various uncertainties and ambiguities. Some uncertainties are not random in nature, and even if others are random, they may not be handled by means of random variables because of lack of statistical data available.

In this paper, an attempt is made to apply the concept of fuzzy sets theory to the reliability analysis of damaged structures. Damage states are represented in terms of fuzzy sets which define several linguistic variables such as "severely damaged", "moderately damaged", "slightly damaged", etc. Information regarding the damage states can be introduced in the formulation of reliability analysis of damaged structures, by coupling with the PNET method proposed by Ang and Ma. Several numerical examples are presented to illustrate the method proposed herein.

## INTRODUCTION

Catastrophic failures of civil engineering structures should be avoided because they could induce a great deal of social, economic and human losses. In order to minimize the potential of catastrophic failures, daily maintenance is important and inevitable. For establishing an appropriate maintenance and repair program, it is necessary to evaluate the reliability of the existing structures, most of which are suffered from damage resulting from corrosions, cracks and other types of deterioration (Yao, 1979, 1982; Frangopol, 1986; Gorman and Moses, 1981). However, the reliability analysis of damaged structures is not an easy task due to the lack of statistical data available and the difficulties in the estimation of damage states of the structure under consideration (Yao, 1985; Shiraishi, Furuta and Sugimoto, 1986; Shiraishi and Furuta, 1986).

On account of these reasons, usual evaluation on the reliability of the existing structures has been performed based on the engineering judgment and intuition of experienced engineers. Although this method is simple and reliable, it has no theoretical basis and no consistency between underlying structures. These problems should be examined from a logical point of view.

In this paper, an attempt is made to derive a simple but well-grounded method for assessing the reliability of damaged structures. The damage states are defined in terms of linguistic variables which are specified by fuzzy sets (Zadeh, 1965, 1975). By using a reduction factor, information regarding the damage states is introduced in the calculation procedure of failure probability. Since the reduction factor is also expressed by a fuzzy set, the failure probability obtained becomes a fuzzy set. This provides a more useful insight for the evaluation of the toughness of each member to damage and the effect of damage grades on the change of dominant failure modes. Emphasis is placed on the redundant structures, because the relationship between the damage grades and the dominant failure modes can be considered important from the practical design point of view. Several numerical examples are presented to illustrate and demonstrate the applicability of the method developed herein.

## RELIABILITY ANALYSIS OF DAMAGED STRUCTURES

As the information sources available in the damage assessment, the followings are considered; 1) design documents or drawings, 2) visual inspections, 3) field testing, 4) laboratory testing, and 5) structural analysis (Yao and Furuta, 1986). However, all the above information cannot be used due to the lack of budget or money. Actual daily maintenance work is carried out on the basis of intuition and engineering judgment of experienced inspectors. Namely, their judgment may possibly be derived through their subjective feelings and insufficient vague data obtained from the limited inquiries.

In this paper, an attempt is made to apply the concept of fuzzy sets theory (Zadeh, 1965) so as to introduce the subjective assessment of engineers into the reliability analysis. Damage states of structures are evaluated by a linguistic variable among "very severe", "severe", "moderate", "slight", and "very slight". These linguistic evaluations are represented by reduction factors which are defined by fuzzy sets as shown in Fig. 1. In Fig. 1, the abscissa u shows u=1 denoting no damage and u=0 denoting failure. For simplicity, the shape of membership functions are assumed to be triangular. When the damage state can be estimated with accuracy, it becomes sharp, otherwise it becomes flat.

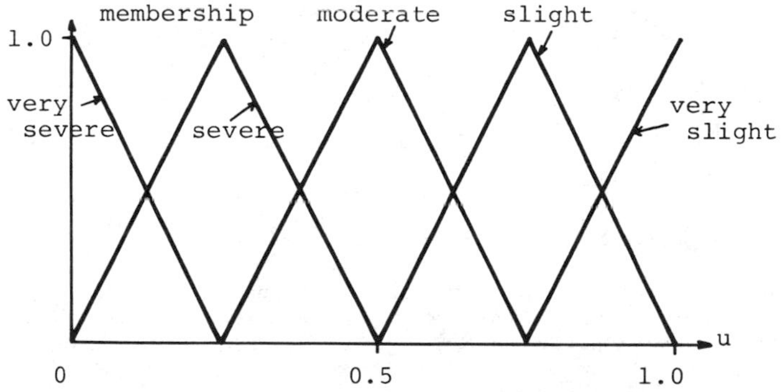


Fig. 1 Membership Functions for Linguistic Evaluations

Suppose that damage does not affect load effect S but member resistance R. Then, safety margin Z is written as

$$\tilde{Z} = \tilde{\phi} R - S \tag{1}$$

where $\tilde{\phi}$ is a reduction factor defined by a fuzzy set (Blockley, 1980; Brown, Furuta, Shiraishi and Yao, 1987). It is noted that the safety margin Z in Eq. 1 is a fuzzy quantity because $\tilde{\phi}$ is a fuzzy quantity. Assuming that R and S are statistically independent and normally distributed, respectively, safety index $\beta$ is calculated as

$$\tilde{\beta} = \frac{\tilde{\phi}\, \mu(R) - \mu(S)}{\sqrt{\tilde{\phi}^2 \sigma(R)^2 + \sigma(S)^2}} \tag{2}$$

Then, the failure probability $p_f$ is obtained as follows:

$$\tilde{p}f = \Phi(-\tilde{\beta}) \quad (3)$$

where $\mu(R)$, $\mu(S)$, $\sigma(R)$, and $\sigma(S)$ are the mean values and standard deviations of R and S, respectively. It should be noted that both $\tilde{\beta}$ and $\tilde{p}f$ in Eqs. 2 and 3 are obtained as fuzzy quantities so that usual arithmetic operations can be no longer used for these calculations. Here, a calculating method called "extension principle" (Dubois and Prade, 1980) is employed for the implementation of Eqs. 2 and 3.

In order to obtain a new quantity $\tilde{C}$ from $\tilde{A}$ and $\tilde{B}$ through the following operation

$$\tilde{C} = f(\tilde{A}, \tilde{B}) \quad (4)$$

the membership function of $\tilde{C}$ is calculated as follows, based on the extension principle.

$$\chi(C)[z] = \sup_{z=f(x,y)} \min(\chi(A)[x], \chi(B)[y]) \quad (5)$$

Although this principle is conceptually applicable to all cases including continuous and discrete variables, its implementation is not easy even if we use a digital computer. Therefore, we utilize an approximate calculation of L and R functions developed by Dubois and Prade (1979).

Representative arithmetic operations are shown as follows:

$$\oplus\ ;\ (m,\alpha,\beta) \oplus (n,\gamma,\delta) = (m+n, \alpha+\gamma, \beta+\delta) \quad (6)$$

$$\ominus\ ;\ (m,\alpha,\beta) \ominus (n,\gamma,\delta) = (m-n, \alpha+\delta, \beta+\gamma) \quad (7)$$

$$\odot\ ;\ (m,\alpha,\beta) \odot (n,\gamma,\delta) = (mn, m\gamma+n\alpha, m\delta+n\beta) \quad (8)$$

$$\oslash\ ;\ (m,\alpha,\beta) \oslash (n,\gamma,\delta) = (m/n, (m\delta+n\alpha)/n^2, (m\gamma+n\beta)/n^2) \quad (9)$$

The symbols $\oplus$, $\ominus$, $\odot$ and $\oslash$ correspond to the usual operations of +, −, • and ÷, respectively. In the above expressions, a fuzzy quantity is expressed by three parameters, for instance, m , $\alpha$ and $\beta$ denote the central value, the scatters of left hand side and right hand side, respectively. Using the expression of L and R functions, any membership function can be defined as follows:

$$\chi(x) = \begin{cases} L((m-x)/\alpha) & \text{for } x \leq m,\ \alpha > 0 \quad (10) \\ R((x-m)/\beta) & \text{for } x \geq m,\ \beta > 0 \quad (11) \end{cases}$$

In order to calculate Eq. 2, it is necessary to newly define the operation of square. Here, we derive the following formula for this operation on the basis of L and R functions (Dubois and Prade, 1979).

$$\textcircled{\surd};\ \sqrt{(m,\alpha,\beta)} \cong (\sqrt{m},\ \alpha/2\sqrt{m},\ \beta/2\sqrt{m}) \quad (12)$$

It is noted that the above formula can be applied for the case with the same-shaped membership functions.

**CALCULATION OF SYSTEM FAILURE PROBABILITY**

Supposing that structural resistance M(j) (j=1, 2,•••••,m) and load effect S(j) (j=1,2,•••••,k) are statistically independent and normally distributed, the safety margin Z(i) of the i-th failure mode is calculated as a normal variable with the mean value μ(Zi), standard deviation σ(Zi) and covariance σ(ZiZj).

$$\mu(Zi) = \sum_{j=1}^{m} a(ij)\,\mu(Mj) - \sum_{j=1}^{l} b(ij)\,\mu(Sj) \quad (i=1,\cdots,n) \tag{13}$$

$$\sigma(Zi)^2 = \sum_{j=1}^{m} a(ij)^2\,\sigma(Mj)^2 + \sum_{j=1}^{l} b(ij)^2\,\sigma(ij)^2 \quad (i=1,\cdots,n) \tag{14}$$

$$\sigma(ZiZj) = \sum_{k=1}^{m} a(ik)a(jk)\,\sigma(Mk)^2 + \sum_{j=1}^{l} b(ik)b(jk)\,\sigma(Sj)^2 \quad (i,j=1,2,\cdots,n;\ i \neq j) \tag{15}$$

Then, the failure probability of the i-th failure mode is calculated similar to Eq. 3.

$$Pfi = \Phi\,(-\mu(Zi)/\,\sigma(Zi)) \tag{16}$$

If a structure is damaged to some extent, Eqs. 14 through 16 can be rewritten as

$$\mu(Zi) = \sum_{j=1}^{ml} \phi\, a(ij)\,\mu(Mj) + \sum_{j=ml+1}^{m} \mu(Mj) - \sum_{j=1}^{l} b(ij)\,\mu(Sj) \tag{17}$$

$$\sigma(Zi)^2 = \sum_{j-1}^{ml} a(ij)^2\,\phi_j^2\,\sigma(Mj)^2 + \sum_{j=ml+1}^{m} a(ij)^2\sigma(Mj)^2 + \sum_{j=1}^{l} b(ij)^2\,\sigma(Sj)^2 \tag{18}$$

$$\sigma(ZiZj) = \sum_{k=1}^{ml} a(ik)a(jk)\,\phi_i\,\phi_j\,\sigma(Mk)^2 + \sum_{j=1}^{l} b(ik)b(jk)\,\sigma(Sj)^2 \tag{19}$$

where m(1) is the number of portions with damage which possibly yield plastic hinges.

The system failure probability of damaged structures is calculated herein using the PNET method proposed by Ang and Ma (1981). However, the PNET method cannot be directly used for the underlying case, because the mean value and variance are given in terms of fuzzy quantities. Here, we attempt to extend the PNET method so as to treat the fuzzy quantities. As mentioned before, pf is represented here in terms of a fuzzy set. For two fuzzy numbers, it is sometimes difficult to determine which number is larger, because fuzzy numbers possess scatters around the central values (Buckley, 1985). Fig. 2 is useful to understand this phenomena. Fig. 2(a) shows that a fuzzy number $\tilde{A}$ is clearly larger than the other fuzzy number $\tilde{B}$, while Fig. 2(b) shows that they have no definite difference. In order to order the fuzzy failure probabilities, three calculating methods are presented herein:

<u>Method 1</u>

In this method, the ordering is carried out by paying attention to their central values. The failure probabilities being less than 10**-6 is not considered in the calculation. The coefficients of correlation are also treated similar to the failure probabilities. This method may provide the same result as that by the usual PNET method.

<u>Method 2</u>

In this method the ordering is performed by paying attention to the sharpness of the membership functions of failure probabilities. The

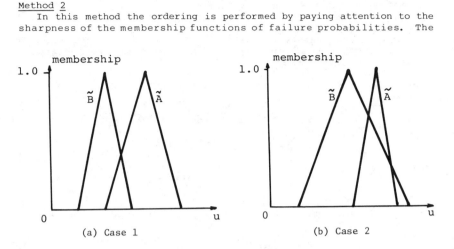

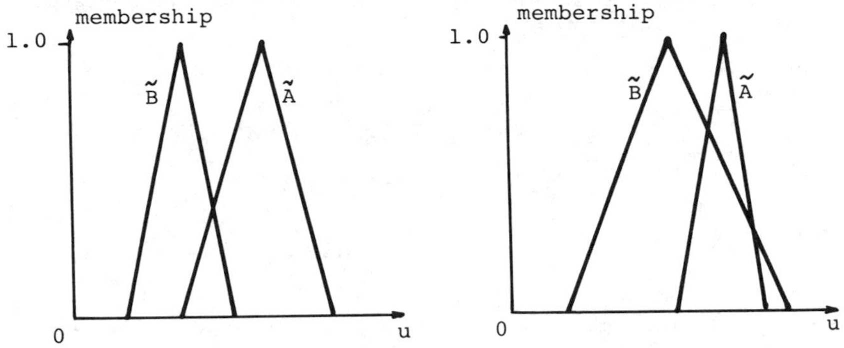


(a) Case 1 (b) Case 2

Fig. 2 Comparisons of Two Fuzzy Numbers

objective of this method is to minimize the ambiguity involved in the estimation of system failure probability. Also, in this method the failure probabilities less than 10**-6 is not considered in the calculation. In the PNET method, possible failure modes are classified into uncorrelated failure modes and correlated failure modes, by comparing their coefficients of correlation $\rho$(ij) with the prescribed value $\rho$(0). $\rho$(ij) is the coefficient of correlation between the i-th and j-th failure modes. In this method, this classification is performed as follows:

Let the minimum values, central values and maximum values of $\tilde{\rho}$(0) and $\tilde{\rho}$(ij) be a and A, b and B, and c and C, respectively. Then, the i-th and j-th failure modes are considered perfectly dependent, if one of the following conditions is satisfied.

1) a $\leq$ A and c $\geq$ C
2) c $\leq$ A
3) a $\leq$ A < c and c < C.

Otherwise, they are considered perfectly independent.

<u>Method 3</u>

In the calculation of the system failure probability, failure modes having the failure probabilities with large right-hand side scatters are considered to be important. This method provides the result in which the ambiguity involved in the region of large values of failure probabilities is emphasized. Similar to Method 2, the classification of failure modes are done as follows:

The i-th and j-th modes are dependent if either condition is satisfied.

1) c < A
2) a > A and c < C
3) a $\leq$ A < and c < C
4) a = A and c = C.

Otherwise, they are independent.

**NUMERICAL EXAMPLES**

As examples, consider a portal frame and a two-story one-bay frame which are shown in Fig. 3 and Fig. 4, respectively. Statistical data are given in Table 1 and Table 2. Their damage patterns considered here are presented in Fig. 5 and Fig. 6. For both examples, $\tilde{\Phi}=0.75$ is employed as a reduction factor. (see Fig. 7) Fig. 8 and Fig. 9 present the results obtained by Method 1, Method 2 and Method 3. In Fig. 8, it is seen that Method 1 and Method 3 give the same result. This is why the portal frame has a few possible failure modes so that there is no difference between these two methods. On the contrary, they provide different results for the two-story frame, as shown in Fig. 9. This means that the two-story frame has sufficient number of failure modes. Comparing the results obtained by Method 2 and Method 3, it is understood that Method 2 presents the system failure probability whose membership function is sharp, while Method 3 presents the system failure probability whose membership function has a large scatter in the right-hand side of the central value.

From these results, it is concluded that Method 2 is appropriate to accurately estimate the failure probability and Method 3 is suitable to estimate the safety of important structures, because this method can cover all possible effects induced by the damage states considered.

Table 1 Statistical Data for Portal Frame

| i | L(m) | R(N m) | S(N) |
|---|---|---|---|
| 1 | 15.0 | 326.431 | 45.0 |
| 2 | 15.0 | 649.708 | 45.0 |
| 3 | 20.0 | 351.616 | 60.0 |
| 4 | 20.0 | 689.707 | 60.0 |

C.O.V. of R = 0.05
C.O.V. of S = 0.2

Table 2 Statistical Data for Two-Story Frame

| | $\mu$ | $\sigma$ | C.O.V. |
|---|---|---|---|
| Mi | 40.0(N•cm) | 8.0(N•cm) | 0.2 |
| H | 0.5(N) | 0.1(N) | 0.2 |
| P | 1.0(N) | 0.2(N) | 0.2 |

i=1,2,••••••,7; L=100 cm

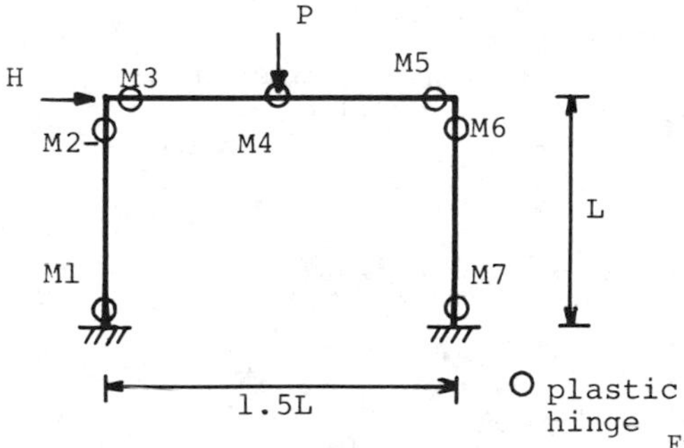


Fig. 3 Portal Frame

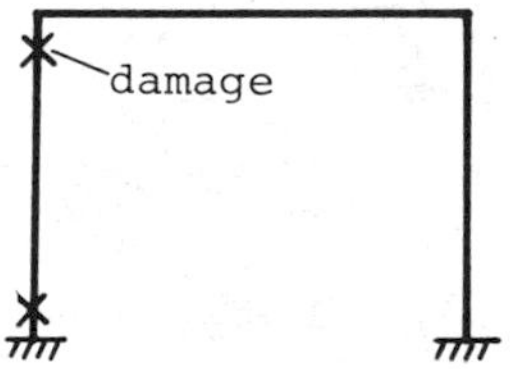


Fig. 5 Damage State of Portal Frame

**SUMMARY AND CONCLUSIONS**

When a structure is damaged, its dominant failure modes may change. Namely, the grade, location and cause of damages greatly affect the overall safety of the structure. However, their accurate estimation is very difficult due to the various constraints. Under the situation, it may be better to accept a vague or imprecise evaluation as a practical and meaningful basis for the safety assessment of the damaged

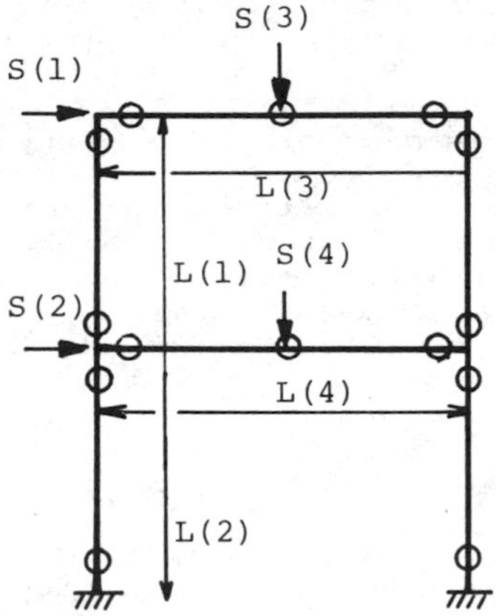


Fig. 4 Two-Story One-Bay Frame

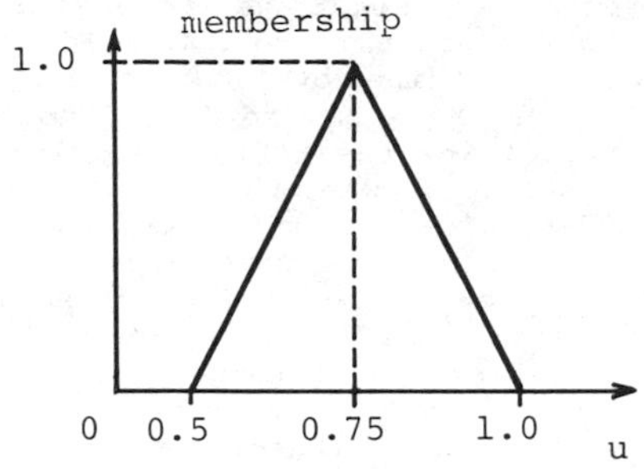


Fig. 7 Reduction Factor $\phi$=0.75

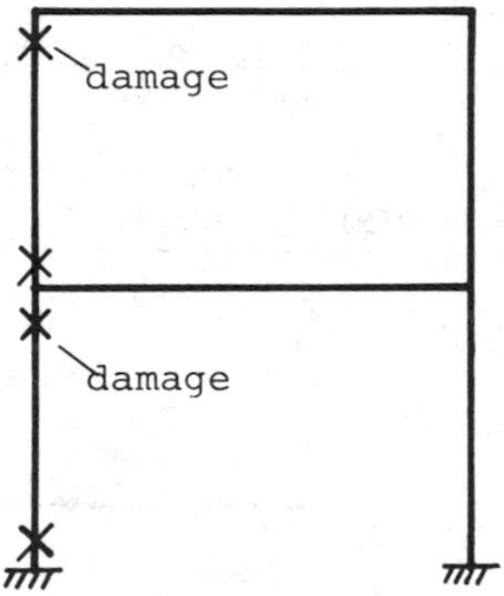


Fig. 6 Damage State of Two-Story Frame

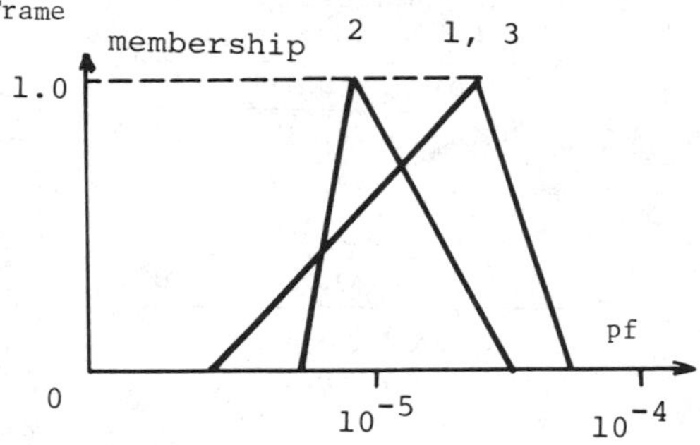


Fig. 8 Numerical Result for Portal Frame

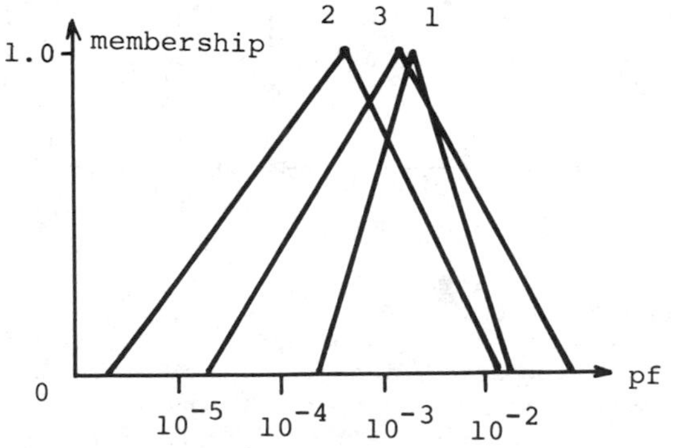


Fig. 9 Numerical Result for Two-Story Frame

structures. For this purpose, fuzzy sets are useful because they can represent the verbal expression of experienced engineers in a clear and informative manner.

In this paper, the PNET method is extensively applied to calculate the system failure probability of damaged structures. In this case, since the failure probabilities and the coefficients of correlation are calculated as fuzzy quantities, some modification is necessary in the calculation process of the system failure probability. Here, three calculating procedures are proposed, which should be used according to the characteristics of the underlying problem.

**REFERENCES**


Ang, A. H-S. and H-F. Ma (1981). "On the Reliability of Structural Systems", Proc. of ICOSSAR '81, Trondheim, Norway, pp.295-314.

Blockley, D. I. (1980). The Nature of Structural Design and Safety, Ellis Horwood, Chichester, England.

Brown, C. B., H. Furuta, N. Shiraishi and J. T. P. Yao (1987). "Civil Engineering Applications of Fuzzy Sets", In J. Bezdeck (Ed.), Proceeding of 1st Int. Conf. on Fuzzy Information Processing, Kauai, Hawaii.

Buckley, J. (1985). "Ranking Alternatives Using Fuzzy Numbers", Fuzzy Sets and Systems, 15, 1-19.

Dubois, D. and H. Prade (1979). "Fuzzy Real Algebra : Some Results", Fuzzy Sets and Systems, 2, 327-384.

Dubois, D. and H. Prade (1980). Fuzzy Sets and Systems : Theory and Applications, Academic Press.

Frangopol, D. M. (1986). "Effects of Redundancy Deterioration on the Reliability of Truss Systems and Bridges", ASCE Convention, Seattle, WA.

Gorman, M. R. and F. Moses (1981). "Partial Factors for Structural Damage", In M. Shinozuka and J. T. P. Yao (Eds.), Proceeding of Symp. on Probabilistic Methods in Structural Engineering, St. Louis,pp.251-257.

Shiraishi, N. and H. Furuta (1986). "Assessment of Structural Durability with Fuzzy Sets", In J. Chameau, C. Brown and J. T. P. Yao (Eds.), Proceeding of NSF Workshop on Civil Engineering Applications of Fuzzy Sets, W. Lafayette, USA, pp.193-218.

Shiraishi, N., H. Furuta and M. Sugimoto (1986). "Integrity Assessment of Bridge Structures Based on Extended Multi-Criteria Analysis", In I. Konishi, A. Ang and M. Shinozuka (Eds.), Proceeding of ICOSSAR-4, pp.I505-I509.

Yao, J. T. P. (1979). "Damage Assessment and Reliability Evaluation of Existing Structures", Jour. of Eng., Struc., 1, 245-251.

Yao, J. T. P. (1982). "Probabilistic Method for the Evaluation of Seismic Damage of Existing Structures", Soil Dynamics Earthquake Eng., 1, 3, 130-135.

Yao, J. T. P. (1985). Safety and Reliability of Existing Structures, Pitman Advanced Publishing Program, Boston, MA.

Yao, J. T. P. and H. Furuta (1986). "Probabilistic Treatment of Fuzzy Events in Civil Engineering", Jour. of Probabilistic Mechanics, 1, 1, 58-64.

Zadeh, L. A. (1965). "Fuzzy Sets", Information and Control, 8, 338-353.

Zadeh, L. A. (1975). "The Concept of a Linguistic Variable and Its Application to Approximate Reasoning - I", Information Science, 8, 199-249.

# FATIGUE ANALYSIS OF REINFORCED CONCRETE DECKS BASED ON FUZZY SETS THEORY

**Hitoshi Furuta*, Yoshinobu Ozaki* and Naruhito Shiraishi***
***Department of Civil Engineering, Kyoto University, Kyoto 606, Japan**

**ABSTRACT**

In this paper, an attempt is made to apply the fuzzy sets theory to the fatigue problem of reinforced concrete decks of bridge structures. The S-N curve is modeled in terms of fuzzy sets instead of probabilistic concept. This is for the reason that the concept of frequency is meaningless for the case with only a few samples. By using the fuzzy regression analysis, it is possible to develop a possibility model for the S-N curve. The concept of possibility distribution is a fundamental basis of the fuzzy sets theory which is a counterpart of the probability theory. Since the possibility model is not based on the concept of frequency, it is useful for the fatigue analysis of concrete bridge decks, in which sufficient amount of data are not available. The use of this model enables us to evaluate their fatigue lives in a more realistic and meaningful manner.

## INTRODUCTION

Recently, many fatigue failures have occurred in the reinforced concrete decks of bridge structures consisting of urban expressways, because of the increase of heavy vehicles and the deterioration of structural materials (Kameda and Morita, 1984; Matsui, 1984). In the fatigue analysis of concrete bridge decks, there are various uncertainties such as experimental and modeling errors as well as the variations of applied loads and structural resistances. These uncertainties are due to the inconsistency between the actual and experimental loading conditions and the inadaptability of the S-N curve or the simple cumulative damage law. Especially, the consistency between the actual and experimental loading conditions is quite important in the fatigue analysis of the concrete bridge decks. Previous studies (Matsui, 1984) have shown that the moving loading is inevitable to realize the actual fatigue failure phenomena in the laboratory testing.

Moreover, even if the moving loading is employed in the experiment, a great deal of experimental data should be collected in order to obtain a reliable S-N curve. However, it is difficult to make a sufficient number of fatigue experiments for concrete bridge decks, mainly because of financial and technical constraints. Namely, although the S-N curve is important to estimate the fatigue life, its accurate estimation is difficult for the concrete bridge decks, because available data are very limited due to the large size of testing pieces and the specific loading condition (Matsui, 1984).

In this paper, an attempt is made to model the S-N curve with fuzzy sets (Zadeh, 1965) instead of probabilistic concepts. This is for the reason that the concept of frequency is useless for the case with only a few data, e.g., about ten samples. By using the fuzzy regression analysis (Heshmaty and Kandel, 1985; Tanaka, 1984), it is possible to develop a possibility model of the S-N curve, which is useful to estimate the fatigue lives of concrete bridge decks in a more realistic and meaningful manner.

**POSSIBILITY MODEL OF S-N CURVE**

In general, the fatigue characteristic of structures under a constant repeated load is expressed in terms of the amplitude of load S and the repeated cycle to fatigue failure N (Itoh, 1977).

$$\log N = C - m \log S \tag{1}$$

where C and m are constants to be determined from experiments. Eq. 1 is called an S-N curve. In this paper the S-N curve is modeled as a possibility model using the fuzzy regression analysis (Heshmaty and Kandel, 1985; Tanaka, 1984). To illustrate the fuzzy regression analysis, its outline is summarized in the following.

Suppose that the following data are given:

$$\left.\begin{array}{l} (y(1),\ x(11),\ \cdots\cdots\cdots,\ x(1n)) \\ \cdots\cdots\cdots\cdots\cdots\cdots \\ \cdots\cdots\cdots\cdots\cdots\cdots \\ \cdots\cdots\cdots\cdots\cdots\cdots \\ (y(m),\ x(m1),\cdots\cdots\ \cdots\cdots,\ x(mn)) \end{array}\right\} \tag{2}$$

where x(ij) and y(j) are input data and output data, and m and n are the numbers of data and variables, respectively. Here, $\tilde{Y}(i)$, the estimate value of y(i), is defined as

$$\tilde{Y}(i) = \tilde{A}(1)x(i1)+\tilde{A}(2)x(i2)+\cdots+\tilde{A}(n)x(in) \tag{3}$$

The above fuzzy parameters $\tilde{A}(j)$ are determined so that y(i) are included in $\tilde{Y}(i)$ with some membership degree. The symbol ~ denotes a fuzzy quantity. Using L and R functions developed by Dubois and Prade (1979), $\tilde{A}(j)$ is specified by the parameters $\alpha(j)$ and c(j) as shown in Fig. 1. All computations on fuzzy quantities are performed based on the extension principle (Dubois and Prade, 1980).

As a measure for the consistency between $\tilde{Y}(i)$ and y(i), we introduce a parameter h which is defined on [0,1]. By using this parameter, a constraint is derived as follows:

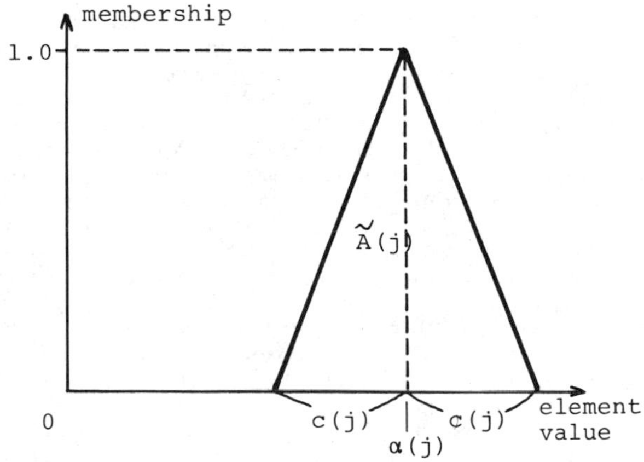


Fig. 1 Membership Functions for $\tilde{A}(j)$

$$\min\ (\ \mu(Yi)[y(i)])\geq\ h \tag{4}$$

The above inequality means that the fuzzy number $\tilde{Y}(i)$ must include y(i) with a membership grade more than or equal to h. Then, the goal is to find $\tilde{A}(j)$ such that the total ambiguity regarding $\tilde{A}(j)$ is minimized:

$$S = c(1)+c(2)+ \cdots\cdots\cdots +c(n) \quad \rightarrow \quad \min \tag{5}$$

The parameter h corresponds to the width of the regression curve. By changing the value of h, it is possible to take the engineering judgment of the decision maker into consideration. Usually, the value of h is determined by experienced engineers through the examination of available experimental data.

Fuzzy regression analysis refers to the following linear programming problem (Tanaka, 1984):

$$\text{objective function : } S = \Sigma\ \ c(j) \rightarrow \ \min \tag{6}$$

$$\text{subject to} \quad (1-h)\,\Sigma\, c(j)\,|x(ij)| + \Sigma\ \ \alpha(j)x(ij) \geq y(i)$$

$$(1-h)\,\Sigma\, c(j)\,|x(ij)| - \Sigma\ \alpha\,(j)x(ij) \geq -y(i) \tag{7}$$

$$c(j) \geq 0$$

The above formulation is applied to the modeling of the S-N curve:

$$\log \tilde{S} = \tilde{A}(0) + \tilde{A}(1) \log N \tag{8}$$

$$\log \tilde{N} = \tilde{A}'(0) + \tilde{A}'(1) \log S \tag{9}$$

In Eqs. 8 and 9, either the load level $\tilde{S}$ or the repeated cycle to fatigue failure $\tilde{N}$ is expressed by a fuzzy set. Since the above formulations of regression analysis are different from the usual formulation, central values of $\tilde{A}(0)(\tilde{A}'(0))$ and $\tilde{A}(1)(\tilde{A}'(1))$,$\alpha(0)(\alpha'(0))$ and $\alpha(1)(\alpha'(1))$, may be different from those obtained from the usual analysis.

Based on the experimental data given in (Kameda and Morita, 1984), an S-N curve is obtained through the fuzzy regression analysis, In Fig. 2, the ordinate of log P/P(d) and the abscissa of log N. P is the axial load of vehicles and P(d) is the axial load yielding the reinforcing steel, respectively. In Fig. 2, P/P(d) is defined as a fuzzy number, whereas N is considered as an ordinal number. This figure corresponds to the possibility model defined by Eq. 8. The solid line provides the central value of the S-N curve, the alternate long and short dash lines show the bounds with h=0.7, and the dash lines show the bounds with h=0.5. As the value of h increases, the width of the S-N curve becomes broader. This figure also indicates that $\tilde{A}(1)$ is a fuzzy number, but $\tilde{A}(0)$ is an ordinal number without scatter. This result implies that the width of the curve becomes larger as N becomes larger. The slope of this line (corresponding to the solid line) is considerably different from that obtained by the usual regression analysis. This is due to the fact that the fuzzy regression analysis has such a different criterion that the width of the line should be minimized.

Fig. 3 presents the result where the abscissa and ordinate are exchanged. In this case N and P/P(d) are considered to be a fuzzy number and an ordinal number, respectively. This case corresponds to the possibility model given by Eq. 9. Alternatively, in this case $\tilde{A}'(1)$

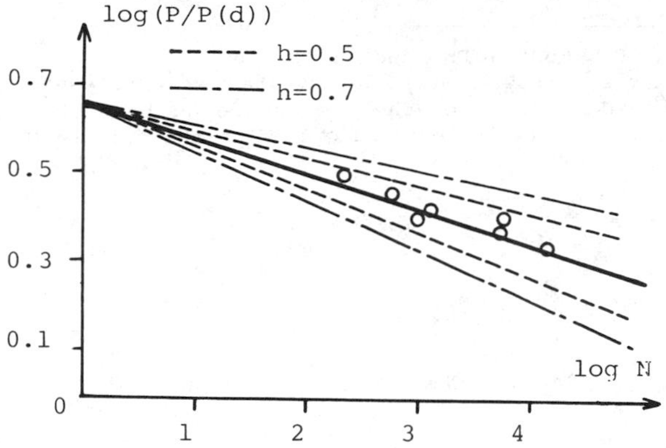


Fig. 2 S-N Curve (1) Obtained by Fuzzy Regression Analysis

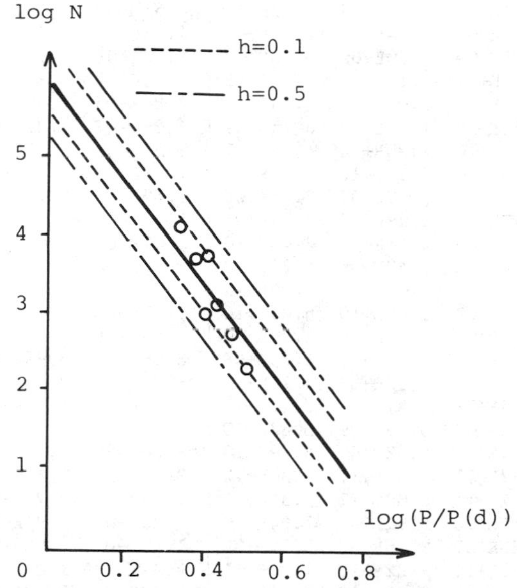


Fig. 3 S-N Curve (2) Obtained by Fuzzy Regression Analysis

and $\tilde{A}'(0)$ are obtained as an ordinal number and a fuzzy number. Therefore, the S-N curve obtained has the same width all over the values of P/P(d). From Figs. 2 and 3, it can be seen that what is a fuzzy number greatly influences on the numerical results.

In this paper, the S-N curve shown in Fig. 3 is employed to estimate the fatigue life of concrete bridge decks. This is why P/P(d) can be obtained with sufficient accuracy if the measurement of loading is done carefully and precisely, while the repeated cycle to fatigue failure cannot be determined definitely even if the loads can be obtained with sufficient accuracy.

**CALCULATION OF FATIGUE LIFE OF RC DECKS**

Based on the Miner's cumulative law (Yao et al., 1986), total damage D is expressed in terms of the occurrence numbers n(i) of each load intensity S(i) and their repeated cycles to the failure N(i).

$$D = \Sigma\ n(i)/N(i) \tag{10}$$

Table 1 Numerical Result of N and D

| Kind of Vehicle | $\tilde{N}(i)$ α | $\tilde{N}(i)$ C(L) | $\tilde{N}(i)$ C(R) | $\tilde{n}(i)/\tilde{N}(i)$ α | $\tilde{n}(i)/\tilde{N}(i)$ C(L) | $\tilde{n}(i)/\tilde{N}(i)$ C(R) |
|---|---|---|---|---|---|---|
| 1 | 7.51E+09 | 6.17E+09 | 3.47E+10 | 4.61E-08 | 2.13E-07 | 3.79E-08 |
| 2 | 5.15E+07 | 4.24E+07 | 2.38E+08 | 4.48E-06 | 2.07E-05 | 3.68E-06 |
| 3 | 7.05E+09 | 5.80E+09 | 3.26E+10 | 8.10E-08 | 3.74E-07 | 6.66E-08 |
| | 2.67E+11 | 2.19E+11 | 1.23E+12 | 2.14E-09 | 9.89E-09 | 1.76E-09 |
| 4 | 3.74E+07 | 3.07E+07 | 1.73E+08 | 2.84E-05 | 1.31E-04 | 2.33E-05 |
| | 1.46E+09 | 1.20E+09 | 6.75E+09 | 7.26E-07 | 3.36E-06 | 5.97E-07 |
| 5 | 3.40E+10 | 2.80E+10 | 1.57E+11 | 1.56E-09 | 7.20E-09 | 1.28E-09 |
| | 3.83E+10 | 3.15E+10 | 1.77E+11 | 1.38E-09 | 6.39E-09 | 1.14E-09 |
| 6 | 4.86E+07 | 3.99E+07 | 2.25E+08 | 1.65E-06 | 6.76E-06 | 1.20E-06 |
| | 5.47E+07 | 3.99E+07 | 2.25E+08 | 1.46E-06 | 6.76E-06 | 1.20E-06 |
| | 5.36E+09 | 4.41E+09 | 2.48E+10 | 4.42E-08 | 2.04E-07 | 3.64E-08 |
| 7 | 0.90E+09 | 7.48E+09 | 4.20E+10 | 3.61E-08 | 1.21E-07 | 2.14E-08 |
| | 1.31E+10 | 1.08E+10 | 6.06E+10 | 1.81E-08 | 8.36E-08 | 1.49E-08 |
| | 5.36E+09 | 1.08E+10 | 6.06E+10 | 1.81E-08 | 8.36E-08 | 1.49E-08 |
| 8 | 0.09E+09 | 7.58E+09 | 4.20E+10 | 5.54E-08 | 2.56E-07 | 4.56E-08 |
| | 5.90E+07 | 4.85E+07 | 2.73E+08 | 8.56E-06 | 3.95E-05 | 7.02E-06 |
| 9 | 1.04E+10 | 8,52E+09 | 4.79E+10 | 4.73E-09 | 2.19E-08 | 3.89E-09 |
| | 1.59E+11 | 1.31E+11 | 7.37E+11 | 3,07E-10 | 1.42E-09 | 2.53E-10 |
| 10 | 8.26E+09 | 6.79E+09 | 3.82E+10 | 1.03E-08 | 4.76E-08 | 8.46E-09 |
| | 1.04E+10 | 8.52E+09 | 4.79E+10 | 8,20E-09 | 3.79E-08 | 6.74E-09 |
| 11 | 2.82E+11 | 2.32E+11 | 1.30E+12 | 3.55E-10 | 1.64E-09 | 2.92E-10 |
| | 9.77E+11 | 8.03E+11 | 4.51E+12 | 1.02E-10 | 4.73E-10 | 8.42E-11 |
| 12 | 3.54E+08 | 2.91E+08 | 1.64E+09 | 6.30E-07 | 2.91E-06 | 5.18E-07 |
| | 1.20E+09 | 9.88E+08 | 5.56E+09 | 1.86E-07 | 8.58E-07 | 1.53E-07 |
| 13 | 2.70E+10 | 2.22E+10 | 1.25E+11 | 3.97E-09 | 1.83E-08 | 3.26E-09 |
| | 3.54E+10 | 2.91E+10 | 1.64E+11 | 3.02E-09 | 1.40E-08 | 2.49E-09 |
| 14 | 3.20E+07 | 2.63E+07 | 1.48E+08 | 2.53E-06 | 1.17E-05 | 2.08E-06 |
| | 4.19E+07 | 3.45E+07 | 1.94E+08 | 1.93E-06 | 8.93E-06 | 1.59E-05 |
| $\tilde{D} = \Sigma\ \tilde{n}(i)/\tilde{N}(i)$ | | | | 5.09E-05 | 2.35E-04 | 4.18E-05 |

Kind of Vehicle: 1=Truck(2 axes) U; 2=Truck(2 axes) L; 3=Truck(3 axes-1) U; =Truck(3 axes-1) L; 5=Truck(3 axes-2) U; 6=Truck(3 axes-2) L; 7=Truck(3 axes-3) U; 8=Truck(3 axes-3) L; 9=Truck(4 axes) U; 10=Truck (4 axes) L; 11=Semi-Trailer(1) U; 12=Semi-Trailer(1) L; 13=Semi-Trailer(2) U; 14=Semi-Trailer(2) L; U=unloaded; L=loaded

Then, the fatigue failure occurs when the total damage D reaches to unity:

$$D = 1 \tag{11}$$

Supposing that the loading condition will not change in the future, fatigue life T can be calculated by D as follows:

$$T = 1 / D \tag{12}$$

Here we try to extend the cumulative law to the case with fuzzy quantities. D is defined as a fuzzy number in terms of fuzzy quantities $\tilde{n}(i)$ and $\tilde{N}(i)$.

$$\tilde{D} = \Sigma\ \tilde{n}(i)/\tilde{N}(i) \tag{13}$$

In Eq. 13, $\tilde{N}(i)$ is considered to be fuzzy as the result of the possibility model derived for the S-N curve.

The criterion of fatigue failure given by Eq. 11 does not possess a strong theoretical basis. Therefore, we consider a more flexible criterion for the fatigue failure, that is, the failure event is defined by a fuzzy set $\tilde{F}$ which fuzzifies the relation of D = 1. This fuzzy relation between D and F gives a new definition of the fatigue failure. An example of $\tilde{F}$ is given in Fig. 4, where the abscissa d=0 means no damage and d=1 means that the fatigue failure is most likely to occur. In this case a being less than 1 has a possibility of failure with a grade of $\mu(a)$, and even when d becomes 1, a failure does not occur, and afterwards when d becomes b being larger than 1, a failure may occur with the possibility of $\mu(b)$. By definition, the fatigue life T is

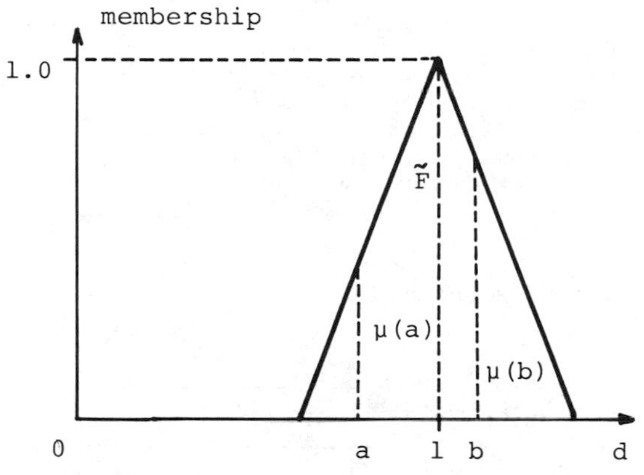


Fig. 4 Membership Function for Ultimate Limit State

expressed as a fuzzy number, by using $\tilde{F}$ and $\tilde{D}$:

$$\tilde{T} = \tilde{F} / \tilde{D} \tag{14}$$

In general, there are two kinds of limit states for the concrete bridge decks; one is the ultimate limit state and the other is the serviceability limit state. The former means the collapse of the deck, whereas the latter means the excessive cracks or deformations. As well as the definition of $\tilde{F}$ (this definition corresponds to the ultimate limit state), the serviceability limit is defined by a fuzzy set $\tilde{F}'$. $\tilde{F}$ and $\tilde{F}'$ may have different membership functions. Based on the data obtained from (Matsui, 1984), $\tilde{F}$ and $\tilde{F}'$ are specified as follows:

$$\tilde{F} = (\alpha(F), C(F), C(F)) = (1.0, 0.1, 0.1) \tag{15}$$

$$\tilde{F}' = (\alpha(F'), C(F'), C(F')) = (0.435, 0.1, 0.1) \tag{16}$$

where $\alpha(F)$ and $\alpha(F')$ denote the central values of the membership functions of $\tilde{F}$ and $\tilde{F}'$, and C(F) and C(F') represent the widths of the membership functions of $\tilde{F}$ and $\tilde{F}'$, respectively. From Eq. 14, the life reaching to the serviceability limit is written as

$$\tilde{T}' = \tilde{F}' / \tilde{D} \tag{17}$$

Table 1 presents the results of the repeated cycles of several kinds of vehicles with different weights to the fatigue failure which are obtained through the fuzzy regression analysis using the data given by (Kameda and Morita, 1984). In this calculation, h is 0.3 and P(d) is 8.0 ton. $\alpha$, C(L), C(R) denote the central value, the widths of scatter for left and right hand sides of N. Namely, $\alpha$ -C(L) is the lower bound and $\alpha$ +C(R) is the upper bound, respectively. In all cases C(R) is larger than C(L), since the membership functions employed for the parameters A(0) and A(1) have triangular shapes on the log scale. Table 2 presents the results of fatigue lives obtained for the cases with different values of h and P(d); h=0.1 and 0.5 and P(d)=8.0 ton and 9.6 ton. For the limit states, the ultimate limit state and the serviceability limit are considered. Naturally, the central value of $\tilde{D}$ varies according to the change of P(d), whereas the values of C(R) and C(L) depend on the value of h. The fatigue life to the ultimate limit (collapse), $\tilde{T}$, is calculated as 4.7 years through 367.6 years for the case of h=0.5 and P(d)=8.0 ton. Although this range seems to be too wide for practical use, it should be noted that every value of year within this range has a membership grade which indicates the degree of reliability or dependability. Namely, the most possible and dependable value of $\tilde{T}$ is 60.4 years. Moreover, it is emphasized that the values less than 60.4 are important from the standpoint of maintenance engineering.

Table 2 Results of Fatigue Lives (year)

| h | P(d) ton | Limit State | $\tilde{T}$ $\alpha$ | C(L) | C(R) |
|---|---|---|---|---|---|
| 0.5 | 8.0 | Ultimate | 60.4 | 55.7 | 307.2 |
| 0.5 | 8.0 | Serviceability | 26.3 | 27.6 | 149.4 |
| 0.5 | 9.6 | Ultimate | 204.9 | 189.0 | 1042.2 |
| 0.5 | 9.6 | Serviceability | 89.1 | 93.8 | 507.0 |
| 0.1 | 8.0 | Ultimate | 60.4 | 43.3 | 107.0 |
| 0.1 | 8.0 | Serviceability | 26.3 | 22.3 | 52.0 |
| 0.1 | 9.6 | Ultimate | 204.9 | 146.9 | 363.0 |
| 0.1 | 9.6 | Serviceability | 89.1 | 75.5 | 176.6 |

On the contrary, the fatigue life to the serviceability limit is calculated as -1.3 years through 175.7 years. For the fatigue life, the negative value is not accepted. This inappropriate result is caused by the assumption of Eq. 16. This model of $\tilde{F}'$ should be revised by making additional experiments. If the depth of the concrete deck is changed to be thicker, that is, P(d) changes from 8.0 to 9.6, $\tilde{T}$ is estimated to be a wider interval such as 15.9 years through 1247.1 years. As well as the result obtained for the ultimate limit state, the values from 15.9 through 1247.1 should be interpreted from the engineering point of view. Also, when the value of h reduces from 0.5 to 0.1, the interval of $\tilde{T}$ becomes narrow. This fact indicates that the effect of h is reflected appropriately in the modeling of the S-N curve.

**CONCLUDING REMARKS**

In this paper we gave an insight for the treatment of uncertainties involved in the definition of limit states, the fatigue experiments, and the cumulative law, which play important roles in the fatigue analysis of reinforced concrete decks of bridge structures. Paying attention to the scarcity of experimental data available for the fatigue analysis of the concrete bridge decks, the concept of possibility distribution (Zadeh, 1978) is introduced into the modeling of the S-N curve. The possibility distribution is a fundamental basis of the fuzzy sets theory which is a counterpart of the probability theory. Since the possibility model of the S-N curve is not based on the concept of frequency, it is useful for the case without sufficient amount of data. The use of this model enables us to evaluate the fatigue life of the concrete decks in a more informative and realistic form. The final results are obtained in terms of fuzzy sets which provide us with all the potential possibilities with corresponding grades.

**REFERENCES**

Dubois, D. and H. Prade (1980). Fuzzy Sets and Systems : Theory and Applications, Academic Press.

Dubois D. and H. Prade (1979). "Fuzzy Real Algebra : Some Results", Fuzzy Sets and Systems, 2, 327-348.

Heshmaty, B and A. Kandel (1985). "Fuzzy Linear Regression and Its Applications to Forecasting in Uncertain Environment", Fuzzy Sets and Systems, 15, 159-191.

Itoh, F. (1977). "Fatigue Life Design Based on Actual Loading", In S. Okamoto (Ed.), Study on Steel Structures, pp.289-328. (in Japanese)

Kameda, H. and S. Morita (1984). "Analysis of Damage Factors and Influence of Live Loads on Fatigue of RC Decks in Urban Expressways, In Report of Hanshin Expressway Corporation, pp.108-146. (in Japanese)

Matsui, S (1984). "Study on Design and Analysis of Fatigue of Concrete Decks of Road Bridges", presented in Partial Fulfillment of Doctor of Engineering , Osaka University. (in Japanese)

Tanaka, H. (1984). "Possibility Model and Its Applications", Systems and Control, Japan, 28, 447-451. (in Japanese)

Yao, J. T. P., F. Kozin, Y.-K. Wen, J.-N. Yang., G. I. Scuëller and O. Ditlevsen (1986). "Stochastic Fatigue, Fracture and Damage Analysis", Structural Safety, 3, 231-267.

Zadeh, L. A. (1965). "Fuzzy Sets", Information and Control, 8, 338-353.

Zadeh, L. A. (1978). "Fuzzy Sets as a Basis for a Theory of Possibility", Fuzzy Sets and Systems, 1, 3-28.

# LOAD COMBINATION ANALYSIS AND RELIABILITY ANALYSIS OF STEEL RIGID-FRAME PIERS SUPPORTING BRIDGES CONSTRUCTED ON URBAN EXPRESSWAY NETWORK

Wataru SHIRAKI, Shigeyuki MATSUHO and Nobuyoshi TAKAOKA

Department of Civil Engineering, Tottori University,
(680) Tottori-shi, Koyama-cho, Japan.

**ABSTRACT**

In this study, a load combination analysis and reliability analysis of steel rigid-frame piers supporting bridges constructed on urban expressway network are performed. Twelve model pier structures and four actual load components (dead, live, temperature and earthquake load) are considered. By numerical calculations, it is pointed that the safety indicies of the pier structures designed by the allowable stress design method differ considerably from each other, depending on the model type. Having recourse to the load factor design method, a procedure is presented to determine the optimal values of load factors, for preselected target safety indicies, for various load combinations.

## 1. INTRODUCTION

A structure is usually subjected to several loads which randomly vary in time and in space during the lifetime of the structure. Therefore, probabilistic evaluation of time-varying loads and their combination is one of the most important problems for the design and/or the reliability analysis of structures.

In the conventional allowable stress design method, consideration of load combination is performed in such a rather rude manner that the individual loads are simply added up while the corresponding allowable stress is augmented by a certain factor, based on engineering judgement and experiences. In the load-factor design method, consideration of load combination is made by introducing load factors which are evaluated by considering the statistical variability of individual loads and experiences obtained in practice.

In recent years, the importance of rational consideration of load combination in structural design has been pointed out, and a lot of studies on this theme have been made using probabilistic methods(1-6).

In this study, a load combination analysis and reliability analysis of steel rigid-frame piers supporting bridges constructed on urban expressway network are performed. Twelve typical types of pier structure are selected out of the existing actual piers on the Hanshin (Osaka-Kobe area) Expressway Network, and four actual load components: dead load D, live load L, temperature effect T and earthquake load E, are considered. They are assumed to be represented by the Borges-Castanheta processes (B-C model). Load combination analysis is made using the Turkstra's rule (7) and reliability analysis is performed using the extended level 2 method based on the Rackwitz-Fiessler's iterative procedure (8). For various loading cases the safety indices are calculated for the twelve model piers which are designed according to the current Design Standards for Hanshin Expressway Bridges (9), based on the allowable stress design method (ASDM). By numerical examples on model pier structures, it is pointed out that the safety indices of the structures designed by the ASDM differ considerably from each other, depending on the model type of pier structures. These examples reveal one of the shortcomings inherent in the current ASDM. Then, having recourse to the load factor design method (LFDM), a procedure is presented to determine the optimal values of load factors, for preselected target safety indices, for various loading cases (load combinations).

## 2. MODELING OF PIER STRUCTURES

As was stated in Introduction above, twelve typical types of pier structures were selected out of the existing actual piers on the Hanshin Expressway Network. The principal dimensions and the configuration of the structures are listed in Table 1 and demonstrated in Figs.1 through 3. The wall thicknesses of beam and column sections, $t_b$ and $t_c$, of these twelve piers, selected taking into consideration the combination of three basic parameters (the span length of superstructure L = 40, 60, 80 m ; the total height of pier H = 10, 20 m ; the total width of pier W = 20, 30 m), are determined, respectively, by the conventional allowable design formats shown in Table 2 (9), and the results of design calculation are summarized in Table 3. In Table 2, $D_n$, $L_n$, $T_n$, $E_n$ = the nominal value of each load component D, L, T and E, respectively; $\alpha_D$, $\alpha_L$, $\alpha_T$, $\alpha_E$ = factors which convert each load component into corresponding stress level; $\phi$ = the augmentation factor of the allowable stress. In the design calculation, four checking points, 1, 2c, 2b and 3 (see Fig.3), are considered. The characteristics steel material used are as follows: the grade of steel = SM50Y; the allowable stress $\sigma_a$ = 2100 kg/cm$^2$ ; the yield stress $\sigma_y$ = 3600 kg/cm$^2$ ; the Young's modulus $E_0$ = 2.1x10 kgf/cm$^2$ ; the linear coefficient of expansion $\alpha$ = 1.2x10$^{-5}$ /°C ; the unit weight $\rho$ = 7.85x10$^{-3}$ kgf/cm$^3$.

Using the model pier structures thus determined, load combination and reliability analysis are carried out in the following sections.

Table 1 Twelve Models of Rigid-Frame Piers

(unit : m)

| Model No. | L | H | W | h | $l$ | a | b | c |
|---|---|---|---|---|---|---|---|---|
| 1 | 40.0 | 10.0 | 20.0 | 9.17 | 18.5 | 2.00 | 1.67 | 1.5 |
| 2 | 〃 | 〃 | 30.0 | 8.75 | 28.0 | 〃 | 2.50 | 2.0 |
| 3 | 〃 | 20.0 | 20.0 | 19.17 | 18.0 | 〃 | 1.67 | 2.0 |
| 4 | 〃 | 〃 | 30.0 | 18.75 | 27.5 | 〃 | 2.50 | 2.5 |
| 5 | 60.0 | 10.0 | 20.0 | 9.17 | 18.5 | 3.00 | 1.67 | 1.5 |
| 6 | 〃 | 〃 | 30.0 | 8.75 | 28.0 | 〃 | 2.50 | 2.0 |
| 7 | 〃 | 20.0 | 20.0 | 19.17 | 18.0 | 〃 | 1.67 | 2.0 |
| 8 | 〃 | 〃 | 30.0 | 18.75 | 27.5 | 〃 | 2.50 | 2.5 |
| 9 | 80.0 | 10.0 | 20.0 | 9.17 | 18.5 | 4.00 | 1.67 | 1.5 |
| 10 | 〃 | 〃 | 30.0 | 8.75 | 28.0 | 〃 | 2.50 | 2.0 |
| 11 | 〃 | 20.0 | 20.0 | 19.17 | 18.0 | 〃 | 1.67 | 2.0 |
| 12 | 〃 | 〃 | 30.0 | 18.75 | 27.5 | 〃 | 2.50 | 2.5 |

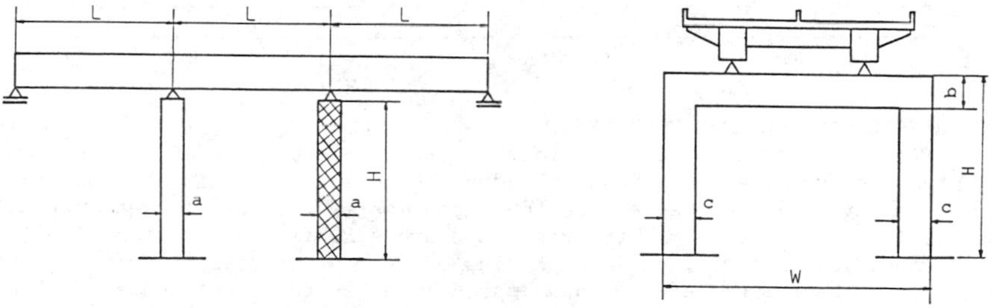


Fig .1 Rigid—Frame Pier Supporting Three—Span Continuous Box Girder Bridge

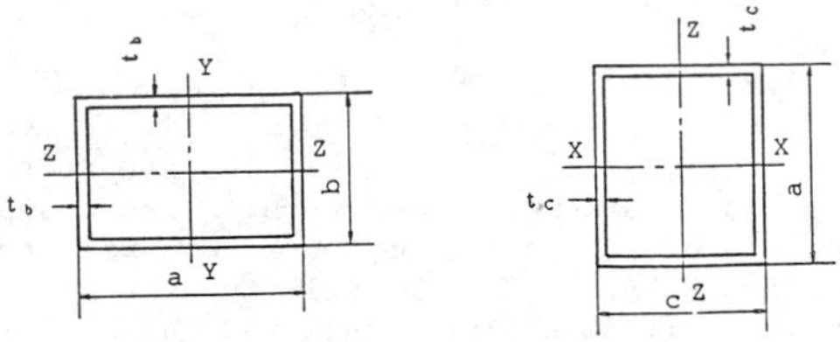


Beam Section

Column Section

Fig . 2 Cross Section of Rigid－Frame Pier

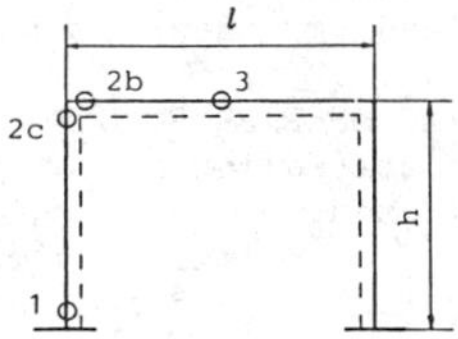


Fig . 3 Analytical Model of Rigid－Frame Pier

Table 2 Current Design Fomulas

| Code | Current Design Formulas | $\phi$ |
|---|---|---|
| 1 | $\alpha_D \cdot D_n + \alpha_L \cdot L_n \leqq \phi \cdot \sigma_a$ | 1.00 |
| 2 | $\alpha_D \cdot D_n + \alpha_L \cdot L_n + \alpha_T \cdot T_n \leqq \phi \cdot \sigma_a$ | 1.15 |
| 3 | $\alpha_D \cdot D_n + \alpha_E \cdot E_n \leqq \phi \cdot \sigma_a$ | 1.50 |
| 4 | $\alpha_D \cdot D_n + \alpha_T \cdot T_n + \alpha_E \cdot E_n \leqq \phi \cdot \sigma_a$ | 1.70 |

Table 3 Results of Design Calculation According to Current Design Code

| Model No. | Beam Section | | | | Column Section | | | | Pier Weight (t) |
|---|---|---|---|---|---|---|---|---|---|
| | Design Section No. | Design Code | $t_b$ (mm) | Unit Length Weight (t/m) | Design Section No. | Design Code | $t_c$ (mm) | Unit Length Weight (t/m) | |
| 1 | $2_b$ | 1 | 22.5 | 1.54 | $2_c$ | 1 | 28.8 | 1.87 | 62.5 |
| 2 | $2_b$ | 1 | 29.0 | 2.43 | $2_c$ | 1 | 39.3 | 2.91 | 118.7 |
| 3 | $2_b$ | 1 | 18.6 | 1.27 | $2_c$ | 1 | 18.5 | 1.38 | 75.6 |
| 4 | $2_b$ | 1 | 24.0 | 2.01 | $2_c$ | 1 | 26.6 | 2.23 | 138.7 |
| 5 | $2_b$ | 1 | 24.4 | 2.12 | $2_c$ | 1 | 31.2 | 2.61 | 86.9 |
| 6 | $2_b$ | 1 | 32.4 | 3.32 | $2_c$ | 1 | 43.1 | 3.99 | 162.6 |
| 7 | $2_b$ | 3 | 20.5 | 1.79 | $2_c$ | 1 | 20.5 | 1.92 | 105.5 |
| 8 | $2_b$ | 1 | 26.7 | 2.74 | $2_c$ | 1 | 29.9 | 3.06 | 189.8 |
| 9 | $2_b$ | 1 | 26.1 | 2.77 | $2_c$ | 1 | 33.5 | 3.43 | 113.8 |
| 10 | $2_b$ | 1 | 35.4 | 4.28 | $2_c$ | 1 | 46.6 | 5.18 | 210.4 |
| 11 | $2_b$ | 3 | 22.4 | 2.37 | $2_c$ | 1 | 22.3 | 2.50 | 138.4 |
| 12 | $2_b$ | 1 | 29.0 | 3.97 | $2_c$ | 1 | 32.7 | 3.97 | 245.3 |
| Total | | | | | | | | | 1648.3 |

## 3. MODELING OF ACTUAL LOAD COMPONENTS

Four load components considered in this study are dead load D, live load L, temperature effect T and earthquake load E. Each load model is assumed to be represented by a Borges-Castanheta (B-C) process (7). Based on an extensive investigation, conducted by the Hanshin Express Public Corporation (10), on actual conditions of various loads acting on urban expressway bridges, the parameters of the B-C process of each load component are determined as follows.

(1) Dead Load, D : As dead load D, only the own weight of structure is considered and it is assumed to be deterministic. To take its variability into

consideration, however, the design value of D is calculated by the formula: $D = D'(1+\delta)$, in which D' = actual weight of the structure calculated on the basis of the unit weight of the material and the volume of the members; $\delta = 0.05$ for the superstructure and 0.10 for pier structure.

(2) Live Load, L : The actual live load is modeled by the mixed type of B-C load model. The probability of occurrence, p, and the basic time intervals, $\tau_L$, are taken as 0.75 and 6 hours, respectively. Given that the load occurs the cumulative distribution function (CDF) of its amplitude $F_L^*(x)$ is expressed as

for span length L = 40 m

$$F_L^*(x) = 1 - \exp[-(x/56.49)^{2.342}]$$

for span length L = 60 m

$$F_L^*(x) = 1 - \exp[-(x/82.81)^{2.730}] \qquad (1)$$

for span length L = 80 m

$$F_L^*(x) = 1 - \exp[-(x/110.97)^{3.073}] \qquad (x>0 \ ; \ \text{unit: ton})$$

(3) Temperature Load, T : Actual temperature load is modeled by the mixed type of B-C load model. The parameters p and $\tau_T$ are taken as 0.75 and 6 hours, respectively. The CDF of the temperature difference (actual temperature of structure minus 15°C), $F_T^*(x)$, is expressed as

$$F_T^*(x) = 0.5 + 0.5\cdot\Phi\{(x-13.2)/4.4\} \qquad (x>0 \ ; \ \text{unit: °C}) \qquad (2)$$

in which (•) = the standard normal distribution function.

(4) Earthquake Load, E : Actual earthquake load is modeled by the limiting spike type of B-C load model. The mean arrival rate of load, $\nu$, is taken as 0.5 $\text{year}^{-1}$. The CDF of the response acceleration spectrum, $F_E^*(x)$, is expressed as

for natural frequency of structure = 0.5 sec

$$F_E^*(x) = 1-\exp[-\{(x-41.28)/34.24\}^{0.913}] \qquad (41.28<x)$$

for natural frequency of structure = 0.7 sec

$$F_E^*(x) = 1-\exp[-\{(x-25.88)/26.12\}^{0.879}] \qquad (25.88<x) \qquad (3)$$

for natural frequency of structure = 1.0 sec

$$F_E^*(x) = 1-\exp[-\{(x-17.91)/18.05\}^{0.850}] \qquad (17.91<x) \ (\text{unit: cm/sec}^2)$$

## 4. LOAD COMBINATION ANALYSIS AND RELIABILITY ANALYSIS

In reliability analysis of the model pier structures under combined action of the four loads components, the Turkstra's rule (7) in connection with the B-C processes described in Section 3 and the extended level 2 method based on Rackwitz-Fiessler's procedure (8) are used. In this study, seven combination cases of actual load components shown in Table 4 are considered.

Assuming that the stress $\sigma^*$ in the ultimate limit state of member is the yield stress $\sigma_y = 3600$ (kgf/cm²), the safety index ß for the combination Case 7 is evaluated as

$$\beta = (\sigma^* - \sigma_D - \sum_{i=1}^{3} C_{X_i}\mu_{X_i}')/\sum_{i=1}^{3} C_{X_i}\sigma_{X_i}'\alpha_i \qquad (4)$$

$$\left.\begin{aligned} &\alpha_i = C_{X_i}\sigma_{X_i}'/k \\ &k = (\sum_{i=1}^{3} C_{X_i}^2\sigma_{X_i}'^2)^{1/2} \\ &\mu_{X_i}' = x_i^* - \Phi^{-1}\{F_{X_i}(x_i^*)\}\cdot\sigma_{X_i}' \\ &\sigma_{X_i}' = \phi[\Phi^{-1}\{F_{X_i}(x_i^*)\}]/f_{X_i}(x_i^*) \\ &x_i^* = F_{X_i}^{-1}\{\Phi(\beta\alpha_i)\} \end{aligned}\right\} \qquad (5)$$

in which $X_1$, $X_2$ and $X_3$ = the live, the temperature and the earthquake load, respectively; $x_i^*$ = the $x_i$-coordinate of the design point; $Fx_i$ and $f_{xi}$ = the CDF and the PDF of $X_i$, respectively; $\phi(\cdot)$ = the standard normal density function; $Cx_i$ = the factor which converts the load $X_i$ into the stress level; $\sigma_D$ = the deterministic stress for the dead load. By solving the Eqs.(4) and (5) iteratively for ß, the safety index ß for the four checking points 1, 2c, 2b and 3 (see Fig.3), can be determined. In this study, the minimum value among the safety indices for these four checking points is considered to be the safety index of the pier system.

For the combination Cases 4 through 7 all of which include earthquake load, the safety index ß is calculated for each of the twelve model pier structures. The results obtained are shown in Table 5 and Fig.4.

As is seen from these results, the safety index ß considerably differs from each other, depending on the model type of pier structure. For the models Nos.3, 7 and 11, the safety indices are very small (ß = 1.3-1.5), while for the models Nos.2, 6 and 10, they are very large (ß = 6.0-6.7).

Table 4
Combination Cases of Actual Lode Components

| Case | Actual Load Conbinations |
|---|---|
| 1 | D + L |
| 2 | D + T |
| 3 | D + L + T |
| 4 | D + E |
| 5 | D + L + E |
| 6 | D + T + E |
| 7 | D + L + T + E |

Table 5 Safety Indices of Twelve Pier Models for Combination Case 4～7

| Model No. | Case 7 (D+L+T+E) | Case 6 (D+T+E) | Case 5 (D+L+E) | Case 4 (D+E) |
|---|---|---|---|---|
| 1 | 4.06 | 4.26 | 4.12 | 4.33 |
| 2 | 6.20 | 6.36 | 6.53 | 6.69 |
| 3 | 1.32 | 1.51 | 1.34 | 1.54 |
| 4 | 3.56 | 3.76 | 3.60 | 3.80 |
| 5 | 3.88 | 4.09 | 3.95 | 4.15 |
| 6 | 6.09 | 6.25 | 6.42 | 6.58 |
| 7 | 1.27 | 1.47 | 1.30 | 1.49 |
| 8 | 3.40 | 3.60 | 3.45 | 3.64 |
| 9 | 3.74 | 3.94 | 3.81 | 4.01 |
| 10 | 6.02 | 6.17 | 6.35 | 6.50 |
| 11 | 1.28 | 1.47 | 1.30 | 1.49 |
| 12 | 3.27 | 3.47 | 3.32 | 3.51 |

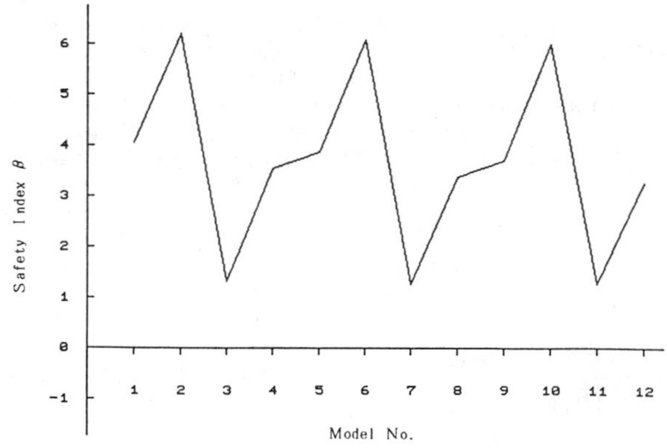


Fig. 4 Comparison of Safety Indices for Twelve Pier Models for Combination Case 7

The reason for this difference lies in the augmentation factor $\phi$ = 1.50 or 1.70 (see Table 2) of the allowable stress which is used when earthquake is to be considered. Using the current design code which is based on the ASDM, the cross-section of the model pier structures are determined for the specified loading cases : D+L, D+L+T, D+E, D+T+E. It is turned out from the obtained results that the first loading case (D+L) is always dominant for the most of the 12 model structures, while in reality the earthquake load E has a significant effect on the reliability of the pier structures. Consequently, the ß values for the models Nos.3, 7 and 11 which is affected significantly by actual load effects due to earthquake are smaller than for other models. The current design code does not insure consistent level of safety for different type of pier structures.

## 5. PROBABILISTIC EVALUATION OF LOAD FACTORS FOR PIER STRUCTURE

In the previous Section, it was pointed out by numerical examples that the conventional allowable design method has some shortcomings. These shortcomings can be greatly reduced by the load factor design method (limit-states design method).

In this Section, let us develop a procedure for calculating optional load factors for a target safety index $\beta_T$ preselected for the ultimate limit state, in such a manner that the preselected value of $\beta_T$ can be maintained regardless of the model type of structure.

Table 6 lists seven formats of load factor design method, used in this study. $\gamma_D$, $\gamma_L$, $\gamma_T$ and $\gamma_E$ are the load factors for load components D, L, T and E, respectively.

The calculation is carried out according to the following procedure:

Step 1: A target safety index $\beta_T$ is preselected.

Step 2: For a load combination case considered, take out the corresponding design format from Table 6, and guess adequately values of the load factors.

Step 3: Using the design format with the load factors guessed in Step 2, cross-sections of the model pier structure i (i = 1,2,...,12; see Table 1) are determined.

Step 4: For the pier structure i thus determined, the actual safety index $\beta_i$ is calculated, under the action of the corresponding loads.

Step 5: Calculate the squared difference $\Omega$ between the values of preselected $\beta_T$ and actual $\beta_i$, defined by

$$\Omega = \sum_{i=1}^{m} (\beta_i - \beta_T)^2 \tag{6}$$

in which m = the number of types of model pier structure (in our study m = 12, see Table 1).

Step 6: Repeat Step 3 and 4 until $\Omega$ becomes minimum, by re-choosing (variating) a set of load-factor values for each iteration.

Table 6 Load Factor Design Formulas

| Case | Load Factor Design Formulas |
|---|---|
| 1 | $\gamma_D \cdot \alpha_D \cdot D_n + \gamma_L \cdot \alpha_L \cdot L_n \leqq \sigma^*$ |
| 2 | $\gamma_D \cdot \alpha_D \cdot D_n + \gamma_T \cdot \alpha_T \cdot T_n \leqq \sigma^*$ |
| 3 | $\gamma_D \cdot \alpha_D \cdot D_n + \gamma_L \cdot \alpha_L \cdot L_n + \gamma_T \cdot \alpha_T \cdot T_n \leqq \sigma^*$ |
| 4 | $\gamma_D \cdot \alpha_D \cdot D_n + \gamma_E \cdot \alpha_E \cdot E_n \leqq \sigma^*$ |
| 5 | $\gamma_D \cdot \alpha_D \cdot D_n + \gamma_L \cdot \alpha_L \cdot L_n + \gamma_E \cdot \alpha_E \cdot E_n \leqq \sigma^*$ |
| 6 | $\gamma_D \cdot \alpha_D \cdot D_n + \gamma_T \cdot \alpha_T \cdot T_n + \gamma_E \cdot \alpha_E \cdot E_n \leqq \sigma^*$ |
| 7 | $\gamma_D \cdot \alpha_D \cdot D_n + \gamma_L \cdot \alpha_L \cdot L_n + \gamma_T \cdot \alpha_T \cdot T_n + \gamma_E \cdot \alpha_E \cdot E_n \leqq \sigma^*$ |

It should be noted that in Step 4 actual loads which appear in the design format used are considered to act on the structure. By thus doing, the defect in the current design code that the safety index ß differs depending on the model types of pier structure can be improved.

Calculation results for load factors are shown in Tables 7 through 10. For the combination cases 4 through 7, in which earthquake load E is included, the values of the load factors $\gamma_L$ and $\gamma_T$ are very small. It may be attributed that the nominal values $L_n$ and $T_n$ in the current design code is overestimated for the case when earthquake is to be considered.

Table 11 shows the results of design calculation using the proposed optimal load factor. As is seen from this Table, most of the actual safety indices $\beta_i$ agree well with the target safety index $\beta_T$ = 2.5. The ratio of the total weight of twelve piers which are designed using the optimal load factors to the total weight according to the current ASDM is 84%, 91% and 101% for $\beta_T$ = 2.5, 3.0 and 3.5, respectively. Because of space limitation, the results for $\beta_T$ = 3.0 and 3.5 are not presented. These results may demonstrate that the developed procedure for calculating optimal load factors is very effective.

Table 7 Load Factors for Case 4 (D+E), $\beta_T$=2.5,3.0,3.5

| $\beta_T$ | $\gamma_D$ | $\gamma_E$ | Ω |
|---|---|---|---|
| 2. 5 | 1. 05 | 1. 66 | 0. 00015 |
| 3. 0 | 1. 05 | 1. 96 | 0. 00008 |
| 3. 5 | 1. 05 | 2. 31 | 0. 00013 |

Table 8 Load Factors for Case 5 (D+L+E), $\beta_T$=2.5,3.0,3.5

| $\beta_T$ | $\gamma_D$ | $\gamma_L$ | $\gamma_E$ | Ω |
|---|---|---|---|---|
| 2. 5 | 1. 08 | 0. 05 | 1. 63 | 0. 00111 |
| 3. 0 | 1. 08 | 0. 05 | 1. 92 | 0. 00102 |
| 3. 5 | 1. 08 | 0. 05 | 2. 28 | 0. 00026 |

Table 9 Load Factors for Case 6 (D+T+E), $\beta_T$=2.5,3.0,3.5

| $\beta_T$ | $\gamma_D$ | $\gamma_T$ | $\gamma_E$ | Ω |
|---|---|---|---|---|
| 2. 5 | 1. 05 | 0. 37 | 1. 66 | 0. 00005 |
| 3. 0 | 1. 05 | 0. 38 | 1. 96 | 0. 00005 |
| 3. 5 | 1. 06 | 0. 30 | 2. 30 | 0. 00001 |

Table 10 Load Factors for Case 7 (D+L+T+E), $\beta_T$=2.5,3.0,3.5

| $\beta_T$ | $\gamma_D$ | $\gamma_L$ | $\gamma_T$ | $\gamma_E$ | Ω |
|---|---|---|---|---|---|
| 2. 5 | 1. 07 | 0. 06 | 0. 50 | 1. 65 | 0. 00041 |
| 3. 0 | 1. 07 | 0. 06 | 0. 50 | 1. 95 | 0. 00033 |
| 3. 5 | 1. 09 | 0. 04 | 0. 29 | 2. 27 | 0. 00011 |

Table 11 Results of Design Calculation According to Proposed Load Factor Design Formulas for $\beta_T$=2.5

| Model No. | Beam Section | | | | Column Section | | | | Pier Weight (t) | Safety Index $\beta$ (Case 7) |
|---|---|---|---|---|---|---|---|---|---|---|
| | Design Section No. | Case No. | $t_b$ (mm) | Unit Length Weight (t/m) | Design Section No. | Case No. | $t_c$ (mm) | Unit Length Weight (t/m) | | |
| 1 | $2_b$ | 7 | 17. 7 | 1. 22 ( 79) | $2_c$ | 7 | 21. 0 | 1. 37 ( 73) | 47. 4 | 2. 51 |
| 2 | $2_b$ | 7 | 18. 4 | 1. 54 ( 63) | $2_c$ | 7 | 23. 6 | 1. 76 ( 61) | 73. 8 | 2. 53 |
| 3 | $2_b$ | 7 | 23. 3 | 1. 59 (125) | 1 | 7 | 21. 9 | 1. 64 (118) | 91. 1 | 2. 48 |
| 4 | $2_b$ | 7 | 20. 1 | 1. 69 ( 84) | $2_c$ | 7 | 21. 0 | 1. 77 ( 79) | 112. 4 | 2. 49 |
| 5 | $2_b$ | 7 | 19. 8 | 1. 73 ( 81) | $2_c$ | 7 | 23. 3 | 1. 96 ( 75) | 67. 7 | 2. 50 |
| 6 | $2_b$ | 7 | 21. 1 | 2. 17 ( 66) | $2_c$ | 7 | 26. 6 | 2. 48 ( 62) | 104. 1 | 2. 52 |
| 7 | $2_b$ | 7 | 25. 9 | 2. 25 (126) | 1 | 7 | 24. 9 | 2. 32 (121) | 129. 1 | 2. 49 |
| 8 | $2_b$ | 7 | 23. 0 | 2. 36 ( 86) | $2_c$ | 7 | 24. 1 | 2. 48 ( 81) | 157. 7 | 2. 48 |
| 9 | $2_b$ | 7 | 21. 7 | 2. 30 ( 83) | $2_c$ | 7 | 25. 5 | 2. 61 ( 76) | 90. 3 | 2. 52 |
| 10 | $2_b$ | 7 | 23. 6 | 2. 87 ( 67) | $2_c$ | 7 | 29. 3 | 3. 28 ( 63) | 137. 5 | 2. 53 |
| 11 | $2_b$ | 7 | 28. 2 | 2. 98 (126) | 1 | 7 | 27. 5 | 3. 08 (123) | 171. 4 | 2. 48 |
| 12 | $2_b$ | 7 | 25. 5 | 3. 10 ( 88) | $2_c$ | 7 | 26. 9 | 3. 26 ( 82) | 207. 4 | 2. 49 |
| Total | | | | | | | | | 1384. 5 (84) | |

( ): Percentage to The Weight Obtained According to The Current Design Code

## 6. SUMMARY AND CONCLUSIONS

A load combination and reliability analysis of steel rigid-frame piers supporting bridges constructed on urban expressway network were performed using statistical data on various loads. Numerical calculations for 12 model pier structures were carried out. The main results of the analysis are as follows.

(1) The safety indices of the pier structures designed by the ASDM differ considerably from each other, depending on the model type of pier structures.

(2) Having recourse to LFDM, a procedure is presented to determine the optimal values of load factors, for preselected target safety indices, for various load combinations.

(3) Most of the safety indices for the model pier structures which are designed using the proposed optimal load factors agree well with the target safety index $\beta_T$.

(4) The ratio of the total weight of 12 model pier structures which are designed using the optimal load factors to the total weight according to ASDM is 84%, 91% and 101% for $\beta_T$ = 2.5, 3.0 and 3.5, respectively.

**Acknowledgements**

This study was made possible by the use of the observed data offered by the Ad hoc Committee on Design Loads, Hanshin Expressway Public Corporation. The authors are thankful to the Committee for kindness and cooperation.

**References**

1) C.J.Turkstra and O.Madsen : Load Combinations in Codified Structural Design, Jour. of the Struct. Div., ASCE, Vol.106, No.ST12, pp.2527-2543, Dec., 1980.
2) R.D.Larrabee and C.A.Cornell : Combination of Various Load Processes, Jour. of the Structural Division, ASCE, Vol.107, No.ST1, pp.223-239, Jan., 1981.
3) T.V.Galambos, B.Ellingwood, J.G.MacGregor and C.A.Cornell : Probability Based Load Criteria : Assessment of Current Design Practice, Jour. of the Structural Division, ASCE, Vol.108, No.ST5, pp.959-977, May, 1982.
4) B.Ellingwood, J.G.MacGregor, T.V.Galambos and C.A.Cornell : Probability Based Load Criteria : Load Factors and Load Combinations, Jour. of the Structural Division, ASCE, Vol.108, No.ST5, pp.978-997, May, 1982.
5) B.Ellingwood : Probability-Based Criteria for Structural Design, Jour. of Structural Safety, Vol.1, No.1, pp.15-26, 1982.
6) A.S.Nowak : Risk Analysis for Code Calibration, Jour. of Structural Safety, Vol.1, No.4, pp.289-304, 1983.
7) P.T.Christensen and M.J.Baker : Structural Reliability and Its Applications, Springer-Verlag, 1982.
8) R.Rackwitz and B.Fiessler : Structural Reliability under Combined Random Load Sequences, Jour. of Comp. Struct., Vol.9, pp.484-494, 1978.
9) Hanshin Expressway Public Corp. : Design Standards (II), 1980. (in Japanese)
10) The Ad Hoc Committee on Design Loads, Hanshin Expressway Public Corporation : Interim Reports on Investigation of Various Loads Acting on Hanshin Expressway Bridges, 1985-1986. (in Japanese)

# STATISTICAL MODELS FOR DEBRIS IMPACT ON BRIDGE PIERS IN AN ARID AREA

M. Nouh
Associate Professor, Department of Civil Engineering, King Saud University, P. O. Box 800, Riyadh 11421, Saudi Arabia.

## ABSTRACT

Statistical models are proposed to estimate the maximum weight of debris that may collide with a bridge pier during its lifetime in a given arid environment. The models differ in the assumption which deals with the seasonal and yearly variation of the number of colliding debris weights. In the models, the probability distribution of the colliding debris weights is taken exponential and that of the number of colliding debris weights is Poisson. The models are verified using data collected at bridge piers in a typical arid area.

## INTRODUCTION

One of the important forces which are given consideration in the design of bridge piers is that arises from debris loading. It may take one of two forms: (a) impact forces resulting from debris colliding with the piers; and (b) hydrodynamic forces on trapped debris being transferred to the pier. Design specifications normally recommend a specified force for each form of debris loading. For example, In respect of impact forces, the Australian Highway Bridge Design Specification (1965) recommends that the designer should allow for a force equivalent to that exerted by a 2 t log, travelling at the normal stream velocity and arrested within distances of 150 mm and 75 mm for column-type and solid-type concrete piers respectively. Current practice within some british consultancy firms is to allow for a force exerted by a 10 t mass travelling at the design streamflow velocity, which is arrested in a distance of 75 mm. In respect to hydrodynamic forces, an allowance for the hydrodynamic force exerted on a minimum depth of 1.20 m of debris is recommended (NAASRA, 1965). The length of debris jam to be applied to a pier should be half of the sum of the adjacent spans up to a maximum of 21.0 m, and the pressure due to the trapped debris is taken as $P = 0.517\ U^2$; where P is the pressure, KN/m$^2$, and U is the approach velocity, m/s.

Previous studies in arid areas (Nouh, 1986) indicate that the impact forces on a bridge pier are much more significant than the hydrodynamic forces on the pier. The main reason is the nature of streamflows which carry large amounts of debris (stones and boulders) during the flash floods. Thus, this study is concerned only with the impact forces. The primary objective of this study was to propose a model by which a design engineer can estimate, in a given arid environment, the maximum weight of debris that may collide with a bridge pier during its lifetimes.

## ANALYTICAL APPROACH

Assume a specified impact force due to debris weight of $w_o$ is considered in the design of a bridge pier. The purpose is to estimate the maximum weight of debris W(T) that may collide with the pier during its life time of T years.

As principles of the proposed models, the distribution of all colliding debris weights which are larger than the specified weight is a conditional distribution and statements of the type "the probability that a debris weight w is > 50 tons, given that it is > 10 tons ( = $w_o$), is 0.20" are made. Such a statement means that 80% of all debris weights which are larger than 10 tons are less than 50 tons but it does not mean that 80% of all debris weights are less than 50 tons. This latter statement is the kind of statement which is required. It is a statement which is unconditional on the value of $w_o$ which, being arbitrary, has no place in the statement finally required. To pass from the conditional to the unconditional statement requires knowledge of the probability of the condition. This transition is expressed as

$$\text{Prob } (A.B) = \text{Prob } (A \mid B) \ \text{Prob}(B) \tag{1}$$

in which Prob denotes probability, B is the event that a debris weight which is larger than $w_o$ ( = 10 tons in the above example) does occur, $A \mid B$ is the event that a debris weight picked from those which are larger than 10 tons also is larger than 50 tons (see the above example) while A.B is the event that any debris weight picked from among all debris weights which are larger than 50 tons (as well as 10 tons).

The quantity Prob $(A \mid B)$ can be obtained from the conditional distribution of debris weights which are larger than the specified weight $w_o$ at a bridge pier. To identify this distribution, debris weights collided with 22 bridge piers in the southwest region of Saudi Arabia were measured, and the debris weights which are larger than a specified value $w_o$ at each of the piers were fitted to different probability distribution functions. Fig. 1 shows the size and shape of these debris at one of the piers. After each flash flood (during the dry period following the flood flows) the volumes of debris collided with each pier were

**Fig. 1. A typical example of size and shape of debris collided with bridge piers in the southwest region of Saudi Arabia [bridge no. 23, road 54, Abha-Al-darb (Nouh, 1986)].**

measured,and then the debris were removed to prepare the site to receive another set of debris during the followed flash flood event. Considering a relative density of debris material equal to 2.70 (checked by 12 tests), these volumes are transferred to debris weights. A specified weight of 100 kg (= $w_o$) was subtracted from these debris weights, and the subtracted weights were then fitted to different probability distribution functions. The two-parameter normal distribution, the three-parameter normal distribution, the two-parameter lognormal distribution, the three-parameter lognormal distribution, the exponential distribution, the two-parameter gamma distribution, the Pearson type 3 distribution, the log-Pearson type 3 distribution, and the extreme value distributions (type 1, 2, and 3) were considered. At 18 (out of 22) bridge piers the exponential distribution was found to best fit the subtracted debris weights. Figs. 2 and 3 show typical examples of fit of subtracted debris weights to an exponential distribution. Based on these results, the exponential distribution is considered the proper function to evaluate Prob (A | B) in Eq. 1.

The quantity Prob (B), the probability of an occurrence of a debris weight which is larger than the specified weight $w_o$, cannot be determined without reference to a time interval because for a given weight $w_o$ the probability of B during an interval of 1 year is less than its probability during 10 years. If for a given $w_o$ the number of debris weights which are larger than $w_o$ in successive years is counted it will be seen that the same number does not in each year; if the year is broken up into seasons then the same number does not occur in each season. These facts regarding Prob (B) are either taken into account or ignored in the proposed various statistical models of debris impact on bridge piers.

In each of the statistical models the conditional distribution of debris weights which are larger than $w_o$ is considered to be exponential. Thus

$$F\,(W \leqq w \mid w \geqq w_o) = 1 - e^{-(w - w_o)/\beta} \tag{2}$$

or in the notation given above

$$\text{Prob}\,(A \mid B) = \text{Prob}\,(W \geqq w \mid w \geqq w_o) = e^{-(w - w_o)/\beta} \tag{3}$$

where F(.) denotes distribution function, and $\beta$ is the distribution parameter.

Three statistical models (which differ from each other in the way the number of debris weights over the specified weight $w_o$ each year is treated) are proposed. Description of these models are given hereafter.

**Model 1:** In this model, it is assumed that the number of debris weights over the specified weight $w_o$ is invariant with either season or year, and a constant number of weight exceedances, $\lambda$, is assumed to occur.

Thus, there are $\lambda$ weight exceedances each year so that there are $\lambda T$ such weight exceedances in T years. Therefore, the T year colliding debris weight occurs once on average among every $\lambda T$ debris weights which are larger than $w_o$ which is equivalent to saying that it has a return period $T' = \lambda T$ sampling units where a sampling unit is a debris weight over the weight $w_o$. Thus, the T year debris weight W(T) is given implicity by

$$F\,(W \leqq W(T) \mid W(T) \geqq w_o) = 1 - 1/\lambda T \tag{4}$$

when the conditional distribution of debris weights is given by Eq. 3 this gives

$$W(T) = w_o + \beta \ln \lambda + \beta \ln T. \tag{5}$$

During a time interval of one year the probability that r of the $\lambda$ exceedances also exceed a higher value w is given by the binomial distribution as

$$\text{Prob}\,(r \mid \lambda) = \binom{\lambda}{r} [\text{Prob}\,(A \mid B)]^{r}\,[1 - \text{Prob}(A \mid B)]^{\lambda - r} \tag{6}$$

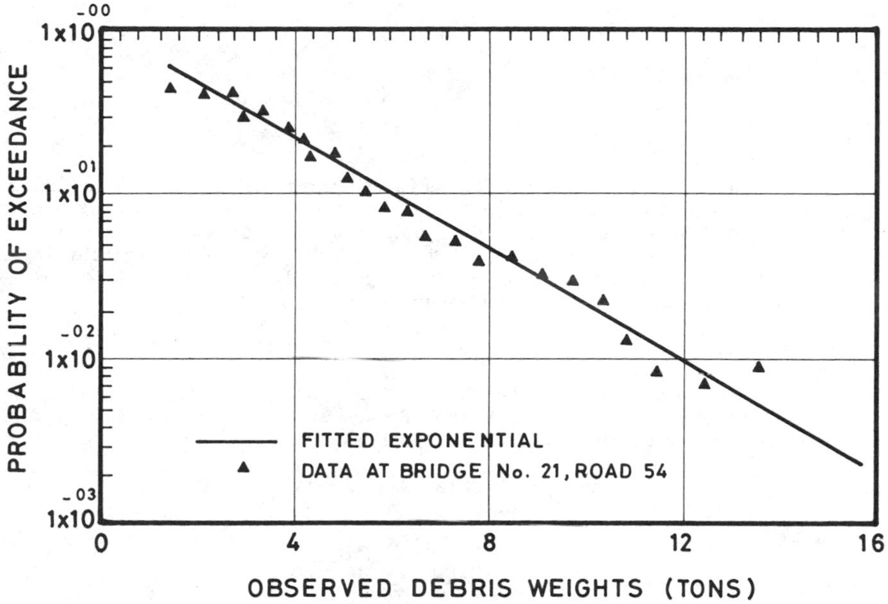


Fig. 2. Fitting of abstracted debris weights to an exponential distribution.

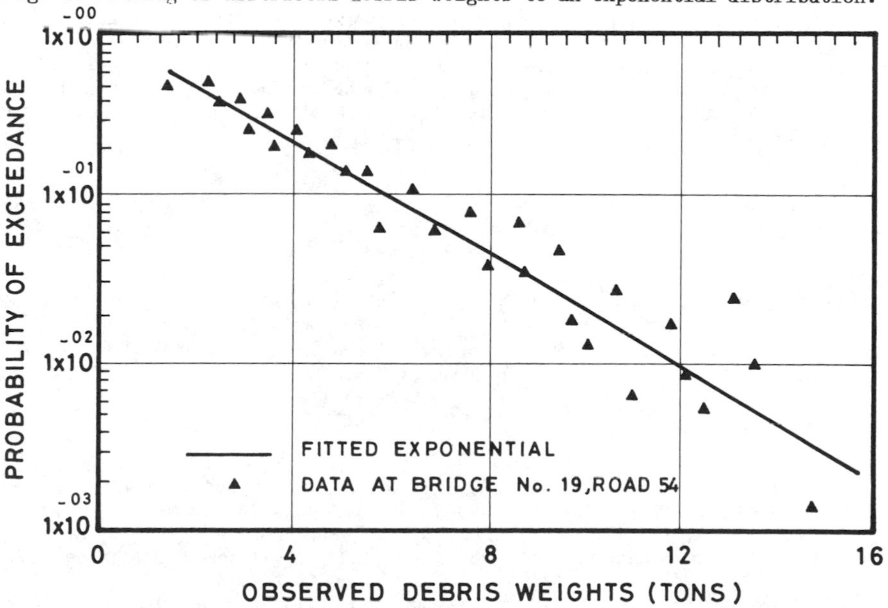


Fig. 3. Fitting of abstracted debris weights to an exponential distribution.

If $r = 0$ the annual maximum debris weight $W_{max}$ is less than $w$. Therefore

$$\text{Prob}\ (W_{max} \leq w) = \text{Prob}\ (0\,|\,\lambda) = [1-\text{Prob}(A\,|\,B)]^{\lambda} \tag{7}$$

and when Eq. 2 gives the distribution of debris weights

$$\text{Prob}\ (W_{max} \leq w) = [1-e^{-(w-w_o)/\beta}\ ]^{\lambda} \tag{8}$$

**Model 2:** In this model the variation between years in the number of debris weights exceeding $w_o$ is considered, but the variation between seasons within the year is ignored. The number of colliding debris weights in a year is considered to be a random variable with mean $\lambda$. Let $p_0, p_1, \ldots, p_\tau$ be the probability of 0, 1 ... $\tau$ debris weights exceeding $w_o$ in a year. If $\tau$ debris weights exceed $w_o$ in a year the probability that r of them exceed $w \geq w_o$ is

$$\text{Prob (r debris weights} > w\,|\,\tau\ ) = \binom{\tau}{r} [\text{Prob}(A\,|\,B)]^r\ [1-\text{Prob}\ (A\,|\,B)]^{\tau-r} \tag{9}$$

This is a conditional probability, conditional on $\tau$ weights $> w_o$ occurring. The r weights $> w$ may occur with any value of $\tau$ providing $r \leq \tau$. The unconditional probability that r weights exceed in a year is therefore

$$\text{Prob (r weights} > w) = \sum_{\tau=r}^{\infty} \text{Prob (r weights} > w\,|\,\tau)\ p_\tau$$

$$= \sum_{T=0}^{\infty} \binom{T+r}{r} [\ \text{Prob}\ (A\,|\,B)]^r\ [1-\text{Prob}\ (A\,|\,B)]^T\ p_{T+r} \tag{10}$$

The number of events exceeding $w_o$ in a year is taken in this study as a Poisson variate. In applications this assumption should be verified using actual data. However, the lifetime of a bridge pier is normally more than 10 years, and for this large return period the mean number of debris weights per year needs to be known but specification of the correct distribution is less important. Nevertheless, if the Poisson distribution is considered, the probability of debris weights over $w_o$ is given as

$$p_\tau = e^{-\lambda}\ \ \lambda^\tau / \tau! \tag{11}$$

Inserting for $p_{T+r}$ in Eq. 10 gives

$$\text{Prob (r weights} > w) = \sum_{T=0}^{\infty} \binom{T+r}{r} \text{Prob}\ (A\,|\,B)^r (1-\text{Prob}(A|B))^T\ \frac{e^{-\lambda}\lambda^{T+r}}{(\ T+r\ )!}$$

$$= \frac{e^{-\lambda\ \text{Prob}(A|\,B)}\ .\ [\ \lambda\,\text{Prob}(A|B)]^r}{r\,!} \tag{12}$$

This indicates that the distribution of the number of debris weights exceeding the higher level w is also a Poisson distribution with parameter $\lambda$Prob(A B). Here, $\lambda$ is the rate per year at which $w_o$ is exceeded and Prob (A| B) is the proportion of these weights which exceed $w_o$ which also exceed the higher level w, as in Eq. 3.

The T year colliding debris weight is found by treating the weight $w > w_o$ as a variable and deriving the value of w which is exceeded on average once in T years. From Eq. 12 it is seen that the number of weights exceeding w each year is a Poisson variate with mean $\lambda$Prob(A|B) and because of the additive property of Poisson variates the number of colliding weights exceeding w during intervals of length $\lambda T$ years is a Poisson variate with mean $\lambda T$ Prob(A|B). If w is such that this last quantity is one then w is the T year colliding debris weight. That is

$$\lambda T \, Prob(A|B) = 1 \tag{13}$$

Inserting for Prob (A|B) from Eq. 3 gives

$$F\,(W \leq W(T) \mid W(T) \geq w_o) = 1 - 1/\lambda T \tag{14}$$

and when F(.) is exponential this reduces to

$$W(T) = w_o + \beta \ln \lambda + \beta \ln T. \tag{15}$$

which is identical to Eq. 5 in model 1. This means that the adoption of a random Poisson model instead of a constant for the number of debris weights exceeding $w_o$ has added nothing in the expression of W(T).

Referring to Eq. 11 the probability that no debris weight exceeds $w_o$ is $p_o = e^{-\lambda}$. This means that in the proportion $e^{-\lambda}$ of years the annual maximum colliding weight is less than $w_o$. Since the distribution of weights is specified for weights exceeding $w_o$ there is no possibility of describing that portion of the distribution of annual maxima in the range $w < w_o$. The distribution of annual maxima which exceed $w_o$ can however be derived. From Eq. 12 the unconditional probability that no debris weights, r=0, exceed the level w in a year can be obtained and this is the probability that the annual maximum is less than w.

$$Prob\,(W_{max} \leq w) = Prob\,(\text{No weights} > w) = e^{-\lambda Prob(A|B)} \tag{16}$$

or

$$Prob\,(W_{max} \leq w) = e^{-\lambda\,[1-F(W \leq w \mid w \geq w_o)]} \tag{17}$$

and if F(.) is exponential as in Eq. 3 this gives

$$Prob\,(W_{max} \leq w) = e^{-\lambda e^{-(w-w_o)/\beta}} \tag{18}$$

**Model 3:** This model takes seasonal variation in the number of debris weights exceeding $w_o$ into account. Let the year be divided into two seasons and let the number of debris weights occurring in the first season have Poisson distribution with mean $\lambda_1$ and let the number occurring in the second season have Poisson distribution with mean $\lambda_2$. Under these assumptions the total number of events is also a Poisson variate with mean $\lambda = \lambda_1 + \lambda_2$ because the sum of any number of Poisson variates is a Poisson variate. Therefore, the results appropriate to model 2 are also appropriate to this model and in particular the T year debris weight is

$$W(T) = w_o + \beta \ln(\lambda_1 + \lambda_2) + \beta \ln T \tag{19}$$

As extension of this is the general time dependent Poisson process where the number of debris weights exceeding $w_o$ in any time interval follows a Poisson law the parameter of which depends on not only the length of the interval but also the time of year in which it begins. If t=0 indicates the beginning of the year let $\Lambda(t_1)$ be the average number of debris weights exceeding $w_o$ between time t=0 and $t=t_1$. Then in any year the probability of r events between t=0 and $t=t_1$ is

$$Prob\,[r \text{ in } (t_0, t_1)] = (e^{-\Lambda(t_1)}[\Lambda(t_1)]^r)/r! \tag{20}$$

If the interval extending from time $t_1$ to $t_2$ is considered, the number of debris weights exceeding $w_o$ is a Poisson variate with mean $\Lambda(t_2) - \Lambda(t_1)$.

For the distribution of annual maxima Eqs. 16 to 18 still hold, with $\lambda$ rep-placed by $\Lambda(t=365)$. Similarly, if $W^s_{max}$ is the maximum in the season its distribution function is

$$\text{Prob } (W^s_{max} \leq w) = e^{-[\Lambda(t_2) - \Lambda(t_1)].[1-F(W \leq w \mid w \geq w_o)]} \tag{21}$$

If the distribution of debris weights is exponential with parameters $w_o$ and $\beta$ then by Eq. 3 the distribution of $W^s_{max}$ can be obtained.

**Estimation of parameters:** Suppose a bridge pier is designed for a colliding debris weight $w_o$, and it is required to estimate the maximum debris weight that may collide with the pier during its lifetime of T years. The proposed models give the annual maximum debris weight, W(T), that exceeds $w_o$ and is expected to collide with the pier during the time of T years, and give also its probability of occurrence.

In order to utilise any of these models in a given environment the distribution of debris weights exceeding $w_o$ and the distribution of the number of weight exceedances should be verified using actual data. In a given environment, and at a site suppose that M exceedances of weights $w_1, w_2, \ldots, w_M$ are measured in N years. Thus, the maximum likelihood method of estimation gives

$$\hat{\lambda} = M/N \tag{22}$$

and

$$\hat{\beta} = \bar{w} - w_o \tag{23}$$

where

$$\bar{w} = \sum_{i=1}^{M} w_i/M$$

Eqs. 22 and 23 estimate the parameters of model 2. For model 3 the exceedances should be evaluated per season. This means that M should be the number of seasonal exceedances and N is the number of seasons within a fixed time interval.

## APPLICATIONS

The proposed models were applied to 22 bridge piers in the southwest region of Saudi Arabia. As it has been mentioned earlier, the debris weights exceeding a specified weight $w_o$ are best fitted by the exponential distribution (see Figs. 2 and 3). The number of weights exceeding $w_o$ is found to vary from season to season, but does not vary from year to year. During the dry season (from April to November) the number of debris weights exceeding $w_o$ is larger than that during the wet season (from December to March). These characteristics of the yearly number of debris weights fit the assumptions of model 3; thus, this model was utilised to evaluate W(T) at bridge number 21 where 3 years of data were collected. Table 1 summarizes the results obtained using different values for $w_o$.

Inspection of the table indicates that the weight of debris that is expected to collide with the pier increases as the return period (taken as the lifetime of the bridge pier) increases, and such weight of debris is more or less independent on the value of $w_o$ Based on the value of the estimated debris weight, the designer can evaluate the various forces on the pier and then determine the risk of the bridge pier failure.

**Table 1. Expected weight of debris at bridge number 21 for various return periods and initial specified weight $w_o$.**

| $w_o$ (tons) | $\lambda_1 + \lambda_2$ ( = $\lambda$ ) | $\beta$ | Return Period "T" ( years ) 5 | 10 | 15 | 25 | 50 | 100 |
|---|---|---|---|---|---|---|---|---|
| 0.10 | 28.6 | 2.14 | 10.720 | 12.204 | 13.071 | 14.164 | 15.647 | 17.131 |
| 0.50 | 18.5 | 2.32 | 11.002 | 12.611 | 13.551 | 14.737 | 16.345 | 17.953 |
| 1.00 | 8.6 | 2.69 | 11.117 | 12.982 | 14.073 | 15.447 | 17.311 | 19.176 |
| 2.00 | 5.5 | 2.83 | 11.378 | 13.340 | 14.487 | 15.933 | 17.895 | 19.856 |
| 5.00 | 3.9 | 2.36 | 12.010 | 13.646 | 14.603 | 15.808 | 17.444 | 19.080 |

## CONCLUSIONS

Three statistical models are proposed to estimate the maximum weight of debris that may collide with a bridge pier during a period of T years. The models help a bridge designer to evaluate the risk of failure of the pier.

Applications of these models in a typical arid area in Saudi Arabia shows that impact forces arise from a debris weight of 15 tons should be considered in the design of a bridge pier having a lifetime up to 25 years. For longer lifetimes (up to 100 years) a debris weight of 20 tons should be considered.

## ACKNOWLEDGEMENTS

This study was supported by the King Abdul-Aziz City for Science and Technology (KACST), operating grant number AR-5-62. The author appreciates the assistance of Mr. O. Abaza (from the Research Center of the College of Engineering, King Saud University) during the computations and data collection.

## REFERENCES

National Association of Australian State Road Authorities.(1965)."Highway Bridge Design Specifications ".

Nouh, M.(1986)."Construction Damages Due to Floods in Wadi Ad-Dilah," Interim Final Report Prepared for the King Abdul-Aziz City for Science and Technology (KACST), KACST, Riyadh, Saudi Arabia, 212p.

# STATISTICAL STRUCTURE OF INITIAL IMPERFECTION BY ENTROPY MODEL

A. Miyamura*, M. Murata* and S. Kato**
*School of Architecture, Meijo University, Nagoya, Japan 468
**Department of Structural Engineering, Toyohashi University of Technology, Toyohashi, Japan 440

ABSTRACT

Although initial imperfections are statistically evaluated in the practical design formula such as the buckling strength curves, their probabilistic structure cannot be analyzed yet because of their complication. The present paper deals with the generation mechanism of initial imperfections by means of the entropy model. This demands the entropy of imperfections maximized under constraint which corresponds to the energy balance equation where the disturbance energy is divided into the control energy to prevent the generation and the residual energy. When these energies can be assumed the elastic ones and the initial imperfections normally distributed, the covariance matrix is expressed in a closed form for the cases of string, rectangular plate, and rotational shell.

## 1. INTRODUCTION

Initial imperfections such as residual stresses, initial deflections or inevitable eccentricities play the important role in the instability behavior of slender structural systems. The buckling curves of centrally loaded column show prominent sensitivity to the initial imperfections. Thus the European column buckling curves take account of the dispersion of all kinds of imperfection from the test results as-delivered with actual imperfections ( Bjorhovde 1972 ). This strength curves, hence, are considered as empirical formulae because of the uncertainty of imperfection characteristics, especially on their probabilistic properties. Moreover, large-scaled shell structures such as reinforced concrete cooling tower, whose stress resultants are intensely influenced by initial imperfections, are not practically designed on their actual distribution. The present paper deals with the probabilistic structure of initial imperfections distributed on the structural systems. To estimate it the entropy model can be applied. The entropy model demands determination of state parameter vector by the maximum entropy criteria instead of the fundamental equations of a system ( Backman 1976, Tai 1978 ). The entropy of initial imperfection should be maximized under certain constraint. The present entropy model is applied to the cases of string, rectangular plate and rotational shell systems. Statistical analysis of actual initial imperfection distributed on welded wide flange members shows a good agreement with the theory.

## 2. ENTROPY MODEL OF INITIAL IMPERFECTION

Based on the mode superposition method the initial displacement vector can be expressed as,

$$\{v^I\}^T = \{u^I(s_1,s_2),\ v^I(s_1,s_2),\ w^I(s_1,s_2)\} \qquad \text{-------------}(1)$$

$$u^I(S_1,S_2) = \sum_{i=1}^{N} \xi_i u_i(S_1,S_2)$$

$$v^I(S_1,S_2) = \sum_{i=1}^{N} \xi_i v_i(S_1,S_2) \qquad \text{-------------(2)}$$

$$w^I(S_1,S_2) = \sum_{i=1}^{N} \xi_i w_i(S_1,S_2)$$

where $u^I$, $v^I$, $w^I$ are initial displacements in $S_1$, $S_2$ and normal directions, respectively ( Fig.1 ). $\xi_i$, $(u_i,v_i,w_i)$ , and $N$ mean the amplitude variable of i-th displacement mode, the displacement field compatible to the boundary condition, and the number of modes. From Eqs.(1) and (2) the probabilistic structure is derived; The auto-correlation and mean functions in each direction define the covariance matrix. The generalized power spectrum density function is obtainable by Wiener-Khintchine relationship.

With regard to the generation mechanism the initial displacement is provided by external disturbance due to the errors of production process such as the production error or observation error. However, all these errors cannot directly contribute to generation, and the practical process demands to prevent occurence of them to some extent by such as strengthening quality control against these errors. Since it becomes difficult to evaluate these effects analytically, herein, the balance of energies due to generation is assumed. The difference between disturbance energy contributed to generation of initial displacement and the control energy contributed to prevention becomes the residual energy which can provide actual occurrence of imperfection. This implies the disturbance energy is partly absorbed by the controlling mechanism and only the rest contributes to generation. More rigorously speaking, the above energy balance may contain residual errors, whose ensemble mean, hence, necessarily eliminates. Thus the following energy balance equation can be obtained.

$$E[V_I] + E[V_C] - E[U_P] = 0 \qquad \text{--------------(3)}$$

where $V_I$ means residual energy, $V_C$, control potential energy and $U_P$, disturbance energy, respectively. In order to evaluate each energy the following assumptions are made; Residual energy is assumed equivalent to the elastic strain energy over all the system. Control potential energy is assumed in terms of forces proportional to the amplitude of initial displacement and its first derivative. The former contributes to retrieve totally generation, whereas the latter, locally. Disturbance energy is due to every errors interacted each other complicatedly, totally and locally. This assumes the existence of both white noise and locally powered noise. Herein for simplicity the band-limited white noise is assumed.

With regard to the residual energy, firstly, the accumulated strain energy on the system becomes

$$V_I = \int_V \frac{1}{2} L^T\{u^I,v^I,w^I\}^T \cdot H \cdot L\{u^I,v^I,w^I\}^T dV \qquad \text{-------------(4)}$$

where $\int_V(\ )dV$ means integration over all the system, $H$, elastic constant matrix. Substituting the assumed displacement Eq.(2) into Eq.(4) then the residual energy becomes

$$V_I = \sum_{i=1}^{N}\sum_{j=1}^{N} A_{ij}\xi_i\xi_j \qquad \text{-------------(5)}$$

where

$$A_{ij} = \frac{1}{2}\int_V L^T\{u_i,v_i,w_i\}^T \cdot H \cdot L\{u_j,v_j,w_j\}^T dV \qquad \text{-------------(6)}$$

The expectation of Eq.(5) is

$$E[V_I] = \sum_{i=1}^{N}\sum_{j=1}^{N} C_{ij}A_{ij} \qquad \text{-------------(7)}$$

The covariance matrix of random variable $C_{ij}$ can be expressed as,

$$C_{ij} = \iint_{-\infty}^{\infty} \xi_i\xi_j P(\xi_i,\xi_j)d\xi_i d\xi_j \qquad \text{-------------(8)}$$

where the mean of variables for each mode is assumed zero. Secondly, the control potential energy is assumed linear, and proportional to the initial displacement and its first derivative in normal direction with respect to $\partial w^I/\partial S_1$ and $\partial w^I/\partial S_2$. Thus,

$$f_{c1} = \mathrm{diag}\{\rho_u(S_1,S_2),\rho_v(S_1,S_2),\rho_w(S_1,S_2)\}\{u^I,v^I,w^I\}^T \qquad \text{-------------(9)}$$

$$f_{c2} = \mathrm{diag}\{\eta_{w1}(S_1,S_2),\eta_{w2}(S_1,S_2)\}\{\frac{\partial w^I}{\partial S_1},\frac{\partial w^I}{\partial S_2}\}^T \qquad \text{------------(10)}$$

where $\rho_u$, $\rho_v$, $\rho_w$, $\eta_{w1}$, and $\eta_{w2}$ are the constants evaluated from process errors during production of the system. The larger these constants become, the lesser the initial displacement occur actually. With Eqs.(2), (9) and (10) the control potential energy becomes

$$V_C = \sum_{i=1}^{N}\sum_{j=1}^{N} \xi_i\xi_j(\alpha_{ij}+\beta_{ij}) \qquad \text{------------(11)}$$

where

$$\alpha_{ij} = \frac{1}{2}\int_V (u_i,v_i,w_i)\begin{bmatrix}\rho_u & & \\ & \rho_v & \\ & & \rho_w\end{bmatrix}\begin{Bmatrix}u_j\\ v_j\\ w_j\end{Bmatrix} dV \qquad \text{-------------(12)}$$

$$\beta_{ij} = \frac{1}{2}\int_V \left(\frac{\partial w_i}{\partial S_1},\frac{\partial w_i}{\partial S_2}\right)\begin{bmatrix}\eta_{w1} & \\ & \eta_{w2}\end{bmatrix}\begin{Bmatrix}\frac{\partial w_j}{\partial S_1}\\ \frac{\partial w_j}{\partial S_2}\end{Bmatrix} dV \qquad \text{-------------(13)}$$

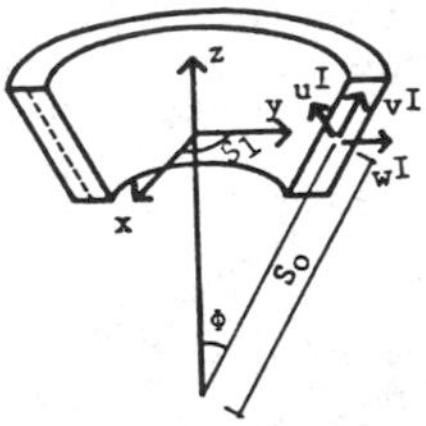


Fig. 1 Coordinate

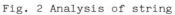

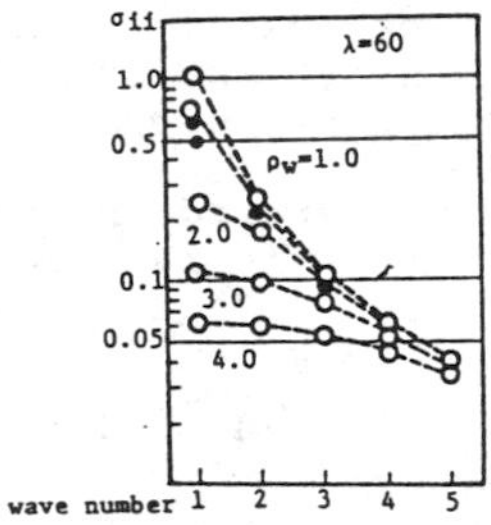


Fig. 2 Analysis of string

The expected control potential is

$$E[V_C] = \sum_{i=1}^{N}\sum_{j=1}^{N} C_{ij}(\alpha_{ij}+\beta_{ij}) \qquad \text{--------------(14)}$$

Lastly, the expected disturbance energy is evaluated by the band-limited white noise as,

$$E[U_p] = \int_V(\bar{N}_u^2 + \bar{N}_v^2 + \bar{N}_w^2)dv = \gamma^2 V \qquad \text{--------------(15)}$$

where

$$\gamma^2 = \gamma_u^2 f_{u1}f_{u2} + \gamma_v^2 f_{v1}f_{v2} + \gamma_w^2 f_{w1}f_{w2} \quad ; \quad V = \int_V dV \qquad \text{--------------(16)}$$

$(f_{u1},f_{u2})$, $(f_{v1},f_{v2})$, and $(f_{w1},f_{w2})$ are the cut-off frequencies of disturbance corresponding to $u$, $v$, and $w$, respectively.
When the entropy of initial displacement is evaluated its covariance can be determined by the maximum entropy criteria. The joint probability density function of random variable in Eq.(2) is assumed the following multivariate normal distribution.

$$P(\xi) = \frac{1}{(2\pi)^{\frac{N}{2}}|C|^{\frac{1}{2}}} \mathrm{EXP}\{-\frac{1}{2}\{\xi\}^T[C]^{-1}\{\xi\}\} \qquad \text{--------------(17)}$$

where $\{\xi\}$ means $\{\xi_1,\xi_2,,\xi_N\}$ vector, $[C]$, its covariance matrix, $|C|$ determinant, $[C]^{-1}$, inverse matrix, respectively. Using the normally distributed joint probability density function, Eq.(17), the entropy of initial displacement can be expressed as,

$$H = -\int\int\cdots\int_{-\infty}^{\infty} P(\xi)\log(P(\xi))d\xi_1 d\xi_2\cdots d\xi_N \qquad \text{---------(18)}$$

When applied the maximum entropy criteria the energy balance, Eq.(3), is adopted as the constraint. Hence, the functional becomes

$$D = \log\{(2\pi e)^{\frac{N}{2}}|C|^{\frac{1}{2}}\} - \lambda\{\sum_{i=1}^{N}\sum_{j=1}^{N}(A_{ij}+\alpha_{ij}+\beta_{ij})C_{ij} - V\gamma^2\} \qquad \text{---------(19)}$$

where $\lambda$ means Lagrange multiplier. Eq.(19) should be stationary with respect to $C_{ij}$ and $\lambda$. Concludingly, the covariance matrix becomes

$$C_{ij}^{-1} = \frac{N(A_{ij}+\alpha_{ij}+\beta_{ij})}{V\gamma^2} \qquad \text{--------------(20)}$$

Eq.(20) predicts the covariance matrix inversely which provides the generalized power spectrum density function matrix by Wiener-Khintchine relationship. Hence, the estimation of probabilistic structure of initial displacement can be accomplished.

## 3. APPLICATION TO STRUCTURAL SYSTEMS

STRING---The present theory is applied to the initial displacement of a string, whose Fourier series becomes

$$w^I(S) = \sum_{i=1}^{N}\xi_i \sin\frac{i\pi S}{L} \qquad \text{--------------(21)}$$

where $\xi_i$ means the amplitude random variable of the i-th mode and $L$, string length ( Fig. 2 ). The expected residual energy along the string becomes

$$E[V_I] = \sum_{i=1}^{N} A_{ii} C_{ii} \qquad (22)$$

where

$$A_{ij} = \frac{EI}{2}\int_0^L \left(\frac{i\pi}{L}\right)^2 \left(\frac{j\pi}{L}\right)^2 \sin\frac{i\pi S}{L}\sin\frac{j\pi S}{L}dS = \frac{EI\pi^4}{4L^3} i^4 \quad (i=j)$$
$$= 0 \quad (i \neq j) \qquad (23)$$

The expected control potential energy can be expressed as,

$$E[V_c] = \sum_{i=1}^{N}\sum_{j=1}^{N} (\alpha_{ij} + \beta_{ij}) C_{ij} \qquad (24)$$

$$\alpha_{ij} = \frac{\rho_w}{2}\int_0^L \sin\frac{i\,S}{L}\sin\frac{j\,S}{L}dS = \frac{\rho_w L}{4} \quad (i=j)$$
$$= 0 \quad (i \neq j) \qquad (25)$$

$$\beta_{ij} = \frac{\eta_w \pi^2 ij}{2L}\int_0^L \cos\frac{i\pi S}{L}\cos\frac{j\pi S}{L}dS = \frac{i^2\pi^2\eta_w}{4L} \quad (i=j)$$
$$= 0 \quad (i \neq j) \qquad (26)$$

where $\rho_W$ and $\eta_W$ mean the constants due to the process errors of string. The expected disturbance energy can be obtained.

$$E[U_p] = L\gamma^2 \qquad (27)$$

By use of Eqs.(23) to (27), Eq.(20) provides the covariance matrix. From statistical analysis of observed data (Aoki 1973) for the welded wide flange members of medium slenderness ratio, there is a good agreement with the theory when the control constant $\rho_w$ becomes approximately unit. Each mode of initial displacement is independent. Furthermore, each covariance becomes inversely proportional to the fourth power of Fourier number.

RECTANGULAR PLATE---The initial displacement of a rectangular plate can be expressed as,

$$w(x,y) = \sum_{i=1}^{N}\sum_{j=1}^{N} \xi_{ij}\sin\frac{i\pi x}{a}\sin\frac{j\pi y}{b} \qquad (28)$$

where $\xi_{ij}$ means the i,j-th amplitude of initial displacement (Fig. 3). The expected residual energy can be expressed as,

$$E[V_I] = \sum_{i=1}^{N}\sum_{j=1}^{N} C_{ij} A_{ij} \qquad (29)$$

where

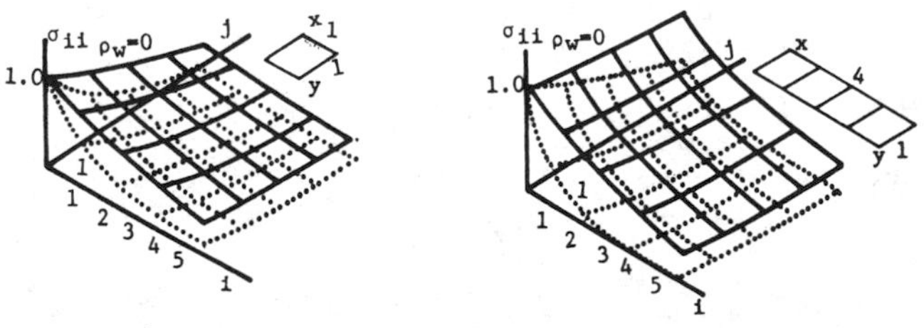


Fig. 3 Analysis of rectangular plates

$$A_{ij} = \frac{1}{8} abD\left(\frac{i^2\pi^2}{a^2} + \frac{j^2\pi^2}{b^2}\right)^2 \qquad \text{--------------(30)}$$

The expected control potential energy is

$$E[V_C] = \sum_{i=1}^{N}\sum_{j=1}^{N} \{\alpha_{ij} + \beta_{ij}\} \, C_{ij} \qquad \text{--------------(31)}$$

where $\alpha_{ij}$ and $\beta_{ij}$ are the control terms proportional to the deflection amplitude and its first derivative, respectively, expressed as,

$$\alpha_{ij} = \frac{1}{8} tab \, \rho_w \qquad \text{--------------(32)}$$

where $\rho_W$ means a parameter providing the extent of diminishing the initial displacement.

$$\beta_{ij} = \frac{1}{8} tab\{(\frac{i\pi}{a})^2 \eta_{w1} + (\frac{j\pi}{b})^2 \eta_{w2}\} \qquad \text{--------------(33)}$$

where $\eta_{W1}$ and $\eta_{W2}$ are the parameters proportional to the first derivatives. The expected disturbance energy can be expressed as,

$$E[U_P] = tab\gamma^2 \qquad \text{--------------(34)}$$

where $\gamma^2$ means the energy constant due to the input disturbance. As a result the covariance matrix can be expressed by Eq.(20). Fig. 3 shows the power spectrum of aspect ratios a/b=1 and 4.

ROTATIONAL SHELL---Although the stress resultants of reinforced concrete cooling tower are significantly sensitive to initial displacements, there are so few observed data available that the artificial generation of initial displacement becomes essential from the engineering design point of view ( Calladine 1972 ). The present theory can provide such simulation. The initial displacement is expressed as,

$$w^I(s,\theta) = w_1^I(s,\theta) + w_2^I(s,\theta)$$

$$w_1^I(s,\theta) = \sum_{i=1}^{N} \xi_i w_i(s)\cos N_i\theta \quad ; \quad N_i = 0,1,\ldots,\bar{N} \qquad \text{--------------(35)}$$

$$w_2^I(s,\theta) = \sum_{j=1}^{N} a_j(s)\cos j\theta$$

where $w_1^I(s,\theta)$ means the initial displacement due to random disturbance and $w_2^I(s,\theta)$, the mean one. s and $\theta$ mean the longitudinal and meridional directions, $w_i$, the initial displacement mode in the normal direction, $\xi_i$, the maximum number of Fourier series, respectively. Thus the residual energy accumulated in the shell becomes

$$V_I = \frac{1}{2}\int_V ( L_t\{^u_v\} + L_b\{w\})^T \cdot H \cdot ( L_t\{^u_v\} + L_b\{w\})dV \qquad \text{-------------(36)}$$

$$L_t\{^u_v\} = \begin{bmatrix} \frac{\partial}{\partial s} & 0 \\ \frac{1}{S_0} & \frac{1}{S_0\sin\phi}\frac{\partial}{\partial\theta} \\ \frac{1}{2S_0\sin\phi}\frac{\partial}{\partial\theta} & \frac{1}{2}(\frac{\partial}{\partial s} - \frac{1}{S_0}) \\ -\frac{\partial\phi}{\partial s}\frac{\partial}{\partial s} - \frac{\partial^2\phi}{\partial s^2} & 0 \end{bmatrix} \{^u_v\}$$

$$\left.\begin{matrix} -\frac{1}{S_0}\frac{\partial\phi}{\partial S} & \Big| \; \frac{\cos\phi}{S_0^2\sin^2\phi}\frac{\partial}{\partial\theta} \\ -\left(\frac{3}{4S_0\sin\phi}\frac{\partial\phi}{\partial S}+\frac{\cos\phi}{4S_0^2\sin\phi}\right)\frac{\partial}{\partial\theta} & \Big| \; \left(\frac{1\partial\phi}{4\partial S}+\frac{3}{4S_0}\frac{\cos\phi}{\sin\phi}\right)\frac{\partial}{\partial S}-\left(\frac{3\cos\phi}{4S_0^2\sin\phi}+\frac{1}{4S_0}\frac{\partial\phi}{\partial S}\right) \end{matrix}\right]$$

$$L_b(w) = \left\{\frac{\partial\phi}{\partial S},\ -\frac{\cos\phi}{S_0\sin\phi},\ 0,\ \frac{\partial^2}{\partial S^2},\ \frac{1}{S_0^2\sin^2\phi}\frac{\partial^2}{\partial\theta^2}+\frac{1}{S_0}\frac{\partial}{\partial S},\ \frac{1}{S_0\sin\phi}\frac{\partial}{\partial\theta}\left(\frac{\partial}{\partial S}-\frac{1}{S_0}\right)\right\}^T\{w\} \qquad \text{------------(37)}$$

$$H = \begin{bmatrix} E_I & 0 \\ 0 & \frac{t^2}{12}E_I \end{bmatrix} \quad E_I = \frac{Et}{1-\nu^2}\begin{bmatrix} 1 & \nu & 0 \\ \nu & 1 & 0 \\ 0 & 0 & 2(1-\nu) \end{bmatrix} \qquad \text{------------(38)}$$

The expectation of Eq.(36) can be expressed as,

$$E[V_I] = \iint_{-\infty}^{\infty} \sum_{i=1}^{N}\sum_{j=1}^{N} B_{ij}\ \xi_i\xi_j P(\xi_i,\xi_j)d\xi_i d\xi_j = \sum_{i=1}^{N}\sum_{j=1}^{N} B_{ij}C_{ij} \qquad \text{--------(39)}$$

$$B_{ij} = \frac{1}{2}\int_V L_b(w_i\cos N_i\theta)H\ L_b(w_j\cos N_j\theta)dV \qquad \text{--------(40)}$$

The control potential energy is assumed in terms of the displacement and its first derivative as,

$$V_C = \sum_{i=1}^{N}\sum_{j=1}^{N}\{{}_1\beta_{ij}+{}_2\beta_{ij}+{}_3\beta_{ij}\}\ \xi_i\xi_j$$

$${}_1\beta_{ij} = \frac{1}{2}\int_V w_i\cos N_i\theta\cdot\rho_w\cdot w_j\cos N_j\theta dV$$

$${}_2\beta_{ij} = \frac{1}{2}\int_V \frac{\partial w_i}{\partial S}\cos N_i\theta\cdot\eta_{w1}\cdot\frac{\partial w_j}{\partial S}\cos N_j\theta dV \qquad \text{--------------(41)}$$

$${}_3\beta_{ij} = \frac{1}{2}N_iN_j\int_V w_i\sin N_i\theta\cdot\eta_{w2}\cdot\sin N_j\theta dV$$

The expectation of control potential becomes

$$E[V_C] = \sum_{i=1}^{N}\sum_{j=1}^{N}\{{}_1\beta_{ij}+{}_2\beta_{ij}+{}_3\beta_{ij}\}\ C_{ij} \qquad \text{--------------(42)}$$

The expected disturbance energy can be expressed as

$$E[U_p] = V\gamma^2 \qquad \text{--------------(43)}$$

Using the maximum entropy criteria under the energy balance in terms of Eqs.(36) to (43) the covariance matrix of initial

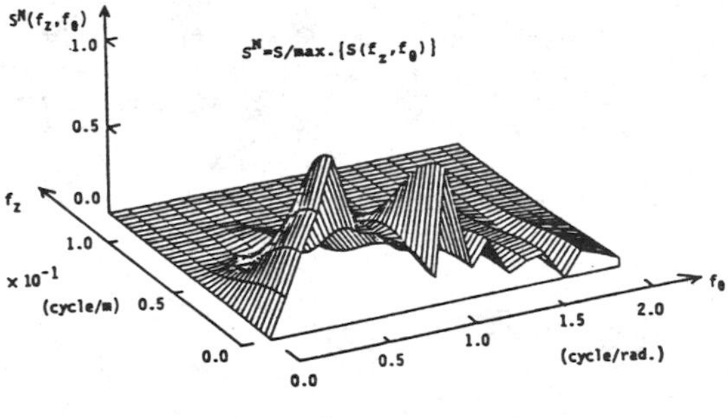


Fig. 5 Spectrum of rotational shell

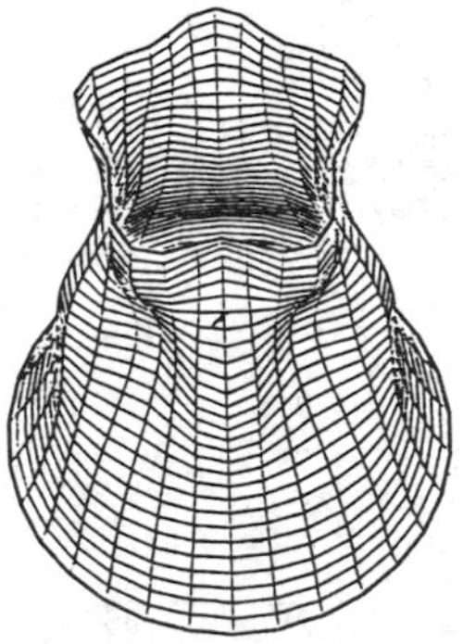

Fig. 4 A simulation result

displacement is

$$C_{ij}^{-1} = \frac{N(B_{ij} + {}_1\beta_{ij} + {}_2\beta_{ij} + {}_3\beta_{ij})}{v\gamma^2} \qquad \text{--------------(44)}$$

Fig. 4 shows one of the initial displacement of concrete cooling tower type shells simulated by Eq.(44) with its averaged standard deviation proportional to shell thickness. Fig. 5 depicts an example of power spectrums. From the numerical analysis the probabilistic structure has the following properties; The higher orders can significantly appear. The spacial distribution of power spectrum becomes considerably uniform regardless in both directions. The components in lower order are insensitive to rather stronger control constants.

5. CONCLUDING REMARKS

The probabilistic structure of initial imperfection distributed on a structural system can be estimated by the present entropy model, which demands the entropy of the initial imperfections maximum under certain constraint. When the initial imperfection is assumed normally distributed and the constraint can be expressed the energy balance equation all over the structural system, then the covariance matrix of initial imperfection is derived in the closed form.

In connection with the functional to be maximized the following remarks are obtainable; Firstly, when the set of amplitude of initial imperfection is not normally distributed it becomes difficult to express the entropy in a simple form like Eq.(18). This implies that the derivation of its derivative with regard to covariance becomes rather complicated. Secondly, the constraint condition, which is, herein, the energy balance equation, is assumed a set of linear combination of covariance, providing rather simple form of the first derivative of constraint equation. However, when this constraint equation becomes nonlinear, though more precisely evaluated itself, then the derivative could not provide analytically simplified solution. Consequently, these two remarks suggest the necessity of numerical analysis to evaluate covariance matrix or power spectrum for the case of more rigorous constraint equation. Moreover especially when chosen a different distribution function from normal one then the first derivative of entropy may not be obtained in a simple form.

REFERENCES

Aoki T. (1973). "Fundamental study on the fluctuation of buckling strength of steel column", Dr. thesis, Nagoya Univ.

Backman B. F. (1976). "The principle of maximum entropy with applications to problems in structural mechanics", PhD thesis, Univ. of Washington

Bjorhovde R. and Tall L. (1972). "Proposed steel column strength criteria", Proc., International Colloq. on Column Strength, Paris, IABSE

Calladine C. R. (1972). "Structural consequences of small imperfections in elastic thin shells of revolution", Int. J. Solids and Structures, Vol. 8

Skolnik M. I. (1970). Radar Handbook, McGraw-Hill

Tai S. (1978). "A study on the assessment and control of water properties by the entropy model", Dr.thesis, Kyoto Univ.

MODELING THE SEISMIC INPUT FOR A STOCHASTIC DYNAMIC STRUCTURAL PROBLEM

L.Faravelli
Department of Structural Mechanics, University of Pavia
I27100 Pavia, Italy

ABSTRACT

Seismic ground acceleration is modeled as a non-stationary stochastic process. All the parameters of the model have a clear seismological meaning. Non stationarity is achieved by making time-dependent the low-frequency corner of the Fourier amplitude spectrum.

The first application of the model is the generation of synthetic time histories. The resulting features are compared with the ones of other seismological and statistical models where a stationary stochastic process is multiplied by a modulating deterministic function.

Stochastic dynamic analysis is then considered. For this purpose the stationary form of the proposed model is shown to be equivalent to five additional first-order differential equations.

The numerical example derives the model for the Southern Italy earthquake of 1980. Artificial ground motions are generated and compared.

1. INTRODUCTION

The definition of the input of dynamical structural problems as a stochastic process is useful in view of either the adoption of stochastic dynamic theory for structural analysis or the simulation of time-histories of the excitation for numerical integration of the equations of motion. In earthquake engineering, several stochastic models were proposed, discussed and analysed from the basic paper by Y.K. Lin (Lin, 1964). Stationary models (generally filtered white-noise) as the Kanai-Tajimi model (Kanai, 1957; Tajimi, 1960) became popular due to both the simple way in which their parameters can be found (Ruiz and Penzien, 1969; Vanmarcke and Lai, 1980) and the advantages they provide in stochastic dynamic analysis. Several researchers are presently focusing their attention on the problem of finding more accurate models (nonstationary in time and in frequency) of the signal recorded in the form of accelerogram (Kozin, 1977; Shinozuka, Ishikawa and Mitsuma, 1979; Spanos, 1983; Shinozuka and Samaras, 1984). These approaches are significant mainly in view of non-linear structural analyses, but they may become cumbersome due to the statistical complication of model inferring. Sometimes they are also inappropriate due to the fact that the model one obtains is not clearly related with the site under investigation, but only idealizes the characteristics of the signals which form the available sample of accelerograms.

If attention is limited within elastic analyses, the engineer decision making is generally well accomplished by stationary models with an appropriate modulating function in order to introduce time non-stationarity. From the seismologist point of view, however, the single time history has to be related to some basic parameters as magnitude, epicentral distance and soil properties. An attempt to mix the features of the Kanai-Tajimi approach with seismological considerations was made in (Chang et al., 1986). A more fascinating approach which provides a stochastic model taking into account source mechanism and wave propagation is the scheme proposed by Boore (Boore, 1985; see also Safak and Boore, 1986). On this line a more complete stochastic earthquake load model is given by (Scherer and Schueller, 1986) and (Lin and Yong, 1986).

In this paper attention is focused on the consequences in structural analysis of the adoption of a seismology-based stochastic model which is developed from Boore's scheme including a more sophisticated source spectrum (Papageorgiou and Aki, 1983). The model can also include nonstationarity. First, linear systems are considered. The classical results of random vibration theory are extended to incorporate this more accurate model of external excitation. Non-linear systems are then considered in the framework of a stochastic equivalent linearization scheme.

Numerical examples illustrate the main aspects of the dynamic analyses to be developed. They are also used in order to compare the results that can be reached by seismology-based models with the response estimations one obtains by adopting a simple Kanai-Tajimi idealization.

2. GOVERING RELATIONS

In the past decade various seismological models for ground motion description have been developed based on the physical parameters of the source and the medium (magnitude, distance, fault dimension, attenuation, and shear wave velocity). In this context the model introduced by Boore (Boore, 1985; Boore 1986), is quite operative: the expression of the Fourier amplitude spectrum A(t) of the ground acceleration is

$$|A(f)| = C\ A_1(f)\ A_2(f)\ A_3(f) \tag{01}$$

where f is the frequency.

The factor C in (01) stands for a scaling factor and it is given by the formula

$$C = R_p\ FV/(4\pi\rho\beta^3)r \tag{02}$$

where $R_p$ is the radiation pattern (Boore and Boatwright, 1984), F accounts for free surface effects (usually F = 2), V is the partition of energy into horizontal components (usually $V=1/\sqrt{2}$), $\rho$ and $\beta$ are the density and shear velocity in the source region and r is the hypocentral distance.

In (01) the factor $A_1(f)$ is the source factor whose commonly used form is

$$A_1(f) = (M_0/(1 + (f_0/f\ )^2))(2\ \pi f_0)^2 \tag{03}$$

where $M_0$ is the seismic moment that can be written in terms of magnitude (Hanks and Kanamori, 1979), and $f_0$ is the corner frequency . $A_2(f)$ denotes an amplification factor to account for both the amplification due to strong impedance contrast of soil layers and the amplification in wave amplitude due to conservation energy for waves travelling through materials with decreasing velocities as the earth's surface is approached. The latter amplification factor is tabulated in (Gusev, 1983 and Boore, 1986).

$A_3(f)$ is a distance diminuition factor whose form has been chosen in (Boore, 1985) as

$$A_3(f) = \exp\ (-\pi fr/Q(f)\beta)\ P(f,f_m) \tag{04}$$

where Q(.) is a frequency dependent attenuation function. In this study the Irpinia earthquake,is considered. Therefore, Q has been assumed proportional to the frequency ($Q = Q_0 f$) as suggested in (Rovelli, 1983). The function P(.) is given by Boore (Boore, 1985) as a high-cut filter with a corner frequency $f_m$ corresponding to the $f_{max}$ of Hanks (Hanks, 1982):

$$P(f,f_m) = (1 + (f/f_m)^8)^{-\frac{1}{2}} \tag{05}$$

Boore showed that the corner frequency $f_m$ is a site effect rather than a source effect, therefore it is independent of the seismic moment.

It is worth noting that in the Boore model, the shape of the source spectrum is governed by two corner frequencies $f_0$ and $f_m$ whose values are given in (Boore, 1985) by:

$$f_m = \text{const} \tag{06}$$

$$f_0 = 4.9 \times 10^{6}\ \beta(\Delta\sigma/M\ )^{1/3} \tag{07}$$

In Eq. (07) $\Delta\sigma$ denotes a scaling parameter with dimension of stress ($\Delta\sigma$ =100bar). Though the relation (07) has been found to lead to predictions in agreement with recorded motions, it is not of general validity for the evaluation of the maximum level $a_0(r)$ of the Fourier amplitude spectrum.

A direct evaluation of the maximum level can be obtained by the Papageorgiou - Aki model (Papageorgiou and Aki, 1983) as

$$a_0\ (r) = (P_0(r)/f_0)^{\frac{1}{2}} = (P_0(r)\ T_r)^{\frac{1}{2}} \tag{08}$$

in which $P_0$ (r) divided by $\pi$ denotes the maximum of the one-sided power spectral density function $G_s(\omega)$ ($\omega=2\pi f$) of the acceleration at the source and $T_r$ is the rupture duration.

The expression of $P_0(r)$ is

$$P_0(r) = \phi\left[\frac{v}{\beta}\right]^2 W\ V\ v^2\left[\frac{24}{7\pi}\ \frac{\Delta\sigma_1}{\mu}\right]^2\left[\frac{R_p}{4\ r}\right]^2 \exp\left(-\frac{2\pi f\ r}{Q(f)\beta}\right) \tag{09}$$

where W is the fault width, V is the velocity of the rupture front along the fault lenght, v is the velocity of rupture spreading within a circular crack, $\Delta\sigma_1$ is the local stress drop, $\mu$ is the rigidity, $\beta$ is the shear wave velocity. The factor $\phi\,(v/\beta)$ is tabulated in (Papageorgiou and Aki, 1983). The coefficients Q , $R_p$ and r have been previously defined.

The seismological models discussed in this section are stationary. In (Safak and Boore, 1986), Safak and Boore included nonstationarity by the classical model

$$a(t) = w(t)\ a_s(t) \tag{10}$$

where $a_s$ (t) is a stationary stochastic process and w(t) is a deterministic time-window.

A nonstationary model based on the Papageorgiou - Aki source model has been developed in (Scherer - Schueller, 1986).

## 3. A SEISMOLOGICAL NON STATIONARY MODEL

In this paper the Boore's model is considered and the attention is focused on the definition of the shape of the source spectrum. In order to avoid the crucial point of the selection of the corner frequency $f_0$ , the following procedure is proposed.

$P_0(r)$ can be evaluated by the Papageorgiou - Aki model (Eq.(08)); it does not account for the source-to-site amplification factor $A_2$ (f). Therefore the relationship between $P_0(r)$ and the maximum of the power spectral density function $G(\omega)$ of the acceleration at the site is given by:

$$P_0(r)\ (A_2(f))^2 = \max G(\omega)\pi \tag{11}$$

$$G(\omega) = |A(f)|^2/\pi T_r \tag{12}$$

From equation (11), (12) and (01), one finds:

$$P_0(r) = \max\ ((C\ A_1(f)\ A_2(f))^2/\pi T_r) \qquad (13)$$

or equivalently, being Q equal to $Q_0 f$ and max $P(f,f_m)=1$

$$\left[\frac{P_0(r)}{\exp(-\pi r/Q_0\beta)}\ T_r\right]^{\frac{1}{2}} = C\ \max\ A_1(f) = (2\pi f_0)^2 \frac{M_0 FV}{4\pi\rho\beta^3} R_p \frac{1}{r} \qquad (14)$$

From Eq.(14) the corner frequency $f_0$ can be easily calculated.

In this way the model losses the scaling law given by equation (07). According to Gusev results, the following scaling law is proposed in this paper:

$$-.33\ (\log M - \log M_0) = \log\ (f) - \log\ (f_0) \qquad (15)$$

where $M_0$ is given, $f_0$ is computed by Eq.(15) and M and f are respectively any value of seismic moment and its corresponding corner frequency. Instead of Eq. (07), Eq.(15) offers the advantage that it can be made site dependent.

Moreover, the author attempted to substitute Gusev's table by an analytical expression for the amplification factor $A_2(f)$:

$$A_2(f) = 1/(1 + (.32/f)^2) \qquad (16)$$

Eq.(16) is accurate for f > 1 Hz, appropriate for .32 Hz <f <1 Hz, wrong for f < .32 Hz. Nevertheless, f < .32 Hz denotes cases without practical interest in common structures. Eq.(16) is therefore adopted in the following with the limitation f > .32 Hz.

The function $G(\omega)$ till now consider is essentially a limited band white-noise; it can be accurate for California seismic events but not for European (Faccioli, Rovelli and Fregonese, 1984) and Russian earthquakes (Gusev, 1983). Although this is a basic point in building a model for seismic excitation, this aspect is not discussed here and $A_1(f)$ is simply corrected by the function:

$$A_1^*(f) = \zeta/(1 + (f/f_1^*)^2)^{\frac{1}{2}} \qquad (17)$$

$\zeta$ being a parameter by which max $(A_1(f)\cdot A_1^*(f))$ is still given by Eq.(14) ($\zeta \cong 1.15$) and with $f_1^* \cong 2$Hz according to (Faccioli, Rovelli and Fregonese, 1984). $P(f,f_m)$ is then modified to have the same decay at high frequencies.

The model is then made nonstationary by introducing the time-dependent (evolutionary) power spectral density function:

$$G(\omega,t) = G(\omega,f_0(t),M_0(t)) = (CA_1(f,f_0(t),M_0(t))A_1^*(f)A_2(f)A_3(f))^2/\pi T_r \qquad (18)$$

where the corner frequency $f_0(t)$ is calculated by Eq.(14).

The seismic moment $M_0(t)$ is supposed: to increase linearly from a value $\bar{M}_0$ to its actual value $M_0$ in the time interval $(0,t_1)$ ($t_1$ is the P and S-waves shift time); to be constant in $(t_1,t_1+\bar{d}_0)$ ($d_0$ is the stationary equivalent duration); to decrease linearly to $\bar{M}_0$ for $t_1 + d_0 < t < d$, d being the actual duration.

The analyses conducted show agreement with the results obtained in (Scherer and Schueller, 1986) and (Safak and Bendimerad, 1986) by the evolutionary spectra models developed by (Priestley, 1965) and (Mark, 1970).

This nonstationary stochastic source model can be easily used to generate artificial acceleration time histories (Augusti, Baratta and Casciati, 1984). Next section is devoted to the use of Eq. (18) in stochastic dynamics.

4. STOCHASTIC EQUATIONS OF MOTION

The response $y(t)$ of a linear system under the excitation $x(t)$ of an evolutionary process is also evolutionary and the relation between the time-varying spectra is given by classical random vibration theory. Eq.(18) can be easily re-written in the form

$$G(\omega,t) = (g(\omega,t))^2\, G(\omega) \tag{19'}$$

being $G(\omega)$ given by Eq.(12) and $g(\omega,t)$ an appropriate deterministic function. The response of a linear system can then be expressed in the same form as Eq.(19') with $g(\omega,t)$ replaced by

$$b(\omega,t) = \int_{-\infty}^{+\infty} h_s(u)\, g(\omega,t-u)\, e^{-i\omega u}\, du \tag{19''}$$

where $h_s(u)$ is the impulse response function of the linear system in question.

The expression of the response of the linear system is strongly simplified assuming the excitation $x(t)$ to be stationary. Let the response $y(t)$ of the system be governed by the differential equations:

$$M\,\ddot{y} + C\,\dot{y} + K\,y = -\,M\,I\,x(t) \tag{20}$$

As the power spectral density function $G(\omega)$ of $x(t)$ has been considered in the seismological model as the product of a constant $G_0 = C^2M_0^2A_3^2/\pi T_r$ by the filters $A_1(f)^2/M_0^2$, $A_1^*(f)^2$, $A_2(f)^2$ defined in the previous section, the excitation $x(t)$ can be regarded as follows: a white-noise is filtered through a first order differential equation system (for $A_1^*$) whose output is filtered in a single-degree-of-freedom force-displacement system with critical damping (for $A_2$); the output acceleration of the second filter is the input of a second force-displacement system with critical damping (for $A_1$) for which $x(t)$ is the output acceleration.

The third filtering $A_1(f)$ can be accomplished by re-writing the differential equations (20) in the form:

$$M\,\ddot{y} + C\,\dot{y} + K\,y + M\,I\,\ddot{z}(t) = 0 \tag{21}$$

$$\ddot{z} + 2\,\omega_1\dot{z} + \omega_1^2\,z = -\,\ddot{u} \tag{22}$$

where $\omega_1/2\,\pi$ is the corner frequency and u is a filtered white noise of PSD $G_0\omega_1^4$. This white noise is twice filtered:

$$\ddot{u} + 2\,\omega_2\dot{u} + \omega_2^2 u = -\,s \tag{23}$$

$$\dot{s} + \omega_1^* s = W \tag{24}$$

with $\omega_2/2\,\pi = .32$ Hz for considering Gusev's correction and $\omega_1^*/2\pi = 2$ Hz for the smothing of high frequency. The stochastic process $W(t)$ is a white noise with constant PSD $G_0\,\omega_1^4\,\omega_1^{*2}$.

Strictly speaking, one has also the high-frequency cut-off filter in Eq.(18), but his direct introduction in the equation of motion can be avoided if the structural system under examination does not involve frequency larger than 10 Hz.

For nonlinear system, equivalent linearization technique (Casciati and Faravelli, 1985) can be adopted on the condition that Eqs. (22)(23)(24) are added to the non linear equations of motion.

5. A NUMERICAL EXAMPLE

The seismic event of Southern Italy of November 1980 has been widely studied from a seismological point of view. With reference to Eqs.(02)(03) and (04) one knows or it is likely to assume that: $R_p$ = .63 (average on the focal sphere), $\rho$ = 2.6 g/cm , $\beta$ = 3.5 Km/s, $T_r$ = 6 sec., $M_0$ = $6.10^{25}$ dyn.cm (Deschamps and King, 1983) and $Q_0$ = 40s (Rovelli, 1983). In Eq.(09) one can assume: W = 12 Km; $v/\beta$ = .8 (i.e. $\phi(v/\beta)$ = 2.19); V = v; $\mu=\rho\beta^2$ and $\Delta\sigma_1$=300 bar.

In particular attention is focused on Bagnoli Irpino where the main shock was recorded at hypocentral distance r = 28 Km (r=22 Km suggested in (Faccioli et al., 1984) was recently updated to the new value). Figure 1 provides the recorded accelerogram, its Fourier amplitude spectrum, the Kanai-Tajimi PSD inferred by the Vanmarcke-Lai approach and a synthetic accelerogram derived by this PSD and Eq.(10) where w(t) has parabolic ramp and exponential decay. The parabolic ramp duration is $t_1$ = 3.8 s (P-S wave shift time) and $d_0$ is 6.1 sec quite close to the rupture duration. It is worth noting that the correction of the synthetic accelerogram is not achieved here by parabolic baseline correction. This method in fact was largely criticized by the experts of accelerogram processing, whose procedure for removing noise is much more accurate. Therefore, after the realization of the filtered white-noise is simulated, it is modulated by (t) and then processed in the frequency space. Note that in this way, removing the very low frequencies,also the undesidered contribution of modulation to this frequency range (Safak and Boore, 1986 b)) is removed.

Figure 2 provides the Fourier amplitude spectrum computed for the accelerogram window between 2.5 and 10 sec. and the Boore's model (01),without Gusev's correction $A_2(f)$,for $f_m$ = 10 Hz and different values of $f_0$: 1) $f_0$ = $1/T_r$ ; 2) $f_0$ from Eq.(07); 3) $f_0$ as computed in (Faccioli-Rovelli and Fregonese, 1984). The synthetic accelerogram is for case 2).

Figure 3 is the same as Figure 2 with the Gusev's correction and its approximation by Eq.(16).

Figure 4 is the same as Figure 3 with the maximum value $P_0$ (r) from Papageorgiou - Aki and the frequency corner from Eq. (14). Three values of $\Delta\sigma_1$ are considered: 200, 250, 300 and 400 bars. Figure 5 provides the model of Figure 4 with the introduction of Eq.(17) and the corresponding synthetic accelerogram, whose peak of acceleration is .153 g for $\Delta\sigma_1$ = 300 bar instead of .267 g for the corresponding curve of Figure 4.

In Figure 5, $f_m$ = 20 Hz is adopted for the filter of Eq.(05).

Figure 6 provides the evolution of the PSD Eq.(18) and the corresponding synthetic accelerogram with $\Delta\sigma_1$ = 300 bar and $M_0$ = $10^{23}$ dyn cm .Comparisons of the effects on linear system of the different PSD models are provided in terms of response spectra in Figure 7. The response spectrum for the non-stationary case is not significantly different from the one obtained for the record of Figure 5b). The Fourier amplitude spectrum, however, shows a larger content of high frequencies.

ACKNOWLEDGEMENT

This paper has been made possible by the award the author obtained in the context of the NSF Visiting Professorship for Woman Program 1986. The researchers met during her stay in the Department of Civil Engineering of Stanford University provided the author fruitful contributions which are here acknowledged.

REFERENCES

Augusti G., Baratta A. and Casciati F. (1984), Probabilistic Methods in Structural Engineering, Chapman & Hall, London

Boore D.M.(1985), The Prediction of Strong Ground Motion, Proc. of NATO Adv.St.Inst. on Strong Motion Seismology, Ankara

Boore D.M.(1986), Short Period P and S-Wave Radiation from Large Earthquake: Implication for Spectral Scaling Relations, BSSA, 76,1,43-64

Boore D.M. and Boatwright J.(1984), Average Body-Wave Radiation Coefficients, BSSA, 74,1615-1621

Casciati F. and Faravelli L.(1985),Methods of Non-Linear Stochastic Dynamics for the Assess. of Struct. Fragility, Nuclear Eng. and Design, 90, 341-356

Chang N.Y., Huang M.J., Lien B.M. and Chang F.K.(1986), EQGEN A User Fr. Art. Earth.Simul.Progr.,Proc. 3rd U.S.Nat.Conf. Earth.Eng.,Charleston, I 439-450

Deschamps A., King G.C.P.(1983), The Campania Lucania (Southern Italy) Earth. of 23 Nov. 1980, Earth and Phisic.Science Letters,62,294-304

Faccioli E.,Rovelli A. and Fregonese R.(1984),A Study of the Spec.Char.of Acc. from Rec.Earth. of Italy and Near.Reg.,Proc.8th WCEE,San Francisco, 361-368

Faravelli L.(1986), Stochastic Modeling of the Seismic Excitation for Struct. Dynamics Purposes,Proc. Euro-China Joint Seminar on Earth.Eng., Beijing

Gusev A.A.(1983), Descr. Stat. Model of Earth. Source Rad. and its Appl.to an Est. of Short-Period Strong Motion, Geophys.J.R.Astr.Soc.,74,787-808

Hanks T.C.(1982), $f_{max}$, BSSA,72,1867-1879

Hanks T.C. and Kanamori H.(1979),A Moment Magn.Scale,J.Geophys.Res.,84,2348-50

Kanai K.(1957), Semi-Emp. Formula for Seismic Characterization of the Ground, Bull.Earth.Res.Inst., Univ.Tokyo,35,309-325

Kozin F.(1977), An App. to Charact., Mod. and Anal. Earth. Exc. Records, in Parkus H.(ed.) Ran.Exc. of Struc. by Earth. and Atm. Turb.,Springer-Verlag

Lin Y.K.(1964),Nonstationary Shot-Noise,J.of Acoust.Soc. of America,36,1,82-84

Lin Y.K. and Yong Y.(1986), Evolutionary Kanai Tajimi Type Earthquake Models, Rep. CAS 86-7, Florida Atl.Univ.

Mark W.D.(1970), Spectral Analysis of the Convolution and Filtering of Nonstationary Stochastic Processes, J. of Sound and Vib., 11, 1, 19-63

Papageorgiou A.S. and Aki K.(1983), A Specific Barrier Model for the Quantitative Description of Inhomogeneous Faulting and the Prediction of Strong Ground Motion - I - Description of the Model, BSSA, 73, 693-722

Priestley M.B.(1981), Spectral Analysis and Time Series, Academic Press

Rovelli A.(1983), Frequency Relationship for Seismic $Q_\beta$ of the Central Southern Italy from Accelerograms for the Irpinia Earthquake 1980, Physics of the Earth and Plan. Int., 32, 209-217

Ruiz P. and Penzien J.(1969), Probabilistic Study for the Behaviour of Structures during Earthquakes, EERC, Univ. of California, Berkeley

Safak E. and Bendimerad F.M.(1986), Time-Varying Spectral Characteristics of Strong Ground Motions: the Imperial Valley, California Earthquake of October, 15, 1979, USGS Open-File Report

Safak E. and Boore D.M.(1986a), On Non-Stationary Stochastic Models for Earthquakes, Proc. 3rd US Nat.Conf. on Earth. Eng., Charleston, I, 137-148

Safak E. and Boore D.M.(1986b), On Low Frequency Error of Commonly Used Ground Motion Models, submited to Eng.Mech.Div.J. of ASCE

Scherer R.J. and Schueller G.I.(1986a), A Stochastic Earthquake Load Model and its Effects on Aseismic Design Procedures, in F.Casciati and L.Faravelli (Eds.) Methods of Stochastic Structural Mechanics, SEAG, Pavia

Scherer R.J. and Schueller G.I.(1986b), The Acceleration Spectrum at the Base Rock Determined from a Nonstationary Stochastic Source Model, Proc.8th ECEE, Lisbon, I.3.3/47

Shinozuka M.,Ishikawa H. and Mitsuma H.(1979), Data-Based Nonstationary Random Processes, Proc.ASCE Spec.Conf. on Prob.Mech. and Str.Rel., Tucson, 39-43

Shinozuka M. and Samaras E.(1984),ARMA Model Representation of Random Processes, Proc.ASCE Spec.Conf.on Prob.Mech. and Str.Rel.,Berkeley, 405-409

Sobczyk K.(1985),Stoc.Diff.Eq.for App.R203,Dept.Civ.Eng.,Tech.Un.of Den.Lyngby

Spanos P.D.(1983),ARMA Alg. for Oc. Wave Mod.,J. En. Res.Techn,105, 300-309

Stagnitto G.(1986),Anal.Mult. di Rischio Sis.(in Ital.), M.D.Thesis, Un. Pavia

Tajimi H.(1960), A Statistical Method of Determining the Maximum Response of a Building Structure During an Earthquake, Proc. 2nd WCEE, Tokyo

Vanmarcke E. and Lai S.P.(1980), Strong Motion Duration and RMS Amplitude Earthquake Records, BSSA, 70-4, 1293-1307

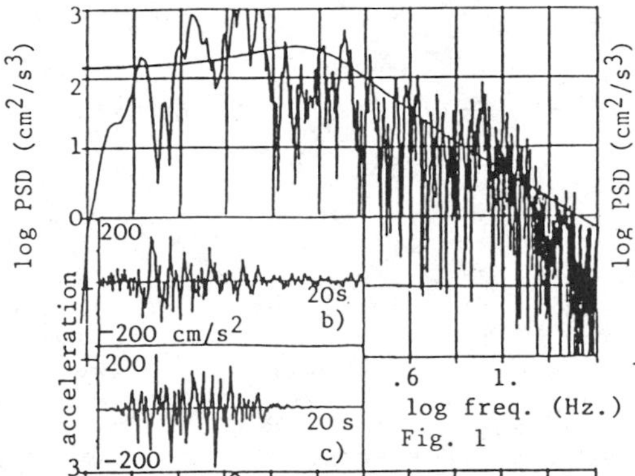

Fig. 1

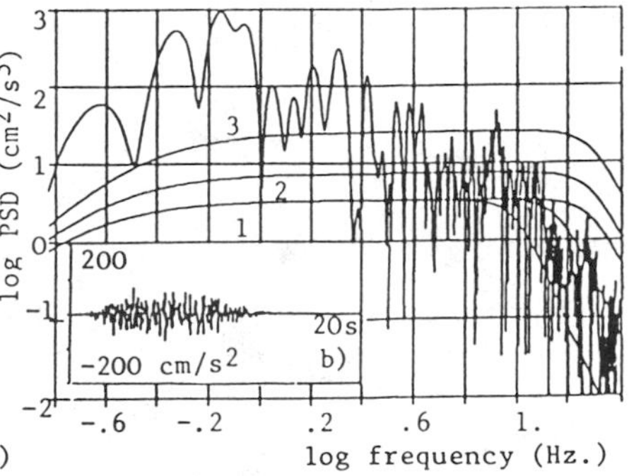

Fig. 2

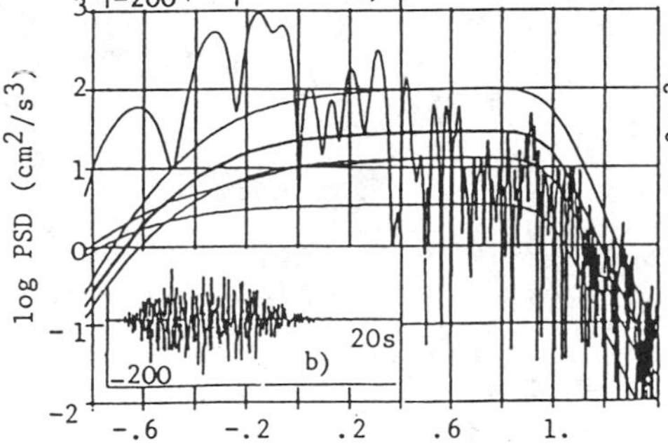

Fig. 3

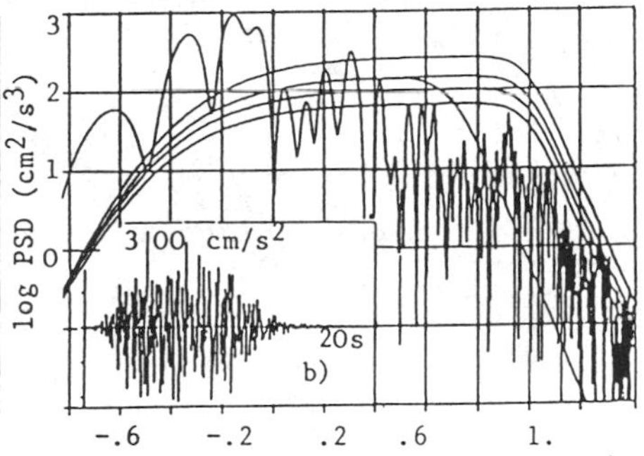

Fig. 4

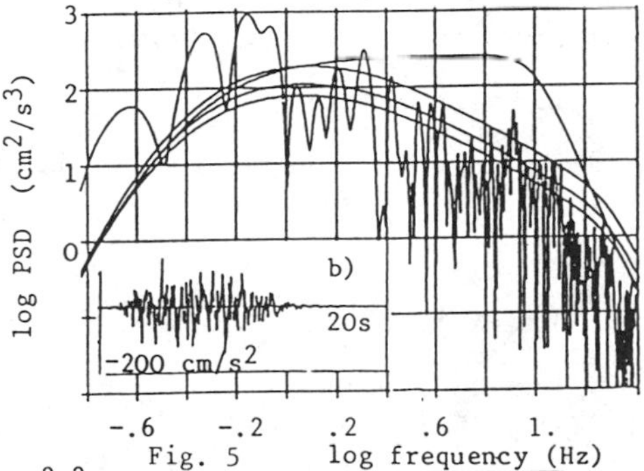

Fig. 5

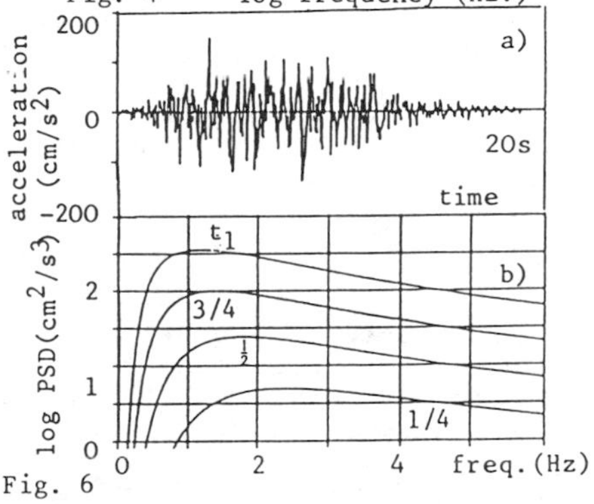

Fig. 6

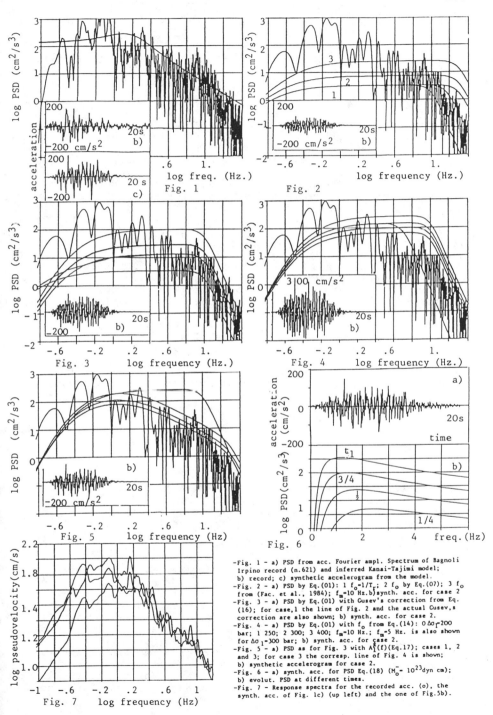

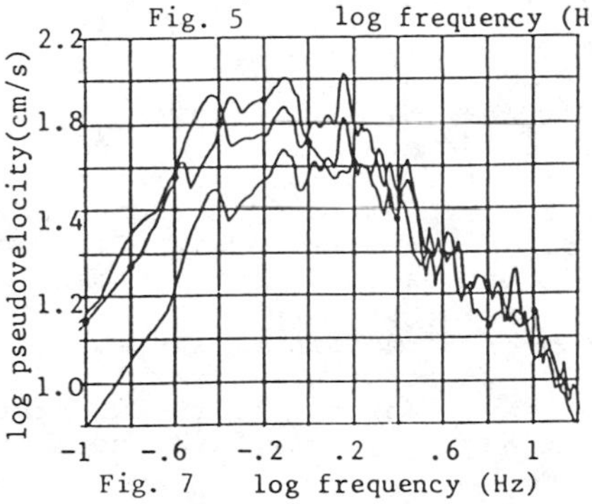

Fig. 7

-Fig. 1 - a) PSD from acc. Fourier ampl. Spectrum of Bagnoli Irpino record (n.621) and inferred Kanai-Tajimi model; b) record; c) synthetic accelerogram from the model.
-Fig. 2 - a) PSD by Eq.(01): 1 $f_o$=1/$T_r$; 2 $f_o$ by Eq.(07); 3 $f_o$ from (Fac. et al., 1984); $f_m$=10 Hz. b) synth. acc. for case 2
-Fig. 3 - a) PSD by Eq.(01) with Gusev's correction from Eq.(16); for case,1 the line of Fig. 2 and the actual Gusev,s correction are also shown; b) synth. acc. for case 2.
-Fig. 4 - a) PSD by Eq.(01) with $f_o$ from Eq.(14): 0 $\Delta\sigma_I$=200 bar; 1 250; 2 300; 3 400; $f_m$=10 Hz.; $f_m$=5 Hz. is also shown for $\Delta\sigma_1$=300 bar; b) synth. acc. for case 2.
-Fig. 5 - a) PSD as for Fig. 3 with $A_I^*(f)$(Eq.17); cases 1, 2 and 3; for case 3 the corresp. line of Fig. 4 is shown; b) synthetic accelerogram for case 2.
-Fig. 6 - a) synth. acc. for PSD Eq.(18) ($\bar{M}_o$= $10^{23}$dyn cm); b) evolut. PSD at different times.
-Fig. 7 - Response spectra for the recorded acc. (o), the synth. acc. of Fig. 1c) (up left) and the one of Fig.5b).

# PROBABILITY-BASED LEVEL-3 STRUCTURAL SYNTHESIS

J.W. Murzewski
Faculty of Civil Engineering, Politechnika Krakowska, Kraków, Poland, 31-155

ABSTRACT

Two hazards are taken into consideration: a local plastic deformation and an elastic buckling of structural members, provided that the stresses have been determined for design loads. The local plastic strength is treated as a log-normal stochastic function and the stress level downcrossing formula helps to characterize the plastic resistance dependent on the length of structural member. The elastic buckling is treated as an independent random event. Statistical estimates of steel properties have given a basis to determine the log-normal distribution parameters of both plastic and critical resistances. Variances of geometrical properties and random imperfections are added to the variance of mechanical properties. A partition of the overall variance into 3 parts is done because there is a strong correlation of the random variables within one subassemblage and a weaker correlation is within the structural system. A four step procedure is elaborated in order to get the probability of failure and hazard function of the weakest element in a subassemblage and the measures of the whole structural system. The hazard functions are additive and a final hazard ratio is taken as the global safety measure. The size and complexity of the structure are taken into account in its safety assessment.

## 1. BASIC IDEAS OF A NEW APPROACH

A new method of reliability assessment of structural systems has been elaborated in the last decade (Murzewski, 1976, 1981, 1982).

It is compatible with usual safety requirements:

I. Any structure of the same design and destination has its bearing capacity B equal or more than the specified design action A*. An actual value B may be verified by a full scale load test,

$$B \geqslant A^* ; \qquad (1)$$

II. Stresses $\sigma_k^*$ due to the design action A* are calculated by means of conventional statics and they shall not exceed the actual limits $R_k$ for k = 1, 2, 3... N, where N is the number of elementary segments of all structural members from the foundation to the roof.

$$\sigma_k^* \leqslant R_k \ . \qquad (2)$$

The point I. allows to perform the stress analysis in a deterministic way since the action A* is fully determined. So are the stresses $\sigma_k^*$ in the simple structures. It is true also for redundant systems if random variations of elastic stiffness are neglected and no plastic redistribution of internal forces is admitted. The condition I. can be satisfied with a probability less than 1 because the resistance and geometrical parameters are random. The probability may be differentiated for 3 or more safety classes.

The point II. allows to treat any structure, simple or redundant, as a series system. However the principle of the weakest link in chain is taken only in a deterministic sense, but not in the probabilistic approach. It means that the joint probability

$$\Omega = \mathcal{P}\left( \sigma_1^* < R_1,\ \sigma_2^* < R_2,\ \ldots\ \sigma_N^* < R_N \right) = \mathcal{P}\left( \min_k R_k/\sigma_k^* > 1 \right) \qquad (3)$$

and not the minimum probability

$$Q = \min_k \left[ \mathcal{P}(\sigma_1^* < R_1),\ \mathcal{P}(\sigma_2^* < R_2),\ \ldots\ \mathcal{P}(\sigma_N^* < R_N) \right] \qquad (4)$$

is taken as a safety measure of a complex structure. Probability $\Omega$ is an auxiliary safety measure. The hazard ratio $1/k$ is a new safety measure (Table 1). It has been derived from system reliability considerations, as well as - from an overall cost optimization solution (Murzewski, 1970, 1984).

$$1/k = B\ h(B) < 1/k^* . \qquad (5)$$

The relation of the hazard function $h(B)$ with the probability density $f(B)$ and the cumulative probability $F(B) = 1-Q$ is as follows

$$h(B) = f(B) / \left[ 1 - F(B) \right] . \qquad (6)$$

The level-3 design strength will be determined by the equation

$$R^*\ h_B(R^*) = 1/k^* . \qquad (7)$$

The maximum stress $\sigma^*$ during the service time of the structure presumably could be derived from the hazard ratio equation as well,

$$\sigma^*\ h_A(\sigma^*) = 1/k^*, \quad \text{where} \quad h(A) = f(A)/F(A) , \qquad (8)$$

but this problem will not be discussed here. Specified factored actions $A^*$ can be taken to the design although a more sophisticated approach will be applied to assess the bearing capacity $B^*$.

Table 1. TENTATIVE VALUES OF THE HAZARD RATIO

| Safety class | I. | II. | III. |
|---|---|---|---|
| k* | 1 | 3 | 15 |

Plastic strengths $R_o(x_1)$ and $R_o(x_2)$ are correlated the stronger the closer are the elementary segments k=1 and k=2. A complex theoretical model is taken to evaluate the size effect:

a) The local plastic strength $R_o(x)$ is supposed to be a stationary stochastic function of coordinates x of cross-sections of a beam or column and $L_o$ is the mean distance between the median $\breve{R}_o$ -level downcrossings (Fig.1 - from Machowski, 1979).

b) Partition of an overall variance $v_R^2$ is accomplished in order to take into account the random variability of mechanical and geometrical properties within the subassemblages of one structure as well as within a series of similar structures.

Mechanical properties: $R_o$ - local plastic strength of the material (Table 2) and E - Young's modulus in stability problems ($\breve{E}$= 200 GPa, $v_E$ = 3%) are taken as the independent random variables. Geometrical properties: L - length of a member, A - area of a cross section, J - moment of inertia etc. are introduced to the calculations as they were non-random. But their variance $v_G^2$ (Table 3) is taken to augment the variance of the leading variables.

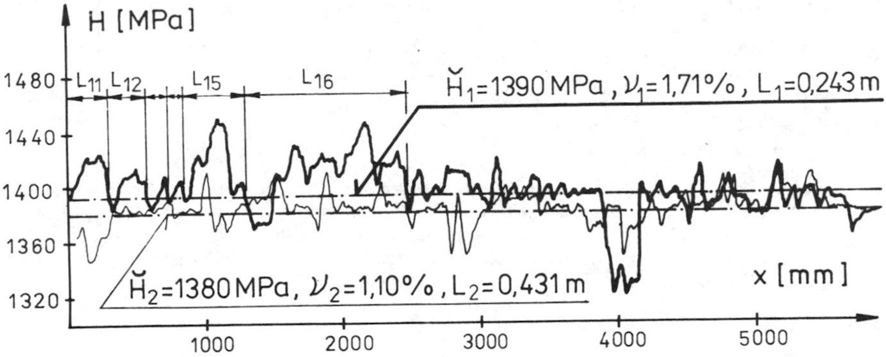


Fig.1 REALIZATIONS OF RANDOM FUNCTION OF STEEL HARDNESS

Numerical values are specified in this paper for steel structures only. Some of the values are estimated on the basis of statistical analyses, the others are derived from comparative designs. The statistical tests were sponsored by the Polish Academy of Sciences. They were performed by the Cracow and Warsaw Polytechnic Universities in 1976-1985. The tests have been representative for Polish structural steels. The origin of steel is usually unknown during designing. Therefore samples were taken for the research project from all metallurgical plants which deliver steel for the national building. Sample sizes were proportional to the mass of steel delivered every year.

Table 2. LOG-NORMAL DISTRIBUTION PARAMETERS OF PLASTIC STRENGTH

| | common | effervescent | killed | manganese | |
|---|---|---|---|---|---|
| | structural carbon steel | | | | |
| $\breve{R}_c$ *) | 290 | 300 | 310 | 410 | MPa |
| $v_R$ | 11.3 | 7.7 | 6.8 | 8.1 | % |

*) to modify (Table 4) unless plates of 5 mm thickness

Table 3. COEFFICIENTS OF VARIATION $v_G$ OF GEOMETRICAL PROPERTIES

| | Tension/Compression | Bending | Buckling | |
|---|---|---|---|---|
| Plates | 2.8 | 5.6 or 2.8 *) | | % |
| Shapes | 3.8 | 3.8 or 5.7 **) | 6.5 or 8.6 ***) | % |
| Bars | 2.8 | 4.2 | | % |
| Pipes | 5.9 | 5.9 | | % |

*) plate girders **) weak-axis bending ***) uncertain free length

3. FAILURE MODES OF STEEL STRUCTURES

A random strength $R_{ij}$ of a column or beam-column is equal to the least stress $\sigma_o$ which causes untolerable effects. At least two effects must be taken under consideration for a steel structure: plastic deformation and elastic buckling of its elements. It should be in the safe domain

$$\sigma_o < R_{ij} = \mathrm{Min}(R_{pl}, R_{cr}) \quad \text{for} \quad \sigma_o = |N|/A, \quad N - \text{axial force.} \tag{9}$$

Log-normal probability distributions are assumed for the random variables $R_{pl}$ and $R_{cr}$. Either median value, $\breve{R}_{pl}$ and $\breve{R}_{cr}$, depends on the length of each structural member under consideration. $\breve{R}_{pl}$ depends also on a thickness t of the steel member because of work-hardening effect during the fabrication process. Discrete classes of thickness are defined in standard specifications. A continuous function seems to be better for probabilistic considerations,

$$\breve{R}_o = c\, R_c \exp(-t/t_o)\ . \tag{10}$$

$\breve{R}_c$ is the basic value indicated in Table 2 for some Polish steels. The parameters c, $t_o$ are given in Table 4. The value $\breve{R}_o$ is identified with a median yield limit of n small specimens in routine tension tests taken from a lot of steel. R may be estimated as the central parameter of the log-normal distribution according to the maximum likelihood rule.

$$\breve{R}_o = \sqrt[n]{\prod_{k=1}^{n} R_k}\ , \qquad n - \text{sample size.} \tag{11}$$

The second distribution parameter, the logarithmic variance v, is close to the square of normal coefficient of variation,

$$v_o^2 = (1/n)\sum_{k=1}^{n} \ln^2 (R_k/\breve{R}_o) \cong (1/n)\sum_{k=1}^{n} (R_k/\bar{R} - 1)^2\ . \tag{12}$$

Table 4. CONVERSION PARAMETERS OF STEEL STRENGTH

| | Carbon steel | | Low-alloy steel | |
|---|---|---|---|---|
| | c | $t_o$ | c | $t_o$ |
| Plates | 1.00 | 0.60 m | 1.00 | 0.90 m |
| Shapes | 1.03 | 0.50 m | 1.01 | 0.70 m |
| Bars | 1.06 | 0.90 m | 1.02 | 0,95 m |
| Pipes | 1.08 | $\infty$ | - | - |
| $L_o$ | 0.30 m | | 0.16 m | |

The probability of failure is considered first as a crossing problem of theory of continuous stochastic processes (Rice, 1944). A logarithmically standarized strength $R_o(x)$ is transformed to a Gaussian stochastic function,

$$\beta_o(x) = -\left[\ln R_o(x) - \ln \breve{R}_o\right]/v_o = \ln \sqrt[v_o]{\breve{R}_o/R_o(x)}\ . \tag{13}$$

The mean level crossing rate $h_o$ is either estimated directly from laboratory tests (Fig.1) or it can be calculated from autocorrelation or spectral functions,

$$h_o = 1/(2L_o) \ . \tag{14}$$

A rate h* of level $\beta^*$ upcrossing is taken in an approximate form which has been applied by Rice,

$$h^* = h_o \exp(-\beta^{*2}/2) \ . \tag{15}$$

An upcrossing probability q* in a structural element of length L′ is formulated as if the upcrossings followed the Poisson process,

$$q^* = \exp(-h^* L') \ . \tag{16}$$

Let apply now the weakest link model to evaluate the probability

$$q^* = \left[\Phi(\beta^*)\right]^{L'/L^*} , \tag{17}$$

where L* is an equivalent length of a link in the discrete model. L* is formulated as the result of comparison of the two formulae (16) and (17),

$$L^* = -\ln \Phi(\beta^*) \exp(\beta^{*2}/2) \, L_o \ , \tag{18}$$

where $\Phi(.)$ – the Laplace function, $\beta^* = \ln \sqrt[v_o]{\breve{R}_o/R^*}$ – the safety index.

The effective length $L' = \kappa L$ of a member , which can fail because of plastic deformation, depends on a stress distribution $\sigma_m(x)$ along the axis x . The stress $\sigma_m(x)$ is due to a simulataneous action of an axial force N and a bending moment M ,

$$\sigma_m(x) = |N(x)|/A + |M(x)|/W \ , \qquad x \in [0, L] \ . \tag{19}$$

$\kappa = 1$ for a uniform stress $\sigma_m = R^*$. Other values $\kappa$ are given elsewhere (Murzewski, 1976). The coefficients $\kappa$ have been evaluated with application of the Weibull asymptotic distribution function of an extreme value R ,

$$F(R) = 1 - \exp(-\sqrt[u]{R/\check{R}}) \ . \tag{20}$$

The Weibull distribution parameters $\check{R}$, u are related with the log-normal distribution parameters. The logarithmic moments give simple proportions

$$\breve{R} = \int_0^\infty \ln R \, dF(R) = \check{R} \exp(-Cu) \ , \quad v^2 = \int_0^\infty \ln(R/\breve{R}) \, dF(R) = \pi^2 u^2/6 \ , \tag{21}$$

where C = 0.5772 – the Euler′s constant.

The weakest link formula for the median plastic strength R of a beam or column is as follows

$$\breve{R}_{pl} = \breve{R}_o (L^*/L')^{u_o} \ , \qquad u_o = (\sqrt{6}/\pi) \, v_{Ro} \ . \tag{22}$$

The formula (22) may be extended to beam-columns by means of a correction coefficient which depends on the excentricity ratio $\eta$ and the relative slenderness ratio $\Lambda$ ,

$$R'_{pl} = R_{pl}\left[1+\eta+\Lambda^2 - \sqrt{(1+\eta+\Lambda^2)^2 - 4\Lambda^2}\right]/2\Lambda^2, \ \eta = (M/N)(A/W) \ , \ \Lambda = \sqrt{\breve{R}_{pl}/\breve{R}_{cr}} \ . \tag{23}$$

The correction is derived from the Ayrton–Perry equation which takes into account second-order moments. The Euler's formula defines a median critical resistance in the case of elastic failure

$$\breve{R}_{cr} = \pi^2 EJ/(AL''^2) \ . \tag{24}$$

L" = $\mu$ L - effective length of an ideally elastic member. $\mu$ depends on end constraints. $\mu$ = 1 for pin-ended columns.

Geometrical imperfections and variable residual stresses influence the coefficient of variation $v_{cr}$ . That is why multiple buckling curves have been specified in some countries. Criteria of selection of one of the 5 buckling curves may be found e.g. in the Recommendations of ECCS (1975). But no equivalent initial excentricity $\eta_o$ is introduced now to the Ayrton-Perry equation as it was suggested when the Eurocodes were under discussion (Boeraeve, Maquoi & Rondal, 1983). The same reduction of the critical strength is obtained here in another way - by a suitable enhancement of the coefficient of variation $v_{cr}$ (Table 6).

The separate treatment of plastic and elastic failure modes is perhaps difficult to comprehend. However, such theoretical model is clear in the probabilistic approach and it is quite simple in calculations since the elastic and plastic strengths of steel elements can be treated as independent random variables.

## 3. PARTITION OF VARIANCE

The logarithmic variance $v_R^2$ of the local plastic strength R (x) of a structural element is less than the overall variance $v^2$ of many tests cumulated by some research institutes. So is the variance $v_E^2$ of buckling strength of slender columns (Fukumoto, 1982). The reason is that the median strength fluctuates from one lot of the material to another. Furthermore, there is a variation of quality among various producers and years of production.

$$v^2 = v_o^2 + v_p^2 + v_s^2 \ . \tag{25}$$

The sum (25) is interpreted for design purposes so that $v_o^2$ is a variance of strength within a subassemblage, $v_p^2$ is a variance of resistances of similar subassemblages and $v_s^2$ is a variance of bearing capacities of structures of the same series. Every component of the sum (25) is augmented because of

a) random geometrical properties : deviations of areas of sections from their nominal value, uncertain free length of columns etc.,

b) random imperfections, i.e. systematic deviation of capacity of a theoretical model from an average capacity of the real structure.

Another partition of the overall variance of plastic capacity of a structure is also useful,

$$v_{pl}^2 = v_R^2 + v_G^2 + v_I^2 \quad \text{or} \quad v_{cr} = v_E^2 + v_G^2 + v_I^2 \ . \tag{26}$$

Table 5 shows approximate values of the partial coefficients of variation of plastic resistance when either criterion of partition is taken into consideration. Table 5 is actual for a particular case of plate girders from an effervescent carbon steel. Changes are necessary in other cases: $v_{oR}$ = 10.0, 5.7, 4.4, 6.2 % - for steels defined in Table 2 ; the mere v is taken to Form.(22) ;

$$v_{oG} = \sqrt{(v_t + \eta v_b)^2/(1+\eta)^2 - 5.86\cdot 10^{-4}} \ , \tag{27}$$

where $v_t$ - for tension, $v_b$ - for bending, (Table 3).

Table 5. TENTATIVE ANALYSIS OF VARIANCE FOR PLASTIC CAPACITY

| Population of | | Coefficient of variation due to random resistance R | geometry G | imperfections I | $\sqrt{v_R^2+v_G^2+v_I^2}$ |
|---|---|---|---|---|---|
| o | segments | 1.1 | 1.1 | 4.0 | 4.4 % |
| p | subassemblages | 5.7 | 1.5 | 1.5 | 6.1 % |
| s | structures | 5.1 | 1.9 | 3.2 | 6.3 % |
| | $\sqrt{v_o^2+v_p^2+v_s^2}$ | 7.7 | 2.8 | 5.4 | 9.8 % |

Table 6 gives partial coefficients of variation when risk of buckling comes into account. Table 6 is actual for annealed steel columns of slenderness ratio $\lambda = 100$ when their end constraints are uncertain. v may be canceled when the end constraints are well determined (Table 3). $v_{oI}$ is adjusted to empirical critical strengths of columns of different slenderness ratios ,

$$v_{oI} = v_c\,(100/\lambda)\ , \qquad \lambda = L''\sqrt{A/J}\ , \tag{28}$$

where $v_c$ = 9.5 , 13.1 , 17.4 % - for buckling curves a, b, c of the ECCS classification, respectively.

Table 6. TENTATIVE ANALYSIS OF VARIANCE FOR ELASTIC STABILITY

| Population of | | Coefficient of variation due to random resistance E | geometry G | imperfections I | $\sqrt{v_E^2+v_G^2+v_I^2}$ |
|---|---|---|---|---|---|
| o | segments | 1.1 | 4.3 | 9.5 | 10.5 % |
| p | subassemblages | 1.4 | 5.7 | 1.5 | 6.1 % |
| s | structures | 2.4 | 4.9 | 3.2 | 6.3 % |
| | $\sqrt{v_o^2+v_p^2+v_s^2}$ | 3.0 | 8.6 | 10.1 | 13.7 % |

## 4. PROBABILISTIC SYNTHESIS OF HAZARDS

Probabilities of no failure $\Omega_{pl}$, $\Omega_{el}$ and hazard functions $h_{pl}$, $h_{el}$ are calculated for the stress $\sigma_{ij}$ determined in every element i = 1, 2, 3 ... $n_j$ of the j-th subassemblage. The safety measures of the weakest element of the subassemblage composed from $n_j$ elements are as follows

$$\Omega_j^{pl} = \prod_{i=1}^{n_j} \Omega_{ij}^{pl} = \prod_{i=1}^{n_j} (1-w_{ij}^{pl}) = 1 - \sum_{i=1}^{n_j} w_{ij}^{pl}\ , \qquad h_j^{pl} = \sum_{i=1}^{n_j} h_{ij}^{pl}\ . \tag{29}$$

and similar formulae - with indices "el" . The $\Omega_j$ and $h_j$ values are collocated with the log-normal curves at the checking point R*

$$\Phi(\ln \sqrt[v_j']{\breve{R}_j'/R^*}) = \Omega_j^{pl}\cdot\Omega_j^{el},\quad (1/v_j')\,\phi(\ln\sqrt[v_j']{\breve{R}_j'/R^*}) = h_j^{pl} + h_j^{el} \;\text{-->}\; \breve{R}_j',\ v_j'\ ; \tag{30}$$

where $\phi(t) = \varphi(t)/\Phi(-t)$ - the Mills function.

$$v_j'' = \sqrt{v_j'^2 + v_p^2}\ ,\quad \beta'' = \ln\sqrt[v_j'']{\breve{R}_j'/R^*},\quad \Omega_j'' = \Omega_j(\beta_j'')\ ,\quad h_j'' = (1/v_j'')\,\phi(\beta_j'')\ . \tag{31}$$

This is the first "randomization". Such calculations shall be done for each subassemblage of the structure, j = 1, 2, ... m, and the safety measures of the weakest one are derived as follows,

$$\Omega''' = \prod_{j=1}^{m} \Omega''_j \;, \qquad h''' = \sum_{j=1}^{m} h''_j \;, \tag{32}$$

$$\Phi(\ln \sqrt[v''']{\breve{R}'''/R^*}) = 0 \;, \quad (1/v''')\phi(\ln \sqrt[v''']{\breve{R}'''/R^*}) = h''' \quad \rightarrow \quad \breve{R}''',\ v''' ; \tag{33}$$

This is the second "minimization". The median strength $\breve{R}'''$ is randomized agaain for any similar structure by means of the same procedure as above

$$v^{IV} = \sqrt{v'''^2 + v_S^2} \;, \quad \beta^{IV} = \ln \sqrt[v^{IV}]{\breve{R}^{IV}/R^*} \;, \quad \Omega^{IV} = \Phi(\beta^{IV}) \;, \quad h^{IV} = (1/v^{IV})\phi(\beta^{IV}) \,. \tag{34}$$

If the hazard ratio obtained in the 4-step procedure is less than the specified value (Table 1), the structure is all right,

$$1/k = (1/v^{IV})\ \phi(\ln \sqrt[v^{IV}]{\breve{R}^{IV}/R^*}) \ < \ 1/k^* \quad \rightarrow \quad \text{the end.} \tag{35}$$

If the inequality (35) is not satisfied, the structure must be redesigned with a lower design strength R**. Usually some sections only may be changed. It is not necessary that $\sigma_{ij}^* < R^{**}$ in every structural element. So, the designer has additional degrees of freedom and he may get savings of time and/or structural materials.

REFERENCES

Boeraeve Ph., Maquoi R. and Rondal J. (1983). "Influence of Imperfections on the Ultimate Carrying Capacity of Centrically Loaded Columns", in J.Melcher (Ed.), Design Limit States of Steel Structures - Preliminary Report, Technical University of Brno, Czechoslovakia, pp. 329-338.

ECCS (1975). "European Specifications for Steel Construction" Vol.II.- Recommendations. European Convention for Constructional Steelwork

Fukumoto Y. (1982). "Numerical Data Bank for the Ultimate Strength of Steel Structures", Der Stahlbau, No.1, pp. 21-27.

Machowski A. (1979). "Experimental Evaluation of Random Function of Hardness for Structural Steel", Bulletin of the Polish Academy of Sciences,27/7, pp. 297-303.

Murzewski J. (1970). "Safety of Building Structures", Polish-Arkady Warszawa; German translation (1974) - Verlag Bauwesen, Berlin.

Murzewski J. (1976). "Random Limit Analysis of Rod Structures", Polish - Studia z zakresu Inzynierii Nr 15, PAN- PWN, Warszawa.

Murzewski J.W. (1981). "Reliability Consideration of Beam Systems" in T.Moan and M.Shinozuka (Eds.), Proceedings of ICOSSAR´81, Elsevier Sci.Publ.Comp., Amsterdam-Oxford-New York, pp. 371-381.

Murzewski J.W. (1982). "Evaluation of Characteristic Strength of Complex Structural Systems" in EUROMECH 155, Reliability Theory of Structural Engineering Systems,DIALOG 6-82, Danmarks Ingenior akademi, Lyngby, pp. 129-142.

Murzewski J.W. (1984). Safety Differentiation Depending on Service Time, Size and Danger", Bulletin of the Polish Academy of Sciences, 32/3-4, pp. 187-192.

Rice S.O. (1944), "Mathematical Analysis of Random Noise", Bell System Technical Journal, 23, pp.282-332.

# LIFETIME PERFORMANCE AND LOAD TESTS OF WOOD STRUCTURES

R. Cunliffe * and J.J. Salinas *

* Dept. of Civil Engineering, Carleton University, Ottawa K1S 5B6

## ABSTRACT

'Design' and 'Performance' environments are defined to evaluate the reliability of wood structures. A structure designed according to building code requirements has a minimum level of safety dictated by the target reliability adopted by the code. The reliability of a structure however, is not constant over time. The strength of the structure tends to degrade with time under load, especially if the structural components exhibit creep rupture behaviour. Damage is accumulated in these materials, shifting the strength distribution down the strength scale and reducing the reliability of the structure.

The service load history, like a proof load, gives indication of a lower bound on the strength distribution. This lower bound is not well defined with wood, because the strength is decreasing with time under load.

Although the actual reliability is decreasing with service life, our confidence in its assessment increases with time.

## INTRODUCTION

For the design of wood structures, the engineer's knowledge of loads and strengths is mostly based on information provided by the building code. The building code prescribes nominal design loads for occupancy, snow, wind, etc., based on load surveys and meteorological information. The code also prescribes allowable stresses or specified strengths for several species groups, based on comprehensive experimental programs.

During an initial stage, the designer determines the load on the structure, selects a convenient strength and proceeds to determine an adequate size or some other geometric property of the member or system under consideration. At this stage the designer implicitly accepts a level of safety targeted by the building code. With some insight into the design process it is possible to estimate this initially accepted level of safety.

After construction, when the structure starts its service life there is improved knowledge of the 'as built' dimensions and sizes which can be used to improve the knowldege about the dead loads. The estimate of actual live loads or material strength is not different from that used in the initial design stage. As time passes, knowledge about the live load will improve if records of occupancy and weather are kept. Although the actual strength of the 'as built' structure is still not known in absolute terms, it is possible to estimate 'relative' changes in strength with time under load by using some damage accumulation model. At this stage, the level of safety under actual field conditions can be estimated and compared with that determined during the initial stage.

This study considers the load and strength parameters under two different sets of conditions: a 'design environment' where loads and strengths have fixed values given by the code for design purposes; and a 'performance environment' where loads and strengths change with time.

THE DESIGN ENVIRONMENT

The nominal capacity of a wood structural element given by CAN3-086.1-M84 can be expressed in the general form:

$$C_n = \phi S_c X_p K* \qquad (1)$$

where $\phi$ = Resistance factor; Sc = Specified strength; Xp = Geometric property of the structural element; K* = Product of strength adjustment factors (moisture content, size, etc).

The nominal load effect calculated by the designer is:

$$B_n = X_g(\alpha_D D_n + \alpha_L L_n) \qquad (2)$$

where: Xg = Geometry factor to convert loads to stresses; $\alpha_D$ = Dead load factor (1.25); $\alpha_L$ = Live load factor (1.50); Dn = Nominal dead load; Ln = Nominal live load.

In a design environment Cn > Bn; substituting Equations (1) and (2) into this 'design inequality', it is possible to find the required size or geometric property:

$$X_p \geq \frac{X_g(\alpha_D D_n + \alpha_L L_n)}{\phi S_c K*} \qquad (3)$$

At this stage, the structural element of size Xp is assumed to have a minimum level of safety close to that targeted by the code. By making some assumptions with regards to the underlying probability density function for the strength values assigned by the code and with regards to the acting loads, it is possible to estimate the level of safety.

THE PERFORMANCE ENVIRONMENT

Once the structure is in service, its performance is dictated by the actual material strength and the imposed loads. The loads are specific realizations of a broad range of values characterized by the nominal values used in the design environment. Within the performance environment the actual capacity is given by:

$$C_a = S_a X_p \qquad (4)$$

and the actual load effect is given by:

$$B_a = X_g(D + L) \qquad (5)$$

where: Sa is the actual material strength; Xp is the geometric property determined with Equation (3); Xg is the geometry factor used in Equation (2); D and L are the acting dead and live loads, respectively.

The material strength, Sa, is a random variable with unknown probability density function. However, it is possible to estimate the parameters of this distribution by assuming that the specified strength given by the code, Sc, corresponds to a 5th percentile value divided by an adjustment factor of 2.1 which includes a factor of safety as well as a load duration factor to bring the short-term test strength to a 'normal' duration. Figure 1 shows a graphic representation of this assumption.

The actual magnitude of the load effect within the performance environment can not be predicted with certainty. National Bureau of Standards Special Publication # 577 gives some recommendations for the selection of the parameters for the probability density functions for loads.

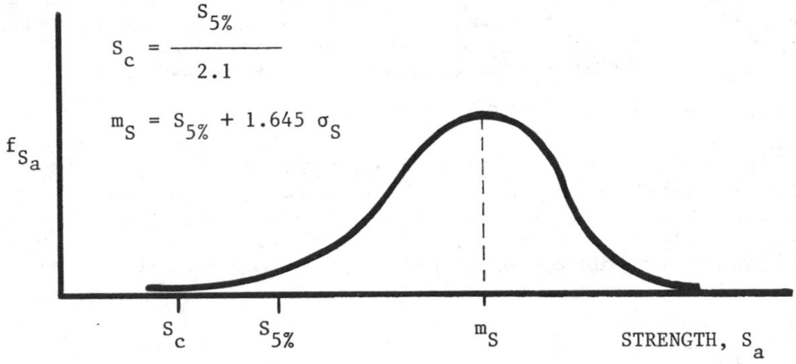


Figure 1 ASSUMED STRENGTH DISTRIBUTION

RELIABILITY CALCULATIONS

The reliability of the system can be formulated in terms of the performance function:

$$G = C - B \tag{6}$$

where C is the capacity and B the load effect. The limiting performance of the system is given by G = 0, which defines a strength limit state. The 'failure state' is given by G < 0 and the 'safe state' by G >0. If the probability density functions for C and B, f and f , are known, the probability of failure can be determined from:

$$P_f = P[G < 0] = \int_{-\infty}^{+\infty} f_B dB \int_{-\infty}^{B} f_C dC = \int_{-\infty}^{+\infty} f_B F_C dB \tag{7}$$

Alternatively, if the probability density function $f_G$ can be derived from $f_B$ and $f_C$ , the reliability index, $\beta$ , is defined as the ratio of the mean to the standard deviation of the derived distribution for G.

$$\beta = \frac{m_G}{\sigma_G} \tag{8}$$

The probability of failure and the reliability index are related by:

$$P_f = 1 - \Phi(\beta) \tag{9}$$

where $\Phi(\beta) =$ Value for the cummulative distribution function of the standard normal distribution.

BASE CASE

To illustrate the concepts discussed here, the following

example will be considered: roof joist system with a 5.5 m span and joist spacing of 400 mm, located in Ottawa. The lumber is S-P-F, No. 2, dry service conditions, no preservative treatment, nominal dead load Dn = 0.5 kPa, live load (snow) Ln = 2.32 kPa, load factors $\alpha_D$ = 1.25 and $\alpha_L$ = 1.50, resistance factor $\phi$= 0.70 (bending). A 38 x 286 mm joist was found to be adequate under these requirements. Substituting Equations (3), (4) and (5) into Equation (6) the performance function takes the form:

$$G = \sum_{i=1}^{3} A_i x_i \qquad 10)$$

where

$$A_1 = \frac{1}{S_c} \qquad x_1 = S_a$$

$$A_2 = -\frac{\phi K*(\frac{D_n}{L_n})}{\alpha_D(\frac{D_n}{L_n})+\alpha_L} \qquad x_2 = \frac{D}{D_n}$$

$$A_3 = \frac{A_2}{(\frac{D_n}{D_L})} \qquad x_3 = \frac{L}{L_n}$$

PERFORMANCE ENVIRONMENT = DESIGN ENVIRONMENT

As a first attempt to estimate the reliability of the system, it will be assumed that the actual material strength and the loads acting on the joist are those used in the design process. Under these conditions, Dn = D; Ln = L; $X_1$ = Sa = 2.1 Sc; $X_2$ = $X_3$ = 1.0. Equation (8) was used to calculate the reliability index and the results are plotted in Figure 2 as a function of the coefficient of variation of the material strength variable, $X_1$ = Sa.

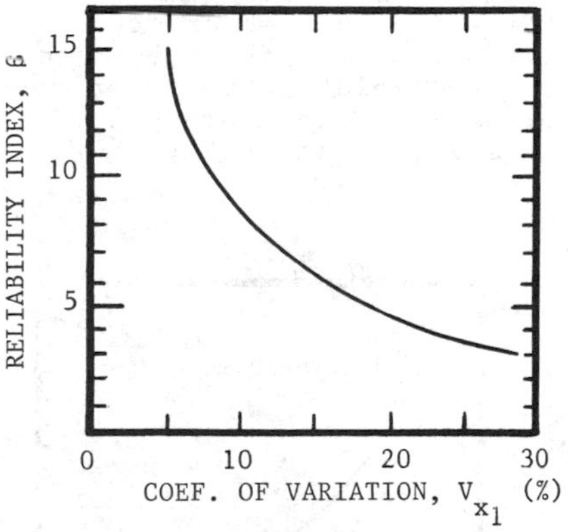


Figure 2 RELIABILITY INDEX FOR
PERFORMANCE ENVIRONMENT = DESIGN ENVIRONMENT

PERFORMANCE ENVIRONMENT ≠DESIGN ENVIRONMENT

Uncorrelated Normal Variates.- The probability density for the material strength during the service life is assumed to be that shown in Figure 1. Within the performance environment it will be assumed that the load variables are uncorrelated and normally distributed. They take the values shown in Table 1 and are based on those reported in NBS Special Publication #577. The reliability index was calculated using Equation (8) and the results are plotted in Figure 3.

Table 1 VALUES FOR STRENGTH AND LOAD VARIABLES

| *VARIABLE* | *MEAN* | *COEFFICIENT OF VARIATION* |
|---|---|---|
| $x_1 = S_a$ | $\frac{2.1S_c}{1-1.645V_{x_1}}$ | $V_{x_1}$ |
| $x_2 = \frac{D}{D_n}$ | 1.00 | 0.10 |
| $x_3 = \frac{L}{L_n}$ | 0.82 | 0.26 |

Correlated Normal Variates.- The material strength, $X_1$ ,and the loads, $X_2$ and $X_3$ , are assumed to be correlated. The strength of wood depends on the applied load history, and the 'load duration' or 'rate of loading' effect plays an important role in determining the strength of wood structures.

The 'size effect' is particularly important in wood engineering. The larger the size of the member, the greater the probability of having a flaw of critical size, which would initiate failure and reduce the assumed strength. The dead load variable, $X_2$ , which includes the self weight of the member,is a function of the member's size, and is therefore correlated to the member's strength, $X_1$ .

Large applied loads,(D+L),call for large member size and hence large dead loads. Therefore, the dead load variable, $X_2$,and the live load variable, $X_3$ , are correlated.

To determine the actual degree of correlation between the variables is a difficult task; for the purpose of comparison in this study, perfect correlation has been assumed between all variables. The reliability index was calculated using Equation (8), and the results are plotted in Figure 3.

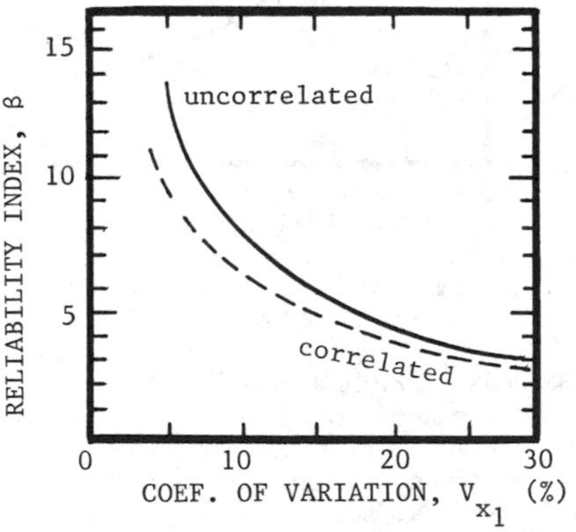


Figure 3 RELIABILITY INDEX FOR PERFORMANCE ENVIRONMENT ≠DESIGN ENVIRONMENT

LIFETIME PERFORMANCE

Time under load reduces the strength of wood members. Damage accumulation models for lumber in bending have been used by Gerhards (1977) and Barrett and Foschi (1978a and 1978b) to study the effect of a load history on the strength of wood members. These studies indicate that weaker members are affected more by the loads than stronger members.

In the examples considered previously, it was assumed that the probability density function for short-term strength was invariant, whereas the loads are assumed to be maximum values over the lifetime of the structure. Salinas and Gillard (1987) have used the concept of 'equivalence' to account for this difference in time-spans when evaluating the reliability of wood structures.

As damage accumulates with time, the probability density function for strength will tend to 'shift' towards the lower end of the scale, increasing the probability of failure and reducing the reliability index with time.

LOAD TESTS

Proof loading is a means for eliminating extraordinarily weak building components before fabrication. Removal of the weak components will alter the low tail of the strength distribution. It will not be truncated at the proof load level because some elements, slightly stronger than the proof load level, will be damaged by it, and their strength reduced. However, the low tail of the probability density function of the surviving components will shift towards the high end of the scale

DISCUSSION

Can the service loads on a structure be considered a proof load? It is difficult to evaluate the two opposite effects on the strength distribution caused by damage accumulation and proof loading. For a single element, proof loading does not eliminate weak components but it does identify a lower limit to the strength distribution. The fact that a structure has survived a known load history gives us improved knowledge of its capacity to accumulate damage without failure.

At this stage, a measure of the residual strength, could be evaluated using damage accumulation models. However, the large variability in lumber strength allows an assessment of the residual strength only within very broad limits.

The evaluation of the reliability of a structure, whose building components do not exhibit a strong creep rupture behaviour, will be more accurate. The maximum imposed load, determined from a load history, would give a lower bound on the strength. If the strength does not degrade with time, a revised probabilty density distribution, with a lower bound equal to the largest applied service load, could be used in the reliability calculation.

A lower bound could not be set in the same manner for a material that exhibits strength degradation with time. The structure could survive a large load early in its service life, but fail at that same load level later on.

An improved characterization of the underlying probability density functions for strength and load variables, within a design environment, proved effective in evaluating the level of safety associated with the wood joist used as a case study in this investigation. Even if the net result is a reduction of the safety index with time, the degree of confidence associated with the knowledge of this parameter will support an affirmative answer to the question of whether service loads on a structure can be considered to be useful in the evaluation of the level of safety.

AKNOWLEDGEMENTS
Financial support from NSERC, in the form of an Operating Grant for the senior author, is gratefully acknowledged.

REFERENCES

Barrett, J.D. and R.O. Foschi (1978a). Duration of Load and Probability of Failure in Wood. Part I. Modelling Creep Rupture. Canadian Journal of Civil Engineering, 5(4), pp.505-514

Barrett, J.D. and R.O. Foschi (1978b). Duration of Load and Probability of Failure in Wood. Part II. Constant, Ramp and Cyclic Loadings Canadian Journal of Civil Engineering 5(4), pp.515-532

Canadian Standards Association (1984). CAN3-086.1-M84. "Engineering Design in Wood (Limit States Design)". CSA 178 Rexdale Blvd., Rexdale, Ontario, M9W 1R3, 222 pp.

Gerhards, C.C. (1977). "Effect of Duration and Rate of Loading on Strength of Wood and Wood-Based Materials". USDA Forest Service Research Paper FPL 283. Forest Products Laboratory, Madison, Wisconsin.

National Bureau of Standards (1980). Special Publication # 577. "Development of a probability based load criterion for American National Standard A58. U.S. Department of Commerce. Superintendent of Documents, U.S. Government Printing Office, Washington, D.C., U.S.A. 20402, 228 pp.

Salinas, J.J. and R.G. Gillard (1987). "Equivalent Criteria in Acceptance Testing". Proceedings of ICASP5, Vancouver, B.C., May 1987.

# PROBABILISTIC FINITE ELEMENTS AND ITS APPLICATIONS*

W. K. Liu, T. Belytschko, A. Mani and G. H. Besterfield
Department of Mechanical Engineering, Northwestern University,
Evanston, Illinois, 60201, U.S.A.

## ABSTRACT

Improved computational procedures are presented for the Probabilistic Finite Element Method (PFEM) for the transient analysis of random field problems of linear and nonlinear continua. The theoretical development of PFEM is reviewed with the inclusion of a transformed uncorrelated random variable. A highly efficient Lanczos algorithm is presented to reduce the PFEM equations to a smaller system of tridiagonal equations. A method based on Fourier analysis is presented for removing secularities from PFEM. The effectiveness of the method presented herein is demonstrated with application to linear elastic and nonlinear elastic/plastic continuum problems. All of the results presented exhibit the excellent performance of PFEM.

## INTRODUCTION

We have developed a methodology which embeds the probabilistic character of both the constitutive properties and loads within a finite element discretization of the random fields (i.e., material uncertainties and load uncertainties as a function of space), (Liu, 1986a,1986b,1987). The corresponding probabilistic character of the **elemental** nodal forces can then be assembled into a description of the probabilistic distribution of the nodal forces for the complete model; and the appropriate mean and covariance responses due to these uncertainties can be determined efficiently. The method is based on a second moment technique but has been found effective in a variety of linear and nonlinear problems.

## EFFICIENT COMPUTATIONAL PROCEDURES

Even though the PFEM formulation is compatible with the element discretization and nodal assembly procedures that characterize finite element theory and software implementation, the number of matrix multiplications is proportional to $q(q+1)/2$ ($q$ is the number of discretized random variables). This would be unacceptably expensive. To remedy this situation, the **full** covariance matrix is transformed to a **diagonal** variance matrix via an eigenvalue orthogonalization. Through this transformation procedure, the number of matrix multiplications is reduced to order $q$. It is shown that a reduced set of the **uncorrelated** variables is sufficient for this PFEM formulation in most cases.

With the random variable transformation the PFEM is quite efficient, but the computations can be decreased further by forming a reduced basis which characterizes the system. The authors suggest constructing a reduced basis from a sequence of Lanczos vectors. The Lanczos basis is formed from the generalized eigenproblem and then it is used to reduce the PFEM equations to a smaller system of tridiagonal equations.

*The support of NASA Lewis Grant No. NAG3-535 for this research and the encouragement of Dr. Christos Chamis are gratefully acknowledged.

The application of PFEM via a sensitivity method for transient problems can result in the emergence of undesirable secular terms. The basic principle of all methods for removing the secular terms consists of expanding the period of oscillation as a perturbation along with the solution. The methods which have been considered include: Lindstedt's frequency expansion, multiple time scales, two-variable expansion, averaging, and Fourier analysis. The above methods have been applied to a single degree-of-freedom random oscillator to numerically remove secularities. The most promising for numerical elimination of secularities is Fourier Analysis using frequency weighting windows. This method can also be extended to multiple degree-of-freedom random systems such as PFEM. Application of these methods to nonlinear random systems present additional problems which need to be dealt with.

## THE DEVELOPMENT OF PFEM FOR TRANSIENT ANALYSIS OF NONLINEAR (BOTH MATERIAL AND GEOMETRICAL) CONTINUA

Based on the linear formulation, the method has been extended to transient analysis of nonlinear continua. The major difference between the linear formulation and the nonlinear formulation is the internal force term. In the linear case, the internal force is directly expressed in terms of the material properties and the kinematic quantities. In the nonlinear case, this is not possible. Furthermore, if the material is elastic/plastic, the internal force exhibits path-dependency.

The variance of the internal force is obtained from its first and second derivatives with respect to the random field variables. These derivatives cannot be directly evaluated for nonlinear continua. However, these derivatives can be evaluated by least squares regression or more simply by finite differences. In this work, the central-difference approximations have been used. The excellent results in many test problems indicate that this method is very effective.

## RESULTS

The computer solutions obtained using these theories have been compared to the Monte Carlo methods. It is found that the performance of the PFEM is superior to the Monte Carlo methods. The Monte Carlo method has many variations and most of these have proven to be very easy to incorporate in deterministic computer codes. The PFEM, though not as simple as the Monte Carlo methods, can also be integrated into many deterministic FEM codes quite easily. The present code can handle linear and nonlinear elastic/plastic problems in both static and transient settings, particularly for random material properties.

The methods presented in this paper are demonstrated by application to a plain strain continuum with a circular hole. The problem statement is presented in Fig. 1 for a linear elastic continuum with 1535 degrees-of-freedom. The continuum is subjected to a uniform in-plane sinusoidal loading which is discretized into 24 random variables with a coefficient of variation of 10% and a correlation length ($L_F$) of 6L, where L is a characteristic length defined in the problem statement. Young's modulus for the material is also discretized into 15 random variables for elements 1 through 15 with a coefficient of variation of 10% and a correlation length ($L_E$) of 3L/2. Adjacent elements which form rings around the hole possess the same statistical material properties. That is, there are only 15 material random variables but all 720 elements are random. Rayleigh stiffness proportional damping is included thereby introducing random damping into the system. The total of 39 random variables are transformed to a set of 6 uncorrelated random variables where the 3 dominant correlated random variables are taken from the random load and material each. The Lanczos basis reduced PFEM (LPFEM) is obtained by using only the first 30 Lanczos vectors in the basis. Results for the secularity elimination scheme (NOSEC) are for a cosine$^2$ weighting window and a range on the weighting window of ±15% of first mode natural frequency. The dominant system characteristics are a first mode natural frequency of 1352 cps and damping ratio equivalent to .6% of first mode. Results obtained are depicted in Figs. 2 through 4.

Two of the more critical design quantities are the time histories for the displacement of node 400 in the y-direction and the stress ($\sigma_{yy}$) in element 15. The expectation and variance of these quantities are plotted in Figs. 2 and 3. Also of design importance is the statistics of the stress ($\sigma_{yy}$) for elements 1 through 15 along the x-axis plotted in Fig. 4. In Fig. 4a, a selected time history for the expectation of stress is depicted. In Fig. 4b the variance of stress is shown and is very similar to the expectation. The spatial stress correlation coefficient along the x-axis with respect to element 7 is plotted in Fig. 4c. In the response statistics, the secularity elimination technique gives transient results devoid of secularities and satisfactory results can be obtained with fewer Lanczos vectors.

Analysis of the computation time required shows the overwhelming numerical advantages of the methodologies presented herein over the Monte Carlo Simulation. The LPFEM solution with 30 Lanczos vectors takes a relative computation time of 6 units, where one unit of computation time is approximately equal to 1 cpu hour on a Harris series 800 computer. The solution without secularities, NOSEC, requires an additional 1 unit of computation time, giving a total of 7 units for a complete analysis. A standard Monte Carlo Simulation with 400 samples for the same time history would require approximately 160 units of computation time. This results in a 96% savings in computation time for the LPFEM and NOSEC over the Monte Carlo Simulation for this problem. This is actually a conservative approximation for the savings in computation time since fewer than 30 Lanczos vectors can be used to obtain accurate results. Of course, the computation time is problem dependent; but in general, a 90% savings can be obtained using the LPFEM and NOSEC in this and many other problems.

To illustrate the capabilities of PFEM in nonlinear continua, the problem in Fig. 1 is analyzed for an elastic/plastic material. In contrast to the previous applications, the uniaxial yield stress is treated as a stationary random field instead of Young's modulus and the load is assumed deterministic. The random yield stress is exponentially correlated in the radial direction with a mean value of 25000.0 psi, a coefficient of variation of 10% and a correlation length of 3L/2. The response statistics for the y-displacement of node 400 and stress ($\sigma_{yy}$) in element 15 are given by Figs. 5 and 6, respectively.

REFERENCES

Liu, W. K., Belytschko, T. and Mani, A. (1986). "Probabilistic Finite Element Methods for Nonlinear Structural Dynamics," Computer Methods in Applied Mechanics and Engineering, 56, pp. 61-81.

Liu, W. K., Belytschko, T. and Mani, A. (1986). "Random Field Finite Elements," International Journal for Numerical Methods in Engineering, 23, pp. 1831-1845.

Liu, W. K., Belytschko, T. and Mani, A. (1987). "Applications of Probabilistic Finite Element Methods in Elastic/Plastic Dynamics," to appear in Journal of Engineering for Industry, ASME.

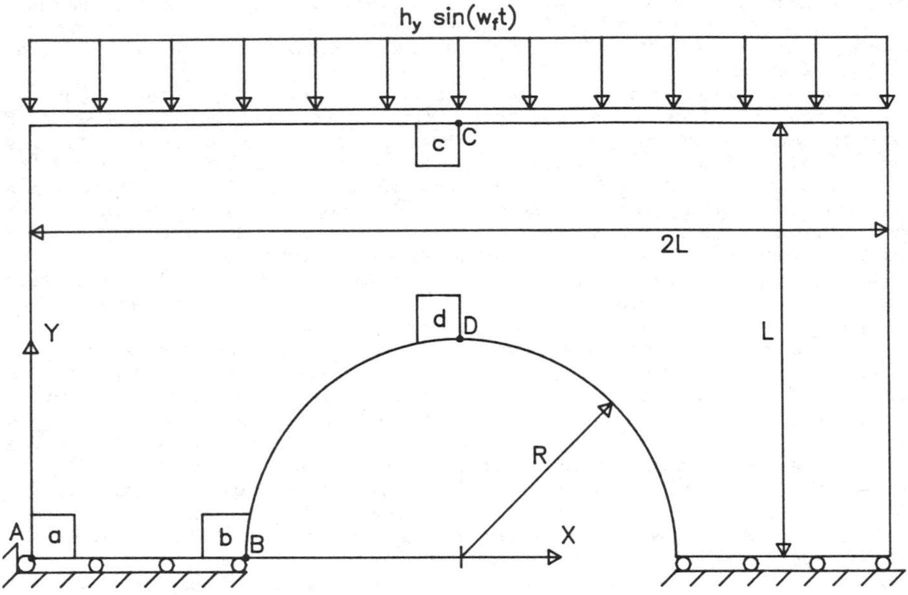


<u>Problem Constants</u>

$E = 3.0X10^7$ lb/in$^2$
Density = 0.3 lb/in$^3$
Thickness = 1.0 in
L = 6.0 in
R = 3.0 in
Poissons Ratio = 0.3
$h_y$ = 2000.0 lb/in
$w_f$ = 1500.0 rad/sec
Delta t = $1.0X10^{-4}$ sec
Rayleigh Damping Parameters
$e_0 = 0.0$ $e_1 = 1.5X10^{-6}$

<u>Random Load</u>

24 Random Variables
Coefficient of Variation = 0.1
Mean Load = 2000.0 lb/in
Spatial Correlation
$R(x_i,x_j) = \exp(-abs(x_i-x_j)/L_F)$

<u>Mesh Data</u>

4 Node 2D Plane Strain Continuum Element in Radial Mesh
784 Nodes, 720 Elements
Point a = Element 1
Point b = Element 15
Point c = Element 346
Point d = Element 360
Point A = Node 1
Point B = Node 16
Point C = Node 385
Point D = Node 400

<u>Random Material</u>

15 Random Variables
Coefficient of Variation = 0.1
Mean Youngs Mod. = $3.0X10^7$ lb/in$^2$
Spatial Correlation
$R(x_i,x_j) = \exp(-abs(x_i-x_j)/L_E)$

Fig. 1. Problem Statement: Plain Strain Continuum with a Circular Hole.

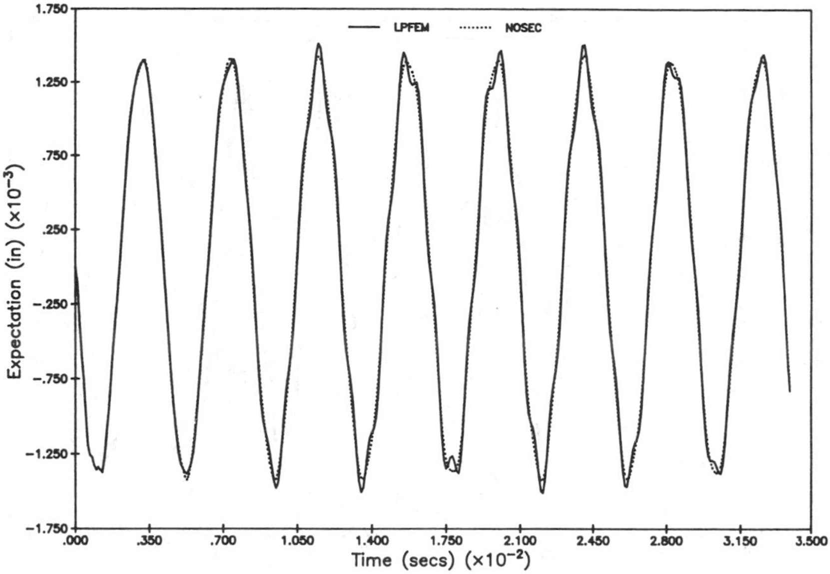


Fig. 2a. Expectation of Node 400 y-Displacement versus Time for LPFEM and NOSEC.

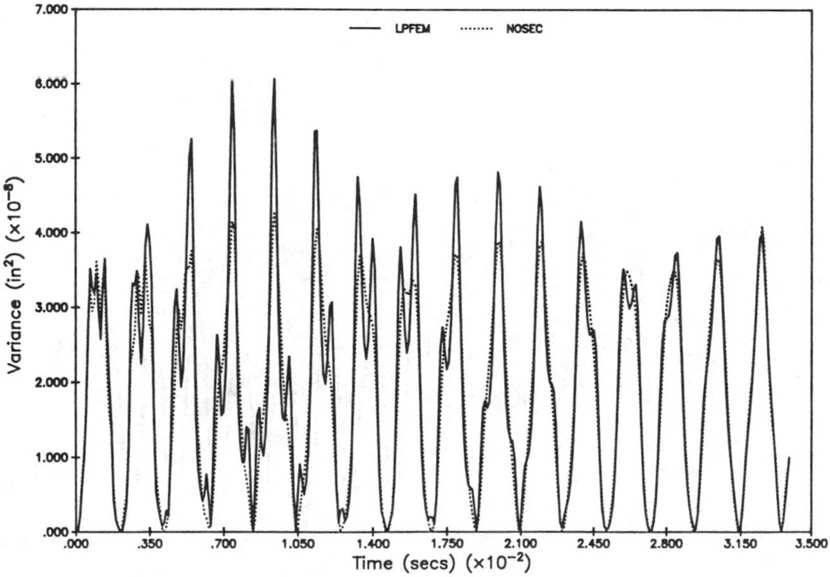


Fig. 2b. Variance of Node 400 y-Displacement versus Time for LPFEM and NOSEC.

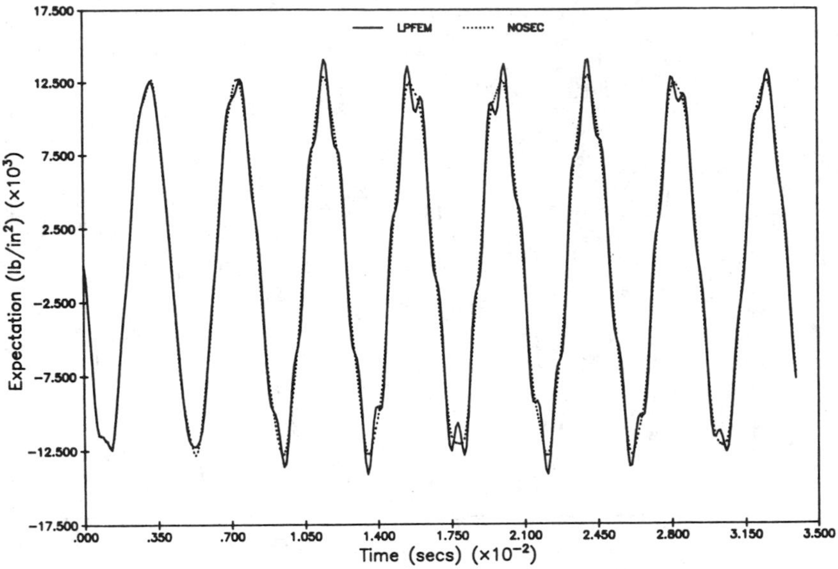


Fig. 3a. Expectation of Stress in Element 15 versus Time for LPFEM and NOSEC.

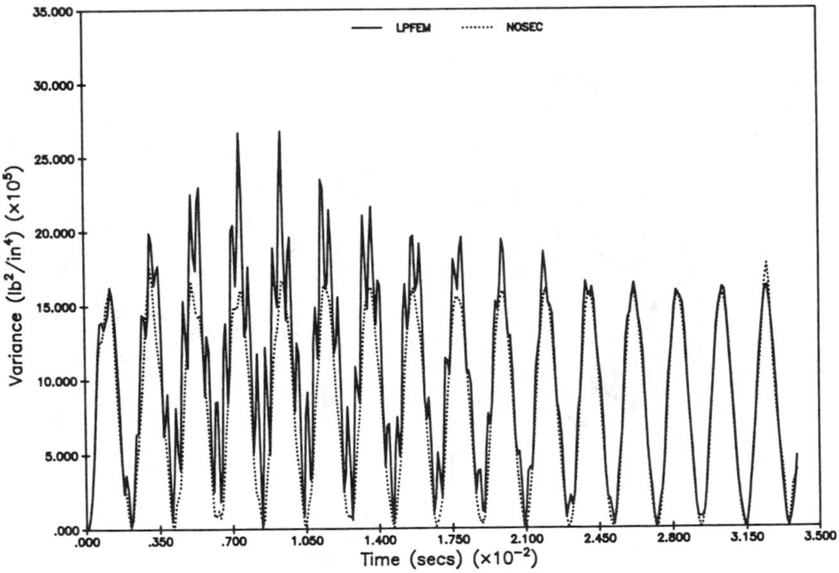


Fig. 3b. Variance of Stress in Element 15 versus Time for LPFEM and NOSEC.

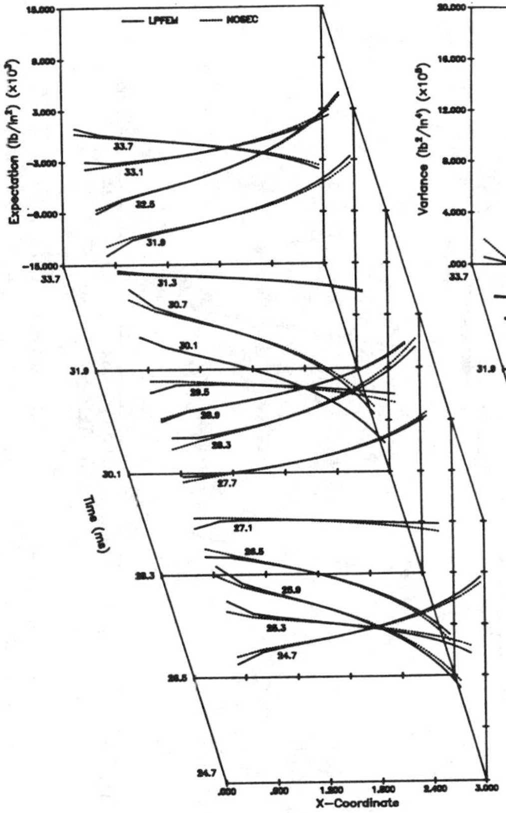


Fig. 4a. Expectation of Stress in Elements 1 to 15 versus Time for LPFEM and NOSEC.

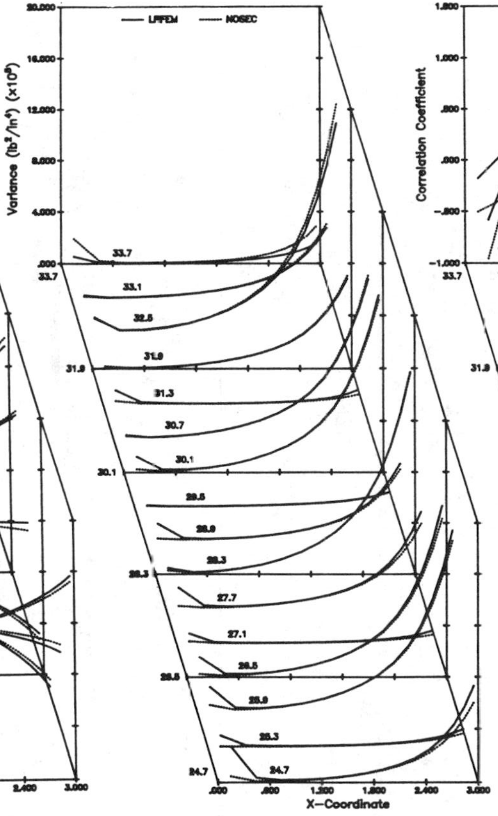


Fig. 4b. Variance of Stress in Elements 1 to 15 versus Time for LPFEM and NOSEC.

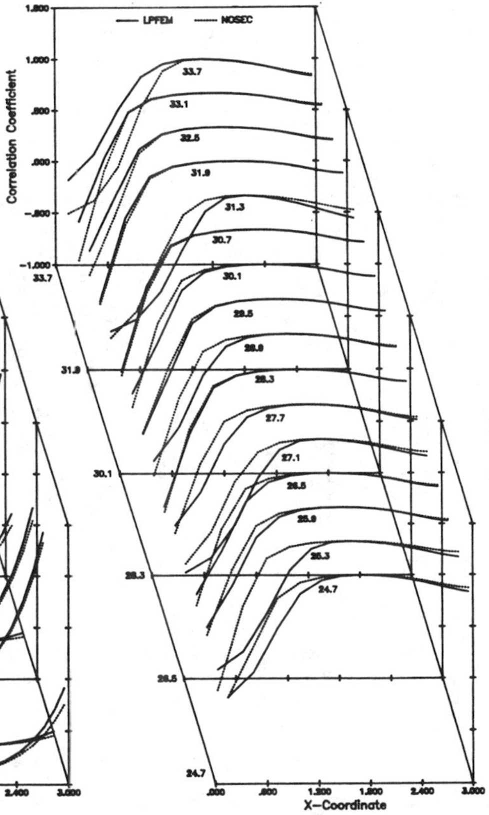


Fig. 4c. Stress Correlation Coefficient in Elements 1 to 15 versus Time for LPFEM and NOSEC.

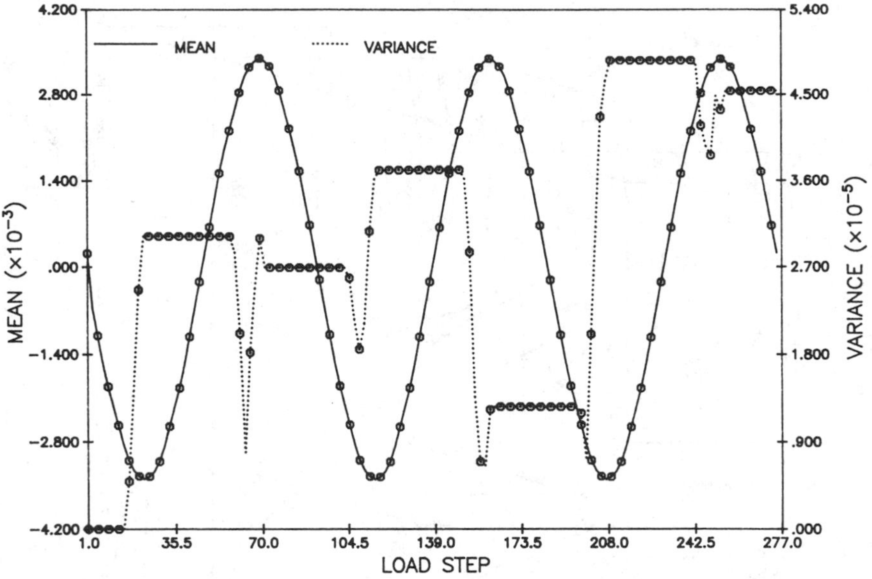


Fig. 5. Mean and Variance of Node 400 y-Displacement versus Load Steps.

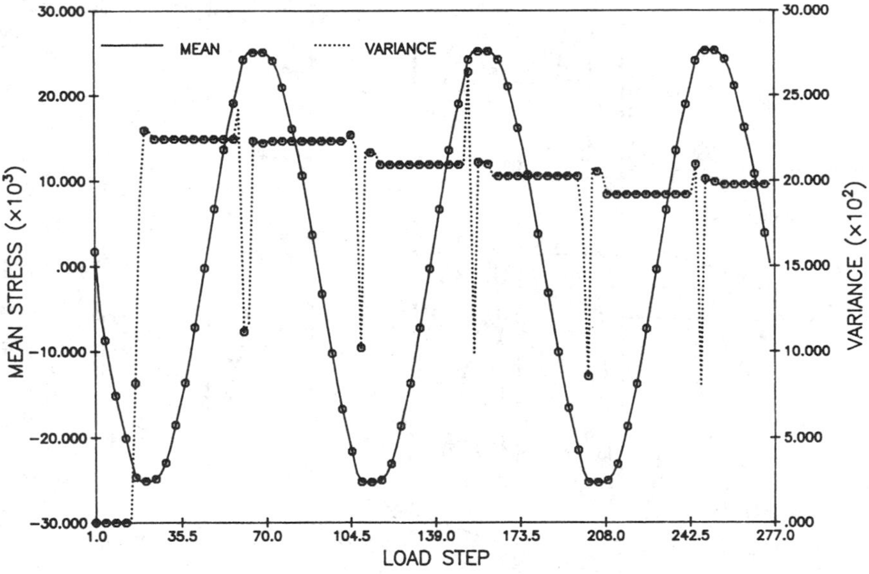


Fig. 6. Mean and Variance of Stress in Element 15 versus Load Steps.

# A NEW METHOD FOR THE EVALUATION OF SYSTEM FAILURE PROBABILITIES

Dr. K. Ramachandran
Department of Civil Engineering, Imperial College,
London SW7 2BU, United Kingdom
Professor P. J. Dowling
Head of Civil Engineering Department, Imperial College,
London SW7 2BU, United Kingdom

## ABSTRACT

Probabilistic safety analysis of civil engineering structures requires the evaluation of multi-normal integrals and these multi-normal integrals can be estimated either from upper and lower bounds on these probabilities or by first-order second-moment approximate methods. In this paper an exact method based on conditional probabilities for the evaluation of parallel systems is presented. Examples are studied to compare the accuracy of this new method with other approximate methods.

## INTRODUCTION

Reliability theory is now widely used in soil and structural engineering to assess the probability of failure of earth slopes (Ramachandran and Hosking 1985), propped cantilevers (Ramachandran 1986), offshore structures (Baker and Ramachandran 1981, Chrysanthopoulos and Dowling 1986) and many other engineering systems. The technique for evaluating the reliability index of a single failure mode is well estabilished and better statistical data are being used in these computations. However, the method of calculating the probability of failure when there are more than three predominant failure modes in a system still lacks vigour, and some times leads to unsafe results. The calculation of system probability of failure requires the evaluation of a multi-normal integral and the current practice is to use bounds on the probability as a means of estimating the system failure probability or to use an approximate method for the evaluation of this multi-normal integral. Although the available bounds (Ramachandran 1984,1986; Rackwitz and Hohenbichler 1984) are reasonably satisfactory, there is a definite need for finding an exact or near exact method for reliable estimation of these multi-normal integrals. In this paper, an exact method is presented for the determination of these failure probabilities.

## PROBLEM DEFINITION

In reliability analysis, each failure mode is represented by a continuous function (safety margin) $g_i(\mathbf{x})$ of the statistical variables $\mathbf{x}$. Usually there are a very large number of possible failure modes in a system; however with little experience, the number of failure modes which have significant effect on the reliability of the system ( predominant modes) can be substantially reduced. The event $g_i(\mathbf{x}) \leq 0$ is referred to as the $i^{th}$ failure mode $F_i$, and its probability of occurrence denoted by $P(F_i)$. The failure of the system is then given by $P(\cup F_i)$ for a series system and by $P(\cap F_i)$ for a parallel system. In this presentation attention is given to the evaluation of $P(\cap F_i)$. The evaluation of $P(\cup F_i)$ is a simple straight-forward extension and will be presented later.

## NEW METHOD

$P(\bigcap_{i=1}^{n} F_i)$ can be expanded as $P(\bigcap_{i=1}^{n-1} F_i | F_n)\, P(F_n)$. Denoting the conditional event $(F_i|F_n)$ as $F_i^n$ , $P(\bigcap_{i=1}^{n} F_i|F_n)$ can be expressed as $P(\bigcap_{i=1}^{n-1} F_i)$

In order to evaluate the probability of occurrence of conditional event $P(F_i^n)$ and the correlation $\rho_{ij}^n$ between the conditional events $F_i^n$ and $F_j^n$ , the following properties of conditional events can be used:

$$P(F_i^n) = P(F_i|F_n) = P(F_i \cap F_n)/P(F_n) \tag{1}$$

$$P(F_i^n \cap F_j^n) = P(F_i|F_n \cap F_j|F_n) \tag{2}$$

$$= P[(F_i \cap F_j)|F_n] \tag{3}$$

$$= P(F_i \cap F_j \cap F_n)/P(F_n) \tag{4}$$

The quantities $P(F_i \cap F_j)$ and $P(F_i \cap F_j \cap F_n)$ can be determined from the first author's computer program. The correlation coefficient $\rho_{ij}^n$ is easily obtainable from the values of $P(F_i^n \cap F_j^n)$, $P(F_i^n)$ and $P(F_j^n)$ by an iterative method. At the end of first step, we get

$$P(\bigcap_{i=1}^{n} F_i) = [P(\bigcap_{i=1}^{n-1} F_i)]\ P(F_n) \tag{5}$$

The probability of the terms within the parenthesis [ ] can now be evaluated by repeating the same process, but conditioning all other events on $F_{n-1}^n$.

$$P(\bigcap_{i=1}^{n-1} F_i) = P(\bigcap_{i=1}^{n-2} F_i^{n-1})\ P(F_{n-1}^n) \tag{6}$$

Note that $F_i^{n-1}$ corresponds to new events $[F_i|F_{n-1}]$, which are obtained from the previous step. The process is repeated till the dimension **n** becomes 3 leading to $P(F_1^4 \cap F_2^4 \cap F_3^4)$. The evaluation of this integral is then carried out numerically. This procedure will give the following result:

$$P(\bigcap_{i=1}^{n} F_i) = P(F_1^4 \cap F_2^4 \cap F_3^4)\ P(F_4^5)\ P(F_5^6)\ \ldots.\ P(F_{n-1}^n)\ P(F_n) \tag{7}$$

This method is an exact method and no approximations are made in any of of the above calculations.

**FIRST-ORDER SECOND-MOMENT METHOD**

The idea of using conditional property to reduce the dimension of a multi-normal inegral is well known and it has appeared in many publications (Hohenbichler 1981; Ditlevsen 1982;Ramachandran 1982,1984). Hohenbichler (1984) used the so-called first-order second-moment method to evaluate the probability of the conditional event and the correlation between the conditional events. As clearly spelled out in Ramachnadran (1986), the first order method tends to give inaccurate values for the correlation coefficients in some cases and examples studied supports this view. Table 1 shows a few results where the first-order second-moment method (FOSM) fails to give satisfactory results for series systems.

**EXAMPLES**

To assess the accuracy and efficiency of this new method, a few known examples are studied and the results are compared with that obtaind by the first-order second-moment method. Table 2 shows the results of equicorrelated systems with the same reliability index $\beta$. The authors' results differ slightly from the exact values possibly due to numerical inaccuracies in the calculation of trivariate integrals.

Table 1. FOSM estimate and bounds

| No of events | RL | RU | FOSM estimate | |
|---|---|---|---|---|
| 3 | 95.372 | 95.372 | 95.468 | $(10^{-2})$ |
| 4 | 0.1749 | 0.1749 | 0.1744 | $(10^{-2})$ |
| 6 | 0.6825 | 0.6834 | 0.6807 | $(10^{-2})$ |

RL - Ramachandran's lower bound; RU - Ramachandran's upper bound

Table 2. Equicorrelated systems

| $\beta$ | correlation coefficient | First-order method | New method | Exact value |
|---|---|---|---|---|
| | 0.5 | 0.0044 | 0.0046 | 0.0046 $(\times10^{-3})$ |
| 3.0 | 0.8 | 0.1192 | 0.1215 | 0.1221 $(\times10^{-3})$ |
| | 0.95 | 0.5322 | 0.5294 | 0.5309 $(\times10^{-3})$ |
| | 0.5 | 0.2017 | 0.2075 | 0.2141 $(\times10^{-3})$ |
| 2.0 | 0.8 | 0.3043 | 0.3052 | 0.3060 $(\times10^{-2})$ |
| | 0.95 | 0.1029 | 0.1010 | 0.1021 $(\times10^{-1})$ |

A few other random examples are also considered and the results are given in table 3. In this case the accuracy of the results are not known and the best available bounds may be used to assess the accuracy.

Table 3. Random examples

| Number of failure modes (N) | First-order method | Exact method |
|---|---|---|
| 4 | 0.000581 | 0.000619 |
| 5 | 0.000142 | 0.000145 |
| 6 | 0.0000011 | 0.0000087 |

**SUMMARY AND CONCLUSIONS**

A new method for the exact evaluation of system reliability using the property of conditional events is presented. Examples are studied and the results are compared with the approximate method. As one can expect this method is much slower than the first-order second-moment method. Because the evaluation of each failure probability $P(F_i)$ for special cases such as nuclear power plants, offshore structures and soil/rock slope stability requires large computer effort, the efficiency of computing $P(\bigcap F_i)$ is not very important to reliability analysts and the main objective is to get the correct failure probabilities.

**REFERENCES**


Baker J. and Ramachandran K. (1981). "Reliability Analysis as a Tool in the Design of Offshore Platforms", Conf. on Integrity of Offshore Structures, Glasgow, Applied Science Publishers, 135-154.

Chryssanthopoulos M.,Baker J. and Dowling P.J. (1986). "A Reliability Approach to the Local Buckling of Stringer-Stiffened Cylinders", OMAE, Tokyo, 2, 64-72.

Ditlevsen O. (1983). "Reliability Bounding by Conditioning", Journal of Engineering Mechanics, ASCE,108,708-718.

Hohenbichler M. (1981). "Approximate Evaluation of the Multinormal Distribution Function", Report Heft 58, Technical University of Munich, Germany, 55-66.

Rackwitz R. and Hohenbichler M. (1984). "First Order Concepts in System Reliability", Structural Safety, 1, 177-188.

Ramachandran K. (1982). "Evaluation of Bivariate Normal Integrals using the First-Order Second-Moment Method", Internal Report, Department of Civil Engineering, Imperial College, London.

Ramachandran K. (1984). "System Bounds- A Critical Study", Civil Engineering Systems, 3, 123-128.

Ramachandran K. and Hosking I. (1985). "Reliability Approach to Stability Analysis of Soil/Rock Slopes", Fifth Int. Conf. on Numerical Methods in Geomechanics, Japan, Balkema, Rotterdam, 1019-1028.

Ramachandran K. (1986). "Bounds for Trivariate Integrals in System Bounds", Journal of Structural Engineering, ASCE, 112, 923-924.

# BAYESIAN INFERENCE IN NONDESTRUCTIVE ON-SITE TESTING OF CONCRETE STRENGTH

Xing Chen*
*Institute for Engineering Structure Research, University of Fuzhou, Fuzhou, Fujian
People's Republic of China

## ABSTRACT

Bayesian inference about strength of concrete in service is proposed for nondestructive on-site testing. The likelihood function is updated in the light of the outcomes of the test. A normal model is developed. The model is simple enough for everyday practice in the case where certain destruction is made to adjust the laboratory-based regression equation to the concrete in question.

## 1. INTRODUCTION

Statistical data on the strength of concrete are often collected by means of destructive testing on standard specimens in a laboratory environment. It is not appropriate to make inference based solely on these data regarding the strength of concrete in service, because of the considerable diversity in workmanship and working conditions. Destructive testing performed directly on the concrete in a structural element may be possible, but the location where a sample is taken must be structurally insignificant, and the sample size is usually too small to assure a reliable inference.

It has been common to conduct nondestructive on-site testing to report the concrete strength of an element. In China, for instance, a nondestructive impact method has been codified and is being practised by quality inspectors. In a test of this nature an investigator measures the responses (physical or chemical) of concrete to an apparatus, feeds them into the associated regression equation and then reports the strength of concrete in equation. A regression equation relates the response to the true strength of concrete, and most of them were derived in the laboratory for the concrete in standard specimens It is generally accepted that the true strength would differ from what an equation gives. This discrepancy has to be taken into account and the regression equation should be adjusted to the concrete of interest.

This paper suggests a Bayesian inference for that purpose. The theoretical development follows the findings by Lindley (1982), Winkler (1981) and Rosenblueth (1984). A normal model is proposed. The model appears to be simple enough for everyday practice when certain on-site destruction is made. Subjective judgement on the part of the investigator is discussed. The model is applicable to similar cases of nondestructive testing other than the concrete strength.

## 2. BASIC CONCEPT

Let $r$ be the strength of concrete of interest to an investigator. Call the value given by a regression equation an indicator of $r$, and denote indicator $i$ by $x_i$, $i = 1,..., s$. The investigator will never know $r$ without the destruction of the concrete, and does not know $x_i$ prior to the nondestructive testing. Both $r$ and $x_i$ are treated as random variables. Define the error for indicator $i$ by $u_i = r - x_i$, then $u_i$ are also random variables. In terms of vectors, the error vector is

$$\underline{u} = r\underline{e} - \underline{x} \tag{1}$$

where $\underline{u} = (u_1, \ldots, u_s)^t$, $\underline{x} = (x_1, \ldots, x_s)^t$ and $\underline{e}$ is a $s \times 1$ unit vector.

The probability density function for $R$, $f_R(r)$, and that for $\underline{U}$, $f_{\underline{U}}(\underline{u})$, are assigned *a priori*. Here a capital letter means that the quantity it refers to is a random variable, while the corresponding lower case is a realization of that variable. Choose

$$f_{\underline{U}}(\underline{u}) \propto g(r-x_1, \ldots, r-x_s) \tag{2}$$

in which $\propto$ signifies "proportional to". $g(\cdot)$ is now understood to be the likelihood function, that is, the conditional probability density function for $\underline{X}$ given $R$. Bayes' formula reads

$$f_{R|\underline{X}}(r; \underline{x}^*) \propto f_R(r) g(r-x_1^*, \ldots, r-x_s^*) \tag{3}$$

where $\underline{x}^*$ stands for the set of indicators that are known after the testing; $f_{R|\underline{X}}(\cdot)$ is the posterior probability density function for $R$. Knowledge about the unknown $r$ is now contained in $f_{R|\underline{X}}(\cdot)$. The investigator may report the estimate of $r$, $\hat{r}$, as the strength of concrete.

The essence behind eq.(3) is that the subjectively assigned $f_R(r)$ is updated upon receiving the test outcomes. The same process of updating should, to be rational, be applied to $f_{\underline{U}}(\underline{u})$ , for it is also subjectively assigned *a priori*. Therefore, take the parameters $\underline{a} = (a_1, \ldots, a_k)^t$ in $g(\cdot)$ as another set of random variables and assign to it a prior joint probability density function $f_{\underline{A}}(\underline{a})$. To update $g(\cdot)$ is to update $f_{\underline{A}}(\underline{a})$.

Eq.(3) should now be written as

$$f_{R|\underline{X}}(r; \underline{x}^*) \propto f_R(r) \int_D g(r-x_1^*, \ldots, r-x_s^*, \underline{a}) f_{\underline{A}}(\underline{a})\, d\underline{a} \tag{4}$$

where $D$ is the domain of $\underline{a}$. Application of Bayes' formula leads to the posterior probability density function

$$f_{\underline{A}|\underline{X}}(\underline{a}; \underline{x}^*) \propto f_{\underline{A}}(\underline{a}) \int_{-\infty}^{\infty} g(r-x_1^*, \ldots, r-x_s^*, \underline{a}) f_R(r)\, dr\ . \tag{5}$$

Knowledge about the parameters, and thus the likelihood function, is improved as the test carries on.

In eq.(5) $r$ is unknown. Situations do occur in practice where $r$ becomes known to the investigator after testing. For example, at certain locations of a structural element the concrete that has been tested by ultrasonic waves is subsequently test to destruction (core sampling), or the standard specimens made while the element was built are destroyed, to adjust the laboratory-based regression equation to the concrete in service. In these instances the true value of $r$ is known, denoted by $r^*$; hence Bayes' formula should be written as

$$f_{\underline{A}|\underline{X},R}(\underline{a}; \underline{x}^*, r^*) \propto f_{\underline{A}}(\underline{a}) g(r^*-x_1^*, \ldots, r^*-x_s^*, \underline{a})\ . \tag{6}$$

Formulas for the posterior probability density function of the parameters are expected to be used repeatedly in the process of updating. The computation may become intractable if $f_{\underline{A}}(\underline{a})$ is not the natural conjugate prior for a given likelihood function. It seems that a natural conjugate prior is a necessity for a model to be useful in everyday practice.

Note that in eq.(6) the natural conjugate prior is for $g(\cdot)$, while in eq.(5) it should be for the integral on the right hand side of the equation.

## 3. A NORMAL MODEL

In this model use is made of eq.(6) for updating. The model applies to a special case in practice where certain destruction is made. It is postulated that the error vector $\underline{U}$ is jointly normal with mean vector $\underline{m}$ and covariance matrix $\underline{v}$. The likelihood function is given by

$$g(r-x_1, \ldots, r-x_s, \underline{m}, \underline{v}) \propto |\underline{v}|^{-\frac{1}{2}}\exp[-\tfrac{1}{2}(r\underline{e} - \underline{x} - \underline{m})^t \underline{v}^{-1} (r\underline{e} - \underline{x} - \underline{m})] \tag{7}$$

The natural conjugate prior for $\underline{M}$ and $\underline{V}$ is found to be the multivariate normal-inverted Wishart density function of the form

$$f_{\underline{M},\underline{V}}(\underline{m}, \underline{v}) \propto |\underline{v}|^{-\frac{1}{2}(n'+s+2)}\exp[-\tfrac{1}{2}(n'-1)tr(\underline{v}^{-1}\underline{v}')-\tfrac{1}{2}n'(\underline{m} - \underline{m}')^t\underline{v}^{-1}(\underline{m} - \underline{m}')] \; . \tag{8}$$

It is not difficult to show that the marginal expectations of $\underline{M}$ and $\underline{V}$ are $\underline{m}'$ and $\underline{v}'$, respectively.

For a noninformative prior $f_R(r) \propto$ constant, the posterior density function of $R$ follows from eq.(4),

$$f_{R|\underline{X}}(r; \underline{x}^*) \propto [b + (r - \overline{R})^2/h]^{-\frac{1}{2}(b+1)} \tag{9}$$

in which

$$b = n' + s \tag{10}$$

$$\overline{R} = \underline{e}^t\underline{v}'^{-1}(\underline{x}^* - \underline{m}') \,/\, (\underline{e}^t\underline{v}'^{-1}\underline{e}) \tag{11}$$

$$h = [(n'^2 - 1)/n' + (\underline{x}^* - \underline{m}' - \overline{R}\underline{e})^t\underline{v}'^{-1}(\underline{x}^* - \underline{m}')] \,/\, (b\underline{e}^t\underline{v}'^{-1}\underline{e}) \; . \tag{12}$$

It is readily seen that $R$ follows a t-distribution with mean $\overline{R}$ given in eq.(11). The investigator may take $\overline{R}$ and $\hat{r}$ and report $\overline{R}$ as the strength of the concrete. Eq.(9) contains more information than just the mean value, and it can be further explored to assist decision making in various contexts.

The joint posterior probability density function for $\underline{M}$ and $\underline{V}$ has the same form as in eq.(8), except that $n'$, $\underline{m}'$, and $\underline{v}'$ are replaced by

$$n'' = n' + 1 \tag{13}$$

$$m'' = (n'\underline{m}' + r^*\underline{e} - \underline{x}^*) \,/\, (n' + 1) \tag{14}$$

$$\underline{v}'' = \underline{v}'(n' - 1)/n' + (r^*\underline{e} - \underline{x}^* - \underline{m}')(r^*\underline{e} - \underline{x}^* - \underline{m}')^t \,/\, (n' + 1) \; . \tag{15}$$

The updated $n''$ , $\underline{m}''$ and $\underline{v}''$ are to be used as $n'$, $\underline{m}'$ and $\underline{v}'$ in the next round of estimating and updating.

It is remarked that in the case of a single indicator, $\overline{R} = x^* - m'$, $n'' = n' + 1$, $m'' = (n'm' + r^* - x^*)/(n' + 1)$, and $v'' = v'(n' - 1)/n'$.

The investigator makes judgements on $n'$, $\underline{m}'$ and $\underline{v}'$. An experienced investigator typically has such knowledge. It can be seen from eq.(8) that if $n'$ is the number of experiments the investigator has practised in the past, then $\underline{m}'$ and $\underline{v}'$ are the sample average and sample covariances of the errors. The investigator's knowledge about $\underline{m}'$ and $\underline{v}'$ may not always come from the experiments, but in any case the investigator should understand what $n'$ and $\underline{m}'$ and $\underline{v}'$ imply.

## 4. CONCLUSIONS

The concept presented in this paper is general. The model can be equally useful in similar cases other than the strength of concrete. The indicators need not be associated with regression equations. They can be expert opinions elicited by the investigator.

An investigator judges certain quantities subjectively. It is interesting to know how a practising engineer would respond to this seemly additional requirement. It would not be surprising if an investigator should feel reluctant to make a personal judgement. In this case, the investigator may set $n' = 0$ and disregard the variance for $n' < 2$.

The posterior probability density function provides more information about $r$ than just a point estimate. Further study could be made on how to relate this information to probabilistic criteria for the acceptance of a product.

## ACKNOWLEDGEMENTS

The theoretical background was prepared while the author served at the Instituto de Ingenieria, Universidad Nacional Autonoma de Mexico, and the Fundacion Barros Sierra, Mexico. The author wishes to express his sincere gratitude to Dr. Emilio Rosenblueth who introduced him to the problem studied in this paper.

## REFERENCES

Lindley D.V. (1982). "The Improvement of Probability Judgements", Journal of the Royal Statistical Society, Series A, 145 (part 1), pp. 117-126.

Rosenblueth E. (1984). "On the Processing of Doubtful Information, Part 1: General Theory", In M. Grigoriu (Ed.), Risk, Structural Engineering and Human Error, University of Waterloo Press, Waterloo, Ontario, Canada.

Winkler R.L. (1981). "Combining Probability Distributions from Dependent Information Sources", Management Science, Vol. 27, No. 4, pp. 479-487.

# RESPONSE OF MASS-COLUMN SYSTEM TO RANDOM EARTHQUAKE EXCITATION

George Tsiatas* and Md. Nurul Huda**

ABSTRACT

The statistical properties of the response of a column supporting a mass under earthquake loading are examined. Particular emphasis is placed on the effect of the vertical component of the ground acceleration. The ground accelerations are modeled as amplitude modulated, nonwhite Gaussian random processes. The equation governing the motion of the system is transformed into an Ito stochastic differential equation. The cumulant truncation scheme is utilized to obtain a closed set of differential equations governing the response moments. A Runge-Kutta method of order four is used to solve this system for the second order moments of displacement and velocity at the top of the column. The effect of the vertical ground acceleration is significant especially when the axial load in the column approaches the critical Euler value. Also, it does not remain constant but it is more pronounced for higher displacements.

## EQUATION OF MOTION

The vertical component of ground motion is usually neglected when studying the lateral response of a structure under earthquake excitation. However, its effect may be significant since it introduces a random axial force which plays the role of parametric excitation making the dynamic characteristics of the system vary with time. This makes ordinary methods of random vibrations such as spectral techniques unsuitable for the solution of this problem.

Gurpinar and Yao (1973) working in the frequency domain examined the case of a massless column carrying a concentrated mass under horizontal and vertical support accelerations. The same system was studied by Lin and Shih (1980) using Markov vector methods. Lin and Shih extended their method for the case of a multistory frame building (1982). Shih (1984) analyzed a linearly tapered column under earthquake excitation. Tsiatas (1984) studied the stability of a simply supported beam-column under combined horizontal and vertical excitation. In these studies the earthquake excitation was modeled as a stationary or nonstationary white noise process.

In the present work, a flexible column carrying a concentrated mass at the top and subjected to the simultaneous action of gravity and earthquake loads is analyzed. The equation governing the motion of the system is (Fig. 1):

---

*Assistant professor, Department of Civil and Environmental Engineering, Washington State University, Pullman, WA 99164-2914.

**Former graduate student, Department of Civil and Environmental Engineering, Washington State University, Pullman, WA 99164-2914.

$$EI \frac{\partial^4 v}{\partial x^4} + [M + m(H - x)](g + \ddot{u}_g) \frac{\partial^2 v}{\partial x^2} - m(g + \ddot{u}_g) \frac{\partial v}{\partial x}$$

$$+ m \frac{\partial^2 v}{\partial t^2} + c \frac{\partial v}{\partial t} = -m\ddot{v}_g \qquad (1)$$

Using a modal framework, the dynamic displacement is set

$$v(x,t) = \sum_{n=1}^{\infty} \phi_n(x)\, y_n(t) \qquad (2)$$

where $\phi_n(x)$ = nth mode shape, and $y_n(t)$ = nth modal coordinate. The natural frequencies and mode shapes of the system are found using the method of finite differences to discretize the continuum. Following the steps of modal decomposition, the equation governing the nth modal coordinate can be shown to be

$$\ddot{y}_n(t) + \frac{C_n}{M_n} \dot{y}_n(t) + \frac{1}{M_n} [K_n - l_n g]\, y_n(t) - \frac{l_n}{M_n} \ddot{u}_g\, y_n(t) = - \frac{m_n}{M_n} \ddot{v}_g \qquad (3)$$

where $C_n$, $M_n$, $l_n$, $m_n$, and $K_n$ are constants depending on the mode shapes and their derivatives as well as on the properties of the system.

The earthquake excitation is considered to be a nonstationary, nonwhite random process. Nonstationarity is achieved by using a modulating function e(t) as follows,

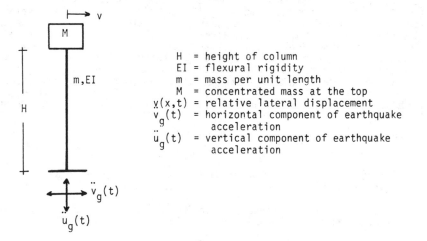

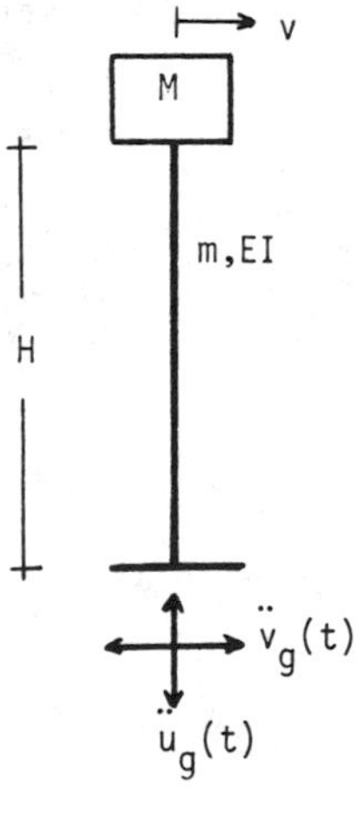


H = height of column
EI = flexural rigidity
m = mass per unit length
M = concentrated mass at the top
$v(x,t)$ = relative lateral displacement
$\ddot{v}_g(t)$ = horizontal component of earthquake acceleration
$\ddot{u}_g(t)$ = vertical component of earthquake acceleration

Figure 1. Column-Mass System

$$\ddot{v}_g(t) = e(t)\, W_1(t) , \qquad \ddot{u}_g(t) = e(t)\, W_2(t) \tag{4}$$

where $W_1(t)$, $W_2(t)$ are Gaussian white noise processes with autocorrelation functions,

$$R_{w_1 w_1}(t) = 2D_{11}\, \delta(t)$$

$$R_{w_2 w_2}(t) = 2D_{22}\, \delta(t)$$

$$R_{w_1 w_2}(t) = 2D_{12}\, \delta(t) = 2\sqrt{D_{11}\, D_{22}}\, \delta(t) \tag{5}$$

and $\delta(t)$ is the Dirac delta function. The envelope function used is

$$e(t) = \sqrt{6.75}\, (e^{-0.25t} - e^{-0.75t}) , \qquad t > 0 \tag{6}$$

Nonwhiteness is achieved by augmenting each modal equation by two filters, as follows,

$$\ddot{y}_{f1} + 2\xi_{f1}\omega_{f\,1}\dot{y}_{f\,1} + \omega_{f\,1}^2 y_{f\,1} = -\ddot{v}_g(t)$$

$$\ddot{y}_{f_2} + 2\xi_{f_2}\,\omega_{f_2}\,\dot{y}_{f_2} + \omega_{f_2}^2\, y_{f_2} = -\ddot{u}_g(t)$$

$$y_n(t) + \frac{C_n}{M_n}\dot{y}_n(t) + \frac{1}{M_n}[K_n - 1_n g]\, y_n - \frac{1_n}{M_n}(\ddot{u}_y + \ddot{v}_{f2}) = -\frac{m_n}{M_n}(\ddot{u}_g + \ddot{y}_{f1}) \tag{7}$$

Introducing the state variables:

$$Z_{n1} = y_n,\ Z_{n2} = \dot{y}_n,\ Z_{n3} = y_{f1},\ Z_{n4} = \dot{y}_{f1},\ Z_{n5} = y_{f2},\ \text{and}\ Z_{n6} = \dot{y}_{f2}$$

Eq. 7 can be written in a matrix form as

$$\dot{\underline{Z}}_n(t) = \underline{f}'(t,\underline{Z}_n(t)) + \underline{G}'(t,\underline{Z}_n(t))\underline{W}(t) \tag{8}$$

Eq. 8 can be transformed using the Wong-Zakai conversion rule into an Ito stochastic differential equation of the form (Arnold 1974):

$$d\underline{Z}_n(t) = \underline{f}(t,Z_n(t))dt + \underline{G}(t,Z_n(t))d\underline{B}(t) \tag{9}$$

where $\underline{B}(t)$ is a two-dimensional Wiener process with intensity matrix $\underline{Q}$ and

$$f_i = f_i' + \tfrac{1}{2} \sum_{j=1}^{6} \sum_{k,l=1}^{2} \frac{\partial G_{ik}'}{\partial z_j} G_{jk}' \, Q_{kl}$$

$$\underline{G} = \underline{G}' \tag{10}$$

The solution of Eq. 9 is a Markov process which is completely defined by solving the associated Fokker-Planck equation for the transition probability density function. For the purposes of the present work, the response moments are considered sufficient. Equations governing the moments can be easily derived using Ito's, lemma and basic properties of Ito calculus.

Let $g(t,\underline{Z}_n(t))$ be a function of the state variables. The expectation of g can be shown to obey the following ordinary differential equation

$$\frac{d}{dt} E[g(t,\underline{Z}_n(t))] = E[\frac{\partial g}{\partial t}] + \sum_{i=1}^{6} E[\frac{\partial g}{\partial Z_{ni}} f_i] +$$

$$+ \tfrac{1}{2} \sum_{i=1}^{6} \sum_{j=1}^{6} E[(\underline{G}\, \underline{Q}\, \underline{G}^T)_{ij} \frac{\partial^2 g}{\partial Z_{ni} \partial Z_{nj}}] \tag{11}$$

By substituting appropriate expressions for the state variables, Eq. 11 gives a set of ordinary differential equations for the moments of the modal coordinates. Unfortunately, these equations form an "infinite hierarchy." Moments of nth order depend on moments of higher order and thus, an explicit solution for moments of any order is not feasible. For an approximate solution the infinite hierarchy must be truncated at some level.

The cumulant truncation scheme is utilized in the present study. Moments of higher order are expressed as functions of lower order moments by setting the corresponding cumulants equal to zero. Then, a closed system of equations is obtained which can be solved for the desired moments. The cumulants of order $K \geq 4$ are assumed to be zero. The fourth order moment can be expressed in terms of lower order moments as follows

$$\begin{aligned} E[x_1x_2x_3x_4] = {} & E[x_1]\, E[x_2x_3x_4] + E[x_2]\, E[x_1x_3x_4] + E[x_3]\, E[x_1x_2x_4] + \\ & + E[x_4]\, E[x_1x_2x_3] + E[x_1x_2]\, E[x_3x_4] + E[x_1x_3]\, E[x_2x_4] + \\ & + E[x_1x_4]\, E[x_2x_3] + 6\, E[x_1]\, E[x_2]\, E[x_3]\, E[x_4] - \\ & - 2\{E[x_1]\, E[x_2]\, E[x_3x_4] + E[x_1]\, E[x_3]\, E[x_2x_4] + \\ & + E[x_1]\, E[x_4]\, E[x_2x_3] + E[x_2]\, E[x_3]\, E[x_1x_4] + \\ & + E[x_2]\, E[x_4]\, E[x_1x_3] + E[x_3]\, E[x_4]\, E[x_1x_2]\} \end{aligned} \tag{12}$$

Using this scheme a system of 83 ordinary differential equations is derived governing the first, second and third order moments of each modal coordinate. This system can be solved for the response moments using standard methods of numerical analysis such as the Runge-Kutta method of fourth order. It should be mentioned that if the third order cumulants are set equal to zero, a system of 27 differential equations for the first and second order moments can be derived, but its solution gives unreasonable results.

Equations governing the cross moments between two modal coordinates can be similarly derived, but the number of equations is very large. In the present work such terms can be neglected.

The moments of the dynamic response are finally calculated using modal superposition but neglecting the effect of the cross moments.

## APPLICATION

In order to demonstrate the analytical formulation of the previous section a column-mass system with the following properties is considered: H = 600 in, E = 30 x $10^6$ psi, I = 7383.5 $in^4$, m = 0.0394 lb·$sec^2/in^2$. The concentrated mass varies so that the ratio of the induced axial force over the critical Euler load of the column ranges from 0.5 to 0.9. The damping ratio is assumed to be 3% for all modes. The 3 first modes are used in the calculations since it can be determined that higher modes do not contribute much in the displacement response. Actually, the first only mode gives very good results for the displacement moments.

The horizontal ground acceleration corresponds to an average earthquake giving $D_{11}$ = 2.85. The vertical component of the ground acceleration is taken as either zero or 2.28. This value corresponds to 80% of the horizontal component and is considered to be on the high end although in certain cases the vertical acceleration has equaled or even exceeded the horizontal one. The filter properties are the same for both acceleration components namely $\xi_{f1} = \xi_{f2}$ = 0.6 and $\omega_{f1} = \omega_{f2}$ = 15.7 rad/sec.

Figures 2 through 4 show the mean square displacement at the top of the column for different concentrated masses. It is clearly seen that the effect of the vertical component of the ground acceleration becomes increasingly significant for higher $P/P_{cr}$ ratios. For a ratio of 0.5 the mean square response increases by 8.7% whereas for a ratio of 0.9 it increases by 65.1%. Also, the difference between parametric and nonparametric loading does not remain constant but the larger the displacements, the more important is the vertical loading.

Figure 5 shows the mean square values of the top displacement and velocity and the correlation between displacement and velocity for $P/P_{cr}$ = 0.7. It should be mentioned that the vertical component of acceleration does not affect much the correlation between displacement and velocity. Also, the first order moments remain zero unless the initial conditions are taken as nonzero.

## ACKNOWLEDGMENT

Support from the National Science Foundation under Grant CEE-8504972 is greatfully appreciated.

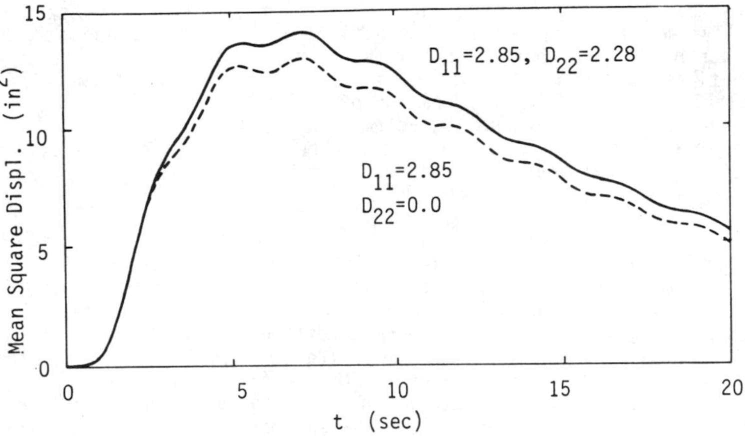


Fig. 2 Mean Square Top Displacement for $P/P_{cr}=0.5$

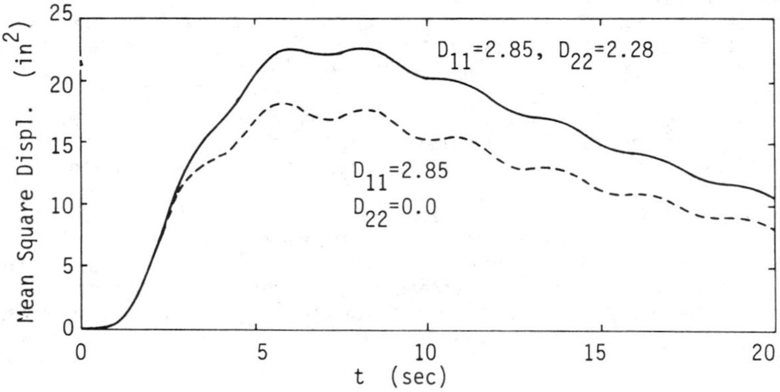


Fig. 3 Mean Square Top Displacement for $P/P_{cr}=0.7$

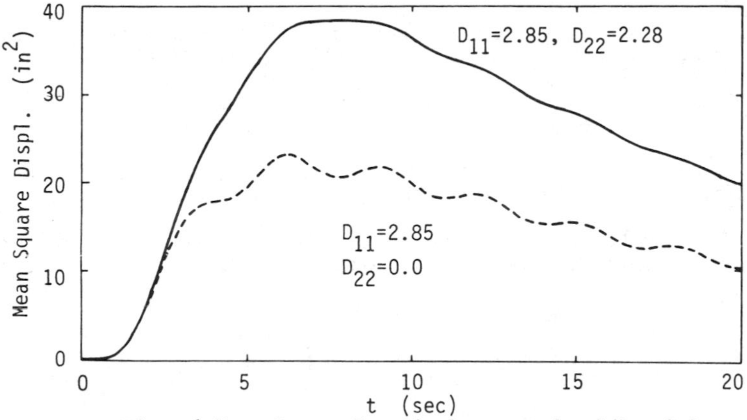


Fig. 4 Mean Square Top Displacement for $P/P_{cr}$=0.9

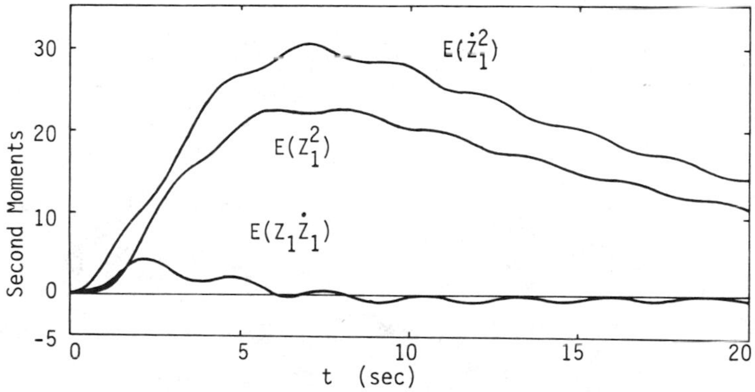

Fig. 5 Second Order Moments for $P/P_{cr}$=0.7
$D_{11}$=2.85, $D_{22}$=2.28

REFERENCES:

Arnold, L. (1974), *Stochastic Differential Equations: Theory and Applications*, John Wiley.

Gurpinar, A. and Yao, J. T. P. (1973), "Design of columns for seismic loads," *J. Struct. Div.*, ASCE, 99(9), pp. 1875-1889.

Lin, Y. K. and Shih, T. Y. (1982), "Vertical seismic load effect on building response," *J. Engrg. Mech. Div.*, ASCE, 107(2), pp. 331-343.

Lin, Y. K. and Shih, T. Y. (1980), "Column response to horizontal vertical earthquakes," *J. Engrg. Mech. Div.*, ASCE, 106(6), pp. 1099-1109.

Shih, T. Y. and Chen, Y. C. (1984), "Stochastic earthquake response of tapered column," *J. Engr. Mech.*, ASCE, 110(8), pp. 1185-1210.

Tsiatas, G. (1984), "Random vibration of nonlinear parametrically excited systems," Ph.D. dissertation, Case Western Reserve University, Cleveland, OH.

# SIMULATED THERMAL RESPONSES OF COMPOSITE SECTIONS

by

Paul C. Hoffman[1] and William M. Fleischman[2]

ABSTRACT

This paper summarizes the first phase of an ongoing study involving the simulation of the thermal responses of reinforced concrete structural sections. The initial phase of the study was a computer simulation of temperature induced deformations for steel-concrete girders. Samples of multi-layered concrete sections with different material properties were randomly generated. The coefficient of thermal expansion, thermal diffusivity and concrete compressive strength were modeled as normal variates. The samples of multi-layered concrete sections were randomly assembled to model a composite section composed of a concrete deck and steel I-beam. One-dimensional heat flow analyses within each section subject to typical thermal boundary conditions were carried out. Curvatures were computed with a modification of the approach based on a uniform flange temperature differential. Midspan deflections were calculated with a numerical application of the second moment area theorem. The coefficient of thermal expansion was found to be the significant random variable with respect to deflections.

## THE THERMAL CONCERN IN BRIDGE ENGINEERING

Deformations due to temperature have always been a design concern in bridge engineering. The considerations have ranged from evaluating longitudinal movements to curvature and stress calculations. Heretofore, analyses have been deterministic, whereas there is substantial randomness in the actual thermal stress problem. The randomness stems from the variable material properties in any bridge superstructure as well as the fluctuations of the thermal boundary conditions.

In this paper we summarize one phase of an ongoing study involving the simulation of thermal responses for steel-concrete composite girders. Such composite girders exhibit a unique thermal compatibility problem. The ratio of thermal diffusivity of steel to concrete is approximately twenty. While the steel I-beam adjusts rapidly to changes in ambient temperature, the concrete lags in response. Subsequently, temperature differentials develop between the concrete and steel which cause deformations and self-equilibrating stress distributions.

The initial phase of our continuing study was a computer simulation of temperature-induced deformations for steel-concrete composite sections. Samples of concrete sections with different thermal properties were randomly generated. One-dimensional heat flow

---

1 Assistant Professor of Civil Engineering, Villanova University, Villanova, PA 19085

2 Associate Professor of Mathematical Sciences, Villanova University, Villanova, PA 19085

analyses were used in conjunction with typical thermal boundary conditions. Curvatures and maximum (midspan) deflections were computed.

## THE THERMAL PROBLEM

The thermal stress design problem in bridge superstructures has two aspects. First, a nonlinear temperature distribution in a cross section gives rise to a curvature/deformation condition. Second, since the temperature distribution is nonlinear and the physical responses (elongation and curvature) are linear, a self-equilibrating stress distribution develops. The significance of the two thermal responses can be evaluated only with respect to the support conditions.

If the girder is statically determinate then the curvature/deformation problem is analogous to the stress-free expansion of a heated axial member. In other words, the girder will bend in response to a nonlinear temperature distribution. Subsequently the residual self-equilibrating stress distribution will be the sole concern.

On the other hand, if the girder is continuous with interior supports the thermal deformations become a concern due to the restraints at the supports. In fact, the stress magnitudes due to the restrained thermal strains would be far more significant than the self-equilibrating stress levels [Hoffman, et al, 1983b].

From the viewpoint of an engineer, the restrained curvature/deformation is the critical design problem. It is reasonable to use a uniform flange temperature differential for the curvature analysis in steel-concrete composite sections [Branson, 1977]. However, the question as to the magnitude of the uniform flange temperature differential must be addressed realistically. With this approach, modifications must be made for possible nonuniform temperature distributions in the concrete slab [Branson, 1977 and Hoffman, et al, 1983b]. This paper explores further whether random nonuniformities in material properties of concrete must be incorporated in a thermal loading specification of uniform flange temperatures.

## TEMPERATURE DISTRIBUTION CALCULATIONS

The temperature problem in a concrete slab and steel I-beam girder can be reasonably modeled using one-dimensional heat flow analysis. Field observations of a segmental reinforced box girder bridge have shown that temperature differentials in the vertical direction exhibit far greater fluctuations in magnitude than in the horizontal direction [Hoffman, et al, 1983a]. The dominant thermal inputs were observed to be solar radiation and ambient air temperature. Subsequently, it was concluded that, for standard bridge configurations and alignments, one-dimensional thermal stress analyses are appropriate.

Even though the temperature problem may be viewed as one-dimensional, the randomness of the problem must also be considered. The purpose of the present study is to investigate whether variation in specific material properties of concrete (thermal diffusivity, coefficient of thermal expansion, and compressive strength) affects temperature distribution and deflection.

The simulation of temperature distributions in a concrete slab was based on a multi-layered concrete section, Figure 1. Each layer was assigned randomly generated material properties (thermal diffusivity, coefficient of thermal expansion, and compressive strength). Surface temperatures, observed in a previous study of a segmental box girder [Hoffman, et al, 1983a], were applied. The temperature distributions in

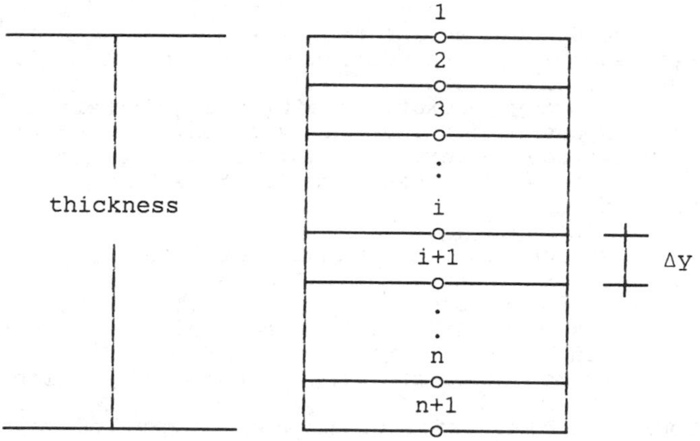


Figure 1: Multi-layered Concrete Section

the multi-layered sections were calculated using a modification of the Crank-Nicolson (implicit) finite difference method applied to the heat conduction equation.

DEFORMATION CALCULATIONS

In addition to modeling the random makeup of the concrete with respect to thickness (multi-layered concrete section), the longitudinal variation of material composition was modeled, Figure 2. Longitudinal spans were modeled as a set of sections, each being composed of a multi-layered concrete section and a steel I-beam. Each section was analyzed with the same thermal boundary conditions.

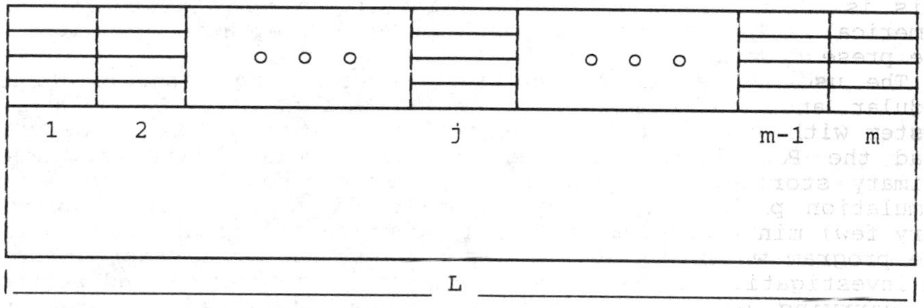


Figure 2: Longitudinal Composition Modeled As m Multi-layered Concrete Sections

The calculated temperature distributions were then used to compute curvatures. The uniform flange temperature method [Branson, 1977] was readily extended for the curvature computation of a multi-layered concrete flange and steel I-beam combination. The equation used was

$$\varphi(j) = [\sum_{i}^{n} E(i,j) \cdot \alpha_e(i,j) \cdot \Delta T(i,j) \cdot b \cdot \Delta y \cdot y(i,j)]/[E(j) \cdot I(j)]$$

where $\varphi(j)$ = curvature of section j.
- $E(i,j)$ = randomly generated modulus of elasticity for layer i, section j.
- $\alpha_e(i,j)$ = randomly generated coefficient of thermal expansion for layer i, section j.
- $\Delta T(i,j)$ = average temperature in layer i, section j minus the ambient temperature.
- $b$ = width of slab.
- $\Delta y$ = nodal spacing.
- $y(i,j)$ = distance from the midpoint of layer i, section j to the neutral axis of the transformed section.
- $E(j)$ = modulus of elasticity for transformed section j.
- $I(j)$ = second moment of area for transformed section j.

The corresponding midspan deflections were determined through application of the second moment area theorem.

COMPUTATIONAL ISSUES

In this section, the computational techniques and computing resources utilized in carrying out the simulation experiments described above are discussed.

The computer programs used for this study were developed in Pascal using the Hewlett-Packard 3.1 Workstation operating system. They were written and run on an H-P Model 310 microcomputer built around a 10-MHz 68010 processor and equipped with 2 megabytes of RAM and two 3 1/2" flexible disk drives but without floating point assist hardware. On this system, the range of integer values is $-2^{31}$ to $2^{31}-1$. Floating point reals are stored with what is effectively a 53-bit mantissa. Thus precision of 15 decimal digits is available. This is more than adequate to maintain reasonable accuracy in the numerical solutions of the heat conduction equation carried out in the present work.

The use of Pascal was an aid in producing programs which are modular and easily read, maintained and modified. The use of a system with a substantial amount (2 megabytes) of RAM allowed us to load the Pascal compiler, editor and other utility programs into primary storage. This enabled us to propose changes to our basic simulation program and have the modified version running within (a very few) minutes. In particular, compilation times for versions of the program which exceed 600 lines of Pascal were under 15 seconds. An investigation has been made verifying the accuracy and feasibility of carrying out these and related calculations on microcomputer systems [Fleischman and Hoffman, 1987].

At the heart of each of the programs used is a sub-program which approximates the solution of the heat conduction equation subject to given initial and boundary conditions. The method implemented is a modification of the Crank-Nicolson method. The modification deals with the treatment of the boundary between two adjacent layers of a vertical section. With the Crank-Nicolson method, a diagonally dominant tridiagonal matrix is used repeatedly to solve systems of linear equations for the vector of temperatures in a one-dimensional 'rod' at time $t+\Delta t$ given the vector of temperatures at time t. See, for example, [Street 1973].

Our modification replaces one of the equations by an equation expressing a compatibility condition at each boundary between layers. The compatibility condition requires that heat flow into the boundary from one layer equals that away from the boundary in the adjacent layer. A standard discretization of this condition yields a single linear equation involving the same three unknowns that occur in the Crank-Nicolson equation being replaced. Thus the modified matrix remains tridiagonal. (It is even diagonally dominant although not strongly so.)

Use of a variant of Crank-Nicolson in preference to the explicit method removes the inconvenient restriction on $\Delta t$ due to the linkage between $\Delta t$ and $\Delta y$ required for stability. In our simulations, we took $\Delta t$ = 10 minutes. The value of $\Delta y$ was ordinarily 0.5 inches although occasionally it was taken as 0.25 inches. Even with the larger of these two values, the explicit method would have required $\Delta t \leq (\Delta y)^2/(2\alpha_d) \leq 1/(8\alpha_d)$ and since a value of $\alpha_d$ as large as 0.3 $in^2$/min. could occur, this would require $\Delta t \leq 5/12$ minutes.

The computational stability of Crank-Nicolson is largely a consequence of the fact that when Gaussian elimination is applied to the Crank-Nicolson matrix, the resulting upper triangular matrix has diagonal elements which are greater than the adjacent super-diagonal elements independent of the ratio of $\Delta t$ to $(\Delta y)^2$. It can be shown mathematically that this property is maintained when the same operations are applied to our modified Crank-Nicolson matrix thus ensuring the stability of our method. In addition, we have verified empirically its stability by repeating selected simulations with progressively smaller values of $\Delta y$ and $\Delta t$.

The pseudo-random number generator used for these simulations is one of the additive type [Knuth 1981]. Its period is at least $2^{55}$. This is comforting considering that a single experiment involving 100 simulations of a 20-section bridge with three layers per section requires 18000 random numbers. It has been subjected to and passed tests for uniformity and for runs.

Random normal deviates were generated by table look-up in a 1001-place table of z-values which correspond to (interpolated) tenths of percentiles of the standard normal distribution. The 0th and 100th percentiles (entries 0 and 1000 in the table) were taken arbitrarily to be the outliers $z = -4$ and $z = +4$ respectively. The precise procedure is first to generate a random integer in the range 0 to 1000 using the additive pseudo-random number generator described above. This value is then used as an index into the table of tenths of percentiles yielding a z-value which can be regarded as a random value selected from the standard normal distribution. Appropriately transformed, these random normal deviates are used to generate values of the thermal parameters $\alpha_d$ and $\alpha_e$ and the strength, $f'_c$, of the concrete comprising each of the layers of each of the vertical sections of the hypothetical bridge being studied. For each layer, the modulus of elasticity was taken as $E = 57000\sqrt{f'_c}$.

In our investigations of the influence of each of these parameters (as well as the number of layers and number of sections) on the maximum deflection of one of our hypothetical structures, we adopted a sample size of forty (although occasionally a sample of size 100 was taken). Random independent samples of size 40 are considered sufficiently large to justify the use of the normal theory (i.e. the use of a z-value derived from sample means and variances) in hypothesis testing or parameter estimation.

PRELIMINARY FINDINGS

As a case study, the midspan deflections of a composite girder (6in. x 72in. concrete deck, and a W 36x150 steel beam) were simulated. Concrete material properties (thermal diffusivity, coefficient of thermal expansion and compressive strength) were randomly generated for each layer of the concrete sections. The findings, except where noted, are summarized for a composite girder, with a simple span equalling 121 ft., divided into 10 sections each consisting of a steel beam and a concrete section of 3 layers. The material properties were modeled as normal variates.

The means and standard deviations of the material properties for concrete were estimated based on previous studies and a brief review of the literature on standard practice, Table 1. While estimates of the means were readily available, the information with respect to standard deviations was limited. Consequently, the standard deviations were estimated using engineering judgement and to avoid random generation of impossible values. For example, at four standard deviations away from the mean a reasonable value should still be expected. In the case of the coefficient of thermal expansion such a consideration resulted in a low value equalling $2 \times 10^{-6}$ in/in - °F and a high value equalling $10 \times 10^{-6}$ in/in - °F.

Sensitivity analyses of the three material properties with respect to midspan deflections were conducted using two approaches. The first approach fixed two of the parameters at their respective means, Table 1, while the mean and standard deviation

Table 1: Concrete Material Properties Parameters

| Property | Mean | Std. Dev. | CV |
|---|---|---|---|
| $\alpha_d$ (in$^2$/min) | 0.16 | 0.03 | 18.8 |
| $\alpha_e$ (in/in · °F) | $6 \times 10^{-6}$ | $1 \times 10^{-6}$ | 16.7 |
| $f'_c$ (psi) | 3600 | 380 | 10.6 |

of the third parameter were varied. The second approach considered two of the material properties to be normally distributed, Table 1, and the response to changes in the mean and standard deviation of the third property were studied.

The sensitivity with respect to thermal diffusivity using both approaches is tabulated in Table 2a and Table 2b. The mean deflections show little variation with respect to changes in the mean value for thermal diffusivity regardless of which approach is taken. In contrast, the standard deviations in Table 2b are considerably larger than those in Table 2a. From these results, we conclude that the variation of thermal diffusivity does not have a significant influence on the variation of midspan deflection.

The sensitivity analyses with respect to the coefficient of thermal expansion indicated a significant influence on the variation of midspan deflection, Table 3a and Table 3b. The mean value for midspan deflection is significantly influenced by the mean value of the coefficient of thermal expansion. The three comparable entries in Table 3a and Table 3b have similar standard deviations for midspan deflection. Furthermore, the standard deviation for deflection responds consistently to changes in the standard deviation for the coefficient (lines 2, 3 and 4 Table 3a).

Sensitivity analysis for concrete compressive strength showed results similar to those for thermal diffusivity. We conclude that the coefficient of thermal expansion is the dominant contributor to the variability of midspan deflections.

The sensitivity to the coefficient of thermal expansion as a uniform variate was tested using the second approach, Table 4.

Table 2a: Sensitivity to Thermal Diffusivity (First Approach)

| $\alpha_d$ (in$^2$/min) | | Deflection (in.) | | |
|---|---|---|---|---|
| Mean | Std. Dev. | Mean | Std. Dev. | C.V. |
| 0.10 | 0.02 | 1.084 | 0.0292 | 2.7 |
| 0.16 | 0.03 | 1.102 | 0.0243 | 2.4 |
| 0.25 | 0.03 | 1.105 | 0.0109 | 1.0 |

Table 2b: Sensitivity to Thermal Diffusivity (Second Approach)

| $\alpha_d$ (in$^2$/min) | | Deflection (in.) | | |
|---|---|---|---|---|
| Mean | Std. Dev. | Mean | Std. Dev. | C.V. |
| 0.10 | 0.01 | 1.086 | 0.0528 | 4.9 |
| 0.16 | 0.03 | 1.106 | 0.0497 | 4.5 |
| 0.25 | 0.03 | 1.101 | 0.0411 | 3.7 |

Table 3a: Sensitivity to Coefficient of Thermal Expansion (First Approach)

| $\alpha_d(in^2/min)$ | | Deflection (in.) | | |
|---|---|---|---|---|
| Mean | Std. Dev. | Mean | Std. Dev. | C.V. |
| 5 | 1 | 0.914 | 0.0464 | 5.1 |
| 6 | 0.5 | 1.097 | 0.0185 | 1.7 |
| 6 | 1 | 1.095 | 0.0485 | 4.4 |
| 6 | 1.4 | 1.105 | 0.0529 | 4.8 |
| 7 | 1 | 1.289 | 0.0485 | 3.8 |

Table 3b: Sensitivity to Coefficient of Thermal Expansion (Second Approach)

| $\alpha_d(in^2/min)$ | | Deflection (in.) | | |
|---|---|---|---|---|
| Mean | Std. Dev. | Mean | Std. Dev. | C.V. |
| 5 | $1 \times 10^{-6}$ | 0.913 | .0528 | 5.8 |
| 6 | $1 \times 10^{-6}$ | 1.106 | .0497 | 4.5 |
| 7 | $1 \times 10^{-6}$ | 1.282 | .0610 | 4.8 |

Table 4: Sensitivity to Uniformly Distributed Coefficient to Thermal Expansion (Second Approach)

| $\alpha_d(in^2/min)$ | | Deflection (in.) | | |
|---|---|---|---|---|
| Mean | Std. Dev. | Mean | Std. Dev. | C.V. |
| 5 | 3 to 7 | .915 | 0.0598 | 6.5 |
| 6 | 4 to 8 | 1.085 | 0.0561 | 5.2 |
| 6 | 3 to 9 | 1.093 | 0.0921 | 8.4 |
| 7 | 5 to 9 | 1.265 | 0.0637 | 5.0 |

The sample statistics for midspan deflection are consistent with those in Table 3b. The results indicate little sensitivity to the assumed probability density function.

We also investigated the midspan response as a function of the number of layers in the model. Table 5 summarizes several experiments, using the second sensitivity approach, in which the number of layers was varied. The conclusion is that as the number of layers increases the mean deflection increases. On the other hand, the standard deviation for deflection decreases as the number of layers increases.

Finally, we investigated the midspan response to changes in the number of sections for five different lengths of span. The second sensitivity approach was used, Table 6. For a given length, there is little variation in mean deflection as the number of sections is changed. In contrast, the standard deviations were observed to decrease as the number of sections increased. As span length increases both the mean and standard deviation increase. In other words, the coefficients of variation seem to be of the same order regardless of girder lengths.

Table 5: Number of Layers Versus Deflection

| | Deflection (in.) | | |
|---|---|---|---|
| No. of Layers | Mean | Std. Dev. | C.V. |
| 1 | 1.016 | 0.0593 | 5.8 |
| 2 | 1.066 | 0.0545 | 5.1 |
| 3 | 1.095 | 0.0485 | 4.4 |
| 6 | 1.136 | 0.0343 | 3.0 |

Table 6: Length Effect

| | | Deflection (in.) | | |
|---|---|---|---|---|
| Length (ft.) | No. of Sections | Mean | Std. Dev. | C.V. |
| 60.5 | 5 | .277 | .0195 | 7.4 |
| 60.5 | 10 | .280 | .0156 | 5.6 |
| 60.5 | 20 | .277 | .0096 | 3.5 |
| 121.0 | 10 | 1.095 | .0485 | 4.4 |
| 121.0 | 20 | 1.108 | .0361 | 3.3 |
| 121.0 | 30 | 1.1 | .0341 | 3.1 |
| 242.0 | 10 | 4.439 | .2296 | 5.2 |
| 242.0 | 20 | 4.417 | .1339 | 3.0 |
| 363.0 | 30 | 10.06 | .2554 | 2.5 |
| 484.0 | 20 | 17.539 | .5719 | 3.3 |

## DIRECTION OF FURTHER STUDY

Currently, we are evaluating the significance of the self-equilibrating stress distributions that may occur due to the variability of material properties. An evaluation of cracking from a probabilistic viewpoint is envisioned. We will investigate the dependence of these effects on cross-sectional dimensions (slab aspect ratios).

A natural extension of these investigations is the introduction of nondeterministic thermal boundary conditions. Certain higher dimensional effects will be considered (such as two dimensional stress analysis).

References


Branson, Dan E. (1977). Differential Shrinkage, Creep, and Temperature in Composite Beams", Chapter 2, in Deformation of Concrete Structures, McGraw Hill, Inc., pp 85-100.

Fleischman, W.M. and Hoffman, P.C. "Microcomputer Solutions of the 1-D Dispersion Equation", (In preparation).

Hoffman, P.C., McClure, R.M. and West, H.H. March/April (1983a). "Temperature Study of an Experimental Segmental Concrete Bridge", PCI Journal, Vol 28, No 2, pp 78-97.

Hoffman, P.C., McClure, R.M. and West, H.H. June (1983b). "Temperature: A Service Design Problem", National Bridge Conference Proceedings, Pittsburgh.

Knuth, Donald E. (1981). Seminumerical Algorithms, vol. 2 of The Art of Computer Programming, 2nd ed., Addison-Wesley, pp 25-37.

Priestley, M.J.N. May (1978). "Design of Concrete Bridges for Temperature Gradients", ACI Journal, Vol 75, No 5, pp 209-217.

Street, Robert L. (1973). Analysis and Solution of Partial Differential Equations, Brooks/Cole, pp 356-372.

# STATISTICAL MODELS FOR SERVICE LIFE STUDY OF METAL CULVERTS

Fabian C. Hadipriono,* Richard E. Larew,*
Oh-Young Lee,* and Pin Chen*
*Department of Civil Engineering, Ohio State University, Columbus, Ohio 43210, USA

ABSTRACT

This paper is concerned with the service life study of corrugated metal culverts. The types of culverts are galvanized, bituminous coated, and bituminous coated and paved culverts. Linear regression analyses were performed to obtain prediction models for expected culvert conditions, then these models were used to estimate service life. As expected, these models indicate the least service life for galvanized culverts and the most for bituminous coated and paved culverts; however each model shows different results. The service life estimates reported herein may be of value to cost engineers performing life cycle cost studies of these types of culverts. However, the prediction equation on which they are based must not be used to predict the service life of a particular culvert. Further research is needed to develop reliable prediction for individual culverts.

## INTRODUCTION

Service life of a culvert is defined by the number of years of relatively maintenance-free performance (TRB, 1978). It also indicates that even if the service life expired, a culvert may last many more years before replacement is necessary. Usually, service life ends when significant deterioration takes place.

Various states in the U.S. have performed studies on the service life of metal culverts used for drainage purposes. However, several of these studies were performed prior to 1950. The State Highway Department of Georgia, for example, performed such a study in 1928 for culverts installed between 1915 and 1924 (Slack and Abercrombie, 1928). The results show an average expected service life of about 18 years for South Georgia and 25 to 34 years for North Georgia Filling and Scouring, respectively. The State Road Commission of West Virginia examined 3765 culverts between 1932 and 1933 (Downs, 1934), among which 1277 were corrugated metal pipe culverts. The study concluded an average service life of 27 years for the metal pipes with an average annual deterioration of 3.64%. About 1590 corrugated metal culvert pipes installed between 1907 and 1928 were investigated by the State of Pennsylvania Department of Highways in 1947 (SPDH, 1950). Assuming that yearly deterioration remains constant, corrugated metal pipes have a life expectancy of 29 years; however, under constant flow, this service life is reduced to 16 to 20 years.

The more recent studies conducted are from the States of Utah and Ohio. The Utah State Department of Highway studied 44 metal culverts in 1974 utilizing regression analysis (Welch, 1974). The study resulted in material selection criteria for various types of culverts. In 1972 and 1984, the Ohio Department of Transportation studied the durability of 685 corrugated metal pipes (Meacham et al, 1982; Hurd, 1984; Hurd, 1985). The study used regression analysis to develop multiplicative regression models for use in predicting metal loss of the culverts. Valuable information may be obtained from such studies, but there is as yet no general agreement concerning variables needed or the form of an appropriate model for the culverts.

The objective of this study is to predict the service life of corrugated metal culverts. The type of failure experienced by the pipes is limited to deterioration or material failures; structural failures are beyond the scope of this study. We use the linear regression to estimate parameters in additive and multiplicative models. Also dummy variables are used for classifying the various categories of the culverts. In order to reach this objective, data of the culverts and important variables affecting the service life of the culverts should first be discussed.

## DATA ANALYSIS

The study performed in this paper is concerned with statistical analyses which include the regression of data on 485 corrugated metal pipes which were provided by the Ohio Department of Transportation (ODOT). Survey and inspection of these data were performed by ODOT (Meacham et al, 1982); only pertinent details are elaborated here. The types of culverts analyzed are the galvanized (GAL), bituminous coated (BCC), and bituminous coated and paved (BCP) culverts.

The pipe rating for each culvert was also performed by ODOT inspectors; for consistency in this study, we will use the same rating procedures. Table 1 shows the rating, number of observations, and the percentage of each type of culverts.

TABLE 1. OBSERVATION AND PROPORTION OF METAL CULVERTS

| RATING | TYPE | NO. OF OBSERV.* | % OF EACH TYPE |
|---|---|---|---|
| 5 | GAL | 58 | 34 |
| | BCC | 4 | 5 |
| | BCP | 11 | 5 |
| 4 | GAL | 33 | 20 |
| | BCC | 12 | 15 |
| | BCP | 13 | 6 |
| 3 | GAL | 48 | 28 |
| | BCC | 16 | 20 |
| | BCP | 50 | 21 |
| 2 | GAL | 29 | 17 |
| | BCC | 40 | 48 |
| | BCP | 90 | 38 |
| 1 | GAL | 1 | 1 |
| | BCC | 10 | 12 |
| | BCP | 70 | 30 |

*Total observations: GAL=169, BCC=82, BCP=234

These observations show that for a pipe rating of 4 (fair) and 5 (poor) the proportion of BC and BCP is very small, warranted unreliable data. For a pipe rating of 1, the proportion of GAL is almost negligible. However, since our analyses emphasize the service life of the culverts (associated with pipe rate 4.5), it is expected that predictions for GAL is far more reliable than the others. The rating and the variables affecting the pipes are described below.

VARIABLES AFFECTING THE CULVERTS

The condition of culverts is usually determined during inspection through rating procedures. If rating indicates significant deterioration, replacement of pipes may take place. Usually, as is also the case in this study, ordinal values are used for this rating. These values are accompanied by linguistic values such as "excellent" which explains "a condition as constructed or no apparent loss of galvanizing." A complete listing of the ratings used for this project is provided in Table 2.

TABLE 2. METAL CULVERT RATING (Meacham et al, 1982)

| RATING | LINGUISTIC VALUE | DESCRIPTION |
|---|---|---|
| 1 | EXCELLENT | Condition as constructed<br>No apparent loss of galvanizing |
| 2 | VERY GOOD | Discoloration but no scaling or corrosion |
| 3 | GOOD | Slight to moderate scale<br>Slight to moderate rust<br>Pitting just started<br>Isolated spots of moderate corrosion |
| 4 | FAIR | Moderate to heavy scale<br>Moderate to heavy rust<br>No geologist's hammer penetration<br>No perforation |
| 5 | POOR | Penetration with geologist's hammer<br>Perforation<br>Loss of invert |

In order to rate the pipe condition, the following variables are considered in this study:

1. Pipe age: time in years from pipe installation through inspection. This variable will be used to predict the expected life of corrugated metal pipes.
2. Pipe size: usually measured in terms of diameter for circular pipes and in terms of rise for other types, such as arch or elliptical pipes.
3. Depth of flow: the depth of water in the pipe measured from the water surface to the bottom of the pipe.
4. Flow velocity: the velocity of water flowing in the pipe. This may be related to loss of pipe protection/material, particularly in cases where there exists a high rate of water velocity. In this study, the rating system for flow velocity consists of 5 descriptive linguistic values. The rating scale ranges from 1 to 5: 1 (rapid), 2 (moderate), 3 (slow), 4 (negligible), 5 (no flow).
5. Presence of sediment or debris: in general, these materials protect the invert of the pipes and slow down the corrosion process.
6. Slope of pipe: the pipe gradient that determines quantity of flow and flow velocity.
7. pH value: results of tests conducted to determine the accidity or alkalinity of the water.
8. Pipe gage: specified thickness for corrugated metal pipe culverts.

The above variables are not exhaustive; they were compiled from various sources and evaluated according to the significance of their contribution to concrete and metal deterioration. In extreme areas, other variables may exist and should be considered. However, these variables represent factors commonly encountered in the analysis of metal pipes and are essential for our analysis and assessment of the service life of drainage pipes. The rating and the above variables are listed in Table 3 as the initial variables used for the regression analyses.

TABLE 3. INITIAL VARIABLES FOR ANALYSES

| VARIABLE | DESCRIPTION | UNIT | RANGE |
|---|---|---|---|
| PRATE | Metal culvert pipe rating | - | 1-5 |
| AGE | Age of pipes | years | 1-50 |
| RISE | Rise or diameter | inches | 24-96 |
| FDEPTH | Flow depth | inches | 0-30 |
| FVEL | Flow velocity rating | - | 1-5 |
| SDEPTH | Depth of sediment | inches | 0-44 |
| SLOPE | Slope of pipes | % | 0.01-15 |
| PH | Accidity/alkalinity of water | - | 3-9.2 |
| GAGE | Thickness of pipes | - | 5-16 |

REGRESSION ANALYSES

We performed analyses using an approach which is different from that of earlier ODOT studies. In this study, linear regression was performed to estimate parameters of additive models. A stepwise regression program was then performed for checking the adequacy of the models. A detailed explanation of the regression procedures was presented in an earlier report on a study of concrete culverts (Hadipriono, 1986). For brevity, only pertinent procedures are presented here. The computer package used was Statistical Analysis System (SAS).

The variables in Table 3 are used for the preliminary model. PRATE is treated as the dependent variable, while the others are independent. Since there are three kinds of corrugated metal pipes, the preliminary model has two dummy variables, P1 and P2, a value of either 0 or 1. If the type of pipe is GAL, then P1 and P2 equal 0. If the pipe is BCC, then only P1 equals 1; and if the pipe is BCP, then only P2 is equal to zero.

Correlation coefficients between PRATE and the independent variables are examined in order to check the significant probability level. The t-tests (to determine whether or not an independent variable contributes any information to the prediction of the culvert rating) for the correlation coefficients reveal that the null hypothesis, Ho:bi=0, is rejected for all variables, except for FDEPTH, SDEPTH, and SLOPE whose probability is greater than the significant probability level determined as 0.05. However, we retain all variables in the prediction model until further analysis since a type 2 error may still occur (Hadipriono, 1986).

The coefficient of determination (R-square) indicates a value of 0.5375 (54%). Despite the rather low value, this yield is expected due to problems with data or unreliable measurement of the variables. For example, ratings on concrete conditions and flow velocity were performed visually, relying only on the inspector's opinion when he/she investigated the pipes. Breakdown of inspection equipment, such as pH meters, has also been reported during observations (Meacham et al, 1982). The F-test (used to test the global utility of the regression model) results in a value of 79.206 (P=0.0001), indicating that the null hypothesis is rejected if the significant level is determined as 0.05. Therefore, at least one of the parameter is nonzero.

Scattergrams (a diagram relating the dependent and independent variables) were also analyzed to determine the general relations between variables. To improve the prediction for PRATE, the natural logarithm is used for PH and this variable is modified to become LPH. For the same reason, and because the t-test for SLOPE fails to reject the null hypothesis, the square root of slope is used and called SQRSL. The square root transform, rather than logarithm, is used because it appears in many empirical design formulae for metal pipes.

The residuals (the difference between the observed and predicted value) for each variable are investigated. The results show no specific problems.

Extra Sums of Square Test (ESST) is performed to test some of the parameters in the model. For this purpose, the model was reduced to include only some of the parameters. The test was performed intuitively by first applying the least square method to fit the full and reduced models, and then by comparing the sums of squares of errors of the full and reduced models. The larger the difference, the more significant is the effect of the excluded variables. The results for SQRSL, FDEPTH, and RISE fail to reject the null hypothesis; hence, their elimination from the regression model is justified. The final regression model is now expressed as follows:

$$\begin{aligned} PRATE = {} & 4.4221 + 0.0589AGE - 0.0696FVEL - 0.0172SDEPTH \\ & - 1.5586LPH + 0.1313GAGE - 0.6323P1 - 1.0016P2 \end{aligned} \qquad \text{......... (1)}$$

This model (Model 1) can be used to estimate the expected service life of the pipes that were installed in environmental conditions similar to those in Ohio. The service life is determined by obtaining AGE from the above equation given PRATE=4.5. Note that 4.5 is a rating between "fair" and "poor." Table 4 below shows an expected service life of about 36, 49, and 54 years for the GAL, BCC, and BCP, respectively.

TABLE 4. EXPECTED SERVICE LIFE FOR METAL CULVERTS

| CORRUGATED METAL CULVERT | EXPECTED SERVICE LIFE (MODEL 1) |
|---|---|
| GALVANIZED CULVERTS (GAL) | 36.22 |
| BITUMINOUS COATED CULVERTS (BCC) | 49.25 |
| BITUMINOUS COATED AND PAVED CULVERTS (BCP) | 54.18 |

ADDITIONAL STUDIES

To further assess the adequacy of the foregoing model, we undertook additional studies. The analysis is the same as the foregoing except that it is performed step-by-step to obtain only the significant variables that fit to the final model. In addition, both additive and multiplicative models were considered.

The initial variables used here are the same as in the foregoing analyses, except for GAGE. As shown in Table 3, the independent variable GAGE is unitless. For the purpose of the following analysis, this variable is given a unit of inches. Information for this transformation is based on the Handbook of Drainage and Construction Products (ARMCO, 1958). Note that this transformation is performed to improve the prediction for PRATE. The variable GAGE is then relabled as: GAGE1=1/(thickness of pipe). Table 3 indicates that the range is between 5 and 16. The data show that they accumulate within GAGE numbers 8, 10, 12, 14, 16, with thickness of 0.16 in. (4.2MM), 0.13 in. (3.4MM), 0.10 in. (2.7MM), 0.07 in. (1.9MM), and 0.06 in. (1.5MM), respectively. The number of the remaining (eight observations) are relatively too few compared to the others, and therefore, removed from the analysis.

The final result for the additive model (Model 2) is shown in the following (R-square=58%, F=70, and P=0.0001):

$$PRATE = 6.1643 - 0.0009AGE*SDEPTH + 0.0064AGE*GAGE1 - 2.0645LPH - 0.2118P1*FVEL + 0.0261P2*AGE + 1.3335P2*LPH + 0.0012RISE*GAGE1 - 0.0179FDEPTH*SQRSL - 4.0855P2 \quad ......... (2)$$

The multiplicative model (Model 3) uses logarithm for the variables (e.g., LPRATE = log PRATE, etc.). The final model is then transfered back into the original variables (R-square=53%, F=534, P=0.0001):

$$PRATE = 0.1796 + \frac{0.2230AGE^{0.3370}\ GAGE1^{0.5303}\ RISE^{0.3113}}{LPH^{0.8929}\ Exp(0.2684P1)\ Exp(0.3966P2)} \quad ......... (3)$$

Using Models 2 and 3, the expected service life of the culverts is found as shown in Table 5.

TABLE 5. EXPECTED SERVICE LIFE FOR METAL CULVERTS

| CORRUGATED METAL CULVERT | EXPECTED SERVICE LIFE (MODEL 2) | EXPECTED SERVICE LIFE (MODEL 3) |
|---|---|---|
| GAL | 40.30 | 39.44 |
| BCC | 62.78 | 95.33 |
| BCP | 46.17 | 155.03 |

CONCLUSIONS

These studies resulted in an additive model (Model 1) and both additive and multiplicative models (Models 2 and 3).

As expected the three models result in small variations of the expected service life for culverts type GAL (36, 39 and 40 years, respectively). These models show expected service lives of 49, 63 and 95 years for BCC and 54, 46, and 155 years for BCP. The variability of BCC and BCP service lifes is too great: we do not have enough data in the fair and poor regions for these two types of culverts.

These models can be used to estimate the expected service life of metal culverts that were installed in conditions representative of those in the State of Ohio. The fact that PRATE (instead of AGE) is used as the dependent variable, prohibits the use of these models to predict the service life of a particular culvert given the knowledge of the independent variables.

The service life estimates may be of value to cost engineers performing life cycle cost studies of these types of culverts. Further studies is needed to develop reliable prediction for individual culverts.

ACKNOWLEDGMENT

The authors wish to thank Mr. John Hurd from the Ohio Department of Transportation who provided data for the regression analyses. Special thanks go to Dr. Paul Thompson from the Department of Statistics of The Ohio State University. The authors appreciate the editorial works performed by Nancy Grace.

REFERENCES

ARMCO (1958). Handbook of Drainage and Construction Products, ARMCO Drainage and Metal Products, Inc., Middletown, Ohio.

Hadipriono F.C. (1986). Durability Study of Concrete Pipe Culverts: Service Life Assessment, A Report Presented to The Army Corps of Engineers, Vicksburg, Mississippi.

Hurd J.O. (1984). "Field Performance of Concrete and Corrugated Steel Pipe Culverts and Bituminous Protection of Corrugated Steel Pipe Culverts," Symposium on Durability of Culverts and Storm Drains, Transportation Research Record 1001, National Research Council, Washington, D.C., pp. 40-48.

Hurd J.O. (1985). Field Performance of Concrete Culverts at Acidic Flow Sites in Ohio," Presented at The 64th Annual Meeting of The Transportation Research Board, Washington, D.C.

Downs W.S. (1934). "A Survey of Culverts in West Virginia," The West Virginia University in Cooperation with The State Road Commission of West Virginia, Morgantown, West Virginia.

Meacham D.G., J.O. Hurd, and W.W. Shisler (1982). "Ohio Culvert Durability Study," Final Report, Ohio Department of Transportation, Columbus, Ohio.

Slack S.B. and W.F. Abercrombie (1928). "Report on Study of Culvert Durability," State Highway Board, Georgia State Highway Department Bureau of Investigations.

SPDH (1950). "Culvert Pipe Study," State of Pennsylvania Department of Highways.

TRB (1978). "Durability of Drainage Pipe," National Cooperative Highway Research Program, Synthesis of Highway Practice 50, Transportation Research Board, National Research Council, Washington, D.C.

Welch B.H. (1974). "Pipe Corrosion and Protective Coatings, Utah State Department of Highways Materials and Tests Division, Research and Development Section, Salt Lake City, Utah.

# PROBABILISTIC ANALYSIS OF LIVE LOAD PROCESSES WITH NONLINEAR STRUCTURAL RESPONSE

Philip A. Thayaparan* and Karen C. Chou**

*Calocerinos & Spina Consulting Engineers, 1020 Seventh North St., Liverpool, NY 13088, U.S.A.

**Department of Civil Engineering, Syracuse University, Syracuse, NY 13244-1190, U.S.A.

ABSTRACT

Study on single structural member reliability subjected to floor live load processes is extended to include material nonlinearity. A probability distribution model is developed here for the number of loads exceeding a predetermined threshold deformation level. The approach presented here is more direct than the one developed in an earlier study. In addition, this approach reduces the numerical error induced and it can also provide greater flexibility in the evaluation of reliability.

## INTRODUCTION

Numerous studies were conducted in the area of structural member reliability due to stochastic load processes. However, most of the studies have generally assumed the member responds linearly, few have considered the nonlinearity rigorously. With the increased emphasis placed on ultimate analysis with partially or fully plastic behavior (ACI, 1977; AISC, 1978), it is essential to consider the nonlinear load effects on structural reliability. A tractable expression for the first moment statistics of load exceedances (number of loads exceeding a predetermined threshold deformation level) for a contiguous rectangular pulse process (e.g., a sustained load process for office floor load) was derived in an earlier study (Chou, Corotis and Karr, 1985). Subsequently, the probability distribution for the number of load exceedances was derived using the first moment obtained (Chou, 1986). The distribution model was good and exact in theory. However, the evaluation of the probability function requires the joint probability density function of two random variables which cannot be obtained readily. Thus, the first term of the Taylor series expansion was used to approximate the derived distribution. The error induced by the approximation increases with threshold level since the coefficient of variation of load exceedances increases respectively. In this study, an alternate approach is presented to reduce the amount of approximation.

As it was discussed by Chou, Corotis and Karr (1985) that the nonlinear response analysis using threshold force is not load history dependent while for response based on the threshold deformation the response becomes load history dependent. Thus, it is necessary to first determine on which domain the threshold level is based. One's choice of threshold criterion depends on the type of failure one is interested in. In this study response based on threshold deformation is considered, and the structural member is assumed to be subjected to a floor live load process which consists of one sustained and one or more extraordinary loads as shown in Figure 1. The sustained load process is assumed to have Poisson arrivals with independent, identically distributed gamma load magnitudes. The extraordinary load process is also assumed to have Poisson arrivals with

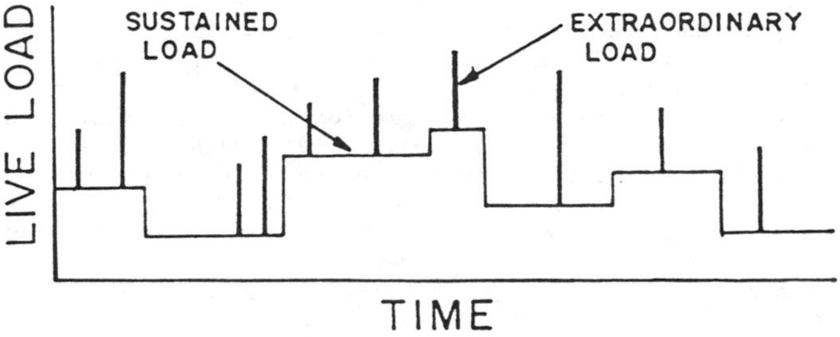


FIGURE 1. FLOOR LOAD HISTORY WITH ONE SUSTAINED AND ONE EXTRAORDINARY LOAD PROCESS.

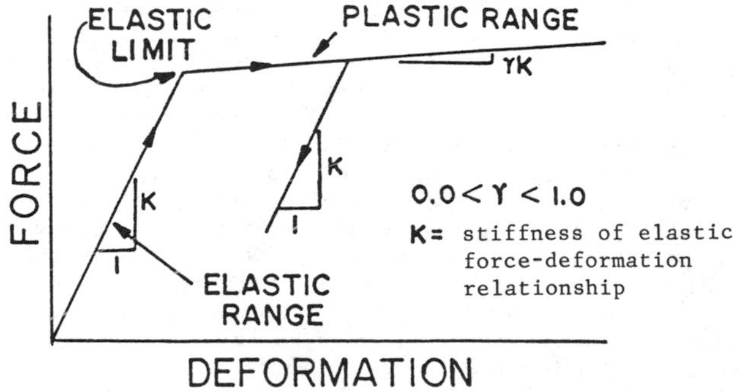


FIGURE 2. FORCE-DEFORMATION RELATIONSHIP

short load durations and iid gamma load magnitudes. In addition, the material is assumed to have a bilinear force-deformation relationship with unloading parallel to the initial elastic range as shown in Figure 2 and the geometric nonlinearity is not included.

LOAD EXCEEDANCES

It was stated in the previous section that the nonlinear response using threshold deformation is load history dependent. For illustration, consider a typical sustained load process and its corresponding nonlinear response shown in Figure 3. The amount of deformation associated with each load depends on the magnitude of the prior load cycles beyond the elastic limit even though the load process is memoryless (a Poisson process in this case). However, if one is only concerned with the occurrences of a load that has deformation greater than a certain level say $\Delta$ (even when $\Delta$ is in the plastic range), then it is unnecessary to know the load history prior to the first excursion of $\alpha_o$ (corresponding to a deformation of $\Delta$) (Chou, Corotis and Karr, 1985). Therefore, for the load process of Figure 3, the magnitude of loads 2, 6 and 8 define the unloading paths b, c and d, respectively, for subsequent loads until a new unloading path is defined. As can be seen from the response, the effective threshold level, force corresponding to the threshold deformation $\Delta$, changes with different unloading path. Thus the load exceedance depends on the effective threshold level which depends on time and the peak load magnitude (the maximum magnitude greater than $\alpha_o$ up to that point in time).

PROBABILITY DISTRIBUTION OF LOAD EXCEEDANCES

In the study by Chou, Corotis and Karr (1985), the number of load exceedances $N_t$ for a contiguous rectangular pulse process was defined as a sum of two exceedance processes, $N_t'$ and $N_t''$. The random process $N_t'$ represents the number of interpeak load exceedances such as loads 3, 5, 7, 9 and 10 of the illustration shown in Figure 3. The random process $N_t''$ represents the number of peak loads such as loads 2, 6 and 8. A tractable first moment statistics for each of the processes $N_t'$ and $N_t''$ was derived. Since the first moment alone is not very informative, the probability mass function (PMF) for the load exceedances was subsequently derived (Chou, 1986) via the PMF of the interpeak exceedance process $N_t'$ and the peak load process $N_t''$. With the load process being assumed to have Poisson arrivals with iid magnitudes, the PMF for the processes $N_t'$ and $N_t''$ are also in the family of Poisson process. Thus, the probability mass functions depend on the expected values of $N_t'$ and $N_t''$. Although the first moments for both $N_t'$ and $N_t''$ were shown to have good agreement with the simulated results (Chou, Corotis and Karr, 1985), but the probability functions evaluated had significant discrepancy with the simulated results especially at high threshold levels. The evaluation of the PMF for the process $N_t'$ requires the joint probability density function of the peak load magnitude $R_t$ and the effective threshold level $A_t$ which is not readily available. The first term of Taylor series expansion was then used to approximate the PMF function. This approximation is the primary source of numerical error in the evaluation of the PMF.

An alternate approach presented herein is based on the fundamental behavior of load exceedances. A load exceedance occurs whenever a load arrives whose magnitude is greater than some threshold level. For a linear structural response, the threshold level remains constant throughout the entire process. Since the floor live loads follow a Poisson process, the exceedance rate is given by

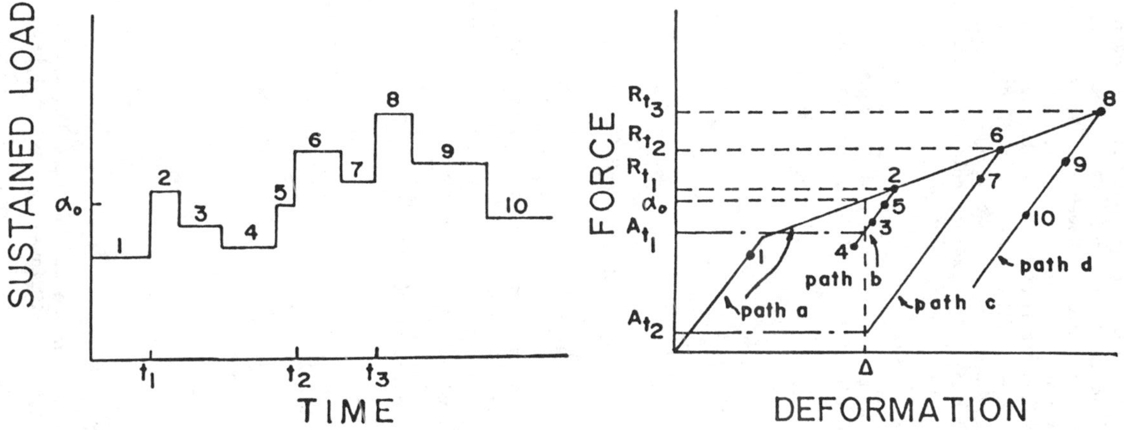


FIGURE 3. SUSTAINED LOAD PROCESS AND THE CORRESPONDING NONLINEAR RESPONSE

$$\text{linear exceedance rate} = \nu_S G_S(\alpha) \tag{1}$$

in which $\nu_S$ = arrival rate of the load process, $G_S(\cdot)$ = the complementary cumulative distribution of the load magnitude and $\alpha$ = predetermined threshold force level. In nonlinear analysis, the fundamental principal of load exceedances remains unchanged. However, the exceedances based on threshold deformation is load history dependent. Thus the threshold force corresponding to the predetermined threshold deformation changes with time. The exceedance rate in this case is no longer constant. In addition, the effective threshold force also depends on the peak load magnitude up to that point in time. The exceedance rate becomes a process,

$$\nu(t,A) = \nu_S \; G_S(A_t) \tag{2}$$

in which $A_t$ = the effective threshold force which depends on time and has a probability density function (PDF) of (Chou, Corotis and Karr, 1985),

$$f_{A_t}(\alpha_t) = \frac{\gamma}{1-\gamma} \nu_S t \; f_S(*) \exp\left[-\nu_S t G_S(*)\right] \tag{3}$$

$$\text{and} \quad * = \frac{\gamma\alpha - \alpha_0}{\gamma - 1} \tag{4}$$

in which $\gamma$ = coefficient of reduced stiffness and $\alpha_0$ = initial threshold level (see Figure 3).

Since the effective threshold level $A_t$ is itself a stochastic process and the load arrivals follow a Poisson process, the load exceedances $N_t$ follow a doubly stochastic Poisson process (Cox, 1980). To find the PMF for $N_t$, it is more convenient to consider the PMF conditioned on the time-dependent threshold level, then followed by the unconditional form (Snyder, 1975). The conditioned rate at any instance time u is

$$\begin{aligned} \nu(u) &= \text{the conditional rate process of } \nu(t,A) \text{ given } A_u = \alpha_u \\ &= \nu_S \; G_S(\alpha_u) \end{aligned} \tag{5}$$

The random process $N_t$ conditioned at $A_t$ becomes a non-stationary Poisson process with a mean (Cinlar, 1975)

$$\begin{aligned} E[N_t \mid A_u = \alpha_u] &= \int_0^t \nu(u)\, du \\ &= \int_0^t \nu_S G_S(\alpha_u)\, du \end{aligned} \tag{6}$$

Note that the value of $\alpha_u$ depends on the time u. The PMF for the non-stationary Poisson process (i.e., conditional PMF for $N_t$) becomes (Cinlar, 1975)

$$\text{Prob}[N_t = k \mid A_u = \alpha_u] = \frac{\left(E[N_t|A_u]\right)^k \exp\left(-E[N_t|A_u]\right)}{k!} \tag{7}$$

By the basic properties in probability, the unconditional PMF for $N_t$ can be found via eqn. (7) as

$$\text{Prob}\ [N_t = k] = \sum_{\text{all } \alpha_u} \text{Prob}[N_t = k \mid A_u = \alpha_u]\ \text{Prob}[A_u = \alpha_u]$$

$$= \int_{\text{all } \alpha_u} \frac{\left(E[N_t \mid A_u]\right)^k \exp\left(-E[N_t \mid A_u]\right)}{k!} f_{A_u}(\alpha_u)\, d\alpha_u \tag{8}$$

It is not anticipated that eqn. (8) can be integrated into a closed form. Numerical integration will be used to perform the calculation for the PMF of $N_t$. Since each term in the integral is well defined. The error induced by the numerical integration will be quite limited.

COMBINED LOAD PROCESSES

Since structures seldom experience one type of load alone, the nonlinear structural response due to a combined process of one sustained and one extraordinary load is investigated. Only the PMF for exceedances due to the extraordinary load is derived because an extraordinary load has a much shorter duration than a sustained load. Thus, a sustained load exceedance yields a significantly different response characteristics from an extraordinary one. As with the sustained load process, the first moment statistics of the extraordinary load exceedances for a combined floor live load process was derived (Chou and Thayaparan, 1987). Only those extraordinary loads whose magnitude combined with the corresponding sustained load is larger than the effective threshold level $A_t$ and the sustained load itself is below $A_t$ are considered as extraordinary load (EOL) exceedances. It should be noted that the interest here is the number of load exceedances, not the magnitude beyond $A_t$. In addition, it was further assumed that the magnitude of EOL exceedances will not define a new unloading path because of its short load duration. Therefore, the EOL exceedances behave linearly similar to the interpeak sustained load exceedances. However, the exceedance rate is not linear because the effective threshold level established by the sustained load is load history dependent. The analysis, nevertheless, is very similar to that discussed in prior sections for sustained load processes. The EOL exceedance rate is given by

$$\nu'(t,A) = \nu_E G_E(A_t - S) \tag{9}$$

in which $\nu_E$ = arrival rate of extraordinary loads, $G_E(\cdot)$ = the complementary cumulative distribution function of the extraordinary load magnitudes and S = the magnitude of the sustained load which is random. The PMF for the EOL exceedances can then be derived via the non-stationary rate process by conditioning eqn. (9) on $A_t$ and S, then followed by the unconditional form.

CONCLUDING REMARKS

An alternate approach is presented here to derive the probability mass function for the total number of load exceeding a predetermined threshold deformation. This approach is attempted to reduce the error incurred during any mathematical approximation as in the case of an earlier study. The calculation necessary for the PMF given here is fairly straight-forward and the computer cost is low. In addition, this approach can also provide more flexibility in reliability study. For instance, if one wishes to evaluate the load exceedances some time after a process has begun, one can obtain the unconditional form of eqn. (6) for the duration $t_1$ to $t_2$ where $t_1$ represents the present time which is greater than or equal to zero; and $t_2$ represents some future time of interest.

REFERENCES

ACI Standard 318-77 (1977). Building Code Requirements for Reinforced Concrete, American Concrete Institute, Detroit, Michigan.

AISC (1978). Specification for the Design, Fabrication and Erection of Structural Steel for Buildings, American Institute of Steel Construction, Chicago, Illinois, November.

Chou, K.C. (1986). "Probabilistic Analysis of Nonlinear Response to Sustained Load Processes", Structural Safety, Vol. 4, No. 1, Oct., pp. 1-13.

Chou, K.C., R.B. Corotis, and A.F. Karr (1985). "Nonlinear Response to Sustained Load Processes", Journal of Structural Engineering, ASCE, Vol. 111, No. 1, Proc. Paper 19432, Jan. pp. 142-157.

Chou, K.C. and P.A. Thayaparan (1987). "Nonlinear Structural Response to Combined Live Load Processes", Journal of Structural Engineering, ASCE (Submitted for review).

Cinlar E. (1975). Introduction to Stochastic Processes, Prentice-Hall, Inc., Englewood liffs, NJ.

Cox, D.R. and V. Isham (1980). Point Processes, Chapman and Hall, NY.

Snyder, D.L. (1975). Random Point Processes, John Wiley & Sons, Inc., New York.

# RELIABILITY OF TALL COLUMNS SUBJECTED TO NONSTATIONARY GROUND MOTIONS

by Richard J. Nielsen* and Anne S. Kiremidjian**

*Dept. of Civil Engineering, University of Idaho, Moscow, Idaho 83843
**Dept. of Civil Engineering, Stanford University, Stanford, California 94305

## ABSTRACT

The reliability of tall cantilever structures subjected to earthquake loads is evaluated using a stochastic dynamic response model which considers the effects of both vertical and horizontal acceleration. Failure is defined as the crossing of the response process over a member strength threshold. The stochastic response model determines both the duration of shaking and the probability distribution for the time to failure. The limit state equation then compares the time to failure to the duration of motion. The reliability of a typical distilling column from an oil refinery is investigated for two limit states, yielding of the anchor bolts and buckling of the supporting skirt. Analyses reveal that the duration of the ground motions significantly affect the probability of failure, whereas vertical acceleration contributes very little to the probability of failure.

## INTRODUCTION

The reliable performance of tall columns under extreme loads can be crucial to the overall safety of industrial facilities. Lateral loads caused by earthquakes or winds gusts are transient phenomena which are usually modeled as nonstationary processes. This paper investigates the reliability of tall columns subjected to nonstationary vertical and horizontal acceleration. Probability of failure is defined as the probability the bending moment process crosses the failure threshold. Analyses are performed by calculating the expected response as a function of time then evaluating the time to cross the member capacity threshold. Numerical calculations are made for a typical structure.

The design of tall columns as outlined by the industrial codes typically considers three modes: (1) yielding of the bolts anchoring the column to the foundation (2) buckling of the supporting skirt (3) tearing of the weld connecting the distilling vessel to the skirt. This list does not include foundation failure modes such as pullout of the anchor bolts from the concrete foundation or liquefaction of the soils under the foundation.

The reliability analysis of the column requires the definition of the limit state equation for the failure mode of interest. Most limit state formulations compare the loads to the resistance . However, for the nonstationary response considered in this model, a more appropriate limit state equation compares the time to failure to the duration of column shaking (cf. Rackwitz, 1985):

$$g(\mathbf{X}) = X_{T_f} - X_{t_{dur}} \qquad (1)$$

where $X_{Tf}$ is the time to failure and $X_{tdur}$ is the duration of the column shaking. Equation 1 implies that if the column fails before it ceases shaking, it enters the failure domain $\omega_f = \{\mathbf{X}: g(\mathbf{X}) < 0\}$. Of interest is the probability, $P_f$, that the structure enters this failure domain:

$$P_f = \int_{\mathbf{x} \in \omega_f} f_{\mathbf{X}}(\mathbf{x})\, d(\mathbf{x}) \qquad (2)$$

where $f_{\mathbf{X}}(\mathbf{x})$ is the joint probability density of the random variables in the limit state equation. The duration of shaking and the time to failure in Eqs. 1 and 2 are determined from nonstationary stochastic response model for the column.

## STOCHASTIC RESPONSE MODEL

The probabilistic response model assumes the horizontal acceleration can be characterized as a filtered nonstationary Gaussian process. If the filter is of the Kanai-Tajimi type, the ground motions are given by (Kanai, 1957 and Tajimi, 1960):

$$\ddot{y}_g = (\ddot{Y}_g + W_1)\, e(t) = e(t)[-\xi_g \omega_g \dot{Y}_g - \omega_g^2 Y_g] \qquad (3)$$

in which $Y_g$ is the relative ground displacement, $\omega_g$ and $\xi_g$ are the natural frequency and damping ratio of the Kanai-Tajimi filter, e(t) is the time varying envelope function described below. $W_1$ is a stationary white noise process whose autocorrelation function is given by $R_{11}(s) = 2D_{11}\delta(s)$ where $\delta(\bullet)$ is the Dirac delta function, and $D_{11}$ is the magnitude of the autocorrelation function. The power spectral density of the ground motion process is the Fourier transform of its autocorrelation function. Thus, the spectral density for the horizontal motion is a constant, $S_1 = D_{11}/\pi$. The expected response values are calculated from the autocorrelation functions. However, the intensities of past earthquakes are more often reported in terms of their spectral densities (e.g. Lai, 1982). Therefore, the spectral density, $S_1$, is used to scale the autocorrelation functions in the numerical analyses.

The envelope function selected for this study has the form of a $\chi^2$-density function (Saragoni and Hart, 1972):

$$e(t) = \beta t^{\gamma} \exp\{-\alpha t\} \qquad (4)$$

where $\beta$, $\gamma$, and $\alpha$ are characterization parameters for the envelope. Saragoni and Hart (1972) relate the expected values of the earthquake duration to the expected duration of the envelope function to find expressions for $\alpha$ and $\gamma$:

$$\alpha = \mu_{dur} / \sigma_{dur}^2 \quad \text{and} \quad \gamma = \left(\mu_{dur}^2 / \sigma_{dur}^2\right) - 1 \qquad (5a\&b)$$

where $\mu_{dur}$ is the mean duration of the earthquake motions and $\sigma^2_{dur}$ is the variance of the duration. In order to simplify the scaling of the ground motion intensity, the parameter $\beta$ is chosen such that the maximum value of the envelope function is one:

$$\beta = (\gamma/\alpha)^{-\gamma} \exp\{\gamma\} \qquad (6)$$

The column response is insensitive to the scaling effects of the filtering process on the vertical accelerations. In fact, it will be shown that the response motions are nearly identical when the vertical accelerations are included or completely ignored. Therefore to simplify the ground motion model, vertical accelerations are assumed to be a white noise process, $\ddot{x}_g = W_2$, with autocorrelation function $R_{22}(s) = 2D_{22}\delta(s)$ and power spectral density $S_2 = D_{22}/\pi$, where $D_{22}$ is the magnitude of the autocorrelation function for vertical acceleration. If the earthquake is assumed to emanate from a point source the vertical and horizontal motions will have the following crosscorrelation function (Shih and Chen, 1984):

$$R_{12}(s) = 2D_{12}\delta(s) = 2\sqrt{D_{11}D_{22}}\,\delta(s) \qquad (7)$$

This ground motion model incorporates the principal characteristics of actual earthquake motions in both the time and frequency domains.

The probabilistic modal response can be written in terms of stochastic differential equations of motion which assumes the loading and response quantities are random processes. In this case, the solution process is said to exist in a mean-squared sense (Lin, 1967). The stochastic differential equations are derived from the deterministic modal equations of motion (Wong and Zakai, 1965). Since the input motions are assumed Gaussian, and the structural response is linear, the output process will be a Gaussian process with independent increments. This is a sufficient condition for the description of the modal response as a Markov vector with components (Lin, 1967):

$$Z_{j1} = q_j(t) \qquad Z_{j2} = \dot{q}_j(t) \tag{8a-d}$$
$$Z_{j3} = Y_g(t) \qquad Z_{j4} = \dot{Y}_g(t)$$

where $q_j(t)$ is the temporal component of the displacement response for mode j. Since a white noise process is the derivative of a Brownian motion process (Karlin and Taylor, 1975), the vertical and horizontal acceleration processes, $W_1$ and $W_2$ are replaced with their corresponding Brownian motion processes, $dB_1/dt$ and $dB_2/dt$. Thus, the relationship between velocity and displacement can be expressed in Itô's form for stochastic differential equations (Nielsen, 1986):

$$d\mathbf{Z}_j = \mathbf{m}_j(\mathbf{Z}_j,t)dt + \mathbf{G}_j(\mathbf{Z}_j,t)d\mathbf{B}(t) \tag{9a}$$

where:

$$\mathbf{Z}_j^T = \left[Z_{j1}, Z_{j2}, Z_{j3}, Z_{j4}\right] \tag{9b}$$

$$\mathbf{m}_j(\mathbf{Z}_j,t) = \begin{bmatrix} Z_{j2} \\ -\omega^{*2} I_{7j} Z_{j1} - 2\beta Z_{j2} + R_{hj}e(t)\omega_g^2 Z_{j3} + 2R_{hj}e(t)\xi_g\omega_g Z_{j4} \\ Z_{j4} \\ -\omega_g^2 Z_{j3} - 2\xi_g\omega_g Z_{j4} \end{bmatrix} \tag{9c}$$

$$\mathbf{G}_j(\mathbf{Z}_j,t) = \begin{bmatrix} 0 & 0 \\ 0 & R_{vj}e(t)Z_{j1} \\ 0 & 0 \\ -1 & 0 \end{bmatrix} \tag{9d}$$

and

$$d\mathbf{B}(t) = \left[dB_1, dB_2\right] \tag{9e}$$

where $I_{ij}$, $\omega^{*2}$, $\beta$, $R_{hj}$, and $R_{vj}$ are the j-th mode normalizing factors for the mode shape, natural frequency, damping, and horizontal and vertical acceleration, respectively (Nielsen, 1986).

The complete statistical properties of $\mathbf{Z}_j$ are uniquely determined by the Fokker-Planck equation associated with Eq. 9a. At present, the solution to the Fokker-Planck equation can only be found for the most trivial cases. However, the statistical expectations for $\mathbf{Z}_j$ can be found by applying Itô's rule for differentiation to Eq. 9a and then taking the expectation of the resulting equation (Jazwinsky, 1970). Since the output processes are Gaussian, their statistical properties are uniquely determined by their first and second order expectations. Defining the quantities $m_i = E[Z_i]$, and $m_{ij} = E[Z_iZ_j]$, the first-order expectations are:

$$dm_1/dt = m_2 \tag{10a}$$
$$dm_2/dt = -\omega^{*2} I_{7j} m_1 - 2\beta m_2 + R_{hj}e(t)\omega_g^2 m_3 + 2R_{hj}e(t)\xi_g\omega_g m_4 \tag{10b}$$

$dm_3/dt = m_4$ (10c)

$dm_4/dt = -\omega_g{}^2 m_3 - 2\xi_g \omega_g m_4$ (10d)

with initial conditions $m_1(0) = m_2(0) = m_3(0) = m_4(0) = 0$. With these initial conditions and the fact that there is no external driving force in Eqs. 10a-d, the first-order moments for these response quantities are all zero throughout the duration of the earthquake.

Given Itô's definition of his stochastic differential equation, the ensemble average, $E[\mathbf{G}d\mathbf{BZ}_j] = 0$ (Jazwinsky, 1970). Therefore, applying Itô's rule for differentiation to Eq. 9a and taking the expectation yields the following system of differential equations for the second-order expectations:

$dm_{11}/dt = 2m_{12}$ (11a)

$dm_{12}/dt = m_{22} - \omega^{*2} I_{7j} m_{11} - 2\beta m_{12} + R_{hj} e(t) \omega_g{}^2 m_{13} + 2R_{hj} e(t) \xi_g \omega_g m_{14}$ (11b)

$dm_{13}/dt = m_{14} + m_{23}$ (11c)

$dm_{14}/dt = m_{24} - \omega_g{}^2 m_{13} - 2\xi_g \omega_g m_{14}$ (11d)

$dm_{22}/dt = 2[R_{vj}{}^2 e^2(t) D_{22} m_{11} - \omega^{*2} I_{7j} m_{12} - 2\beta m_{22} + R_{hj} e(t) \omega_g{}^2 m_{23} +$
$2R_{hj} e(t) \xi_g \omega_g m_{24}]$ (11e)

$dm_{23}/dt = m_{24} - \omega^{*2} I_{7j} m_{13} - 2\beta m_{23} + R_{hj} e(t) \omega_g{}^2 m_{33} + 2R_{hj} e(t) \xi_g \omega_g m_{34}$ (11f)

$dm_{24}/dt = -\omega^{*2} I_{7j} m_{14} - 2\beta m_{24} + R_{hj} e(t) \omega_g{}^2 m_{34} + 2R_{hj} e(t) \xi_g \omega_g m_{44} -$
$\omega_g{}^2 m_{23} - 2\xi_g \omega_g m_{24} + 2R_{vj} e(t) D_{12} m_1$ (11g)

$dm_{33}/dt = 2m_{34}$ (11h)

$dm_{34}/dt = m_{44} - \omega_g{}^2 m_{33} - 2\xi_g \omega_g m_{34}$ (11i)

$dm_{44}/dt = 2(D_{11} - \omega_g{}^2 m_{34} - 2\xi_g \omega_g m_{44})$ (11j)

with initial conditions:

$m_{ij}(0) = 0 ; \quad \text{for } 1 \le i,j \le 4$ (11k)

It is interesting to note that since the first-order moments are mean-zero processes, the crosscorrelation term in Eq. 11g is zero. Thus, the second-order response moments are independent of any crosscorrelation between the horizontal and vertical ground motions. The numerical solution of Eqs. 11a-j allows replacement of the envelope function (Eq. 4) with other types of envelope function if desired (e.g. exponential, trapezoidal).

In order to relate the displacement and velocity response to the actual stresses in the components of the column, the displacement and velocity responses are transformed to bending moment responses. This transformation is performed for the modal responses; the modal responses are then combined to find the total bending moment response. The modal bending moment response along the height of the column is a function of the column displacement:

$E[M_j^2(x,t)] = h_j^2(x) E[q_j^2(t)] = h_j^2(x) m_{11}^{(j)}(t)$ (12a)

where

$h_j(x) = EI\, f_j''(x)$ (12b)

and the superscript $^{(j)}$ denotes the expected response for mode j, and $f_j(x)$ is the shape function for the j-th mode response (Nielsen, 1986). The threshold crossing analysis will also require the derivative of the bending moment response with time which is found in a similar fashion.

Since the combined bending moment response is the sum of the modal bending moment responses, the expected value of the total bending moment response can be expanded into a Taylor series as follows (Shih and Chen, 1984):

$$E\left[M^2(x,t)\right] = \sum_{j=1}^{\infty} E\left[M_j^2(x,t)\right] + 2\sum_{\substack{j=1 \\ j<k}}^{\infty} \sum_{k=1}^{\infty} E\left[M_j(x,t)M_k(x,t)\right] + \ldots \tag{13}$$

Since the modes are sufficiently separated, the cross terms, $E[M_j(x,t)M_k(x,t)]$, are negligible (Nielsen, 1986). A series expansion is also used to find the expected derivative of the bending moment response. These expectations are used to determine both the duration of column motions and the probability distribution for the time to failure in the limit state equation (Eq. 1).

The duration of column motions is assumed to begin when the earthquake arrives at time $t = 0$. Given the exponential decay of the input and response motions, an arbitrary cutoff is needed to determine the end of the response motions. For purposes of this study, the duration cutoff is defined as the time when the expected value of the square of the displacement response ($m_{11}$ in Eqs. 11a-j) has dropped below five percent of its maximum value. It is assumed that the motions after this cutoff will not contribute significantly to the probability of exceeding the threshold; the validity of this assumption is verified through numerical analysis.

The time to failure is defined as the time required for the bending moment response process, $M(x,t)$, to exceed some member strength threshold. For the bolt yield and buckling limit states, failure is assumed to occur at the first upcrossing of the bending moment process over the corresponding member strength threshold, and the probability distribution for time to failure is determined.

**UPCROSSING ANALYSIS** The threshold crossing process is a two-state process. The structure is considered to be in State 0 when the earthquake bending moment response is below the member strength threshold and in State 1 when it is above the threshold. The distribution for the first upcrossing time, $t_1+$, is a function of the upcrossing rate or hazard function. The upcrossing hazard function is in turn a function of the zero crossing rate.

The rate at which the process $M(x,t)$ crosses the zero axis in either direction (i.e., has a zero crossing) is defined by (Cramér and Leadbetter, 1967):

$$\nu_0(t) = 2\left[\frac{\gamma(t)}{\sigma(t)}\right]\sqrt{1-\mu^2(t)}\;\phi^2(0) \tag{14a}$$

where $\phi(\bullet)$ is the standard normal density function and:

$$\sigma^2(t) = E\left[M^2(x_0,t)\right]; \quad \gamma^2(t) = E\left[\left[\frac{\partial M(x_0,t)}{\partial t}\right]^2\right]; \text{ and } \quad \mu(t) = \frac{E\left[M(x_0,t)\dfrac{\partial M(x_0,t)}{\partial t}\right]}{\sigma(t)\gamma(t)}$$

(14b,c&d)

The distance $x_0$ is the height from the base to the critical cross section for the limit state under consideration.

Corotis, et al. (1972) define a nonstationary hazard function for the two-state process. This hazard function determines the rate at which the process enters state 1 in the next increment of time, given that it has been in state 0 up to that time:

$$\alpha(t) = \nu_0(t)\left[\frac{1-\exp\left\{\dfrac{-\sqrt{2\pi}\,u(t)\delta(t)}{\sigma(t)}\right\}}{\exp\left\{\dfrac{u^2(t)}{2\sigma^2(t)}\right\}-1}\right] \tag{15a}$$

where

$$\delta(t) = \sqrt{1 - \mu^2(t)} \tag{15b}$$

and u(t) is the bending moment threshold for the limit state under consideration. For the bolt yield and buckling limit states, the thresholds are constants throughout the duration of the earthquake. However, in general the threshold u(t) can be a time-varying (e.g. deteriorating) function. Equation 15a considers the correlation or "clumping" of outcrossings characteristic of narrow-band processes. Equation 15a also considers the amount of time between upcrossings that is actually spent below the threshold. Thus, the hazard function is valid for both narrow and wide band response processes as well as a range of high and low threshold levels (Corotis, et al. 1972).

The derivation of $\alpha(t)$ assumes that the transition process from state 0 to state 1 is a nonhomogeneous Poisson process . It can be shown that the waiting time between events for both homogeneous and nonhomogeneous Poisson processes is exponentially distributed (Karlin and Taylor, 1975). Since the process is assumed to start in state 0, the probability distribution for the time to first upcrossing, $t_1+$, is exponential with parameter $\mu_+(t_1+)$ given by:

$$\mu_+(t_{1^+}) = \int_0^{t_{1^+}} \alpha(v)\, dv \tag{16}$$

Since failure is defined as the first threshold upcrossing, the time to failure is $t_1+$. Physically, this means that the bolt or skirt will fail the first time the earthquake loads exceed the bolt yield strength or buckling capacity of the column, respectively. For fatigue limit states, failure may not occur until the n-th crossing of the member strength threshold. The time to n-th crossing can be calculated as a function of both the upcrossing and the downcrossing processes (Nielsen, 1986).

**MEMBER STRENGTH THRESHOLDS** The two limit states of concern in this study are: yielding of the anchor bolts and buckling of the supporting skirt. Thus, a resistance threshold level is defined for each limit state. The bolt yield limit state will be exceeded when the applied bending moment due to ground shaking causes inelastic deformations in the anchor bolts. The relationship between the applied bending moment and the strains and stresses in the bolts can be approximately calculated from equilibrium conditions at the base of the column (Nielsen and Kiremidjian, 1986). Since the stresses are calculated at the base of the column, the distance $x_0$ in Eqs. 14b-d is zero for the bolt yield limit state.

The supporting skirt will buckle when the combined compressive stresses due to the weight of the column and the applied bending moment exceed the buckling capacity of the column. The buckling capacity can be found from classical buckling theory combined with experimental data. The uncertainty associated with the buckling capacity is significant therefore the buckling strength threshold is considered a random variable (Nielsen and Kiremidjian, 1986). For this limit state, the critical cross section is conservatively assumed to be located a distance equal to one-half the skirt radius above the base.

The incorporation of the member strength thresholds into the upcrossing analyses determines the probability distribution for the time to first upcrossing. If the time to failure is the only random variable in the limit state equation, the evaluation of Eq. 2 simplifies to:

$$P_f = F_{T_{1^+}}(t_{dur}) = 1 - \exp\left\{-\mu_+(t_{dur})\right\} \tag{17}$$

When variables in addition to the time to failure are considered random variables, the evaluation of Eq. 2 becomes more difficult. In this case, first order reliability methods or numerical simulation may be used. For the buckling limit state, the buckling strength threshold is a random variable. Hence the reliability analysis for this limit state is performed using first order reliability methods.

**NUMERICAL ANALYSIS** The column chosen as an example is a distilling tower from an oil refinery. Although a wide variety of columns are used in refineries, the configuration of this structure is typical for distilling columns. The column is 100 ft. (30.5 m) high and 6 ft. (1.83 m) in diameter. The distilling vessel is a cylindrical steel container which is supported by and welded to a cylindrical steel skirt. The skirt is in turn anchored to the reinforced concrete foundation by twelve mild steel (A307) anchor bolts. These bolts are 1-3/4 in. (4.45 cm) in diameter. The operating weight of the structure is 60 kips (267 kN).

Typical ground motion parameters were also defined for the analysis. The Kanai-Tajimi power spectral density parameters, $\omega_g$ and $\xi_g$, are assumed to be 20.3 rad/sec and 0.32, respectively. These are the mean values for 140 ground motion records reported by Lai (1982). The duration of ground motions is assumed to have a mean of 20 sec and a variance of 100 sec$^2$. These values are based on the statistical properties of several ground motion records reported by Saragoni and Hart (1972). The first two modes of vibration are assumed to dominate the response of the column, and the vertical acceleration intensity is assumed to be one-half of the horizontal acceleration (Penzien and Watabe, 1975).

The reliability analyses of the typical column are presented in the form of fragility curves for the limit states under consideration (Fig. 1). The failure probabilities shown in Fig. 1 are conditional on the intensity of the ground motions as measured by the power spectral density, $S_1$, of the unfiltered white noise acceleration process. The results in Fig. 1 clearly indicate that for a given intensity of ground motions the bolts are more likely to yield than the skirt is to buckle if the skirt is assumed to buckle before the bolts begin to yield. To determine the importance of duration in the bolt yield limit state, the analyses were repeated for a mean duration of 10 and 30 sec with the coefficient of variation of the duration kept at 50%. A comparison with the original analysis with a mean duration of 20 sec is shown in Fig. 2 which indicates that the probability of failure increases with increasing duration of ground motion. A similar analysis was performed neglecting vertical acceleration and the results are also shown in Fig. 2. It can be seen that vertical acceleration has a very small effect on the probability of failure.

## Conclusions

The reliability of tall columns subjected to earthquake ground motions can be calculated using a nonstationary stochastic response model which considers both vertical and horizontal ground motions. Numerical analyses reveal that for a typical distilling column, the bolts are likely to yield before the skirt buckles as assumed in the design process. Vertical acceleration is seen to have a very small effect on the reliability which also confirms design assumptions, however, duration has a significant effect on the probability of failure, but is ignored in the design of most structures including tall columns.

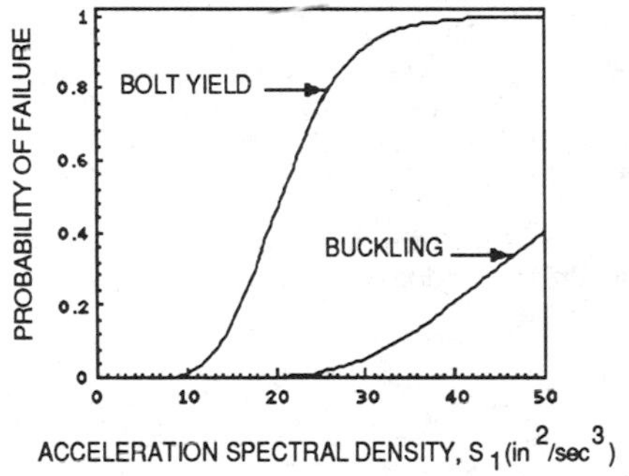


Fig. 1.–Buckling and Bolt Yield Fragility Curves

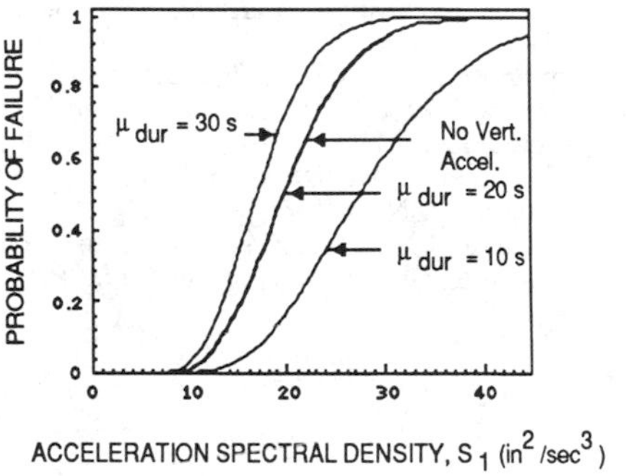


Fig. 2.–Bolt Yield Fragility Curve: Mean Duration = 10, 20 & 30 sec. and No Vertical Acceleration

ACKNOWLEDGEMENTS

The authors would like to gratefully acknowledge the insight provided by Mr. Ben Burke and Mr. Warren W. Mitchell of Chevron, Inc. The research presented in this study was supported by the National Science Foundation through grants No. CEE-8116997 and No. CEE-8400479.

REFERENCES

Corotis, R. B., E. H. Vanmarcke, and C. A. Cornell (1972). "First Passage of Nonstationary Random Processes," *Jour. of the Eng. Mech. Div., Proc. of the ASCE,* Vol. 98, No. EM2, pp. 401-414.

Cramér, H., and M. R. Leadbetter (1967). *Stationary and Related Stochastic Processes.* John Wiley & Sons, Inc., New York.

Donnell, L. H. (1934). "A New Theory for the Buckling of Thin Cylinders Under Axial Compression and Bending," *Trans. of the ASME,* Vol. 56, pp. 795-806.

Jazwinsky, A. H. (1970). *Stochastic Processes and Filtering Theory.* Academic Press, New York.

Kanai, K. (1957). "Semi-Empirical Formula for the Seismic Characteristics of the Ground," *Bull. of the Earthquake Eng. Res. Inst., Univ. of Tokyo.* No. 35. University of Tokyo.

Karlin, S., and H. M. Taylor (1975). *A First Course in Stochastic Processes, 2nd Edition.* Academic Press, New York.

Kircher, C. A., et al. (1978). *Seismic Analysis of Oil Refinery Structures, Part I - Experimental and Analytical Studies of Tall Columns.* J. A. Blume Earthquake. Eng. Ctr., Stanford, CA.

Lai, S. P. (1982). "Statistical Characterization of Strong Ground Motions Using Power Spectral Density Function," *Bull. of the Seis. Soc. of Am.,* Vol. 72, No. 1, pp. 259-274.

Lin, Y. K. (1967). *Probabilistic Theory of Structural Dynamics.* Robert E. Krieger Publishing Company, Malabar, Florida.

Nielsen, R. J. (1986). *Reliability of Tall Columns Subjected to Nonstationary Vertical and Horizontal Ground Motions.* Ph.D. dissertation, Stanford University, Stanford, CA.

Nielsen, R. J. and A. S. Kiremidjian (1986). "Reliability of Tall Columns Under Nonstationary Ground Motions: Model Formulation," paper submitted for publication.

Penzien, J. and M. Watabe (1975). "Characteristics of 3-Dimensional Earthquake Ground Motions," *Earthquake Eng. and Struct. Dyn.,* Vol. 3, pp. 365-373.

Saragoni, G. R. and G. C. Hart (1972). *Nonstationary Analysis and Simulation of Earthquake Ground Motions.* UCLA Earthquake Eng. and Struct. Lab. Report No. UCLA-ENG-7238.

Shih, T. Y. and Y. C. Chen (1984). "Stochastic Earthquake Response of Tapered Column." *Jour. of Eng. Mech.,* Vol. 110, No. 8, pp. 1185-1210.

Tajimi, H. (1960). "A Statistical Method of Determining the Maximum Response of a Building Structure During an Earthquake," *Proc. of the 2nd World Conf. on Earthquake Eng.* Vol. 11. Tokyo, Japan.

Vanmarcke, E. H. (1975). "On the Distribution of the First-Passage Time for Normal Stationary Random Processes," *Jour. of Applied Mech.,* Vol. 42, Series E, No. 1, pp. 215-220.

Vanmarcke, E. H. (1976). "Structural Response to Earthquakes." In *Seismic Risk and Engineering Decisions.* Ed. C. Lomnitz and E. Rosenblueth. Elsevier Scientific Publishing Company, New York.

Wong, E. and M. Zakai (1965). "On the Relation Between Ordinary and Stochastic Differential Equations," *Int. Jour. of Eng. Sci..* Pergamon Press, London, Great Britain

# FATIGUE DAMAGE PREDICTION FOR STATIONARY WIDEBAND RANDOM STRESSES

Keith Ortiz *
Nobel K. Chen **
* Assistant Professor, Aerospace and Mechanical Engineering Department, University of Arizona, Tucson, Arizona 85721
** Reliability Engineer, Electro-Motive Division, General Motors Corporation, Lagrange, Illinois 60525

## ABSTRACT

While there exists a well-known theoretical calculation for the fatigue damage due to stationary narrowband random stresses, there is no such result for wideband stresses. Previous approaches to the problem have sought empirical relations between the bandwidth of the stress process and the fatigue damage factor, which is the ratio of the wideband damage to the equivalent narrowband damage. The current paper presents a theoretical approach to an approximate distribution of wideband random stress cycles and to the corresponding theoretical damage factor. The damage factor is then compared to the results of computer simulations. It is shown that the theoretical damage factor is accurate and easy to apply to design problems.

## FATIGUE DAMAGE DUE TO NARROWBAND RANDOM STRESSES

Fatigue is often the principal mode of failure of structural components subjected to repeated random loadings. When the repeated stresses are of known constant amplitude $S$, fatigue life data is reported as the number of stress cycles, $N$, withstood by the component before failure occurs. The data is usually plotted as the exponential relationship:

$$K = NS^m \tag{1}$$

where $K$ and $m$ are empirical constants. When the repeated stresses are of variable amplitude, Miner's rule is applied as follows. Each cycle of stress, $S_i$ is assumed to contribute incremental damage to the component worth $1/N_i$, where $N_i$ is the number of stress cycles causing failure under constant amplitude loading conditions taken from the S-N curve, Equation (1). The incremental damages are summed to get the total accumulated damage, $D$:

$$D = \sum_{i=1}^{N_T} \frac{1}{N_i} \tag{2}$$

where $N_T$ is the total number of stress cycles in time $T$. Fatigue failure theoretically occurs when the accumulated damage reaches unity.

The fatiguing loadings imposed on many structural components commonly arise from random vibrations. Under these conditions the fatigue damage is a random variable. The expected damage is:

$$E[D] = \frac{1}{K} \nu_0 T \; E[S^m] \tag{3}$$

where $\nu_0$ is the expected rate of zero crossings with positive slope and $T$ is the duration of the loading, that is, the product $\nu_0 T$ equals the number of stress cycles in time $T$. The expected value of $S^m$, $E[S^m]$, is most vital to this calculation.

The case in which the random loading is stationary, narrowband, and Gaussian with a mean of zero, has been thoroughly investigated [e.g., Crandall and Mark, 1963]. In this case, the stress cycle ranges are clearly defined. They have a Rayleigh distribution:

$$f_S(s) = \frac{s}{\theta_{nb}^2} \exp\left[-\frac{1}{2}\frac{s^2}{\theta_{nb}^2}\right] \tag{4}$$

The parameter of the distribution, $\theta_{nb}$, is given by:

$$\theta_{nb} = 2\sigma_X \tag{5}$$

where $\sigma_X$ is the variance of the stress process. It is easily shown that the expected value of $S^m$ is:

$$E[S_{nb}^m] = (2\sqrt{2}\sigma_X)^m \, \Gamma(\frac{m}{2} + 1) \tag{6}$$

where $\Gamma(\cdot)$ is the gamma function. The expected damage in the narrowband case is thus:

$$E[D_{nb}] = \frac{1}{K} \nu_0 T \, (\sqrt{2}\sigma_X)^m \, \Gamma(\frac{m}{2} + 1) \tag{7}$$

## THE WIDEBAND CASE

For the case in which the random loading is wideband, it is much more difficult to calculate the expected damage. A common practical approach to the wideband problem is to calculate the *equivalent narrowband damage,* which is the damage calculated by Equation 7 without regard to either the correct number of stress cycles or their true distribution. Consideration of these effects shows that this approach leads to conservative designs, i.e., the equivalent narrowband damage is more severe than the actual wideband damage.

The correct expected number of stress cycles in a wideband process is $\nu_p T$, where $\nu_p$ is the expected rate of peaking. The expected number of cycles in a wideband process is greater than in a narrowband process with the same variance. This tends to make the wideband damage larger than the equivalent narrowband damage. The ratio of the expected rate (or number) of zero crossings with positive slope to the expected rate (or number) of peaks is called the *irregularity factor,* $\alpha = \nu_0 / \nu_p$, and may be calculated from the moments of the one-sided spectral density function, $G_X(\omega)$, by:

$$\alpha = \left[\frac{m_2^2}{m_0 m_4}\right]^{1/2} \tag{8}$$

where $m_k$ $(k = 0,2,4)$ is the k-th moment given by:

$$m_k = \int_0^\infty \omega^k \, G_X(\omega) \, d\omega \tag{9}$$

The true distribution of wideband stress cycles is unknown. The primary reason for this lack of knowledge is that the wideband stress cycles are not readily identifiable. Fatigue experts currently think that a heuristic algorithm known as rainflow cycle counting [Matsuishi and Endo, 1968] is the best way to count wideband stresses. However, the algorithm cannot be described by a mathematical equation. Furthermore, the true distribution of rainflow cycles is likely to be bimodal. This can be seen by considering the result of adding two narrowband random processes together, one with low-amplitude and high-frequency and the other with high-amplitude and low-frequency. The rainflow stress cycles will tend to form two modes in the distribution: one mode for the many small cycles arising from the high-frequency process and the other mode for the fewer, but larger, cycles arising from the low-frequency process. The upper tail of this bimodal distribution will follow a Rayleigh distribution approximately, but one with a parameter smaller than $\theta_{nb}$.

In any case, it is known that the wideband stress cycles are generally smaller than the equivalent narrowband cycles, so that $E[S_{wb}^m]$ is less than $E[S_{nb}^m]$. This tends to make the wideband damage less. Finally, the smaller $E[S_{wb}^m]$ tends to reduce the wideband damage more than the larger $\nu_p T$ increases it. Therefore, the wideband fatigue damage is less than the narrowband damage, $E[D_{wb}]<E[D_{nb}]$.

## THE DAMAGE FACTOR APPROACH

Lacking a theoretical distribution for $S$, Wirsching and Light [1979] took an empirical approach to determine $E[D_{wb}]$ directly. They performed simulations of random processes with various bandwidths and calculated the fatigue damage for each simulation by both the rainflow and the equivalent narrowband methods. The ratio of the wideband damage to the equivalent narrowband damage called the *rainflow damage factor*, $\lambda$, was calculated for each simulation:

$$\lambda = E[D_{wb}] / E[D_{nb}] \tag{10}$$

The rainflow damage factors were then fit to polynomial functions of bandwidth. Wirsching and Light determined the equations:

$$\lambda_{WL} = a + (1-a)(1-\epsilon)^b \tag{11}$$

$$a = 0.926 - 0.033m \tag{12}$$

$$b = 1.587m - 2.323 \tag{13}$$

where $\epsilon$ is the spectral bandwidth, $\epsilon = \sqrt{1-\alpha^2}$, and $m$ is the slope of the S-N curve. This result is plotted in Figure 1.

Figure 1 also includes the results of simulations performed by Lutes et al. [1984]. It is apparent that Equations (11), (12) and (13) inadequately describe the additional data. Given the poor performance of the standard bandwidth measures, $\alpha$ and $\epsilon$, Lutes et al. suggested that the rainflow damage factor might be a function of an adjustable bandwidth factor, $\beta_b$:

$$\beta_b = \left[ \frac{m_b{}^2}{m_0 m_{2b}} \right]^{1/2} \tag{14}$$

where $m_b$ is the b-th moment of the one-sided power spectral density function. Note that $b=2$ results in $\beta_{b=2} = \alpha$, the irregularity factor, and $b=1$ results in $\beta_{b=1} = \delta$,

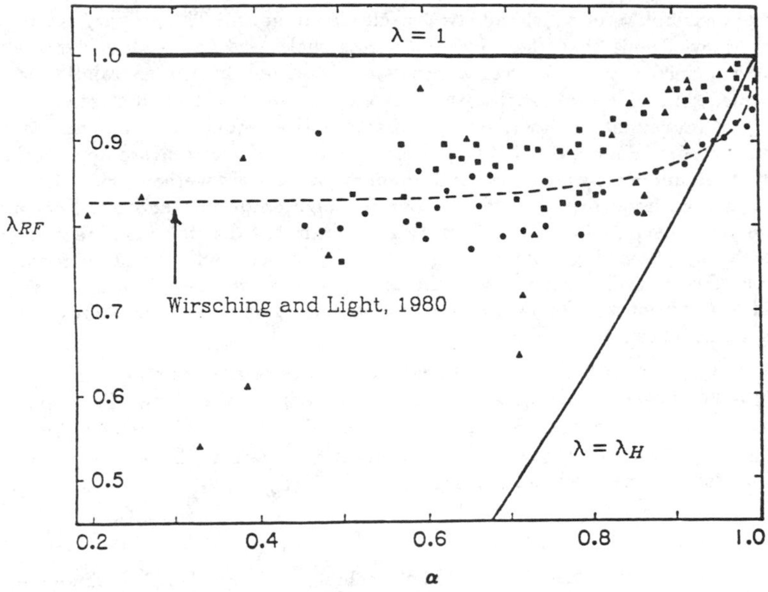


Figure 1 Rainflow Damage Factor, $\lambda$, vs. Irregularity Factor, $\alpha$. (Reproduced from Lutes et al. [1984])

a bandwidth measure defined by Vanmarcke [1972]. Their study found that, given $m$, $b$ can be optimized to produce a linear relationship between $\lambda$ and $\beta_b$, which fits the data with less error than Wirsching and Light's equations. However, the optimum value of $b$ for different values of $m$ is completely unpredictable and, therefore, useless for design.

## A THEORETICAL DAMAGE FACTOR

Ortiz (1985) showed that the heights of the rises or falls, $H$, of a stationary Gaussian process have, approximately, a Rayleigh distribution with parameter, $\theta_H$, given by:

$$\theta_H = 2\sigma_X \alpha \tag{15}$$

Adopting this distribution as the distribution of wideband stress cycles results in the following expected fatigue damage:

$$E[D_H] = \frac{1}{K} \nu_p T \, (\sqrt{2}\sigma_X \alpha)^m \, \Gamma(\frac{m}{2} + 1) \tag{16}$$

From Equations (7), (10) and (16), the corresponding damage factor is:

$$\lambda_H = \frac{\nu_p}{\nu_0} \alpha^m \tag{17}$$

Realizing that $\nu_p / \nu_0 = 1/\alpha$, this equation becomes:

$$\lambda_H = \alpha^{m-1} \tag{18}$$

A plot of this damage factor is also shown in Figure 1. It is obviously much too small, but it suggests another line of reasoning.

Since the cycles from the upper tail of the distribution are the ones that cause the most fatigue damage, it is reasonable to suppose that the rainflow stress cycle ranges follow a Rayleigh distribution similar to that for $H$ described above, at least in the upper tail. Let the parameter of the distribution be $\theta_k$, given by:

$$\theta_k = 2\sigma_X \beta_k \tag{19}$$

where $\beta_k$ is an adjustable bandwidth measure and is defined by:

$$\beta_k = \left[\frac{m_2 m_k}{m_0 m_{k+2}}\right]^{1/2} \tag{20}$$

One might think of this as the ratio of the expected rate of zero-crossings, $\nu_0$, to the expected rate of some arbitrary event, $\nu_k$, i.e., $\beta_k = \nu_0 / \nu_k$. Note that $k=2$ implies $\beta_{k=2} = \alpha$, so $\nu_{k=2}$ equals the expected rate of peaking, $\nu_p$. Also, $k=0$ implies $\beta_{k=0} = 1$, so $\nu_{k=0}$ equals the expected rate of zero-crossings, $\nu_0$.

Analogous to Equation (17) the rainflow damage factor corresponding to this distribution is:

$$\lambda_k = \beta_k^m / \alpha \tag{21}$$

Note that here k = 2 leads to $\lambda_{k=2} = \lambda_H$ and k = 0 to $\lambda_{k=0} = 1$. Thus, $\beta_k$ allows for a smooth transition of $\lambda_k$ from $\lambda_H$ to 1, which appear to be the bounds of most of the data in Figure 1. Using $\lambda_k$, it may be possible to find values of $k$ $(0<k<2)$ which lead to better fits.

## COMPARISON WITH SIMULATIONS

The simulation results of Wirsching and Light [1979] and Lutes et al. [1984] were re-analzed in light of the above discussion. For a given value of $m$, the optimum value of $k$ was determined by minimizing the sum of the squared errors (SSE) of the least squares fit of Equation (21) to the data. Figure 2 shows the typical behavior of SSE as a function of $k$. Figure 3 shows a plot of the optimum regression ($k=0.76$) for $m=3$. These optimum fits are excellent when compared with either of the two previous methods.

Further, plotting $k$ as a function of $m$, as shown in Figure 4, results in the relationship:

$$\log k = \log 2.0 - 0.89 \log m \tag{22}$$

As the sample size of this study is small, the authors recommend the following convenient and conservative (in the design sense) simplification:

$$k = 2/m \tag{23}$$

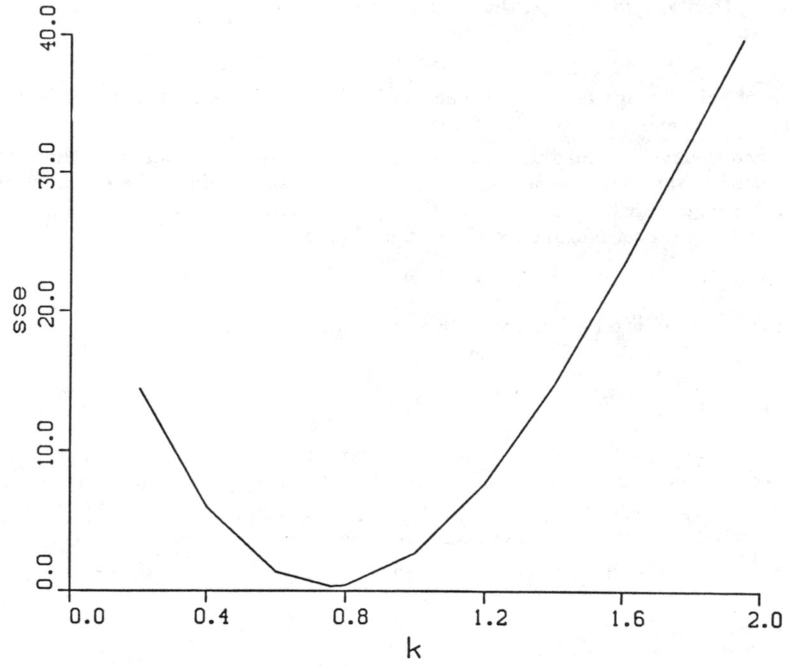


Figure 2 Typical Plot of SSE vs. $k$.

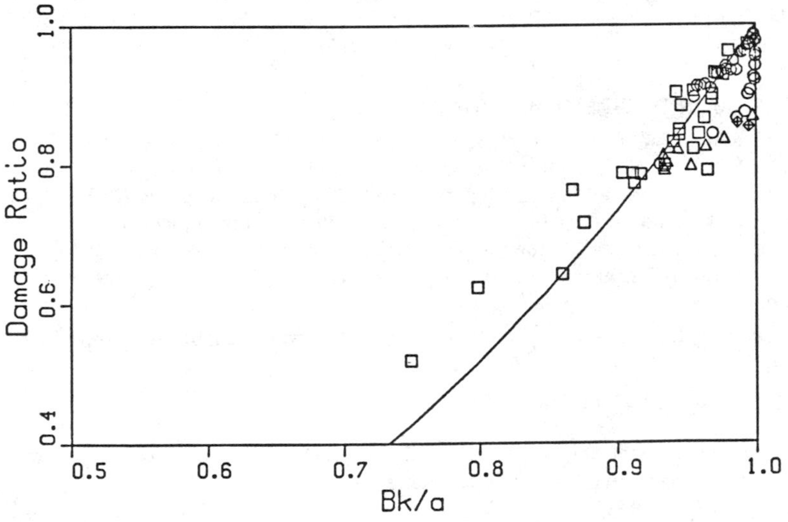


Figure 3 Rainflow Damage Factor, $\lambda$, vs. Adjustable Bandwidth Factor, $\beta_k$. (Actually, $\beta_k / \alpha^{1/m} = \lambda_k^{1/m}$, is plotted, rather than $\beta_k$ itself.)

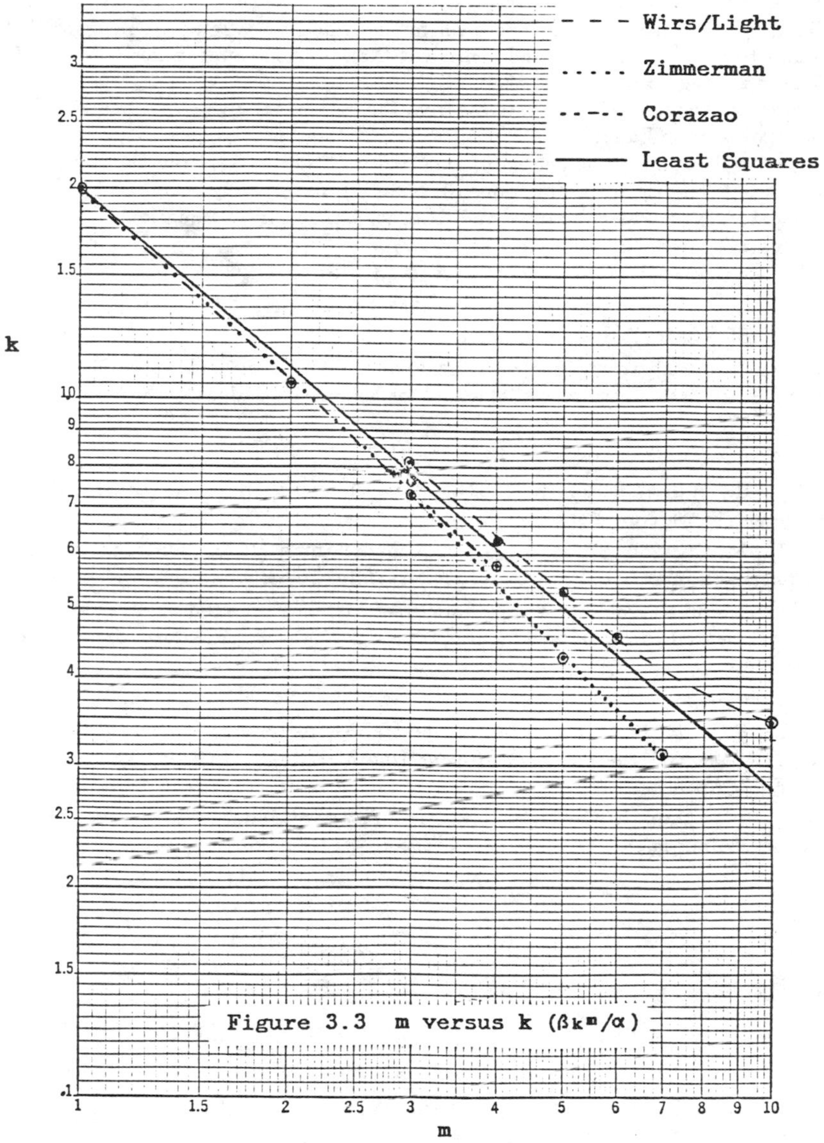


Figure 4 Optimum Values of $k$ vs. $m$.

## SUMMARY

This paper has described an approach to the wideband fatigue problem which has been found to be more accurate and consistent than previous approaches. To use these equations in a design problem one would:

(1) Determine the value of $m$ of interest from the S-N curve.
(2) Calculate $k$ from Equation (23).
(3) Calculate the spectral moments, $m_0$, $m_2$, $m_4$, $m_k$, and $m_{k+2}$, from Equation (9).
(4) Calculate $\alpha$ and $\beta_k$ from Equations (8) and (20), respectively.
(5) Calculate the equivalent narrowband damage, $E[D_{nb}]$, from Equation (7).
(6) Calculate $\lambda_k$ from Equation (21).
(7) Calculate the wideband damage from $E[D_{wb}] = \lambda_k \; E[D_{nb}]$.

## ACKNOWLEDGEMENTS

The authors wish to thank Professors Paul H. Wirsching and Loren D. Lutes for making their simulation results available and for helpful discussions.

## REFERENCES

Crandall, S.H., and W.D. Mark (1963). *Random Vibration in Mechanical Systems,* Academic Press, New York.

Lutes, L.D., M. Corazao, S-L.J. Hu, and J.J. Zimmerman (1984). "Stochastic Fatigue Damage Accumulation," *Journal of the Structural Division,* ASCE, November.

Matsuishi, M., and T. Endo (1968). "Fatigue of Metals Subjected to Varying Stress," paper presented to Japan Society of Mechanical Engineers, Fukuoka, Japan, March.

Ortiz, K. (1985). "On the Stochastic Modeling of Fatigue Crack Growth," Ph.D. Dissertation, Stanford University.

Vanmarcke, E.H. (1972). "Properties of Spectral Moments with Applications to Random Vibrations," *Journal of the Engineering Mechanics Division,* ASCE, Vol. 98, No. EM2, April, pp. 425-446.

Wirsching, P.H., and M.C. Light (1980). "Fatigue Under Wide Band Random Stresses," *Journal of the Structural Division,* ASCE, Vol. 106, No. ST7, July, pp. 1593-1607.

# TRANSIENT RESPONSE OF THREE-DIMENSIONAL LINEAR STRUCTURES TO STOCHASTIC SEISMIC EXCITATIONS

S. Barel* , A. Bernardini* , O. Bursi** , C. Modena*
*Istituto di Scienza e Tecnica delle Costruzioni - University of Padova, via Marzolo, 9 - 35131 PADOVA, ITALY
**Faculty of Engineering- University of Trento
Mesiano di Povo - 38100 TRENTO, ITALY

## ABSTRACT

A numerical procedure to evaluate peack values statistics of the transient response of linear structures to stochastic three-dimensional seismic excitations is presented. Some derived results regarding the response of multi-floors building constructions are discussed with reference to current design code provisions.

## INTRODUCTION

The dynamic analysis of structural systems subjected to seismic action is generally performed in the design practice, when required by the Codes, assuming linear elastic models and adopting simplified rules derived from the modal superposition technique. The assumption that "regular" structures should be designed in seismic zones is made in such Codes.

Gross semplifications are apparently introduced in such design approach, when complex three-dimensional structures and the actual nature of the excitation are taken into account. Such simplifications are not only due to the effects of the inelastic behaviour of the structure during strong earthquakes, usually taken into account by means of simple coefficients assigned for each particular structural typology, but also to the difficulty to calculate with sufficient approximation by means of simplified rules the elastic response.

In some recent research works (Der Kiureghian 1980, Smeby and Der Kiureghian, 1982 ) the stochastic dynamic analysis technique of threedimensional structures has been used to estimate the statistics of peack response parameters and then to derive some improvements of the commonly used procedures.

The seismic action is represented by a stationary Gaussian process, applied to the structure for a limited time duration, during which the response process also is supposed stationary. Three simultaneous traslational components of the ground motion are considered, uncorrelated only along a particular set of orthogonal directions, called principal directions, according to the model proposed by Penzien and Watabe (1975). The effect of the angle between the horizontal principal directions of the ground motion and the principal directions of the structural system, and then of the correlation between the motion components, is taken into account.

Such analyses mainly suggest that the three-dimensional characteristics of the ground motion and the correlation between the modal responses should not be disregarded in the design procedures.

In fact in some recent proposals ( ATC, 1978 ; GNDT, 1985) for new seismic Code two horizontal components of the ground motion are considered, combining the maximum intensity in the unfavourable direction with a reduced (30%) component in the orthogonal direction. Moreover for each direction the well-known "square root of the sum of the squares" rule has been modified when the relative difference between the eigen-periods is less than 10% (GNDT,1985).

Some other aspects of the excitation however could significantly influence the response of the considered linear systems, e.g. particularly the transient phase of the response process and the frequency content of the excitation.

Analyses of actual accelerograms recorded in different countries, for example by Vanmarcke (1983 ) for US accelerograms and by Bernardini and Modena (1986) for italian accelerograms, give values of the equivalent duration of the ground motion stationary process varying in a very large range, mainly from 2 to 15 s . Particularly for the shortest durations, the characteristics of the initial and final not-stationary phases could be of interest.

The frequency content corresponding to the different response spectra shapes given by the Codes or corresponding to excitations generated in different soil condition and/or at different epicentral distances, should be examined.

Usually in the proposed methodologies the transient phase of the response is ignored or treated in a simplified approximate manner, and particular frequency content distributions are considered, allowing simplified or closed form solutions.

The results obtained using linear models should also be compared to the actual responses of structural systems when not-linear behaviour is attended for long return period earthquakes ( as usually for building constructions).

In such cases Montecarlo analyses of the response time-histories of the non linear structures subjected to deterministic eccitations or stochastic dinamic analyses of equivalent linear structures (Park, Wen and Ang, 1986) seem to be the more attractive methods.

The present paper describes the first results of a research program on the described items, regarding particularly the numerical stochastic analysis of the transient response and some derived results regarding the spatial response of multi-floors building constructions.

## NUMERICAL PROCEDURE

The program performs random dynamic analyses in the frequency domain of three dimensional structures. Modal shapes and frequencies of the examined structures are furnished by the general purpose program SAP IV and, for the typical mixed frame-shear walls structures of buildings, by the program ETABS.

The seismic excitation is given as a multidirectional non-stationary gaussian process. Non-stationarity is obtained modulating a stationary process by means of any deterministic time function, numerically or analitically defined.

The power spectral density function of the stationary process can be assigned numerically and analitically, or it can be derived from a given response spectrum or accelerogram.

When a response spectrum is available, the simplification suggested by Vanmarcke (1976) for the calculation of the response variance and peack factors, adopted for example in (Gasparini and Vanmarcke, 1976; Romo-Organista, 1980), are used. They allow in particular to take into account approximately the effect of the transient phase of the response.

Vanmarcke's proposals (1983) are also adopted to derive the power spectral density function from a given accelerogram. In this case the Fourier Transform $A(\omega)$ of the accelerogram is used for the calculation of the Aria's intensity

$$I_0=(1/\pi)_0\int^{\infty}A^2(\omega)d\omega \qquad (1)$$

and of the spectral parameters, derived from spectral moments:

$$\Omega=(\lambda_2/\lambda_0)^{1/2} \quad ; \quad \delta=(1-\lambda_1^2/(\lambda_2\lambda_0))^{1/2} \qquad (2)$$

respectively the center frequency and a measure of the spectral bandwidht, which don't depend on the strong motion duration

$$s_0=I_0/\sigma_0^2=r^2(s_0,p)\ I_0/a_{max}^2 \qquad (3)$$

where $\sigma_0^2$ is the variance and $r(s_0,p)$ the peack factor of the motion process; $a_{max}$ is the maximum value of the given accelerogram and it is assumed that it represents the peack value with a not exceeding probability $p$ equal to 0.5 in the process.

The duration is on the contrary necessary for the evaluation of the power spectral density function $G(\omega)$ , and can be obtained by means of an iterative evaluation of the peack factor through the relation (Vanmarcke, 1976)

$$r(s_0,p)=\{2\ln[(2\Omega s_0)/(-\pi\ \ln p)(1-\exp(-\ \delta^{1+b}(\pi\ln(2\Omega s_0/(-\pi\ \ln p)))^{1/2}))]\}^{1/2} \qquad (4)$$

The Penzien-Watabe model is used to describe the multi-directional nature of the ground motion. The existence of three not correlated orthogonal components of the motion, one of which pratically the vertical, is assumed; the ratios between their intensities are 0.75 and 0.5 respectively for the horizontal components and for the vertical component and the principal direction ( usually the direction of the line connecting the site with the epicenter).

The frequency content and the modulating time function $\zeta$ generally are assumed constant in the different directions; however if data should be available, they could be specified for the three principal directions.

Transient response is evaluated for each selected response displacement integrating numerically the exact expressions of the autocorrelation function

$$R_r(t_1,t_2)=\Sigma_i\Sigma_j\psi_{ir}\psi_{jr}\ {}_0\int^{\infty}G(\omega)M_i(t_1,\omega)M_j^*(t_2,\omega)d\omega \qquad (5)$$

$$M_k(t,\omega)={}_0\int^{t}\zeta(\tau)h_k(t-\tau)\exp(-i\omega\tau)d\tau$$

and of its time derivatives giving the required spectral moments.

Remarkable time computation saving is obtained by the repeated use of the FFT techniques to evaluate the values of .

The cross-correlation between the different modal responses is considered combining all the modes with frequencies in the range from 0.25 to 4 times the frequency of the considered mode. Very slight approximation is in such a way introduced for the usually considered values of the damping factor.

The peack response analysis considers the transient phase

using the expression given by Vanmarcke of the time dependent probability of exceeding a choiced treshold level a , taking into account that the barrier crossings distribution is not poissonian

$$L(t,a)=\exp\{-{}_0\int^t 2\upsilon_0(\tau)[1-\exp(-(\pi/2)^{1/2}a\delta(\tau)/\sigma(\tau))]/[\exp(a^2/(2\sigma^2(\tau)))-1]d\tau\} \qquad (6)$$

where $\upsilon_0$ is the number of zero crossings per unit time. The integration is performed by means of the tenth order Gauss formula, so that the exact values of the functions to be integrated are evaluated in the corresponding Gauss points.

The procedure proposed by Der Kiureghian to determine the value of the angle between the principal directions of the motions and of the buildings maximizing the mean maximum response of any degree of freedom is here extended to analyse not stationary response processes and any value of exceeding probability. The maximum value of the not stationary response variance with respect to such angle is iteratively evaluated; numerical calculations demonstrated in fact that the peack factors only slightly depend on the angle.

NUMERICAL EXAMPLES

The automatic procedure has been tested by comparison (Bernardini and Modena, 1986) with the results published by various authors, in particular Gasparini (1980), Madsen and Krenk (1980) for not stationary process and Smeby and Der Kiureghian (1982) for stationary process.

Some results of the numerical applications are described in the following.

A typical spatial structure is examined, with frames and shear walls systems, considering the effects of irregular distributions of resisting elements.

Analyses are performed deriving power density spectra from the pseudoacceleration response spectrum proposed by GNDT (1985) for stiff soil (type S1), considering different values of the duration and a box-type modulating time function. The considered spectrum corresponds to a not exceeding probability equal to 0.5.

In Fig. 1 the plan distribution of the resisting elements of the six floors examined structure is shown (Structure Type 0).

In structure types 1 and 2 infilled masonry walls are added as schematically indicated in Figs. 2a and 2b. Height irregularities are considered in structure type 3 (Fig. 2c), where the shadowed zone and the reinforced concrete core of the elevator are four storey heigth.

In Fig. 3 the treshold levels of the displacements of the mass center and of the rotation of every floor, computed for a not exceeding probability equal to 0.5 during the strong motion duration, and for the above mentioned critical value of the principal direction of the motion, are compared for structure types 0, 1, 2.

Strong motion durations equal to 5 and 15s were examined; in this case differences are of course negligible.

The important effects of the infilled masonry walls on the response are clearly shown in the figure.

In Figs. 4, 5 and 6 , respectively for strucure types 0, 1, 3, the treshold levels of the same parameters corresponding to not exceeding probabilities equal to 0.5 and 0.9 and 15s duration, are compared with the results of the analyses performed according to the spectral composition rules given by the present Italian Code (where the modal correlation and multidirectional charateristics of the ground motion are ignored) and by the new GNDT proposal.

The frequencies of the first five modes here considered for the calculation of the response are in all cases enough spaced to avoid sensible effect of their correlation. The response calculated according to the Italian Code is generally about 20-30% less than the threshold levels Pr = 0.5; closer values to such levels are obtained with the consideration, in the GNDT proposal, of a reduced (30%) orthogonal component of the ground motion.

Residual, generally unsafe differences appear however in the figures, especially in the case of height irregularities (structure type 3, in fig. 6).

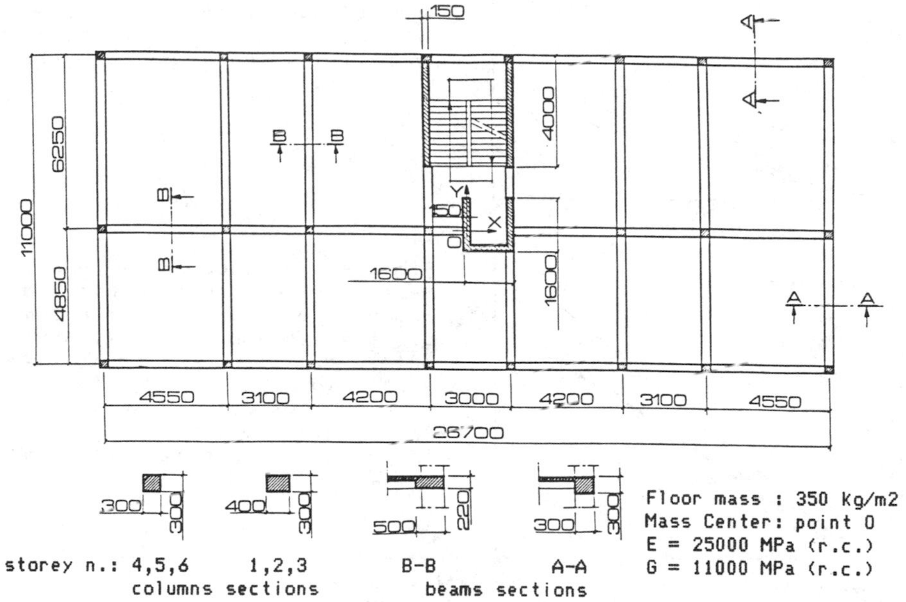


Fig. 1 . Geometrical characteristics of structure type 0

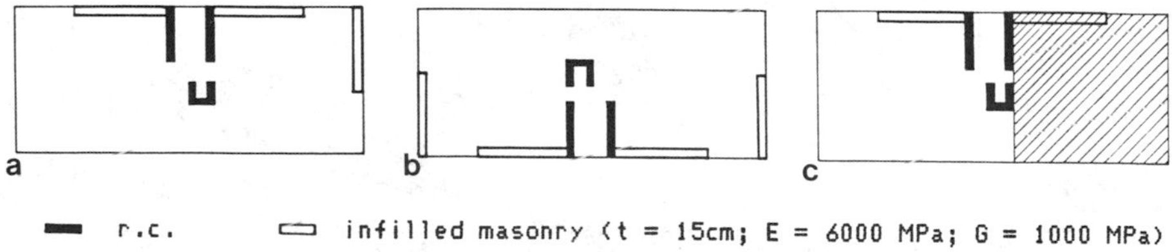


Fig. 2 . Wall distribution in structures types 1(a), 2(b), 3(c)

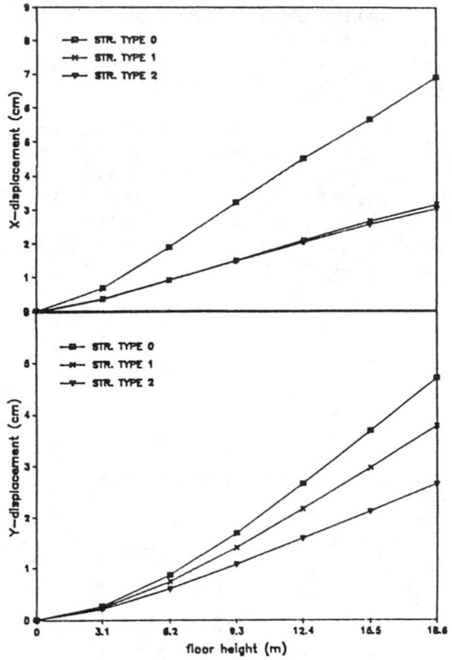


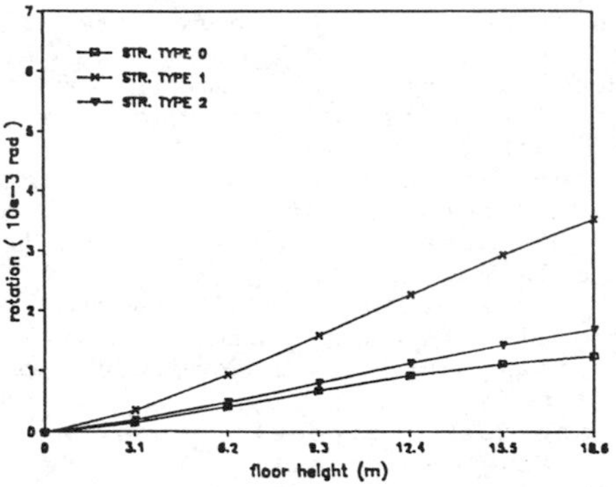


Fig. 3 . Treshold levels of the mass center displacements and of the floor rotations with not exceeding probability equal to 0.5 (15 s duration)

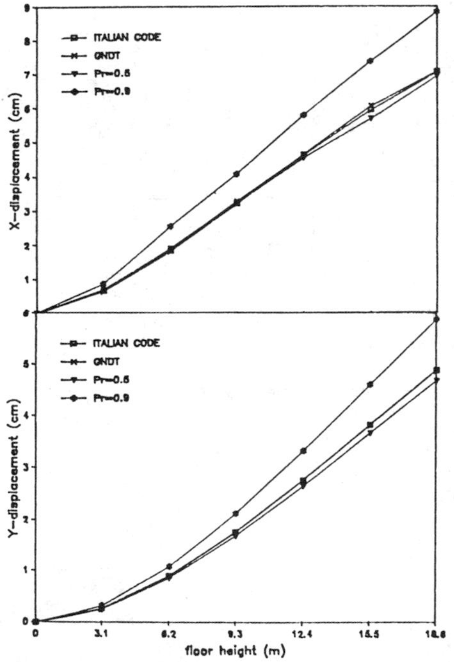


Fig. 4 . Structure type 0 . Mass center displacements and floor rotations: comparison of the treshold levels with not exceeding probability equal to 0.5 and 0.9 with the response calculated according the rules given by (GNDT, 1986) and present Italian Code.

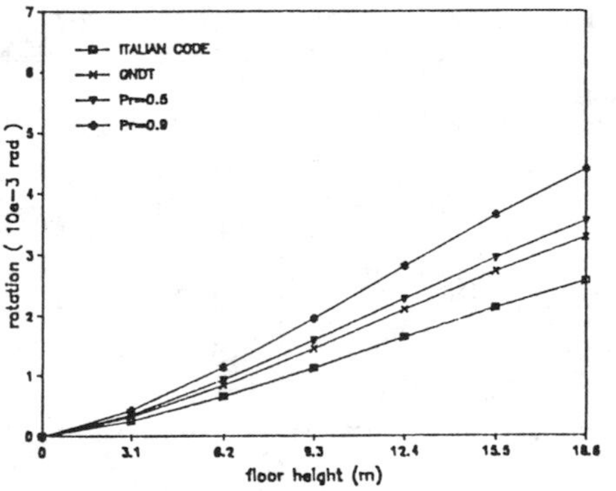

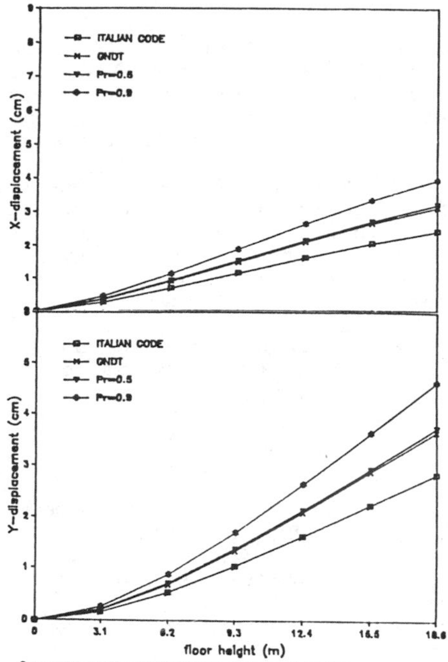


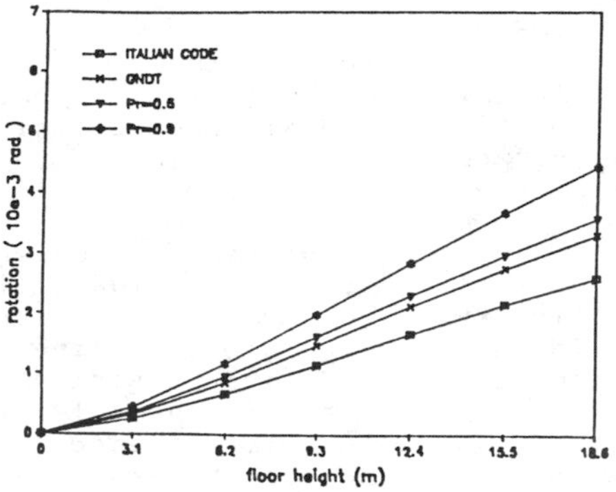


Fig. 5 . Structure type 1 . Mass center displacements and floor rotations: comparison of the treshold levels with not exceeding probability equal to 0.5 and 0.9 with the response calculated according the rules given by (GNDT, 1986) and present Italian Code.

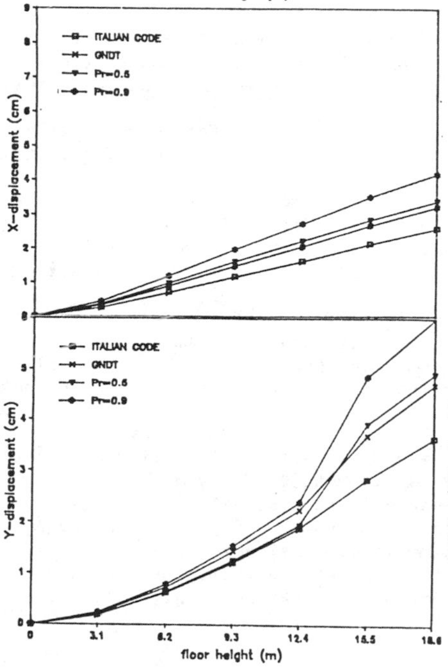


Fig. 6 . Structure type 3 . Mass center displacements and floor rotations: comparison of the treshold levels with not exceeding probability equal to 0.5 and 0.9 with the response calculated according the rules given by (GNDT, 1986) and present Italian Code

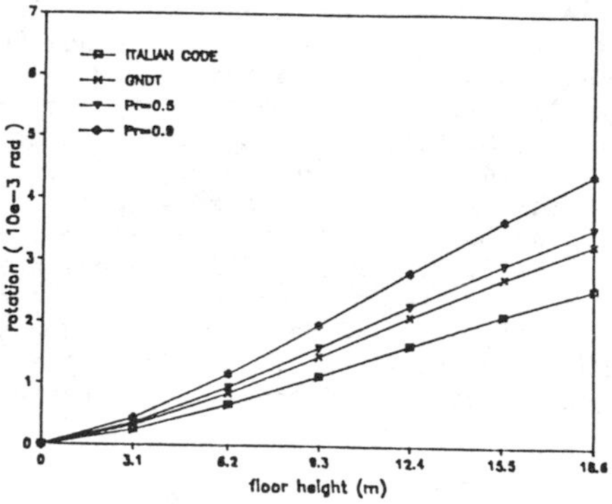

## CONCLUSIONS

A numerical procedure for estimating statistics of peack values of the transient response of linear structures subjected to multidirectional ground motions, also considering the most unfavourable value of the angle between the principal directions of the excitation and of the structure, has been implemented on a computer program.

The program proved to be an efficient tool for a systematic investigation on the actual linear behaviour of complex, and particularly irregular, structures. In a case of a multi-floors building construction, where plant and height irregular distributions of the resisting elements are introduced, the relevant effects of the multidirectional characteristics of the motion have been demonstrated.

Some new design rules introduced in recent Codes to combine the effects of the two horizontal components of the ground motion are justified for the considered structural typology.

## REFERENCES


Applied Technology Council (ATC) (1978). "Tentative provisions for the development of seismic regulations of buildings", ATC Report n. 3-06

Bernardini A. and Modena C. (1986). "Reliability analyses of constructions under seismic actions", Proceeding International Workshop on Engin. Aspects of Earthq. Phenomena, Oxford

Der Kiureghian A. (1980). "A response spectrum method for random vibrations", EERC , Report 80/15, Berkeley, California

Gruppo Nazionale per la Difesa dai Terromoti (GNDT) (1985). "Norme tecniche per le costruzioni in zone sismiche", Ingegneria Sismica, I. R. , n. 1

Gasparini D. A. and Debohaudry A. (1980). "Dynamic response to nonstationary nonwhite excitations", Journ. of the Eng. Mech. Division, ASCE, vol. 106, EM6

Gasparini D. A. and Vanmarcke E. H. (1976). "Simulated earthquake motions compatible wuth prescribed response spectra", MIT, Dpt. of Civil Eng., Pub. n. R76-4, Cambridge, Massachussets, January

Madsen P. H. and Krenk S. (1980). "Stationary and transient response statistics", Danish Center for applied Math. and Mech., Rep. n. 194

Park Y. J., Wen Y. K. and Ang H. S. (1986). "Random vibration of hysteretic systems under bi-directional ground motions", Earthq. Eng. and Structural Dynamics, v. 14, 553-557

Penzien J. and Watabe M. (1975). "Characteristics of threedimensional earthquake ground motions", Earthq. Eng. and Structural Dynamics, v. 3

Romo-Organista M. P. (1980). "PLUSH . A computer program for probabilistic analysisis of response of seismic soil-structure interaction", EERC Report 77/01, Berkeley, California

Smeby W. and Der Kiureghian A. (1982). "Stochastic analysis of response of structures and multiple supported secondary systems to multidirectional ground motions", Det Norske Veritas, Rep. n. 82-0510, Oslo, Norway

Vanmarcke E. H. (1976). "Structural response to earthquake", in "Seismic risk and engineering decisions", chapt. 8, Lomnitz C. and Rosenblueth E. Editors, Elsevier Scient. Publ. Comp., Amsterdam, Netherlands

Vanmarcke E. H. (1983). "Efficient stochastic representation of earthquake ground motions", Proceedings IV Canadian Conf. on Earthq. Eng., Vancouver

EQUIVALENT CRITERIA IN ACCEPTANCE TESTING

J.J. Salinas * and R.G. Gillard **

* Dept. of Civil Eng. Carleton University, Ottawa, Canada K1S 5B6
** Manhire Cunliffe Partnership, Ottawa, Canada, K2A 3X9

ABSTRACT

If the damage accumulated in a structure under a known load history, after time t , is equal to the damage accumulated under a different load history, after time t , the two load histories are assumed to be 'equivalent' at this point. In this study, the concept of 'equivalence' is used to compare different test procedures. A small number of Waferboard I beams were tested using the Canada Mortgage and Housing Corporation (CMHC) load test procedure for floor framing systems and their damage level determined using currently accepted theory. Similar specimens were tested using a short duration ramp load to failure and their damage level determined and compared with that of specimens tested using the CMHC test procedure.

This investigation suggests that the results of the CMHC test procedure can be predicted from short-duration ramp load tests. This 'equivalent' procedure offers significant economies and simplicity in testing.

INTRODUCTION

Acceptance testing of engineered wood products is commonly used to evaluate the performance of floor systems for residential and small buildings. The test procedures currently used face the difficult task of having to determine the stiffness as well as the strength characteristics of structural elements which exhibit complex interactions between two or more constitutive materials. these materials could be: solid lumber, reconstituted wood products, metal plates and metal webs. Acceptance testing procedures tend to be elaborate, time consuming, costly and, in the opinion of some producers, inordinately strict.

The role of the intensity and duration of the test load has been discussed in detail by Duchesne (1980) and Duchesne and Salinas (1984). In order to resist the prescribed test loads, engineered wood systems must have a strength which results in levels of structural reliability considerably higher than those associated with other materials or systems (Salinas, 1979). In an effort to find faster, simpler and more economical performance testing procedures the authors propose the use of the concept of 'equivalence' in damage accumulation modelling. This concept permits us to assess alternate testing procedures and to compare them with standard procedures currently in use.

DAMAGE ACCUMULATION

A damage accumulation model, based upon creep rupture theory, is an analytical tool used to account for the 'load duration' effects in lumber. In general terms, this theory states that failure under a constant load, for long durations, will occur at a load level below that required to produce failure in a short-term test. Based on the work by Barrett and Foschi (1978a and 1978b), the damage accumulated at time T under a given load history can be calculated by Equation (1).

$$\alpha(T) = e^{cT} \int_0^T a[\sigma(t) - \sigma_0]e^{-ct}dt \quad (1)$$

The model parameters a,b and c are determined by calibration with experimental results by assuming that damage equals 1.0 for a time under load equal to the mean time to failure. The values used in this study are $a = 0.11 \times 10 \ hr^{-1}$, $b = 34.2$, $c = 0.00079$ which were found by Barrett and Foschi (1978a and 1978b) for small clear Douglas Fir specimens. The load history represented by $\sigma(t)$ is given as a 'stress ratio' obtained by dividing the load-induced stress by the short-term strength. The 'treshold' stress ratio, $\sigma_o$, corresponds to a load-induced stress below which no damage occurs. For this study the threshold stress ratio was assumed to be 0.20.

Gillard (1986) calculates the total damage at time $T_2$, knowing the damage accumulated up to time $T_1$ using Equation (2).

$$\alpha(T_2) = e^{cT_2}\{\alpha(T_1)e^{-cT_1} + \int_{T_1}^{T_2} a[\sigma(t) - \sigma_0]^b e^{-ct}dt\} \quad (2)$$

Note that for an 'untested' specimen $\alpha(T_1) = 0$ for $T_1 = 0$ and Equation (2) reduces to the form of Equation (1).

EQUIVALENCE

Figure 1 shows two load histories and their corresponding damage curves. Under load history # 1, a constant load $S_1$ is applied to a specimen until it fails at time $t_1$ . Under load history # 2 a ramp load is applied until the specimen fails at a load level $S_2$ in time $t_2$. Consider a specimen ramp-loaded following load history # 2 and failing at point B corresponding to a load level $S_B < S_2$ and time to failure $t_B < t_2$. The damage accumulated up to $t_B$ is $\alpha_B$. If we enter the damage curve corresponding to load history #1 with $\alpha_A = \alpha_B$ we can determine the time $t_A$ required to accumulate this damage as well as point A on load history # 1. It can be said then that point A in load history # 1 is 'equivalent' to point B on load history # 2.

A 'weaker' specimen C in load history # 2 will have an 'equivalent' point A' on load history # 1 which has a lower time to failure $t_{A'} < t_A$. An extension to the equivalence concept is shown in Figure 2 where a specimen is ramp-loaded to failure at point X with corresponding time to failure $t_X$ and damage $\alpha_X$. An equivalent constant stress load history can be found such that the damage at time $t_X$ is the same as that accumulated under the original load history.

CURRENT STANDARD TEST PROCEDURE

To evaluate the performance of some floor systems, Central Mortgage and Housing Corporation (CMHC) recommends the load test procedure shown in Figure 3, for acceptability in construction financed by the National Housing Act of Canada. This procedure is largely based on the Canadian Standard CSA S307-M1980 and is essentially a Pass/Fail test. One shortcoming of the CMHC procedure is that after a specimen has survived the strength test by resisting the maximum load for a period of 24 hours it is not

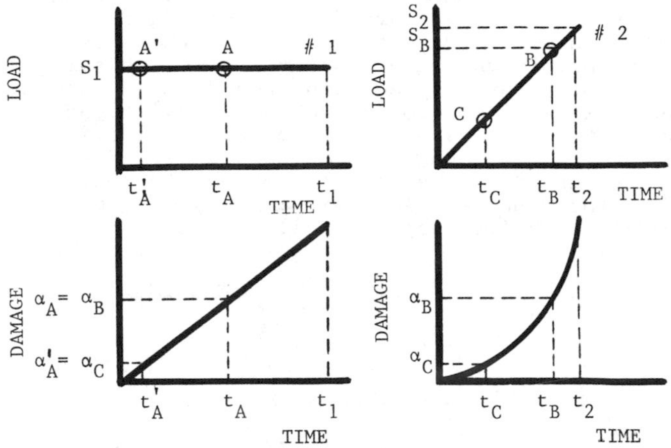


Figure 1 THE CONCEPT OF EQUIVALENCE

required to take this specimen to failure, neglecting to determine its ultimate load capacity. The CMHC procedure requires that three specimens be tested; if all three pass the test, the design is accepted; if one specimen fails, two extra specimens must be tested and pass the test; if two or more specimens fail the test, the system is not acceptable. As shown in Figure 3, it takes a minimum of 48 hours to test each specimen.

TESTING TO FAILURE

Alternate testing procedures which incorporate short-duration load tests to failure are considered in this investigation. These procedures will permit us to evaluate the ultimate load capacity and deformation characteristics of floor systems for strength as well as serviceability limit states.

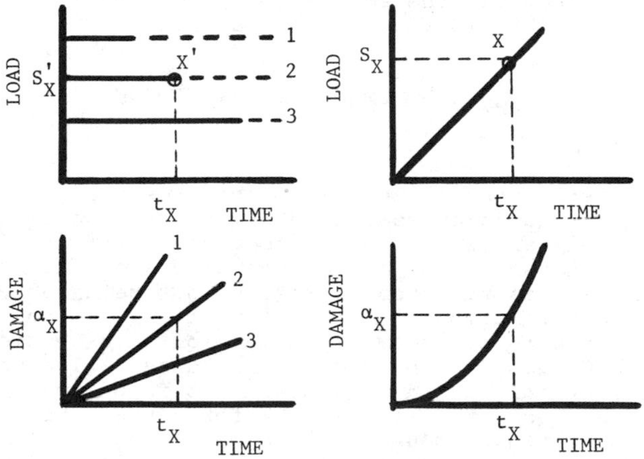


Figure 2 AN EXTENSION OF THE EQUIVALENCE CONCEPT

A significant improvement to the CMHC test procedure would be to add a ramp load to failure for all specimens surviving the basic test. This would determine the ultimate capacity of the specimen and permit an evaluation of the structural reliability of the system. These specimens would have accumulated a considerable amount of damage and their load capacity would be lower than that of 'untested' or 'undamaged' specimens.

By determining the damage accumulated under an alternate test procedure it is possible to use the 'equivalence' concept to look back at the CMHC test load history and determine whether the specimen would have 'passed' or 'failed' the standard test.

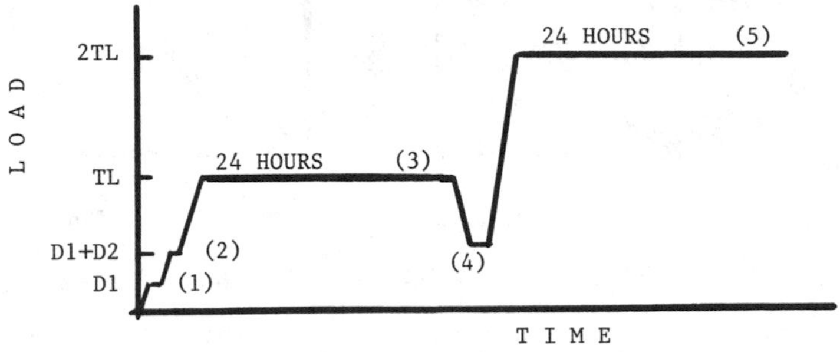


(1) Apply a uniform load of 0.5 kPa (Dead load) and maintain for 5 minutes (D1)

(2) Apply a load of 0.5 kPa (Partition loads) and mantain for 5 minutes (D2)

(3) Apply a load equal to the design live load and mantain this total load (TL) for 24 hours.

(4) Remove the live load and mantain the remaining dead load (D1 + D2) for 5 minutes

(5) Increase the load until twice the total load (2 TL) is reached and mantain for 24 hours

Figure 3 CMHC TEST PROCEDURE

TEST PROCEDURES

Figure 4 shows the three test procedures evaluated in this study. The short-duration ramp load (A) has the obvious advantage of requiring only a few minutes to complete the test. The rate of loading was chosen with a 5-minute time to failure target. Unfortunately it has the disadvantage of not being able to detect creep and other time-related deformations which could be significant for some systems. To allow for this consideration a 'partial' CMHC test (B) up to design load and a 1-hour delay to measure deflections was investigated. It is believed that this would be sufficient allowance for the assessment of serviceability requirements. Finally, the full CMHC test procedure (C) was followed and a ramp load to failure was applied to the surviving specimens.

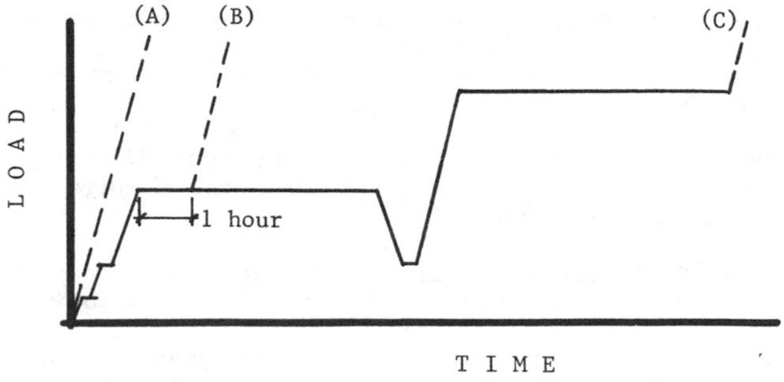


(A) = Ramp load
(B) = Partial CMHC + ramp
(C) = Full CMHC + ramp

Figure 4 TEST PROCEDURES

Figure 5 shows how the equivalence concept is used to assess alternate testing procedures. Consider a specimen A taken to failure by a ramp load, in time $t_A$ and with damage $\alpha_A$ larger than the damage expected from the standard test, $\alpha_C$. Under these conditions it is assumed that the specimen would have passed the strength test. Consider now a 'weaker' specimen B with corresponding time to failure $t_B$ and damage $\alpha_B$. On the damage curve for the standard test this damage corresponds to a time to failure $t'_B$, smaller than the time to failure $t_S$ under the standard test.

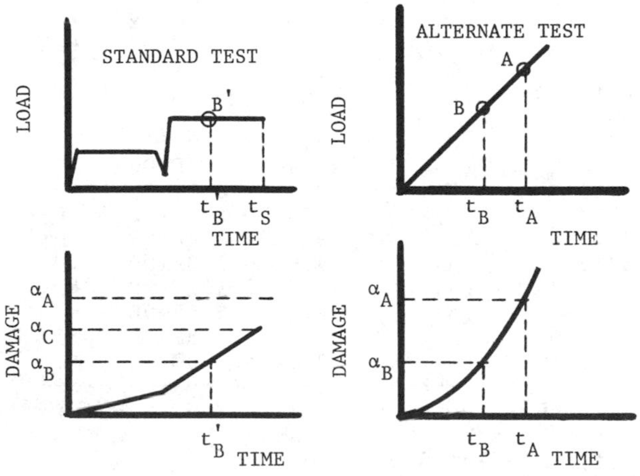


Figure 5 EVALUATION OF ALTERNATE TEST PROCEDURES

Under these conditions it is assumed that the specimen would have failed the standard test. The following procedure can be used to compare standard and alternate testing procedures:

1.- Calculate the damage expected from a standard test procedure, $\alpha_c$, using Equation (2)

2.- Record the load history for an alternate test procedure for a given specimen and calculate the damage $\alpha_T$ accumulated using Equation (1) or (2)

3.- If $\alpha_T > \alpha_c$ the specimen is assumed to have passed the standard test. If $\alpha_T < \alpha_c$ it is assumed to have failed.

Test Specimens.- A total of 40 specimens were tested and grouped into four series with 10 specimens each

WF16 Waferboard I beams, depth 241 mm, span 5 m, chords 38x64 mm
WF20 Waferboard I beams, depth 292 mm, span 6 m, chords 38x89 mm
SJ16 Solid Lumber Joists, span 5 m, cross-section 38x235 mm
SJ20 Solid Lumber Joists, span 6 m, cross-section 38x282 mm

Table 1 RESULTS OF TESTS ON SHORT SPAN SPECIMENS

| SPECIMEN | TEST PROCEDURE | TIME TO FAILURE | DAMAGE | REMARKS |
|---|---|---|---|---|
| WF16-1 | (C) | 1477 | 9.9E-04 | F |
| WF16-2 | (C) | 2964 | 3.3E+04 | P |
| WF16-3 | (A) | 6.4 | 5.4E+05 | *P |
| WF16-4 | (A) | 8.5 | 5.2E+09 | *P |
| WF16-5 | (A) | 6.7 | 1.3E+03 | *P |
| WF16-6 | Not Available | | | |
| WF16-7 | (A) | 5.5 | 5.0E+02 | *P |
| WF16-8 | (A) | 5.4 | 2.2E+03 | *P |
| WF16-9 | (C) | 3015 | 4.8E+04 | P |
| WF16-10 | (C) | 1540 | 3.6E-04 | F |
| SJ16-1 | (C) | 2964 | 1.9E+12 | P |
| SJ16-2 | (C) | 2954 | 6.0E+06 | P |
| SJ16-3 | (C) | 2946 | 2.3E+08 | P |
| SJ16-4 | (C) | 2958 | 4.3E+12 | P |
| SJ16-5 | (C) | 2953 | 4.4E+09 | P |
| SJ16-6 | (A) | 4.6 | 1.3E+09 | *P |
| SJ16-7 | (A) | 1.7 | 1.1E-08 | *F |
| SJ16-8 | (A) | 4.4 | 3.4E+06 | *P |
| SJ16-9 | (A) | 3.7 | 7.3E-01 | *F |
| SJ16-10 | (A) | 3.6 | 1.6E+01 | *P |

(A) = Ramp Load; (C) = Full CMHC + Ramp;
P/F = Pass/Fail CMHC Test
* = Predicted outcome

RESULTS AND DISCUSSION

Tables 1 and 2 show the results of the test program and the application of the principles discussed here to evaluate alternate test procedures. To arrive at the Pass/Fail decision shown in the REMARKS column, the damage accumulated from the test load history, $\alpha_T$, was compared with that expected from the standard test $\alpha_C$ = 0.964, calculated using Equation (2).

The authors believe that a short-duration test with some allowance for delayed elastic or creep deflections such as the test procedure (B) studied here could be used to replace the standard CMHC test in some applications. The resulting economies in time and simplicity of testing may be significant enough to warrant further studies in this direction with a larger sample size.

Table 2 RESULTS OF TESTS ON LONG SPAN SPECIMENS

| SPECIMEN | TEST PROCEDURE | TIME TO FAILURE | DAMAGE | REMARKS |
|---|---|---|---|---|
| WF20-1 | (A) | 2.9 | 4.7E+05 | *P |
| WF20-2 | (B) | 104.3 | 8.3E+03 | *P |
| WF20-3 | (B) | 116.6 | 2.7E+11 | *P |
| WF20-4 | (B) | 103.2 | 5.0E+05 | *P |
| WF20-5 | (B) | 103.9 | 4.4E+05 | *P |
| WF20-6 | (B) | 111.8 | 5.9E+08 | *P |
| WF20-7 | (A) | 3.8 | 9.6E+00 | *P |
| WF20-8 | (A) | 2.8 | 4.4E+03 | *P |
| WF20-9 | (A) | 3.4 | 5.7E+03 | *P |
| WF20-10 | (A) | 3.0 | 7.0E-05 | *F |
| SJ20-1 | (A) | 5.0 | 2.3E-02 | *F |
| SJ20-2 | (A) | 5.9 | 3.3E+03 | *P |
| SJ20-3 | (A) | 5.5 | 3.9E+04 | *P |
| SJ20-4 | (A) | 7.0 | 4.1E+05 | *P |
| SJ20-5 | (A) | 6.7 | 2.3E+07 | *P |
| SJ20-6 | (B) | 105.8 | 8.7E+04 | *P |
| SJ20-7 | (B) | 103.9 | 2.9E-03 | *F |
| SJ20-8 | (B) | 105.7 | 1.9E+04 | *P |
| SJ20-9 | (B) | 103.3 | 4.6E-02 | *F |
| SJ20-10 | (B) | 106.5 | 2.4E+07 | *P |

(A) = Ramp Load; (B) = Partial CMHC + Ramp;
P/F = Pass/Fail CMHC Test
* = Predicted outcome

ACKNOWLDEGMENTS

The financial support of NSERC in the form of an operating grant to the senior author is gratefully acknowledged.

REFERENCES

Barret, J.D. and R.O. Foschi (1978a). Duration of Load and Probability of Failure in Wood. Part I. Modelling Creep Rupture. Canadian Journal of Civil Engineering, 5(4), pp.505-514

Barret, J.D. and R.O. Foschi (1978b). Duration of Load and Probability of Failure in Wood. Part II. Constant, Ramp and Cyclic Loadings Canadian Journal of Civil Engineering 5(4), pp.515-532

Canada Mortgage and Housing Corporation (1983). ME 8309. Load Test Procedure for Floor Framing Systems for Houses and Small Buildings. CMHC, 682 Montreal Road, Ottawa, Ontario, K1A 0P7

Canadian Standards Association (1980). S307-M1980. Load Test Procedures for Wood Roof Trusses for Houses and Small Buildings. CSA, 178 Rexdale Blvd., Rexdale, Ontario, Canada, M9W 1R3

Duchesne, D.P.J. (1980). "An Evaluation of Safety Associated with Testing Timber Trusses". M. Eng. Thesis, Department of Civil Engineering, Carleton University, Ottawa, Canada K1S 5B6,98 pp

Duchesne, D.P.J. and J.J. Salinas (1984). "Evaluation of Truss Testing Procedures". Proceedings of the 4th ASCE Specialty Conference on Probabilistic Mechanics and Structural Reliability. American Society of Civil Engineers, Berkeley, CA January 1984, pp 135-139.

Gillard, R.G. (1986). "Reliability Analysis of Waferboard I Beams, A Damage Accumulation Approach". M.Eng. Thesis, Department of Civil Engineering, Carleton University, Ottawa, Canada K1S 5B6, 141 pp.

Salinas, J.J. (1979). "Performance Criteria and Reliability of Floor Trusses with Metal Webs". Proceedings of the Metal Plate Wood Truss Conference, Forest Products Research Society, St. Louis, MO. November 1979. pp 243-246.

# APPROXIMATE RANDOM VIBRATION OF A NONLINEAR SDOF OSCILLATOR BY NON-GAUSSION CLOSURE AND STATISTICAL LINEARIZATION

H. Davoodi, M.N. Noori, A. Saffar

Worcester Polytechnic Institute,
Worcester, MA. 01609, U.S.A

ABSTRACT. The Non-Gaussian closure technique is applied to a nonlinear SDOF oscillator subjected to a stationary white noise excitation. The nonlinear restoring force in this system has a hyperbolic tangent behavior. Relations between stationary response statistics are generated. These relations are then employed to evaluate a corresponding number of unknown coefficients in a truncated Gram-Charlier density function. Up to the sixth order moments of the response process are obtained. The probability density function predicted by this technique is then compared with the one constructed by exact solution via Fokker-Plank-Kolmogorov equation. A comparison is also made with the density function evaluated by statistical linearization. It is concluded that for the system studied, the Non-Gaussion closure technique does not have significant advantages over statistical linearization.

INTRODUCTION. Since the exact analysis of most nonlinear systems under random excitation is difficult, a variety of approximate techniques for response analysis of nonlinear systems have been explored. These include i) equivalent linearization which was independently introduced by Booton and Caughey (1963); ii) Gaussian and Non-Gaussian closure techniques by Crandall (1980, 1985), and Ibrahim (1985a, 1985b); iii) methods based on the numerical solution of the FPK equations, Spencer and Bergman (1985); and iv) Non-Gaussian techniques based on Wiener-Hermite series expansions Orabi and Ahmadi (1985).

Of these techniques, equivalent linearization has been the most extensively utilized method in the analysis of varies types of nonlinear systems, for the stationary or nonstationary response statistics, Atalik (1976), Baber (1984, 1986), Baber and Noori (1986, 1985,), Iwan (1980), Noori et al (1986, 1987), Spanos (1981).

The objective of this study is to make a comparison between the equivalent linearization and a proposed non-Gaussian closure technique by Crandall (1980).

Herein, an oscillator with nonlinear restoring force is excited by white noise. Stationary response statistics are predicted by the non-Gaussian closure and statistical linearization. These response estimates are then compared with the FPK solution. The approximate random vibration analysis of this system has not been studied before.

RANDOM VIBRATION OF A NONLINEAR SDOF SYSTEM. The system to be studied herein is shown in Fig. 1. This type of nonlinear system has applications in the dynamics of package cushioning, Mindlin (1945).

The governing differential equation of motion for this system of Fig.1 can be written as

$$m\ddot{u} + c\dot{u} + h(u) = f(t) \tag{1}$$

in which m is considered here as unit mass, f(t) is an ideal white noise random with an autocorrelation function

$$R_f(\tau) = 2W\delta(\tau) \tag{2}$$

and h(u) is the nonlinear restoring force which has the form

$$h(u) = \lambda.\tanh(ku/\lambda) \tag{3}$$

where k and $\lambda$ are parameters controlling the rate of stiffness softening and maximum limiting force respectively.

Herein, first the non-Gaussian closure approach, as proposed by Crandall (1980, 1985), will be applied to the nonlinear system defined by Eqs. (1) and (3). In order to evaluate the response statistics, both sides of Eq. (1) are multiplied by a set of arbitary continuously differentiable functions $\phi(u)$. Taking the expected values of the both sides results

$$\{\phi\ddot{u}\} + (c/m)\ E\{\phi\dot{u}\} + (1/m).E\{\phi h(u)\} = (1/m)\ E\{\phi f(t)\} \tag{4}$$

Eq. (4) can be furthered simplified to the form

$$E\{\partial\phi/\partial u\}\ E\{\dot{u}^2\} = 1/m\ E\{\phi h(u)\} \tag{5}$$

It can be shown that

$$E\{\dot{u}^2\} = W/(cm) \tag{6}$$

Substitution of $E\{\dot{u}^2\}$ from Eq. (6) into Eq. (5) results

$$(W/c)\ E\{\partial\phi/\partial u\} = E\{\phi h(u)\} \tag{7}$$

Evaluation of the expected values in Eq. (7) requires a knowledge of the density function for the response. On the other hand, the same equation can be used in producing the relations

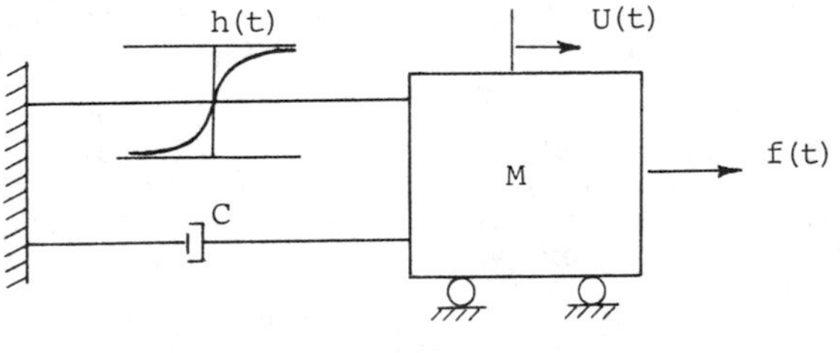


FIG. 1 - SDOF SYSTEM WITH HYPERBOLIC TANGENT RESTORING FORCE.

between the moments. The density function is approximated by a truncated Gram-Charlier expansion

$$P(u) = [1/(\sqrt{2\pi}\,\sigma)] \exp[-(u-\nu)^2/2\sigma^2] .$$
$$\{1+\sum_{n=3}^{N} (C_n/n!)\, H_n[(u-\nu)/\sigma]\} \quad (8)$$

where $\nu$ and $\sigma$ are the mean and the standard deviation of the response, respectively, and $H_n(.)$ are Hermite polynomials defined as

$$H_n(Z) = (-1)^n \exp(Z^2/2)\, d^n/dZ^n[\exp(-Z^2/2)] \quad (9)$$

The coefficients $C_n$ in Eq. (8) can be evaluated as

$$C_n = E\{H_n[(u-\nu)/\sigma]\} \qquad n=3,\ldots,N \quad (10)$$

where the following truncation is used

$$C_n = E\{H_n[(u-\nu)/\sigma]\}=0 \qquad n=N+1,\ N+2,\ldots \quad (11)$$

The density function of Eq. (8) has N unknowns ($\nu$, $\sigma$, $C_3$, $C_4,\ldots,C_N$). In order to find these unknowns, N constraints are needed. Through the selection of appropriate $\phi$'s, Eq. (7) is used to generate a set of simultaneous non-linear equations. The calculations are somewhat simpler if Hermite polynomials are selected as $\phi(u)$ functions.

The non-linear restoring force is an odd function and P(u) given by Eq. (8), is an even function, thus, all odd ordered moments are zero. Substituting $\phi(u) = H_n(u/\sigma)$ into Eq. (7) results

$$(W/c).n/\sigma\ E\{H_{n-1}(u/\sigma)\} = E\{\phi h(u)\} \quad (12)$$

By setting N=6 in Eq. (8) and using Eq. (12)

$$H_n(X) = Wn/c\ (C_{n-1}/\sigma) \quad (13)$$

where

$$X^j = \lambda/(\sqrt{2\pi}\ \sigma^{j+1}) \quad \sum_{i=1}^{4} A_{2(i-1)+j}\ D_i \quad (14a)$$

$$A_i = \int_{-\infty}^{\infty} u^i \tanh(ku/\lambda).\exp(-u^2/2\sigma^2)\ du \quad (14b)$$

and

$$D_1 = 1 + 3C_4/4! - 15C_6/6! \quad (15a)$$
$$D_2 = 45\ C_6/(6!\ \sigma^2) - 6\ C_4/(4!\ \sigma^2) \quad (15b)$$
$$D_3 = C_4/(4!\ \sigma^4) - 15\ C_6/(6!\ \sigma^4) \quad (15c)$$
$$D_4 = C_6/(6!\sigma^6) \quad (15d)$$

For an even i, $A_i$ has a value of zero, so, by setting n=1,3 and 5 in Eq. (12), a set of three independent simultaneous equations are obtained in terms of three unknowns $\sigma$, $C_4$, and $C_6$.

Eq. (14b) can be written as

$$A_i = 2\int_0^\infty u^i \tanh(ku/\lambda).\exp(-u^2/2\sigma^2)\ du \tag{16}$$

A numerical scheme is employed for evaluation of $A_i$ .

For the statistical linearization Eq. (1) is replaced by an equivalent linear system

$$m\ddot{u} + c\dot{u} + k_e u = f(t) \tag{17}$$

The coefficient, $k_e$ of the linear system is found by minimizing the error between Eq. (1) and (17) in the mean square sense. The excitation f(t) is assumed to be zero mean stationary Gaussian white noise with the autocorrelation function as given by Eq. (3). The standard deviation of the response is

$$\sigma_u^2 = W/(ck_e) \tag{18}$$

Since the response is Gaussian, Eq. (18) can provide the probability density function of the response.

The response statistics by NGC and SL compared with FPK solution which is derived following Caughey's approach (1963). It can be shown that for the Eq. (1), the density function of the response is given by

$$P(u) = \eta\ [\cosh(ku/\lambda)]^{-\alpha} \tag{19}$$

where $\alpha = c\lambda^2/(W.k)$ and $\eta$ is a normalizing constant.

NUMERICAL STUDIES. The numerical studies reported herein were performed with the following purposes: (1) To investigate the application of this nonlinear restoring force in random vibration analysis, (2) to explore the relative validity of the NGC technique for the approximate random vibration analysis of this system. Two cases of low and high nonlinearity were considered. In both cases, the maximum restoring force was limited to 1.0. For the low nonlinearity a spring constant parameter of k=0.1; input power spectral density of PSD=0.5; and a dampin coefficient of c=0.5 were chosen. The resulting density functions presented in Fig. 2 shown a very close agreement between both NGC and SL techniques and the FPK solution over the entire space. The SL results show, however, a slightly closer agreement with the FPK at P(0). For a more thorough comparison two additional studies were performed. In the first study, the effect of the change in the spring constant was considered. Fig. 3 shows the results of this investigation. For the value of spring constant in the range of k=0.1-10.0, and the damping value of 0.5, the two approximate techniques show the same trend in predicting the RMS of displacement response. The SL results however, underestimate the response whereas the NGC is in good agreement with the FPK. Beyond k=10.0 where the nonlinearity increases sharply, the FPK solution shows an increase in $\sigma_u$. For this case both NGC and SL results underestimate the FPK solution. Fig. 4 demonstrates the predicted response vs. the variation of damping in the system. Both NGC and SL are in good agreement with FPK solution.

For the case of high nonlinearity, k=10.0, PSD=0.1, c=0.05 where used. The ensuing density functions, as shown in Fig. 5, exhibit deviations of up to 31% at P(0), with NGC technique providing a more precise solution than the one obtained from SL.

A phenomenon observed in this investigation is the presence of an oscillation in the NGC solution. This behavior is not present in

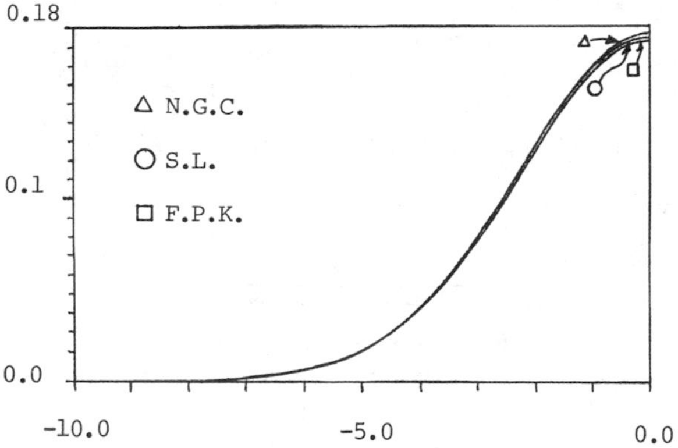


FIG. 2 - DENSITY FUNCTION OF THE RESPONSE FOR THE SYSTEM. (LOW NONLINEARITY).

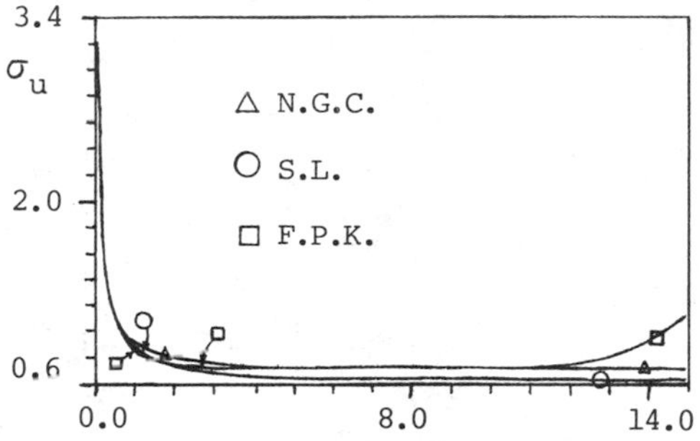


FIG. 3 - RMS DISPLACEMENT RESPONSE VS SPRING CONSTANT (LOW NONLINEARITY).

the FPK or SL. Fig. 6 shows the effect of the variation of the k on the RMS response predicted by the approximate techniques. In this study, c=0.05 was considered. For the spring constant changing from k=0.1 to 7, the two techniques show close agreement with FPK solution. SL results slightly underestimate the response. When k increases beyond a value of 7, there is a sharp disagreement between FPK and the two approximate results. Similar study was done for the RMS response vs. variation of system damping. This is shown in Fig. 7. When the damping is very low, between 0.0-0.03, there is no good agreement between the results. This may stem from the fact that since the system is slightly damped, the stationarity is unlikely. However, for damping value greater than 0.03 both NGC and SL agree very well with FPK results.

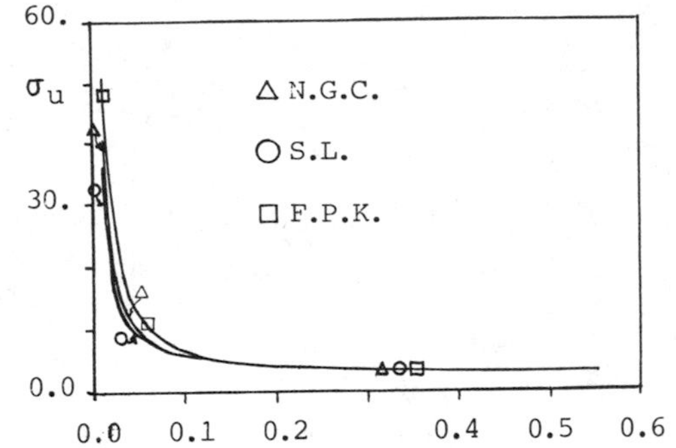


FIG. 4 - RMS DISPLACEMENT RESPONSE VS. DAMPING RATIO (LOW NONLINEARITY).

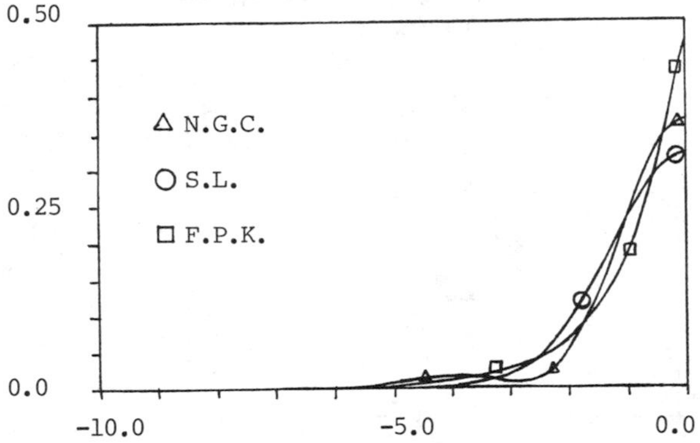


FIG. 5 - DENSITY FUNCTION OF THE RESPONSE FOR THE SYSTEM. (HIGH NONLINEARITY).

SUMMARY AND CONCLUSION. Non-Gaussian Clouser technique is a method for approximating the density function of a given process. It involves an assigned probability density with N unknown coeffecients, the values of which are determined through N independent relationships obtained by using well-known techniques. One such technique was proposed by Crandall. In this approach the assumed probability density function is a truncated Gram-Charlier expansion.

In order to make a comparison between this technique and the statistical linearization, application of both methods to a nonlinear SDOF system is considered. The input to the system is assumed to be a Gaussian white noise.

In deriving the relations between moments several assumptions are made, in particular: (1) The nonlinearity due to the

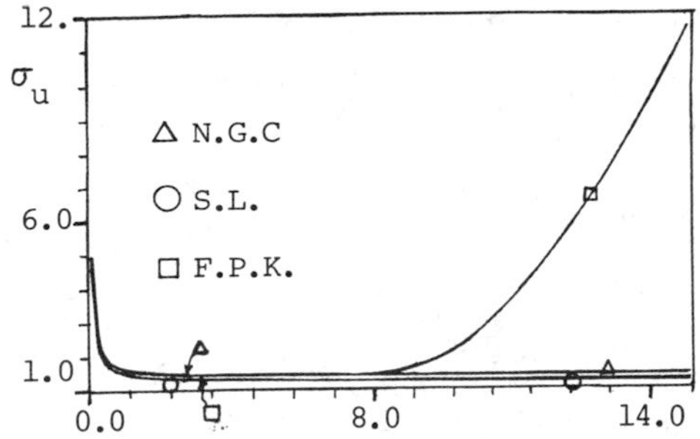


FIG. 6 - RMS DISPLACEMENT RESPONSE VS SPRING CONSTANT (HIGH NONLINEARITY).

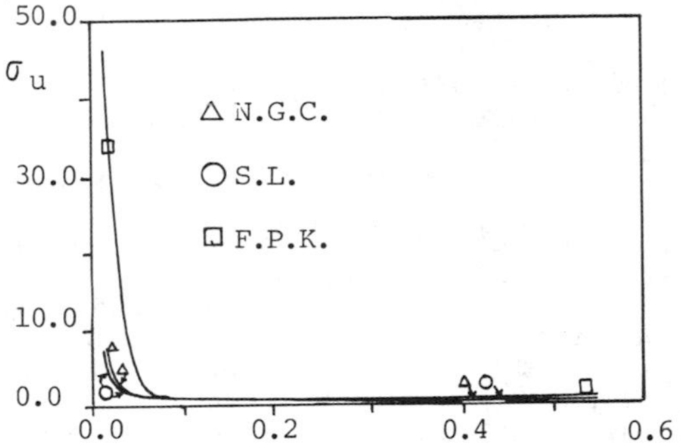


FIG. 7 - RMS DISPLACEMENT RESPONSE VS. DAMPING RATIO (HIGH NONLINEARITY).

restoring force, h(u), should be small and well behaved. It cannot possess discontinuous slope(s); it must be in explicit form and, it cannot be a function of more than one variable; (2) this technique is based on stationary response. The first assumption limits the nonlinearity of the restoring force, and the second one prohibits the inclusion of the transient cases. Other problems with this technique are discused elsewhere (Crandall, 1985; Orabi, 1986).

RMS response statistics for this nonlinear system obtained by statistical linearization are compared with NGC results for two cases of low and high nonlinearity. For the low nonlinearity case, both SL and NGC results are in good agreement with FPK solution. In the case of high nonlinearity, the results obtained by NGC show a slight improvement over the SL results. Considering the hardship associated with the application of NGC technique, and also the computational time required, it is concluded that, for the system studied, the NGC technique does not justify its selection over the SL approach.

ACKNOWLEDGEMENTS. This work was supported in part by Grant No. ECE-8504534 from the National Science Foundation.

REFERENCES

Atalik T.S. and S. Utku (1976). "Stochastic Linearization of Multidegree of Freedom Nonlinear Systems", Earthg. Eng. &Struc. Dyn., 4, 411-420.

Baber T.T. (1984). "Nonzero Mean Random Vibration of Hysteretic Systems", J. Eng. Mech., ASCE, 110, 1036-1049.

Baber T.T. (1986). "Modal Analysis for Random Vibration of Hysteretic Frames", Earthg. Eng. Struc. Dyn., 14, 841-859.

Baber T.T. and M.N. Noori (1986). "Modelling General Hysteresis Behavior and Random Vibration Application", J. Vib., Acous., Stress, and Reli. in Design, October, 411-420.

Baber T.T. and M.N. Noori (1985). "Random Vibration of Degrading, Pinching Systems", ASCE, J. Eng. Mech., 111, 1010-1026.

Caughey T.K. (1963). "Derivation and Application of the Fokker-Plank Equation to Discrete Nonlinear Dynamic Systems Subjected to White Random Excitation", Journal of the Acoustical Society of America, 35, 1683-1692.

Caughey T.K. (1963). "Equivalent Linearization," J. Acous. Society of America, 35, 1706-1711.

Crandall S.H. (1980). "Non-Gaussian Closure for Random Vibration of Non-linear Oscillator", Int. J. Non-Lin. Mechs., 15, 303-313.

Crandall S.H. (1985). "Non-Gaussian Closure for Stationary Random Vibration", Int. J. Non-Lin. Mechs., 20, 1-8.

Ibrahim R.A. (1985). Parametric Random Vibration, John Wiley &Sons Inc. New York.

Ibrahim R.A., A. Soundarajan and H. Heo (1985). "Stochastic Response of Nonlinear Dynamic Systems Based on Non-GaussianClosure", ASME, Winter Annual Meeting, Miami, Florida, Nov. 17-21, Paper No. 85-WA/APM-6.

Iwan W.D. and A.B. Mason, Jr. (1980). "Equivalent Linearization for System Subjected to Non-stationary Random Excitation",Int. Non-Lin. Mech., 15, 71-82.

Mindlin R.D. (1945). "Dynamics of Package Cushioning", Bell System Tech. J., 24, 353-461.

Noori M.N., J.D. Choi and H. Davoodi (1986). "A New Hysteresis Model for Random Vibration of Degrading Systems", Proc. Southeastern Conf. on Theo. & App. Mech., XIII, University of South Carolina, Columbia, South Carolina, USA, 2, 522-530.

Noori M.N., H. Davoodi and J.D. Choi (1987). "Zero and Nonzero Random Vibration Analysis of A New General Hysteresis Model", To Appear in the Journal of Probabilistic Engineering Mechanics.

Orabi I.I. and G. Ahmadi (1985). "Nonstationary Response Analysis of a Duffing Oscillator by the Wiener-Hermite Expansion Method", Report No. MIE-121, Department of Mechanical and Industrial Engineering, Clarkson University, Sept. 1985.

Roberts J.B. (1981). "Response of Nonlinear Mechanical Systems to Random Excitation, Part 2: Equivalent Linearization and Other Methods", Shock and Vibration Digest, 13., 15-29.

Spanos P.D. (1981). "Stochastic Linearization in Structural Dynamics", Appl. Mechs. Revs., 34, 1-8.

Spencer B.F., Jr. and L.A. Bergman (1985). "On the Reliability of a Simple Hysteretic System", J. Eng. Mech., ASCE, 111, 1985, 1502-1514.

# SECOND ORDER UNCERTAINTY MODELLING OVER FINITE AND INFINITE DOMAINS USING ENTROPY

Vicente Solana*,** and Angel Arteaga**
*Department of Civil Engineering, University of Waterloo, Waterloo, Ontario, Canada, N2L 3G1
**Centro Investigacion Matematica y Estadistica, Spanish Council for Scientific Research CSIC, Serrano 123, 28006 Madrid, Spain

ABSTRACT

The maximum entropy formalism is applied as a method for uncertainty modelling. The feasibility of this method for second order uncertainties over finite and infinite $R_1$ and $R_1^+$ domains is examined. A modified representation of second order uncertainty is proposed, using the first absolute moment in addition to mean and variance. The efficiency of the entropy method is demonstrated and families of maximum entropy density models are obtained.

## INTRODUCTION

The modelling of uncertainties in a consistent probabilistic way is a major problem. Uncertainty, or a state of uncertainty about probabilities, may be represented as the partial knowledge of the randomness of one or more variables in that state. Usually this modelling is done by choosing, among all distribution types, one probability distribution model that satisfies the constraints that arise from the partial knowledge about uncertainty.

In civil engineering and other fields, partial knowledge about uncertainty is often available in the form of known values of a few of the moments of the random variables. These values are usually obtained from moment estimates, or they are postulated subjectively.

In many cases only the first two moments, mean and variance, are known and second order methods are then applied. More generally, partial knowledge about uncertainty pertains to a finite sequence of moments. Then there are only two kinds of uncertainty modelling methods available, namely distribution series methods, based on analytical expansion of some initial distributions over different domains, and maximum entropy methods.

Most important distributions series correspond to the classical expansions methods of Gram-Charlier, Edgeworth and Longuet-Higgins, reviewed for applications by Ochi (1986), and the method proposed by Winterstein (1985). Unfortunately these methods are not efficient because they only apply over a limited range of moments. However, the main difficulty with distribution series methods is just the matter of consistency; no justification other than analytical convenience has been given for the choice of initial distributions (second order models), namely the beta, normal and gamma distributions over finite, $R_1$ and $R_1^+$ domains, respectively.

MAXIMUM ENTROPY METHODS. This paper deals with the use of the maximum entropy formalism for uncertainty modelling applied to second order uncertainties. The main purpose of this paper is to examine the feasibility of entropy methods for second order uncertainty modelling over finite and infinite domains.

The formalism is analogous to the entropy maximum principle proposed by Jaynes (1957, 1968), or the equivalent information minimum principle by Evans (1969), based on Shannon's entropy

$$S = - \sum_{i=1}^{n} P_i \log(P_i) \qquad (1)$$

However, it is applied here to continuous distributions so that entropy is defined as the integral

$$H = -\int_R f(x) \log f(x)\, dx \tag{2}$$

Thus the formalism is a variational method in which the density f(x) is selected as a non-negative function maximizing the entropy functional H, subjected to a set of constraints (including normalization $g_o(x) = 1$) usually defined as the functional expectations

$$E[g_j(x)] = \int_R g_j(x) f(x)\, dx \quad ,j = 0,1,\ldots,k \tag{3}$$

The Lagrange multiplier method gives the result that maximum entropy, if it exists, corresponds to the density

$$f(x) = \exp[-\sum_{j=0}^{k} \lambda_j g_j(x)] \tag{4}$$

The entropy functional H was also used by Shannon (1948) who assumed that it is a generalization of the entropy for discrete distributions. However the two entropies are different (Jaynes, 1968; Evans, 1969); extension of Shannon's entropy for discrete distributions to the limiting case of continuous distributions gives expressions that differ from the integral entropy formula (Aczel, 1984).

Since the entropy H also has logarithmic form, it retains many properties of Shannon's entropy for discrete distributions. But, being a different functional, the entropy H lacks two important properties: (1) invariance of the entropy formula in case of non-linear probability-preserving transformations, and (2) having finite positive values. Therefore, unlike Shannon's entropy the integral entropy H cannot be used as a measure of uncertainty.

Particular values of the entropy H for several continuous distributions types are summarized by Mukherjee (1986). Some distributions that maximize entropy among all possible distributions subject to constraints on mean and variance are well known from Shannon (1948). Thus, the Gaussian and the Laplace distributions maximize the entropy H over $R_1$ when the variance or the first absolute moment are given, respectively. The seminormal and the linear exponential distributions correspond to these models respectively for the $R_1^+$ domain, when second moment and mean are given.

SECOND ORDER MAXIMUM ENTROPY DISTRIBUTIONS. Maximum entropy analysis of continuous distributions over $R_1^+$ when the first two moments are known has been previously studied by Wragg and Dowson (1970). These authors stated a theorem on the distribution classes over $R_1^+$ satisfying the inequality $\mu_2' > 2(\mu_1')^2$ or its converse, and they proved that the maximum entropy method breaks down if $\mu_2' > 2(\mu_1')^2$; here $\mu_1'$ and $\mu_2'$ are the first and second moment about the origin. They also gave a table of the parameters of the maximum entropy distributions over $R_1^+$ with unit mean and given second moment satisfying $\mu_2' < 2(\mu_1')^2$.

Dowson and Wragg (1973) extend the analysis to the case of finite domains within $R_1^+$, proving that if the values of $\mu_1'$ and $\mu_2$ are within the range of moments that corresponds to distributions, then a maximum entropy distribution always exists over a finite domain. Therefore, the maximum entropy method only breaks down for infinite domains in $R_1^+$.

An interpretation of the failure of the entropy method was given by Wragg and Dowson (1970). According to these authors the maximum entropy distributions over $R_1^+$ should not always belong to the quadratic exponential density types but rather to a set of distributions with null probabilities over one or more intervals within $R_1^+$. However, this point has not yet been proved, and no distributions were obtained. The same authors (Dowson and Wragg, 1973) studied the limits of the maximum entropy values related to distributions over finite domains. In the case $\mu_2' \geq 2(\mu_1')^2$ in which the method fails, these authors found a finite upper bound of maximum entropy defined by $1 + \log(\mu_1')$.

Maximum entropy distributions over finite domains when different kinds of parameters are prescribed, have been summarized by Kapur (1982), who also analysed the cases of maximum entropy distributions over finite intervals within $R_1^+$, when either mean or second moment are given.

The maximum entropy problem of continuous distributions over finite domains has also been presented by Mukherjee and Hurst (1984) who show that great flexibility may be gained with the maximum-entropy method when the domains are finite. Here an interesting point is the application of the Wragg-Dowson theorem to finite domains; according to Mukherjee and Hurst, the Wragg-Dowson (1970) procedure applies to finite intervals and the maximum-entropy method also breaks down if $\mu_2' > 2(\mu_1')^2$ in case of any finite domain within $R_1^+$. This point will be reviewed in this paper showing in a different way that the maximum entropy method always applies to finite domains and that the Dowson-Wragg (1973) results are correct.

Goodman (1985) applied the maximum entropy formalism to estimate a distribution function of structural fragility over $R_1^+$ and finite domains. He has also studied the problem of the maximum entropy distribution over $R_1^+$ as the first two moments are known; the distributions obtained are the lognormal distribution over $R_1^+$ and a modified lognormal distribution over finite domains within $R_1^+$. However, these maximum-entropy distributions differ from those obtained by Wragg and Dowson (1970) and they are incorrect, being based on an erroneous interpretation of the entropy invariance property.

Families of maximum entropy distributions determining all possible models for second order uncertainties over both finite and infinite domains are obtained in this paper. Such distributions include those obtained by Wragg and Dowson (1970) corresponding to the quadratic exponential density types.

## SECOND ORDER UNCERTAINTY REPRESENTATION

The usual pattern of representing second order uncertainties is reviewed before application of the entropy formalism.

Since an uncertainty may be represented as a finite sequence of moments, it makes sense to define an uncertainty of order k associated with a representation pattern formed by k ordered moments about the origin or the mean. In this way a second order uncertainty is represented by mean and variance.

These patterns are useful in many probabilistic methods providing for successive approximations to different distribution functions.

In the above description of an uncertainty it is implicitly assumed that a representation pattern does not change when uncertainty is defined over different domains. However, this assumption is questionable, and new patterns representing uncertainties are necessary. Here a pattern for second order uncertainty is proposed.

Suppose that a second order uncertainty over $R_1^+$ has the pattern $(\mu_1', \mu_2')$. Consider the classical way to build symmetrical densities f(x) over $R_1$ from the densities f(y) over $R_1^+$, according to the probability-preserving transformation $|x| = y$. Then it is possible to define the symmetrization operation of an uncertainty, in which an uncertainty over $R_1^+$ changes to other over $R_1$ according to this transformation. In this way, the partial knowledge about the new uncertainty corresponds to the moments $\mu_2 = \mu_2'$ and $\mu_1 = 0$ and the first order absolute moment $\beta_1$.

Since this knowledge is to be represented in the above pattern, it reduces to the variance $\mu_2$ and the condition of a centered mean that has been added through the symmetrization operation. However, the knowledge about the first absolute moment is lost in this pattern and consequently the knowledge about the uncertainty is represented incompletely.

The pattern representing a second order uncertainty must therefore be modified to include the first order absolute moment when uncertainties are distributed over the double-infinite domain $R_1$. An analogous pattern is required in the case of finite domains within $R_1$.

Finally, the following representation pattern is proposed for second order uncertainties:

- for asymmetric domains such as $R_1^+$ and $(0, r)$, an uncertainty is completely represented as the mean value $\mu_1'$ and the second moment $\mu_2'$;
- for domains symmetric about the mean such as $R_1$ and $(-r, r)$, the first absolute moment $\beta_1$, centered around the mean, must be given in addition to the mean $\mu_1$ and the variance $\mu_2$ completing the uncertainty representation.

MOMENT RANGES FOR SECOND ORDER UNCERTAINTIES

Once the representation pattern has been fixed, the range of moments must be determined for asymmetric and symmetric domains in order to describe the boundary of all possible second order uncertainties.

Assume that all probabilistic knowledge about a random variable can be derived from a knowledge of the distribution function. In this way, every partial knowledge representing a uncertainty has to agree with the existence of distributions holding such a knowledge.

Consequently, the moments related to a second order uncertainty must lie within the range of moments for which distributions exist. These ranges are different for distributions over different domains. They may be obtained by taking known solutions of the problem of moments in statistics into account (Shohat and Tamarkin, 1943).

In the case of infinite domains $R_1^+$ and $R_1$, solutions of the Stieljes and Hamburger problems are considered, respectively. These problems deal with the existence of distributions having a given infinite sequence of moments. Applying the solutions to second order uncertainties, the following necessary (but not sufficient) conditions for the existence of distributions are obtained:

$$\begin{aligned} &\mu_2' - (\mu_1')^2 \geqslant 0 \text{ and } \mu_1' \geqslant 0, && \text{for } R_1^+ \\ &\mu_2 - \beta_1^2 \geqslant 0 \text{ and } \beta_1 \geqslant 0, && \text{for } R_1 \end{aligned} \tag{5}$$

In the case of finite domains, solutions of the Haussdorf moment problem are considered. Applying these solutions to second order uncertainties, the necessary and sufficient conditions for the existence of distributions are:

$$\begin{aligned} &\mu_2' - (\mu_1')^2 \geqslant 0 \text{ and } \mu_1' r - \mu_2' \geqslant 0, \text{ for } (0,r) \\ &\mu_2 - \beta_1^2 > 0 \ ;\ \beta_1 r - \mu_2 \geqslant 0 \text{ and } r^2 - \mu_2 \geqslant 0, \text{ for } (-r,r) \end{aligned} \tag{6}$$

The moment ranges for second order uncertainties over $(0,r)$ and $(-r,r)$ are given for different values of r in Fig. 1; the moment range for uncertainties over infinite domains $R_1$, and $R_1^+$ corresponds to the region below the parabolic curve in Fig. 1.

In the case of a standardized distribution, necessary conditions for the existence of a distribution over $R_1$ and $(-r,r)$ determine both the range of the first absolute moment $\beta_1$, such that $\beta_1 \geqslant 1$, and the lower limit of finite domains defined by $r \geqslant 1$.

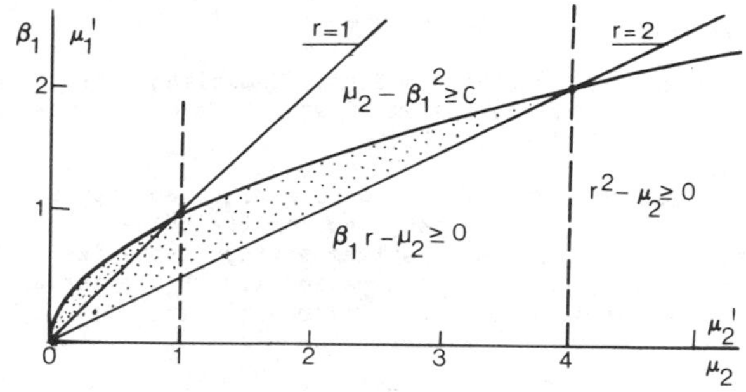


FIG. 1.– Moment Range for Second Order Uncertainty over (−r, r) and (0,r)

MAXIMUM ENTROPY DENSITY OVER A SYMMETRIC DOMAIN

Maximum entropy density functions for second order uncertainty modelling are determined here using standard uncertainties with zero mean value and unit variance.

Given a second order uncertainty over $R_1$ and $(-r, r)$ represented by the moments $\mu_1$, $\mu_2$ and $\beta_1$, the corresponding standard uncertainty is obtained in accordance with the random variable transformation $z = (x - \mu_1) / \sqrt{\mu_2}$. Hence, a standard uncertainty can be described by the reduced first order absolute moment $\beta_o = \beta_1 / \sqrt{\mu_2}$, and extends over $R_1$ and the finite domain $(-r_o, r_o)$ defined by $r_o = r_1 / \sqrt{\mu_2}$.

By applying the maximum entropy formalism to standardized second order uncertainties, it follows from equation (4) that maximum entropy densities correspond to the family of symmetric exponential functions of the form

$$f(z) = \exp(-az^2 - 2b|z| - c) \tag{7}$$

The parameters of the density function in equation (7) must be obtained from the integral equations (3), which in this case are the normalization condition $E(1) = 1$, the constraint on variance $E(z^2) = 1$, and the constraint $E(|z|) = \beta_o$ related to the value of the reduced absolute moment in the range $1 > \beta_o > 0$.

The integration of (3) over the finite domain $(-r_o, r_o)$ when $f(z)$ has the form (7) leads to the following equations:

1. – for the constraints $E(|z|) = \beta_o$ and $E(z^2) = 1$, respectively:

$$2a\beta_o + b = \{1 - \exp[-(ar_o^2 + 2br_o)]\} \exp(-c) \tag{8}$$

$$a + b\beta_o = 1/2 - r_o \exp[-(ar_o^2 + 2br_o + c)] \tag{9}$$

2. – for the normalization condition $E(1) = 1$:

$$\sqrt{(\pi/a)} \exp[(b^2-ac)/a] \, [\mathrm{Erf}[\sqrt{a}\, r_o + (b/\sqrt{a})] - \mathrm{Erf}(b/\sqrt{a})] = 1, \text{ for } a > 0 \tag{10.1}$$

$$\sqrt{(\pi/a)} \exp[(b^2-ac)/a] \, [\mathrm{Erfi}[\sqrt{|a|}\, r_o - (b/\sqrt{|a|})] - \mathrm{Erfi}(b/\sqrt{|a|})] = 1, \text{ for } a<0 \tag{10.2}$$

where Erf(.) and Erfi(.) are integral error functions (Abramowitz, 1965).

As the first parameter of density function (7) equals zero, the integration of constraints $E(1) = 1$ and $E(|z|) = \beta_o$ leads to equations (8) and (9) specialized for $a=0$. In this case integration of $E(z^2) = 1$ also provides another equation of the form

$$b - 2\beta_o + r_o^2 \exp[-(2br_o + c)] = 0, \text{ for } a = 0 \quad (10.3)$$

Therefore the parameters of the standardized maximum entropy densities (7) correspond to the solutions of the system of equations constituted by equations (8) and (9), and either (10.1) or (10.2).

PARTICULAR SOLUTION

FIRST ABSOLUTE MOMENT GIVEN. In this case maximum entropy densities are of the form $f(z) = \exp(-2b|z|-c)$. Although no constraint has been placed on the variance, it makes sense to consider maximum entropy densities as the standard form (unit variance) using (10.3). The parameters of the standardized maximum entropy densities are the solutions of equations (8) and (9), specialized for a=0, and (10.3). By elimination

$$(1/2) - b^2 = [br_o + (br_o)^2][\exp(2br_o)-1]^{-1} \quad (11)$$

Other parameters are given by

$$\beta_o = [(r_o/2) + b][1 + br_o]^{-1} \quad (12)$$

$$\exp(-c) = b[1 - \exp(-2br_o)]^{-1} \quad (13)$$

The limits of the parameter <u>b</u> across the range $r_o \geqslant 1$ follow from (11). When $r_o$ tends to infinity, b equals $\sqrt{2}/2$, which corresponds to the Laplace density; $r_o$ equals $\sqrt{3}$ as b tends to zero, which determines the uniform density. Finally, $r_o$ equals 1, the lowest bound of semi-intervals length, as b tends to $-\infty$ and probability densities tend to be concentrated on the interval ends.

The parameter values of standardized maximum entropy densities over several symmetric domains were calculated, and the maximum entropy H as the first absolute moment has been represented in Fig. 2, where the points representing the Laplace and uniform densities are also drawn in the entropy diagram.

GENERAL SOLUTION. Equations (8), (9) and (10.1) or (10.2) can be simplified by introducing two auxiliary parameters $p = r_o\sqrt{|a|}$ and $q = b/\sqrt{|a|}$ Elimination of <u>b</u>, <u>c</u> and $\beta_o$ results in

$$2a = 1 + 2q^2 - \frac{2[(p-q)\exp(-(p+q)^2) + q\exp(-q^2)]}{[\mathrm{Erf}(p+q) - \mathrm{Erf}(q)]}, \text{ for } a > 0 \quad (14.1)$$

$$2a = 1 - 2q^2 - \frac{p + q - q\exp(-p^2 + 2pq)}{\phi(p-q) + \phi(q)\ \exp(-p^2 + 2pq)}, \text{ for } a < 0 \quad (14.2)$$

where $\phi(.)$ is the Dawson function defined by $\phi(t) = \exp(-t^2)\,\mathrm{Erfi}(t)$ (Abramowitz, 1965).

Other parameters of maximum entropy densities are given by

$$\exp(-c) = a\,[(1/2) + q^2 - a][(p-q)\exp(-p^2 - 2pq) + q]^{-1}, \text{ for } a > 0 \quad (15.1)$$

$$\exp(-c) = \sqrt{|a|}\,\exp(-p^2+2pq)\,[(1/2)-q^2-a][(p+q) - q\exp(-p^2+2pq)]^{-1}, \text{ for } a<0 \quad (15.2)$$

and

$$\beta_o = (1/2a)\,[\exp(-c)[1-\exp(p^2-2pq)]-b], \text{ for } a > 0 \quad (16.1)$$

$$\beta_o = [\exp(-c).[1-\exp(-p^2-2pq)]+b\exp(-p^2+2pq)][2|a|\exp(-p^2+2pq)]^{-1}, \text{for } a>0 \quad (16.2)$$

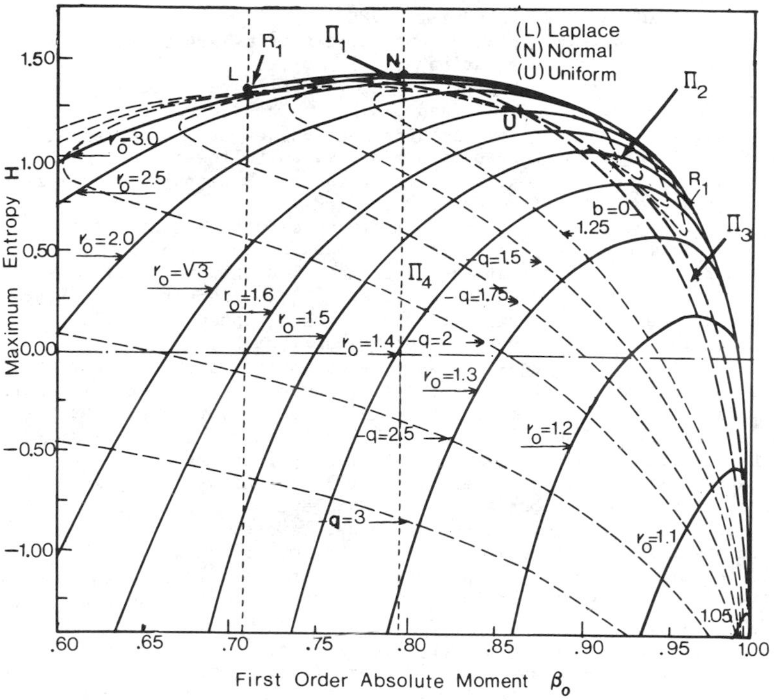

FIG. 2.— MAXIMUM ENTROPY DIAGRAM FOR SYMMETRIC DOMAINS

Maximum entropy values that correspond to these density functions are immediately obtained as $H = a + 2\,\beta_o\, b + c$.

Numerical solutions are found by double iteration as follows. By fixing any value of parameter $q = b/\sqrt{|a|}$, simple equations with the only variables p and $r_o$ may be derived from (14.1) and (14.2); thus, the parameters p, a and b are calculated by iteration according to the given values of $r_o$, and the values of parameters $\beta_o$ and c are immediately obtained from equations (15) and (16). Then a second iteration is made varying the q values until the values of $\beta_o$ fit the initial data.

SECOND ORDER MOMENT GIVEN. In this case standardized maximum-entropy densities are of the form $f(z) = \exp(-az^2 - c)$, and the parameter values result from general solution specialized for b = 0, setting q = 0 in equations (14) to (16).

Limits of the parameter a across the range $r_o \geqslant 1$, are derived from equations (14.1) and (14.2) specialized for q = 0, taking into account the series expansion of the error function and the Dawson function. In this way, when $r_o$ tends to infinity, a equals 1/2 which corresponds to the Gaussian density function; $r_o$ equals $\sqrt{3}$ as a tends to zero, which again gives the uniform density function. Finally, $r_o$ equals 1 as a tends to $-\infty$.

The parameter values of standardized maximum entropy densities were calculated, and the maximum entropy H as the first absolute moment has been represented in Fig. 2, where the Gaussian density point has been drawn.

FIRST ABSOLUTE MOMENT AND SECOND MOMENT GIVEN

In this case standardized maximum entropy densities are of the form (7) and their parameters are given by equations (14.1) to (16.2).

Limits of parameters a and b, across the infinite ranges of auxiliary parameters are obtained from (14.1) and (14.2). These equations and $p=r_o \sqrt{|a|}$ define the family of curves $r_o(p)$ for different values of q (see dashed lines in Fig. 2). Analysis of these curves is summarized as follows:

1. - All curves $r_o(p)$ cross at the limit point $r_o=\sqrt{3}$ as p tends to zero; this point corresponds to the uniform density (Fig. 2).
2. - In the case $a > 0$, $r_o$ tends to infinity as does p what determines the existence of maximum entropy densities over the infinite domain $R_1$. In this case curves $r_o(p)$ show different shapes as they lie into the regions $\pi_1$ and $\pi_2$ (see Fig. 2) defined by inequalities $b > 0$ and $b < 0$, respectively. Every curve into $\pi_2$ ($q<0$) presents a minimum value of $r_o$ below those for uniform density, whereas curves into $\pi_1$ ($q>0$) increase monotonously with p.
3. - In the case $a < 0$, $r_o$ equals 1 as p tends to infinity, and no density over $R_1$ appears in an asymptotic way. Curves $r_o(p)$ show different shapes into regions $\pi_3$ and $\pi_4$ (see Fig. 2) defined by $b > 0$ and $b < 0$. Every curve into $\pi_4$ ($q<0$) presents a maximum value of $r_o$ above the limit value for uniform density, whereas curves into $\pi_3$ decrease monotonously as p increases. Hence the only possibility of maximum entropy densities over $R_1$ existing, is an infinite limit of maximum values on the curves $r_o(p)$. Such a limit appears as q tends to infinite and a equals zero, therefore it corresponds to the Laplace density obtained in the analysis of above-mentioned particular solution.

All finite points on curves $r_o(p)$ determine maximum entropy densities; hence, it results that standardized maximum entropy densities over domains $(-r_o, r_o)$, always exist for $r_o \geqslant 1$ and $1 \geqslant \beta_o > 0$.

Density functions maximizing entropy over $R_1$, may be considered as the limits of maximum entropy densities over finite domains $(-r_o, r_o)$ when $r_o$ tends to infinity. Limits exist for regions $\pi_1$ and $\pi_2$ and they provide maximum entropy densities for different values of the first absolute moment given by $1 > \beta_o \geqslant \sqrt{2}/2$ (see Fig. 2). For regions $\pi_3$ and $\pi_4$, only one limit exists and it corresponds to the standardized Laplace density with $\beta_o = \sqrt{2}/2$. No other density function maximizing entropy over $R_1$ appears for regions $\pi_3$ and $\pi_4$, and one upper bound of maximum entropy values in these regions is just the entropy of Laplace density $= 1 - \mathrm{Ln}(\sqrt{2}/2)$.

The parameter values of standardized maximum entropy densities have been calculated by equations (14.1) to (16.2) as the above-mentioned numerical method. A summary of these calculations corresponds to the maximum entropy diagram in Fig. 2, where the points representing Laplace, Normal and Uniform densities have been drawn.

MAXIMUM ENTROPY DENSITY OVER AN ASYMMETRIC DOMAIN

The density functions that maximize entropy over asymmetric domains are immediately obtained from the densities for standardized uncertainties over symmetric domains.

Consider the second order uncertainty over $R_1^+$ and $(o,r)$ represented as the moments $\mu_1'$ and $\mu_2'$. Maximum entropy densities are of the form $f(y) = \exp(-[a'y^2 + 2b'y + c'])$. They correspond to the standardized uncertainty, transformed as $y = \sqrt{\mu_2'}\,|z|$, defined by $\beta_o = \beta_1/\sqrt{\mu_2'}$ and $r_o = r/\sqrt{\mu_2'}$. Parameters of maximum entropy density are given as those of standardized densities (7) by the equations

$$a' = a/\mu_2' \; ; \; b' = b/\sqrt{\mu_2'} \; ; \text{ and } \mathrm{exc}(-c') = (2/\sqrt{\mu_2'}) \exp(-c) \tag{17}$$

$$H' = H - \log(2/\sqrt{\mu_2'}) \tag{18}$$

## CONCLUSIONS

1. The usual representation of second order uncertainties by the first two moments must be modified when the uncertainties are distributed over the double-infinite domain $R_1$ or finite domains symmetric about the mean. In these cases the first absolute moment must be considered in addition to the mean and second moment in order to complete the representation of uncertainty.

2. The maximum entropy method is very efficient for second order uncertainty modelling. The main reasons are:

2.1 The maximum entropy formalism is well suited to the modified representation of uncertainties. In fact, it may be the only method available for uncertainty modelling when the first absolute moment has to be considered.

2.2 The maximum entropy method applies over all ranges of finite domains in which distributions exist. No truncation of density functions is required for uncertainty modelling over finite domains.

2.3 This method applies only over infinite domains $R_1$ and $R_1^+$ when the conditions $2\beta_1^2 \geqslant \mu_2$ and $2\mu_1'^2 \geqslant \mu_2'$ are satisfied. These conditions are the only limitation of the method. However, they are easily accommodated in practice, either by setting the finite domain as large as desired, or by using the Laplace density function limiting the maximum entropy density.

## REFERENCES


Abramowitz, M. and Stegun, I. (1965). "Handbook of Mathematical Functions", Dover Publications, Inc., New York.

Aczel, J. (1984). "Measuring Information beyond Communication Theory", Aequationes Mathematicae, Vol. 27, pp. 1-19.

Dowson, D.C. and Wragg, A. (1973). "Maximum-Entropy Distributions Having Prescribed First and Second Moments, "IEEE Transactions on Information Theory, September, pp. 689-693.

Evans, R. (1969). "The Principle of Minimum Information", IEEE Transactions on Reliability, Vol. 12-18, Part 3, pp. 87-90.

Goodman, J. (1985). "Structural Fragility and Principle of Maximum-Entropy", Structural Safety, Vol. 3, pp. 37-46.

Jaynes, E.T. (1957). "Information Theory and Statistical Mechanics", Physical Review, Vol. 106, No. 4, pp. 620-630.

Jaynes, E.T. (1968). "Prior Probabilities", IEEE Transactions on System Science and Cybernetics, Vol. 4, No. 3, pp. 227-241.

Kapur, J.N. (1982). "Maximum-Entropy Probability Distributions for a Continuous Random Variate over a Finite Interval", Journal of Mathematical and Physical Sciences, Vol. 16, No. 1, pp. 97-109.

Mukherjee, D. and Hurst, D.C. (1984). "Maximum-Entropy Revisited", Statistica Neerlandica, Vol. 38, No. 1, pp. 1-12.

Mukherjee, D. and Ratnaparkhi, M. (1986). "On the Functional Relationship between Entropy and Variance with Related Applications". Commun. Statist. Theory and Methods, Vol. 37, No. 3, pp. 291-311.

Ochi, M.K. (1986). "Non-Gausian Random Processes in Ocean Engineering". Probabilistic Engineering Mechanics, 1986, Vol. 1, No. 1, pp. 28-33.

Shannon, C.E. (1948). "A Mathematical Theory of Communication", Bell System Technical Journal, Vol. 27, No. 3, pp. 379-423 and pp. 623-656.

Shohat, J.A. and Tamarkin, J.D. (1943). "The Problem of Moments", Mathematical Surveys, No. 1, American Mathematical Society.

Winterstein, S.R. (1985). "Non-Normal Responses and Fatigue Damage", Journal of Engineering Mechanics, ASCE, Vol. 111, No. 10, pp. 1291-1295.

Wragg, A. and Dowson, D.C. (1970). "Fitting Continuous Probability Density Functions over $(0, \infty)$ Using Information Theory Ideas", IEEE Transactions on Information Theory, March, pp. 226-231.



## ACKNOWLEDGMENTS

The authors wish to thank N.C. Lind for helpful comments.

## EVALUATION OF SEISMIC AND WIND DESIGN CRITERIA FOR MODULAR HTGR

**M.K. Ravindra*, R.V. Vasudevan* and F. Swart****

* EQE Incorporated, 3300 Irvine Ave. Suite 345, Newport Beach, California 92660

** Gas Cooled Reactor Associates, 10240 Sorrento Valley Road, Suite 300, San Diego, California 92121-1605

**ABSTRACT**

Seismic and extreme wind (including hurricane and tornado) levels for the design of standard modular high temperature gas-cooled reactor (MHTGR) have been chosen deterministically. This paper describes a study ( Ravindra and Vasudevan, 1986) performed to assess whether the deterministic design levels of the MHTGR conform with the probabilistic requirements on safety and plant investment protection. The goals for risk and plant investment protection are outlined in the Utility/User Requirements and the Overall Plant Design Specifications (OPDS). Since only a conceptual design of the MHTGR was available, a global assessment was performed. The assessment was guided by the results and insights obtained in the post -earthquake, -wind and -tornado investigations, experience gained in performing a number of external event (e.g., seismic and wind) probabilistic risk assessments(PRA) of light water reactors, and studies on fossil and industrial facilities for seismic and wind capabilities. The study concluded that the deterministic design criteria do conform to the probabilistic goals of the MHTGR.

**DETERMINISTIC CRITERIA AND PROBABILISTIC GOALS**

Using the conventional deterministic approach, seismic and extreme wind (tornado, hurricane, and wind) levels for the design of the standard modular high temperature gas-cooled reactor (MHTGR) have been selected for a "reference" site. The reference site is defined as the one for which the seismic and wind hazards are greater than those for at least 85% of the existing nuclear power plant sites in the US.

DETERMINISTIC DESIGN LEVELS: Selected nuclear island(NI) structures, equipment and systems will be designed for an SSE (Safe Shutdown Earthquake) with a peak ground acceleration(PGA) of 0.30g and an OBE (Operating Basis Earthquake) with a PGA of 0.15g. They will also be designed to withstand the effects of the Design Basis Tornado (DBT) specified for Region I in US NRC Regulatory Guide 1.76. The rest of the NI and the balance of plant will be designed to meet the requirements of ANSI A58.1-1982 Zone 3 for seismic loading and 110 mph windspeed.

PROBABILISTIC GOALS: The Utility/Users' document specifies the following for safety and plant investment protection:

1. The calculated equivalent unavailability owing to forced outages caused by external hazards, averaged over the lifetime of the plant shall not exceed 10% (Average of 876 hours./yr).
2. Outages of six months or greater shall not contribute to more than 10% of the total equivalent unavailability from forced outages, including those not expected to occur in an individual plant's lifetime.

3. The calculated annual risk, defined as the sum of the event frequency times consequence over all events, to plant equipment or property when averaged over plant lifetime shall not exceed the annual property damage insurance premium used in economic assessments. The postulated annual premium for property damage from internal and external hazards is $4.5 million.
4. The mean likelihood of exceeding the safety-related design conditions for the MHTGR shall be less than $10^{-5}$ per year.
5. The plant shall be designed to meet the applicable top level regulatory criteria without credit for sheltering or evacuation of the public beyond the plant's exclusion area boundary. This requirement translates to an allowable annual frequency of severe damage to the vessel system (VS), reactor cavity cooling system (RCCS) and reactor building (RB) should be less than $5 \times 10^{-7}$.

**APPROACH AND RESULTS**

REFERENCE SITE: A review of the available seismic and wind hazard studies (e.g., Bernreuter, et al (1985) for the seismic hazard and Changery (1982) for wind hazard) was performed to select the reference site. Figure 1 shows the hazard curves for the reference site.

DAMAGE ESTIMATION: Estimate of the forced outage time as a function of hazard magnitude was made using damage surveys conducted following earthquakes, tornadoes or windstorms, and on the experience gained in the performance of several external event PRAs. Estimate of the property damage cost(i.e., repair and replacement costs) as a function of hazard level was synthesized by assigning damage rates to plant equipment and system inventory and then by compounding the inventory damage costs at each hazard level. Table 1 lists the estimated plant costs at selected hazard levels. In these estimation processes, the MHTGR was assumed to be designed to the deterministic levels stated elsewhere. Figure 2 shows the synthesized forced outage hours for seismic and wind hazards for the MHTGR. By convolving these damage or forced outage functions over the entire range of hazard curves, the mean unavailability and the annualized risk of damage to plant equipment or property due to seismic and wind events were calculated.

EVENT FREQUENCY: The contribution of external events to the frequency of exceeding the safety-related design conditions or 10 CFR 100 limits was calculated by convolving the hazard curves with the plant level fragility curves where fragility is the conditional probability of an event as a function of hazard magnitude. The plant-level fragility was calculated by developing the Boolean expressions for different accident sequences leading to the event of exceeding safety-related design conditions or 10 CFR 100 limits, and quantifying the expressions using component fragilities. The component fragilities were derived from sources such as Budnitz, et al (1985) and were tailored to the MHTGR items. Experience with the actual performance of structures and equipment of power plants and industrial facilities in past major earthquakes and tornadoes has borne out that large conservatisms exist in current design procedures. This fact has been explicitly recognized and used in developing the component fragilities. The calculated event frequencies for exceeding the design conditions and 10 CFR 100 limits are shown in Table 2.

SELECTION OF OBE. The SSE is dictated by regulation, but the choice of an OBE relies on the optimization of initial and future costs __ as seen in figure 3, the initial cost increases with design level while future costs and reliability become constant beyond a certain level (Hitzeman and Ravindra, 1977). These costs are balanced to derive an optimal OBE.

Two OBE levels, 0.07g and 0.15g (i.e., 1/4 SSE and 1/2 SSE) were examined in the study. The forced outage curves for the two OBE designs were developed from actual experience data and convolved with hazard curves to obtain the expected mean forced outage to be 6.7 and 3.2 hours per year. The expected differential cost of replacement power was calculated as 3.5 times $35,000 per hour (= $122,500) and the present value of these annualized expected costs over the life of the plant is $2,830,975 (assuming a discount rate of 3% i.e., interest rate minus inflation rate). Therefore, if the difference between the initial costs for the two designs is larger than $2,830,975, it is economically justified to design for the lower OBE (i.e., 0.07g).

TORNADO DESIGN CRITERIA. The DBT windspeed for the reactor service building (RSB) is 360 mph. This is a steel frame building with metal siding and roofing and the siding is designed to blow off at wind speeds in excess of 160 mph. The steel frame is designed to not collapse at the wind speed of 360 mph because this is adjacent to the inlet and outlet of the RCCS. This requirement of ensuring no collapse against the 360 mph wind results in large steel columns and bracings and substantial increase in initial cost. Therefore, interest lies in reducing the DBT criteria for the RSB.

A total of three design windspeed cases were investigated for the RSB and RCCS. The design windspeeds and the corresponding mean failure frequencies/year are summarized in Table 3. Based on this global and approximate analysis, it is optimal to design the RSB to not collapse at a DBT windspeed of 250 mph and the RCCS to 360 mph in order to satisfy the OPDS requirement.

## CONCLUSIONS

The results of the study (Ravindra and Vasudevan, 1986) on the assessment of the proposed deterministic seismic and wind design levels are :

- The contribution of the seismic and wind events to the mean unavailability due to forced outages is negligibly small.
- The annualized risk of damage to plant equipment or property due to seismic and wind events is small ($9,000) compared to the total annual premium of $4.5 million for property damage from internal and external hazards .

- The mean annual frequency of exceeding the safety-related design conditions due to seismic and wind events is $7 \times 10^{-6}$ which is lower than the OPDS requirement of $1 \times 10^{-5}$.
- The mean annual frequency of exceeding the 10 CFR 100 radiological limits at the site boundary due to seismic events is $7 \times 10^{-6}$; this is larger than $5 \times 10^{-7}$ which is the OPDS requirement for this event.

The selected deterministic seismic and wind design levels show conformance to the probabilistic goals of MHTGR. The magnitude of nonconformance by the deterministic design to meet the OPDS requirement (to satisfy the 10 CFR 100 limits) is within the uncertainty bound of the study. A further study of the RB, VS and RCCS using detailed system and design information is needed to confirm the need to adjust the design criteria.

A global assessment of the conceptual design of the MHTGR for specific seismic and wind design levels was made. The study found that significant cost savings can be realized by reducing the OBE to 1/4 SSE (0.07g) for NI items and by reducing DBT wind speed to 250 mph for RSB. Further optimization of the design criteria can be achieved by performing a detailed PRA of the MHTGR. Such a PRA would identify design weak-links in the plant component and system, and would also enable selecting optimal, deterministic design criteria for structures and components depending on their risk and importance to the plant.

**REFERENCES**


Bernreuter, D.L., J.B. Savy, R.W. Mensing, J.C. Chen, and B.C. Davis (1985). "Seismic Hazard Characterization of the Eastern United States Volume 1: Methodology and Results for Ten Sites", UCID-20421 Vol. 1, Lawrence Livermore National Laboratory, Livermore, CA, April

Budnitz, R.J. et al, (1982) " An Approach to the Quantification of the Seismic Margins in Nuclear Plants," Prepared by the Lawrence Livermore National Laboratory for US Nuclear Regulatory Commission, NUREG/CR-4334, August

Changery, M.J.,(1982) "Historical Extreme Winds for the United States - Atlantic and Gulf of Mexico Coastlines," prepared by the National Oceanic and Atmospheric Administration for US Nuclear Regulatory Commission, NUREG/CR-2639, May

Changery, M.J.,(1982) "Historical Extreme Winds for the United States - Great Lakes and Adjacent Regions ," prepared by the National Oceanic and Atmospheric Administration for US Nuclear Regulatory Commission, NUREG/CR-2830, May

Hitzeman, H.H. and M.K. Ravindra (1977). "Optimal Selection of OBE for Nuclear Plant Design", Presented at the ASCE Spring Convention, Dallas, TX, April

Ravindra, M.K. and R.V. Vasudevan (1986). "Evaluation of Seismic and Wind Design Criteria for Modular HTGR", EQE Report Prepared for Gas Cooled Reactor Associates, San Diego, CA, October

**TABLE 1: DAMAGE COST vs HAZARD MAGNITUDE**

| | DAMAGE COST ( K$ ) AT HAZARD LEVEL | | | | | NOTES |
|---|---|---|---|---|---|---|
| Earthquake, g's | 0.15 | 0.30 | 0.50 | 0.75 | 1.00 | |
| Wind, mph | 110 | 160 | 210 | 260 | 310 | |
| Earthquake===>> | 100 | 1200 | 4150 | 20000 | 63500 | Max |
| | 20 | 550 | 2350 | 10175 | 39600 | Best |
| | 0 | 230 | 750 | 4600 | 18500 | Min |
| Wind=========>> | 225 | 1100 | 4200 | 16100 | 50500 | Max |
| | 85 | 580 | 2100 | 8000 | 40300 | Best |
| | 5 | 180 | 1000 | 3200 | 19060 | Min |

NOTE: The three costs are: Maximum (95%), best (50%) and minimum (5%) estimated damage costs for the item at the earthquake level.

**TABLE 2: ANNUAL FREQUENCIES OF ACCIDENT SEQUENCES**

| EVENT | | SEISMIC | WIND | TOTAL |
|---|---|---|---|---|
| E-1: | a: Conservative (Failure of any item in the NI) | 2.2E-05 | 2.0E-07 | 2.2E-05 |
| | b: Realistic (Failure of RS, VS, or RCCS) | 6.6E-07 | 2.0E-07 | 8.6E-06 |
| E-2: | | 6.8E-06 | 1.0E-07 | 6.9E-06 |

E-1: Mean Annual Frequency of Exceeding Design Conditions
E-2: Mean Annual Frequency of Exceeding 10 CFR 100 limits at the Site Boundary

**TABLE 3: EFFECT OF RSB AND RCCS DESIGN WINDSPEED ON FAILURE FREQUENCY**

| No. | Design Wind Speed | Mean Frequency of Failure/Year | NOTES |
|---|---|---|---|
| 1 | RSB=360 RCCS=360 mph | 2.E-07 | Union of RSB and RCCS |
| 2 | RSB=250 RCCS=360 mph | 7.E-07 | used in all cases |
| 3 | RSB=250 RCCS=250 mph | 1.5E-06 | |

NOTE: RSB is designed to not collapse at this speed. Only exposed portions of RCCS is designed for wind loads

Figure 1: Natural Hazard Curves For the reference site

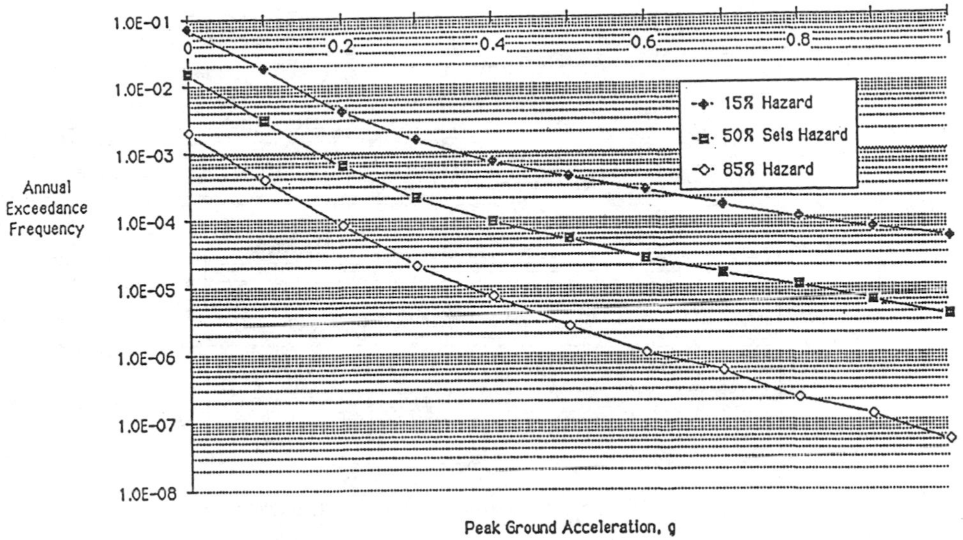


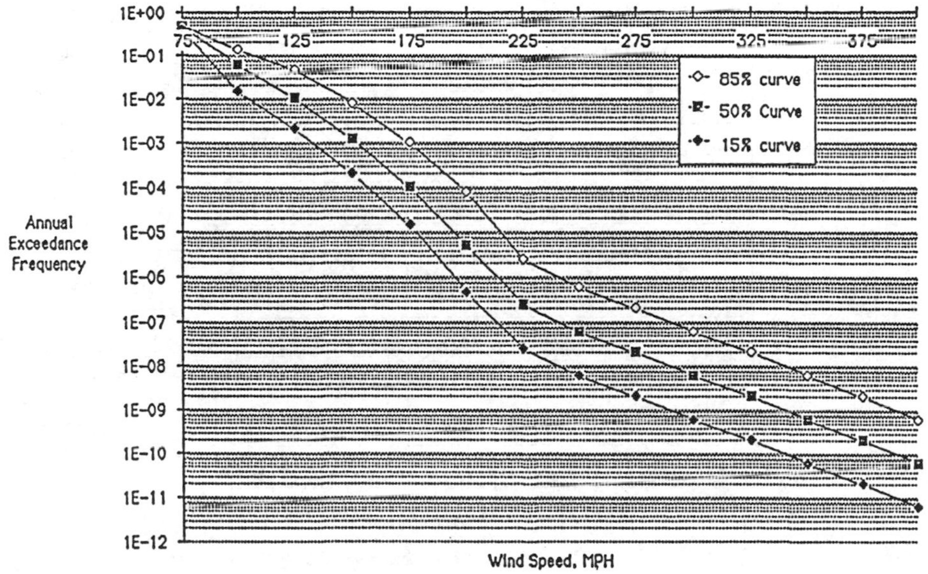

Figure 2: Natural Hazard Vs Forced Outage Functions

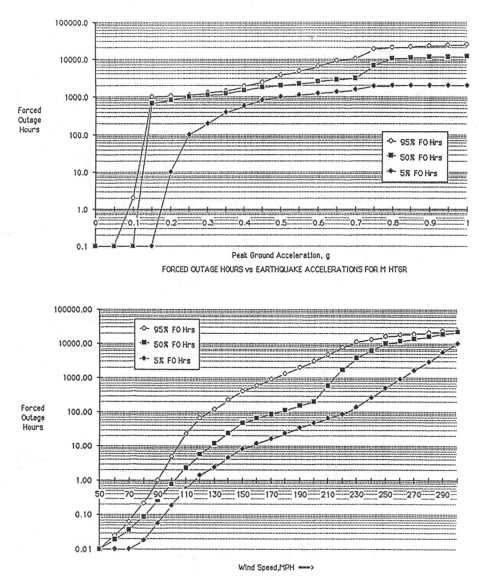

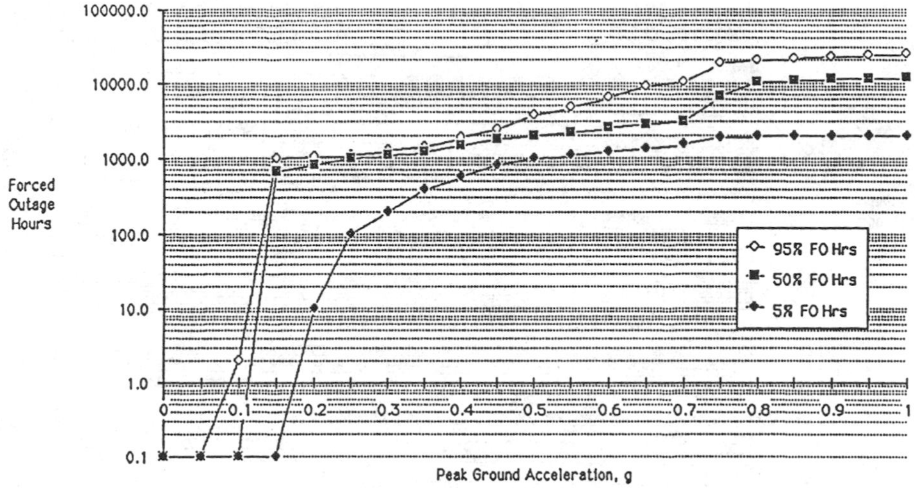


FORCED OUTAGE HOURS vs EARTHQUAKE ACCELERATIONS FOR M HTGR

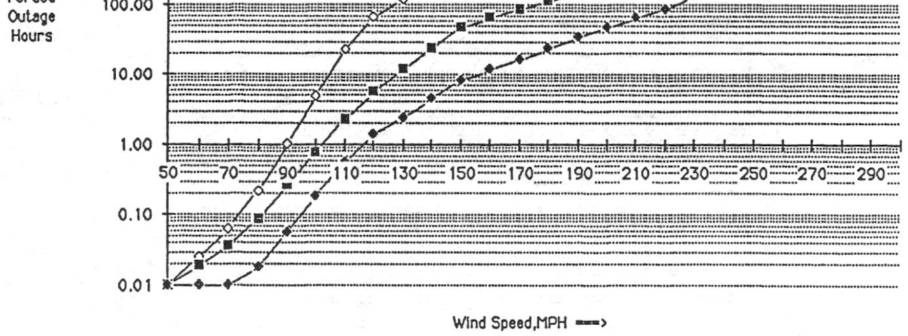


FORCED OUTAGE HOURS vs WIND SPEED FOR M HTGR

Figure 3: Cost Optimization Model for OBE Selection

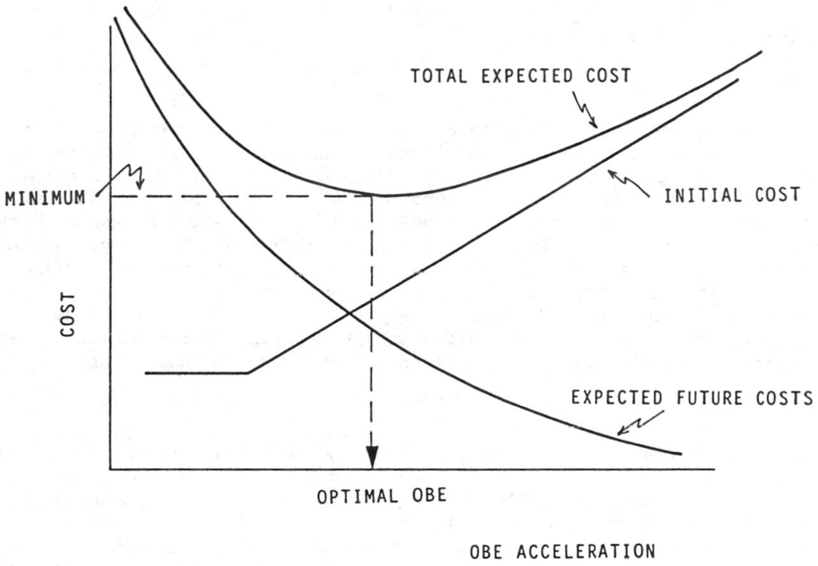

# HAZARD ASSESSMENT IN STRUCTURAL ENGINEERING

N.F. Pidgeon*+
B.A. Turner+
D.I. Blockley*
*Department of Civil Engineering, University of Bristol, Queen's Building, University Walk, Bristol, BS8 1TR, UK.
+Department of Sociology, University of Exeter, Amory Building, Rennes Drive, Exeter EX4 4RJ, U.K.

## ABSTRACT

The development of technological systems with high catastrophic potential has stimulated the development of formal techniques for risk assessment. Today these methods are being increasingly applied to general questions of structural safety. Two contrasting, but not mutually exclusive, approaches to the assessment, and management, of technological hazards are compared. First, the traditional technique of Probabilistic Risk Assessment, based upon the decision analysis philosophy of 'divide-and-conquer', is discussed. Second, System Characteristic Models, based primarily upon systems theory principles, are outlined. Advantages and disadvantages of both methods are noted. It is concluded that, due to the differing underlying philosophies, these two techniques should be seen as complementary, rather than competing.

## INTRODUCTION

The development of technological systems with high energy concentrations, and the potential for irrecoverable catastrophic loss, has raised new issues of safety and social acceptability. In particular, it would be impractical (if not in many cases unethical) to expect to be able to learn about low frequency/high consequence events in these systems merely upon the basis, **ex post**, of operating experience and observed accidents. In consequence, the need has evolved for formal **ex ante** appraisal of the potential hazards in these systems, and this has fostered the development of the discipline of risk assessment. The results of major hazard assessments provide increasingly important inputs to the social decision processes surrounding siting and risk acceptability debates, and to the task of defining appropriate management and control procedures for high risk facilities.

As the techniques of hazard assessment have matured, they have been increasingly utilised to address a wider range of safety and reliability questions. This trend can be observed in civil engineering, both in specific safety assessments for important structures, and in the recent move towards incorporation of probability factors in design codes. The explicit recognition of the importance of uncertainty, in statutory regulations, as well as in the education of the next generation of engineers, is clearly a welcome improvement over some of the more traditional, deterministic, approaches to structural design. However, some difficulties do still exist, and, in particular, we would argue that the debate over the most appropriate techniques for the assessment of safety in civil engineering ought to include the documented strengths and weaknesses of the available methods. It is as a step towards this end that, in this paper, we first discuss the traditional method of Probabilistic Risk Assessment with respect to its applicability to the total process of structural engineering (the technical **and** social aspects of design, construction and use). Second, and in contrast, the discussion will illustrate the more recent developments of System Characteristic Models as practical tools for the assessment and control of potential hazards. The discussion will emphasise throughout that, due to the different underlying philosophies of the two methods, they should be viewed as being complementary, rather than competing.

PROBABILISTIC RISK ASSESSMENT

It is now well over ten years since the publication of the first major study of nuclear safety, the WASH-1400 report (NUREG, 1975). Probabilistic Risk Assessment (PRA) is the principal method used in this study, and most subsequent studies, for the quantification of accident risks from human and environmental sources. In essence, PRA is based upon the 'divide-and-conquer' approach of modern decision analysis (e.g. Raiffa, 1968). By this method, the basic model of system failure is first sub-divided by the analyst into component events, often expressed as logically related event or fault trees. Upon the basis of the available data, probability values are then assigned to the component events that potentially contribute to ultimate failure. In theory, an overall probability of failure can then be computed from an aggregation of these individual probability components. In philosophical terms the 'divide-and-conquer' strategy is in keeping with the tradition of reductionism, identified most closely with the biological sciences, but often taken to be a general paradigm for the conduct of scientific enquiry. The reductionist thesis assumes that the behaviour of complex systems can be studied as no more than the set of properties associated with the system's sub-components. From this perspective, one of the central tasks of science is, therefore, the decomposition, and individual analysis of, system components. A number of the advantages **and** disadvantages of the PRA method can be related to this basic reductionist philosophy.

As a direct result of the experience gained from the major studies performed for nuclear and chemical facilities, the practical strengths and weaknesses of PRA have been highlighted. Particular strengths include the fact that the analyses generally produce some form of quantitative result (which is what most contemporary decision-makers want), and that the mathematical techniques that are used are relatively well formulated. Allied to this, formal PRA can, in theory at least, be subject to rigorous external critique (Fischhoff, Lichtenstein, Slovic, Derby and Keeney, 1981). We believe that the importance of this external accountability cannot be overstressed where sensitive risk issues are in the public domain, and the future of a particular technological development may depend, ultimately, upon its social acceptability. Furthermore, when groups of technical experts disagree about aspects of an analysis this may be an important indicator of limited knowledge about the area, and the need for extensive research before commitment is made to critical decisions. Finally, and perhaps somewhat surprisingly, the most important benefit of performing a PRA appears to be a psychological one. By stimulating creative thought about the structure of the system, the process of analysis may bring to light previously unforeseen failure modes which, if serious, can subsequently be countered by design or operational adjustments (Kunreuther and Linnerooth, 1984). The distinction between the **hypothesis generation** and **hypothesis testing** phases of the scientific method (the contexts of discovery on the one hand, and verification, or criticism, on the other) is one that continually arises within the philosophy of science. By augmenting the process of discovery, PRA can, aside from any specific quantitative results produced, have an important bearing upon the validity of the qualitative modelling of the system.

Several difficulties of PRA have been documented. At a fundamental level Vlek and Stallen (1980) note the basic lack of consensus over an adequate formal, or intuitive, definition of risk. They list at least six formal mathematical definitions of risk, and over thirty other variables thought to influence the intuitive assessment of risk acceptability. It is therefore clearly important to establish whether the conclusions to be drawn from a PRA are sensitive to the risk index employed (e.g. see Otway, 1985). Furthermore, even if an appropriate risk index can be established, such as expected deaths per operating year, problems remain with the probabilistic inputs to the process. First, there are at least four fundamental 'types' of probability defined in the historical literature; classical, frequency, logical, and subjective (Barnett, 1973). While the probability calculus is relatively undisputed for these various 'types', it is far from clear how to justify the use of one 'type' over the other, or the combination of different 'types' (e.g. a subjectively assessed prior adjusted by a well corroborated frequency estimate). A second problem arises from the fact that most practical risk problems are 'open-world', in the sense that even the most comprehensive set of failure scenarios cannot be assumed to be exhaustive. Hence, the probability calculus, which is derived essentially from the closed-world paradigm of games of chance (Hacking, 1975), may force potentially unrealistic modelling assumptions. While this problem may be met in part with some form of sensitivity analysis (Vesely and Rasmuson, 1984), there remains the intractable paradox 'of needing to know completely what one does not know'.

The considerations above force us to recognise the essentially **conditional** nature of all risk assessment, and to question what Watson (1981) has termed the 'phlogiston theory of risk', where risk is characterised as an unique substance, given off by a physical process, and at a rate that can be determined by risk assessment. Whereas, in fact, results of any PRA will be conditional upon, among other things, a range of modelling assumptions introduced by the analyst. As an example of this, Lathrop and Linnerooth (1983) describe how three separate risk assessments for the **same** proposed facility in the USA differed widely in assumptions, presentation, and implied conclusions.

Other difficulties arise with the application of PRA because, as we have argued elsewhere (Pidgeon and Turner, 1986), it is unduly restrictive to talk of structural engineering failures purely in technical terms. To understand many important issues we would do better to consider the total process of engineering as a socio-technical system. Human agency will be involved at all stages of the design, construction, and use of any facility or project. Furthermore, several types of human contribution may underly any significant failure; these may include individual human errors, patterns of interaction in small-groups and predisposing institutional causes. Human reliability analysis (e.g. Swain and Guttman, 1980) may have had modest success in attaching probability estimates to the human errors of individuals, such as operator slips or lapses. However, how one attempts the probabilistic assessment of small-group events, such as communication breakdown, or the more fundamental predisposing institutional factors, such as the safe bounds to a procedure laid down in a code, is an open question. If we combine the technical uncertainty of structural engineering, with such social uncertainties we see that the task of adequately modelling the risk associated with such a system is a daunting one.

The final issues that we shall raise in this short critique of PRA concern the aggregation of the individual probability components into an overall assessment of the probability of failure for accident sequences, or the activity as a whole. First, a quantitative problem arises because probability logic may be inappropriate for conjunctive or disjunctive inference where uncertainties exist with respect to the dependencies between events (Blockley, Pilsworth and Baldwin, 1983). Second, a more critical, qualitative, question concerns the meaning of the overall failure index derived from a complex

PRA. This problem of interpretation arises directly from the distinction, noted earlier, between the different 'types' of probability. With any significantly large problem, the aggregation technique is liable to have confounded, in the singular index, several of the different 'types' of probability. For example, an empirically corroborated frequency estimate for the failure of a safety device might be combined with a human factors specialist's assessment of the probability of the inappropriate operation of the device, together with the guess of the plant manager as to the uncertainties surrounding the environmental conditions under which the device may be required to function. To utilise here a term introduced by Funtowicz and Ravetz (1984), such different inputs will be characterised by differences of **pedigree** (where pedigree is understood to reflect the process of the derivation of the number used as an input, and the dependability of that process). Although sensitivity analysis will provide some indication of the likely bounds on the final calculation, the question still arises as to how one interprets such a statement as "the overall risk to the system is a one chance in one million per year of operation". Is this to be considered as a frequency, as a degree-of-belief, or as a logical statement? The conservative answer would be to treat the overall inference as having no better pedigree than its weakest link. This might help to avoid the well documented effect (Fischhoff et al. 1981) of analysts being over-confident in the results of their analyses, but it might also raise questions about whether some assessments were worth carrying out at all.

## SYSTEM CHARACTERISTIC MODELS

The traditional PRA techniques discussed in the previous section can be contrasted with a number of more recently proposed approaches to the assessment and control of technological hazards. These approaches are based upon a different underlying philosophy to the 'divide-and-conquer' of PRA, and we call them here 'System Characteristic Models' (SCM). For these models, the problem is not segmented into related subsets of potential contributor events. Rather, an attempt is made to identify, in an ongoing technological activity, a set of characteristics associated with the system (technical, individual human, organisational or institutional) that are significant indicators of a potential failure.

Two philosophical assumptions differentiate the SCM approach from PRA, particularly in the context of the analysis necessary with the complex socio-technical systems designed to contain high energy concentrations. The first is the notion, derived from systems theory, that the behaviour of a complex system may exhibit **interactive** properties over and above the sum of the properties of its constituent elements. That is to say, when the relationships between system elements are such that a change in any one element of the system is a function of all the other elements, and this in turn itself **causes** changes in all other elements, then any change necessarily affects the **whole** system. For highly complex socio-technical systems the nature of such interactions may not be easily foreseeable. However, interactivity does not dominate in every type of system: if the relationships are such that each element acts independently then the whole is no more than the sum of its parts. PRA is best at dealing with this latter case, where the problem contains isolated, well understood physical phenomena, the models of which can be established by scientific research. It is not so good at relating such phenomena to their overall context when the total system is complex and not completely understood. Because of this the analyst may often be forced into making artificial assumptions (e.g. by making statistical independence assumptions, or by ignoring the higher order conditionalities). The advantage of a systems approach, on the other hand, is that the dimensions of complexity and interactiveness **per se** can be treated as relevant factors in the failure equation. This is probably a more realistic modelling assumption given that, as suggested by Perrow (1984), the interactive property may be the dominant route to disaster for certain high risk activities.

The second important assumption concerns the underlying characterisation of failure. Turner (1978) describes the important temporal dimension to failure. He argues, as a result of his study of a wide range of contemporary technological disasters, that failure is typically the result of the complex, and unforeseen, compounding of separate undesirable events, often over an 'incubation' period to be measured in years. While the **precise** prediction of the where and how of any specific failure might be impossible (the particular combination of events, and uncertainties, being unique in their manifestation, if not their general characteristics), it does not necessarily follow from this that we cannot prevent some failures. Specifically, prevention may be attained if we can identify an 'incubating' hazard at an early stage. Hence, rather than attempt the difficult task of specifying all possible failure sequences in advance, as in PRA, the SCM approach attempts to identify, using a range of relevant indicators, the point at which a thorough review of the ongoing processes (both technological and social) might be in order. This consideration also focuses our attention upon the control, rather than predictive, orientation of the SCM approach, a feature which arises from the realisation of the ultimate **unpredictability** of many complex socio-technical systems (Collingridge, 1980).

The very nature of complex socio-technical systems inhibits the performance of repeatable and realistic experimental investigations of the potential routes to failure. Hence, SCMs tend to be based upon historical analysis. Failure indicators can be identified by direct analysis of case studies of failure in terms of accident cause sequences, as in the technique of generalised event sequence diagrams, currently being developed at the Universities of Bristol and Exeter (Blockley, 1986). A related technique, first suggested by Schneider (1981), is the use of known hazards to build hazard **scenarios** for a structure. Conversely, indicators might be derived from a theoretical failure model, based upon more extensive case study analysis. In a seminal structural engineering publication, Pugsley (1973) introduces the term 'proneness' to failure, and describes a number of general parameters of significance in accident history; e.g. new materials, the experience of the design and construction teams, the political climate surrounding the project. This approach has been extensively developed by Blockley (1980) in his structural safety studies.

Failure models have also been developed by social scientists who have studied technological failures. Turner (1978) describes a number of significant system characteristics. These include the ways in which human errors combine over time in complex and unforeseen patterns, the organisational factors that compound and amplify the effects of such errors, and the human and organisational conditions, such as Groupthink (Janis, 1972), that prevent the early detection of an incubating disaster. In a related, but much simplified theoretical analysis, Perrow (1984) discusses the important relationships between failure and two characteristics; system complexity, or the extent to which unforeseen interactions will occur, and system coupling, or the extent to which the consequences of undesirable events, once triggered, are likely to propagate throughout the system in an uncontrolled manner. He argues that highly complex and tightly coupled systems present significant control difficulties.

Collingridge (1980) presents a perceptive account of the fallibility of technological decision-making; developing an analysis from observation of the difficulty, noted in our previous section, of specifying all of the potential outcome states associated with a proposed action or event. Under such a constraint, which is likely to be a characteristic of most large socio-technical systems, it follows that any long-range decision-making or forecasting can be characterised as being made under **ignorance** rather than uncertainty. Since any such decision may also consequently be in error, we have to learn to live with this possibility. The key to this, Collingridge argues, is to choose those options which are highly corrigible, in the sense that they can be easily monitored, corrected cheaply, and allow time for correction; they should be easy to control, being responsive and 'well-behaved'; and they should be flexible, so that future options are kept open.

All of the previous examples yield indicators against which an ongoing activity might be evaluated. More importantly, such indicators, by directly describing potentially undesirable features of the system suggest the first step towards formulating appropriate control responses, such as improved checking, diverting more resources towards a particular area of a project, or pointing up desirable interventions by senior engineers.

In conclusion, a number of the advantages and disadvantages of SCM will be noted. By replacing the attempt to predict explicitly using strong probability assumptions with a more general characterisation of hazards, the SCM approach retains flexibility (for example, in the ability to cope with complex interactions), and also avoids the philosophical error of applying overprecise analysis to what in reality may be fuzzy phenomena. Furthermore, by highlighting the fact that alternative hazard assessment methodologies to PRA exist, SCMs caution us against falling into the trap of endorsing the erroneous 'phlogiston theory of risk'. This in turn raises an important social implication. It has been commonplace for some advocates of PRA techniques to describe public objections to certain potentially catastrophic technologies as in some sense 'irrational', or uneducated responses. Of course, such a view presupposes that PRA, or some related technique, is the sole, unchallenged, 'rational' method for hazard assessment. The arguments that we have presented here indicate that such a presupposition is false. It is interesting to note, in this context, that Perrow (1984) discusses the possible correspondence between the 'social rationalities' of laypeople and his characterisation of certain high risk systems.

A further issue of note relates to the fact that the SCM approaches developed to date do not generally give explicit quantitative assessments, and at first sight this might appear to be a distinct disadvantage. However, judgement here should be made in the light of the aims of risk assessment. If the aim is primarily that of the safe management and control of the particular system it may be more critical to ensure realistic qualitative modelling of the situation, rather than to achieve fidelity in numerical calculations.

On the debit side, SCM assessments, unlike those of PRA, may be less readily subject to external critique. A more significant issue, however, is that of hindsight effects. We have noted the predominantly historical aspect to the formulation of system failure models. Although it may seem at first sight to be an easy matter to learn from our past mistakes, the pitfalls of all historical analysis are legion (e.g. see Fischhoff, 1980). Apparent wisdom gained in hindsight does not automatically confer adequate foresight, particularly when dealing with complex phenomena, and multiple causation. Thus, the attempt to build SCMs should be pursued in a methodologically rigorous manner, perhaps including studies of ongoing projects in parallel with those of past failures in an attempt to identify the truly significant variables.

## CONCLUSIONS

Two approaches to the assessment, and control, of technological hazards have been discussed. These are seen to be based upon different underlying philosophies; the 'divide-and-conquer' of PRA contrasting with the systems orientation of SCMs. A number of the advantages and disadvantages of each method of assessment have been outlined. It should be stressed, in conclusion, that due to the differing underlying philosophies the two methods should be seen as being complementary, rather than competing techniques. Indeed, all methods are merely more or less useful for particular purposes, and the choice between them, in any specific instance, requires, in the final analysis, a modelling decision. If the goal of the adequate assessment and management of structural safety is to be properly achieved, then such modelling decisions must be guided by consideration of both the benefits, and the costs, of the currently available techniques.

## ACKNOWLEDGEMENTS

This paper was prepared with the financial support of a grant from the Joint Committee of the Social and Economic, and the Science and Engineering Research Councils of the United Kingdom.

## REFERENCES

Barnett, V. (1973) Comparative Statistical Inference. Wiley, Chichester.

Blockley, D.I. (1980) The Nature of Structural Design and Safety, Ellis Horwood, Chichester.

Blockley, D.I. (1986) 'An A. I. Tool in the Control of Structural Safety'. In A. Nowak (ed) Modelling Human Error in Structural Design and Construction, ASCE, New York.

Blockley, D.I., B.W. Pilsworth and J.F. Baldwin (1983) 'Measures of Uncertainty', Civil Engineering Systems, 1, 3-9.

Collingridge, D. (1980) The Social Control of Technology, Open University Press, Milton Keynes.

Fischhoff, B. (1980) 'For Those Condemned to Study the Past: Reflections on Historical Judgement' in R.A. Shweder and D.W. Fiske (eds), New Directions for Methodology of Behavioural Science: Fallible Judgement in Behavioural Research, Jossey-Bass, San Francisco.

Fischhoff, B., S. Lichtenstein, P. Slovic, S.L. Derby and R. Keeney (1981) Acceptable Risk, Cambridge University Press, Cambridge, U.K.

Funtowicz, S.O. and J.R. Ravetz (1984) 'Policy Related Research: A Notational Scheme for the Expression of Quantitative Technical Information', Department of Philosophy, University of Leeds, U.K. October.

Hacking, I. (1975) The Emergence of Probability, Cambridge University Press, Cambridge, U.K.

Janis, I.L. (1972) Victims of Groupthink, Houghton Mifflin, Boston.

Kunreuther, H. and J. Linnerooth (1984) 'Low Probability Accidents', Risk Analysis, 4(2), 143-152.

Lathrop, J. and J. Linnerooth (1983) 'The Role of Risk Assessment in a Political Decision Process', in P. Humphreys, O. Svenson and A. Vari (eds) Analysing and Aiding Decision Processes, North-Holland Publishing, Amsterdam.

NUREG (1975) 'Reactor Safety Study', WASH-1400, NUREG 75/014, U.S. Nuclear Regulatory Commission, October.

Otway, H. (1985) 'Multidimensional Criteria for Technology Acceptability: A Response to Bernard L. Cohen', Risk Analysis, 5(4) 271-273.

Perrow, C. (1984) Normal Accidents, Basic Books, New York.

Pidgeon, N.F. and B.A. Turner (1986) '"Human Error" and Socio-Technical System Failure in Structural Engineering', in A. Nowak (ed) Modelling Human Error in Structural Design and Construction, ASCE, New York.

Pugsley, A. (1973) 'The Prediction of Proneness to Structural Accidents', The Structural Engineer, 51, 195-196.

Raiffa, H. (1968) Decision Analysis, Addison-Wesley, Reading, Massachusetts.

Schneider, J. (1981) 'Organisation and Management of Structural Safety During Design, Construction and Operation of Structures', In T. Moan and M. Shinozuka (eds) Developments in Civil Engineering 4: Structural Safety and Reliability, Elsevier Science, Amsterdam.

Swain, A.D. and H.A. Guttman (1980) Handbook of Human Reliability Analysis with Emphasis on Nuclear Power Plant Application, NUREG/CR-1278, Washington DC.

Turner, B.A. (1978) Man-Made Disasters, Wykeham, London.

Vesely, W.E. and D.M. Rasmuson (1984) 'Uncertainties in Nuclear Probabilistic Risk Analysis', Risk Analysis, 4(4), 313-322.

Vlek, C. and P-J. Stallen (1980) 'Rational and Personal Aspects of Risk', Acta Psychologica, 45, 273-300.

Watson, S.R. (1981) 'On Risks and Acceptability', Journal of the Society of Radiological Protection, 1, 21-25.

# RELIABILITY OF STRUCTURAL SYSTEMS UNDER TIME VARYING LOADS

Y.K. Wen* and H-C. Chen*
*Department of Civil Engineering, University of Illinois at Urbana-Champaign, Urbana, Illinois 61801, USA

ABSTRACT

An investigation is carried out on the structural system reliability with emphasis on realistic treatment of the time fluctuation of the loads and their interaction with the structure. Currently available methods are critically examined with respect to their theoretical bases, computational ease, and accuracy. New methods based on a consideration of load coincidence and an imbedded Markov Chain representation of the structural damage state are proposed. Extensive Monte-Carlo simulations are carried out to verify the analytical methods. It is found that for brittle parallel systems with equal load distribution among members, the problem can be reduced to a time invariant one using currently available load combination method. If the loads are unequally shared by the members, the system failure domain may be load path dependent and cannot be expressed in terms of the cut set of those of the members. As a result, the outcrossing rate approach inherently underestimates the failure (collapse) rate. The imbedded Markov Chain model adequately treats the deterioration of the system resistance and give satisfactory results for a wide range of load parameters for the simple systems investigated.

## INTRODUCTION

Great progress has been made in structural system reliability in recent years. The attention so far has been on structural configuration (systems in series, parallel or combination thereof), effect of material property (ductile, brittle or of limited ductility), and evaluation of system reliability in terms of those of the members. The loadings have been mostly idealized as time invariant, i.e., as random variables. As most loads fluctuate in time, they need to be treated as such in the reliability study. For time varying loads, a well-known concern is possible dynamic amplification. Even for static (but time varying) loads, the sequence and path of loads have significant effect on the ultimate capacity of the system in sustaining the loads. Also, structural failure (collapse) may be caused by progressive failures of members over a long period of time than a sudden failure of all essential members at one time. Therefore the reliability problem may be significantly different from under time invariant loads. With emphasis on realistic treatment of the time varying nature of the loads, this study examines some of the currently available methods for system reliability. New methods of analysis are also proposed. Extensive Monte-Carlo simulations are carried out to provide common backgrounds against which various approximate methods are compared.

## PROBLEM DEFINITION AND ASSUMPTIONS

The reliability problem investigated is the probability that a structural system, consisting of members (components), reaches a limit state, either a given state of damage or collapse, over a given period of time under the action of one or more time varying loads. As the emphasis is on the system aspect of the problem, to keep the analytical problem tractable, the following assumptions are made:

i) The loadings are assumed to have large scale of fluctuation that the structure will respond statically. Combination of dynamic effects in simple limit state considerations such as those of members or of structures which remain linear elastic can be found in Pearce and Wen (1984). The loadings are modeled by Poisson pulse processes $S(t)$, in which the load occurrence time, duration, and intensity are treated as random variables. The load processes are characterized by a mean occurrence rate $\nu$, a mean duration $\mu_d$, and an intensity random variable X with a density function $f_X(x)$. It is a simple and flexible model which captures the main features of static (but time varying) loads. Details and applications of this model can be found, e.g., in Pearce and Wen (1984) and Larrabee and Cornell (1981).

ii) A partially damaged structure will undergo no repair before the next load application; note if repair is considered the repair time required may vary and loading pattern may also be altered because of repair the reliability analysis therefore will be extremely complex.

iii) The member resistance is assumed to be time invariant, i.e., until the limit state is reached; however, the system resistance deteriorates with time because of the no repair assumption.

iv) The loads are assumed to be statistically independent of one another, i.e., in terms of occurrence time, duration and intensity, unless specifically mentioned (the independence assumption can be relaxed for certain cases).

This paper summarizes results of investigation of simple series systems represented by a ductile frame and parallel systems represented by brittle parallel bars. Details and derivations can be found in Wen and Chen (1986).

TIME VARIANT RELIABILITY OF SERIES SYSTEMS

It is well-known that the plastic collapse of a ductile frame can be treated as the union of all the possible failure modes (mechanism), therefore as a series system. Since the member resistance is assumed to be time invariant, for given (known) resistance of the member $\underset{\sim}{R} = \underset{\sim}{r}_o$, the failure domain for the system is the union of all failure modes

$$F = \bigcup_{i=1}^{\ell} F_i \tag{1}$$

in which $F_i$ = failure domain of i-th mode in the load space $[\underset{\sim}{S} = S_1,S_2,\ldots,S_m]$; $\ell$ = number of failure modes; and m = number of time varying loads. The reliability of tho system at $t = t_o$ is therefore the probability that there is no crossing of the vector load process $\underset{\sim}{S}(t) = [S_1(t),S_2(t),\ldots,S_m(t)]$ into the failure domain in the $\underset{\sim}{S}$ space described by Eq. 1. Note that it is assumed that member resistance is ductile and does not deteriorate from repeated load applications, therefore even without repair, partial damage due to previous load applications would not alter the failure domain. The problem so formulated is that of the first passage probability. The solution is generally difficult. Approximate solution can be obtained based on the outcrossing rate statistics. For example, a Poisson outcrossing assumption would give a good estimate of the reliability as

$$L(t) \approx \exp[-\nu(\underset{\sim}{r}_o)t_o](1 - P_f(o)) \tag{2}$$

in which $\nu(\underset{\sim}{r}_o)$ = the mean outcrossing rate given the resistance $\underset{\sim}{R} = \underset{\sim}{r}_o$. $P_f(o)$ = probability of failure at t = 0, generally negligible. Note in this investigation the load processes are assumed to be independent Poisson pulse processes, the outcrossings can be shown to follow a Poisson law, the solution in Eq. 2 is therefore exact. The crossing rate analysis of a vector pulse process into a union of failure domains, however, is not elementary. The formulation for Poisson square wave (Rackwitz, 1985) has been extended to Poisson pulse process for this purpose (Wen and Chen, 1986). The calculation of the outcrossing rate require evaluations of multivariate normal distribution of order of $2\ell$. When the resistances are unknown and modeled by random variables, Eq. 2 gives the conditional reliability for $\underset{\sim}{R} = \underset{\sim}{r}_o$. The unconditional reliability in principle requires n-fold integration, over the n resistance variables which becomes impractical for n > 3. Numerically efficient approximate methods are therefore necessary under these circumstances. Such methods have been recently developed, e.g., Madsen (1987).

ENSEMBLE OUTCROSSING RATE METHOD. If one includes the resistance variabilities by modeling them as random variables in the outcrossing rate evaluation, one in essence obtains the ensemble average (over the resistance) of the mean outcrossing rate, $\nu$. It is obvious that in connection with this ensemble outcrossing rate the reliability based on the Poisson outcrossing assumption (replacing $\nu(r_o)$ by $\nu$ in Eq. 2) is strictly no longer valid. However, it still can be used as an approximation.

LOAD COINCIDENCE METHOD. Taking advantage of existing methods of time invariant system reliability analysis and the load coincidence method for load combination, Wen (1980) proposed to use Eq. 2 and evaluate the failure (collapse) rate as combination of those due to individual load occurrence and joint occurrence (coincidences) of different loads. Required in this method are the calculation of occurrence and coincidence rates of loads and conditional probabilities of failure (collapse) of the system given the occurrence and coincidence of loads. These conditional probabilities of failure can be evaluated based on state-of-the-art methods of analysis for time invariant system reliability. Therefore, this relatively simple formulation can be applied to rather complex systems using the well developed methodologies for time invariant reliability analysis. Implied in this formulation, however, is the assumption that failures are independent events which is not strictly valid since there is dependence through structural resistance which does not change from occurrence to occurrence of loads. Therefore, the error introduced is similar to that in the ensemble outcrossing rate method.

NUMERICAL EXAMPLES. To compare the accuracies of these methods, numerical examples on the plastic collapse of a simple frame under vertical and horizontal time varying loads (Fig. 1) are carried out. The loadings are sparse Poisson pulse processes representing transient loads. To limit computation time, only three dominant failure modes were used in the ensemble outcrossing rate analysis. Exact solutions are also obtained numerically. The PNET method (Ang and Ma, 1981) is used in the load coincidence method for the calculation of the conditional probability of failure because of its simplicity and good accuracy. The failure rates by both approximate methods compared well with the exact solution. Computationally the load coincidence method is least demanding (in fact done by hand for this particular example). The reliability function using the ensemble failure rate in Eq. 2 consistently underestimates the system reliability (Fig. 2). The error can be significant as time increases. As an independent check of the results of the analytical methods, Monte-Carlo simulations were also carried out. A sample size of 800 is used. The probability of failure (collapse) within the first year based on different methods are compared in Table 1. As expected, the approximate (load coincidence) method overestimates the failure probability, however, the error is small when the failure probability is small.

TIME VARIANT RELIABILITY OF PARALLEL SYSTEMS

Consider a simple structure of two parallel brittle bars under the combined action of a number of time varying system loads $S_1(t), S_2(t) \ldots, S_m(t)$. If there are additional constraints in the system such that the load is equally shared by the members, let the random resistance of the two bars be $R_1$ and $R_2$, respectively. For $R_1 = r_1$ and $R_2 = r_2$ and under the condition $r_2 > r_1$, since the loads are equally shared, member 1 always fails first. Within a time period $t_o$, the system may fail (collapse) according to the sequence shown in either Fig. 3-a or Fig. 3-b, depending on whether $r_2 > 2r_1$. "X" indicates failure of first member and "o" indicates failure of the system. It can be seen that the system collapse can be instantaneous or progressive depending on the resistance. In either case, the event of system collapse within $(o, t_o)$ is described by

$$E = [S_{max} > 2r_1 \cap S_{max} > r_2] \quad (3)$$

in which $S_{max} = \max[S_1(t) + S_2(t) + \ldots, S_m(t) \text{ in } (o, t_o)]$. For $r_2 < r_1$, the sequence of the member failure is reversed, therefore the failure event is

$$E = [S_{max} > 2r_2 \cap S_{max} > r_1] \quad (4)$$

The probability of system collapse is therefore the sum of these two mutually exclusive events. One would recognize that the formulation is identical to that of time invariant problem if the load random variable is replaced by that of the maximum combined value. The same is true for a system with more than two components. Therefore, existing methods of time invariant system reliability analysis can be directly applied to this class of problems. The required maximum combined load probability density can be obtained based on the currently available load combination methods. For example, through the load coincidence method, the dependencies within and between loads can be also included (Wen, 1981).

In a more general and perhaps more realistic parallel system, the distribution of the loads among the member may not be uniform, the sequence of member failure is still more complicated since the weaker member may not fail first. Furthermore, when using an outcrossing formulation, one may not be able to find a time invariant system failure domain. That is, the system failure domain becomes loading path dependent, thus is itself time variant. To illustrate this point consider a simple case with known resistance $R_1 = 1$, $R_2 = 2$. The resultant forces in the members under the action of two time varying loads $S_1(t)$ and $S_2(t)$ are assumed to be $F_1(t) = .3\ S_1(t) + .7\ S_2(t)$ and $F_2(t) = .7\ S_1(t) + .3\ S_2(t)$. The failure surfaces (lines) for each member in the $S_1,S_2$ plane are shown in Fig. 4. The solid lines correspond to the failure sequence of member 1 → 2 and the dashed lines the reversed sequence. It is seen that depending on the load path, the system failure (collapse) (indicated by "o") can be instantaneous or progressive. Also, perhaps more importantly, the failure domain is load path dependent. Disregarding this dependence, the outcrossing result will be in error. For example, if the system failure domain is given by the hatched area (union of cut sets), the failure rate will be underestimated, since for certain load paths the system failure domain is $S_1 + S_2 > 2$. It can be easily seen that under the assumption of uniform load distribution among the members, the failure surfaces are parallel to one another thus the failure domain is independent of the load path. Therefore the results derived from the case of equal load distribution cannot be generalized to the case with unequal load distribution.

IMBEDDED MARKOV CHAIN MODEL. To include the loading path dependence, the sequence of failure of members and the redistribution of loads among the members from application to application needs to be considered.

For a system with known (deterministic) resistance, the state of the system (in terms of the failure or survival of the members) may change only at the occurrence (application) of loads, i.e., either individual load or loads in combination. Since the load intensities are assumed to be independent from occurrence to occurrence within each load and among different loads, the state of the structure at any load application depends only on that at the previous load application and not the ones before; that is, if the dependence of load through the consecutive occurrence of one load during the occurrence of another load is neglected. This dependence is small for most time varying loads. Therefore the Markov Chain would be a good model to describe the change of state of the structure from load application to application. Since the load occurrences are modeled by independent Poisson processes, the occurrence time for the structural state changes is also a Poisson process in which the Markov Chain imbedded. Given the load occurrence (or coincidence), the transition probability from state I to J can be evaluated based on currently available time invariant system reliability method and a load coincidence analysis as follows.

$$P(J,I) = \frac{1}{\lambda}\left[\sum_{i=1}^{m} \lambda_i P_{JI}^{i} + \sum_{i=1}^{m-1} \sum_{j=i+1}^{m} \lambda_{ij} P_{JI}^{ij} + \sum_{i=1}^{m-2} \sum_{j=i+1}^{m-1} \sum_{k=j+1}^{m} \lambda_{ijk} P_{JI}^{ijk}\right] \quad (5)$$

in which $\lambda_i$, $\lambda_{ij}$, and $\lambda_{ijk}$ are occurrence rate and coincidence rate of loads and $P_{JI}^{i}$, $P_{JI}^{ij}$ and $P_{JI}^{ijk}$ are conditional probabilities of transition from state I to J given the occurrence or coincidence of loads. $\lambda$ = overall load occurrence rate. Letting the transition probability matrix be [A] and making use of the well-known Markov and Poisson processes results, one can show (Wen and Chen, 1986) that the structural state probabilities at time $t = t_o$ is given by

$$\{P(t_o)\} = [Q][\diagdown e^{-\lambda t_o(1-u_i)} \diagdown][Q]^{-1}\{P(o)\} \quad (6)$$

in which [Q] = the eigen vector matrix of [A], $[\diagdown \diagdown]$ = diagonal matrix with element $e^{-\lambda t_o(1-u_i)}$; and $u_i$ = the i-th eigenvalue of [A], i.e., the i-th diagonal term of [A], and {P(o)} = the initial structural state probability, i.e., at t = 0. The reliability (no collapse) function and the hazard function at $t = t_o$ can be easily derived from $\{P(t_o)\}$.

Systems with unknown (random) resistance can be handled the same way as in the series systems.

APPROXIMATE OUTCROSSING RATE AND LOAD COINCIDENCE METHOD. If the dependence of system failure domain on load path is disregarded, the outcrossing rate into the failure domain expressed as union of cut sets can be evaluated and would be an underestimate of the failure (collapse) rate. If the system resistance variability is also included in the analysis, the ensemble outcrossing tend to give an overestimate of the failure probability. The same is true when the failure rate is used in conjunction with a Poisson assumption to determine the reliability function. The overall effect is therefore not clear, it may over or underestimate the failure probability.

If the deterioration of the system resistance with time and dependence of loading path are neglected, the failure (collapse) rate can also be evaluated directly based on a load coincidence consideration. The required conditional probabilities of failure are correspondingly the system collapse probabilities given the occurrence or coincidence of loads, and can be evaluated directly based on a method for time invariant problems. Although the theoretical basis for this approach is not strong, the computational aspect is quite attractive, especially for large, complex systems.

NUMERICAL EXAMPLES. To compare the accuracy of the analytical methods, a two-member system with deterministic resistance ($R_1$ = 1.5, $R_2$ = 2.5) under the action of two Poisson pulse processes is considered. The load parameters are: for $S_1(t)$, mean occurrence rate $\nu_1$ = 2/yr, intensity is a normal variate with $\mu_1$ = 2.0, $\sigma_1$ = .4, the corresponding values for $S_2(t)$ are $\nu_2$ = 5/yr, $\mu_2$ = 1.5, $\sigma_2$ = .3. The reliability functions based on the imbedded Markov Chain model, the outcrossing rate method and Monte-Carlo simulation (sample size = 1000) are compared in Fig. 5 for different values of mean load duration $\mu_d$($\mu_{d_1}$ = $\mu_{d_2}$ = $\mu_d$). As expected, for small $\lambda\mu_d$, the Markov assumption is good giving excellent results; the outcrossing rate method is poor and it grossly underestimates the failure probability due to the disregard of the dependence of system failure domain on load path. For relatively large $\lambda\mu_d$, load dependence due to consecutive occurrence of one load during the occurrence of the other load becomes important, the Markov assumption is no longer good and tends to give overestimate of the failure probability; in the outcrossing rate method, the conservative nature of the Poisson assumption (Eq. 2) becomes important and tends to compensate the underestimate of the failure rate, the overall effect is not certain, though the results of this particular example look good.

The results based on a direct application of the load coincidence method are compared with the outcrossing rate method for a wide range of combination of system parameters. It is found that for sparse processes, $\nu\mu_d << 1$, they are almost indistinguishable; for large $\nu\mu_d$, the load coincidence method gives higher estimates.

ACKNOWLEDGMENT

This study is supported by the National Science Foundation under grant NSF DFR 84-14284.

REFERENCES

Ang A.H-S. and H-F. Ma (1981). "On the Reliability of Structural Systems," International Conference on Structural Safety and Reliability, Trondheim, Norway, 295-314.

Larrabee R.O. and C.A. Cornell (1981). "Combination of Various Load Processes," Journal of Structural Division, ASCE, 107, No. ST1, 223-239.

Madsen H.O. (1987). "Fast Integration for Time Variant Reliability," A. S. Varitas Report.

Pearce H.T. and Y.K. Wen (1984). "Stochastic Combination of Load Effects," Journal Structural Engineering, ASCE, 110, 1613-1629.

Rackwitz R. (1985). "Reliability of System Under Renewal Pulse Loading," Journal Engineering Mechanics, ASCE, 111, 1175-1184.

Wen Y.K. (1980). "Method for Reliability of Structures Under Multiple Time Varying Loads," Nuclear Engineering and Design, 60, 61-71.

Wen Y.K. (1981). "Stochastic Dependencies in Load Combination," Proceedings of 3rd International Conference on Structural Safety and Reliability, Trondheim, Norway, 89-102.

Wen Y.K. and H-C. Chen (1986). "System Reliability Under Multiple Hazards," SRS No. 526, Department of Civil Engineering, University of Illinois, Urbana, Illinois, August.

Table 1. System Failure Probability

| Load Parameters ($\mu_{d_1}=\mu_{d_2}=\mu_d$) | Approximate (Load Coincidence) Method | Exact Solution | Monte-Carlo Simulation (n=800) |
|---|---|---|---|
| $\nu_1$=5/yr, $\nu_2$=.2/yr<br>$\mu_d$=0.01 yr | .0097 | .0073 | .0075 |
| $\nu_1=\nu_2$=5/yr<br>$\mu_d$=0.01 yr | .084 | .065 | .060 |
| $\nu_1=\nu_2$=20/yr<br>$\mu_d$=0.01 yr | .37 | .21 | .21 |
| $\nu_1=\nu_2$=20/yr<br>$\mu_d$=0.025 yr | .51 | .27 | .28 |

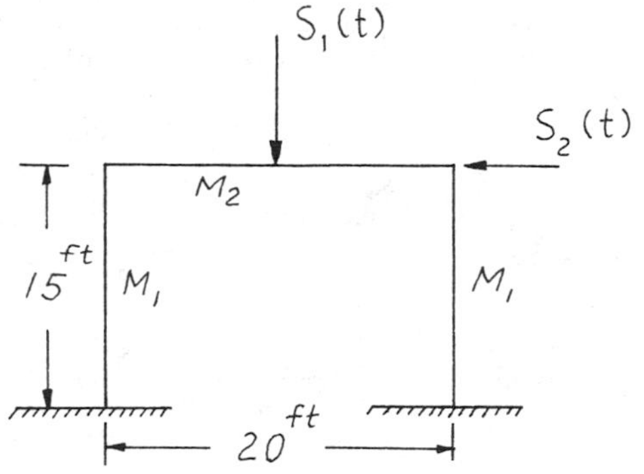


Fig. 1. Problem Geometry and Parameters.
$M_1$=N (360 k-ft, 54 k-ft);
$M_2$=N (480 k-ft, 72 k-ft);
$S_1$=N (100 k, 10 k);
$S_2$=N (50 k, 15 k).

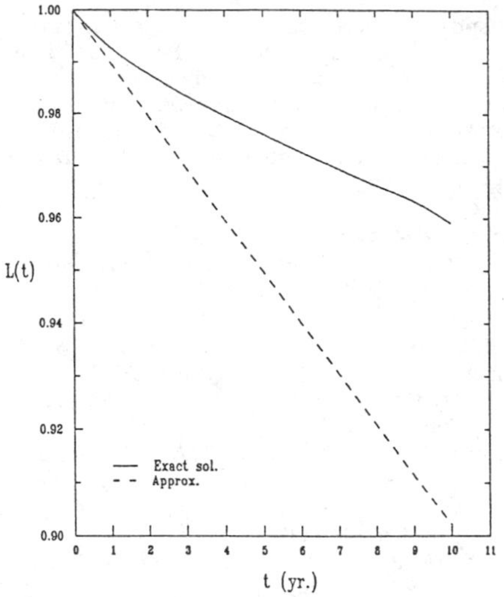


Fig. 2. Error in Using Ensemble Mean Outcrossing Rate.

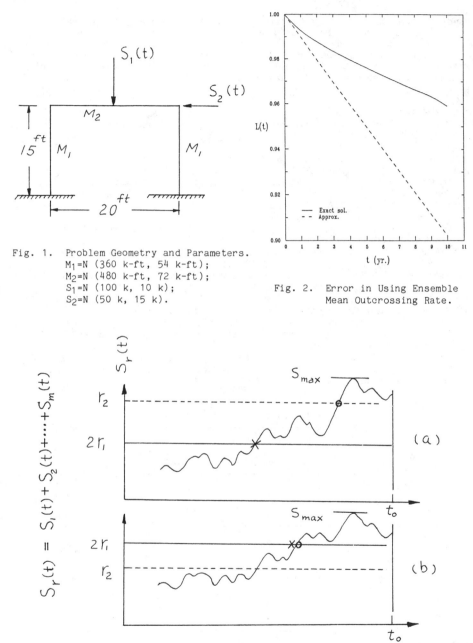

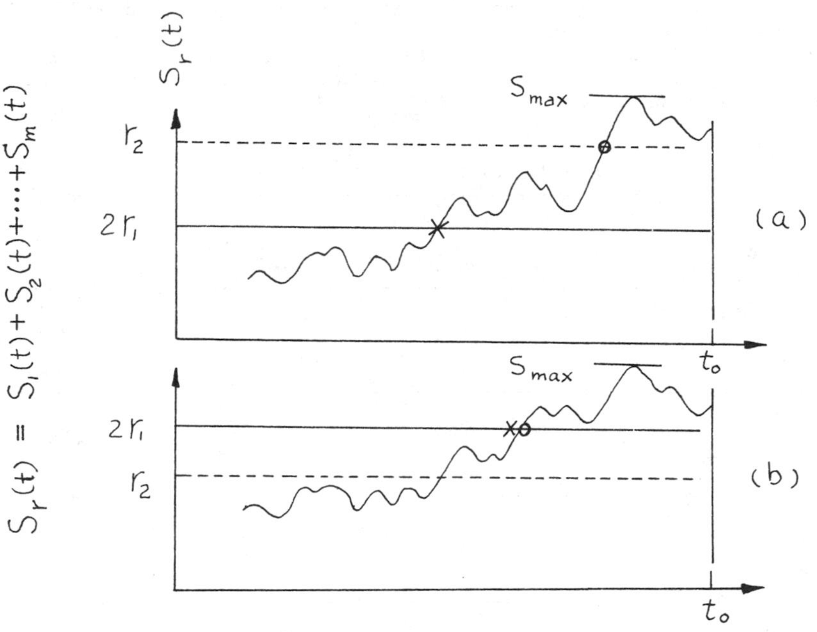


Fig. 3. Sample Time Histories of Damage and Collapse of a Two-Bar System.

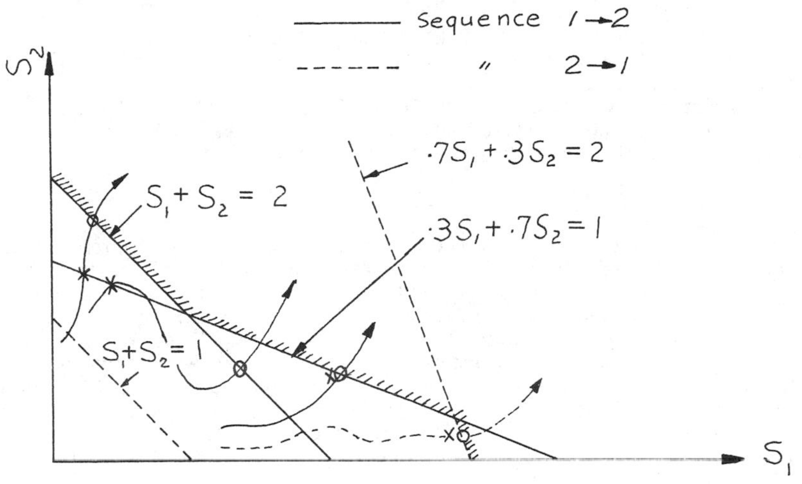


Fig. 4. Dependence of Failure Domain on Member Failure Sequence and Load Path.

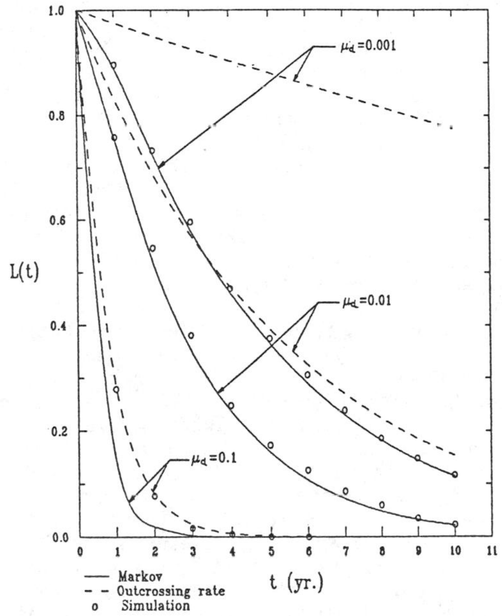


Fig. 5. Comparison of Analytical Method with Monte-Carlo Simulations.

# PROBABILISTIC RESPONSE OF STRUCTURES WITH PARAMETRIC UNCERTAINTIES

Ahsan Kareem* & Wei-Joe Sun**
*Director Structural Aerodynamics and Ocean Systems Modeling Laboratory, Dept. of Civil Engineering, University of Houston, Houston, TX 77004.
**Formerly, Civil Engineering, University of Houston.

## ABSTRACT

This paper addresses several analytical techniques for the implementation of parametric uncertainties in the probabilistic finite element analysis of spatially discrete or distributed structural systems. The analytical concepts are a First-Order Second-Moment approximation, second-order perturbation technique and Galerkin-based weak form discretization of random fields representing the uncertain continuum and/or pressure fluctuations. These methods permit the estimates of the mean values, standard deviation and covariance of structural response in terms of the displacement components or stresses. The methodologies presented herein facilitate parameter studies to delineate the significance of parametric uncertainties on the system dynamic response.

## INTRODUCTION

The treatment of random environmental loading on structures, e.g., wind, waves and earthquakes has been the subject of great interest in structural dynamics for the last few decades. The condition of uncertainty in the loading has been implemented by means of probabilistic or statistical descriptions. In most of the studies the structural systems have been assumed to either have deterministic mechanical characteristics or have been implied that the variations in these properties are sufficiently smaller than those associated with the loading. Indiscriminate utilization of this assumption may lend itself to sizeable effects on the system dynamic behavior. Any uncertainty in material properties lends itself to some statistical variation in the eigenvalues and eigenvectors of the system (for example: Boyce, 1968; Collins and Thomson, 1969; Fox and Kapoor, 1968; Hasselman and Hart, 1972; Schiff and Bagdanoff, 1972; Stetson, 1975; Nelson, 1976; Rudisill, 1974; Kiefling, 1970; Shinozuka and Astill, 1972; Prasthofar and Beadle, 1975). Whilst there have been a number of studies focusing their efforts on delineating the effects of parametric uncertainties in the system dynamic characteristics, limited investigations have been undertaken to examine the influence of uncertainties on the dynamic response of systems. More recently this area has received considerable attention and the subject is being studied systematically by numerous investigators.

Uncertainties originating from both load effects and material characteristics may be implemented in the analysis by utilizing the Monte Carlo simulation directly or in conjunction with variance reduction techniques, e.g., antithetic variates, stratified sampling (Handschin, 1970; Rubenstein, 1979; Kareeem, 1986). The accuracy of any sampling technique improves with an increase in the sample size following the law of large numbers. Therefore, for multi-dimensional problems foregoing simulation technique may become prohibitively expensive. Numerically, the success of the finite element method in the analysis of complex deterministic systems has prompted efforts for implementing uncertainty associated with the system parameter space in the analysis. The desired objective is to formulate a finite element technique which provides estimates of the mean values, standard deviation and covariance of structural response in terms of the displacement components or stresses by taking into consideration the uncertainty associated with structural characteristics and/or applied loading. In the context of the probabilistic or stochastic finite element analysis, analytical and computational concepts such as first- or second-order Taylor series expansions, perturbation techniques, random fields,

Neumann expansion, simulations and Galerkin-based procedures are being utilized for the implementation of uncertainties. The literature related to these studies may be found in the following few sample references (Beacher and Ingra, 1981; Contreras, 1980; Dendrou & Houstis, 1981; Handa & Andersson, 1981; Hisada and Nakagiri, 1985; Kareem & Sun, 1986 and 1987; Lawerence, Liu & Belytschko, 1986; Shinozuka and Dasgupta, 1986; Sun, 1979; Vanmarcke & Grigoriu, 1983; Vanmarcke, Shinozuka, Nakagiri, Scheuller, and Grigoriu, 1986).

In this paper the probabilistic finite element method is presented utilizing the analytical concepts of a second-order perturbation technique, first-order second-moment approximation, and Galerkin-based weak form discretization. The second moment analysis techniques utilizing Taylor series expansion and perturbation are presented for correlated and uncorrelated uncertain material properties of discretized lumped-mass systems. For the Galerkin-based formulation both the loading and material spaces are assumed to be homogeneous random fields. Further details of the formulations and examples may be found in Kareem (1987).

## PROBABILISTIC FINITE ELEMENT METHOD

The propagation of uncertainty to compute the level of uncertainty attributed to the solution utilizing probabilistic finite element method based on the following analytical techniques is presented.

a) Perturbation technique
b) First-Order Second-Moment approximation
c) Galerkin-based formulation

## PERTURBATION TECHNIQUE

As a part of this study the influence of uncertainty in the damping and stiffness matrices has been treated separately. In the case of uncertain stiffness, the stiffness matrix is expressed as a sum of unperturbed mean and a small fluctuation. The small fluctuation is represented by a random variable with zero mean and its variance is derived from the uncertainty associated with the stiffness. The variance of the stiffness may further depend on the physical parameters, e.g., modulus of elasticity, Poisson's ratio, cross-sectional properties, member length and density. The eigenvalues and eigenvectors of the uncertain system are expressed in terms of mean and perturbed values. The variance of the eigen properties are obtained through the Taylor expansion and are expressed in terms of the covariance matrix of the uncertain stiffness.

The covariance matrix of the uncertain stiffness may be formulated based on the knowledge of the make-up of the structure being analyzed. In the absence of the detailed knowledge of the structural make-up one may resort to various assumptions as to the description of the covariance matrix. The assumption of independence appears to be a reasonable starting point, however, the zero correlation implied by this assumption may be too simplistic to justify the physical uncertainty in the stiffness of a continuum. On the other hand for a discrete lumped-mass idealization this assumption may adequately represent the system. Alternatively, one may invoke statistical dependence that decreases with the physical separation between two points in the random medium. An exponential decay model adequately represents such random fluctuation in terms of the distance between the respective locations and a constant that controls the level of correlation. This constant approaching infinity represents correlation equalling zero, i.e., assumption of independence, on the other hand as it approaches zero, it represents perfect correlation. Notwithstanding the attractiveness of the correlation model from qualitative point of view, it may become quite arbitrary from quantitative viewpoint in the absence of information pertaining to the physical make-up of the medium being modeled. The second-order statistics of a random field representing a continuum, or a random space-time loading pattern may also be described in terms of the operational quantities, such as the scale of fluctuation and the variance function (Vanmarcke, 1983).

The equations of motion of a multi-degree-of-freedom system subjected to random base-excitation are given by

$$\underline{M}\,\ddot{\underset{\sim}{X}}(t) + \underline{C}\,\dot{\underset{\sim}{X}}(t) + \underline{K}\,\underset{\sim}{X}(t) = -\underline{M}\,\underset{\sim}{I}\,\ddot{X}_g(t) \tag{1}$$

in which $\underline{M}$ and $\underline{C}$ are deterministic or constant mass and damping matrices, $\ddot{X}_g$ is ground acceleration, $X$ represents relative displacement vector and the number of dots over a quantity represents the corresponding time derivitive, $I$ is a unit column matrix and $K$ is the stiffness matrix with random features that may be described statistically

$$\underline{K} = \underline{\bar{K}}\,(1 + \alpha) \tag{2}$$

in which $\bar{K}$ is a deterministic stiffness matrix and $\alpha$ is a normalized random variable with zero mean and it represents random variation in the stiffness. The variance of eigenvectors and eigenvalues are given by (Kareem & Sun, 1986)

$$\sigma^2_{\lambda_i} = \bar{\Phi}_i^T\,\underline{\Sigma}_{KK}\,\bar{\Phi}_i$$

$$\sigma^2_{\phi_{ki}} = \bar{\Psi}_{ki}^T\,\underline{\Sigma}_{KK}\,\bar{\Psi}_{ki} \tag{3}$$

in which $\Sigma_{KK}$ represents the covariance matrix of the stiffness coefficients and $\Phi_i$ and $\Psi_{ki}$ describe the derivatives of eigenvalues and eigenvectors with respect to the elements of the uncertain stiffness matrix. Further computational details are discussed in Kareem & Sun (1986).

The dynamic response of a multi-degree-of-freedom system is obtained utilizing a modal superposition technique. The modal response is expressed in terms of the powers of the variable used to express fluctuations in stiffness in terms of its zeroth, first and second order perturbations. By ignoring the terms of orders higher than 2, and equating equal order terms, the zeroth-, first- and second order equations corresponding to Eq. 1 are obtained.

Zeroth-Order

$$\tilde{q}_i^o + 2\xi_i\omega_i^o\dot{q}_i^o + \omega_i^{o\,2} q_i^o = \Gamma_i\,\ddot{X}_g \tag{4}$$

First-Order

$$\ddot{q}_i' + 2\xi_i\omega_i^o\dot{q}_i' + \omega_i^{o\,2}\dot{q}_i = \Delta_i X_g - 2m_{1i}\,\ddot{q}_i^o - (C_{1i} - C_{2i})\dot{q}_i^o - (K_{1i} + K_{2i} + \omega_i^{o\,2})\dot{q}_i \tag{5}$$

Second-Order

$$\ddot{q}_i'' + 2\xi_i\omega_i^o\dot{q}_i'' + \omega_i^{o\,2} q_i'' = -2m_{1i}\ddot{q}_i' - (C_{1i} + C_{2i})\dot{q}_i' - (K_{1i} + K_{2i} + \omega_i^{o\,2})q_i'$$

$$- m_{3i}\ddot{q}_i^o - C_{3i}\dot{q}_i^o - (K_{1i} + K_{2i} + K_{3i})q_i^o \tag{6}$$

in which $\underset{\sim}{X} = \sum_{i=1}^{N} \underset{\sim}{\phi}_i\, q_i$; $\underset{\sim}{\phi}_i = \underset{\sim}{\phi}_i^o(\underline{I} + \alpha\underline{\Upsilon})$; $q_i = q_i^o + q_i'\alpha + q_i''\alpha^2 + - - -$;

$m_{1i} = \underset{\sim}{\phi}_i^{o^T} \underline{M}\, \underline{\Upsilon}\, \underset{\sim}{\phi}_i^o$; $m_{3i} = \underset{\sim}{\phi}_i^{o^T} \underline{\Upsilon}\, \underline{M}\, \underline{\Upsilon}\, \underset{\sim}{\phi}_i^o$; $C_{1i} = \underset{\sim}{\phi}_i^{o^T} \underline{C}\, \underline{\Upsilon}\, \phi_i^o$; $C_{2i} = \underset{\sim}{\phi}_i^{o^T} \underline{\Upsilon}\, \underline{C}\, \underset{\sim}{\phi}_i^o$;

$C_{3i} = \underset{\sim}{\phi}_i^{o^T} \underline{\Upsilon}\, \underline{C}\, \underline{\Upsilon}\, \underset{\sim}{\phi}_i^o$; $K_{1i} = \underset{\sim}{\phi}_i^{o^T} \underline{K}\, \underline{\Upsilon}\, \underset{\sim}{\phi}_i^o$; $K_{2i} = \underset{\sim}{\phi}_i^{o^T} \underline{\Upsilon}\, \underline{K}\, \underset{\sim}{\phi}_i^o$; $K_{3i} = \underset{\sim}{\phi}_i^o\, \underline{\Upsilon}\, \underline{K}\, \underline{\Upsilon}\, \underset{\sim}{\phi}_i^o$;

$\underline{C} = (\underset{\sim}{\phi}^{o^T})^{-1}\, \chi\, \underline{\Phi}^{o^{-1}}$; $\chi = \lceil 2\xi\omega^o \rfloor$; $\Gamma_i = -\underset{\sim}{\phi}_i^{o^T}\, \underline{M}\, \underset{\sim}{I}$ and $\Delta_i = \underset{\sim}{\phi}_i^{o^T}\, \underline{\Upsilon}\, \underline{M}\, \underset{\sim}{I}$.

Following random vibration techniques the response at each order may be obtained through the integration of the response power spectral density function which is given by the product of the system transfer function and the spectral description of the input excitation. The integration in this study was carried out utilizing the residue theorem for idealized white noise base excitation. For the filtered white noise, these integrals may be evaluated utilizing either numerical techniques or symbolic operations (Pavelle, 1985). The transfer function at each order and the corresponding closed-form expressions for the response statistics are given in Kareem and Sun (1986). A summary of the second-order statistics is given here

$$\sigma_{X_n}^2 = \underset{\sim}{\Phi}^T \underline{\sum}_{\theta\theta}\, \underset{\sim}{\Phi}^T \tag{7}$$

in which $\sum_{\theta\theta}$ is the covariance matrix of $\underset{\sim}{\theta}$, where $\underset{\sim}{\theta} = [g^o\ (g' + \Upsilon g^o)\alpha\ (g'' + \Upsilon g')\alpha^2]^T$

In the second phase of this part of the study, the dynamic response of a structure to base excitation with uncertain damping characteristics was evaluated; the modal damping ratio was expressed in terms of a mean and perturbed values

$$\xi_i = \xi_i^o\ (1 + \alpha_i) \tag{8}$$

in which $\xi_i^o$ is the mean value of damping and $\alpha_i$ is a small random fluctuation. The preceding perturbation analysis was utilized to ascertain response statistics of a system with uncertain damping (Kareem & Sun, 1986).

Example

A five-story building with uncertain stiffness is considered to illustrate the proposed methodology. The level of uncertainty in stiffness influences the variability in the eigen properties and the system response. The correlation structure of the uncertain stiffness characteristics was assumed to represent either no correlation or a partial correlation beween adjacent stories. The system response is summarized in Table I and the results suggest that the system response is sensitive to the level of correlation, but the effects are not very pronounced for low values of uncertainty in stiffness.

Table I. Standard Deviation of Displacement

| Node | Standard Deviation of Response (inches) | | | | | | |
|---|---|---|---|---|---|---|---|
| | Zero Order | COV of Stiffness | | | | | |
| | Perturbation | 2% | | 5% | | 10% | |
| | | To Ist Order | To Second Order | To Ist Order | To Second Order | To Ist Order | To Second Order |
| 1 | 0.1796 | 0.1801 (0.1801) | 0.1801 (0.1801) | 0.1826 (0.1827) | 0.1830 (0.1831) | 0.1912 (0.1915) | 0.1973 (0.1982) |
| 2 | 0.3416 | 0.3426 (0.3426) | 0.3426 (0.3426) | 0.3481 (0.3484) | 0.3489 (0.3494) | 0.3670 (0.3685) | 0.3800 (0.3832) |
| 3 | 0.4748 | 0.4764 (0.4766) | 0.4765 (0.4766) | 0.4851 (0.4860) | 0.4864 (0.4876) | 0.5147 (0.5182) | 0.5344 (0.5412) |
| 4 | 0.5709 | 0.5731 (0.5734) | 0.5732 (0.5734) | 0.5847 (0.5862) | 0.5864 (0.5883) | 0.6241 (0.6301) | 0.6499 (0.6604) |
| 5 | 0.6222 | 0.6247 (0.6250) | 0.6247 (0.6250) | 0.6377 (0.6396) | 0.6396 (0.6420) | 0.6821 (0.6892) | 0.7111 (0.7234) |

(Numbers in brackets represent correlated case)

SECOND-MOMENT METHOD

The second-moment techniques have provided practical and efficient means of analysing probabilistic engineering mechanics problems (Ditlevsen, 1981; Ang & Tang, 1984; Madsen, Krenk and Lind, 1986). The attractiveness of these techniques rests on the limited statistical information needed to analyze a problem, e.g., only the first two statistical moments of a random variable are sufficient for the analysis. The total uncertainty in a random quantity is characterized by its mean and variance and generally expressed in terms of the coefficient of variation (COV) which is the ratio of the variance and mean value. The expression for response is expanded in terms of the Taylor Series; and only up to the first or second order terms are retained. These approaches may fail to provide satisfactory estimates for large coefficients of variation.

In Kareem and Hsieh (1983), the uncertainty in the dynamic response of a chimney due to parametric uncertainties resulting from both the aerodynamic load effects and structural resistance has been analyzed utilizing the second-moment and the Monte Carlo simulation techniques. In the following, the uncertainty in the structural response to base-excitation in terms of the variances of the uncertain system parameters is given

$$\mathrm{Var}(\sigma_{nx}) = \sum_{i=1}^{M} \{\bar{\phi}_{ni}^2 \bar{\sigma}_{q_i}^2 [\bar{\sigma}_{q_i}^2 \sigma_{\phi_{mi}}^2 + \bar{\phi}_{ni}^2 (\frac{\pi S_o}{2\xi_i \bar{\omega}_i^3}) \sum_{n}^{N} M_n^2 \sigma_{\phi_{ni}}^2 + \frac{9\bar{\Gamma}_i^2 \pi S_o \sigma_{\omega_i}^2}{8\xi_i \bar{\omega}_i^5}]\} / (\sum_{i}^{M} \bar{\phi}_{ni}^2 \bar{\sigma}_{q_i}^2) \qquad (9)$$

in which the participation factor $\Gamma_i = \phi_i^T(-M)I$ (Kareem & Sun, 1986).

Once the mean and variance of frequencies and mode shapes have been evaluated, the $\mathrm{var}(\sigma_{nx})$ may be determined from the previous equation. A similar expression for the variance of the standard deviation of response due to uncertain damping is formulated in Kareem and Sun (1986). The space limitation does not permit discussion of the results based on the Second-Moment analysis, however, details will be presented in a future publication.

GALERKIN-BASED PROBABILISTIC FINITE ELEMENT ANALYSIS

A Galerkin-based probabilistic finite element discretization is utilized to model the dynamic behavior of a shear beam with uncertain material properties; and subjected to spatial white noise. As an extension of this study, the stochastic response of a shear beam to homogeneous random pressure field is estimated. The spatial randomness in stiffness is represented by a homogeneous random field with known scale of fluctuation and the variance function (Vanmarcke, 1983). Therefore, information regarding the spatial scale of random fluctuation is central to this approach, which determines the level of correlation between two spatially separated elements of interest. Whilst the attractiveness of these operational quantities especially for the multidimensional processes is fully realized computationally, but very limited experimental data-base exists to correlate theoretically derived correlation models.

The dynamic response of a shear beam with uncertain properties is obtained by utilizing a Galerkin-based weak form in which the basis function is expressed in terms of the random fluctuation in the material, spatial excitation and interpolation functions. The excitation $f(x,t;\omega)$ is assumed to be independent of the random rigidity of the beam. The weak form of the equation of motion is given as

$$\bar{G}E[(W^h_{,x},U^h_{,x})] + CE[(W^h,\dot{U}^h)] + mE[(W^h,\ddot{U}^h)] = E[(W^h,f)] - E[W^h(L) \cdot \int_0^L \frac{1}{G(X)} f \cdot dx]\bar{G} \tag{10}$$

in which the inner product (f,g) is defined as $(f,g) = \int_0^L fg\,dx$, $W^h$ and $U^h$ are the test and trial functions, respectively. A trial solution is defined as a linear combination of given shape functions and unknown time dependent nodel values

$$U^h(x,t;\omega) = \sum_j^N \sum_k^N a_{jk}(t)\, \Delta B_j(\omega)\, G_k(x)\, \theta_k(x) \tag{11}$$

in which N = total number of elements, $\Delta B_j(\omega)$ - jth increment of Brownian process defined by $\Delta B_j(\omega) = [B(jh;\omega) - B((j-1)h;\omega)]$ and $d/dx\, B(x,t;\omega) = f(x,t;\omega) = \alpha(t)B'(x;\omega)$, $G_k(x)$ = average rigidity over the kth element and $\theta_k(x)$ are linear interpolation functions. The details of the rest of this formulation far exceeds the permitted length of this paper. The details are available in (Kareem and Sun; 1987) and will be presented in a future paper. The stochastic partial differential equation of the system are reduced to $N^2$ ordinary differential equations with unknown nodal values $a_{nk}(t)$. These equations are amenable to traditional numerical methods in Finite element analysis. The covariance matrix of various response components, e.g., displacement, velocity and acceleration are evaluated (Kareem, Sun; 1987).

CLOSURE

This paper addresses several analytical techniques for the implementation of uncertainties in the probabilistic finite element analysis of spatially discrete and/or distributed structural systems. The formulations presented herein permit parametric studies to delineate the significance of parametric uncertainties on the system dynamic response. Further details of the foregoing formulations, computational procedures and results will be presented in forthcoming papers.

AKNOWLEDGEMENTS

Support of this work was provided in part by the National Science Foundation Grants Nos. CEE-8019392 and ECE 8352223 and several industrial sponsors under the PYI-84 award to the senior author. Their support is gratefully acknowledged. Any opinions, findings, and conclusions or recommendations expressed in this paper are the writers' and do not necessarily reflect the views of the sponsors.

REFERENCES

Ang, A. H-S. and Tang, W.H., Probability Concepts in Engineering Planning and Design, Vols. I & II, John Wiley, 1984.

Beacher, G.B., Ingra, T.S., "Stochastic Finite Element Method in Settlement Predictions," Journal of the Geotechnical Engineering Division, Vol. 107, No. GT4, April 1981.

Boyce, W.E., "Random Eigenvalue Problems," Probabilistic Methods in Applied Mathematics, Vol. 1, Ed., A.T. Bharucha-Reid, Academic Press, 1968.

Collins, J.D., Thomson, W.T., "The Eigenvalue Problem for Structural Systems with Statistical Properties," AIAA Journal, Vol. 7, No. 4, April 1969.

Contreras, H., "The Stochastic Finite-Element Method," Computers and Structures, Vol. 12, 1980.

Dendrou, B.A., and Houstis, E.N., "Uncertainty Finite Element Dynamic Analysis," Applied Mathematic Modelling, Vol. 3, No. 4, 1979.

Ditlevsen, O., Uncertainty Modeling with Applications to Multidimensional Civil Engineering Systems, McGraw-Hill, 1981.

Fox, R.L. and Kapoor, M.P., "Rate of Change of Eigenvalues and Eigenvectors," AIAA Journal, Vol. 6, No. 12, 1968.

Handa, K., and Andersson, K., "Application of Finite Element Methods in the Statistical Analysis of Structures," Proc. 3rd Int. Conf. on Structural Safety and Reliability, 1981.

Handschin, J.E., "Monte Carlo Techniques for Prediction and Filtering of Non-Linear Stochastic Processes," Automatica, Vol. 6, 1970.

Hasselman, T.K., Hart, G.C., "Modal Analysis of Random Structural Systems," Journal of the Engineering Mechanics Div., ASCE, Vol. 98, No. EM3, June 1972.

Hisada, T., Nakagiri, S., "Role of the Stochastic Finite Element Method in Structural Safety and Reliability," Proceedings, Fourth International Conference on Structural Safety and Reliability, Kobe, Japan, May 1985.

Kareem, A., "Effect of Parametric Uncertainties on Wind Excited Structural Response," University of Houston, Department of Civil Engineering, Research Report No. UHCE 8614, 1986.

Kareem, A., "Mapping and Synthesis of Random Pressure Fields," University of Houston, Department of Civil Engineering, Research Report No. UHCE 86-16, 1986.

Kareem, A., Hsieh, J., "Reliability Analysis of Concrete Chimneys under Winds," Department of Civil Engineering, University of Houston, Report No. UHCE 83-4, May 1983.

Kareem, A. and Sun, W.J., "Stochastic Response of MDOF Systems with Statistical Uncertainties in Their Stiffness," University of Houston, Department of Civil Engineering, Research Report UHCE 86-18, 1986.

Kareem, A. and Sun Wei-Joe, "Probabilisitic Finite Element Analysis of Structures with Parametric Uncertainties," University of Houston, Civil Engineering Department Research Report, UHCE 87-1, 1987.

Kiefling, L.A., "Comment on the Eigenvalue Problem for Structural Systems with Statistical Properties," AIAA Journal, Vol. 8, No. 7, 1970.

Lawrence, M., Liu, W.K., and Belytschko, T., "Stochastic Finite Element Analysis for Linear and Nonlinear Structural Response," Structural Congress '86, (Abstract), 1986.

Madsen, Henrick O., Krenk, S., and Lind, N.C., Methods of Structural Safety, Prentice Hall, 1986.
Nelson, R.B., "Simplified Calculation of Eigenvector Derivatives," AIAA Journal, Vol. 14, No. 9, 1976.
Pavelle, R., "MACSYMA: Capabilities and Applications to Problems in Enginering and the Sciences," Applications of Computer Algebra, Kluwer Academic Publishers, Boston, 1985.
Prasthofer, P.H., Beadle, C.W., "Dynamic Response of Structures with Statistical Uncertainties in Their Stiffness," Journal of Sound and Vibration, Vol. 42, No. 4, 1975.
Rudisill, C.S., "Derivatives of Eigenvalues and Eigenvectors for a General Matrix," AIAA Journal, Vol. 12, No. 5, 1974.
Rubenstein, R.Y., Simulation and Monte Carlo Method, Wiley Interscience, 1981.
Schiff, A.J., Bagdanoff, J.L., "An Estimator for the Standard Deviation of a Natural Frequency - Part I and Part II, Journal of Applied Mechanics, Vol. 39, 1972.
Shinozuka, M., Astill, J., "Random Eigenvalue Problems in Structural Analysis," AIAA Journal, Vol. 10, 1972.
Shinozuka, M., and Dasgupta, G., "Stochastic Finite Element Methods in Dynamics," Proceedings of the Third Conference on the Dynamic Response of Structures, ASCE, N.Y., 1986.
Stetson, K.A., "Perturbation Method of Structural Design Relevant to Holographic Vibration Analysis," AIAA Journal, Vol. 13, No. 4., April 1975.
Sun, T.C., "A Finite Element Method for Random Differential Equations with Random Coefficients," SIAM Journal of Numerical Analysis, Vol. 16, 1979.
Vanmarcke, E., Random Fields: Analysis and Synthesis, MIT Press, Cambridge, Mass., 1983.
Vanmarcke, E. and Grigoriu, M., "Stochastic Finite Element Analysis of Simple Beams," Journal of Engineering Mechanics, ASCE, Vol. 109, No. 5, 1983.
Vanmarcke, E., Shinozuka, M., Nakagiri, S., Schueller, G.I., and Grigoriu, M., "Random Fields and Stochastic Finite Elements," Structural Safety, Vol. 3, Nos. 3 & 4, 1986.

RELIABILITY UNDER A NONLINEAR DAMAGE ACCUMULATION LAW:
AN APPLICATION TO WOOD ELEMENTS.

R. O. Foschi and Z. C. Yao,
Department of Civil Engineering, University of British Columbia,
Vancouver, B.C., Canada, V6T 1W5

ABSTRACT

The Rackwitz-Fiessler algorithm is applied to the study of the reliability of a structural element subject to strength degradation and controlled by a nonlinear damage accumulation law. The failure surface corresponding to a sequence of load cycles is not approximated well by a single hyperplane and offers several design points. The probability of failure is underestimated if the lowest reliability index β is used. An alternate procedure is discussed which leads to an efficient use of the algorithm and to accurate results, which compare well with Montecarlo simulations.

INTRODUCTION

This paper considers the calculation of the reliability, after a period of service, of a structural element exhibiting nonlinear strength degradation as a function of the time under load. As a particular example, we discuss the case of a wood member in bending under a combination of dead (permanent) and live (snow) loads.

The introduction of reliability-based design to wood structures requires the consideration of the effect of load history on the degradation of strength over time. It is well known that wood exhibits static fatigue in bending. Thus, a member may not fail immediately following the application of a load but it may collapse if the same load is sustained for some time. The experimental data available from tests under constant load have shown that simple, linear damage accumulation models (like Miner's rule) cannot represent the experimental trend in a satisfactory manner. On the other hand, damage accumulation models which define the rate of damage growth as a function of both stress level and the amount of damage already accumulated have been shown to be much more effective to represent the data (Foschi and Barrett, 1982). This paper considers a model of this type, and then studies its application to reliability calculations using the Rackwitz-Fiessler algorithm for the reliability index β at the end of the service life. An application of the model to reliability of wood systems has been discussed by Foschi (1984), using computer simulation.

DAMAGE ACCUMULATION

Damage $\alpha$ is a variable normalized to take the value $\alpha = 0$ at the beginning of loading and $\alpha = 1$ at failure. The rate of growth of $\alpha$ is postulated to obey the relationship

$$\frac{d\alpha}{dt} = a\,[\,\tau(t) - \sigma_o \tau_s\,]^b + c\,[\,\tau(t) - \sigma_o \tau_s\,]^n\,\alpha \qquad (1)$$

in which: 1) a, b, c and n are model parameters, random variables determining the variability in growth rate among structural elements; 2) $\tau(t)$ is the stress history; 3) $\sigma_o$ is a threshold stress ratio; and 4) $\tau_s$ is the standard, short-term bending strength of the element.

Damage is assumed to accumulate only when the applied stress $\tau(t)$ exceeds the threshold stress ($\sigma_o \tau_s$), and both the threshold stress ratio $\sigma_o$ and the short-term strength are random variables. The latter is normally measured in a ramp load test of short duration.

The damage accumulation relationship of Eq.(1) can be integrated for any given stress history $\tau(t)$, and the corresponding time-to-failure $T_f$ can then be derived from the failure condition $\alpha = 1$. In particular, when this integration is performed for the standard, short-term bending test, one of the model parameters (for example, a) can be determined as a function of the value $\tau_s$ and the remaining model parameters b, c, n and $\sigma_o$.

One of the characteristics of this damage model is that the first term on the right-hand side of Eq.(1), only dependent on stress level, controls growth rate at the beginning of loading. As damage increases, the second term, both stress level and damage-dependent, introduces an exponential, accelerated damage growth which eventually brings about the element's failure. Thus, even for a constant load, damage grows nonlinearly with time, and this permits the representation of experimental trends for wood in a manner which cannot be duplicated with linear accumulation models.

Table 1 shows values for the model parameters resulting from the model's calibration to bending tests of Hemlock lumber. These same data are shown by Foschi and Barrett (1982). All parameters, as well as the short-term strength $\tau_s$, have been assumed lognormally distributed.

TABLE 1. DAMAGE MODEL PARAMETERS

| Parameter | Mean | Standard Deviation |
|---|---|---|
| b | 35.20 | 6.59 |
| c | $0.156 \times 10^{-6}$ | $0.962 \times 10^{-7}$ |
| n | 1.43 | 0.14 |
| $\sigma_o$ | 0.58 | 0.16 |
| $\tau_s$ | 47.84 MPa | 19.54 MPa |

LOADING SEQUENCE AND THE LIMIT STATE

The loading function considred is a superposition of dead (permanent) and live (snow) loads. In the example, the snow is assumed to fall within a five month period every year. The probability distribution for the annual maximum load is known, but the shape of the five-month snow cycle is generally not available from weather records. It will be assumed that the snow load takes on constant values over each of NS segments making up the period of five months. The individual segment loads are assumed equally distributed and independent from each other. Their distribution can be derived from the condition that the distribution for the largest load in the NS segments be the same as the distribution for the annual maximum load.

If $\alpha(NY)$ is the damage accumulated after a service life of NY years, the limit state can be studied using the failure function

$$G = 1.0 - \alpha(NY) \tag{2}$$

which satisfies $G < 0$ when failure occurs within the NY years.

If NS live load segments are considered per year, the variables in the problem are: NSxNY live loads, the dead load plus five damage model parameters.

The reliability index β corresponding to the limit state G = 0 can be calculated using Rackwitz-Fiessler's algorithm (RF). For a set of variables, the value of the function G and its gradient can be efficiently derived by a recursive scheme, obtained from the integration of the damage model over each of the constant load segments. Thus, for the cycle shown in Fig. 1,

$$\alpha_{i+1} = \alpha_i K_o(i) + K_1(i) \tag{3}$$

and

$$\frac{d\alpha_{i+1}}{dz} = \frac{d\alpha_i}{dz} K_o(i) + \alpha_i \frac{dK_o(i)}{dz} + \frac{dK_1(i)}{dz} \tag{4}$$

in which z represents any one of the variables in the problem and

$$K_o(i) = e^{c\,[\,\tau_i - \sigma_o \tau_s\,]^n \,\Delta_i}, \tag{5}$$

$$K_1(i) = \frac{k\,(b+1)}{c\,[\,\tau_i - \sigma_o \tau_s\,]^{(n+1)}} \left( \frac{\tau_i - \sigma_o \tau_s}{\tau_s \quad \sigma_o \tau_s} \right)^{(b+1)} [K_o(i) - 1] \tag{6}$$

$\Delta_i$ is the duration of the constant load segment and k is the loading rate for the standard test used to obtain $\tau_s$.

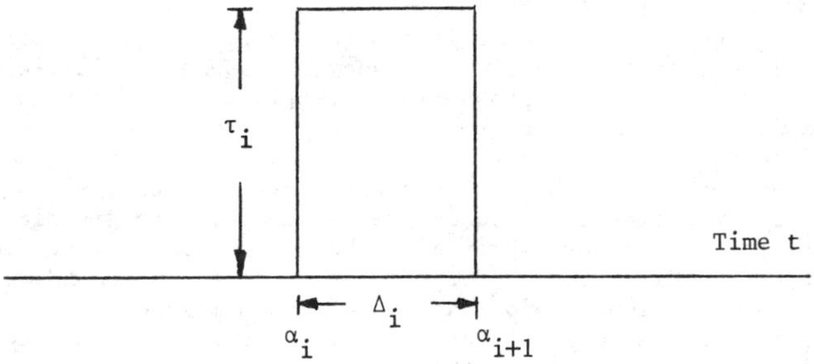


FIGURE 1. LOAD CYCLE

The cycle stress $\tau_i$ is produced by the combination of dead load D and the live load L. Let us assume that the nominal (design) values $D_N$ and $L_N$ of these loads are such that the following design equation is satisfied,

$$\alpha_D D_N + \alpha_L L_N = \phi R \tag{7}$$

where $\alpha_D$ and $\alpha_L$ are the corresponding load factors and R is a characteristic capacity of the element. $\phi$ is the performance factor applied to R.

The cycle stress $\tau_i$ can then be written

$$\tau_i = \frac{\phi R}{\alpha_D \gamma + \alpha_L} ( \gamma d + x_i ) \tag{8}$$

in which d and $x_i$ are, respectively, the dead and live load variables normalized with respect to their corresponding design values. The factor $\gamma$ is the ratio between the design dead load and the design live load:

$$\gamma = D_N / L_N \tag{9}$$

If a particular load sequence over the NY years produces stresses below the threshold no damage is accumulated during the service life. For all such cases G = 1.0. In general, the accumulated damage is much smaller than 1.0 except in those cases in which failure is achieved during the service period. Thus, the failure function G has a plateau G = 1.0 or G ≅ 1.0 over most of the safe domain and abruptly drops to G = 0 at the limit state, taking on very large negative values over the unsafe domain. Because of the presence of the plateau, and the required calculation for the gradient of G, convergence of the RF algorithm is dependent upon an appropriate choice for the initial vector, and this must be chosen as close as possible to the limit state G = 0.

In the application described in this paper, the algorithm was modified to maintain, during the iterations, the tangent point between the hyperplane and the G surface close to the intersection G = 0. If an intermediate design point was obtained for which G (in absolute value) was greater than 0.001, the live loads were increased and the short-term strength $\tau_s$ was decreased until the condition on G was satisfied. The modified design point was then adopted to continue the iterations in the algorithm.

## RESULTS

Convergence of the RF algorithm, modified as described above, was quite fast even for a service life of NY = 30 years and NS = 10 load segments per year. However, convergence to different design points was obtained depending on the choice for the initial vector. The G = 0 surface offers several local minima for the distance to the origin, and these different design points corresponded to loading sequences with specific characteristics. Each one contained a high load segment while all others had an equal and smaller live load, approximately equal to the average of the live load distribution. The difference between these design points' load sequences was the timing of the high load segment: this could occur at the beginning, at any time in between or at the end of the service life.

When the lowest value for the reliability index $\beta$ was chosen to calculate the probability of failure $P_f$ ,

$$P_f = \Phi(-\beta) \tag{10}$$

it was found that the result underestimated the true probability content of the failure domain, as obtained by Montecarlo simulations. Following determination of the $\beta$'s for all design points, it was found that the simulation results were bounded by Ditlevsen's bounds but that these, narrow at the beginning of the service life, became wider and not too useful if longer service periods were considered.

These difficulties would suggest that the estimation of $P_f$ by means of the reliability indices computed with the RF algorithm, although fast, would not be sufficiently accurate. The alternative of Montecarlo simulations is tedious and expensive, and the following section presents an approximate procedure which showed good agreement with simulation results for different periods of service.

## AN APPROXIMATE PROCEDURE

Montecarlo simulation results showed that the probability of failure after NY years of service increased if the number of load segments NS per year was reduced. Thus, shorter load periods produced less damage than longer ones. This suggests that the difference between the actual probability of failure and the one computed from Eq.(10), using the lowest $\beta$ for the realistic situation of NS > 1, could be made up by considering fictitious load segments with the same probability distribution but of longer duration. In particular, one could take the most conservative case of NS = 1.

Fig.2 shows results for the case of snow loads corresponding to the city of Quebec, Canada. The annual maximum load obeyed an Extreme Type I (Gumbel) distribution, and the design snow load corresponded to a 30-year return period. The dead load was assumed normally distributed with a coefficient of variation 0.10, and the design dead load was equal to the mean.

The results of Fig.2 correspond to a performance factor $\phi$ = 0.80 and a ratio $\gamma$ = 0.40. The probability of failure is represented by the corresponding reliability index $\beta$ , according to Eq.(10), and was obtained by Montecarlo simulation using a sample of 100,000 replications.

Fig.2 clearly shows: a) that the reliability decreases as a function of the service life; and b) that shorter load cycles (NS = 10) produce a lower probability of failure than NS = 1 (when the load cycle equals five months of constant snow load). Clearly, NS = 10 is a closer approximation to the actual shape of the annual snow cycle, but if the RF algorithm is run for NS = 1 and the corresponding lowest index $\beta$ is adopted in conjunction with Eq.(10), very good approximations to the simulation results for NS = 10 are obtained.

The approximate procedure is then based on ignoring the actual shape of the live load cycle and adopting, for purposes of calculation, a constant (more severe) load cycle with the maximum duration. The probability distribution of this constant load equals that for the annual maximum, and the lowest index $\beta$ thus obtained from the RF algorithm would provide a good approximation to the probability of failure for the actual cycle shape.

While it is difficult to generalize these conclusions, research on cases of other types of live loads, or combinations of live loads, is continuing.

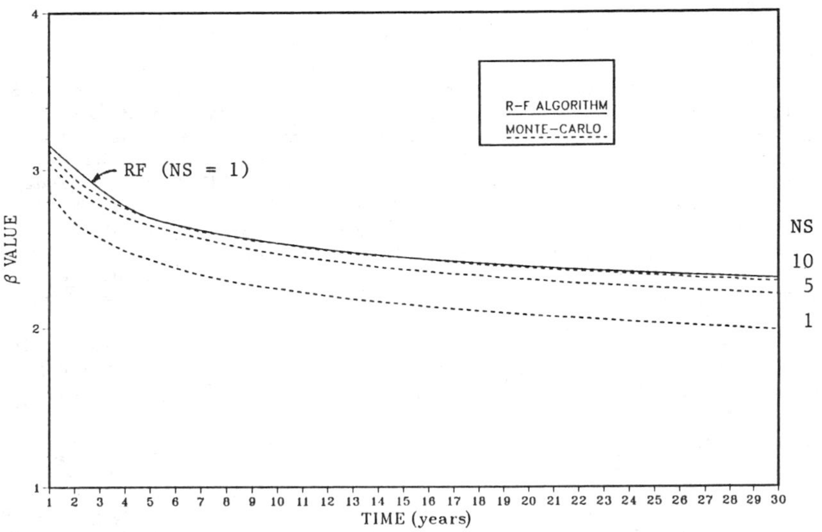


FIGURE 2. NUMERICAL RESULTS

CONCLUSIONS

The reliability of a structural element subject to strength degradation and controlled by a nonlinear damage accumulation law has been considered, using wood in bending as an example. The application of the Rackwitz-Fiessler algorithm to the calculation of the reliability index showed that the failure function offered several design points, each corresponding to different loading sequences over the service life of the structure. A single hyperplane is not a good approximation to this surface, and the lowest β results in an underestimation of the probability of failure. Comparisons with Montecarlo simulations showed that an approximate procedure could be used by choosing the lowest β when this is obtained for loading sequences which are more severe: with constant load levels over the maximum cycle duration, ignoring the actual cycle shape. Application of the Rackwitz-Fiessler algorithm in this manner proved very efficient and, in the example considered, sufficiently accurate.

REFERENCES


Foschi R.O. and Barrett, J.D. (1982). "Load Duration Effects in Western Hemlock Lumber", ASCE Journal of the Structural Division, 108, ST7, pp. 1494-1510.

Foschi, R.O. (1984). "Reliability of Wood Structural Systems", ASCE Journal of Structural Engineering, 110, 12, pp. 2995-3013.

# RESULTANT LOADS FOR RANDOM SYSTEM LOADS

V.N. Latinovic*

## ABSTRACT

The work deals with random system loads defined by space force vectors and their respective points of application; each vector varying in magnitude within a given range and constant in direction relative to the frame attached to the mechanical system. The statistics of the resultant loads - the force and the moment with respect to the frame are investigated first for a general three-dimensional case then for a system of cutting forces exerted on a multi-edge cutting tool. Equations for the deviations from the mean magnitude and direction for the force resultant as well as from the mean magnitude for the resultant moment are derived by use of the limit method. These general equations are checked by a computer simulation technique using a large sample size.

The results reveal that for a case of a small magnitude of the force resultant the deviations from the means are conservative for both the magnitude and the direction. The same conclusion was deduced for the magnitude of the resultant moment.

## INTRODUCTION

As the computer era began the designers have relied on the computation of those elements which arise from the practical problems and have a statistical basis, but for which no closed-form theory exists, by applying simulation technique of a Monte Carlo type. Typically, a set of random numbers can be generated from a uniform distribution in the interval 0,1. This can be enormous in length without repetition and can be created using one or more seed integers. This set can then serve to create random numbers from other distributions through the user programming. From the central limit theorem it is known that the sum or difference of variates of any distribution approaches a Gaussian or normal distribution as the number of variates increases. Provided that a sufficient sample size is used, the simulation can provide the designer very rapidly with desired means and deviations for the joint variable (Haugen, 1986).

The problem which prompted the present investigation has arised from a study of stability conditions for a multi-edge cutting tool of a BTA** type for deep-hole machining. Since it seemed from the literature survey that a closed-form theory was not available an attempt was made to come out with general relations which could lead to a quick estimate of the statistics of the joint variables. These were identified to be the most representative value of the force resultant magnitude R (mean) and the deviations from the mean $\Delta R$, the mean and the the deviations from the mean for the direction of the force resultant vector and finally the most representative value of the resultant moment M and the deviations from the mean $\Delta M$ (Mischke, 1986). The solution was sought in a general form applicable to any random system loads with an immediate application to the cutting force resultant necessary for a multi-edge cutting tool guidance.

---

* Department of Mechanical Engineering, Concordia University
Montreal, Quebec, Canada H3G 1M8

**Boring and Trepanning Association

From the basic principle of these boring tools it has been deduced that their performance and stability heavily depend on prediction of the cutting force resultant transmitted to the bore-wall through the two carbide guiding pads (Osman and Latinovic, 1976; Latinovic et al, 1979). Furthermore, from the measurements of the axial cutting force component and the torque which is directly proportional to the tangential cutting force component it has been concluded that both exhibit probability characteristics of a random phenomenon, Gaussian or normally distributed. This has been verified by a probability density analysis using the FFT analyser to obtain the probability density plots over a frequency range of 0-1000 Hz (Chandrashekhar, 1984). A typical sample of the results is shown in Fig. 1, for the axial force component. It clearly indicates a strong central tendency which can be approximated by a Gaussian

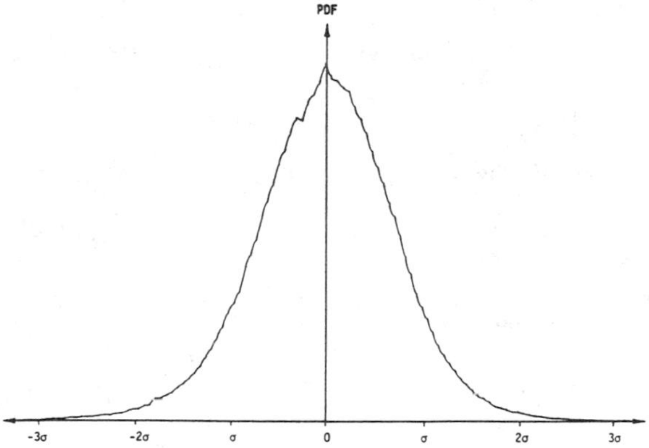


Fig. 1 PDF of Axial Force at 150 mm/min Feed for Single-Edge 7/8"DIA Solid Boring Tool

distribution. Furthermore, the variable was found stationary and ergodic in a weak sense; it was found uncorrelated and finally from the spectral density analysis it was idealized as a band limited white noise bounded by 0 and 350 Hz frequency. It has been assumed that all above probabilistic characteristics can be extended to the radial and tangential cutting force components which were not measured and that they are also true for the cutting force components in the multi-edge cutting where such an experimental measurement was not feasible.

DERIVATION OF GOVERNING EQUATIONS

The force resultant and the resultant moment for a system of forces which are random in magnitude but deterministic in direction must be random variables of a certain mean magnitude and direction. But in the reliability problems it is important to know how much the extreme values deviate from the means, in other words what is the expected range of change for the force resultant magnitude and its direction as well as the resultant moment magnitude. This is an analytical attempt for n forces given by mean values $F_i$ and deviations $\pm \Delta F_i$ as well as their direction cosines $\cos \phi_i$, $\cos \psi_i$ and $\cos \theta_i$ with respect to the Cartesian coordinate axes x, y, and z respectively.

The means for the force resultant and the resultant moment with respect to the origin are determined from the equilibrium conditions

$$\vec{R} = \sum_{i=1}^{n} \vec{F}_i \qquad\qquad i = 1,2,\ldots,n \qquad (1)$$
$$\vec{M} = \sum_{i=1}^{n} (\vec{r}_i \times \vec{F}_i)$$

where $\vec{r}_i$ are location vectors of the application points of forces $\vec{F}_i$ with respect to the origin.

RANGE OF CHANGE FOR THE FORCE RESULTANT

The force resultant of (1) can be written in the familiar form

$$\vec{R} = R_x\vec{i} + R_y\vec{j} + R_z\vec{k} = \sum_{i=1}^{n} |\vec{F}_i|(\cos \phi_i\vec{i} + \cos \psi_i\vec{j} + \cos \theta_i\vec{k}) \qquad (2)$$

In further text writing of the magnitude of vectors will be simplified to

$|\vec{F}_i| = F_i$, $|\vec{R}| = R$, $|\Delta\vec{F}_i| = \Delta F_i$, $|\Delta\vec{R}| = \Delta R$ and so on.

The mean amplitude of the force resultant is calculated from

$$R = \left[\left(\sum_{i=1}^{n} F_i \cos \phi_i\right)^2 + \left(\sum_{i=1}^{n} F_i \cos \psi_i\right)^2 + \left(\sum_{i=1}^{n} F_i \cos \theta_i\right)^2\right]^{\frac{1}{2}} \qquad (3)$$

The mean direction of the force resultant is determined by the three angles of the line of action with respect to x, y and z axes

$$\lambda_x = \cos^{-1}\left[\sum_{i=1}^{n} F_i \cos \phi_i/R\right] = \tan^{-1}\left[\sum_{i=1}^{n} F_i \sin \phi_i/\sum_{i=1}^{n} F_i \cos \phi_i\right]$$
$$\lambda_y = \cos^{-1}\left[\sum_{i=1}^{n} F_i \cos \psi_i/R\right] = \tan^{-1}\left[\sum_{i=1}^{n} F_i \sin \psi_i/\sum_{i=1}^{n} F_i \cos \psi_i\right] \qquad (4)$$
$$\lambda_z = \cos^{-1}\left[\sum_{i=1}^{n} F_i \cos \theta_i/R\right] = \tan^{-1}\left[\sum_{i=1}^{n} F_i \sin \theta_i/\sum_{i=1}^{n} F_i \cos \theta_i\right]$$

which must satisfy condition

$$\cos^2 \lambda_x + \cos^2 \lambda_y + \cos^2 \lambda_z = 1 \qquad (5)$$

As the mean magnitude and direction for the force resultant are determined the next step is to determine the extreme deviations from the means. But before this step is undertaken some assumptions about the individual forces entering into the above summations must be made. In fact the forces are considered to be uncorrelated and furthermore, the peak values in each of the constituent forces are assumed to be sample functions of a stochastic stationary process with possibly Gaussian distribution. Equations (3) and (4) are then valid provided that $F_i$ and R are taken to represent the mean value of the respective variables which vary within the range of $\pm\ \Delta F_i$ and $\pm\ \Delta R$.

According to equations (2) and (3) it can be written

$$R^2 = R_x^2 + R_y^2 + R_z^2 = \left(\sum_{i=1}^{n} F_i\cos \phi_i\right)^2 + \left(\sum_{i=1}^{n} F_i\cos \psi_i\right)^2 + \left(\sum_{i=1}^{n} F_i\cos \theta_i\right)^2 \qquad (6)$$

Applying the limit method the upper limit of the force resultant squared may be written as follows

$$(R + \Delta R)^2 = \sum_{i=1}^{n} (F_i + \Delta F_i) \cos \phi_i ]^2 + \sum_{i=1}^{n} (F_i + \Delta F_i) \cos \psi_i ]^2$$

$$+ [\sum_{i=1}^{n} (F_i + \Delta F_i) \cos \theta_i ]^2 \tag{7}$$

Equation (7), according to the limit method, implies that upper limit of the sum of random variables is the sum of upper limits of the individual random variables. Though the limit method yields too conservative results, it is used here to establish the relationship between the extreme deviations of the force resultant and the force components.

By Performing the indicated operations and introducing,

$$\Delta R_x = \sum_{i=1}^{n} |\Delta F_i \cos \phi_i| \; ; \quad \Delta R_y = \sum_{i=1}^{n} |\Delta F_i \cos \psi_i| \; ; \quad \Delta R_z = \sum_{i=1}^{n} |\Delta F_i \cos \theta_i| \tag{8}$$

equation (7) reduces to a quadratic equation in $\Delta R$ which readily could be solved for $\Delta R$

$$(\Delta R)^2 + 2R\Delta R = 2R_x \Delta R_x + (\Delta R_x)^2 + 2R_y \Delta R_y + (\Delta R_y)^2 + 2R_z \Delta R_z + (\Delta R_z)^2 \tag{9}$$

It is not difficult to show that equations (8) will hold even if the assumption that all terms under summation in equation (7) are positive is not true. If some of the terms are negative, by the limit method, these terms must be taken at minima $(F_i - \Delta F_i)$ and, since they come with negative sign, their contribution to $\Delta R_x$ $\Delta R_y$ and $\Delta R_z$ will be positive values $\Delta F_i \cos \phi_i$, $\Delta F_i \cos \psi_i$ and $\Delta F_i \cos \theta_i$ respectively. To prevent subtraction of the terms with negative cosine the absolute values of all terms under the summation must be taken. Hence, equations (8) are always valid. It is appropriate to assume that equation (9) will be valid regardless what values of component deviations $\Delta R_x$, $\Delta R_y$ and $\Delta R_z$ are. If so we can examine the assumption that all positive terms under summation are in maxima and all negative terms in minima. Obviously such an assumption is too conservative and we would prefere to apply the probabilistic method. Accordingly we recall the theorem which defines the variance of a sum of random variables as the sum of individual variances and get the extreme deviations of the three components of the force resultant from

$$\Delta R_x = [\sum_{i=1}^{n} (\Delta F_i \cos \phi_i)^2]^{\frac{1}{2}}; \quad \Delta R_y = [\sum_{i=1}^{n} (\Delta F_i \cos \psi_i)^2]^{\frac{1}{2}}; \quad \Delta R_z = [\sum_{i=1}^{n} (\Delta F_i \cos \theta_i)^2]^{\frac{1}{2}} \tag{10}$$

By solving quadratic equation (9) with values (10) substituted into it one would get $\Delta R$, the value of the extreme deviation from the mean magnitude of the force resultant. It is important to notice that this value is still conservative because the limit method has been applied to the sum of the three component vectors. Unfortunately there is no probabilistic method substitute for this step and $\Delta R$ calculated from (9) is the closest safe approximation for the deviation from the mean magnitude of the force resultant.

Finally, since the solution to the force system is independent of choice of the reference system one might wish to transform the coordinate system such that say x-axis is parallel to the force resultant vector. This could be conveniently done by series of homogeneous transformations (Adams and Billow, 1986). The final result of this step allows us to write for the new coordinate system $R = R_x$, $R_y = 0$, $R_z = 0$. Then equation (9) written in the standard format of quadratic equation simplifies to

$$(\Delta R)^2 + 2R_x\Delta R - [2R_x\Delta R_x + (\Delta R_x)^2 + (\Delta R_y)^2 + (\Delta R_z)^2] = 0 \tag{11}$$

The two roots of equation (11) are

$$\Delta R = -R_x \pm \sqrt{(R_x + \Delta R_x)^2 + (\Delta R_y)^2 + (\Delta R_z)^2} \quad (12)$$

The negative root is deemed infeasible and the positive root is the solution for the extreme deviation from the mean magnitude of the force resultant. It is possible to give graphical interpretation of the result as shown in Fig. 2. $\Delta R$ can be identified as the difference of magnitudes of the upper limit and the mean force resultant vector as follows

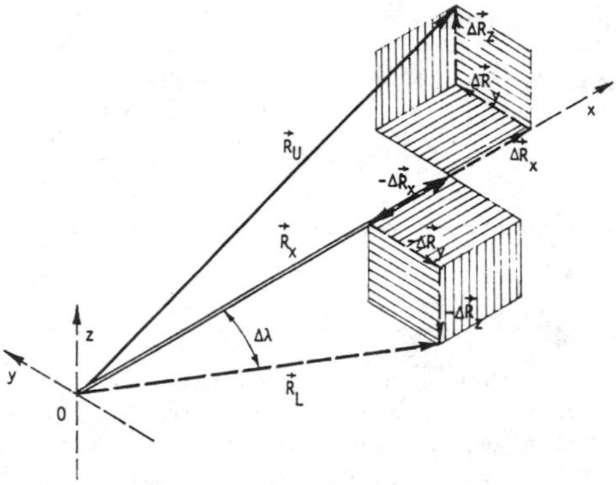


Fig. 2. Graphical Representation of Deviations from Mean Magnitude and Direction

$$\Delta R = R_U - R_x \quad (13)$$

where

$$R_U = \sqrt{(R_x + \Delta R_x)^2 + (\Delta R_y)^2 + (\Delta R_z)^2} \quad (14)$$

After the homogeneous transformation of the coordinates, according to equations (4) and (5), the line of action of the force resultant in the transformed system is

$$\lambda_x = \lambda = 0 \; ; \quad \lambda_y = \pi/2 \; ; \quad \lambda_z = \pi/2 \quad (15)$$

The angular deviation of the force resultant vector from the above direction can be readily written. If the limit method is applied, according to Fig. 2, the extreme deviation is

$$\Delta\lambda = \tan^{-1} \left[\frac{\sqrt{(\Delta R_y)^2 + (\Delta R_z)^2}}{R_x - \Delta R_x}\right] \quad (16)$$

The angular deviation calculated from (16) is a conservative approximation because the maximal perpendicular deviation and minimal magnitude of the force resultant are assumed. Hence, the range of swing of the force resultant is $\pm \Delta\lambda$ from the zero mean with respect to x-axis. This greatly simplified determination of $\Delta\lambda$ with respect to the zero mean by itself justifies the transformation of the coordinates.

## RANGE OF CHANGE FOR THE RESULTANT MOMENT

The resultant moment of equation (1) can be written in the familiar form

$$\vec{M} = M_x\vec{i} + M_y\vec{j} + M_z\vec{k},\ \text{where}$$

$$M_x = \sum_{i=1}^{n} (y_i\ F_i\ \cos\ \theta_i - z_i\ F_i\ \cos\ \psi_i)$$

$$M_y = \sum_{i=1}^{n} (z_i\ F_i\ \cos\ \phi_i - x_i\ F_i\ \cos\ \theta_i) \tag{17}$$

$$M_z = \sum_{i=1}^{n} (x_i\ F_i\ \cos\ \psi_i - y_i\ F_i\ \cos\ \phi_i)$$

The mean magnitude of the moment can be calculated from

$$M^2 = [\sum_{i=1}^{n} (y_iF_i\ \cos\ t_i - z_iF_i\ \cos\ \psi_i)]^2 + [\sum_{i=1}^{n} (z_iF_i\ \cos\ \phi_i - x_iF_i\ \cos\ \theta_i)]^2$$

$$+ [\sum_{i=1}^{n} (x_iF_i\ \cos\ \psi_i - y_iF_i\ \cos\ \phi_i)]^2 \tag{18}$$

Under the same assumptions as for equation (7) it can be written

$$(M + \Delta M)^2 = [\sum_{i=1}^{n}\ y_i(F_i + \Delta F_i)\ \cos\ \theta_i - z_i(F_i + \Delta F_i)\ \cos\ \psi_i]^2$$

$$+ [\sum_{i=1}^{n}\ z_i(F_i + \Delta F_i)\ \cos\ \phi_i - x_i(F_i + \Delta F_i)\ \cos\ \theta_i]^2 \tag{19}$$

$$+ [\sum_{i=1}^{n}\ x_i(F_i + \Delta F_i)\ \cos\ \psi_i - y_i(F_i + \Delta F_i)\ \cos\ \phi_i]^2$$

Subtracting (18) from (19) and performing all indicated operations as it was done for the forces, we get

$$2M\ \Delta M + (\Delta M)^2 = (2M_x + \Delta M_x)\ \Delta M_x + (2M_y + \Delta M_y)\ \Delta M_y + (2M_z + \Delta M_z)\ \Delta M_z \tag{20}$$

$M_x$, $M_y$ and $M_z$ are defined by (17) and $\Delta M_x$, $\Delta M_y$ and $\Delta M_z$ represent the extreme deviations from the mean magnitudes for the three Cartesian components of the resultant moment. All terms under the summation are taken positive, because by the limit method, negative terms must be taken at minima in order to get maximum joint deviation. The absolute values of all terms, however, must be taken to prevent negative sign due to negative values of cosines. As in the case of force resultant we know that these values are too conservative, and therefore, they should be calculated according to the probabilistic method as follows

$$\Delta M_x = [\sum_{i=1}^{n} (y_i\Delta F_i\cos\ \theta_i)^2 + (z_i\Delta F_i\ \cos\ \psi_i)^2]^{\frac{1}{2}}$$

$$\Delta M_y = [\sum_{i=1}^{n} (z_i\Delta F_i\cos\ \phi_i)^2 + (x_i\Delta F_i\ \cos\ \theta_i)^2]^{\frac{1}{2}} \tag{21}$$

$$\Delta M_z = [\sum_{i=1}^{n} (x_i\Delta F_i\cos\ \psi_i)^2 + (y_i\Delta F_i\ \cos\ \phi_i)^2]^{\frac{1}{2}}$$

Again for the sake of simplicity the coordinate system can be transformed by a set of homogeneous transformations and the problem simplified such that the the resultant moment vector is parallel to say x-axis. Then, the following is true

$$M = M_x\ ,\qquad M_y = 0\ ,\qquad M_z = 0$$

With these substituted into equation (20) it reduces to

$$(\Delta M)^2 + 2M_x \, \Delta M - \left[2M_x \, \Delta M_x + (\Delta M_x)^2 + (\Delta M_y)^2 + (\Delta M_z)^2\right] = 0 \qquad (22)$$

The negative root of quadratic equation (22) is deemed infeasible and the positive root is the solution for the extreme deviation from the mean magnitude of the resultant moment and it can be calculated from

$$\Delta M = -M_x \pm \sqrt{(M_x + \Delta M_x)^2 + (\Delta M_y)^2 + (\Delta M_z)^2} \qquad (23)$$

Equation (23) has been derived for the sake of completeness. However, the need for its application is remote, because in most practical problems the coordinate system is selected conveniently relative to the component so that the three Cartesian components of the resultant moment are already the torques or bending moments with respect to a critical sections of the component and hence these are directly used for the stress calculation and the reliability assessment. Even if the resultant moment vector is known it would be decomposed into the three Cartesian components selected conveniently with respect to the component axes. Therefore, equations (21) have more significance and better chance of application in engineering practice than equation (23).

It is important to notice that the quantities $\Delta R_x$, $\Delta R_y$, $\Delta R_z$, $\Delta R$, $\Delta\lambda$, $\Delta M_x$, $M_y$, $\Delta M_z$ and $\Delta M$ represent the extreme positive or negative deviations from the means of respective variables. In practice forces $F_i$ are specified in terms of the maxima and minima encountered in a given time interval. It appears reasonable to assume that, within the time interval, the two extreme values are six standard deviations apart which for a Gaussian distribution of the peak values encompasses 99.73 percent of all possible instantaneous values likely to occur within the time of interest. In this contest, then, the extreme deviations derived become synonymous with three standard deviations of the respective variables and we can, in general, assume that the same confidence level applies to the joint variables. Obviously, all relations hold for one standard deviation and, hence, all theorems related to the variance apply to the squares of deviations from means as equations (10) and (21) imply.

## APPLICATION TO THE SYSTEM OF CUTTING FORCES

With the assumptions already stipulated the equations derived can be applied to the problem of cutting force resultant transmitted to the bore-wall and deviations from the means for both magnitude and direction can be calculated. Two tool designs have been proposed; an unsymmetrical multi-edge boring head and a multi-edge boring head with staggered cutters. Though different in basic concept both tools have one thing in common, a multi-edge feature; each edge located at a different angle $\phi_i$ and acted upon by a cutting force $F_i$.

The cutting forces which affect the force resultant transmitted to the bore-wall are the components perpendicular to the tool axis. These forces are distributed along cutting edges and do not act in a single plane, but in this analysis they are approximated by a system of concurrent forces acting in a mean plane perpendicular to the tool axis. If z-axis is aligned with the tool axis then the force components act in the x-y plane, and they are radial forces $F_{Ri}$ and tangential forces $F_{Ti}$ acting upon a cutter i located at angle $\phi_i$:

Equations (3) and (4) for the general three-dimensional case apply. They could be used for calculating support reaction $R_s$ and its angular location $\lambda$ and then aligning the x-axis with $\vec{R}_s$ by rotating the coordinate system for $\lambda$ in counter-clockwise direction. Instead, the cutting edges are located angularly and radially in such a way that the force reaction $R_s$ has a predetermined value and it is aligned with x-axis. This is achieved by a direct search optimization on the computer and it is beyond scope of this work (Latinovic et al, 1979).

However, the final outcome is the same as if $R_s$ and $\lambda$ where first determined and then the homogeneous tranformations of the coordinates performed to align $\vec{R}_s$ with x-axis. Therefore, equations (10), (12) and (16) apply. Because of $R_z = 0$ and $\Delta R_z = 0$ for a system of concurrent forces they simplify to

$$\Delta R_x = \left[\sum_{i=1}^{n} (\Delta F_{Ri} \cos\phi_i)^2 + (\Delta F_{Ti} \sin\phi_i)^2\right]^{\frac{1}{2}}$$

$$\Delta R_y = \left[\sum_{i=1}^{n} (\Delta F_{Ri} \sin\phi_i)^2 + (\Delta F_{Ti} \cos\phi_i)^2\right]^{\frac{1}{2}} \tag{24}$$

$$\Delta R = -R_x \pm \sqrt{(R_x + \Delta R_x)^2 + (\Delta R_y)^2} \tag{25}$$

$$\Delta\lambda = \tan^{-1}\left[\Delta R_y/(R_x - \Delta R_x\right] \tag{26}$$

Since equations (25) and (26) have resulted from the limit method the values of $\Delta R$ and $\Delta\lambda$ calculated from them are on the conservative side. To find out how much they are on a safe side a Monte Carlo simulation has been programmed in FORTRAN and ran on the computer for a sample size of 1000. This sample size practically eliminated any uncertainty interval associated with means R and $\lambda$. The computer package, besides the main program, included seven subroutines.

A large number of tool optima has been evaluated to test the model for a multi-edge trepanning head with three cutters designed for a hole size of 4.145" DIA and a core size of 49 mm. The feed was 0.22 mm/rev and workpiece material AISI H11 tempered to 40 - 42 RC with ultimate strength 110 - 124 $KN/cm^2$ (160-180 ksi). The results calculated from equations (25) and (26) and those obtained by the simulation were compared for two different sets of cutting force ranges, the first ± 10 percent for both radial and tangential components and the second ± 21.5 percent for radial components and 8 percent for tangential components; both ranges reported as the resultants of experimental measurements (Latinovic et al, 1979). The comparison was made of the relative deviation $\Delta R/R$ and $\Delta\lambda$, the first being the triple value of the respective coefficient of variation ($\sigma/\mu$). The tool was optimized for force resultant R taking values 0.5 kN to 4.0 kN in increaments of 0.5 kN. These discrete data were plotted on the computer by smoothing the curves as a cubic spline. The computer plotted charts are shown in Figs. 3 and 4. Fig. 3 gives the relative deviation in magnitude and Fig. 4, gives the deviation in direction versus the force resultant for range of change of 21.5% for radial and 8% for tangential components.

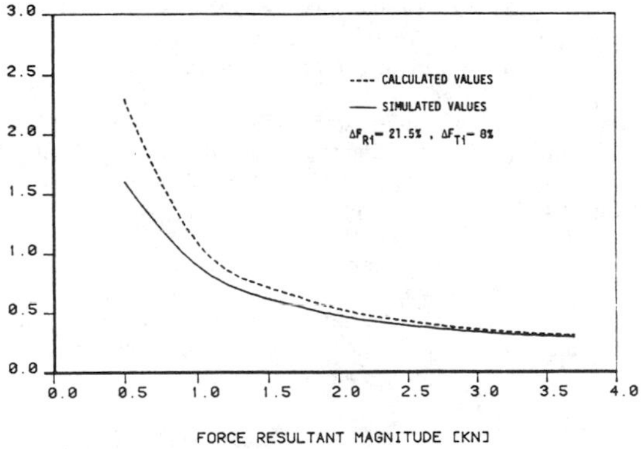


Fig. 3 Relative Deviation $\Delta R/R$ vs Force Resultant R for 4.145"DIA Three-Edge Trepanning Tool

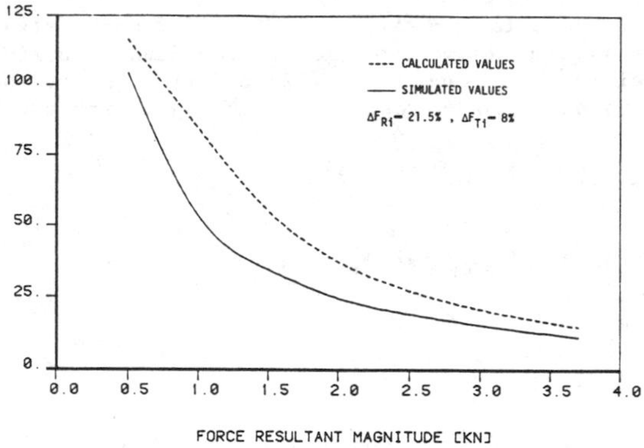


Fig. 4 Deviation $\Delta\lambda$ vs Force Resultant R for 4.145"DIA Three-Edge Trepanning Tool

The charts reveal consistant trends of change of deviations in magnitude and direction; both tend to the infinity as the force system approaches equilibrium (R = 0) and as the force resultant increases $\Delta R/R$ and $\Delta\lambda$ decrease. Also, the differences in calculated and simulated values of $\Delta R$ and $\Delta\lambda$ deminish as R increases. Eventually, as the force system approaches a system of parallel concurrent forces these differences disappear. This is also evident from equations (25) and (26) which in this case simplify to $\Delta R = \Delta R_x$ and $\Delta\lambda = 0$, both values being the correct for the system of parallel forces.

Another evidence obtained during the program testing is the probability density function for both force resultant magnitude and direction yielded by the simulation.

A 3.375"DIA solid boring head with two BTA 24 trepanning cutters and a 11.760"DIA trepanning head with two trepanning cutters (BTA 21 and BTA 31) were optimized for 6.5 kN and 7.0 kN force resultant respectively and the deviations from these means calculated.

The probability density functions (PDF) have been plotted by a computer line plotter. Fig. 5 gives the PDF plot of the force resultant magnitude for the trepanning tool and ± 21.5% range for radial and ± 8% range for tangential components. Fig. 6 gives PDF plot of the force resultant direction for the same tool and the same range of cutting force components.

The PDF values for the sample were first sorted in increasing order and plotted over the range of 8 standard deviations. Each point was found by counting the number of occurances within the interval of 0.1 for the standard variable, resulting in 80 discrete points.

Though only two cutters are used resulting in a system of four forces, the plots reveal that the PDF is centered with respect to the means and exhibits a strong central tendency and the Gaussian distribution. This equally holds for both the magnitude and the direction. All tests have been run for a sample size of 1000.

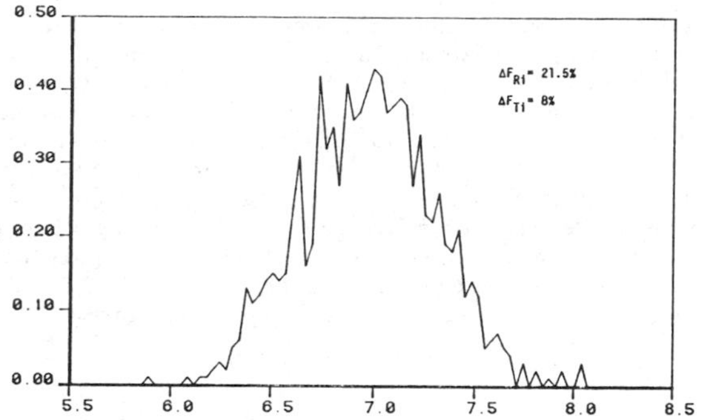


Fig. 5. PDF of Force Resultant Magnitude of 11.760"DIA Two-Edge Trepanning Tool with Staggered Cutters

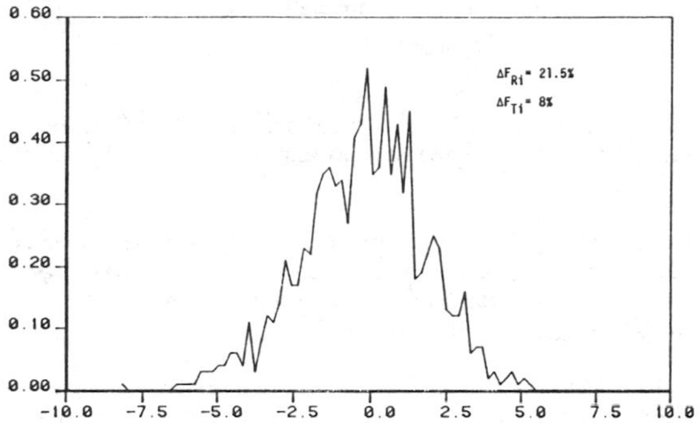


Fig. 6. PDF of Force Resultant Direction of 11.760"DIA Two-Edge Trepanning Tool with Staggered Cutters

CONCLUSIONS

From this study, it can be concluded that the equations derived analytically based on the limit approach are conservative solutions to the problem of statistics for random system loads. The calculated range of change in magnitude and direction for force resultant and resultant moment compared to those yielded by the simulation technique using a large sample size show the largest error as the force resultant approaches zero, and no error at all as the system loads approach parallel directions, the latter meaning that the vector summation is replaced by the algebraic summation. This means the error deminishes as the force resultant increases in magnitude to a maximum possible value when the error vanishes. Consequently there is a force vector magnitude beyond which the calculated values are close enough to those obtained by the simulation and always on the conservative side. It is recommended that this limit be selected at the average loads magnitude, otherwise the calculated ranges are too conservative. The results also show that analytical approach in some special cases yields the exact solutions. It should be noticed that the calculated deviations in direction are always more conservative than deviations in magnitude as Figs. 3 and 4 indicated.

Finally, it can be concluded that the Monte Carlo simulation yields correct solutions provided the sample size is large enough. Hence, it is recommended to use the simulation technique whenever there is a doubt about probabilistic characteristics of the resultant load. Though the equations have been derived under the assumption that the random system loads are Gaussian or normally distributed and all verification has been done for a system which does exhibit such probabilistic characteristics, it is believed that, according to the central limit theorem, the equations are applicable to any distribution provided that number of loads is large enough. In this case applying the simulation technique would require generation of events by finding random numbers from other distributions, hence preparing a user's program for a given distribution, which may be of a histogram type.

ACKNOWLEDGEMENT

The financial support of the National Science and Engineering Research Council of Canada and Formation de chercheurs et d'action concertee of the Government of Quebec, is greatfully acknowledged.

REFERENCES

Adams, J.A. and L.M. Billow, (1986), "Combining Descriptive and Computational Geometry", Computers in Mechanical Engineering, ASME Journal, Vol. 4, No. 6, pp. 69-76.

Chandrashekhar, S., (1984), "An Analytical and Experimental Stochastic Modeling of the Resultant Force System in BTA Deep-Hole Machining and its Influence on the Dynamics of the Machine Tool-Workpeice System", Ph.D. Thesis, Concordia University, Montreal, pp. 124-146.

Haugen, E.B., (1986), "Statistical Considerations in Design and Interpretation of Data", Standard Handbook of Machine Design, Chapter 2, Edited by J.E. Shigley and C.R. Mischke, McGraw-Hill Book Co., pp. 2.1-2.29.

Latinovic, V., R. Blakely and M.O.M. Osman, (1979), "Optimal Design of Multi-Edge Cutting Tools for BTA Deep-Hole Machining", ASME J. Eng. for Design, Vol. 101, pp. 281-290.

Mischke, C.R., (1986), "Computational Considerations in Design", Standard Handbook of Machine Design, Chapter 5, Edited by J.E. Shigley and C.R. Mischke, McGraw-Hill Book Co., pp. 5.1-5.33.

Osman, M.O.M. and V. Latinovic, (1976), "On the Development of Multi-Edge Cutting Tools for BTA Deep-Hole Machining", ASME Trans., J. Eng. for Industry, Vol. 98, No. 2, pp. 474-480.

# SEMIVARIOGRAM ANALYSIS AND KRIGING ESTIMATION OF THE STRENGTH OF STRUCTURAL COMPONENTS

Bilal M. Ayyub* and Richard H. McCuen*
*Department of Civil Engineering, University of Maryland
College Park, Maryland 20742, USA

## ABSTRACT

The objective of this paper is to demonstrate the use of semivariogram analysis and kriging estimation in nondestructive testing for strength evaluation of structural components. These methods provide the basis for establishing guidelines for developing a sampling scheme that balances the cost of collecting data and the required accuracy. Two examples on the strength evaluation of columns and slabs are presented in the paper. The sample points that are needed for the strength evaluation of columns may consist of a one-dimensional vector along the axis of the column; while the sample points for slabs may consist of a two-dimensional matrix. The relative error variances of the point and mean values for columns and slabs, respectively, are determined.

## INTRODUCTION

Given the recent examples of failed structures, there is concern for public safety with respect of the integrity of existing structures. Nondestructive testing provides one means of assessing the risk of failure of an existing structure. An important element of the nondestructive testing process is the identification of significant variation in the strength of structural components. Such identification is an integral part of developing guidelines for detecting high risk structural components.

Semivariogram analysis provides a means of characterizing the randomness in the strength of a structural component. Such an analysis is desirable because it provides for a systematic assessment of strength variation and a basis for developing a mathematical model from which guidelines for nondestructive testing can be developed. Semivariogram analysis is intended to be used in cases involving the spatial or temporal variation of a single random variable. For a structural component in good condition, the strength characteristics will be homogeneous in the space of the component, while any variation in measurements will be due to the random nature of the material rather than deterioration in the strength. Thus, a first step towards developing guidelines for the evaluation of existing structural components is to characterize the nature of this random variation. This is necessary in order to be able to distinguish between a sound structural component and one that has deteriorated over a portion of the component. Deteriorated structural components would have much greater variation near any deteriorated portion; thus, a comparison of the random variation in a structural component with that identified for a component in good condition can be used to identify the existence of deterioration. On the other hand, semivariogram analysis provides the means of selecting the number and location of the necessary sampling points in the space of a structural component to achieve a specified confidence level on the estimated property, e.g., the mean structural strength of the component.

Semivariogram can be used part of the kriging estimation or prediction process. Kriging estimation is used to determine which sample points should be considered in the estimation and what weight factor should be given to each sample point.

SEMIVARIOGRAM MODELING AND KRIGING ESTIMATION

In order to develop guidelines for the spacing requirements in nondestructive testing, assumptions about the properties of the structure must be made. For a structural member without decay we can assume that the member is homogeneous. However, recognizing that the properties of the member vary on the micro level, the properties must be viewed as random variables, with the value of a property assumed stationary over the structural member. For columns subjected to nondestructive testing, the cross sectional dimensions are small relative to the longitudinal dimensions and the property being assessed by the nondestructive measuring device is averaged at a cross section. Therefore, the random variable can be assumed to be one dimensional, and the random variation along the length of the member is the only stochastic characteristic of interest. For slabs subjected to nondestructive testing, the thickness of the slab is small relative to its width and length. Therefore, the random variable in this case can be assumed to be two dimensional, i.e., a field, and the random variation in this field is the only stochastic characteristic of interest.

Semivariogram analysis provides the tools for describing the stochastic structure of the random variables such as the strength properties of structural components. Kriging estimation, which uses the results of the semivariogram analysis as input, provides the means for making the best linear unbiased estimates of the property. The combination of semivariogram analysis and kriging estimation can then be used to describe the stochastic structure of the properties so that guidelines for nondestructive testing can be developed.

SEMIVARIOGRAM ANALYSIS. The property of a structural component at any location $\underline{X}$ in the space of the component is denoted as $z(\underline{X})$. The same property has a value $z(\underline{X}+\underline{h})$ at any distance h from the initial point measured at $\underline{X}$. For relatively small separation distances, the values $z(\underline{X})$ and $z(\underline{X}+\underline{h})$ are probably autocorrelated; for large separation distances, the autocorrelation is zero, i.e., the values $z(\underline{X})$ and $z(\underline{X}+\underline{h})$ are independent. For very small h, the autocorrelation is large, and it decreases to zero as h increases. At some point, the value $z(\underline{X})$ will be independent of $z(\underline{X}+\underline{h})$; this point is called the range of influence and is denoted as r.

Of interest in assessing the stochastic structure of a property is the variability between the two values separated by distance h. The variogram, which is denoted as $2\gamma(h)$, characterizes the variability of the property z between the two points:

$$2\gamma(h) = \frac{1}{n} \sum_{i=1}^{n} [z(\underline{X}_i) - z(\underline{X}_i + \underline{h})]^2 \tag{1}$$

in which n is the number of measurements made at separation distance h, and $\underline{X}_i$ is the location of a point with respect to some reference point. Equation 3 has the form of the expected value and is actually the expected value of the random variable $[z(\underline{X}) - z(\underline{X}+\underline{h})]^2$:

$$2\gamma(h) = E([z(\underline{X}) - z(\underline{X}+\underline{h})]^2) \tag{2}$$

In order to quantify the variogram, realizations of the property must be available. A sample estimate of $2\gamma(h)$ is denoted as $2\bar{\gamma}(h)$. In application of

Eqs. 1 and 2, we assume that the intrinsic hypothesis is valid; this hypothesis states that the value of the variogram depends only on the separation distance h and not the location $\underline{X}$ of the sample points. In other words, Eqs. 1 and 2 assume that the difference $(z(\underline{X}) - z(\underline{X}+\underline{h}))$ is a random variable with second-order stationarity.

Equations 1 and 2 define the variogram. Dividing these values by 2 yields the semivariogram $\gamma(h)$. The semivariogram is used in the second phase of the problem, i.e., the estimation problem with kriging. Just as probability functions are fit using sample data that may be presented as a histogram, a sample semivariogram computed with Eq. 1 can be used to fit a semivariogram function, or model. The most frequently used semivariogram model is called a spherical model and has the form:

$$\gamma(h) = \begin{cases} \gamma_r & \text{where } h > r \quad (3a) \\ \frac{\gamma_r}{2}\left[\frac{3h}{r} - \left(\frac{h}{r}\right)^3\right] & \text{where } h \le r \quad (3b) \end{cases}$$

in which $\gamma_r$ is a semivariogram model parameter called the sill; it is often quantified using the variance of the sample measurements $z(\underline{X})$. The spherical model is just one of many models used to represent a semivariogram; it is widely used because its properties are easily computed and it has the shape and scale properties that characterize many data measurements.

A semivariogram is usually estimated for the length of a column or the spatial field of a slab. The resulting semivariogram for a column is called the core-semivariogram $\gamma_c(h)$ and determined by averaging the sample-pointsemivariogram $\gamma(h)$. The core-semivariogram is smaller than the point-semivariogram. The concept is not new if one views it in light of the standard error of the mean value of a sample consisting of n points. The standard error of the mean is $S/\sqrt{n}$ which is smaller than the standard error of the sample points, i.e., S. The difference between the point-sill $\gamma_r$, and core-sill $\gamma_{rc}$, which are based on the point semivariogram and core-semivariogram, respectively, is given by the following core auxiliary function for one-dimensional samples with a length L for the spherical model:

$$\gamma(z,z) = \begin{cases} \frac{\gamma_r L}{20r}\left(10 - \frac{L^2}{r2}\right) & \text{for } L \le r \quad (4\text{-a}) \\ \frac{\gamma_r}{20}\left(20 - \frac{15r}{L} + \frac{4r^2}{L^2}\right) & \text{for } L > r \quad (4\text{-b}) \end{cases}$$

The field auxiliary function that is analogous to the core auxiliary function can also be calculated for a slab. The calculations involve the evaluation of tedious integrations. For a slab which has length L and width W, the function is given in Table 1 (McCuen and Synder, 1986). For a given radius of influence and slab of specified length and width, the value of the slab auxiliary function of the standardized spherical model can be read from the appropriate table entry and multiplied by the sample-sill $\gamma_r$ to get the

As the sample size increases, the first part of the error variance will decrease because of the greater level of confidence associated with larger samples. Therefore, the within sample variation must be subtracted from the point sample variation because it reflects variation that is not part of the total error variation. The within sample variation is the weighted average semivariogram value between each point in the sample. Therefore, the error variance, $S_e^2$, is given by:

$$S_e^2 = 2 \sum_{i=1}^{n} w_i \, \gamma(h_i) - \sum_{i=1}^{n} \sum_{j=1}^{n} w_i w_j \, \gamma(h_{ij}) \tag{6}$$

in which $h_{ij}$ is the separation distance between sample points i and j. The second term on the right-hand side of Eq. 6 is the variance that is internal to the sample points.

THE ERROR VARIANCE OF THE MEAN. The other objective of the analysis problem is to provide a means of estimating the mean value of a property of a structural component, i.e., strength or resistance. An estimate of the mean value of the strength of a structural component is given by the either the arithmetic mean, i.e.,

$$\bar{z} = \frac{1}{n} \sum_{i=1}^{n} Z(\underline{X}_i) \tag{7}$$

or the weighted mean which is given in Eq. 5. The weighted mean is used in the kriging estimation, while the arithmetic mean is used in this section.

For a sample that consists of a vector of n points and the criterion of Eq. 7, the error variance of the mean value is given by

$$S_e^2 = 2\,\gamma(S,z) - \gamma(z,z) - \gamma(S,S) \tag{8}$$

The variance component $\gamma(S,z)$ is the average semivariogram value between each of the n sample points and the line:

$$(S,z) = \frac{1}{n} \sum_{i=1}^{n} (S_i,z) \tag{9}$$

The computation of each component $\gamma(S_i,z)$ is complicated and involves integration. For a spherical semivariogram model and a sample point located at a distance d from one end of a column of length L, there are two line segments, with one having a length d and the other a length L-d. The variance component $\gamma(S_i,z)$ is given by

$$\gamma(S_i,z) = \frac{1}{L} [d\,\chi(d) + (L-d)\,\chi(L-d)] \tag{10}$$

value of the field auxiliary function. The slab-sill $\gamma_{rs}$ equals the difference between $\gamma_r$ and the slab auxiliary function.

The objectives of the analysis problem are to provide a means of estimating the property of a structural component at any point $\underline{X}$ within the space of the element and/or estimating the average (mean) value of the property. In addition to the best estimate of the property, we are interested in the accuracy of the estimate.

| L/r | W/r 0.1 | 0.2 | 0.3 | 0.4 | 0.5 | 0.6 | 0.7 | 0.8 | 0.9 | 1.0 |
|---|---|---|---|---|---|---|---|---|---|---|
| 0.10 | 0.078 | 0.120 | 0.165 | 0.211 | 0.256 | 0.300 | 0.342 | 0.383 | 0.422 | 0.457 |
| 0.20 | 0.120 | 0.155 | 0.196 | 0.237 | 0.280 | 0.321 | 0.362 | 0.401 | 0.438 | 0.473 |
| 0.30 | 0.165 | 0.196 | 0.231 | 0.270 | 0.309 | 0.349 | 0.387 | 0.424 | 0.460 | 0.493 |
| 0.40 | 0.211 | 0.237 | 0.270 | 0.305 | 0.342 | 0.379 | 0.415 | 0.451 | 0.484 | 0.516 |
| 0.50 | 0.256 | 0.280 | 0.309 | 0.342 | 0.376 | 0.411 | 0.445 | 0.479 | 0.511 | 0.541 |
| 0.60 | 0.300 | 0.321 | 0.349 | 0.379 | 0.411 | 0.443 | 0.476 | 0.507 | 0.538 | 0.566 |
| 0.70 | 0.342 | 0.362 | 0.387 | 0.415 | 0.445 | 0.476 | 0.506 | 0.536 | 0.565 | 0.591 |
| 0.80 | 0.383 | 0.401 | 0.424 | 0.451 | 0.479 | 0.507 | 0.536 | 0.564 | 0.591 | 0.616 |
| 0.90 | 0.422 | 0.438 | 0.460 | 0.484 | 0.511 | 0.538 | 0.565 | 0.591 | 0.616 | 0.640 |
| 1.00 | 0.457 | 0.473 | 0.493 | 0.516 | 0.541 | 0.566 | 0.591 | 0.616 | 0.640 | 0.662 |
| 1.20 | 0.520 | 0.534 | 0.551 | 0.572 | 0.593 | 0.616 | 0.638 | 0.660 | 0.682 | 0.701 |
| 1.40 | 0.572 | 0.584 | 0.600 | 0.618 | 0.637 | 0.657 | 0.677 | 0.697 | 0.716 | 0.733 |
| 1.60 | 0.614 | 0.625 | 0.639 | 0.655 | 0.673 | 0.691 | 0.709 | 0.727 | 0.744 | 0.760 |
| 1.80 | 0.650 | 0.659 | 0.672 | 0.687 | 0.703 | 0.719 | 0.736 | 0.752 | 0.767 | 0.782 |
| 2.00 | 0.679 | 0.688 | 0.700 | 0.713 | 0.728 | 0.743 | 0.758 | 0.773 | 0.787 | 0.800 |
| 2.50 | 0.735 | 0.743 | 0.752 | 0.763 | 0.775 | 0.788 | 0.800 | 0.813 | 0.824 | 0.835 |
| 3.00 | 0.775 | 0.781 | 0.789 | 0.799 | 0.809 | 0.820 | 0.830 | 0.841 | 0.851 | 0.860 |
| 3.50 | 0.804 | 0.810 | 0.817 | 0.825 | 0.834 | 0.843 | 0.852 | 0.861 | 0.870 | 0.878 |
| 4.00 | 0.827 | 0.832 | 0.838 | 0.845 | 0.853 | 0.861 | 0.870 | 0.878 | 0.885 | 0.892 |
| 5.00 | 0.860 | 0.864 | 0.869 | 0.874 | 0.881 | 0.887 | 0.894 | 0.901 | 0.907 | 0.913 |

| L/r | W/r 1.2 | 1.4 | 1.6 | 1.8 | 2.0 | 2.5 | 3.0 | 3.5 | 4.0 | 5.0 |
|---|---|---|---|---|---|---|---|---|---|---|
| 0.10 | 0.520 | 0.572 | 0.614 | 0.650 | 0.679 | 0.735 | 0.775 | 0.804 | 0.827 | 0.860 |
| 0.20 | 0.534 | 0.584 | 0.625 | 0.659 | 0.688 | 0.743 | 0.781 | 0.810 | 0.832 | 0.864 |
| 0.30 | 0.551 | 0.600 | 0.639 | 0.672 | 0.700 | 0.752 | 0.789 | 0.817 | 0.838 | 0.869 |
| 0.40 | 0.572 | 0.618 | 0.655 | 0.687 | 0.713 | 0.763 | 0.799 | 0.825 | 0.845 | 0.874 |
| 0.50 | 0.593 | 0.637 | 0.673 | 0.703 | 0.728 | 0.775 | 0.809 | 0.834 | 0.853 | 0.881 |
| 0.60 | 0.616 | 0.657 | 0.691 | 0.719 | 0.743 | 0.788 | 0.820 | 0.843 | 0.861 | 0.887 |
| 0.70 | 0.638 | 0.677 | 0.709 | 0.736 | 0.758 | 0.800 | 0.830 | 0.852 | 0.870 | 0.894 |
| 0.80 | 0.660 | 0.697 | 0.727 | 0.752 | 0.773 | 0.813 | 0.841 | 0.861 | 0.878 | 0.901 |
| 0.90 | 0.682 | 0.716 | 0.744 | 0.767 | 0.787 | 0.824 | 0.851 | 0.870 | 0.885 | 0.907 |
| 1.00 | 0.701 | 0.733 | 0.760 | 0.782 | 0.800 | 0.835 | 0.860 | 0.878 | 0.892 | 0.913 |
| 1.20 | 0.736 | 0.764 | 0.788 | 0.807 | 0.823 | 0.854 | 0.876 | 0.892 | 0.905 | 0.923 |
| 1.40 | 0.764 | 0.790 | 0.811 | 0.828 | 0.842 | 0.870 | 0.890 | 0.904 | 0.915 | 0.931 |
| 1.60 | 0.788 | 0.811 | 0.829 | 0.845 | 0.858 | 0.883 | 0.901 | 0.914 | 0.924 | 0.938 |
| 1.80 | 0.807 | 0.828 | 0.845 | 0.859 | 0.871 | 0.894 | 0.910 | 0.921 | 0.931 | 0.944 |
| 2.00 | 0.823 | 0.842 | 0.858 | 0.871 | 0.882 | 0.903 | 0.917 | 0.928 | 0.936 | 0.948 |
| 2.50 | 0.854 | 0.870 | 0.883 | 0.894 | 0.903 | 0.920 | 0.932 | 0.941 | 0.948 | 0.957 |
| 3.00 | 0.876 | 0.890 | 0.901 | 0.910 | 0.917 | 0.932 | 0.942 | 0.950 | 0.955 | 0.964 |
| 3.50 | 0.892 | 0.904 | 0.914 | 0.921 | 0.928 | 0.941 | 0.950 | 0.956 | 0.961 | 0.969 |
| 4.00 | 0.905 | 0.915 | 0.924 | 0.931 | 0.936 | 0.948 | 0.955 | 0.961 | 0.966 | 0.972 |
| 5.00 | 0.923 | 0.931 | 0.938 | 0.944 | 0.948 | 0.957 | 0.964 | 0.969 | 0.972 | 0.977 |

Table 1. The Field Auxiliary Function

THE ERROR VARIANCE AT A POINT. If we have a value of the property $z(\underline{X})$ measured at a single point $\underline{X}$ within the space of the components, then assuming other information is not available, our best estimate of the property at a point $(\underline{X}+\underline{h})$ is $z(\underline{X})$. The variogram defines the accuracy of the estimate. That is, if we have a single point estimate of the property $z(\underline{X})$ at a point, then our best estimate of the property at any other point $(\underline{X}+\underline{h})$ is $z(\underline{X})$ and the accuracy of $z(\underline{X}+\underline{h})$ is the error variance $\gamma(h)$. The standard error of estimate $S_e$ would be the square root of the error variance.

If instead of a single point sample, we collect a sample of n measurements within the space of the component, then our best estimate of the property at a given point would be a weighted mean value of the individual points:

$$\bar{z} = \sum_{i=1}^{n} w_i \, z(\underline{X}_i) \tag{5}$$

in which $w_i$ is a weight factor for $z(\underline{X}_i)$ that reflects the importance of measurement $z(\underline{X}_i)$. The error variance of z is no longer $2\gamma(h)$ because the larger sample size, i.e., n rather than one, should be expected to reduce the error variance. The reduction in the error variance depends on the number of points in the sample and the relative independence of the sample points.

To develop an expression for the error variance when the sample consists of n measurements, with each sample point having a weight factor $w_i$, both the error variance associated with each sample point and the point to be estimated and the error variance among the sample points must be assessed. The first source of the error variance would be the weighted average variogram value between sample point i and the point to be estimated, $2 \Sigma w_i \gamma(h_i)$, where $h_i$ is the separation distance between sample point i and the point to be estimated.

where the values of $\chi(d)$ and $\chi(L-d)$ are computed from the following equation using either d or L-d as the argument:

$$\chi(d) = \begin{cases} \dfrac{0.125\ \gamma_r d\ (6 - d^2/r^2)}{r} & \text{For } d \leq r \quad (11\text{-a}) \\[2ex] 0.125\ \gamma_r\ (8 - \dfrac{3r}{d}) & \text{For } d > r \quad (11\text{-b}) \end{cases}$$

The second variance component of Eq. 8 is computed using the core auxiliary function of Eq. 4. The third variance component of Eq. 8 is the average semivariogram value for every pair of points in the sample and can be computed using Eq. 3.

If the sample that consists of n points is used to estimate the mean strength value of a slab of length L and width W, the error variance is given by Eq. 8 with a different definition of the three variance components $\gamma(S,z)$, $\gamma(z,z)$ and $\gamma(S,S)$. The first component is the average semivariogram value between each of the n sample points and the field as given by Eq. 9. The computation of each component $\gamma(S_i,z)$ is complicated and involves integration. For a sample point located within the slab, the slab is divided by the sample point into four fields, each of length and width of $L_i$ and $W_i$, i = 1,2,3 and 4, respectively. The component $\gamma(S_i,z)$ is given by

$$\gamma(s_i,\ z) = \frac{\gamma_r}{4} \left[ F(\frac{L_1}{r}, \frac{W_1}{r}) + F(\frac{L_2}{r}, \frac{W_2}{r}) + F(\frac{L_3}{r}, \frac{W_3}{r}) + F(\frac{L_4}{r}, \frac{W_4}{r}) \right] \quad (12)$$

in which $F(L_i/r, W_i/r)$, i = 1,2,3, and 4 is given in Table 2 for a spherical semivariogram model. The second variance component of Eq. 8 is computed using the slab auxiliary function of Table 1. The third variance component of Eq. 8 is the average semivariogram value for every pair of points in the sample and can be computed using Eq. 3.

| L/r \ B/r | 0.1 | 0.2 | 0.3 | 0.4 | 0.5 | 0.6 | 0.7 | 0.8 | 0.9 | 1.0 |
|---|---|---|---|---|---|---|---|---|---|---|
| 0.10 | 0.114 | 0.177 | 0.243 | 0.310 | 0.374 | 0.436 | 0.494 | 0.546 | 0.593 | 0.633 |
| 0.20 | 0.177 | 0.227 | 0.285 | 0.346 | 0.406 | 0.464 | 0.518 | 0.568 | 0.613 | 0.651 |
| 0.30 | 0.243 | 0.285 | 0.336 | 0.390 | 0.445 | 0.499 | 0.550 | 0.597 | 0.639 | 0.674 |
| 0.40 | 0.310 | 0.346 | 0.390 | 0.439 | 0.489 | 0.539 | 0.586 | 0.629 | 0.668 | 0.701 |
| 0.50 | 0.374 | 0.406 | 0.445 | 0.489 | 0.535 | 0.580 | 0.623 | 0.663 | 0.698 | 0.728 |
| 0.60 | 0.436 | 0.464 | 0.499 | 0.539 | 0.580 | 0.621 | 0.660 | 0.697 | 0.728 | 0.755 |
| 0.70 | 0.494 | 0.518 | 0.550 | 0.586 | 0.623 | 0.660 | 0.696 | 0.729 | 0.757 | 0.781 |
| 0.80 | 0.546 | 0.568 | 0.597 | 0.629 | 0.663 | 0.697 | 0.729 | 0.758 | 0.783 | 0.805 |
| 0.90 | 0.593 | 0.613 | 0.639 | 0.668 | 0.698 | 0.728 | 0.757 | 0.783 | 0.806 | 0.826 |
| 1.00 | 0.633 | 0.651 | 0.674 | 0.701 | 0.728 | 0.755 | 0.781 | 0.805 | 0.826 | 0.843 |
| 1.20 | 0.694 | 0.709 | 0.729 | 0.751 | 0.774 | 0.796 | 0.818 | 0.837 | 0.855 | 0.869 |
| 1.40 | 0.738 | 0.751 | 0.767 | 0.786 | 0.806 | 0.825 | 0.844 | 0.861 | 0.875 | 0.888 |
| 1.60 | 0.771 | 0.782 | 0.797 | 0.813 | 0.830 | 0.847 | 0.863 | 0.878 | 0.891 | 0.902 |
| 1.80 | 0.796 | 0.806 | 0.819 | 0.834 | 0.849 | 0.864 | 0.879 | 0.892 | 0.903 | 0.913 |
| 2.00 | 0.817 | 0.826 | 0.837 | 0.850 | 0.864 | 0.878 | 0.891 | 0.902 | 0.913 | 0.921 |
| 2.50 | 0.853 | 0.860 | 0.870 | 0.880 | 0.891 | 0.902 | 0.913 | 0.922 | 0.930 | 0.937 |
| 3.00 | 0.878 | 0.884 | 0.891 | 0.900 | 0.909 | 0.918 | 0.927 | 0.935 | 0.942 | 0.948 |
| 3.50 | 0.895 | 0.900 | 0.907 | 0.914 | 0.922 | 0.930 | 0.938 | 0.944 | 0.950 | 0.955 |
| 4.00 | 0.908 | 0.913 | 0.919 | 0.925 | 0.932 | 0.939 | 0.945 | 0.951 | 0.956 | 0.961 |
| 5.00 | 0.927 | 0.930 | 0.935 | 0.940 | 0.946 | 0.951 | 0.956 | 0.961 | 0.965 | 0.969 |

| L/r \ B/r | 1.2 | 1.4 | 1.6 | 1.8 | 2.0 | 2.5 | 3.0 | 3.5 | 4.0 | 5.0 |
|---|---|---|---|---|---|---|---|---|---|---|
| 0.10 | 0.694 | 0.738 | 0.771 | 0.796 | 0.817 | 0.853 | 0.878 | 0.895 | 0.908 | 0.927 |
| 0.20 | 0.709 | 0.751 | 0.782 | 0.806 | 0.826 | 0.860 | 0.884 | 0.900 | 0.913 | 0.930 |
| 0.30 | 0.729 | 0.767 | 0.797 | 0.819 | 0.837 | 0.870 | 0.891 | 0.907 | 0.919 | 0.935 |
| 0.40 | 0.751 | 0.786 | 0.813 | 0.834 | 0.850 | 0.880 | 0.900 | 0.914 | 0.925 | 0.940 |
| 0.50 | 0.774 | 0.806 | 0.830 | 0.849 | 0.864 | 0.891 | 0.909 | 0.922 | 0.932 | 0.946 |
| 0.60 | 0.796 | 0.825 | 0.847 | 0.864 | 0.878 | 0.902 | 0.918 | 0.930 | 0.939 | 0.951 |
| 0.70 | 0.818 | 0.844 | 0.863 | 0.879 | 0.891 | 0.913 | 0.927 | 0.938 | 0.945 | 0.956 |
| 0.80 | 0.837 | 0.861 | 0.878 | 0.892 | 0.902 | 0.922 | 0.935 | 0.944 | 0.951 | 0.961 |
| 0.90 | 0.855 | 0.875 | 0.891 | 0.903 | 0.913 | 0.930 | 0.942 | 0.950 | 0.956 | 0.965 |
| 1.00 | 0.869 | 0.888 | 0.902 | 0.913 | 0.921 | 0.937 | 0.948 | 0.955 | 0.961 | 0.969 |
| 1.20 | 0.891 | 0.907 | 0.918 | 0.927 | 0.935 | 0.948 | 0.956 | 0.963 | 0.967 | 0.974 |
| 1.40 | 0.907 | 0.920 | 0.930 | 0.938 | 0.944 | 0.955 | 0.963 | 0.968 | 0.972 | 0.978 |
| 1.60 | 0.918 | 0.930 | 0.939 | 0.945 | 0.951 | 0.961 | 0.967 | 0.972 | 0.975 | 0.980 |
| 1.80 | 0.927 | 0.938 | 0.945 | 0.952 | 0.956 | 0.965 | 0.971 | 0.975 | 0.978 | 0.983 |
| 2.00 | 0.935 | 0.944 | 0.951 | 0.956 | 0.961 | 0.969 | 0.974 | 0.978 | 0.980 | 0.984 |
| 2.50 | 0.948 | 0.955 | 0.961 | 0.965 | 0.969 | 0.975 | 0.979 | 0.982 | 0.984 | 0.987 |
| 3.00 | 0.956 | 0.963 | 0.967 | 0.971 | 0.974 | 0.979 | 0.983 | 0.985 | 0.987 | 0.990 |
| 3.50 | 0.963 | 0.968 | 0.972 | 0.975 | 0.978 | 0.982 | 0.985 | 0.987 | 0.989 | 0.991 |
| 4.00 | 0.967 | 0.972 | 0.975 | 0.978 | 0.980 | 0.984 | 0.987 | 0.989 | 0.990 | 0.992 |
| 5.00 | 0.974 | 0.978 | 0.980 | 0.983 | 0.984 | 0.987 | 0.990 | 0.991 | 0.992 | 0.994 |

Table 2. The Auxiliary Function for Eq. 12

ESTIMATION BY KRIGING. Using the weighted mean value of Eq. 5, the estimate of the error variance is given by

$$S_e^2 = 2 \sum_{i=1}^{n} w_i \; \gamma(S_i, z) - \sum_{i=1}^{n} \sum_{j=1}^{n} w_i w_j \; \gamma(S_i, S_j) - \gamma(z, z) \qquad (13)$$

If we want unbiased model, we must impose the constraint that the sum of the weights, $w_i$, equals one. The objective function is to minimize:

$$S_e^2 - \lambda \left[ \left( \sum_{i=1}^{n} w_i \right) - 1 \right] \qquad (14)$$

in which $\lambda$ is an unknown. It should be apparent that the solution procedure for kriging is an example of Lagrangian optimization, with $\lambda$ being the Lagrangian multiplier. There are (n + 1) unknowns (i.e., the n values of $w_i$ and $\lambda$), and there are (n+1) equations. The solution provides the weights that yield the minimum error variance as defined by Eq. 13.

EXAMPLE 1 - STRENGTH EVALUATION OF COLUMNS

Consider a column of length L and a spacing between the sample points of h, the relative error variance between the sample points is shown in Fig. 1. The error variance of the points is determiend using Eq. 6.

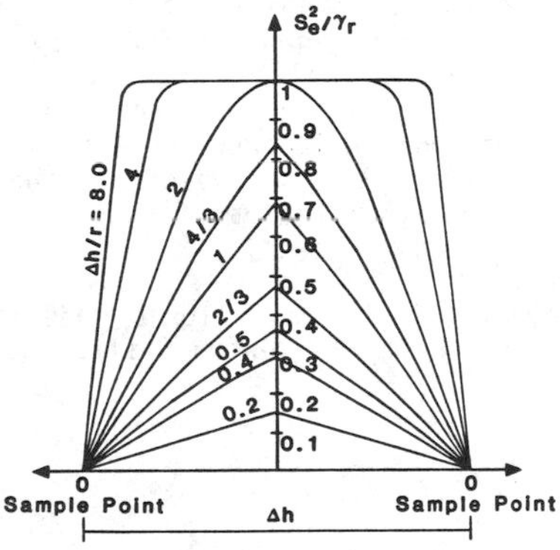


Fig. 1 The Error Variance for a Column

EXAMPLE 2 - STRENGTH EVALUATION OF SLABS

For a slab of dimensions L x L, the mean strength value can be estimated using Eq. 7. The relative error variance for the four cases of Fig. 2 are determine using different L/r ratios and summarized in Fig. 3. The error variance of the mean value is determined using Eq. 8. The error variance of case 4 can be reduced by having the sample points scattered, i.e., not on a straight line.

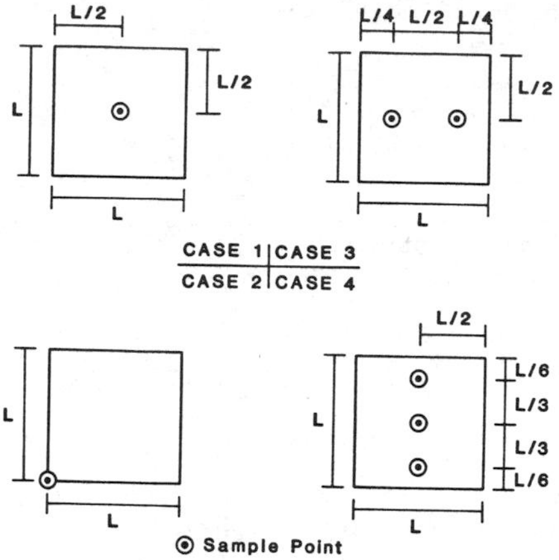


Fig. 2 The Four Cases of Sampling

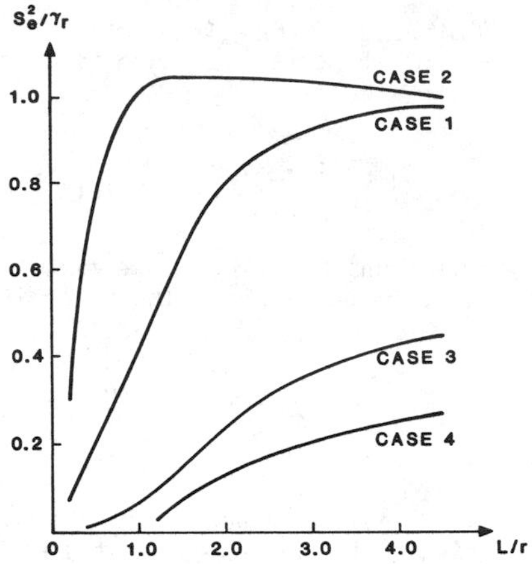


Fig. 3. The Error Variance for a Slab

SUMMARY AND CONCLUSIONS

The objective of this paper is to demonstrate the use of semivariogram analysis and kriging estimation in nondestructive testing for strength evaluation of structural components. These methods provide the basis for establishing guidelines for developing a sampling scheme that balances the cost of collecting data and the required accuracy. Two examples on the strength evaluation of columns and slabs are presented in the paper. The sample points that are needed for the strength evaluation of columns may consist of a one-dimensional vector along the axis of the column; while the sample points for slabs may consist of a two-dimensional matrix. The relative error variances of the point and mean values for columns and slabs, respectively, are determined.

REFERENCES

McCuen, R.H. and W.M. Snyder (1986). Hydrologic Modeling: Statistical Methods and Applications, Prentice Hall, Englewood Cliffs, NJ.

# BASIS FOR EARTHQUAKE-RESISTANT DESIGN WITH TOLERABLE STRUCTURAL DAMAGE

A.H-S. Ang*
*Department of Civil Engineering, University of Illinois at Urbana-Champaign, Urbana, Illinois 61801

ABSTRACT

A basis for earthquake-resistant design with an explicit tolerable degree of damage is developed. The approach is based on the damage model developed earlier (Park and Ang, 1985) in which structural damage is expressed as a function of the maximum deformation and dissipated hysteretic energy. The tolerable degree of damage is defined through calibration with observed damages from past major earthquakes. The effectiveness of the design approach is illustrated for reinforced concrete buildings.

## INTRODUCTION

Some level of damage to structures during a strong-motion earthquake is inevitable. Therefore, aseismic design of low-rise and medium-rise buildings, especially under severe ground shakings, should permit some level of structural damage. Current aseismic codes, however, do not have explicit provisions for tolerable damage.

A basis for design is formulated that explicitly limits the potential structural damage to a tolerable level by properly selecting the strength and ductility of building components. Structural damage is expressed quantitatively in terms of the damage index (Park and Ang, 1985), and a tolerable damage index is defined for reinforced concrete buildings on the basis of calibration with past earthquake damage data (Park, Ang and Wen, 1985).

As evidenced by laboratory experiments of building components tested under inelastic loading reversals (e.g., Popov and Pinkney, 1969), increasing the component strength by merely changing the structural parameters, such as the longitudinal steel ratio and the shear span ratio, could drastically decrease the corresponding deformation capacity. In the proposed design formulation, the potential ductility of a structural component is expressed as an explicit function of several structural parameters and the tolerable damage level, and a practical scheme is proposed to verify the adequacy of available ductility against the required ductility defined as a function of the ground motion intensity and base shear coefficient.

## BACKGROUND CONCEPTS

DAMAGE INDEX FOR BUILDING COMPONENTS. Damage of structural components under earthquake loading is generally caused by the combination of repeated stress reversals and high stress excursions; this may be expressed in terms of a damage index, D,

$$D = \frac{\delta_m}{\delta_u} + \frac{\beta}{Q_y \, \delta_u} \int dE \qquad (1)$$

where:

- $\delta_m$ = maximum response deformation under an earthquake;
- $dE$ = incremental dissipated hysteretic energy;
- $\delta_u$ = ultimate deformation capacity under monotonic loading;
- $Q_y$ = yield strength; and
- $\beta$ = non-negative constant.

Structural damage, therefore, is a function of the response $\delta_m$ and $\int dE$, that are dependent on the loading history, and the parameters $\beta$, $\delta_u$, and $Q_y$ that specify the structural capacity. Values of the damage index, D, are such that $D \geq 1.0$ signifies collapse or total damage.

Available laboratory data for beams and columns, that were tested to ultimate failure, were analyzed to evaluate the parameters, $\beta$ and $\delta_u$, as well as the probability distribution of the damage index at collapse. A regression analysis was performed on data for 402 reinforced concrete components of rectangular cross-sections (Park, Ang and Wen, 1984). The minimum-variance solutions for reinforced concrete components are as follows:

$$\frac{\delta_u}{\ell}(\%) = 0.52\ (\ell/d)^{0.93}\ \rho^{-0.27}\ \rho_w^{0.48}\ n_o^{-0.48}\ f_c^{-0.15} \qquad (2)$$

and, $\beta = 0.05$; in which,

$\ell/d$ = shear span ratio;
$\rho$ = $p_t f_y/f_c$, the normalized steel ratio;
$\rho_w$ = confinement ratio, in percent (replaced by 0.4% if $\rho_w < 0.4\%$);
$n_o$ = $P/bdf_c$, normalized axial stress (replaced by 0.05 if $n_o < 0.05$);
$f_c$ = concrete strength, in ksi; and
$f_y$ = yield strength of steel reinforcement, in ksi.

Using the above expressions for the respective parameters, damage indices for 402 reinforced concrete test specimens were evaluated with Eq. 1 at the appropriate failure points. The aggregate results are plotted on lognormal probability paper as shown in Fig. 1, indicating that the distribution of D is reasonably lognormal with a mean of 1.0 and a c.o.v. of 0.48. The high degree of scatter (c.o.v.) in the damage capacity should be expected as the capacity under cyclic loadings is much less predictable than under monotonic loadings (Park and Ang, 1985).

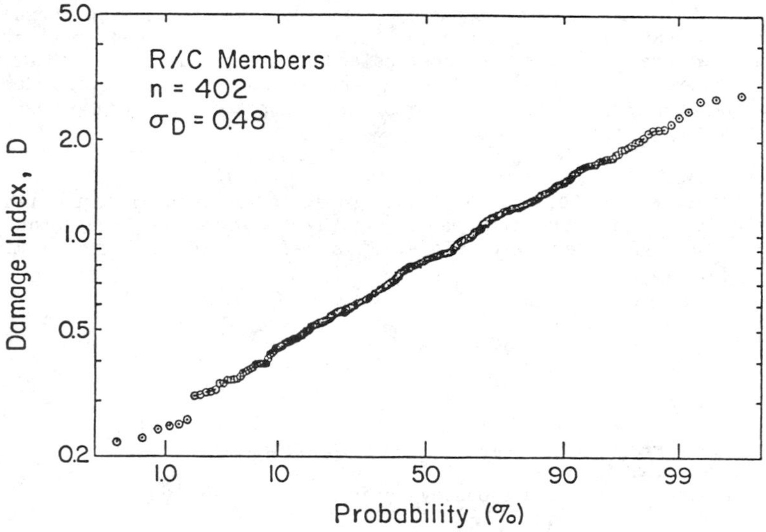

Fig. 1. Damage Index of R/C Members Plotted on Lognormal Probability Paper.

DESTRUCTIVE POTENTIAL OF EARTHQUAKE GROUND MOTION. Based on the above damage model, the damage potential of an earthquake ground motion may be defined by the following "characteristic intensity,"

$$I_c = \sigma_G^{1.5} \, t_o^{0.5} \tag{3}$$

where:

$\sigma_G$ = the rms ground acceleration, and
$t_o$ = the duration of the strong phase motion.

The mean damage index can be shown to be linearly related with the ground motion defined in terms of $I_c$, as illustrated in Fig. 2. The above intensity, $I_c$, therefore may be used as a reasonable measure of the actual destructive potential of seismic ground motions.

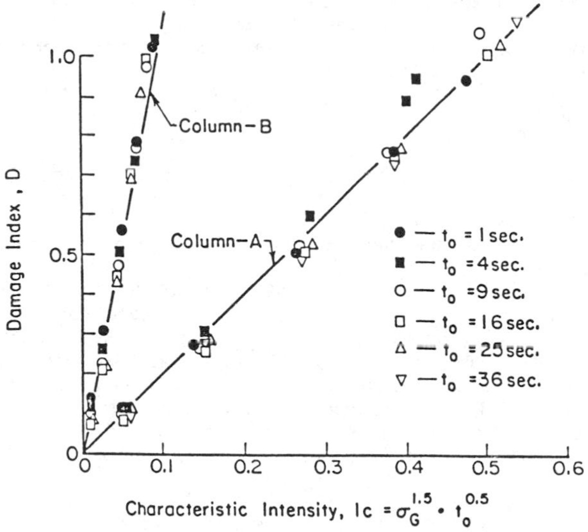


Fig. 2. Characteristic Intensity vs. Damage Index.

DAMAGE ANALYSIS OF BUILDINGS. Based on the foregoing damage model, the response quantities in Eq. 1, $\delta_m$ and $\int dE$, required for assessing building damage under a given earthquake can be obtained through a random vibration method for nonlinear-hysteretic systems (Wen, 1980). For such nonlinear response analyses, special idealization and discretization of a structural system are necessary (see Park, Ang and Wen, 1985).

The ultimate deformation, $\delta_u$, in the damage index for each story is determined so that the potential energy up to ultimate condition is equal to the sum of those of the constituent members. This may be approximated by the following,

$$\delta_u^s = \frac{\sum_i Q_{y_i} \delta_{u_i}}{\sum_i Q_{y_i}} \tag{4}$$

in which,

$\delta_u^s$ = the ultimate deformation of each story;

$Q_{y_i}$ = the yield strength of the constituent members; and

$\delta_{u_i}$ = the ultimate deformation of the constituent members.

In addition to the damage description at the member and story-level, an indicator of the overall damage sustained by a building would be useful. Such an indicator should reflect the damage concentration in the weakest part of a building, e.g., the first story or top story as frequently observed, as well as the distribution of damage throughout a building. It is well recognized that the damage distribution is closely correlated with the absorbed energy (Akiyama, 1980). Therefore, the overall damage may be expressed as the sum of the damage indices of each story, $D_i$, weighted by the corresponding energy contribution factor, $\lambda_i$; namely,

$$D_T = \sum \lambda_i D_i \tag{5}$$

where,

$\lambda_i = E_i/\sum E_i$;

in which $E_i$ is the total absorbed energy in the i-th story. $D_T$ may be called the "overall damage index."

CALIBRATION OF DAMAGE INDEX FOR REINFORCED CONCRETE BUILDINGS. In formulating a rational criterion for design, the tolerable damage level, besides the ultimate state (i.e., building collapse) needs to be identified. For this purpose, the proposed damage index is calibrated with respect to the observed damage of nine reinforced concrete buildings that were moderately or severely damaged during the 1971 San Fernando and the 1978 Miyagiken-Oki earthquakes. The buildings are listed in Table 1 with the observed damage description (more details can be found in Park, Ang and Wen, 1984). Table 1 also gives the

Table 1. List of Damaged Buildings

| Name of Building | Number of Stories | Observed Damage | Ground Motion, $I_c$ | Damage Index, $D_T$ |
|---|---|---|---|---|
| A. Olive View Hospital | 6 | Collapse* | 0.31 | 1.47 |
| B. Taiyo Gyogyo Building | 3 | Collapse* | 0.23 | 1.05 |
| C. Tohoku Togyo University | 4 | Moderate* | 0.12 | 0.48 |
| D. Saigo School | 2 | Minor | 0.19 | 0.22 |
| E. Tonan High School | 3 | Moderate* | 0.19 | 0.39 |
| F. Kinoshita Menko Building | 3 | Severe* | 0.23 | 0.85 |
| G. Obisan Office Building | 3 | Collapse* | 0.23 | 1.25 |
| H. Fukushi Kaikan Building | 2 | Very Minor | 0.12 | 0.02 |
| I. Izumi High School | 3 | Minor | 0.23 | 0.27 |

*Subsequently demolished

calculated overall damage index, $D_T$, for each building and the corresponding ground motion intensity defined in terms of $I_C$. The same results are also portrayed in Fig. 3, which are used as the basis for calibrating the damage index D and defining the practical significance of D. In light of these calibration results and the subsequent decisions on the respective buildings (to repair or demolish) after the respective earthquakes, an overall damage index of $D_T \leq 0.4$ may be considered to be repairable, whereas $D_T > 0.4$ represents damage beyond repair, and $D_T \geq 1.0$ represents total collapse.

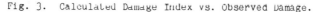

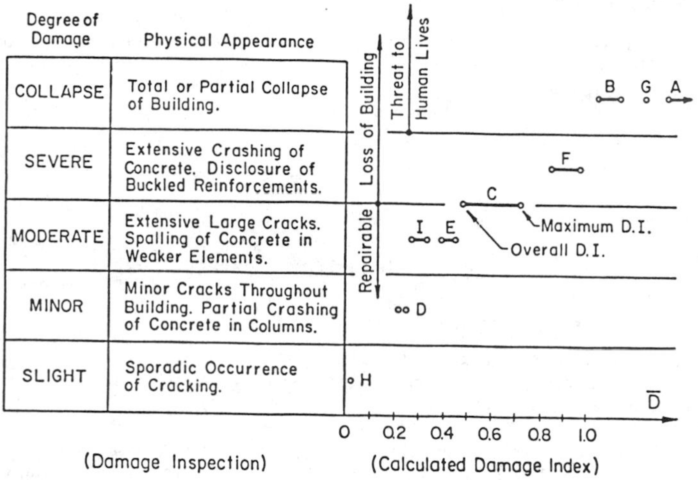


Fig. 3. Calculated Damage Index vs. Observed Damage.

PROPOSED BASES FOR DAMAGE-LIMITING DESIGN

On the basis of the above calibration results, it appears reasonable to define an overall damage level of $D_T = 0.4$ as the limit of tolerable damage in the aseismic design of reinforced concrete buildings. A damage-limiting design approach may then be formulated to achieve a tolerable damage of $D \leq 0.4$ by properly selecting both the strength and ductility of the structural members.

In the proposed design approach, the base shear coefficient, $C_B$ is regarded as the basic variable determining the required strength of a design. Following the strength specification, the degree of structural ductility (necessary to limit the damage to $D = 0.4$) is determined according to the selected value of $C_B$ and the design earthquake intensity. Thus, the designer may select a "high strength-low ductility" design or a "high ductility-low strength" design.

STRENGTH REQUIREMENT. For weak-column type buildings, the assumption of a linear mode shape would lead to a linear lateral force distribution (as in the UBC); i.e., for the i-th floor, the interstory shear force is

$$Q_i = C_B \overline{W} \frac{\sum_{j=i}^{n} w_j h_j}{\sum_{j=1}^{n} w_j h_j} \tag{6}$$

in which,

$C_B$ = the selected base shear coefficient;

$\overline{W}$ = total weight of the building;

$h_i$ = height of the i-th floor from the base; and

$w_i$ = weight of the i-th floor.

Time-history response analyses of several low-rise and medium-rise buildings show that the linear variation with height of the floor response is approximately achieved when both the story strengths and story stiffnesses are proportioned according to the shear force distribution of Eq. 6.

In the case of weak-beam type buildings, a near-linear mode shape of the floor responses may also be expected due to interstory couplings. However, the strength requirement should be applied to the entire building (instead of each story); thus, yielding

$$\sum M_i = h_e \, C_B \, \overline{W} \tag{7}$$

in which,

$h_e = \dfrac{\sum w_i \, h_i^2}{\sum w_i \, h_i}$, the equivalent height of the building; and

$M_i$ = the yield moment at a plastic hinge.

When weak-beam type and weak-column type frames are combined within a building, the strength of the constituent members may be proportioned so that failure in the beams is more likely at every story, and the columns or walls remain elastic (or near-elastic) with the exception of possible flexural failure of the columns at the bottom of the first story.

DUCTILITY REQUIREMENT. With the prescribed linear mode shape for both weak-beam type and weak-column type buildings, a multistory building can be represented by an equivalent SDF system defined with the following parameters:

$$\overline{W}_e = \frac{(\sum w_i \, h_i)^2}{\sum w_i \, h_i^2} \text{, the equivalent building weight} \tag{8}$$

$$Q_e = C_B \, \overline{W} \text{, equivalent SDF strength} \tag{9}$$

$$u_e = h_e \, R \text{, equivalent SDF response} \tag{10}$$

in which, R = the rotational deformation of the building corresponding to the linear mode shape.

Using the damage index, D of Eq. 1, the maximum earthquake response of the equivalent SDF system may be expressed in terms of the "equivalent maximum response" $\delta'_m$ (which includes the cyclic loading effect) as

$$\delta'_m = \delta_m \left(1 + \frac{\beta}{Q_y \, \delta_m} \int dE\right) \tag{11}$$

The responses of 132 SDF systems were calculated to determine the $\delta'_m$ corresponding to several discrete values of the parameters, namely, the fundamental natural period, T, the predominant period of excitation, $T_G$, the effective strength of a SDF system, $C_e = C_B \, \overline{W}/\overline{W}_e$, the damping coefficient of the ground,

$\zeta_G$, and the characteristic intensity, $I_c$. The ranges of the parameter values examined are as follows:

$I_c$ = 0.1 to 0.2;
$T$ = 0.2 to 2.0 sec;
$T_G$ = 0.4 to 1.2 sec;
$C_c$ = 0.1 to 0.6; and
$\zeta_G$ = 0.9

Multiple regression analysis of the results yielded the following expression for the response rotation $R_d = \delta'_m/h_e$,

$$R_d = \frac{40\, I_c\, T^{1.5}}{h_e\, C_e^{\,0.67-0.42\, \ell n(T/T_G)}} \qquad (12)$$

in which $C_e = C_B\, \overline{W}/\overline{W}_e$.

A comparison of the calculated maximum response rotations and those obtained with Eq. 12 is shown in Fig. 4. The (model) error associated with Eq. 12 is relatively small (c.o.v. = 0.12).

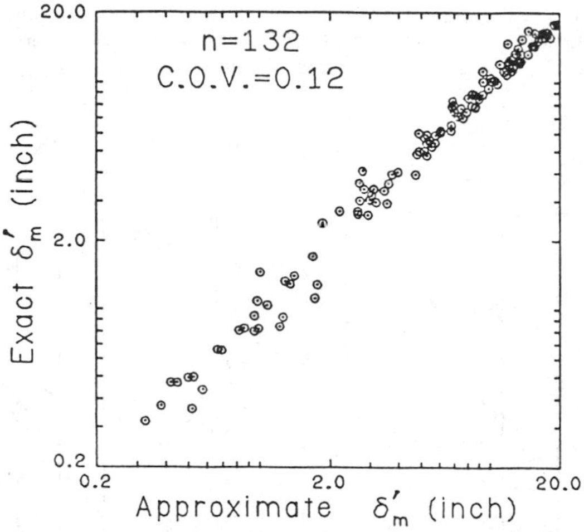


Fig. 4. Response of Equivalent SDF Systems.

Since the objective is to achieve a uniform damage distribution with a limiting value of D = 0.4, the potential damage to the constituent components should also satisfy the same tolerable limit of D = 0.4. With Eqs. 1 and 11, the allowable rotation of a member, $R_i$, can be expressed as (Park, Ang and Wen, 1984),

$$R_i = \frac{0.4}{(1 + \sigma_D^2)} R_u = 0.325\, R_u \qquad (13)$$

in which,

$R_u = \delta_u/\ell$, the ultimate rotational capacity of Eq. 2; and
$\sigma_D = 0.48$, the standard deviation of the ultimate damage index (see Fig. 1).

Using the formulation of Eq. 4, the required overall ductility (capacity) of each story of a weak-column type building may be obtained as,

$$R_T = \frac{\sum Q_i \; R_i}{\sum Q_i} \tag{14}$$

and such that $R_T \geqq R_d$. For weak-beam type buildings, the required ductility may be obtained for the whole structure as

$$R_T = \frac{\sum M_i \; R_i}{\sum M_i} \tag{15}$$

again, such that $R_T \geqq R_d$.

DESIGN EXAMPLES

Based on the concepts described above, a design procedure has also been developed (Park, Ang and Wen, 1987). To illustrate the effectiveness of the approach, two 5-story 3-bay reinforced concrete frames are designed and evaluated. The general dimensions of the frames are shown in Fig. 5a. One structure is a weak-column type building, whereas the other represents a weak-beam type structure. All frames have a uniform story weight of 560 kips and equal interstory height of 12 feet.

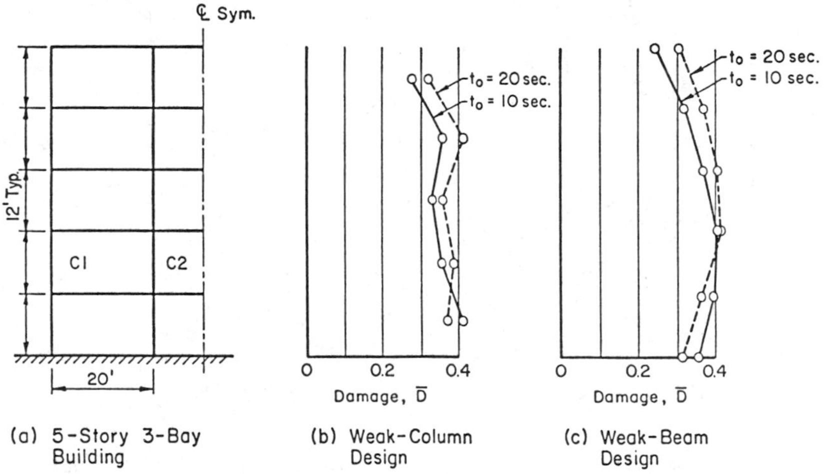


Fig. 5. Interstory Damages of Designed Frames.

Both frames are designed for a seismic load of characteristic intensity $I_c$ = 0.15. This corresponds to a peak acceleration of about 0.4g for California earthquakes (Park, Ang and Wen, 1984). The predominant period of the ground motion is assumed to be $T_G$ = 0.4 sec (representing medium soil condition). Nominal concrete strength of $f_c$ = 3 ksi and reinforcing steel yield strength of $f_y$ = 50 ksi are prescribed.

Damage analyses were performed for both frames in order to appraise the proposed design approach. For this purpose, strong-motion durations of $t_o$ = 10 sec and $t_o$ = 20 sec were used; the corresponding rms accelerations (consistent with $I_c$ = 0.15) are 0.131g and 0.104g, respectively. The calculated story damages for the two frames are plotted in Figs. 5b and 5c, which show that for both the weak-column type and weak-beam type frames, the damages are approximately uniform for all stories and the criterion of $\overline{D} \leqq 0.4$ is satisfied at all story levels.

LIMITATION AND RELIABILITY

Because the proposed design approach is based on the assumption of a linear mode shape, it is limited to buildings up to around seven stories. For such buildings, a near uniform damage for all stories can be obtained for both weak-beam and weak-column type frames.

In the proposed approach, the mean potential damage is limited to a tolerable level of D = 0.4 under a specified design seismic load, $I_{c,des}$. Structures designed on the basis of the proposed approach has certain reliability against collapse, $D \geqq 1.0$; that is, there is an underlying probability of collapse, $P(D \geqq 1.0)$, which includes the effect of uncertainties in the random response and structural capacity. Figure 6 shows the (median) probability of collapse, $P(D \geqq 1.0)$, as a function of the characteristic intensity

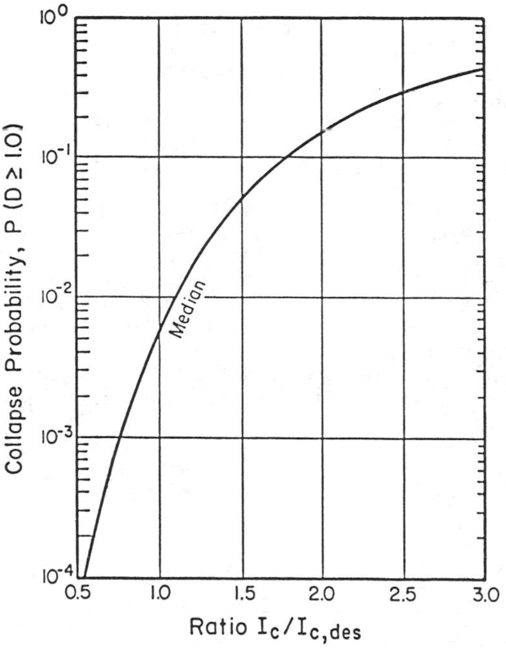


Fig. 6. Reliability of Design Approach.

of ground motion (given in multiples of $I_{c,des}$). On this basis, it can be observed that at the design intensity, $I_{c,des}$, the median collapse probability is of the order of $10^{-3}$.

CONCLUSIONS

The basis for aseismic design of buildings with an explicit tolerable damage is proposed. Expressing structural damage as a function of the maximum deformation and the effect of cyclic loadings, an explicit damage-limiting design approach has been developed for reinforced concrete buildings. Based on calibration with past earthquake damage of the resulting damage index, D, the tolerable damage may be defined as $D \leqq 0.4$. Accordingly, the design limits the potential damage at $D = 0.4$ by properly selecting both the strength and ductility of the structural members. For buildings up to seven stories, the approach will yield structures with nearly uniform story damage, within the specified limiting damage of $D = 0.4$ when subjected to the design earthquake, and a median probability of collapse of around $10^{-3}$.

ACKNOWLEDGMENTS

The studies reported herein were conducted as part of a research program supported by the National Science Foundation, Earthquake Mitigation Program, under grants CEE 82-13729 and ECE 85-11972, monitored by Dr. S. C. Liu. These supports are gratefully acknowledged.

This paper is based on the results of work obtained by the author and his colleagues Professor Y. K. Wen and Dr. Y. J. Park. It serves only to highlight the main significance of the proposed approach; details can be found in the references cited.

REFERENCES

Akiyama H. (1980). "Aseismic Ultimate Design of Building Structures," Tokyo University Press, Tokyo, Japan.

Park Y.J., A.H-S. Ang and Y.K. Wen (1984). "Seismic Damage Analysis and Damage-Limiting Design of R. C. Buildings," Civil Engineering Studies, SRS No. 516, University of Illinois at Urbana-Champaign, Urbana, IL, October.

Park Y.J. and A.H-S. Ang (1985). "Mechanistic Seismic Damage Model for Reinforced Concrete," Journal of Structural Engineering, ASCE, 111, No. ST4, 722-739.

Park Y.J., A.H-S. Ang and Y.K. Wen (1985). "Seismic Damage Analysis of Reinforced Concrete Buildings," Journal of Structural Engineering, ASCE, 111, No. ST4, 740-757.

Park Y.J., A.H-S. Ang and Y.K. Wen (1987). "Damage-Limiting Aseismic Design of Buildings," EERI Earthquake Spectra (scheduled for publication).

Popov E.P. and R.B. Pinkney (1969). "Cyclic Yield Reversal in Steel Building Connections," Journal of the Structural Division, ASCE, 95, No. ST3.

Wen, Y.K. (1980). "Equivalent Linearization for Hysteretic Systems Under Random Excitations," Journal of Applied Mechanics, 47, No. 1, 150-154.

# ANALYSIS OF OVERHEAD TRANSMISSION STRUCTURES BY PROBABILISTIC METHODS

S. (Samy) G. Krishnasamy*
*Ontario Hydro Research Division, 800 Kipling Avenue, Toronto, Ontario, Canada, M8Z 5S4.

ABSTRACT

In this paper the application of probabilistic methods to uprating overhead transmission structures is described. First the necessary probability density models for wind, ice and wind-on-ice loads are derived from meteorological data. The probability density models and probabilistic methods are then used to calculate the uprating options for a proposed future 500 kv transmission line. Weather information from four meteorological stations along the line route have been used in calculations. The final results are expressed in terms of return period values for different combinations of span and conductor size for the estimated meteorological loading conditions on the line route. The results show that the line under consideration can be uprated by using larger conductors without modifying the tower structures. However, to maintain the same reliability the tower spacings have to be reduced.

## 1.0 INTRODUCTION

The ever increasing cost of building power systems has created a need for designing lines more effectively and economically. The major shortcomings of the currently used deterministic approach are its limited ability to assess quantitatively the system reliability and the possibility of over conservative designs in many cases. Because of these inherent limitations, the current design methods may not be sufficient to meet the requirements.

Power system designers are seeking alternative methods. Among these alternatives, the most attractive one is the probability-based method, because it represents more realistically the load on a system and the strength of the system than the present deterministic design methods. The probability-based design method has the potential for producing designs at a reduced cost. In this paper the probabilistic method is first applied to derive probabilistic models (Probability Density Functions) for wind and ice loads which in turn are used in the uprating of transmission towers.

## 2.0 PROBABILITY DENSITY FUNCTIONS FOR WIND, ICE AND WIND-ON-ICE LOADS ON A CONDUCTOR

In order to apply the probability based method to overhead transmission lines the design parameters should be represented on a probabilistic basis. This section of the paper deals with the derivation of probabilistic models (Probability Density Functions) for wind, ice and wind-on-ice loads from meteorological data and transmission line details.

## 2.1 Probability Density Function For Transverse Wind Load On A Conductor

The basic calculation procedure for the transverse wind load on a conductor $L_W$ is explained below:

$$L_W = CSv_g^2 \frac{DL}{12} \tag{1}$$

where

$L_W$ = wind load (lb)
S = span factor
L = span length (ft)
$v_m$ = mean wind speed (mph)
C = constant (=0.0025 or 0.003)
D = conductor diameter (in)
$v_g$ = gust speed = 1.29 $v_m$ + 5.

For a given conductor diameter and span, the conductor wind load is a function of wind speed. Meteorological measurements (Simu et al, 1979) indicate that the annual extreme wind data can be closely represented by an extreme Gumbel's Type I probability distribution function. The wind speed distribution can be transformed into transverse wind load distribution (Fig. 1) by making use of the transverse load relationship (Eq (1)) as shown in (Krishnasamy, 1985). The procedure for deriving wind load distribution from wind speed distribution and span details is outlined below:

STEP 1 - Since in general the mean conductor height and the height at which the wind speed is measured are different, the wind data are extrapolated to the same height by means of a suitable relationship.

STEP 2 - The extrapolated annual extreme wind speed values from Step 1 are transformed into the wind speed probability density function (PDF).

STEP 3 - The wind speed PDF in combination with the transverse wind load relationship is transformed into the wind load PDF.

## 2.2 Probability Density Function For Ice Load On A Conductor

The basic calculation procedure for developing the PDF for ice load is similar to the one for wind load. The ice load on a conductor is given by:

$$L_I = \frac{\omega\pi}{576} [(D + 2t)^2 - D^2] L \tag{2}$$

where

$\omega$ = density of ice (lb/cu ft)
t = equivalent radial ice thickness (in)
D = conductor diameter (in)
$L_I$ = ice load (lb)
L = span length (ft)

The following are the various steps in developing ice load distribution:

STEP 1 - The annual extreme ice PDF is derived from ice data using the procedure used for wind in (Krishnasamy, 1985). The annual extreme ice data are also assumed to conform to the Gumbel's Type I extreme distribution.

STEP 2 - The ice PDF developed in Step 1 is combined with the ice load relationship to derive the ice load PDF.

### 2.3 Probability Density Function For Wind-On-Ice Load On A Conductor

The meteorological data used in calculating the wind-on-ice load are different than those used for developing separate wind and ice load disributions. The ice accretion and the maximum wind speed observed during an ice storm, and also for that part of the 24 hour period following the storm during which the temperature remains below freezing, are used in calculating the wind-on-ice load.

Knowing the radial ice thickness t and the maximum wind speed during an ice storm the wind-on-ice load can be calculated by

$$L_{WI} = CSv_g^2 \frac{(D + 2t)}{12} L \tag{3}$$

where

$C$ = constant (=0.0025 or 0.003)
$v_g$ = maximum gust speed during an ice storm (mph)
$t$ = equivalent radial ice thickness (in)
$S$ = span factor (=1)
$D$ = conductor diameter (in)
$L$ = span length (ft)
$L_{WI}$ = load due to wind-on-ice (lb)

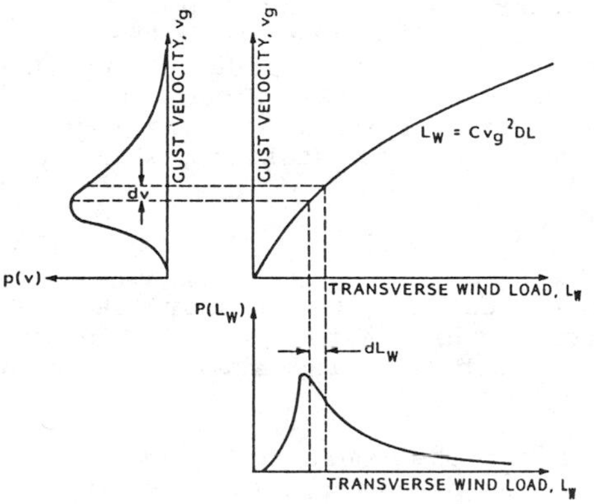


Fig. 1. Transformation of Wind Probability Density Function into Load Probability Density Function.

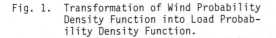

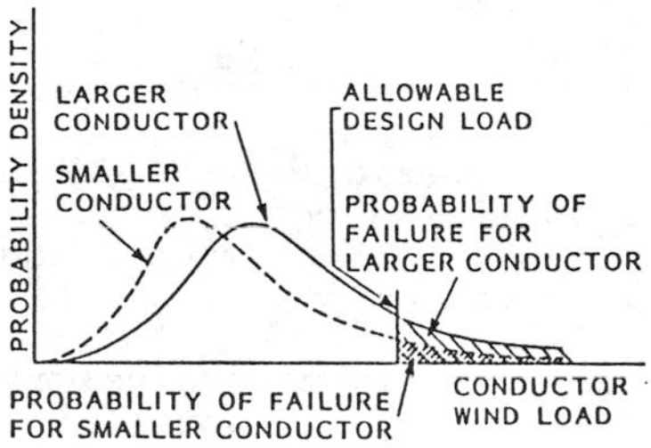


Fig. 2. Concept of Relative Probability of Failure.

Using Eq (3) a number of wind-on-ice loads ($L_{WI}$) are calculated for any given location and from these $L_{WI}$ values a wind-on-ice load PDF is developed. The following are the various steps in developing the wind-on-ice load distribution (Krishnasamy, 1985).

STEP 1 - Calculate the equivalent radial ice thickness from the available ice data.

STEP 2 - Calculate the wind-on-ice loads from the equivalent radial ice (Step 1) and the corresponding wind speed by applying Eq (3).

STEP 3 - For the calculated wind-on-ice loads in Step 2 fit a Gumbel's Type I equation.

The procedures developed above for deriving probability density functions will be applied in the next section to an overhead transmission line considered for possible uprating.

## 3.0 APPLICATION OF PROBABILISTIC METHODS TO TRANSMISSION LINE UPRATING

Increasing electrical loads, coupled with constraints of rights-of-way acquisition, lead to consideration of uprating existing transmission lines. One of the approaches often proposed is the uprating of transmission lines by increasing the conductor cross-section. In this case, the basic environmental factors such as wind, ice and combined wind-on-ice do not change; however, it results in higher conductor loads on the tower arms and shorter return periods for specific loads. A method proposed in an earlier paper (Krishnasamy, Ford and Orde, 1981) is applied to a proposed future 500 kV overhead transmission line in Ontario, Canada to verify whether it can be upgraded by increasing the conductor size without decreasing the line reliability below specified levels. The proposed line was originally evaluated assuming identical weather loads for all parts of the Province of Ontario. The emphasis in this work is on utilizing weather data from four weather stations along the line route.

### 3.1 Basic Theory Of Line Uprating

The basic method will be illustrated for the transverse wind load on the conductors. Conductor loads due to ice and wind-on-ice are accommodated using similar methods. The transverse wind load on the conductors is given by (Eq 1).

For a given wind velocity and span, the conductor wind load is directly proportional to the conductor diameter. In terms of the statistical weather data used in the conventional design procedure, this proportionality results in a shift in the wind load probability density distribution (Fig. 2) corresponding to a change in conductor diameter. These curves are obtained by transforming it to load as explained earlier in this paper and by the technique described in (Krishnasamy, Ford and Orde, 1981).

Referring to Fig. 2, the probability of conductor wind loads above a certain value is given by the area of the shaded tail region. In the present case, a useful value of strength to compare with conductor wind loads is the allowable design load at the end of each arm (Fig. 3), since conductor wind loads greater than this value contribute to structural failure. The allowable design load at the end of each arm includes consideration of simultaneous loads on the tower. The tail area, where conductor wind load exceeds the allowable design load at the end of each arm, is the probability of failure due to wind load. The return period of structural failure is a function of this quantity. The statistical variation of the allowable design load at the end of each arm could be included in the analysis, however, the simpler assumption of a single deterministic value has been made to simplify the concepts and to make the analysis as compatible as possible with present techniques.

The relative performance of a new uprated design compared with an existing design is given by the ratio (Fig. 2 and 3):

$$\text{Relative Performance} = \frac{\text{Probability of failure for new line}}{\text{Probabilty of failure for existing line}}$$

These relationships can be used to calculate individual relative performance ratios or relative return periods for conductor loads due to wind, ice and wind-on-ice.

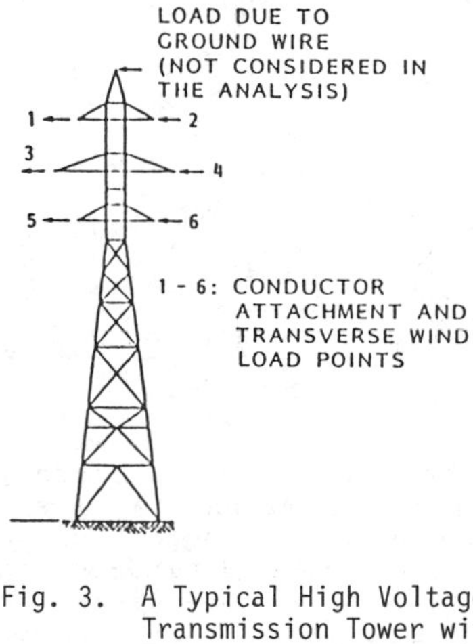


Fig. 3. A Typical High Voltage Transmission Tower with Transverse Wind Loading Points.

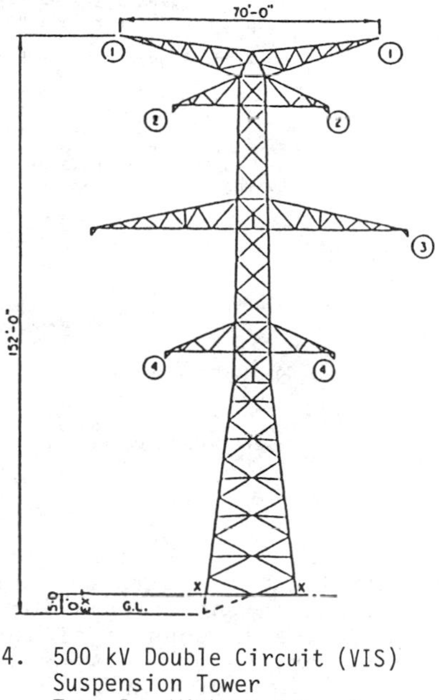


Fig. 4. 500 kV Double Circuit (VIS) Suspension Tower
Type I: Without Extension
Type II: With 15 ft Extension

## 3.2 A Case Study

The method is applied to a proposed future 500 kV overhead double circuit line to assess its reserve strength, if any, for possible upgrading of the line by increasing the conductor size. It should be noted here that the current design technique assumes identical weather loads for all parts of the Province of Ontario and the proposed method will account for variations in local weather conditions.

### 3.2.1 Line Details And Meteorological Data

The 500 kV double circuit line has four conductor bundles and runs through fairly smooth farm lands with few pockets of wooded area. Since the line runs approximately parallel to the shores of Lake Huron, at some locations it can be exposed to strong winds. The span and conductor details of the line are given in Table 1. A typical 500 kV, double circuit, type V1S suspension tower used in the proposed line is shown in Fig. 4. The various conductor sizes, span lengths, span factors, tower heights, etc., used in the upgrading calculations are given in Table 2.

TABLE 1

SPAN AND CONDUCTOR DETAILS FOR THE 500 kV DOUBLE CIRCUIT LINE

| | |
|---|---|
| Tower Structure Type | - V1S (Fig. 4) |
| Average Tower Height | - 147 ft |
| Original Conductor | - 0.95 in (585 kcmil) ACSR, four conductor bundle |
| Horizontal Span | - 950 ft |
| MAXIMUM TENSION (due to 3/4" ice and 10 PSF wind at 0°F) | |
| Conductor | - 12670 lbs |
| Ground Cable | - 10970 lbs |
| Maximum Transverse Load at Each Conductor Attachment | - 8225 lbs |
| Maximum Vertical Load at Each Conductor Attachment | - 39480 lbs |
| Average Conductor Sag | - 22 ft |

TABLE 2

INFORMATION USED IN THE PROPOSED UPGRADING CALCULATIONS

| | |
|---|---|
| Conductor Sizes Considered: | 1.05 in (714.7 kcmil), 1.15 in (856.5 kcmil), 1.108 in (795 kcmil), 1.2 in (932.7 kcmil) |
| Span Lengths Considered: | 800, 850 and 900 ft |
| Tower Heights Considered: | 152 ft (Type I, without extension), and 172 ft (Type II, with 20 ft extension). |

Meteorological data from four weather stations - London, Centralia, Goderich and Paisley - along the proposed route are utilized in the calculations. The meteorological data for London and Centralia consist of information on wind, ice and wind-on-ice while for the other two stations only wind data are available. A typical set of wind, ice and wind-on-ice data for the London weather station is given in Table 3. The wind data were obtained from historical records while the ice and wind-on-ice data were calculated from ice-accretion models, using weather data such as wind velocity, temperature, preciptiation, etc. (Brown and Krishnasamy, 1984).

The various structural and other relationships used to calculate the load on the conductor are discussed in (Krishnasamy, Ford and Orde, 1981).

TABLE 3

METEOROLOGICAL DATA FOR LONDON
(Period of Record: 31 Years)

| | | |
|---|---|---|
| Annual Maximum Hourly Mean Wind Velocity (mph) | | 40,44,45,38,55,40,55,40,40,40,40,62, 58,43,39,40,50,45,42,36,40,42,44, 41,39,54,38,35,32,42,35 |
| Annual Maximum Equivalent Radial Ice (in) | | 0.3,0.4,0.2,0.3,0.2,0.3,0.6,0.4,0.5,0.3, 0.3,0.3,0.5,0.5,0.8,0.7,0.3,0.1,0.4,0.7, 0.5,0.6,0.4,1.1,0.2,0.4,0.4,0.3,0.1,0.3,0.3 |
| Annual Maximum Wind-On-Ice (Paired Values) | (a) Equivalent Radial Ice (in) | 0.3,0.4,0.1,0.3,0.1,0.2,0.6,0.4,0.5, 0.1,0.3,0.3,0.5,0.5,0.8,0.6,0.3,0.1, 0.4,0.7,0.5,0.6,0.4,1.1,0.1, 0.3, 0.0,0.3,0.1,0.2,0.3 |
| | (b) Hourly Mean Wind Velocity (mph) | 36,34,30,36,34,40,29,30,39,40,35,33,38, 35,30,26,23,26,32,27,20,22,35,28,39,26, 26,26,23,32,34 |

## 3.3 Analysis And Discussion Of Uprating Options

A computer program has been developed to calculate the relative performance indices and relative return periods corresponding to different upgrading options. The computed relative performance indices for two typical spans are given in Table 4. These indices could be used in the upgrading calculations as explained below.

Based on the historical line maintenance records and the experience of the operating engineers, the absolute performance indices for an existing line considered for upgrading can be calculated. If it is not possible to assess the absolute performance indices (or return periods) of the existing line from the maintenance records or if they are for a new line like the one being considered in this paper then they could be directly calculated in terms of return period values of critical weather loads Table 4. Such values can then be used to calculate the performance of different upgrading options. Since, in this paper, the method is applied to a proposed future 500 kV overhead line to verify whether it can be upgraded without modification to the tower structures the absolute performance indices for the various upgrading options are calculated in terms of return period values.

The performance indices shown in Table 4 show that the governing design load for this part of the province is due to wind and the effects of ice load and wind-on-ice load are not significant. The return period values shown in Table 5 for London and Centralia indicate that if the 60 year return period is taken as the base value, then various combinations of span length and conductor size, eg, 800 ft span and 1.2 in conductor,

900 ft span and 1.10 in conductor etc, can be used for upgrading the existing line without modifying the proposed tower structures, Types I and II. The appropriate conductor-span combination can be chosen, based on the type of terrain, availability of materials, cost, etc.

It should be noted here that the original allowable design loads on the existing tower arms remain the same and the loads on different conductors considered for upgrading are kept below the allowable values. The proposed method essentially utilizes the potential reserve strength of the existing towers which were designed assuming identical weather loads for all parts of the Province of Ontario.

TABLE 4

RELATIVE AND ABSOLUTE PERFORMANCE INDICES OF VARIOUS CONDUCTORS BASED ON WEATHER DATA FROM LONDON, CENTRALIA, PAISLEY AND GODERICH

(Tower Type - I: Span Length = 900 ft)

| Conductor Diameter (in) | Relative Performance Indices: Wind Load | Ice Load | Wind-On-Ice Load | Absolute Performance Indices (Return Period In Years)*: Wind Load | Ice Load | Wind-On-Ice Load |
|---|---|---|---|---|---|---|
| | | | CENTRALIA | | | |
| 0.950 | 1.000 | 1.000 | 1.000 | 350 | 50000 | 2010 |
| 1.050 | 0.508 | 0.690 | 0.626 | 180 | 50000 | 1260 |
| 1.108 | 0.359 | 0.566 | 0.487 | 130 | 50000 | 980 |
| 1.150 | 0.283 | 0.492 | 0.408 | 100 | 50000 | 820 |
| 1.200 | 0.217 | 0.418 | 0.334 | 80 | 50000 | 670 |
| | | | LONDON | | | |
| 0.950 | 1.000 | 1.000 | 1.000 | 2790 | 50000 | 1220 |
| 1.050 | 0.435 | 0.663 | 0.688 | 1210 | 50000 | 840 |
| 1.108 | 0.283 | 0.532 | 0.562 | 790 | 50000 | 690 |
| 1.150 | 0.211 | 0.456 | 0.488 | 590 | 50000 | 600 |
| 1.200 | 0.153 | 0.382 | 0.414 | 430 | 50000 | 510 |
| | | | PAISLEY | | | |
| 0.950 | 1.000 | ** | ** | 50000 | ** | ** |
| 1.050 | 0.215 | | | 50000 | | |
| 1.108 | 0.097 | | | 50000 | | |
| 1.150 | 0.057 | | | 50000 | | |
| 1.200 | 0.031 | | | 50000 | | |
| | | | GODERICH | | | |
| 0.950 | 1.000 | ** | ** | 50000 | ** | ** |
| 1.050 | 0.355 | | | 46950 | | |
| 1.108 | 0.208 | | | 27500 | | |
| 1.150 | 0.145 | | | 19150 | | |
| 1.200 | 0.097 | | | 12760 | | |

* Values above 50,000 years are not calculated.
** Ice and wind-on-ice data not available.

TABLE 5

RETURN PERIOD VALUES FOR VARIOUS SPANS AND CONDUCTOR SIZES BASED ON WEATHER DATA FROM LONDON, GODERICH AND CENTRALIA *

| Tower Type | Span (ft) | Conductor Diameter (in) | Return Period (Years): Centralia | Goderich | London |
|---|---|---|---|---|---|
| I | 800 | 0.950 | 810 | 478300 | 7870 |
| | | 1.050 | 400 | 159570 | 3250 |
| | | 1.108 | 270 | 90480 | 2060 |
| | | 1.150 | 210 | 61640 | 1510 |
| | | 1.200 | 160 | 40080 | 1070 |
| | 850 | 0.950 | 520 | 244390 | 4580 |
| | | 1.050 | 260 | 84250 | 1940 |
| | | 1.108 | 180 | 48580 | 1250 |
| | | 1.150 | 140 | 33480 | 930 |
| | | 1.200 | 110 | 22050 | 660 |
| | 900 | 0.950 | 350 | 132160 | 2790 |
| | | 1.050 | 180 | 46950 | 1210 |
| | | 1.108 | 130 | 27500 | 790 |
| | | 1.150 | 100 | 19150 | 590 |
| | | 1.200 | 80 | 12760 | 430 |
| II | 800 | 0.950 | 560 | 275310 | 5040 |
| | | 1.050 | 280 | 94470 | 2130 |
| | | 1.108 | 200 | 54350 | 1370 |
| | | 1.150 | 150 | 37390 | 1010 |
| | | 1.200 | 120 | 24590 | 720 |
| | 850 | 0.950 | 370 | 143110 | 2980 |
| | | 1.050 | 190 | 50700 | 1290 |
| | | 1.108 | 130 | 29660 | 840 |
| | | 1.150 | 100 | 20630 | 630 |
| | | 1.200 | 80 | 13740 | 450 |
| | 900 | 0.950 | 250 | 78620 | 1840 |
| | | 1.050 | 130 | 28680 | 820 |
| | | 1.108 | 90 | 17030 | 540 |
| | | 1.150 | 70 | 11970 | 400 |
| | | 1.200 | 60 | 8060 | 290 |

* The return periods for Paisley are over 50,000 years for all the combinations of span and conductor diameter.

| | |
|---|---|
| Current Span Length: | 950 ft |
| Existing Conductor Diameter: | 0.95 in |
| Allowable Transverse Load on Existing Tower: | 8225 lbs |
| Allowable Vertical Load on Existing Tower: | 39480 lbs |

## 4.0 SUMMARY AND CONCLUSIONS

A probabilistic method is used to assess the various upgrading options for a proposed future 500 kV overhead line along the shores of Lake Huron in Ontario, Canada. The proposed line was originally evaluated assuming identical weather loads for all parts of Ontario without accounting for variation in local weather conditions. The probabilistic method does take into consideration the statistical variability in local weather data.

Weather data from four meteorological stations - London, Centralia, Paisley and Goderich - along the line route are used in the upgrading calculations. The probability density distributions for wind, ice and wind-on-ice loads are derived from weather data by using models developed in this paper. The 500 kV double circuit tower structures considered for the proposed line are shown in Fig. 4. The existing conductor bundle has four 0.95 in (505 kcmil) ACSR conductors and the proposed alternative four-conductor bundles are 1.05 in (714.7 kcmil), 1.108 in (795 kcmil), 1.15 in (856.5 kcmil) and 1.2 in (932.7 kcmil). The original span is 950 ft and the proposed spans are 800, 850 and 900 ft. The upgrading calculations are done for various combinations of span and conductor using data from all the four weather stations. The performance indices of the different combinations are expressed in terms of return period for the wind, ice and wind-on-ice loading conditions. These values allow the designer to choose the span-conductor combination appropriate for local conditions and to take into account the availability and cost of hardware, etc.

The upgrading calculations for the 500 kV line show that the proposed span length of 950 ft with a four (0.95 in) conductor bundle can be replaced by a span of 900 ft with a 4 x 1.12 in conductor bundle if the design life of the line is assumed to be 60 years and the tower with a 10 ft extension is used. If a longer life span of 100 years is required the above span-conductor combination can be used with the standard tower (Type I).

In conclusion, the application of the proposed upgrading method shows that it is a useful and simple tool to verify the reserve capacity of lines designed on the basis of 'global' rather than local weather data. The application of this method to the 500 kV line shows that the line can be upgraded by using larger conductors without modifying the proposed tower structures. However, to maintain the same reliability the tower spacings have to be reduced.

REFERENCES

Brown R., and Krishnasamy, S.G., (1984). "Climatological ice accretion modelling", Canadian Climate Centre Report No. 89-10, Atmospheric Environment Service, Downsview, Ontario, Canada.

Krishnasamy S.G. (1985). "Wind and ice loading in Ontario Hydro", Proceedings of the Fifth US National Conference on Wind Engineering, Texas Tech University, Lubbock, Texas.

Krishnasamy S.G. (1985), "Assessment of Weather Induced Transmission Line Loads on a Probabilistic Basis," IEEE Transactions, PAS Vol. 104, No. 9.

Krishnasamy S.G., Ford, G.L., and Orde, C.I., (1981). "Predicting the structural performance of transmission lines uprated by reconductoring", IEEE Transactions, PAS Vol 100, No. 5.

Simiu E., M.J. Changery and J.J. Filliben (1979), "Extreme Wind Speeds at 129 Stations in the Contiguous United States," NBS Building Science Series 118, US Department of Commerce.

# PROBABILITY-BASED DESIGN OF WOOD STRUCTURES

Bruce Ellingwood, Erik Hendrickson, and Joseph F. Murphy
*Department of Civil Engineering, The Johns Hopkins University, Baltimore, MD 21218-2699 USA
**National Bureau of Standards, Gaithersburg, MD 20899 USA
***Structural Reliability Consultants, P.O. Box 56164, Madison, WI, 53705 USA

## ABSTRACT

Methods are presented for calculating limit state probabilities of engineered wood structural members, considering load duration effects due to stochastic dead, snow and occupancy live load. These methods are used to conduct reliability studies of existing wood design criteria. When realistic load processes are considered, it is found that the importance of load duration and gradual damage accumulation has been somewhat overstated. One possible probability-based design method that should be useful in future code development work also is presented.

## INTRODUCTION

Structural codes governing design of engineered wood structures do not yet include concepts embodied in probability-based limit states design. As a naturally occurring construction material, wood presents problems that have not been encountered in steel and concrete construction. The strength of wood is highly variable and is unusually sensitive to the rate and duration of structural loading. The dependence of the strength of wood structures on load history means that random process models of structural loads, rather than random variable models, are required to analyze their performance and reliability. The possibility that failure occurs by progressive accumulation of damage (creep rupture) rather than by once-in-a-lifetime overloading must be considered. The analysis of stochastic damage accumulation in wood requires (1) description of loads as stochastic processes; (2) probabilistic models of strength; (3) cumulative damage models, and (4) reliability analysis methods to synthesize the load and damage accumulation data.

## STOCHASTIC LOAD MODELS

Previous probability-based studies of steel and reinforced concrete have focused on the distribution of the maximum load to occur during a convenient period of reference, often assumed to be 50 years. However, the variation of load in time may be as important as the maximum load for evaluating failure by creep rupture in wood structures. Thus, a stochastic characterization of the entire load process is required. The dead, occupancy live and snow loads are assumed to be statically equivalent uniformly distributed loads (Ellingwood, et al., 1982), in which the spatial variation of the actual load is taken into account.

The dead load is assumed to be random in intensity but invariant in time, and is modeled simply by a normal random variable. Live loads acting on floors and snow loads acting on roofs are modeled as Poisson or Bernoulli pulse processes. The occupancy live load is assumed to have two components. The sustained live load arises from the weight of people normally on the floor, their possessions, furniture and moveable equipment. The parameters needed to describe the sustained live load process can be obtained from surveys of live loads in buildings. The extraordinary, or intermittent, live load is caused by temporary crowding during parties, remodeling or emergencies, and its parameters are based on load event scenarios. Roof snow loads are determined from basic climatological data and surveys of snow accumulation on roofs. The benchmark statistics on snow loads describe the annual extreme roof load. Thus, the snow load pulse intensities are determined so as to be consistent with the assumed pulse occurence parameters and the (known) distribution of the annual extremes. Table 1 summarizes statistical data on the occurrence and intensity of dead, live and snow loads used in this paper. The sensitivity of damage accumulation and limit state probabilities to load pulse occurrence parameters will be examined subsequently.

Table 1. Load Process Parameters

| Load | Occurrence | | Intensity | | |
|---|---|---|---|---|---|
| | Mean Rate/yr | Duration | Mean* | COV | CDF |
| Dead | | 50 yr | 1.0Dn | 0.10 | normal |
| Sustained Live | 0.125 | 8 yr | 0.3Ln | 0.57 | gamma |
| Extraord. Live | 1 typ. | 1 wk typ. | 0.19Ln | 0.52 | gamma |
| Snow | 6 typ. | 2 wk typ. | 0.20Sn** | 0.87** | lognormal |

*$D_n$, $L_n$, $S_n$ from A58.1-1982 **annual extreme

PROBABILISTIC MODELS OF STRENGTH

The structural members in this study are glued-laminated (glulam) beams that are part of the main load-bearing system of a floor or roof. Most available data for glulam members have been derived from tests of simply supported beams in flexure. These standard tests determine the modulus of rupture (MOR), $F_r$, are conducted by loading the beams to failure over approximately 5 to 10 minutes and do not take load duration effects into account. Two sets of beam test data are examined: one set is based on beam tests conducted in Canada, while the second is based on tests conducted at the U.S. Forest Products Laboratory. The test results all were normalized by the allowable bending stress, $F_b$, at standard conditions in the United States: beams with 12-inch depth, 12 percent moisture content, uniform load and a span-to-depth ratio of 21:1. The data were fitted by Weibull probability distributions:

$$F(x) = 1 - \exp\left[-\left(\frac{x-x_o}{\eta}\right)^{\gamma}\right]; x \geq x_o; \; x_o, \eta, \gamma > 0 \qquad (1)$$

in which $\gamma$, $\eta$, and $x_o$ are, respectively, the shape, scale and location parameters.

Data reported by Sexsmith and Fox (1978) consist of 56 beams. A two-parameter Weibull distribution was found to give the best fit to these data, with $\eta = 3.39\ F_b$ and $\gamma = 6.82$. The 103 beams tested at the U.S. Forest Products Laboratory were specifically fabricated to have near-minimum quality for their respective grades (Moody, 1977; Marx and Moody, 1981). A three-parameter Weibull distribution provided the best fit to these data, with $x_o = 0.87F_b$, $\eta = 1.91\ F_b$, and $\gamma = 4.09$.

DAMAGE ACCUMULATION MODELS

The strength of wood depends on the rate at which load is applied and the time that it is held at a constant load intensity. Other factors being equal, high constant loads cause failures to occur sooner than low constant loads. The so-called "Madison" curve has been used for many years to take load duration into account. However, it is based on tests of small clear specimens and has been criticized for not modeling load duration effects accurately in members of structural size (Madsen, 1975). Several improved models of damage accumulation in structural lumber have been developed at the U.S. Forest Products Laboratory (Gerhards and Link, 1986) and at Forintek (Barrett and Foschi, 1978). Gerhards' model takes the form,

$$d\alpha/dt = \exp(-A + B\sigma) \tag{2}$$

in which $d\alpha/dt$ = damage accumulation rate; $\alpha$= damage state variable ($\alpha$= 0 when undamaged; $\alpha$= 1 at failure); $\sigma$ = stress ratio, the ratio of the applied stress to the stress causing failure in a conventional strength test. Equation 2 is denoted an exponential damage rate model (EDRM) and does not include a damage threshold. Load duration curves for two series of FPL tests obtained by solving Eqn 2 for time to failure, $T_f$, under constant stress ratio, $\sigma$, are compared to the Madison curve in Figure 1. Figure 1 demonstrates the sensitivity of $T_f$ to small changes in applied stress; this sensitivity arises from the magnitude of B in Eqn. 2. Most damage models proposed recently are fairly close to one another at stress ratios above about 0.75 (Hendrickson, Ellingwood and Murphy, 1987), where most load duration data also fall.

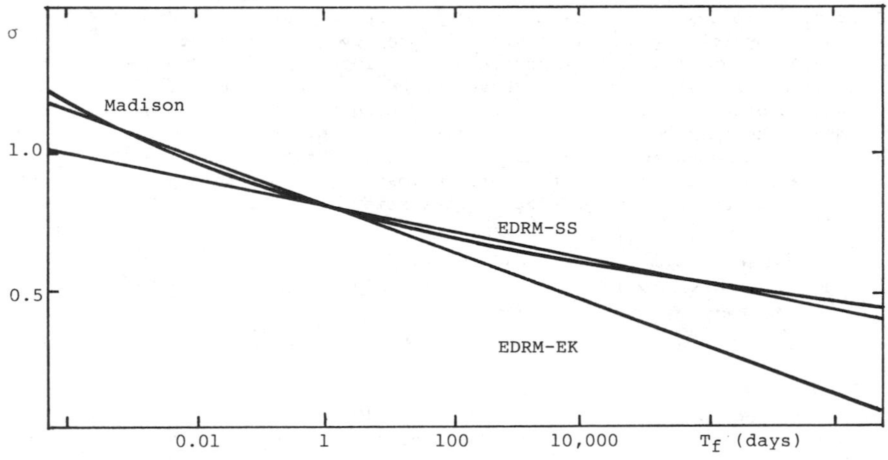


Figure 1. Load Duration Models

RELIABILITY ANALYSIS

Damage accumulates stochastically as structural loads and applied stresses vary randomly in time:

$$\alpha(t) = \int_0^t (d\alpha/dv)\ dv \tag{3}$$

Failure is assumed to occur when $\alpha(t) = 1$. The limit state probability during period T (in this paper, T = 50 years) is,

$$P_f = P(\alpha(T) \geq 1) \tag{4}$$

A generalized reliability index, $\beta$, can be determined as,

$$\beta = \Phi^{-1}(1 - P_f) \tag{5}$$

The probability, $P_f$, cannot be determined in closed form without oversimplifying the damage accumulation process and has been determined by Monte Carlo simulation using the statistics for the loads and MOR presented earlier.

Consider, first, a simply supported glulam beam designed to support a roof, for which nominal snow load, $S_n$, is 20 psf (1 kPa) and nominal dead load, $D_n$, is 5 psf (0.24 kPa). (Load sharing is not addressed explicitly, and failure of the beam does not necessarily imply collapse of the roof). The stress ratio during snow load, $\sigma_i$, is the applied stress divided by the MOR, $F_i/F_r$, in which $F_i$ is,

$$F_i = c(D + S_i)/Z \tag{6}$$

c = analysis factor, D and $S_i$ = random dead and snow loads, and Z = section modulus in bending. If the beam is designed according to existing allowable stress design procedures,

$$Z = c(D_n + S_n)/(1.15F_b) \tag{7}$$

where the factor 1.15 accounts for the 15% increase currently permitted for combinations involving snow load. Table 2 presents reliability estimates for beams with different pulse durations.

Table 2. Reliability Measures for Snow Load

| Pulse duration | p | $P_f$ | $\beta$ |
|---|---|---|---|
| 2 weeks | 0.4 | 0.0156 | 2.16 |
| 1 month | 0.4 | 0.0168 | 2.13 |
| 1 month | 1.0 | 0.0176 | 2.11 |
| 2 months | 0.4 | 0.0186 | 2.09 |

The results show that approximately the same $P_f$ and $\beta$ are obtained for a range of durations from 2 weeks to 2 months. When the probability, p, that the snow load pulse intensity is nonzero is 1.0 rather than 0.4 (i.e., the snow load process is always "on" during the 6-month winter season), the reliability estimates are almost the same, so the choice of p also appears to be noncritical.

Next, consider a floor in which the glulam beams support dead and live loads distributed over an influence area of 800 $ft^2$ ($74m^2$). The nominal live load in this case is 39 psf (1.9 kPa) (ANSI A58.1-1982), and the dead load is assumed to be 10 psf. The results of the reliability analyses of these floor beams is given in Table 3, in which $\tau_e$ = mean duration of extraordinary live load pulses. It may be observed that the reliability

Table 3. Reliability Measures for Live Load

| $\tau_e$ | $P_f$ | $\beta$ |
|---|---|---|
| 1 day | 0.00532 | 2.56 |
| 3 days | 0.00613 | 2.51 |
| 1 week | 0.00708 | 2.46 |
| 2 weeks | 0.00798 | 2.42 |
| 1 month | 0.00913 | 2.36 |

decreases slightly, as might be expected. However, neither reliability measure is sensitive to $\tau_e$ within a range that is reasonable for scenarios giving rise to extraordinary live loads.

The insensitivity of the reliabilities to the temporal parameters of the snow or live load processes is a consequence of the highly nonlinear characteristics of $d\alpha/dt$ in Eqn 2. Small changes in $\sigma_i$ cause variations in damage increment of many orders of magnitude, and damage increments increase from 0 to 1 over a very narrow range of $\sigma_i$. The behavior of $\alpha(t)$ during stochastic loadings reveals that virtually all damage accumulates during the occurrence of the largest load pulse (occasionally, the largest two load pulses) in 50 years. Thus, we conclude that gradual progressive damage accumulation as a failure mechanism in wood may actually occur relatively infrequently. Moreover, the reliability measures are not sensitive to the damage accumulation model selected because the models are all about the same at high stress (load) levels of significance.

## PROBABILITY BASED CODIFIED DESIGN

The design requirement for a floor or a roof subjected to dead, snow and live loads can be written in a "load and resistance factor design format" as,

$$(\lambda_L \text{ or } \lambda_s)\psi F_n Z > c\,[1.2D_n + 1.6(L_n \text{ or } S_n)] \quad (8)$$

in which $F_n$ = specified nominal strength, $\psi$ = resistance factor on structural action, and $\lambda_i$ = load duration factors. The resistance factor, $\psi$, depends on the nature of the particular limit state of interest. The factor, $\lambda_i$, takes into account the fact that adjustments in design resistance are necessary if the structure is to have the same reliability for load combinations involving loads with different temporal characteristics, such as live and snow load. The specified nominal strength is selected as the 5 percent exclusion limit of the MOR, a value easily determined from laboratory tests. The load side of Eqn 8 is from the A58 Standard (ANSI A58, 1982).

Factors $\psi$ and $\lambda_s$(and $\lambda_L$) can be determined as follows. First, a set of beams is designed as a function of $\lambda_s\psi$ and the variation in $\beta$ with $\lambda_s\psi$ is determined, taking creep rupture into account. This is illustrated in Figure 2. Next, the reliabilities of the same beams are evaluated by assuming that the limit state is reached if the maximum applied moment in 50 years exceeds the modulus of rupture; this second analysis parallels that performed when developing LRFD for steel and reinforced concrete, and ignores creep rupture. This analysis provides a second relation between $\lambda_s\psi$ and $\beta$, also shown in Figure 2. However, $\lambda_s$ equals unity in this second case because creep rupture is not considered. Finally, for a particular target $\beta$, $\lambda_s$ and $\psi$ can be

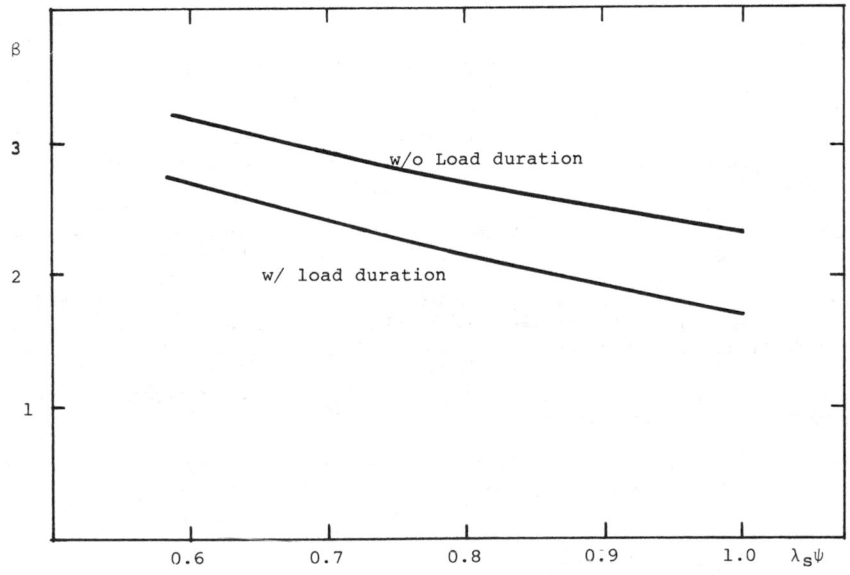


Figure 2. Design for Dead Plus Snow (EDRM-SS)

determined as the ratios of the two curves. For example, if $\beta$ = 2.5, then $\psi$ for overload = 0.89; $\lambda_s\psi$ for creep rupture = 0.64 and so $\lambda_s$ = 0.72. Similarly, $\lambda_L$ = 0.8 for live load.

ACKNOWLEDGMENT

Support for the load modeling aspects of this study was provided, in part, by National Science Foundation Grant No. MSM 8306334, which is gratefully acknowledged.

REFERENCES

American National Standard Minimum Design Loads for Buildings and Other Structures, ANSI A58.1-1982, American National Standards Institute, New York, 1982.

Barrett, J.D. and Foschi, R.O., "Duration of Load and Probability of Failure in Wood: Part I - Modeling Creep Rupture, and Part II - Constant, Ramp and Cyclic Loadings," Canadian Journal of Civil Engineering, Vol. 5, No. 4, December 1978.

Ellingwood, B., et al., "Probability Based Load Criteria: Load Factors and Load Combinations," Journal of the Structural Division, ASCE, Vol. 108, No. ST5, May 1982.

Galambos, T.V., et al., "Probability Based Load Criteria: Assessment of Current Design Practice," Journal of the Structural Division, ASCE, Vol. 108, No. ST5, May 1982.

Gerhards, C.C. and Link, C.L., "Effect of Loading Rate on Bending Strength of Douglas-fir 2 by 4's," Forest Products Journal. Vol. 36, No. 2, 1986.

Hendrickson, E., Ellingwood, B., and Murphy, J.F., "Limit State Probabilities for Wood Structural Members," Journal of Structural Engineering, ASCE, Vol. 112, No. 1, January 1987.

Madsen, B., "Strength Values for Wood and Limit States Design," Canadian Journal of Civil Engineering, Vol. 2, No. 3, September 1975.

Marx, C. and Moody, R., "Strength and Stiffness of Small Glued-Laminated Beams with Different Qualities of Tension Laminations," FPL Report 381, U.S. Forest Products Laboratory, Madison, WI, 1981.

Moody, R., "Improved Utilization of Lumber in Glued-Laminated Beams," FPL Report 292, U.S. Forest Products Laboratory, Madison, WI, 1977.

Sexsmith, R.G. and Fox, S., "Limit State Design Concepts for Timber Engineering," Forest Products Journal, Vol. 28, No. 5, May 1978.

EFFECT OF TRANSVERSE DEFLECTION PROFILE ON THE FAILURE LOAD OF LAMINATED WOOD BRIDGES

Leslie G. Jaeger* and Baidar Bakht**
* Technical University of Nova Scotia, Halifax, N.S., Canada B3J 2X4
** Ministry of Transportation and Communications, Downsview, Ontario Canada M3M 1J8

ABSTRACT

It is already well established that the expectation of the failure load of a laminated wood bridge is less than the failure load which is obtained by assuming that the longitudinal Young's Modulus ($E_L$) and Modulus of Rupture (MOR) of all the laminates are the same and equal to the means of the statistical distributions for the species of wood concerned. It is shown in this paper that this diminution is characterized for all practical purposes by the variabilities of $E_L$ and MOR and by the ratio of the maximum to mean deflection at a representative transverse section of the bridge. A functional relationship is developed for the above diminution in terms of the ratio of the maximum to mean deflections. It is suggested that this functional relationship, which is little affected by the transverse profile of the bridge, will be of particular value in the framing of design criteria for laminated wood bridges.

INTRODUCTION

The cross section of a typical laminated wood bridge is shown in Fig. 1. The main load carrying components of this type of bridge are wood laminates whose orientation is shown in Fig. 1. The laminates are either glued together, or held together by nails or transverse prestressing (Csagoly and Taylor, 1980).

Some aspects of the problem of the failure load of laminated wood bridges have been dealt with by Jaeger and Bakht (1986a), who have shown that these failure loads, treated as random variables, have smaller mean values than those obtained by assuming that all laminates have the same $E_L$ and MOR. The scope of their work is extended in this paper to investigate the effect on the failure loads of different transverse profiles of deflection.

THE CONCEPT OF THE FAILURE LOAD. If a bridge comprising many laminates is subjected to a steadily increasing load, the failure of the first laminate does not necessarily mean the collapse of the entire bridge. On the contrary, as is intuitively obvious, the remaining laminates are usually still capable together of withstanding heavier loads. As more and more laminates fail,

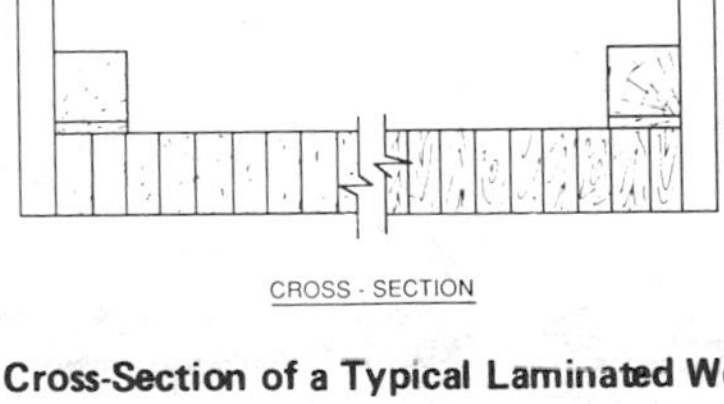


**Figure 1/ Cross-Section of a Typical Laminated Wood Bridge**

however, a maximum load carrying capacity is reached beyond which the failureof one more laminate will result in a reduction. The maximum load which the bridge can sustain is here called the "failure load;" it is thus seen to be the ultimate, or collapse load of the bridge.

Because of the manner in which the various laminates are glued, or otherwise secured, together, the failure .of a few laminates in random locations is unlikely to render the bridge unserviceable.

ASSUMED BEHAVIOUR OF A LAMINATE UP TO FAILURE. It is assumed that a laminate behaves linear elastically until its MOR is reached, at which time it abruptly ceases to be able to carry any load.

## REVIEW OF PREVIOUS WORK

The problem of the probabilistic assessment of the failure loads of laminated wood bridges has been tackled by plotting $E_L$ and MOR data for a given species of wood on axes of $E_L/(E_L)_{mean}$ and $MOR/(MOR)_{mean}$ (Jaeger and Bakht, 1986a). The subscript to $E_L$ and MOR refers to their respective mean values. For a given species of wood, it is found that the scatter of points can be approximated by a probability function within an annular sector as shown in Fig. 2. The probability function $p(r,\theta)$ was assumed to be representable as the product of a variation with respect to r, f(r), and a variation with respect to $\theta$, $\phi(\theta)$, i.e.:

$$p(r,\theta) = f(r) \times \phi(\theta) \qquad (1)$$

This assumption was found to be in reasonable agreement with the test data for Red pine used by Jaeger and Bakht (1986 a and b) with angle $\alpha$ shown in Fig. 2 being about 28°, and the function $\phi(\theta)$ being of the form:

$$\phi(\theta) = c\ (\sin 2\theta - \sin 2\alpha) \text{ for } \alpha \leqslant \theta\ (90°-\alpha) \qquad (2)$$

Fig. 3 shows in plan view the same annular sector of the probability function $p(r,\theta)$ with the addition of a failure boundary line at an angle $\beta$ from the $E_L/(E_L)_{mean}$ axis. For uniform deflection of the cross-section, the phenomenon of gradually increasing the load, and hence the deflection of a bridge, can be shown to be the same as the clockwise rotation of a radial line which starts on the $E_L/(E_L)_{mean}$ axis, and with the angle $\beta$ being related to the uniform

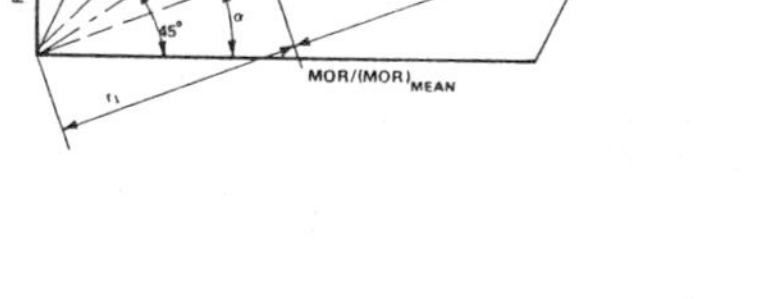

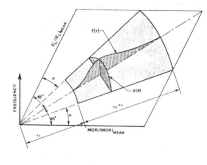

Figure 2/ The Probability Function $p(r,\theta)$

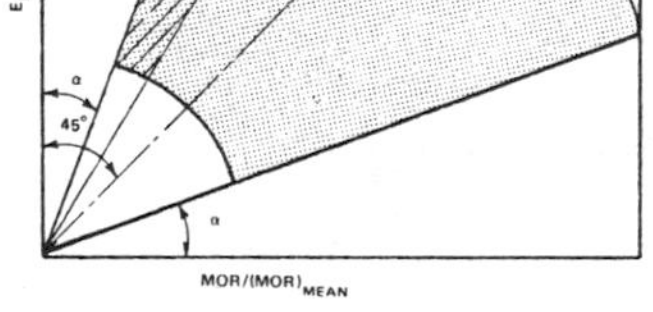

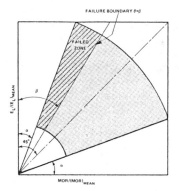

Figure 3/ Representation of The Failed Elements

deflection of the bridge cross-section by:

$$\tan\beta = w/\bar{w}_{mean} \tag{3}$$

where $\bar{w}_{mean}$ is the deflection at which a laminate having values of $(E_L)_{mean}$ and $(MOR)_{mean}$ would fail. Clearly, no laminate fails as long as $\beta$ is less than $\alpha$; however, when $\beta$ exceeds $\alpha$, then the laminates in the zone identified as the "failed zone" in Fig 3, will have failed.

For a given $p(r,\theta)$, it is a straightforward matter to find the value of $\beta$ corresponding to maximum load acceptance by the bridge and to express the expected failure moment M as:

$$M = M_T\, k(\beta) \tag{4}$$

where M is the expected failure load; $M_T$ is the failure load for the deterministic case in which all laminates have $(E_L)_{mean}$ and $(MOR)_{mean}$; and $k(\beta)$ is a reduction factor affected by the distribution of $E_L/(E_L)_{mean}$ and $MOR/(MOR)_{mean}$. For a bridge with N laminates:

$$M_T = N\,(M_{ult})_{mean} \tag{5}$$

where $(M_{ult})_{mean}$ is the mean ultimate moment of resistance of a population of laminates. For data corresponding to Red Pine (Jaeger and Bakht, 1986a), $k(\beta)$ is found to be about 0.609.

EXTENSION OF THE WORK TO ANY TRANSVERSE PROFILE

The above described approach can also be applied to the case where the deflections across a transverse section vary in the manner shown in Fig. 4. In this figure, the transverse co-ordinate y is represented in a non-dimensional form by $\lambda$ and the deflection of a representative point is related to $\bar{w}_{mean}$ by a factor $\psi(\lambda)$.

It has been shown by Jaeger and Bakht (1986b) that f(r) has little influence on the failure load, so that the two-dimensional distribution $p(r,\theta)$ can be replaced, without loss of accuracy, by a one-dimensional distribution on a z-axis, where z is defined by:

$$z = \left\{\frac{MOR}{(MOR)_{mean}}\right\} \Big/ \left\{\frac{E_L}{(E_L)_{mean}}\right\} \tag{6}$$

A suitable probability function for purposes of analysis is shown in Fig. 5.

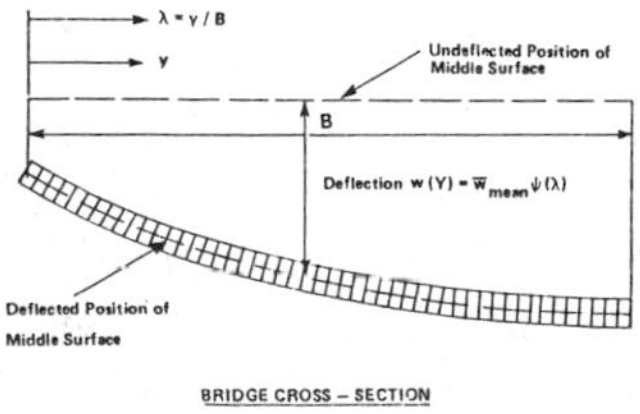


**Figure 4/ Cross-Section Having Variable Deflection**

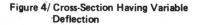

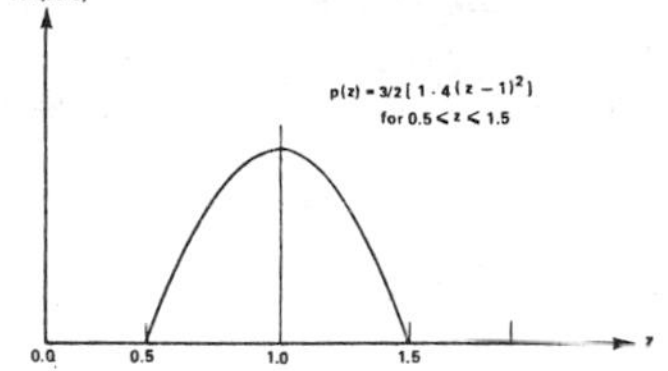


**Figure 5/ A Frequency Distribution for Purposes of Analysis**

This distribution represents fairly closely the variability of Red Pine. For a species with a larger scatter of properties the valid range of z will become somewhat larger. It is emphasized that the actual distribution of p(z) can be readily employed in the solution with the help of numerical methods.

The use of the one-dimensional distribution is a considerable simplification; it is valid provided that $(E_L)_{mean}$ of still unbroken laminates does not depart significantly from the $(E_L)_{mean}$ of the entire population. Extensive checking has shown this to be closely the case.

The clockwise rotation of the radial line in Fig. 3 representing the gradual increase of load, can now be shown to be the same as the left-to-right movement of a vertical line along the z-axis. The co-ordinate z is also available as a one-dimensional measure of deflection. Thus, as shown in Fig. 6, if a laminate has a non-dimensional deflection z, its probability of being still unbroken is given by g(z).

LINEAR VARIATION OF DEFLECTION. The case of the bridge with linearly varying transverse deflection profile, as shown in Fig. 7(a) is first considered. It is assumed that the non-dimensional deflection $z(\lambda)$ is given by:

$$z(\lambda) = Z\,(1 + c\lambda) \tag{7}$$

where Z is the non-dimensional deflection of the left hand element. The expectation of load acceptance by a laminate is proportional to zg(z) and the expected moment M accepted by the bridge is given by:

$$M = M_T \int_0^1 zg(z)\, d\lambda \tag{8}$$

As deflection increases, the integral in Eq. (8) increases until it reaches a maximum. This maximum, which is always less than unity, represents the factor by which $M_T$ must be multiplied in order to get the expected failure load.

For smaller values of c, all values of z of the cross-section at maximum load condition fall within the range $0.5 < z < 1.5$, and the integral of Eq. (8) is evaluated to give the following expression.

$$\int_0^1 zg(z)d\lambda = \frac{Z^2}{2c}[3\ \{(1+c)^3-1\}\ \ -3Z\{(1+c)^4\ -1\}\ +\frac{4Z^2}{5}\ \{(1+c)^5-1\}] \tag{9}$$

For any given value of c, the value of Z that will maximize M, is readily obtained. If the maximum of right hand side of Eq. (9) is denoted by $F_1$, then:

$$M = F_1 M_T \tag{10}$$

It is noted that Eq.(10) is valid for values of c upto about 0.9; for higher values of c the value of Z falls below 0.5 so that some laminates have still a

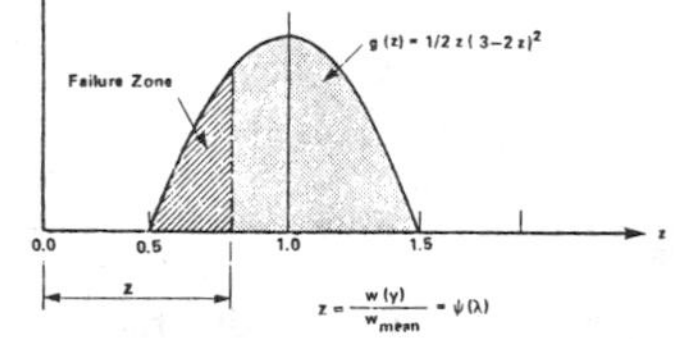


**Figure 6/ Probability of a Laminate Being Still Unbroken**

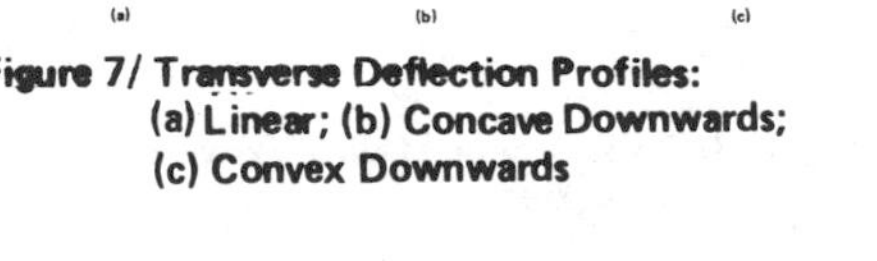

**Figure 7/ Transverse Deflection Profiles: (a) Linear; (b) Concave Downwards; (c) Convex Downwards**

zero probability of having failed when the maximum load carrying capacity is reached.

For a bridge in which all laminates have $(E_L)_{mean}$ and $(MOR)_{mean}$ and the deflection profile of which is defined by Eq. (7), the ultimate momement of resistance, $M_D$, is given by:

$$M_D = M_T/F_2 \qquad (11)$$

where $F_2$ is the ratio of maximum to mean deflections and is given by:

$$F_2 = 2(1+c)/(2+c) \qquad (12)$$

The product of $F_1$ and $F_2$ is the Reduction Factor R which relates the expected failure moment M to the deterministic failure moment $M_D$ which is obtained by assuming that all laminates have $(E_L)_{mean}$ and $(MOR)_{mean}$:

$$M = R\, M_D \qquad (13)$$

Values of R are calculated using Eqs. (9) and (12) and are plotted against $F_2$ in Fig. 8 as the curve which is identified as "linear".

PARABOLIC VARIATION OF DEFLECTION. Two cases in which the transverse deflection profile varies parabolically are now considered: In one case, which is shown in Fig. 7b, the profile is concave downwards; for this case the non-dimensional deflection $z(\lambda)$ is given by:

$$z(\lambda) = Z\,(1 + c\lambda^2) \qquad (14)$$

and for the other case, for which the profile, as shown in Fig. 7(c), is convex downwards by:

$$z(\lambda) = Z\,(1 - c\lambda^2) \qquad (15)$$

For these two cases also the values of the Reduction Factor R can be calculated by using procedures similar to those used for the linear profile case. Thus obtained values of R are also plotted in Fig. 8 against $F_2$. It can be seen that the Reduction Factor curves for the three very different transverse profiles shown in Fig. 7, lie within a relatively narrow band implying that the earlier-mentioned diminution of the failure load depends more on the ratio of maximum to mean deflections, i.e., $F_2$, than on the shape of transverse deflection profile for the bridge.

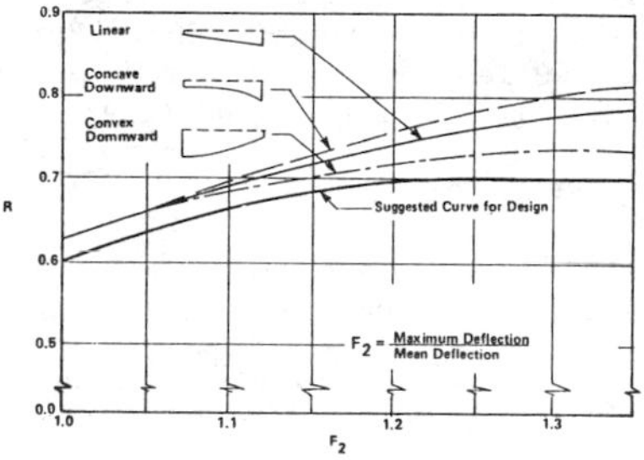


**Figure 8/ Reduction Factor R Plotted Against $F_2$**

PROPOSED DESIGN CRITERION

As concluded above, R is characterized fairly closely by $F_2$ with, however, some tendency for R to decrease with increasing downward convexity of the profile.

After extensive calculations it was concluded that a single lower-bound curve for R can be used not only for all deflection profiles but also for all species of softwood used in North America for bridge construction. The following two factors influence the selection of such a single curve.

(a) The value of $(E_L)_{mean}$ of still unbroken laminates is slightly smaller than that of the entire population, resulting in a slight decrease of R.

(b) For a species of wood for which the scatter of properties is larger than that for Red Pine, the R curves would lie somewhat lower than the corresponding curves shown in Fig. 8.

With these two aspects in mind, a suggested design curve of R plotted against $F_2$ is also shown in Fig. 8. As can be seen, in this case the value of R ranges between 0.6 and 0.7. This curve can be used to get safe estimates of the expectation of failure loads in laminated bridges constructed out of all commonly used species of wood.

ESTIMATION OF $F_2$. The ratio of the maximum to mean deflection, i.e., $F_2$, can clearly be obtained by a rigorous linear elastic analysis in which all the laminates are assumed to have the mean values of E. Alternatively, when these bridges are analyzed by simplified methods such as those specified in the AASHTO specifications (1984) or the Ontario Highway Bridge Design code (OHBDC, 1983). The following procedure can be used.

According to the methods given in AASHTO and Ontario codes, the analysis of a laminated wood bridge subjected to design loading is simplified to that of a longitudinal strip of the bridge subjected to one line of loading multiplied by a fraction (S/D). The quantity S is the width of the strip which is usually taken as one unit, and D has either a prespecified value for all laminated bridges (AASHTO, 1984), or is obtained by a semi-graphical procedure (OHBDC, 1983). The quantity D, which has units of length, is given by:

$$D = M_w/(M_x)_{max} \tag{16}$$

where $M_w$ is the beam moment at the transverse section under consideration due to one line of wheels of the design vehicle, and $(M_x)_{max}$ is the maximum intensity of longitudinal moment at the same transverse section. The mean value of $M_x$, denoted as $(M_x)_{mean}$, is given by

$$(M_x)_{mean} = n\ M_w\ RF/B \tag{17}$$

where n is the No. of lines of wheels on the bridge, RF is reduction factor for multi-lane loading and B is the bridge width. For single-lane bridges n is 2 and RF is 1.0; for two-lane bridges n is 4 and RF is 1.0 for AASHTO loading and 0.90 for OHBDC. From Eqs. (16) and (17):

$$(M_x)_{max}/(M_x)_{mean} = B/(n\ D\ RF) \tag{18}$$

It can be shown that the ratio of the maximum to mean deflections is fairly close to the ratio of the maximum to mean intensities of longitudinal moments. Thus:

$F_2 \approx B/(nD\ RF)$ (19)

By using Eq. (19), the value of $F_2$ can be obtained without performing a rigorous analysis.

SUGGESTED PROCEDURE. The expectation of the failure moment of the bridge can be obtained as follows.

(a) Obtain $F_2$ either by rigorous linear elastic analysis or by Eq. (19) in which the value of D is obtained by the code specified simplified method.
(b) Calculate the failure moment, $M_D$, of the bridge by assuming that all laminates have $(E_L)_{mean}$ and $(MOR)_{mean}$, using Eq. (11).
(c) Find R from the curve identified for design in Fig. 8 for the relevant value of $F_2$.
(d) Obtain the estimated collapse moment M from Eq. (13).

## MOR VALUE USED IN CALCULATIONS

It is common practice to use a certain percentile (usually 5th) value of the MOR in design calculations rather than the $(MOR)_{mean}$ on which the R-curves of Fig. 8 are based. Account for using a different value of MOR than $(MOR)_{mean}$ can be easily made as follows. Let the ratio of $(MOR)_{mean}$ and MOR value used in the calculation of $M_d$ be denoted by k. For the 5th percentile MOR, the value of k will be typically about 2.5. The revised values of R can be obtained by simply multiplying the values of Fig. 8 by k. It can be appreciated that if the 5th percentile MOR is used in the calculation of $M_D$ then R will be larger than 1.0 indicating that the expected failure load in this case is larger than the deterministically obtained value.

## CONCLUSIONS

It has been demonstrated that the expected failure load in a laminated timber bridge is significantly different than the deterministically obtained failure load; and that the expectation of the failure load is characterized by the variabilities of $E_L$ and MOR and the ratio of the maximum to mean deflections at at representative transverse section of the bridge. A simple procedure, which is independent of the species of wood, is proposed to calculate the expected failure load from the results of a deterministic analysis.

## ACKNOWLEDGEMENTS

The research which led to the writing of this paper has been supported by the Ministry of Transportation and Communications of Ontario and the Natural Sciences and Engineering Research Council of Canada. This support is gratefully acknowledged.

REFERENCES

American Association of State Highway and Transportation Officials. (1984). Standard Specifications for Highway Bridges. Washington, D.C.

Csagoly, P.F. and Taylor, R.J. (1980). A Structural Wood System for Highway Bridges. International Association for Bridge and Structural Engineering Proceedings P-35/80, pp.157-183.

Jaeger, L.G. and Bakht, B. (1986a). Probabilistic Assessment of the Failure of Laminated Timber Bridges. Transportation Research Record 1053. Transportation Research Board, Washington, D.C., U.S.A.

Jaeger, L.G. and Bakht, B. (1986b). Analysis of Failure Loads of Timber Bridges. Structural Research Report STR-86-02. Ministry of Transportation and Communications, Downsview, Ontario, Canada.

Ontario Highway Bridge Design Code. (1983). Ministry of Transportation and Communications. Downsview, Ontario.

# RELIABILITY DEGRADATION OF WOOD FLOOR SYSTEMS

R.G. Gillard * and J.J. Salinas **

* Manhire Cunliffe Partnership, Ottawa, Canada K2A 3X9
** Dept. of Civil Eng. Carleton University, Ottawa, Canada K1S 5B6

## ABSTRACT

The structural reliability of floor systems using Waferboard I beams and conventional solid lumber joists was evaluated over life spans of 5 to 30 years. The reliability index was used to characterize the systems' reliability, first by using an approximate formulation, and second by using a damage accumulation approach. A Monte Carlo technique was used to simulate the intensity and duration of dead and live service loads and their variations with time.

Results indicate that a conventional approach fails to account for a possibly significant degradation of the reliability index with time. This condition is evaluated for two different spans allowing to evaluate a 'size effect'. This technique was also used to evaluate the structural reliability of conventional solid lumber joist systems and compare it with that of engineered systems such as the Waferboard I beams.

## INTRODUCTION

The reliability analysis of single failure mode systems can be formulated as a 'supply-demand' problem where the supply is characterized by the structural capacity of the system, represented by the resistance variable R, and the demand is characterized by the load variable L. The performance function for this system is given by:

$$Z = R - L \tag{1}$$

The limiting performance of the system is given by Z = 0 which defines a 'limit state' in which there is no failure nor excess capacity in the system. The 'failure state' is given by Z < 0 and the 'safe state' by Z > 0. The probability of failure for the system can be calculated by determining the probability of occurrence of the 'failure state', Z < 0. If the probability density functions for R and L, $f_R$ and $f_L$, are known, the probability of failure is given by:

$$P_f = P[Z < 0] = \int_{-\infty}^{+\infty} f_L dL \int_{-\infty}^{L} f_R dR = \int_{-\infty}^{+\infty} f_L F_R dL \tag{2}$$

The probability density function for Z, $f_Z$, can be derived from $f_R$ and $f_L$ and the reliability index, $\beta$, can be defined by the ratio of the mean to the standard deviation of the derived distribution for Z.

$$\beta = \frac{m_Z}{\sigma_Z} \tag{3}$$

The probability of failure and the reliability index are related by:

$$P_f = 1 - \Phi(\beta) \tag{4}$$

where $\Phi(\beta) =$ Cumulative distribution function of the standard normal distribution.

CONVENTIONAL APPROACH (AN APPROXIMATION)

If the actual probability density functions for R and L are approximated by lognormal curves that fit in the significant tails, CSA S408-1981 suggests the following approximation for the reliability index:

$$\beta = \frac{\ln(m_R/m_L)}{\sqrt{V_R^2 + V_L^2}} \tag{5}$$

where 'm' refers to the mean and 'V' to the coefficient of variation. In the case of a joist floor system the resistance variable R can be used to represent either the strength or the stiffness of the system. The load variable L represents the total load effects including dead, live and extraordinary loads.

Based on earlier work by the authors (Salinas, et al, 1985; Gillard, 1986) the resistance and load variables can be defined:

$$R = \frac{F_T K_{DL}}{K_{DT}(D_n + L_n)} \tag{6}$$

$$L = \frac{\overline{D} + \overline{L}}{D_n + L_n} \tag{7}$$

The mean and coefficient of variation of these random variables are obtained from the application of the basic definition of expectation and variance as shown in the references mentioned above. The terms used in Equations (6) and (7) are explained below

Test Failure Load, $F_T$

The resistance variable used in this study was based on experimental results from bending tests to failure of Waferboard I beams and solid lumber joists grouped into four series, each with 10 specimens:

WF16 Waferboard I beams, depth 241 mm, span 5 m, chords 38x64 mm
WF20 Waferboard I beams, depth 292 mm, span 6 m, chords 38x89 mm
SJ16 Solid Lumber Joists, span 5 m, cross-section 38x235 mm
SJ20 Solid Lumber Joists, span 6 m, cross-section 38x282 mm

The test failure load is a random variable with mean and standard deviation determined from the test data.

Load Duration Factors, $K_{DT}$ and $K_{DL}$

Rate of loading has a significant effect on wood structures. It has been known for a long time that wood appears to be stronger when loaded rapidly. Stress adjustment factors are commonly used in the design of wood structures to account for the duration of the design load. These factors are incorporated into the code of practice and are based in the work by Wood (1951). Figure 1 shows the variation of the load duration factor with time. For this study $K_{DT}$ refers to a test load duration typically between 5 minutes and 1.5 hours for short-duration tests and around 48 hours for other performance or acceptability testing procedures such as that recommended by Canada Mortgage and Housing Corporation. The factor $K_{DL}$ refers to a lifespan of time under service which ranges from 5 years to 30 years.

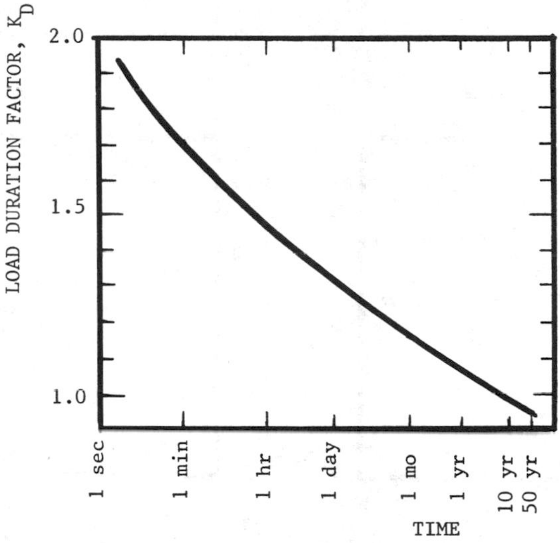


Figure 1 LOAD DURATION FACTOR

Nominal Design Loads, Dn and Ln

Dead loads are normally well defined for most conventional building systems. Live loads are prescribed by codes of practice and are based on load surveys or meteorological data. For this study the following values were used: Dn = 1 kPa and Ln = 1.9 kPa.

Actual Loads, $\bar{D}$ and $\bar{L}$

According to the National Bureau of Standards special publication # 577 the a ratio of the mean acting live load to the nominal live load is $\bar{L}/Ln = 0.70$ with a coefficient of variation of 0.30. Similarly the ratio of acting dead load to the nominal dead load is $\bar{D}/Dn = 1.05$ with a coefficient of variation of 0.10.

Reliability Index,

Equation (5) was used to calculate the reliability index for a range of lifetimes from 5 years to 30 years and the results plotted in Figure 2.

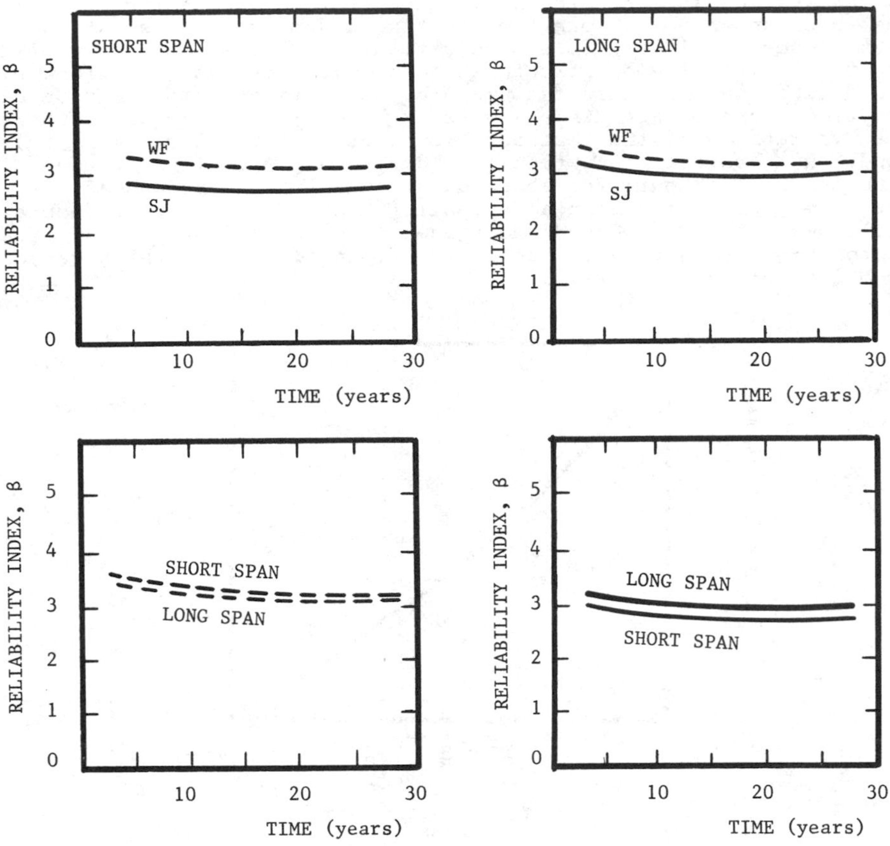


Figure 2 RELIABILITY INDEX VS TIME. CONVENTIONAL APPROACH

DAMAGE ACCUMULATION APPROACH

Due to the action of the loads, damage will accumulate on the system with time, reducing its capacity and increasing its probability of failure. As time increases, the load duration factor, $K_{DL}$, in Equation (6) decreases as shown in Figure 1, reducing the capacity of the system.. There is no such explicit time effect on the load variable given by Equation (7) and the reliability index does not show much change with time, as shown in Figure 2. In the second phase of this study, the reliability index was calculated from Equation (4) and the probability of failure from Equation (2) using a Monte Carlo process to generate the required probability density functions, $f_R$ and $f_L$ .

Background

Based on a model proposed by Barrett and Foschi (1978 a & b), Gillard (1986) calculates the total damage accumulated at time $T_2$

knowing the damage accumulated up to time $T_1$, using Equation (8).

$$\alpha(T_2) = e^{\lambda T_2}\{\alpha(T_1)e^{-\lambda T_1} + \int_{T_1}^{T_2} a[\sigma(t) - \sigma_0]^b e^{-\lambda t} dt\} \tag{8}$$

When determining the damage accumulated through a discontinuous load history Equation (8) is applied from $T_1 = 0$, $\alpha(T_1) = 0$ and evaluated over those regions where the load function is continuous. A 10-point Gaussian quadrature numerical procedure was used to evaluate the integral.

Resistance Variable, R

For each specimen tested, the test load history was recorded and used to evaluate the damage using Equation (8). An equivalent constant stress load history was then found which would result in the same damage. This was assumed to be the characteristic strength for each specimen. A two-parameter Weibull distribution was then fitted to the set of characteristic strengths for each test series and used as the underlying probability density function for the resistance variable, $f_R$. A Kolmogorov-Smirnoff goodness of fit test indicated this distribution to be significant at the 95 % confidence level.

Load Variable, L

Based on the work by Chalk and Corotis (1980) and Corotis and Jaria (1979) the total load was modelled with a dead load component and a live load component.

Dead Load.- This load consists of the weight of the floor joist itself, floor sheathing, covering, ceiling, partitions and non-loadbearing walls supported by the floor system. This load component is fairly constant over the life of the structure and it is assumed to have an underlying Normal probability density function with mean value 0.48 kPa and coefficient of variation of 0.10.

Live Load.- This load component is assumed to remain unchanged between certain points in time but changes its magnitude to reflect changes in use or occupancy. Chalk and Corotis (1980) give parameters for the instantaneous sustained live load for residential buildings based on load surveys. A mean load of 0.29 kPa and a standard deviation of 0.16 kPa were used in this study. The underlying distribution for this load component was assumed to be a Type I, extreme value distribution.

Simulation.- A Monte Carlo simulation was performed to generate the load components described above over lifetimes ranging from 5 to 30 years. Figure 3 shows a typical load history generated for a lifespan of 10 years using this technique. The spikes in this load history correspond to extraordinary live loads of short duration, generated using a Type I, largest value, distribution used in another phase of this study and not included here.

Damage Accumulation.- For each load history generated for a given lifespan (5,10,20 and 30 years) the damage accumulated by the end of the period was calculated using Equation (8). An equivalent constant stress load history resulting in the same damage was then found and the corresponding stress level was assumed to be the characteristic load for each load history. This process was repeated 100 times for each lifespan and the resulting data points were fitted to a two-parameter Weibull distribution which was assumed to be the underlying probability density function for the load variable, $f_L$ .

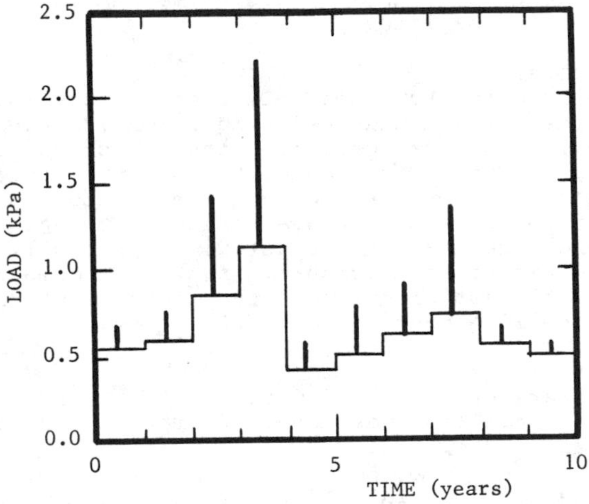


Figure 3 TYPICAL LOAD HISTORY OBTAINED FROM THE MONTE CARLO SIMULATION

Reliability Index,

The probability of failure and the safety index were calculated with Equations (2) and (4). The results are plotted in Figure 4.

DISCUSSION

Both methods of analysis show acceptable levels of structural reliability for short-term duration (5 years) for both systems studied, Waferboard I beams and solid joists. This is indicated by values of the reliability index between 3 and 4, as shown in Figures 2 and 4.

Using the conventional approach there is no strong evidence of a difference in structural reliability between the Waferboard I beam system and the solid joists.

No strong evidence of a size effect, as characterized by span length, could be seen for either system.

Using a damage accumulation approach with Monte Carlo simulation, there is significant evidence of a reduction of the reliability index for lifespans near 30 years, for all cases studied, as shown in Figure 4.

The reliability index for the solid joists with long spans is betwen 10 % and 30 % higher than that of the Waferboard I beams.

Both systems show a significant reduction of the reliability index, with time under load.

Size effect appears to be negligible for Waferboard I beams but significant for solid joists.

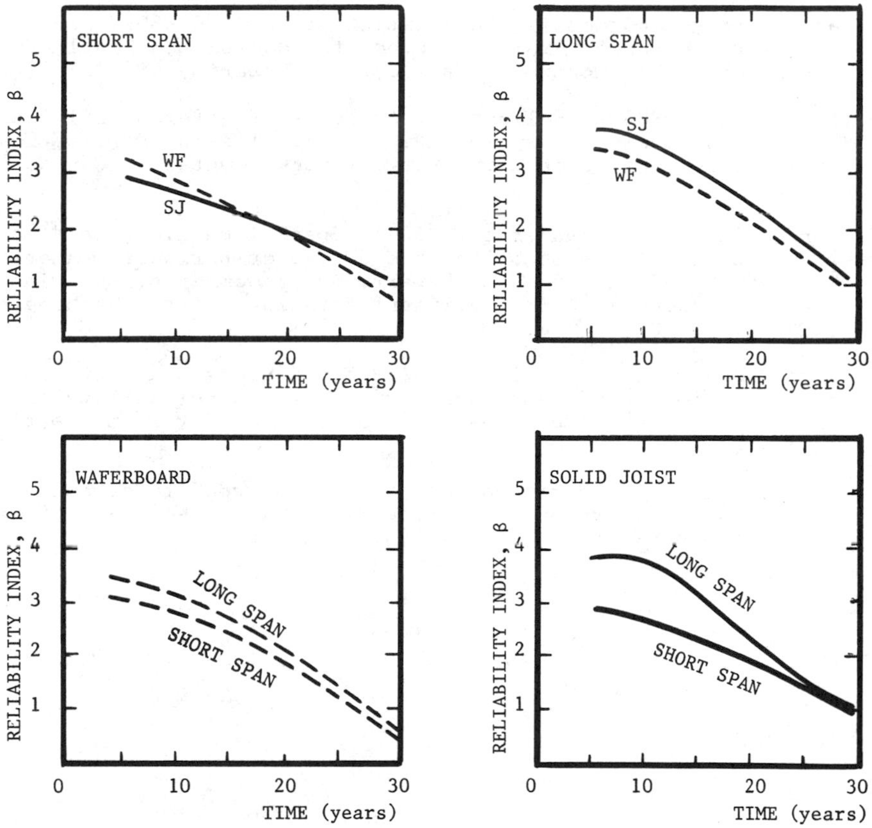


Figure 4 RELIABILITY INDEX VS TIME. A DAMAGE ACCUMULATION APPROACH

ACKNOWLEDGEMENTS

Financial support from NSERC in the form of an Operating Grant for the senior author is gratefully acknowledged.

REFERENCES

Barret, J.D. and R.O. Foschi (1978a). Duration of Load and Probability of Failure in Wood. Part I. Modelling Creep Rupture. Canadian Journal of Civil Engineering, 5(4), pp.505-514

Barret, J.D. and R.O. Foschi (1978b). Duration of Load and Probability of Failure in Wood. Part II. Constant, Ramp and Cyclic Loadings Canadian Journal of Civil Engineering 5(4), pp.515-532

Canada Mortgage and Housing Corporation (1983). ME 8309. Load Test Procedure for Floor Framing Systems for Houses and Small Buildings. CMHC, 682 Montreal Road, Ottawa, Ontario, K1A 0P7

Gillard, G.R. (1986). "Reliability Analysis of Waferboard I Beams. A Damage Accumulation Approach". M.Eng. Thesis. Dep. of Civil Engineering, Carleton University, Ottawa, Ontario, Canada K1S 5B6, 141 pp.

National Bureau of Standards (1980). Special Publication # 577. "Development of a probability based load criterion for American National Standard A58. U.S. Department of Commerce. Superintendent of Documents, U.S. Government Printing Office, Washington, D.C., U.S.A. 20402, 228 pp.

Salinas, J.J. and R.G. Gillard (1985). "Strength and structural safety of longspan light wood roof trusses. Reliability analysis using safety index". Canadian Journal of Civil Engineering, 12 (1) pp 114-125.

Wood, L. (1951). "Relation of strength of wood to duration of load". U.S. Department of Agriculture, Report No. 1916, Forest Products Laboratory, Madison, Wisconsin.

A STOCHASTIC MODEL FOR LOADS DUE TO CAR PARKING

P. Gross and R. Rackwitz*
*Lehrstuhl fuer Massivbau, Technical University of Munich, Munich, FRG

ABSTRACT

Loads due to cars in parking houses or similar facilities are modelled by a rectangular wave renewal process whose parameter can be adjusted to the special type of use of the facility. A table collecting parameters derived from a statistical survey by judgement is given. The extreme value distribution of certain load effects is derived as well as the random point-in-time distribution. The proposed model is compared with an earlier model.

INTRODUCTION

A special case of traffic loading is the loading due to parking cars on parking decks. Koenig/Marten (1975) have studied this type of loading and whom we follow as concerns the data.

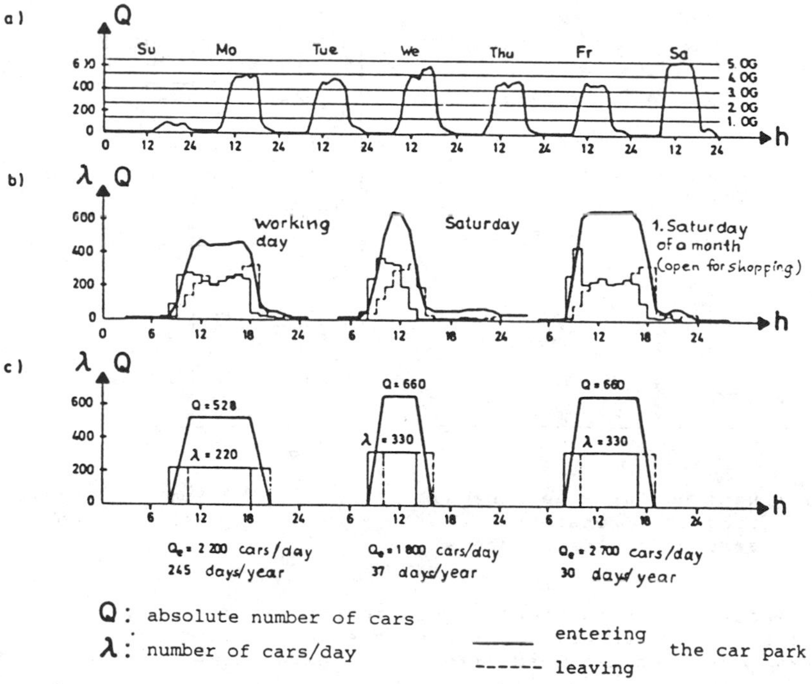


Figure 1: Example of daily and weekly fluctuations of vehicles in a car park (Konstabler Wache, Frankfurt - after Koenig/ Marten, 1975)

Figure 1 shows the typical pattern of temporal fluctuations in a parking house in a downtown commercial area. Q denotes the total number of cars in the car park as a function of time, λ denotes the number of cars per hour entering (thin solid line) and leaving (thin dashed line). In this case the maximum capacity of the parking house is $Q_{max}$ = 660 cars. It is seen that there are characteristic fluctuations during the day and less significant changes from day to day. In the morning of a day there is intense inflow of cars until the capacity of the parking house is reached or is nearly reached. This period is followed by an almost stationary phase of reduced inflow and outflow until the end of the busy period of the day. Then, the outflow of cars dominates the inflow. Nights are rather quiet periods.

## THE MODEL

The existence of those stationary periods at (almost) exhausted parking house capacities suggests to model the fluctuations of cars in parking houses as a simple stationary renewal process. In neglecting the small changes in the weight of a vehicle at arrival and departure the temporal characteristics of the loads

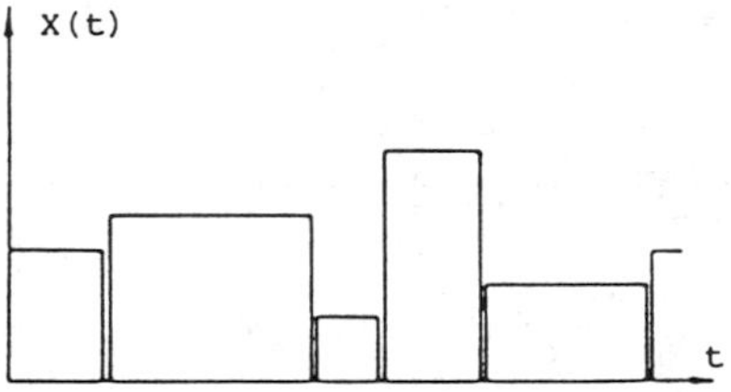


Figure 2a: Rectangular wave renewal process returning to zero before each renewal

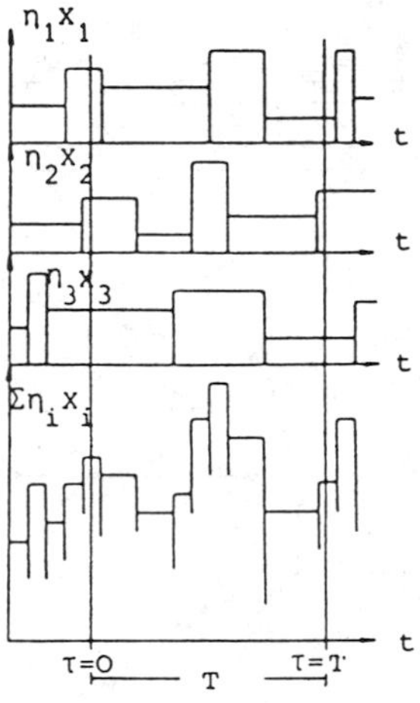


Figure 2b: Sum of three vehicle loads

at the individual parking units can accurately be modelled as rectangular wave renewal load processes of the type shown in figure 2a. Any scalar load effect at a given time instant is given by

$$S(t) = \sum_{i=1}^{n} \eta_i X_i(t) \qquad (1)$$

if the individual car loads are represented by a concentrated force at the center of gravity of the cars acting at a (usually) predefined location. They include orthogonal, oblique or other arrangements of parking units. The $\eta_i$'s are the corresponding (deterministic) influence factors. Car loads in different parking units may be assumed to be independent. Their amplitudes follow approximately a Gaussian distribution.

The following table collects the observations by Koenig/Marten (1975) on renewal rates and other relevant characteristics but also proposes some reasonable estimates for other types of parking houses.

If the size of the cars admitted to the facility is limited to usual passenger cars, station wagons and small trucks a reasonable estimate for the mean weight is 10 KN. The coefficient of variation is about 30%. These numbers may vary from country to country. If larger cars (trucks) are allowed to enter the facility a mixed Gaussian distribution is appropriate. The lower part of that distribution models the weights due to light traffic. The upper part takes account of trucks. In more sophisticated studies it may be necessary to distinguish between loaded and unloaded trucks.

Table 1: Tentative parameters of load model for different types of parking facilities

| Parking areas | Number of busy days per year $t_y$ [days] | Busy period per day $t_d$ [h] | Mean dwell time $T_\mu$ [h] | $\bar{\mu}$ [cars/day] |
|---|---|---|---|---|
| in down town | 245[1] | 8 | 2.4 | |
| | 37[2] | 4 | 2 | |
| commercial areas | 30[3] | 7 | 2 | |
| | 312[4] | | | 3.2 |
| at railway stations, airports, etc. | 360 | 14 - 18 | 10 - 14 | 1.3 |
| Public assembly halls, concert halls, sport facilities | 50 - 150 | 2.5 | 2.5 | 1.0 |
| for large office buildings, factories,....[5] | 260 | 8 - 12 | 8 - 12 | 1.0 |
| adjoined to residential areas[6] | 360 | 17 | 8 | 2.1 |

[1] normal week days
[2] saturdays
[3] exceptional
[4] average day
[5-6] see text for proper interpretation

In first approximation the load process associated with a parking unit can be assumed to be a Poisson renewal rectancular wave process. Note that each renewal is associated with a return of the load amplitude to zero (a car must leave the unit before another car can occupy it, see figure 2b).

EXTREME VALUE DISTRIBUTION

Of primary interest is the extreme value distribution for load effects. The upcrossing rate of a level s by S(t) during a stationary busy period is (Breitung/Rackwitz, 1982):

$$v(s) = \sum_{i=1}^{n} \mu_i\{[P(S^{-}>s) - P(\{S_i>s\}\cap\{S_i^{-}>s\})]$$

$$+ [P(S_i^{+}>s) - P(\{S_i>s\}\cap\{S_i^{+}>s\})]\} \qquad (2)$$

with $\mu_i = \mu = 1/T_\mu$. The first term in square brackets is associated with cars leaving a unit and is only present when negative influence coefficients have to be considered. The second term in square brackets is for cars entering a free parking unit. For all $\mu_i$'s being positive, there can be an upcrossing only if a new car enters the parking unit. The intersection terms usually can be neglected. Then, in good approximation and with due regard of the central limit theorem if the load amplitudes are not Gaussian the probabilities $P(S_i^{+}>s)$ are:

$$P(S_i^{+}>s) \approx 1 - \Phi\left(\frac{s - \sum_{i=1}^{n} \eta_i E[X]}{(\sum_{i=1}^{n} \eta_i^2 Var[X])^{1/2}}\right) \qquad (3)$$

The extreme load effect during a day is (asymptotically)

$$F_{\max_{[0,t_d]} S}(s) \backsim \exp[-v(s)t_d] \qquad (4)$$

and assuming independence of the stochastic characteristics in different days for t years

$$F_{\max_{[0,t]} S}(s) \backsim \exp[-v(s)t_d t_y t]$$

$$= \exp[-\bar{\mu}(\sum_{i=1}^{n} P(S_i^{+}>s))t_y t] \qquad (5)$$

where $\bar{\mu} = \mu\, t_d$.

RANDOM POINT-IN-TIME DISTRIBUTION

The random point-in-time distribution can also be given by assuming the load amplitude as a typical on/off renewal process. The mean fraction of busy periods is $m_b = t_d t_y/365$. The load amplitude may be assumed to be constant in time during a busy period equal to $\Sigma \eta_i X_i$ or even as a fixed value equal to the mean $\Sigma \eta_i E[X]$. Hence, its density is

$$f_S(s) \approx \begin{cases} 1 - m_b & \text{for } s=0 \\ m_b & \text{for } s = \sum_{i=1}^{n} \eta_i E[X] \end{cases} \qquad (6)$$

DISCUSSION

The above model does not apply to car parks for office buildings, factories or residential houses if each parking unit can be attributed to a specific user. The treatment of this case, however, appears straightforward insofar as it may be assumed that a parking unit is used by a particular user and time-variations are only caused by changes of the user and/or replacements of his car.

Theoretically more interesting is the case where the capacity of the parking house is rarely exhausted so that an extreme loading situation may also occur at partially occupied states of the parking house. Filtered Poisson processes might be appropriate to model this situation. This case is not considered herein because it appears to be of little practical interest.

Finally, it is easy to derive equivalent uniformly distributed loads (EUDL in [KN/m$^2$]) for any given type and size of influence surface and probability level along the lines adopted for usual occupancy loads (Peir/Cornell, 1973).

Let $p^*$ be the specified probability level. Then, with eq. (5) the EUDL can be determined from

$$P(\text{EUDL } A\, \Sigma\eta_i \leq s^*) = P(\max_{[0,t]} \{\Sigma\mu_i S_i\} \leq s^*) = F_{\max_{[0,t]} S}(s^*) = p^* \qquad (7a)$$

or

$$\text{EUDL} = s^*/(A\, \Sigma\eta_i) = F^{-1}_{\max_{[0,t]} S}(p^*) \qquad (7b)$$

Some numerical examples are given in figure 3 from which characteristic or design value loads can be derived. It is recognized that the parameters $t_y$ and $\bar{\mu}$ have only moderate effect. Also, the type of influence line is not significant from a practical point of view. But there is considerable area dependence of the EUDL and, of course, strong dependence on the parameters of the distribution of vehicle weights, especially on the mean.

The model presented before differs from the one proposed by Koenig/Marten (1975) in several aspects. Probably most important is that Koenig/Marten assume spatial correlation of vehicle weights which, however, does not appear to be supported by their own observations. Even if there is, in fact, spatial correlation of vehicle weights, it is suggested that eq. (2) should be modified according to the developments in Rackwitz (1985) rather than to use a spatial process model similar to the one proposed by Peir/Cornell (1973). Numerically, the two models differ by almost a factor of 2, i.e. the Koenig/Marten-model is conservative with respect to the model presented before. The above model appears to be operationally simpler than the Koenig/Marten-model. It permits immediate adjustment to other data.

LOADS ON DRIVE WAYS

The loads on drive ways can be modelled very much in the same manner as the loads for (short) bridges. In general, dynamic effects can be neglected due to the limited and small car velocities. Since the affected influence areas rarely exceed a few multiples of the car size it appears justified to assume that there is almost no superposition of load effects due to different cars. Then, it suffices to determine the extreme car weight whose probability distribution is (one way drives assumed):

$$F_{\substack{\max S \\ [0,t]}}(s) = \exp[-\bar{\mu} Q t_y t\, \Phi(-\frac{s+m_S}{\sigma_S})] \qquad (8)$$

If instationarity of the traffic needs to be considered $\bar{\mu}t_d$ must be replaced by the integral over $\bar{\mu}(\tau)$ between $[0,t_d]$. EUDL's are again easily derived in analogy to eq. (7). For example, assuming $\bar{\mu} = 3.2$, $t_y = 312$, $t = 50$ and $Q = 660$ one obtains a design value for the concentrated load of $s^* = 25.3$ KN or, related to an area of $2.4 \times 5.0 = 12m^2$, EUDL = 2.11 KN/m$^2$. This is, of course, a higher load than for parking units due to the greater frequency of load pulse changes.

REFERENCES

Breitung, K. and Rackwitz, R. (1982). "Nonlinear combination of load processes", Journal of Structural Mechanics, 10(2), pp. 145-166

Koenig, G. and Marten, K. (1975). "Zum wirklichkeitsnahen Erfassen von Nutzlasten", Bautechnik, 8, pp. 275-281

Peir, J.-C. and Cornell, C.A. (1973). "Spatial and temporal variability of live loads", Journal of Structural Division, ASCE, 99, pp. 903-922

Rackwitz, R. (1985). "Reliability of systems under renewal pulse loading", Journal of Engineering Mechanics, ASCE, 111(9), pp. 1175-1184

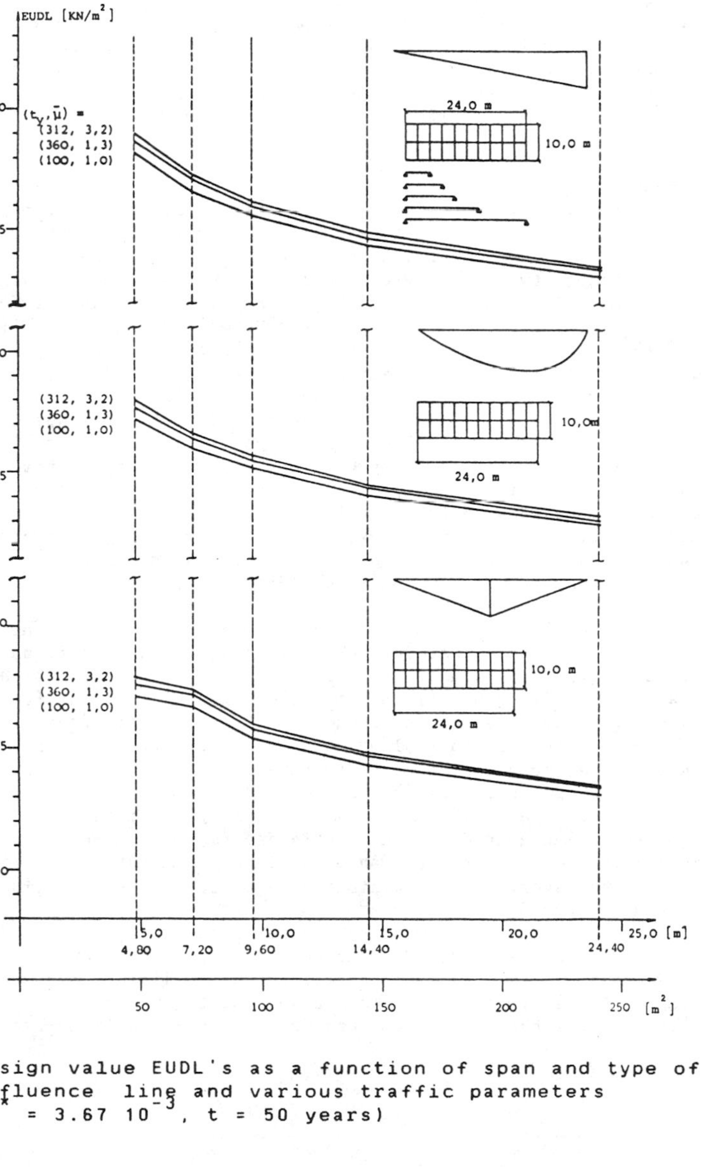


Figure 3: Design value EUDL's as a function of span and type of influence line and various traffic parameters ($p^* = 3.67\ 10^{-3}$, t = 50 years)

# RELIABILITY ANALYSIS OF DEFLECTION-DRIFT LIMITED STRUCTURES

Dan M. Frangopol* and Rachid Nakib**
*Associate Professor, Department of Civil Engineering, University of Colorado, Boulder, CO 80309-0428, U.S.A.
**Research Assistant, Department of Civil Engineering, University of Colorado, Boulder, CO 80309-0428, U.S.A.

## ABSTRACT

Deflections, structural deteriorations, floor vibrations and other serviceability criteria are naturally random with respect to their magnitudes. A realistic analysis of serviceability limit states therefore requires the consideration of risk of unserviceability. Isosafety functions are proposed here for analyzing the influence of different parameters on the reliability levels with respect to limit states associated with deflection and drift conditions.

## INTRODUCTION

Structural systems are typically multifunctional in nature, required to perform a combination of ultimate and serviceability limit state constraints. While this basic design philosophy has been accepted for some time, the area of serviceability limit state research has not enjoyed the same development as the ultimate limit state area. The Ad Hoc Committee on Serviceability Research, Committee on Research of the Structural Division (1986) recognized that the problems in the area of serviceabilty limit states are more difficult to define and analyze, they are not necessarily safety related, the basic data are more available to the practitioner than to the researcher, and the current code treatment of serviceability issues is limited or inadequate. It is also important to recognize that during the past decade the desire to reduce structural weight and rigidity has been a strong driving force behind the development of serviceability limit states procedures. Today, the need for reliability-based structural optimization via weight reduction provides further motivation for the development of serviceability procedures that are consistent with the concepts of probability-based limit states design.

The papers by Turkstra and Reid (1981) and Galambos and Ellingwood (1986) deserve special attention in view of the information on probabilistic design for serviceability. Turkstra and Reid (1981), recognized the problems of subjectivity, discretization, load-time history, and optimization and developed a general approach to analyze these problems for codification purposes. Galambos and Ellingwood (1986), treated deflection and drift as random variables using the first-order second-moment reliability theory. Both of these papers indicate that in reality there are not distinct sets of serviceability limit states; they depend on subjective factors (e.g., the perceptions of the building occupants). However, as pointed out by Galambos and Ellingwood (1986), there are indicators providing some guidelines as to what behavior might be expected at different static deformations. For example, at a deflection limit of 1/300 of the span of a flexural member, or a drift limit of 1/300 of the story height, visible damages to ceiling and flooring, and cracking in reinforced walls are expected.

From the broad spectrum of common serviceability problems discussed by Galambos and Ellingwood (1986) as well as the Ad Hoc Committee on Serviceability Research (1986), this paper deals with two limit states related to excessive static deformation: deflection and drift. These serviceability requirements are simultaneously accounted for in the reliability-based analysis process. The deflection and drift limit states for a structure acted on by random loads are defined here as isosafety functions in the space of the mean values of the loads (i.e., isosafety loading functions). The space of the mean values of deformations is also used for defining isosafety functions against unserviceability by excessive deflection and drift (i.e., isosafety deformation functions). A parametric analysis is conducted to study the effect of various parameters on both the isosafety loading and deformation functions.

RELIABILITY WITH RESPECT TO DEFLECTION AND DRIFT

The problem considered in this paper is to find the reliability of a deterministic structure acted on by random service loads with respect to both deflection and drift. In particular, aspects of the problem such as the influence of the input parameters on the reliability associated with deflection and drift, and the individual contribution of loads to the global safety with respect to deformation are also considered.

The following assumptions are made: (a) deflection and drift computations correspond to an idealized elastic deterministic structure with fixed geometry and rigidity; (b) the service static loads acting on the structure are random variables with known statistical properties for a given serviceability reference period (e.g., eight years according to Galambos and Ellingwood (1986)); (c) the positions of loads are deterministic; (d) the allowable (vertical) deflection, $\Delta_v^{allow}$, and the allowable (horizontal) drift, $\Delta_h^{allow}$, are deterministic limits specified by the designer; (e) the statistical dependencies between the service loads are accounted for through correlation coefficients; (f) consistent with a first-order second-moment reliability theory, the necessary statistical information is given in terms of service load vectors (mean values and coefficients of variation) and service load correlation matrix (coefficients of correlation among loads); (g) on the same basis, of a first-order second-moment reliability approach, regardless of the probability distributions of the individual loads, the reliability of the structure with regard to (vertical) deflections is given as

$$\beta_v = 1/V(g_v) \tag{1}$$

and with regard to (horizontal) drift is given as

$$\beta_h = 1/V(g_h) \tag{2}$$

where $\beta_v$ and $\beta_h$ are safety indices,

$$g_v = \Delta_v^{allow} - \Delta_v \tag{3}$$

$$g_h = \Delta_h^{allow} - \Delta_h \tag{4}$$

are the reserve safety margins (also termed performance functions) with respect to deflection and drift, respectively, and $V(g_v)$ and $V(g_h)$ are the coefficients of variations of the safety margins $g_v$ and $g_h$, ($\Delta_v$ and $\Delta_h$ in (3) and (4) are the (vertical) deflection and the (horizontal) drift due to service static loads); and (h) the global safety of a structure with regard to both deflection and drift (i.e., deformation serviceability) is given as

$$\beta_{system} = 1/V\ (g_{system}) \tag{5}$$

where the global safety (generalized system reliability) index is defined as the reciprocal of V ($g_{system}$) = the coefficient of variation of the unserviceability mode expression (i.e., $g_{system}$ = reserve safety margin of the system with respect to deformation) including both deflection and drift.

The safety indices (1), (2) and (5) provide an exact probability of unserviceability with respect to deflection, drift, and system deformation, respectively, if the loads are normally distributed. In this case

$$P_{f,v} = \Phi(-\beta_v) \quad (6)$$

$$P_{f,h} = \Phi(-\beta_h) \quad (7)$$

$$P_{f,system} = \Phi(-\beta_{system}) \quad (8)$$

where $\Phi(.)$ is the standard normal probability distribution function.

If a structure under a given service load combination has m critical sections with respect to vertical deflections and n critical sections with respect to lateral deflections (drift), the occurrence of $\Delta_v^{allow}$ or $\Delta_h^{allow}$ or both, in any of these sections will constitute loss of deformation serviceability of the system. The probability of system unserviceability, therefore, is

$$P_{f,system} = P\,(A_1 U \ldots U A_i U \ldots U A_m U B_1 U \ldots U B_j U \ldots U B_n) \quad (9)$$

where the unserviceability events $A_i$ and $B_j$ represent the occurrence of $\Delta_v^{allow}$ and $\Delta_h^{allow}$ in the critical sections i and j, respectively, and the symbol U represents the union of the individual unserviceability events. Exact evaluation of (9) is usually impractical or impossible because of numerical difficulties. However, because (9) is based on the "weakest-link" concept, boundary techniques similar to those used for calculating the overall collapse probability of plastic structures could be used (see, for example, the computer program described in Frangopol and Nakib (1986)).

SAFETY INDEX WITH RESPECT TO UNSERVICEABILITY OF RIGID FRAME

As an example, reliability analysis of a rigid frame with respect to deflection and drift was performed. The steel frame shown in Fig. 1 has fixed geometry ($\ell$ = 10m, h = 4m) and uniform flexural rigidity (EI = 20525.6 $kNm^2$), and is acted on by two random service loads with a given serviceability reference period. The coefficients of variation of the loads are V(H) = 0.15 and V(P) = 0.20; the loads are assumed to be independent $\rho(P,H) = 0$. The two critical sections of the frame with respect to loss of serviceability due to excessive flexural deflection, $\Delta_v$, and drift, $\Delta_h$, are the sections 1 and 2, respectively. Both the (vertical) deflection $\Delta_v$ and the (horizontal) drift $\Delta_h$ have two components as follows:

$$\Delta_v = \Delta_v^P + \Delta_v^H \quad (10)$$

$$\Delta_h = \Delta_h^H + \Delta_h^P \quad (11)$$

where $\Delta_v^P$ = the component of the (vertical) deflection due to P, $\Delta_v^H$ = the component of the (vertical) deflection due to H, $\Delta_h^H$ = the component of the (lateral) drift due to H, and $\Delta_h^P$ = the component of the (lateral) drift due to P. The influence of different combinations of the mean values of service loads ($\overline{P},\overline{H}$) on the safety indices $\beta_v$ (see Eq.(1)) and $\beta_h$ (see Eq. (2)) is shown in Fig. 2. The allowable deflection and drift limits are $\Delta_v^{allow} = \ell/300$ = 3.33 cm and $\Delta_h^{allow}$ = h/200 = 2cm. In Fig. 2 the results are given for four different values of the mean vertical load $\overline{P}$ (50, 60, 70 and 80 kN) while the mean lateral load $\overline{H}$ is increased from 0 to 150 kN. The decrease in the drift

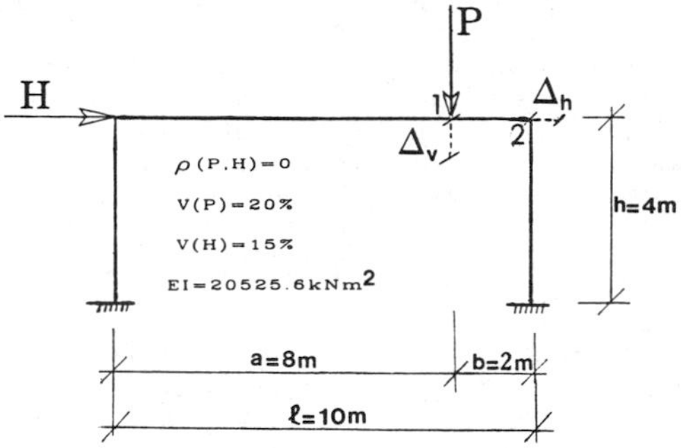


Fig. 1. Rigid Portal Frame under Random Loads.

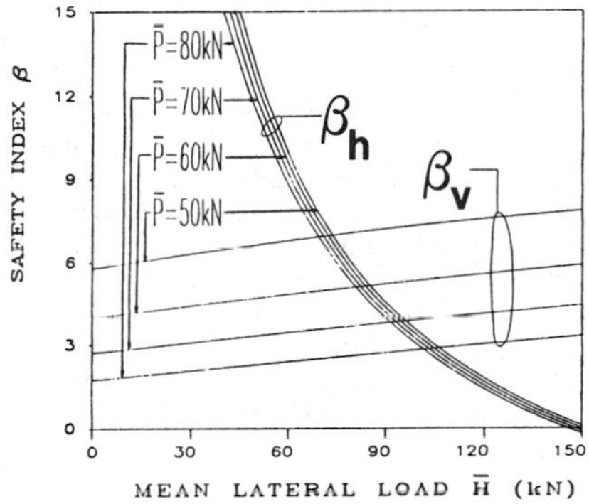


Fig. 2. Deflection and Drift Safety Indices.

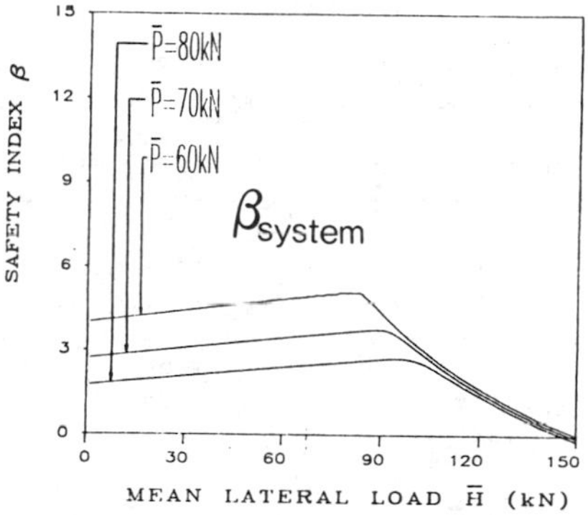


Fig. 3. Global Deflection - Drift Safety Indices.

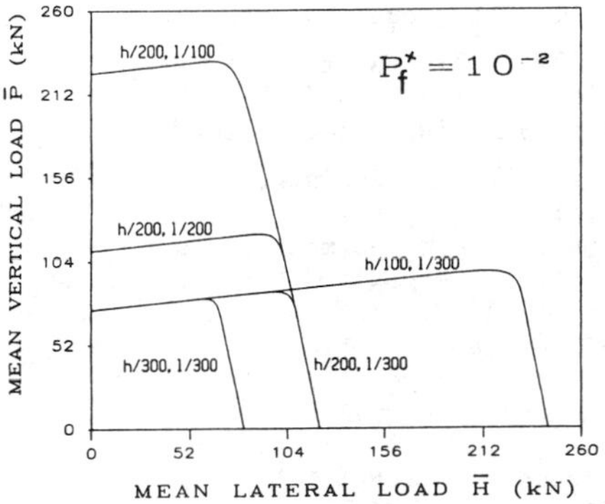


Fig. 4. Mean Load Space; Influence of Allowable Deflection and Drift Limits.

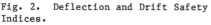

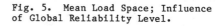

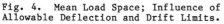

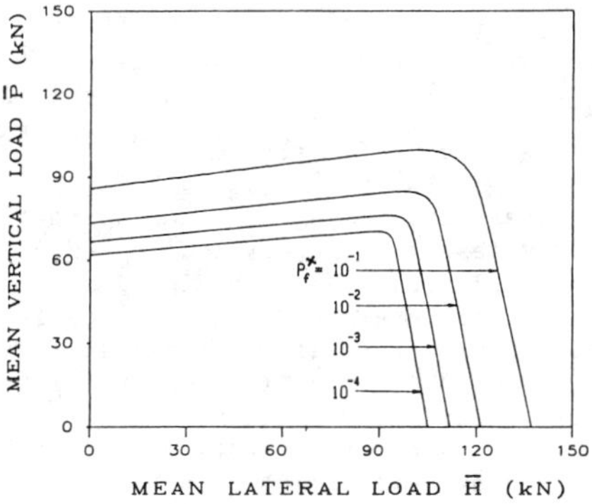


Fig. 5. Mean Load Space; Influence of Global Reliability Level.

safety index, $\beta_h$, with increasing $\overline{H}$ and/or $\overline{P}$ is due to the fact that $\overline{H}$ and $\overline{P}$ have the same effect on $\Delta_h$ (i.e., $\Delta_h^H > 0$ and $\Delta_h^P > 0$). On the other hand, the increase in the deflection safety index, $\beta_v$, with increasing $\overline{H}$ and/or decreasing $\overline{P}$ is due to the fact that for this particular position of the vertical load (a = 8m) $\overline{H}$ and $\overline{P}$ have opposite effects on $\Delta_v$ (i.e., $\Delta_v^H < 0$ and $\Delta_v^P > 0$). As expected, it appears that changes in the mean value of the vertical load, $\overline{P}$, show considerable influence on the safety index associated with vertical deflection $\beta_v$ and almost no influence on the safety index associated with drift $\beta_h$. This is because $|\Delta_v^P| \gg |\Delta_v^H|$ in (10), and $\Delta_h^P \ll \Delta_h^H$ in (11).

The influence of different combinations of the mean values of loads $(\overline{P},\overline{H})$ on the global safety index $\beta_{system}$ (see Eq. (5)) of the frame shown in Fig. 1 is illustrated in Fig. 3. The global safety index in Fig. 3 corresponds to independent deflection and drift safety margins, $\rho(g_v,g_h) = 0$; this assumption conforms to the upper bound method proposed by Cornell (1967). It is important to observe that $\beta_{system}$ increases as $\overline{P}$ decreases. However, $\beta_{system}$ becomes less sensitive to $\overline{P}$ than to changes in $\overline{H}$ when the unreliability with respect to drift becomes dominant (i.e., $\beta_h < \beta_v$); it is clear (see Fig. 2) that this refers to large values of $\overline{H}$ (e.g., $\overline{H} > 110$ kN).

## ISOSAFETY LOADING FUNCTIONS IN MEAN LOAD SPACE

Each combination of mean values of service loads acting on a structure represents a point in the mean service load space. An incremental mean loading technique is used to obtain different isosafety loading functions in the space of mean values of service loads. Each isosafety loading function with respect to deflection-drift corresponds to a specified value of the global reliability index $\beta_{system}$ (see Eq. (5)). Therefore, each point on such a function represents a combination of the mean values of the service loads leading to a specified value of $\beta_{system}$ (i.e., $\beta_{system} = \beta^*_{system}$). The set of mean service load combinations leading to a prescribed reliability value $\beta^*_{system}$ forms an isosafety function against deflection-drift. Using Eq. (8), it is clear that

$$P^*_{f,system} = \Phi(-\beta^*_{system}) \qquad (12)$$

Therefore, we may view each isosafety loading function against deflection-drift, as the set of mean service load combinations leading to a prescribed value of the global probability of deflection-drift unserviceability, $P^*_{f,system}$. In general, an isosafety loading function cuts the mean load space into two regions: the safe loading region (where $\beta_{system} > \beta^*_{system}$ or $P_{f,system} < P^*_{f,system}$) and the unsafe loading region (where $\beta_{system} < \beta^*_{system}$ or $P_{f,system} > P^*_{f,system}$). The set of mean service load combinations that satisfy the equation $\beta_{system} = \beta^*_{system}$ or $P_{f,system} = P^*_{f,system}$ are points on the isosafety loading function against unserviceability.

Examples of isosafety loading functions in the space of mean loads $(\overline{P},\overline{H})$ of the portal frame shown in Fig. 1 are illustrated in Figs. 4,5,6 and 7. Figs. 4 and 5 show the sensitivity of the isosafety loading functions against deformation unserviceability to changes in the allowable deflection-drift limits and the global probability of system failure, respectively; the isosafety functions in these figures correspond to independent normal distributed deflection and drift safety margins (i.e., $\rho(g_v,g_h) = 0$). Figs. 6 and 7 show the effects of load correlation and methods for global reliability evaluation, respectively, on the isosafety loading functions corresponding to

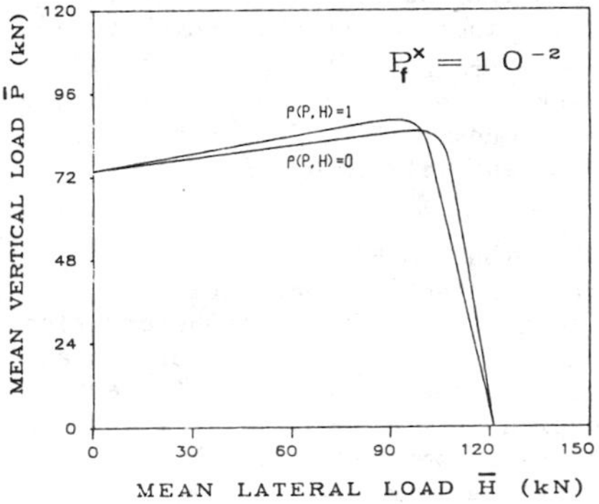


Fig. 6. Mean Load Space; Influence of Load Correlation.

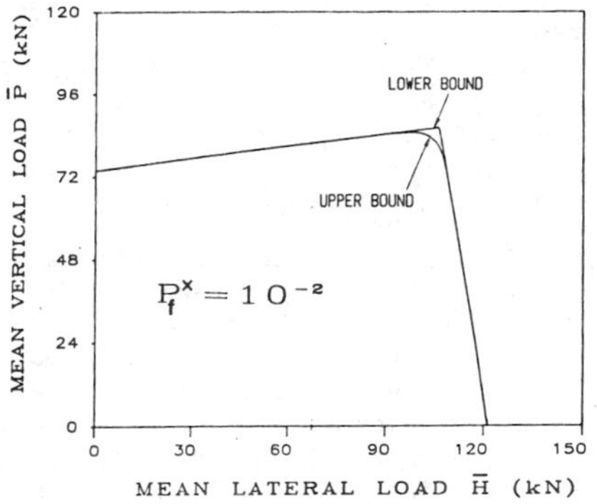


Fig. 7. Mean Load Space; Influence of Method for Global Reliability Evaluation.

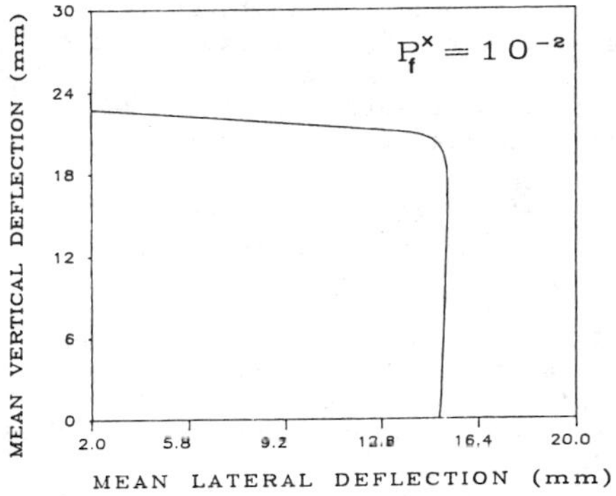


Fig. 8. Isosafety Deflection-Drift Function in Mean Deformation Space.

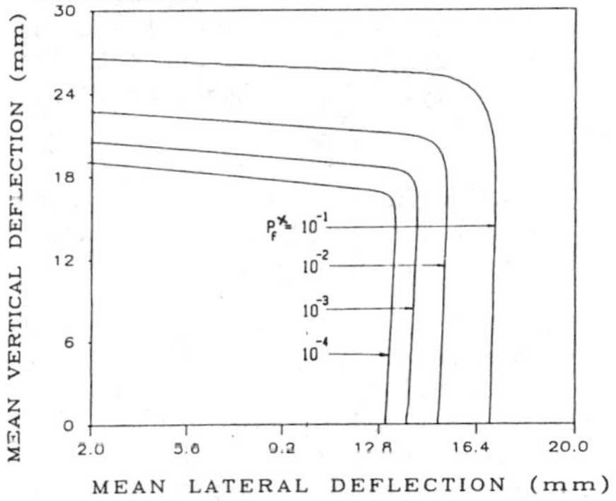


Fig. 9. Mean Deformation Space; Influence of Global Reliability Level.

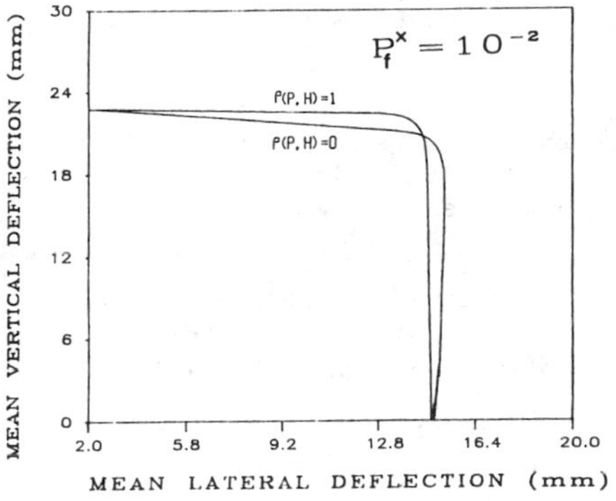


Fig. 10. Mean Deformation Space; Influence of Load Correlation.

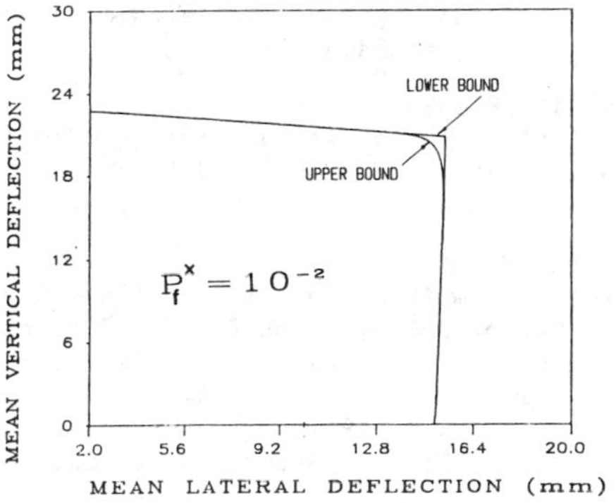


Fig. 11. Mean Deformation Space; Influence of Method for Global Reliability Evaluation.

a specified value of the probability of deformation unserviceability of the frame $P^*_{f,system} = 10^{-2}$ ($\beta^*_{system} = 2.32$). It is important to observe that the isosafety loading function is sensitive to the correlation between loads (Fig. 6) and almost insensitive to the correlation between deflection and drift safety margins; the lower and the upper bounds in Fig. 7 correspond to perfectly correlated ($\rho(g_v,g_h) = 1$) and independent ($\rho(g_v,g_h) = 0$) safety margins, respectively.

## ISOSAFETY DEFORMATION FUNCTIONS IN MEAN DEFORMATION SPACE

Each combination of mean values of vertical (deflection) and lateral (drift) deformations of a structure represents a point in the mean deformation space. An incremental mean deformation technique, similar to the incremental technique used for the mean service load space, is used to obtain different isosafety deformation (deflection-drift) functions in the mean deformation space. Each point on such a function represents a combination of the mean values of deformations leading to a specified value of $\beta_{system}$ (i.e., $\beta_{system} = \beta^*_{system}$) and $P_{f,system}$ (i.e., $P_{f,system} = P^*_{f,system}$).

Examples of isosafety deformation functions in the space of mean deformations ($\overline{\Delta}_v$, $\overline{\Delta}_h$) of the portal frame acted on by the normal distributed loads P and H shown in Fig. 1 are illustrated in Figs. 8, 9, 10 and 11. The allowable deflection and drift limits are $\ell/200 = 3.33$ cm and $h/200 = 2$ cm, respectively. The reliability level against unserviceability is the same in Figs. 8, 10 and 11: $P^*_{f,system} = 10^{-2}$. The influence of the prescribed reliability level on the isosafety deformation functions is shown in Fig. 9. Figs. 10 and 11 present the sensitivity of the isosafety deformation functions to changes in correlation between loads and methods for global reliability evaluation, respectively.

## CONCLUSION

Isosafety loading and deformation functions of structural systems against unserviceability with respect to both excessive deflection and drift are briefly examined in this paper. From the results it can be concluded that the proposed isosafety functions allow deflection and drift conditions to be considered simultaneously in the reliability analysis process. This makes it possible to approach the serviceability limit states related to excessive static deformations in a much more integrated manner than is possible with the conventional approach in which deformation unserviceability conditions are checked independently.

## ACKNOWLEDGMENTS

This research was partially supported by the Graduate School of the University of Colorado and by the National Science Foundation under Grant ECE-8609894. This support is gratefully acknowledged.

## REFERENCES

Ad Hoc Committee on Serviceability Research, Committee on Research of The Structural Division (1986). "Structural Serviceability: A Critical Appraisal and Research Needs", Journal of Structural Engineering, ASCE, Vol. 112, pp. 2646-2664.

Cornell, C.A. (1967). "Bounds on the Reliability of Structural Systems", Journal of the Structural Division, ASCE, Vol. 93, pp. 171-200.

Frangopol, D.M. and R. Nakib (1986). "Isosafety Loading Functions in System Reliability Analysis", Computers and Structures, Vol. 24, No. 3, pp. 425-436.

Galambos, T.V. and B. Ellingwood (1986). "Serviceability Limit States: Deflection", Journal of Structural Engineering, ASCE, Vol. 112, pp. 67-84.

Turkstra, C.J. and S.G. Reid (1981). "Structural Design for Serviceability", In M. Shinozuka and J.T.P. Yao (Eds.), Probabilistic Methods in Structural Engineering, ASCE, New York, pp. 81-101.

# A STATISTICAL CONSIDERATION ON HIGHWAY TRAFFIC LOAD MODEL FOR DESIGN CODE

Toshiyuki SUGIYAMA* and Yozo FUJINO**
*Department of Civil Engineering, Yamanashi University, Kofu, Yamanashi Pref., Japan.
**Department of Civil Engineering, University of Tokyo, Bunkyo-ku,Tokyo, Japan.

ABSTRACT

The way to prescribe the highway traffic load for design code is discussed based on computer simulations. Simulations of traffic loads are carried out with inclusion of the effect of the congested traffic flow passing over bridges. The maximum values of both moments and shears produced by traffic loads in a single-lane are calculated for five types of superstructures whose bridge length is between 20m and 200m. It is found that both a concentrated load and a uniform load are required to prescribe the highway traffic loads for design code. The design value of a concentrated load is suitable to be taken as a constant regardless of the span length for moments or shears or both. On the other hand that of a uniform load should be determined corresponding to what stress is considered. And the result shows that these two design values should be estimated taking account of the effect of the congested traffic flow passing over bridge. It has been also revealed that traffic load model for moments and that for shears should be adopted separately if the accurate estimation of the maximum stress produced by traffic load id required.

## 1.INTRODUCTION

Highway traffic load, one of the principal loads act on the highway bridges, has large uncertainties. This depends on the variations of vehicle weight, headway distance of two successive vehicles, constitutions of traffic, and so on. Therefore it is very difficult to estimate the design traffic load of highway bridge at design stage.

In the current design code for highway bridges in Japan (JHA, 1980), both of a concentrated load and a uniform load are used for representing a highway traffic load. And their design values are calculated as the function of the breadth and the span length of bridge. In other countries, almost the same way as used in Japan is adopted for prescribing the design traffic loads.

Although many studies discuss the probability-based highway traffic load model ( Nishimura, 1956; Nakagawa, 1966 ; and so on), few of them are concerned with whether both a concentrated load and a uniform load are required to express the traffic loads and/or whether it is suitable to calculate its design values as the function of span length. Furthermore most of these works choose only the maximum bending moment at the center of simple beam as the subject of study.

The purpose of this contribution is to discuss the way to prescribe the highway traffic load for design code based on computer simulations. Simulations of traffic loads are carried out with inclusion of the effect of the congested traffic flow passing over bridges. Maximum values of both moments and shears produced by traffic loads in a single-lane are calculated for five types of superstructures whose bridge length is between 20m and 200m.

## 2.SIMULATION OF TRAFFIC LOADS

### 2.1.Highway traffic flow

In the simulation of traffic loads, the vehicle weight and the headway distance between two successive vehicles are considered as random variables. And the type of vehicles in the array is determined by Monte Carlo simulation.

For simplicity, the vehicles are lumped into five categories as shown in Fig.1 (Miki et al.,1985). Table 1 presents the constitution of traffic (ratio of various vehicles) used here, one of the field measured date taken on the Tomei Expressway in Japan (JHPC et al.,1983).

The distributions of the weights of five types of vehicles are listed in Table 2. These distributions are the same as used in Miki et al.'s study (1985). The weight of vehicle is distributed to each axle in proportion to the ratio presented in Fig.1.

The distribution of the headway distance between two successive vehicles, accurately the distance between the tail of a vehicle and the top of the next one, is assumed to be log-normal distribution whose parameters are as follows (PWRI, 1984): mean value = 2.0m, coefficient of variation = 0.5, maximum value = 6.0m, minimum value = 0.5m.

About 5 km length of the congested traffic flow passes over the bridge in each simulation.This length corresponds to the case that a heavy traffic jam continues for about an hour.

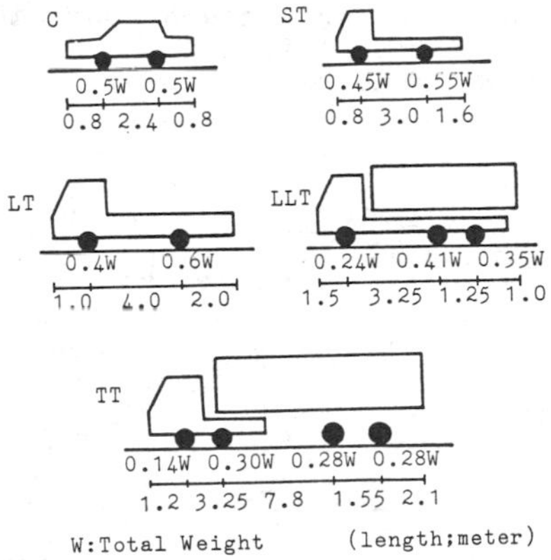


Fig.1 Configurations and Axle Weight Distributions of Model Vehicles

Table 1 Constitution of Traffic (%)

| C | ST | LT | LLT | TT |
|---|---|---|---|---|
| 10 | 5 | 25 | 50 | 10 |

Table 2 Distribution of Vehicle Weight

| Vehicle Type | Distribution Type | Mean value [tonf] | C.O.V. | Maximum Value[tonf] | Minimum Value[tonf] |
|---|---|---|---|---|---|
| C | Normal | 1.2 | 0.645 | 4.0 | 0.5 |
| ST | Normal | 3.1 | 0.577 | 8.0 | 0.8 |
| LT | Normal | 8.1 | 0.395 | 30.0 | 1.0 |
| LLT | Normal | 17.7 | 0.345 | 45.0 | 2.0 |
| TT | Log-Normal | 22.2 | 0.432 | 66.0 | 6.0 |

2.2.Types of superstructure

Five types of superstructure shown in Fig.2 are taken up in this study. The bridge length is between 20m and 200m. As illustrated in Fig.2, the span ratio of two span continuous beam is 1:1, and those of three span continuous beam and Gerber (cantilever) beam are 3:5:3 and 2:1:3:1:2, respectively. Those values are commonly used in practice in Japan (Tachibana et al.,1979).

The maximum values of the bending moment or the shear force or both at the points shown in Fig.3 are calculated in each simulation. These points are the positions where the maximum stress is produced by the congested traffic flow passing over bridge. Then the mean values at each point are computed after the required repetition number of simulations.

The maximum repetition number of simulations is fifty because the stable results were obtained by more than forty times of repetition.

Fig.4 shows the flow of computer simulations.

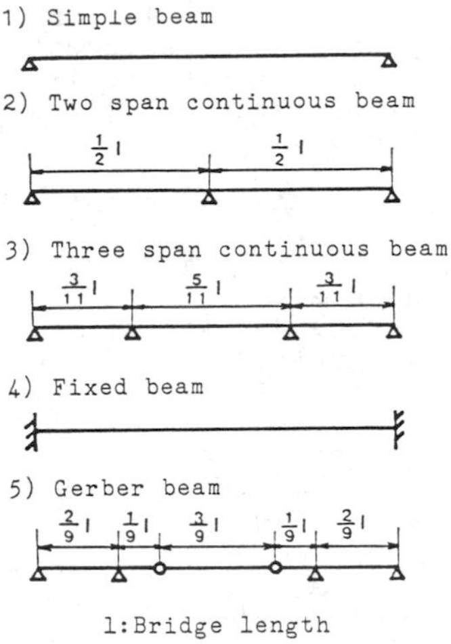


Fig.2 Types of Superstructure and Span Ratio

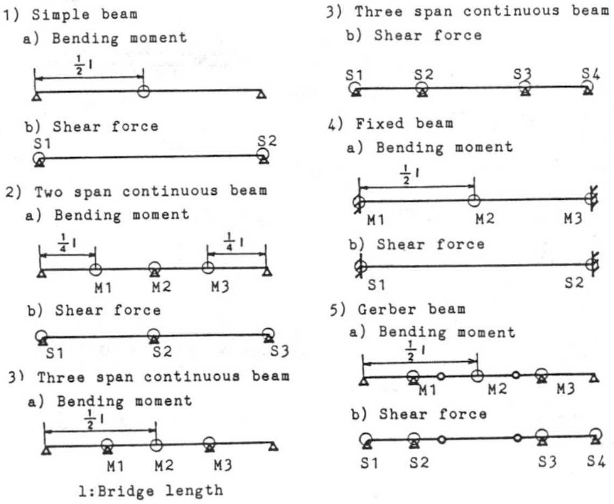


Fig.3 Points where Maximum Stress Resultant is computed (marked by the symbol "o")

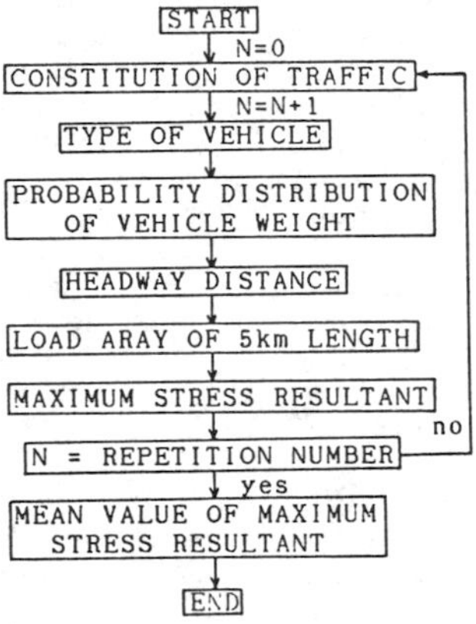


Fig.4 Flow of Simulation

## 3.OPTIMAL WAY TO PRESCRIBE THE DESIGN TRAFFIC LOAD FOR MAIN GIRDER

Assume that the design highway traffic load is prescribed by a concentrated load or a uniform load or both and that this(these) design load(s) is(are) placed on the superstructure to produce the maximum stress in the member under consideration. Furthermore each design value of a concentrated load and a uniform load is assumed to be defined by the function of span length. Both loads are considered as uniformly distributed over a 2.75 meter width on a lane normal to the center line of the lane. The following six pairs of functions are considered;

| | | |
|---|---|---|
| Pair No. 1 : | $P=0$ | $W=a(1/L)^b$ |
| Pair No. 2 : | $P=Const.$ | $W=Const.$ |
| Pair No. 3 : | $P=Const.$ | $W=a(1/L)^b$ |
| Pair No. 4 : | $P=kL+C$ | $W=0$ |
| Pair No. 5 : | $P=kL+C$ | $W=Const.$ |
| Pair No. 6 : | $P=kL+C$ | $W=a(1/L)^b$ |

where P : design concentrated load, W : design uniform load,
L : span length, a, b, k, c : constants.

Among these six ones, the optimal pair of functions to prescribe the design highway traffic load is determined as follows;

1) using the least squares method, determine the constants $k_j$, $c_j$, $a_j$, $b_j$ included in j-th pair of functions so as to obtain close agreement between calculated maximum moments and/or shears by each pair of functions and the maximum values obtained from simulations;

2) calculate the bending moment and/or shear force at the points under consideration by each of six pairs of functions obtained at step 1) and compute the root mean square error R defined by

$$R=\sqrt{\{\sum_{i=1}^{n}(1-Mo/Mi)^2\}/(n-1)} \qquad (1)$$

where n: number of data,
$M_i$ : bending moment or shear force obtained from simulation
$M_o=A_i \times W_j+B_i \times P_j$ : bending moment or shear force calculated by the j-th pair of functions
$P_j=k_jL_i+C_j$ : a concentrated load for j-th pair (2)
$W_j=a(1/L_i)^{b_j}$ : a uniform load for j-th pair (3)
$A_i$ : influence area corresponding to the loaded length for a uniform load
$B_i$ : value of the influence line at the point where a concentrated load is placed
$L_i$ : span length

3) find the optimal pair whose root mean square error given by Eq.(1) becomes smaller than other pairs.

It should be noticed that the span length $L_i$ used in Eqs.(2) and (3) is the aggregate of the lengths of the portion where the value of influence line is not zero.

Table 3 Bridge Length used in Simulations

| Type of Superstructure | Bridge Length [m] | | | | | | | | | |
|---|---|---|---|---|---|---|---|---|---|---|
| | 20 | 40 | 60 | 80 | 100 | 120 | 140 | 160 | 180 | 200 |
| Simple beam | * | * | * | * | | | | | | |
| 2-span continuous beam | * | * | * | * | * | * | | | | |
| 3-span continuous beam | | | * | * | * | * | * | * | * | * |
| Fixed beam | * | * | * | * | * | | | | | |
| Gerber beam | * | * | * | * | * | * | * | | | |

Though simulations are carried out for five types of superstructures and for ten span lengths, i.e. 20m, 40m, 60m, 80m, 100m, 120m, 140m, 160m, 180m, and 200m, it is necessary to discuss which type of superstructure is used frequently and how long the application limit of each superstructure is. However, there is not enough information to do so at present, the data corresponding to the span length marked by the symbol "*" in Table 3 are used uniformly with reference to Tamada's study (1979) and JOMC's work (1982).

4.NUMERICAL RESULTS AND DISCUSSIONS

Root mean square errors of six pairs of functions given by Eq.(1) are presented in Table 4. Columns (a), (b) and (c) in Table 4 correspond to the following cases.

(a) root mean square errors in the case only for bending moments.

(b) root mean square errors in the case only for shear forces.

(c) root mean square errors in the case for both bending moments and shear forces.

Table 4 Root Mean Square Errors

($\times 10^{-4}$)

| Pair No. | M (a) | S (b) | M+S (c) |
|---|---|---|---|
| 1 | 1255 | 1910 | 1914 |
| 2 | 702 | 847 | 809 |
| 3 | 511 | 856 | 837 |
| 4 | 5892 | 4296 | 6932 |
| 5 | 676 | 855 | 857 |
| 6 | 505 | 855 | 811 |

From Table 4, it can be found that the values of root mean square error for pair number 1 and 4 are remarkably larger than other four values in all cases. This means that both a concentrated load and a uniform load are required to prescribe the design value of the highway traffic load.

Though not shown in figures, the values of moments and shears become maximum when a considerably heavy vehicle passes through the point under consideration. This fact shows that the data of maximum bending moments and shear forces should be obtained not from the simulations in which some types of vehicles are randomly distributed on the bridge but from those where the effect of the congested traffic flow passing over the bridge is taken into account.

In the case only for the bending moments, pair number 3 and 6 can be selected as the optimal one. As regards a concentrated load, the design value is constant in the former and is the function of the span length in the latter. On the other hand the design value of a uniform load is defined as the function of span length in both pairs. There is no significant difference between these two values of root mean square error. To discuss why this result was obtained, the functions included in both pairs are sketched graphically in Fig.5. In this figure the abscissa is the span length L and the ordinate is a concentrated load for one lane P (Fig.5 (a)) and a uniform load for a single lane W (Fig.5 (b)). From Fig.5, it is found that both functions with regard to W take approximately the same values for L. On the other hand, the value of P of pair number 6 decreases linearly as L increases and is larger than that of pair number 3 when L is smaller than 100m. The difference of P between two functions is at most 1.5

ton/lane, however. This fact indicates that a bending moment is not sensitive to the value of P. Therefore it can be concluded that pair number 3, in which a concentrated load is constant and a uniform load is the function of span length, is best from the standpoint of designer's convenience.

In the case only for the shear force, root mean square errors for pair number 2, 3, 5 and 6 take nearly the same values. Thus in the same way as used above, the functions of each pair are presented in Fig.6. This figure suggests that design highway traffic load for shear force can be prescribed by the constant values of P and W. These characteristics does not agree with those for the bending moment.

In the case that both moments and shears are considered simultaneously, root mean square errors of pair number 2 and 6 are smaller than others. Fig.7 shows the relations between the values of P or W and L with respect to these two pairs. The relations for pair 3 and 5 are also presented in this figure because of their relatively small root mean square errors. Comparing Fig.7 with Figs.5 and 6, it can be found that the values of pair 2 and 6 are nearly equal to those of pair 2 shown in Fig.6 and pair 6 presented in Fig.5, respectively. In other words, pair 2 has close agreement mainly with the maximum shear forces, while the maximum bending moments are made a fairly good approximation with pair 6. By comparing pair 2 with pair 5 or doing pair 3 with pair 6 in Fig.7, it can be concluded that both a bending moment and a shear force are not so sensitive to the value of P. Therefore pair 2 may be

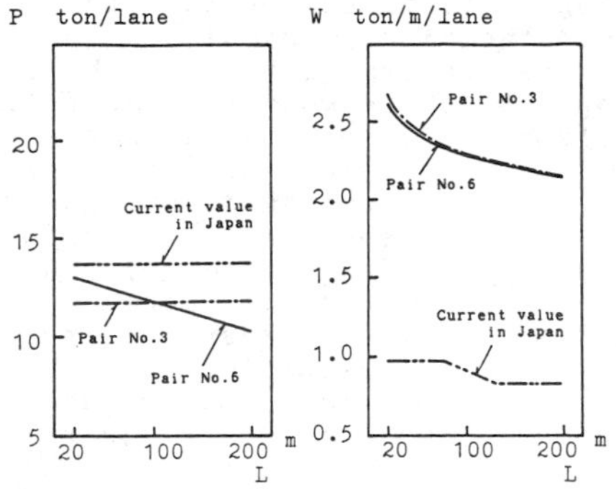


Fig.5 Graphical Sketches of Eqs.(2) and (3) (Case for only Moments)

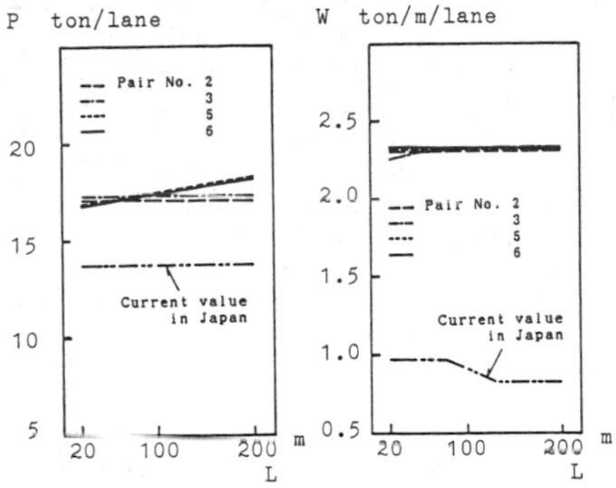


Fig.6 Graphical Sketches of Eqs.(2) and (3) (Case for only Shears)

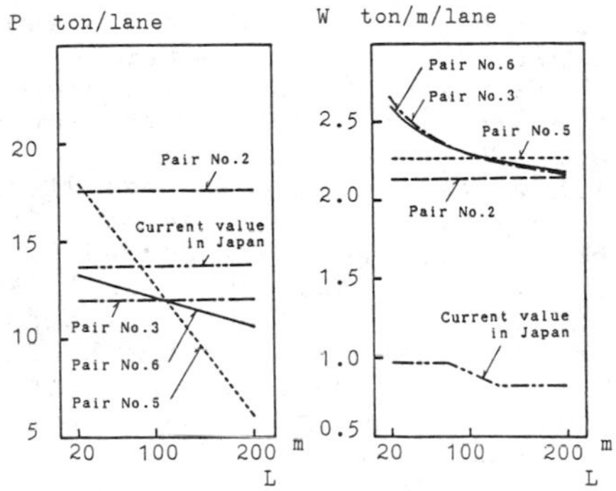


Fig.7 Graphical Sketches of Eqs.(2) and (3) (Case for both Moments and Shears)

adopted to prescribe the highway traffic load in the design code from the standpoint of designer's convenient at design stage.

The values listed in the columns (a), (b), (c) and (d) in Table 5 correspond to the following cases;

column (a):root mean square errors when the bending moments are calculated by the functions determined for both a bending moment and a shear force;

column (b):root mean square errors when the bending moment calculated by the functions determined for only a bending moment;

column (c):root mean square errors when the shear forces are calculated by the functions determined for both a bending moment and a shear force;

column (d):root mean square error when the shear forces are calculated by the functions determined for only a shear force.

It is found from Table 5 that root mean square errors listed in columns (b) and (d) are smaller than those in columns (a) and (c), respectively. This means that traffic load model for moments and that for shears should be used separately if the accurate estimation of each maximum value produced by traffic load is required.

Table 5 Root Mean Square Errors

($x10^{-4}$)

| Pair No. | Moment | | Shear | |
|---|---|---|---|---|
| | M+S (a) | M (b) | M+S (c) | S (d) |
| 1 | 1256 | 1255 | 2343 | 1910 |
| 2 | 706 | 702 | 892 | 847 |
| 3 | 512 | 511 | 1039 | 856 |
| 4 | 5898 | 5892 | 7779 | 4296 |
| 5 | 685 | 676 | 984 | 855 |
| 6 | 512 | 505 | 1000 | 855 |

## 5.CONCLUDING REMARKS

The way to prescribe the highway traffic load for design code has been discussed based on computer simulations. Simulations of highway traffic load is carried out with inclusion of the effect of the congested traffic flow passing over the bridge. Maximum values of both a bending moment and a shear force produced by traffic loads in a single lane are calculated for five types of superstructures whose bridge length is between 20m and 200m.

It is found that both a concentrated load and a uniform load are required to prescribe the highway traffic loads for design code. The design value of a concentrated load is suitable to be taken as a constant regardless of span length for moments or shears or both. On the other hand, that of a uniform load should be determined corresponding to what stress resultant is considered. And the result shows that these two design values should be estimated taking account of the effect of the congested traffic flow passing over bridge. It has been also revealed that traffic load model for the bending moment and that for the shear force should be adopted separately if the accurate estimation of the maximum values of stress resultant produced by traffic loads is required.

ACKNOWLEDGMENT

The work reported in this paper was partially supported by the Grant-in Aids for Scientific Research including No.60302059 and No.61750430 from the Japanese Ministry of Education, Science and Culture.

REFERENCES

JHA (1980). Design Code for Highway Bridges, Japan Highway Association, Chiyoda-ku, Tokyo.

JHPC et al. (1983). Report on the Measurements of Traffic Loads on the Tomei Expressway, Japan Highway Public Corporation, Chiyoda-ku, Tokyo.

JMOC (1982). Annual Report of Statistics of Highway, Japanese Ministry of Construction, Chiyoda-ku, Tokyo.

Miki C. et al. (1985). Computer Simulation Studied on the Fatigue Load and Fatigue Design of Highway Bridges, Proc. of JSCE Structural Eng./Earthquake Eng., Vol.2, No.1, pp. 37-46.

Nishimura A. (1957). Effect of Traffic Load on the Safety of Highway Bridges, Proc. of JSCE, No.43, pp.23-28 (in Japanese).

Nakagawa K. (1966). Stochastic Study on Equivalent Uniform Live Load, Proc. of JSCE, No.127, pp.1-8 (in Japanese).

PWRI (1984). Research on the Actual Condition of Traffic, Public Works Research Institute, Tsukuba, Ibaraki.

Tachibana Y. et al. (1979). Bridge Engineering, Kyoritsu-Shuppan Co., Bunkyo-ku, Tokyo.

Tamada H. (1979). Transition of Long-Span Bridges in the World, The 50th Anniversary Book of Akatsuki-kai at Kobe University.

ON HAZARD - TOLERANCE CRITERIA FOR MARINE STRUCTURES

T. Moan*
*Department of Marine Technology, The Norwegian Institute of Technology, N- 7034 - Trondheim -NTH, NORWAY

SUMMARY

A general methodology for assessing the probability of failure of structural systems, considering random variabilities, uncertainties relating to lack of knowledge and human errors, is briefly outlined. The effect of human faults are accounted for in terms of abnormal loads and strength. The sensitivity of the systems failure probability to small damages is applied to deduce progressive limit state criteria to the structure, while other risk control measures are suggested to cope with more severe damage potentials. A tension-leg system of a TLP is applied to demonstrate the procedure more specifically.

INTRODUCTION

Rational planning of constructed facilities should be based on probabilistic measures of structural failure. Up to now codes have focused upon measures for component failure modes, mainly due to convenience. The systems failure probability is important because potential consequences, especially in terms of fatalities, in many structures depend strongly upon systems performance, see, e.g. (ISSC, 1985; Pfrang, 1986).

Optimal decision-making about safety issues requires a broad approach, recognizing the various initial causes of structural failure; i.e., load effects exceed resistances due to:

- normal variabilities and uncertainties
- errors and omissions in design, fabrication and operation
- unknown phenomena

and the risk control measures available:

- control of man-induced hazards (event control)
- structural design for strength and ductility.

In the present structural engineering approach man-made hazards are treated primarily through their effect in terms of abnormal loads and strength.

The purpose is to show how risk control measures, especially direct progressive limit state criteria, JCSS (1981) can be derived through structural risk assessment, and thereby extend the currently most versatile safety assessment approaches used for marine structures, NPD (1981). The following is largely based on Moan (1987).

SYSTEMS FAILURE PROBABILITY

The systems failure probability $p_{fSYS}$ is determined by considering contributions from natural hazards, $H'_j$ (wind, waves, earthquake, ice ...) and man-made hazards, $H_j$ (ship collisions, explosions, ..., abnormal strength ...) by:

$$p_{fSYS} = \sum_{j'} p_{fSYS|H'_j} \cdot p_{H_j'} + \sum_{i} p_{fSYS|D_i} \cdot p_{D_i} \qquad (1)$$

where $p_{fSYS|H_j}$ denotes $p_{fSYS}$ conditional upon the event $H_j$. The first sum accounts for extreme natural events, while man-made hazards properly combined with natural hazards, are implicit in the damage state $D_i$ of the second sum. The infrequent occurrence and short duration of the accidental action due to $H_j$, often justifies considering an extreme $H_j$ in conjunction with an expected value of an actual set of $\{H_j'\}$.

The probabilities $p_{fSYS}$ may be annual or lifetime values, both are necessary in the decision making. In the present paper only lifetime values are referred to.

The probabilities $p_{fSYS|Hj}$ in the first sum of Eq. (1) are determined by structural reliability analysis, Ditlevsen and Bjerager (1986) based on, e.g., a hazard $H'_j$ with return period, e.g., 100 years, and $p_{Hj'}$ the corresponding lifetime exceedance probability of the hazard.

$p_{fSYS|Di}$ is also determined by structural reliability theory, however, as indicated in the example case later, uncertainties beyond those normally inherent in load effects and resistances will contribute to the probability content in this case.

The damage $D_i$ is measured by strength reduction and buoyancy loss for structural failure and sinking/capsizing, respectively, and is characterized by its type (depth, crack, ... flooding), extent, and location. For a given hazard $H_j$ and location of $D_i$, the damage extent can be related to the magnitude ($IH_j$) of the hazard. If the relation between exceedance probability $Q_{IHj}(I)$ and magnitude of the hazard is known, a similar relationship between $Q_{Di|Hj}(d) = Q_{Dij}(d)$ and d, can be established for the damage. The contribution $p_{Dij}$ to $p_{Di}$ from this hazard can then be determined as the $Q_{Dij}(d)$ that yields the maximum $p_{fSYSij} = p_{fSYS|Di}(d) \cdot p_{Dij}(d)$.

In some cases, $H_j$ may be defined as the joint occurrence of hazards (e.g., fires and explosions) to account for the correlation or dependence existing between them.

While system failures due to extreme natural hazards $H_j$ normally are assumed to occur at the time (t=0) when the hazard acts, system failure due to a man-made hazard $H_j$ may take place when $H_j$ acts, or later, in a time period T when the natural hazards are higher than at t=0. The period T itself may be a random variable, and depend upon the likelihood of detecting the actual damage, delay of repair after detection due to weather conditions, etc.; and may last for a storm period and up to months or even years for smaller damages. Damage detection depends, for instance, upon the nature of the damage, i.e., whether there is evidence of its occurrence such as given by accidental loads, or not; and the damage extent itself. The time aspect of the failure suggests that the $p_{fSYS|Di}$ may be expressed as the sum of two contributions:

$$p_{fSYS|Di} = p_{fSYS|Di,0} + (1 - p_{fSYS|Di,0}) \cdot p_{fSYS|Di,T} \tag{2}$$

For a given hazard $H_j$, $Q_{Di}(d)$ for the damage at location i, may be displayed together with $p_{fSYS|Di}(d)$ and the product $p_{fSYSij}(d) = p_{fSYS|Di}(d) \cdot Q_{Dij}(d)$ for a proper set $\{H'_j\}$ as shown in Fig. 1.

Besides the inherent variability of $IH_j$ accounted for by the $Q_{IHj}$ - $IH_j$ relationship, there are normally significant model uncertainties associated with this relationship and that between $IH_j$ and the extent of damage, d. This will not be pursued further in the present paper.

## PROGRESSIVE LIMIT STATE CRITERION

Risk control measures can be assessed with reference to the systems failure probability versus level of potential damage, d (Fig. 1a) as follows:

- excessive $p_{fSYSij}$ relating to d=0 is dealt with by component limit state criteria, possibly accounting for a systems factor.
- excessive $p_{fSYSij}$ relating to $0>d>\bar{d}$, $\bar{d}$ being a small quantity, is handled by progressive limit state (PLS) criteria, to ensure that small damages do not yield disproportionately large consequences.
- excessive $p_{fSYSij}$ relating to intermediate damage levels are dealt with by combined measures.
- excessive $p_{fSYSij}$ relating to d>d* requires event control measures, including siting and orientation of the structure, specification of

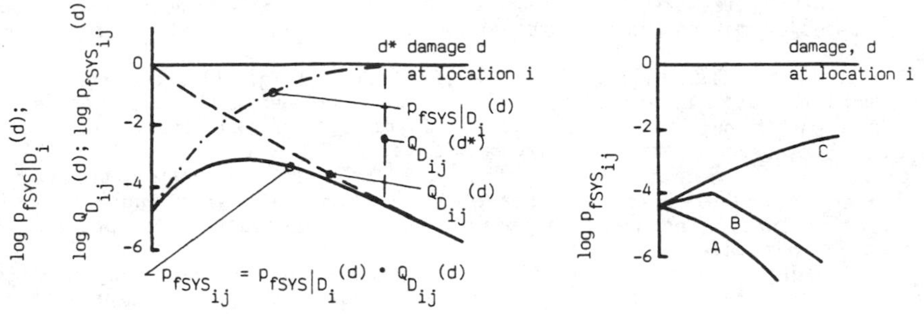


a) $p_{fSYS|Di}(d)$ and $Q_{Dij}(d)$

b) Typical variation of $p_{fSYSij}(d)$ versus d.

Fig. 1. Exceedance probability $Q_{Dij}(d)$, $p_{fSYS|Di}(d)$ and $p_{fSYSij}(d)$ vs. damage, d due to a man-made hazard, $H_j$, and an associated set of natural hazards $\{H'_j\}$.

equipment, operational procedures, distance between hazardous area and main load carrying structure, etc.

**Damage-** and **hazard-tolerance** (robustness) in relation to man-made hazards may in a strict sense be measured by $\partial p_{fSYS|Di}(d)/\partial d$ and $\partial p_{fSYSij}(d)/\partial d$ at $D_i$=0, respectively. A positive and negative $\partial p_{fSYSij}(d)/\partial d$ correspond to hazard fragile and robust behaviour, respectively.

The limiting probabilities $p_{fSYS}(0) = p_{fSYS|Di}(0)$; and $p_{fSYSij}(d^*) = p_{Dij}(d^*)$ and its sum over ($H'_j$, $H_j$), provide measures for target levels for intermediate damage levels, i.e., also for PLS criteria.

Assuming that the $p_{fSYS}(0)$ represents a target safety level, curve A in Fig. 1b shows a case of inherent hazard robustness and no additional safety measures would be necessary. Safety improvement may be obtained by PLS requirements in the hazard fragile Case B. For Case C in Fig. 1b the most efficient risk control measure may be event control.

The hazard robustness/fragility check should be accomplished for all hazards and for various damage locations to determine whether PLS criteria are necessary, and if so, establish the damage condition and associated natural load conditions and partial factors that yield the target safety level.

In general, the procedure outlined must be accomplished on a case by case basis, however, using an authoritative data basis especially on the probabilities of initial events relating to man-made hazards, such as ship collisions, blow-outs, etc.

EXAMPLE CASE

GENERAL REMARKS. The methodology outlined is applied on a TLP structure as shown in Fig. 2. While in general the risk assessment should include all subsystems, the present example is limited to the mooring system, typically consisting of four tension - legs, each with, e.g., 1 to 6 tethers. This substructure normally would comprise of a series of 10-15m long tubulars, joined by screw connections. The tethers are pretensioned by excess buoyancy to a level equal to 0.3-0.4 of the ultimate strength.

As the failure of a tension-leg implies large overall transient motions and a probability close to 1.0 for overload failure of the remaining active tethers, system failure is modelled as failure of one tension-leg, which can be initiated by failure of individual tethers or be caused by a common mode failure of all tethers, as expressed in fault/event trees, Moan (1987).

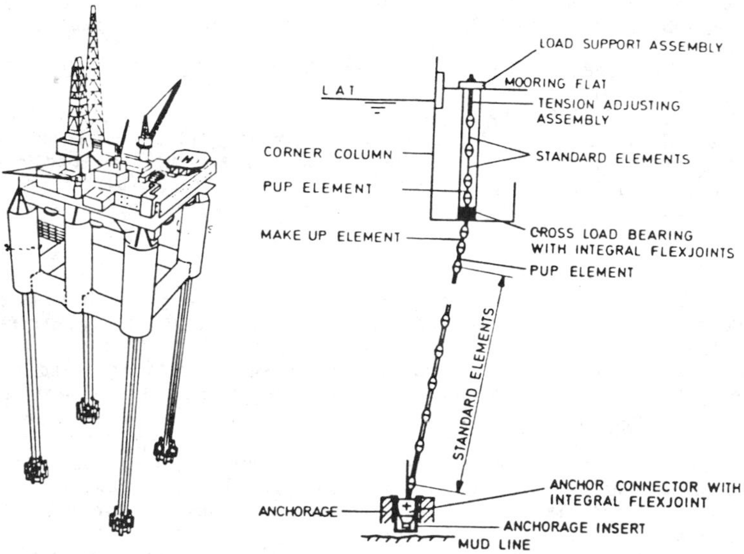


a) System b) Tether

Fig. 2. Tension-leg platform.

The failure due to environmental overload of such a system has previously been studied by, e.g., Guenard (1984).

For tension-legs complying precisely with current codes, the lifetime probability $p_{fSYS}(0)$ of overload and slack due to natural hazards $H'_J$, is estimated to be of the order 0.001 to 0.01 and 0.01 to 0.04, respectively.

Similarly, for systems which exactly fulfill the relative restrictive fatigue requirements to tethers, the lifetime failure probability may be of the same order, 0.001 to 0.01. Which component limit state criterion will be governing depends upon environmental conditions, water depth, diameter/thickness ratio of tethers, etc.

The high correlation between load effects, and partly between resistances in the tethers of a tension-leg, and the general dominance of load effect uncertainties on the safety margins, make the failure of the tethers in a leg a common mode failure, especially for the overload case, see, e.g., Guenard (1984).

A PLS criterion may be introduced for a tension-leg if the system failure probability implied by a single tether failure exceeds the target level. Such a requirement may be expressed as an overload criterion for the tension-leg with one tether failed, and would imply lower stress levels and hence reduced failure probabilities for the component limit states of the intact structure, especially for tension-legs with few tethers.

If the systems failure probability corresponding to initial failure of more than one tether is excessive, risk control through event control of the related hazards should primarily be considered.

In the following two of the man-made hazards that carry most risks are used to illustrate the features of risk control measures for the tension-leg system. These are:

- overload failure initiated by fracture of an individual tether ($D_1$) due to the combined effect of fabrication fault, deficient inspection, and crack growth.
- slack in a tension-leg due to buoyancy loss ($D_2$) caused by collision-induced flooding.

OVERLOAD INITIATED BY FRACTURE IN ONE TETHER. The damage, d in this case is defined as the number, $n_f$ of tethers being in an initial failure state. The location (i) and hazard (j) are denoted by i=1 and j=1, respectively. The purpose in the following therefore is to establish $p_{fSYS11}(n_f)$ vs. $n_f$.

The probability of fracture, $p_{D11}$, in (any) one tether is expressed as:

$$p_{D11} = p(a) \cdot p(T_r > T|a) \tag{3}$$

where p(a) and $p(T_r > T|a)$ are the probability of through-thickness crack, and the probability that the time ($T_r$) from crack penetration to repair/replacement exceeds the time (T) from crack penetration to final fracture.

Fractures will most likely occur in the screw connections or adjacent welds. Monitoring of cracks and subsequent replacement of tethers are here based on the leak-before-break principle, and hence, the effect of possibly monitoring shallow cracks, is not accounted for.

The probability p(a) depends upon the flaw sensitivity of the fabrication and inspection methods (which in turn will be thickness dependent), volume or surface area of material susceptible to initial cracking, dynamic stress level (as influenced, e.g., by conventional fatigue design checks), etc. p(a) is intended to reflect abnormal defects induced by fabrication and design, and may be 5 to 50 times the probability of fatigue failure due to normal variabilities and uncertainties, i.e., of the order 0.005 to 0.5.

The uncertainties in $T_r$, e.g., due to delayed replacement of tether after crack detection and in T, e.g., due to model and data uncertainties associated with the predicted crack growth, are represented by lognormal random variables. Example calculations for tethers in a typical North Sea deepwater TLP indicate a $p(T_r > T|a)$ in the range of 0.02 to 0.2 for a median T and $T_r$ equal to 0.8, and 0.2 to 0.4, respectively, and c.o.v.'s of $T/T_r$ in the order 0.6 to 0.85.

Hence, $p_{D11}$ is of the order $10^{-1}$ to $10^{-4}$ in the present example.

$p_{fSYS|D1}$ may be calculated by Eq. (2), with

$$p_{fSYS|D1,0} = P[MQ_o > R_y] \tag{4}$$

where $Q_o$ and M signify the load level in a tether at fracture and M the load amplification due to load shedding, respectively. The instantaneous redistribution of loads among tethers implies that the external loads remain the same during the load shedding as at fracture, and that there will be a dynamic magnification. Under certain assumptions, M is found, Moan (1987), to be $(4n+3)/(4n-3)$, where n is the number of tethers in a tension-leg. $Q_o$ can be expressed by $\alpha R_y$, where the factor $\alpha$ can be determined by fracture mechanics analysis, and is typically in the range 0.4 to 0.6 for tethers. $R_y$ is the ultimate strength, which for the pure tension case normally is represented by yield strength times net cross section area. With a median ($MQ_o$) and c.o.v. of 0.4 to 0.6; and 0.25, respectively, and a c.o.v. of $R_y$ equal to 0.1, $p_{fSYS|D1,0}$ lies in the range 0.02 to 0.30 for n=4, and 0.004 to 0.130 for n=6.

The time after the fracture may be split in two periods:

- one of a few hours (storm duration) with increased pretension and wave load effects of the order n/(n-1) due to the failure of one tether.
- one representing a winter season, with remedial actions taken to reduce the pretension, to or even below the value before the failure.

The total contribution to $p_{fSYS|D1,T}$ from these intervals may be of same order as, or, most often, less than $p_{fSYS|D1,0}$.

The joint probability of fracture of two or more tethers is estimated to be smaller than $10^{-4}$.

With $p_{fSYS11}(1) = 3 \cdot 10^{-2}$ to $2 \cdot 10^{-6}$ and typically $2 \cdot 10^{-3}$ (n=4); $p_{fSYS11}(1) = 1.3 \cdot 10^{-2}$ to $4 \cdot 10^{-7}$ and typically $10^{-3}$ (n=6); $p_{fSYS11}(2) < 10^{-4}$; and $p_{fSYS}(0) = 10^{-2} - 10^{-3}$ taken as the target level, systems with n equal to 4 or 6 often seem to be hazard-tolerant (Case A in Fig. 1b). However, in some cases, especially with n smaller than 4, the situation represented by Case B in Fig. 1b may occur, and PLS requirements of the type indicated above, may then be desireable. Such criteria can be calibrated over actual tension-leg configurations, including variations of n, to yield a safety level corresponding as closely as possible to the target level. This point is discussed further in Moan (1987).

SLACK OF A TENSION/LEG DUE TO BUOYANCY LOSS. Slack may be caused by loss of buoyancy alone or in combination with environmental loads. As mentioned above, only the fault-tree branch involving collision-induced buoyancy loss will be pursued herein. The damage, d in this case may be defined as the buoyancy loss, BL as a fraction, $\eta$ of the pretension ($T_0$) in each tension-leg. This failure mode of all tethers is denoted i=2, and the initiating ship-collision hazard is termed j=2. Hence, the aim in the following is to relate $p_{fSYS22}(\eta)$ vs. $\eta$.

Collisions may be caused by ships of various types: supply vessels, offshore tankers, fishing vessels or general shipping, due to errant or blind navigation or maneuvering, or due to loss of steering or power, DEn (1986). Collision damage is commonly estimated on the basis of the kinetic energy transformed into deformation energy, and based on determination of energy absorption in the platform and ship.

The geometry of TLP's implies that the ship impact damage of interest can be confined to the columns.

The probability $p_{D22}(\eta)$ or $Q_{D22}(\eta)$ is first determined by a probabilistic description of the collision energy for given impact configurations. By using relationships between deformation energy and extent of structural damage, and between structural damage and buoyancy loss, the required relationship may be obtained.

The exceedance probability, $Q_E(e)$ for the deformation energy, for a given collision configuration (head-on, sideways) may be obtained from:

$$Q_E(e) = p_C \cdot p_{L|C} \sum_i \sum_j Q_{E|Si,CMj}(e|S_i, CM_j) \cdot p_{Si} \cdot p_{CMj|Si} \tag{5}$$

where $p_C$ and $p_{L|C}$ are the striking probability, and conditional probability of hitting a given location of the structure, respectively. $p_{Si}$ and $p_{CMj|Si}$ signify the relative frequency of a vessel type, and crusing mode given the ship type, respectively. $Q_{E|Si,CMj}$ is obtained from the expression:

$$E = \alpha \tfrac{1}{2} mv^2 \tag{6}$$

conveniently assuming log-normal variables: $\alpha$ (fraction of kinetic energy transformed into deformation energy), m (vessel mass, including added mass) and v (relative velocity between vessel and platform). An example of $Q_E(e)$ vs. e relationship is presented in Fig. 3, considering collisions with passing vessels. The actual $Q_E(e)$ vs. e curve will vary depending on site, traffic composition, etc. For instance, the annual $p_C$ varies between $8 \cdot 10^{-2}$ and $10^{-6}$ for North Sea sites, DEn (1986).

The extent of the damage, i.e., penetration of one, or more compartments, may be related to the energy and impact location using the penetration depth as an indirect measure. Given the access of water, the magnitude of the flooding depends for instance upon the location of the flooding opening, sea-state, and subdivision in compartments and arrangement of piping in the TLP column.

| Ship type | Cruising Mode | Prob. | | Velocities | |
|---|---|---|---|---|---|
| | | $p_{S_i}$ | $p_{CM_j \mid S_i}$ | Median (m/s) | C.O.V |
| $S_1$ | $CM_1$ | 0.7 | 0.3 | 3 | 0.2 |
| | $CM_2$ | | 0.7 | 1 | 0.3 |
| $S_2$ | $CM_1$ | 0.2 | 0.1 | 3 | 0.1 |
| | $CM_2$ | | 0.9 | 0.5 | 0.2 |
| $S_3$ | $CM_1$ | 0.1 | 0.85 | 4 | 0.1 |
| | $CM_2$ | | 0.15 | 1 | 0.2 |

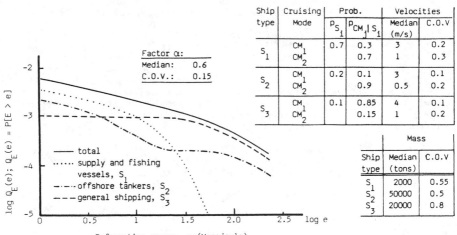

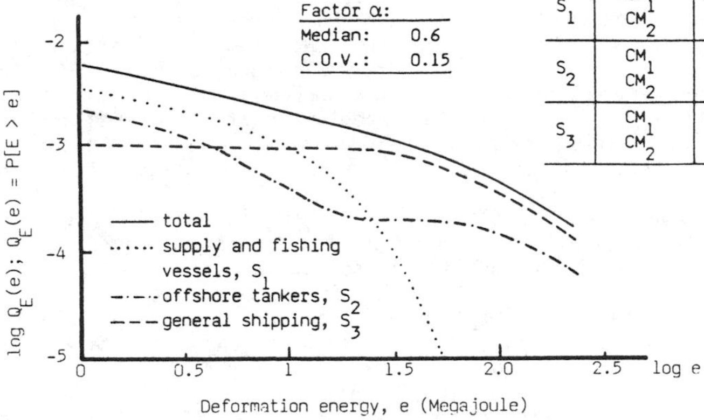


| Ship type | Mass | |
|---|---|---|
| | Median (tons) | C.O.V |
| $S_1$ | 2000 | 0.55 |
| $S_2$ | 50000 | 0.5 |
| $S_3$ | 20000 | 0.8 |

Fig. 3. Probability of exceedance, $Q_E(e)$ vs. energy, e for head-on collisions by passing vessels at a North Sea site, with a lifetime $p_C p_{L|C} = 10^{-2}$.

Smaller compartments are, for example, commonly used along the outer column shell in the splash zone to limit the buoyancy loss.

Table 1 shows an example relation between deformation energy and structural damage. Obviously, such relations will be subject to significant model uncertainties, corresponding to, e.g., a C.O.V. of 0.5 on energy estimates.

Table 1. Relationship between median deformation energy and buoyancy loss for head-on collisions and an example TLP column.

| | Buoyancy loss, BL = $\eta \cdot T_0$, with $T_0$ being the pretension of a tension-leg, $\eta$: | | | | Structural failure of the column |
|---|---|---|---|---|---|
| | 0.2 | 0.5 | 0.75 | 1.0 | |
| Energy (MJ) | 15 | 60 | 100 | 150 | 200 |

Based on the results in Fig. 3 and information such as that in Table 1, the relationship between $Q_{D22}(\eta)$ vs. $\eta$ can be achieved.

Given the extent of flooding ($\overline{BL}$), the conditional probability of slack can be determined by:

$$p_{fSYS|D2}(\eta) = P[T_0 - \overline{BL} - E^- < 0 | BL] \quad (7)$$

where $T_0$, $\overline{BL}$ and $E^-$ are the "given" pretension of a leg, buoyancy loss in the column above the leg, and $E^-$ the "minimum" environmental load in a wave through. $E^-$ (and BL) are random variables.

The contribution from $p_{fSYS|D2,0}(\eta)$ is small because collisions with passing vessels are only weakly correlated to environmental loads. The mean exposure time (T) for the steady-state phase is taken to be a winter season. A particular uncertainty is associated with whether corrective actions (deballasting) can be undertaken or not in the period T. The likelihood of such remedial actions is expected to decrease with the extent of damage. The probability of slack, $p_{fSYS|D2,T}(\eta)$, may be of the order 0.01, 0.1 and 1.0 for $\eta$ = 0.2, 0.4 and 0.6, respectively.

By combining the information about $p_{D22}(\eta)$ and $p_{fSYS|D2}(\eta)$, it is found that $p_{fSYS22}(\eta)$ is smaller than the assumed target level, $p_{fSYS}(0)$ in this example, but that it increases with $\eta$. The implication is that slack of tethers due to this hazard may not require risk control measures in the example presented. However, considering the fact that there are offshore fields where the probability of striking, $p_c$ may be 30 times higher than in the present case, and that the relative frequency of large ships also may be higher, risk control actions, especially in terms of event control (ship traffic surveillance, alertness systems onboard, etc.) may be necessary.

## CONCLUDING REMARKS

A method has been outlined for establishing structural hazard-tolerance requirements to ensure that small damages do not yield disproportionately large consequences (i.e., systems failure), and event control measures to avoid structural failures due to severe hazards.

The use of the structural risk assessment procedures on two hazards relating to the tension-leg system of a TLP has been briefly demonstrated. However, the main idea is to include all hazards, and thus achieve a balanced view of hazard-tolerance.

By applying the method to an actual platform at a given site, uncertainties included to show variations among platform concepts and sites, vanish.

The design damage condition and associated load condition for PLS design check should be determined by this procedure at a conceptual design stage, preceeding the engineering stage, to ensure that a consistent safety basis for making decisions about layout and member sizes, is laid.

## REFERENCES


DEn (1986). UK Department of Energy Report OTH 86 217, "The Risk of Ship/Platform Collisions in the Area of the UK Continental Shelf," Technica, UK.

Ditlevsen, O. and Bjerager, P. (1986). "Methods of Structural Systems Reliability," Structural Safety, Vol. 3, pp. 195-229.

Guenard, Y.F. (1984). "Application of Systems Reliability Analysis to Offshore Structures," Report No. 71, John A. Blume Earthquake Engineering Center, Stanford University.

ISSC (1985). "Report of Committee IV.1 on Design Philosophy," Int. Ship Structures Congress, Genova.

JCSS (1981). "General Principles on Reliability for Structural Design," Joint Committee on Structural Safety, Part II of Volume 35.

Moan, T. (1987). "Probabilistic Structural Risk Assessment," Report to appear at the Div. of Marine Structures, the Norwegian Institute of Technology.

NPD (1981). "Guidelines for Safety Evaluation of Platform Conceptual Design," the Norwegian Petroleum Directorate, Stavanger.

Pfrang, E.O. et al. (1986). "Building Structural Failures - Their Cause and Prevention," IABSE Periodica 3, S-35.

# ON THE CALCULATION OF A CLASS OF IMPROPER INTEGRALS

P D. Spanos
Brown School of Engineering, Rice University
Houston, P.O. Box 1892, TX. 77251

## ABSTRACT

A versatile formula is presented for the calculation of a class of improper integrals frequently encountered in random vibration analyses and in other technical fields. This formula is derived in connection with the response of a time-invariant linear dynamic system under a stationary random excitation. Its usefulness is demonstrated by considering a particular numerical application.

## INTRODUCTORY REMARKS

A class of integrals often encountered in random vibration calculations and other technical areas is considered. These integrals can be related to the statistics of the stationary response of a stable, linear, and time-invariant dynamic system excited by a stationary stochastic process. A pertinent formula is derived which yields as a special case the well-known James et al. (1965) integral of control engineering and random vibration applications which has also been derived by Spanos (1983) using an alternative approach; the latter approach is extended in the present paper.

An example of application of the derived general formula is given. It involves an excitation with autocorrelation which decays linearly over a finite interval from its peak value to zero. Also, it is pointed out that this formula has purely mathematical merit irrespective of random vibration analyses interpretations.

## MATHEMATICAL PRELIMINARIES

Consider the response of a linear system of order m to stochastic stationary excitation w(t) which is described by the equation

$$[\lambda_m D^m + \lambda_{m-1} D^{m-1} + \lambda_{m-2} D^{m-2} + \ldots + \lambda_o] x(t) = w(t) \quad . \tag{1}$$

The symbol D represents the operator of differentiation, and $\lambda_k$, k=o, ... m, are time-invariant constants. Denote by $R_w(\tau)$ and $S(\omega)_w$ the autocorrelation and the spectral density of w(t), respectively. Further, assume that the values of $\lambda_k$ are such that x(t) becomes as $t \to \infty$, stationary with autocorrelation $R_x(\tau)$

and power spectrum $S_x(\omega)$. Obviously, $S_x(\omega)$ and $S_w(\omega)$ are related by the equation

$$S_x(\omega) = \frac{S_w(\omega)}{|\Lambda(s)|^2} . \tag{2}$$

The symbol $|.|$ denotes the modulus of a complex number,

$$s = i\omega, \tag{3}$$

$$i = \sqrt{-1} \tag{4}$$

and

$$\Lambda(s) = \lambda_m s^m + \lambda_{m-1} s^{m-1} + \ldots + \lambda_o . \tag{5}$$

Based on the formulas

$$\langle x(t) D^k x(t-\tau) \rangle = (-1)^k D^k R_x(\tau) \tag{6}$$

and

$$\langle w(t-\tau) D^k x(t) \rangle = D^k R_{xw}(\tau) \tag{7}$$

it can be shown that

$$[\lambda_m D^{\ell+m} + \lambda_{m-1} D^{\ell+m-1} + \ldots + \lambda_o D^{\ell}] R_{xw}(\tau) = D^{\ell} R_w(\tau), \quad \ell = o, 1, .. \tag{8}$$

and

$$[\hat{\lambda}_m D^{n+m} + \hat{\lambda}_{m-1} D^{n+m-1} + \ldots + \hat{\lambda}_o D^n] R_x(\tau) = D^n R_{xw}(\tau), \quad n = o, 1, \ldots \tag{9}$$

where

$$\hat{\lambda}_k = (-1)^k \lambda^k, \quad k = o, \ldots \tag{10}$$

and

$$R_{xw}(\tau) = \langle x(t) w(t-\tau) \rangle \tag{11}$$

is the cross-correlation of $x(t)$ and $w(t-\tau)$ Note that equations (8) and (9) are valid assuming that the orders $\ell$ and n of differentiation result in a meaningful, ordinary or generalized, functional interpretation of the derivatives of $R_w(\tau)$. Also, note that the stationary system response can be expressed in terms of the impulse response function $h(\tau)$

$$x(t) = \int_o^{\infty} h(u)w(t-u)du \quad . \tag{12}$$

Assume for simplicity that $\Lambda(s)$ has simple roots, that is

$$\Lambda(s) = \alpha(s+s_1)(s+s_2)....(s+s_m), \; s_1 \neq s_2 \neq s_3 ... \neq s_m \tag{13}$$

where $\alpha$ is a constant. Then (Korn and Korn, 1968),

$$h(t) = \sum_{k=1}^{m} h_k e^{-s_k t}, \tag{14}$$

where

$$h_k = [\ 1 \ / \ \frac{d\Lambda(s)}{ds}\ ]_{s} = -s_k. \tag{15}$$

Note that the case in which $\Lambda(s)$ has multiple roots is treated in Spanos (1987).

## CORRELATION EQUATIONS

Multiplying equation (12) by $w(t-\tau)$ and ensemble averaging gives

$$R_{xw}(\tau) = \int_o^{\infty} h(u)R_w(\tau-u)du. \tag{16}$$

Substituting $\tau = o$ in this equation yields

$$R_{xw}(o) = \int_o^{\infty} h(u)R_w(u)du. \tag{17}$$

Further, differentiating equation (16) with respect to $\tau$ and substituting $\tau = o$ gives

$$D^k R_{xw}(o) = \int_o^{\infty} R_w(u)D^k h(u)du, \; k=o,\ 1,\ ... \tag{18}$$

Observe that

$$R_x(\tau) = 2\int_o^{\infty} S_x(\omega)\cos(\omega\tau)d\omega \tag{19}$$

and define

$$M_{2k} = (-1)^k D^{2k} R_x(o) \tag{20}$$

Then, substituting equation (20) into equation (8) for $k=\ell=m-1, m-2,\ldots,o$ and taking into consideration equation (18) gives

$$\begin{array}{l} \lambda_{m-1}M_{2m-2} - \lambda_{m-3}M_{2m-4} + \lambda_{m-5}M_{2m-6} - \cdots\cdots = r_{m-1} \\ -\lambda_m M_{2m-2} + \lambda_{m-2}M_{2m-4} - \lambda_{m-4}M_{2m-6} + \cdots\cdots = r_{m-2} \\ \quad 0 \qquad . \qquad . \qquad \cdots\cdot = . \\ \quad . \qquad . \qquad . \quad -\lambda_2 M_2 + \lambda_o M_o = r_o \end{array} \tag{21}$$

where

$$r_k = \int_o^\infty R_w(u)D^k h(u)du, \; k=o,\ 1,\ \ldots,\ m-1. \tag{22}$$

Therefore, given $r_o$. $r_1$ ... $r_{m-1}$ the values of $M_{2k}$ can be calculated by the solution of the system of equation (21). Specifically, in terms of determinants

$$M_{2k} = \frac{\det \Gamma_k}{\det \Gamma} \tag{23}$$

where

$$\Gamma = (\underline{\gamma}_{m-1}, \underline{\gamma}_{m-2}, \ldots, \underline{\gamma}_o) \tag{24}$$

is the coefficient matrix of equation (21) with columns $\underline{\gamma}_{m-1}$, $\underline{\gamma}_{m-2}$, ..., $\underline{\gamma}_o$, and $\tilde{\Gamma}_k$ is the matrix obtained by replacing the $(m-k)^{th}$ column of $\Gamma$ by the vector

$$\underline{r} = (r_{m-1},\ldots, r_o)^T, \tag{25}$$

where T represents the operation of transposition.

Having determined $M_{2k}$, $k=o, \ldots., m-1$, for $k>m-1$ equations (9) and (20) yield

$$\hat{\lambda}_m(-1)^{\frac{m+k}{2}} M_{m+k} + \hat{\lambda}_{m-1}(-1)^{\frac{m+k-1}{2}} M_{m+k-1} + \ldots + \hat{\lambda}_o(-1)^{\frac{k}{2}} M_k = D^k R_{xw}(o). \tag{26}$$

Note that the term $D^k R_{xw}(o)$ $k>m-1$ can be calculated recursively from equation (9) in terms of $r_n$, $n<k$. That is,

$$\lambda_m r_{\ell+m} = \lambda_m D^{\ell+m} R_{xw}(o) = D^\ell R_w(o) - \lambda_{m-1} r_{\ell+m-1} - \ldots - \lambda_o r_\ell, \quad \ell=k+1-m=1,2,\ldots \tag{27}$$

A CLASS OF IMPROPER INTEGRALS

Consider the integral

$$I_m = \int_{-\infty}^{\infty} \frac{\Xi_m(\omega)}{|\Lambda(i\omega)|^2} S_w(\omega)d\omega \tag{28}$$

where

$$\Xi_m(\omega) = \xi_{m-1}\omega^{2m-2} + \xi_{m-2}\,\omega^{2m-4} + \ldots + \xi_o \tag{29}$$

and $\xi_o$, ..., $\xi_{m-1}$ are arbitrary constants. Then, it can be readily shown that

$$I_m = \xi_{m-1}M_{2m-2} + \xi_{m-2}M_{2m-4} + \ldots \xi_o M_o. \tag{30}$$

Further, combining equations (23) and (30) and taking into consideration the nullity of a determinant with two identical columns gives

$$I_m = \frac{\det \tilde{\Gamma}}{\det \Gamma} -1 \tag{31}$$

where

$$\tilde{\Gamma} = \begin{vmatrix} \lambda_{m-1}+\xi_{m-1}r_{m-1} & -\lambda_{m-3}+\xi_{m-2}r_{m-1} & \lambda_{m-5}+\xi_{m-3}r_{m-1} & \cdot\;\cdot & \cdot & \cdot \\ -\lambda_m+\xi_{m-1}r_{m-2} & \lambda_{m-2}+\xi_{m-2}r_{m-2} & -\lambda_{m-4}+\xi_{m-2}r_{m-2} & \cdot\;\cdot & \cdot & \cdot \\ \xi_{m-1}r_{m-3} & -\lambda_{m-1}+\xi_{m-2}r_{m-3} & \lambda_{m-3}+\xi_{m-2}r_{m-3} & \cdot\;\cdot & \cdot & \cdot \\ \xi_{m-1}r_{m-4} & \lambda_m\;+\xi_{m-2}r_{m-4} & -\lambda_{m-2}+\xi_{m-2}r_{m-4} & \cdot\;\cdot & \cdot & \cdot \\ \xi_{m-1}r_{m-5} & \xi_{m-2}r_{m-4} & \lambda_{m-1}+\xi_{m-2}r_{m-5} & \cdot\;\cdot & \cdot & \cdot \\ \cdot & \cdot & \cdot & \cdot\;\cdot & \cdot & \cdot \\ \cdot & \cdot & \cdot & \cdot\;\cdot & \cdot & \cdot \\ \xi_{m-1}r_o & \xi_{m-2}r_o & \cdot & & -\lambda_2+\xi_1 r_o & \lambda_o+\xi_o r_o \end{vmatrix} \tag{32}$$

and

$$\Gamma = \begin{vmatrix} \lambda_{m-1} & -\lambda_{m-3} & \lambda_{m-5} & \cdot\ \cdot\ \cdot\ \cdot \\ -\lambda_m & \lambda_{m-2} & -\lambda_{m-4} & \cdot\ \cdot\ \cdot\ \cdot \\ 0 & -\lambda_{m-1} & \lambda_{m-3} & \cdot\ \cdot\ \cdot\ \cdot \\ 0 & \lambda_m & -\lambda_{m-2} & \cdot\ \cdot\ \cdot\ \cdot \\ 0 & 0 & \lambda_{m-1} & \cdot\ \cdot\ \cdot\ \cdot \\ \cdot & \cdot & \cdot & \cdot\ \cdot\ \cdot\ \cdot \\ \cdot & \cdot & \cdot & \cdot\ \cdot\ \cdot\ \cdot \\ \cdot & \cdot & \cdot & \cdot\ \cdot\ -\lambda_2\lambda_o \end{vmatrix} \tag{33}$$

Note that if w(t) is a white noise process with

$$S_w\ (\omega) = 1,\ -\infty < \omega < \infty\ . \tag{34}$$

and

$$R_w(\tau) = 2\pi\delta(\tau) \tag{35}$$

where $\delta(\tau)$ is a two-sided delta function, equations (18), (22) and (34) yield

$$r_k = D^k R_{xw}(o) = o,\ k=o,\ \ldots,\ m-2 \tag{36}$$

and

$$r_{m-1} = D^{m-1} R_{xw}(o) = \frac{\pi}{\lambda_m}\ . \tag{37}$$

Substituting equations (36) and (37) into equation (31) leads to the well known integral given in Gradshteyn and Ryzhik (1965) and determined by two independent approaches in James et al. (1965) and Spanos (1983).

AN APPLICATION

Assume that w(t) has the power spectrum

$$S_w(\omega) = \frac{\tau_o}{2\pi}\left[\frac{\sin(\omega\tau_o/2)}{(\omega\tau_o/2)}\right]^2, \quad -\infty<\omega<\infty \tag{38}$$

where $\tau_o$ is a positive constant. This spectral form relates to the useful class of stationary processes with autocorrelation function decaying from the peak value, at $\tau$=o, to zero at $|\tau|=\tau_o$. The autocorrelation function of w(t) is non-zero only in the interval $[-\tau_o, \tau_o]$. It can be written as

$$R_w(\tau) = 1-\frac{|\tau|}{\tau_o} \tag{39}$$

Therefore, in determining the integrals which appear in equation (22) it is necessary to calculate the values of the integrals

$$\bar{I}_q = \int_o^{\tau_o} (1-\frac{\tau}{\tau_o})\, \tau^q e^{-s_k\tau} d\tau \tag{40}$$

The value of this definite integral can be determined by relying on the identity (Gradshteyn and Ryzhik, 1965)

$$\int \tau^n e^{\alpha\tau} d\tau = e^{\alpha\tau}\left[\frac{\tau^n}{\alpha} + \sum_{k=1}^{n} (-1)^k \frac{n(n-1)\ldots(n-k+1)}{\alpha^{k+1}}\tau^{n-k}\right] \tag{41}$$

where n is a positive integer. Further, since the roots $s_k$ are assumed to be simple, equations (40) and (41) yield

$$\bar{I}_o = \frac{1}{s_k}\,(1+\frac{e^{-s_k\tau_o}-1}{s_k\tau_o}) \tag{42}$$

Thus, the elements of the vector $\underline{r}$ are given by the expression

$$r_\mu = -\sum_{k=1}^{m} h_k(-s_k)^{\mu-1}(1+\frac{e^{-s_k\tau_o}-1}{s_k\tau_o}), \quad \mu=o,\ 1,\ \ldots \tag{43}$$

For exemplification, consider the stochastic dynamics problem described by the equation of motion

$$\ddot{x} + \dot{x} + x = w(t), \tag{44}$$

where the power spectrum of w(t) is given by equation (38) with $r_o$=1. Clearly

$$\Lambda(s) = s^2+s+1 = (s+s_1)(s+s_2) \tag{45}$$

with

$$s_1 = \frac{1 + i\sqrt{3}}{2}, \tag{46}$$

and

$$s_2 = \frac{1 - i\sqrt{3}}{2}, \tag{47}$$

Thus, using equation (42) one obtains

$$r_o = 1 - \exp(-\tfrac{1}{2})\left[\frac{\sqrt{3}}{3}\sin\left(\frac{\sqrt{3}}{2}\right) + \cos\left(\frac{\sqrt{3}}{2}\right)\right] = .1262 \tag{48}$$

and

$$r_1 = 1 - \frac{2\sqrt{3}}{3}\exp(-\tfrac{1}{2})\sin\left(\frac{\sqrt{3}}{2} + \frac{1}{3}\right) = 0.3403 \tag{49}$$

Further, equation (27) gives

$$r_2 = R_w(o) - r_o - r_1 = 0.5335 \tag{50}$$

Then, equation (21) yields

$$M_2 = \frac{2}{\pi}\int_{-\infty}^{\infty} \frac{\sin^2(\omega/2)}{\omega^4+(\omega^2-1)^2}\, d\omega = r_1 = 0.3403 \tag{51}$$

and

$$M_o = \frac{2}{\pi}\int_{-\infty}^{\infty} \frac{\sin^2(\omega/2)}{\omega^2[\omega^4+(\omega^2-1)^2]}\, d\omega = M_2 + r_o = 0.4665 \tag{52}$$

Next, combining equations (26), (50) and (51) gives

$$M_4 = \frac{2}{\pi}\int_{-\infty}^{\infty} \frac{\omega^2\sin^2(\omega/2)}{\omega^4+(\omega^2-1)^2}\, d\omega = M_2 + r_2 = 0.8738 \tag{53}$$

Note, that the values of $M_o$, $M_2$ and $M_4$ which are given by equations (51)-(53) have been verified by relying on a standard numerical quadrature algorithm and on relevant analytical results. Further, observe that the recursive procedure used to determine $M_4$ can be followed to calculate higher order quantities $M_{2k}$, $k>2$.

## CONCLUSION

Equation (31) has been derived by using the properties of the response autocorrelation, and of the response with excitation cross-correlation of a linear time-invariant dynamical system. It yields as a special case the James et al. (1965) formula which is used extensively in random vibration and control calculations. Clearly, this is a quite powerful formula. In fact the developed formula is applicable as long as the elements of the vector $\underline{r}$ are available. Note that these elements involve integrals with exponentially decaying, in general, integrands. Therefore, in many cases, they can be determined analytically. Further, they lend themselves to routine numerical quadrature schemes. A more comprehensive discussion of this aspect is given in Spanos (1987).

## ACKNOWLEDGMENT

The financial support of this research by a PYI-84 grant from the National Science Foundation and a group of industrial firms is gratefully acknowledged.

## REFERENCES

Gradshteyn, I.S. and Ryzhik, I.M. (1965). Table of Integrals, Series and Products, Academic Press, NY.

James, H.M., Nichols, N.B. and Philips, R.S. eds. (1965). Theory of Servomechanisms, Dover, NY.

Korn, A.G. and Korn, T.M. (1968). Mathematical Handbook for Scientists and Engineers, McGraw-Hill, NY.

Nigam, N.C. (1983). Introduction to Random Vibrations, The MIT Press, Cambridge, MA.

Spanos, P-T.D. (1983). "Spectral Moments Calculation of Linear System Output", Journal of Applied Mechanics, ASME, Vol. 50, pp. 901-903.

Spanos, P.D. (1987). "An Approach to Calculating Random Vibration Integrals", Journal of Applied Mechanics, ASME (in press).

# *Probability of instability of semi-elliptical cracks Application to the reliability of an offshore structure*

*G. Lebas & D. Bergez & Y. Guenard*
elf aquitaine -64108 PAU -FRANCE-

**ABSTRACT**

In structural steels commonly used for truss type structures, it is extremely difficult to measure a valid KIc value and the Charpy V test is often the only one enabling the sensitivity of the material to notching to be characterized. Should one wish later to apply the concepts of fracture mechanics to obtain either the load resulting in the instability of a given crack, or the tolerable defects dimensions, one must use an empirical relationship between the Charpy V and the KIc.

Now, all the relationships proposed are the outcome of scattered measurements and the values of the Charpy V measured on a materiel can themselves be highly scattered. Because of this, when placing oneself systematically «on the side of safety», one arrives either at the instability loads that are unrealistic, or at critical defect dimensions which are well below the threshold of detectability. When the structure studied has been existing for many years, the estimated values then appear unrealistic.

The probabilistic approach that we propose takes into account the scatters observed on Charpy V measurements and the relationships between Charpy V and KIc values. It also enables the random character of the stresses to be taken into consideration. Starting from the assumption that any connection of one member to another comprises a defect, the distributions of depths and widths are jointly estimated from the statistics published by DUFRESNE (2).

Next, these dimensions and external loads are converted into distributions of stress level factors by means of various semi-empirical formulae taken from the literature.

At the other end of the chain, we present statistical analyses of Charpy V tests carried out on test-pieces sampled from the structure. This study shows that a probabilistic approach is necessary, since the conventional approach taking parameters with a safety margin would lead to results that are quite unrealistic.

Next we follow the statistical study of the experimental correlations published in the literature between the Charpy V and KIc values. Lastly, since all the randomnes of uncertain variables are described by their statistical distribution, the probability of brittle fracture is determined by Monte-Carlo simulation.

Comparing the probability of sudden fracture thus estimated to the probability induced by another failure mode, one can determine, with a certain degree of realism, which members must be reinforced, which require inspection at regular intervals and which involve no immediate danger.

**INTRODUCTION**

At some stage it was decided to drill new wells from an existing platform with a new drilling system different from the one the structure was originally designed for. It was therefore decided to document the safety of the new installation.

As a first step samples were taken from beams of the substructure. Charpy V tests performed on those samples showed very low impact strengths, and the problem of the substructure safety against brittle fracture arised. In particular, the following questions were raised: are brittle failures likely to occur, and what are the consequences of such failures on the integrity of the substructure?

In order to answer those questions, it was decided to perform a probabilistic study taking into account the various sources of uncertainties (loads ans resistances) and the redundancy of the structure.

## STATISTICAL ANALYSIS OF TEST DATA

### Statistical analysis of the parameters

The scatter of the results (Charpy V impact values) was very large (Figure 1), and in order to carry out a statistical analysis we had to check if the temperature or/and the specimen had an influence on the results. In order to show the effect of a parameter, we looked for the residual scatter by a variance analysis. This method allowed us to test whether a fixed parameter had an effect on the results or not. Morever this analysis allowed us to say wether this influence was significant.

It was found that the temperature has a large influence but not the specimen type. The conclusion is that, for a given temperature, all the samples can be mixed and that therefore only two studies could be carried out (one for each temperature -5°C and 15°C).

### Distributions of Charpy V test results

For each temperature we built the histogram of the Charpy V test value, KCv. One such histogram is shown on Figure 1. It reflects a bi-modal distribution. It was hence necessary to use two laws for a good fitting.

$$Fkcv(x) = p \quad F1kcv(x) + (1-p) \quad F2kcv(x)$$

with

$$Fikcv(x) = 1 - \exp\left(-\left(x/ti\right)^{bi}\right)$$

where ti is a scale parameter, bi a shape parameter and p is the proportion of data in the first population. The results are (in J):

*-5° C, p = 88 %* t1=22, b1=1.55, t2=215, b2=4.8
*15° C, p = 39 %* t1=48, b1=3.74, t2=210, b2=3.9

In each case, these two populations seem to correspond to a brittle and to a ductile population. As expected we observe a translation of the populations as the temperature changes. Note that many other laws have been fitted, and that Chi-square and Kolmogorov-Smirnov tests showed the best fittings with Weibull laws.

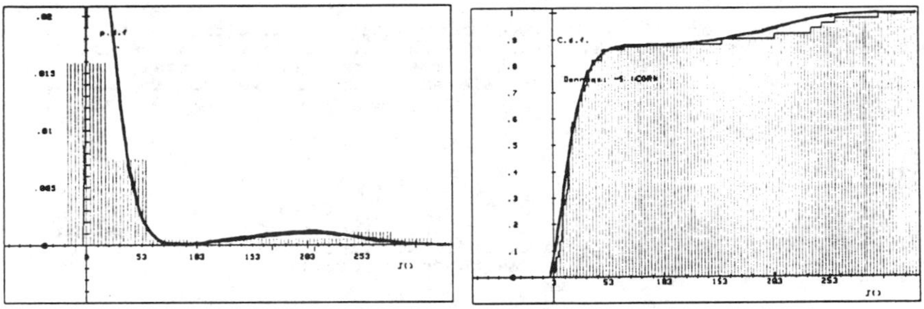

Figure 1. Charpy V test histogram and fitting by a Weibull law: Temperature -5°C.

### Yield stress distribution.

The scatter is not very large so that we decided to choose a Log-Normal distribution. The mean yield stress is 287 N/mm² and the standard deviation equal to 30 N/mm² (coefficient of variation = 10%).

## Crack dimensions

Different welds of the substructure have been inspected in order to detect existing defects. The results of the inspection showed: no detectable defect. However, in order to perform the study of the influence of the brittleness of the material on the reliability of the substructure, we assumed that *each weld contained one defect*. Of course since none had been detected, this hypothesis is very conservative.

Based on the conclusions of two papers, (10) and (11), devoted to crack detection on offshore structures, the two following hypotheses were made:

- *all the defects are located at the weld toe*
- *all are semi-elliptical surface cracks* .

Regarding the statistical distribution of the defect dimensions, the one given in (2) (see Figure 2 on page 4) was chosen. It results from a statistical analysis of defects measured in nuclear pressure vessels, i.e. in structure of better quality than offshore structures as far as welding is concerned. Nevertheless the most probable crack dimension (length and depth) agree well with those given in (10) and in (11).

## Stress intensity factors

Different relations have been proposed in the literature to compute the stress intensity factors in semi-elliptical surface cracks. Different formulae are given below. Most of them give the stress intensity factor at the intersection with the surface. This point seems to be the most critical. Roughly speaking, the stress intensity factor K can be written as follows:

$$K = \sigma \sqrt{\pi \frac{a}{Q}}\, F \qquad [1]$$

The unknown functions Q and F depend on a, b and h (see Figure 2 on page 4 for notations).

***Function Q:*** Unless otherwise specified, Q is given by:

$$Q = 1 + 1{,}464 \left(\frac{a}{b}\right)^{1{,}65} \quad \text{if } a/b \le 1 \qquad Q = 1 + 1{,}464 \left(\frac{b}{a}\right)^{1{,}65} \quad \text{if } a/b > 1$$

***Function F:*** While F can be obtained from any of the following:

*Irwin (5):* F = 1.1, this relation can only be applied if a/h < 0.5 and a/b < 1.

*Paris and Sih (8):* This relation can only be applied if a/h < 0.75 and a/b < 1.

$$F = \left[1 + 0{,}12\left(1 - \frac{a}{b}\right)\right]\sqrt{\frac{2hQ}{\pi a}\, tg\left(\frac{\pi a}{2hQ}\right)}$$

*Anderson, Holms and Orange (1):* This relation can only be applied if a/h < 1. and a/b < 1.

$$F = \left[1 + 0{,}12\left(1 - \frac{a}{b}\right)\right]\sqrt{\frac{2h}{\pi a}\, tg\left(\frac{\pi a}{2h}\right)}$$

*Newman and Raju (7):* The equation given for F in the case a/b < 0.03 is not the one proposed by Newman and Raju but the one, more accurate, given by Tada (12). The former has been retained because it does not contain any limitation on the ratio a/h.

$$M1 = 1{,}13 - 0{,}1\left(\frac{a}{b}\right) \quad \text{if } 0.03 \le a/b \le 1 \qquad M1 = \sqrt{\frac{b}{a}}\left(1 + 0{,}03\,\frac{b}{a}\right) \text{ if } a/b > 1$$

$$M2 = \sqrt{\frac{\pi}{4}} \quad \text{if } a/b \le 1 \qquad M2 = 1 + \frac{b}{a}\left(\sqrt{\frac{\pi}{4}} - 1\right) \quad \text{if } a/b > 1$$

$$F = \sqrt{\frac{2h}{\pi a}\, tg\, \frac{\pi a}{2h}}\; \frac{0{,}752 + 2{,}02\left(\frac{a}{h}\right) + 0{,}37\left(1 - \sin\frac{\pi a}{2h}\right)^3}{\cos\left(\frac{\pi a}{2h}\right)} \qquad \text{for } a/b \le 0.03$$

$$F = M_1 + \left(\sqrt{Q\frac{b}{a}} - M_1\right)\left(\frac{a}{h}\right)^P + \sqrt{Q\,\frac{b}{a}}\,\left(M_2 - 1\right)\left(\frac{a}{h}\right)^{2P} \qquad \text{for } a/b > 0.03$$

$$P = \sqrt{\pi}$$

*Dufresne (2):*

Deepest point $F = \sqrt{Q}\left\{\left[1,14 - 0,48\ \frac{a}{b}\right] + \frac{1}{0,2 + 4,9\left(\frac{a}{b}\right)^{1,2}}\left(\frac{a}{h}\right)^2\right\}$ for $a/b \leq 1$

Surface point $F = \sqrt{Q\ \frac{a}{b}}\left\{1,3 - 0,57\ \frac{a}{b} + \left(1,8 - 1,46\ \frac{a}{b}\right)\left(\frac{a}{h}\right)^2\right\}$

## PROBABILISTIC APPROACH OF THE BRITTLE FRACTURE

### Relationship between KCv and KIc

The result of a Charpy V test, KCv, is not the fracture toughness KIc. However, these parameters are correlated. Using the data given by G.Leclerc (6) we performed a linear regression by the least square method (see Figure 3) between the two parameters Xi=log(KCv) and Yi=log(KIc). The following relationship was obtained:

$$KIc = 10\ KCv^{.64}\ R \quad [2]$$

In order to account for the model uncertainty, we looked for the distribution of the residual values Ri, Ri being calculated for each point Xi, Yi from [2]. The value R is well fitted by a normal distribution with a mean equal to 1.01 and a variance equal to 0.021.

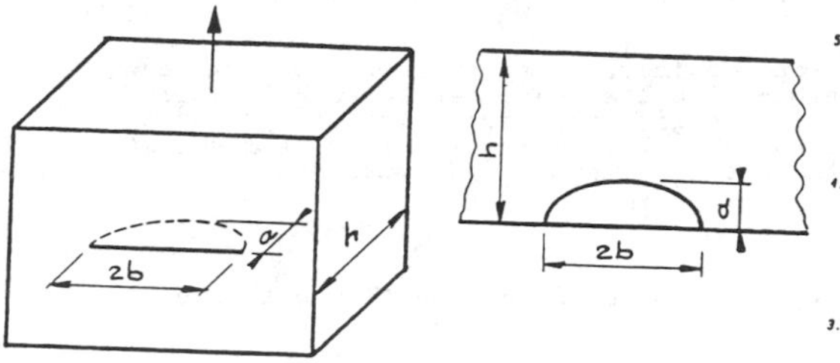


Figure 2. Dimensional characteristics of a semi-elliptical crack.

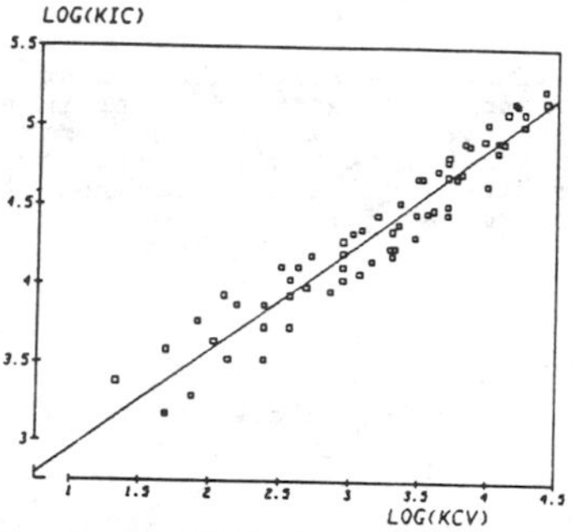


Figure 3. Charpy V test results and fracture toughness

### Defect size distribution

From the data given by Dufresne (2), the crack length (in mm) distribution was well fitted by an exponential law with a scatter parameter equal to .7 and a location parameter equal to 1.5 mm. It was assumed that all crack length were greater than 1.5 mm. For each class of crack length, we built the empirical distribution of the crack depth, b, as shown by Figure 4 on page 5. By a Monte carlo simulation of f(a), we estimated by interpolation the distribution of b and simulated f(b|a). Figure 5 on page 5 shows the scatter diagram of 3000 defects size.

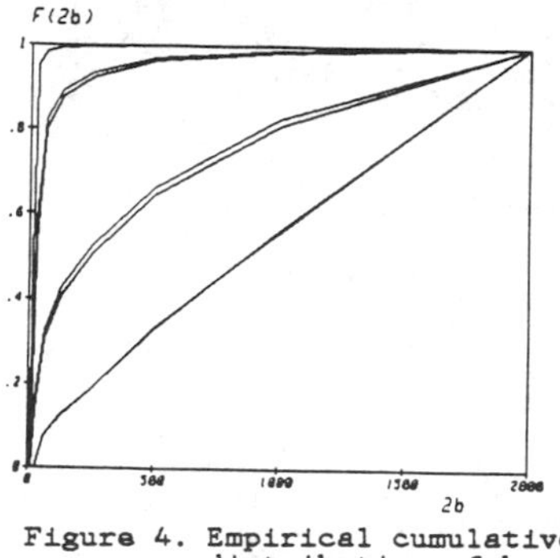


Figure 4. Empirical cumulative distribution of b.

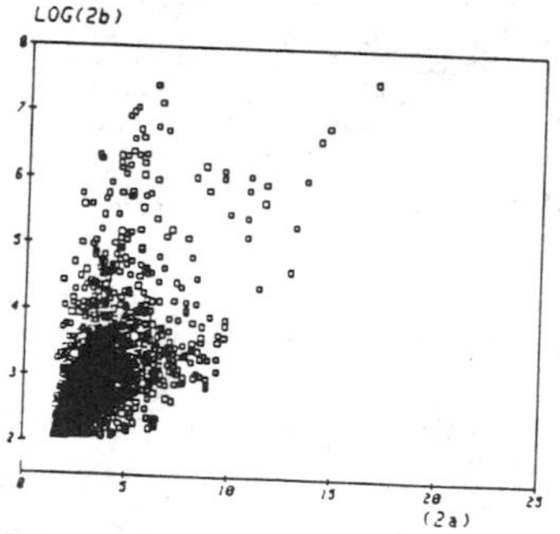


Figure 5. Scatter diagram of the size of 3000 defects.

***Definition:*** From [1], «***the brittle strength***» (MPa) was defined as follows:

$$Sbrit = \frac{KIc}{(K/S)} = \frac{10\ \ KCv\ \ .\ R^{.64}}{\sqrt{10^{-3}\pi a\ /\ Q(a,b)}\ F(a,b,h)}$$

KCv is a random variable, which characterizes the random properties of the material. R is a random variable characterizing the model uncertainty. The size of an unknown defect is defined by two random variables, the length a and the depth b, which are correlated. Expressions for F varies from one author to the other. We retained the six most frequently used, (see "Function F" on page 3) and for each couple (a,b), and for each thickness h, the maximum value of the six was chosen.

***Distribution:*** Thus, for a given temperature, and for a given beam thickness h, we could obtain by a Monte carlo simulation the distribution of Sbrit. We chose to perform the simulation for h varying from 8mm to 22mm for each value of the temperature. This results in 30 esimulations of 3000 crack dimensions each.

As expected the Sbrit showed two modes, corresponding to the two populations of the Charpy V test results. Each population was fitted by a Weibull law (example is shown by Figure 6 on page 6) and the resulting distribution could be writen as:

$$F(\ Sbrit\ ) = p\ \ \ F1(\ Sbrit\ ) + (1-p)\ \ \ F2(\ Sbrit\ )$$

Note that when h increases, all the parameters of the distribution tend to constant values. Also, the smaller the thickness, the more detrimental the distribution of Sbrit is. More precisely the scale and shape parameters could be expressed as functions of the inverse of the thickness ***y = 1/h*** as shown on the example of Figure 7 on page 6 .

$$t = (a - b.y - c.\ y^2)\ \rightarrow 0\quad \text{for } h \rightarrow +\infty$$

## Probability of failure

The probability of failure is the probability of having a stress greater or equal to the brittle strength

$$Pf = P(\ S \geq Sbrit) = \int_{-\infty}^{+\infty} Fs(x)\quad fr(x)\quad dx$$

Where fr(x) is the probability density function (pdf) of the brittle strength. Noting f1(x) and f2(x) the pdf of the two populations, this expression becomes:

$$Pf = p \int_0^{+\infty} Fs(x)\ f1(x)\ dx + (1-p) \int_0^{+\infty} Fs(x)\ f2(x)\ dx$$

In a first approximation, and especially for a low temperature (-5°C), the second term can be neglected. In other word the probability of failure is almost the probability of being in the first population AND of having a stress greater than the brittle strength.

$$Pf \rightarrow p\ \ P1(\ S \geq Sbrit\ )$$

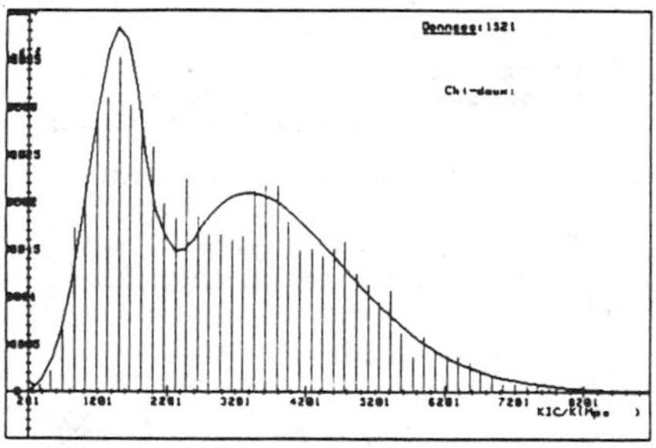


Figure 6. Brittle strength distibution T=15°C and H=21mm.

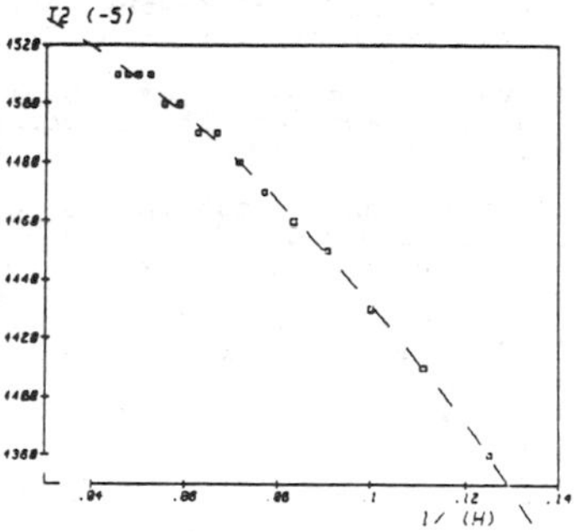


Figure 7. Scale parameter as a function of the inverse thickness.

## STRUCTURAL SYSTEM RELIABILITY ANALYSIS

### Structural model

A global view of the structural model is shown on Figure 8 on page 7.

### Methodology

A complete description of the methodology can be found in (4). Each failure mode is described by an equation $g(X)=0$ such that failure occurs if $g(X)\leq 0$, where X is a vector of parameters such as internal forces and moments, material properties, and geometrical characteristics. Estimating individual probabilities of failure is the first step of a structural system reliability analysis. Once a member has failed, the structure stiffness is modified and the load initially carried by the failed member has to be redistributed among other members. The load redistribution may trigger another member failure which itself can lead to other failures until the structure cannot satisfactorily support the loads applied to it. Identifying the most critical failure sequences and estimating their probabilities of occurrence is the second and main step of a structural system reliability analysis. In this study the probabilities of failure are replaced by ***safety indices*** called

### Definitions of failure modes and general assumptions

Failure modes accounted for in this analysis and the corresponding equations were:

1. Buckling (Bu): $Fcr - Fx = 0$
2. Plastifiction (P): $1 - Fx/Np - Mz/Mp = 0$
3. Brittle fracture Sbrit (Br): $SCF(Fx/A + Mz/(I/v)) = 0$

Fx and Mz are respectively the internal axial force and bending moment. The following parameters were assumed to have a lognormal distribution with a coefficient of variation noted Cv:

- the total dead load resultant, (Cv=10%)
- the total live load resultant,(Cv=10%)
- the wind load, (Cv=30%)
- the compressive strength Fcr, (Cv=17% (3))
- the plastic axial strength Np, and the plastic moment, Mp, (Cv=10% see "Yield stress distribution." on page 3)

The others parameters were:

- the section area A and the elastic section modulus I/v (deterministic).
- the stress concentration factor at the tension web connection SCF (deterministic to 1.7) (see (9)).
- Sbrit defined in the part entitled "Distribution" on page 5, (note the large Cv: more than 50%).

The results consist mainly in a listing of the critical failure sequences and of the associated safety indices. They are presented on failure trees (see Figure 9 on page 7) with the following conventions:

- each branch represents a beam failure in one of the three possible failure modes (Br, Bu or P)
- the numbers indicated on the branches are the beam numbers
- the numbers indicated at the nodes are the safety indices corresponding to the probability of the structure being in the damaged state associated to that node.

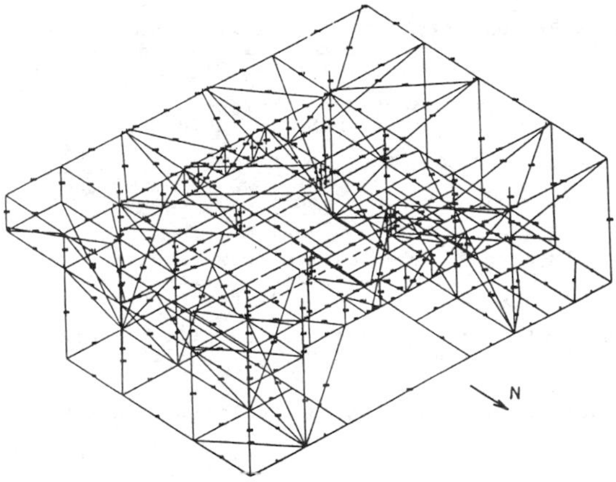


Figure 8. Global view of the structural model

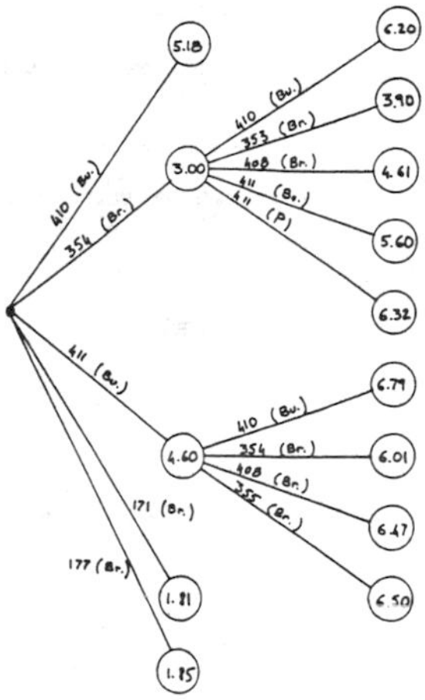


Figure 9. Failure tree

COMMENTS.

The first comment that must be made about these results is that brittle failure modes are predominant. This is mainly due to the large uncertainty associated to the random variable Sbrit but also to the conservative assumptions made about this failure mode:

1. one elliptical crack at each weld
2. a stress concentration factor equal to 1.7

The second comment is about the redundancy of the structure. Eventhough brittle failure modes predominate, the structure shows a large amount of redundancy. This can be inferred from the significant increase in safety index that shows up between every two consecutive failures.

In conclusion, the substructure is higly redundant and hence a sudden catastrophic sequence of failures is very unlikely, and the structure was considered safe. It was however recommended to periodically inspect visually the most critical beams identified and look for potential fractures.

REFERENCES


(1) ***Anderson, Holms R. and Orange T.***. Stress intensity magnification for deep surface cracks in sheets and plates. NASA TN D-6054, 1970.

(2) ***Dufresne J.***. Probabilistic application of fracture mechanics, ICF5 Vol 2, 1981, pp 517-531.

(3) ***Fjeld S.***. Reliability of Offshore Structures, OTC paper 3027, 1977.

(4) ***Guénard Y.***. Application of Structural System Reliability Analysis to Offshore Structures, PhD thesis, Stanford University, 1984.

(5) ***Irwin G.***. Journal of applied mechanics, Vol. 29, N° 4, 1962,pp 651-654.

(6) ***Leclercq G., Marandet B. and Sanz G.*** . Evolution de la tenacité des marériaux à partir de paramètres issus d'essais mécaniques simples, Rapport IRSID REP 123, mai 1975.

(7) ***Newman J. and Raju I.***. Analysis of surface cracks in finite plates under tension or bending loads, NASA TP, 1978.

(8) ***Paris P. and Sih G.***. ASTM STP 381, 1965, pp 30-83.

(9) ***Peterson R.E.***. Stress Concentration Factors, John Wiley & Sons, 1974.

(10) ***Rodrigues, Wong and Rogerson***. Weld defect distribution in offshore platforms and their relevance to reliability studies, quality control and in-service inspection. OTC Paper 3693.

(11) ***Rogerson and Wong***. Weld defect distributions in offshore structures and their influence on structural reliability. OTC Paper 4237.

(12) ***Tada H., Paris P. anf Irwin G.***. The stress analysis of cracks handbook, DEL Research Corporation, 1973.

# TIME-VARIANT RELIABILITY OF STRUCTURAL SYSTEMS SUBJECT TO FATIGUE

F. Guers and R. Rackwitz
Technical University Munich
Munich, FRG

ABSTRACT
A model is presented for the reliability calculation of so-called time variant redundant systems subject to a Gaussian load-process accounting for the possibility of failure under fatigue reduced resistances. The upcrossing approach together with the well-known Poisson limit theorem is used for the derivation of the distribution function of individual times to failure. The numerical part is facilitated by modern FORM/SORM techniques. Especially informative are parameters computed for the most likely failure state. The times up to and between individual failures resulting from these calculations can be used for the design of appropriate inspection and repair strategies.

## 1. INTRODUCTION

Fatigue-induced deterioration of offshore platforms and other structures is an important source of diminished structural performance and can even cause structural collapse. A reliability analysis of deteriorating structures is especially interesting for redundant structures as it can help to design suitable inspection and repair strategies and/or to quantify the remaining time of safe use of the structure. However, reliability models so far have primarily been developed for failure of structural components and systems under extreme loading and only a few studies are directed towards the reliability analysis of structural components subject to fatigue (see, for example, Martindale/Wirsching, 1983).

Recently, a reliability formulation has been proposed (Guers et al.,1987) which leads to approximate "time-variant" reliabilities of redundant structures whose componential resistance properties are still time-invariant. It models structural deterioration by considering explicitely the consecutive states of degradation in time as descibed by the sequence of componential failures. It is particularly suited for high reliable structures.

In this paper that formulation is generalized to include fatigue deterioration. It is based on some earlier studies on structural component reliability under fatigue where the so-called upcrossing approach (Guers/Rackwitz, 1985) has been found to be feasible and sufficiently accurate, especially in the context of modern FORM/SORM techniques. It enables a unified reliability approach for both extreme-value failure and fatigue rupture. It will be shown that those concepts directly carry over to structural systems.

## 2. BASIC MECHANICAL AND STOCHASTIC ASSUMPTIONS

Assume a linear-elastic, statically reacting, redundant structural system where M control points (bars, cross sections, hot spots, etc.) have been preselected as prone to failure. For simplicity of

presentation but also sufficiently realistic in many cases, the load on the structure is taken as a stationary scalar Gaussian process $L(\tau)$ with mean $m_L$ and standard derivation $\sigma_L$. Further, the load process obeys certain regularity conditions, that is continuous differentiability of sample paths and ergodicity (see Cramer et al.1967). The load-effects in the control points are then given by $S_m(\tau) = a_m L(\tau)$ where the $a_m$'s are certain determin-istic coefficients. The m-th control point is said to fail when a large load "wave" causes $S_m$ to exceed a possibly deteriorated control point resistance $R_m$ for the first time.
This event (upcrossing of $R_m(\tau)$ by $S_m(\tau)$) is followed by a more or less abrupt change of the mechanical properties of the control point. The change is assumed as perfectly brittle as concerns the remaining resistance after failure. The corresponding load re-distribution, however, is supposed to occur sufficiently slowly such that, firstly, no dynamic effects need to be considered at the surviving hot spots and, secondly, the new stress regime in the structure is reached at the earliest in the next loading cycle. This means that the same resistance thresholds are relevant during the very wave that caused control point failure or, potentially, multiple control point failure resp. multiple threshold crossings. It is then possible in any state of the system to assign a critical threshold $R_m(\tau)/a_m$ to each non-failed control point and failure of one or more elements in a large wave can be treated by the out-crossing approach formulated in the same load space.

The resistance parameters in the control points, in general, must be assumed as uncertain. Therefore, control point failure is first considered conditional on a realisation of the vector $\underline{Q}=\underline{q}$ of un-certain resistance parameters.In a second step these conditions must be removed by integration according to the total probability law.

The other limiting case of immediate stress redistribution can be dealt with in a similar manner at the price of slightly more invol-ved computational operations (see Guers, 1987). With some restrict-ions it is also possible to consider dynamic overshooting of load effects in non-failing control points (Rackwitz/Guers,1986) and even damped load redistribution. These and other refinements of the approach are presently still under study.

## 3. OUTCROSSING APPROACH FOR FATIGUE-INDUCED DETERIORATION

### 3.1 INDIVIDUAL FAILURE TIMES

It has been shown (Guers, et al.,1987) that a probabilistic de-scription of the time-variant reliability of redundant systems can be based on the distributions of the conditional times to individu-al failures. For the highly reliable structures under consideration the distribution of the time $T_i^{(l)}$ to failure of (time) component i under a single large "wave" is well approximated by an exponential distribution. In each structural state (l) such a time component is the result of the almost simul-taneous failure of j control points, i.e. it comprises control points $i = (i_1,...,i_j)$. The following well-known asymptotic formula is valid

$$F_{T_i^{(1)}}(T) = 1 - \exp[-\int_0^T \nu_i^{(1)}(\tau)d\tau] = 1 - \exp[-I_i^{(1)}(T)] \qquad (3.1)$$

where $\nu_i^{(1)}(\tau)$ is the time-dependent upcrossing rate of $L(\tau)$ of the considered thresholds and $I_i^{(1)}(T)$ denotes the integral over $\nu_i^{(1)}(\tau)$ in the time interval $[0,T]$. For simplification of notation, the index (1) is omitted. It is further well known that (Madsen et al., 1985)

$$\nu_i(\tau) = \omega_o \varphi(\gamma_i(\tau)) \Psi(\dot{r}_i(\tau)/\omega_o) \qquad (3.2)$$

where

$$r_i(\tau) = (R_i(\tau) - a_i m_L)/(a_i \sigma_L) \qquad (3.3)$$

is the standardised threshold, $\dot{r}(\tau)$ its derivative, $\omega_o^2$ the variance of the derivative of the normalized load process, and $\Psi(x) = \varphi(x) - x\phi(-x)$ with $\varphi$ the density and $\phi$ the distribution function of a standard normal variable, respectively. The function $\Psi$ frequently can be approximated by the constant $(2\pi)^{-1/2}$. By introducing an auxiliary standard normal variable $U_{T_i}$ by the identity $F_{T_i}(T) = F_{U_{T_i}}(u) = \phi(u)$, the variable $T_i$ can be expressed as

$$T_i = I_i^{-1}[-\ln \phi(-U_{T_i})] \qquad (3.4)$$

Herein, $I_i^{-1}[.]$ represents the inversion of the integral in eq. (3.1) with respect to the upper integration limit. A simple, fairly accurate formula for the evaluation of the upcrossing rate integral which makes use of Laplace's approximation (Copson, 1965), and a suitable numerical inversion algorithm has been derived in (Guers/Rackwitz ,1986). It is recognized that the failure probability can now be determined from

$$P_f = P(T_i - T \leq 0) \qquad (3.5)$$

which is precisely the formulation needed for the application of FORM/SORM-techniques.

## 3.2 SYSTEM FORMULATION

Structures can fail in one of K failure sequences which are formed by a series of individual random failure times. At the end of each time step a time component is said to fail. Each time component is associated with a single failure or multiple failures of control points. The total time to structural failure is obtained by adding up the time component failure times. Hence, structural collapse occurs in a given sequence during the reference period [0,T], if

$$\sum_{i=1}^{i_m} T_i - T \leq 0 \qquad (3.6)$$

where the complete set of consecutive failures of time components $i=1$ to $i=i_m$ imply collapse. In contrast to the case of time-independent resistances, the values of the thresholds of the non-failed control points at the beginning of every time step are dependent on the previous time-step lengths and the already failed control points due to the different deterioration regimes of the accumulation of damage along that sequence. This implies a dependency between the $T_i$'s. It is conveniently represented by the sequence of conditional distribution functions of failure times. The corresponding Rosenblatt-transformation necessary for application of FORM/SORM for these failures times given a realisation of the resistance variables can be written as (Hohenbichler/Rackwitz, 1981):

$$F_{T_1}(T_1) = 1 - \exp[-\int_0^{T_1} \nu_1(\tau)d\tau] = \phi(U_{T_1})$$

$$F_{T_2}(T_2|T_1) = 1 - \exp[-\int_0^{T_2} \nu_2(\tau|T_1)d\tau] = \phi(U_{T_2})$$

$$F_{T_{i_m}}(T_{i_m}|T_1,\dots,T_{i_m-1}) = 1 - \exp[-\int_0^{T_{i_m}} \nu_{i_m}(\tau|T_1,\dots,T_{i_m-1})d\tau]$$

$$= \phi(U_{T_{i_m}}) \qquad (3.7)$$

Again, performing the integrations in eq. (3.7) and inverting them as described above and inserting the failiure times into eq. (3.6) yields a representation of the failure event in the standard space.

Consider now a general system with K possible failure paths to system collapse. The number of time steps in the k-th path is $L_k$. In order to completely define the failure sequence in that path, an ordering of the reduced resistances must be performed for each of the time steps and the elements must be grouped into components failing at the end of each time step. The probability of occurrence of the k-th failure sequence during [0,T] can be written as:

$$P(F_k) = \int_{\underline{Q}=\underline{q}} P_k(T|\underline{Q}=\underline{q})\ P\Big(\underset{\substack{l=1\\ \uparrow\\ \text{for each}\\ \text{time step}}}{\overset{L_k}{\cap}}\ \underset{\substack{i=1\\ \uparrow\\ \text{for all}\\ \text{present}\\ \text{elements}}}{\overset{I_k^l}{\cap}} r^l_{n_{kl}(i)} \le r^l_{n_{kl}(i+1)}\Big)dF_{\underline{Q}}(\underline{q}) \qquad (3.8)$$

The second probability corresponds to the specific ordering.In numerical calculations the variables r are represented by their Rosenblatt-transformations.The first probability is:

$$P_k(T|\underline{Q}=\underline{q}) = P^k\ P\Big(\sum_{l=1}^{L_k} T_l^k(r^l_{n_{kl}(1)}) \le t\Big) \qquad (3.9)$$

where the second term corresponds to eq. (3.6) with new notation. The first probability is the probability to be on path k. In these equations, the following notations are used:

* $\underline{I}_k^l$ denotes the numbers of the control points in the k-th path surviving at the beginning and along the l-th time step.
* $n_{kl}(i)$ is an integer function which assigns in ascending order the numbers of the reduced thresholds during the l-th time step.

* $P^k = \prod_{l=1}^{L_k} P_k^l$ is the weighting probability of being on the k-th failure path where

$$P_k^l = \frac{\nu^l_{n_{kl}(i_{kl})} - \nu^l_{n_{kl}(i_{kl}+1)}}{\nu^l_{n_{kl}(1)}}$$

is the weighting probability for the l-th time step which ends at the upcrossing of $i_{kl}$ thresholds corresponding to the elements $n_{kl}(1)$ to $n_{kl}(i_{kl})$ without upcrossing the $n_{kl}(i_{kl}+1)$-th level.Again, the corresponding events are expressed in the standard space by auxiliary standard normal variables making use of $P_k^l = \phi(U_k^l)$ (see Guers et al.,1987, for details)

* $T_l^k(r^l_{n_{kl}(1)})$ is the time to the first upcrossing of the lowest relevant level for the l-th time step, which is also the length of this time step.

The total failure probability can finally be obtained by integration over the uncertain resistance vector $\underline{Q}$, i.e. from

$$P_f(T) = \int_{\underline{q}} P(\bigcup_{k=1}^{K} F_{k|\underline{Q}=\underline{q}})\, dF_{\underline{Q}}(\underline{q})$$

where $F_{k|\underline{Q}=\underline{q}}$ is the failure event in the k-th sequence conditional on $\underline{Q} = \underline{q}$.

## 4. MODEL FOR FATIGUE DETERIORATION OF STRUCTURAL ELEMENTS

Fatigue phenomena in metallic structural elements can suitably be modelled by assuming a certain crack initiation period which is followed by the crack propagation period. During the first period there is no substantial reduction of strength against extreme value loading. In the second period a gradual reduction of residual strength takes place. For simplicity of presentation it is here assumed that the crack initiation period is negligibly short (see Guers/Rackwitz, 1986 for a more rigorous, general formulation). A number of crack propagation models have been proposed. It must, however, be recognized that due to the lack of data relatively simple relationships such as the one proposed by Paris-Erdogan usually is accurate enough. For this model and many other alternatives such as the so-called Feddersen scheme it is possible to assess a decreasing threshold function in the load effect space (stress space). This function usually has the form

$$R(\tau) = R(o)[1-K\, E[\sum_{[o,\tau]} (\Delta S_i)^c]]^d \qquad (4.1)$$

where R(o) is the initial resistance and K, c and d are possibly uncertain material properties. The $(\Delta S_i)$ denote the damage relevant stress cycle amplitudes. The damage accumulation term $\Sigma(\Delta S_i)^c$ in that equation depends on the counting method of damage relevant stress cycles. If the loading process is fairly narrow banded it is simply $\Delta S_i$ = max $S_i$ - min $S_i$. Then, the expectation term in eq. (4.1) can be written out explicitely. A slight generalisation is achieved if one adopts certain empirical adjustments proposed by Yang (1979). Eq. (4.1) can then be written as

$$R(\tau) = R(o)\ [1 - \frac{X\ K}{R(o)^c}\ \tau]^{1/c} \qquad (4.2)$$

with $X\ K = A^c\ K\ (2\sqrt{2})^B\ \Gamma(1+B/2)$ and A and B some additional, usually uncertain parameters also obtainable from fatigue tests.
An important characteristic of that model is the assumption of a slowly deterministically decreasing resistance, which can be verified theoretically and experimentally for high cycle fatigue (Guers/Rackwitz, 1986). The value of the threshold depends primarily on the past load history and only negligibly on the instantaneous stress cycle. The independence of threshold and load process as another consequence of the high cycle assumption together with the limitation to high-reliable systems is equally important for the outcrossing approach because it allows to assume Poisson-distributed conditional upcrossing events.

5. APPLICATION FOR A 4-ELEMENT DANIELS SYSTEM
The ideal-brittle Daniels system (Daniels, 1944) is known for its simple mechanics. On the other hand, the degree and efficiency in redundancy of this system is exceptional due to its symmetry. As a consequence it requires more involved reliability calculations than most of the more common structures. For the purpose of illustration of the foregoing concepts a Daniels system with 4 elements is assumed (fig. 1). The tension strengths $R_i$ of the different tendons are assumed to be normally distributed and equicorrelated. The following simple resistance model then holds:

$$R_i = E[R_i] + D[R_i](\sqrt{\rho}\ U_o+\sqrt{1-\rho}\ U_i)$$

where $U_o$ and the $U_i$'s are independent standard normal variables.
For the numerical calculations with this example the following values have been chosen

$$R_i \sim N(E[R_i] = 0.9; D[R_i] = 0.2)$$
$$L(\tau) \sim N(0.5;0.1)$$
$$\rho = 0.3$$
$$\nu^+T = 10^6$$

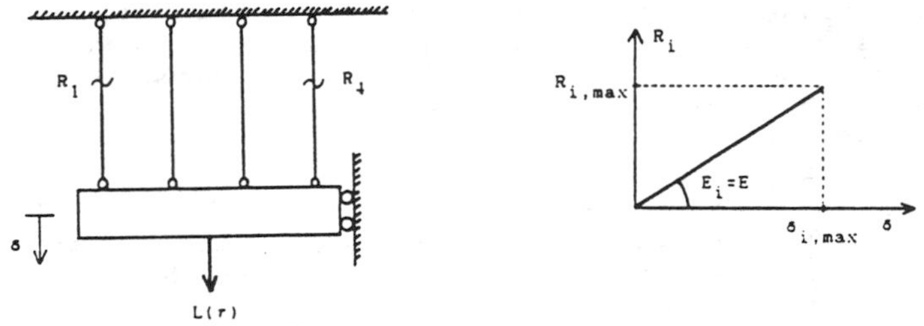


Figure 1: 4 elements Daniels system

The two parameters in eq.(4.2) are assumed to be lognormally distributed with means E[XK] = $10^{-3}$ resp. E[c] = 4 and a coefficient of variation COV = 0.2. B is deterministic, i.e. B = 3. The method of the order statistics is used to calculate the distributions of the ordered resistances $\hat{R}_1 < \hat{R}_2 < \hat{R}_3 < \hat{R}_4$ (Hohenbichler/Rackwitz, 1982). The failure sequences are represented by the ruptures of elements $\hat{1},\hat{2},\hat{3}$ and $\hat{4}$, repectively, and differ only by the composition of the components failing at the end of each time step.

The failure tree of the system without deterioration, i.e. for E[XK] = 0 is given in fig. 2. The second-order safety indices are shown in parenthesis at every step in the failure tree after the last failed component.The values of the variables at the expansion point for FORM/SORM can be interpreted as the most likely parameter values for the considered failure sequence. In particular, the most likely times between failures can be computed providing important information about the remaining redundancy in the system and, thus, also for further inspection and repair actions. The numbers just above the same component are the time step lenghts in the most likely failure state given as fractiles of the total lifetime. An ordering of the failure sequences is possible. As expected due to the assumption of delayed load redistribution, the sequences with several time steps and thus load redistributions are the most likely to occur (see fig. 2).

In figure 3 the failure tree with fatigue deterioration of the resistances is shown. It can be observed that the safety indices now are generally smaller. The safety index for the sequence $\hat{1},\hat{2}\cap\hat{3}$, for example drops down from 4.72 to 4.10. Also, the system most likely spends comparatively more time in the first time steps when the resistances are less deteriorated. In the previously mentioned sequence, the time spent in the intact state increases from 26.4% to 58.2%. Of course, the total lifetime is reduced (compare the $\beta$-values).

## 6. DISCUSSION

As mentioned in section 4, the independence of the upcrossing events is a basic condition for the calculation of the first crossing time. This assumption will be more and more violated for the lower thresholds, i.e. at the end of the lifetime of the structure. However, it has been found that because the later times are short as compared to the preceeding ones, the error made remains negligible.

The deterioration model proposed before is adequate for preliminary investigations. It can be easily improved for special cases, for example, by using Vanmarcke's (1975) improvement for the upcrossing rate of narrow-band processes or by using more sophisticated models for componential residual strength.

The application of this methodology to more complicated truss or frame structures does not imply essential changes. Only ordering conditions as in eq. (3.9) of the thresholds then have to be included (Guers et al.,1987). The case of unequal fatigue constant,i.e. where the thresholds can cross others during he lifetime, can also be solved by introducing truncated distributions for the first crossing times.

REFERENCES

Cramer H. Leadbetter,M.R. (1967). Stationary and Related Stochastic Processes. Wiley, New York.

Copson E.I. (1965). Asymptotic Expansions, Cambridge University Press, Cambridge.

Daniels H.E. (1945). The Statistical Theory of the Strength of Bundles of Threads, Part I, Proc. Roy. Soc., A 183, pp.405-435.

Guers F. (1987). Zur Zuverlässigkeit redundanter Tragsysteme bei Ermüdungsbeanspruchung durch zeitvariante Gaußsche Lasten, München.

Guers F. Dolinski K. Rackwitz R. (1986), Progressive Failure of Brittle, Redundant Structural Systems in Time, Technische Universität, München.

Guers F. Rackwitz R. (1968) On the Calculation of Upcrossing Rates for Narrow-Band Gaussian Processes Related to Structural Fatigue, Berichte zur Zuverlässigkeitstheorie der Bauwerke, SFB 96, Technische Universität Muenchen, Heft 79.

Hohenbichler M. Gollwitzer S. Kruse W. Rackwitz, R., (1984) New Light on First-and Second-Order Reliability Methods, Submitted for Publication to Structural Safety.

Hohenbichler M. Rackwitz R. (1981) Non-Normal Dependent Vectors in Structural Safety, Journ. of the Eng. Mech. Div., ASCE, Vol. 1o7, No. 6, pp. 1227-1249.

Madsen H.O. Krenk S. Lind N.C. (1968) Methods of Structural Safety, Prentice Hall, Englewood Cliffs.

Martindale S.G. Wirsching P.H. (1983) Reliability-Based Progressive Fatigue Collapse, Journ. of Struc. Eng., Vol. 1o9,No.8.

Vanmarcke E.H. (1975) On the Distribution of the First-passage Time for Normal Stationary Random Processes, J. Appl. Mech., Vol. 42, pp.215-220.

Yang J.N. Lin M.D. (1977) Residual Strength Degradation Model and Theory of Periodic Proof Tests for Graphite/Epoxy Laminates, J. Composite Materials, 11, pp. 176-203.

$(26.2;\underset{\wedge}{5}2.2;21.6)$
$\hat{3}(3.95) - \hat{4}(3.95)$  3.95  I

$(2.8;67.2)$  $(23.8;50.3;25.9)$
$\hat{2}(3.68)$  $\hat{3}n\hat{4}(4.73)$  4.73  IV

$(100)$
$\hat{1}(2.79)$  $(26.4;73.6)$
$\hat{2}n\hat{3}(4.72)$  $\hat{4}(4.72)$  4.72  III

$(22.6;77.4)$
$\hat{2}n\hat{3}n\hat{4}(5.62)$  5.62  VII

$(82.2;17.8)$
$\hat{3}(4.62)$  $\hat{4}(4.62)$  4.62  II

$(100)$
$\hat{1}n\hat{2}$ $(4.44)$

$(77.\underset{\wedge}{5};22.5)$
$\hat{3}n\hat{4}(5.32)$  5.32  V

$(100)$
$\hat{1}n\hat{2}n\hat{3}$ $(5.52) - \hat{4}(5.52)$  5.52  VI

$(100)$
$\hat{1}n\hat{2}n\hat{3}n\hat{4}$ $(6.44)$  6.44  VIII

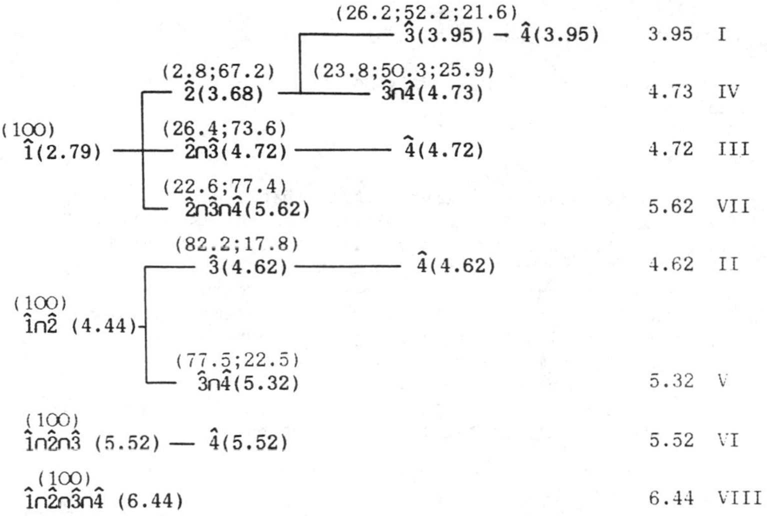

Figure 2: Failure tree for Daniels system with time-invariant
resistances

$(51.4;37.5;11.1)$
$\hat{3}(2.84)$  $\hat{4}(2.84)$  2.84  I

$(58.6;41.4)$  $(53.3;37.9;8.8)$
$\hat{2}(2.63)$  $\hat{3}n\hat{4}(3.96)$  3.96  II

$(100)$
$\hat{1}(1.98)$  $(58.2;41.8)$
$\hat{2}n\hat{3}(4.10)$  $\hat{4}(4.10)$  4.10  III

$(57.8;42.2)$
$\hat{2}n\hat{3}n\hat{4}(5.22)$  5.22  VI

$(90.7;9.3)$
$\hat{3}(4.20)$  $\hat{4}(4.20)$  4.20  IV

$(100)$
$\hat{1}n\hat{2}$ $(4.08)$

$(91.7;8.3)$
$\hat{3}n\hat{4}(5.01)$  5.01  V

$(100)$
$\hat{1}n\hat{2}n\hat{3}$ $(5.35) - \hat{4}(5.35)$  5.35  VII

$(100)$
$\hat{1}n\hat{2}n\hat{3}n\hat{4}$ $(6.38)$  6.38  VIII

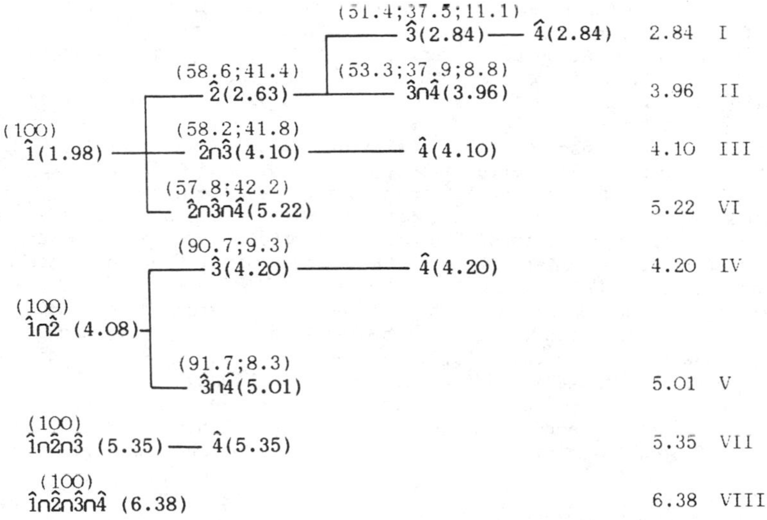

Figure 3: Failure tree for Daniels system with deteriorating
resistances

# BASIC ISSUES IN STOCHASTIC FINITE ELEMENT ANALYSIS

M. Shinozuka*
*Department of Civil Engineering, Columbia University, NY, NY 10027, USA

ABSTRACT

This paper provides an overview of various methods that are efficiently used within the framework of finite element analysis, for the estimation of structural response variability arising from spatial variation of material properties. Interpreting these variations to constitute stochastic fields, the variability is measured in terms of covariances of the structural response quantities. Emphasis is placed on the perturbation and Neumann expansion methods. With a numerical example, the efficiency and accuracy of these methods are compared. Appropriate comments are made on the size of finite elements, non-Gaussianess of stochastic fields, variability under dynamic and nonlinear conditions, structural reliability assessment, and one-dimensional structures where the problem of stochastic fields can be reduced to that of random variables.

## INTRODUCTION

Recently, the structural variability due to spatial variation of material properties has attracted considerable attention among engineers and researchers. The effort in this direction appears to be well justified if one recognizes the following: some engineering materials such as soils are known to have large spatial variability in their mechanical properties and hence a response analysis based on the average values of such properties may not provide sufficient engineering information on the response behavior and performance of structures under prescribed loading conditions. There is also a question of under what conditions the degree of response variability due to material property variation is more than, equal to or less than that due to possible randomness involved in the loading conditions.

The present paper focuses on methods for evaluating the response variability in terms of the expected value and covariance of the structural response. For this purpose, the material property variations are interpreted as stochastic fields, and the perturbation and Neuman expansion methods are used, in conjunction with the finite element method, for the analysis. A numerical example is also worked out.

Appropriate comments are made on (a) the size of finite elements, (b) the possible non-Gaussianess of stochastic fields, (c) dynamic and nonlinear response analysis, (d) structural reliability assessment, (e) one-dimensional structures where the problem of stochastic fields can be reduced to that of random variables and (f) comparison of the effect of material property variation on structural response variability with that arising from the randomness of loading conditions.

While a number of researchers contributed to the state-of-the-art of structural variability evaluation due to material property variation (e.g., Gambou, 1971; Astill, Nosseir and Shinozuka, 1972; Beacher and Ingra, 1981; Handa and Andersson, 1981; Vanmarcke and Grigoriu, 1983; Der Kiureghian, 1985; Liu, Belytschko and Mani, 1985; Hisada and Nakagiri, 1981 and 1985), the present paper is primarily based on the work by Yamazaki, Shinozuka and Dasgupta (1985a and 1985b), Yamazaki and Shinozuka (1987) and Bucher and Shinozuka (1986).

## DISCRETIZATION OF STOCHASTIC FIELDS

Mathematical models and their digital simulation for multivariate and multidimensional Gaussian and non-Gaussian stochastic fields have been developed by a number of researchers including the present author and his associates (e.g., Shinozuka and Jan, 1972; Vanmarcke, 1981; Shinozuka, 1985 and Yamazaki and Shinozuka, 1986). A discretized version of such a stochastic field, whether homogeneous or nonhomogeneous, can be constructed by decomposing the corresponding covariance matrix.

In the context of stochastic finite element analysis, a structure is first divided into the appropriate number of finite elements. The size of each finite element must be small enough from the spatial variability of the material properties as well as strain and stress gradients points of view. From the former point of view, it must be small enough so that the property values can be considered approximately constant within each element. Hence, if there are n finite elements in total and m material property parameters which exhibit random variability, then there are N = n x m material property values to be considered. Thus, the multivariate multidimensional stochastic field is discretized and reduced to a random vector, $\boldsymbol{\alpha}$, of N dimensions as

$$\boldsymbol{\alpha} = [\alpha_1(\mathbf{x}_1)\ \alpha_1(\mathbf{x}_2)\ldots\alpha_1(\mathbf{x}_n)\ldots\alpha_m(\mathbf{x}_1)\ \alpha_m(\mathbf{x}_2)\ldots\alpha_m(\mathbf{x}_n)]^T \tag{1}$$

where $\alpha_i(\cdot)$ and $\mathbf{x}_k$ indicate the i-th material property and position vector of the centroid of the k-th element, respectively.

The correlational characteristics of these N values in their standardized forms can be specified in terms of their covariance matrix $\mathbf{C}_{\boldsymbol{\alpha\alpha}}$ as

$$\mathbf{C}_{\boldsymbol{\alpha\alpha}} = \begin{bmatrix} \mathbf{C}^{11}_{\boldsymbol{\alpha\alpha}} & \mathbf{C}^{12}_{\boldsymbol{\alpha\alpha}} & \ldots & \mathbf{C}^{1m}_{\boldsymbol{\alpha\alpha}} \\ \mathbf{C}^{21}_{\boldsymbol{\alpha\alpha}} & \mathbf{C}^{22}_{\boldsymbol{\alpha\alpha}} & \ldots & \mathbf{C}^{2m}_{\boldsymbol{\alpha\alpha}} \\ \ldots & \ldots & \ldots & \ldots \\ \mathbf{C}^{m1}_{\boldsymbol{\alpha\alpha}} & \mathbf{C}^{m2}_{\boldsymbol{\alpha\alpha}} & \ldots & \mathbf{C}^{mm}_{\boldsymbol{\alpha\alpha}} \end{bmatrix} \tag{2}$$

and each sub-matrix represents

$$\mathbf{C}^{ij}_{\boldsymbol{\alpha\alpha}} = \begin{bmatrix} \mathrm{Cov}[\alpha_i(x_1),\alpha_j(x_1)] & \mathrm{Cov}[\alpha_i(x_1),\alpha_j(x_2)] & \ldots & \mathrm{Cov}[\alpha_i(x_1),\alpha_j(x_n)] \\ \mathrm{Cov}[\alpha_i(x_2),\alpha_j(x_1)] & \mathrm{Cov}[\alpha_i(x_2),\alpha_j(x_2)] & \ldots & \mathrm{Cov}[\alpha_i(x_2),\alpha_j(x_n)] \\ \mathrm{Cov}[\alpha_i(x_n),\alpha_j(x_1)] & \mathrm{Cov}[\alpha_i(x_n),\alpha_j(x_2)] & \ldots & \mathrm{Cov}[\alpha_i(x_n),\alpha_j(x_n)] \end{bmatrix} \tag{3}$$

From the auto- and cross-correlation functions of the underlying stochastic field, the kℓ-component of the sub-matrix is

$$\mathrm{Cov}[\alpha_i(x_k),\alpha_j(x_\ell)] = R_{\alpha_i\alpha_j}(\boldsymbol{\xi}_{k\ell}) \tag{4}$$

with $\boldsymbol{\xi}_{k\ell} = \boldsymbol{\alpha}_\ell - \boldsymbol{\alpha}_k$ representing the separation vector between the centroids of elements k and ℓ. The covariance matrix, $\mathbf{C}_{\boldsymbol{\alpha\alpha}}$, is always symmetric because of the following relationship:

$$R_{\alpha_i\alpha_j}(\boldsymbol{\xi}_{k\ell}) = R_{\alpha_j\alpha_i}(\boldsymbol{\xi}_{\ell k}) \tag{5}$$

Once the covariance matrix is constructed, the eigenvalues and eigenvectors of $\mathbf{C}_{\boldsymbol{\alpha\alpha}}$ are obtained by solving the following eigenequation

$$\mathbf{C}_{\boldsymbol{\alpha\alpha}}\boldsymbol{\Phi}_{\boldsymbol{\alpha}} = \boldsymbol{\Phi}_{\boldsymbol{\alpha}}\boldsymbol{\Lambda}_{\boldsymbol{\alpha}} \tag{6}$$

in which $\boldsymbol{\Phi}_{\boldsymbol{\alpha}} = [\boldsymbol{\phi}_1,\boldsymbol{\phi}_2,\ldots,\boldsymbol{\phi}_N]^T$ is the modal matrix whose column vectors are orthogonal to each other having the Euclidean length of 1:

$$\Phi_\alpha^T \Phi_\alpha = I \tag{7}$$

where **I** = identity matrix. Also, $\Lambda_\alpha$ is a diagonal matrix consisting of the (real) eigenvalues $\lambda_1 \geq \lambda_2 \geq \cdots \geq \lambda_N$ along its diagonal.

A random Gaussian vector $\mathbf{Z} = [Z_1\ Z_2 \cdots Z_N]^T$ whose components are independent of each other and have mean zeros and variances $\lambda_i$ (i=1,2,...,N) can easily be generated. In this case, the covariance matrix of **Z** is obviously given by $\Lambda_\alpha$. Then, the Gaussian random vector $\alpha$ can be generated by

$$\alpha = \Phi_\alpha Z \tag{8}$$

It can be easily shown that $\alpha$ given by Eq. 8 has the covariance matrix $C_{\alpha\alpha}$. If $\alpha$ exhibits non-Gaussian characteristics, the simulation technique developed by Yamazaki and Shinozuka (1986) for non-Gaussian fields may be useful for sample function generation.

Equation 8 may be approximated by its truncated form using only the first M modes (M < N) and corresponding independent random variables as

$$\alpha = [\Phi_1, \Phi_2, \ldots, \Phi_M][Z_1, Z_2, \ldots, Z_M]^T \tag{9}$$

The error caused by truncation can be evaluated by

$$P_\lambda(M) = \left(\sum_{k=1}^{M} \lambda_k\right) / \left(\sum_{k=1}^{N} \lambda_k\right) = \sum_{k=1}^{M} \lambda_k / N \tag{10}$$

which indicates the accuracy of the variance of samples generated using Eq. 9. It may happen that M is much smaller than N, since eigenvalues for higher-order modes may rapidly become smaller. Such a truncation of modes contributes to better numerical efficiency in generating sample functions.

The decomposition of $\mathbf{C}_{\alpha\alpha}$ above is often referred to as spectral decomposition and has been used in many applications.

Another method that is also often used for the same purpose is the Cholesky decomposition method. In this case, $\mathbf{C}_{\alpha\alpha}$ is decomposed into $\mathbf{QQ}^L$:

$$C_{\alpha\alpha} = QQ^T \tag{11}$$

where **Q** is a lower triangular matrix. Then, it can be shown that the random vector $\alpha$ is expressable as

$$\alpha = QZ \tag{12}$$

This method does not permit truncation of the **Z** vector, however.

SOLUTION BY PERTURBATION METHOD ($\varepsilon$ METHOD)

The stochastic finite element method for static problems based on the perturbation technique has been developed by several researchers. All these techniques are basically the same, although the work by Hisada and Nakagiri (1981 and 1985) is well-organized and covers a wide range of structural and mechanical problems. The application of the perturbation method to static problems is briefly described here following Hisada and Nakagiri's notation.

The equation of equilibrium is represented by

$$\mathbf{KU} = \mathbf{F} \tag{13}$$

and the stiffness matrix **K** involves the random variables $\alpha_i$ (i=1,2,...,N) which represent the spatial variation of the material properties. **K** can be expanded in the following form with the assumption that each $\alpha_i$ is small enough and has zero-mean

$$\mathbf{K} = \mathbf{K}^0 + \sum_{i=1}^{N} \mathbf{K}_i^I \alpha_i + \frac{1}{2} \sum_{i=1}^{N} \sum_{j=1}^{N} \mathbf{K}_{ij}^{II} \alpha_i \alpha_j + \cdots\cdot \tag{14}$$

in which N is the number of random variables, $\mathbf{K}^0$ is the stiffness matrix evaluated at $\boldsymbol{\alpha} = [\alpha_1\ \alpha_2\ \ldots.\ \alpha_n]^T = \mathbf{0}$: and

$$\mathbf{K}_i^I = \left.\frac{\partial \mathbf{K}}{\partial \alpha_i}\right|_{\boldsymbol{\alpha}=\mathbf{0}} \qquad \mathbf{K}_{ij}^{II} = \left.\frac{\partial^2 \mathbf{K}}{\partial \alpha_i \partial \alpha_j}\right|_{\boldsymbol{\alpha}=\mathbf{0}} \tag{15}$$

The unknown displacement vector $\mathbf{U}$ is also assumed to be expanded in a similar form as

$$\mathbf{U} = \mathbf{U}^0 + \sum_{i=1}^{n} \mathbf{U}_i^I \alpha_i + \frac{1}{2} \sum_{i=1}^{n} \sum_{j=1}^{n} \mathbf{U}_{ij}^{II} \alpha_i \alpha_j + \cdots\cdot \tag{16}$$

in which the coefficient vectors $\mathbf{U}^0$, $\mathbf{U}_i^I$ and $\mathbf{U}_{ij}^{II}$ can be represented by the following set of recursive equations

$$\mathbf{U}^0 = (\mathbf{K}^0)^{-1}\mathbf{F} \tag{17}$$

$$\mathbf{U}_i^I = -(\mathbf{K}^0)^{-1}(\mathbf{K}_i^I \mathbf{U}^0) \tag{18}$$

$$\mathbf{U}_{ij}^{II} = -(\mathbf{K}^0)^{-1}(\mathbf{K}_i^I \mathbf{U}_j^I + \mathbf{K}_j^I \mathbf{U}_i^I + \mathbf{K}_{ij}^{II} \mathbf{U}^0) \tag{19}$$

The strain and stress of the e-th element are calculated using $\mathbf{u}_e$, a part of the solution vector $\mathbf{U}$ related to the e-th element. In fact, utilizing the standard finite element technique, the strain-displacement relationship is described as

$$\boldsymbol{\varepsilon}_e = \mathbf{B}_e \mathbf{u}_e \tag{20}$$

where $\mathbf{B}_e$ is the matrix which is determined by the assumed shape functions and geometric conditions of an element and does not involve randomness of the material properties. Hence, the strain vector for the e-th element $\boldsymbol{\varepsilon}_e = [\varepsilon_{xxe}\ \varepsilon_{yye}\ \varepsilon_{xye}]^T$ can be written as

$$\boldsymbol{\varepsilon}_e = \boldsymbol{\varepsilon}_e^0 + \sum_{i=1}^{n} \boldsymbol{\varepsilon}_{ie}^I \alpha_i + \frac{1}{2} \sum_{i=1}^{n} \sum_{j=1}^{n} \boldsymbol{\varepsilon}_{ije}^{II} \alpha_i \alpha_j + \cdots\cdot \tag{21}$$

with the relationship

$$\boldsymbol{\varepsilon}_e^0 = \mathbf{B}_e \mathbf{U}_e^0 \qquad \boldsymbol{\varepsilon}_{ie}^I = \mathbf{B}_e \mathbf{U}_{ie}^I \qquad \boldsymbol{\varepsilon}_{ije}^{II} = \mathbf{B}_e \mathbf{U}_{ije}^{II} \tag{22}$$

where $\mathbf{U}_e^0$, $\mathbf{U}_{ie}^I$ and $\mathbf{U}_{ije}^{II}$ are the appropriate sub-vectors of $\mathbf{U}^0$, $\mathbf{U}_j^I$, $\mathbf{U}_{ij}^{II}$, respectively.

The stress vector for the e-th element $\boldsymbol{\sigma}_e = [\sigma_{xxe}\ \sigma_{yye}\ \sigma_{xye}]^T$ is then represented by the stress-strain relationship

$$\boldsymbol{\sigma}_e = \mathbf{D}_e \boldsymbol{\varepsilon}_e \tag{23}$$

where $\mathbf{D}_e$ is the elasticity matrix of the e-th element and can be represented in series form using the random variable of the e-th element, $\alpha_e$, as

$$\mathbf{D}_e = \mathbf{D}_e^0 + \mathbf{D}_e^I \alpha_e + \frac{1}{2} \mathbf{D}_{ee}^{II} \alpha_e^2 + \cdots \tag{24}$$

where $\mathbf{D}_e^0$ is the elasticity matrix evaluated at $\alpha_e = 0$, $\mathbf{D}_e^I$ and $\mathbf{D}_{ee}^{II}$ are such that

$$\mathbf{D}_e^I = \left.\frac{\partial \mathbf{D}_e}{\partial \alpha_e}\right|_{\alpha_e=0} \qquad \mathbf{D}_{ee}^{II} = \left.\frac{\partial^2 \mathbf{D}_e}{\partial \alpha_e^2}\right|_{\alpha_e=0} \tag{25}$$

Introducing Eqs. 21 and 24 into Eq. 23, $\boldsymbol{\sigma}_e$ is obtained as

$$\boldsymbol{\sigma}_e = \boldsymbol{\sigma}_e^0 + \sum_{i=1}^{n} \boldsymbol{\sigma}_{ie}^I \alpha_i + \frac{1}{2} \sum_{i=1}^{n} \sum_{j=1}^{n} \boldsymbol{\sigma}_{ije}^{II} \alpha_i \alpha_j + \cdots \tag{26}$$

with the relationship

$$\boldsymbol{\sigma}_e^0 = \mathbf{D}_e^0 \boldsymbol{\varepsilon}_e^0 \qquad \boldsymbol{\sigma}_{ie}^I = \mathbf{D}_e^0 \boldsymbol{\varepsilon}_{ie}^I + \delta_{ie} \mathbf{D}_e^I \boldsymbol{\varepsilon}_e^0$$

$$\boldsymbol{\sigma}_{ije}^{II} = \mathbf{D}_e^0 \boldsymbol{\varepsilon}_{ije}^{II} + 2\delta_{je} \mathbf{D}_e^I \boldsymbol{\varepsilon}_{ie}^I + \delta_{ie} \delta_{je} \mathbf{D}_{ee}^{II} \boldsymbol{\varepsilon}_e^0$$

in which $\delta_{ie}$ and $\delta_{je}$ denote Kronecker's deltas.

One of the purposes of the stochastic finite element method is to evaluate first and second moments (expected values and covariances) of the response. The first-order approximation for the displacement is obtained by truncating the right-hand side of Eq. 16 after the second term as

$$\mathbf{U} = \mathbf{U}^0 + \sum_{i=1}^{n} \mathbf{U}_i^I \alpha_i \tag{27}$$

with expected value

$$E^1[\mathbf{U}] = \mathbf{U}^0 \tag{28}$$

and covariance matrix

$$\mathrm{Cov}^1[\mathbf{U},\mathbf{U}] = E\left[\{\mathbf{U} - E^1[\mathbf{U}]\}\{\mathbf{U} - E^1[\mathbf{U}]\}^T\right] = \sum_{i=1}^{n} \sum_{j=1}^{n} \mathbf{U}_i^I (\mathbf{U}_j^I)^T E[\alpha_i \alpha_j] \tag{29}$$

The second-order approximation for the displacement is obtained by truncating the right-hand side of Eq. 16 after the third term as

$$\mathbf{U} = \mathbf{U}^0 + \sum_{i=1}^{n} \mathbf{U}_i^I \alpha_i + \frac{1}{2} \sum_{i=1}^{n} \sum_{j=1}^{n} \mathbf{U}_{ij}^{II} \alpha_i \alpha_j \tag{30}$$

with expected value

$$E^2[\mathbf{U}] = E^1[\mathbf{U}] + \frac{1}{2} \sum_{i=1}^{n} \sum_{j=1}^{n} \mathbf{U}_{ij}^{II} E[\alpha_i \alpha_j] \tag{31}$$

and covariance matrix

$$\mathrm{Cov}^2[\mathbf{U},\mathbf{U}] = \mathrm{Cov}^1[\mathbf{U},\mathbf{U}] + \tag{32}$$

$$+ \frac{1}{4} \sum_{i=1}^{n} \sum_{j=1}^{n} \sum_{k=1}^{n} \sum_{\ell=1}^{n} \mathbf{U}_{ij}^{II}(\mathbf{U}_{k\ell}^{II})^T \{E[\alpha_i\alpha_\ell]E[\alpha_j\alpha_k] + E[\alpha_i\alpha_k]E[\alpha_j\alpha_\ell]\} \tag{33}$$

In the process of obtaining $\mathrm{Cov}^2[\mathbf{U},\mathbf{U}]$ or $\mathrm{Var}^2[\mathbf{U}]$, the following well-known relationship of Gaussian random variables is used.

$$E[\alpha_i\alpha_j\alpha_k] = 0 \tag{34a}$$

$$E[\alpha_i\alpha_j\alpha_k\alpha_\ell] = E[\alpha_i\alpha_j]E[\alpha_k\alpha_\ell] + E[\alpha_i\alpha_\ell]E[\alpha_j\alpha_k] + E[\alpha_i\alpha_k]E[\alpha_j\alpha_\ell] \tag{34b}$$

If the α's are not Gaussian, those higher-order moments must be determined by other methods.

The equations for evaluating the first- and second-order moments of the displacement are equally applied to obtain the first- and second-order moments of the strains and stresses just by replacing $\mathbf{U}^0$, $\mathbf{U}_i^I$, $\mathbf{U}_{ij}^{II}$ respectively with $\boldsymbol{\varepsilon}_e^0$, $\boldsymbol{\varepsilon}_{ie}^I$, $\boldsymbol{\varepsilon}_{ije}^{II}$ or with $\boldsymbol{\sigma}_e^0$, $\boldsymbol{\sigma}_{ie}^I$, $\boldsymbol{\sigma}_{ije}^{II}$ because of the identical forms of Eqs. 16, 21 and 26.

SOLUTION BY NEUMANN EXPANSION METHOD (Δ METHOD)

The equilibrium equation formulated by the finite element method can obviously be solved by taking the inverse of the stiffness matrix as

$$\mathbf{U} = \mathbf{K}^{-1}\mathbf{F} \tag{35}$$

However, it is well known that matrix inversions require a large amount of CPU time. Also, $\mathbf{K}^{-1}$ is no longer banded, although $\mathbf{K}$ is usually narrowly banded. Hence, the multiplication on the right-hand side of Eq. 35 cannot be performed efficiently if the number of degrees of freedom is large.

The alternative way to solve Eq. 13 directly is to first take the Cholesky decomposition of $\mathbf{K}$ and obtain the lower triangular matrix L as

$$L\, L^T = \mathbf{K} \tag{36}$$

and then to solve the following equations for the unknown $\mathbf{X}$ and $\mathbf{U}$ in turn.

$$L\mathbf{X} = \mathbf{F} \qquad\qquad L^T\mathbf{U} = \mathbf{X} \tag{37}$$

It is important to note that, since the lower triangular matrix L preserves the same bandwidth as $\mathbf{K}$, $\mathbf{X}$ and $\mathbf{U}$ can be solved from Eq. 37 very efficiently.

Under the assumption that $\mathbf{K}$ contains parameters which are subject to spatial variabilities, decompose $\mathbf{K}$ into two matrices,

$$\mathbf{K} = \mathbf{K}_0 + \Delta\mathbf{K} \tag{38}$$

where $\mathbf{K}_0$ represents the stiffness matrix in which the spatially varying parameters are replaced by their representative values and $\Delta\mathbf{K}$ consists of the components representing deviatoric parts of the corresponding components in $\mathbf{K}$: $\Delta\mathbf{K} = \mathbf{K} - \mathbf{K}_0$. The solution $\mathbf{U}_0$ which corresponds to $\mathbf{K}_0$ can be obtained as

$$\mathbf{K}_0\mathbf{U}_0 = \mathbf{F} \qquad \text{or} \qquad \mathbf{U}_0 = \mathbf{K}_0^{-1}\mathbf{F} \tag{39}$$

The Neumann expansion of $\mathbf{K}^{-1}$ takes the following form

$$\mathbf{K}^{-1} = (\mathbf{K}_0+\Delta\mathbf{K})^{-1} = (\mathbf{I} - \mathbf{P} + \mathbf{P}^2 - \mathbf{P}^3 + \cdots\cdot)\mathbf{K}_0^{-1} \tag{40}$$

in which $\mathbf{P} = \mathbf{K}_0^{-1}\Delta\mathbf{K}$. Introducing Eq. 40 into Eq. 35 and using Eq. 39, the solution vector $\mathbf{U}$ is represented by the following series as

$$\mathbf{U} = \mathbf{U}_0 - \mathbf{P}\mathbf{U}_0 + \mathbf{P}^2\mathbf{U}_0 - \mathbf{P}^3\mathbf{U}_0 + \cdots\cdot = \mathbf{U}_0 - \mathbf{U}_1 + \mathbf{U}_2 - \mathbf{U}_3 + \cdots\cdot \tag{41}$$

This series solution is equivalent to the following recursive equation

$$\mathbf{K}_0\mathbf{U}_i = \Delta\mathbf{K}\mathbf{U}_{i-1} \qquad (i=1,2,\ldots) \tag{42}$$

Thus, once the Cholesky decomposition of $\mathbf{K}_0$ is obtained as $\mathbf{L}_0\mathbf{L}_0^T = \mathbf{K}_0$, and once $\mathbf{U}_0$ is obtained using the algorithm represented by Eq. 37, then the same algorithm can be used to obtain $\mathbf{U}_i$ iteratively with the aid of Eq. 42. The expansion series in Eq. 41 may be terminated after a few terms if convergence of the series is numerically confirmed.

The most outstanding feature of this approach in the case of the Monte Carlo simulation for the spatial variation of material properties is that the matrix factorization is only required once for all samples, and the rest of the computational process can fully utilize the banded characteristic of $\Delta\mathbf{K}$ and $\mathbf{L}_0$. Therefore, the computational time and costs may be reduced considerably.

It is well known that the Neumann expansion shown in Eq. 41 converges if the absolute values of all the eigenvalues of the product $\mathbf{K}_0^{-1}\Delta\mathbf{K}$ are less than 1. However, this convergence criterion can be easily met irrespective of how large in absolute value each component of the deviation matrix $\Delta\mathbf{K}$ is in comparison with the corresponding component of $\mathbf{K}$. For the details of this statement, the reader is referred to Yamazaki, Shinozuka and Dasgupta (1986b).

It is important to note that first-order and second-order approximations for the expected values and variances of response quantities similar to those obtained from the perturbation method can also be obtained within the context of the Δ method (Shinozuka and Dasgupta, 1986). These approximations based on the Δ method involve lengthy but straightforward algebra. An example of a first-order approximation based on the Δ method was presented by Deodatis and Shinozuka (1986a) in evaluating the response variability of a prismatic bar due to material property variation.

## NUMERICAL EXAMPLES

A computer program was developed by which the response variability due to material property variation can be estimated. This program estimates the expected value and standard deviation of the response by means of Monte Carlo techniques. In doing so, two different Monte Carlo methods are used for the solution: the direct method uses Eq. 35, while the Neumann expansion method uses the iterative scheme in the form of Eq. 42. A number of sample global stiffness matrices are constructed on the basis of sample stochastic fields generated by means of Eq. 9. Then, the direct Monte Carlo solution (direct M.C.S.) is obtained using Eq. 35 repeatedly, each time employing one of the sample global stiffness matrices and taking statistics on the resulting response quantities. On the other hand, the simulation method based on the Neumann expansion, referred to as the Neumann expansion Monte Carlo simulation (expansion M.C.S.) uses Eq. 42 for Monte Carlo purposes. Another program based on the perturbation method, which involves first- and second-order perturbation approximations, is also developed. Numerical examples are presented here in order to examine the accuracy and efficienty of these methods.

The finite element model shown in Fig. 1 is adopted as an example. The particular structural geometry and loading conditions are chosen so that the response variability can be clearly highlighted by the material property variability. The model consists of 100 plane-stress square finite elements with

121 nodes. Nodal displacements in the y-direction are constrained along the lower edge and the nodal displacements in both directions are constrained at the lower left corner node. Under these boundary conditions, the number of degrees-of-freedom (DOF) of this structural system is 230. A uniformly distributed load is applied along the upper edge.

In the following, it is assumed that Young's modulus E(x,y) is truncated Gaussian and the deviatoric component $\alpha(x,y)E_0$ is introduced so that

$$E(x,y) = E_0[1 + \alpha(x,y)] \tag{43}$$

where $E_0$ is the expected value of E(x,y). Obviously, the expected value of $\alpha(x,y)$ is zero and its standard deviation $\sigma_\alpha$ represents the coefficient of variation of E(x,y). As mentioned earlier, each element size is made so small that E(x,y) and hence $\alpha(x,y)$ are considered constant within each element, being equal to $E_e$ and $\alpha_e$, respectively. For example,

$$E_e = E(x_e^c, y_e^c) \qquad \alpha_e = \alpha(x_e^c, y_e^c) \tag{44}$$

where $x_e^c$ and $y_e^c$ are the x and y coordinates of the centroid of element e. Then

$$E_e = E_0(1 + \alpha_e) \tag{45}$$

where $\alpha_e$ is assumed to be truncated Gaussian with mean zero defined over the following domain of $\alpha_e$

$$-1 < \alpha_e < 1 \tag{46}$$

The stochastic field $\alpha_0(x,y)$ is introduced and assumed to be homogeneous and Gaussian and characterized by the following spectral density with $d = d_x = d_y = 2.0$ and $\sigma_0$ = = standard deviation of $\alpha_0(x,y)$.

$$S_{\alpha_0\alpha_0}(\kappa_x,\kappa_y) = \sigma_0^2 \frac{d_x d_y}{4\pi} \exp\{-[(\frac{d_x\kappa_x}{2})^2 + (\frac{d_y\kappa_y}{2})^2]\} \tag{47}$$

Our experience indicates that the element size in Fig. 1 is considered to be small enough in view of the fact that d = 2.0 in this case; the element size is one-half the scale of correlation (Harada and Shinozuka, 1986). The question of "in what sense is it small enough" is an important matter to be studied as was done by Shinozuka and Deodatis (1986). As mentioned earlier, however, the major concern of the present study is to examine the accuracy of the various analytical and numerical methods of variability prediction. Thus, once the random field is discretized in the manner indicated above, the accuracy problem can be dealt with as an issue separate from that of the mesh size.

Discretization of the stochastic field and digital generation of sample fields were done in this study with the aid of Eq. 9 while the field was characterized by Eq. 47. Note also that only those sample fields that satisfy Eq. 46 for all the elements were used for the Monte Carlo analysis. These are the sample functions associated with the truncated Gaussian field $\alpha(x,y)$. The quantity $\sigma_0$ in Eq. 47 is closer to $\sigma_\alpha$, if it is smaller.

The results of the numerical example will be shown at locations where large output values are expected, i.e., node 121 for displacements $U_y$ and element 96 for strain $\varepsilon_{yy}$.

In Fig. 2, the standard deviation of $\varepsilon_{yy}$ is shown to increase linearly when estimated by the first-order perturbation method. This represents a considerable underestimation of the standard deviation, which can be only slightly improved by the implementation of the second-order perturbation approximation as also observed in Fig. 2. This result obtained from the second-order perturbation approximation is disappointing, particularly because it requires an enormous amount of computational time as well as memory space. In contrast to the results provided by the perturbation methods, the standard deviation estimated by the Monte Carlo methods is shown in Fig. 2 to have an accelerated rate of increase as $\sigma_0$ increases. When the direct M.C.S. method is used, the estimated standard deviation is somewhat larger than that estimated by the expansion M.C.S. method, most notably when $\sigma_0$ is larger than 0.2. Obviously, these two results can be made closer if we use a higher-order Neumann expansion at the expense of additional computer time.

It is observed in Fig. 2 that the perturbation methods, whether first- or second-order, underestimate the response variability for large values of $\sigma_0$ for which such a response variability analysis is particularly significant. It is important to note that this result is consistent with the earlier results as demonstrated, for example, by Shinozuka and Astill (1972).

Referring to the CPU time, Table 1 compares the CPU time on a Vax 11/750 in estimating the expected value and standard deviation for all the response quantities (displacement vector as well as stress and strain tensors). The direct M.C.S. method requires more time than the expansion M.C.S. method does. How much more, however, depends on many factors including the order of expansion, variability of input ($\sigma_0$), desired level of accuracy, number of DOF of the system, and bandwidth of the stiffness matrix. In the present example, the convergence of each sample solution in the expansion M.C.S. is considered to have been attained if the relative increment of the nodal displacement is less than or equal to 1% at all nodes. This criterion requires third-order expansion for the expansion M.C.S. method on the average. On the basis of counting the number of units of add-multiply operations involved in the algorithm mentioned earlier, it can be shown that, if the order of the Neumann expansion is fixed and not too large, the expansion method will be more advantageous in terms of CPU time, as the number of DOF increases; For example, the ratio of CPU time required for the expansion M.C.S. method to that for the direct M.C.S. method is of the order of 1/50, when the sample size = 100, the order of expansion = 3, the number of DOF = 10,000 and the bandwidth = 1,000 ~ 2,500 (Deodatis, 1985).

Table 1 also indicates that the first-order perturbation method requires the least amount of CPU time, as expected. However, the second-order perturbation approximation, even for only one element, reuqires by far the greatest amount of CPU time, suggesting tha this approximation method is quite impractical.

The response variability when 1/E, log E or $\nu$ is considered to form a homogeneous Gaussian field is estimated by Yamazaki, Shinozuka and Dasgupta (1986a). In these cases, the agreement among the response variabilities estimated by the four methods mentioned above is much better than the case when E itself is a stochastic field. In fact, the agreement is good even when the coefficient of variation of 1/E, log E or $\nu$ is relatively large. Therefore, for the Gaussian variability of 1/E, log E or $\nu$, the first-order perturbation method is found to be quite efficient. The reader is reminded that the strain $\varepsilon_{yy}$ distributes as Gaussian in approximation when 1/E is a Gaussian field. It can also be demonstrated that the same is true when log E or $\nu$ is a Gaussian field. This is the reason for the first-order perturbation method working fairly well under those conditions. Even in these cases, however, it is necessary to perform a direct or expansion M.C.S. at least once for each problem, in order to verify the accuracy of the perturbation analysis.

SOME BASIC ISSUES

Some basic analytical and numerical issues of stochastic finite element analysis that have not been adequately addressed above are considered here.

(a) SIZE OF FINITE ELEMENTS. Comparison of the analytical solution for stochastic field problems for one-dimensional structures (Shinozuka, 1986 and Bucher and Shinozuka, 1986) with the finite element solution (Shinozuka and Deodatis, 1986) confirms the earlier statement that if the finite element size is much smaller than the scale of corelation, the size may be considered small enough. Rigorously speaking, however, whether or not the same conclusion applies to two-dimensional structures remains to be seen (Harada and Shinozuka, 1986).

(b) NON-GAUSSIANESS. If the underlying stochastic field and hence $\boldsymbol{\alpha}$ exhibit homogeneous but non-Gaussian characteristics, the simulation technique developed by Yamazaki and Shinozuka (1986) can be used for discretization of the stochastic fields and generation of $\boldsymbol{\alpha}$. The technique requires knowledge of the one-dimensional distribution fucntion and the power spectral density function of the non-Gaussian field.

(c) DYNAMIC AND NONLINEAR RESPONSE ANALYSES. The iterative algorithm demonstrated in conjunction with the $\Delta$-method is perfectly suitable for dynamic and nonlinear response analyses involving stochastic fields. Within each increment of time or load, the iterative algorithm can be used to solve the problem incrementally with numerical efficiency.

(d) STRUCTURAL RELIABILITY ASSESSMENT. The structural response variability due to material property variations can be evaluated in terms of such quantities as expected values and variances of the response with the aid of the methods considered in this paper and elsewhere. Knowledge of these quantities certainly paves the way towards the reliability assessment of structures. It is recognized, however, that these quantities are obtained under various assumptions. Further assumptions needed for tractability of the reliability analysis may necessitate careful interpretation of the results. For example, a reliability assessment based on a linear structural analysis may be meaningful only for those less significant limit states that do not cause real concern over structural safety. At this time, it appears, real safety issues can be adequately dealt with only by Monte Carlo simulation methods with the aid of the iterative algorithm indicated in (a), when material property variation is involved.

(e) ONE-DIMENSIONAL STRUCTURES (Bucher and Shinozuka, 1986). One-dimensional and generally staticaly indeterminate structures such as rigid frames are considered. For the analysis of these structures, statically indeterminate forces are introduced in order to satisfy the boundary conditions. These statically indeterminate forces can be written in the form of integrals where the integrands involve stochastic fields representing the material property variations. Choosing the simplest case for the purpose of illustration, the deflection of w(x) of a beam of span length L having one degree of statical indeterminancy, with a fixed end on one side and a simple support on the other can be written, under uniform load p, as

$$w(x) = w_0(x) - \frac{w_0(L)}{w_1(L)} w_1(x) = X_1 - \frac{X_2}{X_4} X_3 \tag{48}$$

where

$$w_0(x) = \frac{p}{2E_0 I} \int_0^x (x-\bar{x})(L-\bar{x})^2[1+\alpha(\bar{x})]d\bar{x} \tag{49}$$

and

$$w_1(x) = -\frac{1}{E_0 I}\int_0^x (x-\bar{x})(L-\bar{x})[1+\alpha(\bar{x})]d\bar{x} \tag{50}$$

In order to derive these equations, however, an assumption is made that the flexibility $1/E(x)$, rather than Young's modulus $E(x)$, is interpreted as constituting a stochastic field in such a way that

$$\frac{1}{E(x)} = f(x) = \frac{1}{E_0}[1+\alpha(x)] \tag{51}$$

where $1/E_0$ is the expected value of $1/E(x)$.

The most important point, however, is that $w(x)$ can now be written as a function of random variables $X_1 = w_0(x)$, $X_2 = w_0(L)$, $X_3 = w_1(x)$ and $X_4 = w_1(L)$. This interpretation provides various new avenues of analysis for structural response variability estimation arising from spatial material property variation. For example, if the reliability is to be estimated, the various mathematical methods developed so far by numerous researchers for finding the limit state probability can be used directly, since usually these methods can only handle limit state conditions expressed in terms of random variables. Obviously, in engaging in such an analytical exercise, the comments made in (d) above must be remembered.

(f) COMPARISON OF EFFECT OF MATERIAL PROPERTY VARIATION ON RESPONSE VARIABILITY WITH THAT ARISING FROM RANDOMNESS OF LOADING CONDITIONS. One-dimensional structures such as those considered in (e) above allow, with considerable ease, comparison of the effect of material property variation on structural response variability with that arising from some type of random loading conditions. For example, if p in Eq. 49 is interpreted as random in such a way that

$$p(x) = qp_D(x) \tag{52}$$

where $q$ is a random variable and $p_D(x)$ a deterministic function of $x$. Then

$$w(x) = qw_D(x) \tag{53}$$

in which $w_D(x)$ is the deflection due to the deterministic loading $p_D(x)$. Considering the spatial variation of the elastic properties of the beam, both the quantities $q$ and $w_D(x)$ in Eq. 53 are random variables. Since their randomness pertains to different physical quantities, $q$ and $w_D(x)$ are assumed to be statistically independent. Hence the statistical moments of $w(x)$ may be easily obtained once the respective moments of $q$ and $w_D(x)$ are known. Eventually, the coefficient of variation $V_w$ of $w(x)$ is found to be given in terms of $V_q$ and $V_{w_D}$ (coefficients of variation of $q$ and $w_D$, respectively):

$$V_w^2 = V_{w_D}^2 + V_q^2 + V_{w_D}^2 V_q^2 \tag{54}$$

If $V_q$ is considerably larger than $V_{w_D}$, then the coefficient of variation of the deflection $V_w$ will hardly be influenced by $V_{w_D}$, i.e.,

$$V_w \doteq V_q \qquad \text{if } V_q >> V_{w_D} \tag{55}$$

Similar conclusions can be obtained for two- and three-dimensional structures.

CONCLUSION

The applicability of the perturbation and Neumann expansion techniques to, and their numerical efficiency in, stochastic finite element analysis were reviewed. It was pointed out that the perturbation technique is the least time-consuming when the first-order approximation is made, which, however, may not provide adequate accuracy for the solution, particularly when the material property variation is of considerable magnitude. The second-order perturbation approximation is impractical because of the unrealistic amount of computational time required and at the same time because of the disappointing level of improvement it produces over the first-order approximation. This conclusion is primarily based on the assumption that the rigidity (Young's modulus) forms a (truncated) Gaussian stochastic field. However, when the flexibility (inverse of Young's modulus) and Poisson's ratio are considered to form Gaussian stochastic fields, the first-order perturbation approximation provides substantially better results (Yamazaki, Shinozuka and Dasgupta, 1986a).

The Neumann expansion method was also used in conjunction with the Monte Carlo solution technique for the estimation of structural response variability. The iterative algorithm used to upgrade the solution recursively was found to be highly efficient in the Monte Carlo simulation environment. The algorithm is essential for response variability estimation under dynamic and nonlinear conditions. It was pointed out that the Neumann expansion method becomes more efficient than the direct Monte Carlo simulation method as the number of degrees of freedom associated with the finite element system increases.

Comments and suggestions were also made on the following issues: finite element size, non-Gaussianess of stochastic fields, structural reliability assessment, reducibility of stochastic field problems to random variable problems for one-dimensional structures, and comparison of the effect of material property variation on structural response variability with that arising from randomness in loading conditions.

ACKNOWLEDGEMENT

This work was partially supported by NSF Grant No. ECE-85-15249 and partially by Sub-contract No. NCEER-86-3033 under the auspices of the National Center for Earthquake Engineering Research under NSF Grant No. ECE-86-07591

REFERENCES

Astill, C.J., B. Nosseir, and M. Shinozuka (1972). "Impact Loading on Structures with Random Properties," Journal of Structural Mechanics, 1, 1, 63-77.

Baecher, G.B. and T.S. Ingra (1981). "Stochastic FEM in Settlement Predictions," Journal of the Geotechnical Engineering Division, ASCE, 107, GT4, 449-463.

Bucher, C. and M. Shinozuka (1986). "Structural Response Variability II," Technical Report, Department of Civil Engineering and Engineering Mechanics, Columbia University.

Deodatis, G. (1985). "Number of Operations Required for the Solution of Linear Systems: Comparison of Direct and Expansion Methods," Technical Report, Department of Civil Engineering and Engineering Mechanics, Columbia University.

Der Kiureghian, A. (1985). "Finite Element Methods in Structural Safety Studies," Proceedings of the Structural Safety Studies Symposium in conjunction with the ASCE Convention in Denver, Colorado.

Gambou, B. (1971). "Application of First-Order Uncertainty Analysis in the Finite Element Method in Linear Elasticity," Proceedings of the 2nd International Conference on Applications of Statistics and Probability in Soil and Structural Enginering.

Handa, K. and K. Andersson (1981). "Application of Finite Element Methods in the Statistical Analysis of Structures," Proceedings of the 3rd ICOSSAR, pp. 409-417.

Harada, T. and M. Shinozuka (1986). "The Scale of Correlation for Stochastic Fields," Technical Report, Department of Civil Engineering and Engineering Mechanics, Columbia University.

Hisada, T. and S. Nakagiri (1981). "Stochastic Finite Element Method Developed for Structural Safety and Reliability," Proceedings of the 3rd ICOSSAR, pp. 395-408.

Hisada, T. and S. Nakagiri (1985). "Role of the Stochastic Finite Element Method in Structural Safety and Reliability," Proceedings of the 4th ICOSSAR, pp. 385-394.

Liu, W-K., T. Belytschko and A. Mani (1985). "A Computational Method for the Determination of the Probabilistic Distribution of the Dynamic Response of Structures," ASME PVP-98-5, 243-248.

Shinozuka, M. (1985). "Stochastic Fields and Their Digital Simulation," Lecture Notes for the CISM Course on Stochastic Methods in Structural Mechanics, Udine, Italy.

Shinozuka, M. and C.J. Astill (1972). "Random Eigenvalue Problems in Structural Mechanics," AIAA Journal, 10, 4, 456-462.

Shinozuka, M. and C-M. Jan (1972). "Digital Simulation of Random Processes and Its Applications," Journal of Sound and Vibration, 25, 1, 111-128.

Shinozuka, M. and G. Deodatis (1986). "Response Variability of Stochastic Finite Element Systems," Technical Report, Department of Civil Engineering and Engineering Mechanics, Columbia University.

Shinozuka, M. and G. Dasgupta (1986). "Stochastic Finite Element Methods in Dynamics," Keynote Lecture, in G.C. Hart and R.B. Nelson (Eds.), Proceedings of the 3rd ASCE EMD Specialty Conference on Dynamic Response of Structures, University of California at Los Angeles, pp. 44-54.

Vanmarcke, E. and M. Grigoriu (1983). "Stochastic Finite Element Analysis of Simple Beams," Journal of the Structural Division, ASCE, 109, 5, 1203-1214.

Yamazaki, F. and M. Shinozuka (1986). "Digital Simulation of Non-Gaussian Stochastic Fields," Technical Report, Department of Civil Engineering and Engineering Mechanics, Columbia University.

Yamazaki, F. and M. Shinozuka (1987). "Safety Evaluation of Stochastic Systems by Monte Carlo Simulation," to appear in the Proceedings of the 9th SMiRT, Lausanne, Switzerland.

Yamazaki, F., M. Shinozuka and G. Dasgupta (1986a). "Structural Response Variability Due to Material Property Variations," Technical Report, Department of Civil Engineering and Engineering Mechanics, Columbia University.

Yamazaki, F., M. Shinozuka and G. Dasgupta (1986b). "Neumann Expansion for Stochastic Finite Element Analysis," Technical Report, Department of Civil Engineering and Engineering Mechanics, Columbia University; to appear in the Journal of Engineering Mechanics, ASCE.

Table 1 Comparison of CPU time (230 DOF Model)

Computer : VAX/VMS 11/750 $\sigma_0$=0.30

| Monte Carlo Simulation ( sample size = 100 ) | | Perturbation Method | |
|---|---|---|---|
| Direct Method | Expansion Method | 1st-order Approx. | 2nd-order Approx. |
| 00:15:05 | 00:09:01 (1st)<br>00:10:10 (2nd)<br>00:11:19 (3rd) | 00:03:58 | 04:46:09 for One Element |

( hr : min : sec )

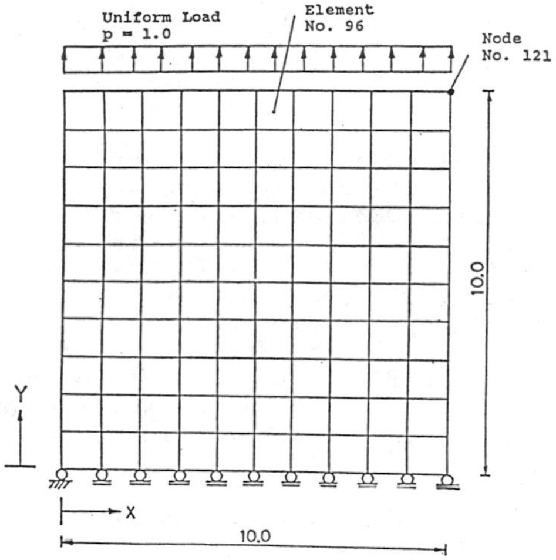


Fig. 1 Finite Element Model with 100 Elements

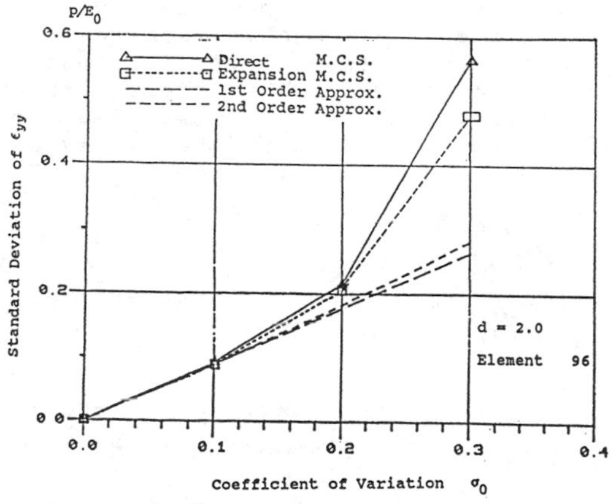


Fig. 2 Comparison of Standard Deviation of $\epsilon_{yy}$ (Variation of E)

# TIME-VARIANT COMPONENT RELIABILITIES BY FORM-SORM AND UPDATING BY IMPORTANCE SAMPLING

M.Fujita, G.Schall and R.Rackwitz
Technical University of Munich

ABSTRACT
The methods to compute failure probabilities based on the upcrossing approach for structural components where a part of the basic uncertainties is presented by a stationary and ergodic Gaussian vector process is reviewed. It is demonstrated that for a consistent application of the concepts one needs two alternate algorithms. Updating of those results by importance sampling is proposed so that arbitrarily accurate results can also be obtained in the non-asymptotic case. A numerical example is given.

## INTRODUCTION

The theory and the numerical methods of time-variant reliability of structures and their components appear to be well developed due to the advances in first-order (FORM) and second-order (SORM) reliability methods and the recently proposed updating procedures by importance sampling (Breitung, 1984, Hohenbichler et al. 1985, Hohenbichler/Rackwitz, 1986). Much less developed are both theory and numerics when part of the uncertainty vector must be modelled by a vector process. Even if one restricts the class of random vector processes to ergodic and differentiable Gaussian vector processes the results are limited, i.e. when using the well-known outcrossing approach only an upper bound and an asymptotic formula for the failure probability in terms of the conditional crossing rate of the process out of the domain of safe structural states is known. On the other hand, the presence of some Gaussian processes and other time-invariant variables is just the cse which frequently is met in practical applications, for example, in wind, bridge, earthquake and ocean engineering where the loading that is wind, waves, ground accelerations, vehicles respectively, and their load effects can well be represented by Gaussian vector processes while the system properties (stiffnesses, geometrical quantities, resistances) are modelled by random vectors with given distribution function.
In this paper the well-known FORM/SORM concepts are extended to include an importance sampling update for time-variant reliability problems as described before. With this update highly accurate results can be obtained within the theoretical concept.

## 2. Time-variant failure probabilities

Let $\underline{Y} = (Y_1,\dots,Y_n)^T$ be the vector of time-invariant random variables with distribution function $F_{\underline{Y}}(\underline{y})$ and

$\underline{X}(\tau) = (X_{n+1}(\tau),\dots,X_m(\tau))^T$ be a stationary and ergodic Gaussian vector process with mean $\underline{m}_{\underline{X}}$ and covariance function

$\underline{\underline{C}}_{\underline{X}}(\theta)$ $(\theta=|\tau_1-\tau_2|)$. It is assumed that $\underline{X}(\tau)$ is stochastically independent of $\underline{Y}$ which appears reasonable in almost all applications.

Further, let $V = \{g(\underline{x},\underline{y}) \leq 0\}$ define the failure domain of a structural component with $\partial V = \{g(\underline{x},\underline{y}) = 0\}$ the failure surface separating the safe and the failure domain. Then, the following bound and asymptotic formula for the failure probability in a time interval $[0,t]$ is well known

$$P_f(t) \leq E_{\underline{Y}}[\nu^+(\underline{y})t]$$
$$\sim 1 - E_{\underline{Y}}[\exp[-\nu^+(\underline{y})t]] \qquad (1)$$

The conditional outcrossing rate $\nu^+(\underline{y})$ is given by the generalized Rice formula (Veneziano et al.,1977)

$$\nu^+(\underline{y}) = \int_{\partial G} E_o^\infty[\underline{n}^T(\underline{x},\underline{y})\dot{\underline{X}}|\underline{X}=\underline{x}]f_{\underline{X}}(\underline{x})\, ds(\underline{x}) \qquad (2)$$

where $\underline{n}(\underline{x},\underline{y})$ is the outwards directed unit normal vector at $(\underline{x},\underline{y})$ on the surface $\partial G = \partial V(\underline{x}|\underline{y})$, $X(\tau) = (X_{n+1}(\tau).....X_m(\tau))^T$ the vector derivative process of $X(\tau)$ and $f_X(\tau)$ the Gaussian probability density of $\underline{X}(\tau)$. $ds(\underline{x})$ means surface integration. For simplicity of notation, reference to $\tau$ is dropped in the sequel. While the scalar variants of formulae (1) and (2) are relatively easy to compute there are considerable difficulties when $\underline{X}$ and/or $\underline{Y}$ are multidimensional and $\partial G$ is an arbitrary surface, e.g. representing v. Mises yield criterion or some multivariate criterion of crack instability. Of course, this is due to the integrations to be performed in eq. (1) and (2). Those integrations can, however, be facilitated very much by applying FORM/SORM concepts if approximate results are sufficient. The possible error implied by these methods can be quantified by a certain importance sampling procedure if necessary.

In order to facilitate the following derivations a transformation $\underline{X}\rightarrow\underline{U}$ is performed such that $\underline{U}$ becomes a standard normal process with independent components, i.e. with $E[\underline{U}] = \underline{O}$, $\underline{\underline{C}}_{\underline{U}}(O) = \underline{\underline{R}} = \underline{\underline{I}}$, $E[\dot{\underline{U}}] = \underline{O}$, $E[\underline{U}(O)\dot{\underline{U}}^T(O)] = \dot{\underline{\underline{R}}}$ and $E[\dot{\underline{U}}(O)\dot{\underline{U}}^T(O)] = \ddot{\underline{\underline{R}}}$ (Hohenbichler/Rackwitz, 1986). Further, the Rosenblatt-transformation for $\underline{Y}$ is $\underline{Y} = \underline{T}_{\underline{Y}}(\underline{Z})$ with $\underline{Z} = (Z_1,...,Z_n)^T$ a standard normal vector. Next, we introduce the identity

$$P_f(t) = F_T(t) = 1 - E_{\underline{Z}}[\exp[-\nu^+(\underline{z})t]] = \phi(U_T) \qquad (3)$$

with $F_T(t)$ the distribution of the first-passage time T and $U_T$ an additional, auxiliary standard normal variable. It follows that eq. (3) can be written as

$$P_f(t) = \int\{T(\underline{z}) - t \leq O\}\, dF_{\underline{Z}}(\underline{z}) \qquad (4)$$

with

$$T(\underline{z}) = -\frac{1}{\nu^+(\underline{z})} \ln \phi(-U_T) \qquad (5)$$

This is precisely in the form required for FORM or SORM. Using the term in brackets in eq. (4) as the new failure domain, the failure probability can be computed from:

$$P_f(t) \approx \phi(-\beta)\ C\ K \qquad (6)$$

$\phi(-\beta)$ corresponds to the FORM-result where

$$\beta = \|\underline{z}^*\| = \min\{\|\underline{z}^*\|\} \text{ for } \{\underline{z}: g(\underline{z}) = T(\underline{z}) - t \leq 0\} \qquad (7)$$

the first-order safety index. If corrected by

$$C = \prod_{i=1}^{m} (1-\kappa_i \varphi(-\beta))^{-1/2} \qquad (8)$$

where $\varphi(-\beta) = \varphi(\beta)/\phi(-\beta)$ and $\kappa_i$ the main curvatures of $g(\underline{z}) = 0$ in $\underline{z}^*$, the SORM-result is obtained (Breitung, 1984 a). Finally, if corrected by (Hohenbichler,1984)

$$K = \frac{1}{N} \sum_{k=1}^{N} \frac{\phi(h(\underline{s}_k))}{\phi(-\beta)} \exp\left[-\frac{1}{2}\varphi(-\beta) \sum_{i=1}^{n-1} \kappa_i\ s_{ik}^2\right] \qquad (9)$$

where $h(\underline{s}_k)$ is the solution of $g(s_{1k},\ldots,s_{nk}) = 0$ with respect to $s_{nk}$, an arbitrarily exact result can be obtained by importance sampling. The $\underline{s}_k = (s_{1k},\ldots,s_{n-1,k})^T$ are independent, zero mean Gaussian variables with variance $(1-\varphi(-\beta)\kappa_i)^{-1}$ to be simulated. For simplicity of notation, we have performed an orthogonal transformatiom $\underline{z}\rightarrow\underline{s}$ such that the $\beta$-point lies on the positive $s_n$-axis and all mixed derivatives $\partial^2 g(\underline{s})/(\partial s_i \partial s_j)$ vanish (Fiessler,et al. 1979). It should be mentioned that for numerical reasons the failure criterion in eq. (4)

$$V = \{-\frac{1}{\nu^+(\underline{z})} \ln \phi(-U_T) - t \leq o\}$$

should be replaced by the equivalent criterion

$$V = \{-\ln \nu^+(\underline{z}) - \ln(-\ln \phi(-U_T)) - \ln t \leq 0\}$$

Eq. (2) now reads

$$\nu^+(\underline{z}\ ) = \int_{\partial G} E_o^{\infty}[\underline{n}^T(\underline{u},\underline{z})\dot{\underline{U}}\,|\,\underline{U}=\underline{u}]\varphi_{\underline{U}}(\underline{u})ds(\underline{u}) \qquad (10)$$

Unfortunately, very few exact results exist for eq. (10) (see, for example, Veneziano et al., 1977). However, if $\partial G$ is linearized by a hyperplane

$$\partial L = \{\underline{\alpha}^T(\underline{z})\underline{U} + \beta(\underline{z}) = 0\} \qquad (11)$$

where, as before, $\beta(\underline{z}) = -\underline{\alpha}^T(\underline{z})\underline{u}^*(\underline{z}) = \|\underline{u}(\underline{z})\|$ with $\underline{u}^*(\underline{z})$ the solution point ($\beta$-point) for which

$$\beta(\underline{z}) = \min\{\|\underline{u}(\underline{z})\|\} \text{ for } \{\underline{u} \in \partial V(\underline{u},\underline{z})\} \qquad (12)$$

and $\underline{\alpha}^T(\underline{z})$ the normalized gradient ($\|\underline{\alpha}(\underline{z})\| = 1$) of $\partial V(\underline{u},\underline{z})$ in $\underline{u}^*(\underline{z})$, the following result is exact (Ditlevsen, 1983):

$$\nu^+(\underline{z}) = \frac{(\underline{\alpha}^T(\underline{z})\ \ddot{\underline{\underline{R}}}\ \underline{\alpha}(\underline{z}))^{1/2}}{(2\pi)^{1/2}} \varphi(\beta(\underline{z})) \qquad (13)$$

Breitung (1984 b) showed that an asymptotic result for the outcrossing rate ($\beta(\underline{z}) \rightarrow \infty$) can also be derived which is given here for easy reference.

$$\nu^+(\underline{z}) = \frac{\varphi(\beta(\underline{z}))}{(2\pi)^{1/2}} \prod_{i=n+1}^{m} (1-\beta(\underline{z})\kappa_i(\underline{z}))^{-1/2} [\sigma^2(\underline{z}) + \tau^2(\underline{z})]^{1/2} \qquad (14)$$

where

$$\sigma^2(\underline{z}) = \underline{n}^T(\underline{z},\underline{u}^*)\ (\ddot{\underline{\underline{R}}} - \dot{\underline{\underline{R}}}\ \dot{\underline{\underline{R}}}^T)\ \underline{n}(\underline{z},\underline{u}^*)$$

$$\tau^2(\underline{z}) = \underline{n}^T(\underline{z},\underline{u}^*)\ \dot{\underline{\underline{R}}}^T \underline{\underline{D}}\ \dot{\underline{\underline{R}}}\ \underline{n}(\underline{z},\underline{u}^*)$$

and

$$\underline{\underline{D}} = \{\delta_{ij} + \frac{\partial^2 g(\underline{u}^*,\underline{z})}{\partial u_i \partial u_j} \|\text{grad } g(\underline{u}^*,\underline{z})\|^{-1}\}$$

with $\delta_{ij}$ Kronecker's delta. This formula is based on a parabolic approximation of $\partial V(\underline{u},\underline{z})$ in $\underline{u}^*(\underline{z})$. It is worth noting that the above mentioned $\beta$-point $\underline{u}^*(\underline{z})$ is the asymptotically correct expansion point.

It is also possible to derive an importance sampling scheme for updating either eq. (13) or (14). This is even more justified as the rates according to eq. (13) or (14) based on approximations of $\partial G$ in the $\beta$-point appear to be less reliable than the corresponding results for volume integrals. That this is so is easily explained by the fact that rotational symmetry which was a necessary presupposition for the volume integral approximations according to FORM/SORM usually cannot be achieved simultaneously for $\underline{U}$ and $\dot{\underline{U}}$. In the following reference to the condition $\underline{Z} = \underline{z}$ is now temporarily omitted. The outcrossing rate is written as

$$\nu^{+} = \nu^{+}_{\partial G} \frac{\nu^{+}_{\partial G}}{\nu^{+}_{\partial A}} = \nu^{+}_{\partial A}\ H \qquad (15)$$

where H is a correction in the order of unity. Again, for simplicity of notation, an orthogonal transformation $\underline{u} \rightarrow \underline{v}$ is performed such that the $\beta$-point lies on the $v_m$-axis and all mixed derivatives $\partial^2 g(\underline{v})/((\partial v_i \partial v_j)$ of $\partial G$ vanish in $\underline{v}^*$. Then,

$$\partial L = v_m - \beta = 0 \qquad (16a)$$

$$\partial Q = v_m - \beta + \frac{1}{2} \sum_{i=n+1}^{m-1} \kappa_i v_i^2 = 0 \qquad (16b)$$

$$\partial G = v_m - f(\tilde{\underline{v}}) = 0 \qquad (16c)$$

with $\tilde{\underline{v}} = (v_{n+1},\ldots,v_{m-1})^T$. Using the explicit form for the surface $\partial F$

$$v_m = f(\tilde{\underline{v}}) \qquad (16d)$$

eq. (2) can be rewritten as

$$\nu^{+}_{\partial F} = \int_{\partial F} E_o^{\infty}\, [\underline{n}^T(\underline{v})\dot{\underline{V}} \,|\, \underline{V} = \underline{v}]\ \varphi(\underline{v})\ \Big(1+ \sum_{i=n+1}^{m-1} \big(\frac{\partial v_m}{\partial \tilde{v}_i}\big)^2\Big)^{1/2} d\underline{v} \qquad (17)$$

where the expectation term is (Ditlevsen, 1983)

$$E_o^{\infty}\ [\underline{u}^T(\underline{v})\dot{V} \,|\, \underline{V} = \underline{v}] = m\ \Phi(\frac{m}{\sigma}) + \sigma\ \varphi(\frac{m}{\sigma})$$

with

$$m = -\underline{\alpha}^T(\underline{v})\ \dot{\underline{\underline{R}}}\ \underline{v} \qquad (18)$$

$$\sigma^2 = \underline{\alpha}^T(\underline{v})(\ddot{\underline{\underline{R}}} - \dot{\underline{\underline{R}}}\ \dot{\underline{\underline{R}}}^T)\ \underline{\alpha}(\underline{v}) \qquad (19)$$

This leads to:

$$H \approx \frac{\frac{1}{M}\sum_{l=1}^{M} E_o^{\infty}[\underline{n}^T_{\partial G}(\underline{v}_l)\dot{\underline{V}} \,|\, \underline{V}=\underline{v}_l]\ \|\mathrm{grad}\ \partial G(\underline{v}_l)\|\ \dfrac{\varphi(\underline{v}_l)}{\varphi(\underline{v}_l)}}{\frac{1}{M}\sum_{l=1}^{M} E_o^{\infty}[\underline{n}^T_{\partial A}(\underline{v}_l)\dot{\underline{V}} \,|\, \underline{V}=\underline{v}_l]\ \|\mathrm{grad}\ \partial A(\underline{v}_l)\|\ \dfrac{\varphi(\underline{v}_l)}{\overline{\varphi(\underline{v}_l)}}} \qquad (20)$$

$$\approx \frac{1}{M}\sum_{l=1}^{M} \frac{E_o^{\infty}[\underline{n}^T_{\partial G}(\underline{v}_l)\dot{\underline{V}} \,|\, \underline{V}=\underline{v}_l]\ \|\mathrm{grad}\ \partial G(\underline{v}_l)\|}{E_o^{\infty}[\underline{n}^T_{\partial A}(\underline{v}_l)\dot{\underline{V}} \,|\, \underline{V}=\underline{v}_l]\ \|\mathrm{grad}\ \partial A(\underline{v}_l)\|}\ \frac{\varphi(\underline{v}_l)}{\varphi(\underline{v}_l)} \qquad (20a)$$

$\partial A$ is an approximating surface. Either $\partial L$ or $\partial Q$ may be chosen. As before, $\varphi(\underline{v})$ is the sampling distribution, i.e. has density

$$\varphi(\underline{v}) = \varphi(v_m) \prod_{i=n+1}^{m-1} \frac{1}{\sigma_i} \varphi\left(\frac{\tilde{v}_i}{\sigma_i}\right) \qquad (21)$$

with $\sigma_i^2 = (1-\varphi(-\beta)\kappa_i)^{-1}$. The zero mean variables $\tilde{V}_i$ are to be simulated and $v_m$ is obtained from relationships of the form eq. (16d). This result is believed to be derived here for the first time.

## 3 COMPUTATION ALGORITHM

It is easy to design an algorithm for the computation of failure probabilities on the basis of section 2. Two alternate ß-point searches are required. The first search only determines a conditional ß-point $\beta(\underline{z})$ to be used to compute the outcrossing rates. The second algorithm removes that condition. The following steps must be carried out:

1. Select starting vector $\underline{z}^{(i)}$; i=0
2. Compute estimate $\nu^+(\underline{z}^{(i)})$ by eq. (13) or better by eq. (14) using FORM and SORM, respectively.
3. Compute better approximation point $\underline{z}^{(i+1)}$ in eq. (4) using FORM.
4. Compare $\underline{z}^{(i+1)}$ with $\underline{z}^{(i)}$ according to some appropiate convergence criteria. In the non-convergent case repeat steps 2. and 3. with $\underline{z}^{(i)} := \underline{z}^{(i+1)}$ in step 2.
5. Evaluate H by eq. (20) and set $\nu^+(\underline{z}^{(i)}) := \nu^+(\underline{z}^{(i)})\ H$
6. Evaluate C by eq. (8)
7. Evaluate K by eq. (9)
8. Compute $\phi(-\beta)$ C K

## 4. DISCUSSION

There are three points to be discussed:

i. the choice of the expansion point for the computation of the outcrossing rate
ii. the choice of the conditional approximation surface given by eqs. (16))
iii. the assumption of exponentially distributed first-passage times used in eq. (1)

As concerns item i. the authors also studied expansions at the point of maximum local outcrossing rate (ML-point) proposed by Breitung/Rackwitz(1982). Since, for $\beta(\underline{z})\rightarrow\infty$, this point converges to the $\beta$-point used before, there cannot be any preference in the (almost) asymptotic case. For moderate and small $\beta(\underline{z})$ one, in fact, finds that the ML-point gives slightly better approximations. Also, the coefficient of variation of the corresponding correction factor H is slightly smaller than for expansions in the $\beta$-point. But the gain in accuracy is small so that the $\beta$-point is generally recommended for consistency reasons.
The choice of the linear (eq. (16a)) or quadratic (eq. (16b))

approximation in eq. (20) again is uncritical in the asymptotic case. The correction factor for eq. (16b) has smaller coefficient of variation if the quadratic form is used as compared to the linear form. However, the expectation term in Breitung'formula (14) is an approximation. Therefore, only the use of the linear form yields an unbiased correction factor in eq. (20).
More serious is the assumption of exponentially distributed failure times. This well-known asymptotic result appears hard to improve without making use of higher-order crossing rates which are extremely difficult to compute. A small improvement may be obtained by following Ditlevsen (1971), i.e. by starting from

$$P_f(t) \sim 1 - E_{\underline{Y}}[(1-P_f(o))\exp[-\nu^+(\underline{y})t/(1-P_f(o))]]$$

where $P_f(o)$ is the initial failure probability determined by FORM/SORM. The effect of the randomness in failures times is in our formulation captured by the variable $U_T$ in eq.(4). Numerical calculations show that at the expansion point $u_T^*$ is always close to zero implying that only the central part of a firstpassage time distribution is significant. This in turn implies that it is not very important to use the "exact" form of the distribution function since they resemble each other very much in the central parts. The results obtained by the foregoing, approximating approach, therefore, should be fairly accurate as long as the failure probabilities are sufficiently small.

5.EXAMPLE

Let $U_Q$ and $U_M$ be two dependant Gaussian processes of shear force and bending moment, respectively, in a simply supported, widespan beam subjected to a moving train of Gaussian shot noise causing dynamic effects (Gross/Rackwitz,1987). Mean value and covariance matrices of $U_Q$, $U_Q$, $U_M$ and $U_M$ are given in Table 1. The limit state function is given by the well-known v.Mises yield criterion where $\sigma_F$ is the yield stress. It is assumed log-normally distributed. Its mean value and its coefficient of variation is given in Table 1. The length of the reference period t in eq. (4) is set equal to 10. The results for FORM/SORM and the important sampling update are given in Table 2.

| Variable | $m_{\underline{X}}$ | $\underline{\underline{C}}_{\underline{X}}$ | | | |
|---|---|---|---|---|---|
| $U_Q$ | 23.5 | 1940 | -7940 | 0 | -22.4 |
| $U_M$ | 94.6 | -7940 | 32600 | 22.4 | 0 |
| $U_Q$ | 0 | 0 | -22.4 | 114000 | -403000 |
| $U_M$ | 0 | 22.4 | 0 | -403000 | 1780000 |
| $\sigma_F$ | 72 | | 7.2 | | |

Table 1: Random variable parameters

| Method | $\nu^+$ | $\beta(\underline{u}^*)$ | $u_T^*$ | $z^*$ | $\sigma_F^*$ | ß | Comp. time |
|---|---|---|---|---|---|---|---|
| FORM | $5.648\cdot10^{-3}$ | 4,312 | -1,599 | -1,515 | 61,6 | 2,2o3 | 1 |
| SORM | $5.650\cdot10^{-3}$ | 4,312 | -1,599 | -1,515 | 61.6 | 2.175 | 2 |
| i.s.*) | $5.611\cdot10^{-3}$ | 4.209 | -1,599 | -1,515 | 61.6 | 2.185 | 16 |

Table 2: Numerical results *) importance sampling

REFERENCES

Breitung, K. (1984a). Asymptotic Approximations for Multinormal Integrals, Journ. of the Eng. Mech. Div., Vol. 11O, No.3, pp. 357-366.

Breitung, K. (1984b). Asymptotic Approximations for the Outcrossing Rates of Stationary Gaussian Vector Processes, University of Lund, Dept. of Math. Statistics.

Breitung, K., Rackwitz, R. (1982). Nonlinear Combination of Load Processes, Journ. of Struct. Mech., Vol. 1O, No.2, pp. 145-166.

Gross, P., Rackwitz,R. (1987). Spectral Approach for Dynamic Response of Bridges Under Moving Vehicles on Rough Surfaces, Technical University of Munich.

Fiessler, B., Neumann, H.-J., Rackwitz, R. (1979). Quadratic Limit States in Structural Reliability, Journ. of the Eng. Mech. Div., ASCE, Vol. 1O5, EM4, pp. 661-676.

Hohenbichler, M. (1984). Numerical Evaluation of the Error Term in Breitung's Formula, in: Berichte zur Zuverlaessigkeitstheorie der Bauwerke, Technical University of Munich, SFB 96, Heft 69, pp. 49-58.

Hohenbichler, M., Gollwitzer, S., Kruse, W., Rackwitz, R. (1984). New Light on First- and Second-Order Reliability Methods, Submitted for publication to Structural Safety.

Hohenbichler, H.,Rackwitz, R., (1986). Improvement of Second-Order Estimates by Importance Sampling, submitted to ASCE.

Veneziano, D., Grigoriu,M. Cornell, C.A. (1977). Vector-Process Models for System Reliability, Journ. of Eng.Mech.Div.,ASCE, Vol. 1o3, EM 3, pp. 441-460.

# BOUNDARY ELEMENT METHOD IN STRUCTURAL RELIABILITY

Ole Vilmann* and Peter Bjerager**

*ABSTRACT*

Application of boundary element methods (BEM) in analyses of structures having uncertain properties is studied. The reliability calculations are based on first–order reliability methods (FORM). A theoretical formulation of a Mindlin plate analysis, which involves uncertain geometrical parameters is given . In particular, an infinite plate with a hole of uncertain shape and position is considered. As an example, the upper tail of the probability distribution of a stress concentration factor in the boundary of the hole is addressed.

## 1. INTRODUCTION

The performance of a structural system is typically evaluated by relating the stress field or the displacement field in the structure to the capacity of the system. In general, the solution for the stress field or the displacement field can not be obtained in closed form, but must be calculated approximately. Particularly useful and rather general methods in this respect are the finite element method (FEM), the finite difference method, the boundary element method (BEM) and related methods, all based on a discretized model of the structure.

The finite element method has in recent years gained interest for reliability analysis of structures, see e.g. [Der Kiuregian and Ke, 1985; Hisada and Nakagiri, 1985; Vanmarcke, et al, 1986]. The method is well suited for dealing with random spatial variations in the material properties due to the segmentation of the structure into elements, each of which may be represented by its own properties.

In stochastic finite element analysis two different approaches have been applied. The first approach focuses on the second moment representation of the output vector (stress or displacement), whereas the second approach focuses on the determination of probabilities, e.g. the probability that the stresses in the structure exceed some (random) limit values. For typical structural reliability problems this probability is of a rather small order and is, in general, not very well determined on the basis of the second moment representation of the problem variables.

The first approach is often referred to as the mean–centered perturbation method since all expansions of non–linear functions are performed at the mean point. Such a stochastic finite element method has been developed for geotechnical analysis in [Baecher and Ingra,

---

* Visiting Scholar, Dept. of Civil Engrg. and Engrg. Mech., Columbia University, New York 10027, USA

** Research Associate, Dept. of Strc. Engrg., Tech. Univ. of Denmark, DK-2800 Lyngby, Denmark

1981] as well as linear structural analysis in [Handa, 1975; Handa and Anderson, 1981; Hisada and Nakagiri, 1981; Hisada and Nakagiri, 1985]. In the reported FEM applications the expansion of the stiffness matrix and the solution (the displacements) is at most of second order. Another mean-centered FEM formulation is the one in [Shinozuka and Dasgupta, 1986] where the second-moment representation in found by a Monte Carlo method. This approach also applies to non-linear structures. For all the mean-centered methods, the inversion of the stiffness matrix needs only to be performed once.

The second approach is based on the first and second order reliability method (FORM/SORM) [Der Kiuregian and Taylor, 1983; Der Kiuregian and Ke, 1985]. Here, the attention is on determining a probability $p = P[g(\mathbf{U}) \leq 0]$ where $g$ is some performance function and the standard Gaussian vector $\mathbf{U} = \mathbf{T}(\mathbf{R}, \mathbf{S}(\mathbf{X}))$ is the image of the set of random resistance variables $\mathbf{R}$ (e.g. strengths) and the set of load effect variables $\mathbf{S}$ (e.g. stresses or displacements) given by a solution procedure in terms of the basic physical variables $\mathbf{X}$, comprising loads and some material properties of the structure. Applying FORM essentially implies that the multi-dimensional integral for $p$ is replaced by an optimization problem for determining the (set of) most likely failure point(s) in $\mathbf{U}$-space [Madsen, Krenk and Lind, 1986]. In order to efficiently find a solution to this optimization problem, the gradient vector $\nabla g(\mathbf{U})$ is required. For linear elastic structures, the vector can conveniently be determined using the element partial derivatives stiffness matrices and load vectors [Der Kiuregian and Taylor, 1983; Der Kiuregian and Ke, 1985]. In principle, the identification of the most likely failure point requires that a finite element calculation has to be performed for each step of an iterative algorithm. Some methods of computational reductions are suggested in [Der Kiuregian and Taylor, 1983; Der Kiuregian and Ke, 1985].

From deterministic analysis it is known that for some problems significant computational savings are gained with BEM, see e.g. [Banerjee and Butterfield, 1983; Brebbia and Walker, 1980], as compared to an analysis based on FEM. Furthermore, BEM may apply to problems (e.g. some problems with infinite bodies) where a finite element approach is not suitable.

In this paper the application of BEM in structural reliability analysis is addressed. In particular, the boundary element method is used together with FORM in static response analysis of linear structures. As opposed to the finite element analysis the boundary element approach seems ill suited for dealing with problems of random spatial variations in the material properties. The boundary element method is particularly useful when geometrical imperfections in the boundary of the body (uncertain shape of the boundary) are present. For some problems this uncertainty may significantly influence the performance of the structure. In the present paper use of FORM-BEM is examplified by analysing a Mindlin plate [Mindlin, 1951] containing a hole of uncertain shape and position. In particular, the influence of the uncertainty in the stress concentration factor around the hole is considered.

## 2. FIRST ORDER RELIABILITY METHOD (FORM)

A structural reliability model of the random variable type is considered. The model is described by the random vector $\mathbf{Z} = (Z_1, Z_2, ..., Z_n)$ together with the limit state or performance function $G(\cdot)$, such that failure of the system is assumed for outcomes $\mathbf{z}$ for which $G(\mathbf{z}) \leq 0$. For other outcomes the structure is assumed safe. $G(\mathbf{z}) = 0$ defines the limit state surface in $z$–space.

For random vectors $\mathbf{Z}$ having a (multivariate) continuous probability distribution a transformation exists

$$\mathbf{U} = \mathbf{T}(\mathbf{Z}) \tag{1}$$

such that $\mathbf{U}$ is a vector of independent and normalized Gaussian variables, see [Madsen, Krenk and Lind, 1986]. By the transformation the limit state surface is mapped into a corresponding surface in the standardized $u$–space, defined by $g(\mathbf{u}) = 0$.

For smooth and rather flat limit state surfaces the reliability index

$$\beta = \Phi^{-1}(1 - p_f) \tag{2}$$

where $p_f = P\{g(\mathbf{U}) \leq 0\}$ is the probability of failure and $\Phi(\cdot)$ is the standard normal distribution function, may with sufficient accuracy for practical purposes be determined by the probability content of the half–space outside the hyperplane at the point $\mathbf{u}^*$ on the limit state surface closest to the origin. This is due to the rapid decay with distance from the origin of the rotational symmetric standardized normal density function together with the small sensitivity of $\beta$ to variations of $p_f$ in the region of small order probabilities of failure common in structural reliability problems. Improvements on FORM results can be obtained by second order reliability methods (SORM), see [Hohenbichler et al, 1986], or by simulation. Moreover, FORM/SORM calculations may include a number of sensitivity factors.

The formulation of the FORM–BEM method thus includes a transformation of the basic variables into the standardized space, as well as an identification of the point closest to the origin in this space. The transformation $\mathbf{T}(\cdot)$ is here linear since all basic random variables $\mathbf{X}$ are assumed normally distributed. The vector $\mathbf{X}$ comprises the radii from the center to the nodes at the hole in the infinite Mindlin plate, Fig. 1. The transformation $\mathbf{T}(\cdot)$ can thus be expressed as

$$\mathbf{X} = \mathbf{L}\ \mathbf{U} + \mathbf{E}[\mathbf{X}] \tag{3}$$

where $\mathbf{L}$ is the (lower triangular) Cholesky decomposed matrix of the covariance matrix $\mathbf{C_X} = \mathbf{L}\ \mathbf{L^T}$. The correlation coefficients are assumed to be given by

$$\rho_{ij} = k_0\ e^{-k_1 d_{ij}^2} \tag{4}$$

where $d_{ij}$ is the distance between the $i^{th}$ and the $j^{th}$ node.

The point $\mathbf{u}^*$ closest to the origin in $u$–space is the solution to a standard optimization procedure for which a number of numerical methods can be used. In the present calculation the solution has been found by the modified HL–RF algorithm suggested in [Liu and Der Kuireghian, 1986]. This method is based on a positive definite merit function, and in each step of the algorithm a Newton–Raphson minimization in a calculated direction is carried out. Compared to the original algorithm, this scheme has improved the convergence properties.

The gradient vector of the limit state function is needed in the computation. This vector is computed numerically. Whereas an analytical expression of the gradient vector can be obtained in a FORM–FEM calculation ( through the derivative stiffness matrices etc. as mentioned in the introduction ), this is not possible in a BEM analysis. A formulation of an integral equation expressing the derivatives of the boundary displacements in the BEM needs to be based on a deterministically prescribed variation of the boundary. The computation of the derivatives of the boundary displacements, is comparable with calculation of the stresses in the boundary, which can not be obtained directly [Brebbia and Walker, 1980; Banerjee and Butterfield, 1983].

The limit state function considered in the following is

$$G(\mathbf{z}) = k_2 - \frac{m_{ss_{max}}}{m_0} \tag{5}$$

where $m_{ss}$ is a bending moment perpendicular to the hole near (in) the boundary of the plate, $m_0$ is the plate bending moment at infinity and $k_2$ is a constant describing the limit value of the stress concentration factor $\frac{m_{ss_{max}}}{m_0}$.

## 3. MINDLIN PLATE THEORY

In this section the Mindlin plate theory will briefly be reviewed. A more thorough treatment can be found elsewhere.

The Mindlin plate theory [Mindlin, 1951] was originally developed to demonstrate a comprehensive two–dimensional theory of flexural motions of plates (analogous to Timoshenko's one–dimensional theory for beams [Timoshenko, 1937] ) in order to capture a wider range of wave velocities (compared to the classical Kirchoff formulation). This theory describes both the flexural motion with wavelengths having an upper limit of three–dimensional Rayleigh surface waves and with wavelengths corresponding to long waves (compared to the plate thickness). The classical theory of plates can reproduce only wave velocities associated with long waves, compared to the thickness of the plate.

In this paper only the static solution is considered. This includes the contribution of the transverse shear deformation to the generalized displacements and leads to three natural boundary conditions rather than the two of classical plate theory. Other higher–order plate theories, e.g. Reissner's plate theory [Reissner, 1944; Reissner, 1985] and Hencky's plate theory [Hencky, 1947], also include these latter conditions.

Consider an isotropic, elastic plate as a three–dimensional body $V$ enclosed by the boundary $A$ in a cartesian coordinate system $x_i$ $(i = 1,2,3)$. The midplane $V_p$ of the plate intersect the outer boundary along the curve $A_p$ (which is termed the boundary of the plate in a two–dimensional sense). The equations of equilibrium are expressed in the undeformed state and the material is assumed to be linearly elastic and isotropic. Definitions from classical theory of the plate–stress relations are used,

$$m_{\alpha\beta} = \int_{-\frac{h}{2}}^{\frac{h}{2}} \sigma_{\alpha\beta} x_3 dx_3 \tag{6}$$

$$q_\alpha = \int_{-\frac{h}{2}}^{\frac{h}{2}} \sigma_{\alpha 3} dx_3 \tag{7}$$

In eqs. 6 and 7 lowercase greek letters are used as subscript characters to indicate the implied summation convention $(\alpha, \beta = 1, 2)$. The components of the section forces $m_{\alpha\beta}$ are the bending moments when $\alpha = \beta$, otherwise they constitute the twisting or torsional moments. The components $q_\alpha$ are the transverse shear forces.

The fundamental assumption that leads to the deduction of the Mindlin plate theory, is the assumption that the displacements $u_\alpha$ are proportional to $x_3$, while $u_3$ is assumed to be independent of $x_3$, i.e.

$$u_\alpha = \hat{u}_\alpha + x_3\theta_\alpha = \hat{u}_\alpha(x_\alpha) + x_3\theta_\alpha(x_\alpha) \tag{8}$$

$$u_3 = w = w(x_\alpha) \tag{9}$$

where $\hat{u}_\alpha$ are inplane displacements in the plates midplane, $\theta_\alpha$ are rotations of the cylindrical surface of the plate and $w$ is the transverse displacement of the plate.

To derive the bending moments, the twisting moment and the transverse shear forces the definition of these components are used, i.e.

$$m_{11} = \int_{-\frac{h}{2}}^{\frac{h}{2}} \sigma_{11} x_3 dx_3 = D[\theta_{1,1} + \nu\theta_{2,2}]$$

$$m_{22} = \int_{-\frac{h}{2}}^{\frac{h}{2}} \sigma_{22} x_3 dx_3 = D[\theta_{2,2} + \nu\theta_{1,1}]$$

$$m_{12} = \int_{-\frac{h}{2}}^{\frac{h}{2}} \sigma_{12} x_3 dx_3 = D\frac{(1-\nu)}{2}[\theta_{1,2} + \theta_{2,1}]$$

$$q_1 = \int_{-\frac{h}{2}}^{\frac{h}{2}} \sigma_{13} dx_3 = Gh_k[w_{,1} + \theta_1]$$

$$q_2 = \int_{-\frac{h}{2}}^{\frac{h}{2}} \sigma_{23} dx_3 = Gh_k[w_{,2} + \theta_2] \tag{10}$$

where $D$ is the plate flexural stiffness coefficient expressed in terms of the Poisson's ratio $\nu$, the plate thickness $h$, the Young's modulus of elasticity $E$ and the modulus of rigidity $G$. The reduced plate height $h_k = \kappa^2 h$ is the actual plate height multiplied by a factor $\kappa^2$ expressing the distribution of the shear stress across the plate thickness. This factor can be calculated by considering the wave velocities of short and long waves, as mentioned above.

The stress component $\sigma_{33}$ is not assumed to be zero as in some other theories but the adopted procedure reveals that an average effect of $\sigma_{33}$ is neglected.

## 4. BOUNDARY ELEMENT METHOD (BEM)

The BEM for Mindlin plates is formulated as a direct boundary element method based on Maxwell–Betti's reciprocal theorem, [Nielsen and Vilmann, 1983]. The reciprocal theorem applied to Mindlin plates, is expressed in generalized quantities according to the principle of virtual work, yielding

$$\int_{V_p} q_i^{(1)} u_i^{(2)} dV + \int_{A_p} t_i^{(1)} u_i^{(2)} dA - \int_{V_p} \sigma_{i\alpha}^{0(1)} \epsilon_{i\alpha}^{(2)} dV$$

$$= \int_{V_p} q_i^{(2)} u_i^{(1)} dV + \int_{A_p} t_i^{(2)} u_i^{(1)} dA - \int_{V_p} \sigma_{i\alpha}^{0(2)} \epsilon_{i\alpha}^{(1)} dV \tag{11}$$

where $q_i$ is the generalized load $q_i = \{p, m_1, m_2\}^T$, $m_1$ and $m_2$ are distributed bending moments, $p$ is a distributed transverse load and $u_i$ are the generalized displacements $u_i = \{w, \theta_1, \theta_2\}^T$. $t_i$ are the generalized tractions $t_i = \{q_\alpha n_\alpha, m_{1\beta} n_\beta, m_{2\beta} n_\beta\}^T$, $n_\beta$ is the outward normal to the boundary, $\sigma_{i\alpha}^0$ are the initial generalized stresses,

$$\sigma_{i\alpha}^0 = \begin{bmatrix} q_1^0 & q_2^0 \\ m_{11}^0 & m_{12}^0 \\ m_{21}^0 & m_{22}^0 \end{bmatrix} \tag{12}$$

and $\epsilon_{i\alpha}$ are the generalized strains

$$\epsilon_{i\alpha} = \begin{bmatrix} w_{,1} + \theta_1 & w_{,2} + \theta_2 \\ \theta_{1,1} & \theta_{1,2} \\ \theta_{2,1} & \theta_{2,2} \end{bmatrix} \tag{13}$$

The two equilibrium states, i.e. $\sigma_{i\alpha}^{(1)}, u_i^{(1)}, \epsilon_{i\alpha}^{(1)}$ due to the loading $q_i^{(1)}, \hat{t}_i^{(1)}, \hat{u}_i^{(1)}$ and $\sigma_{i\alpha}^{0(1)}$, and $\sigma_{i\alpha}^{(2)}, u_i^{(2)}, \epsilon_{i\alpha}^{(2)}$ due to the loading $q_i^{(2)}, \hat{t}_i^{(2)}, \hat{u}_i^{(2)}$ and $\sigma_{i\alpha}^{0(2)}$ are exact equilibrium states due to the corresponding loads. The hat symbol denotes that the values are prescribed.

The state (1) will be substituted with the fundamental solution ( denoted here with an asterisk ) and the state (2) $\sigma_{i\alpha}, u_i, \epsilon_{i\alpha}$ is the exact equilibrium state due to the loading $q_i, \hat{t}_i, \hat{u}_i$ and $\sigma_{i\alpha}^0$.

It is shown in [Vilmann, 1987] that the integral equation (which is the basis of the boundary element method) for Mindlin plates can be written as

$$C_{ij} P_i^* u_j(x_i^*) + \int_{A_p} t_i^* u_i dA = \int_{V_p} q_i u_i^* dV + \int_{A_p} t_i u_i^* dA - \int_{V_p} \sigma_{i\alpha}^0 \epsilon_{i\alpha}^* dV \tag{14}$$

where the integrals should be interpreted in a Cauchy principal value sense. The $P_i^*$ expresses the magnitude of the concentrated generalized load of the fundamental solution.

The magnitudes of $C_{ij}$ are evaluated by rigid body displacements, e.g. [Van der Weeen, 1983].

In this paper the integrals with respect to $V_p$ can be omitted, since it is assumed that $q_i = \{0,0,0\}^T$ and $\sigma^0_{i\alpha} \equiv 0$.

The boundary of the plate or a part of the boundary will be segmented into a number ($N_{el}$) of boundary elements. In this paper isoparametric cubic one–dimensional elements [Zienkiewicz, 1977] are used, i.e.

$$u_i(x_\alpha) = [N^k]\ \{v_i^u\}\quad x_\alpha\ on\ A_p^E$$
$$t_i(x_\alpha) = [N^k]\ \{v_i^t\}\quad x_\alpha\ on\ A_p^E \tag{15}$$

where $A_p^E, \{v_i^u\}, \{v_i^t\}$ and the matrix $[N^k]$ is the boundary of the element, the $i^{th}$ nodal displacements of the element, the $i^{th}$ nodal tractions of the element and the coefficients of the interpolation matrix, respectively. In this paper $k = 4$ because an isoparametric cubic serendipity element is used. Only the part of the boundary that gives contributions to the integral equation should be subdivided into boundary elements.

By use of the above given interpolation matrices the integral equation can be assembled into a set of $N$ linear equation, where $N$ is the number of nodes in the system, i.e.

$$\mathbf{B}\ \mathbf{Y} = \mathbf{F} \tag{16}$$

where $\mathbf{Y}$ is the vector with the unknown boundary parameters, $\mathbf{B}$ is the corresponding interaction coefficient matrix and $\mathbf{F}$ is the vector of the generalized node forces obtained through the known boundary parameters and the corresponding interaction coefficients.

By solving eq. 16 one can obtain all the boundary parameters at the nodes in the system.

## 5. STRESS CONCENTRATION FACTOR

The expression of the generalized plate stresses near (in) the boundary can be obtained through the definitions of the generalized plate stresses, the section forces. In this section only the bending moment perpendicular to the hole near the boundary is established. The five generalized stresses are the two shear forces $q_n, q_s$, the bending moments $m_{nn}, m_{ss}$ and the torsional moment $m_{ns}$. The $n$ and $s$ indicates a cartesian frame located along the outward normal and along the tangent to the surface (hole), respectively.

The generalized boundary parameters that are known after the solution of eq. 16 (and after a transformation) are the generalized plate stresses $\{q_n, m_{ns}, m_{nn}\}$ and the generalized plate displacements $\{w, \theta_n, \theta_s\}$. The bending moment $m_{ss}$ is obtained by rewriting the definition from eq. 10 in the new boundary cartesian frame, i.e.

$$m_{ss} = D(\theta_{n,n} + \nu\theta_{s,s})$$

and

$$m_{nn} = D(\theta_{s,s} + \nu\theta_{n,n})$$

to

$$m_{ss} = \nu m_{nn} + D(1 - \nu^2)\theta_{s,s} \tag{17}$$

The computation of $\theta_{s,s}$, the only remaining unknown, is acomplished through the interpolation of the generalized node parameters by the coefficients (eq. 15) and their derivatives, [Vilmann, 1987].

## 6. EXAMPLE FORMULATION

The analytical solution of an infinite plate with a circular hole loaded with a constant bending moment at infinity is available in [Reissner, 1944; Goodier, 1946] for the Reissner plate model and for the classical plate model, respectively. The load at infinity consists of

$$\begin{aligned} q_r &= 0 \\ m_{rr} &= m_0 cos^2\varphi \\ m_{r\varphi} &= m_0 \frac{sin2\varphi}{2} \end{aligned} \tag{18}$$

while the boundary of the hole is load free. The shear force and the moments are expressed in cylindrical coordinates. The solution of the Reissner plate is in close agreement with the Mindlin plate solution. A BEM discretized model of the plate with 8 elements (24 nodes) is shown in Fig. 1. The stress concentration factor was captured within 1 percent with the discretized latter BEM model.

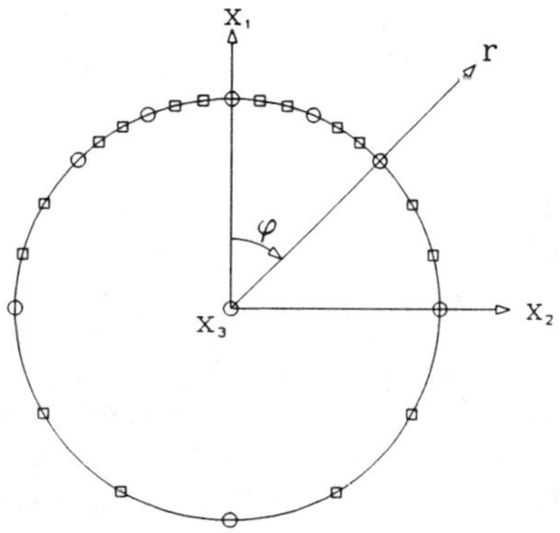


Fig. 1. The boundary element discretized plate model with 8 elements. The ○ defines the element intersection nodes, while ◇ defines the internal element nodes.

The BEM equations, with vanishing terms at infinity, are obtained by splitting the generalized displacements and the generalized plate forces into two parts. One part (1) is the parameters in an infinite plate and the second part (2) is the parameters in the infinite plate due to the hole, i.e. some of the generalized plate parameters

$$\begin{aligned} q_r &= q_r^{(1)} + q_r^{(2)} \\ m_{rr} &= m_{rr}^{(1)} + m_{rr}^{(2)} \\ m_{r\varphi} &= m_{r\varphi}^{(1)} + m_{r\varphi}^{(2)} \end{aligned} \tag{19}$$

The boundary of the hole is load free, i.e. the boundary conditions are all zero. Only the field (2) is solved by the BEM giving non-zero boundary parameters on the boundary of the hole, whereas the boundary conditions at infinity and their contribution to the BEM equations vanish. Therefore, only BEM discretization of the boundary of the hole is necessary in this analysis.

## 7. CONCLUSION

Application of a boundary element method within structural reliability analysis has been addressed. The method is used together with a first-order reliability method. The following conclusions can be drawn:

- As a (rather) general structural analysis tool the boundary element method can be used in reliability analysis of structures
- In the BEM formulation the gradient vector of the limit state function can not, as in the case of a FEM formulation, be determined directly but must be computed numerically
- However, compared to a finite element analysis the boundary element method may provide an efficient alternative. This is especially so for problems where the volume/surface ratio is relatively large or where infinite bodies are dealt with.

## REFERENCES


Baecher, G.B. and Ingra, T.S., 'Stochastic FEM in Settlement Predictions', Journal of Geotechnical Division, ASCE, Vol. 107, No. GT4, (1981)

Banerjee, P.K. and Butterfield, R., 'Boundary Element Methods in Engineering Science', McGraw–Hill Book Company, UK, (1983)

Der Kiuregian, A. and Taylor, R.L., 'Numerical Methods in Structural Reliability', Proc. of Fourth International Conference on Applications of Statistics and Probability in Soil and Structural Engineering, Florence, Italy, (1983)

Der Kiuregian, A. and Ke, J.–B., 'Finite–Element Based Reliability Analysis of Frame Structures', Proc. of 4th International Conf. on Structural Safety and Reliability, Kobe, Japan, (1985)

Goodier, J.N., 'The Effect of Transverse Shear Deformation on the bending of elastic plates', J. Appl. Mech., Vol. 13, (1946)

Handa, K., 'Application of the FEM in the Statistical Analysis of Structures', Division of Structural Design, Chalmers University of Technology, Gothenburg, Report No. 1975:6, (1975)

Handa, K. and Anderson, K., 'Application of the Finite Element Method in the Statistical Analysis of Structures', Proc. of Third International Conference on Safety and Reliability, Moan, Ang and Shinozuka (Eds.), Trondheim, Norway, (1981)

Hencky, H., 'Über die berücksichtigung der shubverzerrung in ebenen Platten', Ing-Archiv, Band 16, (1947)

Hisada, T. and Nakagiri, S., 'Stochastic Finite Element Method Developed for Structural Safety and Reliability', Proc. of 3rd International Conf. Structural Safety and Reliability, Moan, Ang and Shinozuka (Eds.), Trondheim, Norway, (1981)

Hisada, T. and Nakagiri, S., 'Role of the Stochastic Finite Element Method in Structural Safety and Reliability', Proc. of 4th International Conf. on Structural Safety and Reliability, Kobe, Japan, (1985)

Hohenbichler, M., Gollwitzer, S., Kruser, W. and Rackwitz, R., 'New Light on First and Second-Order Reliability Methods', Submitted to Structural Safety, (1986)

Lui, P-L and Der Kiureghian, A., 'Optimization Algorithms for Structural Reliability Analysis', Report No. UCB/SESM-86/09, Struct. Engrg. and Struct. Mech., Dept. of Civil Engrg., Univ. of California, Berkeley, (1986)

Madsen, H.O., Krenk, S. and Lind, N.C., 'Methods of Structural Safety', Prentice-Hall Inc., (1986)

Mindlin, R. D., 'Influence of Rotatory Inertia and Shear on Flexural Motions of Isotropic, Elastic Plates', J.Appl. Mech., (1951)

Nielsen, L.O. and Vilmann, O., 'Om randelementmetoden til spændingsberegning', Bygningsstatiske meddelelser, Vol. 54, No. 4, (1983)

Rackwitz, R. and Fiessler, B., 'Non-Normal Vectors in Structural Reliability', Berichte zur Zuverlässigkeittheorie der Bauwerke, Heft 29, LKI, Technische Universität München, (1978)

Reissner, E., 'On the theory of bending of elastic plates', J. Math. Phys., Vol. 23, (1944)

Reissner, E., 'Reflections on the theory of elastic plates', Appl. Mech. Rev., Vol. 38, (1985)

Shinozuka, M. and Dasgupta, G., 'Stochastic Finite Element Methods in Dynamics', Proc. of Third ASCE Conf. on Dynamic Response of Strc., Hart and Nelson (Eds.), Los Angeles, (1986)

Timoshenko, S., 'Vibration problems in engineering.', D. van Nostand Company, Inc., Sec. ed., (1937)

Timoshenko, S. and Woinowsky-Krieger, S., 'Theory of Plates and shells', McGraw-Hill, New York, (1959)

Van der Weeen, F., 'Randintegraalvergelijkingen voor het plaatmodel van Reissner', Ph.D. thesis , State University of Ghent, Belgium, (1981)

Vanmarcke E., Shinozuka, M., Nakagiri, S., Schueller, G.I. and Grigoriu, M., 'Random Fields and Stochastic Finite Elements', Structural Safety, Vol. 3, (1986)

Vilmann, O., 'Boundary element techniques applied to the Mindlin plate theory', Draft Ph.D. thesis , Dept. of Structural Engineering, Technical University of Denmark, (1987).

Vilmann, O. and Dasgupta, G., 'A Perturbation Expansion of the Fundamental Solution for Mindlin Plates', Report No. OV1, Dept. of Civil Engrg. and Engrg. Mech., Columbia University, (1986)

Zienkiewicz, O.C., 'The Finite Element Method', McGraw-Hill Book Compagny, (1977)

# RISK UNCERTAINTIES IN SAFETY DECISIONS: DEALING WITH SOFT NUMBERS

M.E. Paté-Cornell
Department of Industrial Engineering and Engineering Management
Stanford University, Stanford, CA, 94305

## ABSTRACT

The form of risk assessment results that is required for public safety decisions depends on the intended use. In this paper we examine three levels of assessment of uncertainties in risk analysis: the worst-case approach, the probabilistic (Bayesian) approach, and the probabilistic method in which the risk uncertainties are made explicit in the results using notions of secondary probability. For each type of analysis and results, we examine the risk assessment problems and the risk management implications (conservativeness, cost-effectiveness, and equity of regulatory policies). We raise two major issues of public safety decision making: the inconsistency of risk management policies among regulatory agencies, and the existence and adequacy for regulatory decisions of an aversion towards analytical uncertainty in addition to classical risk aversion.

## INTRODUCTION

In the United States, the legislation increasingly requires probabilistic risk analysis for public sector safety decisions. This is true for example for nuclear safety and, more recently, for the regulation of the chemical industry. Some building codes are also based on probability.

One of the difficulties in assessing and reporting the risks is to communicate the firmness of the risk assessment results. In the classical framework of decision theory, this notion is considered unnecessary: the uncertainty about probability for a given lottery is not part of the preference structure. In practice, it is clear that instead of maximizing an expected utility, the regulatory agencies and the administrators prefer to act on "conservative estimates" when they believe that they are using "soft numbers". Mixing assessment and risk aversion, however, is dangerous to the extent that it can lead to the overestimation of some risks (by an unknown amount), to a reversal of risk management priorities, and to a misallocation of safety funds.

In this paper, we describe the problems of treatment of uncertainties in risk assessment. We examine first how different regulatory bodies treat risk uncertainties in safety decisions. We discuss management implications of different assessment methods in terms of economic efficiency, conservativeness, and equity in individual safety. Strict economic efficiency means that the maximum expected number of people are saved for a given level of investment. Equity in safety means that individuals' protection is independent of the potential number of victims in an accident.

## LEVEL 0: THE WORST-CASE APPROACH

EXISTENCE OF A HAZARD. This is the most basic level of risk identification. No risk assessment is required. The hazard must simply be detected. There is, in particular, no attempt at exposure assessment. For example, a reservoir has been constructed, drowning is a possibility, and swimming is simply forbidden. In spite of the intention the goal of absolute safety is seldom reached in practice. No attention is paid to risk displacement, to trade-offs in choices, and to the consistency of safety regulations.

WORST-CASE ANALYSIS. This approach relies on the notion of maximal loss and maximal exposure. For example, the absolute upper bound of property damage in an earthquake in San Francisco is simply the total value of all the buildings, assuming that they are totally vulnerable to ground motions. This method is seldom used in practice because it leads to such an overestimation of the risk that this information is of little value for management decisions.

QUASI-WORST-CASE ANALYSIS. This approach represents an attempt either to assess an upper bound of the risk (losses or probability of death or accident) when there is some uncertainty as to what the worst case might be, or to obtain an evaluation of the worst possible conditions that can be "reasonably" expected. The analysis results in a quasi-upper bound based on a "conservative" interpretation of existing statistics with some give and take in the risk assessment itself to support decisions that look economically and politically viable.

In hydrology, an example of this philosophy is the popular concept of Probable Maximum Flood (PMF). The PMF is based on the Probable Maximum Precipitation (PMP) and on an assumption of worst possible conditions such as an already saturated soil (National Research Council, 1985). The PMP itself is deduced from the worst historical record adjusted to reflect the worst possible conditions and its position on the tail of the precipitation distribution is unclear. Consequently, the return period of the PMF probably varies from site to site. Using the PMF therefore does not allow any consistency in flood risk assessment from site to site, or any analytical coherence in analyses where a flood may be one of several types of initiating events of an accident (for example, floods and earthquakes can both be initiators of failure of dams.) Because using the PMF to judge the spillway adequacy of some dams seems to lead to an inefficient allocation of safety funds, some federal and state agencies use a fraction of the PMF, with the value of this fraction depending on the size of the dam (a surrogate for the consequences of failure). The goal is to provide a more reasonable criterion, but what actual level of safety is reached by this method is unclear.

The Maximum Credible Earthquake (MCE) used to judge the safety of some civil structures design relies on a similar concept (National Research Council, 1985). It is an attempt to reach an upper bound of the magnitude of earthquakes that can affect a given site. It is defined by the U.S. Army Corps of Engineers as "the earthquake that would cause the most severe vibratory ground motion or foundation dislocation capable of being produced at the site under the currently known tectonic framework". There is no place in this analysis, however, for the potential existence of other seismic mechanisms than those already known (e.g., as yet unidentified faults). Another method of quasi-upper bound computation is used to obtain the Safe Shutdown Earthquake (SSE), which is the peak ground acceleration used as a basis for the seismic design of nuclear power plants (National Research Council, 1985). It is the maximum earthquake intensity that can be generated by rupture of (nearly) the full length of the neighboring faults. Again the notion of absolute upper bound was softened to yield an economically reasonable figure but without indication of the actual safety level that is implied: the return period (or the annual probability) of the SSE is unknown, but probably varies from site to site.

In the quasi-worst-case approach, the criteria of risk management are imbedded in the risk assessment itself but in a manner that does not give the decision maker any information about the probability of exceeding the risk estimates. There is an obvious intention of risk aversion and a general desire to accomodate to some extent economic realities by *ad hoc* adjustments of the quasi-upper bound. It is impossible, however, to know the level of conservativeness of the final decision and to ensure the coherence of risk management decisions.

The major problem is therefore a serious lack of consistency and economic efficiency. Some minute environmental risks might be regulated at great expense (Graham and Vaupel, 1981), or some dams may be equipped with very large spillways, thus absorbing considerable efforts into marginal risk reductions when resources could be better used elsewhere. In the quasi-worst-case approach, although safety decisions might appear conservative case-by-case, the order of priorities among risk mitigation needs could well be reversed leading to essentially unconservative overall effects. This reversal of priorities may occur within a given project (for instance, floods vs earthquakes as potential causes of dam failures), or project-to-project within a single agency such as EPA, or area-to area (e.g., EPA versus NRC).

LEVEL 1: PROBABILISTIC APPROACH

This method is based on logic and probability. Uncertainty about basic mechanisms, models, and parameter values is represented by probability distributions for the spectrum of models, and for parameter values given each model. In the end, however, the estimation of these uncertainties is reduced to an expected value representing the final probability attached to each outcome, for example, the probability of exceeding a given level of losses in a given time period.

This method of risk analysis corresponds to the axioms of decision theory and to the maximization of expected utility (von Neuman and Morgenstern, 1947; Raiffa, 1968; Howard, 1984). The rationale of aggregation of uncertainties in a single probabilistic estimate regardless of the "softness" of the probabilities involved relies on the decomposition axiom that requires the aggregation of all uncertainties by virtue of the structure of preferences. Under this scheme, there is no distinction between risk and uncertainty. This axiom implies indifference between two lotteries represented by the same probability distribution for the outcomes regardless of the amount of evidence that supports the probability assessment. Another key feature of this definition of rationality is the separation of risk assessment (models and probabilities) and risk management (utilities). The utility for an outcome is independent of the probability of this outcome.

In public sector safety decisions one encounters theoretical as well as practical difficulties in adapting the decision analysis methodology to essentially collective decisions. This requires collective aggregation of sometimes conflicting sources of information into one probabilistic estimate, and the use of collective preferences in the evaluation of the possible outcomes (Paté, 1986). One of the critical steps is to obtain an agreement about a probability distribution for a spectrum of possible models when basic mechanisms are poorly known. This problem arises, for example, in the analysis of carcinogenicity or seismicity. Classical decision analysis is seldom used in public sector decisions. In the nuclear power industry where PRA was developed in the early 1970's (USNRC, 1975), numerical safety goals based on means of probabilitis and frequencies have been recently approved (Atomic Energy Clearing House, 1986). Yet, full computation and display of risk uncertainties is required by the NRC for PRA studies. In practice, it seems that the "softness" of probabilities does enter the actual decision criteria.

The Bayesian method has important advantages over the worst-case approach or simple sensitivity analysis in the management of risks. Maximization of the expected value of the outcomes (or minimization of the expected value of losses) is the only criterion that leads to strict economic efficiency and to equity in protection from risks. This is why this rule has often been recommended for public sector decisions. Risk aversion, when desired, can be introduced in the utility function independently from risk assessment and the decision maker can then be consistent in his preferences. Risk aversion, however, implies a risk premium, i.e., a willingness to make additional payment to avoid losses in large single events beyond what is spent to avoid the same losses in several smaller accidents. For this reason, it also leads to inequities among individuals because protection depends on the size of the potential accidents to which people are exposed.

LEVEL 2: RECOGNITION OF RISK UNCERTAINTY

The next level of uncertainty analysis involves a probability distribution for the probability (or future frequency) of failure, accident, death, or disease which leads to a distribution of risk curves for the description of the associated number of fatalities. In the nuclear power industry, it was judged from the beginning that a single estimate of a failure probability or a single probability distribution of the potential losses gave insufficient support to regulatory decisions. The need for a thorough treatment and communication of analytical uncertainties in PRA was emphasized in the review of the Reactor Safety Study by the Lewis Committee (USNRC, 1978). Uncertainties about future frequencies, probabilities, and models are assigned for the input variables, propagated in the analysis, and displayed in the results (Kaplan et al. 1981; Vesely and Rasmuson, 1984).

One interesting example of this method is the treatment of uncertainties in seismic PRA which requires analysis of uncertainties about seismic hazard as well as system fragility (Kennedy et al., 1980,). In the United States, the information regarding seismicity is substantial in some western parts of the country but much more limited in the East where the seismic mechanisms themselves are often poorly known. The Bayesian method consists of identifying all the possible underlying seismic mechanisms and assessing a probability distribution to this set of possible models and parameter values.

The seismic PRA for the Limmerick power station provides an interesting illustration of this method. In this study, six different combinations of seismic mechanisms and parameter values are identified leading to a set of six probability distributions for the annual maximum effective peak ground acceleration and their six probabilities, i.e., a degree of belief based on experts' opinions (USNRC, 1983). The next step is to compute the effect of the uncertainty in seismic hazard and in fragility analyses on the future frequency of core melt. The future frequencies of core melts caused by earthquakes, fires, or other initiating events, are represented and compared through their probability distributions. Obviously, internal consistency in the analysis of possible models and parameters values is needed to make meaningful comparisons about the relative contribution of each type of initiating event to the overall probability of core melt.

Finally, the question is to assess the effect of these uncertainties on the probability distribution of losses. Instead of a single cumulative distribution function, the results are presented as a family of cumulative distributions representing the range of analytical uncertainties. For each number of fatalities, these curves give a partial representation (e.g., by chosen fractiles) of the marginal probability distribution of the frequency of exceedence per reactor-year. An important use of these curves is to compute the effects on the potential losses of possible risk mitigation measures. This information can be a major input in safety decisions. This representation allows the analyst to communicate analytical uncertainties as part of the results.

In part because of large risk uncertainties, PRA is currently used by the NRC only "as a supplement to the regulatory process" and not as sole basis for decisions (Bernero, 1984). For problems such as nuclear safety, the decision analysis paradigm seems insufficient to capture the preferences expressed within the regulatory agencies where there seems to be a definite preference for "hard" probability estimates (e.g., low uncertainty in core melt probability or loss distributions). The information given by the level 1 described above seems too densely aggregated. It is thus important to examine how risk uncertainties affect regulatory decisions in order to identify the level of analysis that provides the corresponding results.

Uncertainty in decisions involving risk can be separated into two types: the analytical uncertainty, which can be further refined between modelling and parametric uncertainties, and the observational uncertainty that would always remain even if the characteristics of the system were perfectly known. In other fields, the same distinction is sometimes made under the names of "ambiguity" and "risk" (Yates and Zukowski, 1976). The spectrum of uncertainties is continuous. Analytical uncertainties reflect the limitations of the information available in many parts of the analysis ranging, for example, from small sample sizes upon which to base parameter estimates to current limitations in the study of human errors. To assess risk uncertainties, it is necessary to represent under one form or another a probability of a probability.

This notion of secondary probability is anchored in the definition of Bayesian probability in which a probability distribution can be attributed to the parameters (e.g., mean or standard deviation) of a probability distribution representing observational uncertainty. In Bayesian decision theory, however, the axioms of rationality imply that it is the mean value of this distribution of the probability itself that actually represents "the" probability of an event for decision purposes (Savage, 1954; Raiffa, 1968).

There are several possible interpretations of the apparent desire of the regulators and other interested parties to gain information about risk uncertainty beyond the expected values of probability. First, they may want to understand the results better and displaying uncertainties in the results adds some perspective. In some sectors, where there is great reluctance even to change from worst-case concept to probability for fear of going further than what the scientific knowledge permits, developing methods that involve not only a level 1 but a level 2 of uncertainty analysis might alleviate the concern that probabilistic risk analysis can give a false impression of certainty.

Second, the different parties involved may want to be able to anticipate future changes in the risk estimates. Indeed, in the field of nuclear safety, it might well be that, in addition to earthquakes themselves, the outcomes of interest in the future include new estimates of seismic risk that may prompt additional plant retrofits. Third, the uneasiness of the decision makers about using means of "soft distributions" and, therefore, about the von Neuman definition of rationality, suggests that they may be unwilling to follow literally the classical axioms of decision theory. In addition to an attitude towards risk (e.g., risk aversion), they seem to have a separate aversion towards analytical uncertainties.

This phenomenon, known as the Ellsberg paradox (Ellsberg, 1961), implies that they do not necessarily value equally two lotteries in which the distributions of the final outcomes are identical. They may indeed be willing to pay an additional premium to reduce the uncertainty about probabilities themselves. This concept escapes the classical notion of value of information (Howard, 1966) which relies on the anticipated change in the distribution of the outcomes (based on mean probabilities) and, therefore, on the reduction of analytical uncertainties only to the extent that it results in a change in this outcome distribution and affects the expected utility. Although ambiguity avoidance has been documented in the literature (e.g., Curley et al. 1986), invoking the Ellsberg paradox raises a host of uncomfortable issues, such as the existence of mutiple levels of uncertainties.

One of the reasons for this uncertainty attitude may be the collective nature of regulatory decisions. Bayesian probability as well as utility theory are based on individual notions of preferences and degree of belief that are difficult to translate into elements of collective decisions. Reaching an agreement about a collective degree of belief in a probability and making a collective value judgment about the outcomes may require a higher degree of confidence in the results than individual decision making, and, therefore, imply a greater willingness to pay for analytical information.

There is a gap between the level of sophistication of the uncertainty analysis performed in some sectors, such as the nuclear power industry, and the theoretical understanding of the actual management implications of acting on the "softness" of the numbers. On one hand, the decision makers are told that "rationality" implies that the softness of the results does not matter. They are urged to focus on probability based on expected future frequencies (or classical Bayesian probabilities) because it contains all relevant description of uncertainties. On the other hand, they express the need for additional information to reduce analytical uncertainties. Gaining information about risk uncertainties for the sake of a better perspective is unquestionable. The appropriateness of including the second level of uncertainty in the decision criteria depends on the axioms of choice that one wants to adopt.

## CONCLUSION

There are large discrepancies among the different risk assessment methods used by the different regulatory bodies in the U.S. Risk uncertainties are currently analyzed at three levels.

Level 0 (the worst-case approach) does not account for uncertainties beyond upper bound or quasi-upper bound notions and mixes risk assessment and value judgments. It has the advantage of simplicity but may lead to inconsistent and costly decisions, and to reversals of management priorities. Level 1 relies on a single probability distribution of annual losses. The probabilities involved are based on the expected value of future frequency (or probability) of the considered event. This is the level of uncertainty analysis that is required by the axioms of decision theory and allows introduction of the desired risk attitude in the utility for the outcomes. Level 2 results in a family of risk curves or cumulative probability distributions for the potential annual losses. This formulation of the results allows the decision maker to judge the "softness" of the information and, if he wants to do it, to introduce in his preference structure an element of "uncertainty aversion" that goes beyond the classical risk aversion of utility theory.

It is important to adopt consistent risk assessment methods across agencies for reasons of equity and efficiency. In particular, it is essential that the role of analytical uncertainty in management decisions be examined from a fundamental point of view. If uncertainty aversion is really a paradox, it must be eliminated from regulatory practice. If it is a desirable feature of public sector risk management, it must be treated consistently across economic sectors.

## REFERENCES

Atomic Energy Clearing House. "The Nuclear Regulatory Commission voted to adopt a policy statement on nuclear power plant safety goals". AECH, Vol. 32, No. 26, pp.23-31, 1986.

Bernero, R.M. "Probabilistic Risk Analysis: NRC Programs and Perspectives". Risk Analysis. Vol. 4, No. 4, December 1984, pp. 287-297.

Curley S. P., J.F. Yates, and R.A. Abrams. "Psychological Sources of Ambiguity Avoidance". Organizational Behavior and Human Decision Processes. Vol. 38, pp. 230-256, 1986.

Ellsberg, D. "Risk, Ambiguity, and the Savage Axioms". Quarterly Journal of Economics. Vol.71, pp.643-669, 1961.

Graham, J. D. and J. W. Vaupel. "Value of a life: What difference does it make?" Risk Analysis, Vol.1, No. 1, pp. 89-95, March 1981.

Howard, R. A. "Information Value Theory". IEEE Transactions on Systems, Man, and Cybernetics. Vol. SSC-2, No.1, pp.22-26, 1966.

Howard, R. A. "Risk Preference" in Principles and Applications of Decision Analysis, Vol. 2, pp. 627-664, Strategic Decisions Group, Menlo Park, California, 1984.

Kaplan, S., G. Apostolakis, B. J. Garrick, D. C. Bley, and K. Woodard. "Methodology for Probabilistic Risk Assessment of Nuclear Power Plants". Irvine, California: Pickard, Lowe and Garrick, Inc., June 1981.

Kennedy, R. P., C. A. Cornell, R. D. Campbell, S. Kaplan, and H. F. Perla. "Probabilistic Seismic Safety Study of an Existing Nuclear Power Plant". Nuclear Engineering and Design. Vol. 59, No. 2, pp. 315-338, Aug. 1980.

National Research Council. Safety of Dams: Flood and Earthquake Criteria. Committee on Safety Criteria for Dams. Washington, DC: National Academy Press, 1985.

Paté, M. E. "Probability and Uncertainty in Nuclear Safety Decisions". Nuclear Engineering and Design, Vol. 93, pp. 319-327, 1986.

Raiffa, H. Decision Analysis. Reading, MA: Addison-Wesley, 1968.

Savage, L. J. The Foundations of Statistics, New York: Wiley,1954.

U. S. Nuclear Regulatory Commission. Reactor Safety Study. WASH-1400 (NUREG-75/014), Washington, DC, October 1975.

U. S. Nuclear Regulatory Commission. Risk Assessment Review, Group Report to the U. S. Nuclear Regulatory Commission. NUREG/CR-0400, Washington, DC, 1978.

U. S. Nuclear Regulatory Commission. Probabilistic Risk Assessment; Limmerick Generating Station. Docket 50-352, Washington, DC, 1983.

Vesely, W. E. and D. M. Rasmuson. "Uncertainties in Nuclear Probabilistic Risk Analysis". Risk Analysis, Vol. 4, No. 4, December 1984, pp. 313-322.

von Neuman, J. and O. Morgenstern. Theory of Games and Economic Behavior. Princeton, NJ: Princeton Univ., 1947.

Yates, J.F. and L.G. Zukowski. "Characterization of Ambiguity in Decision Making". Behavioral Science, Vol. 21, pp. 19-25, 1976.

# OUTCROSSING RATES OF STATIONARY MARKED POISSON CLUSTER PROCESSES IN STRUCTURAL RELIABILITY

Karl Schrupp* and Ruediger Rackwitz**
*Siemens AG, 8000 Munich, FRG
**Technial University of Munich, 8000 Munich, FRG

ABSTRACT

A marked Poisson cluster load process (PCP) is defined as a suitable model for live loads in buildings and other types of jump-like stochastic phenomena. The crossing rate for a function of several such processes out of a safe domain of structural states is derived and structural failure probabilities are determined. For the equilibrium process a Poisson limit theorem for the failure probability and an asymptotic approximation for the outcrossing rate is given.

## INTRODUCTION

Various attempts have been made to realistically describe structural loads by appropriate stochastic models and to solve the corresponding combination problem when calculating structural reliability. The class of marked jump processes has been found useful to describe certain loading phenomena. Most of these models rest on the assumption that load occurence, intensity and duration of the load pulses are independent random variables. However, real loading phenomena oftenly exhibit pronounced dependencies of various kinds. One of the more important dependencies is occurence clustering first studied by Wen (1981). Therein and in Wen/Pearce (1981) a number of examples can be found where such clustering can be observed in reality and, therefore, needs to be modelled adequately.

In this paper a more general clustering phenomenon is described by a marked point process. The maximum lifetime distribution of sums or more complicated functions of such processes is approximated by the well-known outcrossing rate method.

A formal description and several properties of the unmarked Poisson cluster point process are presented first. Then, a special marked Poisson cluster process (PCP) is defined. Its crossing rate out of safe domains of structural states is given. The results are extended to sums of such processes. Finally, the Poisson convergence theorem leading to a simple formula for failure probabilities is applied together with an asymptotic formula for the crossing rate out of arbitrary domains.

## OUTCROSSING RATES AND FAILURE PROBABILITIES

There exists no direct approach to the failure probability of structural components under general individual or multivariate marked jump processes. However, the outcrossing approach although yielding only an upper bound and an asymptotic approximation for the failure probability has proved to be efficient (see, for example, Breitung/Rackwitz, 1982).

Denoting by $P_F(t) = P(T \leq t)$, $t \geq 0$, the distribution function of the time T to first failure, i.e. the entrance of a marked point process X(t) into the failure domain F, a well-known upper bound to the failure probability is (Bolotin, 1981)

$$P_F(t) \leq P_F(0) + E[M(t)] = P_F(0) + \int_0^t \kappa(\sigma)d\sigma \qquad (1)$$

where $P_F(0)$ is the initial failure probability, $E[M(t)]$ the mean value of the point process $M(t)$ of exits of $X(t)$ into $F$ and $\kappa(\sigma)$ the instantaneous crossing rate of $M(t)$ into $F$. The asymptotic approximation (Bolotin, 1981)

$$P_F(t) \sim 1 - \exp[- E[M(t)]] \qquad (2)$$

valid under certain conditions frequently is of even greater practical interest. It will be the basis for a simple and general formula for the failure probability to be described below in some detail.

THE UNMARKED CLUSTER POINT PROCESS

In the context of point process theory clustering means that points which occur along a time scale can be separated into main points, the cluster centers, and subsidiary points, the points within a cluster.

For our purposes the following point process is introduced

$$N(t) = \begin{cases} 0 & \text{for } N_c(t) = 0 \\ \sum_{i=1}^{N_c(t)} N_p(\tau_i;t) & \text{for } N_c(t) \in \mathbb{N} \end{cases} \qquad (3)$$

where

i) $N_c(\sigma)$ is a homogenous Poisson counting process with intensity parameter $\lambda > 0$ and jump-times $\tau_i$, $i \in \mathbb{N}$ $(\tau_o = 0)$ and,

ii) $N_p(\sigma;t) = \sum_{j=1}^{Z(\sigma)} I(\{\varrho_j^\sigma \in (\sigma,t]\})$

is a process counting the number of events of a renewal process in the interval $(\sigma,t]$ with renewal times $\varrho_j^\sigma$, $j \in \mathbb{N}_o$ $(\varrho_o^\sigma = \sigma)$ and continuous waiting time distribution function $F(u)$, $u \geq 0$,

$$P(\Delta \leq u) = P(\Delta_j \leq u) = P(\varrho_{j+1}^\sigma - \varrho_j^\sigma \leq u) = F(u), \quad j \in \mathbb{N}_0$$

which has expectation $E[\Delta] = \mu$.

The renewal process is assumed to be finite, i.e. there exists a probability distribution with

$$P(Z(\sigma) = k) = p_k, \quad k \in \mathbb{N}_o, \quad \sum_{k \in \mathbb{N}_o} p_k = 1 \text{ and } E[Z] < \infty. \qquad (4)$$

The process (3) is similar to the Bartlett-Lewis point process (Lewis, 1964). Cluster centers are the starting points $\tau_i$ of the subsidiary processes $N_p(\tau_i;\infty) = Z(\tau_i)$. The clusters are the points in each subsidiary process. For the derivation of some important stochastic properties of the subsidiary process $N_p(\sigma;t)$ and the cluster process $N(t)$ it is assumed that the random variables $\tau_i$, $\rho_j^\sigma$ and $Z(\tau_i)$ are mutually independent for $i,j \in N$.

The process (3) is instationary and evolves with after-effects. Stationarity for the cluster process can be regained by using a limit operation common in renewal theory. Instead of using the process (3) which starts at time instant zero, another point process is considered which starts in the infinite past. The resulting point process which is observed at time zero, the so-called equilibrium point process, then is stationary.

All further derivations are restricted to this equilibrium point process. For easy reference some characteristics of this equilibrium point process are cited here (see Lewis, 1964, for an extensive discussion and further results).

The number of subsidiary processes D which are active at time instant $\sigma$ has Poisson distribution with parameter $\lambda_e = \lambda\mu E[Z] = \lambda E[\Delta]E[Z]$, i.e.

$$P(D = k) = q_k = \exp(-\lambda_e)\,\lambda_e^k/k! \quad , k \in \mathbb{N}_0 \tag{5}$$

The distribution function of the lifetime of a cluster is given by

$$P(L \leqslant l) = \frac{1}{\mu E[Z]} \int_0^l R(u)du, \quad l \geqslant 0 \tag{6}$$

and the distribution function of the forward recurrence time in the equilibrium process can be shown to be:

$$P(\gamma \leqslant h) = \frac{1}{\mu} \int_0^h (1 - F(u))du, \quad h \geqslant 0 \tag{7}$$

Now, if $E[\Delta]E[Z] < 1/\lambda$, the expected length of a cluster does not exceed the expected waiting time for the next cluster and, thus, the clusters usually are separated. This process is similar to the one studied by Wen (1981). The probability that clusters overlap is small. For $E[\Delta]E[Z] = 1/\lambda$, the expected number of $Z_\sigma$ is one, i.e. there is always one subsidiary process active at time instant $\sigma$ and the clusters change with the same rate as the cluster centers. This resembles very much the well-known case of a Poisson square wave process. For $E[\Delta]E[Z] > 1/\lambda$ the clusters overlap, but in the equilibrium case, the expected number of $Z_\sigma$ is finite, provided that $E[\Delta]E[Z] < \infty$. This is exactly the condition ensuring the existence of the stationary process.

## THE MARKED POISSON CLUSTER PROCESS

The previous point process model can be generalized by assigning a mark to each renewal. The marks are independent, identically distributed (iid) random vectors which assume values in a mark space. Formally, the following definition for the Poisson cluster process (PCP) holds

$$X(t) = \sum_{i=1}^{N_c(t)} \sum_{j=1}^{\infty} A_j^i \; I(\{N_p(\tau_i;t) = j\}) \; I(\{L(\tau_i) \geqslant t\}) \tag{8}$$

with $A_j^i$ iid random vectors with distribution $V(A) = V(A_j^i)$. It is further assumed that $A_j^i$, $\tau_i$, $\varrho_j^\sigma$ and $Z(\sigma)$ are mutually independent. In structural reliability the interpretation of eq. (8) is as follows: Load changes occur according to the point process eq. (3). To each change there is associated a random vector which characterises the load, for example, by attributes such as amplitude, oscillator frequency, pulse shape. By assuming a failure domain F, the structure fails if the process (8) enters this domain. A typical realisation of the PCP with square wave marks is shown in figure 1. This is also the only process to be dealt with herein.

As shown in Schrupp (1986), the outcrossing rate $\kappa$ of the stationary equilibrium PCP is given by

$$\kappa = b \sum_{k=0}^{\infty} q_k \; B(F,k) + \frac{1}{E[Z]E[\Delta]} \sum_{k=1}^{\infty} k \; q_k D(F,k)$$

$$+ \frac{1}{E[\Delta]} \sum_{k=1}^{\infty} k \; q_k \; C(F,k) \qquad (9)$$

with $q_k = \exp(-\lambda_e)\lambda_e{}^k/k!$.

$\lambda_e = \lambda E[\Delta]E[Z]$ and $b = \lambda(1-p_0) \; f(\lambda(1-p_0))$

with f denoting the Laplace-transform of the waiting time density function.

The factors B, C and D denote the probability contribution of a jump from the safe domain $\bar{F}$ into the failure domain F and are given by

$$B(F,k) = P(A^{k^*} \in \bar{F}, \; A^{(k+1)^*} \in F),$$

$$C(F,k) = P(A^{k^*} \in \bar{F}, \; A^{k^*} \in F) \text{ and} \qquad (10)$$

$$D(F,k) = P(A^{k^*} \in \bar{F}, \; A^{(k-1)^*} \in F).$$

$A^{k^*}$ is the superposition of the marks of k active clusters. If the mark space is strictly positive, then, there cannot be an outcrossing due to the dying out of a subsidiary process. In this case, the last summation term in eq. (9) disappears. For $\lambda_e >> \lambda$, the second summation term is dominant. The numerical calculation of (9), in general, is quite involved. Explicit formulae have been derived for Gaussian and gamma distributed marks (see Schrupp, 1986). An asymptotic approximation is given in the last chapter.

SUPERPOSITION OF POISSON CLUSTER PROCESSES

Eq. (8) can easily be generalized to the superposition of several PCP's (Schrupp, 1986).

The combination of load processes results in summations over the different components in accordance with or in good approximation to the physical context. Here, the superposition of $s \in \mathbb{N}$

iid copies of a PCP defined in the foregoing section is investigated first which yields a simple generalisation.

Let

$$X(t) = \sum_{v=1}^{s} X_v(t)$$

$$= \sum_{v=1}^{s} \sum_{i=1}^{N_c(t)} \sum_{j=1}^{\infty} A_j^{i,v} \; I(\{N_p^v(\tau_i;t)\}) I(\{L^v(\tau_i) \geq t\}) \tag{11}$$

be the superposition of s iid PCPs' $X_v(t)$. The calculation of the crossing rate of eq. (11) is rather straightforward. The only difference to the univariate case is that the number of active processes at instant $\sigma$ needs to be considered. Observing that

$$D = \sum_{v=1}^{s} D^v \tag{12}$$

with $D^v$ the number of active clusters in the component $v$, and using the iid-condition it follows that V(D) is Poissonian with parameter $s\lambda_e$ with $\lambda_e$ from eq. (4). Thus, the results of the last section apply with this slight modification.

More generally, the process N(t) is defined as in eq. (3). All variables are independent but, the cluster processes $N_p^v$ have different distributions. This can be described by different waiting time distributions $V(\Delta^v)$ or different occurrence distributions $V(Z^v)$ in the component processes $v=1,...,s$. Both results in a modification of $V(D) = V(\sum_{v=1}^{s} D^v)$. V(D) is still Poissonian but with parameter $\lambda = \sum_{v=1}^{s} \lambda_v$ and $\lambda_v = E[Z^v]$ as in eq. (4) with the obvious modifications. Somewhat more subtle is the change of the intensity functions when calculating the crossing rate $\kappa(\sigma)$ which cannot be discussed here. The crossing rate $\kappa$ of the superposition process (11) for different distributions of $N_p^v$ can then be shown to be

$$\kappa = \sum_{v=1}^{s} r_v \; b^v \sum_{k=0}^{\infty} q_k \; B(F,k)$$
$$+ \sum_{v=1}^{s} r_v \; d^v \sum_{k=1}^{\infty} k \; q_k \; D(F,k) \tag{13}$$
$$+ \sum_{v=1}^{s} r_v \; c^v \sum_{k=1}^{\infty} k \; q_k \; C(F,k)$$

with

$$r_v = \frac{\lambda_v}{\lambda} \text{ and } b^v = \lambda(1-p_o^v)\hat{f}^v(\lambda(1-P_o^v))$$

The last case to be considered here is when $V(A_j^{i,\nu}) \neq V(A_k^{l,\mu})$, i.e. the distribution of the marks in the processes are different. In this case we obtain different compositions of the convolution factors in eq. (10). The rather complicated factors are derived explicitly in Schrupp (1986).

## POISSON CONVERGENCE FOR THE EQUILIBRIUM PROCESS AND AN ASYMPTOTIC APPROXIMATION FOR THE OUTCROSSING RATE

Using eq. (1) and the results of the last two chapters an upper bound for the failure probability is obtained. We now discuss another approach by using the fact that under some special conditions the equilibrium point process of crossings $M_F(t)$ has an asymptotic Poisson distribution. This limit distribution can be used to approximate the failure probability $P_F(t)$, a procedure which is also common when deriving limit distributions for the extreme values of stochastic processes.

Under the mixing condition, i.e. the dependence of the events within and between the PCP's vanish asymptotically, we obtain the limit result mentioned already earlier

$$P_F(t) = 1 - P(M_F(t) = 0) \sim 1 - \exp(-\kappa t) \qquad (14)$$

where $\kappa$ is given in the last chapter.

Practical application of eq. (14) still requires the laborous calculation of the outcrossing rate. The most difficult part is the determination of the factors B, C and D in eq. (10) especially for non-linear combinations of several processes. However, for standard normally distributed marks and failure domains which have twice differentiable boundaries asymptotic approximations for these factors can be derived on the basis of a concept used in Breitung (1984). If the marks are not standard normal a suitable probability preserving transformation will always reduce the problem to the standard one (Hohenbichler/Rackwitz, 1981).

Let the failure domain F for k active clusters be given by

$$F_k = \{\underline{x} \in R^k \mid g_k(\underline{x}) < 0\} \qquad (15)$$

and the safe domain S by

$$S_k = \{\underline{x} \in R^k \mid g_k(\underline{x}) > 0\} \qquad (16)$$

with $g_k : R^k \to R$ a twice differentiable function. With these notations the factors in eq. (10) can also be written as:

$$B(F,k) = P(\{X(t-) \in S_k\} \cap \{X(t) \in F_{k+1}\})$$

$$B(F,0) = I(\{0 \in \bar{F}\})\, P(X(t) \in F_1)$$

$$C(F,k) = P(\{X(t-) \in S_k\} \cap \{X(t) \in F_k\}) \qquad (17)$$

$$D(F,k) = P(\{X(t-) \in S_k\} \cap \{X(t) \in F_{k-1}\})$$

$$D(F,1) = P(X(t) \in \bar{F})\, I(\{0 \in F\})$$

X(t-) and X(t) are the left- and right-limits at time-instant t of the PCP, respectively.

Asymptotic approximations for eq. (17) can then be developed following closely the arguments in Breitung (1984). Making use of

$P(A \cap B) = P(B) - P(\bar{A} \cap B)$ and neglecting the second intersection probability asymptotically one obtains (Schrupp/Rackwitz, 1986):

$$B(F,k) \approx \Phi(-\beta_{k+1}) \prod_{j=1}^{k} (1 - \varrho_j^{k+1}), \quad k \in \mathbb{N}$$

$$B(F,0) \approx \Phi(-\beta_1)$$

$$C(F,k) \approx \Phi(-\beta_k) \prod_{j=1}^{k-1} (1 - \varrho_j^{k}), \quad k \in \mathbb{N} \tag{18}$$

$$D(F,k) \approx \Phi(-\beta_{k-1}) \prod_{j=1}^{k-2} (1 - \varrho_j^{k-1}), \quad k > 2$$

$$D(F,1) \approx 0$$

Herein, $\beta_k$ is the minimal distance of $g_k(\underline{x}) = 0$ to the origin

$$\beta_k = \|\underline{x}_k^*\| = \min \{\|\underline{x}\| \mid \underline{X} \in R^k,\ g_k(\underline{x}) = 0\} \tag{19}$$

and $\varrho_j^k$ the main curvatures of $g_k(\underline{x}) = 0$ at $\underline{x} = \underline{x}_k^*$. For large values of $\beta_k$ these approximation can be used in eq. (17). As shown by Breitung (1984) the limit result (14) remains valid when using these approximations.

A final remark appears suitable. An obvious difficulty in practical computations is the infinite summation required for the calculation of exact or even asymptotic outcrossing rates. Observing that the factors B, C and D are not greater than unity and using the bounds

$$\sum_{k \in N_0} q_k < \sum_{k=K+1}^{\infty} q_k \equiv \varepsilon_1$$

and

$$\sum_{k \in N} kq_k < \sum_{k=K+1}^{\infty} kq_k = \lambda_e \sum_{k=K}^{\infty} q_k \equiv \varepsilon_2$$

the error of a finite summation, up to K, say, can be bounded by:

$$r(K) \leqslant b \quad \varepsilon_1 + \left(\frac{1}{E[Z]E[\Delta]} + \frac{1}{E[\Delta]}\right) \varepsilon_2 \equiv \varepsilon.$$

Thus, for given $\varepsilon > 0$ we can find a $K = K(\varepsilon, \lambda_e)$ such that the rest of the series is smaller than $\varepsilon$.

## REFERENCES

Bolotin V.V. (1981). Wahrscheinlichkeitsmethoden zur Berechnung von Konstruktionen, VEB Verlag fuer Bauwesen, Berlin.

Breitung K. (1984). Asymptotic Approximations for the Maximum of the sum of Poisson Square Wave Processes, Berichte zur Zuverlaessigkeitstheorie der Bauwerke, 69, Technische Universitaet Muenchen, Muenchen.

Hohenbichler M. and R. Rackwitz (1981). "Non-normal dependent vectors in structural safety", Journ. Eng. Mech. Div. ASCE, EM6, pp. 1227-1238.

Lewis P.A.W. (1964). A Branching Poisson Process Model for the Analysis of Computer Failure Patterns, J.R. Statist. Soc. B, 26.

Schrupp K. (1986). Austrittsraten von markierten Poissonschen Clusterprozessen und ihre Anwendung in der Zuverlaessigkeitstheorie, Berichte zur Zuverlaessigkeitstheorie der Bauwerke, 77, Technische Universitaet Muenchen, Muenchen.

Schrupp K. and R. Rackwitz (1986). "Outcrossing Rates of Marked Poisson Cluster Processes in Structural Reliability", submitted to Applied Mathematical Modelling.

Wen Y.K. (1981). "A Clustering Model for Correlated Load Processes", Journ. of the Struct. Div., ASCE, 107, ST5, pp. 965-983.

Wen Y.K. and H.T. Pearce (1981). Stochastic Models for Dependent Load Processes, University of Illinois, Urbana, Illinois.

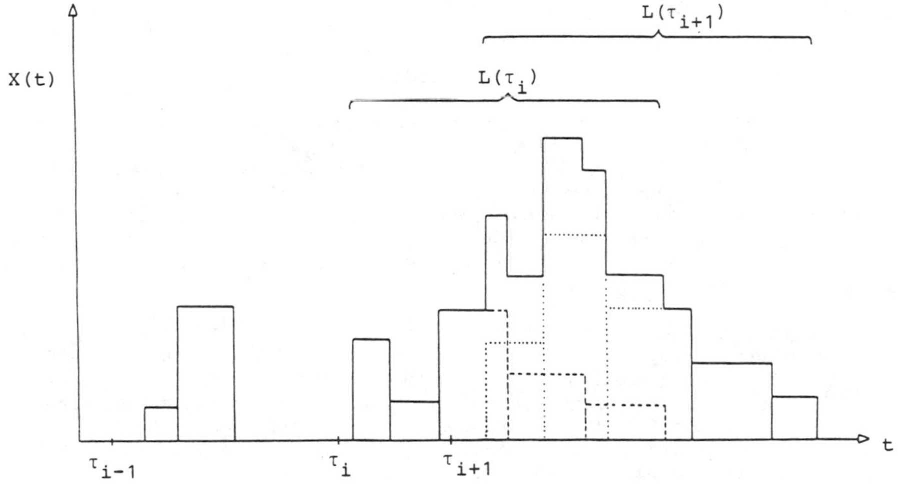


Figure 1: The Poisson cluster process (PCP)

# COLLISION RISK TO BRIDGES

Robert G. Sexsmith
Principal
Buckland and Taylor Ltd.
North Vancouver, Canada

## ABSTRACT

Collision by ships is one of the leading causes of damage to or failure of bridges. Because of the variety of situations and performance objectives, collision cannot be treated by simple load specifications or by prescribed safety levels. Consideration of the elements of decision analysis is recommended as the only way to achieve reasonable balance between protection costs and consequences.

A variety of situations, involving different sources of risk and different mechanical models of response, can arise. The following discussion is intended to illustrate the elements of three such situations using examples based on risk studies carried out on bridges in the Vancouver area. In each case the treatment is based on discrete probabilities estimated from a small data base, with simple mechanical models of collision. Despite the many approximations, the results provided the owners with definitive guides to decisions on protective measures.

## INTRODUCTION

A number of dramatic ship collision accidents have occurred in recent years, and these appear to be on the increase as a result of larger ships, heavier traffic, and more structures in exposed locations. Frandsen (1983) collected case histories covering up to the year 1982, several of which are noted in Table 1. The table illustrates several situations representative of the type of accidents that have occurred. It is by no means a complete list, but it does provide convincing evidence of the need to consider ship collision.

In response to the growing interest in the ship collision problem, and the fact that several major crossings are under detailed study around the world, the International Association for Bridge and Structural Engineering (IABSE) organized a colloquium entitled "Ship Collision with Bridges and Offshore Structures", held in Copenhagen in 1983. The resulting publications (IABSE 1983) provide an excellent reference to the state of the art, and form the basis for further developments. The colloquium covered case studies of collisions, navigation, probabilistic studies, collision behaviour, consequences, acceptance criteria, and design assumptions.

The purpose of this paper is to illustrate the application of ship collision risk principles to each of three bridges in the Vancouver area. In each

TABLE 1. Examples of Collision Events

| | |
|---|---|
| Bridge: | Maracaibo Bridge, Venezuela |
| Struck: | 1964 |
| Damage: | 3 - 235 m spans collapsed, \$5 - \$10 million damage |
| Vessel: | 36,000 dwt "Esso Maracaibo" |
| Cause: | Steering Malfunction |
| | |
| Bridge: | Chesapeake Bay Bridge and Tunnel, Virginia USA |
| Struck: | 1967, 1970, 1972 |
| Damage: | Several spans of 23 m damaged or destroyed each incident |
| Vessel: | Various tugs, cargo ship |
| Cause: | Storm driven vessels adrift |
| | |
| Bridge: | Tasman Bridge, Hobart Tasmania, Australia |
| Struck: | 1975 |
| Damage: | 3 - 42 m spans collapsed, 15 fatalities |
| Vessel: | 7200 dwt "SS Lake Illawara" |
| Cause: | Steering fault |
| | |
| Bridge: | Almo Bridge, Sweden |
| Struck: | 1980 |
| Damage: | 280 m arch collapsed, 8 fatalities |
| Vessel: | 27,000 dwt "Star Clipper" |
| Cause: | Steering difficulties in poor weather |
| | |
| Bridge: | Sunshine Skyway, Florida USA |
| Struck: | 1980 |
| Damage: | 400 m of 3 main spans fell, 35 fatalities |
| Vessel: | 35,000 dwt "Summit Venture" |
| Cause: | Poor visibility and rough weather |
| | |
| Bridge: | Second Narrows Railway Bridge, Vancouver |
| Struck: | 1979 |
| Damage: | 152 m lift span and its anchor span severely damaged |
| Vessel: | 22,000 dwt "Japan Erika" |
| Cause: | Dense Fog |

case, the owners faced decisions regarding design, modification, or control. These decisions were facilitated by the results of the risk assessments.

The examples demonstrate the need to consider each type of problem from basic principles. No single methodology could have been used for the three cases.

## DESIGN DECISIONS

The risk assessment has to be tailored to the situation, including the kind of design or control decisions that may be considered. Before embarking on a probabilistic modelling project, the alternative decisions should be considered. This usually implies a discrete breakdown of the possible options. Once the options have been identified, the types of mechanical models that are to be employed can be refined, and the necessary input to them can be identified. It is only at this stage that the data search and model assumptions can be generated.

The probability of a ship collision is estimated by breaking the collision event into a chain of events. The "causation" probability is the probability that a given vessel will suffer a loss of control. Worldwide data on this figure is available (Frandsen and Langso 1980). It is about $2 \times 10^{-4}$, but estimates should be made in particular cases. Two of the following examples involve a river, where it is reasonable to assume a higher probability of loss of control than in a harbour.

The conditional probability that a vessel out of control will strike a target must be estimated by considering the geometry of the situation (Larsen 1983, Leslie, 1979). An array of equally likely postulated trajectories, drawn from an assumed loss of control point, will provide an idea of the geometrical probability of a collision, given a loss of control incident. The product of the causation probability and the geometric probability is the probability of collision per vessel transit. The probability of a collision multiplied by the number of transits per unit time (eg per annum) is then a good estimate of the probability of a collision per unit time.

The probability of collision is the first element of the problem, and it is obvious that it is highly approximate. The next stage is an estimate of the energy of a collision, or, in some cases, the force of the collision. In each of the three examples that follow, the energy of the moving vessel is a critical parameter. The speed and vessel sizes are therefore required. Ship data can provide good estimates of size or tonnage, but generally the speeds are difficult to obtain. The requirement is for the speed at the time of impact, for a vessel out of control. A joint distribution of vessel mass and speed yields the kinetic energy distribution. One recent case involved a rigid bridge pier, and the crushing force for the ship hull had to be provided for (Frandsen and Langso 1980, Minorsky 1983). Other cases, discussed below, involve energy dissipation.

Consequences and control or warning strategies should be considered carefully. In the Lions' Gate and Alex Fraser Bridge examples discussed below, consequences were measured in terms of dollars assigned to the catastrophic event of collapse. The protection provided made the expected value of these consequences virtually negligible, and optimal decisions were not sensitive to the value of consequences. In the New Westminster Rail Bridge example, Consequences were measured in terms of economic disruption as well as structural costs. Experienced economists were retained to assess consequences.

Control of ship traffic and of bridge traffic should be a consideration. Ship control reduces the risk of collision, while bridge traffic control may reduce or eliminate the possibility of traffic driving onto a partially collapsed bridge, or may stop traffic when a ship loses control and before it strikes the bridge. Ship collision accidents can take several minutes between initial loss of control and actual collision with the structure. In a heavily travelled waterway the event can be monitored and radio controlled barriers can be activated.

The variety of situations possible, including the three examples that follow, illustrate that it is not realistic to specify collision loads in a bridge code, or to prescribe safety targets. Ship collision is well suited to individual decision analysis approaches.

## LIONS' GATE BRIDGE NORTH PIER

The Lions' Gate Bridge, a 450 m main span suspension bridge, is located at the entrance to First Narrows, Vancouver. The North Pier is a pair of heavy concrete pedestals founded upon a deep concrete caisson. The pedestals stand in one metre of water at high tide, and are protected by a drying beach at low tide. The tide range is about five metres. Because the Narrows is the only entrance to a busy harbour, a decision was made by the owner, the British Columbia Ministry of Transportation and Highways (MOTH) to assess the risk and carry out protective measures if required.

The first stage of the project was to determine whether there was a plausible risk. It was easily established that if a vessel of moderate size, say 20,000 deadweight tonnes (dwt), travelled at a speed of about 6 knots (3m/s), it could ride up the beach and strike the pier pedestal. The force required to overturn the pedestal was crudely calculated and found to be small compared with the possible force exerted by the ship. Since several thousand vessels pass the narrow harbour entrance each year, it was clear that some risk existed.

It was decided that because the pedestals were constructed of unreinforced concrete, and could overturn with a force that was small compared with the bow crush load of most oceangoing vessels, the risk would be estimated as the risk of collision with a pedestal. The consequences of a collision were assumed to be catastrophic.

In order for a collision to occur, a vessel transiting the Narrows would have to get out of control at a significant speed, take on a collision course for the pedestals, and then run up on the beach far enough to reach the pedestals. The beach runup is clearly affected by the tidal elevation, and is a function of the kinetic energy of the vessel as it strikes the beach.

The probability assessment is based on a crude, discrete analysis. First, a histogram of vessel sizes was constructed. The corresponding draft for loaded, half loaded, and empty vessels was determined, and these were assumed equally likely. A set of three approach angles were considered, and assigned likelihoods. For each approach angle, vessel speeds were assumed, based on discussions with pilots and consideration of current in the Narrows. All of this data was used in an event tree, Figure 1, that was constructed to determine the conditional probability of a vessel hitting the pedestal, given that it has grounded on a collision course. Before the event tree could be constructed, the mechanics of collision had to be estimated.

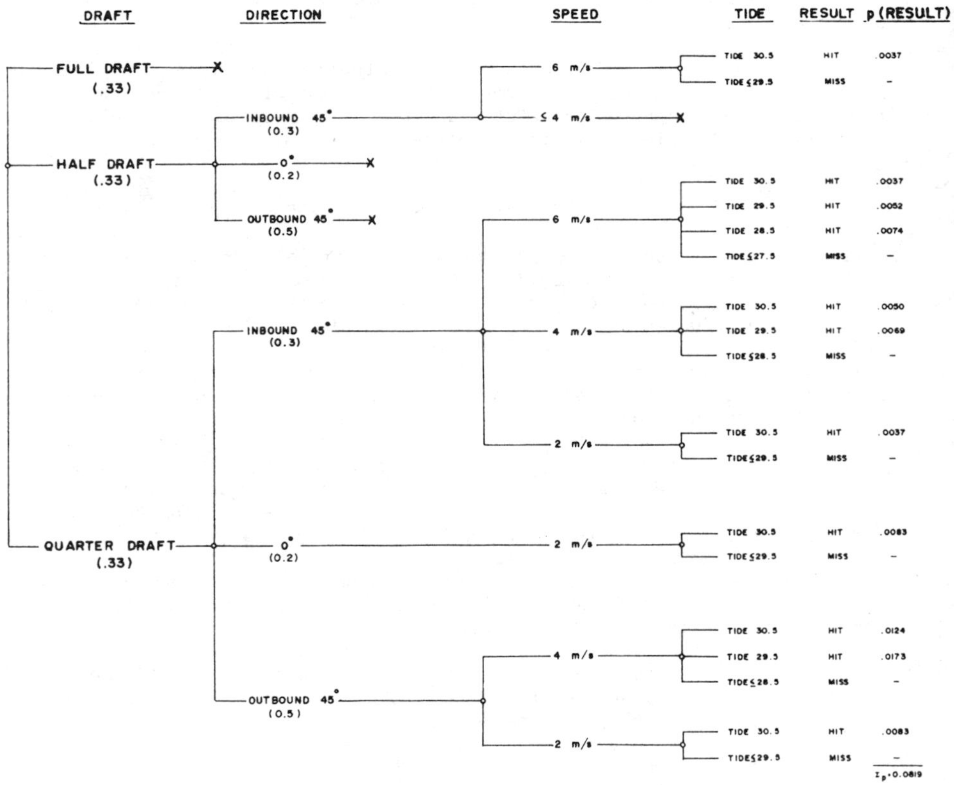


Figure 1. Event Tree

When a ship grounds on a beach, it will slide on the surface, or plough into the beach, dissipating its kinetic energy through friction at the contact zone and earth pressure on the frontal area (Minorsky 1983). With suitable assumptions regarding friction coefficient of the steel hull on earth, and passive pressure coefficients for the earth, a deterministic model of each of the two modes, sliding and ploughing, was developed. The model was programmed to facilitate rapid calculation. Later model studies by the Canadian Coast Guard (Eryuzlu 1986) verified the analysis.

The grounding model showed that the penetration to the pedestal was a strong function of ship speed, angle of attack on the beach, and tide elevation, but was almost independent of ship size for a given load condition. When the penetration results are plotted as the velocity required to penetrate to the pedestal, versus ship displacement tonnes, the curves are flat for any chosen draft condition. This is a fortunate result, partly due to the slope of the beach, which determines the penetration distance from the point of grounding to the pedestal.

Figure 2 is an example plot of ship size versus required velocity to strike the pedestal for two tidal elevations. The figure provides plots for ships of full, half, and quarter draft, corresponding to full load, half load, and empty. The sliding and the penetration models are plotted, and a solid line follows the minimum of these, on the assumption that this represents the probable behaviour.

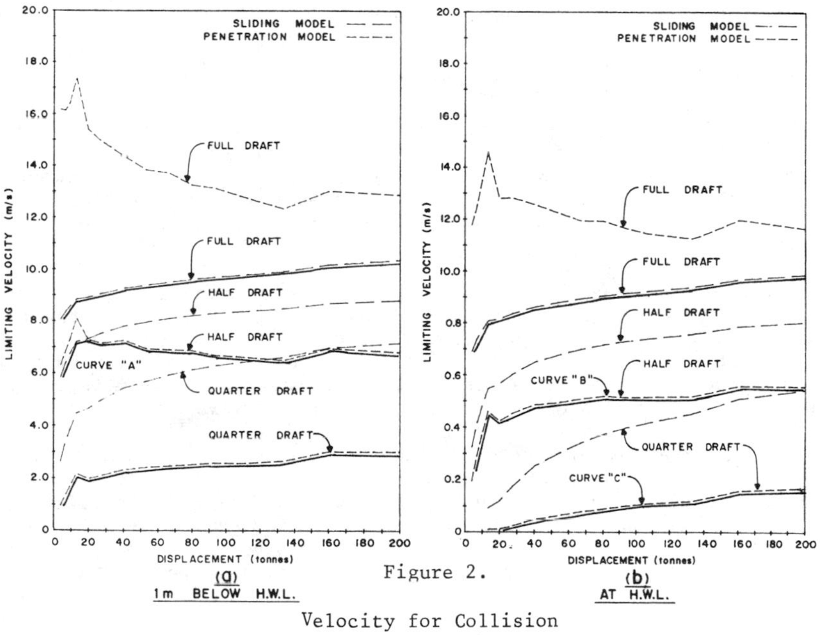


Figure 2.

Velocity for Collision

Curve A of Figure 2 is an example. It shows that small vessels, in the range 20,000 to 40,000 displacement tonnes, require about 7m/s velocity in order to strike the pedestal at this tide elevation. Larger vessels require just over 6 m/s. The curve is flat enough to justify the deterministic statement that a half draft vessel at 6 m/s will miss the pedestal; this is a terminal event on the event tree.

Similar plots were made for the various angles of approach. The event tree of Figure 1 summarizes the results. The very crude discrete division of events is consistent with the general level of accuracy. The event tree shows that the conditional probability of a collision given that a vessel grounds on the beach on a collision course is 0.08.

The resulting annual risk to the pier was consistent with other structural risks normally accepted, but a consideration of the consequences led to the conclusion that protective measures were justified. The expected present value of future consequences, when the cost in present dollars is $C_f$ and the event is Poisson in time with annual rate u, assuming a true discount rate i and u<<i, (Sexsmith 1983), is

$$C_o = C_f \, u/(i+u)$$

This figure is large compared with the cost of the proposed protective action which was to construct a gravel and rock berm around the pier. The grounding studies were repeated for the berm and no conditions of draft or tide led to striking the pedestals. The berm was constructed in 1986.

## ALEX FRASER BRIDGE

The Alex Fraser Bridge (formerly called the Annacis Bridge) crosses the Fraser River near New Westminster, B.C. At 465 m, the main span, completed in 1986, is the world's longest cable stayed bridge. The massive towers are near the shore, but within the natural water course of the Fraser River. Large vessels transit the river at the crossing, known as Mungo Bend on the charts.

The need for an assessment of the ship collision risk and the means to mitigate it was recognized early in the design planning. With towers unprotected in the river, the collision problem is one of energy accounting. The kinetic energy of the ship must be dissipated in a collision by a force acting through a displacement. If the pier is not to move, the displacement must be from deformation of the vessel or of a protective barrier.

Design alternatives considered included no protection, dolphins located at protective positions, and a protective island surrounding the tower bases. Dolphins have been used effectively elsewhere (Hahn and Rama 1982), but where currents are strong, the dolphin is a source for scour. In this case the practical alternatives are either a strong tower pier, or a protective berm. For either of these, the risk can be assessed by considering the energy of collision.

A vessel traffic survey was conducted with the help of pilotage records. Again, discrete measures were used to simplify the problem. Histograms of vessel size and of vessel speed were constructed. A joint probability mass function (pmf) of size and speed was then derived, from which a pmf of vessel energy was developed.

The energy capacity of the pier or berm was calculated using a deterministic model similar to the sliding/ploughing model discussed for the Lions' Gate Bridge. The uncertainty of the problem is primarily in the vessel traffic characteristics, thus a crude deterministic resistance model is realistic.

The pier reliability was then estimated by considering each of the discrete design energy capacities in turn, finding the annual probability of demand exceeding this capacity, and expressing this as return period or reliability in 50 or 100 years. When this is done for two or more possible design capacities, the cost of reducing risk by increasing capacity can be estimated, and an optimal decision made.

In this case a berm was constructed that reduced the risk to a negligible amount (return period of the order of 10,000 years).

There are many refinements possible with a model of this type, however the actual construction cost of the protection turned out to be small compared with the insurance value that it provided. Thus while the probabilistic part of the problem is treated crudely, it does lead to sensible design decisions that are not sensitive to details of the analysis.

## NEW WESTMINSTER RAIL BRIDGE

The New Westminster Rail Bridge crosses the Fraser River upstream of the Pattullo Bridge in New Westminster. The owner, Public Works Canada, required a risk study that would provide a basis for a number of decisions related to ship traffic control and protection measures on specific parts of the bridge. The ship collision risk problem in this case is similar in principle to the Alex Fraser Bridge, except that the assessment had to be broken down to several vessel types, several environmental conditions, and several different piers and spans.

For each combination of the above features, a distribution of ship energies, and a resulting risk of damage or failure, was calculated using principles similar to those employed for the Alex Fraser Bridge. The interesting added feature, however, was the identification of risk from the various individual causes and to the various "targets". Further, the effect on these values on the expected value of damage, with various control or design strategies, was identified.

The key to the treatment was to separate each of the categories of vessel type, environment type, and target into sets of mutually exclusive and exhaustive events. The risk or the expected present value of damage is conditional on the specific combination. The theorem of total probability was then invoked to generate the risk or expected damage unconditioned on any set of categories.

Because the risk was rather high in some of the categories (the bridge has been hit on a number of instances), it was possible to identify the sensitivity of the results to the different control strategies.

Results were obtained for such quantities as the expected value of damage per transit of a particular vessel category travelling upstream.This corresponds to the fair insurance premium for the passage. The effect of control on transit conditions, and the identification of high risk vessel types, was determined.

## SUMMARY

The three examples outlined above serve to illustrate a variety of approaches to the collision risk and decision problems. They have in common the simplicity of coarse discrete probability models and simple mechanical models. These provided effective aids to decision making in all cases.

## ACKNOWLEDGEMENTS

The author acknowledges with thanks the cooperation of the British Columbia Ministry of Transportation and Highways (MOTH), owner of Lions' Gate and Alex Fraser Bridges, and Public Works Canada (PWC), owner of the New Westminster Rail Bridge.

Buckland and Taylor Ltd. performed the risk assessment for MOTH on the Lions' Gate Bridge. CBA-Buckland and Taylor Ltd. were the consultants for design, including ship risk assessment, of the Alex Fraser Bridge. Buckland and Taylor Ltd. were subconsultants, for the probabilistic aspects of the risk study, to Crippen Consultants, engineers for Public Works Canada on the New Westminster Rail Bridge study.

## REFERENCES

Eryuzlu (1986). Unpublished correspondence.

Frandsen (1983). "Accidents Involving Bridges", Introductory Report, IABSE Colloquium on Ship Collision with Bridges and Offshore Structures - Copenhagen, IABSE, Zurich.

Frandsen and Langso (1980). "Ship Collision Problem", Proceedings, IABSE, Zurich.

Hahn and Rama (1982). "Cofferdam Protecting New York Bridges from Ship Collisions, Civil Engineering, American Society of Civil Engineers, Feb 1982.

IABSE (1983). IABSE Colloquium on Ship Collision with Bridges and Offshore Structures - Copenhagen, Introductory Report, Preliminary Report, and Final Report, IABSE, Zurich.

Larsen (1983). "Ship Collision Risk Assessment for Bridges", "Introductory Report, IABSE Colloquium on Ship Collision with Bridges and Offshore Structures - Copenhagen, IABSE, Zurich.

Leslie (1979). "Ships and Bridges", 3rd International Conference on Applications of Statistics and Probability in Soil and Structural Engineering, Sydney.

Minorsky (1983). "Evaluation of Ship-Bridge Pier Impact and of Islands as Protection", "Introductory Report, IABSE Colloquium on Ship Collision with Bridges and Offshore Structures - Copenhagen, IABSE, Zurich.
Sexsmith (1983). "Bridge Risk Assessment and Protective Design for Ship Collision", "Preliminary Report, IABSE Colloquium on Ship Collision with Bridges and Offshore Structures - Copenhagen, IABSE, Zurich.

# MODEL UPDATING IN RELIABILITY THEORY

Henrik O. Madsen
Chief Scientist, A.S Veritas Research, P. O. Box 300, N-1322 Hovik, Norway.

## ABSTRACT

Structural reliability methods are successfully applied for design analysis in soil and structural engineering. Fundamentals of structural reliability analysis are well developed and accurate and efficient numerical methods are available for reliability calculations. The use of reliability methods in decision making for existing structures is in progress. Such decisions may concern extended life time, repair or demolition, and inspection planning.

A coupling of the design reliability analysis with additional information is presented. The conceptual formulation of the coupling is described and the notion of an event margin is introduced. Numerical techniques for computing updated reliaibilities or updated distributions for the entering basic variables are developed. The analysis is illustrated through several practical examples with additional information obtained from proof loading, deformation measurement, quality control and inspection.

## INTRODUCTION

A general framework for structural reliability theory is well developed and accepted, and the capabilities and limitations are widely appreciated. Structural reliability methods are applied in the design processes of individual and fleets of structures as well as for calibration of technical standards. A major reason for the widespread use of structural reliability techniques is the development of efficient and accurate numerical tools for reliability calculation. This makes the reliability evaluation a matter of routine for many engineers, who in turn can concentrate their efforts on the mechanical and physical modeling together with the uncertainty modeling. The fundamentals of structural reliability theory are briefly reviewed based on the concepts of limit state and safety margin.

The design process is only one element in assuring safe and reliable structures. In fabrication and service several other safety elements are introduced such as statistical quality control, proof loading, inspection, instrumented monitoring, and repair. Each of these provide information about the structure additional to the information available at the design state. The reliability aspects of each of these elements appear not as well understood as for the design process itself and very few studies of their interaction are available. The interaction is of particular interest in situations in which decisions have to be made concerning e.g., extended life time, alternative use, repair/strengthening or demolition, and inspection planning.

A formal framework in which the design information is coupled to subsequent information from fabrication and service is presented. The concept of an event margin is introduced similar to the safety margin. The reliability evaluation involves conditional probabilities and the numerical techniques available for safety margins are extended. These extensions basically make the reliability evaluation a matter of routine also in this case.

The reliability formulation is presented for a number of situations. Numerical results are presented for inspection of fatigue cracks in metal structures and for deflection measurements on concrete beams subjected to concrete creep and shrinkage.

## LIMIT STATE AND SAFETY MARGIN

A fundamental assumption in structural reliability analysis is that a structure can always be classified as being in a failed state or a safe state. The failure state may correspond to actual failure or to some undesired state. The state of the structure depends on quantities such as loads, material strengths, dimensions, and workmanship. These quantities are modeled by a finite set of variables, called the *basic variables*, z. Based on structural analysis models it is possible for each set of values of the basic variables to state whether or not the structure fails. This leads to a unique division of the basic variable space into two sets called the *safe set* $S$ and the *failure set* $F$, respectively. The two sets are divided by the *limit state surface* which may be determined through an equation

$$g(z) = 0 \quad \textit{limit state surface} \tag{1}$$

The function $g(\,)$ is a *limit state function*, for which the following sign convention is adopted

$$\begin{aligned} g(z) > 0 \quad z \in S \\ g(z) < 0 \quad z \in F \end{aligned} \tag{2}$$

In structural analysis failure is generally described in terms of individual failure modes. Each system failure mode may involve failure of one or more structural elements, which again can have one or more failure modes. As a consequence of this, the limit state function for the system is often expressed in terms of limit state functions for individual element or system failure modes. The following options for the failure set and the corresponding limit state function are well known from system reliability analysis of electrical systems

*Parallel system:*

$$\begin{aligned} F &= \bigcap_{i=1}^{n} \{z \mid g_i(z) \leqslant 0\} \\ g(z) &= \max_{i=1}^{n} g_i(z) \end{aligned} \tag{3}$$

*Series system:*

$$\begin{aligned} F &= \bigcup_{i=1}^{n} \{z \mid g_i(z) \leqslant 0\} \\ g(z) &= \min_{i=1}^{n} g_i(z) \end{aligned} \tag{4}$$

*Parallel system of series subsystems (minimal path set representation):*

$$\begin{aligned} F &= \bigcap_{i=1}^{k} \bigcup_{l=1}^{m_i} \{z \mid g_{il}(z) \leqslant 0\} \\ g(z) &= \max_{i=1}^{k} \min_{l=1}^{m_i} g_{il}(z) \end{aligned} \tag{5}$$

*Series system of parallel subsystems (minimal cut set representation):*

$$\begin{aligned} F &= \bigcap_{i=1}^{k} \bigcup_{l=1}^{m_i} \{z \mid g_{il}(z) \leqslant 0\} \\ g(z) &= \max_{i=1}^{k} \min_{l=1}^{m_i} g_{il}(z) \end{aligned} \tag{6}$$

A general system, modeled e.g. in terms of fault or event trees, can be represented by equivalent minimal path set and minimal cut set representions. The same applies to structural systems. A major problem in structural system reliability analysis is, however, to determine all or the most important failure or survival modes.

At the design state the values of all basic variables are only rarely known. A description of different sources of uncertainty as well as uncertainty in the structural models can be found in Madsen et al (1986) and Ditlevsen (1982). Some elements in the basic variable vector z are therefore modeled as random variables. A *safety margin* $M$ is now obtained from the limit state function by replacing z by the random vector Z

$$M = g(\mathrm{Z}) \tag{7}$$

$M$ is a random variable and the *failure probability* $P_F$ is

$$P_F = P(g(\mathrm{Z}) \leqslant 0) = P(M \leqslant 0) \tag{8}$$

A *reliability index* $\beta_R$ is defined uniquely in terms of the failure probability as

$$\beta_R = -\Phi^{-1}(P_F) \tag{9}$$

where $\Phi(\ )$ is the standardized normal distribution function. In applications of structural reliability analysis not only the value of $P_F$ or $\beta_R$ is of interest, but the derivatives with respect to either deterministic limit state parameters or statistical parameters in the distributions of the basic variables are equally informative. Such derivatives are called *parametric sensitivity factors.*

## EVENT MARGIN

The reliability analysis can be updated when additional information becomes available. It is convenient to introduce concepts similar to the concepts of limit state and safety margin for this purpose. The additional information is described in the form

$$\begin{aligned} h_i(\mathrm{z}) &\leqslant 0, \quad i=1,2,\cdots,r \\ h_i(\mathrm{z}) &= 0, \quad i=r+1,r+2,\cdots,r+s \end{aligned} \tag{10}$$

The vector z contains the basic variables in the reliability problem plus variables related to the additional information. Three examples are included for illustration:

1. A structural element is proof loaded and survives the load $q_{proof}$ . In this case

$$h(\mathrm{z}) = q_{proof} - r \leqslant 0 \tag{11}$$

since the resistance $r$ is demonstrated to be larger than the proof load.

2. A structural monitoring of a structure determines the angular frequency for the first eigen mode as $\Omega_0$. In this case

$$h(\mathrm{z}) = \omega_0(\mathrm{z}) - \Omega_0 = 0 \tag{12}$$

where the angular frequency of the first eigen mode $\omega_0$ is a function of basic variables describing stiffness and mass. Measurement uncertainty is accounted for by modeling $\Omega_0$ as a random variable in the reliability analysis.

3. A material is known to have passed a compliance control in which $r$ specimens were tested. The distribution parameters for the resistance distribution are unknown. The acceptance decision in the control is taken if the average value falls above a limit $a$ and no values fall below a value $b$, (Rackwitz and Schrupp, 1985). In this case

$$\begin{aligned} h_i(\mathrm{z}) &= b - z_{,i} \leqslant 0, \quad i=1,2,\cdots,r \\ h_{r+1}(\mathrm{z}) &= a - \frac{1}{r}\sum_{i=1}^{r} z_{,i} \leqslant 0 \end{aligned} \tag{13}$$

where $z_{,i}$ are sample values with the same distribution and (unknown) distribution parameters as the basic variable $Z$.

Corresponding to each additional information in the form of a function $h(\mathrm{z})$, an *event margin* $H$ is defined as

$$H = h(\mathrm{Z}) \tag{14}$$

Event margins are thus of the same fundamental form as safety margins.

With the additional information the updated failure probability becomes

$$P(M \leqslant 0 \mid H_1 \leqslant 0 \cap \cdots \cap H_r \leqslant 0 \cap H_{r+1} = \cdots = H_{r+s} = 0) \tag{15}$$

$$= \frac{\dfrac{\partial^s P(M \leqslant 0 \cap H_1 \leqslant 0 \cap \cdots \cap H_r \leqslant 0 \cap H_{r+1} - x_{r+1} \leqslant 0 \cap \cdots \cap H_{r+s} - x_{r+s} \leqslant 0)}{\partial x_{r+1} \cdots \partial x_{r+s}}}{\dfrac{\partial^s P(H_1 \leqslant 0 \cap \cdots \cap H_r \leqslant 0 \cap H_{r+1} - x_{r+1} \leqslant 0 \cap \cdots \cap H_{r+s} - x_{r+s} \leqslant 0)}{\partial x_{r+1} \cdots \partial x_{r+s}}}$$

where the partial derivatives are evaluated at x=0.

The distribution of the basic variables is updated in a similar manner. To determine the value of the updated distribution function $F_Z(z)$, the safety margin $M$ in (15) is replaced by

$$M = Z - z\,, \quad \textit{updating of distribution function} \tag{16}$$

By varying the value of $z$ the complete distribution function can be updated. Even when the basic variables are initially independent the updating generally introduces dependence. To determine the updated joint distribution function of e.g. $Z_1$ and $Z_2$ the event $M \leqslant 0$ in (15) is replaced by

$$\{M_1 = Z_1 - z_1 \leqslant 0\} \bigcap \{M_2 = Z_2 - z_2 \leqslant 0\} \tag{17}$$

The evaluation of the updated failure probability or basic variable distributions thus requires evaluation of parametric sensitivity factors for systems. This is described in the next section for a safety margin $M$ corresponding to a single failure mode of an element. In this case parametric sensitivity factors for two parallel systems are needed. A generalization to the system representations in (3-6) is straightforward.

## RELIABILITY EVALUATION

Presently available general purpose computer programs for structural reliability evaluation are based on either a Monte Carlo simulation method or on first- and second-order reliability methods, with programs based on the latter methods being the most efficient. Both techniques can be applied to compute the updated failure probability, but here the emphasis is on the use of first-order reliability methods, which is briefly reviewed for parallel systems. For a more thorough description see Madsen et al (1986). The failure probability of a parallel system with $k$ elements is according to (3,8)

$$P_F = P(M_1 \leqslant 0 \cap M_2 \leqslant 0 \cap \cdots \cap M_k \leqslant 0) \tag{18}$$

The first step in the first-order reliability method is a transformation of the vector of basic variables into a vector of standardized and independent normal variables U. The transformation is denoted T and the transformed space is called the normal space.

$$\mathrm{U} = \mathrm{T}(\mathrm{Z}) \tag{19}$$

A good choice for T is a transformation, which uses the conditional distribution functions $F_i(z_i \mid z_1, \ldots, z_{i-1}) = P(Z_i \leqslant z_i \mid Z_1 = z_1, \cdots, Z_{i-1} = z_{i-1})$ of the basic variables as suggested by Hohenbichler and Rackwitz (1981).

$$\begin{aligned}
U_1 &= \Phi^{-1}(F_1(Z_1)) \\
U_2 &= \Phi^{-1}(F_2(Z_2 \mid Z_1)) \\
&\;\;\vdots \\
U_i &= \Phi^{-1}(F_i(Z_i \mid Z_1, Z_2, \cdots, Z_{i-1})) \\
&\;\;\vdots \\
U_n &= \Phi^{-1}(F_n(Z_n \mid Z_1, Z_2, \cdots, Z_{n-1}))
\end{aligned} \tag{20}$$

The limit state surfaces for the individual elements are expressed in terms of $\mathbf{u}$ as

$$g_i(\mathbf{z}) = g_i(\mathrm{T}^{-1}(\mathbf{u})) = g_{u,i}(\mathbf{u}) = 0, \quad i=1,2,\cdots,k \tag{21}$$

The second step in a first-order reliability analysis consists in determining the joint design point $\mathbf{u}^*$, which is the point on the limit state surface closest to the origin. $\mathbf{u}^*$ is thus found as the solution of a constrained minimization

$$\begin{aligned} &\min |\mathbf{u}| \\ &g_{u,i}(\mathbf{u}) \leqslant 0, \quad i=1,2,\cdots,k \end{aligned} \tag{22}$$

provided that $g_{u,i}(0)>0$ for at least one $i \in \{1,...,k\}$. Standard optimization techniques can be applied to solve this problem. All constraints are not necessarily active at the joint design point, i.e., $g_{u,i}(\mathbf{u})=0$ is not necessarily valid for all $i$. Let $l \leqslant k$ denote the number of active constraints.

The third step in a first-order reliability method consists in a linearization of the element limit state surfaces for the active constraints at the joint design point. In normalized form the corresponding linearized safety margins are

$$M_i = \beta_i - \alpha_i^T \mathrm{U} \tag{23}$$

where $\alpha_i$ is a unit vector and $\beta_i$ is the first-order reliability index for element $i$ of the parallel system linearized at the joint design point. The correlation coefficient $\rho_{ij}$ between the safety margins $M_i$ and $M_j$ is

$$\rho_{ij} = \rho[M_i, M_j] = \alpha_i^T \alpha_j \tag{24}$$

The failure probability of the parallel system is now approximated by the probability content in the set bounded by the linearized element limit state surfaces

$$P_F \approx \Phi_l(-\beta;\rho) \tag{25}$$

where $\beta=\{\beta_i\}$, $\rho=\{\rho_{ij}\}$ and only the $l$ active elements are included. The asymptotic result as $|\mathbf{u}^*| \to \infty$ is (Hohenbichler, 1984a)

$$P_F \sim \Phi_l(-\beta;\rho)\,[\det(\mathbf{I}-\mathbf{D})]^{-1/2}, \quad |\mathbf{u}^*| \to \infty \tag{26}$$

where $\mathbf{I}$ denotes the unit matrix and $\mathbf{D}$ is a matrix determined by the coordinates of the design point and the gradients and second order derivatives of the limit state functions at the design point. For a single element the asymptotic result for the corresponding reliability index $\beta_R$ is derived in Breitung (1984)

$$\beta_R \sim \beta, \quad \beta = |\mathbf{u}^*| \to \infty \tag{27}$$

A generalization of this result to a parallel system yields

$$\beta_R \sim -\Phi^{-1}(\Phi_l(-\beta;\rho)), \quad |\mathbf{u}^*| \to \infty \tag{28}$$

To compute the updated failure probability in (15) two parallel systems must be analyzed. The optimization, however, must be cast in a slightly different form than (22) with the constraints corresponding to event margins $H_i=0$ changed to equality constraints. In addition, linearized safety margins for inactive constraints should be included as described in Hohenbichler et al (1986). The vector of reliability indices and the correlation matrix for the normalized safety and event margins in the numerator of (15) are

$$\begin{bmatrix} \beta \\ \beta_1 \\ \beta_2 \end{bmatrix}, \quad \begin{bmatrix} 1 & \rho_1^T & \rho_2^T \\ \rho_1 & \rho_{11} & \rho_{21}^T \\ \rho_2 & \rho_{21} & \rho_{22} \end{bmatrix} \tag{29}$$

where $\beta$ refer to the safety margin, an index 1 to the normalized event margins of type $H_i \leqslant 0$ and an index 2 to the normalized event margins of type $H_i = 0$. The dimension of $\boldsymbol{\beta}_1$ is $r$ (since inactive constraints have been included) and the dimension of $\boldsymbol{\beta}_2$ is $s$. The vector of reliability indices and the correlation matrix for the denominator are similarly

$$\begin{bmatrix} \boldsymbol{\beta}_1' \\ \boldsymbol{\beta}_2' \end{bmatrix}, \quad \begin{bmatrix} \rho_{11}' & \rho_{21}'^T \\ \rho_{21}' & \rho_{22}' \end{bmatrix} \tag{30}$$

The joint design point for the parallel system in the denominator is generally different from the design point of the parallel system in the numerator which is emphasized by the prime. The dimension of $\boldsymbol{\beta}_1'$ is $r$ and the dimension of $\boldsymbol{\beta}_2'$ is $s$.

In Hohenbichler (1984b) the asymptotic result for the parametric sensitivity factor for $\beta_R$ of an element has been derived:

$$\frac{\partial \beta_R}{\partial p} \sim \frac{\partial \beta}{\partial p}, \quad |\mathbf{u}^*| \to \infty \tag{31}$$

For the failure probability then follows

$$\frac{\partial P_F}{\partial p} = \frac{\partial \Phi(-\beta_R)}{\partial p} = -\phi(\beta_R)\frac{\partial \beta_R}{\partial p} \sim -\phi(\beta)\frac{\partial \beta}{\partial p}, \quad |\mathbf{u}^*| \to \infty \tag{32}$$

Generalizing this result to the parallel system in the numerator of (15) yields

$$\left.\frac{\partial^s P(M \leqslant 0 \cap H_1 \leqslant 0 \cap \cdots \cap H_r \leqslant 0 \cap H_{r+1} - x_{r+1} \leqslant 0 \cap \cdots \cap H_{r+s} - x_{r+s} \leqslant 0)}{\partial x_{r+1} \cdots \partial x_{r+s}}\right|_{\mathbf{x}=0} \tag{33}$$

$$\sim \frac{\partial^s \Phi_{r+s+1}\left(-\begin{bmatrix} \beta \\ \boldsymbol{\beta}_1 \\ \boldsymbol{\beta}_2 \end{bmatrix}; \begin{bmatrix} 1 & \rho_1^T & \rho_2^T \\ \rho_1 & \rho_{11} & \rho_{21}^T \\ \rho_2 & \rho_{21} & \rho_{22} \end{bmatrix}\right)}{\partial \beta_{r+1} \cdots \partial \beta_{r+s}}$$

$$= \phi_s(-\boldsymbol{\beta}_2; \rho_{22})\, \Phi_{r+1}\left(-\left\{\begin{bmatrix} \beta \\ \boldsymbol{\beta}_1 \end{bmatrix} - \begin{bmatrix} \rho_2^T \\ \rho_{21}^T \end{bmatrix} \rho_{22}^{-1} \boldsymbol{\beta}_2\right\}; \left\{\begin{bmatrix} 1 & \rho_1^T \\ \rho_1 & \rho_{11} \end{bmatrix} - \begin{bmatrix} \rho_2^T \\ \rho_{21}^T \end{bmatrix} \rho_{22}^{-1} [\rho_2 \;\; \rho_{21}]\right\}\right)$$

where standard results for the conditional multivariate normal distribution have been applied since the vectors of linearized safety margins are joint normally distributed. Furthermore $\partial \beta_i / \partial x_i = -1$ has been used, which is valid since $Var[M_i] = 1$. The conditional probability in (15) now becomes

$$P(M \leqslant 0 | H_1 \leqslant 0 \cap \cdots \cap H_r \leqslant 0 \cap H_{r+1} = \cdots = H_{r+s} = 0) \tag{34}$$

$$\sim \frac{\phi_s(-\boldsymbol{\beta}_2; \rho_{22})}{\phi_s(-\boldsymbol{\beta}_2'; \rho_{22}')} \; \frac{\Phi_{r+1}\left(-\left\{\begin{bmatrix} \beta \\ \boldsymbol{\beta}_1 \end{bmatrix} - \begin{bmatrix} \rho_2^T \\ \rho_{21}^T \end{bmatrix} \rho_{22}^{-1} \boldsymbol{\beta}_2\right\}; \left\{\begin{bmatrix} 1 & \rho_1^T \\ \rho_1 & \rho_{11} \end{bmatrix} - \begin{bmatrix} \rho_2^T \\ \rho_{21}^T \end{bmatrix} \rho_{22}^{-1} [\rho_2 \;\; \rho_{21}]\right\}\right)}{\Phi_r(-\boldsymbol{\beta}_1' + \rho_{21}'^T(\rho_{22}')^{-1}\boldsymbol{\beta}_2'; \; \rho_{11}' - \rho_{21}'^T(\rho_{22}')^{-1}\rho_{21}')}$$

## EXAMPLES

Examples involving quality control and proof testing can be found in Rackwitz and

Schrupp (1985), while examples for offshore structures are presented in Diamantidis (1987). Here results are presented for two practical applications related to creep and shrinkage of concrete structures and to crack propagation in metal structures. A similar application in soil engineering relates to measurement of consolidation settlements.

**Creep and Shrinkage Effects in Concrete Structures.** The uncertainty in creep and shrinkage properties for concrete is larger than the uncertainty in parameters related to strength. Uncertainties in creep and shrinkage effects are consequently large at the design stage. The importance of this is amplified by the design practice attempting to prestress or post-tension in such a way that creep and deflection deformations become minimal. A probabilistic design analysis is thus relevant together with a follow-up in service. Additional information in service may be available based on, e.g., deflection measurements on the actual structure or on control specimens.

As an example consider the prestress loss in a prestressed concrete beam.

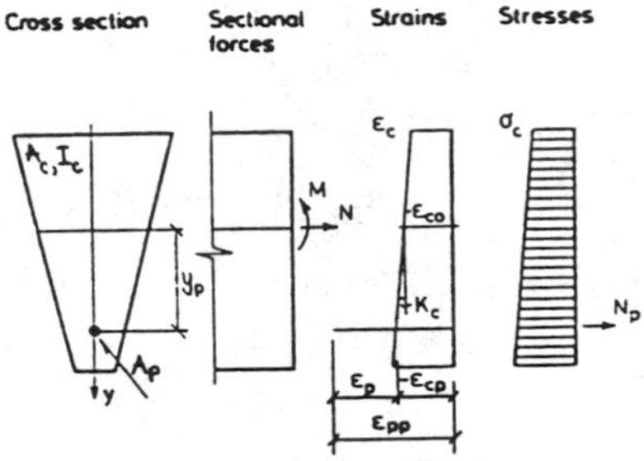


Fig. 1 Prestressed Beam

Using a matrix formulation (Madsen, 1979) the steel force $N_p$ at different times is collected in the vector $\mathbf{N}_p$. $\mathbf{N}_p$ is computed from

$$\mathbf{N}_p = A_p E_p \left[ \mathbf{I} + \left( \frac{A_p}{A_c} + \frac{A_p y_p^2}{I_c} \right) E_p \mathbf{E}_c^{-1} \right]^{-1} \left\{ \epsilon_{pp} + \epsilon_{sh} + \mathbf{E}_c^{-1} \left( \frac{\mathrm{N}}{A_c} + \frac{\mathrm{M} y_p}{I_c} \right) \right\} \qquad (35)$$

where $A_p$ = area of prestressing steel, $E_p$ = modulus of elasticity of prestressing steel, I= unit matrix, $A_c$ = area of concrete, $y_p$ = distance from centroidal axis of concrete cross section to prestressing cable, $I_c$ = moment of inertia of concrete cross section, $\mathbf{E}_c$ = creep matrix determined from compliance function, $\epsilon_{pp}$ = prestress strain, $\epsilon_{sh}$ = shrinkage strain, N=cross section axial force, and M= cross section bending moment. $\mathbf{E}_c$ and $\epsilon_{sh}$ depend on basic variables Z including uncertain humidity and temperature conditions, uncertain concrete composition and strength, and model uncertainties in creep and shrinkage formulas. Other basic variables may refer to the prestress strain and the sectional forces.

$N_p(t)$ decreases with time and corresponding to a value $n_p$ a safety margin is defined as

$$M = N_p(T) - n_p \qquad (36)$$

where $T$ is the length of the considered period, e.g., the anticipated life time, and $N_p(T)$ is an element of the vector $\mathbf{N}_p$. Different deterministic values of $n_p$ is selected and an analysis is carried out for each value. In this way the cumulative distribution function of $N_p(T)$ is determined.

Figure 2 shows the cumulative distribution function for T=10,000 days. Eight basic variables have been introduced: humidity $h$, cement content in kg / m$^3$, C, water-cement

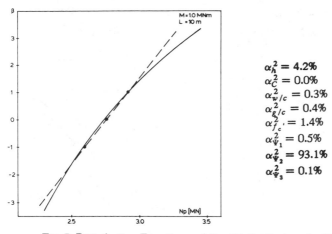

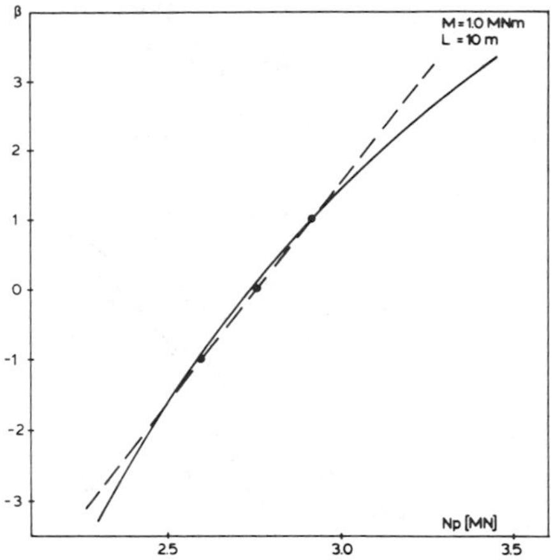


$\alpha_h^2 = 4.2\%$
$\alpha_C^2 = 0.0\%$
$\alpha_{w/c}^2 = 0.3\%$
$\alpha_{g/c}^2 = 0.4\%$
$\alpha_{f_c'}^2 = 1.4\%$
$\alpha_{\Psi_1}^2 = 0.5\%$
$\alpha_{\Psi_2}^2 = 93.1\%$
$\alpha_{\Psi_3}^2 = 0.1\%$

**Fig. 2 Distribution Function and Sensitivity Factors for Steel Force at $T$=10,000 days, $L$=10 m, $M$=1 MNm**

ratio $w/c$, gravel-cement ratio $g/c$, 28-days cylinder compressive strength $f_c'$, model uncertainty in shrinkage formula $\Psi_1$, model uncertainty in basic creep formula $\Psi_2$, and model uncertainty in drying creep formula $\Psi_3$. The BP models (Bazant and Panula, 1978, 1979) have been used for shrinkage and creep. All eight basic variables have been assigned a normal distribution with mean values and coefficients of variation as suggested in Madsen and Bazant (1983). The plot is on normal probability paper and $\beta$ represents the number of standards deviations from the mean value. It is observed that the distribution of $N_p(T)$ deviates significantly from a normal distribution. Also shown in the figure are three dots representing the mean value and the mean value plus and minus one standard deviation obtained by the point estimation method applied in Madsen and Bazant (1983). A good agreement between the two sets of results is observed. The sensitivity factors $\alpha_i^2$ are a by-product of the first-order reliability analysis. These sensitivity factors divide the total uncertainty on the eight basic variables. The sensitivity factors for $n_p$=2.5$MN$ are shown in the figure, and the major source of uncertainty is identified as the model uncertainty in the formula for basic creep.

The curvature $\kappa$ at the cross section at different times is collected in the vector $\kappa$

$$\kappa = E_c^{-1} \frac{M - N_p y_p}{I_c} \tag{37}$$

Let the mid-point deflection $\delta$ be given by

$$\delta = \frac{5}{48} \kappa L^2 \tag{38}$$

where $L$ is the length of the beam. Deflection measurements can be used to update the distribution of the steel force. As an example let the measurement refer to the mid-point deflection one day after loading $t_0$ and at a later time $t_0+t_1$. An event margin becomes

$$H_1 = \frac{5}{48}(\kappa(t_0+t_1) - \kappa(t_0+1))L^2 - \Delta = 0 \tag{39}$$

where $\Delta$ is the measured difference in deflection. Due to measurement uncertainty $\Delta$ is modeled as a random variable. The updated distribution function becomes

$$P(N_p(T) \leqslant n_p \mid \delta(t_0+t_1)-\delta(t_0)=\Delta) = P(M \leqslant 0 \mid H_1=0) \tag{40}$$

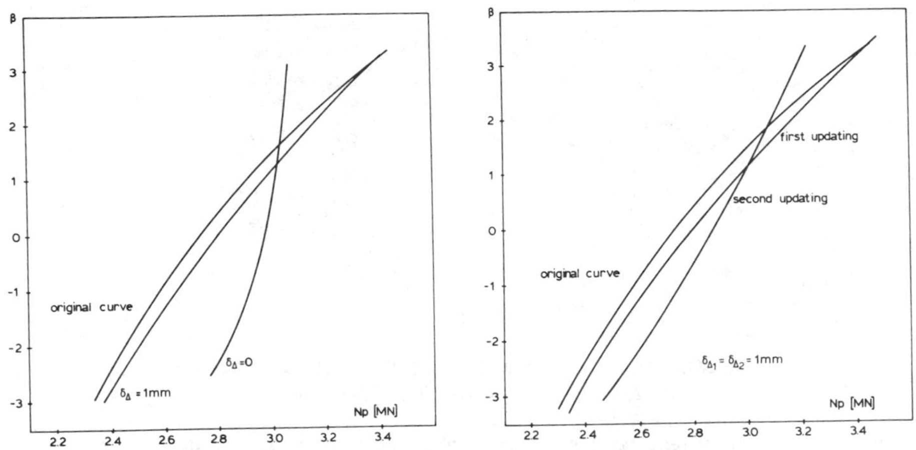


**Fig. 3** Updated Distribution Function for Steel Force at
$T=10{,}000$ days, $L=10$ m, $M=1$ MNm

Figure 3 shows the updated distribution function for $t_1=1$ year, a mean value of $\Delta$ of -4 mm, and a standard deviation $\sigma_\Delta$ equal to zero or 1 mm. When the deflection measurement has no uncertainty, i.e. $\sigma_\Delta=0$, the reduction in variance of the distribution for $N_p(T)$ is very large, while for $\sigma_\Delta=1$ mm the standard deviation is almost unchanged. With a second deflection measurement at $t_1=10$ years a further updating can be carried out. Figure 3 also shows such results for $\sigma_\Delta=1$ mm for both measurements, and with statistically independent measurement errors. With this second piece of additional information the uncertainty in $N_p(T)$ is significantly reduced.

**Fatigue Crack Growth in Metal Structures.** Fatigue crack growth and subsequent failure is important for many steel and aluminum structures under cyclic loading. Failure may refer to leakage, brittle fracture or plastic collapse. Parameters affecting the crack growth phase generally have a large uncertainty at the design state.

For illustration crack growth in a panel is considered. The Paris and Erdogan equation determines the crack growth rate and the stress intensity factor is computed by linear elastic fracture mechancis. The safety margin $M$ is defined as (Madsen, 1985)

$$M = \int_{a_0}^{a_C} \frac{da}{Y(a,\mathrm{Y})^m (\sqrt{\pi a})^m} - C\, S^m\, n \tag{41}$$

where $a_0$=initial crack length, $a_C$=critical crack length, $Y(a,\mathrm{Y})$=geometry function, $C, m$=material parameters, $S$= stress range, and $n$=number of stress cycles. The life time distribution is described through the distribution function for the number of cycles $N$ at failure.

As an example a geometry function

$$Y(a\,\mathrm{Y}) = \exp(Y_1(a/50)^{Y_2}) \tag{42}$$

is considered and statistics for the basic variables are taken as in Madsen (1985). Figure 4 shows on normal probability paper the distribution function for $N$, and sensitivity factors for $n = 1.5 \cdot 10^6$ stress cycles.

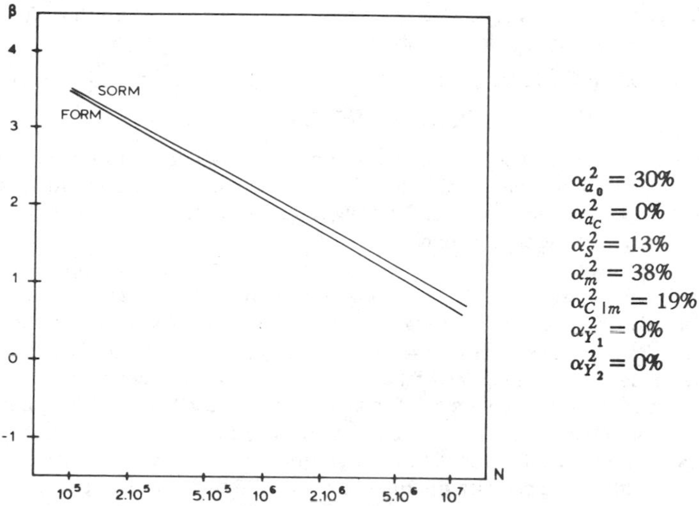


Fig. 4 Distribution function for number of cycles to failure - first- and second-order approximation and sensitivity factors

Structures in service are often inspected to detect cracks before they become critical. Let a crack be detected after $n_j$ stress cycles and its length measured as

$$a(n_j) = A_j \tag{43}$$

$A_j$ is generally random due to measurement error and/or due to uncertainties in the interpretation of a measured signal as a crack length. Measurements of the type (43) can be envisaged for several times corresponding to different values of $n_j$. For each measurement (43) an event margin can be defined as

$$H_j = \int_{a_0}^{A_j} \frac{da}{Y(a,\mathrm{Y})^m (\sqrt{\pi a})^m} - C\, S^m\, n_j = 0, \quad j = 1,2,\cdots,s \tag{44}$$

These event margins are zero due to (43).

A second type of inspection result is that no crack is detected. For an inspection at a time corresponding to $n_i$ stress cycles this implies

$$a(n_i) \leqslant A_{di} \tag{45}$$

expressing that the crack length is smaller than the smallest detectable crack length $A_{di}$. $A_{di}$ is generally random since a detectable crack is only detected with a certain probability depending on the crack length and on the inspection method. The distribution of $A_{di}$ is the distribution of non-detected cracks. Information of the type (45) can also be envisaged for several times. If $A_{di}$ is deterministic, however, and the same for all inspections, the information in the latest observation contains all the information of the previous ones. For each measurement (45) an event margin $M_i$ can be defined as

$$H_i = C\, S^m\, n_i - \int_{a_0}^{A_{di}} \frac{da}{Y(a,\mathrm{Y})^m (\sqrt{\pi a})^m} \leqslant 0, \quad i = 1,2,\cdots,r \tag{46}$$

These event margins are negative due to (45).

A general situation is considered where no crack is detected in the first $r$ inspections at a location, while a crack is detected by the $r+1$'th inspection and its length is measured at this and the following $s-1$ inspections. The updated distribution function for the number of cycles to failure is in this case

$$P(N \leqslant n \mid a(n_1) \leqslant A_{d1}, \cdots, a(n_r) \leqslant A_{dr}, a(n_{r+1}) = A_{r+1}, \cdots, a(n_{r+s}) = A_{r+s}) \quad (47)$$
$$= P(M \leqslant 0 \mid H_1 \leqslant 0 \cap \cdots \cap H_r \leqslant 0 \cap H_{r+1} = \cdots = H_{r+s} = 0)$$

A more general situation involves simultaneous consideration of several locations with potentially dangerous cracks for which inspections are carried out. The updating procedure still applies when due consideration is taken to the dependence between basic variables referring to different locations.

Consider the situation where a crack is found in an inspection after $n_1=10^5$ stress cycles and a crack length of 3.9 mm is measured. The measurement error is assumed to be normally distributed with standard deviation $\sigma_A$. Assume that the crack is not repaired but a second inspection at $n=2\cdot10^5$ stress cycles is required. Let the inspection method be the same as in the first inspection and let the measured crack length be 4.0 mm. The measurement error is again assumed to be normally distributed with standard deviation $\sigma_A$ and the two measurement errors are assumed to be statistically independent. Figure 5 shows the updated distribution function for the number of cycles to failure after this second inspection. Different inspection qualities lead to quite different results.

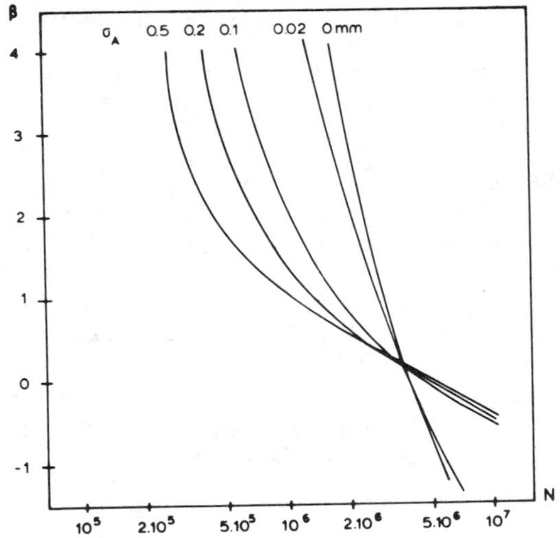


Fig. 5 Updated distribution function after two inspections with crack length measurements 3.9 mm and 4.0 mm

Consider now a situation where the first inspection does not result in crack detection. The quality of the inspection is reflected in the distribution of non-detected cracks. An exponential distribution is assumed with a mean value $\lambda$. Cracks initially present are cracks which have passed the inspection at the production site either because they were not detected or because they were below the acceptance level. If no cracks were accepted in fabrication, the fabrication inspection therefore corresponds to $\lambda=1$.

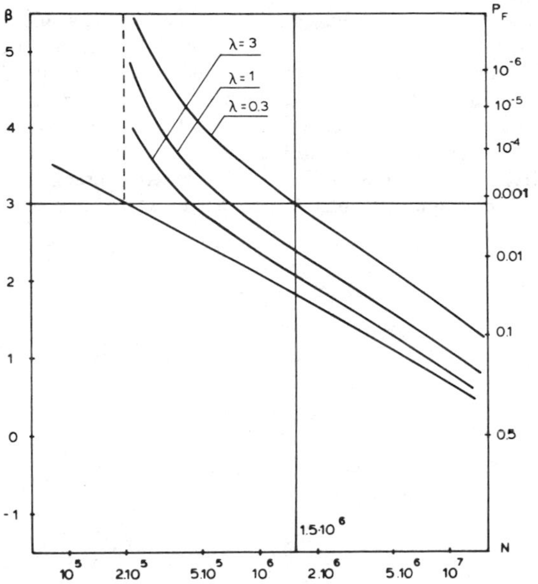


Fig. 6 Updated distribution function after one inspection with no crack detection

Figure 6 shows the initial distribution function for $N$ and updated distribution functions for three inspection qualities. Let the requirement be that $\beta \geqslant 3$ throughout the life time corresponding to $n=1.5 \cdot 10^6$ stress cycles. The best inspection quality $\lambda=0.3$ is better than the fabrication inspection quality and if no crack is found with this method, the increase in reliability is sufficient to make further inspections unnecessary. For the two other inspection qualities, periods are determined until the next inspection.

The interest is now on updating after repair and it is assumed that a repair takes place after $n_{rep}$ stress cycles when a crack length $a_{rep}$ is observed. An event margin $H_{rep}$ is defined as

$$H_{rep} = \int_{a_0}^{a_{rep}} \frac{da}{Y(a,\mathrm{Y})^m \, (\sqrt{\pi a}\,)^m} - C\, S^m \, n_{rep} = 0 \tag{48}$$

The crack length present after repair and a possible inspection is a random variable $a_{new}$ and the material properties after repair are $m_{new}$ and $C_{new}$. The safety margin after repair is $M_{new}$

$$M_{new} = \int_{a_{new}}^{a_C} \frac{da}{Y(a,\mathrm{Y})^{m_{new}} \, (\sqrt{\pi x}\,)^{m_{new}}} - C_{new}\, S^{m_{new}} \, (n - n_{rep}) \tag{49}$$

and the distribution function for $N$ after repair is

$$P(N \leqslant n \mid repair \ at \ n_{rep}) = P(M_{new} \leqslant 0 \mid H_{rep}=0) \tag{50}$$

The results of a reliability analysis following a repair of a detected crack is illustrated in Fig. 7. It is assumed that a crack with length $a_{rep}=8$ mm is repaired after $n_{rep}=2 \cdot 10^5$ stress cycles. The distribution of the initial crack length after repair $a_{new}$ is taken as an exponential distribution with a mean value of 1 mm, i.e., as the same initial distribution as after fabrication. Two situations are considered with either identical or independent material properties before and after repair. When independent properties are assumed the same distribution is used for the properties before and after repair. If follows from the results that there is an immediate increase in reliability after repair, but the reliability quickly drops to a level below the level obtained for the calculations before repair. This reflects the possibility that the cause for the large repaired crack length is a larger than anticipated loading of the crack tip, which is also acting after the repair.

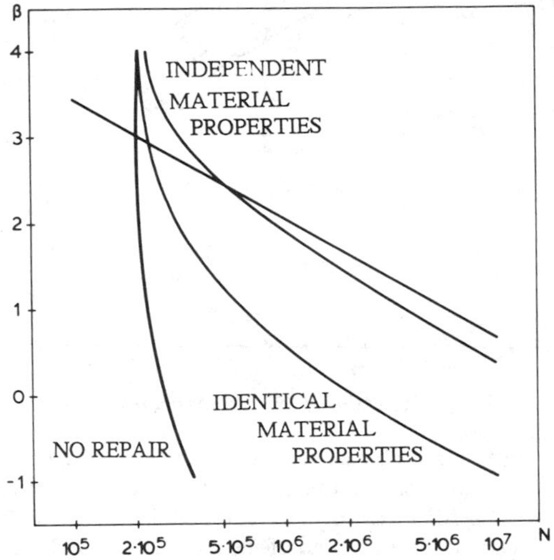


**Fig. 7 Updated first-order reliability index after repair of an 8 mm crack at $N = 2{\cdot}10^5$ stress cycles**

## CONCLUSIONS

The following conclusions can be stated:

- Reliability analysis procedures combining information available at the design state with information becoming available during fabrication and service are of significant practical relevance for decisions concerning extended life time, repair or demolition, and inspection planning.
- A general formulation for reliability updating has been formulated. The formulation introduces the concept of an event margin, and combines this concept with the limit state and safety margin concepts of reliability analysis in design.
- The updating procedure requires the evaluation of parametric sensitivity factors for parallel systems. Full compatibility with first-order reliability methods is established and demonstrated through examples.

## REFERENCES

Bazant, Z. P. and L. Panula (1978, 1979). "Practical Prediction of Time-Dependent Deformations of Concrete", Materials and Structures, Research and Testing (RILEM, Paris), 11, 307-328, 11, 415-434, 12, 169-183.

Breitung, K. (1984). "Asymptotic Approximations for Multinormal Integrals", Journal of the Engineering Mechanics Division, ASCE, 110, 377-386.

Diamantidis, D. (1987). "Reliability Assessment of Existing Structures", Engineering Structures, 10.

Ditlevsen, O. (1982). "Model Uncertainty in Structural Reliability", Structural Safety, 1, 73-86.

Hohenbichler, M. (1984a). "An Asymptotic Formula for the Probability of Intersections", Berichte zur Zuverlassigkeitstheorie der Bauwerke, Heft 69, LKI, Technische Universitat Munchen, Munich, West Germany, 21-48.

Hohenbichler, M. (1984b). "Mathematische Grundlagen der Zuverlassigkeitsmethode Erste Ordnung und Einige Erweiterungen", Doctoral Thesis at the Technical University of Munich, Munich, West Germany.

Hohenbichler, M. and R. Rackwitz (1981). "Nonnormal Dependent Vectors in Structural Reliability", Journal of the Engineering Mechanics Division, ASCE, 107, 1227-1238.

Hohenbichler, M., Gollwitzer, S., Kruse, W., and R. Rackwitz (1986). "New Light on First- and Second-Order Reliability Methods", Manuscript, Technical University of Munich, Munich, West Germany.

Madsen, H. O. (1985). "Random Fatigue Crack Growth and Inspection", in Structural Safety and Reliability, Proceedings of ICOSSAR"85, Kobe, Japan, IASSAR, 1, 475-484.

Madsen, H. O. and Z. P. Bazant (1983). "Uncertainty Analysis of Creep and Shrinkage Effects in Concrete Structures", American Concrete Institute Journal, 80, 116-127.

Madsen, H. O., Krenk, S. and N. C. Lind (1986). Methods of Structural Safety, Prentice-Hall Inc., Englewood Cliffs, New Jersey.

Madsen, K. (1979). "Matrix Formulation for Practical Solution of Concrete Creep Problems", DIALOG 1-79, Danish Engineering Academy, Lyngby, Denmark.

Rackwitz, R. and K. Schrupp (1985). "Quality Control, Proof Testing and Structural Reliability", Structural Safety 2, 239-244.